COMPUTER DICTIONARY

by
Charles J. Sippl
and
Charles P. Sippl

HOWARD W. SAMS & CO., INC.
THE BOBBS-MERRILL CO., INC.
INDIANAPOLIS · KANSAS CITY · NEW YORK

International Standard Book Number: 0-672-20943-8
Library of Congress Catalog Card Number: 72-91729

Printed in the United States of America.

Preface

A new and distinct language has come upon us in the "Age of the Computer." This language takes strange forms—it is part mathematics, part logic, part English, part electronics, and part machine nomenclature—and it is constantly changing and growing.

At the present time management is in the midst of a sweeping cultural and methodological change due to the advances of computer science and the systems approach to organization and problem solving. The impact of the computer on production, education, military science, and information processing has been truly revolutionary. This new science cuts across many previously unrelated disciplines. One authoritative writer has projected that the number of computers will level off at somewhere near ten or fifteen computers per 100 persons.

This dictionary is designed to aid in identifying, classifying, and interpreting terms and concepts concerned with Electronic Data Processing, Information Technology, Automation, and Computer Science. Its purpose is to identify and explain—not to standardize. Several governmental and professional groups have the standardization of terms as their task. In this book, the terms have been presented as they are presently being used; however, the authors are pleased to cooperate and aid in standardization efforts relating to terms, symbols, and languages.

New technological breakthroughs in hardware, software, and systems bring forth new terms, trade names, and even advertising phrases which become part of the jargon and then integral parts of the language itself. "Computerese" is thus a dynamic language concerning a revolutionary new way of conducting business, transforming education, and revitalizing the methodology of scientific inquiry and discovery. Despite its awkward origin and formulation, the language must be mastered, at least in part, by teachers, scientists, business personnel, students, computer personnel, and alert people of all trades and professions.

After more than five years of research and teaching computer technology in several colleges and universities, it was found it to be practically impossible to lecture with any degree of speed and comprehension unless the student has some previous knowledge of the many new terms and concepts. Many students become lost during the first few college lectures or in-service training sessions without the aid of a dictionary or glossary to guide them. Whole lectures can be totally missed or become terribly confused when even a few basic terms are not clearly understood. The first edition of this dictionary was then written to provide the necessary guidance. Now, in this edition, many new terms have been added and the definitions of other terms have been revised to reflect current usage. "Computerese" is a rapidly expanding and changing language.

A glossary of information processing terms and concepts is indispensable to avert confusion and mental obsolescence. The reference dictionary must be kept as complete as possible and as up-to-date as time permits. It then becomes a necessary and most valuable tool for the growing hundreds of thousands of computer students and users, as well as the developers of the instruments themselves. While the development of this book is quite obviously college oriented and tested, it will also provide a valuable tool for high school students and all people who come in contact with the computer.

The reader is invited to forward any newly developed terms, acronyms, concepts, explanations, jargon, abbreviations, coined words, and other items, with information concerning origin, extent of use, and concise definition, for inclusion in future editions.

CHARLES J. SIPPL
CHARLES P. SIPPL

ABOUT THE AUTHORS

Charles J. Sippl has taught marketing, mathematics of finance, economics, statistics, quantitative analysis for business and economics, and several computer introductory, programming, and application courses. His teaching appointments include: California State College at Los Angeles, Long Beach, San Fernando Valley, and Fullerton, as well as the University of California at Los Angeles (Ext.). He has been a member of the Curriculum Planning Committee at the University of California Extension at Los Angeles and has taught several computer "crash" courses for various management groups. He has conducted Computer Industry Structure and Investment Opportunity seminars and lectures for the financial community in twenty major cities in the United States and is a SEC registered investment advisor. He received his B.Sc. degree from the University of Wisconsin, M.A. degree from the University of Miami, and completed Ph. D. work (except dissertation) at the University of California at Los Angeles and Berkeley. He is presently teaching at Chapman College in Orange, California.

Charles P. Sippl received his B.A. degree in Economics from the University of California, at Irvine (summa cum laude). In 1969 he was awarded a full scholarship to the University of Wisconsin's Graduate School of Business and in 1971 a scholarship to the University of Pennsylvania's Wharton Graduate School of Finance and Commerce. He has worked as a financial analyst, has been accredited by the National Association of Securities Dealers to write and publish financial analyses and securities recommendations, and has completed NASD's General Securities Examination, 1970. He has written, edited, and compiled many articles, newsletters, and consulting reports pertaining to the computer industry.

ACKNOWLEDGEMENTS

The author wishes to express his thanks and appreciation to practically every major firm in the computer industry for their willingness to cooperate in supplying information necessary for the completion of this text. Some individuals and firms were especially generous in supplying manuals, photographs, and other miscellaneous materials. I welcome the opportunity to list some of their names: R. P. (Bud) Hurst, Robert F. Korinke, and R. S. Cecil all of IBM; Don Sanden and Henry Lee of GE; Michael Frawley and H. R. Wise of NCR; Harold Clark of the Union Bank of LosAngleles;C. H. Simmons and W. M. Aamoth of UNIVAC; Henry J. Meier, Jr., of Burroughs; Robert G. Strayton of Honeywell; Thomas I. Bradshaw of RCA; Richard F. Musson and Jerry Murphy of Digital Equipment Co.; Thomas Buchholz of Control Data Corporation; Clyde C. Ball of Philco. Some of my academic colleagues who were of particular assistance are Dr. Herbert Stone, California State College at Long Beach; Dr. Donald Moore, California State College at Los Angeles; Dr. Taylor Meloan, University of Southern California; Dr. Harold Somers and Dr. William Allen, University of California, Los Angeles; and Thomas Badger and Marion Sapiro, University of California Extension.

How To Use This Book

The dictionary section of this book follows the standards accepted by modern lexicographers. All terms of more than one word are treated as one word. For example, "check, duplication" appears between "check, dump" and "check, echo." Abbreviations are also treated alphabetically; the letters "BOS" follow "borrow" rather than appearing at the beginning of the B's.

For ease in quickly locating a specific term, the first and last entires on each page appear as catch words at the top of the pages.

Extensive cross-referencing has been used as an aid in locating terms which you might look for in more than one place. For example, "transverse check" may also be located in "check, transverse." If you are not sure whether you want "memory" or "storage," check both.

A

ABA—Abbreviation for American Bankers Association.

abacus—1. A device for performing calculations by sliding beads or counters along rods. 2. An early (3000 B.C.) form of biquinary calculator.

ABA number—A coding number assigned to banks by the American Bankers Association to assist in check clearing.

Abnormal statement—The optional Abnormal statement permits increased optimization of object programs. Where common subexpressions occur within a statement, it is obviously desirable to evaluate each subexpression only once. Where the common subexpressions contain function references, however, there is a possibility that the function will produce a different result upon successive references with the same arguments. Because of this possibility, most FORTRAN systems are forced to re-evaluate subexpressions containing function references at each occurrence. FORTRAN V permits all functions that can produce different results from identical sets of arguments to be designated Abnormal. All common expressions except those that reference Abnormal functions are evaluated only once. When the Abnormal statement does not appear at all in a program, all function references are considered Abnormal and are re-evaluated at each occurrence, as in most other FORTRAN systems.

abort—A procedure to terminate execution of a program when an irrecoverable error, mistake, or malfunction occurs.

abrasiveness—The quality or characteristic of being able to abrade, scratch, or wear away a material. An important factor in optical character recognition where damage to the read screen may affect the reading process detrimentally and cause a large reject rate.

absolute address—1. An actual location in storage of a particular unit of data; address that the control unit can interpret directly. 2. The label assigned by the engineer to a particular storage area in the computer. 3. A pattern of characters that identifies a unique storage location or device without further modification. (Synonymous with machine address.)

absolute addressing—A method of signalling or addressing which has the address part of an instruction as the actual address to be specified, and in which the address part is called the absolute address.

absolute code—See code, absolute.

absolute coding—Coding in which instructions are written in the basic machine language; i.e., coding using absolute operators and addresses. Coding that does not require

processing before it can be understood by the computer.

absolute error—The magnitude of the error disregarding the algebraic sign, or if a vectorial error, disregarding its direction.

absolute instruction—See instruction, absolute.

absolute language—Same as machine language.

absolute programming—Also called absolute language programming. The writing of a computer program in which all addresses are referred to by their actual code numbers in the computer system.

absolute value—A particular quantity, the magnitude of which is known by the computer, but the algebraic sign is not relevant.

absolute-value computer—A computer that processes all data expressed in full values of all variables at all times. (Contrasted with incremental computer.)

absorbency—An important property of paper, when used in optical character recognition, pertaining to the distribution of fibers and their effect on the document's readability.

abstract—1. A short form or summary of a document. 2. To shorten or summarize a document.

abstracting, automatic—Searching for the criteria by which human beings judge what should be abstracted from a document, as programmed.

abstracting service—An organization that provides summary information or documents in a given subject field.

abstract symbol—See symbol, abstract.

ACC—Abbreviation for accumulator.

acceleration period—The period of time in which a card reader and/or punch physically move (s) the card into a position where the data can be read.

acceleration time—The time between the interpretation of instructions to read or write on tape, and the transfer of information to or from the tape into storage, or from storage into tape, as the case may be. (Synonymous with start time.)

access—Concerns the process of obtaining data from or placing data in storage.

access-address, second-level—Same as indirect address.

access, arbitrary—See arbitrary access.

access arm—A mechanical device or unit which positions another device or portion of itself in proper alignment or position relative to operations as designed, i.e., a reading head when positioned properly to read or record information.

access-coding, minimal—The reference to programming which is done in order to locate the data in such a manner as to reduce the access time and minimize the amount of time required to transfer words from auxiliary storage to main memory.

access-control registers—*See* registers, access control.

access control words—*See* control words I/O access.

access, direct—A memory device which allows the particular address to be accessed in a manner independent of the location of that address; thus, the items stored in the memory can be addressed or accessed in the same amount of time for each location. Thus, access by a program is not dependent upon the previously accessed position.

access, disk—*See* disk, access.

access display channel, direct—*See* direct access channel display.

access, immediate—Pertaining to the ability to directly obtain data from, or place data in, a storage device or register without serial delay due to other units of data, and usually in a relatively short period of time.

access instantaneous—*Same as* access, immediate.

access, magnetic drum — *See* drum access, magnetic.

access memory, faster — Various storage media which obtain or release data faster through the use of two or more differing storage devices or media. Examples: magnetic core storage is the faster access memory in equipment where both magnetic core storage and magnetic disk storage are built in.

access method — The software link between the program and the data that must be transferred in or out of memory by the program. It is defined by both the file structures and programming language elements involved.

access mode—In COBOL, a technique that is used to obtain a specific logic record from, or place a specific logic record into, a file assigned to a mass-storage device.

access, multiple—Reference to a system from which output or input can be received or dispatched from more than one location.

accessory—An additional part or an added feature which is designed to increase the function or add to the value or capacity of equipment without redesigning or altering the basic function of the equipment.

access, parallel—The process of obtaining information from storage or placing information in storage, where the time required for such access is dependent on the simultaneous transfer of all elements of a word from a given storage location. (Synonymous with simultaneous access.)

access, queried—Referencing to an automatic sequencing of the transfer of data among the peripherals under the control of the program.

access, random—1. Pertains to the process of obtaining information from or placing information in storage, where the time required

for such access is independent of the location of the information most recently obtained or placed in storage. 2. Pertaining to a device in which random access, as defined in definition 1, can be achieved without effective penalty in time.

access, random sequential—A random sequential-access storage device is one in which the information storage medium is grouped in strips. The computer can gain random access to any one strip as easily as any other, but it is then necessary to scan sequentially along the strip to find the desired word. An example of a random sequential-access storage device is a magnetic drum. There are a large number of magnetic heads along the cylinder, each having access to a circular strip, or track, of the magnetic coating. There are many storage locations around each track. Any magnetic head can be selected at random, but the words in a track pass by sequentially.

access, remote batch—Remote access to information and remote access for information are the keys that have pushed data communications to its position of growth and controversy at the present time. The time-sharing concept in its broadest definition also includes message switching, data acquisition, intercomputer communication, data bank, and the transfer and servicing of large amounts of lower-priority and lower cost "stacked-job" processing.

access, removable random—Describes a feature of storage devices such as disk packs, tape strips, or card strips which can be physically removed and replaced by another, thereby allowing for a theoretically unlimited storage capacity.

access scan—A procedure for receiving data from the files by searching each data item until the desired one is obtained.

access, sequential—*See* sequential, access storage.

access, serial—Pertains to the process of obtaining information from or placing information in storage, where the time required for such access is dependent on the necessity for waiting while nondesired storage locations are processed in turn.

access, simultaneous—*See* access, parallel.

access storage devices, direct—Units of computer equipment which have capabilities of direct and rapid access to storage.

access storage, immediate access—*See* storage, immediate access.

access time—1. The time interval between the instant at which information is called for storage and the instant at which delivery is completed, i.e., the read time. 2. The time interval between the instant at which data are ready for storage and the instant at which storage is completed, i.e., the write time.

access time, reading—*See* reading access time.

access time storage, zero—*See* storage, zero access.

access, zero—The capability of a device to transfer data in or out of a location without undue delays, i. e., due to other units of data. The transfer occurs in a parallel fashion or simultaneously and not serially.

accounting—Some executive systems include an accounting function which maintains an accurate and equitable record of machine-time usage. This information, logged on an appropriate output unit, is available to the user for his own purposes.

accounting center, cost—*See* cost center, accounting.

accounting checks—Accuracy controls on input data that are based on such accounting principles as control totals, cross totals, or hash totals.

accounting function—Some executive systems include an accounting function which maintains an accurate and equitable record of machine-time usage. This information, logged on an appropriate output unit, is available to the user for his own purposes (some computers).

accounting machine—A machine that reads information from one medium, e.g. cards, paper tape, and magnetic tape, and produces lists, tables, and totals on separate forms or continuous paper.

accounting machine, distribution—A machine which sets amounts into categories and accumulates the totals of each category.

accounting machine, magnetic strip—A machine in which data recorded on the magnetic strip at the back of the ledger card can be read by the machine and recorded on a document without manual keyboarding.

accumulated total punching—A control device that sums the contents of a deck of cards, that are processed repeatedly, as a quick check against a known sum to detect if an item has been dropped from the file.

accumulating reproducer—A piece of equipment that reproduces punched cards and has limited additional capabilities of adding, subtracting, and summary punching.

accumulator—1. A part of the logical-arithmetic unit of a computer. It may be used for intermediate storage, to form algebraic sums, or for other intermediate operations. 2. The zero-access register (and associated equipment) in the arithmetic unit in which are formed sums and other arithmetical and logical results; a unit in a digital computer where numbers are totaled, i.e., accumulated. Often the accumulator stores one quantity and upon receipt of any second quantity, it forms and stores the sum of the first and second quantities. *See* register.

accumulator, decimal—Registers 12 through 15 of a register block, used as a single, 16-byte register (some computers).

accumulator jump instruction—An instruction that tells the computer to leave the established program sequence at or after the time the accumulator has reached a certain status.

accumulator register—That part of the arithmetic unit in which the results of an operation remain, and into which numbers are brought from storage, and from which numbers may be taken for storage.

accumulator, running—A memory device which has been programmed so as to make the next item of data retrieved the one that was put in most recently. This method of retrieval is also called the push-down list.

accumulator shift instruction—A computer instruction that causes the contents of a register to be displaced by some specific number of digit positions left or right.

accuracy—Freedom from error. Accuracy contrasts with precision; e.g., a four-place table, correctly computed, is accurate; a six-place table containing an error is more precise, but not accurate.

accuracy-control system—A system of error detection and control.

ac dump—The intentional, accidental, or conditional removal of all alternating current or power from a system or component. An a-c dump usually results in the removal of all power, since direct current is usually supplied through a rectifier or converter.

ac erasing—To erase magnetic recording material by using a device that is powered with alternating current.

acetate base—Magnetic tapes that have a transparent backing of cellulose acetate film.

ACM—Abbreviation for Association for Computing Machinery.

ACM-GAMM—Association for Computing Machinery-German Association for Applied Mathematics and Mechanics, related to the development of ALGOL.

A-conversion—A Fortran instruction to transmit alphanumeric data to and from variables in storage.

acoustic delay line—A device using regenerated shock waves in a conducting medium (for example, mercury) for storing information.

acoustic memory—Computer memory that uses a sonic delay line.

acoustic storage—*See* storage, acoustic.

acquisition, data—*See* data acquisition.

acquisition system, data—*See* data acquisition system.

acronym—A word formed from the first letter or letters of the words in a name, term, or phrase; e.g., SAGE from Semi-Automatic Ground Environment, and ALGOL from ALGOrithmic Language.

action cycle—Refers to the complete operation performed on data. Includes basic steps of origination, input, manipulation, output, and storage.

action line—When a cathode ray storage tube is operating in a serial mode, it refers to that line of the raster which is used during the active period.

action period—*See* period, action.

action, rate—A type of control action in which the rate of correction is made proportional to how fast the condition is going awry. This is also called derivative action.

action spot—In a cathode-ray tube, it is the spot of the raster on the face of the tube used to store the digit or character.

activate key (button)—See button, initiate.

active element—A circuit or device that receives energy from a source other than the main input signal.

active file—A file which is being used and to which entries or references are made on a current basis.

active master file—A master file containing items which are relatively active as contrasted to static or reference items.

active master item—The most active items on a master file measured by usage of the data.

activity—1. A term to indicate that a record in a master file is used, altered, or referred to. 2. A measure of the changes made concerning the use of files of data; e.g., the part of the file or the number of records.

activity level—The value taken by a structural variable in an intermediate or final solution to a programming problem.

activity ratio—When a file is processed, the ratio of the number of records that have activity to the total number of records in that file.

actual address—See address, actual.

actual coding—Same as coding, absolute.

actual decimal point—A decimal point used for "display" purposes; e.g., when a numeric value is listed on a printed report, the decimal point will often appear as an actual printed character. When specified for data to be used within a computer, it requires an actual space in storage.

actual instruction—See instruction, actual.

actual key—In COBOL, a data item that may be used as a hardware address and which expresses the location of a record on a mass-storage medium.

actual time—Same as time, real.

actuating signal—A particular input pulse in the control circuitry of computers.

acyclic feeding—A system employed by character readers in character recognition which senses the trailing edge of the preceding document and triggers automatically the feeding of the following document. This system allows character recognition of varying sized documents.

ADAPSO—An important association of United States and Canadian data processing service organizations, and which now includes a software developer and marketing group as well.

ADAPT (Adaptation of APT)—ADAPT is a program for design calculations and preparation of control tapes for numerically controlled (N/C) machine tools. ADAPT provides through the multilevel copy logic, the ability to generate, relocate, and alter copies of patterns of hole and cut sequences. (GE)

adapter, communication-line—The communication-line adapter (CLAT) for teletype is a semiautomatic device used to link buffer units with the remote teletype units. The CLAT is incorporated within the buffer cabinet, which is located with the processor at the central site. The purpose of the CLAT is to receive data in serial bit form from the remote inquiry station and convert the data to parallel bit form for use in the inquiry buffer unit. Similarly, data transmitted from the buffer to a remote inquiry station is converted by the CLAT from parallel to serial bit form.

adapter, on-line—See on-line adapter.

adapters, dataphone—Transceivers, transmitters, and receivers are dataphone adapters or components of digital-plotting communication systems. They enable high-speed digital incremental plotting of digital computer outputs at remote locations—either nearby or thousands of miles from the data source. The dataphone adapter drives the plotter over regular telephone lines using standard telephone company dataphone terminals. For the nominal service charge of a regular telephone call, the computer may "talk" directly to a remote plotter or, on a conference hookup, to many remote plotters simultaneously, at any place where there is a standard telephone. Dataphone-adapter installation options can provide two-way communications between stations.

adapter, transmission—The transmission adapter (XA) provides for the connection of remote and local devices to the data adapter as well as the necessary controls to move data to or from the processing unit via the XIC (Transmission Interface Converter). A number of data adapters are available to allow attachment of various remote devices through their communication facility as well as the attachment of various local devices.

adapter unit, data (communications)—The data-adapter unit greatly expands the input/output capabilities of the system. It provides direct connection of a variety of remote and local external devices to a system. These devices include the data-collection system, the data-communication system, process-communication system, telegraph terminals, telemetry terminals, and control and data-acquisition equipment. It can be attached either to a selector channel or to the multiplexor channel of the system.

adapter unit, display—See display adapter unit.

adapting—This concerns the ability of a system to change its performance characteristics in response to its environment.

adapting, self—The ability of a computer system to change its performance characteristics in response to its environment.

adaptive control action—Various types of control actions by which automatic means are used to change the type and/or influence of control parameters in such a way as to improve the performance of the control system.

ADCON (address constant)—A value or expression used to calculate the real or virtual storage addresses.

add, Boolean—Same as OR in set theory. *Same as* OR Gate, positive.

addend—The number or quantity to be added to another number or quantity (augend) to produce the result (sum).

adder—A device that forms as an output, the sum of two or more numbers presented as inputs. Often no data retention feature is included; i.e., the output signal remains only as long as the input signals are present. (Related to accumulator, definition 2.)

adder, analog — An amplifier (analog computer) with output voltage which is the weighted sum of the input voltages. The heights correspond to the positional significance of a given numbering system and would be proportional to the conductances of the circuit elements in the input leads.

adder, anticipated carry—A parallel adder in which each stage is capable of looking back at all addend and augend bits of less significant stages and deciding whether the less significant bits provide a "0" or "1" carry in. Having determined the carry in it combines with its own addend and augend to give the sum for that bit or stage. Also called fast adder or look ahead carry adder.

adder, digital—*See* digital adder.

adder full (parallel)—A parallel full adder can be developed from as many three-input adders as there are digits in the input words. The carry output of each operation is connected to one input of the three-digit adder corresponding to the next significant digit position.

adder full (serial)—A serial full adder may be formed from a three-input adder with a digit delay element connected between the carry output and one of the three inputs.

adder, half—A logic element that has two input channels to which signals may be applied and which represent two input digits, the addend and the augend. The two output-channels from which the signals may-emerge are those which represent the sum and carry digits.

adder, half (parallel)—As regards half adders, parallel half adders can be developed from as many two-input adders as there are digits in the words, with the carry output of each connected to the addend input of the two-input adder corresponding to the digit position of next higher significance.

adder, half (serial)—When serial representation is used, a serial half adder may be formed from a two-input adder with a digit delay element connected to the carry output. The output of the delay element is combined with the addend input, where the addend is assumed to be the number containing the single non-zero digit.

adder, one-digit—*Same as* half-adder.

adder, ripple—A binary adding system simliar to the system most people use to add decimal numbers: i.e., add the units column, get the carry, add it to the 10's column, get the carry, add it to the 100's column, and so on.

adder, soft—An adder used in incremental computers with a resulting output which is equal to minus the sum of the inputs.

adder-subtracter—A logic element designed to act as an adder or a subtracter as ordered by the control signal applied to it.

adder, three input—A device that forms as an output, the sum of two or more numbers presented as inputs. Often no data retention feature is included because the output signal remains only as long as input signals are present.

adder, two input—*Same as* adder, half.

add, false—This is addition without carries; the performance of a logic add.

addition—In data processing, that function of combining quantities according to various circuitry designs, specific machine rules regarding changes in values, and types of carryover operations.

additional character—A character which is neither a letter or a number, but which is usually a punctuation mark, %, *, #; i.e., a member of a specialized alphabet. Specific meanings are assigned to this character to use it to convey special information.

addition, destructive—The sum appears in the location previously occupied by the augend which is thus lost. The addend remains in its original location.

addition item—An item that is to be added at a specific place to an already established file. Addition master item would be the proper term if file is a master file.

addition, nondestructive — The first operand placed in the arithmetic register is the augend, the next operand is the addend, and the sum replaces the augend and thus becomes the augend for a subsequent addition.

addition record—A record that results in the creation of a new record in the master file that is being updated.

addition, serial—A special addition procedure in which the corresponding digit pairs of the numbers added are processed individually beginning with the low-order digits. Carries, in general, are propagated as they occur.

addition table—The area or core storage that holds a table of numbers to be used during the table-scan concept of addition.

addition, zero access—Similar to immediate access. Addition is performed by adding a number to one already stored in an accumulator, and the sum is formed in the same accumulator. The sum is thus available for the next operation and no access time is involved for the addend or the sum storage.

add, logical—A Boolean algebra operation on two binary numbers. The result is one if either one or both numbers are a one; if both digits are zero, then the result is zero.

add operation—An add instruction in which the result is the sum, and the result is usually apparent in the storage location previously occupied by one of the operands.

address—1. A label, name, or number identifying a register, location, or unit where information is stored. 2. The operand part of an instruction. 3. In communications, the coded representation of the destination of a message. 4. To call a specific piece of information from the memory or to put it in the memory.

addressable register—A temporary storage location with a fixed location and address number.

address, absolute—An address that indicates the exact storage location where the referenced operand is to be found or stored in the actual machine-code address numbering system. (Synonymous with specific address, and related to absolute code.)

address, actual—The real or designed address built into the computer by the manufacturer as a storage location or register. Adjacent addresses usually have adjacent numbers. It is the specific or machine address that is used particularly in diagnosing machine faults.

address, arithmetic—A technique of assembly language which appends an address modifier, consisting of a sign and from one to four decimal digits, to a symbolic tag in order to designate a memory location address location which relates to the location represented by the tag. See relative address.

address, base—1. A number that appears as an address in a computer instruction, but which serves as the base, index, initial or starting point for subsequent addresses to be modified. (Synonymous with presumptive address and reference address.) 2. A number used in symbolic coding in conjunction with a relative address.

address, binary-coded—An address which is expressed in binary form—sometimes lacking the absolute or machine address.

address, calculated—An address most often generated or developed by machine instructions contained in the program which uses the address. This address may be determined as a result of some program or process and it may depend upon some set of criteria or condition.

address, checking file program—A program to check addresses, when macros instruct to write on the file, to see that the program is not writing on the wrong area.

address code, single—See code, single address.

address code, zero—See code, zero address.

address comparator—A device used to verify that the correct address is being read. The comparison is made between the address being read and the specified address.

address computation—A computation that produces or modifies the address portion of an instruction.

address, constant—See address, base.

address conversion—The translation of the symbolic addresses or relative addresses into absolute addresses by using the computer and an assembly program or by manual means.

address, counter program register—Same as address program counter.

address, direct—An address that indicates the location where the referenced operand is to be found or stored with no reference to an index register or B-box. (Synonymous with first-level address.)

address, direct reference—A virtual address that is not modified by indirect addressing, but may be modified by indexing.

address, double—Same as address two level.

address, dummy—An artificial address used for illustration or instruction purposes.

addressed location, specific—To aid in random access, data may be directly stored and retrieved from a specific addressed location without the need for a sequential search as is necessary with magnetic tape.

addressed location, specified—Same as addressed location, specific.

addressed memory—Memory sections containing each individual register.

address effective—1. A modified address. 2. The address actually considered to be used in a particular execution of a computer instruction. 3. An address obtained by the combination of the contents of a specific index register with the address of an instruction. 4. The address used for the execution of an instruction. This may differ from that of the instruction in storage.

address, effective virtual—The virtual address value after only indirect addressing and/or indexing modifications have been accomplished, but before memory mapping is performed.

addresses of address—Programming technique used mainly with subroutines.

address, external device (ED)—The ED address specifies to which external device a particularly instruction is referring. Sixty-four different external devices can be specified (some computers).

address, first-level—Same as address direct.

address, floating—Formerly, an address written in such a way that it could easily be converted to a machine address by indexing, assembly, or by some other means.

address format—The arrangement of the address parts of an instruction. The expression "plus-one" is frequently used to indicate that one of the addresses specifies the location of the next instruction to be executed, such as one plus one, two plus one, three plus one, four plus one.

address, four—A method of specifying the location of operands and instructions; the storage location of the two operands and the storage location of the results of the operation are cited, and the storage location of the next instruction to be executed is also cited.

address, four plus one—An arrangement of the address parts of an instruction. The use of "plus" is to indicate that one of the addresses states or specifies the location of the next instruction to be executed, such as, one "plus" one, two "plus" one, etc.

address, functional instruction—*See* address instruction, functional.

address, general register—A value in the range 0 through 15 that designates a register in the current register block, whether by means of the R field of the instruction word, or by means of an effective virtual address (some computers).

address, generated — *Same as* address, calculated.

address, immediate—An instruction address in which the address part of the instruction is the operand. (Synonymous with zero-level address.)

address, indexed—An address that is to be modified or has been modified by an index register or similar device. (Synonymous with variable address.)

address, indirect—1. An address that specifies a storage location whose content is either an indirect address or another indirect address. 2. A single instruction address that is at once the address of another address. The second address is the specific address of the data to be processed. This is classified as single-level indirect addressing. But, the second address could also be indirect, which is then second-level indirect addressing. This same process could develop third, fourth, fifth, and other levels of indirect addressing.

address, indirect reference—A reference address in an instruction that contains a 1 in bit position 0; the virtual address of the location that contains the direct address. If indirect addressing is called for by an instruction, the reference address field is used to access a word location that contains the direct reference address; this then replaces the indirect reference address and is used as an operand address value. Indirect addressing is limited to one level and is performed prior to indexing (some computers).

addressing—Any memory location can be addressed in any one of three formats: direct, indirect, or indexed addressing. The use of binary addressing eliminates the necessity of complex machine-language coding schemes to represent memory addresses in expanded configurations. Index-register usage is by no means restricted; indexed addressing is possible in all instruction formats. In addition, indexed addressing is simplified by a convenient loop-control technique that automatically increments and tests index register contents.

addressing, deferred—Preferred term for indirect addressing in which the address part

specifies a location containing an address, and which in turn specifies a location containing an address, etc., until the specified location address is eventually found. A preset or conditioned number of iterations is set by a termination indicator.

addressing, direct—A procedure for specifically citing an operand in the instruction by the operand's location in storage. The direct address is the number representing the storage location.

addressing, disk file—The operation which locates information on a random access file.

addressing, file pockets—In a random file, a small area or pocket in which one or more records are kept. This is an economical method of holding a small number of records.

addressing, fixed-position—Permits selective updating of tape information, as in magnetic disk or drum storage devices. Units as small as a single computer word may be stored or recorded on tape without disturbing adjacent information. Data blocks are numbered and completely addressable. Interrecord gaps are eliminated, thereby increasing tape-storage capacity.

addressing, (hashing) hash—A calculation of the approximate address of a record in a file by some semi-empirical function.

addressing, immediate—A particular system of specifying the locations of operands and instructions in the same storage location, i.e., at the same address. This is contrasted with normal addressing in which the instruction word is stored at one address or location and contains the addresses of other locations in which the operands are stored.

addressing, implied—*Same as* addressing repetitive.

addressing, indirect—1. A method of computer cross reference in which one memory location indicates where the correct address of the main fact can be found. 2. Any level of addressing other than the first level of direct addressing. 3. Translation of symbolic instructions into machine-language instructions on a computer other than that for which the program was written.

addressing level — A determination of the number of steps of indirect address which have been applied to a particular program. First level is direct addressing, i.e., the address part of the instruction word has the address of the operand in storage. In second level addressing (indirect), the address part of the instruction word gives the storage location where the address of the operand may be found.

addressing, multilevel—*Same as* address, indirect.

addressing, one-ahead — *Same as* addressing repetitive.

addressing, real-time—*Same as* addressing, immediate.

addressing, relative—A procedure or method of addressing in which the absolute address is obtained by means of the address modification, either simulated or actual, and is performed by the addition of a given number to the address part of an instruction, i.e., the address part of the presumptive instruction is known as the relative address.

addressing, repetitive—A specific method of addressing for some computers which have a variable instruction format. Instructions which have a zero address instruction format, for example, refer again automatically to the location affected by the last instruction executed.

addressing, self-relative—In relative addressing, the number added corresponds to the address of the insruction under consideration.

addressing, specific—A procedure or method of addressing in which the address part of an instruction is the actual address to be specified, i.e., the address part is known as the specific address or the absolute address.

addressing, stepped — See addressing, one-ahead.

addressing, symbolic—The procedure for using alphabetic or alphanumeric labels to specify various storage locations for particular programs, i.e., before program execution, the symbolic address is converted to an absolute address.

addressing system—The procedure used to label storage locations in a computer. On a magnetic storage drum, storage locations might be identified by four digit addresses which are numbered consecutively in each band as follows:

First band	0000-0199
Second band	0200-0399
Third band	0400-0599
* * *	* *
Twenty-fourth band	4600-4799
Twenty-fifth band	4800-4999

The consecutively numbered band addresses begin with 0000, to which increments of 200 are added until the address of the last band, 4800, is reached. Within each band, particular locations might be consecutively numbered from 0 to 199 to give each location an address indicative of a position on the drum or drum level. This level is added to the band address to produce the address of a particular storage location. In a magnetic-core storage unit, the locations might be addressed consecutively from 0000 to 4,095.

addressing, three-level — Instruction words contain the address which specifies the storage location of the address which, in turn, has the address of the storage location which contains the address of the operand; i.e., 3 references to storage locations for obtaining the desired operand.

addressing, two-level—A procedure for addressing in which the instruction word changes addresses designating the storage locations where the addresses of the operands

are to be found. If two references in storage locations need to be obtained, this will use an indirect address and a second level address.

addressing, virtual—Same as addressing, immediate.

addressing, zero-level—Same as addressing, immediate.

address, instruction—The address of the storage location where the instruction word is stored. The next instruction to be performed is determined by the control program of the instruction addresses, and the machine control automatically refers to these addresses sequentially unless otherwise directed to skip or branch, or directed by other schemes.

address instruction, functional — An instruction that has no particular operation part since the operation is specified by the address parts, i.e., some two addresses which are specified might designate storage locations having contents which are always added.

address instruction, immediate — A specific instruction which contains the value of the operand in its address part rather than the address of the operand. It is used most often for incrementing a count by a fixed amount, or for masking a partial-word field of data, or for testing a special character for identical characteristics with the immediate character in the instruction.

address instruction, operational — Same as address instruction, functional.

address instruction, three — See instruction, three address.

address instruction three-plus-one—Same as address four.

address instruction, two-plus-one — See instruction, two-plus-one address.

addressless instruction format—A particular instruction format which contains no address part, used either when no address is required, or when the address is in some way implicit.

address, machine—An absolute, direct, unindexed address expressed as such, or resulting after indexing and other processing has been completed.

address modification — 1. The process of changing the address part of a machine instruction by means of coded instruction. 2. A change in the address portion of an instruction or command such that, if the routine containing the instruction or command is repeated, the computer will go to a new address or location for data or instructions. See address computation.

address, multiple—A type of instruction that specifies the addresses of two or more items which may be the addresses of locations of inputs or outputs of the calculating unit, or the addresses of locations of instructions for the control unit. The term multiaddress is also used in characterizing computers; e.g., two-, three-, or four-address machines. (Synonymous with multiaddress.)

address, Nth-level—An indirect address which might be second level, third level addresses, etc., that specify addresses of desired operands.

address one—*Same as* single address.

address, one-level—*Same as* direct address.

address, one plus one—An instruction system having the property that each complete instruction includes an operation and two addresses, one for the location of a register in the storage containing the item to be operated upon, and one for the location containing the next instruction.

address, operand—In indirect addressing, the address of the instruction refers to a location whose content is not the operand but rather the address of the operand. The address of the operand is called the indirect address, usually signalled as an indirect address by the presence of an extra flag bit.

address, operand effective—An address obtained at the time of execution by the computer to give the actual operand address.

address, P—Location to which the program branches, or to which data is transposed (certain equipment).

address, page—The eight-high-order bits of a virtual address or an actual address, which represent a page of memory (some computers).

address part—The part of an instruction word that defines the address of a register or locations.

address, presumptive—*See* address, base.

address, program counter—A register in which the address of the current instruction is recorded.

address, Q—A source location in internal storage of some types of equipment, from which data is transferred.

address, quadruple—Same as address-four.

address, real-time—Same as address, immediate.

address, reference—A number that appears as an address in a computer instruction, but which serves as the base, index, initial or starting point for subsequent addresses to be modified. (Synonymous with presumptive address.)

address, regional—A specific address usually set within a series of consecutive addresses, such as in the A region of consecutive addresses.

address register—A register in which an address is stored.

address, register field—The portion of an instruction word that contains a register address.

address register, memory—*See* register memory address.

address registers, instruction—*See* instruction-address registers.

address, relative—A label used to identify a word in a routine or subroutine with respect to its position in that routine or subroutine. Relative addresses are translated into absolute addresses by the addition of some spe-

cific "reference" address, usually that at which the first word of the routine is stored; e.g., if a relative-address instruction specified an address N, and the address of the first word of the routine is K, then the absolute address is N + K.

address, result—That address into which the results of an arithmetic process are transferred.

address, second-level—*Same as* address indirect.

address, single—A system of machine instructions in which each complete instruction explicitly describes one operation and involves one storage location. (Related to one-address instruction.)

address, single-level—*Same as* direct address.

address size—The maximum number of binary digits in an instruction used in directly addressing memory.

address source, instruction—*Same as* address instruction, functional.

address, specific—An address that indicates the exact storage location where the referenced operand is to be found or stored in the actual machine-code address numbering system. (Related to absolute code.)

address storage, display lights—The various indicator lights on the control panel that specify the bit pattern in a selected address.

address switches, manual—*See* switches, manual address.

address, symbolic—1. A label chosen to identify a particular word, function, or other information in a routine, independent of the location of the information within the routine; floating address. 2. A label, alphabetic or alphameric, used to specify a storage location in the context of a particular program. Often, programs are first written using symbolic addresses in some convenient code which is then translated into absolute addresses by an assembly program.

address, synthetic—*Same as* address calculated.

address system, one-over-one—A machine-language system that uses two addresses; one of these may be a reference for date.

address, third-level—As in an indirect or multilevel addressing system; the third address sought in the attempt to arrive at the location of an operand. The machine interprets the contents of the first two storage locations as addresses rather than as operands.

address, three—A method of specifying the location of operands and instruction in which the storage location of the two operands and the storage location of the results of the operations are cited, and in which the location or address of the next instruction to be executed is also to be specified; e.g., addend, augend, and sum addresses all specified in one instruction word.

address, three-plus-one—*Same as* address, four.

address, triple—*Same as* address, three.

address-two—An instruction that includes an operation and specifies the location of an operand and the result of the operation.

address two-level—*Same as* address, indirect.

address, variable—An address that is to be modified or has been modified by an index register or similar device.

address, virtual—*Same as* address, immediate.

address, zero-level—An instruction address in which the address part of the instruction is the operand.

add, special—This is similar to double-precision addition in that it concerns addition of numbers having twice as many digits as the particular computer register is capable of containing.

add-subtract time—The time required to perform an addition or subtraction, exclusive of the time required to obtain the quantities from storage and put the sum or difference back in storage.

add time—*See* time, add.

add to storage—The process which immediately enters the final sum of the accumulator into the computer memory.

add without carry gate—*Same as* gate, exclusive OR.

ADIS—Abbreviation for a data interchange system.

adjacency—1. Relates to character recognition and printing conditions. Reference lines designate spacing between two consecutive characters. 2. A condition in character recognition in which two consecutive characters, either printed or handwritten, are closer than the specified distance.

adjacent channel—A channel whose frequency band is adjacent to that of the reference channel.

adjacent-channel interference—Such interference or "noise" occurs when two modulated carrier channels are situated or placed too close together in frequency so that one or both sidebands extend from one channel into the other.

adjacent-channel selectivity—Receivers have characteristics which govern their ability to reject signals or channels adjacent to that of the desired signals.

adjustment, character — The address adjustment in which the literal used to modify the address has reference to a specific given number or group of characters.

administrative data processing — An expression usually meaning business data processing such as the recording, classifying, or summarizing of transactions, activities, events, etc. Usually of a financial nature, or the collection, retrieval, or control of such items.

admissable mark—*See* mark, admissable.

ADP (Automatic Data Processing)—1. This acronym pertains to equipment such as EAM (Electronic Accounting Machines) and EDP (Electronic Data Processing) equipment units, or systems. 2. Data processing performed by a system of electronic or electrical machines so interconnected and interacting as to reduce to a minimum the need for human assistance or intervention.

ADPE—Abbreviation for automatic data processing equipment.

ADPS—Abbreviation for automatic data processing system.

advance feed tape—Those perforated tapes that have leading edges of feed holes directly in line wtih the leading edges of the intelligence holes. This is a Western Union exclusive feature to aid in differentiating between the "front end" and the "tail end" of an uninterpreted tape. Most new installations no longer use it. *See* center-feed tape.

advance item—This is a technique to group records for operating successively on different records in memory.

advantages, simulation—*See* simulation advantages.

AED—An abbreviation for automated engineering design system. An MIT-developed extension of ALGOL.

AESOP (An Evolutionary System for On-Line Processing)—An on-line inquiry system based prinicipally on the use of display screens and light pens.

A except B gate—*Same as* gate, A AND-NOT B.

AFCAL — Abbreviation for Association Francaise de Calcul, a French computing association.

AFIPS—Abbreviation for American Federation of Information Processing Societies, an association of American data processing groups formerly called AFID.

agenda—The set of control-language statements used to prescribe a solution path or run procedures; an ordered list of the major operations constituting a procedure (for a solution or computer run. (This usage corresponds roughly to the ordinary "agenda" for a meeting.)

agendum—The body of code called for execution by a control-language statement (agendum call card).

agendum call card—A single agendum name and its parameters punched on one card in a stylized form; one item of the agenda—a control-language statement calling for the execution of the named agendum. A set of agendum call cards is used to control a linear programming system, thus forming an agenda.

Aid—Aid, the utility and debugging package for XDS Series computers, consists of a group of commonly used routines controlled by an on-line supervisory program through which the user requests assistance. Aid contains minimal format restrictions and helps the programmer perform direct, on-line program checkout.

A ignore B gate, negative—*See* gate B ignore A negative.

A implies B gate—*Same as* gate B OR-NOT A.

A implies B gate, negative—*Same as* gate, A AND-NOT B.

alarm—A signal, by display or audio device, which signifies that an error has occurred, or an emergency condition exists that is interfering or could interfere with the proper execution or completion of a program.

alarm, audible—This is an audio signal which indicates that a predetermined condition has been met or detected, that a malfunction has occurred in the equipment, or that a program error or a problem condition exists.

alarm display—A visual display signal such as on a CRT or radar screen which would alert the operator to conditions which require attention.

alarm-repeated transmission—An audible alarm which sounds after 3 successive failures to transmit (or receive) a line.

alertor—A device to watch the man who watches the machine. The alertor consists of a small box connected to a large floor pad laced with wires. Any movement on the pad keeps the box content. But, should there be no movement from the operator during a suspicious interval of time, the alertor concludes he is either inattentive or napping, and sounds an alarm.

algebra, Boolean—*See* Boolean algebra.

algebraic expression—A statement expressed in various symbols, signs, and abbreviations following mathematical rules and syntax to designate variables, constants, functions, and rules.

algebraic language—*See* language, algebraic.

algebraic language, international—*See* language international algebraic.

ALGOL—1. ALGOrithmic Language. A data-processing language used to express problem-solving formulas for machine solution. 2. ALGebraic Oriented Language (some authors). The international procedural language. 3. An arithmetic language by which numerical procedures may be precisely presented to a computer in a standard form. The language is intended not only as a means of directly presenting any numerical procedure to any suitable computer for which a compiler exists, but also as a means of communicating numerical procedures among individuals. The language itself is a result of international cooperation to obtain a standardized algorithmic language. The International Algebraic Language is the forerunner of ALGOL.

algorithm—1. A fixed step-by-step procedure for accomplishing a given result; usually a simplified procedure for solving a complex problem, also a full statement of a finite number of steps. 2. A defined process or set of rules that leads and assures development of a desired output from a given input. A sequence of formulas and/or algebraic/logical steps to calculate or determine a given task; processing rules.

algorithm, convergence—An algorithm is said to converge if it is certain to yield its solu-

tion in a finite number of steps. It is a much stronger requirement than the mathematical convergence of the sequence of obtained function values.

algorithmic—Pertaining to a constructive calculating process usually assumed to lead to the solution of a problem in a finite number of steps.

algorithmic language—*Same as* ALGOL.

algorithmic routine — That specific routine which directs the computer in a program to solve a problem in a finite or specified number of steps, but not relying on a trial and error procedure. The solution and solution method are exact and must always reach the specific answer.

algorithm, scheduling—A set of rules that is included in the scheduling routine of the executive program. The scheduling algorithm determines the length of a user's quantum and the frequency with which this quantum is repeated.

algorithm translation—Various sets of rules, specific methods, or procedures used to obtain translations from one language to various others. Often this is done by the computer using computational methods to solve the algorithm.

alias—1. A label which is an alternate for something of the same nature type for which it is being used. Various primary or secondary names are used in computer slang such as red tape, GIGO, kludge, etc., which may be aliases for the basic or primary term. 2. Alternate entry point where program execution is allowed to begin.

A-light—A control panel light which monitors the A-register and signals parity check errors.

allocate—To assign storage locations to the main routines and subroutines, thereby fixing the absolute values of any symbolic address.

allocate storage—The assignment of specific storage areas for exact purposes, such as holding Input/Output data, constants, specific routines, scratchpad storage, stored routines, priority or executive instructions, housekeeping, or end programs.

allocation—The assignment of blocks of data to specified blocks of storage.

allocation and loading program—Relocatable binary elements produced by compilation are linked together for execution or for future use by an allocation program which is resident in the system at all times. An extensive selection of subroutines is directly available from the system library, enabling the allocator to incorporate them dynamically as the compiled elements are being constructed into a program. The relocatable element is the common-denominator output of processors, allowing applications to be programmed in several different languages, compiled, and properly linked at execution time (some systems).

allocation, dynamic core—A storage allocation procedure used in multi-programming for the more efficient utilization of core by shifting units of work from location to location within the core.

allocation, dynamic-storage — Each time a subroutine is called using this feature, the unique storage area for that subroutine is assigned to the first storage available. Thus, all subroutines called on the same level will share the same storage area. This results in a significant storage saving in many cases. In addition, a recursive subroutine call is possible because a new storage area is assigned each time a subroutine is entered. This feature, together with in-line symbolic coding, provides real-time capability.

allocation of hardware resources, time-sharing—See time sharing, allocation of hardware resources.

allocation, resource—A program which integrates the allocation of resources (men, machines, materials, money, and space) with scheduling, by time period, of project activities.

allocation storage—The process of reserving blocks of storage to specified blocks of information.

allocator—The allocator does most of the work of program construction. Embodied within the allocator is a set of selection rules that allows it to choose the proper elements to be included in the program. By submitting the name of the main or controlling part of a program to the allocator on an execute (XQT) card, the complete program, including subroutines, system interfaces and communication linkages will be produced automatically. The allocator will also apply relocatable patches to any elements to be included in the program. (UNIVAC)

allocator, dynamic—The dynamic allocator is responsible for taking runs set up by the coarse scheduler and allotting storage space according to the needs of the individual tasks of a run. Each run may be thought of as being made up of tasks, where a task is defined to be a single operation of a system processor or the execution of a user program. All tasks for a given run will be processed serially; however, tasks of separate runs will be interleaved.

When time-sharing of central storage is appropriate, the dynamic allocator is also responsible for initiating "storage swaps," i.e., the writing-out of one program to drum, and replacing it temporarily in central storage with another program. Such action is taken only to provide reasonable response time to remote demand-processing terminals.

The CPU dispatching routine is a third level of scheduling which selects among the various tasks currently occupying storage whenever it is appropriate to switch the commitment of the CPU from one to another. Under normal circumstances, a batch program is allowed to use the CPU until it either becomes interlocked against some

event, or until some higher priority program is freed of all of its interlocks. (UNIVAC)

allocator, library—The allocator, when constructing a program, searches the table of contents of the program complex file for elements needed to complete a program. If all the elements are not in the program complex file, the allocator will then search the table of contents of the system library in exactly the same manner. Each installation may build up one or more system libraries, tailored for specific needs, in the same way a programmer builds a program complex file. A routine called LIBRY transcribes a library to the system library area on drum. (UNIVAC)

allotting—A process of selection in which the objects are given assignments before the actual selecting procedure is initiated.

all-purpose computer—A computer combining the specific talents heretofore assigned solely to a general-purpose or special-purpose computer (scientific or business).

alpha—The first letter of the Greek alphabet, and thus, a symbol representing first. 2. An abbreviation for Alphanumeric. 3. A feature of representation of data in alphabetical characteris in contrast to numerical.

alphabet—A specific kind of character set excluding numerals, i.e., the character set most frequently used in a natural language. (Clarified by character set.)

alphabetic—Using only letters of the alphabet and the special characters of period, comma, asterisk, and others.

alphabetic addressing — The procedure for using alphabetic or alphanumeric labels to specify various storage locations for particular programs; i.e., before program execution the alphabetic address is converted to an absolute address.

alphabetic code—A system of alphabetic abbreviations used in preparing information for input to a machine; e.g., Boston, New York, Philadelphia, and Washington may in alphabetical coding be reported as BS, NY, PH, WA. (Contrasted with numeric code.)

alphabetic-numeric—The characters that include letters of the alphabet, numerals, and other symbols, such as punctuation or mathematical symbols.

alphabetic string—A string or group of characters all of which are letters. A string is a one dimensional array of characters, letters, etc., ordered by references to the relations between adjacent numbers.

alphabetic word—A specific word entirely of characters of an alphabet or special signs and symbols.

alphameric—A contraction of alphanumeric and alphabetic-numeric.

alphameric characters—A generic term for numeric digits, alphabetic characters, and special characters.

alphanumeric — A contraction of alphabetic-numeric.

alphanumerical — A coding system capable of representing alphabetical characters and other symbols as well as numbers.

alphanumeric character set—Special character set of letters and digits and other special characters including especially punctuation marks.

alphameric code — *Same as* code, alphanumeric.

alphanumeric instruction — The name given to instructions that can be used equally well with alphabetic or numeric kinds of data.

ALPS—Advanced Linear Programming System. An advanced Honeywell operations research technique that can be used to maximize the efficiency of any real world problem capable of being expressed as a set of linear equations. For example, ALPS can be used to maximize profit in a manufacturing plant by determining the scheduling of men, machines, and materials that achieves maximum use of these resources. Applications include sales forecasting, materials blending, advertising, transportation and other multi-factor problems.

alteration switch—A switch on the console of a computer which may be set to ON or OFF. Statements may be included in a program to test the condition of these switches and to vary program execution based on these settings.

altering—An operation for inserting, deleting, or changing information.

altering errors—Internal, machine-generated errors resulting from incorrect data transfer within the machine.

alter mode—A program condition which permits changing or updating data in storage.

alternate optima—Distinct solutions to the same optimization problem.

alternate routine—Assignment of a secondary communications path to a destination if the primary path is unavailable.

alternate routing — A communications term relating to the assignment of other communications paths to a particular destination if the primary path has become unavailable.

alternation—A technique which uses two or more input/output units in an attempt to speed up input and output operations. Examples might be: two to four card readers which serve the same control or input buffer, accepting data from each reader in sequence. Double feed hoppers and duo reading stations are examples of this type of alternation which is designed for increased reading volume.

alternation gate—*Same as* gate, OR.

alternation, tape—A selection, usually controlled automatically by a program, of first one tape unit and then another, normally during input or output operations, which permits successive reels of a file to be mounted and removed without interrupting the program.

alternative denial gate — *Same as* gate, NAND.

ALTRAN—A language for symbolic algebraic manipulation in FORTRAN, by Bell Laboratories.

ALU—Arithmetic and Logical Unit—The portion of the hardware of a computer in which arithmetic and logical operations are performed. The arithmetic unit generally consists of an accumulator, some special registers for the storage of operands and results, supplemented by shifting and sequencing circuitry for implementing multiplication, division, and other desired operations.

ambiguity—Having more than one meaning or interpretation. In computer processing, ambiguity is often the result of changes of state in various systems.

ambiguity error—A gross error, usually transient, occurring in the reading of digits of numbers and imprecise synchronism which causes changes in different digit positions, such as in analog-to-digital conversion. Guard signals can aid in avoiding such errors.

AMBIT—A programming language for algebraic symbol manipulation.

Amble's method—An analog computer term relating to a connection devised by O. Amble, such that the output of an integrator contributes through an adder to its own input to solve differential equations of a specific form.

American National Standards Institute—The name of the organization which compiles and publishes standards in the U.S.

amplifier—An unidirectional device which is capable of putting out an enlargement of the waveform of the electric current, voltage, or power that is supplied to the input.

amplifier, buffer — An amplifier designed to isolate a preceding circuit from the effects of a following circuit.

amplifier, computing — This amplifier combines functions of amplification and performance of operations. Computing amplifiers are often summing amplifiers, *analog* adders, or sign reversing amplifiers.

amplifier, differential — This amplifier has two signal-input channels and one signal output channel, which has characteristics such as instantaneous output signals which are directly proportional to the difference between the instantaneous values of the input signals.

amplifier, differentiating — An amplifier infrequently used in analog computers whose output voltage is proportional to the derivative of the input voltage with respect to time.

amplifier, direct-coupled—*Same as* amplifier, direct-current.

amplifier, direct-current — A specific analog computer amplifier which uses resistors for coupling signals in and out of the active elements; i.e., a vacuum tube or transistor. It is then capable of amplifying input signal currents despite how slowly the input signals might vary in time.

amplifier, drift-corrected—A specific "direct-coupled" analog computer amplifier which reduces or stops drift; i.e., the output voltage does not change in value without a corresponding change in input signal voltage.

amplifier, operational — *Same as* amplifier, computing.

amplifier, see-saw—*Same as* amplifier, sign-reversing.

amplifier, sign-reversing—A specific analog computer amplifier which has output voltage equal to the input voltage but opposite in sign.

amplifier, valve control—Some systems have integrating amplifiers which accept analog signals from time-sharing valve output modules, provide memory and conditioning for the signal, and generate control output signals.

amplitude, pulse—The maximum instantaneous value of a pulse.

A/M station (automatic/manual operator station)—In a process control, a device which is designed to enable the process operator to manually position one or more valves. A single-loop station enables manual positioning of a single valve, a shared station enables control of multiple valves, and a cascade station provides control of paired loops.

AMTRAN—Abbreviation for automatic mathematical translation.

AMVER—Data from the crafts of 55 nations are forwarded to a computer located in New York City. With this information, AMVER personnel (Atlantic Merchant Vessel Report) keep track of ships and airplanes that cross the Atlantic. When a craft is in distress, the system is activated. The SOS signal is picked up, its location fed into the computer, and almost instantly the machine indicates the ships traveling the Atlantic that are near enough to effect rescue operations.

analog—The representation of numerical quantities by means of physical variables; e.g., translation, rotation, voltage, or resistance. (Contrasted with digital.)

analog adder—Also known as a summer in analog representation; a unit with two or more input variables and one output variable which is equal to the sum, or a specific weighted sum, of the input variables.

analog assignment of variables—Consists of deciding which quantities on the computer will represent which variables in the problem. The user must know the mathematical laws controlling the variables in the problem as well as the laws controlling the currents, voltages, and reactances in the computer. He then matches those quantities which are analogous to each other; that is, quantities which obey the same mathematical laws. For example, water pressure can be analogous to voltage, while water flow can be analogous to current.

analog back-up—A designed alternate method of process control most often used by conventional analog instruments in the event of a failure in the computer system.

analog channel—A channel on which the information transmitted can take any value between the defined limits of the channel.

analog comparator—Performs range checking on digital values developed by the ADC (analog-to-digital converter). The high and low limits are selectively obtained from the processor-controller (P-C) for those values to be checked. When values are determined to be out-of-limit, then an interrupt informs the P-C. Only one P-C cycle is required for each value to be limit checked. (IBM)

analog computer—*See* computer analog.

analog data—*See* data, analog.

analog device—A mechanism that represents numbers by physical quantities; e.g., by lengths, as in a slide rule, or by voltage currents, as in a differential analyzer or a computer of the analog type.

analog-digital-analog converter system — This system performs fast, real-time data conversion between digital and analog computers. Maximum sample rate for D/A conversion is 200kc; for A/D and interlaced conversions, 100kc. Digital word length is 10 bits. Actual conversion times are 5 microseconds for A/D and 2 microseconds for D/A. Semiautomatic features enable the converter system to perform many of the functions that a computer normally performs for other converter interfaces (some computers).

analog divider—A unit with two input variables and one output variable which is proportional to the quotient of the input variables, provided that all the variables are within the operating range of the unit. An analog multiplier unit can be used in the feedback path of an operational amplifier to perform division. These two units combined become an analog divider.

analog input—Units feature modular packaged equipment used to convert voltage or current signals into digital values. The modules used to accomplish the conversions include analog-to-digital converters, multiplexors, amplifiers, and other signal conditioning equipment.

analog input expander—This unit allows a complete analog input system to be configured around the data-adapter unit.

analog input module—In some systems, devices which convert analog input signals from process instrumentation into a digit code for transmission to the computer.

analog input operation—Various modes are available for the selection of analog input points, conversion of the selected analog signal to a digital value, and then the transfer of the digital value to the processor-controller (P-C).

There are three basic modes for the input of analog data: (1) programmed, (2) chained sequential, and (3) random. Essentially the programmed mode requires the execution of at least one XI/O (executive input/output) instruction for each value that is read into the P-C. The chained sequential mode uses one data channel and allows any number of groups of sequentially addressed values to be read into the P-C with the execution of one instruction (XI/O). Sequentially addressed values are those which are developed from multiplexor addresses in sequence (some systems).

analog multiplexer/R—A relay multiplexer to provide low-level differential switching of analog input signals to allow use of a common amplifier and analog-to-digital converter. High-level signals can also be handled. Up to 100,000 points-per-second switching rate can be attained, with a maximum 50,000 point-per-second repetition rate (per point).

analog multiplexer/S (HLSE)—A solid-state, high-level single-ended (HLSE) multiplexer to provide high-speed switching of analog input signals to allow use of a common analog-to-digital converter. Switching rates up to 100,000 points-per-second are possible.

analog multiplier—A unit which generates analog products from two or more input signals. The output variable is proportional to the product of the input variables.

analog network—A circuit or circuits that represent(s) physical variables in such a manner as to permit the expression and solution of mathematical relationships between the variables, or to permit the solution directly by electric or electronic means.

analog processor-controller (P-C)—The processor-controller (P-C) can be used for editing, supervisory control, direct control, or data analysis. A control and data path provides for the attachment of the system where more powerful supervision is required. For example, the system may be used to integrate the commercial aspects of an application with the controlling operations exercised by an analog computer. Some multiprocessor system capabilities enable the handling of real-time applications of any size or complexity.

analog representation—A representation that does not have discrete values but is continuously variable.

analog-to-digital conversion—The conversion of analog signals from a voltage level to digital information is accomplished by an analog-to-digital converter (ADC). Such converters, however, are complex enough so that if multiple sources of analog signals are to be converted, they share the use of one ADC. The switching is accomplished by a multiplexer. The data path from sensor or transducer to processor is shown in various diagrams.

analog-to-digital converter—A device that changes physical motion or electrical voltage into digital factors; e.g., turns of a shaft into a number input.

analog-to-digital programmed control—Using the programmed control mode of operation, two execute input/output (XIO) instructions are used. The first XIO instruction (write) addresses the multiplexer and selects the analog input point which is to be converted. Upon completion of multiplexing, an internal signal is sent to the ADC (analog-to-digital converter) to start the point conversion. When the ADC has completed the conversion, an interrupt signal is sent from the ADC to the P-C (processor-controller). The P-C initiates a subroutine to determine the cause of interrupt, if necessary, and provides the second XIO instruction (read) to transfer the data to storage. This mode of converting data from analog signal to digital value in storage is a discrete addressing method; that is, two instructions result in the acquisition of data from one input point (some computers).

analog to digital sensing—Physical measurements must be monitored and quantified with greater speed and accuracy than ever before. The collection of analog data and its conversion for presentation to the digital processor-controller is the function of the analog input features.

A physical phenomenon is first sensed and converted to an analog electrical signal by sensors or transducers, such as thermocouples or strain gauges. Electrical signals from sensors or transducers may be in the millivolt, volt, or milliampere range. Low voltage signals (less than 1 volt) must be amplified to a level acceptable for conversion to digital form. All customer lines from transducers are terminated at the control system on screw-down terminals. The signals are also conditioned at the terminals, including the filtering of extraneous signals, known as noise (some computers).

analysis—The methodological investigation of a problem by a consistent procedure, and its separation into related units for further detailed study.

analysis area—An area of core into which data required to monitor or debug programs are written. A log of interrupts, program identifications, or macro trace data are written in the analysis area.

analysis block—A relocatable part of the computer storage in which program testing or statistical data are stored which can later be utilized to analyze the performance of the system. During program testing there may be an analysis block for each transaction in the system, and when the transaction leaves the system this block is dumped into a file or tape.

analysis, contour—*See* contour analysis.

analysis, file—The examination, study, and resolution of file characteristics to determine similarities, number and type of redundancies, and to check labeling and listing of documents which affect data elements contained in files.

analysis, hybrid problem—Programs in the problem analysis group help the hybrid programmer decide which parts of the problem to solve on a digital computer and the mathematic techniques that should be used. For example, multivariable function generation that may be difficult to perform on the analog computer is well-suited to digital solution.

analysis, logic—The delineation or determination of the specific steps required to produce the desired computer output or derive the intelligence information from the given or ascertained input data or model. Such logic studies are completed for many computer processes, programs, or runs.

analysis mode — A mode of operation in which special programs monitor the performance of the system for subsequent analysis. Program testing data or statistical data may be automatically recording when the system is running in the analysis mode.

analysis, numerical—The study of methods of obtaining useful quantitative solutions to mathematical problems, regardless of whether an analytic solution exists or not, and the study of the errors and bounds on errors in obtaining such solutions.

analysis, operations — The use of scientific method procedures to solve operational problems. Management thus uses quantitative bases for developing optimal decisions and predictions. Some of these procedures are: linear programming, probability information, game theory, PERT, queuing, and statistical theory.

analysis, procedure—The analysis of a business activity to determine precisely what must be accomplished, and how it is to be accomplished.

analysis, statistical—One of the four main techniques of operations research. Data gathering, arranging, sorting, sequencing, and evaluating are all common statistical analysis. Three other techniques are linear programming, queuing theory, and simulation. Statistical analysis combines mathematical techniques and computer technology to handle a wide range of business and scientific problems wherever large amounts of information or data must be evaluated and analyzed.

analysis, systems—The examination of an activity, procedure, method, technique, or a business to determine what must be accomplished and how the necessary operations may best be accomplished.

analyst — An individual who is skilled and trained to define problems and to analyze, develop, and express algorithms for their solution, especially algorithms that may be resolved and implemented by a computer.

analyst, business programmer — Employees who investigate and analyze business systems within the company for possible adaptation to electronic data processing and develop the computer programs and associated documentation necessary to implement such systems.

analyst, lead systems—Usually considered as the assistant manager of systems analysis, or has full technical knowledge of the activity comparable to a senior but also has supervisory duties of instructing, directing, and checking the work of other system analysts, including the senior systems analysts.

analyst, methods—Designs systems and supervises their implementation. He also plans, controls, and coordinates conversion to new systems.

analyst, procedure—Develops improved clerical and manual office procedures.

analyst, programmer—Has capability in programming as well as analysis of problems, systems, and specific specialities as desired.

analyst, research—Investigates and reviews operations and identifies those suitable for data processing.

analyst, systems—A person who designs information-handling procedures which incorporate computer processing. The systems analyst is usually highly skilled in defining problems and developing algorithms for their solution.

analytic aid to research, time sharing — See time sharing, analytic aid to research.

analytical engine—The name Charles Babbage gave to one of his primitive computer devices. Conceived in 1833, the analytical engine was the first general-purpose automatic digital computer. It embodied all the fundamental principles of the modern digital computer. It was theoretically capable of executing any mathematical operation; it stored sequences of instructions in memory, and it was to use punched cards modeled after those used in the Jacquard loom as mass memory for storage of mathematical tables. Babbage's concept of the analytical engine is one of the truly great intellectual achievements of all time.

analytical function generator—See generator, analytical function.

analytic relationship—The relationship which exists between concepts and corresponding terms, by virtue of their definition and inherent scope of meaning.

analyzer—A computer routine whose purpose is to analyze a program written for the same or a different computer. This analysis may consist of summarizing instruction references to storage and tracing sequences of jumps.

analyzer, differential—A computer (usually analog) designed and used primarily for solving many types of differential equations.

analyzer, digital differential — 1. A specific device that resolves differential equations in digital data form and is constructed with the differential analyzer. 2. In some incremental computers (computing the changes *in* variables rather than *of* variables) the principal type of computing unit is a digital integrator which is similar in operation to an integrating unit or mechanism, and especially in England, integrators have been called differential analyzers which begets the term digital differential analyzer.

analyzer, electronic differential—Electronic circuitry is used in this differential analyzer, usually an analog computer, to solve differential equations, i.e., integration or summation and differentiation (differencing). Electronic analogs of the mechanical parts are used to distinguish this from the mechanical analyzer.

analyzer, mechanical-differential—A form of analog computer using inter-connected mechanical surfaces to solve differential equations; e.g., the Bush differential analyzer developed by Vannevar Bush at M.I.T. which used differential gear boxes to perform additions, and a combination of wheel-disk spherical mechanisms to perform integration.

analyzer, network—An analog device designed primarily for simulating electrical networks. (Synonymous with network calculator.)

analyzer, program—See analyzer.

analyzer, routine—See analyzer.

analyzer, subroutine—Same as analyzer.

ancillary equipment — Same as equipment, peripheral.

AND—1. The Boolean operator that gives a truth table value of true only when both of the variables connected by the logical operator are true. 2. A logical operator that has the property that if P is a statement and Q is a statement, then P AND Q are true if both statements are true, false if either is false or both are false. Truth is normally expressed by the value 1, falsity by O. The AND operator is often represented by a centered dot (P·Q), by no sign (PQ), by an invered "u" or logical product symbol (P∩Q), or by the letter "X" or multiplication symbol (P×Q). Note that the letters AND are capitalized to differentiate between the logical operator and the word *and* in common usage. 3. The logical operation which makes use of the AND operator or logical product.

AND circuit—Same as gate, AND.

AND gate—See gate AND.

AND gate, positive—Same as gate, AND.

AND-NOT gate—Same as gate, A AND-NOT B or B AND-NOT A gate.

AND operator—1. A logical operator that has the property that if P is a statement and Q is a statement, then P AND Q are true if both statements are true, false if either is false or both are false. Truth is normally expressed by the value 1, falsity by 0. The AND operator is often represented by a centered dot (P·Q), by no sign (PQ), by an inverted "u" or logical product symbol (P∩Q), or by the letter "X" or multiplication symbol (P×Q). Note that the letters AND are capitalized to differentiate between the logical operator and the word *and* in common usage. 2. The logical operation that makes use of the AND operator or logical product.

AND unit—Same as gate, AND.

anglicize—Usually means to translate from programming language to English phrases; i.e., to state the precise meaning of various coded statements in exact and understandable language.

annex memory—Small memory unit used as a go-between for the input and output units and the main memory. Better known as a buffer.

annex storage—Same as associative, storage.

annotate—To include explanations or descriptions as remarks to portions of programs. Information or data to clarify relations, significance, or priorities.

annotation—The added descriptive comments or explanatory notes.

answer, inquiry (remote)—See inquiry answer (remote).

anticipated carry adder—See adder, anticipated carry.

anticipation mode—A visual means of represent binary information. One binary digit is represented by a line, and the binary digit in the opposite state is represented by the absence of a line.

anticoincidence gate—Same as gate, exclusive OR.

anti-setoff powder—See powder, anti-setoff.

any-sequence queue—A collection of items in the system which are waiting for the attention of the processor. The any-sequence queue is organized so that items may be removed from the collection without regard to the sequence in which they entered it.

A OR-NOT B gate—See gate, A OR-NOT B.

AOSP (Automatic Operating and Scheduling Program)—The AOSP assigns memory locations eliminating the need for the human programmer to keep track of instruction or data locations in the memory. In the computer field, wide use is made of programming systems, maintenance systems, debugging aids, confidence checking, and diagnostic routines. These are often separate systems, and the burden of integrating them falls on a program-scheduling department in the user's organization. The scheduling of all service programs is included within the AOSP of Burroughs' systems.

aperture—The opening or port in a card or mask for allowing passage or viewing of portions of information.

aperture card—A card designed to hold microfilm image film. The card is designed to also accept punched information that is helpful in sorting and data retrieval.

APL/360 (A Programming Language on the 360)—An on-line version of a subset of Iverson's language on IBM 360 systems.

application—The system or problem to which a computer is applied. Reference is often made to an application as being either of the computational type, wherein arithmetic computations predominate, or of the data-processing type, wherein data-handling operations predominate.

application, computer—*See* computer operation.

application criterion, computer—The test or rule of thumb used to define a computer in the business and applications areas, and distinguish between computers and sophisticated calculators. Under the computer application criterion, a computer may be defined as a general-purpose, internally programmed machine which can do business as well as scientific jobs, including such applications as payroll, billing, and other processing.

application, inquiry—*See* inquiry application.

application package—A series of interrelated routines and subroutines designed to perform a specific task.

application programmer—*See* programming, application.

application, real time—*See* real-time application.

application, scientific—*Same as* computer, scientific.

application, slave—A fail-safe or backup system (application) whereby a slave or second computer performs the same steps of the same programs so that if the master computer fails or malfunctions, the slave computer continues without a deterioration of operations. Various space or urgent real-time applications require this double-precision or double safety feature.

applications, processor-controller—See processor-controller applications.

applications, programming — *See* programming applications.

applications programs — Mathematical routines, including sine, cosine, tangent, arc sine, square root, natural logarithms, and exponential functions.

application, standby — An application in which two or more computers are tied together as a part of a single over-all system, and which, as in the case of an inquiry application, stand ready for immediate activation and appropriate action.

applications study—1. The development of the design and sequence of an integrated or specific system relating and ordering processes and equipment to perform individual and integrated data processing. 2. The detailed process of determining a system or set of procedures for using a computer for definite functions or operations, and establishing specifications to be used as a base for the selection of equipment suitable to the specific needs.

approach, brute-force—To try to undertake with existing equipment the mass of problems that do not use precise computations or logical manipulation (as accounting problems and scientific problems do).

approach, heuristic—An approach that encourages further experimentation and investigation. An intuitive trial-and-error method of attacking a problem as opposed to the algorithmic method.

approach, systems—A systems approach pertains to looking at the over-all situation rather than the narrow implications of the task at hand, particularly looking for inter-relationships between the task at hand and other functions which relate to it.

APT (Automatically Programmed Tools)—APT can cut only straight lines; however, its use is not restricted. These straight lines may be as short as $\frac{1}{1000}$ of an inch. Therefore, any conceivable shape can be cut. But the machine has to be told by the computer to cut each of these tiny segments, demonstrating the tediousness of the programming of the operation of the tool. But once this is accomplished, there can be endless repetition of the procedure with no added instruction, or the tape can be stored for later use. The great step forward that APT has made is to perform work better than can be done with a human operator. APT has made possible a production run of one—as opposed to thousands or millions of items.

APT III—APT is a system for the computer-assisted programming of numerically controlled machine tools, flame cutters, drafting machines, and similar equipment. It is production-oriented, that is, it was written to simplify the effort, time and money needed to take full advantage of numerically controlled techniques in engineering and manufacturing. In addition to providing machine-tool programming capabilities virtually impossible by manual methods, APT enhances most of the usual advantages found in numerical control: reduced lead time; greater design freedom and flexibility; lower direct costs; greater accuracy; improved production forecasting; lower tooling costs; better engineering control of the manufacturing process; and simplified introduction of changes. The APT III program represents over one hundred man years of development and testing.

arbitrary access—Equal access time to all memory locations, independent of the location of the previous memory reference. *See* random access.

arbitrary-function generator — *See* generator arbitrary function.

arbitrary sequence computer—A specific type of sequential or consecutive computer (having capability of performing and storing parts or sequences of problems or computations) in which the sequence of execution of computer instructions is not part of the logic design of the computer. Each instruction determines the location of the next instruction to be executed.

area, analysis—*See* analysis area.

area, clear—*Same as* band, clear.

area, common-storage — FORTRAN programs and other programs may specify that data storage is to occupy a common area. This allows programs to share temporary storage, and FORTRAN-coded programs may communicate with hand-coded routines by using a common data storage. The system loader automatically allocates common area when it is loading programs. Common storage occupies the same memory space during execution as the system loader does when loading programs. This allows effective utilization of memory storage since the space taken up by the loader can be used by the programs during execution.

area, constant—A part of storage designated to store the invariable quantities required for processing.

area, fixed—The area on a disk where data files or image programs may be stored and protected.

area, fixed-product—*See* fixed product area.

area, input—A section of internal storage of a computer reserved for the receiving and processing of input information.

area, input/output—*Same as* storage, working.

area, instruction—1. A part of storage allocated to receive and store the group of instructions to be executed. 2. The storage locations used to store the program.

area, output—A section of internal storage reserved for storing data which are to be transferred out of the computer.

area search—The examination of a large group of documents to select those that pertain to one group, such as one category, class, etc.

areas in storage—The assignment of characters, fields, or words in processor storage in order to complete program editing, printing, read-in, punching, constants, write-out, and other procedures.

areas, overflow file—*See* overflow areas, file.

area, storage—*See* storage area.

area, working—*See* storage working.

a-register—*See* register, arithmetic.

argument—1. The known reference factor necessary to find the desired item (function) in a table. 2. A variable upon whose value the value of a function depends. The arguments of a function are listed in parentheses after the function name, whenever that function is used. The computations specified by the function definiton occur using the variables specified as arguments.

ARGUS—Automatic Routine Generating and Updating System. This is an integrated automatic programming system for the Honeywell computers which include a symbolic assembly language, an assembly program, automatic inclusion of library tapes and routines, file maintenance of a library of unchecked programs, a checkout system, and a produuction scheduling and operating system.

arithmetic address—Specific locations which are used for the results of computations.

arithmetical operation—An operation completed according to arithmetical rules, i.e., the operands are the addend and augend, the result is the sum.

arithmetic check—A verification of arithmetic computation; e.g., multiplying 4 by 2 to check against the product obtained by multiplying 2 by 4.

arithmetic expression—An expression containing any combination of data-names, numeric literals, and named constants, joined by one or more arithmetic operators in such a way that the expression as a whole can be reduced to a single numeric value.

arithmetic, external—Operations performed outside of the computer itself as by peripheral or ancillary units but which may or may not become part of the total problem or program on interrupt basis.

arithmetic, fixed-point—1. A method of calculation in which operators take place in an invariant manner, and in which the computer does not consider the location of the radix point. This is illustrated by desk calculators or slide rules, with which the operator must keep track of the decimal point. Similarly with many automatic computers, in which the location of the radix point is the programmer's responsibility. (Contrasted with floating-point arithmetic.) 2. A type of arithmetic in which the operands and results of all arithmetic operations must be properly scaled so as to have a magnitude between certain fixed values.

arithmetic, fixed-point double word-length—Many arithmetic instructions produce two word results. With fixed-point multiplication, a double-length product is stored in two A registers of control storage for integer and fractional operations. Integer and fractional division is performed upon a double-length dividend, with the remainder and the quotient retained in the A registers.

arithmetic, floating-decimal—A method of calculation which automatically accounts for the location of the radix point. This is usually accomplished by handling the number as a signed mantissa times the radix raised to an integral exponent; e.g., the decimal number $+88.3$ might be written as $+.883 \times 10^2$; the binary number $-.0011$ as $-.11 \times 2^{-2}$. (Contrasted with fixed-point arithmetic, definition 1.)

arithmetic, floating point operation—*See* floating point arithmetic operation.

arithmetic instruction—The operator part of this instruction specifies an arithmetic operation; add, subtract, multiply, divide, powers, or square-root. Not a logical operation such as logic sum, logic multiply, or compare.

arithmetic, internal—The computations performed by the arithmetic unit of a computer.

arithmetic, multiple—A procedure for performing arithmetic on a digital computer in which several parts of one or more numbers are used in arithmetic operations which yield several results.

arithmetic, multiprecision—A form of arithmetic similar to double precision arithmetic except that two or more words may be used to represent each number.

arithmetic operation—Any of the fundamental operations of arithmetic; e.g., the binary operations of addition, subtraction, multiplication and division, and the binary operations of negation and absolute value.

arithmetic operation, binary — Digital computer operations such as add and subtract performed with operands with output results in binary notation.

arithmetic organ — *Same as* arithmetic unit.

arithmetic, parallel — A process in which simultaneous operations are performed on all digits of a number and in which partial sums and numbers are formed or shifted.

arithmetic partial—*See* arithmetic, multiple.

arithmetic point—The point is a true character in positional notation and can be expressed or implied. It separates the integral part of the number or expression from the fractional part using a decimal or binary point. The position of the point is programmed in the logic section of the computer usually falling between the zero and the minus-one power of the base and/or is implied to be at the right end of the integer. Same as base point or radix point.

arithmetic product—A result developed as two numbers are multipled as in decimal notation, $6 \times 10 = 60$. In data processing, the product is the result of performing the logic AND operation.

arithmetic register—*See* register, arithmetic.

arithmetic section—The portion of the hardware of a computer in which arithmetic and logical operations are performed. The arithmetic unit generally consists of an accumulator, some special registers for the storage of operands and results supplemented by shifting and sequencing circuitry for implementing multiplication, division, and other desired operations. (Synonymous with ALU.)

arithmetic, serial — This is an operation in which each number is divided into digits to be operated upon singly usually in the adder-subtracter or a comparator. The same number of addition operations are required as there are binary digits in the operands; a simpler and slower operation than parallel arithmetic.

arithmetic shift—1. A shift of digits to the left or right within a fixed framework in order to multiply or divide by a power of the given number base equivalent to the number of positions shifted. 2. To multiply or divide a quantity by a power of the number base; e.g., if binary 1101, which represents decimal 13, is arithmetically shifted twice to the left, the result is 110100, which represents 52, which is also obtained by multiplying 13 by 2 twice; on the other hand, if the decimal 13 were to be shifted to the left twice, the result would be the same as multiplying by 10 twice, or 1300. (Related to shift, and cyclic shift.)

arithmetic, signed-magnitude—Some systems use signed-magnitude computers; that is, all the arithmetic operations are accomplished by the process of addition and subtraction of magnitudes. Since multiplication and division can be broken down into a series of additions and subtractions, respectively, the computer will perform these operations as well. Operations with signed-magnitude numbers are identical with algebraic addition using a pencil and paper.

arithmetic, significant digit — A particular arithmetic system which uses a modified form of floating-point representation in which representation is standardized fully, partly, or not at all depending on the accuracy of the operands, the degree of precision, and the number of significant digits at any stage of the calculation.

arithmetic statement—A type of FORTRAN statement that specifies a numerical computation.

arithmetic trap mask—The bit, in the program status doubleword, that indicates whether (if 1) or not (if 0) the fixed-point arithmetic trap is in effect.

arithmetic trap mask, decimal — The bit, in the program status doubleword, that indicates whether (if 1) or not (if 0) the decimal arithmetic trap is in effect.

arithmetic unit—The portion of the hardware of a computer in which arithmetic and logical operations are performed. The arithmetic unit generally consists of an accumulator, some special registers for the storage of operands and results, supplemented by shifting and sequencing circuitry for implementing multiplication, division, and other desired operations.

arithmetic units, fractional—Arithmetic units operated with the decimal point at the extreme left, thus all numbers having a value of less than one.

ARM (Automated Route Management)—This is a program which provides output of daily sales and production reports for dairies, bakeries, and other business operations with route distribution operations. (IBM)

arm, access—*See* access arm.

arm, disk (moving)—*See* disk, moving arm.

armed interrupt—*See* interrupt, armed.

ARQ — An automatic system which provides error correction by utilizing a constant ratio code and a closed loop to request retransmission of mutilated characters as indicated by receipt of nonconstant ratio characters.

array—A series of items arranged in a meaningful pattern.

array, closed—An array that can only be extended if the newly added elements do not alter the value of the entire array.

array, data—A representation of data in the form of signs or symbols recorded on tape, cards, etc.

array pitch—*See* pitch row.

ART-assembly system — The ART-assembly system accepts information written in an

English-language shorthand and produces a running (object) program complete with facility assignments. It provides for error detection, print-out, error correction, debugging, and edited hardcopy outputs. It also provides automatic library building, maintenance, and retrieval. ART includes the Univac-developed software concept "PROC" (Procedure) which is an advanced form of the variable MACRO concept.

artificial cognition—The optical sensing of a displayed character in which the machine or equipment selects from its memory the shape of the character that is closest to the character being displayed.

artificial intelligence—1. Research and study in methods for the development of a machine that can improve its own operations. The development or capability of a machine that can proceed or perform functions that are normally concerned with human intelligence as learning, adapting, reasoning, self-correction, automatic improvement. 2. The study of computer and related techniques to supplement the intellectual capabilities of man. As man has invented and used tools to increase his physical powers, he now is beginning to use artificial intelligence to increase his mental powers. In a more restricted sense, the study of techniques for more effective use of digital computers by improved programming techniques.

artificial language — A language specifically designed for ease of communication in a particular area of endeavor, but one that is not yet natural to that area. This is contrasted with a natural language which has evolved through long usage.

artificial perception—See artificial cognition.

ASA (American Standards Association)—Now changed to American National Standards Institute (ANSI). This is an association which developed American Standards for: optical character recognition, coded character sets, data transmission, programming languages, computer definitions, magnetic ink, character recognition, and others.

ASA code—An information-interchange seven-level code recently adopted as standard code by the American National Standards Institute.

ASA FORTRAN — Standardized FORTRAN specified by ANSI.

ascending sort—A sort in which the final sequence of records is such that successive keys compare greater than, less than, or equal to.

ASCII—American Standard Code for Information Interchange.

ASIS—Abbreviation for American Society for Information Science, formerly American Documentation Institute.

ASIST (Advanced Scientific Instruments Symbolic Translator)—ASI's Symbolic Translator, ASIST, is an assembly program that provides a powerful, flexible programming tool. ASIST features assembly control, pseudo-

operation, and macrostatements. (Advanced Scientific Instruments)

ASLIB—Abbreviation for Association of Special Libraries and Information Bureaus.

aspect card—A card on which is entered the accession numbers of documents in an information-retrieval system. Such cards often contain identity numbers of various documents or data elements and their relation to the problem or programmed concept. They are used for coordinate indexing, and accession numbers can be represented as holes or edge-punched cards.

aspect indexing—See indexing aspect.

ASPER (Assembly System for the PERipheral processors)—The ASPER programs are separated by control cards which represent information to the loader for use at execute time, cause the system to assign a peripheral processor, and cause the ASPER routine to be loaded. (Control Data Coorporation)

ASR—Automatic Send-Receive set. A combination teletypewriter, transmitter, and receiver with transmission capability from either keyboard or paper tape. Most often used in half-duplex circuit.

assemble—1. To prepare an object language program from a symbolic language program by substituting machine operation codes for symbolic operation codes and absolute or relocatable addresses for symbolic addresses. 2. To integrate subroutines (supplied, selected, or generated) into the main routine, by adapting or changing relative and symbolic addresses to absolute form or incorporating, or placing in storage.

assembler—A computer program that operates on symbolic input data to produce from such data, machine instructions by carrying out such functions as: translation of symbolic-operation codes into computer-operating instructions, assigning locations in storage for successive instructions, or computation of absolute addresses from symbolic addresses. An assembler generally translates input symbolic codes into machine instructions, item for item, and produces as an output the same number of instructions or constants that were defined in the input symbolic codes.

assembler directive commands — Assembler directive commands provide the programmer with the ability to generate data words and values based on specific conditions at assembly time. The instruction operation codes are assigned mnemonics which describe the hardware function of each instruction.

assembler directives — The symbolic assembler directives control or direct the assembly processor just as operation codes control or direct the central computer. These directives are represented by mnemonics.

assembler, macro—A two-pass assembler on some computers is available with subprogram, literal, and powerful macrofacilities. It resembles the standard SDS Meta-Symbol assembler. The output, which can be directly processed by the debugging program (DDT) provides symbol tables for effective program checkout in terms of the source language symbols (some systems).

assembler, macrofacilities—An assembler is available for use in the operating system in assembling object programs from source programs written in a flexible but easy-to-use symbolic language. The assembler language is a versatile machine-oriented language that can be used for a variety of applications, both commercial and scientific. A number of facilities for assisting the programmer are provided by the assembler. These include macrofacilities as well as facilities for defining constants, for defining data-storage areas, for referring to files and storage locations symbolically, and for using literals.

assembler, one-to-one — A straight forward translating program which generally produces only one instruction in the object language for each instruction in the source language.

assembler operators — *See* assembler program.

assembler program—The assembler is an assembly program for a symbolic-coding language. It is composed of simple, brief expressions that provide rapid translation from symbolic to machine-language relocatable-object coding for the computer. The assembly language includes a wide and sophisticated variety of operators which allows the fabrication of desired fields based on information generated at assembly time. The instruction-operation codes are assigned mnemonics which describe the hardware function of each instruction. Assembler-directive commands provide the programmer with the ability to generate data words and values based on specific conditions at assembly time.

assembler, symbolic—The symbolic assembler lets the programmer code instructions in a symbolic language. The assembler allows mnemomic symbols to be used for instruction codes and addresses. Constant and variable storage registers can be automatically assigned. The assembler produces a binary object tape and lists a symbol with memory allocations and useful diagnostic messages.

assembler, two-pass—An assembler which requires scanning of the source program twice. The first pass constructs a symbol table, and the second pass does the translation.

assembling—The process of composing or integrating instructions into subroutines or main routines for acceptance and use by computing units.

assembly—The translation of a source program written in a symbolic language into an object or target program in a machine language.

assembly control, IF statement—This feature allows for bypassing sections of an object program at assembly time under control of external indications, such as the sense switches.

assembly-control statements — These statements instruct the assembly program in the performance of a wide variety of functions related to creating an object program.

assembly language—1. A machine-oriented-language for programming, such as ARGUS or EASY, which belongs to an assembly program or system. 2. In writing instructions using the assembly language, the programmer is primarily concerned with three fields: a label field, an operation field, and an operand field. It is possible to relate the symbolic coding to its associated flowchart, if desired, by appending comments to each instruction line or program segment.

assembly language coding—*See* coding, assembly language.

assembly-language output—A symbolic assembly-language listing of the binary object program output of the compiler is optional at compile time. The listing contains the symbolic instructions equivalent to the binary code output from the compiler. This assembly-language output listing is useful as a debugging aid. By including certain pseudo-operations codes in in-line assembly language, the assembly-language output can be assembled by the assembler. This will allow modification of programs at the assembly-language level.

assembly language processor — A language processor that accepts words, statements, and phrases to produce machine instructions. It is more than an assembly program because it has compiler powers. The macroassembler permits segmentation of a large program so that positions may be tested separately. It also provides extensive program analysis to aid in debugging.

assembly line balancing—A specialized program allowing production control management to plan most efficient and profitable man-work element relationship in an assembly line operation.

assembly list—A printed list which is the by-product of an assembly procedure. It lists in logical-instruction sequence all details of a routine, showing the coded and symbolic notation next to the actual notations established by the assembly procedure. This listing is highly useful in the debugging of routines.

assembly print-wheel—*See* print-wheel assembly.

assembly program—*See* assembly routine.

assembly routine—1. A procedure that directs the conversion of a program which is written in relative or symbolic form into a machine-language program, most often on an instruction-by-instruction design. 2. A computer program that operates on symbolic input data to produce from such data machine instructions by carrying out such functions as: translation of symbolic-operation codes into computer-operating instructions; assigning locations in storage for successive instructions; or computation of absolute addresses from symbolic addresses. 3. An assembler generally translates input symbolic codes into machine instructions item for item, and produces as output the same number of instructions or constants which were defined in the input symbolic codes. (Synonymous with assembly program, and related to compiler.)

assembly, selective—A procedure which run tapes contain a specific program selected by the programmer from both an input deck of new programs and a tape file of previously processed symbolic programs.

assembly, symbolic—The first level of language described for a class of processor programs.

assembly system — 1. An automatic system (softwear) that includes a language and machine-language programs. Such supplementary programs perform such programming functions as checkout, updating, and others. 2. An assembly system comprises two elements, a symbolic language and an assembly program, that translate source programs written in the symbolic language into machine language.

assembly, system, symbolic—A program system developed in two parts; a symbolic-language program, and a computer program (processor). The processor translates a source program developed in symbolic language to a machine object program.

assembly testing—The testing of a group of functionally related programs to determine whether or not the group operates according to specifications. The programs may be related in that they have access to common data, occupy high-speed storage simultaneously, operate under common program control, or perform an integrated task.

assembly unit—1. A device that performs the function of associating and joining several parts or piecing together a program. 2. A portion of a program that is capable of being assembled into a larger whole program.

assertion—Relates to flow charting as a presumption or anticipation of a condition or some content concerning the data design, program, or processing.

assignment, facilities (Executive) — The assignment of memory and external facilities to meet the requirements which are defined symbolically in a job program selected for initiation. Executive maintains a list of all allocatable facilities which is updated to reflect release of facilities by programs during, or at termination of, a run.

assistant manager of data processing—Under general direction, assists the manager in planning, organizing, and controlling the various sections of the department. Usually has departmental line responsibility but, in certain instances, may only have departmental staff responsibility. Participates in research and procedural studies.

association indexing—A study following two approaches — the automatic generation of word association maps based on lists of words from the text, and representations based on the number of times words appear in the text.

associative memories—With associative-memory capability, high-speed memory searches within computers are based on content or subject matter rather than being limited to locating data through specified "addresses."

associative storage—A storage system or device such that storage locations are identified by their contents. Such systems are often considered synonymous with parallel search and content-addressed storage.

assumed decimal point—The point within a numeric item at which the decimal point is assumed to be located. When a numeric item is to be used within a computer, the location of the assumed decimal point is considered to be at the right, unless otherwise specified in the appropriate record description entry. It will not occupy an actual space in storage, but it will be used by the computer to align the value properly for calculation.

asterisk protection—The insertion of a series of asterisks on the left of the most significant digit. This scheme is commonly used in check protection systems.

asynchronous—1. Pertaining to a lack of time coincidence in a set of repeated events where this term is applied to a computer to indicate that the execution of one operation is dependent on a signal that the previous operation is completed. 2. A mode of computer operation in which performance of the next command is started by a signal that the previous command has been completed. Contrast with synchronous, characterized by a fixed time cycle for the execution of operations.

asynchronous computer — A computer in which the performance of each operation starts as a result of a signal either that the previous operation has been completed, or that the parts of the computer required for the next operation are now available. (Contrasted with synchronous computer.)

asynchronous-data transmission—In this type of data transmission, each character consists of information bits, 5, 6, 7, or 8 depending on the code structure, preceded by a start bit (zero condition) and followed by a stop bit (one condition). Each bit in a data character is of equal time duration, with the exception of the stop bit which may be one, one and one half, or two times as long as the other bits in the data character. An asynchronous input CLT recognizes the initial change of state from the one condition as the start of a data character. It then looks at the condition of the line facilities at time intervals corresponding to the middle of each of the following information bits in order to transfer a complete data-character into the assembly register (some systems).

asynchronous device—A unit which has an operating speed not related to any particular frequency of the system to which it is connected.

asynchronous machine—Machines which have operating speeds not related to any fixed or specific frequency of the system. Since no fixed period or interval signals the next event, it may begin at the end of a prior one, without regard to the time it might take.

asynchronous operation—The method of processing in which one operation is completed before the next operation is initiated.

asynchronous operator—See asynchronous.

asynchronous output (transmission)—Timing on asynchronous output-data transfers is not time critical. Since each output-data character is preceded by a start bit and followed by a stop bit, the time interval between characters will appear to the transmission facilities as nothing more than an extra-long stop bit. Although no information is lost if a data character is not transferred from the central processor to the asynchronous output CLT within the "character availability interval," a failure to do so will result in a reduced transmission rate (some systems).

asynchronous signalling—Codes used in signalling, in which characters provide their own start and stop indicators.

asynchronous working—See asychronous.

asyndetic—1. Omitting conjunctions or connectives. 2. Pertaining to a catalog without cross references.

atomic symbols—See symbols, atomic.

ATS—Abbreviation for administrative terminal system.

attached support processor (ASP)—The utilization of multiple computers, usually two, connected via channel-to-channel adaptors, to increase the efficiency in processing many short duration jobs.

attended operation—In data set applications, individuals are required at both stations to establish the connection and transfer the data sets from talk (voice) mode to data mode.

attention device—A device programmed to indicate a new display on a screen of lasting displays by some different shapes, sizes, or light intensity, or by making older displays smaller, dimmer, or of another shape.

attenuate—To reduce the amplitude of an action or signal.

attenuation—1. Fractional part or reduction of energy of an action or signal. Measurement may be made as units, decibels, or percentages. 2. The loss between delivered and received power due to transmission loss through equipment, lines or other devices.

audible alarm—See alarm, audible.

audio—Frequencies that can be heard by the human ear (usually 15 cycles to 20,000 cycles per second).

audio response—A form of output which uses verbal replies to inquiries. The computer can be programmed to seek answers to inquiries made on a time-shared on-line system and then to utilize a special audio response unit which elicits the appropriate pre-recorded response to the inquiry. Of course, inquiries must be of the nature for which the audio response has been prepared.

audio-response unit—1. A device that can link a computer system to a telephone network to provide voice responses to inquiries made from telephone-type terminals. The audio response is composed from a vocabulary prerecorded in a digitally coded voice on a disk storage device. 2. The audio response unit can be attached to various computer systems through their multiplexer channels. It links the processor with a telephone network to provide a recorded voice response to inquiries made from telephone-type terminals. The audio response is assembled from a vocabulary that is prerecorded in a digitally coded voice on a disk storage file connected to the computer. Inquiries to the unit are received as a series of digits either dialed or keyed from an ordinary telephone. The unit buffers each digit. Then these digits are transferred to the processor's core storage and assembled into a complete message. After processing the message, the computer assembles a digitally coded voice response which is transferred to the audio response unit. The unit converts it to actual voice signals and sends it to the inquiring party as an audio response. The unit has two basic input/output lines, but it can be expanded to eight lines or more.

audit—The operations developed to corroborate the evidence as regards authenticity and validity of the data that are introduced into the data-processing problem or system.

audit-in-depth—Detailed examination of all manipulations performed on a single transaction or piece of information.

auditing—Source data, methodology, and report conclusions and sums are checked for accuracy and validity as well as credibility in the auditing process through the use of studied techniques and information sources.

audit program—A program designed to enable use of the computer as an auditing tool.

audit trail—1. The trail or path left by a transaction when it is processed. The trail begins with the original documents, transactions entries, posting of records and is complete with the report. Validity tests of records are achieved by this method. 2. An audit trail must be incorporated into every procedure; provision for it should be made early so that it becomes an integral part. In creating an audit trail it is necessary to provide: (A) Transaction documentation which is detailed enough to permit the association of any one record with its original source document. (B) A system of accounting controls which provides that all transactions have been processed and that accounting records are in balance. (C) Documentation from which any transaction can be recreated and its processing continued, should that transaction be misplaced or destroyed at some point in the procedure.

augend—The number or quantity to which another number or quantity (addend) is added to produce the result (sum).

augment—To increase a quantity in order to bring it to its full value.

augmenter—The quantity added to another to bring it to its full value. An augmenter is usually positive; however, when "added," a negative quantity is also called an augmenter.

autoabstract—1. A collection of words selected from a document, arranged in a meaningful order, commonly by an automatic or machine method. 2. Preparation of abstracts from larger bodies of information are often completed by the use of programs which select key words as key word in context (KWIC) indexes which are then printed out with titles or the articles or reports.

autocode—Use of the computer itself to develop the machine-coded program from macro codes; i.e., the conversion of symbolic codes for operations and addresses. Mnemacrocodes; i.e., the conversion of symbolic simplify programs for more efficient use by the computer and programmer.

autocoder—An IBM programming language.

AUTOCOMM (Business System)—Designed for commercial data-processing problems, AUTOCOMM provides a method of quick and easy translation of business problems into solutions. It includes all input/output, move, compare, and edit routines. In addition, AUTOCOMM is decimally oriented and uses powerful instructions to minimize programming time. (Control Data Corporation)

auto-man—A type of locking switch which indicates and controls methods of operation, such as automatic or manual.

automata theory—The development of theory which relates the study of principles of operations and applications of automatic devices to various behaviorist concepts and theories.

automated data medium—*Same as* data, machine readable.

automated question answering, time sharing — *See* time sharing, automated question answering.

Automath—A Honeywell scientific computer program that translates mathematical notation into machine instructions. The Automath 800 will accept FORTRAN II language as will Automath 400 and 1400. Automath 1800 (which also runs on large H-800 systems) accepts FORTRAN IV.

automatic abstracting—Searching for the criteria by which human beings judge what should be abstracted from a document, as programmed.

automatically programmed tools (APT)—APT is a system for the computer-assisted programming of numerically controlled machine

tools, flame cutters, drafting machines, and similar equipment. It is production-oriented, written to simplify the effort, and to reduce time and money needed to take full advantage of numerically controlled techniques in engineering and manufacturing.

automatic carriage—A device on a printer that moves continuous-form paper under machine control.

automatic character generation—In addition to automatic line generation, the display hardware can display characters specified by 6-bit codes. Each character is displayed in an average of 15 μsec (some systems).

automatic check—A provision constructed in hardware for verifying the accuracy of information transmitted, manipulated, or stored by any unit or device in a computer. (Synonymous with built-in check, built-in automatic check, hardware check, and related to program check.)

automatic checking — Processors are constructed and designed for verification of information transmitted, computed, or stored. The procedure is complete when all processes in the machine are automatically checked, or else the check is considered a partial verification. Partial checking concerns either the number or proportion of the processes that are checked, or the number and proportion of the machine units that are assigned to checking.

automatic checking, inadmissible character—Numerous internal checks continually monitor the accuracy of the system and guard against incipient malfunction. Typical are the parity and inadmissable character check, i.e., an automatic read-back of magnetic tape and magnetic cards as the information is being recorded. The electronic tests which precede each use of magnetic tape or magnetic cards ensure that the operator has not inadvertently set switches improperly. These internal automatic tests are supplemented by the TEST instruction which may be programmed to ensure proper setup of certain units prior to their use. Console switches are designed to protect against inadvertent or improper use, and interlocks are provided on peripheral units to guard against operator error (some systems).

automatic check, interrupts — *See* interrupts, automatic check.

automatic checkout systems — *See* checkout systems, automatic.

automatic code—A code that allows a machine to translate or convert a symbolic language into a machine language for automatic machine or computer operations.

automatic coding—1. A technique by which a machine translates a routine written in a synthetic language into coded machine instructions, e.g., assembling is automatic coding. 2. Various techniques and methodology by which a computer is utilized to translate programs from formats which are quick and easy for programmers to produce, into formats which are convenient and efficient for the computer to execute.

automatic coding language—A technique, device, or language, such that the computer is assisted in doing part of the coding task.

automatic computer—1. A computer configuration that includes a general-purpose stored-program digital computer often generally considered to be simply an electronic computer. 2. A computer that performs long sequences of operations without human intervention.

automatic control—See control, automatic.

automatic controller—See control, automatic.

automatic corrections—See correction, automatic error.

automatic data medium—See data, machine readable.

automatic data processing (ADP)—Data processing performed by a system of electronic or electrical machines so interconnected and interacting as to reduce to a minimum the need for human assistance or intervention.

automatic data-processing equipment — See data processing equipment, automatic.

automatic data-processing system—See automatic data processing.

automatic data-switching center — A data-switching center which senses contents of messages and relays such information without human handling or intervention. Same as automatic message switching.

automatic dictionary—The component of a language-translating machine that will provide a word for word substitution from one language to another. In automatic searching systems, the automatic dictionary is the component that substitutes codes for words or phrases during the encoding operation. (Related to machine translation.)

automatic electronic data-switching center—A communications center designed for relaying digitized information by automatic electronic means.

automatic error-correction — A technique, usually requiring the use of special codes and/or automatic retransmission, that detects and corrects errors occurring in transmission. The degree of correction depends upon coding and equipment configuration.

automatic error detection—The program itself, or the program embedded in a more complicated system, is usually designed to detect its own errors, print them out with the cause and, if so designed, take steps to correct them.

automatic exchange—An exchange in which communication between subscribers is effected without the intervention of operators, and is completed by means of devices and equipment set in operation by the originating subscriber's instrument.

automatic feed punch—See punch, automatic feed.

automatic hold—In an analog computer, attainment of the hold condition automatically

through amplitude comparison of a problem variable, or through an overload condition.

automatic interrupt—An automatic program-controlled interrupt system that causes a hardware jump to a predetermined location. There are five types of interrupt: (1) input/output, (2) programmer error, (3) machine error, (4) supervisor call, and (5) external (for example, timer turned to negative value, alert button on console, external lines from another processor). There is further subdivision under the five types. Unwanted interrupts, such as an anticipated overflow, can be "masked out" (some computers).

automatic message—Incoming messages are automatically directed to one or more outgoing circuits, according to intelligence contained in the message.

automatic message-switching center—A center in which messages are automatically routed according to information in them.

automatic plotting—See plotting, automatic.

automatic program-interrupt—The ability of computers to put "first things first"; abandon one operation, temporarily, when a priority operation arises, do that one, and go on from there. The interruption is caused by a specific predetermined condition.

automatic program-interruption and time sharing—See time sharing and automatic program interruption.

automatic programming—1. A technique by which a machine converts the definition of the solution of the problem into a series of ordered procedures and operations that can be automatically coded. 2. The method or technique whereby the computer itself is used to transform or translate programming from a language or form that is easy for a human being to produce, into a language that is efficient for the computer to carry out. Examples of automatic programming are compiling, assembling, and interpretive routines.

automatic programming language—A device, technique, or language which permits the computer to aid in doing part of the coding and programming.

automatic programming, mnemonic — See mnemonic automatic programming.

automatic punch—See punch, automatic feed.

automatic recovery program — See program, automatic recovery.

automatic routine—A routine that is executed independently of manual operations, but only if certain conditions occur within a program or record, or during some other process.

automatic segmentation and control—Automatic segmentation and control means that the computer can efficiently handle programs which exceed the core memory capacity of a particular system configuration. Without reprogramming, the computer automatically adapts its operational procedures to allow processing of any program on any system configuration. Thus, the user is not forced to install a system of maximum-memory capacity to accommodate one long program; he need not purchase more equipment than he normally needs for efficient operation. Segments of all programs concurrently being executed are "fitted" into available memory space for execution. (Available on some computers.)

automatic send-receive—*See* ASR.

automatic-sensing display flags—Control state or mode permits the visual display to jump, conditioned on the states of its own flags (light pen flag, edge flag, stop flag, etc.). This reduces the number of program interrupts (some systems).

automatic sequence-controlled calculator—A computer using Babbage's principle of sequential control; it is very similar in principle to the analytical engine. Called the Mark I, it was completed in 1944.

automatic sequencing—The ability of equipment to put information in order or in a connected series without human intervention.

automatic sequential operation—To develop a series or family of solutions from a set of equations, various initial conditions are recalculated with other parameters.

automatic stop—An automatic halting of a computer processing operation as the result of an error detected by built-in checking devices.

automatic switch over—An operating system which has a stand-by machine that is capable of detecting when the on-line machine is faulty and once this determination is made, to switch this operation to itself.

automatic tape punch—*See* punch, automatic tape.

automatic tape transmitter—*See* tape transmitter, automatic.

automatic transaction recorder—1. Routines or systems are developed for recording several facts about each transaction with minimum manual input; e.g., worker and job identification are picked up from plates or individual cards, start-stop times are checked by clock notations, completions are developed by recording dials at inquiry stations throughout plants. 2. This data capture method is used in mechanical payroll systems using badge readers and a digital clock for capturing employee working hours.

automation—A machine designed to simulate chines that are self-acting with respect to predetermined processes; e.g., making automatic the process of moving work from one machine to the next. The implementation of processes by automatic means. 2. The theory, art, or technique of making processes self-acting. 3. The investigation, development, or application of procedures toward making automatic, the processes of self-movement and self-control. 4. The generalized term used to convey the dedicated use or exploitation of automatic machines or devices designed to control various processes, such as

control machines, machine tools, routine office procedures, accounting, and several thousand other applications.

automation, source-data—The many methods of recording information in coded forms on paper tapes, punched cards, or tags that can be used over and over again to produce many other records without rewriting. (Synonymous with SDA.)

automation—A machine designed to simulate the operations of living things, or to respond automatically to predesigned programs, stimuli, or signals. An automatic or self-acting or reacting system, often with capability to form logic decisions on the basis of programmed criteria, guides, or rules of its designers. Some automatons mimic living organisms and are responsive to environmental conditions.

automonitor—1. To instruct an automatic computer to make a record of its information-handling operations. 2. A program or routine for this purpose.

automonitor routine—A particular executive program or routine which develops a selective record of a computer's execution of another program to be completed.

autonomous devices—Some computer systems consist of processors, memories, and input/output devices. Since each device is autonomous (no device is dependent upon another for its timing), a system configuration can include memory modules of different speeds, processors of different types sharing the same memory modules, and standard or unique input/output devices.

autonomous working—1. A specific type of concurrent or simultaneous working; i.e., the carrying out of multiple instructions at the same time. 2. The initiation and execution of a part of a computer or automation system independent of a computer, or automation system independent and separate from other operations being performed on other parts of the system. The independent set of operations on various data are themselves often only monitored.

autopiler—A specific automatic compiler.

autoplotter—The autoplotter system was designed as a "plot report generator." Several distinct goals were set forth in the design of the autoplotter system. It was designed to allow the user to automatically generate a variety of plotted information with a minimum of control information, and to accept data in a wide variety of input formats. A variety of output formats is allowed to meet the needs of most users. This flexibility is required in order to represent, in condensed graphical form, the mountains of data present in the work of engineers, scientists, mathematicians, analysts, and management personnel. Autoplotter will allow a user who has no knowledge of computers or of the mechanics of plotting to achieve the desired plotted results. The only requirements for successful use are the generation of a few control parameters that are similar to the data which would be required in the planning phase for hand plotting. Growth, development, and compatibility are the important yardsticks by which an application must be measured. The autoplotter system is independent of the output device except for the plotter control routines. It is a modular program so that as new plotters and new generations of computers arrive, the logic changes required for their utilization are minimal. The language is one which might be adapted to any computer-plotter system. Bar graphs, histograms, point and line plots are the components of most graphical displays. Graphical data processing can condense pages of numerical data into plots on which the user can instantly determine areas requiring more comprehensive study (some systems).

autopolling—This refers to a party-line type circuit with equipment that provides for automatic transmission from station to station by predetermined programming or arrangement.

AUTOPROMT — Abbreviation for automatic programming of machine tools, which is a programming technique developed by IBM for directing the operations of machine tools.

auxiliary console—A console other than the main console.

auxiliary data—See data, auxiliary.

auxiliary equipment—The peripheral equipment or devices which may or may not be in direct communication with the central processing unit of a computer.

auxiliary operation—An operation performed by equipment not under continuous control of the central processing unit.

auxiliary processors—Contained within the executive system is a set of auxiliary processors for performing functions complementing those of the source language processors such as FORTRAN. This set of processors includes the collector for linking relocatable subprograms, the procedure definition processor for inserting and modifying procedure definitions in a library, the COBOL library processor for manipulation of COBOL library elements, and the data definition processor for introducing data descriptions.

auxiliary routine—A routine designed to assist in the operation of the computer, and in debugging other routines.

auxiliary storage—Same as storage external.

auxiliary storage, random access, (time-sharing) — See time sharing, random access auxiliary storage.

availability—1. The ratio or percent of the time, during a certain period, that a piece of equipment is operating correctly, to the total time in that period. Also called operating ratio. 2. The ratio of total service time to the total of fault time, supplementary time, and serviceable time.

available machine time—1. Time during which a computer has the power turned on, is not under maintenance, and is known or believed to be operating correctly. 2. The elapsed time when a computer is in operating condition, whether or not it is in use.

available-next—An address register of available blocks of core storage that are chained together for use by the line control computer for the allocation of incoming information.

available storage list—Same as storage list, uncommitted.

average calculating operation—See calculating operation, average.

average-edge line—An imaginary line, in optical character recognition, that traces and smoothes the form of the printed or handwritten character to better convey the intended form.

average-effectiveness level—See level, average-effectiveness.

average, moving — A moving average performed on data in which some of the values are more heavily valued than others.

average operation time—See operation time, average.

average transmission rate—Same as data transfer rate, average.

awaiting repair time—The interval of time from when the operator reports a fault or failure until the time when the engineer or maintenance man starts to repair the unit. If no fault is found, this time interval is called operating delay.

axis, reference—A line that is fixed or permanent—either horizontal or vertical—that is used as a reference for character design specification, location and shape, for optical character recognition purposes.

azimuth rate computer—A device that computes the rate of change of the horizontal angle from a fixed base line.

B

Babbage, Charles (1792-1871)—The British mathematician whose "analytical engine" anticipated the automatic digital computer by more than a century. Babbage was also interested in the fields of geology, archeology, and astronomy, besides being an early exponent of the science of operations research. After working on several earlier calculating machines, Babbage conceived of his analytical engine in 1833 and devoted the rest of his life to its development. It was the first general-purpose automatic digital computer, was theoretically capable of executing any mathematical operation, could store sequences of instructions in memory, and used punched cards as mass memory for storage of mathematical tables. Unfortunately, Babbage's ideas were developed in a world without sophisticated electronic devices, so most of his work was scorned by his contemporaries. Nevertheless, Babbage's concept of the analytical engine ranks with the greatest intellectual achievements of all time.

background — In time-sharing and multiprogramming the lower-priority work done by the computer when real-time, conversational, high-priority, or quick-response programs are inactive.

background processing—Work which has a low priority and is handled by the computer when higher priority or real-time entries are not occurring. Batch processing such as inventory control, payroll, housekeeping, etc., are often treated as background processing but can be interrupted on orders from terminals or inquiries from other units.

background program—A program that is not time-dependent. This program is of a lower priority than the foreground or main program and is at halt or standby while the main program runs.

background reflectance — See reflectance, background.

backgroup, hands-on—The prior work experience developed by actually operating the hardware and often used as a criteria of programmer capability and knowledge.

backing storage—Same as storage, auxiliary.

back-roll—A system that will restart the program after a system failure. Snapshots of data and programs are stored at periodic intervals and the system rolls back to restart at the last recorded snapshot.

backspace—To move one unit in the reverse or backward direction as opposed to moving one unit in the forward direction; e.g., to move back one record or file on an I/O device.

backspace character — See character, backspace.

backspace key — That specific push button which causes a selected tape unit to backspace one record.

back-up—Relates to on-site or remote equipment which is designed and available to complete the operation or redo the operation in the event of primary equipment failure.

back-up system—Such systems combine several sophisticated error detection and correction techniques which spot and correct equipment and transmission errors.

back-up system library—See library back-up system.

backus-naur form — Same as backus normal form.

backus normal form (BNF) — A formal language structure for syntax parsing used in Design of ALGOL-60.

backward-forward counter—A counter having both an add and subtract input, and capable of counting in either an increasing or a decreasing direction.

backward read—See read backward.

badge reader—See reader, badge.

balance check mode—In some specific computers, the computing units can be adjusted to remove the unbalance.

balanced circuits—Circuits that are terminated by a network whose impedance balances the impedance of the line so that the return losses are infinite.

balanced error—An error relating to a range which has a balance of zero, or a mean value of zero. A measure of balance in which the range of errors are equally probable, i.e., the highest and lowest values in the range are equal in value but have opposite signs.

balanced error, range of—1. A range of error in which the maximum and minimum possible errors are opposite in sign and equal in magnitude. 2. A range of error in which the average value is zero.

balanced sorting—A technique used in a sort program to merge strings of sequenced data. The power of the merge is equal to $T/2$.

balancing error—A specific error which in effect balances or offsets another error, i.e., two offsetting errors of equal values or same numbers of opposite signs could exist and would be most difficult to detect or correct because the various check totals would agree or compare favorably.

band—1. A cylindrical recording area on a magnetic drum. 2. Range of frequency between two defined limits. 3. A group of recording tracks on a magnetic drum or tape.

band, clear—For documents to be used in optical character recognition, certain areas must be kept clear of ink or marks. The clear band is used by the OCR equipment and must be free of unrelated printing.

B AND-NOT A gate—See gate B AND-NOT A.

BANKPAC—A comprehensive group of generalized programs to serve the needs of banks automating demand deposit accounting, installment loan accounting, savings accounting, transit, and personal trust accounting functions. Bankpac programs minimize programming effort and conversion time.

banner word—The first word in a file record.

BAP (basic assembler) — A basic assembler, permitting the user to write machine-language programs using symbolic instructions. (Utilizes a self-contained program loader.) Input may be from cards, paper tape, or magnetic tape. Output is a machine code, relocatable binary-object program. (Honeywell)

bar-code, optical scanner—See optical scanner, bar-code.

bar-code scanner—An optical scanning unit that can read documents encoded in a special bar code, at a 50 character-per-second speed, is an element in data stations. The scanner opens up various system concepts for such tasks as billing, couponing, retail item control, and other forms of returnable media. The scanner can read either lithographed or computer-printed bar codes at speeds of 30 to 45 documents per minute. As it scans, it transfers the encoded data to a buffer for direct transmission, or to punched paper tape and printer for pre-transmission editing (some systems).

bar, fixed type—A type bar on a printer which cannot be removed by an operator and therefore the printer unit has a fixed alphabet.

bar, interchangable type—A printer type bar which can be removed by the operator to change from one alphabet to another.

bar printer—*See* printer, bar.

bar, type—*See* printer type bar.

base—*See* number base.

base address—1. A number that appears as an address in a computer instruction, but which serves as the base, index, initial or starting point for subsequent addresses to be modified. (Synonymous with presumptive address and reference address.) 2. A number used in symbolic coding in conjunction with a relative address.

base address relocation—The ability to augment memory references by the contents of a specific base register, alterable only in the supervisor mode.

base data — The set of data or information from which conclusions can be drawn. This is the set of data that is internally accessible to the computer and on which the computer performs operations.

base-displacement addressing system—A system that uses a displacement-base to designate all core-storage locations and provides abilities to: (1) easily relocate a program at load time, (2) address a very large amount of storage with relatively few address bits in each instruction, and (3) conveniently address three-dimensional arrays.

base management data—*See* data, base management.

base-minus-ones complement — A number representation that can be derived from another by subtracting each digit from one less than the base. Nines complements and ones complements are base-minus-ones complements.

base notation—*See* notation, base.

base notation, mixed—A method of expressing a quantity by using two or more characters, where each character is of a different radix.

base number—*See* number, base.

base point—*Same as* arithmetic point.

base register—*Same as* index register.

base registers, time-sharing—*See* time sharing, base registers.

BASIC — Beginner's All-purpose Symbolic Instruction Code; a procedure-level computer language that is well-suited for time-sharing. BASIC, developed at Dartmouth College, is probably one of the easiest computer programming languages to learn and master. These attributes have allowed BASIC to be instrumental in the spread of time-sharing to businesses that are not within the computer industry.

basic access method — BAM is an access method in which each input/output statement causes a machine input/output operation to be performed.

basic autocoder—An autocode developed by IBM originally for the IBM 7070 computer system and now widely used on other IBM and competing systems.

basic code—*Same as* code, absolute.

basic coding—*See* absolute coding.

basic linkage—A linkage which is used repeatedly in one routine, program, or system and which follows the same set of rules each time. *See* linkage.

batch—A group of records or documents considered as a single unit for the purpose of processing.

batch data processing—*See* batch processing.

batching with a control total—In batching with a control total, some data field that is common to all items or documents is accumulated for the control total which then becomes the basis for balancing operations during processing. The control field may be an amount, a quantity, an item code, an account number, etc.

batching with a document or item count—In batching data with a document or an item count, the items or documents are counted instead of numbered; an indication of the count accompanies the group. This technique can be used to control data both before and after it is punched into cards; e.g., requisitions, changes, receiving reports, and punched cards for various analysis reports.

batch process—A sequential-processing procedure that uses an accumulation or group of units; this is in contrast to on-line processing, during which each unit of data or information is processed immediately at the time of presentation to the top of the processing sequence.

batch processing—1. A technique by which items to be processed must be coded and collected into groups prior to processing. 2. A systems approach to processing where a number of similar input items are grouped for processing during the same machine run.

batch-processing interrupt — An outstanding feature of any real-time system is its capacity to process real-time and batch-processing applications concurrently. This real-time data-processing innovation is made possible through a unique feature that permits remote external units with information of high precedence to interrupt computer processing. Whenever transaction data for a real-time problem are entered into a remote external unit, the computer's batch-processing program may be interrupted to permit handling the high priority real-time transaction and the sending of processed results back to the external unit.

batch-processing mode — Card systems may have full batch-processing capabilities. Intermixed compilations, assemblies, and executions may be processed in a continuous sequence. The only restriction is that no load-and-go jobs may be processed since no intermediate storage unit is available for binary object programs. For continuous processing, the monitor remains in memory at all times. The compiler, assembler, system loader (with executive), and utility routines are loaded and executed by the monitor. The monitor itself is loaded into memory by a "preset" operation. The operations performed upon a program are determined from the absolute binary decks placed in the card reader (some systems).

batch processing, real-time — *See* real-time, batch processing.

batch, remote—The method of entering jobs for the computer to perform through a remote terminal as opposed to normal batch processing, where inputting the job must take place in the computer center.

batch ticket—A control document that summarizes the control totals and identifies the appropriate group of source documents.

batch total—1. The sum of certain quantities, pertaining to batches of unit records, used to verify accuracy of operations on a particular batch of records; e.g., in a payroll calculation, the batches might be departments, and batch totals could be number of employees in the department, total hours worked in the department, total pay for the department. Batches, however, may be arbitrary, such as orders received from 9 A.M. to 11 A.M. on a certain day. 2. Each or any of a number of sums that can be calculated from a series of records which are intended to serve as aids to check the accuracy of computer operations.

batch transaction files — Transactions accumulated as a batch ready for processing against the master file.

Batten check—*See* check, Batten.

Batten system — 1. An information-retrieval system that uses peek-a-boo cards; i.e., cards into which small holes are drilled at the intersections of coordinates (column and row designations) to represent document numbers. (Synonymous with cordonnier system, and related to aspect card.) 2. A method for coordinating single words to identify a document, and developed by W. E. Batten. Sometimes referred to as the peek-a-boo system.

baud—1. A unit of signalling speed equal to the number of code elements per second. 2. The unit of signalling speed equal to twice the number of Morse code dots continuously sent per second. 3. A technical term, originally used to express the capabilities of a telegraph transmission facility in terms of "modulation rate per unit of time . . ." For practical purposes, it is now used interchangeably with "bits per second" as the unit of measure of data flow. It was derived from the name Baudot, after whom the Baudot Code was named. Example: If the duration of audit is 20 milliseconds, the modulation rate is 50 bauds.

Baudot code—The standard five-channel teletypewriter code consisting of a start impulse and five character impulses, all of equal length, and a stop impulse whose length is 1.42 times all of the start impulse. Also known as the 1.42 unit code. The Baudot code has been used by the telegraph industry for about 100 years.

bauds, data transmission—The measure of the speed of a transmission. A baud is equal to one signal element per second.

bay, patch—In an analog computer, a concentrated assembly of electrical tie points that offers a means of electrical connection between the inputs and outputs of computing elements, multiples, reference voltages, and ground.

B-box—*Same as* index register.

BCD (Binary Coded Decimal) — A numerical representation in which decimal digits are represented by binary numerals. The most common binary code is the 8-4-2-1. In binary coded decimal the number 14 would be 0001 0100.

BCD coding—A system of representing decimal equivalents by a series of four binary digits.

BCO (Binary Coded Octal) — In this system, binary numbers are used to represent octal digits of an octal number. In the common 4-2-1 octal code 101 equals octal 5.

BCS—British Computer Society.

beam storage—Storage units which use one or more beams of electrons or light to gain access to individual storage cells for operation, most often cathode ray tube storage.

beat—1. One of the fundamental states of the control unit of a computer or the duration of such a state. A beat might be designed to set up a correct circuit to perform a function, and execution of it might be the next beat. The duration might be a single word period. 2. A time measurement for a given computer word to pass a given point as in serial storage delay-lines. All of the bits of a word must pass through the input control gate; the beat is then the sum of all the bit times.

bed, card—A mechanical device for holding cards to be transported past the punching and reading stations.

BEEF (Business and Engineering Enriched Fortran)—BEEF enriches FORTRAN to overcome FORTRAN'S limitations as a data-processing language and to enhance its abilities as a scientific processor. The scientific enrichment is in the form of subroutines for mathematical functions, matrix arithmetic, and other standard engineering requirements. To enrich FORTRAN as a data-processing language, FORTRAN was augmented with a package of callable subroutines suitable for management-information systems and business-data processing. Thus, enriched FORTRAN now serves a dual purpose suitable for a large spectrum of applications in either science or business. The advantages to the user in being able to standardize on one compiler language are obvious. Developed by Westinghouse Electric Corporation, Baltimore Defense and Space Center, Baltimore, Maryland.

begin—A procedure delimiter in the ALGOL language.

beginners algebraic symbolic interpretive compiler (BASIC)—This language, originally developed at Dartmouth College, is also available on many systems. Designed as a simple FORTRAN-like language, it can be learned by the average non-computer oriented mathematician or engineer in a few hours.

beginning file label—A label which appears at the beginning of a file describing the contents of the file.

beginning-of-information marker (BIM) — A reflective spot on the back of a magnetic tape, 10 feet from the physical beginning of the tape which is sensed photoelectrically to indicate the point on tape at which recording may begin.

beginning of tape control—See beginning of information marker (BIM).

beginning of tape marker—See beginning of information marker (BIM).

beginning tape label — A description which appears at the beginning of a tape describing the content of the tape.

bell signal—A yellow lamp that glows whenever the bell signal is detected by a re-perforator. As long as it glows, the position has priority in establishing cross-office connection.

BEMA (Business Equipment Manufacturers Association)—A large respected trade association of business equipment, data processing equipment, and office supplies and furniture manufacturers, and a sponsor of Standards Institute Sectional Committee X3 on Information Processing.

benchmark—A point of reference from which measurements can be made.

benchmark problem—1. A problem to evaluate the performance of computers relative to each other. 2. A routine used to determine the speed performance of a computer. One method is to use one-tenth of the time required to perform nine complete additions and one complete multiplication. A complete addition or a complete multiplication time includes the time required to procure two operands from storage, perform the operation and store the result, and the time re-

quired to select and execute the required number of instructions to do this.

benchmark routine—A set of routines or problems which will help determine the performance of a given piece of equipment.

BEST (Business EDP Systems Technique) — BEST is a concept for designing and implementing total business systems; it provides a systems-oriented approach to programming. BEST is a responsive computer programming technique that employs tools familiar to the systems man. Systems people have a means of translating their logic flowcharts directly into running computer programs. (NCR)

B EXCEPT A gate—Same as gate, B AND-NOT A.

bias—1. The departure from a reference value of the average of a set of values. 2. The average d-c voltage maintained between the cathode and control grid of a vacuum tube. 3. An unbalanced range of error; i.e., having an average error that is not zero. 4. An operating voltage applied to elements of a transistor or vacuum tube to set the operating characteristics.

bias check—A means of testing circuits for incipient or intermittent failures developed by varying the voltages applied to the circuit. Such marginal or bias checks are helpful prior to extended run periods.

bias distortion—1. Bias distortion or bias of start-stop teletypewriter signals is the uniform shifting of the beginning of all marking pulses from their proper positions in relation to the beginning of the start pulse. 2. Distortion affecting a two-condition (or binary) modulation (or restitution), in which all the significant intervals corresponding to one of the two significant conditions have longer or shorter durations than the corresponding theoretical durations.

biased exponent—See exponent, biased.

bias, internal (teletypewriter)—The bias, either marking or spacing, that may occur within a start-stop teletypewriter receiving mechanism, and which will have the same effect on the margins of operation as a bias which is external to the receiver.

bias, marking—A bias distortion which lengthens the marking impulse by advancing the mark-to-space transition.

bias, ordering—1. A check on the exactness of the order of alphabetic words or numerals. 2. A unique characteristic of a sequence which keeps it away from or toward a needed order, a designed, or desired order. In consequence, some degree of effort is required to achieve the desired order other than would normally be expected, say, from a random distribution.

bias, spacing—A bias distortion which lengthens the spacing impulse by delaying the space-to-mark transition.

bias test—See bias check.

bias testing—See testing, marginal.

biax memory—The trade name of a nondestructive read-out memory of the Philco Division of the Ford Motor Company. The biax memory is constructed from small ferrite cores containing multiple orthogonal apertures.

bibliography—1. A list of documents pertaining to a given subject or author. 2. An annotated catalog of documents.

BICEP—General Electric Co. language for process control procedures.

biconditional gate—*Same as* gate, exclusive NOR.

biconditional statement — A logic condition that exists when two conditions are either both true or both false; a logical AND or NAND gate.

bidirectional flow—Flow that can extend over the same flow lines in either direction as in flowcharting by being represented by a single flowline.

bidirectional operation — An operation in which reading, writing, and searching may be conducted in either direction, thus saving time and providing easy access to stored information.

bifurcation—A logic condition where only two states are possible. This is the basic logic pattern of binary digital computers.

B ignore A gate—*See* gate, B ignore A.

B ignore A gate, negative—*See* gate, B ignore A negative.

billibit—One billion bits. *Same as* kilomegabit.

billicycle—One billion cycles. *Same as* kilomega.

billisecond—*Same as* nanosecond.

BIM—*See* beginning of information marker.

bimag—A magnetic core possessing two states of magnetization. The core consists of a thin metallic ribbon of high-retention properties spirally wound on a ceramic bobbin. Bimags are used principally as shift-register elements.

B implies A gate, negative—*Same as* gate B AND-NOT A.

binary—1. A numbering system based on 2's rather than 10's which uses only the digits 0 and 1 when written. 2. A characteristic, property, or condition in which there are but two possible alternatives; e.g., the binary number system using 2 as its base and using only the digits zero (0) and one (1). (Related to binary-coded decimal, and clarified by number systems.)

binary arithmetical operation—An arithmetical operation with operands and results represented in binary notation.

binary arithmetic operation—*See* arithmetic operation, binary.

binary card—*See* card, binary.

binary card, row—See card, row-binary.

binary cell—1. A cell of one binary digit capacity. 2. A one-bit register or bit position.

binary chain—A series of binary circuits existing in one of two possible states and so arranged that each circuit can affect or modify the condition of the circuit following it.

binary, Chinese—*Same as* binary column.

binary code—1. A coding system in which the encoding of any data is done through the use of bits; i.e., 0 or 1. 2. A code for the ten decimal digits, 0, 1, . . ., 9 in which each is represented by its binary, radix 2, equivalent; i.e., straight binary.

binary code, cyclic—*Same as* code, cyclic.

binary-coded address — *See* address, binary-coded.

binary-coded character—One element of a notation system representing alphameric characters such as decimal digits, alphabetic letters, and punctuation marks, by a predetermined configuration of consecutive binary digits.

binary-coded decimal (BCD)—1. Pertaining to a decimal notation in which the individual decimal digits are each represented by a binary code group; i.e., in the 8-4-2-1 coded decimal notation, the number twenty-three is represented as 0010 0011. In pure binary, notation twenty-three is represented by 10111. 2. Describing a decimal notation in which the individual decimal digits are represented by a pattern of ones and zeros; e.g., in the 8-4-2-1 coded decimal notation, the number twelve is represented as 0001 0010 for 1 and 2, respectively, whereas in pure or straight binary notation it is represented as 1100.

binary-coded decimal notation—A method of representing each figure in a decimal number by a four-figured binary number.

binary-coded decimal number — A number usually consisting of successive groups of figures, in which each group of four figures is a binary number that represents, but does not necessarily equal arithmetically, a particular figure in an associated decimal number; e.g., if the three rightmost figures of a decimal number are 262, the three rightmost figure groups of the binary coded decimal number might be 0010, 0110, and 0010.

binary-coded decimal representation (BCD)—A system of representing decimal numbers. Each decimal digit is represented by a combination of four binary digits (bits), as follows:

Binary	Decimal	Binary	Decimal
0 0 0 0	0	0 1 0 1	5
0 0 0 1	1	0 1 1 0	6
0 0 1 0	2	0 1 1 1	7
0 0 1 1	3	1 0 0 0	8
0 1 0 0	4	1 0 0 1	9

binary-coded digit—One element of a notation system for representing a decimal digit by a fixed number of binary positions.

binary code, dense—Particular binary coding system which uses all possible binary representations and positions. The binary-coded-decimal notation does not use 6 of the 16 possible patterns and thus, in effect, wastes valuable computing space.

binary-coded octal—A coding system in which binary numbers are used to represent the octal digits of an octal number.

binary column—Concerns binary representation of data on punched cards such that adjacent positions in a column correspond to adjacent bits of the data. Example: each column in a 12-row card may be used to represent 12 consecutive bits of a 36-bit word.

binary counter—1. A counter that counts according to the binary number system. 2. A counter capable of assuming one of two stable states.

binary deck—A punched card deck containing data, information, and instructions in binary codes.

binary digit (bit)—1. A numeral in the binary scale of notation. This digit may be zero (0), or one (1). It may be equivalent to an on or off condition, a yes, or a no. Often abbreviated to (bit). 2. The kind of number that computers use internally. There are only two binary digits, 1 and 0, otherwise known as "on" and "off." Follow the table below by progressing geometrically per column right to left, and add the column values where one appears, i.e.; 7 is 1, 2, 4, 0, right to left.

COLUMN VALUES

		8	4	2	1
0	is	0	0	0	0
1	is	0	0	0	1
2	is	0	0	1	0
3	is	0	0	1	1
4	is	0	1	0	0
5	is	0	1	0	1
6	is	0	1	1	0
7	is	0	1	1	1
8	is	1	0	0	0
9	is	1	0	0	1

binary digits, equivalent—A comparison to establish an equivalency of the number of binary digit places which are necessary to represent a given number in another radix, such as decimal or 10. Decimal, octal, binary-coded-decimal, and straight binary are expressed with the same values but each requires a different number of digit places for the same values.

binary element—An element of data which may assume either of two values or states, i.e., 0, 1, or +, −.

binary half-adder—*Same as* half-adder

binary incremental representation — In this type of incremental representation, the value of an increment is limited to one of the two values plus one or minus one for each quantum step. The maximum positive rate of change is represented as a continuous string of plus ones, and the maximum negative of change is a continuous string of minus ones.

binary logic — Digital logic elements which operate with two distinct states. The two

states are variously called true and false, high and low, on and off, or 1 and 0. In computers they are represented by two different voltage levels. The level which is more positive (or less negative) than the other is called the high level, the other the low level. If the true (1) level is the most positive voltage, such logic is referred to as positive true or positive logic.

binary mode—Operations using basic machine arithmetic may use binary mode, i.e., the number system with a base 2, allowing only the digits 0 and 1, in contrast to the decimal system of base 10 with digits, 0, 1, 2 . . . . . 9.

binary normal—*Same as* binary.

binary notation—*See* number, binary.

binary number—A number, usually consisting of more than one figure, representing a sum in which the individual quantity represented by each figure is based on a radix of two. The figures used are 0 and 1.

binary number, system—*See* number, binary.

binary numeral—The binary representation of a number; e.g., 0101 is the binary numeral and "V" is the roman numeral of the number of fingers on one hand.

binary one—There are two possible binary digits; the numeral 1 has the value of unity and is represented by the presence or absence of a punched hole in a card or tape, by voltage flip-flop, etc. It has the same value as a decimal 1 differing only in the weights of values assigned to positions of the digits.

binary operation — An operation which depends on the applications and the strict adherence to the rules of Boolean algebra, i.e., any operation in which the operands and results take either one of two values or states such as logic operations on single bits.

binary ordinary—*See* binary.

binary pair—A circuit which is binary, has two states, each requiring an appropriate trigger for excitation and transition from one state to the other.

binary point—That point in a binary number which separates the integral from the fractional part. It is analogous to the decimal point for a decimal number.

binary, pure—*Same as* binary.

binary, reflected—A code using the binary 0 and 1, and so constructed that each successive code is derived from its predecessor by inverting only one bit. Reflected binary is a particular form of gray code.

binary row—This concerns binary representation of data on punched cards in which adjacent positions in a row correspond to adjacent bits of the data. Example: each row in a 80-row card may be used to represent 80 consecutive bits of two 40-bit words.

binary scale (or numbering system)—A numbering system having a radix (base) of two. Thus, only two symbols (0 and 1) are needed.

binary search—1. The procedure for finding an element of an order table by successively halving a search interval to then evaluate the remaining half where that element is known to exist. 2. A search in which a set of items is divided into two parts, where one part is rejected, and the process is repeated on the accepted part until the item with the desired property is found. (Synonymous with dichotomizing search.)

binary signaling—A communications mode in which information is passed by the presence and absence, or plus and minus variations, of one parameter of the signaling medium only.

binary, straight—*Same as* binary.

binary-to-decimal conversion—Conversion of a binary number to the equivalent decimal number; i.e., a base two number to a base ten number.

binary unit distance code—*See* code, unit distance.

binary variable—A variable which assumes values in a set containing exactly two elements, often symbolized as 0 and 1. This is often confused with double-value variable; e.g., $y = \pm \sqrt{x}$. (Synonymous with two-state variable.)

binary-weighted error-detection system — This system is based upon the concept of assigning binary-one values to all marking pulses or each code combination.

binary zero — Contrasted to the only other binary representation, 1, the binary zero represents the lack of magnitude, and is represented as the presence or absence of a punched hole in a card or tape, a metallic spot, a current or lack of current, etc.

bin, tape — A magnetic tape storage device with movable read/record heads or fixed heads for each loop. The heads and loops can move to particular or selected locations on a tape, thus providing more rapid access time than for plain serial reels of tape which must be rewound.

bionics—The application of knowledge gained from the analysis of living systems to the creation of hardware that will perform functions in a manner analogous to the more sophisticated functions of the living system.

biosensor — A mechanism for detecting and transmitting biological data from an organism in a way which permits display or storage of results.

bipolar (unipolar)—When a logical "true" input is represented by an electrical voltage polarity opposite to that representing a logical "false" input, the signal is defined as bipolar. If both "true" and "false" inputs are represented by the same electrical voltage polarity, the signal is defined as unipolar.

biquinary — A two-part representation of a decimal digit consisting of a binary portion with values of 0 or 5, and a quinary portion with values of 0 through 4; e.g., the number 7 is coded as 12 which implies 5 and 2.

biquinary code—*See* code, biquinary.

biquinary number—*See* number, biquinary.

biquinary system—*See* code, biquinary.

BISEC—A General Electric Co. process control language.

bistable—1. The capability of assuming either of two stable states, hence of storing one bit of information. 2. Pertaining to devices capable of assuming either one of two stable states.

bistable magnetic core (Bimag)—The bimag is a bistable magnetic core useful in digital systems because of its ability to store binary information. Bimag cores are magnetic cores having low coercive force, rectangular hysteresis loops, and switching times in the microsecond range. These properties are controlled by the type of material used and the manufacturing process.

Bimags have been used in switching circuits, shift registers, pulse transformers, high-frequency magnetic amplifiers, blocking oscillators, scalers, and fixed program memories. This, however, by no means exhausts the application to which bimag cores may be put.

bit—1. An abbreviation of binary digit. 2. A single character in a binary number. 3. A single pulse in a group of pulses. 4. A unit of information capacity of a storage device. The capacity in bits is the logarithm to the base two of the number of possible states of the device. (Related to storage capacity.) 5. A binary digit; hence, a unit of data in binary notation. In the binary numbering system, only two marks (0 and 1) are used. Each of these marks is called a binary digit. 6. The smallest element of binary machine language represented by a magnetized spot on a recording surface or a magnetized element of a storage device. Whether the bit represents a 0 or a 1 is determined by ascertaining whether the magnetism was created by a positive or negative electrical charge.

bit check—A binary check digit; often a parity bit. (Related to parity check and self-checking number.)

bit combination—*Same as* bit pattern.

bit density—A measure of the number of bits recorded per unit of length or area.

bit guard—A bit which indicates whether a core or disk memory word, or group of words is to be filed.

bit, information—In data communication, bits which are genuine data source bits and not those used for error control or checking procedures.

bit location—A storage position on a record capable of storing one bit.

bit, parity — A check bit that indicates whether the total number of binary "1" digits in a character or word (excluding the parity bit) is odd or even. If a "1" parity bit indicates an odd number of "1" digits, then a "0" bit indicates an even number of them. If the total number of "1" bits, including the parity bit, is always even, the system is called an even-parity system. In an odd-parity system, the total number of "1" bits, including the parity bit, is always odd.

bit pattern—A combination of N binary digits to represent 2 to the N possible choices; e.g., a 3-bit pattern represents 8 possible combinations.

bit, presence — An individual sentinel bit which appears in the descriptor to indicate that information which is being referenced is in the high-speed storage area.

bit rate—1. The speed at which bits are transmitted. 2. The rate at which binary digits, or pulses representing them, pass a given point on a communications line or channel. (Clarified by baud and channel capacity.)

bit, serial-by—*See* serial-by-bit.

bit, sign—A binary digit used as a sign draft.

bit significance—The presence or absence of a bit in a certain location of an instruction word which designates the instruction to be of certain type, for example, zero vs. one-address instruction.

bits, information—Bits that are generated by the data source and which are not used for error-control by the data-transmission system.

bit site—A location on magnetic recording media where a bit of information is stored.

bits, packing—*See* packing.

bits, punctuation — The use of a variable-length data format requires that there be a method of indicating the actual length of a unit of information. This requirement is fulfilled by two punctuation bits associated with each memory location. These bits can constitute a word mark—used to define the length of a field; an item mark—used to define the length of an item; or a record mark—used to define the length of a record.

bits, service—Such overhead bits which are not check bits, as for example, request for repetition, numbering sequence, others.

bit stream—This is a term used regularly in conjunction with transmission methods in which character separation is accomplished by the terminal equipment, and the bits are transmitted over the circuit in a consecutive line of bits.

bit stream transmission — The method of transmitting characters at fixed time intervals. No stop and start elements are used and the bits making up the characters follow each other without pause.

bits, string of—It is most common and conventional to add a string of bits at the end of a block, in magnetic tapes, to allow a parity check in the columns of the entire block or record.

bit string—A one-dimensional array of bits ordered by reference to the relations between adjacent numbers.

bit, zone—1. One of the two left-most bits in a commonly used system in which six bits are used for each character. Related to overpunch. 2. Any bit in a group of bit positions that are used to indicate a specific class of items; e.g., numbers, letters, special signs, and commands.

black box—1. A generic term used to describe an unspecified device which performs a special function or in which known inputs produce known outputs in a fixed relationship (computer). 2. A generic term for any integral unit or device, but most often used to refer to electronic devices; i.e., a kludge (slang) (computer).

blank—1. A regimented place of storage where data may be stored; e.g., a location in a storage medium. (Synonymous with space.) 2. A character on a printer used to indicate an output space in which nothing is printed. 3. A condition of "no information at all" in a given column of a punched card or in a given storage medium. In the case of tape, the feed hole is perforated but no intelligence is perforated into the same vertical column. In some cases, however, processing equipment may be programmed to recognize a blank and perform certain functions as with other codes.

blank character—Any character or characters used to produce a character space on an output medium.

blank-column detection, double-punch — *See* double-punch and blank-column detection.

blank deleter—A device which eliminates the receiving of blanks in perforated paper tape.

blank form—*See* form, blank.

blank instruction—*See* instruction, dummy.

blank medium—*See* form, blank.

blank, switching—A specific range of values in which the incoming signal can be altered without also changing the outgoing response. (Synonymous with dead space, dead zone, and similar to neutral zone.)

blank tape—*See* form, blank.

blank-transmission test—This feature allows the checking of any data field for all blank positions. As a computer control, it can be used to prevent the destruction of existing records in storage, indicate when the last item from a spread card has been processed, skip calculation if a rate or factor field is blank, etc.

blast—The release of various specified areas or blocks of either main or auxiliary storage no longer needed by an operational program. This type program will execute a blast macroinstruction which causes the control program to return the address of the area blasted to its list of storage available for use by future operational programs.

bleed, ink—*See* ink bleed

blind (unblind)—The selective controlling of a transmission printer or reperforator. Example: used to prevent prices from typing on a receiving teletypewriter.

B-line—*Same as* index register.

block—1. A group of consecutive machine words or characters considered or transferred as a unit, particularly with reference to input and output. (Contrast with record.) 2. A collection or group of words, records, or characters which are handled as a single unit. In real-time systems, blocks are used to describe input/output or working storage areas in main storage. A file storage block is often called a "physical record." 3. An aggregate or group of characters, words, or information developed or considered as a unit. It is often considered a synonym for grouped records on tapes. 4. The set of locations or tape positions in which a block of words, as defined above, is stored or recorded. 5. A circuit assemblage which functions as a unit; e.g., a circuit building block of standard design, and the logic block in a sequential circuit.

block analysis—A relocatable part of the computer storage in which program testing or statistical data are stored which can later be used to analyze the performance of the system. During program testing there may be an analysis block for each transaction in the system, and when the transaction leaves the system this block is dumped into a file or tape.

block chaining—Associating a block of data in core with another block, in order to allow an item or queue of items to occupy more than one block. The blocks may be linked by programming, but some machines do it automatically.

block control—A storage location which contains information in condensed, formalized form necessary for the control of a task, function, or operation.

block, data-set control—See data-set control block.

block diagram—1. A chart setting forth the particular sequence of operations to be performed for handling a particular application. Used as a tool in programming. 2. A sequential, graphic representation of operations of the various computer machines through the use of symbols which represent functional steps rather than the physical structural details. The block diagram is usually the gross or macro diagram for the entire integrated system or large application areas. Flow charts then provide the specific detail of various operations. 3. The graphic representation of the logic of a sequence of methodological or procedural steps; a data-processing chart. 4. A graphical representation of the hardware in a computer system. The primary purpose of a block diagram is to indicate the paths, along with information and/or control flows, between the various parts of a computer system. It should not be confused with the term flow chart. 5. A coarser and less symbolic representation than a flow chart.

block-entry—See entry block.

blockette—A subdivision of a group of consecutive machine words transferred as a unit, particularly with reference to input and output.

block event control—A unique information (control) block designed to control status of

operations which are waiting for an act or special signal to happen, i.e., processing may be halted until one or more events occur. Usually a WAIT macroinstruction is involved.

block gap—The space and/or distance between particular blocks of data or instructions on a tape or other storage medium left blank in order to separate blocks of data. Insertion of such blanks by programmers or by automatic means are to fix block lengths. Tapes can be stopped, for example, or they can be brought up to standard speed again, within such gaps.

block ignore character—See character, block ignore.

blocking—1. Combining two or more numbers (records) into one block. 2. To efficiently decrease the number of starts and stops; a combining of two or more items or groups of items.

blocking factor—The limit of the data records which can be contained in a given block on tape.

block, input—1. A section of internal storage of a computer reserved for the receiving and processing of input information. (Synonymous with input area.) 2. An input buffer. 3. A block of computer words considered as a unit and intended or destined to be transferred from an external source or storage medium to the internal storage of the computer.

block length—The total number of records, words, or characters contained in one block.

block loading—A technique for program loading in which the control sections of the program or program segment are loaded into adjacent positions in the main memory.

blockmark—A storage-indicator mark which indicates the end of a block of data that would be written on tape for a processor that handles variable-length blocks on tape.

block, message reference—The storage areas and working storage set aside by the system when more than one message is being processed in parallel by the system. This message reference block is associated with that message so long as it registers in the computer for processing.

block, order—A group of computer words or a record being transferred out of the equipment. A section of storage reserved to handle such outputs.

block, output—1. A block of computer words considered as a unit and intended or destined to be transferred from an internal storage medium to an external destination. 2. A section of internal storage reserved for storing data which are to be transferred out of the computer. (Synonymous with output area.) 3. A block used as an output buffer.

block parity system—A system of using an additional bit to a block of information to detect single-bit errors in the whole block.

block record—A specific storage area of fixed size which usually contains a main memory or file storage, organized into standard blocks to allow more flexibility in storage allocation and control.

block, register—The set of 16 general registers referenced by the current value of the register pointer (some computers).

blocks—Records are transferred to and from magnetic tapes in the form of blocks (sometimes called physical records). A block (physical record) may contain one or more records (logical). Records may be reduced to blocks on tape to reduce the acceleration and deceleration time.

block sort—1. A sort of one or more of the most significant characters of a key to serve as a means of making workable sized groups from a large volume of records to be sorted. 2. Sorting by separation of the entire field on the highest order portion of the key, usually implying separate ordering of these segments and then adjoining the entire file.

block, standby—A location always set aside in storage for communication with buffers in order to make more efficient use of such buffers.

block, storage—A portion or section of storage usually within a storage area. A storage block is considered a single element for holding a specific or fixed number of words.

block structure—A technique allowing program segmentation into blocks of information or subroutines of a total program.

block, table—A distinct portion or subset of a table of data or instructions, usually specifically identified for more convenient access.

block transfer—The conveyance of a group of consecutive words from one place to another.

block, variable—In a variable block the number of characters in the block is determined by the programmer (usually between some practical limits).

blue ribbon program—*Same as* program, star.

BNF—Abbreviation for backus normal form.

board—An electrical panel which can be altered with the addition or deletion of external wiring. Also known as a plugboard, panel, or wire board.

board, control—*Same as* control panel.

board, plotting—The flat surface unit of a plotter; that part of a plotting machine or unit on which plots, curves, or displays of lines, diagrams, symbols, etc., are transferred or transformed. The plotting board is the output section of the total plotter machine displaying the results of the plotters manipulation of analog or digital data, usually for human use.

board, plug—*See* plugboard computer.

board, problem—*See* plugboard computer.

board, wiring—*See* plugboard computer.

bobbin core—A magnetic memory device that is made by wrapping magnetic tape on a core. The completed device resembles a bobbin.

book—A particular large segment of memory most often used in virtual memory addressing.

book, documentation — All the material needed, to document a computer application, including problem statement, flowcharts, coding and operating instructions.

bookkeeping operation—*See* operation, bookkeeping.

book, run—*Same as* book documentation.

Boolean—1. Pertaining to the processes used in the algebra formulated by George Boole. 2. Pertaining to the operations of formal logic.

Boolean add—*Same as* gate, OR.

Boolean algebra—1. An algebra named for George Boole. This algebra is similar in form to ordinary algebra, but with classes, propositions, one-of-circuit elements, etc., for variables rather than data values. It includes the operators AND, OR, NOT, EXCEPT, IF, THEN. 2. A binary system of algebra; hence, a useful tool for logical analysis of binary computers. Has been instrumental in the development and design of original computer units and continues to be useful not only for students in developing binary concepts, but also for continuous technological research.

Boolean calculus—Boolean algebra modified to include time. Thus, such additional operators as after, while, happen, delay, before, etc., are provided. It is concerned with binary-state changes with time (triggers, delay lines).

Boolean complement—*Same as* gate, NOT.

Boolean connective—A symbol between two operands or before the operands. Such symbols are for exclusion, conjunction, non-equivalence, disjunction, etc.

Boolean logic — A mathematical analysis of logic. Applications of Boolean logic include information retrieval and circuit-switching designs.

Boolean operation—A logic or math manipulation, association, or operation which uses or applies the rules of Boolean algebra. The operands, states, or results assume either one of two values, conditions, or states when determined or evaluated as to which of such two states is in being or to be assumed, by either of the two variables or expressions, such as on/off; go/no-go, zero/one; etc.

Boolean operation, binary — A specific Boolean operation on two operands, the result of which depends upon both of them. The results from each of four possible combinations of values p and q form a truth table, or Boolean operation table.

Boolean operation, dyadic—An operation in Boolean algebra performed on or with two operands and in which the result is dependent upon both of them. Operations on or with two operands are usually represented with connective symbols written between them. . . . as "union" or other Boolean connectives. Such connective operands or operations are most often related to Boolean truth tables.

Boolean operation, monadic — An operation performed on one operand.

Boolean operation table — A table which shows the value of the results from each of four possible combinations of values p and q. This is synonomous with truth table, but Boolean operation table is the preferred use in electronic data processing procedures.

Boolean variable — The use of two-valued Boolean algebra to assume either one of the only two values possible. Examples: true or false; on or off; open or closed. Basically, all digital computers use the two-state or two-variable Boolean algebra in construction and operation.

bootleg program—*See* program, bootleg.

bootstrap—1. A technique or device designed to bring itself into a desired state by means of its own action. For example, a machine routine whose first few instructions are sufficient to bring the rest of itself into the computer from an input device. This usually involves either the manual entering of a few instructions, or the use of a special key on the console. 2. A brief developer subroutine which, while in storage, controls the computer to read in other data such as a loading routine, after control has been transferred to it.

bootstrap input program—Very popular programs which have simple preset computer operations to facilitate information or program input reading and which also contain instructions to be read until the program is assembled or executed, i.e., one instruction pulls other preset instructions.

bootstrap loader — A subroutine which is usually automatic and built into the hardware of the computer, which is capable of initiating the reading of another subroutine whose first instructions are designed to bring in the rest of the subroutine and thus initiate the total program schedule.

bootstrap loading routine—*See* loading routine (bootstrap).

bootstrap memory—The bootstrap memory is a time-saving device built into the main computer. It consists of sixteen 30-bit words of wired storage. It is programmed (wired) to fit the specialized needs of various computer users. The program and words in the bootstrap memory cannot be altered by the computer but can be manually changed when necessary. The purpose of the bootstrap memory is to provide for the automatic reading of new programs into the computer, with protection against erasing its vital instructions (some computers).

bootstrap routine, tape — Some load tapes have, as the first block, a bootstrap routine which serves to bring in the remainder of the resident and various other parts of the system. The bootstrap routines also provide a simple card load routine, a panic dump,

and a method of patching the resident system prior to writing it to drum.

border-punched card — *Same as* margin-punched card.

bore—Inside diameter of the hub on a tape reel.

B OR-NOT A gate—*See* gate, B OR-NOT A.

borrow—An arithmetically negative carry. It occurs in direct subtraction by raising the low order digit of the minuend by one unit of the next higher order digit; e.g., when subtracting 67 from 92, a tens digit is borrowed from the 9, to raise the 2 to a factor of 12; the 7 of 67 is then subtracted from the 12 to yield 5 as the units digit of the difference; the 6 is then subtracted from 8, or 9-1, yielding 2 as the tens digit of the difference.

BOS—Abbreviation for basic operating system. Disk-oriented, this is a more powerful extension of tape basic programming support.

BOSS—BOSS, the Raytheon Monitor and I/0 Control System, provides automatic control of the operations. BOSS achieves its goal of enabling efficient "hands off" operation by: 1. Supervising the running of separate jobs; permitting linkage control between and among the programs in the library. 2. Calling system programs needed to translate symbolic programs of compiler language to machine language. 3. Supervising loading of programs and library subroutines. 4. Supervising the printing of diagnostic and memory dumps.

bound—The upper or lower limit of values that can be permitted.

boundary, byte—In an IBM 360 system, any core address within the computer.

boundary, character—1. A real or imaginary rectangle which serves as a boundary, in character recognition, between consecutive characters or successive lines on a source document. 2. A character recognition term indicating the largest rectangle with a side parallel to the reference edge of the document. Each of the sides of this rectangle is tangent to the printed outline of a particular character.

boundary, double-word—Any address ending in 000, which is divisible by 8 in the IBM 360 System, a natural boundary for 8-byte double-word items.

boundary, full-word—In the IBM 360 system, an address which ends in 00 and which is divisible by binary 4, is a natural boundary for a 4-byte machine word.

boundary, half-word—In the IBM 360 Computer Series, any address ending in a 0 which is divisible by binary 2 denotes a natural boundary for an item of 2 bytes length. Items of this type must be referenced by an address falling on a boundary of the corresponding type.

boundary, page—*See* page, boundary.

boundary register—A special register used in a multi-programmed system to designate the upper and lower addresses of each user's program block in the core memory.

bound, tape—*Same as* tape limited.

box—In a programming flow chart, a logical unit of computer programming surrounded by a rectangle and treated as a unit.

box-B —*See* index register.

box, connection — An electrical distribution panel similar in purpose to that of a plugboard, which permits distribution or altering of destinations of signals. Most often found in punch card machines with mechanical sensing. Wires can be disconnected and changed to different terminals to achieve specific design purposes.

box, decision—The symbol used in flow charting to indicate a choice or branching in the information-processing path.

box, loop—A specific register used as an index register but only to modify instructions immediately prior to their execution. Example, a number or symbol is addended to an instruction as the last step before the instruction is executed and the instruction is thus modified, but without changing the instruction as it is stored in memory.

box, stunt—A device used in teleprinters to perform nonreadout functions such as carriage return, line feed, ring signal bell, answer cdc's and tsc's, etc.

box, universal button—*See* button box, universal.

BPS — Abbreviation for basic programming support. BPS card and BPS tape systems are the two simplest and smallest operating systems available for main-line IBM System 360 computers.

branch—1. To depart from the normal sequence of executing instruction in a computer. (Synonymous with jump.) 2. A machine instruction that can cause a departure as in definition 1. (Synonymous with transfer.) 3. A sequence of instructions that is executed as a result of a decision instruction. 4. The selection of one, two, or more possible paths in the flow of control based on some criterion. The instructions which mechanize this concept are sometimes called branch instructions; however the terms transfer of control and jump, are more widely used.

branch calling—*Same as* calling sequence.

branch, computed—A common example is the GO TO $N_1N_2N_3 \ldots N_1$. Branching occurs to N_1, depending on the computed current value of 1. Assigned branches of the form GO TO 1, where 1 is an assigned address, may also be available.

branch, conditional—1. An instruction which is interpreted as an unconditional transfer if a specified condition or set of conditions is satisfied. If the condition is not satisfied, the instruction causes the computer to proceed in its normal sequence of control. A conditional transfer also includes the testing of the condition. 2. A specific instruction will depend upon the result of some arithmetical or logical operation or the state of some

switch or indicator as to whether or not that instruction will cause a jump or skip to another preset instruction.

branch controller, remote real-time—This is a multiplexing unit which permits up to 16 accounting machines at a remote location to communicate with a real-time buffer over a single telephone circuit (some systems).

branching—1. A computer operation, similar to switching, where a selection is made between two or more possible courses of action depending upon some related fact or condition. 2. Method of selecting the next operation for the computer to execute while the program is in progress, based on the computer results. Adds greatly to program flexibility.

branch instruction—An instruction to a computer that enables the programmer to instruct the computer to choose between alternative subprograms, depending upon the conditions determined by the computer during the execution of the program. (Synonymous with transfer instruction.)

branch instruction test—Most such instructions are of the testing type, i.e., if some arithmetic relation is satisfied, such as, X being greater than A, or less than A, then a jump or branch will occur to some specified instruction, where X is usually the contents of a machine register.

branch-on indicator—*See* indicator, branch-on.

branch-on switch setting—Branching is often designed by the use of certain memory locations or index registers to set the value of the switches. The presetting of a switch may cause the program to branch to the appropriate one of N points, where N is the number of possible switch settings.

branchpoint—A point in a routine where one of two or more choices is selected under control of the routine.

branch, unconditional—An instruction which switches the sequence of control to some specified location. (Synonymous with unconditional jump, and unconditional transfer of control.)

breadboard—This bit of jargon usually refers to an experimental or rough construction model of a process, device, or construction.

break—To break, in a communication circuit, the receiver user interrupts the sending user and takes control of the circuit. The term is used especially in connection with half-duplex telegraph circuits and two-way telephone circuits equipped with voice-operated devices.

breakpoint—1. A point in a program as specified by an instruction, instruction digit, or other condition, where the program may be interrupted by external intervention or by a monitor routine. 2. A point in a computer program at which conditional interruption, to permit visual check, printing out, or other analyzing, may occur. Breakpoints are usually used in debugging operations.

breakpoint, conditional — A breakpoint at which the routine may be continued as coded if desired conditions are satisfied.

breakpoint instruction — 1. An instruction which will cause a computer to stop or to transfer control in some standard fashion to a supervisory routine that can monitor the progress of the interrupted program. 2. An instruction which, if some specified switch is set, will cause the computer to stop or take other special action.

breakpoint instruction, conditional — A conditional jump instruction, which if some specified switch is set, will cause the computer to stop, after which either the routine may be continued as coded, or a jump may be forced.

breakpoint switch — A manually operated switch which controls conditional operation at breakpoints; it is used primarily in debugging.

breakpoint symbol — A symbol which may be optionally included in an instruction, as an indication, tag, or flag, to designate it as a breakpoint.

break, sequence (sorting) — That point in a file between the end of one string and start of another.

break, string — The point at which a sort can find no more records with sufficiently high control keys to fit on the current output string.

breakthrough — An interruption in the intended character stroke in optical character recognition.

break, transcription — A flow-chart symbol or device that shows the relation between two files. The symbol is directional and suggests the flow of information from one file to the file that is affected by the information. The operation symbol should be on the history lines of the file that is affected.

B-register — *Same as* register index.

BRIDGE — A Honeywell (Liberator) program which performs direct translation from the machine language of competitive systems to the machine language of various Honeywell computers.

bridge, central-office — Like the data sets and lines, the central-office bridges are supplied and installed by the telephone company. A bridge, located in the telephone company central office, combines lines from several offices into one line to provide optimum transaction loads for each line going to the processing center. Up to nine offices can be combined into one line, with a corresponding reduction in line and data set costs.

bridge limiter — A limiter is a unit intended to prevent a variable from exceeding specified limits. A diode bridge can be used as a bridge limiter.

brightness — The average reflectance of paper, in character recognition, measured in relation to a standard surface.

broadband — As applied to data transmission, it is used to denote transmission facilities capable of handling frequencies greater than those required for high-grade voice communications; i.e., higher than 3 to 4 kc.

broadband, single-station (communications) — A single broadband station can be connected to a CTS (communication terminal station) by a leased Telpak A line. Leased Telepak A line operation permits continuous data exchange between two fixed locations at a maximum transfer rate of 5100 characters per second. Data transfer can be initiated by either device, providing the remote hardware can handle such an operation. The data format will be such that character parity, start and end of message limits, message parity, and character synchronization will be established. The CTS will be prepared to receive the data at all times.

These modes of operation reflect the influence of presently available communications tariff offerings. The CTS design and packaging philosophy will allow for future higher-speed operation (up to 100,000 bits/sec) and also for operation with communications hardware using more advanced techniques.

broadcast — Some control stations have the ability to broadcast messages simultaneously to all stations on a circuit. This is accomplished by using a call which is common to all stations.

brush — An electrical conductor for reading data from a punch card.

brush-compare check — In a machine that punches cards, an operation which reads a character that has just been punched, compares it with the desired character, and signals if there is any disagreement.

brushes, comparing — *See* comparing brushes.

brush readers — Method of reading characters in punch cards by interpreting the electronic signals as each row on the card passes between the brushes and the roller.

brush station — A location in a device where the holes in a punched card are sensed by brushes sweeping electrical contacts.

Brussels classification — *See* universal decimal classification.

brute-force approach — To try to undertake with existing equipment the mass of problems that do not use precise computation or logical manipulations (as accounting problems and scientific problems do).

BSI (British Standards Institution) — A British institution corresponding somewhat to the American National Standards Institute. It publishes various standards including a glossary of terms used in data processing.

B-store — *Same as* index register.

bubble sort — A sorting technique which exchanges a pair of numbers if they are out of order.

bucket — 1. A slang expression used to indicate some portion of storage specifically reserved for accumulating data, or totals; e.g., "throw it in bucket #1" is a possible expression. Commonly used in initial planning. 2. A general term for a specific reference in storage; e.g., a section of storage, the location of a word, a storage cell, etc.

bucket, double—*See* double bucket.

buffer—1. A word which often implies buffer storage. 2. An isolating circuit used to avoid any reaction of a driven circuit upon the corresponding driving circuit. 3. The auxiliary data-storage device which holds data temporarily and which may also perform other functions in conjunction with various input/output machines. 4. A storage device used to compensate for a difference in rate of flow of data, or time of occurrence of events when transmitting data from one device to another. 5. An extremely temporary storage device of relatively small capacity capable of receiving and transmitting data at different rates of speed. Used as an equalizer when positioned between any set of components that operate at different speeds than the computer itself, such as a card reader and a card punch. 6. A logical OR circuit. 7. An isolating component designed to eliminate the reaction of a driven circuit on the circuits driving it; e.g., a buffer amplifier. 9. A diode.

buffer amplifier—An amplifier designed to isolate a preceding circuit from the effects of a following circuit.

buffer, card-punch—A parity check is performed on all data transmitted to the card-punch buffer. The correctness of the punching is checked by the circuitry built into the card punch. If for any reason the card punch does not punch (hopper empty, stacker full, misfeed, etc.) after receiving data from the buffer, it will enter an inoperative status.

buffer, data—*Same as* buffer.

buffer, drum—A magnetic drum unit which accepts data from various input circuits, modules, or devices and retains these data for future use either because the computer mainframe is not ready to accept it or because it will use it for later processing.

buffered computer—A computing system with a storage device which permits input and output data to be stored temporarily in order to match the slow speed of input/output devices with the higher speeds of the computer. Thus, simultaneous input/output computer operations are possible. A data-transmission trap is essential for effective use of buffering, since it obviates frequent testing for the availability of a data channel.

buffered input/output—Magnetic-core buffers outside the main processor memory compensate for speed differences between slower electromechanical input/output devices and processor speeds. Operations are overlapped, with all units operating simultaneously at rated speeds. Buffering eliminates the need for more expensive, multiple I/O channels —and eliminates complex I/O timing considerations from the programming job.

buffered input/output channels—*See* input/output section, buffered.

buffered input/output section—*See* input/output section, buffered.

buffer, full-word I/O—Since output data characters are located in the lower half of output data words, while input data characters are found in the upper half of input data words, it is possible to use the same computer word in core storage for both input and output buffers. Since each buffer is controlled by its own buffer control word, there need be no relationship between the input and output buffers other than that they use the upper and lower halves of the same computer words.

buffer gate—*Same as* gate, OR.

buffer, half-word I/O—If, for reasons of previous program compatibility or to facilitate systems design, it becomes desirable to use the upper half of the computer word for both input data characters and output data characters, this arrangement can be made when the system is ordered. This technique leaves the lower half of the buffer area words free to be used for some entirely unrelated purpose such as the storage of constants.

buffering exchange—A technique for input/output buffering which prevents or avoids the internal movement of data. Buffers are either filled, empty, or actively in use, by an input/output device. Exchange buffering relates to distinct areas set aside for work and for buffering.

buffer, input—Magnetic core buffers outside the main processor memory compensate for speed differences between slower electromechanical input/output devices and processor speeds; operations are overlapped with all units operating simultaneously at rated speeds.

buffer, input/output—Permits data-word transfers to and from memory to proceed without main program attention. May be programmed so that when input/output transfer is complete, the computer generates an internal interrupt.

buffer, inquiry—Also included in the computer system is an inquiry buffer with a 17-digit storage capacity. This unit is intended primarily for communication through a 359-1 Communication Line Adapter (CLA) with the bank window machine used in savings and loans institutions (some computers).

buffer, media conversion—Small, tightly coded subroutines operating under control of the executive system perform on-line conversion of data between card, printer, punch, and tape equipment concurrently with other programs. Low-speed devices use a magnetic drum as a large buffer area between themselves and operating programs. Use of the magnetic drum as a buffer provides increased throughput capability as programs using these drum buffers effectively "read" or "print" information at drum-transfer speeds.

buffer memory register—*See* register, memory buffer.

buffer output—A buffer developed to receive and store data being transmitted into a computer, and which usually includes instructions.

buffer, overlapped-operations — Magnetic core buffers outside the main processor memory compensate for speed differences between slower electromechanical input/output devices and processor speeds. Operations are overlapped, with all units operating simultaneously at rated speeds. Buffering eliminates the need for more expensive, multiple I/O channels, and eliminates complex I/O timing considerations from the programming job.

buffer register, output—*See* register, output buffer.

buffer size, display—The minimum and maximum number of words reserved for display units and used, with automatic refreshing, to present a flicker-free picture.

buffers, peripheral—*See* peripheral buffers.

buffer storage—1. Any device which temporarily stores information during a transfer of information. 2. Secondary storage used exclusively for assembly and transfer of data between internal and external storage. 3. Storage used to facilitate transfer of data between any two storage devices whose input and output speeds are not synchronized. 4. A synchronizing element between two different forms of storage, usually between internal and external. 5. An input device in which information is assembled from external or secondary storage and stored ready for transfer to internal storage. 6. An output device into which information is copied from internal storage and held for transfer to secondary or external storage. Computation continues while transfers between buffer storage and secondary or internal storage, or vice versa, take place.

buffer storage locations—A set of locations used to compensate for a difference in rate of flow of data, or time of occurrence of events, when transmitting data from one device to another.

bug—1. Any mechanical, electrical or electronic defect that interferes with, or "bugs up" the operation of the computer. It can also be a defect in the coding of the program. (If you're diffident about using this word, call it a malfunction.) 2. A mistake in the design of a routine or a computer, or a malfunction.

BUIC, (Back-Up Interceptor Control)—A modular computing system developed by Burroughs Corp. for military systems and currently being used in surveillance air defense systems.

building block principle—A system which permits the addition of other equipment units to form a larger system. Also called modularity.

built-in checks (automatic) — Built-in checks should be taken advantage of and not duplicated by wired, programmed, or manual controls. They function as a result of internal machine circuitry and are, therefore, performed automatically. Some of these checks are common to all machines. For example, all machines have checks which stop the machine for a timing error, a blown fuse, or an operation that is impossible or in conflict with another. Computers utilize input/output checks, instruction checks and parity checks. The input check insures that all data is read and coded correctly into machine language; the output check insures that the output characters are correctly set up for punching and printing. The instruction check permits the execution of only those instructions having a valid operation code and instruction format. The parity check verifies each character in the computer on the basis of an odd or even bit configuration. To insure accuracy in disk-storage write operations, internal circuitry automatically compares the written record against the one from which it was written, or requires that a compare instruction doing this be executed before another disk-storage operation. In magnetic-tape operations, each character and each channel within a record must pass a validity check for an odd or even number of bits; the system determines whether the bit count is odd or even.

built-in controls—Various error-checking techniques built into EDP equipment by the manufacturer.

built-in storage—*See* storage ,internal.

built-in tracing structure—*See* tracing structure, built-in.

bulk eraser—A device which erases or destroys the magnetic information on a reel of tape without removing the tape from the reel.

bulk storage—Storage of large-volume capacity used to supplement the high-speed storage which can be made addressable, such as disks, drums, or remain nonaddressable with magnetic tapes. Other names for this type of storage are external or secondary storage.

bulk testing—*See* testing, saturation.

bureau, service—*See* service bureau.

burst—The separation of sheets of a continuous form.

burst, error—A data transmission technique using a specified number of correct bits interspersed with designed error bits. The last erroneous bit in a burst and the first erronous bit in the successive burst are separated by the specified number of correct bits. The group of bits in which two successive erroneous bits are always separated by less than a specific number of correct bits.

burst mode—A mode of communications between the processor and I/O devices. When a signal from an I/O device operating through the multiplexer channel indicates burst mode, the receiving unit continues to fetch bits until the unit is finished.

bus—1. A circuit over which data or power is transmitted. Often one which acts as a common connection among a number of locations. (Synonymous with trunk.) 2. A path over which information is transferred, from any of several sources to any of several destinations.

bus check—*See* check, bus.

bus, digit-transfer — *Same as* trunk, digit transfer.

bus drivers, output—All major output signals from the standard computer used in programmed and data-break information transfers are power amplified by bus-driver modules to allow them to drive a very heavy circuit load.

bus hub—A location on the control panel which permits several entries or exits of pulse signals.

business application—Close groupings of related activities for treatment as specific units; e.g., inventory-control processes, order and sales entires, customer-credit reports and accounting, automated purchasing models, and others may be treated as units for conversion to electronic data processing and operating systems.

business-data processing — 1. The almost boundless variety of commercial applications from actual transactions (in contrast to problem solutions). Such processes involve and concern file processing, manipulations, and reporting, plus planning procedures for operating or quality control, capital, and project budgeting. 2. Data processing for business purposes; e.g., recording and summarizing the financial transactions of a business.

business programmer analyst — *See* analyst, business programmer.

bust—The malperformance of a programmer or machine operator.

button, activate—*Same as* button, initiate.

button box, universal—A coined term for a set of push buttons whose functions are determined by the computer program.

button, emergency—Some units contain a button which, when depressed, is designed to prevent further destruction or malady in the event of a current failure, or when the operator knows no other corrective act.

button, initiate—A control panel switch which causes the first step of a subroutine or sequence of programmed steps to be started to perform the cycling or movement of operations.

button, intervention—*Same as* button, emergency.

button, panic—*See* button, emergency.

buttons, function—The small typewriter-key-like buttons found on many specialized input/output terminals which are used to query the system or have it perform certain operations. For example, on the remote-inquiry terminal used in a stock quotation system, a three letter combination identifies any stock, and by punching the right function button, earnings, sales, dividends, volume, etc., can be displayed.

button, start—*Same as* button, initiate.

bypass procedure—A procedure used to get the most vital information into the main computer when the line control computer fails. The few direct control lines into the main computer are frequently switched to maximize different terminal input. Teleprinters, paper tape punches, telephones, etc., are used to provide by-pass.

byproduct—Data in some form developed without additional effort from a device whose basic purpose is to perform some other operation.

byte—1. A generic term to indicate a measureable portion of consecutive binary digits; e.g., an 8-bit or 6-bit byte. 2. A group of binary digits usually operated upon as a unit. 3. A sequence of adjacent binary digits operated upon as a unit and usually shorter than a word.

byte boundary—In an IBM 360 system, any core address within the computer.

byte, effective—The byte actually accessed in an operation on a single byte or byte string.

byte, effective location—The actual storage location pointed to by the effective virtual address of a byte addressing instruction.

byte manipulation—The ability to manipulate, as individual instructions, groups of bits such as characters. A byte is considered to be eight bits in most cases, and forms either one character or two numerals.

byte mode—An alternate mode of communications between the processor and I/O devices. The multiplexer channel accepts one character at a time from an input device unless the I/O unit itself signals burst mode. Byte mode allows the multiplexer channel to accept data from multiple low-speed devices simultaneously.

C

cable—Assembly of one or more conductors within an enveloping protection sheath so constructed as to permit the use of conductors separately or in groups.

cable, combination—A cable that has conductors grouped in combinations, such as pairs and quads.

cable, composite—In communications use, a composite cable is one in which conductors of different gauges, or types, are combined under one sheath.

cable, flat—*See* cable, tape.

cable, paired—A particular cable in which all of the conductors are arranged in the form of twisted pairs, none of which are arranged with others to form quads.

cables, noise—When digital equipments are cabled together, care must be taken to minimize crosstalk between the individual conductors in the cables. Because of the fast rise and fall times characteristic of digital signals, these individual conductors can often generate significant amounts of noise.

cable, tape—A cable containing flat metallic ribbon conductors, all lying side by side in the same plane and imbedded in a material which insulates and binds them together.

cache memory—An IBM developed, limited-capacity, very fast semiconductor memory which can be used in combination with lower cost, but slower large-capacity core memory, giving effect to a larger and faster memory. Look-ahead procedures are required in the progress of the programs to affect locating and depositing the right information into the fast memory when it is required.

CAL — Abbreviation for conversational algebraic language.

calculated address—*See* address, calculated.

calculating—The computation as a result of multiplication, division, addition, subtraction, or by a combination of these operations. A data-processing practice.

calculating, card-programmed — Card-programmed calculating uses many connected or separate machines. That is, an accounting machine reads from punched cards the various factors for calculating, and the codes instruct the machines about calculations to be made, thus, involving multiple steps of data processing.

calculating operation, average—An indication of the calculating speed of the computer determined by taking the mean time for nine additions and one multiplication.

calculating operation, representative—*Same as* calculating operation, average.

calculating punch—A type of punched card device which reads data from cards and performs various arithmetic or logic operations as well. The results are then punched on another card, or if desired, on the same card.

calculating time, representative — *See* time, representative computing.

calculation, double or reverse—Double or reverse calculation is the calculation, recalculation, and then comparison of the two results to prove accuracy. It is commonly used in payroll and other calculations for which no predetermined control total can be developed. In the recalculation, factors are reversed; the original multiplier becomes the multiplicand and the original multiplicand becomes the multiplier. When processing with unit record equipment, if the recalculation is performed in a separate run, then punching of the result can also be verified.

calculation, fixed point — A calculation of numbers in which the arithmetic point, binary or decimal, is assumed to be or is held at a specific relative position for each number. *See* arithmetic, fixed point.

calculation, floating point—A calculation of numbers in which the arithmetic point, binary or decimal, is movable not necessarily the same for each number. *See* arithmetic, floating decimal.

calculator—1. A device that performs primarily arithmetic operations based upon data and instructions inserted manually or contained on punch cards. It is sometimes used interchangeably with computer. 2. A particular device for performing arithmetic usually requiring frequent manual intervention. Generally, a device or machine used to carry out logical and arithmetic digital calculations of any type.

calculator, network—An analog device designed primarily for simulating electrical networks.

calculator, remote — Desk calculator allows simultaneous on-line computing service for many engineers, scientists, and mathematicians from their home or office. In a time-sharing system, the remote calculator provides direct, remote access to the computer. Remote connections can be made anywhere, via standard telephone channels, through the common-user dial network. Through the common-user dial network, users query the computer from a keyboard containing conventional functions and symbols of mathematics . . . answers are immediately shown on the remote calculator display panel. All features of the powerful digital computers can be made instantly available at low cost.

calculus, Boolean—An extension of Boolean algebra which includes other variables, such as time, step functions, changes of state, delay.

calculus of variations — A specific calculus which relates to the maxima/minima theory of definite integrals. The integrands are functions of dependent variables, independent variables, and their derivatives.

call—The branching or transfer of control to a specified closed subroutine.

call card, agendum—A single agendum name and its parameters punched on one card in a stylized form; one item of the agenda—a control-language statement calling for the execution of the named agendum. A set of agendum call cards is used to control a linear programming system, thus forming an agenda.

call direction code(CDC)—An identifying call, usually of two letters, which is transmitted to an outlying receiver and which automatically turns on its printer (selective calling).

call in—To temporarily transfer control of a digital computer from a main routine to a subroutine which is inserted in the sequence of calculating operations to fulfill a subsidiary purpose.

calling branch—*Same as* calling sequence.

calling, selective—This is a form of a teletypewriter communications system. A particular loop may include several machines, but with selective calling, only the machine selected will respond. The device that controls the individual machines in response to a selective call (CDC) is called a stunt box.

calling sequence—1. A basic set of instructions used to begin or initialize or to transfer control to a subroutine, but usually to complete the return of control after the execution of a subroutine is finished. 2. The instructions used for linking a closed routine with the main routine; i.e., basic linkage and a list of the parameters.

call instructions—A call is an operation which brings into action a specific subroutine generally consisting of specific entry conditions which jump to the entry point of the subroutine. The operation begins with the execution of just one instruction referred to as a call instruction.

call number—1. A group of characters identifying a subroutine and containing: (a) information concerning parameters to be inserted in the subroutine, (b) information to be used in generating the subroutine, or (c) information related to the operands. 2. A call word, if the quantity of characters in the call number is equal to the length of a computer word.

call, operand—1. The function of the operand call syllable is to obtain an operand and place it in the top of the stack. The method by which this is accomplished varies according to the kind of data word addressed. When an operand call addresses an operand, the operand is brought to the top of the stack; the processor automatically checks the flag bit and finding it 0, terminates the oper-and-call operation leaving the operand in the top of the stack. 2. A principal method of obtaining values from a PRT (Production Run Tape), using the relative addressing technique, is through use of the operand call syllable. An instruction is referred to as a

syllable, and one word accommodates four syllables. Each operand-call syllable contains the relative address of the location from which it is to obtain information (some computers).

calls, error—Too many subroutines have been called by the program. A maximum of fifty subroutines may be called by an object program (some systems).

calls, subroutine—*See* subroutine calls.

call word—*See* word, call.

Cambridge Polish—Used in the LISP language, the Polish operators = and × are allowed to have more than two operands.

camp-on—A special method for holding a call for a line that is in use, and signaling when it becomes free.

cancel character—A specific control character designed to indicate that the data with which it is associated are erroneous or are to be disregarded.

capability, stand-alone—A multiplexer designed to function independently of a host or mastercomputer, either some of the time or all of the time.

capacity—1. The limits, both upper and lower, of the items or numbers which may be processed in a computer register—in the accumulator. When quantities exceed the capacity, a computer interrupt develops and requires special handling. 2. The total quantity of data that a part of a computer can hold or handle, usually expressed as words per unit of time. 3. The capability of a specific system to store data, accept transactions, process data, and generate reports.

capacity, channel—1. The maximum number of binary digits or elementary digits to other bases which can be handled in a particular channel per unit time. 2. The maximum possible information-transmission rate through a channel at a specified error rate. The channel capacity may be measured in bits per second or bauds. (Clarified by bits rate and baud.)

capacity, circuit—The number of communications channels which can be handled by a given circuit simultaneously.

capacity, computer—*See* capacity.

capacity, exceed—The generating of a word or number the magnitude or length of which is too great or too small to be represented by the computer; such as an attempt to divide by zero.

capacity, memory—The number of elementary pieces of data that can be contained in a storage device. Frequently defined in terms of characters in a particular code or words of a fixed size that can be so contained.

capacity, output—The number of loads that can be driven by the output of a circuit.

capacity, processing—Often the maximum limitation of places of a number that can be processed at any one time.

capacity, register—The number of digits, characters, or bits that a register can store.

capacity, storage—The number of elementary pieces of data that can be contained in a storage device. Frequently defined in terms of characters in a particular code or words of a fixed size that can be so contained.

capacity, system—*See* capacity.

capacity, word—The number of characters in a machine word. In a given computer, the number may be constant or variable.

capstan—The rotating shaft on a magnetic-tape handling unit which is used to impart uniform motion to the magnetic tape when engaged.

carbon, spot—Carbon paper that is designed to allow only selected areas to be carbonized and thereby only reproduce certain areas of the original.

card—1. The paperboard material formed in uniform size and shape which is punched or marked in various arrays to be sensed electronically or visually by brushes or feelers or by photoelectric pickup. The standard card is $7\frac{3}{8}$ inches long by $3\frac{1}{4}$ inches wide and contains 80 columns and 12 punch positions. 2. An internal plug-in unit for printed-circuit wiring and components.

card, aperture—*See* aperture card.

card, aspect—A card on which is entered the accession numbers of documents in an information-retrieval system. The documents are judged to be related in an important fashion to the concept for which the card is established. (Related to peek-a-boo system, uniterm system, docuterm, and uniterm.)

card bed—A mechanical device for holding cards to be transported past the punching and reading stations.

card, binary — The fundamental punched card containing binary numerals representing numbers, characters, or control symbols in columns and rows.

card, border-punched—*Same as* card, edge punched.

card checking—After the synchronizer has completed transferring the data from a card, the number of memory accesses is checked to verify that an entire card image has been transferred to memory. Only the image from the second read station is transmitted to memory. The hole counts from the two read stations are compared. A modulo-3 check is made on each word that is transferred. If any of these checks detects an error, a program-testable indicator is set, and an automatic program interrupt occurs (some systems).

card code—The combinations of punched holes which represent characters (letters, digits, etc.) in a punched card.

card column—1. One of the vertical lines of punching positions on a punched card. 2. One of twenty to ninety single-digit columns in a tabulating card. When punched, a column contains only one digit, one letter, or one special code.

card, composite—A card, often multipurpose, which contains data needed in the processing of various applications.

card, continuation—A punched card which continues data that has been started on a previous card. This is allowed in many compilers such as Fortran.

card, control—A card which contains input data or parameters for a specific application of a general routine.

card, CRAM—A strip of oxide coated mylar, $3\frac{1}{4}'' \times 14''$, on which information may be placed in the form of magnetically polarized spots. (NCR)

card cycle — The time required to read or punch a card.

card, detail—A punched card which contains data which is part of a total, i.e., individual transaction card.

card, double entry—A punched card which contains data for entry into two different accounts such as a card containing both payroll and labor distribution information.

card, dual purpose — Punched cards which contain printed as well as punched information.

card, ducol punched—A punched card with 12 rows of punching positions in each column. Zero through 9, to represent numerals zero to 99 using multiple punching in each column, and a punch or no punch in the x and y positions.

card, duo purpose—A Hollerith card containing information recorded on the card as well as the punched equivalent of such data. Such a card often serves as a source document for punching and is contrasted with a transcript card.

card, edge-notched—A card of any size provided with a series of holes on one or more edges for use in coding information for a simple mechanical search technique. Each hole position may be coded to represent an item of information by notching away the edge of the card into the hole. Cards containing desired information may then be mechanically selected from a deck by inserting a long needle in a hole position and lifting the deck to allow the notched cards to fall from the needle. Unwanted cards remain in the deck.

card, edge-perforated—*Same as* card, edge-punched.

card, edge-punched—A card of fixed size into which information may be recorded or stored by punching holes along one edge in a pattern similar to that used for punch tape. Hole positions are arranged to form coded patterns in 5, 6, 7, or 8 channels and usually represent data by a binary-coded decimal system.

card editor—A special subroutine relating to the reading of information contained on punched cards with built-in specific capabilities.

card, eighty (80) column—A punch card with 80 vertical columns representing 80 characters. Each column is divided into two sections, one with character positions labeled zero through nine, and the other labeled eleven (11) and twelve (12). The 11 and 12 positions are also referred to as the X and Y zone punches, respectively. (Related to punch card, and ninety-column card.)

card face—The printed side of a punched card. If both sides are printed, the side of major importance is the face.

card feed—A mechanism which moves cards into a machine one at a time.

card feed, interchangeable—A device which usually converts an 80 column card feed to a 51 column card feed.

card field—A fixed number of consecutive card columns assigned to a unit of information; e.g., card columns 15-20 can be assigned to an identification number.

card, header—A card containing information necessary for the processing of the data on cards to follow.

card, Hollerith—A common name for the standard punched card, 3¼ by 7⅜ inches, usually divided into 80 columns of punch hole sites. A combination of punches in a column zone (and field) can represent letters, digits, or symbols. The card was named in honor of Dr. Herman Hollerith who invented it in 1889.

card hopper—A mechanism that holds cards preparatory to feeding.

card, IBM—A type of card that may have information recorded on it by means of punched holes, and which may be read by a computer.

card image—1. A representation in storage of the holes punched in a card, in such a manner that the holes are represented by one binary digit and the unpunched spaces are represented by the other binary digit. 2. In machine language, a duplication of the data contained in a punch card.

card input—A method of introducing data to an input device by the use of punched cards; the card reader proper; data read from punched cards by the machine; the mechanical method by which data is read from punched cards and fed into a machine.

card input magazine—See magazine.

card jam—A pile-up of cards in a machine.

card leading edge—That edge of a punched card which is most forward as regards the direction of motion of the card. Any of the edges may be used to enter the machine first depending on the machine requirements.

card loader—A routine generated automatically according to a programmer's specification and included in an object program to perform, respectively, program-loading operations and a printout of memory content upon request.

card, magnetic—A card, usually with a rectangular flat surface, of any material coated with a magnetic substance on which data is recorded, such that it can be read by an automatic device.

card, margin-perforated—Same as card, edge-punched.

card, margin-punched—Same as card, edge-punched.

card, master—A card containing fixed or indicative information for a group of cards. It is usually the first card of that group.

card mode—The status of the computer while cards are being read or punched.

card, ninety (90)-column—1. A punch card with 90 vertical columns representing 90 characters. The columns are divided in half horizontally, such that the vertical columns in the upper half of the card are numbered 1 through 45, and those in the lower half, 46 through 90. Six punching positions may be used in each column; these are designated, from top to bottom, to represent the digits 0, 1, 3, 5, 7, and 9, by a single punch. The digits 2, 4, 6, and 8 by other characters may be represented by a combination of two or more punches. 2. The standard Remington Rand card contains 90 columns. Alphabetical or numerical data is recorded in these columns in combinations of punched holes which Remington Rand punched-card equipment can sense and translate to produce desired results or reports. The card can be divided into fields made up of any combination of columns and designed exclusively to meet a customer's requirements.

The punched card is a mobile, permanent unit record that can be automatically interpreted, sorted, reproduced, interfiled, collated, segregated, computed and tabulated at high speeds to insure accurate data processing. Once punched and verified, cards become unit records which can be arranged in any desired sequence to produce reports in convenient and usable form.

card, powers—An alternative to the Hollerith card is 3¼ by 7⅜ inches, but divided into two sections, each of which contains 45 of the 90 total alphanumeric characters or symbols. The card, using 0, 1, 3, 5, 7, 9 code, is compatible with Remington Rand Univac equipment.

card, printed-circuit—A card, usually of laminate or resinous material of the insulating type, which is used for the mounting of an electrical circuit. Together the base and circuit make up the card.

card processing, short—Short cards are used as store-sales checks, gasoline sales checks, account receivable transmittal advices, and so forth. Short cards can be processed with full-size name and address cards of account balance cards. The short cards are fed by a processor equipment with a short card feed; the full size cards by a read-punch unit. Reproduction of short cards into standard size cards is not necessary.

card-programmed—1. The capability of being programmed by punch cards. 2. The capability of performing sequences of calculating operations according to instructions contained in a stack of punch cards.

card-programmed calculating—A card-programmed calculating process makes use of several connected machine units. An accounting unit reads from punched cards the factors for calculating, and the codes instruct the machines about calculations to be made. A multiple step data-processing operation is thus involved.

card programmed calculator—A unit in a group of conventional electronic accounting machine (EAM) equipment, often associated with a tabulator to read punched cards.

card-programmed computer—An older type or new "mini" sized computer which is limited in input operation to obtaining information from punched, or magnetic cards.

card punch—The item of peripheral equipment for punching holes (data) into cards, such as hand punches, keyboard printpunches, high-speed punches, paper tapeto-card punches, magnetic tape-to-card conversion units.

card-punch buffer—A parity check is performed on all data transmitted to the cardpunch buffer. The correctness of the punching is checked by the circuitry built into the card punch. If for any reason the card punch does not punch (hopper empty, stacker full, misfeed, etc.) after receiving data from the buffer, it will enter an inoperative status.

card, punched—The common input/output medium used for digital computers.

card punching—This is the basic method for converting source data into punched cards. The operator reads the source document and by depressing keys, converts the information into punched holes. See keypunch.

card punching, 90-column card—This punch is used when the information to be punched into a tabulating card is both alphabetical and numerical. Individual holes are not punched as the keys are depressed since the key action automatically "sets up" the information in the machine (similar to the setting of keys on an adding machine) and upon the depression of the strip key, all holes are perforated simultaneously. Thus, any corrections can be made before the card is punched, eliminating the necessity of removing an incorrectly punched card and repunching a new one.

card-punch unit—A machine that punches cards in designated locations to store data that can be conveyed to other machines or devices by reading or sensing the holes.

card reader—1. A device which senses and translates into internal form the holes in punched cards. 2. This peripheral unit converts holes punched in cards into electrical impulses, and transmits the data to the memory of the computer for processing.

card reader, high-speed (HSR)—See reader, high-speed.

card reader-punch—That peripheral unit which reads and punches data on cards and usually has an input hopper, a card feed, a

read station, a punch station, and two output card stackers.

card-reader unit—An input device, consisting of a mechanical punch-card reader and related electronic circuitry, that transcribes data from punch cards to working storage or magnetic tape.

card, ready-read—A punched card which has a preprinted, often copyrighted format which contains the alphabetic equivalent to the punched hole as well as end of message.

card receiver—1. A receptacle that accumulates cards after they have passed through a machine. 2. A hopper.

card reproducer—A device that reproduces a punch card by punching another similar card.

card row—One of the horizontal lines of punching positions on a punched card.

card, row-binary — A punched card which contains data in binary numbers.

card sensing-punching unit—In the card sensing-punching unit, cards containing variable values for entry into the computing unit are sensed. Subsequently, the results of the program of computing are punched into them. This unit has provision for 90 card columns of input or output.

cards, load—The punched cards which contain the program instructions and the constant values.

card stacker—1. A receptacle that accumulates cards after they have passed through a machine. 2. A hopper. (Synonymous with hopper.)

card strips—Materials used in random access devices that have removable or replaceable storage, in contrast to fixed storage. Card strips, disk packs, or tape strips can be physically removed and replaced. This allows for a theoretically unlimited storage capacity. However, there is a setup time in replacing a disk, card, or strip.

card systems—Systems having card equipment with no mass storage device have an operating system contained in binary card decks. The system operation is determined by the operator. The binary decks are of two types —formatted binary and absolute binary. Formatted binary programs are loaded by the system loader. Absolute binary programs may be loaded by the monitor or by a "preset" operation.

card-to-card (communications) — The operation of transferring data in punched-card form at one location into the same form at another location.

card-to-disk conversion—An operation which consists of using a utility program to load the data from a deck of cards into a disk.

card-to-tape—Pertaining to equipment which transfers information directly from punched cards to punched or magnetic tape.

card-to-tape (communications)—The operation of conversion from the 12-unit Hollerith code of tab cards into perforated-tape code, usually into the five-unit Baudot code (some systems).

card-to-tape converter—A device which converts information directly from punched cards to punched or magnetic tape.

card-to-tape conversion—An operation that uses a utility program to load the data from a deck of cards onto a magnetic tape.

card track—The part of the card peripheral device which moves or guides cards through the machine from the input hopper to the output stacker. Such machines with card tracks are: card readers, punches, tabulators, sorters, keypunches, etc.

card trailing edge—The edge of cards which is opposite to the direction in which the card moves as it passes along the card track of various card processing devices. The trailing edge enters the machine last.

card transceiver—A peripheral device which has four capabilities; it can read data from a punched card, transmit it, receive data, and punch a card. This card-to-card converter is used for rapid card information transmission. Such machines are usually located at each end of the communication net and can each receive or transmit.

card, transcript—That specific card which is key-punched from a source document other than the card itself.

card, transfer—A card, used in the loading of a deck of program cards, which causes the termination of loading and initiates the execution of the program. (Synonymous with transfer of control card.)

card, transfer of control—*Same as* card, transfer.

card transition—*Same as* card, transfer.

card transmission terminal—The transmitting machine which reads data from punched cards and transmits it over telephone circuits to a receiving machine.

card unit speed—The rate, in cards per minute, at which cards are read or punched by the unit.

card unit type—Indicates the unit function: read only (RD), punch only (PN), or read-punch combination (RP).

card, verge-perforated—*Same as* card, edge-punched.

card, verge-punched — *Same as* card, edge-punched.

card verifying—This is a means of checking the accuracy of key punching. It is a duplication check. A second operator verifies the original punching by depressing the keys of a verifier while reading the same source data. The machine compares the key depressed with the hole already punched in the card.

caret—A symbol (an inverted v) used to indicate the location of an insertion.

carriage—A control mechanism for a typewriter or other listing device that can automatically control the feeding, spacing, skipping, and ejecting of paper or preprinted forms.

carriage, automatic—The device which automatically controls the console typewriter to feed forms, paper, provide spacing, skipping,

tabulating, and other operations to display information, program progress, and diagnostics.

carriage control tape—This tape contains the control codes related to the movement of the carriage of the printer and controls the vertical and horizontal positioning of the carriage as well as the paper feed unit.

carriage restore key — A button which returns the printer carriage to the start or home position.

carriage return—The operation that causes printing to be returned to the left margin with or without line advance.

carriage space key—A specific push button which advances the hard copy one or more lines in various type printers.

carrier, data—The selected medium used to transport or carry data or information such as punched cards, magnetic tapes, and punched paper tapes.

carry—1. A signal, or expression, produced as a result of an arithmetic operation on one digit place of two or more numbers expressed in positional notation and transferred to the next higher place for processing there. 2. A signal or expression, as defined in (1) above, which arises in adding, when the sum of two digits in the same digit place equals or exceeds the base of the number system in use. If a carry into a digit place will result in a carry out of the same digit place, and if the normal adding circuit is bypassed when generating this new carry, it is called a high-speed carry, or standing-on-nines carry. If the normal adding circuit is used in such a case, the carry is called a cascaded carry. If a carry resulting from the addition of carries is not allowed to propagate, e.g., when forming the partial product in one step of a multiplication process, the process is called a partial carry. If it is allowed to propagate, the process is called a complete carry. If a carry generated in the most significant digit place is sent directly to the least significant place, e.g., when adding two negative numbers using nine complements, that carry is called an end-around carry. (Synonymous with cascaded carry, complete carry, end-around carry, high-speed carry, and partial carry.) 3. A signal or expression in direct subtraction, as defined in (1) above, which arises when the difference between the digits is less than zero. Such a carry is frequently called a borrow. (Related to borrow.) 4. The action of forwarding a carry. 5. The command directing a carry to be forwarded.

carry cascaded—*See* cascaded carry.

carry, complete—1. A carry which is allowed to propagate. 2. *Same as* carry, definition 2.

carry-complete signal—A signal generated by a digital parallel adder, indicating that all carries from an adding operation have been generated and propagated, and that the addition operation is completed.

carry, end-around—1. A carry from the most significant digit place to the least significant place. 2. A carry sent directly from the high-order position to the least significant place; e.g., using 9's complement addition to subtract numbers. 3. *Same as* carry, definition 2.

carry, high-speed—1. A type of carry in which a carry into a column results in a carry out of that column, because the sum without carry in that column is 9; and instead of normal adding processes, a special process is used which takes the carry at high-speed to the actual column where it is added. Also called standing-on-nines carry. 2. A technique in parallel addition for speeding up carry propagation; e.g., standing-on-nines carry. 3. *Same as* carry, definition 2.

carry, partial—1. The technique in parallel addition wherein some or all of the carries are stored temporarily instead of being allowed to propagate immediately. 2. *Same as* carry, definition 2.

carry, ripple-through — *Same as* carry, high-speed.

carry, standing-on-nines—A carry out of a digit position generated by a carry into the digit position, and the normal adding circuit is by-passed.

carry time—1. The time required for transferring a carry digit into the higher column and there adding it. 2. The time required for transferring all the carry digits to higher columns and adding them for all digits in the number.

CART (Computerized Automatic Rating Technique)—A new type of computer technique developed by Honeywell's electronic data-processing division. When used with one of the firm's computers, CART will automatically select the correct freight rate for any common carrier shipment from the more than 110,000 applicable tariffs of the Interstate Commerce Commission (ICC). It will also determine the best delivery route and monitor the movement of freight shipments from the time they are picked up until they are delivered. (Honeywell)

cartridge—An aluminum cannister used to physically insert and remove a CRAM deck into and out of the chamber of a CRAM unit. (NCR)

cascade control—An automatic control system in which various control units are linked in sequence, each control unit regulating the operation of the next control unit in line.

cascaded carry—1. A carry using the normal adding circuit rather than any special or high-speed circuit. 2. In parallel addition, a carry process in which the addition of two numerals results in a sum numeral and a carry numeral which are in turn added together, this process being repeated until no new carries are generated. 3. Same as carry, definition 2. (Contrast with high-speed carry.)

cascade merging—A technique used in a sort program to merge strings of sequenced data and performed a $T-1$ on part of the data

$T/2$ on parts of the data, and so on. Strings of sequenced data are distributed in a Fibonacci series on the work tapes preceding each merge. The effective power of the merge varies between $T-1$ and $T/2$.

case, test—*See* test case.

casting-out-nines check—*See* check, casting-out-nines.

CASTOR (College Applicant Status Report)—CASTOR enables a personnel department to keep abreast of dynamic college recruiting activities. It records and maintains comprehensive information concerning the college recruiting program and prepares reports showing the disposition and status of all applications. Reports from the system are provided for use as feedback to college placement officers and to the cognizant managers involved in the college program. CASTOR totals job offers, acceptances and rejections, and analyzes the salaries being offered. Acceptances and rejections are correlated with salary offers to produce the timely information essential in evaluating the posture of a company's salary program. This quick feedback enables management to make appropriate adjustments in salary offers while the most qualified applicants are still available.

CASTOR provides a comprehensive review of the variable college recruiting situation and allows for compensating action during the program, when such action is found to be desirable. College applications that are initially introduced through CASTOR are input to Prospect, which maintains each applicant's record for future consideration. (Honeywell)

catalog—1. A list of items with descriptive data, usually arranged so that a specific kind of information can be readily located. 2. To assign a representative label for a document according to a definite set of rules.

cataloged procedure—A group of control cards placed in a cataloged data set.

catalog, union—Often meant to merge a compiled list of the contents of two or more tape libraries.

catastrophic failure—*See* failure, catastrophic.

category—1. A natural classification. 2. A logical grouping of associated documents.

category, display—*See* display catagory.

catena—A chain, a series, especially a connected series.

catenate—*See* concatenate.

cathode follower—A vacuum-tube circuit in which the input signal is applied to the control grid and the output is taken from the cathode. Electrically, such a circuit possesses high-input and low-output impedance characteristics. The equivalent circuit using a transistor is called an emitter follower.

cathode-ray tube—1. An electronic vacuum tube containing a screen on which information may be stored by means of a multigrid modulated beam of electrons from the thermionic emitter storage effected by means of charged or uncharged spots. 2. Abbreviated CRT. A vacuum tube in which a beam of electrons can be focused to a small point on a luminescent screen and can be varied in position and intensity to form a pattern. 3. A storage tube. 4. An oscilloscope tube. 5. A picture tube.

cathode-ray tube display—There are binary displays on many computer operator's consoles. One display bit indicates the memory word parity; other display bits may indicate: (a) The next instruction. (b) The contents of any memory location. (c) The contents of the accumulator. (d) The contents of index registers. (e) The status of the traps. When the computer halts, the display register will indicate the next instruction word, while a register will contain the address of the halt instruction that stopped the computer. To display anything else, the appropriate pushbutton display switch must be pressed. When the display-M button is pressed, the contents of the memory location specified by a register will be displayed. When either the display or other buttons are pressed, the contents of other registers or the condition of the traps are displayed. The display register is also used as an entry register. Push-buttons which may clear all or various parts of the display register, are provided. The contents of the display register may be entered in any memory location. Pushing any of the entry buttons will accomplish entry of the display register contents into the appropriate memory location or register.

cathode-ray tube storage—See storage, cathode-ray tube.

CC process code—When the terminal is in the program mode, the user can execute a single statement that he does not want included in the active program. By typing process code CC in columns 1 and 2 and an arithmetic assignment statement or an output statement in columns 7 through 72, the user indicates to the system that the statement is to be executed immediately, but not retained as part of the program (some computers).

CDC (Call Direction Code) — An identifying call, usually two letters, which is transmitted to an outlying receiver and automatically turns on its printer (selective calling).

cell—1. The storage for one unit of information, usually one character or one word. 2. A location specified by whole or part of the address and possessed of the faculty of store. Specific terms such as column, field, location, and block, are preferable when appropriate.

cell, binary—1. A cell of one-binary digit capacity. 2. A one-bit register or bit position.

cell disturbed—A magnetic cell which has received one or more partial drive pulses in the opposite sense since it was set or reset.

cell, magnetic — 1. Fundamental unit of memory capable of storing a single bit or representing the site of a no bit area where

an existing bit will represent a magnetic field or direction of a magnetic force. 2. A binary storage cell in which the two values of one binary digit are represented by different patterns of magnetism, and in which means of setting and sensing the contents are stationary with respect to the magnetic material.

cells, core storage—That storage using an array of storage cores as cells which are usually arrayed in three dimensions, the plane containing corresponding bits of every word.

cells, dedicated trap — See trap, dedicated cells.

center, automatic-switching — Communications center designed specifically for relaying digitized data by automatic electronic methods.

center, cost accounting—See cost center, accounting.

center, data-processing—A computer installation providing data-processing service for others, sometimes called customers, on a reimbursable or nonreimbursable basis.

center, data switching—See switching center.

center, EDP—Electronic data processing center, a complete complex including one or more computers.

center-feed tape — Perforated paper tape which has feed holes centered directly in line with the centers of the intelligence holes. The most common method in use today.

centerline stroke—Printed character specification drawings and a line used to designate the position and shape of the locus of character stroke midpoints.

center, relay—A system in which data transmissions between stations on different circuits within a network are accomplished by routing the data through a central point. (Synonymous with message switching center.)

center, semiautomatic message-switching—A location where an incoming message is displayed to an operator who directs the message to one or more outgoing circuits according to information read from the message.

center, store-and-forward switching—A message-switching center in which the message accepted from the sender, whenever he offers it, is held in a physical store and forwarded to the receiver, whenever he is able to accept it.

center, switching—A location in which incoming data from one circuit is transferred to the proper outgoing circuit.

center, torn-tape switching—A location where operators tear off the incoming printed and punched paper tape and transfer it manually to the proper outgoing circuit.

central character, font-change — Same as character, font change.

central communications controller—See communications, central controller.

central computer, input/output — Communication between the central computer and the peripheral units of some computer systems may be performed over all input/output channels. Each of the several channels allows bidirectional transfers of data and control signals between the central computer and the peripheral devices.

central control panel—*See* control panel.

central control unit—*See* control unit, central.

central file, on-line—*See* file, on-line (Central).

central, hybrid hardware — The hardware control program group provides the control and communication between various elements of the hybrid system. The programmer can control analog computer modes and operation of automatic features of the analog device.

central input/output control—Input/output operations are performed by a request to the monitor Central Input/Output routine (CIO). CIO initiates the operation specified and returns control to the program. The program may continue operation simultaneously with the input/output operation. When the input/output operation is complete the program is interrupted. The interrupt is processed and control is returned to the object program. The program that performs the input/output operations is called an input/output driver. When a call is made for input/output, CIO processes the call and determines which driver is needed to perform the operation. The driver is determined from the logical equipment number specified in the call. The monitor contains a table of physical equipment and drivers, called a Physical Equipment Table (PET). A logical equipment number specifies an entry in PET. From this entry, CIO sets the necessary parameters and executes the driver. The driver initiates the operation upon the external device and sets up an interrupt-processing routine. Control is then returned to CIO which restores the program conditions and returns to the calling program (some systems).

centralized control—In a computer, the control of all processing by a single operational unit.

centralized data processing—Data processing performed at a single, central location on data obtained from several geographical locations or managerial levels. Decentralized data processing involves processing at various managerial levels or geographical points throughout the organization.

centralized input/output coordination, time sharing—See time sharing, centralized input/ output coordination.

central office bridge—Like the data sets and lines, the central office bridges are supplied and installed by the local telephone company. A bridge, located in the telephone company central office, connects lines from several offices into one circuit-line to provide optimum transaction loads for each line going to the processing center. Up to

nine offices can be bridged into a circuit-line. (A circuit-line is the same kind of line as the lines from each office to the bridge. The term circuit-line is used to distinguish the total line going into the processing center from the lines coming from each office.)

central office exchange—1. The place where a communication common carrier locates the equipment which interconnects subscribers and circuits. 2. A common-carrier facility which performs the necessary circuit-switching functions required in the operation of communication networks.

central processing unit (CPU)—1. The unit of a computing system that contains the circuits that control and perform the execution of instructions. 2. The central processor of the computer system. It contains the main storage, arithmetic unit, and special register groups.

central processing, unit loop—The main routine or a control program and that which is associated with the control of the internal status of the processing unit, in contrast to those control programs of routines developed with terminals and file storage input-output.

central processor—*See* central processing unit.

central processor organization—The computer can be divided into three main sections: arithmetic and control, input/output, and memory. The arithmetic and control section carries out the directives of the program. The calculations, routing of information, and control of the other sections occur in this part of the central processor. All information going in and coming out of the central processor is handled by the input/output section. It also controls the operation of all peripheral equipment. The memory section is the heart of the central processor; it provides temporary storage for data and instructions. Because of its importance, the total cycle time of the memory is the main determining factor in the overall speed of the processor.

central scanning loop—A loop of instructions which determines which task is to be performed next. After each item of work is completed, control is transferred to the central scanning loop which searches for processing requests in order to determine the next item to be processed. The computer may cycle idly in the central scanning loop if no item requires its attention, or it may go into a wait state which is interrupted if the need arises. The central scanning loop is the nucleus of a set of supervisory programs.

central terminal unit (CTU)—This unit supervises communication between the teller consoles and the processing center. It receives incoming messages at random intervals, stores them until the central processor is ready to process them, and returns the processed replies to the teller consoles which originated the transactions (bank application).

CEPS (Civil Engineering Problems)—CEPS enables the engineer to express solutions in a language approximately the same as he would use in describing his solution to another engineer. CEPS is problem oriented, modular, and with an expandable instruction repertoire. (CDC)

certifier tape—A peripheral device or unit designed to locate defects in magnetic tape before use, such as oxide emissions, unevenness, bubbles, etc.

CF—*See* control footing.

CH—*See* control heading.

chad—That piece of material removed in punching a hole in perforated tape.

chadded—Pertaining to the punching of tape in which chad results.

chadded tape—Perforated tape with the chad completely removed.

chadless—A type of punching of paper tape in which each chad is left fastened by about a quarter of the circumference of the hole, at the leading edge. This mode of punching is useful where it is undesirable to destroy information written or printed on the punched tape, or it is undesirable to produce chads. Chadless-punched paper tape must be sensed by mechanical fingers, for the presence of chad in the tape would interfere with reliable electrical or photolectric reading of the paper tape.

chadless paper tape—A paper tape with the holes partially punched. It is commonly used in teletype operations.

chads — The chips or cuttings which are punched away from paper tape.

chain—1. Any series of items linked together. 2. Pertaining to a routine consisting of segments which are run through the computer in tandem, only one segment being within the computer at any one time and each segment using the output from the previous program as its input.

chain additions program—An instruction set that will permit new records to be added to a file.

chain, binary—A series of flip-flops (binary circuits) which exist in either one of two states, but each circuit can affect or change the following or next circuit.

chain code—An arrangement in a cyclic sequence of some or all of the possible different N-bit words, in which adjacent words are linked by the relationship that each word is derived from its neighbor by displacing the bits one digit position to the left or right, dropping the leading bit, and inserting a bit at the end. The value of the inserted bit needs only to meet the requirement that a word must not recur before the cycle is complete; e.g., 000 001 010 011 111 100 000 . . . .

chained file—*See* file, chained.

chained list—*See* list, chained.

chained record—Physical records, located randomly in main or auxiliary memory modules, that are linked or chained by means of

a control field in each record which contains the address of the next record in the series or chain. Long and complete waiting lists or files can be connected or chained in this way.

chaining—1. A system of storing records in which each record belongs to a list or group of records, and has a linking field for tracing the chain. 2. The capability of an object program to call another object program for execution after its own execution has been performed.

chaining, command—The execution of a sequence of I/O commands in a command list, under control of an IOP, on one or more logical records.

chaining core blocks—The linking together of uncommitted or available core blocks to form queues which may be called uncommitted storage lists.

chaining, data—The gathering (or scattering) of information within one physical record, from (or to) more than one region of memory, by means of successive I/O commands.

chaining search—A particular search key is chosen and when a search of an interconnected set is made whose key matches the search key, the content of the address includes the key matching the search key. It also contains either the item itself or the location of the item sought—or another address is sought and found in the content, the process being repeated, until either the item is found or the chain is terminated.

chain maintenance program—An instruction set that will permit the deletion of records from a file.

chain printer—*See* printer, chain.

chain reaction — The initiation of multiple levels of address modification with few instructions.

chain search—A search key is used and is transformed to bring out an initial address. If the contents of the initial address contain the key matching the search key, the contents contain the sum or other information sought. If unsuccessful, another address is found in the contents, and the process is repeated until the item is found or the chain ends. Thus, a chain search operates in a file of unordered but related or interconnected data.

changeable storage—*See* storage, changeable.

change, control—*See* control change.

change dump—A print-out or output recording of the contents of all storage locations in which a change has been made since the previous change dump.

change file—A list of transactions processed against the master file.

change record—A record which results in changing of some of the information in the corresponding master file record.

changes, pending — Occurrences of various types have prevented successful processing of transactions such as: program errors, records deleted from files, data mistakes, "frozen" accounts, and others. Such deviations from the normal require hold-ups or delays pending decisions resulting in changes.

change, step—The change from one value to another in a single increment in negligible time.

change tape—A paper tape or magnetic tape carrying information that is to be used to update filed information. This filed information is often on a master tape. (Synonymous with transaction tape.)

channel—1. A path along which signals can be sent; e.g., data channel, output channel. 2. The portion of a storage medium that is accessible to a given reading station, e.g., track, band. 3. A unit which controls the operation of one or more I/O units. 4. One or more parallel tracks treated as a unit. 5. In a circulating storage, a channel is one recirculating path containing a fixed number of words stored serially by word. (Synonymous with band.) 6. A path for electrical communication. 7. A band of frequencies used for communication.

channel adapter—A device which permits the connection between data channels of differing equipment. The device allows data transfer at the rate of the slower channel.

channel, analog—A channel on which the information transmitted can take any value between the limits defined by the channel. Voice channels are analog channels.

channel capacity—1. The maximum number of binary digits or elementary digits to other bases which can be handled in a particular channel per unit time. 2. The maximum possible information-transmission rate through a channel at a specified error rate. The channel capacity may be measured in bits per second or bauds.

channel, Class-D—The Class-D channel can be used to transmit punched paper tape at approximately 240 words per minute, depending upon the code element (5-, 6-, 7-, or 8-level code) employed. It could also be used to transmit 80-column punched cards at the rate of 10 to 11 per minute.

channel, Class-E — The Class-E data channel is capable of transmission rates up to 1200 baud. The channel will also accept polar-pulse input conforming to EIA standards, and will deliver signals at the destination having the same characteristics.

channel control, input/output—The transfer of data between external devices and the associated assembly registers proceeds under the control of the external device. Input/output channels may transfer data simultaneously in multichannel operation. The access to main memory from the in/out channel is made available as needed, subject to channel priority. This provided by channel priority logic, which selects the channel of highest priority requesting transfer, that is, the lowest numbered channel requesting transfer data. The data rate and active channels are not restricted except that the program must not require data transfer which exceeds a peak word rate of 525 kc considered over all input/output channels (some computers).

channel controllers—Units which allow several central elements in the computer to share, in a changing manner, a pool of millions of characters of main memory that can be partitioned into numerous (at least 8) different memories.

channel, data—The bidirectional data path between the I/O devices and the main memory in a digital computer that permits one or more I/O operations to take place concurrently with computation.

channel, dedicated—A specific channel that has been reserved or committed or set aside for a very specific use or application.

channel, direct-access display—This provides automatic collection of data and control information from core memory with a single instruction. This indexible address register contains the memory address of the next display control or data word in memory. Termination of the transfer is controlled by the stop bit which signals the computer upon completion of plotting. The stop bit's location may be determined by examining the contents of the channel register (some systems).

channel, duplex—A channel providing simultaneous transmission in both directions.

channel, four-wire—A two-way circuit where the signals simultaneously follow separate and distinct paths, in opposite directions, in the transmission medium.

channel, half-duplex—A channel capable of transmitting and receiving signals, but in only one direction at a time.

channel, information—The transmission and intervening equipment involved in the transfer of information in a given direction between two terminals. An information channel includes the modulator and demodulator and any error-control equipment irrespective of its location, as well as the backward channel, when provided.

channel, input — The channel which first brings in or introduces signals or data to a computing device.

channel, input/output — A specific channel which permits simultaneous communications, and independently so, between various storage units or any of the various input or output units. Such a channel is the control channel for most peripheral devices and quite often performs various checks on data transfers such as validity checks, etc.

channel, multiplexor—See multiplexor, channel.

channel, multiplexor mode—See multiplexor channel mode.

channel operation, multiplexor — See multiplexor channel operation.

channel, output—That particular or dedicated channel reserved for removal or carrying of data from a peripheral device.

channel reliability—The percentage of time that the channel meets the arbitrary standards established by the user.

channels — In perforated tape, channels are longitudinal rows where intelligence holes may be punched along the length of the tape. Also known as levels or tracks.

channel scheduler—A program whose function is to see that a list of requests for input/output operations are executed in a desirable sequence. The channel scheduler program sequentially initiates the next operation on the list after it has completed one operation on a channel.

channel, selector—The selector channel is designed primarily for such devices as tape units and disk files. When the selector channel is directed to make connection with one input or output unit, all other units on that channel are locked out until the first unit is released. The selector channel is capable of handling high-speed units overlapped with processing, so that a stream of data can be fed to storage while the processing unit is performing arithmetic or logic operations for another phase of the program.

channel, simplex—A channel which permits transmission in one direction only.

channels, input/output multiplexing—See input/output channels, multiple.

channels, overlapped—Although processors improved in internal performance, the added speed and power were not always utilized to full advantage. For example, processing and computing operations had to be suspended during I/O operations because the circuits in the processor were being used to handle the input/output data. To solve this problem, overlapped channels were developed.

Overlapped channels (several channels can be serviced simultaneously) in many ways act like a small computer that can take over I/O operations and free the processor for other jobs. This development represented a major step in the utilization of system capabilities.

channels, paper tape — See tape channels, paper.

channels, read/write—The degree of peripheral simultaneity in any computer system depends on the number of read/write channels in the system. A read/write channel is a bi-directional data path across an interface between the main memory and a peripheral device. Whenever an input/output operation is to be performed, a programmer-assigned read/write channel completes the path betwen the required peripheral device and the main memory.

channels tape, punched-paper—The parallel tracks along the length of the tape.

channel status routine (BSY)—BSY (busy) is called by drivers to determine the status of a channel. A driver cannot use a channel until the channel is free. When BSY is called, it retains control until the channel is free. The status of each channel available to the system is contained in the channel status table (CST). This table contains one entry for each channel. Each time a driver is called, it waits for the necessary channel to be free. When an input/output operation is initiated, the driver sets the channel status at busy. Upon completion of the interrupt, the channel status is set at not busy.

channel status table (CST) — The channel status table (CST) is used by input/output drivers to wait until a specific channel is available prior to using it. CST is composed of separate entries for each channel available to the system. Each entry corresponds in order to the address of the channel. That is, entry 0 corresponds to channel 0, entry 1 to channel 1, etc. The size of the table varies according to the number of channels. Each CST entry is one 24-bit word of the following format: CS is the channel status. If CS is zero, the channel is busy. If CS is nonzero, the channel is free and CS is the number of words last transferred via the channel (some computers).

channel switching — Same as input/output switching.

channel synchronizer—The channel synchronizer, housed with the peripheral control unit in a single cabinet, provides the proper interface between the central computer and the peripheral equipment. Other control functions of the channel synchronizer include: primary interpreting of the function words; searching, by comparison of an identifier with data read from a peripheral unit; and providing the central computer with peripheral-unit status information.

channel, time-derived—Any of the channels obtained by time-division multiplexing of a channel.

channel-to-channel connection—A device for rapid data transfer between two computers. A channel adapter is available that permits the connection between any two channels on any two systems. Data is transferred at the rate of the slower channel. See direct-control connection.

channel waiting queue—The group of items in the system needing the attention of the channel scheduler program which executes the items in queue in a desirable sequence.

chapter—Programs are often divided into self-contained parts, most often called segments or sections, and often times chapters, in order to be able to execute the program without maintaining it in its entirety in the internal storage medium at any one time. Other program divisions are pages, paragraphs, books.

character—1. One symbol of a set of elementary symbols such as those corresponding to the keys on a typewriter. The symbols usually include the decimal digits 0 through 9, the letters A through Z, punctuation marks, operation symbols, and any other single symbols which a computer may read, store, or write. 2. The electrical, magnetic, or mechanical profile used to represent a character in a computer, and its various storage and peripheral devices. A character may be represented by a group of other elementary marks, such as bits or pulses.

character, additional — Same as character, special.

character adjustment — The address adjustment in which the literal used to modify the address has reference to a specific given number or group of characters.

character, alphameric—A generic term for numeric digits, alphabetic characters, and special characters.

character-at-a-time—A printer which prints only one character at a time, as contrasted with the line-at-a-time printer, which can print 100 or considerably more characters at a time.

character, backspace — One which creates action of the printing mechanism without printing. The backspace character causes a spacing backwards of one character width.

character, binary-coded—An element of notation which represents alphanumeric characters as decimal digits, letters, and symbols by a set configuration of consecutive binary digits.

character, blank — A specific character designed and used to separate groups of characters. In some computers an actual symbol such as * is used to signify a blank and thus assurance is positive that a blank space did not develop from machine malfunction or keypunch operator error.

character, block ignore — One of the many control characters which indicates that an error in data preparation or transmission has occurred and certain predetermined amounts of data should be ignored. In some particular cases the amount to be ignored is a partial block of characters back to the most recently occurring block mark.

character boundary—A real or imaginary rectangle which serves as a boundary, in character recognition, between consecutive characters or successive lines on a source document.

character, check—See check character.

character checking, inadmissable—Numerous internal checks continually monitor the accuracy of the system and guard against incipient malfunction. Typical are the parity and inadmissable characters check; an automatic read-back of magnetic tape and magnetic cards as the information is being recorded. The electronic tests which precede each use of magnetic tape or magnetic cards ensure that the operator has not set switches improperly.

character check, tape—The tape character is most commonly recorded as a 7-bit code across the tape which contains only 6 bits

of information, the 7th being a parity check or bit. Where odd parity is specified the number of ones in a character will be odd, and where even parity is specified, the number will be even. This allows for error checking when reading or writing on tape.

character, code—A particular arrangement of code elements used in a code to represent a single value or symbol.

character, coded—A character represented by a specific code.

character, coded extension—A distinct character designed to indicate that succeeding characters are to be interpreted using a different code.

character code, forbidden—In the binary coding of characters, a bit code which indicates an error in coding.

character, command—Characters, when used as code elements, can initiate, modify, or stop a control operation. Characters may be used, for example, to control the carriage return, etc., on various devices or control the devices themselves.

character, control—See character, command.

character, controlled, generator—See generator, character-controlled.

character crowding—The effect of reducing the time interval between subsequent characters read from tape, caused by a combination of mechanical skew, gap scatter, jitter, amplitude variation, etc. Also called packing.

character density—Same as packing density.

character, device control—A specific control character to switch devices on or off, usually in telecommunications systems, but also used with other data processing equipment.

character edge—In optical character recognition, there is an imaginary edge which runs along the optical discontinuity between the printed area and the unprinted area of a printed symbol or character. The optical discontinuity is observed by a change in the reflectivity along this imaginary line which is transverse to the character edge.

character emitter—An electromechanical device which emits a timed pulse or group of pulses in some code.

character, end-of-message — Some programmers use specific characters or groups of characters such as: OUT, ROGER, EOM to indicate the end of a message.

character, erase—A character which most often represents a character to be ignored or signifies that the preceding or following item is to be ignored as prescribed by some fixed convention of the machine or as programmed. It may signify that some particular action is to be prevented, or it may signify an erase or destroy action on a tape or disk.

character, error—One of the control characters used to indicate that an error in data preparation or transmission has occurred. It also usually signifies that a certain predetermined amount of coming or recently transmitted data should be ignored.

character, escape—1. The control characters with a time-sequence characteristic which serves to assign, either temporarily or permanently, various new or different meanings to specific coded representations. Examples are: locking-shift characters, nonlocking shift characters, shift-out or shift-in characters, font-change characters, etc. Thus, escape characters permit a limited code to represent a wide range of characters since it assigns more than one meaning to each character representation. 2. A character used to specify that the succeeding one or more characters are expressed in a code different from the code regularly or currently in use.

character fill—1. A procedure of storing the same character or symbol in storage locations, in a group of storage locations, or even in a complete storage unit of a computer. 2. To replace all data in a particular storage device in a group of locations by bringing all the cells to a prescribed or desired state.

character, font-change—A control character which causes the next character to determine which type font is to be used until the next font-change character comes up.

character, forbidden—*Same as* character, illegal.

character, format—A specific control character used to control a key printer. This character does not print but may cause backspacing, tabulating, new lines, etc.

character format memory — Memory storing technique of storing one character in each addressable location.

character, form-feed — The character which controls the printer or demands action of the printer, in this case to feed forms.

character functional — *See* character, command.

character generation, automatic — *See* automatic character generation.

character, ignore—*See* ignore.

character ignore block—The character which indicates that an error in data preparation or transmission has occurred and certain predetermined amounts of coming or recently transmitted data should be ignored. In this particular case, the amount to be ignored is a partial block of characters back to the most recently occurring block mark.

character, illegal—A character or combination of bits which is not accepted as a valid representation by the machine design or by a specific routine. Illegal characters are commonly detected and used as an indication of machine malfunction.

character, improper—*Same as* character illegal.

character instruction — *See* character command.

characteristic—The integral part of a logarithm; the exponent of a normalized number.

characteristic distortion—1. A fixed distortion which results in either shortened or lengthened impulses. It generally does not change in degree from day to day. 2. Distortions caused by transients which, as a result of the modulation, are present in the transmission channel and depend on its transmission qualities.

characteristic overflow — A situation developed in floating-point arithmetic if an attempt is made to develop a characteristic greater than a specified number.

characteristics, noise—*See* noise characteristics.

characteristic underflow—A situation developed in floating-point arithmetic if an attempt is made to develop a characteristic less than a specified number.

character, layout—A specific control character used to control a printer. This character does not print but may cause back-spacing, tabulating, new lines, etc.

character, least significant—The character in the rightmost position in a number or word.

character, locking shift—A common control character which causes all characters which follow to shift to a different character set until the shift character representative of that set is met, whereupon reversion is then made to the original character set. A shift-out character makes the change, while the shift-in character changes the character set back to the original. This action is somewhat analogous to shifting to capital letters on a typewriter by pressing the lock and shift keys.

character, magnetic—*See* magnetic character.

character misregistration — The improper state of appearance of a character, in character recognition, with respect to a real or imaginary horizontal base line in a character reader.

character mode (display) — This mode provides a rapid means for displaying alphanumeric characters. Three characters or symbols are contained in each 18-bit word with provision for a 128-character alphabet. Characters or symbols may be displayed in one of three sizes. The character generator is capable of performing carriage-return functions upon specific characterlike commands. Escape from the character mode is accomplished with another characterlike code (some systems).

character, most significant—The character in the leftmost position in a number or word.

character, new-line—A particular functional character which controls or demands action of the printer, in this case, a new-line.

character, nonlocking shift—A special control character which causes one (sometimes more) characters following to shift to that of another total set of characters, for example, to caps, or italics. Similar to a nonlocking shift key on a typewriter.

character, nonprinting — *See* nonprinting character.

character, numeric—*Same as* digit.

character operational — *See* character command.

character outline — The graphic pattern formed by the stroke edges of a handwritten or printed character in character recognition.

character, pad—Character introduced to use up time while a function (usually mechanical) is being accomplished, e.g., carriage return, form eject, etc.

character, paper throw—A character which controls or demands action of the printer; in this case a paper-throw.

character parity check (communications) — During transmission as the core storage readout is being converted from parallel to serial bit form, the data line terminal at the transmitting end functions to add a parity bit, where necessary, to make each data character odd or even parity. As the data characters are being received, the data line terminal makes a parity check as the conversion from serial to parallel bit form takes place for the storage entry. The parity and synchronizing bits are dropped off at this time. If the wrong parity is detected, an error is signalled by the receiving computer.

character pitch—*See* pitch, character.

character, print control — A specific control character used to affect printing operations such as feeding, spacing, font selection.

character printer—A printer in which only a single character is composed and determined within the device prior to printing.

character, protection—A character selected by the programmer or built into the machine which replaces a zero which has been suppressed to avoid error or false statements. Such characters are usually symbols, such as an ampersand or an asterisk.

character reader—1. A scanning device for identifying characters on documents by computer or humans. Magnetic-ink (MICR) readers work with specifically shaped characters printed in metallic ink that is magnetized before reading. Optical readers use letter configuration analysis and comparison techniques. 2. A specialized device which can convert data represented in one of the type fonts or scripts read by human beings directly into machine language. Such a reader may operate optically; or if the characters are printed in magnetic ink, the device may operate magnetically or optically.

character reader, optical—This unit reads numerical data printed in widely used type styles on paper or card documents at the rate of up to 480 characters/second, and documents at 400 per minute. The printed data is automatically translated into machine language for direct input to the processor (some units).

character recognition—1. Identifying, reading, or encoding a printed character by the various means which include magnetic, optical, mechanical, and others. 2. The technology of using a machine to sense and encode into a machine language, characters which are written or printed to be read by human beings.

character, redundant—A character specifically added to a group of characters to insure conformity with certain rules which can be used to detect computer malfunction.

character, separating — One of the control characters designed to setout various hierarchies in data structures, i.e., to separate the parts or units. For example, SP might mean space between words, while S1 might mean spaces between sentences; S2 meaning space between paragraphs; S4 meaning space between pages; etc. Other separating characters might indicate parenthetical or bracketed matter in context or mathematics.

character, serial-by—*See* serial-by character.

character set—An agreed set of representations, called characters, from which selections are made to denote and distinguish data. Each character differs from all others, and the total number of characters in a given set is fixed; e.g., a set may include the numerals 0 to 9, the letters A to Z, punctuation marks and a blank or space. (Clarified by alphabet.)

character, shift-in — *See* character, locking shift.

character, shift-out—*Same as* character, locking shift.

characters, idle — Control character interchanged by a synchronized transmitter and receiver to maintain synchronization during nondata periods.

character size—The number of binary digits in a single character in the storage device.

character skew—A form of character misregistration, in character recognition, such that the image to be recognized appears in a skewed condition with respect to a real or imaginary horizontal base line.

characters, machine readable—The symbols (printed, typed or written) that can be interpreted by both people and optical character recognition equipment.

character-spacing reference line—An optical character recognition term related to a vertical line used to determine the horizontal spacing of characters. It may equally divide the distance between the sides of a character boundary or it may coincide with the centerline of a vertical stroke.

character, special—Special characters which are neither numerals nor letters but may be symbols, such as /,*/$,=,or ?.

characters, throw-away—In tape which is transmitted over a telegraph channel, certain functions which require more time than is allowed between successive characters in the transmission. Examples of these functions are from feedout, duplicating of card fields, etc. In order to prevent reception of an intelligence character while the machine is in the midst of performing such a function, a calculated number of "throw-away" characters must be inserted into the tape immediately following the function code and ahead of the next printing or function code. Letter codes are usually used as "throw-away" codes.

character string—1. A group of characters in a one dimensional array in an order due to the reference of relations between adjacent numbers. 2. A sequence or group of connected characters, connected by codes, key words, or other programming or associative techniques.

character stroke—Optical character recognition (OCR) lines, points, arcs, and other marks are often used as parts or portions of graphic characters. Even the dot over the letter, or the cross of a t is a stroke.

character style—In optical character recognition (OCR) a distinctive construction, with no restriction as to size, that is common to a group of characters. Different sizes of a given character style are proportional in all respects.

character subset—A smaller set of certain characters from a larger or universal set, all with specified common features. If all men is one set, tall men would be a subset; both sets being men and the subset being a smaller group with the common characteristic.

character, tabulation—A specific character which controls the printer or demands action. In this case a tabulation character to begin tabulation.

character transfer—The normal mode of communication is by sequential transmission of 6-bit (in parallel) characters with provision for computer specification of the number of words to be transferred. The basic operation of the character input communication cycle is as follows: After an external device (ED) has been addressed and commanded to perform a specific input operation by an ED instruction, four characters are input to the assembly register of the communication channel. The word is then stored in memory at the location specified by a register (some systems).

character, transfer rate—The speed at which data may be read from or written to the unit, exclusive of seek or latency delays.

character, transmission control—Some characters may be interspersed with regular data characters, but in effect are so designed or coded to control an operation such as recording, interpreting, transferring, or some type of processing. A character controlling transmission is one of these types.

charactron—A specifically constructed cathode-ray tube which is capable of displaying alphanumeric characters and other special symbols on its screen. Used as a form of output device.

charge, storage—*See* storage charge.

charge storage tube—An early computer memory device that stored a single charge in a tube. The presence or absence of a

charge in the tube was equivalent to a binary digit.

chart, detail—A flowchart in minute detail of a sequence of operations. (The symbols of the detail chart usually denote an individual step or computer operation.) A detail chart is more detailed than a logic chart, usually reflects the particular computer characteristics and instructions, and facilitates the actual coding of the program in the manner intended by the programmer preparing the chart.

chart, flow—A graphical representation of a sequence of operations using symbols to represent the operations, such as compute, substitute, compare, jump, copy, read, write, etc.

chart, grid—A representation of the relations between inputs, files, and outputs in matrix form.

chart, logic—A flowchart of a program or portions of a program showing the major logical steps intended to solve a problem. The symbols of the logic chart usually denote routines and subroutines and should represent the computer run in terms of highlights and control points. The level of detail in a particular logic chart may vary from one run to another and from one program to another, depending on the requirements of the program, and at the prerogative of the person preparing the chart.

chart, logical flow—A detailed solution of the work order in terms of the logic, or built-in operations and characteristics, of a specific machine. Concise symbolic notation is used to represent the information and describe the input, output, arithmetic, and logical operation involved. The chart indicates types of operations by use of a standard set of block symbols. A coding process normally follows the logical flowchart.

chart, plugboard—A diagramatic chart showing where plugs or wires are to be inserted into a plugboard. Other information displayed relates to placement and setting of switches, digit emitters, and other specific uses of the plugboard.

chart, process—*Same as* flowchart.

chart, run—A flowchart of one or more computer runs in terms of input and output.

chart, spacing—A form for developing a layout and spacing or general design of printed output, as well as the preparation of the carriage control tape.

chart, system—A symbolic representation of the main data flows and operations indigenous to an information-handling procedure.

chart, systems flow—A schematic representation of the flow of information through the components of a processing system.

chart, Veitch—A table or chart which shows all the information contained in a truth table (Set Theory). It displays columns and rows headed with the combinations of variables in Gray code groupings, and sequences in straight binary number sequence.

check—1. A means of verifying the accuracy of data transmitted, manipulated, or stored by any unit or device in a computer. 2. A process of partial or complete testing of the correctness of machine operations, the existence of certain prescribed conditions within the computer, or the correctness of the results produced by a program. A check of any of these conditions may be made automatically by the equipment or may be programmed.

check, accounting—An accuracy control on input data that is based on an accounting principle such as control totals.

check, arithmetic—A check which uses mathematical identities or other properties, occasionally with some degree of discrepancy being acceptable; e.g., checking multiplication by verifying that $A \times B = B \times A$.

check, automatic—A provision constructed in hardware for verifying the accuracy of information transmitted, manipulated, or stored by any unit or device in a computer. (Synonymous with built-in check, built-in automatic check, hardware check.)

check, Batten—A simple check performed by sighting through the holes of a stack of punched cards. If the card deck is aligned and held toward a light source the accuracy of punching, sorting, or commonality of punched holes can be verified.

check bias—See bias, check.

check bit—A binary check digit; often a parity bit. (Related to parity check, and self-checking number.)

check, brush-compare — See brush-compare check.

check, built-in — A provision constructed in hardware for verifying the accuracy of information transmitted, manipulated, or stored by any unit or device in a computer.

check, built-in automatic—A provision constructed in hardware for verifying the accuracy of information transmitted, manipulated, or stored by any unit or device in a computer.

check bus—Relates to a set or group of parallel lines for transmission of data to a particular checking device or unit such as a check register, a parity checker, or a comparator.

check, casting-out-nines—A check devised for arithmetic operations by using the remainder obtained from the operand and dividing by nine, performing the same operation on the remainders as are performed on the operands. The remainder can be obtained by dividing by nine or by adding the digits. The remainders of both should be the same.

check character—One or more characters carried in such a fashion that if a single error occurs (excluding compensating errors) a check will fail, and the error will be reported.

check code—To isolate and remove mistakes from a routine.

check, consistency — A process for verifying that a piece of data is consistent with the rules prescribed for its handling.

check, copy—See check, transfer.

check, diagnostic—A specific check used to locate a malfunction in a computer.

check digit—See digit, check.

check digit, parity—If a check bit is added to a string or if its complement is added, it is called a parity bit. If the check bit is appended, it is called an even parity check. If the complement is added, the string contains an odd number of ones and the check is called an odd parity check.

check digit, sum—A check digit produced by a sum check.

check, dump—A check which usually consists of adding all the digits during dumping, and verifying the sum when retransferring.

check, duplication—A check which requires that the results of two independent performances, either concurrently on duplicate equipment or at different times on the same equipment, of the same operation be identical.

check, echo—A check of accuracy of transmission in which the information which was transmitted to an output device is returned to the information source and compared with the original information, to ensure accuracy of output.

check, even-odd—See check digit, parity.

check, even parity—1. One or more redundant digits in the word as a self-checking or error-detecting code to detect malfunctions of equipment in data-transfer operations. (Related to forbidden-combination check and parity check.) 2. An extra or redundant digit related to the group of digits to be checked by a specific rule for double check.

check, false code—See check, forbidden combination.

check, forbidden-combination—A check, usually automatic) that tests for the occurrence of a nonpermissible code expression. A self-checking code or error-detecting code uses code expressions such that one or more errors in a code expression produces a forbidden combination. A parity check makes use of a self-checking code employing binary digits in which the total number of 1s or 0s in each permissible code expression is always even or always odd. A check may be made either for even parity or odd parity. A redundancy check employs a self-checking code that makes use of redundant digits called check digits. Some of the various names that have been applied to this type of check are forbidden-pulse combination, unused order, improper instruction, unallowable digits, improper command, false code, forbidden digit, nonexistent code, and unused code.

check, forbidden-digit—Same as check, forbidden-combination.

check, hardware—A provision constructed in hardware for verifying the accuracy of information transmitted, manipulated, or stored by any unit or device in a computer. (Synonymous with built-in check, built-in automatic check.)

check, illegal-command—*See* check, forbidden combination.

check, improper-command—*See* check, forbidden combination.

check indicator—A device which displays or announces that an error has been made or that a failure has occurred.

check-indicator instruction — An instruction which directs a signal device that is turned on to call the operators' attention to the fact that there is some discrepancy in the instruction now in use.

check indicator, overflow — *See* indicator, overflow check.

check indicator, read/write — *See* indicator, read/write check.

check indicator, sign — *See* indicator, sign check.

checking and recovery error—Parity is computed or checked on all references to central store. If a parity error occurs, the computer will interrupt to the proper location, an alarm will sound, and the appropriate fault lights will be flashed on the operator's console. For all real-time applications, the system will attempt to recover. Once the computer has satisfactorily recovered, the system will continue normal operation.

checking, automatic — Numerous internal checks continually monitor the accuracy of the system and guard against incipient malfunction. Typical are the parity and inadmissible-character check, automatic readback of magnetic tape and magnetic cards as the information is being recorded, the electronic tests which precede each use of magnetic tape or magnetic cards to ensure that the operator has not inadvertently set switches improperly. These internal automatic tests are supplemented by the instructions which may be programmed to ensure proper setup of certain units prior to their use. Console switches are designed to protect against inadvertent or improper use, and interlocks are provided on peripheral units to guard against operator error.

checking card—*See* card, checking.

checking characters, inadmissable (automatic)—*See* character checking, inadmissable.

checking code, error—*See* code, error checking.

checking loop—A method of checking the accuracy of transmission of data in which the received data are returned to the sending end for comparison with the original data, which are stored there for this purpose.

checking, module—*Same as* module testing.

checking program—A specific type of diagnostic (error-discovering) program which examines programs or data for the most obvious mistakes, such as misspelling in key-punching, or misskeypunching, but which does not cause execution of the program itself.

checking, redundant — The specific use of added or extra digits or bits in order to diagnose, detect, or cause errors which can arise as a result of unwarranted dropping or gaining of digits or bits.

checking, sequence—*See* sequence checking.

check, instruction—*See* check, forbidden combination.

check light—A control panel indicator light which indicates parity errors or arithmetic overflow conditions.

check, limit—A type of check on the input for the purpose of ensuring that only valid codes or transaction types are permitted. If, for instance, there are only four transaction types, the limit check will reveal an error situation if a transaction other than the four is encountered. A limit check will detect transposition errors as in the case where an 83 was mistakenly input as a 38. In such a case the 38 would show up as an error.

check, longitudinal—An even or odd parity check at fixed intervals during data transmission.

check, machine—This is a functional check to determine the proper operating characteristics of equipment to ensure that all instructions are being properly decoded and arithmetic operations are being performed properly. The use of check or parity bits to determine proper operation of storage units.

check, marginal—A preventive maintenance procedure in which certain operating conditions are varied about their normal values in order to detect and locate incipient defective units; e.g., supply voltage or frequency may be varied. (Synonymous with marginal test, and high-low bias test, and related to check.)

check, mathematical—*Same as* check, arithmetic.

check mode, balance — *See* balance check mode.

check, modulo-N—1. A check that makes use of a check number that is equal to the remainder of the desired number when divided by N; e.g., in a modulo-4 check, the check number will be 0, 1, 2, or 3 and the remainder of A when divided by 4 must equal the reported check number B, otherwise an equipment malfunction has occurred. 2. A method of verification by congruences, e.g., casting out nines. (Related to self-checking number.)

check, nonexistence code — *See* check, forbidden combination.

check number—A number composed of one or more digits and used to detect equipment malfunctions in data-transfer operations. If a check number consists of only one digit, it is synonymous with check digit. (Related to check digit.)

check, odd-even—*See* check digit, parity.

check, odd parity—*See* check digit, parity.

checkout—A general term used to describe a set of routines developed to provide the programmer with a complete evaluation of his program under operating conditions. Checkout routines are provided by most manufacturers of equipment.

checkout, program—A standard run of a program on a computer to determine if all designs and results of a program are as anticipated.

checkout systems, automatic—Static and dynamic tests on components and subsystems of aircraft and submarine simulators, aircraft weapons complexes, missiles, etc., require automatic test facilities. Checkout of each element yields an evaluation of the overall system operation and provides data fundamental to the logical troubleshooting of defective systems and components.

check, overflow—*See* overflow check.

check, page—A procedure for controlling the accuracy of data by verifying that the value of a piece of data falls between certain preestablished maximum and minimum values.

check, parity—*See* parity check.

check parity, longitudinal (communications)—*See* parity check, longitudinal (communications).

checkpoint—1. In a machine run, a point in time at which processing is momentarily halted to make a magnetic tape record of the condition of all the variables of the machine run, such as the position of input and output tapes and a copy of working storage. Checkpoints are used in conjunction with a restart routine to minimize reprocessing time occasioned by functional failures. 2. A position in a routine or program at which information or data is stored which permits the computation from that position or point.

checkpoint and restart procedures—Checkpoint and restart procedures, which are techniques associated with computers, make it possible, in the event of an error or interruption, to continue processing from the last checkpoint rather than from the beginning of the run. These techniques are included in applications which require many hours of processing time, since heavy machine scheduling and deadlines generally do not permit a complete rerun. To establish checkpoints, processing intervals are determined, each being based upon a certain number of items, transactions, or records processed. At each interval or checkpoint, the stored program identifies input and output records and then records them along with the contents of important storage areas such as counters and registers; at the same time, accuracy of processing up to that point is established. Restart procedures are the means by which processing is continued after an error or interruption. Each set of restart procedures includes the necessary operator and stored-program instructions for (1) locating the last checkpoint, (2) reading

the machine for reprocessing, and (3) entering the main routine at that point.

checkpoint routine—A series of instructions that generate information for further verification.

checkpoint sorting—Also, restart point. The point at which a restart (or rerun) can be initiated. Memory, registers, and the position of tapes are recorded at this point.

check problem—A problem chosen to determine whether the computer or a program is operating correctly.

check, program—The technique for observing program errors and malfunction through the use of sample data about which there are known results.

check, programmed—1. A system of determining the correct program and machine functioning either by running a sample problem with similar programming and known answer, including mathematical or logical checks such as comparing A times B with B times A, and usually where reliance is placed on a high probability of correctness rather than built-in error-detection circuits, or by building a checking system into the actual program being run and utilized for checking during the actual running of the problem. 2. A procedure for checking which is specifically designed to be an integral part of the total program.

check, range—A procedure for controlling the accuracy of data by verifying that the value of a piece of data falls between certain preestablished maximum and minimum values.

check, read-back—*Same as* check, echo.

check, read/write—An accuracy check on reading, writing, sensing, and punching, by comparing what has been written, usually by running the originals and the newly printed or punched cards through a comparator to check for errors.

check, redundancy—A specific or automatic check which is based on the systematic insertion of components or characters developed especially for checking purposes. (Related to parity check.)

check, redundant—1. A check which makes use of redundant characters. (Related to parity check, and forbidden-combination check.) 2. A check which attaches one or more extra digits to a word according to rules that if any digit changes, the malfunction or mistake can be detected.

check register—A register used to temporarily store information where it may be checked with the result of a succeeding transfer of this information.

check reset key—A push button that acknowledges an error and resets the error detection mechanism indicated by the check light. This is required to restart a program after an error has been discovered in batch mode.

check, residue—*Same as* check, modulo-N.

check, routine—*Same as* check, programmed.

check row—A specific check on input from punched tape which treats each row as if it represented a symbol, and thus a check row on a tape can represent or replace a check symbol.

check, selection—A check, usually automatic, to verify that the correct register or other device has been selected in the performance of an instruction.

check, sequence—A data-processing operation designed to check the sequence of the items in a file assumed to be already in sequence.

check, sight—*See* sight check.

check, sign indicator—An error-checking device, indicating no sign or improper signing of a field used for arithmetic processes. The machine can, upon interrogation, be made to stop or enter into a correction routine.

check solution—A solution to a problem obtained by independent means to verify a computer solution.

checks, photocell light—Checks performed on data read from cards passing through a card reader.

check, static—An equipment setup check performed by comparing measurements taken in the reset mode or hold mode for a single value of the independent variable, and including initial rates of change, with the results received from some alternative method of computation. This type of check reveals the static errors and often times reveals the ihstantaneous values of dynamic errors.

check sum—The sum used in a summation check.

check, summation—A check in which groups of digits are summed, usually without regard for overflow, and that sum checked against a previously computed sum to verify that no digits have been changed since the last summation.

check symbol—A symbol for representation of a check sum, which is normally attached or appended to the original string and is copied along with it. Such a check on copying is usually completed by recomputing and then matching this sum with the original sum.

check, system—A check on the overall performance of the system, usually not made by built-in computer check circuits, e.g., control totals, hash totals, and record counts.

check total—One of a number of totals or sums which can be correlated in some procedure or manner as a check for consistency of reconciliation in a set of calculations.

check, transfer—1. A check which verifies that information is transferred correctly from one place to another. It is usually done by comparing each character with a copy of the same character transferred at a different time or by a different route. 2. A check on transmitted data by temporarily storing, retransmitting, and comparing.

check, transmission longitudinal—An even or odd parity check at fixed intervals during data transmission.

check, transverse—A system of error-control based on the check that some preset rules for the formation of characters are observed.

check trunk—A set or group of parallel lines for transmission of data to a particular checking device or unit such as a check register, a parity checker, or a comparator.

check, twin—A continuous duplication check achieved by duplication of hardware and automatic comparison.

check, unallowable code—*See* check, forbidden combination.

check, unallowable instruction — *See* check, forbidden combination.

check, validity—A check based upon known limits or upon given information or computer results; e.g., a calendar month will not be numbered greater than 12, and a week does not have more than 168 hours.

check word—A machine word is often used to represent a check symbol and this is appended and printed to the block, thus signifying the check.

chief keypunch operator—Employees who assign work to, and expedite and review the work of keypunch operators. In addition they perform keypunch, verification, and specialized E.A.M. functions as required.

chief operator, computer — Employs who instruct, guide, and assign work to a group of at least five computer operators, performing the duties listed in computer console operator classification in addition to performing the actual work operations of the assigned group. The chief computer operator is responsible for the progress, correctness, and completeness of the work assigned to the group.

Chinese binary — A code used with punch cards in which successive bits are represented by the presence or absence of punches on contiguous positions in successive columns as opposed to rows. Column-binary code is widely used in connection with 36-bit word computers where each group of 3 columns is used to represent a single word.

chip box—A receptacle on a card punch that accepts and retains the pieces of the punched card that were removed during punching.

Chomsky Type II—Similar to backus normal form, a meta-language.

cinching—Longitudinal slippage between the layers of tape in a tape pack when the roll is accelerated or decelerated.

CIOCS — An abbreviation for communication input/output control system.

circuit—1. A system of conductors and related electrical elements through which electrical current flows. 2. A communications link between two or more points.

circuit, AND—*See* AND circuit.

circuit, bistable—A circuit which is binary, has two states, each requiring an appropriate trigger for excitation and transition from one state to the other. Also called, binary pair, rigger pair, and flip-flop.

circuit capacity—The number of communications channels that can be handled by a given circuit at the same time.

circuit, clear-to-send — *See* clear-to-send circuit.

circuit, coincidence—*Same as* gate, AND.

circuit, data telephone—A specific telephone circuit permitting the transmission of digital data, for example, through use of the Dataphone developed by American Telephone and Telegraph Company.

circuit dropout—The momentary interruption of a transmission because of the complete failure of a circuit.

circuit, equality—A device whose output signal represents one only when signals representing identical n-bit numbers are applied to both its inputs.

circuit, monostable—A circuit which has one stable state, and one unstable state, and which undergoes a complete cycle of change in response to a single triggering excitation.

circuit, nanosecond—Computer logic circuits, or other electronic circuits, which have gradient pulse rise or fall times measured in billionths of a second or less. A nanosecond is 1 billionth of a second.

circut, NOT—*Same as* gate, NOT.

crcuit, OR—*See* gate, OR.

circuit, received-data—Signals on this circuit are originated by the receiving-signal converter, in response to signals received over the communication media. This circuit is not required for send-only messages. In half-duplex service, the receiving-signal converter shall hold marking condition on the received-data circuit when the remote data has its send-request circuit in the 'off'' condition. Optionally, in half-duplex service, the received-data circuit may be used to monitor transmitted signals, e.f., for local copy.

circuit reliability—The percentage of time the circuit meets arbitrary standards set by the user.

circuitry, arithmetic — High-speed arithmetic unit which provides fixed and floating-point operations in one computer.

circuits, balanced—A circuit terminated by a network whose impedance losses are infinite.

circuits, control—The circuits which cause the computer to carry out the instructions in proper sequence, and which can control by permitting only the coded conditions to continue or function.

circuit, send-request—Signals on this circuit are originated in the data-terminal equipment to select whether the signal converter is to be conditioned to transmit or to receive. For half-duplex service, when the signal on the send-request circuit is switched to the "on" condition, the signal converter shall switch to the transmit condition, without regard to any signals that may be received from the communications facility. When this signal is switched to the "off" condition, the signal converter shall switch

to the receive condition, without regard to any signals on the transmitted-data circuit. Data-terminal equipment intended for use with send-only service shall hold the send-request circuit in the "on" condition at all times. Data-terminal equipment intended for use with receive-only service shall hold the send-request circuit in the "off" condition at all times. This circuit is not required for full-duplex service.

circuit shift—*See* shift, circular.

circuit, side—One of two physical circuits in a phantom group.

circuit, single—A telegraph circuit capable of nonsimultaneous two-way communications.

circuits, instruction control—*Same as* circuits, control.

circuits, priority—The priority circuits of the control unit grant memory access to the various units of the system in a sequence that enables each input/output device and system running-time to be used most efficiently. The priority circuits receive, store, and grant requests for access to memory made by the input/output synchronizers and the central processor. When simultaneous requests are made, the priority circuits select the synchronizer that is to be granted memory access according to the relative data-transfer rate of the input/output device controlled by each synchronizer. A synchronizer that controls a unit with a relatively slow transfer rate, such as the card-punch unit, requires access to memory less often than a synchronizer that controls a unit with a relatively fast transfer rate, such as a tape unit; thus, the card-punch unit synchronizer has a lower priority than the tape-unit synchronizer. The central processor has the lowest priority, since delaying a central-processor request for memory access will not disrupt the execution cycle or cause loss of information (some systems).

circuit switching—A system in which stations on different circuits within a network are joined by connecting the two circuits together.

circuit, transmitted-data—Signals on this circuit are originated by the data-terminal equipment for transmission on the data-communication channel. This circuit is not required for receive-only service.

circuit, tributary—A circuit which connects an individual drop, or drops, to a switching center.

circuit, trunk—A circuit which connects two switching centers.

circuit, way-operated—A circuit shared by three or more stations on a "party line" basis. One of the stations may be a switching center. May be a single or duplex circuit.

circular shift—*See* shift circular.

circulating memory — A register or memory consisting of a means for delaying the information (delay line) and a means for regenerating and reinserting it back into the delay line.

circulating register—*See* register, circulating.

circulating storage—A device or unit which stores information in a train or pattern of pulses, where the pattern of pulses issuing at the final end is sensed, amplified, reshaped and reinserted into the device at the beginning end.

citation — A reference statement relating to other sources of data or special notes concerning the data on punched cards.

citation index—*See* index, citation.

CIU (Computer Interface Unit)—A CIU is a device which interfaces with the central processing unit and peripheral devices such as disks or printers.

clamper—When used in a broadband transmission, a clamper reinserts low-frequency signal components which were not faithfully transmitted.

class—1. A set of individuals, documents, data, etc., with similar characteristics. 2. A subdivision of a category.

Class-D channel—A transmission circuit which can transmit punched paper tape at the rate of 240 words per minute, or punch card data at the rate of approximately 10 cards (80 columns) per minute.

Class-E channel—A data transmission circuit which can transmit data at the rate of 1200 bits per second.

classification — An arrangement of data in classes or groups. This is required to produce summary reports.

classification, concept—A particular type of classification for retrieving information from storage units based on specific concepts or images. Concepts may be identified by a word or a group of words, but they define the concept, and when concepts are assigned to documents they are then identified during searches.

classify—The arrangement of data into classes or groups according to a definite plan or method.

clause—A part of a statement in COBOL. It may describe structures, give initial values to items, or redefine data defined by a previous clause.

clean hole punching — Same as chad tape, which has punched holes entirely detaching the disk from the paper.

clear—1. The replacement of information in a storage unit with zeros or blanks; the passing of a data medium through a station; e.g., the clearing of punched cards through a reading station or the clearing of the output card stackers. 2. To erase the contents of a storage device by replacing the contents with blanks, or zeros. (Contrasted with hold, and clarified by erase.)

clear area—Any area to be kept free, by designation, of printing or any markings in character recognition.

clear band—In optical character recognition (OCR) a specified area that is to be kept free of printing or any other markings not related to machine reading.

clear-to-send circuit—Signals on this circuit are originated in the signal converter. For send-only and full-duplex service, the signal converter shall hold the clear-to-send circuit in the "on" condition at all times. This circuit is not required for receive-only service. For half-duplex service when the send-request signal is switched to the "on" condition, the clear-to-send circuit shall be switched to the "on" condition after a time delay sufficient to effect the reversal of direction of transmission equipment. When the send-request circuit is switched back to the "off" condition, the clear-to-send circuit shall be switched back to the "off" condition.

clerk, control—This individual is responsible for the integrity of the data received, processed, and dispatched from the data processing department. Sometimes this function is performed by one of the operators. Control clerks also perform activities such as batch reconciliation, checking the validity of the data, zero balancing, and other control activities.

clerk, data-examination—Maintains accuracy, correctness, and appropriateness of input/ output data.

clerk, input preparation—Prepares accurate and properly coded information which is to be put into the system.

clock—A time-keeping, pulse-counting, frequency-measuring or synchronizing device within a computer system. Such clocks are of various types: real-time clock, which measures the past or used time in the same analogous scale as external events it will be used to describe; a master clock, which is the source of pulses required for computer operation; programmable clock, whose time values are transmitted into a clock register and which may be accessed as determined by clock instructions in the program.

clock, control — The electronic clock usually contained in the hardware which times the instruction sets, and times the flow and manipulation of the data.

clock counter—A memory location that records the progress of real time, or its approximation, by accumulating counts produced by a (clock) count pulse interrupt.

clock-count word, real-time—The contents of this 36 bit address are decremented by one, approximately every millisecond. Decrementation is performed by the index adder circuitry. When the clock count word has been reduced to zero, an internal interrupt is generated and the program then executes the instruction programmed at the real-time clock-interrupt address (some systems).

clock, day—A system feature particularly suited to real-time problems is the 24-hour day clock. As an auxiliary device, this electronic clock causes an external interrupt of computer processing once every minute.

Thus "keeping time" is placed completely under the programmer's direction. Since program control is shifted once every minute to a set address in the computer, the day clock can be used to initiate a variety of subroutines. For example, by using a compare routine on the address reserved for timing purposes, reports can be generated at any desired time of the day, week, or month. These reports could provide up to the minute information and analysis of company status. Error-checking routines, trace routines, output conversions, maintenance routines, and memory dumps are just some of the many routines which can be initiated by the day clock (some systems).

clock, delta—This "program-setable" clock counts up to 32,768 milliseconds. Upon reaching its upper limit, the delta clock unconditionally interrupts the computer at the end of the instruction being handled, regardless of the type of instruction. The delta-clock count is maintained in core storage. One of the primary uses of this clock is timing subroutine operations. If a momentary fault throws the computer into a closed programming loop, or if a fault occurring during the execution of an instruction halts the computer, the delta clock restarts the computer by means of an interrupt, thus providing automatic fault recovery. The interrupt can be programmed to notify the operator that a closed loop has occurred. If completing an operation takes longer than desired, this clock is also used to interrupt the computer and thereby allow program attention to be diverted to items of more immediate importance (some systems).

clock frequency—The master frequency of periodic pulses which schedule the operation of the computer. (Clarified by synchronous computer.)

clocking, data set—A time base oscillator supplied by the data set for regulating the bit rate of transmission. This is referred to by IBM as external clocking.

clocking, external—*See* clocking non-data set.

clocking, internal—*See* clocking non-data set.

clocking, nondata set—A time base oscillator supplied by the business machine for regulating the bit rate of transmission. This is referred to by IBM as internal clocking and by the common carrier as external clocking.

clocking external—*See* clocking data set.

clock, master—*See* master clock.

clock pulse—*See* pulse, clock. pulse.

clock rate—1. The time rate at which pulses are emitted from the clock. The clock rate determines the rate at which logical or arithmetic gating is performed with a synchronous computer. 2. The rate at which a word or characters of words (bits) are transferred from one internal computer element to another. Clock rate is expressed in cycles (if a parallel-operation machine—words: if a serial operation machine—bits) per second.

clock, real-time—A clock which indicates the passage of actual time, in contrast to a fictitious time set up by the computer program; such as, elapsed time in the flight of a missile, wherein a 60-second trajectory is computed in 200 actual milliseconds, or a 0.1 second interval is integrated in 100 actual microseconds.

clock, real-time (time-sharing) — *See* time sharing, real-time clock.

clock signal—A fundamental repetitive signal which times or controls most operations in electronic data processing equipment.

clock-signal generator—This is the basic unit of the clock which controls the timing of EDP equipment. The input to the generator could be from an oscillator.

clock, time of day—Records time in hours, minutes, seconds, over 24-hour range and sends time to central processor upon command.

clock track—A specific track upon which a desired pattern of digits has been recorded and thus provides a clock signal.

closed array—An array which cannot be extended at either end.

closed loop—1. A group of instructions which are repeated indefinitely. 2. Pertaining to a system with feedback type of control, such that the output is used to modify the input.

closed-loop system—A system in which the computer controls an external program or process without human intervention. An example of a closed-loop process-control system would be the computer connected directly to instrumentation through a digital-to-analog converter to complete the feedback loop. The computer could then take control directly to the process by setting controllers, activating switches, valves, etc.

close-down, disorderly — A system stoppage due to an equipment error wherein it is impossible to do an orderly close-down. Special precautions are necessary to prevent the loss of messages and duplication in record updating.

close-down, orderly—The stopping of the system in such a way that ensures an orderly restart and no destruction of messages. When a system is forced to stop, an orderly close-down provides that all records are updated that should be updated and that no records are erroneously updated again when the restart is made. Furthermore, all incoming and outgoing transmissions are completed, with a message sent to the terminals which notifies the operators of the close-down.

closed routine—A routine which is not inserted as a block of instructions within a main routine, but is entered by basic linkage from the main routine.

closed shop—1. A computing installation at which all computer programming, coding, and operating functions are performed by members of a regular computing group. 2. The operation of a computer facility where programming service to the user is the responsibility of a group of specialists, thereby effectively separating the phase of task formulation from that of computer implementation. The programmers are not allowed in the computer room to run or oversee the running of their programs. (Contrasted with open shop.)

closed subroutine—*See* subroutine, closed.

CLT identifier—The CLT identifier is used in all standard communication subsystem function words (computer generated instructions to the subsystem). Each pair of input/output CLTs in a standard communication subsystem has a unique seven-bit address (CLT identifier) which enables a central processor to distinguish it from other input/output pairs in the subsystem (some systems).

CLT, unattended operation—Most telephone company data sets can be equipped for unattended operation. This means that the data set will automatically answer any incoming calls which are directed to it. The data set, however, has no way of recognizing the termination of the transmission, and for this reason, the signal to disconnect must come from the associated CLT (Communications Line Terminals). Similarly, when the central processor dials a remote location, the CLT must signal its associated data set to disconnect after the transmission is completed.

Automatic calling units, supplied by the telephone company, must be disconnected from their associated transmission lines between every call. The CLT-dialing must signal the automatic calling unit to disconnect after a connection has been established. The ability to hang up or disconnect is provided on output CLTs only; however, the function of hanging up after input data transmission can be performed by an output CLT (some systems).

coalesce—The act of combining two or more files into one.

COBOL—1. COmmon Business Oriented Language. This is a common procedural language designed for commercial data processing as developed and defined by a national committee of computer manufacturers and users. 2. A specific language by which business-data processing procedure may be precisely described in a standard form. The language is intended not only as a means for directly presenting any business program to any suitable computer for which a compiler exists, but also as a means of communicating such procedures among individuals.

COBOL compiler—The compiler is completely modularized into relocatable elements and is handled as any program in the system, thus providing for easy expandability and maintenance. Likewise, the COBOL processor produces as its output relocatable binary elements stored on the drum or mass storage, which are indistinguishable from other elements in the system. Other outputs from the

compiler include extensive diagnostic messages, source-language listings, machine-language listings, and special cross-reference listings of name definitions and their references. The machine-language listings consists of side by side procedure division statements and the corresponding generated symbolic machine code (some systems).

COBOL, data division—The data division describes the data to be processed by the object program. It contains a file section which describes the files used. There may be a working storage section which allocates memory space for the storage of intermediate results.

COBOL, environment division—The environment division describes the computer on which the source program is to be compiled, the computer on which the object program is to be executed, and the relationship between data files and input/output media. The configuration section contains three paragraphs which deal with the overall specifications of the computer involved and equates actual hardware names with mnemonic names supplied by the programmer. The input/output section consists of two paragraphs which identify each file and specify input/output techniques, respectively.

COBOL, identification division—Identifies the source program and provides optional documentation information.

COBOL language — The English-language statements of COBOL provide a relatively machine-independent method of expressing a business-oriented problem to the computer. Commonly used nouns, verbs, and the connectives are used in the procedural portion of a COBOL program to construct easily understood sentences. The excellent documentation provided by COBOL—problem definition as well as a method of solution—enables more than one programmer to work on a particular problem with minimal duplication of effort.

COBOL library—A COBOL library processor is available to store and retrieve data and procedure division descriptions, and it provides dynamic dumps of specified data areas to facilitate program checkout.

COBOL, procedure division—The procedure division describes the procedures to be used in processing the data described in the data division; it contains all the necessary steps to solve a given problem. Procedures are written as sentences that are combined to form named paragraphs. Likewise, paragraphs may be combined to form sections. Paragraph and section names are assigned by the programmer so that control may be transferred from one section or paragraph to another.

COBOL processor—The COBOL processor is a 6-phase compiler requiring a drum, 32K core, and an input device (tape, drum, or card) for source programs. The compiler is completely modularized into relocatable elements and is handled as any object program in the system, thus providing for easy expandability and maintenance. Likewise, the COBOL processor produces as its output relocatable binary elements stored on the drum, which are indistinguishable from other elements in the system. Other outputs from the compiler include extensive diagnostic messages, source-language listings, machine-language listings, and special cross-reference listings of name definitions and their references. The machine-language listing consists of side by side procedure-division statements and the corresponding generated symbolic-machine code. The compiler diagnostics are of four categories: Precautionary —print warning message and continue compilation. Correctable—try to correct the error, print explanatory message and continue compilation. Uncorrectable—if intent of programmer cannot be determined, print a diagnostic message, reject the clause or statement and continue compilation. Catastrophic—when so many errors have occurred that no more useful diagnostic information can be produced, terminate the compilation (some systems).

COBOL segmentation—COBOL programs can be segmented by use of priority numbers on procedural sections.

COBOL word—A word given a preassigned meaning in COBOL language, including both optional and key words that must be used in their prescribed context; also called "reserve words." The standard list of COBOL reserved words is supplemented by a manufacturer's list for each machine with a COBOL compiler.

CODASYL—Conference on data systems languages. Organized by the Department of Defense, computer users, and manufacturers.

code—1. A system of symbols for meaningful communication. (Related to instruction.) 2. A system of symbols for representing data or instruction in a computer or a tabulating machine. 3. To translate the program for the solution of a problem on a given computer into a sequence of machine language or psuedo instructions and addresses acceptable to that computer. (Related to encode.) 4. The translating and writing of information in the form of abbreviations and specific notation to develop machine instructions or symbolic instructions from the statement of a problem. 5. To express a program in a code that a specific computer was built or programmed to interpret and execute.

code, absolute—A code using absolute addresses and absolute operation codes; i.e., a code which indicates the exact location where the referenced operand is to be found or stored. (Synonymous with one-level code and specific code, and related to absolute address.)

code, access control — Used in conjunction with the memory map option, that determines whether or not a CPU operating in

the slave mode may read from, obtain instructions from, or write into a given page of virtual addresses.

code, alphabetic—A system of alphabetic abbreviations used in preparing information for input into a machine; e.g., Boston, New York, Philadelphia, and Washington may in alphabetical coding be reported as BS, NY, PH, WA. (Contrasted with numeric code.)

code, alphanumeric—The code of the set of characters used, i.e., both letters and digits.

code, ASA—An information interchange seven-level code recently adopted as a standard code by the American Standards Association.

code, augmented operation — A particular code which is further defined or limited by information found in another position of an instruction, i.e., an instruction word but one which has addresses considered as the operation code.

code, automatic—A code which allows a machine to translate or convert a symbolic language into a machine language for automatic machine or computer operations.

code basic—*Same as* code, absolute.

code, Baudot—The standard five-channel teletypewriter code consisting of a start impulse and five character impulses, all of equal length, and a stop impulse whose length is 1.42 times the start impulse. Also known as the 1.42 unit code. The Baudot code has been used by the telegraph industry for about 100 years.

code, binary—1. A coding system in which the encoding of any data is done through the use of bits; i.e., 0 or 1. 2. A code for the ten decimal digits, 0 through 9, in which each is represented by its binary, radix 2, equivalent, i.e., straight binary.

code, biquinary—A two-part code in which each decimal digit is represented by the sum of the two parts, one of which has the value of decimal zero or five, and the other the values zero through four. The abacus and soroban both use biquinary codes. An example follows.

Decimal	Biquinary	Interpretation
0	0 000	0+0
1	0 001	0+1
2	0 010	0+2
3	0 011	0+3
4	0 100	0+4
5	1 000	5+0
6	1 001	5+1
7	1 010	5+2
8	1 011	5+3
9	1 100	5+4

code, card—The combinations of punched holes which represent characters (letters, digits, etc.) in a punched card.

code chain—An arrangement in a cyclic sequence of some or all of the possible different N-bit words, in which adjacent words are linked by the relation that each word is derived from its neighbor by displacing the bits one digit position to the left or right, dropping the leading bit, and inserting a bit at the end. The value of the inserting bit needs only to meet the requirement that a word must not recur before the cycle is complete; e.g., 000 001 010 101 011 111 110 100 000 . . .

code, character—A particular arrangement of code elements used in a code to represent a single value or symbol.

code character, extension—A distinct character designed to indicate that succeeding characters are to be interpreted using a different code.

code check—To isolate and remove mistakes from a routine.

code, check, false—See check, forbidden combination.

code-checking time—The time spent checking out a problem on the machine, making sure that the problem is set up correctly, and that the code is correct.

code, Chinese-binary — A code, used with punch cards, in which successive bits are represented by the presence or absence of punches on contiguous positions in successive columns as opposed to rows. Column-binary code is widely used in connection with 36-bit word computers where each group of 3 columns is used to represent a single word.

code, column-binary — A code used with punch cards in which successive bits are represented by the presence or absence of punches on contiguous positions in successive columns as opposed to rows. Column-binary code is widely used in connection with 36-bit word computers where each group of 3 columns is used to represent a single word.

code, command—See code operation.

code, comment (CF)—This code is used to keep programs for the remote-computing system compatible with source programs for other FORTRAN processors. The remote-computing system will process statements beginning with comment code CF as though the CF were not there. Other FORTRAN processors will regard those statements as components. The remote computing system will automatically supply process code CF for all program statements that are not valid FORTRAN IV statements.

code, computer—1. A system of combinations of binary digits used by a given computer. (Synonymous with machine code.) 2. A repertoire of instructions.

code, computer instruction — An instruction code designed for specific computers.

code, condition—A 4-bit code, in the program status double-word, that indicates the nature of the results of an instruction executive (some computers).

code, conditional progression — See code, cyclic permuted.

code, constant ratio—A code in which all characters are represented by combinations having a fixed ratio of ones to zeros.

code, continuous progressive—Same as code, unit distance.

code conversion—A process for changing the bit groupings for characters in one code into the corresponding character bit groupings for a second code.

code CP—See code, unit distance.

code, cyclic—A binary code in which sequential numbers are represented by expressions which are the same, except in one place, and in that place differ by one unit; e.g.,

Decimal	Binary	Gray
0	000	000
1	001	001
2	010	011
3	011	010
4	100	110
5	101	111

thus, in going from one decimal digit to the next sequential digit, only one binary digit changes its value. (Synonymous with gray code.)

code cyclic permuted—See code, unit distance.

coded—Relates to decimal notation in which the individual decimal digits are each represented by a group of binary digits; e.g., in the 8-4-2-1 binary-coded decimal notation, the number twenty-three is represented as 10111.

code data—Sets of symbols which are used to represent various data items for data elements on a one-for-one basis. A single number or symbol might represent a particular week or month.

code, data conversion — The translation of alphanumeric data into a form acceptable to the computer. This is usually done by the computer during the input of the data.

coded character—See character, coded.

coded decimal—Describing a form of notation by which each decimal digit separately is expressed in some other number system; e.g., in the 8-4-2-1 coded decimal notation, the number twelve is represented as 0001 0010, for 1 and 2; whereas in pure or straight binary notation it is represented as 1100. Other coded decimal notations used are the 5-4-2-1, the excess three, and the 2-3-2-1 codes.

coded decimal notation—A method of representing each figure in a decimal number by a character or group of characters.

code, dense binary—A code in which all possible states of the binary code are used.

code, dictionary—An alphabetical arrangement of English words and terms, associated with their code representations. (Related to reverse-code dictionary.)

code, direct—A code which specifies the use of actual computer command and address configurations.

code-directing character — One or several routing indicators at the start of a message that determine message destination.

coded program—A program which has been expressed in the code or language of a specific machine or programming system.

coded stop—A stop instruction built into the routine.

code element — The elemental unit from which a code is constructed; e.g., Baudot code is a binary representation of the alphabet and numerals in which a grouping, presence or absence of five elements expresses the code information.

code, end-of-file—It is usually conventional to terminate a set of blocks as indicated by an end-of-file code preceded by 3.75 inches of blank tape. The presence of this code may be tested by appropriate branch instructions. Usually a tape is read in terms of words when a word is a constant number of characters for a fixed-word-length machine.

code, end-of-loop—Loops are terminated by letting the cards run out and restarting the machine, or by using preset values in cards or tapes, or by testing on branches or values in counters, etc. When certain columns, never used for data, are reserved for end of loop codes, loop endings are preprogrammed. Such codes terminate loops when counters reach preset values, causing branching to occur.

code error—Illegal control code on a binary card.

code, error-checking — A designed code for either detecting or correcting errors in the information as represented and used particularly in transmission or storage of data in computers. Various types of check bits are the main components of such codes.

code, error-correcting — 1. A code in which each telegraph data signal conforms to rules on construction, so that departures from this construction in the received signal can be automatically detected ,and which permits the automatic correction, at the receive terminal, of some or all of the errors. Such codes require more signal elements than are necessary to convey the basic information. 2. An error-detecting code in which the forbidden-pulse combination produced by gain or loss of a bit indicates which bit is wrong.

code, error-detecting—A code in which errors produce forbidden combinations. A single error-detecting code produces a forbidden combination if a digit gains or loses a single bit. A double error-detecting code produces a forbidden combination if a digit gains or loses either one or two bits and so forth. (Synonymous with self-checking code, and related to self-checking number.)

code, excess-three—A binary-coded decimal code in which each digit is represented by the binary equivalent of that number plus three, for example:

Decimal Digit	XS 3 Code	Binary Value
0	0011	3
1	0100	4
2	0101	5
3	0110	6
4	0111	7
5	1000	8
6	1001	9
7	1010	10
8	1011	11
9	1100	12

A binary-coded decimal system that represents each decimal digit as the corresponding binary number plus three. For example, the decimal digits 0, 1, 9, are represented as 0011, 0100, 1100, respectively. The nines complement of the decimal digit corresponds (also in excess-three code) to the ones complement of the four binary digits.

code extension character—A distinct character designed to indicate that succeeding characters are to be interpreted using a different code.

code, external device (ED)—All external devices are connected to the processor by a "common cable" that carries an external device address code and a code which specifies what operation is to be performed. Only that device whose address is on the lines will respond to an instruction on the common cable. No instruction will be initiated unless it is accompanied by a start signal. When a device recognizes its address and receives a start signal, it will store the essential information from the operation code in flip-flops and initiate the specified operation. When the operation is complete, the external device will interrupt the computer program if it was instructed to do so by the operation code. Otherwise, the external device just becomes not busy when it has completed its operation. It is then available for further instruction.

code, false—See character, illegal.

code, fieldata—A standardized military data transmission code, containing seven data bits plus one parity bit.

code, forbidden—Same as code ,illegal.

code, forbidden character — Same as code illegal.

code, four-address — See instruction, four-address.

code, gray—See code, cyclic.

code, group—A form of minimum-distance code in which a valid representation comprises a set of digits (data) just sufficient to identify and distinguish the representation, and a set of check digits arranged to give the required minimum signal distance between any two valid representations.

code, Hamming—One of the error-correction code systems in use today, named after the inventor.

code holes—See holes, code.

code, identifying—A code placed in perforated tape or punched cards to identify the contents therein, or their origin.

code, illegal — A code character or symbol which appears to be the proper element but really is not a true member of the defined alphabet or specific language. If forbidden patterns, characters, or symbols present themselves, they are judged to be mistakes or the results of malfunctions.

code, improper—*Same as* code, illegal.

code, input instruction—A code designed for the convenience of programmers which has mnemonic symbols or groupings which appear somewhat like the actual operations to be performed, i.e., MPY for multiply, etc. The computer then translates these into actual machine instructions for execution.

code, instruction—1. The list of symbols, names and definitions of the instructions which are intelligible to a given computer or computing system. 2. An artificial language for describing or expressing the instructions which can be carried out by a digital computer. In automatically sequenced computers, the instruction code is used when describing or expressing sequences of instructions, and each instruction word usually contains a part specifying the operation to be performed and one or more addresses which identify a particular location in storage. Sometimes an address part of an instruction is not intended to specify a location in storage, but is used for some other purpose. 3. If more than one address is used, the code is called a multiple-address code.

code, internal—This is a system of character-word structure that is now used by the IBM 360 computer series to replace the bit/block relationship of older systems. Data representation is character- or word-oriented:

 byte = 8 bits plus a check bit.
 halfword = 2 bytes.
 word = 4 bytes.
 instruction = 1, 2, 3, halfwords.
 internal code = 8-bit character.

code, interpreter—An interim, arbitrarily designed code which must be translated to computer coding in order to function as designed, usually for diagnostic or checking purposes.

code, interpretive—A routine which decodes and immediately executes instructions written as pseudocodes. This is contrasted with a compiler which decodes the pseudocodes into a machine-language routine to be executed at a later time. The essential characteristic of an interpretive routine is that a particular pseudocode operation must be decoded each time it is executed.

code, letters—In the Baudot code, the function which causes machines to shift to lower case. This code is used to "rub out" errors in tape, as it is made up of intelligence pulses in each of the five channels, and causes receiving machines to print nothing.

code line—A single instruction, usually written on one line, in a code for a specific computer to solve a problem. This instruction is usually stored as a whole in the program register of the computer while it is executed, and it may contain one or more addresses of registers or storage locations in the computer where numbers or machine words are to be obtained or sent, and one or more operations to be executed. (Synonymous with program line.)

code, line-feed—A function code which causes printers or similar devices to rotate the platen up one line.

code machine—The absolute numbers, names or symbols assigned by the machine designer to any part of the machine.

code, machine instruction—*Same as* code, instruction.

code, machine-language—1. A system of combinations of binary digits used by a given computer. (Synonymous with computer code.) 2. A repertory of instructions.

code, macro—A coding system that assembles groups of computer instructions into single code words. The system, therefore, requires interpretation or translation so that an automatic computer can follow it.

code, MICR—In magnetic ink character recognition, the special code consists of a set of 10 numeric symbols and four special symbols standardized as Font E-13B developed for the American Bankers Association. The characters are visually readable through the use of magnetic sensing heads in various types of magnetic ink recognition equipment. The special symbols mentioned above are: amount, dash, transit number, and on us.

code, micro- —1. An instruction written by a programmer or systems analyst in a source program to specify and execute a routine to be extracted from the computer library to give the processor program information and instructions required to regularize the routine to fit into the specific object program. 2. A system of coding making use of sub-operations not ordinarily accessible in programming; e.g., coding that makes use of parts of multiplication or division operations. 3. A list of small program steps. Combinations of these steps, performed automatically in a prescribed sequence to form a macro operation like multiply, divide, and square root.

code, minimum-access—A system of coding which minimizes the effect of delays for transfer of data or instructions between storage and other machine components. (Related to optimum code, minimum-latency code, and minimum-access coding.)

code, minimum distance — A specific code which uses words to represent signal distance between any two words but which does not fall below a specified minimum amount or value.

code, minimum-latency—*See* code minimum-access.

code, mnemonic—An instruction code using conventional abbreviations instead of numeric codes in order to facilitate easy recognition. Examples: MLT for multiply, SUB for subtract, instead of "12."

code, m out of n—A form of fixed weight binary code in which m of the n digits are always in the same state.

code, multiple-address—An instruction code in which an instruction word can specify more than one address to be used during the operation. In a typical instruction of a four-address code, the addresses specify the location of two operands, the location at which the results are to be stored, and the location of the next instruction in the sequence. In a typical three-address code, the fourth address specifying the location of the next instructions is dispensed with, the instructions are taken from storage in a preassigned order. In a typical two-address code, the addresses may specify the locations of the operands. The results may be placed at one of the addresses or the destination of the results may be specified by another instruction.

code, N-ary—A code employing N distinguishable types of code elements.

code, nonexistent—*See* character, illegal.

code, nonexistent check—*See* check, forbidden combination.

code, nonprint (NP code)—The third case of a teleprinter, in which functions may be performed and signals passed through without printing or spacing taking place. The nonprint code is the function code which triggers this condition.

code, nonreproducing—Codes (punched into master tapes) that cause functions to be performed but are not reproduced in the product tape.

code, numeric—A system of numerical abbreviations used in the preparation of information for input into a machine; i.e., all information is reduced to numerical quantities.

code, object—The code produced by a compiler or special assembler which can be executed on the target computer.

code, one-address — *See* instruction, one-address.

code, one-level—See code, absolute.

code, operation—1. The symbols that designate a basic computer operation to be performed. 2. A combination of bits specifying an absolute machine-language operator, or the symbolic representation of the machine-language operator. 3. That part of an instruction that designates the operation of arithmetic, logic, or transfer to be performed.

code, operation field—The portion of an instruction word that contains the operation code.

code, optimum—A computer code which is particularly efficient with regard to a particular aspect; e.g., minimum time of execution, minimum or efficient use of storage space, and minimum coding time. (Related to minimum-access code.)

code, order—*See* code, operation.

code, own—A code developed and made a part of a standard routine to extend or change the routine to accomplish specific jobs or tasks.

code, permuted cyclic—*See* code, cyclic permuted.

code, PI—Program indicator code. When two or more programs are used in the same program tape, the use of PI codes permits automatic selection of programs and permits switching from one program to the other.

code position—The positions or sites in various data recording media in which data may be entered or recorded such as hole positions, magnetic spot, etc. Conventions have been adopted to standardize the locations of code positions in almost all media.

code, print restore (PR)—The function which causes a printer to resume printing when it has been in a nonprint case. The PR code triggers this function.

code, pseudo- —1. A code which expresses programs in source language; i.e., by referring to storage locations and machine operations by symbolic names and addresses which are independent of their hardware-determined names and addresses. (Contrasted with machine-language code.) 2. An arbitrary code, independent of the hardware of a computer and designed for convenience in programming, that must be translated into computer code if it is to direct the computer.

code, pulse—1. A code in which sets of pulses have been assigned particular meanings. 2. The binary representations of characters.

code, punched-tape—A particular code consisting of patterns of punched holes in tapes so arranged that each character uses one row of holes (or several) to represent a character, the holes corresponding to binary digits. Such codes include, Standard Teletype, Flexowriter, Fieldata, and the USA Standard.

code, quibinary — A binary-coded decimal code for representing decimal numbers in which each decimal digit is represented by seven binary digits which are coefficients of 8, 6, 4, 2, 0, 1, 0, respectively.

coder—A person who prepares instruction sequences from detailed flow charts and other algorithmic procedures prepared by others, as contrasted with a programmer who prepares the procedures and flow charts.

code, redundant—A code using more signal elements than necessary to represent the intrinsic information; used for checking purposes.

code, reflected binary—*See* code, cyclic.

code register, return—A particular register used to store data which controls the execution of follow-on of subsequent programs.

code, relative—A code in which all addresses are specified or written with respect to an arbitrarily selected position, or in which all addresses are represented symbolically in a computable form.

code repertory—*Same as* code, instruction.

code, reproduction—Function codes in a master tape which are carried through the data-processing operations and also appear in the product tape. *See* nonreproduction codes.

code, self-checking—A code in which errors produce forbidden combinations. A single-error detecting code produces a forbidden combination if a digit gains or loses a single bit. A double-error detecting code produces a forbidden combination if a digit gains or loses either one or two bits and so forth. (Related to self-checking number.)

code, self-complimenting—A unique memory system in which the compliment of the numbering system used equals the compliment of the decimal equivalent.

code, self-demarcating—A code in which the symbols are so arranged and selected that the generation of false combinations by interaction of segments from two successive codes is prevented.

code set—A complete or closed set or group representation defined as a code, such as a group of three-letter sets for codes of various military or government bureaus.

codes, function—Codes which appear in tape or cards to operate machine functions, such as carriage return, space, shift, tabulate, etc.

code, short—A system of instructions that causes an automaton to behave as if it were another, specified automaton.

code, single-address—An instruction which contains the location of the data and the operation or sequence of operations to be performed on this data.

codes, instruction operation—The instruction operation codes are assigned mnemonics which describe the hardware function of each instruction. Assembler directive commands provide the programmer with the ability to generate data words and values based on specific conditions at assembly time.

code, skeletal—The framework of a routine which is completed by a generalized routine using input parameters.

code, skip—A functional code which instructs the machine to skip certain predetermined fields.

codes, mnemonic operation—The writing of operation codes in a symbolic notation which is easier to remember than the actual operation codes of the machine. This code must be converted to actual operation codes before execution, which is done as part of any assembly, interpretive, or compiling routine.

codes, nonreproducing — These are various punched hole patterns in paper tapes which cause functions to be performed but are not reproduced in the product or output tape.

code, space—An NCR 315 character (binary 00 1100) used to denote intentional separations in data.

code, specific—*See* code, absolute.

codes, process (remote-computing system)— Some types of program statements are also useful for manipulating the values of a user's program. When the terminal is in the program mode, the user may insert special characters, called "process codes," into the first two columns so that these statements can be used as commands. For example, CC preceding a statement has the following effect: the statement is immediately executed with all the effects of normal execution, but no new variable names are created; the statement is then discarded and does not become a part of the program. Thus, the user may insert values into parameters at any time, thereby creating completely new testing situations without having to build their presence into the logic of the program or attempting to anticipate the debugging operations required.

code, stop—A code, which when read in the reader of tape-operated equipment (other than tape-to-card converters), stops the reader and suspends machine operations. On some machines (like Flexowriter) it is normally nonreproducing. On teletype it is usually reproducing.

code, straight-line—The repetition of a sequence of instructions, with or without address modification, by explicitly writing the instructions for each repetition. Generally straight-line coding will require less execution time and more space than equivalent loop coding. If the number of repetitions is large, this type of coding is tedious unless a generator is used. The feasibility of straight-line coding is limited by the space required as well as by the difficulty of coding a variable number of repetitions.

codes, transmission systems, cyclic—A group of error-checking codes used to detect bursts of errors.

codes, transmission systems, fixed ratio codes—Error detection codes that use a fixed ratio of one bit to the total number of bits.

codes, transmission systems, recurrent — Codes in which checks symbols are used to detect against the burst type of error.

codes, transmission systems, spiral parity checking—A method used to detect single bit errors. Each check character is obtained by shifting the level for each successive checking character.

code, symbolic—A code that expresses programs in source language; i.e., by referring to storage locations and machine operations by symbolic names and addresses which are independent of their hardware-determined names and addresses.

code, systematic error checking—A form of minimum-distance code in which a valid representation comprises a set of digits (data) just sufficient to identify and distinguish the representation, and a set of check digits arranged to give the required minimum signal distance between any two valid representations.

code, telephone—*Same as* code, Baudot.

code teletype—*See* code, Baudot.

code, ternary—A code in which only three states are considered.

code, thirty-nine feature—A code which is designed for punched cards to represent numerals from 0 to 39 but with no more than two punches in any column.

code, three-address—*See* address, three.

code track—A track of a paper tape other than the feed track.

code, transmitter-start—Usually, a two-letter call that is sent to an outlying machine to automatically turn on its tape transmitter.

code twenty-nine feature—A code which is designed for punched cards to represent numerals from 0 to 29 but with no more than two punches in any one column.

code, two-out-of-five—A system of encoding the decimal digits 0, 1, . . . 9, where each digit is represented by binary digits of which 2 are zeros and 3 are ones or vice versa.

code, unitary—A code having only one digit; the number of times it is repeated determines the quantity it represents.

code, unit distance—A specific code in which characters are represented by words of a fixed number of bits, but which are arranged in a sequence so that the signal distance between consecutive words is 1 or unity. Also called; cyclic permuted code or C.P. code.

code, unused—*See* character, illegal .

code, zero address—An instruction code which contains no instruction code for the next address.

coding—1. The act of preparing in code or pseudocode a list of the successive computer operations required to solve a specific problem: also, the list itself. 2. The ordered list in computer code or pseudocode, of the successive computer operations for solving a specific problem. 3. Writing instructions for a computer either in machine or nonmachine language.

coding, absolute, relative, or symbolic—Coding in which one uses absolute, relative, or symbolic addresses, respectively; coding in which all addresses refer to an arbitrarily selected position, or in which all addresses are represented symbolically.

coding, actual—*Same as* coding, absolute.

coding, alphabetic—A system of abbreviation used in preparing information for input into a computer such that the information is reported in the form of letters; e.g., New York as NY, carriage return as CN, etc.

coding, assembly language—Assembly languages are used to avoid coding directly into machine code; mnemonics are used for both the command instructions and the operands, and it is usually not necessary to label the address for every instruction. In an instruction such as, ADD Y, Y is a mnemonic for

a location. Assembly programs generate in a one-to-one fashion a set of machine-coded instructions as contrasted to a compiler, or macro language wherein one compiler instruction can generate many machine instructions, i.e., such as FORTRAN, COBOL, etc.

coding, automatic—Any technique in which a computer is used to help bridge the gap between some "easiest" form, intellectually and manually, of describing the steps to be followed in solving a given problem and some "most efficient" final coding of the same problem for a given computer; two basic forms are compilation routines and interpretation routines.

coding, direct—*Same as* coding, absolute.

coding, ECD—A system of representing decimal equivalents by a series of four binary digits.

coding, fixed-form—Specific coding instructions with a fixed field assigned to particular labels, operations codes, and operand parts of the instruction.

coding, forced—*Same as* programming, minimum access.

coding format, symbolic—In writing instructions using the assembly language, the programmer is primarily concerned with three fields; a label field, an operation field, and an operand field. It is possible to relate the symbolic coding to its associated flow-chart, if desired, by appending comments to each instruction line or program segment.

coding, in-line—A portion of coding which is stored in the main path of a routine. *See* open subroutine.

coding line—A single command or instruction for a computer to solve.

coding, machine—This coding uses the machine order code, which is directly interpreted by the instruction register. For a decimal machine, an example of a code might be 600141 1100, which would be the order to put the contents of location 141 into the upper arithmetic accumulator and then go to location 1100 to get the next instruction, whereas in a binary machine, an example of an order code might be 0000100000000000020, which might be interpreted as adding the contents of memory location 20 (in binary) to the arithmetic accumulator.

coding, machine language—Coding in the form in which instructions are executed by the computer.

coding, minimum-access—The process of developing or applying a minimum-access code. (Related to optimum code and minimum-latency code.)

coding, minimum delay — *Same as* programming, minimum access.

coding, minimum latency—*Same as* programming, minimum access.

coding, nonnumeric—Relates to the various nonnumeric abbreviations used to prepare information for input to computers and closely akin to mnemonic coding.

coding, numeric—A system of abbreviation used in preparation of information for machine acceptance by reducing all information to numerical quantities; in contrast to alphabetic coding.

coding, optimum—The preparation of a programming routine with a view toward optimizing or idealizing the specific situation.

coding, out-of-line — A portion of coding which is stored away from the main path of a routine. *See* closed subroutine.

coding, own (sorting) — Special coding provided by the programmer, which is integrated with sort/merge coding.

coding, pence—*Same as* coding, single-column pence.

coding, relative—Coding in which all addresses refer to an arbitrarily selected position, or in which all addresses are represented symbolically.

coding sheet—A form upon which computer instructions are written prior to being punched into cards.

coding, single-column pence—A punched card code with relative addresses in the program instructions. *See* code, relative.

coding, skeletal—A generalized routine consisting only of the framework that is to be completed by a generator.

coding, specific—Coding in which all addresses refer to particular registers and locations.

coding, straight line—*See* straight line code.

coding, symbolic—*See* symbolic coding.

coefficient—A number or factor put before and multiplying another.

coefficient, floating point—That specific part of a floating point number or representation that expresses the number of times that the number base with exponent is to be multiplied, i.e., the number 5.06 in the number 5.06×10^{18}, is the floating-point coefficient. This means it will be expanded by 10^{18}.

coefficient matrix—The matrix of left-hand side coefficients in a system of linear equations. It is to be distinguished from the matrix obtained by appending the right-hand side, which is called the "augmented matrix" of the system. It may be thought of as including a full set of logical vectors to convert inequality constraints to equations. In the case of the modified simplex array it also contains the objective function coefficients.

coefficient scale—*Same as* scale factor.

coefficient unit, multiplier — *See* multiplier, coefficient unit.

COGENT—Argonne National Laboratory List Processor.

cognition, artificial—The optical sensing of a displayed character in which the machine or equipment selects from memory the shape of the character that is closest to the character being displayed.

cognition, machine — Certain machines have the capability to sense optically a displayed character and to select from a given repertory of characters, the specific character which is nearest in shape to the character which is displayed. The various shapes of characters are based on statistical norms, and if different shapes arise new characters join the repertory. This suggests a type of artificial learning because perception and interpretation are based on experience.

COGO (COordinated GeOmetry)—1. Coordinated geometry program. 2. A higher-level language originated by Prof. C. L. Miller and his staff at MIT in association with the staff of the Puerto Rico Dept. of Public Works, Bureau of Highways. The COGO system is designed to be used for civil engineering applications.

coil, blank paper-tape—A coil of paper tape that has been punched with the feed holes and can be punched with a pattern of holes that represent data.

coil, paper tape—A roll of paper tape that is used to record data and may be virgin, blank, or punched with data.

coincidence circuit—*Same as* gate, AND.

coincidence error—The difference in time for switching of different integrators to the compute mode or the hold mode.

coincidence gate—*Same as* gate, AND.

coincident-current selection—The selection of a magnetic core, for reading or writing, by the simultaneous application of two or more currents.

collate—1. To merge two or more ordered sets of data, or cards, in order to produce one or more ordered sets which still reflect the original ordering relations. The collation process is the merging of two sequences of cards, each ordered on some mutual key, into a single sequence ordered on the mutual key. 2. To produce a single sequence of items, ordered according to some rule (that is, arranged in some orderly sequence), from two or more ordered sequences. The final sequence need not contain all of the data available in the original sets. If, for example, two sets of items are being matched, items that do not match may be discarded. *See* merge.

collate programs and tape sort—Generalized programs that adapt themselves, as directed by programmer-specified parameters, to operate in a particular configuration to sort and collate data into a particular format.

collating sequence—A sequence of characters as arranged in the order of their relative precedence. The collating sequence of a particular computer is determined as part of its design; each character acceptable to the computer has a preassigned place in this sequence. A collating sequence is used primarily in comparing operations.

collating unit—Collating is the process of interfiling two decks of cards in numerical sequence. This machine can also be used to interfile two decks of cards on a match or nonmatch basis only, disregarding numerical sequence.

collation sequence—1. The sequence in which the characters acceptable to a computer are ordered. 2. The relative ranking of permissible graphic symbols or their representations.

collator—1. A device designed to compare data from two decks of punched cards and to sequence-check them, merge them, and/or select cards from them based on this data. 2. A device used to collate or merge sets or decks of cards or other units into a sequence. A typical example of a card collator has two input feeds, so that two ordered sets may enter into the process, and four output stackers, so that four ordered sets can be generated by the process. Three comparison stations are used to route the cards to one stacker or the other on the basis of comparison of criteria as specified by plugboard wiring.

collection and analysis, data—Process data are collected by processor controller for mathematical analysis. Current performance figures are compared with those obtained in the past, and the results are printed for process operator and management evaluation.

collection, data—The act of bringing data from one or more points to a central point. May be in-plant or out-plant.

collection, factory data—See data collection stations.

collection stations, data—See data collection stations.

colon—1. A delimiter indicating a pause, break, or stop. 2. The symbol used to separate items in the colon classification system. 3. One of the character or digit positions in a positional-notation representation of a unit of information; columns are usually numbered from right to left column, zero being the right-most column if there is no point, or the column immediately to the left of the point if there is one.

color—In optical character recognition (OCR), the spectral appearance of the image dependent upon the spectral reflectance of the image. The spectral response of the observer and the spectral composition of incident light.

column—1. A character or digit position in a positional-information format, particularly one in which characters appear in rows, and the rows are placed one above another; e.g., the rightmost column in a five decimal place table, or in a list of data. 2. A character or digit position in a physical device, such as punch card or a register, corresponding to a position in a written table or list; e.g., the right-most place in a register, or the third column in an eighty-column punch card.

column binary—A code used with punch cards in which successive bits are represented by the presence or absence of punches on contiguous positions in successive columns as opposed to rows. Column-binary code is widely used in connection with 36-bit word

computers where each group of 3 columns is used to represent a single word.

column-binary card—A card in which the columns are contiguous components of a binary vector.

column-binary code—See code, column-binary.

column, card—A vertical line of punched positions on a card where holes may be punched that will represent data.

column, comment — Usually column 1 on punched cards is reserved for comments, especially in FORTRAN programming.

column, continuation—Usually column 6 is reserved for a non-zero numerical punch which indicates that the card is a continuation of a statement from a previous card, especially in FORTRAN programming.

column, digit—1. The position of a digit in a numeral, such as the 9 in 209. 2. The vertical grouping of computer elements handling the particular position of a number in a computer.

columns, FORTRAN statement — Columns 7 through 72 are most often reserved for the FORTRAN statement.

column split — A device for distinguishing pulses corresponding to an 11 or 12 punch from those corresponding to numeric punches in a card column, and making them separately available while reading or punching a card.

column split hub—An electrical jack connection which splits pulses on a control panel.

columns, statement number — Usually columns 1-5 are reserved on punched cards for statement numbers, especially in FORTRAN programming.

combinational logic element—A device having at least one output channel and one or more input channels, all characterized by discrete states, such that the state of each output channel is completely determined by the contemporaneous states of the input channels.

combination bit—Same as bit pattern.

combination, forbidden — Same as character illegal.

combination hub—An electrical jack connection which will emit or receive electrical impulses on a control panel.

combined print and punch—The simultaneous printing and punching of data onto a punched card.

combined print and read—A specific procedure or process in which the printing unit cooperates at the same speed as the reading unit. In this process of simultaneous reading and printing, the computer system does not require storage or buffering due to the uniform synchronization of speeds.

combined print, read, and punch—The synchronized process of reading by a card reader and punching and printing onto a new punched card.

combined read and punch—The reading and punching of record for record by a piece of equipment.

combined read/write head — A particular magnetic head which is used to read and to write.

combiner—A functional block which groups several inputs which are separated by space to form a single output.

comb printer—A device utilizing a set of characters mounted on a bar which faces a paper form. As the bar makes a left-to-right pass over the paper, hammers strike the selected characters onto the form. The bar returns when it reaches the right edge of the form.

COMIT String—A manipulation and pattern matching language by MIT, Massachusetts Institute of Technology.

command—1. An electronic pulse, signal, or set of signals to start, stop, or continue some operation. It is incorrect to use command as a synonym for instruction. 2. The portion of an instruction word which specifies the operation to be performed.

command chaining—The execution of a sequence of I/O commands in a command list, under control of an IOP, on one or more logical records.

command character—*See* character, command.

command check, illegal—*Same as* check, forbidden combination.

command check, improper—*Same as* check, forbidden combination.

command check, unused — *See* check, forbidden combination.

command code—*See* code command.

command control program—A program that handles all commands addressed to the system from the user-consoles. These commands would include requests to log in or out, a request to use the edit program, requests to have a program placed on the run queue, requests to load a program, etc.

command decoder — The command decoder preprocesses commands from the user-console. This program is used to convert parameters, etc., before the command is sent to the program for which the command is intended.

command double-word—A double-word that contains detailed information concerning a portion of an input/output operation.

command functions—Instructions used by the central processor to govern the circuitry to carry out some particular action.

command, illegal—*See* character, illegal.

command, language—*See* language, command.

command list—A sequence of steps, generated by the CPU, pertaining to the performance of an I/O operation.

command mode—When no program is active at a given terminal, that terminal is in the command mode; and, conversely, when a user enters a command statement, he will destroy the active image of his program.

command mode, remote-computing system— When no program is active at a given terminal, that terminal is in the command mode; and, conversely, when a user enters a command statement, he will destroy the active image of his program. Since no program can be active at the terminal and statements cannot be retained, they must be processed immediately. Consequently, the user may employ only the general operating statements, the program defining statements, or a limited form of the arithmetic-assignment statement. This latter provision allows the terminal to be used as a fast, versatile symbolic calculator. In this mode, the user enters a statement of the form $X = e$, where e is any expression consisting of constants and built-in functions, and the system immediately evaluates the expression and prints the result at the user's terminal.

command mode, time sharing—*See* time sharing, command mode.

commands, system (time sharing)—*See* time sharing, system commands.

command, transfer—*See* transfer command.

command, unused—*See* character, illegal.

comment—An expression which explains or identifies a particular step in a routine, but which has no effect on the operation of the computer in performing the instructions for the routine.

comment code CB—This code indicates that the remainder of the line is a comment. If a program is active for the terminal when this comment code is entered, the comment will be retained as part of the active program. (The B indicates a blank.)

comment code CF—This code is used to keep programs for the remote-computing system compatible with source programs for other FORTRAN processors. The remote-computing system will process statements beginning with comment code CF as though the CF were not there. Other FORTRAN processors will regard those statements as comments. The remote computing system will automatically supply process code CF for all program statements that are not valid FORTRAN IV statements.

comment code CV—This code indicates that the remainder of the line is a comment. The remote-computing system does not retain comments identified with this comment code. Comment code CV can be used to print comments that are useful during program construction, but that need not be part of the active program.

comment codes—Various types of comments can be entered from a terminal when it is in the program mode. Each type of comment is identified by a different comment code.

comment column—*See* column, comment.

common area — FORTRAN programs and other programs may specify that data storage is to occupy a common area. This allows programs to share temporary storage, and FORTRAN-coded programs to communicate with assembly-coded routines by using a common data storage. The system loader automatically allocates common area when it is loading programs. Common storage occupies the same memory space during execution as the system loader does when loading programs. This allows effective utilization of memory storage, since the space taken up by the loader can be used by the programs during execution.

common assembler directive—*See* assembler directive commands.

common business oriented language — *See* COBOL.

common control unit—The unit is that portion of the terminal whose primary function is to control and coordinate the flow of data between the data device (s) and the communication facility.

common error—The maximum size of common was not specified in the first loaded program.

common field—A field accessible to two or more routines.

common hub—A common connection such as a ground voltage that provides this voltage to other circuits that are connected.

common language—1. A technique which reduces all information to a form that is intelligible to the units of a data-processing system. This enables units to talk with one another. 2. A language in machine-sensible form that is common to a group of computers or users of computers. 3. A language or macro code which can be read or written by many different machines or by various groups of users. 4. A single code used by devices—typewriters, calculators, transmitters, and others—manufactured by different companies.

common language, OCR—*See* language, common (OCR).

common machine language—A machine-sensible information representation which is common to a related group of data-processing machines.

common storage—Since COBOL programs can be chained (an executive function), intermediate data results can be maintained between programs using the common storage provision of UNIVAC COBOL.

communality—That proportion of one correlated variance held in common with other measures in the same set.

communication—The process of transferring information in the various media from one point, person, or device, to another.

communication channel—Voice, mail, messenger, telephone, telegraph, microwave, teletype, and other media are available for transmitting business data over short or very great distances; e.g. a Telpak or microwave channel is a communication channel with data-transmission rates up to 100,000 characters per second.

communication, data — The transmission of data from one point to another.

communication data sets, unattended — *See* CLT, unattended operation.

communication data systems—Real-time systems that interface between teletype stations and the computer. These are ideal for multi-user computer time-sharing, message-switching systems, and data-collection processing systems. A variety of systems are available for half-duplex and full-duplex operation with 64 stations and up.

communication, display registers—The contents of the x-y position registers and the display-address counter can be read into the accumulator via IOT (input/output transfer) instructions. Likewise, the display used for starting the display or setting up certain control conditions.

All of the features tend to make the programming job for a given application easier. The programmer not only has a powerful computer to generate the display, to control interfaces to external-data sources, or to handle real-time requests, but he also has a powerful display that can operate at a high degree of independence from the computer.

communication, external device—Up to 16 bits of data may be sent directly to any external device as an operation code. This direct communication is under direct program control and requires no buffered communication channel. The operation code may also be used to specify one of up to 16,000 control lines to be signaled. Here again, no buffered channel is required and the communication is under direct program control.

An optional programmed input/output channel which is independent of all the buffered I/O channels is available. Four computer instructions allow direct input and output of words containing 24 bits or less to and from the accumulator under program control. This input and output can be programmed to occur regardless of external conditions, or with a "wait" for an external READY signal (some computers).

communication, intercomputer (I/C)—Data is transmitted from one computer to another so that the data can be reprocessed in order to facilitate handling and to increase transmission speed.

communication-interface modules—Modules are provided to interface CLTs (Communication Line Terminals) with currently available modems in addition to telegraph facilities for which no modem is necessary. Where required, interface modules conform to EIA specifications. The modular concept of the standard communication subsystem permits the addition of new interface modules as new offerings are made available by the common carriers. Jacks are provided on each telegraph interface module which permit a teletypewriter to monitor all data passing through the interface. (Interface means synchronize or mesh with other modules or units.)

communication lights—These lights located on the keyboard for easy operator visibility, indicate power on (to punch), punch on, low

85

tape supply, exceed capacity or zero proof warning, and others.

communication line adapter—The Communication Line Adapter for Teletype (CLAT) is a semiautomatic device used to link the buffer units with the remote teletype units. The CLAT is incorporated within the buffer cabinet, which is located with the processor at the central site. The purpose of the CLAT is to receive data in serial bit form from the remote inquiry station and convert the data to parallel bit form for use in the inquiry buffer unit. Similarly, data transmitted from buffer to remote inquiry station is converted by the CLAT from parallel to serial bit form.

communication line terminals (CLT)—*See* terminals, communication line.

communication link—The physical means of connecting one location to another for the purpose of transmitting and receiving information.

communication modes—Each channel is capable of operating in three different communication modes: input, output, or function. The input and output modes are employed when transferring data to or from the central computer. The function mode is the means by which the central computer establishes the initial communication path with a peripheral subsystem. During this mode of transmission, the central computer sends one or more function words to a peripheral subsystem. These function words direct the units to perform the desired operation (some computers).

communication multiplexer—The communication multiplexer functions as the link between the processor and the CLTs and is available in modules to handle 4, 8, 16, 32, or, 64 CLTs. In each of these modules, an equal number of input and output CLT positions are provided. For example, a 64-position communication multiplexer can accommodate up to 32 input and up to 32 output CLTs (some systems).

communication multiplexer switching-time priority—The communication multiplexer contains priority logic which enables it to determine on a priority basis, which CLT in the subsystem should be served first. Thirteen microseconds elapse from the time the communication multiplexer is freed from its previous CLT, by receiving either an input-acknowledge or an output acknowledge signal from the central processor, until it is able to make the next input/data request or output-data request. During this 13 microsecond interval, the communication multiplexer must analyze the status of all CLTs in the subsystem, determine which CLT requesting service is connected to the highest number multiplexer position, and perform all of the necessary switching to permit the data transfer (some systems).

communication, operator-monitor—Direct communication between the monitor system and the computer operator is transmitted via the "operator message device." This device is normally the console typewriter. Operator messages are listed by the system on this device. The operator directs the system operation through this device with system directives. Operator information may be supplied through the device with operator requests. When job information is input via the console typewriter, the system is in the operator mode of operation. The system operates in either of two modes, operator mode or batch-processing mode. The mode is determined by the input device for job control information. This device is the console typewriter in the operator mode. In the batch-processing mode, the input device is a logical unit called the system input unit (SI). This unit may be assigned as a card reader, magnetic-tape unit, or paper-taper reader. This assignment of SI and the mode of operation is controlled with system directives. If a system has no console typewriter, the system always operates in the batch-processing mode. A directive to enter the operator mode in this type of system consists of a halt of computer operations. The system is initialized by loading the monitor with a bootstrap loader. The bootstrap loader is loaded into memory with a preset operation (some computers).

communication, process system—*See* process communication system.

communication, real-time processing—To close the gap in time between the actual transaction and its recognition by the processing system, a basic concept has been devised—real-time processing. A real time system is a combined data processing and communications system which involves the direct communication of transaction data between remote locations and a central computer, via communication lines, and allows the data to be processed while the business transaction is actually taking place. A real-time system may be thought of as a communications-oriented data-processing system which is capable of performing batch-processing functions while concurrently processing inquiries or messages, and generating responses in a time interval directly related to the operational requirements of the system.

communications and inquiry systems—Systems are now provided for diversified on-site and long-distance inquiry and data-communications networks. Centralized records and data-processing operations can be tied in with information sources at remote locations, and will provide instant on-line response to interrogations and data from a large number of inquiry stations. Communication networks may include up to 5,985 standard teletype stations and up to 120 electric-typewriter stations (some computers).

communications, audio—*See* audio response unit.

communications buffer—In a computer communications network, a buffer is a storage device used to compensate for a difference in the rate flow of data received and transmitted along the numerous communication lines converging on the data processing center. The communications buffer orders information from many operators and controls the information so it can be processed by the computer without confusion. The buffer has memory and control circuitry of its own for storing incoming messages that the computer is not ready to process and storing outgoing messages which have to be delayed because of busy lines.

communications, central controller—This permits party-line techniques to be employed. Multiple sending and receiving units may share the same communication line. With this type of installation, several hundred remote units may be on-line. This system permits a wide array of on-line units to be employed—on-line window posting machines, adding machines, teletype machines, and other remote devices.

The central controller provides simultaneous communications and processing. Up to 100 messages may be flowing in and out of memory simultaneously—and this may be time-shared with the processing of an independent program. The control center provides built-in accuracy. All transmission is checked for accuracy. Improper signals are detected immediately. When transmission errors exist, the controller demands that the data be retransmitted. All data entering the computer memory has been "edited" to assure accuracy and completeness. Each segment of data entering memory is automatically identified as to its source. Whether the system employs private or party-line facilities, all data is routed to its proper destination by the central controller.

communications control—See ESI communications control.

communications control, QUIKTRAN — See QUIKTRAN communication control.

communications, data-adapter unit — See data-adapter unit, communications.

communications device, input/output — Any subscriber (user) equipment which introduces data into or extracts data from a data-communications system.

communications, executive — See executive communications.

communications input/output control system (CIOCS)—A communications IOCS that allows the customer's problem program to communicate with remote terminals in the same general manner in which the program utilizes basic IOCS to communicate with magnetic tape or other standard I/O devices.

communications interface—See interface communications.

communications intersystem—See intersystem communications.

communications linkage — Common-carrier equipment provided by such companies as American Telephone and Telegraph, Western Union, and American Cable and Radio provide high-speed communication facilities for two-way transmission of data between the central computer site and remotely located input-output units. Transactions originating at these remote points are conveyed along wires directly to the computer where they are immediately evaluated and processed. Then the result is returned to the originator and other appropriate distant points. The whole transaction is handled in a matter of seconds, i.e., time current.

communications, message switching, (time sharing)—See time sharing, message switching communications.

communications multiplexer—Same as multiplexer priority communications.

communication software—Sets of software for monitoring communication activities include the following routines: Interrupt—Upon a program interrupt, this routine directs data transfer between the communication control unit and the central processor and then returns control to the main program; Message Queuing—Controls the order in which messages are stored, processed, and transmitted; Error Control—Corrects errors in messages received from other communication stations.

communications processing — The transmission of data to the central computer for processing from a remote terminal as opposed to a terminal connected directly to the central computer.

communications, QUIKTRAN — See QUIKTRAN communications.

communications system—A computer system which handles on-line, real-time applications. A typical communications system would consist of the following: a teletype, visual display, or audio answer-back device connected to an ordinary telephone line through a communication multiplexor, a device which converts the keyed-in characters to electronic pulses for transmission over the telephone line. An interface device in the computer center translates these pulses into binary code and delivers the character to computer storage. After receipt of the entire message, the central computer searches or stores the requested information and sends back the appropriate response.

An important element of any communications system are the modems (MODulator/DEModulator) which connect the communications multiplexor from the remote output to the interface device in the computer center. On the transmission end, the modulator converts the signals or pulses to the right codes and readies them for transmissions over a communication line. On the receiving end a demodulator reconverts the signals for communication to the computer via the computer interface device.

communications system equipment, dataphone—*See* dataphone communications system equipment.

communications terminal module controller (CTMC)—The communications terminal module controller functions as the link between the processor and the CTMs and CLTs (communication line terminal). A CTMC can handle 16 CTMs; this means that a maximum of 32 inputs and 32 outputs can be handled by a single CTMC.

The CTMs may request access to the central processor via the communications terminal module controller in random sequence. The CTMC automatically assigns priority among CTMs requesting access and identifies to the central processor the particular CTM granted access. This process is automatic and self-controlled on the system through externally specified indexing (ESI) on each I/O channel (some systems).

communications terminal modules (CTM'S)—There are three basic types of input and output CTMs; low speed (up to 300 bps), medium speed (up to 1600 bps), and high speed (200-4800 bps). Each is easily adjusted to the speed and other characteristics of the type of line with which it is to operate. Each CTM accommodates two full duplex communications lines, or two input and two output simplex communications lines. A CTM requires one position of the CTMC (Communications Terminal Module Controller).

In addition to the CTMs, parallel and dial communication-line terminals (CLTs) may be connected to the CTMC. The parallel CLT receives and transmits in a bit-parallel mode rather than bit serial. The CLT enables the central processor to automatically establish communications with remote points via the common carrier's switching network (some systems).

communication subsystem — The standard communication subsystem enables the real-time system to receive and transmit data via any common carrier in any of the standard codes and at any of the standard rates of transmission, up to 4800 bits per second. It is a communication system that can receive data from or transmit data to low-speed, medium-speed, or high-speed lines in any combination. The subsystem consists of two principal elements, the Communication Line Terminals (CLTs), which make direct connection with the communication facilities, and the communication multiplexer through which the CLTs deliver data to and receive data from the central processor. A communication multiplexer may be connected to any general purpose computer channel, or two or more multiplexers may be connected to two or more channels. If required, a number of multiplexers may be connected through a scanner selector to the same general purpose channel. The total number of multiplexers which can be connected to a general pur-

pose channel is dependent on the number and speed of the communication systems linked to the multiplexers by their CLTs (some systems).

communication subsystem control — The standard communication subsystem is controlled by function words which activate external function control lines and instruct a specific CLT (communication line terminal) to perform a particular action. The use of program-generated function words, rather than processor instructions, in controlling the standard communication subsystem, allows the processor logic to be completely independent of the subsystem logic.

communications, unattended — Connections established through the common carrier's dial switching network for the purpose of data transmission are in many ways identical to similar connections for voice communication. A telephone number must be dialed and the called party must answer before any transmission or conversation can take place. When the transmission or the conversation is finished, both the calling and the called party must hang up before another call can be made or received.

Some standard communication subsystems can be equipped automatically to dial remote locations using CLT-dialing, and automatically to hang up upon the completion of a data transmission by using the unattended operation feature (which is a button) on many output CLTs.

communication switching unit — This unit, like the magnetic-tape switching unit, can also perform two switching functions. Two processors share the same lines. The communication switching unit allows any two processors to share a group (one to eight) of communications lines. One processor shares different lines. Additionally, a switching unit enables one processor to switch between different groups of communication lines. Additional expansion features can provide a group switching capability of up to 63 lines (some computers).

communications word, arrangements — The standard communication subsystem accommodates four types of computer input/output words. They are the function word, input-data word, output-data word, and output-data request word.

communication system, process—One process communication system is a TELE-PROCESSING terminal designed for on-line data transmission between remote process locations and a central system. Connection to the system is made by a data adapter unit or transmission control.

communication system, standard—*See* standard communications subsystem.

commutator pulse—*See* pulse commutator.

COMPACT—COMputer Planning And Control Technique is a management tool, developed by Honeywell, to aid those directly responsible for the installation of a computer in the planning and scheduling of a computer installation, and for programming new applications.

compacting, storage—*See* storage compacting.

compaction, curve fitting—A specific method of data compaction developed by substituting analytical expressions for data to be stored or transmitted. An example is the breaking of curves into straight line segments, and then transmitting only the slope, intercept, and acceptable range for each line segment.

compaction, curve-pattern—*See* compaction, curve-fitting.

compaction, data—*See* data compaction.

compaction, floating point—Data compaction which uses exponents to specify the scale or range, such as to set the decimal point of a number, or set of numbers. In this system, each number is expressed as a number, and a coefficient which is to be multiplied by a power of ten to express the actual magnitude. An example is the number, 32,760,000 which can be expressed as 3276×10^4, or 3276 (4).

compaction, frequency-analysis — A form of data compaction using specific coded expressions to represent a number of different frequencies of different magnitudes to express, compare, or indicate a curve or geometric configuration. Only identifiable coefficients might be necessary to compare and thus transmit a whole series of fundamental frequencies.

compaction, incremental — A procedure for data compaction using only the initial value, and all subsequent changes in storage for transmission. A saving in time and space is achieved when only the changes at specific intervals are transmitted or processed.

compaction of file records—The reduction of space required for records by compressing or compacting the records by means of specialized coding and formating under a programmed routine. A balance, though, must be maintained in a system between processing time and core storage, and the reduction of file size and channel utilization.

compaction, slope-keypoint—A data compaction procedure using statements of specific points of departure. Direction or slope of departure is transmitted until the deviation from a prescribed condition exceeds a specified value, and at that point, a new slope or keypoint is signalled.

compandor—A device, for use on a telephone channel, designed to improve the voice and crosstalk performance. The input is effectively compressed for transmission and then expanded to near original form at the receiving end. A compander may distort some types of data signals.

companion keyboard—An auxiliary keyboard device which is usually located remotely from the main unit.

comparand—A word or number used for a comparison to another word or number.

comparator—1. A device for comparing two different transcriptions of the same information to verify the accuracy of transcription, storage, arithmetic operation, or other processes, in which a signal is given dependent on some relation between two items; i.e., one item is larger than, smaller than, or equal to the other. 2. A form of verifier. 3. A circuit that compares two signals and indicates agreement or disagreement; a signal may be given indicating whether they are equal or unequal.

comparator-sorter—A unit of punch card equipment which has the capability of sorting and selecting particular cards, sequence checking them, and making comparisons between stored data and these new items.

comparator, tape — A machine which automatically compares two tapes which are expected to be identical. The comparison is row by row and the machine shops when a discrepancy occurs.

compare—1. To determine whether a particular quantity is higher, equal to, or lower than another quantity, or to determine whether one piece of data is exactly like another. 2. To examine the representation of a quantity to discover its relationship to zero, or to examine two quantities usually for the purposes of discovering identity or relative magnitude.

compare and print—A specified number of records from each of two tapes are compared, record for record, with all nonidentical records printed in either alphanumeric or octal mode.

compare check, brush — *See* brush-compare check.

compare facility—The ability of a machine to execute set instructions depending upon the outcome of various possible combinations.

comparing—Comparing, as a control technique, permits data fields to be machine-checked against each other to prove the accuracy of machine, merging, coding, balancing, reproducing, gang punching, record selection from magnetic drum, disk, and tape storage. In wired control-panel machines this is accomplished with comparing magnets, and in a stored-program machine it is accomplished with a compare instruction.

comparing brushes—Reading brushes within the read hopper. Their main function is to read the data card and compare it with the data punched into the new card to ensure accuracy.

comparing unit—1. An electromechanical device which compares two groups of timed pulses and signals, either identity or nonidentity. 2. Comparing is the automatic checking of cards on a match or nonmatch basis. With this machine, feeding, punching, and segregating are controlled by comparing cards from two separate files for a match on nonmatch condition. Comparison of both alphabetical and numerical data may be made on selected columns or fields, or on entire cards.

comparison—1. The act of comparing and, usually, acting on the result of the comparison. The common forms are comparison of two numbers for identity, comparison of two numbers for relative magnitude, and comparison of two signs, plus or minus. 2. Determining the identity, relative magnitude, and relative sign of two quantities and thereby initiating an action.

comparison indicators—Three comparison indicators are: high, low, and equal and they are set on the basis of comparisons of operands in the arithmetic or index registers with operands in memory. The equal indicator is also set and reset by add and subtract instructions. If the result of an addition or subtraction is zero, the equal indicator is set. If the result is not zero, the equal indicator is reset (some computers).

comparison, logic—*See* comparator.

comparison, logical — The operation concerned with the determination of similarity or dissimilarity of two items; e.g. if A and B are alike, the result shall be "1" or yes, if A and B are not alike or equal, the result shall be "0" or no, signifying "not alike."

comparison-of-pairs sorting—The comparison of the keys in two records and placement of the higher value ahead of the smaller value for descending sequences.

compatibility—The quality of an instruction to be translatable or executable on more than one class of computer.

compatibility, equipment—The characteristic of computers by which one computer may accept and process data prepared by another computer without conversion or code modification.

compatibility, program—1. A distinctive feature of programming aids is that they and the object programs which they produce are operationally compatible with one another. This property enables the operating system to draw all elements into an integrated whole. Object programs produced by program preparation aids (other than conversion programs), as well as programs from the software library itself, may all be intermixed on run tapes and processed by the program loading, updating, and selection. 2. Complete program and data compatibility is a built-in feature of many processors. A single machine language is used with all models, enabling the user to run a program written for any smaller system on any larger system. Programs for a minimum computer model for example, can also run on any other larger processor, usually with a considerable gain in performance because of faster cycle times and increased peripheral simultaneity.

compatibility, systems — In complex systems applications, modules are often completely compatible electrically, logically, and mechanically with other systems components, which include digital computers, a complete line of input/output devices, and analog interface equipment.

compatability test—Specific tests run to check acceptability of both software and hardware as a system.

compatible—That particular characteristic of a device, program, etc., which makes it acceptable to a computer or another device, i.e., a suitable tape width, similarity of operating speeds, etc.

compatible hardware—Components, peripheral equipment, or other devices which can be used on more than one system with little or no adjustment.

compatible software—Languages which can be used on more than one computer system.

compendium—An abbreviated summary of the essentials of a subject.

compilation, program—*See* program compilation.

compile—1. The conversion of relatively machine-independent source program into specific machine-language routines. 2. To develop or produce a logically or sequentially ordered machine-language program from a series of mnemonic or symbolic operation codes or statements. Special compilers (programs) are utilized to perform this transformation from nonmachine language to machine language. 3. To produce a machine-language routine from a routine written in source language by selecting appropriate subroutines from a subroutine library, as directed by the instructions or other symbols of the original routine, supplying the linkage which combines the subroutines into a workable routine, and translating the subroutines and linkage into machine language. The compiled routine is then ready to be loaded into storage and run; i.e., the compiler does not usually run the routine it produces.

compiler—1. A program-making routine which produces a specific program for a particular problem by determining the intended meaning of an element of information expressed in pseudocode, selecting or generating the required subroutine, transforming the subroutine into specific coding for the specific problem, assigning specific storage registers, etc., and entering it as an element of the problem program, maintaining a record of the subroutines used and their position in the problem program and continuing to the next element of information in pseudocode. 2. A computer program more powerful than an assembler. In addition to its translating function which is generally the same process as that used in an assembler, it is able to replace certain items of input with series of instructions, usually called subroutines. Thus, where an assembler translates item for item and produces as output the same number of instructions or constants which were put into it, a compiler will do more than this. The program which results from compiling is a translated and expanded version of the original. (Synonymous with compiling routine, and related to assembler.)

compiler, beginner's algebraic symbolic interpretive—*See* BASIC.

compiler, COBOL—The compiler is completely modularized into relocatable elements and is handled as any program in the system, thus providing for easy expandability and maintenance. Likewise, the COBOL processor produces as its output relocatable binary elements stored on the drum or mass storage, which are indistinguishable from other elements in the system. Other outputs from the compiler include extensive diagnostic messages, source-language listings, machine-language listings, and special cross-reference listings of name definitions and their references. The machine-language listing consists of side by side procedure division statements and the corresponding generated symbolic machine code.

compiler-compiler — A machine-independent language which generates compilers for any specific machine.

compiler, diagnostics—The compiler diagnostics are of four categories: Precautionary; print warning message and continue compilation. Correctable; try to correct the error, print explanatory message and continue compilation. Uncorrectable; if intent of programmer cannot be determined, print a diagnostic message, reject the clause or statement, and continue compilation. Catastrophic; when so many errors have occurred that no more useful diagnostic information can be produced, terminate the compilation.

compiler generator—*See* generator, compiler.

compiler, incremental (time sharing) — *See* time sharing, incremental, compiler.

compiler, input/output—The source-language input to the compiler can be on paper tape, cards, magnetic tape, or the on-line typewriter. The output of the compiler is a binary executable object program. The output of the compiler may be paper tape, cards, or magnetic tape with the option of obtaining a source language listing on the on-line printer or the on-line typewriter. The memory map is listed on the same device as the source-language listing. The assembly-language listing may be on any output device other than that used for the binary output. The compiler operates as part of the monitor system. All input/output device assignments can be easily changed at compile time.

compiler-level languages — High-level languages that are normally supplied with the computer by the computer manufacturer. ALGOL and COBOL are compiler-level languages.

compiler, MAYBE—*See* MAYBE compiler.

compiler, (NEAT)—Compiler is an automatic programming system which will greatly reduce the time and effort required to prepare programs for the NCR computers. The programmer can use mnemonics and symbolic and relative references to write: a source program independent of fixed memory locations, control instruction to direct the compiling process, and macroinstructions to call upon an expandable library of macro subroutines. The compiler will process the source program, assign memory locations to all instructions and data, generate and insert subroutines where indicated by macroinstructions, and produce a complete object program in the language of the NCR computer.

compile routine—*See* routine, compile.

compiler, Programming Language/1 (PL/1)—A compiler is provided in the special support system for use in compiling object programs from source programs written in PL/1. This language has some features that are characteristic of FORTRAN and also incorporates some of the best features of other languages, such as string manipulation, data structures, and extensive editing capabilities. The PL/1 compiler translates a PL/1 program to a machine-usable (binary) language as do other compilers, i.e., FORTRAN compilers. The new programming language for the special support system provides the facilities for the operating system. This new language is designed to provide the programmer with a flexible problem-oriented language for programming problems that can best be solved using a combination of scientific and commercial computing techniques.

compiler system, FORTRAN—The FORTRAN compiler system consists of two basic elements: a source language (FORTRAN IV) whose structure closely resembles the language of mathematics, and a compiler which translates the statements and formulas written in the source language into a machine-language program.

compiling computer—The computer which is used to translate a particular program into the machine language of another computer; such a computer is often called the source computer while the computer for which the translation (compiling) is being done is called the target or object computer.

compiling duration—The time necessary to translate one computer program into an acceptable language for another computer, or to transform or translate to an assembly program, and often to generating and diagnostic programs.

compiling phase—The time used to translate one computer program into another equivalent program in an acceptable assembly, structure, and language.

compiling program—A translating program designed to transform, to assemble, or to structure programs expressed in other languages into same or equivalent programs expressed in terms of the particular computer language for which a particular machine was designed. Compiling programs or compilers most often include assemblers (or programs) as well as diagnostic and generating programs within them. The computer which is using the compiling program or compiler is called the source computer or compiling computer, and the computer in which the program is used or is to be used is called the object computer or target computer. The occasion or run of compilation or translation is called the compiling phase, while the use of the newly translated program is the run. Time to translate is compile duration.

compiling routine—A computer program more powerful than an assembler. In addition to its translating function which is generally the same process as that used in an assembler, it is able to replace certain items of input with series of instructions, usually called subroutines. Thus, where an assembler translates item for item, and produces as output the same number of instructions or constants which were put into it, a compiler will do more than this. The program which results from compiling is a translated and expanded version of the original. (Related to assembler.)

compiling technique, fully automatic — *See* FACT (fully automatic compiling technique).

complement—1. A quantity expressed to the base N, which is derived from a given quantity by a particular rule; frequently used to represent the negative of the given quantity. 2. A complement on N, obtained by subtracting each digit of the given quantity from N—1, adding unity to the least significant digit, and performing all resulting carrys; e.g., and two's complement of binary 11010 is 00110; the tens complement of decimal 456 is 544. 3. A complement on N—1, obtained by subtracting each digit of the given quantity from N—1; e.g., the ones complement of binary 11010 is 00101; the nines complement of decimal 456 is 543. (Synonymous with radix-minus-1 complement, and radix complement.)

complementary operations—In any Boolean operation, a complementary operation is the negation of the result of the first or original operation. In computing, it is represented when 0 is substituted for 1 and 1 is substituted for 0 in the tabulated values for r for the first or original operation.

complementary operator—An operator whose results are the NOT of a given operator, i.e., NOR or NAND.

complementation Boolean — *Same as* gate, NOT.

complement, Boolean—*Same as* gate, NOT.

complement, diminished — *Same as* complement, radix minus one.

complementer—A device which is designed to reverse a signal, state, or a condition into its opposite, or in some cases, alternate.

complement instruction — A built-in feature

designed to provide a number of instructions for each programmed instruction.

complement, nines — A decimal system in which each decimal digit in the subtrahend is first subtracted from 9.

compliment, noughts—*Same as* complement, radix.

complement, ones — A numeral in binary which is derived from another binary number when it is the result of a change in the sense of every digit, i.e., the sum of a number and its one complement is a number of all 1-bits. A number 110, 101, 100, 011 when added to its ones complement, 001, 010, 011, 100 has a sum of 111, 111, 111, 111.

complement on N—An expression meant to make a determination of the radix complement.

complement on N-1—An expression meant to make a determination of the radix-minus-one complement.

complement, radix—*Same as* complement.

complement, radix-minus one — *Same as* complement.

complement, tens—The radix complement of a numeral whose radix is ten. The tens complement is obtained by subtracting each digit of a number from 9, and adding 1 to the least significant of the resultant number. For example, the tens complement of 2456 is 7544.

complement, true—*Same as* complement.

complement, twos—For binary numbers, a value divided by subtracting an original number from the base number (or a power of the base number). For decimal numbers the equivalent of the twos complement would be the tens complement.

complement, zero — *Same as* complement, radix.

complete carry—When a carry resulting from the addition of carries is not allowed to propagate it is called a partial carry. When it is allowed to propagate it is called a complete carry.

complete instruction — A specific instruction which takes in a complete computer operation including the execution of that operation.

completeness—The contrast to programs that are incomplete due to transfers to nonexistent statement numbers, improper DO nesting, illegal transfer into the range of a DO loop, etc.

completeness errors—*See* errors, completeness.

completeness errors, remote-computing system—*See* errors, completeness (remote computing system).

complete operation — An operation that includes obtaining the instruction, obtaining all operands from storage, performing the operation, and returning the results to storage.

complete routine—A routine that does not require modification before it is used. Such routines are usually in company or manufacturer libraries.

complex utility routines, error messages— *See* utility routines, complex (CUR).

component—A basic part. An element.

component derating—To ensure reliable system operation under extremely adverse conditions and with limit-value components, components used in circuit modules are derated far below manufacturers' specification.

component, quadrature—Reactive component of a current or voltage due to inductive or capacitive reactance in a circuit.

components, monitor system — *See* monitor system components.

component, solid-state—A component whose operation depends on the control of electric or magnetic phenomena in solids, e.g., a transistor, crystal diode, or ferrite.

components, operating system—*See* monitor system components.

composite card—A card, often multipurpose, which contains data needed in the processing of various applications.

composition errors—Errors that are detected as soon as the user enters the offending statement. He may immediately substitute a correct statement.

composition file—The filing of records within a storage unit.

composition (remote computing system) errors—*See* errors, composition (remote computing system).

compound condition — A number of simple logic conditions such as AND, NOT, or OR logic gates that can be combined to form compound logic operations.

compound logical element — Computer circuitry which provides an output resulting from multiple inputs.

compression, data—*See* data compaction.

compression digit—*See* digit compression.

compression, zero—That process which eliminates the storage of insignificant leadings zeros, and these are to the left of the most significant digits. For clarification, *see* zero suppression.

Comptometer—A trade name for a particular key-driven calculator.

computation address — A computation that produces or modifies the address portion of an instruction.

computational stability—That particular degree to which a computational process remains valid and reliable when subjected to various conditions which tend to produce errors, mistakes, or malfunctions.

computation, implicit—Computation using a self-nulling principle in which, for example, the variable sought first is assumed to exist, after which a synthetic variable is produced according to an equation and compared with a corresponding known variable and the difference between the synthetic and the known variable driven to zero by correcting the assumed variable. Although the term applies to most analog circuits, even a single

operational amplifier, it is restricted usually to computation performed by the following circuits. 1. Circuits in which a function is generated at the output of a single high-gain dc amplifier in the feedback path. 2. Circuits in which combinations of computing elements are interconnected in closed loops to satisfy implicit equations. 3. Circuits in which linear or nonlinear differential equations yield the solutions to a system of algebraic or transcendental equations in the steady state.

computed branch—*See* branch, computed.

compute limited—A restriction in computing equipment limiting the output because operations are delayed awaiting completion of a computation operation.

compute-limited switching — *See* switching, compute-limited.

computer—A device capable of accepting information, applying prescribed processes to the information, and supplying the results of these processes. It usually consists of input and output devices, storage, arithmetic, and logical units, and a control unit.

computer, absolute-value—A computer which processes all data expressed in full values of all variables at all times. (Contrasted with incremental computer.)

computer administrative records—These records provide the source of statistics that tell how the computer use is distributed—that is, by department, by programmer, by time, and by application.

computer-aided design (CAD) — The adaptation of the computer for automated industrial, biological, statistical, (etc.) design through visual devices.

computer-aided instruction (CAI)—An educational concept which places the student in a conversational mode with a computer which has a preprogrammed study plan. The programmed course selects the next topic or phase of study according to previous responses from the student, allowing each student to progress at a pace directly related to his learning capability.

computer, all-purpose—A computer combining the specific talents heretofore assigned solely to a general purpose or special-purpose computer, scientific or business.

computer, analog—1. A computer which represents variables by physical analogies. Thus, any computer that solves problems by translating physical conditions such as flow, temperature, pressure, angular position, or voltage into related mechanical or electrical quantities, and uses mechanical or electrical equivalent circuits as an analog for the physical phenomenon being investigated. In general, it is a computer which uses an analog for each variable and produces analogs as output. Thus, an analog computer measures continuously, whereas a digital computer counts discretely. (Related to data-processing machine.) 2. A computer which calculates by using physical analogs of the variables. Usually a one-to-one correspondence exists between each numerical variable occurring in the problem and a varying physical measurement in the analog computer. The physical quantities in an analog computer are varied continuously instead of in discrete steps as in the digital computer; for example, as in the speedometer on a car.

computer application criterion—The test or rule of thumb used to define a computer in the business and applications areas and distinguished between computers and sophisticated calculators. Under the computer application criterion, a computer is defined as a general-purpose, internally programmed machine which can do business as well as scientific jobs, including such applications as payroll, billing, and order processing.

computer applications — The versatile multi-memory computer with its wide range of capabilities is readily adaptable to many typical and specialized applications such as: tactical data systems, command and control systems, digital communications and switching systems, data reduction and analysis, logistics, scientific computation, traffic control, reservation systems, computation analysis, inventory and scheduling systems, intelligence systems, systems simulation, missile and satellite dynamics, and process control.

computer, asynchronous — A computer in which the performance of each operation starts as a result of a signal that the previous operation has been completed, or that the parts of the computer required for the next operation are now available. (Contrasted with synchronous computer.)

computer, automatic—A computer which performs long sequences of operations without human intervention.

computer, buffered — A computing system with a storage device which permits input and output data to be stored temporarily in order to match the slow speed of input/output devices with the higher speeds of the computer. Thus, simultaneous input/output computer operations are possible. A data-transmission trap is essential for effective use of buffering since it obviates frequent testing for the availability of a data channel.

computer, card-programmed — See card-programmed computer.

computer center—See EDP center.

computer code—1. A system of combinations of binary digits used by a given computer. (Synonymous with machine code.) 2. A repertoire of instructions.

computer, compiling — See compiling computer.

computer, concurrent—A specifically designed computer which executes two or more instructions simultaneously, such as read, search, and compute. Such action is program controlled in some cases, but is built in or automatic, depending upon the specific purpose for which the mainframe was designed.

computer configuration—The particular set of equipment so connected to form a single computer center or system for various computer runs.

computer, consecutive — Same as computer, sequential.

computer, control—See control computer.

computer control mode — Analog computers offer several specific and selectable control modes. In reset mode, the integrators are inoperable and the required initial conditions are reapplied. The compute or operate modes cause the connecting of signals to the computing units including integrators. All various modes, including the hold mode, are computer control modes.

computer-dependent language — See language, computer-dependent.

computer, digital—A computer which processes information represented by combinations of discrete or discontinuous data, as compared with an analog computer for continuous data. More specifically, it is a device for performing sequences of arithmetic and logical operations, not only on data, but also on its own program. Still more specifically, it is a stored-program digital computer capable of performing sequences of internally stored instructions, as opposed to calculators, such as card programmed calculators, on which the sequence is impressed manually. (Related to data-processing machine.)

computer, duplex—A pair of usually identical computers operating so that if and when one is shut down for maintenance, improvements, checkouts, etc., the other can operate without a reduction in capability of the total system. Use of each computer might alternate, to provide time for preventive maintenance, or one might run relatively low priority problems or act as a slave to the other.

computer efficiency—The ratio of the number of hours of correct machine operation to the total hours of scheduled operation; e.g., on a 168-hour week scheduled operation, if 12 hours of preventive maintenance are required and 4.8 hours of unscheduled down time occurs, then the operation ratio is (168-16.8)/168, which is equivalent to a 90% operation ratio.

computer equation (machine equation)—An equation derived from a mathematical model for more convenient use on a computer.

computer, first generation — Refers to the technological era of development of the computer when the vacuum tube was the main electronic element. First generation equipment was predominantly manufactured in the years 1953-1960 and included the Univac I, IBM 704, RCA Bizmac, and the Honeywell D-1000. The second generation of computer equipment began in about 1959 and was characterized by the utilization of transistors instead of vacuum tubes. The third generation of computer equipment began in about 1964 and featured microcircuits or miniaturization of components. There is not yet a clear consensus as to the definition of a fourth generation of equipment.

computer, fixed-point — Some systems use fixed-point computers, which means the binary point of each operand is always in the same location in the registers. A good example of a fixed-point computer is the office adding machine which has a fixed decimal point located between the second and third column for the right (0,000,000,000.00) in order to show one-hundredths of the dollar.

computer, fixed-program — A computer in which the sequence of instructions are permanently stored or wired in, and perform automatically and are not subject to change either by the computer or the programmer except by rewiring or changing the storage input. (Related to wired-program computer.)

computer, floating point—A computer that is designed to represent data as an agreement and exponent. An example would be 1234 represented by $.1234 \times 10^4$ in the computer.

computer, general-purpose—A computer designed to solve a large variety of problems; e.g., a stored-program computer which may be adapted to any of a very large class of applications.

computer, host—*See* host computer.

computer, hybrid—A computer designed to perform both analog and digital computing for distinct or special purposes. Many are used in automated production.

computer, incremental—A computer in which changes in the variables, rather than the variables themselves, are represented. Those changes correspond to a change in an independent variable as defined by the equations being solved. (Contrasted with absolute-value computer.)

computer-independent language — A programming language which is not a computer language, but one which requires translation or compiling to any one of a variety of computer languages. The language which is a particular language of that machine or one which has compilers for translating to its own machine language.

computer installation — A single computer configuration, facility, center, or system consisting of one or more mainframes and endless potential combinations of peripheral, communications, input/output, and other types of support devices.

computer instruction—A machine instruction for a specific computer.

computer instruction code — An instruction code designed for specific computers, i.e., the machine language.

computer instruction set—A particular set of computer instructions which usually require no compiling and work directly to and within the computer.

Computer Interface Unit (CIU)—A CIU is a device which interfaces (matches and connects to) a central processing unit and/or peripheral devices such as disks, printers, and terminals.

computerized operations research—*See* operations research, computerized.

computer language — A programming procedure or language in which instructions are computer instructions only. A machine language as contrasted to a problem-oriented language, which must be compiled to a computer language before a machine can use it directly.

computer language symbols (standard)—Prescribed graphical shapes used to represent special meanings or functions in any computer program.

computer learning—That process by which computers modify programs according to their own memory or experience, i.e., changes of logic paths, parameter values. An example is a chess-playing computer. 2. In process-control, an analog computer can alter its parameters by a continuous process according to temperatures, or other reports it receives.

computer limited—A specific condition of a computer in which the time required for computation exceeds the time required for some other type of operation such as card or tape reading and punching. This happens quite frequently with computers that perform scientific types of calculations, and especially if computers permit concurrent reading, computing, writing, etc. If the computing time is less than that required for other operations then the computer might be limited by other procedures, i.e., input-output limited, etc.

computer logic — The logical operations of the computer, consisting generally of five operations—add, subtract, multiple, divide, and compare. This simple processing logic is enough to allow the computer to accomplish the majority of its tasks when properly programmed.

computer, logic-controlled sequential—A specific sequential computer with the capability of executing instructions in a sequence designed by particular built-in logic, i.e., fixed-sequence, but one which can be overridden or changed by an instruction; a highly unique and almost single purpose computer with little or no concurrent action.

computer manager—The professional charged with the responsibility of co-ordinating EDP with the other functions of a business. The computer manager must not only be technically qualified, but he must also have a thorough grasp of all the activities of his firm. He must be able to manage the programmers, systems engineers, and systems analysts who translate the ideas of management into a language the computer can understand and follow.

computer, master/slave — *See* master/slave system.

computer, message switching — A computer designed to perform communication control functions such as reception of messages, message validation, message storage, logging of messages, and message transmission.

computer, multiple address — Computers in which the instruction word contains more than one address. For example, the National Bureau of Standards' SWAC is a four-address machine, as is Raytheon's RAYDAC. In such a machine, three addresses are used as in a three-address machine, and the fourth gives the location of the next instruction word. *See* three addresses.

computer, multiple-operation—Depending on the work to be done, the multiplexor channel can provide linkage for a few or a great many communications lines. Up to 248 communications lines can, for instance, be connected to the processing unit through some eight transmission control units. Each line can hold a great many separate terminals.

Many computers are equipped with a multiplexor channel. Multiplexor operation is a collateral function for the logic circuits. That is, circuits are borrowed from normal duties as each character is taken into the processing unit, then returned to the program being run at the time. This interleaving of functions provides both logic and channel functions with the same circuits. The multiplexor channel consists of circuits reserved for this function.

A large installation might employ one of the more powerful models as a central processing system while a smaller model services communications inquiries. The two systems could be linked through their channels or through a file. The effect would be to have the smaller model predigest communicated messages which would then be passed to the large model's domain for storing, record updating, information retrieval or special program processing.

computer network — Basically, two or more interconnected computers with the advantage of permitting geographical distribution, and thus economy, of computer operations. Such a network also permits parallel processing, time-sharing combinations of send-receive communications, multipoint remote entry and output, and locally controlled and maintained data banks and switching centers.

computer, next sequential—Requires that the address of the next instruction be contained in the prior instruction. Opposite of sequential computer.

computer, object—*See* object computer.

computer operation—1. The electronic action resulting from an instruction. In general, it is a computer manipulation required to secure results. 2. One of many designed or predetermined operations which are built-in or performed directly, i.e., jump, subtract.

computer operation, multiple—*See* multiple computer operation.

computer operations manager—*See* manager, operations.

computer operator—*See* operator, computer.

Computer Optimization Package (COP)—COP is comprised of a group of routines which efficiently automate program testing, operating, and maintenance. COP includes monitoring and scheduling routines to facilitate parallel processing, program test systems, thoroughly tested library routines, sort routines, tape handling, maintenance routines, and simulator routines. (Honeywell)

computer-oriented language—A related term for a programming language requiring a low degree of translation. Such programs usually run very efficiently on a related computer but require very extensive translation or compiling on another variety of computer.

computer-output microfilm (COM)—A microfilm printer that will take output directly from the computer, thus substituting for line printer or tape output.

computer, parallel—A computer in which the digits or data lines are handled concurrently by separate units of the computer. The units may be interconnected in different ways, as determined by the computation, to operate in parallel or serially. Mixed serial and parallel machines are frequently called serial or parallel according to the way arithmetic processes are performed. An example of a parallel computer is one which handles decimal digits in parallel although it might handle the bits which comprise a digit either serially or in parallel. (Contrasted with serial computer.)

computer program—A plan or routine or set of instructions for solving a problem on a computer, as contrasted with such terms as fiscal program, military program, and development program.

computer, program-controlled sequential — *See* computer, logic-controlled sequential.

computer programming language—The machine language that the computer was designed to understand. This is contrasted with compiler systems such as FORTRAN or COBOL.

computer, remote—A system which has four principal components; a central processor, a communications linkage, a terminal device, and a user. These components interact in some environment to carry out a task.

computer run—*See* run.

computer science — The entire spectrum of theoretical and applied disciplines connected with the development and application of computers. Contributions have come mostly from such fields as mathematics, logic, language analysis, programming, computer design, systems engineering, and information systems.

computer, scientific — Scientific problems are characterized by a minimum of input, a maximum of compute, and a maximum of integration. Management-science applications partake of these attributes, plus massive data loads of the contrasting commercial applications. The requirements for a computer to handle these special applications are: a very large memory, extremely high-speed arithmetic, and a large variety of floating-point arithmetic commands.

computers, coupled—An installation in which computers are joined to carry out special applications, such as two computers operating in parallel and used as a check on one another, or when they are coupled or joined so that the off-line computer is programmed to watch the on-line computer and if needed switch operation to itself.

computers, design augmented (DAC-1)—The initial goal of the design augmented by computers project was the development of a combination of computer hardware and software which (a) would permit conversational man-machine graphic communication and (b) would provide a maximum programming flexibility and ease of use for experimentation. This goal was achieved in early 1963. The over-all objective of the image processing system was to achieve the equivalent of what is possible with graphical man-to-man communication while utilizing drawings. The IBM 7094 computer which GM is using to control the DAC-1 system was modified to permit it to handle the CRT and Image Processing System while multiprogramming a background job.

computer, second generation — A computer belonging to the era of technological development when the transistor replaced vacuum tubes. Machines using transistors occupy much less space, operate faster, require less maintenance, and are more reliable. The second generation computer was prominent in the years 1959-1964 and included the IBM 1401, the Honeywell 800, the RCA 501, and the Remington Rand Solid-State 80.

computer-sensitive language — See language computer-sensitive.

computer, sequential—A computer which executes instructions individually and sequentially without any concurrent activities such as simultaneous reading, writing, and computing.

computer, serial—A computer in which digits or data lines are handled sequentially by separate units of the computer. Mixed serial and parallel machines are frequently called serial or parallel according to the way arithmetic processes are performed. An example of a serial computer is one which handles decimal digits serially, although it might handle the bits which comprise a digit serially or in parallel. (Contrasted with parallel computer.)

computer service organization — 1. Various companies which offer and contract maintenance and operation of computers not owned or leased by them for charges and fees commensurate with the size and complexity of the system. 2. Organizations which

provide either personnel or total systems planning, operation, and other related support for customers. The national organization is ADAPSO (Association of Data Processing Service Organizations).

computer, signed-magnitude — In a signed-magnitude computer, all the arithmetic actions are accomplished by the process of addition and subtraction of magnitudes. Since multiplication and division can be broken down into a series of addition and subtraction, respectively, the computer will perform these operations as well. Operations with signed-magnitude numbers are identical when algebraic addition using a pencil and paper.

computer, simultaneous—A computer that is organized in such a way that a separate unit is available to execute each portion of the computation, usually overlapping portions, and therefore executing operations somewhat concurrently.

computer, slave—A fail-safe or backup system (application), whereby a slave or second computer performs the steps of the same program so that if the master computer fails or malfunctions, the slave computer continues without a deterioration of operations.

computer, solid-state—A computer built primarily from solid state electronic circuit elements; e.g. transistors, diodes, monolith circuits, ets.

computer, source—This computer system has a specific task of translating or compiling a source program into the output program. It is used in the final phase of computing.

computer, special-purpose—A computer designed to solve a specific class or narrow range of problems.

computer store—See storage.

computer, stored-program — A digital computer capable of performing sequences of internally stored instructions as opposed to calculators on which the sequence is impressed manually. Such computers usually possess the further ability to operate upon the instruction themselves, and to alter the sequence of instructions in accordance with results already calculated.

computer, switch control—A computer designed to handle data transmission to and from remote computers and terminals.

computer, synchronous—1. A calculating device in which the performance of any operation does not start as a result of a signal that the previous operation has been completed. 2. A calculating device in which the performance of all operations is controlled with equally spaced signals from a master clock.

computer systems, distributed—The arrangement of computers within an organization, in which the organization's computer complex has many separate computing facilities all working in a cooperative manner, rather than the conventional single computer at a single location. Versatility of a computer system is often increased if small computers in geographically dispersed branches are used for simple tasks and a central computer is available for larger tasks. Frequently an organization's central files are stored at the central computing facility, with the geographically dispersed smaller computers calling on the central files when they need them. Such an arrangement lessens the load on the central computer and reduces both the volume and cost of data transmission.

computer, target — 1. The specific computer configuration needed for a particular program. 2. The computer which is not designed to use a particular program, but which must have another computer translate such a program for its ultimate use, is called a target or object computer.

computer, variable word length—A computer designed to treat information having a variable number of bits.

computer, wired-program—A computer in which the instructions that specify the operations to be performed are specified by the placement and interconnection of wires. The wires are usually held by a removable control panel, allowing flexibility of operation, but the term is also applied to permanently wired machines which are then called fixed-program computers. (Related to fixed-program computer.)

computer word—*See* word, computer.

computing—A generic term for all mathematical and logical operations carried out according to precise rules of procedure.

computing amplifier — This amplifier combines functions of amplification and performance of operations. Computing amplifiers are often summing amplifiers, analog adders, or sign reversing amplifiers. Most are used in analog computing systems.

computing element—A computer component that performs the mathematical operations required for problem solution.

computing machinery—Systems of equipment capable of processing data in accordance with the design of the devices and the programming and instructions of the total system. Such systems usually consist of interconnected input/output, storage, communications, and other specific-purpose units.

computing, multiaccess — This implies that more than one identical input/output terminal may be directly used with the system; usually they are remote such as teletype or other typewriter-like units.

computing, remote-batch—*See* remote-batch computing.

computing, remote system command mode—*See* command mode, remote-computing system.

computing systems, remote consistency errors—*See* errors consistency (remote computing system).

computing unit—Computing entails the arithmetical processes of addition, subtraction, multiplication, and division, and the ability to make comparisons and logical decisions based upon a predetermined program or the results of previous operations. The punched-card computers handle complex problems of business record keeping and scientific mathematics in fractions of seconds. Processing up to 9000 cards an hour, each machine makes a series of computations and logical choices.

Each computer is comprised of two units:
 (1) The card sensing-punching unit
 (2) The electronic computing unit

computyper—A data processing system comprised of a typewriter input and output of either hard copy, punched tape, or punched cards. This system is marketed by FRIDEN, INC.

concatenate—To unite in a series; to link together; to chain.

concatenated data set — A data set temporarily formed by uniting the data contained in several independent data sets in a specific sequence.

concentrator—A device used in data communications to multiplex numerous low-speed communications lines on to a single high-speed communications line.

concept-coordination — A term used to describe the basic principles of various punched-card and mechanized information-retrieval systems which involve the multidimensional analysis of information and coordinate retrieval. In concept coordination, independently assigned concepts are used to characterize the subject contents of documents, and the latter are identified during searching by means of either such assigned concepts or a combination of the same.

concept cylinder—The concept that data on all tracks above and below the one currently being used are available by merely switching read/write heads. Allows access to large amounts of information with no extra movement of the access device.

conceptual modeling—A method of making a model to fit the results of a biological experiment, then conducting another experiment to find out whether the model is right or wrong. The models are created continuously, and are tested and changed in a cycles manner. The physical sciences have developed through the years in this way, but there has been little use of the approach in biology, mainly because the kind of mathematics that developed is not well suited to biology. But now computers can get around this problem, and the important technique of conceptual modeling is beginning to be used in biology.

concordance—An alphabetic list of words and phrases appearing in a document, with an indication of the place where those words and phrases appear.

concordant—A specific type or arrangement of information or data into fixed or harmonious locations on particular documents.

concurrency, executive-system — The executive system is a multiprogramming control system with the capabilities of running (scheduling, loading, executing) one or more programs based on store and peripheral availability and requirements. The system provides for the sequential execution of data-dependent jobs while allowing job sequences to be run in parallel with other unrelated sequenced jobs or unsequenced jobs. Job schedules may be entered as far in advance as necessary with provision to allow late-entered jobs to be selected in advance of previously submitted lower-priority jobs. The executive system controls all input/output and interrupt handling as well as providing automatic loading, facility assignments, dynamic timesharing between jobs, terminal actions, and job time accounting records. The executive system's ability to maximize the utilization of the internal speeds of the computer by timesharing both internal and external storage with many programs, its ability to dynamically assign facilities (central store, magnetic tapes, etc.) to new jobs as they become available, and its complete control of the entire system assures efficiency in total system throughout.

concurrency, operations (real-time)—The great point is that the real-time system is at no moment necessarily committed to real time operations or to batch processing operations exclusively. Both may proceed concurrently and several kinds of each may proceed concurrently under the control of an internally stored executive program. But the real-time operations always have priority and the system will assign its facilities as these priorities require, relinquishing them to other activities, such as engineering calculations or normal business processing tasks, as soon as they are no longer needed to keep pace with real-time events.

In this way, maximum use may be made of the components of any desired configuration of the real-time system; and the advantages of its enormous storage capacity, speed, flexibility, and communications capabilities may be obtained at a low cost per unit of work accomplished. Experience indicates that the real-time system will quite probably outperform by a wide margin any other system of its kind in a wide range of applications.

concurrency, real time—Real-time is a mode of operation in which data, necessary to the control and/or execution of a transaction, can be processed in time for the transaction to be affected by the results of the processing. Real-time processing is most usually identified with great speed, but speed is relative. The essence of real time is concurrency . . . simultaneity. Real-time is the ultimate refinement in the integration of data-processing with communications. Real-time eliminates slow information-gathering procedures, dated reporting techniques, and lax communications; insures that facts within the system are as timely as a prevailing situation, as current as the decisions which they must support. Real-time provides answers when answers are needed, delivers data instantly

whenever the need for that data arises. Incoming information is edited, updated and made available on demand at every level of responsibility. Imminent departures from established standards are automatically detected, management notified in time for action.

concurrent—The occurrance of two or more events within the same time period, i.e., two computers or programs operating simultaneously.

concurrent computer—A specifically designed computer which executes simultaneously two or more instructions, such as read, search, compute. Such action is program controlled in some cases, but is built in or automatic depending upon the specific purpose for which the mainframe was designed.

concurrent control system—This environment allows for the concurrent operation of many programs; it allows the system to react immediately to the requests, and demands of many different users at local and remote stations; it allows for the stringent demands of real-time applications; it is able to store, file, retrieve, and protect large blocks of data; and it makes optimum use of all available hardware facilities, while minimizing job turn-around time.

concurrent conversion — Some computer designs eliminate the need for off-line conversion equipment. Conversion of programs from cards or paper tape to magnetic tape can be done concurrent with normal program running. Users at peripheral teleprinters can simultaneously prepare and debug their programs on line.

concurrent input/output — See input/output concurrent.

concurrent operating control—Operating systems provide the ability for several programs to share the computer at the same time. Concurrent operations include job processing while performing inquiry of peripheral utility operations, time sharing, and multiprogramming. For example, in the operation mode, a teleprocessing application (servicing terminals) can be under way concurrently with both stacked-job batch processing and peripheral utility-type operations.

concurrent operation—This term is used to refer to various methods in electronic data processing in which multiple instructions or operations of different instructions are executed simultaneously. Concurrent operation refers to computers working as contrasted to computer programming. This concept is one of the basic tenets of time-sharing, priority processing, etc.

concurrent processing—1. The ability to work on more than one program at the same time. This is a valuable feature of the new large scale computer systems. The result is a better utilization of time by taking full advantage of the high speed of the central processor. 2. Concerns the processing of more than one independent task simultaneously by a single computing system involving interlaced time-sharing of at least one section of hardware, which is generally the control unit and memory-address register or the multiplexing unit, for selecting individual control units and memory-address registers for each task. 3. The operation of a computer which has some or all of the program for more than one run stored simultaneously in its memory, and which executes these programs concurrently by time-shared control. *See* multiprogramming.

concurrent processing, peripheral — *See* peripheral processing, concurrent.

concurrent real-time processing—To close the gap in time between the actual transaction and its recognition by the processing system, a new concept has been devised, real-time processing. A real-time system is a combined data-processing and communications system which involves the direct communication of transaction data between remote locations and a central computer, via communication lines, and allows the data to be processed while the business transaction is actually taking place. A real-time system may be thought of as a communications-oriented data-processing system which is capable of performing batch-processing functions while concurrently processing inquiries or messages, and generating responses in a time interval directly related to the operational requirements of the system.

concurrent working—This term is used to refer to various methods in electronic data processing in which multiple instructions or operations of different instructions are executed simultaneously. Concurrent working refers to computer operation as contrasted to computer programming. This concept is one of the basic tenets of time-sharing, priority processing, etc.

condense—A routine which acecpts an object-program deck produced by an assembler, each card of which contains a single instruction, and produces a condensed deck containing several instructions per card. A typical deck is compressed to about one-fifth its original size (some computers).

condensed deck — *See* condensed instruction deck.

condensed instruction deck—The card output from an assembly program in which several instructions per card are punched in machine language. Input to the assembly program may consist of one instruction per card; thus, the name condensed is used for output.

condensing routine—A routine used to convert the machine language, i.e., the one-instruction-per-card output format, from an assembly program or system into several instructions per card.

condition—In the COBOL system one of a set of specified values that a data item can assume; the status of a switch as specified in the special-names paragraph of the en-

vironment division; a simple conditional expression. *See* conditional expression.

conditional — Subject to various constraints; i.e., the result of a comparison made during the program or subject to human intervention.

conditional branch—*See* branch, conditional.

conditional breakpoint — A breakpoint at which the routine may be continued as coded if desired conditions are satisfied.

conditional-breakpoint instruction—A conditional-jump instruction which, if some specified switch is set or situation exists, will cause the computer to stop, after which either the routine may be continued as coded, or a jump may be forced.

conditional dump — *See* branch, conditional.

conditional expression—In the COBOL language, an expression which has the particular characteristic that, taken as a whole, it may be either true or false, in accordance with the rules.

conditional macroexpansion — *See* macroexpansion, conditional.

conditional transfer—*See* branch, conditional.

conditional transfer instruction—*See* branch, conditional.

conditional transfer of control — *Same as* branch.

condition code—A 4-bit code, in the program status double-word, that indicates the nature of the results of an instruction executive (some computers).

condition code, initial—In analog computing, the integrators are inoperative, and the required initial conditions are applied or re-applied, as contrasted to the operate mode when the input signals are connected to the computing units including integrators, for the generation of the solution.

condition, compound — A number of simple logic conditions such as AND, NOT, or logic gates that can be combined to form compound logic operations.

condition, entry—A necessary and specified requirement, in computer programming, that must be met before a subroutine can be entered; for example, the use of a counter.

conditioning, signal—To process the form or mode of a signal so as to make it intelligible to, or compatible with, a given device, including such manipulation as pulse shaping, pulse clipping, digitizing, and linearizing.

condition, initial—The value of a variable at the start of computation.

condition name—1. A name assigned by the programmer to a value representing one of several conditions which may be assumed by a data item. 2. In a source language, programmers often tentatively or conditionally assign names to one or more possible values or ranges of values, which any particular item might represent. An item called month may have values 1 through 12 and may be referred to by such condition names as January, March, etc.

conditions—Expressions that, when taken as a whole, may assume one of a number of states. In programming it is the result of a test, e.g., greater than, less than, overflow, negative, etc.

confidence unit—*Same as* gate, AND.

configuration—A group of machines that are interconnected and are programmed to operate as a system.

configuration, computer—The particular set of equipment so connected to form a single computer center or system for various computer runs.

configuration, object — *See* object configtion.

configuration target—*Same as* object configuration.

conjunction — The logical operation which makes use of the AND operator or logical product. The conjunction of two variables, or expressions, may be written as $A \cdot B$, $A \wedge B$, $A \cap B$, or just plain AB. These may also be described as an intersection when using Venn diagrams. (Clarified by AND operator, AND gate, and contrasted with disjunction.)

conjunction gate—*Same as* gate, AND.

conjunctive search—A search defined in terms of a logical product, i.e., conjunctive form, in contrast to a disjunctive form, or logical sum.

connecting cable—The cable used to transfer electrical impulses between two pieces of equipment.

connection box — An interchangeable preset mechanical distributing device, for use with various punched-card machines for determining the destination and significance of data—a purpose quite similar to a plugboard.

connection, channel-to-channel—A device for rapid data transfer between two computers. A channel adapter is available that permits connection between any two channels on any two systems. Data is transferred at the rate of the slower channel.

connective—Related to Boolean algebra, it is that specific symbol which signifies the operation to be performed, i.e., in computing, usually between the operands.

connective, logical—Most logical connectives are Boolean operators, such as AND, OR, etc. Particular words which make new statements from given conditional statements; the calculation of the truth or falsity of new statements plus the logical meaning of the connective, such as AND, OR, NEITHER, NOR. Truth tables are of considerable aid in showing the equivalence of the logical connectives.

connective word—A COBOL reserved term to denote the presence of a qualifier. It may also be used to form a compound condition.

connector—1. A symbol to represent the junction of two consecutive lines of flow on a flow chart or block diagram. 2. An operator to indicate the relationship between two parts of a logical statement. 3. In a flow chart, the means of representing the convergence of more than one flow line into one, or the divergence of one flow line into more than one. It may also represent a break in a single flow line for continuation in another area.

connector, fixed — Used in flowcharting to indicate that only the result indicator can exist after a process completion.

connector, flowchart—The symbol representing the junction of two consecutive lines of flow on a flowchart, block diagram, or logic diagram.

connector, multiple—A connector to indicate the merging of several lines of flow into one line, or the dispersal of one line to flow into several lines.

connector, variable — 1. A flowchart symbol representing a sequence connection which is not fixed, but which can be varied by the flowchart procedure itself. 2. The device which inserts instructions in a program corresponding to selection of paths appearing in a flowchart. 3. The computer instructions which cause a logical chain to take one of several alternative paths. (Synonymous with N-way switch and programmed switch.)

connect time — The amount of time that elapses while the user of a remote terminal is connected to a time-shared system. Connect time is usually measured by the duration between sign-on and sign-off.

consecutive computer—*Same as* computer, sequential.

consecutive sequence computer — A specific type of computer (having capability of performing and storing parts or sequences of problems or computations) which executes computer instructions according to the logic design of that particular computer, but which is still controllable by programs and special instructions.

consistency, (remote-computing system) errors—*See* errors consistency (remote-computing system) .

consistent unit—A specific unit which contrasts from a linear unit in which all input and output variables are represented in the same way, for example, by voltages only.

console—1. The unit of a computer where the control keys and certain special devices are located. This unit may contain the start key, stop key, power key, sense switches, etc., as well as lights which display the information located in certain registers. 2. A portion of the computer which may be used to control the machine manually, correct errors, determine the status of machine circuits, registers, and counters, determine the contents of storage, and manually revise the contents of storage.

console, auxiliary — As contrasted to main consoles, some computers or units have additional banks of controls, displays, switches, and other devices for operator manipulation or visual access to operations.

console, data-station — *See* data-station console.

console debugging—*See* debugging console.

console devices, terminal—The terminal device or console supplies input to and receives output from the central computer. Most initial time-sharing systems have some form of electric typewriter as a terminal device. The principal choices have been Teletypes Models 33 and 35, Western Union TELEX units, and modified IBM Selective typewriters.

console display—1. A visual display unit that provides a "window into the computer." It can display a message of thousands of characters of information, or tables, charts, graphs and the lines and curves of drawings as a series of points. A "light pen" (stylus), available with the display, can detect information that has been displayed on the screen and enables the operator to change information under program control. 2. There are binary displays on many computer operator's consoles. One display bit indicates the memory work parity; other display bits may indicate:

1. The next instruction.
2. The contents of any memory location.
3. The contents of the accumulator.
4. The contents of index registers.
5. The status of the traps.

When the computer halts, the display register will indicate the next instruction word, while a register will contain the address of the halt instruction that stopped the computer. To display anything else, the appropriate push-button display switch must be pressed.

When the display-M button is pressed, the contents of the memory location specified by a register will be displayed. When either the display or other buttons are pressed, the contents of other registers or the condition of the traps are displayed.

The display register is also used as an entry register. Push-buttons that are provided may clear all or various parts of the display register. The contents of the display register may be entered in any memory location.

Pushing any of the entry buttons will accomplish entry of the display-register contents into the appropriate memory location or register.

console, display register—*See* register, console display.

console, duplex—A switchover console connecting two or more computers and used to govern which computer is to be on-line.

console, graphic—*See* graphic console.

console keyboard, display — 1. A keyboard which makes possible interpretive operations. Its function for a particular job is assigned by the computer program and the keys for that job are identified by removable illuminated overlays. 2. An operator control panel

for those processors where the display is used in place of the typewriter control console.

console, message-display — The message-display console, which contains a symbol generator and CRT, was designed without specialized memory and control in a form widely adaptable to a variety of data sources. Displayed symbols are presented in a typewriter format on a 21-inch CRT in the order received. A flicker-free message is displayed under full daylight ambient light conditions. The 64-symbol repertoire is placed in a format of 18 lines of 80 symbols each. Control logic and memory are contained within a modular data-processing system, which provides the overall automatic supervision of the message processing system (some systems).

console, operator—*See* operator console.

console optical-display plotter—*See* optical-display plotter.

console printer—An auxiliary output printer used to relay messages to the computer operator.

consoles, teller—Teller consoles accept keyboard-indexed messages for transmission to the processing center, and print processed replies received from the center to passbooks, tickets, and transaction journal.

console, supervisory—The supervisory console includes the operator's control panel, a keyboard and type-printer, and a control unit for the keyboard and type-printer. Optionally, a paper-tape reader and punch may be connected through the same control unit. The transfer of information between the computer and any of these devices is performed on a character basis over the input and output channels assigned to the console auxiliaries. Two switches mounted on the control unit permit selection of the paper-tape reader or the keyboard and the paper-tape punch or the type printer (some systems).

console to console consulting, time sharing—*See* time sharing, console to console consulting.

console typewriter (monitor) — The console typewriter is a standard feature of most computers. The primary function of the typewriter is to monitor system and program operations. Such system conditions as Add Overflow, Exponent Overflow, etc. and program conditions as Syntax Error, Symbol Length, Integer Size, etc. are brought to the operator's attention via the typewriter. The typewriter also may be programmed to request information from the operator. The typewriter also may be used to enter programs and data into the central processor and to type out the results in lieu of other peripheral equipment specifically designed for these functions.

console, uniset—The uniset console is a keyboard device specifically designed to meet point-of-sale operating requirements. Connected on-line with the computer, this device interrogates the system for desired information. Indicator lamps display requested information as well as the computer's reply. Relevant information is stored on a series of transparent cards. When inserted in the uniset console by its operator, this information is identified to the computer.

console, utility control—A computer console that is primarily used to control utility and maintenance program.

console, visual-display—*See* display console.

constant(s) — 1. The quantities or messages that will be present in the machine and available as data for the program, and which usually are not subject to change with time. 2. A character or group of characters usually representing a value, key or standard, used by the computer to identify, locate, measure, or test in order to make a decision.

constant address—*See* address, base.

constant area—A part of storage designated to store the invariable quantities required for processing.

constant, figurative—One of several constants which have been prenamed and predefined in a COBOL processor so that they can be written in the program without having to be described in the data division.

constant instruction—An instruction not intended to be executed as an instruction, written in the form of a constant. (Related to dummy instruction.)

constant multiplier coefficient unit—*Same as* scaler quantity.

constants (FORTRAN)—When used in computations, a constant is any number that does not change from one execution of the program to the next. It appears in its actual numerical form in the statement. For example, in the following statement, 3 is a constant since it appears in actual numerical form:

$$J = 3*K$$

Two types of constants may be written: integer constants and real constants (characterized by being written with a decimal point). The rules for writing each of these constants are given in various manuals. (FORTRAN)

constants, integer (FORTRAN) — An integer constant is written without a decimal point, using the decimal digits 0, 1, . . . 9. A preceding + or − sign is optional. An unsigned integer constant is assumed to be positive.

constants, real (FORTRAN)—A real constant is written with a decimal point, using the decimal digits 0, 1, . . . 9. A preceding + or − sign is optional. An unsigned real constant is assumed to be positive. An integer exponent preceded by an E may follow a real constant. The exponent may have a preceding + or − sign. An unsigned exponent is assumed to be positive.

constants, system—System constants are permanent locations contained in the monitor.

These locations contain data used by system programs. Some contain data that may be used by object programs.

constant storage—A part of storage designated to store the invariable quantities required for processing.

constant words—Descriptive data that is fixed and does not generally appear as an element of input.

constraint—An equation or inequality relating the variables is an optimization problem. A feasible (primal) solution must satisfy all the constraints including column-type restrictions (bounds, non-negativity, etc.)

constraint matrix — In linear programming, the augmented matrix of the constraint equations; it is the matrix formed by the coefficient columns, or left-hand sides, and the column of constants.

consultant, systems—This individual supplies technical assistance and direction with specific emphasis on problem identification, organization analysis, conversion planning, forms control and analysis, and reports control.

content — Data, characters, words, or other units which are held specifically addressable in some storage unit are said to be its content.

content-addressed memory — A memory where the storage locations are identified by their contents rather than their addresses. Enables faster interrogation to retrieve a particular element.

content-addressed storage—*See* storage, content-addressed.

contention—1. A condition on a multipoint communication channel when two or more locations try to transmit at the same time. 2. A real-time method of terminal transmission control. If the channel is not free, the requesting terminal will have to queue. The queue of contention is solved either on a first come first served basis or by a prearranged sequence.

contents—1. A phrase frequently represented by parentheses enclosing an address and used to denote the contents of the corresponding storage location; e.g., the contents of storage location "M" is written (M). 2. The information stored in any storage medium. Quite prevalently, the symbol ( ) is used to indicate "the contents of"; whose address is m; (A) indicates the contents of register A; (T_2) may indicate the contents of the tape on input/output unit two, etc.

context—The words or data directly before and after a word that influences its meaning.

contiguous—Adjacent or adjoining.

contingency interrupt—The program is interrupted if any of the following events occur at the operator's console: the operator requests use of the keyboard to type in information; a character has been typed in or out; a type-in has been completed; or the operator requests a program stop.

Contingency interrupt also occurs if an arithmetic operation resulted in an overflow, an invalid operation code was specified, or the clock was addressed after clock power was removed.

continuation card — A punched card which continues data that has been started on a previous card. This is allowed in many compilers such as FORTRAN.

continuation column — *See* column, continuation.

continue, FORTRAN—A statement which does not generate machine code. It is useful as the last statement in a DO loop.

continuous forms — Any source information, for character recognition, that is contained in reel form such as cash-register receipts.

continuous optimization program (COP)—A continuous program using quasi-linearization linear programming technique. (IBM)

continuous processing — The technique of constantly processing input items. This is sometimes referred to as on-line or real-time processing and is contrasted to batch processing.

continuous progression code—*Same as* code, unit distance.

continuous stationary readers — The special class of character readers for optical character recognition, which process only forms of predefined dimensions such as a tally roll of recorded cash-register receipts.

continuous system diagnosis, time sharing —*See* time sharing continuous system diagnosis.

continuous systems modeling program — A digital simulated analog system.

contour analysis—A reading technique, in optical character recognition, which uses a roving spot of light to trace the outline of a character by bouncing around the edges. This system is usually used for handwritten material because of the nonstandardized appearance of the input. The result of the contour tracing is compared to a complete character set within a library in an attempt to determine which character has been traced.

CONTRAN (CONtrol TRANslator)—CONTRAN is an advanced compiler-level language combining the most desirable features of FORTRAN IV and ALGOL 60. It is a concept in multiprogrammed, time-shared, real-time programming problems normally encountered in the following: the uses of a shared primary memory with an auxiliary bulk memory, linkages to executive control, responses to asychronous external interrupts, interprogram communication, compilation and debugging of both related and unrelated programs while the system is performing on-line control. (Honeywell)

contrast—*See* reflectance, background.

control—1. The part of a digital computer or processor which determines the execution and interpretation of instructions in proper sequence, including the decoding of each

instruction and the application of the proper signals to the arithmetic unit and other registers in accordance with the decoded information. 2. Frequently, it is one or more of the components in any mechanism responsible for interpreting and carrying out manually initiated directions. Sometimes it is called manual control. 3. In some business applications, a mathematical check. 4. In programming, instructions which determine conditional jumps are often referred to as control instructions, and the time sequence of execution of instructions is called the flow of control.

control, access code — Used in conjunction with the memory map option, that determines whether or not a CPU operating in the slave mode may read from, obtain instructions from, or write into a given page of virtual addresses.

control accuracy—Degree of correspondence between the controlled variable and the ideal value.

control, automatic — Control is achieved by electronic devices which receive signals of measurements of particular variables involved in the process or program. The devices automatically regulate or control processes or perform calculations with the variables to direct or correct actions of a process which is programmed for control under constraints or guides.

control, beginning of tape—*See* beginning-of-information marker.

control block—A storage location which contains information in condensed, formalized form necessary for the control of a task, function, operation, or quantity of information.

control block event — A unique information (control) block designed to control status of operations which are waiting for an entry or special signal, i.e., processing may be halted until one or more events occur. Usually a WAIT macroinstruction is involved.

control board—*See* control panel.

control card—A card which contains input data or parameters for a specific application of a general routine. Such cards are punched (coded) to cause segregation of various groups of cards, to cause changes in or startups of computer or peripheral machine operations.

control carriage—The control device which regulates the feed of continuous paper forms through a printer or typewriter unit.

control carriage tape—A paper or magnetic tape which contains punches (coded) for peripheral machine operations as, vertical spacing start of page, first and last line of printing, and other functions.

control, cascade—An automatic-control system in which various control units are linked in sequence, each control unit regulating the operation of the next control unit in line.

control center, input/output—*See* input/output control center.

control center, program—This feature directs and controls the computer through all phases of its operation. Each program control center may contain programs for four or more separate applications. It obsoletes externally attached control bars and other single job programming devices.

control, centralized—The control of all processing by a single operational unit.

control change—When the last of items is to be added, for example, and the computing function is then changed by the program to sorting or printing, a control change has occurred. Such functional changes in cards are represented by changes in the control field.

control change, minor—When control changes of different levels of significance are used, they can be given distinguishing titles such as a minor control change, then intermediate, or next major—to establish a hierarchy related to the importance of the data.

control character—See character command.

control character device—See character, device control.

control character, print—See character, print control.

control character, separating—One of a set of control characters used to delimit hierarchic units of data. The first separating character in a hierarchy might be used between words, paragraphs, or for nested brackets, etc.

control circuits—The circuits which cause the computer to carry out the instructions in proper sequence.

control circuits, instruction—Same as control circuits.

control clerk—See clerk, control.

control clock—The electronic clock, usually contained in the hardware, which times the instruction sets and the flow of and manipulation of the data.

control, closed loop—See closed loop.

control command, program — See command control program.

control communications, ESI—See communications control.

control computer — A computer which, by means of inputs from and outputs to a process, directly controls the operation of elements in that process.

control, concurrent operating — See concurrent operating control.

control, concurrent-operations—An operating system, like the executive, provides the ability for several programs to share the computer at the same time. Concurrent operations and control include job processing while performing inquiry or peripheral utility operations, time sharing, and multiprogramming. For example, in this operation mode, a teleprocessing application (servicing terminals) can be under way concurrently with both stacked-job batch processing and peripheral utility-type operations.

control console—The control console of the electronic data-processing system enables the operator to centrally control and monitor all processing functions. The panel is designed for efficient supervision and provides what is necessary for the operator, as the needs of the service engineers often have been placed within individual components of the system.

An electric typewriter provides direct communication with the processor memory. Data can be entered into the memory through the typewriter keyboard. The processor can transmit data to the typewriter for output through the typewriter printer. Thus, through the console typewriter, the operator can interrogate the memory, input programs, and enter instructions to modify a program (some computers).

control console, utility—A computer console that is primarily used to control utility and maintenance programs.

control counter—The device which contains or retains the address of the next instruction word.

control cycle—A particular cycle of a punch card machine's main shaft during which the feeding is stopped due to a control change, i.e., a choice is often given the user as to how many intercycles arise for a control change, which may or may not be determined within the machine.

control data—See data, control.

control, data initiated — See data initiated control.

control devices, communications—Communication lines and data devices can be attached directly to the system channel via a control unit that performs character assembly and transmission control. The control unit may be either the data-adapter unit or the transmission control.

control, direct—When one unit of peripheral equipment is under the control of another unit without human intervention, the controlling unit is then on-line to the second unit, which is under direct control of the first. If human intervention is necessary, the controlling unit is said to be off-line to the second, but the controlling unit has indirect control over the second unit while an operator acts as the link in the control sequence.

control, display—This unit permits up to eight display units to operate in an economical time-sharing configuration. It has a keyboard which makes possible interpretive operations. Its function for a particular job is assigned by the computer program, and the keys for that job are identified by removable illuminated overlays (some systems).

control dump, monitor—See dump, monitor-control.

control, dynamic—Operating a digital computer in such a manner that the computer can alter the instructions as the computation proceeds, or during the sequence in which the instructions are executed, or both.

control equipment, remote—*See* remote control equipment.

control, ESI—A feature that provides communications control for many systems is ESI (externally specified index). ESI makes it possible to handle a substantial number of computer channels, using buffers in memory. This buffer control permits other transactions to run without interruption. Communications instructions that involve other memory areas interrupt other programs for a minimum period of time, measured in microseconds, because subsequent instructions are in a "ready" position at all times. Real-time circuitry provides tight, accurate operations in rapid succession, handling a vast number of instructions in real-time, communications, and batch-processing modes simultaneously, or with logical priorities (some systems).

control, execution (program) — *See* program execution control.

control, executive-language — *See* language, executive-control.

control, executive system—Primary control of the executive system is by control information fed to the system by one or more input devices which may be either on-line or at various remote sites. This control information is similar in nature to present control-card operations, but allows additional flexibility and standardization.

control, external device (EXD)—*See* external device control (EXD).

control, feedback—A type of system control obtained when a portion of the output signal is operated on and fed back to the input in order to obtain a desired effect.

control field—A constant location where information for control purposes is placed; e.g., in a set of punch cards, if columns 79 and 80 contain various codes that control whether or not certain operations will be performed on any particular card, then columns 79 and 80 constitute a control field.

control, floating normalize—The bit, in the program status double-word, that indicates whether (if 0) or not (if 1) the result of a floating-point operation is to be normalized.

control, floating significance—The bit, in the program status double-word that indicates whether (if 0) or not (if 1) the result of a floating-point operation is checked for significance.

control, floating zero—The bit, in the program status double-word, that indicates whether (if 0) or not (if 1) the result of a floating-operation is stored if the characteristic is reduced below zero.

control, flow—*See* flow control.

control footing—A summary or total at the end of a control group or for various control groups, i.e., a minor total.

control, format—Controlling the arrangement of data in an individual medium.

control function—An operation to control a device, i.e., the starting or stopping of a

carriage, or a font change, rewind, or transmission reading.

control group—The number of people from one on up required to spend their full time in decision making when a system is being programmed. The group reads, modifies, evaluates, monitors the developing program, and then approves the changes necessary as they occur to prevent the build up of a queue of work.

control heading—A title or short definition of a control group of records which appear in front of each such group.

control hole—*See* control punches.

control, indirect—When one peripheral unit controls another through various types of electronic ties, but a human is part of the chain of control with necessary intervention, the first unit is said to be in indirect control of the second.

control, input/output channel—The transfer of data between external devices and their associated assembly registers proceeds under the control of the external device.

Input/output channels may transfer data simultaneously in multichannel operation. The access to main memory from the in/out channel is made available as needed, subject to channel priority. This is provided by channel priority logic which selects the channel of highest priority requesting transfer, that is, the lowest numbered channel requesting transfer of data. The data rate and active channels are not restricted except that the program must not require data transfer which exceeds a peak word rate of 525 kc considered over all input/output channels (some computers).

control, input/output real-time—*See* input/output, real time control.

control, input/output (unit)—There are several portions of control which direct interactions between the processing unit and input and output equipment. One control is written to control actions with tape, card, and printer equipment. A second control is specifically designed for random processing of records stored on direct-access devices. It is a separate control in order to minimize seek times.

control instructions—The instructions in this category are used to manipulate data within the main memory and the control memory, to prepare main memory storage areas for the processing of data fields, and to control the sequential selection and interpretation of instructions in the stored program.

control instruction transfer—*Same as* instruction transfer.

control, job flow—Job flow control includes: input/output transition between jobs and job segments, unit assignments, initial loading and initialization when the computer is first turned on; control between jobs; and control over the type of operation made, ranging from simple stacked jobs through teleprocessing systems performing concurrent operations.

control, job-processing — The job-processing control is the portion of the control program which starts job operations, assigns input/output units, and performs functions needed to proceed from one job to another.

control keys, tape-punch—Control functions such as power on, feeding tape at beginning and end of reel, tape error, and punch on and off.

control language, linear programming—The language used to prescribe the course of a linear programming run on a computer. The language consists mainly of verbs (agendum names) which call in a body of code (program or subroutine) embodying the desired algorithm for execution.

controlled head gap—A microscopic gap is maintained between read/write heads and the disk surface—with absolute reliability. A "fail-safe" head-retraction mechanism prevents any contact with the disk. Heads are completely self-adjusting (some units).

controlled machine tools, numerically — See APT.

controlled variable—A quantity, condition, or part of a system which is subject to manipulation, regulation, or control by computer.

controller, automatic—See automatic control.

controller, central communications—See communications, central controller.

controller, dual channel—This controller increases the sorting and merging powers of the systems by permitting simultaneous tape reading and/or writing. All tapes may be accessed from either channel.

controller, floating—A controller in which the rate of change of the output is a continuous or piecewise continuous function of the actuating error signal.

controller, input/output — See input/output controller.

controllers, channel—Channel controllers allow several central elements in the computer to share, in a changing manner, a pool of millions of characters of main memory that can be partitioned into numerous (at least 8) different memories (some computers).

control line—The randomly or sequentially timed cycle control that tells each terminal in a reel when to start transmitting. A method of communication line and terminal control.

controlling elements, forward — Those elements in the control system which change a variable in response to the actuating signal.

controlling system—Usually refers to a feedback control system; i.e., that portion which compares functions of a directly controlled variable and a set point and adjusts a manipulated variable as a function of the difference. It includes the reference input elements, summing point, forward and final controlling elements, as well as feedback elements (including sensing element).

control logic—The sequence of steps or events

necessary to perform a particular function. Each step or event is defined to be either a single arithmetic or a single Boolean expression.

control logic and interrupts — See interrupts and control logic.

control, manual—The direction of a computer by means of manually operated switches.

control marks (CM)—The central mark (any one-slab block) supplies special control features which can be utilized by the programmer. However, several specified CM configurations have been reserved for particular features on data tapes, as FF for end of file, etc.

control, master — 1. An application-oriented routine usually applied to the highest level of a subroutine hierarchy. 2. A computer program to control operation of the system, designed to reduce the amount of intervention required of the operator. Master control schedules programs to be processed, initiates segments of programs, controls input/output traffic, informs operator and verifies his actions, and performs corrective action on program errors or system malfunction.

control-message display — A device which shows in plain language form a particular sequence of events. The sequence of events represent events that have occurred in the past, events presently taking place, and/or events that will take place in the future.

control-message error, illegal — See error, illegal control-message.

control, minor—The least significant or lowest category of report grouping of basic detail.

control mode—The state that all terminals on a line must be in to allow line discipline, line control, or terminal selection to occur. When all terminals on a line are in the control mode, characters on the line are viewed as control characters performing line discipline, that is, polling or addressing.

control module, input/output — See input/output control module.

control module, interface—Same as compiler, COBOL.

control nondata i/o operations — Processes which relate to input/output operations as differentiated or exclusive of data manipulation, such as tape rewinding.

control, nonlinear—See nonlinear control.

control number — This is the quantity or number (value) which must be the result of a process or problem in order to prove the accuracy of the process or problem.

control, numeric — That field of computer activity which centers around the control of machine tools by mechanical devices, e.g., a computer can control assembly-line tools for machining.

control, numerical—Descriptive of systems in which digital computers are used for the control of operations, particularly of automatic machines; e.g., drilling or boring machines, wherein the operation control is applied at discrete points in the operation or process. (Contrasted with process control, in which control is applied continuously.)

control, operating (concurrent) — Operating systems provide the ability for several programs to share the computer at the same time. Concurrent operations include job processing while performing inquiry or peripheral utility operations, time sharing, and multiprogramming. For example, in the operation mode, a teleprocessing application, servicing terminals can be under way concurrently with both stacked-job batch processing and peripheral utility type operations.

control, operator—A central control console provides supervision of the computer system. Through the console, the operator can control the processor and peripheral units, observe, and monitor processing functions. A console typewriter provides direct communication with the processor memory.

control, orthotronic — The Honeywell correction technique which employs a frame parity check, a longitudinal check, and the two orthotronic words. The check is made as information is transferred from magnetic tape to memory.

control, orthotronic error—Accuracy of information on magnetic tape is orthotronic control which provides unique orthocorrection—the automatic detection and correction of erroneous data. Basically, orthotronic control can be compared to the accounting technique of crossfooting, in which a zero balance in rows and columns of figures confirms accuracy and a nonzero balance indicates an error. When information is written on tape, a special checking digit, called a parity bit, is automatically computed and placed at the end of frames (rows) of data in an information word.

control panel—1. An interconnection device, usually removable, which employs removable wires to control the operation of computing equipment. It is used on punch-card machines to carry out functions which are under control of the user. On computers it is used primarily to control input and output functions. 2. A device or component of some data-processing machines, which permits the expression of instructions in a semifixed computer program by the insertion of pins, plugs, or wires into sockets, or hubs in the device, in a pattern to represent instructions, and thus making electrical interconnections which may be sensed by the data-processing machine. (Synonymous with plugboard and related to pinboard.) 3. A part of a computer console that contains manual controls. 4. A removable wiring panel on EDP equipment on which external wiring may be performed to complete connections between the equipment's internal circuits.

control panel, automatic—A panel of indicator lights and switches on which are displayed a particular sequence of routines, and from which an operator can control the operation of these routines.

control panel, maintenance—A panel of indicator lights and switches on which are displayed a particular sequence of routines, and from which repair men can determine changes to execute.

control panel, operator's—*See* operator's control panel.

control panel, operator's request—A panel consisting of indicator lights and switches by which an operator can request the computer to perform particular functions.

control panel or console—Two methods of operator control are provided in conjunction with the control unit: a control panel, or an operator's console. Either method provides a visual indication of the status of the entire system and permits manual intervention in the system's operation. The control panel contains various control switches by which the operator can start and stop the machine and can load and interrogate both main and control-memory locations. "Sense" switches may be used in conjunction with programmed instructions to stop processing or to select predetermined program paths, thereby increasing the flexibility of a program.

control panel, programming — A panel consisting of indicator lights and switches by which a programmer can enter or change routines in the computer.

control panel, system — The system control panel is divided into three major sections: operator control section, which contains only those controls required by the operator when the processor is operating under full supervisory control; operator intervention section, which contains additional controls required for the operator to intervene in normal programming operation; and the customer engineering section, which contains controls intended only for customer engineering use in diagnostics and maintenance. Manual control operations are held to a minimum by the system design and operating system. The result is fewer operator errors.

control pen—*See* light pen.

control print character — A specific control character used to affect printing operations such as feeding, spacing, font selection.

control printing—A list of the control group for purposes of identification without the list of the detail records.

control, process — Descriptive of systems in which computers, most frequently analog computers, are used for the automatic regulation of operations or processes. Typical are operations in the production of chemicals wherein the operation control is applied continuously, and adjustments to regulate the operation are directed by the computer to keep the value of a controlled variable constant. (Contrasted with numerical control.)

control, production—As applied by computers, a data acquisition system from the floor of a production line or process for the speed up and simplification of the flow of production information for management.

control program—A sequence of instructions which prescribe the series of steps to be taken by a system, a computer, or any other device.

control program, command — A program to handle all commands addressed to the system from the user-consoles. These commands would include requests to log in or out, a request to use the edit program, requests to have a program placed on the run queue, requests to load a program, etc.

control, program-execution—See program execution control.

control program, master—Same as program, master control.

control programs—Control programs contain many routines that would otherwise have to be put into each individual program. Such routines include those for handling error conditions, interruptions from the console, or interruptions from a communications terminal. There are also routines for handling input and output equipment. Because these routines are prewritten, the programmer is saved a good deal of effort and the likelihood of programming-errors is reduced.

control, proportional—A method of control in which the intensity of action varies linearly as the condition being regulated deviates from the prescribed condition.

control punches—In the broadest sense, control punches are used to alter the performance of the program in some manner. For instance, it is customary to identify different types of cards with significant control punches, and to use these punches to route the program in different directions for the various types of cards. One example of this distinction might be to identify a header card with a 1-punch in column 1 and a detain card with a 3-punch in column 1.

control, real-time input/output — See real-time control, input/output.

control register—See register, control.

control registers, access—See registers, access control.

control register, sequence—See register, sequence control.

control routine—Same as executive routine.

control schedule, record — A type of master record or schedule designating all activities involved regarding disposition of business records, i.e., transfers, retention, etc.

control section—Nerve center of the electronic brain. It prescribes a chain of instructions (a program) for every bundle of facts that enters the system. It can send the stored data when it's needed during the program. It can examine the results of any step to select the following step or steps. When one bundle of facts has been processed, the control section usually issues orders to start all over again with the next one.

control section, input/output—See input/output control section.

control, selection—The control device that assists the instruction control unit in performing the selection of instructions to be executed.

control sequence—The normal order of selection of instructions for execution. In some computers, one of the addresses in each instruction specifies the control sequence. In most other computers, the sequence is consecutive except where a transfer occurs.

control sequence processing—See processing, control sequence.

control, sequential—A mode of computer operation in which instructions are executed in consecutive order by ascending or descending addresses of storage locations, unless otherwise specified by a jump.

control, serial number — Messages are controlled by assigning a number at the time of origination and adding additional numbers as the message passes through specific points.

controls, executive program—The program execution controls determine relative priority of programs that are ready to run, and load other programs into storage. They handle the allocation and protection of main storage blocks, the interval timer, error diagnostic routines, and checkpoint procedures.

control signals—Various control signals are provided to control and to insure the orderly flow of information words between the central computer and the peripheral subsystems. These signals do not transmit data, but are used to command and to identify the transfer of information words at the proper times and in the proper sequence. These control signals travel over the control lines of the input/output channel. A listing of these control signals and their respective functions is provided.

controls, peripheral—Peripheral controls regulate the transfer of data between the central processor and peripheral devices. Specifically, they reconcile the mechanical speeds of the peripheral devices with the electronic speed of the central processor, and minimize the interruption of central-processor activity due to peripheral data transfers.

control state (display)—All modes can specify that the display enter the control state in which 12-bit words are decoded as instructions to change display parameters, change mode, or change the address of access to the computer memory (some systems).

control statement, job—Individual statements used to direct an operating system in its functions, as contrasted to information needed to process a job but not intended directly for the operating system itself.

control statements—1. A statement which is used to direct the flow of the program, either causing specific transfers or making transfers dependent upon meeting certain specified conditions. 2. Instructions which convey control information to the processor, but do not develop machine-language instructions, i.e., symbolic statements.

control statements, assembly—*See* assembly control statements.

control station—A switching network station directing operations such as polling, averting, recovering, selecting.

control store, thin-film—*See* thin film (control store).

control supervisor—A control system furnishing data to a centralized location, allowing the operator to supervise or monitor the controlling of a process, operation, or calculation.

control supervisory—A control system which furnishes intelligence, usually to a centralized location, to be used by an operator to supervise the control of a process or operation.

control switch operation—*See* switch, operation control.

control, symbiont—*See* symbiont control.

control symbiont, with I/O—*See* symbiont control with I/O.

control system—A system of the closed-loop type in which the computer is used to govern external processes.

control system and data acquisition—*See* data acquisition and control system.

control system, concurrent—This environment allows for the concurrent operation of many programs; it allows the system to react immediately to the inquiries, requests and demands of many different users at local and remote stations; it allows for the stringent demands of real-time applications; it is able to store, file, retrieve, and protect large blocks of data; and it makes optimum use of all available hardware facilities, while minimizing job turn-around time.

Only through central control of all activities can this environment of the combined hardware and software systems be fully established and maintained to satisfy the requirements of all applications; this responsibility for efficient, flexible, centralized control is borne by the executive system. The executive system controls and coordinates the functions of this complex internal environment, and by presenting a relatively simple interface to the programmer, allows him to use the system easily, while relieving him of concern for the internal interaction between his program and other coexistent programs.

control system or section operator—A portion of the controlling equipment which is readily available to operators for controlling the systems equipment; this is usually a major portion of the console.

control system, real-time—*See* real-time control system.

control systems, internal—Programmed controls built into the system to govern the flow of computer operations.

control tape—A paper or plastic tape used to control the carriage operation of some printing output devices. Also called carriage tape.

control tape mechanism—That part of the printer which controls the printing carriage to permit desired and designed hard copy printout, i.e., the specific device which reads paper tape containing particular instructions for controlling the carriage operations.

control tape sequence—*See* program, tape.

control total—1. The summation of some field from each record in an arbitrary grouping of records; the number is often used for checking machine and program data reliability. 2. A sum of numbers in a specified record field of a batch of records determined repetitiously during the processing operation, so that any discrepancy from the control indicates an error. A control total often has some significance in itself, but may not, as for example, when a control total is determined as the sum of identification numbers of records. (Related to hash total.)

control, traffic—A method of optimizing the flow of work through a factory by means of a computer.

control, transfer—To copy, exchange, read, record, store, transmit, transport, or write data.

control transfer instruction—*See* branch.

control transfer instruction, conditioned—*See* branch, conditional.

control, transfer of—*See* branch.

control transfer instruction, conditional—*See* conditional.

control, transmission—The system can communicate directly with various types of communication terminals. Examples of terminals include the data-collection system, the data-communication systems, the process-communication system and telegraph terminals, including terminals using the new American Standard Code for Information Interchange.

Terminal attachments can be made via common carrier-leased private telegraph, voice- or subvoice-grade lines. Accommodations also include attachment via privately owned voice-grade communication lines and common carrier-switched voice and data networks.

Up to 248 communication lines can be attached to the system through appropriate transmission control units. Multiple terminals can be attached to each communication line. However, the limiting number of terminals per line is determined by the addressing capability of that particular terminal. Each communication line is under the system channel control (some systems).

control, trap settings—Trap settings controls which interrupt signals will be allowed to interrupt a program in process. If a trap is armed, then the associated interrupt conditions will be permitted to interrupt the main program when they occur. A trap that has not been armed, or has been disarmed, inhibits the occurrence of interrupt signals.

control, unconditional transfer of—*See* branch, unconditional.

control unit—1. A portion of the hardware of an automatic digital computer that directs sequence of operations, interprets coded instructions, and initiates proper commands to computer circuits to execute instructions. 2. An auxiliary component of a computer located behind the "mainframe" and other component equipment such as tape units, printers and card readers, for the purpose of controlling these components.

control unit, central—*Same as* central processing unit.

control unit, common—This unit is that portion of the terminal whose primary function is to control and coordinate the flow of data between the data device(s) and the communication facility.

control unit, data communications—*See* data communications control unit.

control unit, hypertape—*See* hypertape control unit.

control unit, input/output—*See* input/output control unit.

control unit, line—A multiplexor or line control computer—a special purpose computer for controlling input and output from communication lines when these lines are not directly accessed to the computer.

control unit, peripheral—An intermediary control device which links a peripheral unit to the central processor, or in the case of off-line operation, to another peripheral unit.

control unit, register system—One hundred twenty-eight words of high-speed and word-addressable locations, consisting of arrays of bistable integrated circuit registers, constitute the control unit. Multiple accumulators, index registers, input/output access-control words, an addressable binary clock, and high-speed auxiliary-storage registers are contained in the control unit.

The control unit is the functional heart of the system since it provides the program with multiple index and accumulator locations and allows each channel to transfer data words to and from central storage without program supervison. Simultaneity of input/output transfers, zero time indexing and address modification, and high-speed arithmetic functions are made possible by this versatile register system (some systems).

control units, punch-card—These units contain all logic, control, and power electronics to make card formats compatible with other formats. One unit is for use with an 800 card-per-minute reader and a 250 card-per-minute punch, while the other unit has a self-contained 200 card-per-minute reader and operates a 100 card-per-minute punch (some computers).

control word—1. A word, usually the first or last of a record, or first or last word of a block, that carries indicative information for the following words, records, or blocks. 2. A word which is used to transmit processing information from the control program to the operational programs, or between operational programs. Most systems normally contain the several significant fields within the record.

control words, I/O access—There are thirty-two locations in film storage that are used to maintain control over data transfers between the central computer and its peripheral equipment. Sixteen of these locations are used for input access-words and sixteen locations are used for output access-control words. These words, along with the function words, are necessary to initiate input/output data transfers (some systems).

CONTRON—A FORTRAN process control language developed by Control Data Corp.

conventional equipment—That equipment which is generally considered to be part of the computer system but which is not specifically part of the computer itself. Various card handling devices, tape handlers, and disk units, if not built in to the mainframe or wired in, would be conventional equipment, i.e., a teletype device.

conventions—Standard and accepted procedures in programs and systems analysis. The abbreviations, symbols, and their meanings as developed for particular systems and programs.

convergence, algorithm—An algorithm is said to converge if it is certain to yield its solution in a finite number of steps. It is a much stronger requirement than the mathematical convergence of the sequence of obtained function values.

conversational algebraic language (CAL)—It is primarily aimed at small numerical problems in a highly interactive environment. It relieves the user of all burdens of storage allocation for both programs and data and offers a problem-oriented language for conversational use (some computers).

conversational compilers, time sharing—*See* time sharing, conversational compilers.

conversational guidance, time sharing—*See* time sharing, conversational guidance.

conversational language—A language utilizing a near-English character set which facilitates communication between the computer and the user. For example, BASIC is one of the more commonly used conversational languages.

conversational mode—1. This mode of operation means that real-time man-machine communications are maintained. In this mode the system is used exclusively for servicing remote terminals. 2. The term given to the man-machine communicating technique that is the great dream of the future. This permits the user to "talk" to the machine locally instead of operating with the present restriction of having to tell the machine precisely what it is to do.

conversational mode operation—In this mode the system is used exclusively for servicing remote terminals. Real-time man-machine communications are maintained.

conversational processing—The user is said to be communicating with the system in a "conversational" manner when each statement he enters through the terminal is processed (translated, verified, and, if desired, executed) immediately. The system then sends a reply to the terminal. The information contained in the reply varies. For example, it might be a message indicating that the previous statement contained an error. Operations in the conversational manner must be in either of two possible modes: the program mode or the command mode.

conversational programming — A technique used in instructing the computer to perform its operations, whereby common vocabulary can be utilized by the user to describe his procedures most accurately. If a statement cannot be understood by the computer, it asks the user for a clarified instruction. This conversational procedure continues until the user has selected the series of statements in the proper sequence which will solve his problem. Conversational programming saves the user the inconvenience of having to study other programming languages extensively before he can solve his problem.

conversational time-sharing — The simultaneous utilization of a computer system by multiple users at remote locations, each being equipped with a remote terminal. The user and the computer usually communicate by way of a higher-level, easy-to-learn computer language.

conversion—1. The process of changing information from one form of representation to another; such as, from the language of one type of machine to that of another, or from magnetic tape to the printed page. (Synonymous with data conversion.) 2. The process of changing from one data-processing method to another, or from one type of equipment to another; e.g., conversion from punch-card equipment to magnetic-tape equipment.

conversion, A—A FORTRAN instruction to transmit alphanumeric to and from variables in storage.

conversion, binary to decimal—The process of converting a number written to the base of two to the equivalent number written to the base of ten.

conversion, code—A process for changing the bit groupings for characters in one code into the corresponding character bit groupings for a second code.

conversion, concurrent—Some computer designs eliminate the need for off-line conversion equipment. Conversion of programs from card or paper tape to magnetic tape can be done concurrent with normal program running. Users at peripheral teleprinters can simultaneously prepare and debug their programs on line.

conversion, data—The process of changing information from one form of representation to another; such as from the language of one type of machine to that of another, or from magnetic tape to the printed page.

conversion, data code — The translation of alphanumeric data into a form acceptable to the computer. This is usually done by the computer during the input of the data.

conversion, decimal to binary—The process of converting a number written to the base of ten, or decimal, into the equivalent number written to the base of two, or binary.

conversion device — A particular device or piece of peripheral equipment which converts data from one form into another form or medium, but without changing the data, content, or information.

conversion equipment—The equipment that is capable of transposing or transcribing the information from one type of data-processing medium to render it acceptable as input to another type of processing medium.

conversion F—One of the three types of format specifications in Fortran. F-conversion is used to convert floating-point data for input/output operation.

conversion, file—The transformation of parts of customer account records, employee records, and the like from their original documents into magnetic files by the computer.

conversion, media—*See* media conversion.

conversion mode—Communication between a terminal and the computer, in which each entry form the terminal elicits a response from the computer and vice versa.

conversion program, peripherals—This program handles all those jobs normally done by a separate peripheral processor. The priority interrupt system and multiple memory accumulators in the computer eliminate virtually all loss in running time. Such processing is done through the arithmetic processor.

conversion programs—These programs enable users of several competitive systems to take advantage of the superior throughput and cost performance characteristics of computers without incurring prohibitive programming costs.

conversion program, symbolic—*See* symbolic conversion program.

conversion routine—A flexible and generalized program which can be used by a programmer to change the presentation of data from one form to another such as from card to disk.

conversion time—The length of time required to read out all the digits in a given coded word.

convert—1. To change numerical information from one number base to another. 2. To transfer information from one recorded medium to another.

converter—1. A device for transferring data from one storage medium to another; for example, a punched-card to magnetic-tape converter. 2. A device that converts the representation of information, or which permits the changing of the method for data processing from one form to another; e.g., a unit which accepts information from punch cards and records the information on magnetic tape, and possibly including editing facilities.

converter, analog-digital-analog — Performs fast, real-time data conversion between digital and analog computers. Maximum sample rate for D/A conversion is 200kc; for A/D and interlaced conversion, 100kc. Digital word length is 10 bits. Actual conversion times are 5 microseconds for A/D and 2 microseconds for D/A. Semiautomatic features enable the converter system to perform many of the functions that a computer normally performs for other converter interfacts (some systems).

converter, analog-to-digital—This converter transforms an analog voltage to a binary number, selectable from six to eleven bits. Conversion time varies, depending on the number of bits and the accuracy required. Twenty-one combinations of switching-point accuracy and number of bits can be selected on the front panel (some systems).

converter, card-to-tape—A device which converts information directly from punched cards to punched or magnetic tape.

converter, (frequency)—In heterodyne reception, a converter is the portion of the receiver which converts the incoming signal to the intermediate frequency.

converter, language—*See* language converter.

converter, tape-to-card—A device which converts information directly from punched or magnetic tape to cards.

converter, tape-to-tape — *See* tape-to-tape converter.

converter, (telegraphy)—A telegraph repeater in which the input and output signals are formed according to the same code, but not according to the same type of electrical modulation.

converter, ticket—A device that reads data on prepunched tickets, such as for retail sales, and punches the data on punched cards for computer processing.

converting — A device used for transferring data from one form to a different form.

convex programming — *See* programming, convex.

cooperation index — *See* index, cooperation.

cooperative installation—An agreement by a group of users to band together and install a single computer to service all of them. The advantages are that they can afford a larger computer, have access to more capability, and achieve maximum economy and maximum service. The disadvantages are those associated with having many masters with differing priorities.

coordinate indexing—1. A system of indexing individual documents by descriptors of equal rank, so that a library can be searched for a combination of one or more descriptors. 2. An indexing technique where the interrelations of terms are shown by coupling individual words. 3. An indexing scheme by which descriptors may be correlated or combined to show any interrelationships desired for purposes of more precise information retrieval.

coordinate paper—Marginally punched, continuous-form graph paper normally used for printout on an XY plotter.

coordinate retrieval—*Same as* concept coordination.

coordinate storage—*See* storage, coordinate.

coordination, concept—*See* concept coordination.

coordinator of data processing—Coordinates activities of the electronic data-processing operations with the other organization departments. Usually has only departmental staff responsibility.

COP—Abbreviation for continuous optimization program.

copy—1. To reproduce information in a new location replacing whatever was previously stored there and leaving the source of the information unchanged. 2. To transfer data to a new location within a machine without destroying or changing either the content or the location or the data copied.

copy and correct—*See* correct and copy.

copy check—*See* check transfer.

copy, hard—A printed copy of machine output, e.g., printed reports, listings, documents, and summaries.

CORAL—Abbreviation for graphical communications and control language.

cordless plugs—On patchcords, if connectors do not include a flexible portion, they are termed cordless plugs.

cordonnier check—*See* check, Batten.

cordonnier system—*See* Batten system.

core—A configuration of magnetic material that is placed in a spatial relationship to current-carrying conductors, and whose magnetic properties are essential to its use. It is used to concentrate an induced magnetic field as in a transformer, induction coil, or armature, to retain a magnetic polarization for the purpose of storing data, or for its nonlinear properties as in a logic element. It may be made of such material as iron, iron oxide, or ferrite, and in such shapes as wires, tapes, toroids, or thin film.

core allocation—Since the core is in the immediate access working memory, its liimted capacity must provide or allocate core space for (a) programs permanently in core, (b) programs temporarily in core, (c) space for data permanently in core, (d) space for temporary data, and (e) working space.

core-array—A rectangular grid of cores containing a given number of words each of a given number of bits making up the rectangular array.

core bank—A stock of a specific number of core arrays and the associated electronics that make up a functional unit of digital computer memory.

core blocks, chaining—The linking together of uncommitted or available core blocks to form queues that may be called uncommitted storage lists.

core, bobbin—*See* bobbin core.

core dump—A listing of the contents of a storage device or selected parts of it. (Synonymous with memory dump and memory printout.)

core image—The images of ones and zeros as represented by polarized magnetic cores as formed or stored in other media. Each binary digit is represented as on or off in some media, by direction in magnetic type devices, or by magnetized spots on the surface of a magnetic storage drum.

core-image library—A grouping of computer programs stored on a mass-storage device in easily accessible form.

core, magnetic—A magnetic material capable of assuming and remaining at one or two or more conditions of magnetization, thus capable of providing storage, gating or switching functions, usually of toroidal shape and pulsed or polarized by electric currents carried on wire wound around the material.

core magnetic storage — *See* magnetic-core storage.

core memory—A storage device composed of ferromagnetic cores, or an apertured ferrite plate, through which select lines and sense windings are threaded. *See* memory, and thin-film memory.

core memory, high speed — A high-speed, random-access storage device, utilizing matrix arrays of ferrite cores which are most often used as the computer's working memory.

core memory, re-entrant routines — *See* re-entrant routines, core memory.

core memory, resident — *See* resident core memory.

core memory, thin-film—The magnetic film storage of the computer provides high-speed internal storage. By using this thin-film storage area as an auxiliary, temporary storage medium, faster computation can be obtained. Any one of the addresses in control store can be accessed as quickly as 167 nanoseconds, and have a complete cycle time of 667 nanoseconds. Because of this high speed, thin-film is one of the frequently used portions of the computer's internal-storage area; it may be referenced three times in the same time that it takes to make one reference to the core-storage area. The high access and internal switching times of thin-film store make it ideal for use as temporary storage of operands while the actual computation of data is taking place. Special address assignments for arithmetic registers, index registers, and other purposes are provided. These special addresses have dual accessibility in most instructions; that is, they can be referenced directly by the base operand (U), address of an instruction word, or by a special (A) designator within the word (some systems).

core, multiple aperture—A specific magnetic core with multiple holes through which wires can pass to create more than one magnetic closed path and used in nondestructive reading.

core plane—That particular plane or grid which houses the wires and magnetic cores, most commonly used for memory or program storage, in parallel, and which contains the bit positions or addresses.

core-rope memory—*See* memory, core-rope.

core-rope storage—*See* storage, core-rope.

core stock—A number of core arrays adjacent to one another that are treated as a unit.

core storage—*See* storage, core.

core, switch—A magnetic core in a switching device used to route signals to a selected destination.

core tape—A ferromagnetic ribbon, foil, or other material used to make a tape-wound core. The ribbon is usually wound on bobbins for sturdier support.

core, tape-wound—A magnetic core consisting of a plastic or ceramic toroid around which is wound a strip of thin magnetic tape possessing a square-hysteresis-loop characteristic. Also known as bimag, a tape wound core is used principally as a shift-register element.

corner cut—A corner removed from a card for orientation purposes.

correct and copy—A designated record is copied from one tape to another with specified corrections. In manipulating magnetic tapes, either a record-counting method or a file-identification method may be employed. The file option provides added convenience in that it permits operation over an entire tape or file, rather than over a specified number of records.

correcting signal—In synchronous systems, a special signal that may be sent recurrently for correction of data.

correction—A quantity (equal in absolute value to the error) added to a calculated or observed value to obtain the true value.

correction, automatic — *See* error correction, automatic.

correction, automatic error — A technique, usually requiring the use of special codes and/or automatic retransmission, which detects and corrects errors occurring in transmission. The degree of correction depends upon coding and equipment configuration.

correction, error (transmission)—*Same as* error correction, automatic.

corrective maintenance — *See* maintenance, corrective.

corrective routine, error—A series of computer instructions programmed to correct a detected error.

correlation, fact—*See* fact correlation.

correlative indexing—*Same as* indexing, coordinate.

COS (compatible operating system)—Not a true operating system but a series of programs which allow IBM 1401 programs to be operational along with IBM 360 programs and BOS and DOS.

cost center accounting—A type of financial accounting where charges of all kinds are recorded, keypunched, edited, sorted, and posted. The information is then used as input to the computer to post the required formal ledgers.

count—The consecutive or successive increase or decrease of a common cumulative total of the number of times an event appears; e.g., the count of the number of iterations already completed or which remain to be completed.

count check, hole—An accuracy checking feature which performs a count of the number of punched holes at the particular read station and compares that total with that of a subsequent reading/station total in column by column fashion.

count, dropout—The number of dropouts detected in a given length of tape. In digital recording, the length specified is normally that of the complete roll.

counter—1. A device for storing a number and allowing the number to be increased or decreased as directed by the instructions needed. An adding wheel or device. 2. A device, such as a register or storage location, used to represent the number of occurrences of an event.

counter, binary—1. A counter which counts according to the binary number system. 2. A counter capable of assuming one of two stable states.

counter, control—*Same as* register, control.

counter, cycle—*See* cycle counter.

counter, decade—A counter which counts to 10 in one column, or place of a decimal number, or one which counts to nine and resets to zero at the next count.

counter, delay—In the central unit of some computers, a counter that can temporarily delay a program long enough for the completion of an operation.

counter, forward-backward—A counter having both an add and subtract input, so that it is capable of counting in either an increasing or a decreasing direction.

counter inhibit — The bit, in the program status double-word, that indicates whether (if 1) or not (if 0) all (clock) count zero interrupts are inhibited.

counter, instructions—*Same as* register, control.

counter, locations—*Same as* register, control.

counter, modulo-N—A counter which in a recurring sequence counts and stores up to a value of N and then reverts to zero. For example, a modulo-5 counter stores $0,1,2,3,4,5$, $0,1,2,3,4,5$ . . . in sequence as it counts.

counter, origin—The circuitry which develops the location of the start of the next instruction by adding the instruction word length to the initial value and to the running total after each instruction.

counter, printing—The printing counter of the magnetic tape terminal advances by one

for each tape block transmitted or received. At the end of transmission, the total number of tape blocks for the run is printed automatically. During a run upon the detection of an error block when receiving, the number of that tape block is printed.

counter, program—*Same as* register control.

counter, program-address — A register in which the address of the current instruction is recorded. (Synonymous with instruction counter.)

counter, repeat—The repeat counter is used to control repeated operations, such as block transfer and repeated search commands. To execute a repeated instruction "k" times, the repeat counter must be loaded with "k" prior to the execution of the instruction. A repeated sequence may be suspended to process an interrupt, with circuitry providing for the completion of the repeated sequence after the interrupt has been processed.

counter, reversible—When the number stored in a counter is capable of being increased or decreased according to the value of various types of control signals, it is termed a reversible counter.

counter, ring—A loop of bistable elements interconnected so that one and only one is in a specified state at any given time and such that, as input signals are counted, the position of the element in the specified state moves in an ordered sequence around the loop.

counter, sequence—*Same as* register sequence control.

counter, step—A counter used in the arithmetical unit to count the steps in multiplication, division, and shift operation.

counter, subsequence—A specific type of instruction counter designed to step through or count microoperations, i.e., part of larger operations.

count modulo-N—When a number stored in a counter reverts to zero in the counting sequence after reaching a maximum value of (N-1), the counter is said to count modulo-N.

count zero interrupt—An interrupt level that is triggered when an associated (clock) counter pulse interrupt has produced a zero result in a clock counter.

coupled computers—An installation in which computers are joined to carry out special applications such as two computers operating in parallel and used as a check on one another, or when they are coupled or joined so that the off-line computer is programmed to watch the on-line computer and, if needed, switch operation to itself.

coupling, cross-talk—*See* talk, cross.

CPC—1. An abbreviation for each of the following: card programmed calculator, clock pulsed control, cycle program counter, cycle program control, and computer process control. 2. Electronic calculators that read punched cards of data or instructions for its own performance or for that of other units.

CP code—*Same as* code, unit distance.

CPM—Abbreviation for cards per minute.

CPP—Abbreviation for card-punching printer.

cps—Abbreviation for both "characters per second" and "cycles per second."

CPU—1. Central Processing Unit. The central processor of the computer system. It contains the main storage, arithmetic unit, and special register groups. 2. The principal unit of the computer which controls the processing routines, performs the arithmetic functions, and maintains a quickly accessible memory. It also contains the console in some computers.

CPU time — The actual computational time necessary to process a set of instructions in the arithmetic and logic units of the computer.

CRAFT—CRAFT is an acronym for Computerized Relative Allocation of Facilities Technique. Possible applications include office layout to reduce order-picking labor, and even layout of hospitals to reduce movement of patients and materials to and from various rooms, such as X-ray rooms, laboratories, operating rooms, and so forth. (IBM).

CRAM—The National Cash Register Company's Card Random Access Memory (CRAM) is a unique device which provides a single practical unit for both random and sequential processing.

CRAM card—A strip of oxide-coaded mylar, $3\frac{1}{4}'' \times 14''$, on which information may be placed in the form of magnetically polarized spots. (NCR)

CRAM deck—A set of 256 CRAM cards (numbered 000 through 255). (NCR)

CRAM track—A lane on a CRAM card for the writing of a block of information. (NCR)

crippled leap-frog test—A variation of the leap-frog test, modified so that it repeats its tests from a single set of storage locations rather than a changing set of locations.

criteria, sequencing (sorting)—The field in a record which determines, or is used for determining, the sequence of records in a file.

criterion—A value used for testing, comparing, or judging; e.g., in determining whether a condition is plus or minus, true or false; also, a rule or test for making a decision in a computer or by humans.

criterion, cycle—*See* cycle criterion.

critical path—The longest time path in a project which has to be done as quickly as possible. Because the overall time required to complete the project cannot be less than that required along the critical path, it requires the most careful monitoring. Any delay along this path causes the project to be delayed, while minor delays along noncritical paths do not. *See* PERT network.

Critical Path Method (CPM)—The XDS, CPM package offers a flexible tool for computer users requiring a project scheduling and process evaluation system. The XDS, CPM package has the following features: optimum schedules can be developed, including total project duration and cost constraints; process can be monitored throughout the project, with critical paths flagged for attention downstream; change and current status information can be incorporated easily without total rescheduling; calendar data, including holiday effects, are automatically reported. (XDS)

critical path scheduling—A monitoring system that continuously checks progress in programming needs of an operating system to report and prevent slippage. Reports generated by this monitoring of computer programming needs in which jobs to be done are sorted will indicate the most critical items on the critical path of the computer.

cross bar—An automatic telephone-switching system using movable switches mounted on bars. The dialed information is received and stored by common circuits which select and test the switching paths and control the operation of the switching mechanisms.

cross-channel switching — This optional feature permits direct program access to attached input/output devices through two channels.

crosscheck—To check the computing by two different methods.

crossfire — Interference from one telegraph circuit to another telegraph circuit or into telephone circuits.

crossfoot—1. The addition of several horizontal fields of information from cards or across a document. 2. To add several horizontal fields of numeric information, usually for checking or totalling purposes. 3. The process whereby numbers in different fields of the same punch card are added or subtracted and the result punched into another field of the same card. Or, a check in which totals secured by one method in a given problem are compared with totals obtained by another method. The totals should be equal if no error has been made.

crossfooting — Crossfooting is the addition and/or subtraction of factors in a horizontal spread to prove processing accuracy. It can be used on a payroll register to prove that the final totals of net pay and deductions equal the final total earnings; this provides control on report preparation as well as calculating and card-punching operations. In posting transactions to records that are stored in a computer (e.g., accounts receivable), crossfooting is used to prove the accuracy of posting either as each transaction is posted, or collectively at the end of the run, or both.

cross isle—A location where operators tear off the incoming printed and punched paper tape and transfer it manually to the proper outgoing circuit.

cross-sectional testing—A series of tests to get a representative sampling of system performance. These tests are usually one-pass tests such as an acceptance test.

cross tracking—A crosslike array of bright dots on the display, used for locating points and lines or for drawing curves.

cross-validation — The verification of results by replicating an experiment under independent conditions.

crowding, character — The reduction of the time or space interval on magnetic tape between characters.

CRT—*See* cathode-ray tube.

CRT display—The display plots data point by point on a 16-inch cathode-ray tube in a raster 9⅜ inches square having 1024 points on a side, and separate variables 10-bit X and Y coordinates. Includes program intensity control. Plotting rate is 35 microseconds per point (some systems).

CRT display, precision — This is a 16-inch random-position, point-plotting cathode-ray tube with magnetic deflection and focusing. It is useful for conversion of digital computer data into graphic and tabular form without the greater flexibility afforded by the ultraprecision CRT display.

CRT display, ultraprecision—This is a five-inch random-position, point-plotting cathode-ray tube designed to meet the particular needs of those requiring a high degree of accuracy, stability, and resolution. It is especially suited for photographic recording of digital output data and for use in combination with a photomultiplier as a precision programmed spot scanner for the input of photographic data to digital computers. Discrete points may be plotted in any sequence on its 3-inch by 3-inch raster at a 20-kilocycle rate (1 point every 50 microseconds) (some systems).

CRT inquiry display—Information is placed into the computer through the alphanumeric keyboard and is simultaneously displayed on its four-inch-square (or larger) screen (CRT). The unit then displays a reply to the inquiry on its screen.

CRT storage—*See* storage, electrostatic.

CRT, X, Y coordinates (display) — Precision CRT display is a 16-inch random-position, point-plotting cathode-ray tube which permits rapid conversion of digital computer data into graphic and tabular form. A self-contained unit with built-in control and power supplies, the CRT requires only logic level inputs for operation and thus may be easily connected to any digital system. Location of any desired point may be specified by any of the 1024 X and 1024 Y coordinate addresses contained in a 9⅜ inch square on the tube face. X and Y coordinate information in two ten-bit words is received from the computer, and, on command, displayed as a spot of light on the tube face. Discrete points may be plotted in any sequence at a 20-kilocycle rate (one point every 50 microseconds). Magnetic deflection and focusing techniques result in uniform resolution over the entire usable area of the tube face and maximum spot size of approximately .012 inch when measured by raster techniques (some systems).

cryogenic element—Various high speed circuits which use the superconductivity characteristics of materials operating at or near absolute zero temperatures.

cryogenic memory — *Same as* cryogenic storage.

cryogenics—The study and use of devices utilizing properties of materials near absolute zero in temperature. At these temperatures large current changes can be obtained from relatively small magnetic-field changes.

cryogenic storage—This type of storage depends for its operation on the properties of specific materials, which can become superconductive when their temperatures and the magnetic fields in which they are situated fall below certain very low temperatures. Since superconductors have zero resistance, they have the ability to maintain or store a current permanently.

cryostat—A device that uses evaporative and condensing cycles to achieve extremely low temperatures, and often used to liquify gases.

cryotron — A device utilizing properties assumed by metals at near absolute zero temperature so that large current changes can be obtained by relatively small magnetic-field changes.

CSL—Abbreviation for computer sensitive language.

CSMP — Abbreviation for continuous systems modeling program. A digital simulated analog system.

CTC—Abbreviation for conditional transfer of control.

cue—An instruction, address, or miscellaneous statement containing a key used to initiate entry into a closed subroutine at a specified entry point.

Culler-Fried—An on-line symbol manipulation system developed by Culler and Fried, of TRW, Inc.

cumulative indexing—*See* indexing, cumulative.

current-instruction register—The control section register that contains the instruction currently being executed after it is brought to the control section from memory. Also called instruction register.

current time—*See* time, real.

curtate—A certain horizontal division of the hole rows on a punched card. Example: if the rows of possible code positions are designated 1 to 24 from bottom to top of the punched card, then rows 19 to 24 may form the upper curtate and rows 1 to 18 the lower curtate.

curve—The graphical representation of the relationship between two variables (line, points, bar graphs, histograms).

curve fitting—*See* compaction, curve fitting.

curve follower—A peripheral unit which reads data that is represented in graphs.

curve-pattern compaction—*See* compaction, curve fitting.

customer engineering section—Those pieces or sections of equipment which remain unavailable to programmers or operators but which are intended for exclusive use, maintenance, or operations by the engineers employed by the equipment manufacturer.

cutoff—The frequency of transmission at which the loss exceeds by 10 decibles that observed at 1000 cycles.

cyberculture—A composite word derived from cybernetics and culture.

cybernetics—1. The field of technology involved in the comparative study of the control and intracommunication of information-handling machines and nervous systems of animals and man in order to understand and improve communication. 2. The theory of control and communication in the machine and the animal.

cycle—1. A self-contained series of instructions in which the last instruction can modify and repeat itself until a terminal condition is reached. The productive instructions in the loop generally manipulate the operands, while bookkeeping instructions modify the productive instructions and keep count of the number of repetitions. A loop may contain any number of conditions for termination. The equivalent of a loop can be achieved by the technique of straight-line coding, whereby the repetition of productive and bookkeeping operations is accomplished by explicitly writing the instructions for each repetition. 2. A nonarithmetic shift in which digits dropped off at one end of a word are returned at the other end in circular fashion; e.g., cycle left and cycle right. 3. To repeat a set of operations indefinitely, or until a stated condition is met. The set of operations may be subject to variation on each repetition, as by address changes obtained by programmed computation, or by use of devices such as index register. 4. An occurrence, phenomenon, or interval of space or time that recurs regularly and in the same sequence; e.g., the interval required for completion of one operation in a repetitive sequence of operations. 5. To repeat a set of operations a prescribed number of times including, when required, supplying necessary address changes by arithmetical processes or by means of a hardware device, such as a cycle counter, B-box, or index register.

cycle availabiilty—That specific time period during which stored information can be read.

cycle, card—The time required to read or punch a card.

cycle count—The increase or decrease of the cycle index by a unit or by an arbitrary integer.

cycle counter—The accumulator or counter of a cycle index.

cycle criterion—1. The number of times a cycle is to be repeated. 2. The register in which that number is stored.

cycled interrupt—The charge, by sequence or specific operation cycle of control, to the next or specific function in a predetermined manner or order.

cycle, execution—That portion of a machine cycle during which the actual execution of the instruction takes place. Some operations need a large number of these cycles to complete the operation and the normal instruction/operation alteration will be held up during this time.

cycle, grandfather—The period during which magnetic-tape records are retained before reusing, so that records can be reconstructed in the event of loss of information stored on a magnetic tape.

cycle, in action—Refers to the complete operation performed on data. Includes basic steps of origination, input, manipulation, output, and storage.

cycle index—The number of times a cycle has been executed, or the difference or negative of the difference between the number that has been executed and the number of repetitions desired.

cycle, instruction—The steps involved in the processing of an instruction.

cycle, intermediate—An unconditional branch instruction may address itself, i.e., a branch command is called, executed, and a cycle is set up, which may be used for stopping a machine.

cycle, machine—The shortest period of time, in the operation of a digital computer, for a sequence of events to repeat itself.

cycle, major—1. The maximum access time of a recirculating serial storage element. 2. The time for one rotation of a magnetic drum or of pulses in an acoustic delay line. 3. A number of minor cycles.

cycle, memory—1. The process of reading and restoring information in magnetic-core memory. 2. The time required to complete this process.

cycle, minor—The time interval between the appearance of corresponding parts of successive words in a storage device which provides serial access to storage positions.

cycle, null—The time necessary to cycle through a program without introducing data. This establishes the lower bound for program processing time.

cycle reset—The return of a cycle index to its initial or some preselected condition.

cycle, search—The sequence of events or time interval needed for the occurrence of a fixed number of events required to complete a single search operation, such as carrying out a comparison.

cycle shift—Removal of the digits of a number (or characters of a word) from one end of a number or word and their insertion, in the same sequence, at the other end.

cycle-stealing, data acquisition—*See* data acquisition, cycle stealing.

cycle stealing, data channels—Data channels give the processor-controller (P-C) the ability to delay the execution of a program for communication of an I/O device with core storage. For example, if an input unit requires a memory cycle to store data that it has collected, the data channel with its "cycle stealing" capability makes it possible to delay the program during execution of an instruction and store the data word without changing the logical condition of the P-C. After the data is stored, the program continues as though nothing had occurred. This capability should not be confused with interrupt which changes the contents of the instruction register. Cycle stealing by the data channels can occur at the end of any memory cycle. Maximum delay before cycle stealing can occur is one memory cycle time.

cycle, storage—1. A periodic sequence of events occurring when information is transferred to or from the storage device of a computer. 2. Storing, sensing, and regeneration form parts of the storage sequence.

cycle time—The interval between the call for, and the delivery of, information from a storage unit or device.

cycle time, processor—The computer can be divided into three main sections: arithmetic and control, input/output, and memory. The arithmetic and control section carries out the directives of the program. The calculations, routing of information, and control of other sections occur in this part of the central processor. All information going in and out of the central processor is handled by the I/O section. It also controls the operation of all peripheral equipment. The memory section is the heart of the central processor; it provides temporary storage for data and instructions. Because of its importance, the total cycle time of the memory is the main determining factor in the overall speed of the processor.

cycle time storage (in microseconds)—For core storage, the total time to read and restore one storage word. For drum or other random storage, the total time for one revolution.

cycle, work—The time necessary for a sequence of events, steps, or operations required for tasks.

cyclically magnetized condition—The condition found in a magnetic core after it has been under the influence of a magnetizing force varying between two specific limits, until the flux density has the same value in successive cycles each time the force is increased or decreased in value.

cyclic code—*See* code, cyclic.

cyclic code (permuted)—*Same as* CP code, gray code, unit distance code, and reflected binary code.

cyclic feeding—A system used by character recognition readers, in which each individual input document is issued to the document transport at a predetermined and constant rate.

cyclic permuted code—*See* code, unit distance.

cyclic shift—*See* shift, circular.

cyclic storage—*Same as* storage, circulating.

cyclic storage access—*See* storage access, cyclic.

cyclic transfer—This optional channel provides continuous cyclic word communication with from one to four equal-length blocks of memory. The blocks are contiguous and contain from one to 4,096 words. Both input and output modes are accommodated. The cyclic feature of this channel is beneficial in such applications as telemetry or other high-speed repetitive operations because once initiated, this channel continues to function without the need of a program instruction to start each cycle (some computers).

cycling tape—An updating procedure which creates a new tape file.

cylinder—For disk units with multiple read-write heads, all of the data tracks under the read-write heads can be accessed without mechanical movement of the heads. If each disk surface has one read-write head, the tracks under them can be thought of as a cylinder consisting of one track from each disk.

cylinder concept—The concept that data on all tracks above and below the one currently being used is available by merely switching read/write heads. Allows access to large amounts of information with no extra movement of the access device.

D

DAB—An abbreviation for display assignment bits, and for display attention bits.

dagger operation—*Same as* gate, NAND.

DAM—An abbreviation for data association message, and for descriptor attribute matrix.

damping—A characteristic built into electrical circuits and mechanical systems to prevent rapid or excessive corrections which

may lead to instability or oscillatory conditions; e.g., connecting a register on the terminals of a pulse transformer to remove natural oscillations or placing a moving element in oil or sluggish grease to prevent mechanical overshoot of the moving parts.

Dartmouth, ALGOL—The Dartmouth ALGOL is essentially ALGOL-60 with only a few restrictions and extensions made to allow operation within the BASIC system time-sharing framework.

DAS—Abbreviation for digital-analog simulator.

DASD (direct access storage devices) — *See* storage, direct access.

data—1. A general term used to denote any or all facts, numbers, letters and symbols that refer to or describe an object, idea, condition, situation, or other factors. It connotes basic elements of information which can be processed or produced by a computer. Sometimes data are considered to be expressible only in numerical form, but information is not so limited. (Related to information.) 2. Plural of the term datum. Collectively used to designate alphabetic or numeric material serving as a basis of discussion.

data acquisition (DA)—Process data are acquired by the DA system, converted into digital information, and printed to provide: (a) operating records for accounting and supervisory purposes, or (b) a record of experimental data in process research.

data acquisition and control system (DAC)— The system is designed to handle a wide variety of real-time applications, process control, and high-speed data acquisition. Each system is individually tailored with modular building blocks that are easily integrated to meet specific system requirements. A large family of real-time process input/output (I/O) devices is included, such as analog input, analog output, contact sense, and contact operate, as well as data processing I/O units, such as magnetic tape, disk storage, line printer, graph plotter, card and paper tape input and output. Data are received and transmitted on either a high-speed cycle-steal basis or under program control, depending on the intrinsic data rate of the I/O device.

data acquisition, cycle-stealing—The display receives data and control words from the memory unit via the data-break channel. The data-break channel is a high-speed, direct-access channel that passes words to the program in execution.

data-acquisition system — A system designed to gather data from multiple remote locations at a certain computing facility.

data-adapter unit (communications) — The data-adapter unit greatly expands the input/output capabilites of the system. It provides direct connection of a variety of remote and local external devices to a system. These devices include the data-collection system, the data-communication system, process-communication system, telegraph terminals, telemetry terminals, and control and data-acquisition equipment.

data, analog—The physical representation of information so that the representation bears an exact relationship to the original information. The electrical signals on a telephone channel are an analog-data representation of the original voice.

data analysis, display—The precision CRT display can significantly aid in the analysis and evaluation of stored, digital data. In the many cases where a visual presentation is useful but where hard-copy output is neither needed nor desired, the unit offers a rapid presentation of reference data to the user either in text, graphical, or tabular form, without the normal processing delays associated with mechanical print-out devices.

The display is particularly useful when observing data variations over a period of time. By providing dynamic, on-line observation of data, interpretation of a series of print-outs is eliminated and data evaluation is simplified.

data array—A representation of data in the form of signs, symbols as recorded on tape, cards, etc.

data auxiliary—That data which is associated with, but not a distinct part of, the main data. Data related to dates, locations, operator names, and such other items not in themselves associated with computations.

data base—The set of data or information on which operations and conclusions can be based. This is the set of data that is internally accessible to the computer and on which the computer performs.

data base management — A systematic approach to storing, updating, and retrieval of information stored as data items, usually in the form of records in a file, where many users, or even many remote installations, will use common data banks.

data base management and reporting, time sharing—*See* time sharing, data base management and reporting.

data, biased—A distribution of records in a file which is nonrandom with respect to the sequencing or sorting criteria. Biased data affects sorting time, depending on the technique used during the first pass on the data.

data buffer—*Same as* buffer.

data capture, speech synthesis—Any method of using speech as a direct form of data input.

data carrier—The selected medium used to transport or carry (communicate) data or information. Punched cards, magnetic tapes, and punched paper tapes are examples. Most often data is easily transported independently of the devices used in reading or interpreting such data or information.

data cell—The smallest unit of data which cannot be further subdivided such as a magnetic bit.

data cell drive—A random-access device that can store millions of alphanumeric characters of decimal digits. Multiple drives, providing a storage capacity of billions of characters of information, can be linked to the computer system.

data chaining—The gathering (or scattering) of information within one physical record, from (or to) more than one region of memory, by means of successive I/O commands.

data channel — The bidirectional data path between the I/O devices and the main memory in a digital computer that permits one or more I/O operations to happen concurrently with computation.

data channel multiplexer—The multiplexer option expands the data-break facilities of the computer to allow large numbers of input/output devices to transfer data directly with the core memory, via the memory buffer register. Simultaneous data-break requests are serviced by the multiplexer according to prewired priority.

data circuit, transmitted—Signals on this circuit are originated by the data terminal equipment for transmission on the data communication channel. This circuit is not required for receive-only service.

data-code conversion — The translation of alphanumeric data into a form acceptable to the computer. This is usually done by the computer itself during the input of the data.

data code, numeric—A digital code used to represent numerals and some special characters.

data collection—The act of bringing data from one or more points to a central point.

data collection and analysis—Process data are collected by the P-C (processor-controller) for mathematical analysis. Current performance figures are compared with those obtained in the past, and the results are printed for process analysis and management evaluation.

data collection, factory—*See* data collection stations.

data collection stations—Devices installed on production floors which allow a company to collect detailed data about the time employees have worked on each job, for payroll purposes. When an employee starts or stops work on a job, he punches in or out at the nearest data collection station. His employee number, the job number, and the time are recorded on a punched paper tape in the machine to form computer-readable records of employee time by job.

data-collection system—This system gathers manufacturing information from electronic in-plant reporting stations and transmits it directly to the computer. The information is processed as it is received. Reports can be produced which indicate, for example, job cost or machine utilization. Information can enter the processor in several ways, including punched card, plastic badge, keyboard or data cartridge. The latter logs production data on a pocket-sized recording device that the employee maintains at his work station.

DATACOM (Data Communications) — DATACOM is a system that is a culmination of many individual steps. This is a global network, that took three years to build, and is one of the largest and most advanced digital

systems now in operation. It transmits the equivalent of 12 million punched cards between 300 locations. Individual stockpiling of supplies by Air Force units has become outmoded, as any one of them can feed its requirement into DATACOM. The requisition is received immediately, the order is filled from a supply depot, and the shipment is sent, via air, on the same day.

data communication—The transmission of the representation of information from one point to another.

data-communications control unit (DCCU) — This unit scans the CTU (central terminal unit) buffers for transaction messages, transfers the next message to the central processor when requested, and returns the processed relay to the same CTU buffer. The DCCU and CTU greatly simplify central processor programming since the program has been freed of communications, control, queuing, and storage of messages and replies (some computers).

data communications, I/O exchange — Through the I/O exchange the communication control unit (DCCU) has full data-communications network control capabilities. Dial TWX, teletype, inquiry typewriter, and other terminal units may be specified.

data-communication system—These are real-time systems which interface between teletype stations and the computer. They are ideal for multiuser computer time-sharing, message-switching systems, and data-collection processing systems. A variety of systems are available for half-duplex and full-duplex operation with 64 stations and up.

data-communication terminal—A data station is an all-purpose remote communication terminal which can be used for a broad range of applications involving direct, on-line data transmission to and from the company. Branch offices, warehouses, remote reporting locations throughout a plant, or any other company outpost can communicate directly with a centrally located computer via the data station. When not being used for actual on-line transmission (remote mode), the data station can be used off-line (local mode) for activities such as data preparation and editing.

data compaction—A series of techniques used for the reduction of space, bandwidth, cost, transmission, generating time, and the storage of data. These techniques are designed for the elimination of repetition, removal of irrelevancies, and employment of special coding techniques.

data compression—*See* data compaction.

data, control—The items of data which are used to identify, select, execute or modify another routine, record, file, operation or data value.

data control clerk—A clerical-type employee in computer centers whose job it is to see that the right data are used properly and correctly. For instance, in a program checkout the output of one program is usually verified by the data control clerk before it is used as input for another program.

data control group—The people in the accounting or other parts of an organization who have the responsibility for submitting all data to be processed by the computer and for receiving all the results produced. The data control group must verify that authorization for certain types of transactions is satisfactory before the transactions are key punched, and be responsible for verification that output and postings are consistent with the original information. This procedure is effective, because if no data enters or leaves the machine except with control group approval, and if adequate accounting checks exist to guide the control group, very little can go wrong.

data conversion—A series or program of different types of processes which result in a change from the original form of data representation such as a card-to-tape conversion.

data conversion, display—The incremental display provides a fast, direct method of converting line drawings, photographs, and other written data into digital information when used with a photomultiplier system. In such a system, the incremental plotter is used as a programmed spot-scanning source of light in combination with a lens system to focus the raster being scanned on the film being read. The photomultiplier gathers the light passing through the film and signals the computer whenever light is sensed. In this manner, a digital record of the photograph being scanned is accumulated in the computer memory.

data definition (DD) statement—Control card used to describe a data set that is to be used by a job step in IBM OS/360 and other systems.

data delay—1. The measured time concerned in the delay or waiting period for information before another process would be performed. 2. A delay attributable to some contingency within the data itself.

data description—An entry in the data division of a COBOL program describing the characteristics of a data item in terms of level, name, length, and alphanumeric content.

data descriptors—A data descriptor, as its name implies, describes data (i.e., a data area) by pointing to one or more contiguous data locations. Consequently, a particular data descriptor may be concerned with many memory locations. More than this, however, a data descriptor is also concerned with the presence, in core, of the data it describes. This is necessarily so particularly because of the data-overlay capabilities of the computer. A descriptor is concerned with many aspects of storage. These aspects are indicated by various bits in the descriptor.

data design—A particular layout or format of

computer storage or machine storage allocation, i.e., for input and output. Often related to flow charts and diagrams to define procedures and practices for problem solution.

data, digital—Information represented by a code consisting of a sequence of discrete elements, i.e., a zero or a one.

data display module—An optional device which stores computer output and translates this output into literal, numerical, or graphic signals which are distributed to a program-determined group of lights, annunciators, and numerical indicators for use in operator consoles and remote stations.

data division—1. A division of a COBOL program describing the characteristics of data (files, records, and data elements). 2. Data division describes the data to be processed by the object program. It contains a file section which describes the files used. There may be a working storage section which allocates memory space for the storage of intermediate results.

data element—1. A group of characters that specify an item at or near the basic level. An elementary item; e.g., "hour"—contains no subordinate item. A group item; e.g., "date", which consists of day, month, and year—contains items that may be used separately and therefore treated as elementary items. 2. A specific item of information appearing in a set of data; e.g., in the following set of data, each item is a data element: the quantity of a supply item issued, a unit rate, an amount, and the balance of stock items on hand. 3. The smallest unit of information to which reference is made, such as customer code, invoice number, unit price, etc.

data, end of—The signal that is read or generated when the final record of a file has been read or written.

data entry—The writing, reading, or posting to a coding form or to a terminal or processing medium, of information or instructions. A datum or item which is usually entered on one line, a single entity of processing.

data error—A deviation from correctness in data, usually an error, which occurred prior to processing the data.

data evaluation—The examination and analysis of data to make an assessment of its inherent meaning, probably accuracy relevancy and its relation to given situations or context.

data-examination clerk—Under direct supervision maintains accuracy, correctness, and appropriateness of input/output data.

data-exchange system—The fundamental operation of the data-exchange system is to accept data from a number of input channels, sort the data according to priority and destination, perform any necessary translation functions, and retransmit the data as output channels become available. Concurrently, the system may perform a variety of housekeeping chores, such as checking for errors, maintaining message logs or maps, and keeping track of the source and number of messages that flow through the system.

data-exchange unit, data transmission—The data-exchange unit (DEU), is a multiformat input/output buffering device which provides an interface capability to place the computing system at the heart of communications networks, as the Gemini project, for example. During booster guidance, fifteen 24-bit words of trajectory data are forwarded,, via the DEU, each half-second of a computation cycle to the Manned Spacecraft Control Center (MSCC) for distribution to various monitoring displays. In addition, simultaneous links are maintained with several other computer complexes. The DEU aids in the guidance, recording, displaying, and transmitting of information to a variety of users by providing the multiformat buffering capability to enable the computer to communicate in real time among many centers (some computers).

data facilities, storage — *See* data storage facilities.

data field — An area located in the main memory which contains a data record.

data files—Aggregations of data sets for definite usage. The file may contain one or more different data sets. A permanent data file is one in which the data is perpetually subject to being updated; e.g., a name and address file. A working data file is a temporary accumulation of data sets which is destroyed after the data has been transferred to another form.

data files, working—*See* data files.

data flowchart—A flowchart showing the path of the data step by step of a problem solution or through a system.

data flow, external device—The transfer of data between external devices and their associated assembly registers proceeds under the control of the external device. Input/output channels may transfer data simultaneously in multichannel operation. The access to main memory from the in/out channel is made available as needed, subject to channel priority. This is provided by channel priority logic which selects the channel of highest priority requesting transfer, that is, the lowest numbered channel requesting transfer of data. The data rate and channels active are not restricted except that the program must not require data transfer which exceeds a peak word rate considered over all input/output channels.

data-formatting statements — These statements instruct the assembly program to set up constants and reserved memory areas and to punctuate memory to indicate field boundaries.

data frames — Data frames are written on some tapes at a density of either 200 or 556 bits per inch. Data block length is not specified. When the end of a block is reached and no more data is transmitted, the tape comes to a stop. After the last block in the

file (related group of blocks), the end-of file sentinel (tapemark) is written to indicate the termination of the file (some systems).

data gathering—*Same as* data collection.

data group generation—*See* generation, data group.

data handling—1. The production of records and reports. 2. The performance of those data-processing chores common to most users such as sorting, input/output operation, and report generation.

data hierarchy — Structuring data into the subsets within a set, such as bit, byte, character, word, block, record, file, and bank.

data-initiated control—Jobs can be initiated and run automatically, according to preset rules, upon receipt of a signal or message from an external source using data. For example, in a teleprocessing application. jobs are performed upon receipt of messages from remote terminals. Data from a remote terminal can initiate loading of a program from the library; the program then processes the data and makes appropriate response to the originating terminal. Messages can be logged and queued on a secondary device, routed, and transmitted to other terminals. Inquiry by name, account number, or other key data can initiate a search of files stored in the system, find the requested information, and respond to the requester.

data input—1 Any data upon which one or more of the basic processing functions are to be performed, such as coding, sorting, computing, summarizing, and reporting, recording, and communication. 2. Data ready for processing and on the input channel of an input device such as an optical reader, card reader, logic element or gate.

data item—1. Sometimes called a datum. A single unit of information of a specific kind pertaining to a single thing. 2. A specific member of a data set denoted by a data element; for instance Monday, the name of a specific member of the set of the days of a week. The week is the data element. Monday the data item, and 05 could be the data code.

data layout—1. A predetermined arrangement of characters, fields, lines, punctuation, page numbers, etc. 2. A defined ararngement of words, totals, characters, stubs, headings, etc. for a desired clear presentation of data or print-output, such as a financial record.

data level—A rank or reference number used to indicate to a compiling program the position of data in a particular hierarchy.

data link — Equipment which permits the transmission of information in data format.

data location—*See* location.

data, machine readable—Being able to be sensed or read by a specific device, i.e., information on tapes, cards, drums, disks, etc., that is capable of being read by a machine.

data management (DM) — A term referring collectively to all OS/360 routines that give access to data, enforce storage conventions, and regulate the use of each individual I/O device.

data management programming system—A system of programs designed to provide a human operator with the capability for querying, augmenting, and manipulating large computer-stored data bases in a natural language.

data manipulation—The performance of those data-processing chores common to most users, such as sorting, input/output operations, and report generation.

data, mass—An amount of data too great to store in the central processing unit (CPU) at any given time, usually stored in a mass data auxiliary unit.

data, master—A set of data which is altered infrequently and supplies basic data for processing operations. The data content of a master file. Examples include: names, badge numbers, or pay rate in personnel data, or stock numbers, stock descriptions, or units of measure in stock-control data.

datamation—A shortened term for automatic data processing; taken from data and automation.

data, mechanized — The device or material which is used to convey data to a sensing device or unit, i.e., punched cards, tapes.

data media—*See* continuous forms.

data medium, automated—*See* data, machine readable.

data medium, parallel—A medium for recording or entering data and also an input/output media for computers such as cards, tapes, paper, and disks.

data name — A single word or a group of words signifying an item of data; it may be a tag or a label.

DATANET—A General Electric model that can be used for production control. A message exchange which receives and transmits automatically. Another use is a data-collection system for the purpose of transmitting data from a remote station to a central unit. Still another use permits an operator to dial and send perforated-tape data over a phone line.

data organization — Also known as data-set organization. Pertains to any one of the data management conventions for the spatial or physical arrangements of the records of a data set. The five data management organizing methods are sometimes defined as: 1. sequential 2. partitioned 3. indexed sequential 4. direct 5. telecommunications.

data origination—1. The translation of information from its original form into a machine-sensible form. 2. The act of creating a record in a machine-sensible form, directly or as a by-product of a human-readable document.

data output — Data obtained or obtainable from a device, such as a logic element, or the output channel of a logic element.

dataphone—1. A word used by A.T.&T. to designate any of a family of devices used to permit data communications over telephone

channels. 2. A generic term to describe a family of devices available to facilitate data communication.

dataphone adapters—Transceivers, transmitters, and receivers of digital-plotting communication systems. They enable high-speed digital incremental plotting of digital-computer outputs at remote locations—either nearby or thousands of miles from the data source. The data phone adapter uses regular telephone lines using standard telephone dataphone terminals. For the nominal service charge of a regular telephone call, the computer may "talk" directly to a remote plotter, or on a conference hook-up to many remote plotters simultaneously, any place there is a standard telephone. Dataphone-adapter installation options can provide two-way communications between stations.

dataphone, communications system equipment—The Bell Systems 201A or 201B dataphone data sets as used with the many data communications systems provide "half-duplex" capability. They are used for sending and receiving but not simultaneously for both operations.

The data set at the transmitting end takes the character pulses from the data-line terminal and converts them to modulated information-bearing signals that can be transmitted over the telephone line.

The data set at the receiving end converts the signals from the telephone line back to the same character pulses as those delivered by the transmitting data-line terminal and delivers these pulses to the receiving data-line terminal.

dataplotter—A dataplotter provides fast, accurate, automatic plotting of digital information in the form of points, lines, or symbols. Inputs may come from magnetic tape, punched card or tape, manual keyboard, or direct analog voltages.

data preparation—The process of converting data into a medium suitable for input to and processing by the computer.

data preparation clerks—A staff of clerical personnel who operate keypunch devices, or who gather, collate, select, or adjust data so that it can be easily input to the computer.

data processing—1. Any procedure for receiving information and producing a specific result. 2. Rearrangement and refinement of raw data into a form suitable for further use. 3. The preparation of source media which contain data or basic elements of information, and the handling of such data according to precise rules of procedure to accomplish such operations as classifying, sorting, calculating, summarizing, and recording. 4. The production of records and reports. (Synonymous with data handling.)

data-processing center—1. A grouping of automatic data-processing equipment and operating personnel in a separate area under the control of a single management group for the purpose of centralizing and controlling data-processing service for others, sometimes called customers, on a reimbursable or nonreimbursable basis.

data processing, centralized—The processing of all data involved with a given activity at a given location and usually in one building housing the equipment configuration.

data processing, decentralized—The housing of data by individual subdivisions of an organization or at each geographical location of the parts of an organization.

data processing, electronic—Data processing by way of electronic equipment, such as an internally stored program, electronic digital computer, or other automatic data processing machine.

data processing equipment, automatic — A machine, or group of interconnected machines consisting of input, storage, computing control, and output devices that uses electronic circuitry in the main computing element to perform arithmetic and/or logical operations automatically by means of internally stored or externally controlled programmed instructions.

data processing, graphic—A letter or other drawn, diagrammed (or an omission of such) character or figure which can be reproduced or transmitted in some way through an electronic data system, usually by an ordered set of pulses.

data processing, in-line—Data processing in which all changes to relevant records and accounts are made at the time that each transaction or event occurs. The process usually requires random access storage.

data processing, integrated—The processing of data on an organized, systematic, and correlated basis throughout some area of interest as opposed to a series of disjointed operations.

data processing, line finder—See line finder (data processing).

data processing, low activity—The processing of a limited number of input transactions against very large master files.

data-processing machine — A general name for a machine that can store and process numeric and alphabetic information. (Related to analog computer, digital computer, and automatic data-processing equipment.)

data processing machine, electronic—See data processing equipment, automatic.

data processing, non-numerical—Specific languages developed by symbol manipulation and used primarily as research tools rather than for production programming. Most have proved valuable in construction of compilers and in simulation of human problem solving. Other uses have been generalized and verification of mathematical proofs, pattern recognition, information retrieval, algebraic manipulation, heuristic programming, and exploration of new programming languages.

data processing, on-line—See on-line processing.

data processing, paper-type — A processing system in which the message is typed in hard-copy form on a machine that simultaneously punches a paper tape. Then the tape is placed in a Teletype transmitting machine for transmission over the wire at maximum transmitting speed.

data processing, scientific—The processing of data involved with solving mathematical functions or equations.

data processing, specialized—Various types of automatic data processing have become distinct enough to be designated by proper names. Among these are: business data processing, automated production management, administrative data processing, and others.

data-processing system—A network of machine components capable of accepting information, processing it according to a plan, and producing the desired results.

data processor—1. A device capable of performing operations on data, such as a digital computer, analog computer, or a desk calculator. 2. A person processing data. 3. A standardized term representing any and all devices which have the capability of performing the reduction, summarizing, processing, or input and output of data or information, and including calculators, punched card equipment, computers, and subsidiary systems.

data protection, printing—Operation of the printers is checked automatically to insure that they respond correctly to control-unit printing signals. If this check fails, an indicator, which can be tested by a programmed instruction, is automatically set.

data purification—The reduction of the number of errors, as much as possible, prior to using data in an automatic data-processing system.

data, raw—Data that have not been processed. Such data may or may not be in machine-sensible form.

data record—A record containing data to be processed by a program.

data reduction—1. The art or process of transforming masses of raw test or experimentally obtained data, usually gathered by instrumentation, into useful, ordered, or simplified intelligence. 2. The process of transforming raw data into intelligible form by smoothing, adjusting, scaling and ordering experimental readings.

data reduction, on-line—The processing of information as rapidly as the information is received by the computing system, or as rapidly as it is generated by the source.

data reduction, real-time—The reduction of data as speedily as it is received at the processor or computer, or as rapidly as it is generated by the source, if the transmission time is not overbearing. The computer must process (reduce) immediately since by storing and then reducing, operations would be online but not real-time.

data reference external (time-sharing)—*See* time sharing, external data reference.

data reliability—A ratio that relates the extent to which data meets a specific or given standard, usually concerning the accuracy of data, or the degree to which data is error free. Other examples relate to the probabilities of the correctness of data, i.e., the degree to which data is unchanged after transmission or recording operations.

data retrieval—The retrieval or return of data by selecting, searching, or retransmission of information from a file, data bank, or storage device.

data rules—The unique group of conditions surrounding data elements, sets, and files, and the action to be taken when the conditions are satisfied. The rules are usually expressed in tabular form, rather than narrative, to insure complete, consistent, and accurate documentation of the processing methodology, and at the same time to provide flexibility for change.

data select—A special selection operation in which one set of items is taken for printing or punching from several sets presented on tape.

data (display) selection and modification—By using the light pen in conjunction with incremental display, data of interest stored in the computer memory may be easily selected and modified. Pointing the light pen at a selected displayed point causes the pen to signal the computer. The computer program may then operate on the data selected in a manner previously determined, or under the immediate control of the user, via switch inputs on the console.

data set—A collection of similar and related data records that is recorded for use by a computer. A recordable medium such as a data file.

data set clocking—A time base oscillator supplied by the data set for regulating the bit rate of transmission. This is referred to by IBM as external clocking.

data set, concatenated—A data set temporarily formed by uniting the data contained in several sets in a specific sequence.

data-set control block (DSCB)—A standard-format control block specifying the parameter, for one data set, needed to describe and manipulate the data set in a direct-access device.

data set, indexed sequential—A particular data set organization which combines the efficiency of sequential organization with the ability to rapidly access records out of sequence but used only on direct-access devices.

data set, partitioned—When a single data set is divided internally into a directory and when one or more sequentially organized subsections (members) reside on a direct access basis for each device, a partitioned data set is developed and is most commonly used for storage or for program libraries. Each member of any individual partitioned data

set has the same record format and organization, but the internal structure may differ from one partitioned data set to another.

data sets—Unique combinations or aggregations of data elements. Examples are the sales order, accounts-receivable ledger card, sales summary report, payroll register, etc. It should be noted that a data set is a potential combination of data elements. Not all data elements need be present at one time. For example, a payroll-register entry for a given employee may contain only one or two of several possible deductions.

data set, telephone line—A standard telephone data set. For example, Model 202D dataphone is often used at each end of the telephone line. In each office the data set connects the remote terminal unit to the telephone line and converts that unit's signal into "tones" for transmission over the line. Conversely, the data set converts "tones" received over the line from the processing center into signals for the remote terminal unit. At the processing center, other data sets perform the same conversions for the central terminal unit.

data signalling rate—An expression in bits per second relating to data transmission capacity of a particular channel.

data sink—Relating to a data transmission system; data sink often refers to equipment which accepts data.

data, source—1. Data created by the individual or organization generating or originating the data. 2. The data transmission equipment supplying the data.

DATASPEED—A copyright term of the Bell System used to describe a series of terminal input/output paper-tape devices.

data station—1. This unit has a broad range of operating characteristics and high speed; it can combine several input and output devices into a single console for use either online to a centralized computer system, or off-line for local data preparation. It can thus handle a variety of transmission applications, such as inquiries, field reporting, and data collection. The connected optical scanner can read documents encoded in a special bar code. As it scans, it transfers the encoded data to a buffer for direct transmission, or to punched tape for pretransmission editing. Various numbers of terminals include high- and medium-speed paper-tape punches and readers. The data station uses the ASCIL (American Standard Code for Information Interchange) code for all transmission. Errors are detected by parity and channel-checking features. Through control programs in the remote computer, the data station can be turned on or off, specific peripheral units can be activated and deactivated, and full transmission cycles can be executed, including correction or retransmission. The computer system can thus timeshare by running several programs simultaneously and independent of its core memory (some systems).

data-station console — Some consoles are equipped with specialized devices that perform three basic functions: document reading, information printing, and data transmission and reception. Document reading is done by an optical scanner that reads information, printed in a special bar-code, by means of a beam of light. A teleprinter terminal is used to simultaneously print information and punch it onto paper tape for data transmission to the primary computer. A communications device to send and receive data is also part of the console. The console provides each office with its own data-collection system, which, via conventional lines, can be directly linked to the centralized computer to provide an integrated information-processing system. Principal users of the unit are retail firms, educational systems, government agencies, manufacturing firms, insurance companies and other geographically dispersed organization as branches, warehouses, remote plants, etc. Transmission errors are detected by parity and channel checking, and corrected by automatic retransmission of the data (some systems).

data-station console, remote — See remote data station console.

data stations, remote — See remote data stations.

data-storage facilities real-time — Since the real-time system applies transaction data to the master-file information as the transaction data occurs, the system employs extensive data-storage facilities which are capable of storing entire master files of information. In addition, these facilities are of the random-access type allowing immediate access to the master-file information. Real-time systems provide for internal core, drum, disk, and tape memories.

data switching — 1. A location at which incoming data from one circuit is transferred to the proper outgoing circuit. 2. A location where an incoming message is automatically or manually directed to one or more outgoing circuits, according to the intelligence contained in the message.

data switching center — See switching center.

data switching center, automatic — See switching center.

data systems communications — See communication data systems.

data telephone circuit — A specific telephone circuit permitting the transmission of digital data, for example, through use of the Dataphone developed by American Telephone and Telegraph Company.

data terminal — 1. A device which modulates and/or demodulates data between one input/output device and a data-transmission link. 2. Various typewriter, audio, or visual devices for inputting or receiving output of computers.

data terminal equipment — The modem, device, or unit, at either end of a data communication channel.

data terminal, multiplex — A unique data transmission device which modulates and demodulates, encodes and decodes, between two or more input/output devices and data transmission stations.

data terminal, remote — See remote data terminal.

data, test — A set of data developed specifically to test the adequacy of a computer run or system. The data may be actual data that have been taken from previous operations, or artificial data created for this purpose.

data time — The unit of measurement relating to the time necessary to fulfill a single instruction.

data, transaction — A set of data in a data-processing area, a record of occurrence of a new event or transaction, in which the incidence of the data is essentially random and unpredictable. Hours worked, quantities shipped, and amounts invoiced are examples from, respectively, the areas of payroll, accounts receivable, and accounts payable.

data transcription — A standard process for copying information from one type data transcribing media to a dissimilar type, such as from magnetic tape to punched cards.

data transfer, programmed — Normally, data are transferred between the computer accumulator and an external device under program control. An input bus allows each device to clear the computer accumulator before transferring data into it.

data transfer rate — A particular rate at which data is transmitted through a channel, but measured during the time data is actually being transmitted, i.e., tape transfer rates are measured in terms of characters per second, discounting gaps between blocks, words, etc.

data transfer rate, average — A particular rate of data transmission through a channel over a relatively long period of time to include gaps between blocks, words, or records. Also included in this time are regeneration time and other items not subject to program control. Starting, stopping, rewinding, searching, or other programmed control items are not included.

data transfer rate, effective — Same as data transfer rate, average.

data transfer register — The temporary storage device which eases the communication or movement of data within the computer.

data transmission — The sending of data from one part of a system to another part.

data transmission, bands — The measure of the speed of a transmission. A band is equal to one signal element per second.

data-transmission equipment — The communications equipment used in direct support of data-processing equipment.

data transmission, synchronous — In this type of data transmission, each character consists of 5, 6, 7, or 8 information bits depending on the code structure. There are no start and stop bits. Timing is derived through synchronizing characters at the beginning of each message or block of data.

data transmission system—A series of circuits, modems, or other devices which transfer or translate information from one site or location to another.

data-transmission trap—Usually a conditional (unprogrammed) jump to a specific location activated automatically to provide communication or signals between specific input/output routines and the related programs.

data-transmission utilization measure—The ratio of useful data output of a data transmission system, to the total data input.

data transmission, video display units—Any type of input/output equipment with a special feature of displaying information on a screen, usually a cathode-ray tube.

data-trap transmission — See data transmission trap.

data unit—A set of one or more related characters which is treated as a whole. Often used in place of field to specify a particular unit of information.

data use identifier—A title or name for the use of the data items for a data element, for instance, an occurrence date such as the employment date of an employee that is used for data base information.

data validity—A relation or measure of verifiability of data, i.e., the results of specific tests performed on the data such as the forbidden code check. Such tests and checks verify the reliability of the data and thus its validity or degree of acceptability.

data word—1. A word which may be primarily regarded as part of the information manipulated by a given program. A data word may be used to modify a program instruction, or to be arithmetically combined with other data words. 2. A data word often consists of 36 bits (or six 6-bit characters). Data is transferred on a word basis, 36 bits in parallel (some computers).

date, delivery—The date of physical delivery, on-site, of the components of the computer configuration without regard to whether or not they have been unpacked, placed in final position, or interconnected. Delivery of equipment carries no connotation of operational status.

date, installation—The date new equipment is ready for use. The commencement of rental normally begins on the day following the date on which the contractor officially notifies the using organization that the equipment is installed and ready for use, subject to the acceptance and standard of performance provisions of the applicable contract.

dating routine — A routine which computes and/or stores, where needed, a date such

as current day's date, expiration date of a tape, etc.

dating subrouting—See subroutine, dating.

datum—Signifies a single computer word or unit of information.

day clock—See clock, day.

dc coupled — The connection by a device which passes the steady state characteristics of a signal and which largely eliminates the transient or oscillating characteristics of the signal.

dc dump—1. The intentional, accidental, or conditional removal of all direct-current power from a system or component. 2. The condition that results when direct-current power is withdrawn from a computer using volatile storage.

dc erasing head—A device which causes the removal of magnetic bits from magnetic tape by the use of a magnetic field developed from a direct current.

d-character — A specific character which is used to modify the operations code in some equipment.

dc signaling—A transmission method which utilizes direct current.

DD — Abbreviation for delay driver, digital data, digital display, decimal display, data demand.

DDA — Abbreviation for digital differential analyzer, digital differential and digital display alarm.

DDC—Abbreviation for direct digital control.

DDCE—Abbreviation for digital data conversion equipment.

DDG—Abbreviation for digital display generator.

DDGE—Abbreviation for digital display make-up (U.S. Air Force).

DDP—An abbreviation for digital data processor.

DDS—Abbreviation for digital display scope.

DDT—See debugging package.

DEACON—A program for direct english and control, developed by General Electric Co.

dead band—A specific range of values in which the incoming signal can be altered, without also changing the outgoing response. (Synonymous with dead space, dead zone, switching blank, and similar to neutral zone.)

dead file—A file that is not in current use but is retained.

dead halt—See halt, dead.

dead space—Same as dead band.

dead time—1. Any definite delay deliberately placed between two related actions in order to avoid overlap that might cause confusion or to permit a particular different event, such as a control decision, switching event, or similar action, to take place. 2. The delay between two related actions, measured in units time for efficiency study.

dead zone—The specific area in various types storage media which is not reserved for data store. An example is the space between the bit sites on magnetic tapes.

debatable time—When there is no proof as to what difficulty has caused a delay, such time is labeled debatable time, and a search for evidence ensues to determine if a program mistake, operating mistake, or perhaps a transient fault has occurred.

deblocking—A procedure for reducing a data block into its component records for further processing.

debug—1. To locate and correct any errors in a computer program. 2. To detect and correct malfunctions in the computer itself. (Related to diagnostic routine.) 3. To test a program on a computer to find whether it works properly. If mistakes are revealed, they must be traced to their source and corrected.

debugging—The process of isolating and correcting all malfunctions and/or mistakes in a piece of equipment or a program of operations.

debugging-aid routine—A routine to aid programmers in the debugging of their routines. Some typical routines are: storage, print-out, tape print-out, and drum print-out.

debugging aids—A set of routines to aid the programmer in checking out a particular program by furnishing him with the contents of selected areas of memory.

debugging aids, reference—A set of routines which provides a means of utilizing the computer to assist the programmer in debugging his programs. Among the routines included are the following: (a) changed-word post mortem, a routine to compare the contents of program or data areas with a selected image area; (b) address reference search, a routine to detect all words in the computer memory which reference a particular address; (c) dump selected memory area, a routine to provide the contents of all locations within a specified memory area.

debugging, console—The programmer may debug at the machine console or at a remote console by slowly stepping the machine through each instruction and observing the contents of appropriate registers and memory locations.

debugging package (DDT)—Permits the user to examine, search, change, insert breakpoint instructions, and stop/trace his program at the symbolic level. DDT permits the use of literals in the same manner as the assembler. It can load both absolute and relocatable assembler-produced files. Its command language is geared to rapid interactive operations by the on-line user (some systems).

debugging, program—This process is mainly one of making corrections to the program. It is followed by documentation, (which is really a continuing process). The programmer must keep precise records of the entire programming procedure; documentation includes a brief description of the problem, the program, its results, and the process which was used to obtain them.

debugging, remote—The use of remote terminals in a mode suitable for testing of programs, most frequently found in systems devoted to scientific or engineering computation.

debugging, snapshot—A type of diagnostics and debugging technique in which the programmer specifies the start and end of program segments where he wishes to examine the contents of various registers and accumulators. The snapshot tracing may indicate the contents not only of the various accumulators and registers but also of specified memory locations.

debugging, source-language—Debugging information is requested by the user and displayed by the system in a form consistent with the source programming language.

debugging statements—The operating statements provide a wide and flexible variety of methods for manipulating the program itself. The user may: (a) insert or delete statements; (b) execute selectivity; (c) print changes of values as the change occurs and transfer control as the transfer occurs; (d) obtain a static printout of all cross-reference relationships among names and labels, and dynamic exposure of impartial or imperfect execution.

debugging, symbolic—Symbolic commands or macroinstruments are utilized to assist in the debugging procedure.

debug macroinstruction—A macroinstruction which generates a debugging or program testing capability within a particular program.

debug macros—Aids built into a program by the applications programmer, in addition to those supplied by the supervisory program. Debugging macros are a type of unit testing.

debug on-line—Same as debug, except the computer is performing on-line functions, utilizing another routine which has previously been checked out.

decade—A group or assembly of ten units; e.g., a counter which counts to ten in one column, or a resistor box which inserts resistance quantities in multiples of powers of 10.

decade counter—See counter, decade.

decay time—The time in which a voltage or current pulse will decrease to one-tenth of its maximum value. Decay time is proportional to the time constant of the circuit.

deceleration time—1. The time which elapses between completion of reading or writing of a tape record, and the time when the tape stops moving. (Synonymous with stop time.) 2. The time required to stop a tape after reading or recording the last piece of information from a record on that tape.

decentralized data processing—See data processing, decentralized.

decibel—A unit measurement of transmission loss, gain, or relative level. The formal definition is 1 db = 10_{10} log P_2/P_1; P_1 and P_2 are measurements of power and are expressed in watts. It is also a convenient general practice to speak of voltage or current gains in "db."

deciding—An operation whose function is to accept or reject certain items of information. One input is the information, while the other is a fixed reference. The two inputs are combined by the appropriate logical rule to give the output.

decimal—1. Pertaining to a characteristic or property involving a selection, choice, or condition in which there are ten possibilities. 2. Pertaining to the number-representation system with a radix of ten.

decimal accumulator — Registers 12 through 15 of a register block, used as a single, 16-byte register (some computers).

decimal, binary-coded—See binary coded decimal.

decimal, binary-coded representation — See binary-coded decimal representation.

decimal, coded—Describing a form of notation by which each decimal digit is separately expressed in some other number system; e.g., in the 8-4-2-1 coded-decimal notation, the number twelve is represented as 0001 0010, for 1 and 2; whereas in pure or straight binary notation it is represented as 1100. Other coded decimal notations used are the 5-4-2-1, the excess three, and the 2-3-2-1 codes.

decimal-coded digit—A digit or character defined by a set of decimal digits, such as a pair of decimal digits specifying a letter or special character in a system of notation.

decimal digit—See digit, decimal.

decimal notation—See number, decimal.

decimal number—See number, decimal.

decimal numbering system—A system of reckoning by 10 or the powers of 10 using the digits 0 through 9 to express numerical quantities.

decimal, packed—The storage of two digits in an area which usually stores an alphabetic letter or special character.

decimal point—That base point (radix 10) in decimal numbers which separates integers from fractional values, i.e., values to the left of the point are positive powers of 10, while values to the right of the point are negative powers of 10.

decimal point, actual — A decimal point for "display" purposes: e.g., when a numeric value is listed on a printed report, the decimal point will often appear as an actual printed character. When specified for data to be used within a computer, it requires an actual space in storage.

decimal point, assumed—The point within a numeric item at which the decimal point is assumed to be located. When a numeric item is to be used within a computer, the location of the assumed decimal point is considered to be at the right unless otherwise specified in the appropriate record-description entry. It will not occupy an actual space in storage, but it will be used by the computer to align the value properly for calculation.

decimal-to-binary conversion—The process of converting a number written to the base of ten, or decimal, into the equivalent number written to the base of two, or binary.

decision—1. Usually by comparison, a verification is completed concerning the existence or nonexistence of a given condition as a result of developing an alternative action. 2. The computer operation of determining if a certain relationship exists between words in storage or registers, and taking alternative courses of action. This is effected by conditional jumps or equivalent techniques. Use of this term has given rise to the misnomer "magic brain;" actually, the process consists of making comparisons, by use of arithmetic, to determine the relationship of two terms (numeric, alphabetic or a combination of both), e.g., equal, greater than, or less than.

decision box—1. The symbol used in flow charting to indicate a choice or branching in the information-processing path. 2. A flow-chart symbol whose interior contains the criterion for decision or branching.

decision element—A circuit that performs a logical operation on one or more binary digits of input information (represent "yes" or "no") and expresses the result in its output.

decision instruction—See branch.

decision logic—See logic decision.

decision, logical — The choice or ability to choose between alternatives. Basically, this amounts to an ability to answer yes or no with respect to certain fundamental questions involving equality and relative magnitude; e.g., in an inventory application, it is necessary to determine whether or not there has been an issue of a given stock item.

decision-making (game theory)—Game theory is a mathematical theory dealing with decision-making in a competitive situation in which both parties are active and have an effect on the final outcome. The object is to arrive at an optimal course of action by consideration of all possible moves and chance happenings.

decision-making system — One of the basic uses of an on-line, real-time system is to find an optimum answer to every demand according to decision rules which have been previously established, or according to a simulation model.

decision mechanism—The component part of a character reader, in character recognition, that receives the finalized version of the input character and makes a determination as to its probable identity.

decision plan—A system or procedure used for making managerial decisions; i.e. rules either prepared in advance of specific events or developed at the time or on the scene and applied by men, machines, or combinations of these. Such plans include the exception principle, internal decision-making procedures, manual interrupt and intervention, variable or stochastic processing, and various adaptive and heuristic plans.

decision rules — The programmed criteria which an on-line, real-time system uses to make operating decisions. It is important to periodically review the decision rules which are being used by a system, because the nature of the problems to be solved changes over time and because new situations may have arisen which were not at first anticipated.

decision rules, time-sharing—*See* time sharing decision rules.

decision table—*See* table, decision.

deck—A collection of cards, commonly a complete set of cards which have been punched for a definite service or purpose.

deck, condensed-instruction—The card output instructions per card are punched in machine language. Input to the assembly program may consist of one instruction per card; thus, the name condensed is used for output.

deck, executive—A deck of punched cards containing executive programs, routines, and subroutines.

deck, instruction—A deck of punched cards containing the data that defines the operations to be performed by a data processing system. The instructions comprising a program may be in machine language code or in the form of a compiler.

deck, symbolic—A deck of punched cards containing programs written in symbolic language as opposed to programs written in binary language, or a computer language.

deck, tape—The device or mechanism which is designed to control the movement of tape.

declaration—A declaration is represented by one or more instructions which specify the type, characteristics, or amount of data associated with identifiers.

declarative operation — 1. Coding sequence consisting of a symbolic label, a declarative operation code, and an operand. It involves writing symbolic labels and operation codes for data and constants. 2. The process or procedures which provide the object program with various input, output, work ideas, and other constants which may be designed or required.

declaratives—Statements made to a symbolic processor to control the specifics of an assembly.

declarative statement—Instructions in symbolic coding, or systems used to define and designate areas, constants, and symbols.

decode—1. To apply a code so as to reverse some previous encoding. 2. To determine the meaning of individual characters or groups of characters in a message. 3. To determine the meaning of an instruction from the set of pulses which describes the instruction, command, or operation to be performed. 4. To translate coded characters to a more understandable form.

decoded operations—*See* decoding.

decoder—1. A device that determines the meaning of a set of signals and initiates a computer operation based thereon. 2. A matrix of switching elements that selects one or more output channels according to the combination of input signals present. (Contrasted with encoder, and clarified by matrix.) 3. A specific device capable of ascertaining the significance or meaning of a group of signals and initiating a computer event based on these signals.

decoder, command—The command decoder preprocesses commands from the user-console. This program is used to convert parameters, etc., before the command is sent to the program for which the command is intended.

decoder, operation—A decoder used to examine and interpret the part of the instruction word specifying the operation to be performed and which sends signals to the circuitry executing the specified operation.

decoding—1. Performing the internal operations by which a computer determines the meaning of the operation code of an instruction; also sometimes applied to addresses. 2. In interpretive routines and some subroutines, an operation by which a computer determines the meaning of parameters in the routine. 3. Translating a secretive language into the clear.

decollate—The act of separating the parts of a multipart form and the removal of the carbons to then disperse cards or other information or data.

decollator—A device which combines the removal of carbon paper and separation of various copies of a standard multi-part continuous form.

decrement—1. The quantity by which a variable is decreased. 2. A specific part of an instruction word in some binary computers; thus, a set of digits.

decrement field—A portion of an instruction word set aside specifically for modifying the contents of a register or storage location.

decryption—A procedure for the interpretation or deciphering of coded data.

dedicated storage—*See* storage, dedicated.

dedicated trap cells—*See* trap, dedicated cells.

deferred addressing—*See* addressing deferred.

deferred entry/deferred exit — An asynchronous event causes the deferred entry by passing the central processing unit control to a subroutine or to an entry point. This transfer causes a deferred exit from the program having control previously.

deferred processing—Processing which can be delayed or is considered low priority, and is completed when computer time is at non-peak periods.

define—To establish a value for a variable or symbol or to establish what the variable represents.

definition—1. The resolution and sharpness of an image, or the extent to which an image is brought into sharp relief. 2. The degree with which a communication system reproduces sound images or messages.

definition, index—The number of times a loop operation is to be repeated. This Fortran specification can appear in either do, read, or write statements. It is specified by the starting value, the limit value, and the incremental value.

definition, problem — The art of compiling logic in the form of general flow charts and logic diagrams which clearly explain and present the problem to the programmer in such a way that all requirements involved in the run are presented.

definition, recursive—A definition which defines something partly in terms of itself.

deflection sensitivity — Used in connection with cathode-ray tubes, the quotient of the change in displacement of the electron beam at the place of impact, divided by the change in the deflecting field. It is usually expressed in millimeters per volt when applied between the deflection electrode plates for electrostatic-field deflection, or in millimeters per gauss for magnetic-field deflection.

degradation—A special condition when the system continues to operate but at reduced levels of service. Such circumstances are usually caused by unavailability of various equipment units or subsystems.

degradation, graceful—*See* fail softly.

degradation testing — Measurement of performance of a system at the extreme operating limits. Tests are performed to determine the gradual changes in performance characteristics.

degree of multiprogramming—Refers to the number of transactions handled in parallel by the systems involved in a multi-program.

delay—1. The length of time after the close of a reporting period before information pertaining to that period becomes available. Delay may also cover the time to process data, and to prepare and distribute reports. 2. The retardation of the flow of information in a channel for a definite period of time.

delay coding, minimum—*Same as* programming, minimum access.

delay counter—In the control unit of some computers, a counter that can temporarily delay a program long enough for the completion of an operation.

delay, data—*See* data delay.

delay differential—The difference between the maximum and the minimum frequency delays occurring across a band.

delay digit—A logic element which delays its input signal by one digit period.

delay distortion—Also termed envelope delay or phase delay. Distortion resulting from nonuniform speed of transmission of the various frequency components of a signal through a transmission medium.

delayed-output equipment—Equipment which removes the data from the system after processing has been completed or while in process, but which holds it for further instructions or later use.

delay element—The circuitry or electronic mechanism which accepts data temporarily, and emits the same data after a specific interval.

delay envelope—Characteristics of a circuit which result in some frequencies arriving ahead of the others even though they were transmitted together.

delay, external — Compute down time attributable to circumstances not the fault of the computer system, and beyond the reasonable control of the system operator or maintenance engineer. An example of an external delay would be a failure of the electrical power to the building.

delay line—A device capable of retarding a pulse of energy between input and output, based on the properties of materials, circuit parameters, or mechanical devices. Examples of delay lines are material media such as mercury, in which sonic patterns may be propagated in time; lumped-constant electrical lines; coaxial cables; transmission lines; and recirculating magnetic-drum loops.

delay line register—*See* register delay line.

delay-line storage — A storage technique in which data is stored by allowing it to travel through some medium such as mercury.

delay loop stores—A method of storing information by transmitting bits or no bits serially through a loop.

delay, operating—During repair time to discover suspected faults, if the investigation shows the equipment to be free of faults, the time lost should count as an operating delay.

delay, output—The typical delay of the circuit measured at the 50 percent signal levels, with half of rated d-c load and half of the specified wiring capacity. Greater loading and less wiring capacity generally decrease the delay. The mean of the turn-off and turn-on delays is given.

delay register line—*See* register delay line.

delay time—The amount of elapsed time between the end of one event and the beginning of the next sequential event.

deleave—1. The reversing of the collation operation by separating the members of a collated sequence and obtaining a dispersal. 2. Separating the files of a multipart form.

delete—To remove or eliminate; e.g., to remove a record from a master file.

deleted representation—Similar to an erase character, i.e., a particular representation to which any other representation can be converted by further operation or recording. In paper tape, which does not lend itself to erasure or deletions, deleted representation consists of a code hole in all of the code positions. Often called null representation. In graphics, the absence of information can be deleted representation.

deletion record—A record, which when matched with a master file, results in one or more corresponding records being deleted from the master file.

delimit—To fix the limits of; to bound.

delimiter—A character that limits a string of characters, and therefore cannot be a member of the string.

delta—The difference between a partial-select output of a magnetic core in a 1 state, and a partial-select output of the same core in a 0 state.

delta clock—One of the primary uses of this clock is timing subroutine operations. If a momentary fault throws the computer into a closed programming loop, or if a fault occurring during the execution of an instruction halts the computer, the delta clock restarts the computer by means of an interrupt, thus providing automatic fault recovery. The interrupt can be programmed to notify the operator that a closed loop has occurred. If completing an operation takes longer than desired, this clock is also used to interrupt the computer and thereby allow program attention to be diverted to items of more immediate importance.

delta noise—The difference between the 1-state and the 0-state half-selected noise.

demand—An input/output coding technique in which a read or write order is initiated as the need to read a new block or write a new block of data occurs. Operations do not take place in parallel.

demand processing—See processing, demand.

demand processing time-sharing — See time-sharing, demand processing.

demodulation—1. The process of retrieving an original signal from a modulated carrier wave. 2. A procedure for retrieving original signals from modulated carrier waves. Such a technique is utilized to make communication signals compatible with business-machine signals.

demodulator—1. A device which receives tones from a transmission circuit and converts them to electrical pulses, or bits, which may be accepted by a business machine. 2. A device which detects the modulating signals, then removes the carrier signal and reconstitutes the intelligence. (Clarified by modulation code, and contrasted with modulator.)

demonstration testing — An exhibition to show the basic system capabilities and limitations.

demultiplexing — Dividing one or more information streams into a larger number of streams. Contrasted with multiplexing.

denial gate, alternative — Same as gate, NAND.

denial gate, joint—Same as gate NOR.

dense binary code—A code in which all possible states of the binary code are used.

density—The closeness of space distribution on a storage medium such as a magnetic drum, magnetic tape, or cathode-ray tube.

density, bit—The number of binary digits that are stored in a given linear area or volume.

density, character—Same as packing density.

density, packing—See packing density.

density recording—The number of bits per a given unit length of a linear track in a recording medium.

density, storage—See storage density.

density, track — The number of adjacent tracks per unit distance measured in a direction perpendicular to the direction of individual tracks. The inverse of track pitch.

departure time—The time at which control is returned to the supervisory program when a segment of an application program is completed.

dependent variable—See variable, dependent.

derail—An instruction to go to a subroutine.

derating, component—To ensure reliable system operation under extremely adverse conditions and with limit-value components, components used in circuit modules are derated far below manufacturers' specification.

descending sort—A sort in which the successive keys compare less-than or equal-to.

description, data—See data description.

description, problem—A statement of a problem, possibly a description of the method of its solution, or the solution itself. The transformations of data and the relationship of procedures, data, constraints, environments, etc. may also be included.

description record—See record description.

descriptor—1. A significant word that helps to classify the components of a document. 2. An elementary term, word, or simple phrase used to identify a subject, concept, or idea.

descriptor, data — A data descriptor, as its name implies, describes data (i.e., a data area) by pointing to one or more contiguous data locations. Consequently, a particular data descriptor may be concerned with many memory locations. More than this, however, a data descriptor is also concerned with the presence, in core, of the data it describes. This is necessarily so particularly because of the data overlay capabilities of the computer. A descriptor is concerned with many aspects of storage. These aspects are indicated by various bits in the descriptor.

descriptor, procedure — The procedure descriptor is a program descriptor uniquely marked as a descriptor that will cause subroutine entry when addressed by an operand call syllable.

design—The specification of the working relations between the parts of a system in terms of their characteristic actions.

design and monitoring simulation—See simulation, monitoring and design.

designating device—A device on certain tabulators which allows the first item of a series of similar data to be printed, and inhibits some or all printing of the rest of the series.

designation number—See number designation.

designation numeral—*See* number designation.

designation punch—*Same as* control punches

designation punches—*See* control punches.

designation register—A register into which data is being placed.

designator—A property of part of an entity serving to classify the entity, such as, the speed of a computer determining whether it is a high-, medium-, or low-speed system.

designators, instruction format—*See* instruction format (designators).

design, functional—Logic is a discipline which deals with the principles relating to switching theory and other techniques as regards design of data processing equipment. The application of this logic between the working relations and basic principles is without primary regard for the equipment used. A type of block diagram is formed using logic symbols, and the practical or working relations between all parts of the system is called the functional design.

design, item—The specification of what fields make up an item, the order in which the fields are to be recorded, and the number of characters to be allocated to each field.

design, logic—The analytical detail of the working relations between the parts of a system in terms of symbolic logic and without primary regard for its hardware implementation.

design, logical—1. The planning of a data-processing system prior to its detailed engineering design. 2. The synthesizing of a network of logical elements to perform a specified function. 3. The results of definitions 1 and 2, frequently called the logic of a computer or of a data-processing system.

design, objective—The planned or projected performance goal or expectation based on or chosen prior to the developed operations. The technical estimates of performance requirements awaiting confirmation.

design, operational—The description in logical, mathematical, or operating terms of how system tasks are to be performed. This also refers to the development of methods to accomplish system tasks.

design, problem system—*See* system, design problem.

design programmer—*See* programmer, design.

design, solid-state—The solid-state components and circuitry of the real-time system offer numerous advantages including standardized production of components and the reduction of maintenance procedures. In addition to ease of maintenance, solid-state circuits also impart a high degree of operating reliability to the computer and reduce the power, cooling, and space requirements of the system at the same time.

design, systems—*See* systems design.

design verification—The experimental tests and original experiments to determine that the design meets the required specifications.

design, worst-case—The worst-case design approach is an extremely conservative one in which the circuit is designed to function normally even though all component values have simultaneously assumed the worst possible condition that can be caused by initial tolerance, aging, and a temperature range of 0°C to 100°C. Worst-case techniques are also applied to obtain conservative derating of transient and speed specifications.

desk check—A procedure of analyzing or inspecting a written program or specific instructions for errors in logic or syntax without the requirement or use of computing equipment.

destination file—A CRAM deck or magnetic tape designated to receive the file of information that is output from a computer run.

destination source instruction—*See* instruction, source destination.

destination warning marker (DWM)—A reflective spot on the back of a magnetic tape, 18 feet from the physical end of the tape, which is sensed photoelectrically to indicate that the physical end of the tape is approaching.

destructive addition—*See* addition, destructive.

destructive read—To take information from a storage device and, by doing so, destroying the information in that device.

destructive reading—A reading process that destroys the data in the source.

destructive readout—*See* read, destructive.

destructive storage—*See* storage, destructive.

destructive test—*See* test, destructive.

detab-X—Decision Tables, Experimental; a programming language that combines decision tables with COBOL.

detachable plugboard—*See* plugboard, detachable.

detail—Most often a file of present or current transactions in the processing plan, such as a record from a file.

detail card—A punched card containing data which is a part of a total, i.e., an individual transaction card.

detail chart—A flowchart in minute detail of a sequence of operations. The symbols of the detail chart usually denote an individual step or computer operation. A detail chart is more detailed than a logic chart, usually reflects the particular computer characteristics and instructions, and facilitates the actual coding of the program in the manner intended by the programmer preparing the chart.

detail file—*See* file, detail.

detail printing—*See* printing detail.

detail record—The specific listing of data which is a unit part of a major classification of larger segments or a total classification of data.

detecting code, error—*See* code, error detecting.

detection, error (transmission)—Transmission errors are detected by parity and long (channel) checks.

detection, execution errors—Those errors detected during the execution of the user's program.

detection, mark—A type of character recognition system which detects certain intelligence or information from marks placed in areas on paper or cards, called site areas, boxes, or windows. Mark reading results from optical character recognition or mark sensing systems which seek out the presence or absence of pencil marks or graphite particles, such as in college or school exams, census returns, etc.

detector—A circuitry which produces a designed output upon receipt of specific corresponding patterns or patterns of input.

detector (primary element) — The first system element that performs the initial measurement operation and responds quantitatively to the measured variable, i.e., the primary element performs the initial conversion of measurement energy.

detector, property—An optical character recognition (OCR) term which represents the component of a character reader that has the normalized signal for use in extracting a set of characteristic properties on the basis of which a character can be identified.

device—1. That which is devised, invented, or formed by design. 2. A mechanical contrivance or appliance.

device, analog—A mechanism that represents numbers by physical quantities; e.g., by lengths, as in a slide rule, or by voltage currents as in a differential analyzer or a computer of the analog type.

device, attention — A device programmed to indicate a new display on a screen of various lasting displays by using some different shape, size, or light intensity, or conversely by making older displays smaller, thinner, or of another shape.

device control character — See character, device control.

device, conversion—See conversion device.

device, designating — A device on certain tabulators which allows the first item of a series of similar data to be printed and inhibits some or all printing of the rest of the series.

device, external code. — See code, external device.

device, film optical-sensing — A piece of equipment capable of reading the contents of a film by optical methods; i.e., a system consisting of a light source, lenses, photocells and a film-moving mechanism. The output of the device is digitized and transferred directly to an electronic computer. An example of such a device is the FOSDIC system developed jointly by the Bureau of Census and the National Bureau of Standards.

device handlers I/O—The input/output device handlers are responsible for controlling the activities of all input/output channels and peripheral equipment.

device, input—The mechanical unit designed to bring data to be processed into a computer; e.g., a card reader, a tape reader, or a keyboard.

device, input/output—See input/output device.

device, input/output (communications)—Any subscriber (user) equipment which introduces data into or extracts data from a data-communications system.

device, interconnecting — See interconnecting device.

device, output—That part of a machine which translates the electrical impulses representing data and processed by the machine, into permanent results, such as printed forms, punched cards, and magnetic writing on tape.

device, read-out—See read-out device.

device ready/not ready—The ability to inform the central computer that an I/O device is prepared to accept data.

device, remote — An input/output unit, or other piece of equipment, which is removed from the computer center but connected by a communication line. In a typical on-line, real-time communications system, the remote device is usually a teletypewriter, an audio answer back device, or a CRT visual display unit.

devices (control) sorting—See sorting devices (control).

device status, external—See external device status.

device status word (DSW)—The device status word contains one bit of information for each indicator within the device. These generally fall into four categories: (1) error or exception interrupt conditions; (2) normal data, or service required interrupts; (3) routine status conditions; (4) process-interrupt indicators. If a device contains interrupt requests which are connected to more than one interrupt level, all of the routine status indicators and the interrupt conditions of the DSW are placed in the accumulator. These indicators are reset (depending upon the device) when sensed. Normally all indicators which place a "1" in the accumulator are considered to be on and would be reset (some systems).

devices, terminal console—See console devices, terminal.

device, storage—A device into which data can be inserted, retained, and retrieved.

device, universal-interconnecting—See interconnecting device.

Dewey decimal system—A classification system, developed by Mevil Dewey, to indicate the arrangement of books.

diagnosis—The process of locating and explaining detectable errors in a computer routine or hardware component.

diagnosis, continuous system (time sharing) —*See* time sharing, continuous system diagnosis.

diagnostic—Pertaining to the detection, discovery, and further isolation of a malfunction or a mistake.

diagnostic check—A specific routine designed to locate a malfunction in a computer.

diagnostic routine—1. A routine used to locate a malfunction in a computer, or to aid in locating mistakes in a computer program. Thus, in general, any routine specifically designed to aid in debugging or troubleshooting. (Synonymous with malfunction routine, and related to debugging, definition 2.) 2. A program that facilitates computer maintenance by detection and isolation of malfunctions or mistakes.

diagnostics — Another part of the executive system is an integrated system of diagnostic routines designed to provide the programmer with information of maximum utility and convenience in checking out programs. The programmer can be highly selective about what is to be printed, and may receive diagnostic listings with source-code symbolics collated with the contents of both registers and central store. Both dynamic (snapshot) and post-mortem (PMD) dumps of registers and central store are provided.

diagnostics, compiler—The compiler diagnostics are of four categories:

precautionary—Print warning message and continue compilation.

correctable—Try to correct the error, print explanatory message, and continue compilation.

uncorrectable—If intent of programmer cannot be determined, print a diagnostic message, reject the clause or statement, and continue compilation.

catastrophic—When so many errors have occurred that no more useful diagnostic information can be produced, terminate the compilation.

Other outputs from the compiler include extensive diagnostic messages, source-language listings, machine-language listings, and special cross-reference listings of name definitions and their references.

diagnostics, error—*See* error diagnostics.

diagnostics error, time sharing — *See* time-sharing, error diagnostics.

diagnostics, on-line—The running of diagnostics on a system while it is on-line but off-peak to save time and to take corrective action without closing down the system.

diagnostics program—A program used by the supervisory program or the computer operator to check malfunctions and to locate faulty components.

diagnostics, system — A program resembling the operational program rather than a systematic logical-pattern program which will detect overall system malfunctions rather than isolate or locate faulty components.

diagnostic structure — Errors committed by the user may be classified in two broad categories; syntactic and semantic. *See* errors.

diagnostics unit—A unit diagnostic program used to detect malfunctions in units as the input/output and the arithmetic circuitry.

diagnostic system, executive—A comprehensive diagnostic system is available within the executive system to aid the checkout of user programs. Both allocation time and compilation or assembly time commands are available to trigger snapshot dumps. Postmortem dumps are also available through the executive control statement.

diagnostic test—The running of a machine program or routine for the purpose of discovering a failure or a potential failure of a machine element, and to determine its location or its potential location.

diagnotor—A combination diagnostic and edit routine which questions unusual situations and notes the implied results.

diagram—1. A schematic representation of a sequence of subroutines designed to solve a problem. 2. A coarser and less symbolic representation than a flow chart, frequently including descriptions in English words. 3. A schematic or logical drawing showing the electrical circuit or logical arrangements within a component.

diagram, block—1. A graphical representation of the hardware in a computer system. The primary purpose of a block diagram is to indicate the paths along which information and/or control flows between the various parts of a computer system. It should not be confused with the term flow chart. 2. A coarser and less symbolic representation than a flow chart.

diagram, dynamic flow — A diagram that shows the operational aspects of a computer program as a function of time. All references to pertinent items, such as, tables, index registers, subroutines, etc.

diagram, flow—A graphic representation of the major steps of work in process. The illustrative symbols may represent documents, machines, or actions taken during the process. The area of concentration is on where or who does what, rather than how it is to be done. (Synonymous with process chart.)

diagram, functional — 1. A specific type of block diagram which represents the functional design and special symbols called functional symbols. Functional design relates to the specification between all parts of a system, including the logic design and equipment used. A graphic representation showing the operational aspects of a system.

diagram, logical—A diagram that represents the logical elements of a system and their interconnections, without necessarily expressing construction, engineering, or electrical-schematic circuit details.

diagram, run—*See* run diagram.

diagram, setup — A graphic representation showing how a computing system has been prepared and the arrangements that have been made for operation.

diagram, Veitch—*See* chart, Veitch.

diagram, Venn—A diagram in which each point represents an individual. Sets are represented by closed regions including all members of the set and excluding all nonmembers. The diagram is used to facilitate determination whether several sets include or exclude the same individuals.

DIAL—Dial Interrogation And Loading. A Honeywell system that enables the user to locate information on, print the contents of, and load and unload, disks.

dialectic sensors—A method used in reading data from paper tape by a special sensor.

DIALOG—A conversational programming system with graphical orientation.

dial, print-timing—The control knob on the printer which is an adjustment for the printing quality.

dial-up—The service whereby a dial telephone can be used to initiate and effect station-to-station telephone calls.

diamond switch—*Same as* storage, core-rope.

dibit—A group of two bits. In four-phase-modulation, each possible dibit is encoded as one of four unique carrier phase shifts. The four possible states of a dibit are 00, 01, 10, 11.

di-cap storage—A device capable of holding data in the form of an array of charged capacitors, or condensers, and using diodes for controlling information flow.

dichotomizing search—A search in which the series of items is divided into two parts, one of which is rejected, and the process repeated on the unrejected part until the item with the desired property is found. This process usually depends upon the presence of a known sequence in the series.

dichotomy—A division into subordinate classes; e.g., all white and all nonwhite, or all zero and all nonzero.

dictionary—1. A book or list of code names or keys used in a program, routine, or system with the description or identification of their designed or intended meaning in that program, routine, or system.

dictionary, automatic—The component of a language-translating machine which will provide a word for word substitution from one language to another. In automatic-searching systems, the automatic dictionary is the component which substitutes codes for words or phrases during the encoding operation. (Related to machine translation.)

dictionary code—An alphabetical arrangement of English words and terms associated with their code representations. (Related to reverse-code dictionary.)

dictionary, electronic—*Same as* dictionary automatic.

dictionary external symbol—*See* external symbol dictionary.

dictionary, relocation—1. The part of an object progam that identifies all of the ad-

dresses of a program that must be changed when the program is to be relocated. 2. Part of a load module containing directions which enable a fetch program to initialize properly all relocatable address constants within the text section by accounting for the actual starting address of the load module in storage and the incremental difference between the required address and the initial address of the module.

dictionary, reverse-code—An alphabetic or numeric-alphabetic arrangement of codes, associated with their corresponding English words or terms. (Related to dictionary code.)

difference—The number or quantity resulting when one number or quantity (minuend) has another (subtrahend) subtracted from it.

difference engine—A machine capable of computing mathematical tables automatically. It was built in 1812 by Charles Babbage.

difference gate—*Same as* gate, exclusive OR.

difference reports—A report noting resulting changes from an original computer program and a program change.

differential analyzer—*See* analyzer, electronic differential.

differential analyzer, digital—*See* digital differential analyzer.

differential analyzer, mechanical—*See* analyzer, mechanical differential.

differential delay—The difference between the maximum and the minimum frequency delays occurring across a band.

differential modulation—A type of modulation in which the choice of the significant condition for any signal element is dependent on the choice of the previous signal element.

differentiator—A device whose output function is proportional to a derivative, i.e., the rate of change, of its input function with respect to one or more variables.

DIGIPRINT microfilm display—The DIGIPRINT system, consisting of a symbol generator, line generator, CRT, and memory, is a low-cost alphanumeric and graphic-information recording system that operates from any digital-data source. Computer-generated data consisting of symbol and format commands are converted by the DIGIPRINT system to a CRT display which is photographed with the system's special digitally controlled 16-mm microfilm camera (35-mm option). The camera can also simultaneously photograph an overlay that contains basic continuing entries. Up to 10 overlays can be stored. Thus, when the recorded information is retrieved, it is printed on the forms or maps that were used as overlays. The unit is compatible with 63-kc tape drives on a real-time basis. A camera/monitoring system is provided to permit quick confidence checks during long runs. Slave monitors are also available in the form of display consoles using 10-inch, 16-inch, or 21-inch cathode-ray tubes. The DIGIPRINT system supplies its own page formatting without burdening the data source with this requirement. It provides automatic positioning of 135 symbols per line, up to 80 lines per page. (Burroughs)

digit—1. One of the n symbols of integral value, ranging from 0 to n-1 inclusive, in a system of numbering with radix n; for example, the ten digts 0, 1, 2, 3, 4, 5, 6, 7, 8, 9 in the decimal system; 0, 1 in the binary system. 2. One of the ideographic characters 0, 1 ... 9 ... used to designate a quantity smaller than n for the base n number system. 3. A sign or symbol used to convey a specific quantity of information either by itself or with other numbers of its set; e.g., 2, 3, 4, and 5 are digits. The base or radix must be specified and each digit's value assigned.

digital—Pertaining to the utilization of discrete integral numbers in a given base to represent all the quantities that occur in a problem or a calculation. It is possible to express in digital form all information stored, transferred, or processed by a dual-state condition; e.g., on-off, open-closed, and true-false.

digital adder—A unit capable of developing the representation of the sum of two or more numbers represented by signals applied to its inputs. Note definitions of half-adders, full-adders, etc.

digital-analog decoder—An analog computer device which translates digital data into variable electrical flow.

digital back-up—A specially designed alternate method of digital process control initiated through the activation of special purpose digital logic in the event of a failure in the computer system.

digital clock—Clocks which have output signals in digital representation.

digital computer—1. A computer that operates by using numbers to express all the quantities and variables of a problem. In most digital computers, the numbers, in turn, are expressed by electrical impulses. 2. A computer that processes information represented by combinations of discrete or discontinuous data as compared with an analog computer for continuous data. More specifically, it is a device for performing sequences of arithmetic and logical operations, not only on data but also on its own program. Still more specifically it is a stored program digital computer capable of performing sequences of internally stored instructions, as opposed to calculators, such as card-programmed calculators, on which the sequence is impressed manually. (Related to machine, data-processing.)

digital computer, serial—*See* computer, serial.

digital control, direct — *See* control, direct digital.

digital data—Information which is expressed in discreet or noncontinuous form. Opposite of analog data.

digital differential analyzer — *See* analyzer, digital differential.

digital display (DD)—1. A display of digitally oriented numerals. 2. A visual display, generally on a cathode-ray tube, of alphabetic, numeric, or graphic material.

digital divider—A unit capable of generating a quotient and a remainder from the representation of two numbers.

digital incremental plotter — *See* plotter, digital incremental.

digital multiplier — A specific device which generates a digital product from the representation of two digital numbers, by additions of the multiplicand in accordance with the value of the digits in the multiplier. It is necessary only to shift the multiplicand and add it to the product if the multiplier digit is a one, and just shift the multiplicand without adding, if the multiplier digit is a zero, for each successive digit of the multiplier.

digital multiplier unit—A unit which is capable of generating a product from the representations of two numbers, often formed by repeated additions of the multiplicand or multiples of it. See adders, subtracters, etc.

digital recorder—A peripheral device that records data as discreet numerically defined points.

digital representation — A representation of variables as data, by means of digits or discrete quantities, as determined by their appearance or nonappearance.

digital sort—An ordering or sorting according to the least significant digit, followed by a resort on each next higher order digit until the items are completely sorted, most often used in punched card sorting.

digital subtracter—A unit with the capability of developing the representation of the difference between two numbers represented by signals applied to its inputs.

digit, binary—A whole number in the binary scale of notation; this digit may only be 0 (zero) or 1 (one). It may be equivalent to an "on" or "off" condition, a "yes" or a "no," etc. The word "bit" is a contraction of binary digit.

digit, binary-coded—*See* binary-coded digit.

digit, check—1. One or more redundant digits in a character or word, which depend upon the remaining digits in such a fashion, that if a digit changes, the malfunction can be detected; e.g., a given digit may be zero if the sum of other digits in the word is odd, and this (check) digit may be one, if the sum of other digits in the word is even. 2. One or more redundant digits carried along with a machine word and used in relation to the other digits in the word as a self-checking or error-detecting code to detect malfunctions of equipment in data-transfer operations. (Related to forbidden-combination check, and parity check.)

digit, check-sum—A check digit produced by a sum check.

digit-coded voice—Inquiries are received as a series of digits, dialed or keyed from a telephone. The audio-response unit buffers each digit. Then these are transferred to the processor's core storage and assembled into a complete message. After processing the message, the computer assembles a digitally coded voice-output response which is transferred to the ARU (audio response unit). The ARU converts it to actual voice signals and sends it to the inquiring party as the audio response. The ARU has two basic input/output lines, but can be expanded to eight lines (some systems).

digit compression—1. A specific packing process in which an assigned area contains additional digits. Example: storing three digits in two character positions containing six bits. In some computers, a four-bit pattern represents a single decimal digit. Then two six-bit character positions can accommodate twelve-bits or three four-bit digits. 2. Any of a number of techniques used to pack digits.

digit decimal—A single character which represents an integer, i.e., in decimal notation, one of the characters, 0 through 9.

digit, decimal-coded—A digit or character defined by a set of decimal digits, such as a pair of decimal digits specifying a letter or special character in a system of notation.

digit delay—A logic element which delays its input signal by one digit period.

digit delay element—A specific delay element that introduces a delay in a line of signals or pulses of one digit period duration.

digit emitter—1. A character emitter which generates and emits only digits to the exclusion of all other characters, signs, and symbols. 2. A character emitter limited to the twelve row pulses in a punched card.

digit emitter, selective—A section or part of the control mechanism of a punched card reader which the operator can use to select which rows of a punched card are to be read.

digit filter—A particular punched card unit which can be manually set to permit a machine to recognize the occurrence of a specific designation punch in one card column. It thus relates to control functions.

digit forbidden—*Same as* character, illegal.

digit, function—A unique computer code digit that describes the arithmetic or logical operation which is to be carried out.

digit, gap—Digits that are not used to represent data, but are included in a computer word for engineering or convenience purposes, such as spaces.

digit, guard—A low-order hexadecimal zero appended to each operand fraction in a single-word floating-point arithmetic addition or subtraction operation.

digit, high-order—A digit that occupies a more significant or highly weighted position in a numeral or positional notation system.

digitize—1. To assign digital numbers to characters and words according to fixed rules of ordering. 2. To convert an analog measurement of a physical variable into a numerical

value, thereby expressing the quantity in digital form. (Synonymous with quantize.)

digitizer — A device that converts an analog measurement into digital form.

digit, least significant (LSD)—The digit contributing the smallest quantity to the value of a numeral.

digit, low-order—A digit that occupies a low weighted position in a numeral in a positional notation system.

digit, most significant (MSD)—The significant digit contributing the largest quantity to the value of a numeral.

digit, noisy—A specific digit that is chosen to be inserted into the units position of a mantissa during left-shifting manipulation.

digit operation, serial — The capability of handling digits one following another regardless as to whether the bits can be handled in serial or parallel fashion.

digit period—The time interval between the occurrence of successive digit signals.

digit place—The site of a digit in a numeral in various positional notation systems.

digit plane—A specific array of cells which are arranged in order to affect three dimensions. The plane therefore contains corresponding bits of every word.

digit position punching — The area on a punched card onto which a decimal digit may be punched.

digit pulse—A particular drive pulse common to magnetic cells corresponding to a one digit position in some or all the words in a storage unit. In some techniques it may always be an inhibit pulse or always an enable pulse which are more acceptable names for the general term.

digit-punching position — The area on a punched card onto which a digit may be punched.

digit selector — 1. A device that separates a card column into individual pulses corresponding to punched-row positions. 2. A particular punched card unit which can be manually set to permit a machine to recognize the occurrence of a specific designation punch in one card column.

digit(s), equivalent-binary — The number of binary digits required to express a number in another base with the same precision; e.g., approximately $3\frac{1}{3}$ binary digits are required to express in binary form each digit of a decimal number. For the case of coded decimal notation, the number of binary digits required is usually 4 times the number of decimal digits.

digit, sexadecimal—A digit that is a member of the set of sixteen digits: 0 thru 9 and then K, S, N, J, F, and L used in a numerical notation system using a radix of 16.

digit, sign—A character, frequently a single bit, used to designate the algebraic sign of the quantity. (Synonymous with sign bit.)

digit(s), significant—A set of digits, usually from consecutive columns beginning with the most significant digit different from zero and ending with the least significant digit whose value is known and assumed relevant; e.g., 2300.0 has five significant digits, whereas 2300 probably has two significant digits; however, 2301 has four significant digits and 0.0023 has two significant digits.

digits, octal—The symbol 0, 1, 2, 3, 4, 5, 6, or 7 used as a digit in the system of notation which uses 8 as the base or radix. (Clarified by number systems.)

digit sorting method, reverse—Sorting which begins with the units position of a given field and proceeds one column at a time (from right to left) until the field is completely sorted.

digit-transfer bus—The main wire or wires used to transfer numerical and other information (but not control signals) among the various registers in a digital computer.

digit transfer trunk—*See* trunk, digit transfer.

digit, unallowable instruction — *Same as* character, illegal.

DIMATE—A language for automatic equipment testing.

diminished complement—*Same as* complement, radix-minus-one.

diminished radix complement—*Same as* complement, radix-minus-one.

direct access—The ability to read or write information at any location within a storage device in a constant amount of time. Every site available for data storage on a direct access-device is identified by its own unique, numeric address.

direct-access channel display — This display provides automatic collection of data and control information from core memory with a single instruction. This indexible address register contains the memory address of the next display control or data word in memory. Termination of the transfer is controlled by the stop bit which signals the computer upon completion of plotting. The stop bit's location may be determined by examining the contents of the channel register.

direct access inquiry — A storage method which allows direct information inquiry from temporary or permanent storage devices.

direct-access library—The "librarian" portion of the control programs keeps track of library programs of the operating system. The library may be stored on a single secondary-storage unit, or it may be distributed over several different storage units for more efficient operation. The library is initially established by selection and editing of a complete set of programs to produce a specially tailored program library that fits the needs of the individual user. The librarian keeps this set of programs up to date by adding, deleting, and modifying as required. User-written application programs can be incorporated into the library along with subroutines, the control program, compilers, sort-merge, and utility programs. Most effi-

cient operation is possible when the program library is stored on a direct access device.

direct-access storage—A type of storage device wherein access to the next position from which information is to be obtained is in no way dependent on the position from which information was previously obtained.

direct access storage inquiry — A process through which information can be directly requested from temporary or permanent storage devices.

direct address—1. A machine-instruction address of the data to be processed. 2. An address that indicates the location where the referenced operand is to be found or stored, with no reference to an index register or B-box. (Synonymous with first-level address.)

direct addressing—*See* addressing, direct.

direct-address processing—Reading or writing of data from a sector whose address is given.

direct code—A code that specifies the use of actual computer command and address configurations.

direct coding—*Same as* coding, absolute.

direct control—*See* control, direct.

direct control connection—A device that permits two systems to be coupled together for control purposes bypassing the channels. Control information can be sent across the connector by a single instruction in each computer.

direct data capture—A technique employed in cash registers, or on sales slips whereby customer account numbers, the amount of the purchase, and other information are automatically recorded, read by an optical reading device, and sent to the computer to be processed. The desirability of using direct data capture depends on two factors—the urgency of processing the transactions, and the increased costs of data capture devices compared to manual data preparation.

directing character code — One or several routing indicators at the start of a message that determine message destination.

direct insert subroutine — A subroutine inserted directly into the linear operational sequence, not entered by a jump. Such a subroutine must be recopied at each point that it is needed in a routine.

direct instruction—An instruction which contains an operand for the operation specified by the instruction.

direction—In flowcharting, the antecedent-to-successor relation, indicated by arrows, lines, or other conventions, between operations on a flowchart.

direction, flow — The antecedent-to-successor relation, indicated by arrows or other conventions, between operations on flow charts.

direction, grain — The arrangement (direction) of the fibers in the paper in relation to the route or manner in which a document travels through the character reader.

direction, normal flow—*See* flow, normal direction.

directive — An instruction (pseudo-instruction) in a program which has the same general form as a computer instruction but is actually used to control translation.

directives, assembler — The symbolic assembler directives control or direct the assembly processor just as operation codes control or direct the central computer. These directives are represented by mnemonics.

direct or on-line system—*See* on-line.

directory—A file with the layout for each field of the record which it describes; thus a directory describes the layout of a record within a file.

direct output—*See* output, direct.

direct reference address — A virtual address that is not modified by indirect addressing, but may be modified by indexing.

disable—A suppression of an interrupt feature.

disabled interrupt—*See* interrupt, armed.

disarmed interrupt—*See* interrupt, armed.

discrete — Pertains to separate and distinct parts of data such as holes in a card, or graphic characters.

discrete programming — A class of optimization problems in which the values of all the variables are restricted to integers. Normally, the optimization problem without this integer restriction is linear programming, additional adjectives indicate variations; for example, integer quadratic programming, etc.

discrimination—The skipping of various instructions as developed in a predetermined set of conditions as programmed. If a conditional jump is not used, the next instructions would follow in the normal proper sequence. *See* branch, conditional.

discrimination instruction—A more acceptable term for jump or branch instruction. Also called decision instruction. *See* branch.

disjunction — The logical operation which makes use of the OR operator or the logical sum. The disjunction of two variables, or expressions, may be written as A+B, AVB, or AUB. These may also be described as a union when using Venn diagrams. (Clarified by OR operator, OR gate, and contrasted with conjunction.)

disjunction gate—*Same as* gate, OR.

disjunctive search—A search defined in terms of a logical sum; i.e., disjunctive form, in contrast to a conjunctive form or logical product.

disk—A circular metal plate with magnetic material on both sides, continuously rotated for reading or writing by means of one or more read/write heads mounted on moveable or fixed arms; disks may be permanently mounted on a shaft, or as a package, they may be removable and others placed on the shaft.

disk access — Disks are usually stacked with each disk rotating in a horizontal plane, as they may be permanent or exchangeable.

Access to each disk is by one or more arms which move to definite radial locations on a rotating disk. They are random accessed only in the sense that the read/write heads on the arms move to definite tracks or portions of the disk, and, within a given track, data are transferred in a sequential manner.

disk file addressing — The operation which locates information on a random-access file.

disk file, on-line—The powerful advanced systems concepts of the computer are fully complemented by the on-line disk file subsystem. With its "head-per-track" design, the disk file provides all-electronic access to any record throughout the file in an average of 20 milliseconds. File organization, programming, and use are simplified because access is entirely by electronic switching, with no moving arms, card drops, or the like. Each record segment is equally available regardless of physical location on the disks. Multiple segments can be transferred with a single instruction. Module size is four disks totalling 9.6 million alphanumeric characters of information capacity. Up to 100 of these modules may be used with the computer, effectively extending the memory of the computer system by almost a billion characters. Transfer rate is 100,000 characters per second (some systems).

disk file optimizer—*See* optimizer, disk file.

disk file, random-access (banks)—The account records and related information, such as holds and no-book transactions, are stored in the random-access disk file. Since access time to the disk file is so fast (average of 1/50 of a second), its storage provides a virtually unlimited extension of core memory. Consequently, there are virtually no limits to the number of tellers for whom proof totals can be maintained, the variety of transactions which can be handled, the variations in transaction processing that individual institutions require, and the variety of passbook formats that are used. The extreme reliability and extremely fast access of the disk file stems from its head-per-track design. There is no positioning of arms or read/write heads since each track has its own read/write device (some systems).

disk files—A type of storage medium consisting of numbers of disks that rotate; each disk has a special coating for retaining stored information.

disk, magnetic—A storage device on which information is recorded on the magnetized surface of a roating disk. A magnetic-disk storage system is an array of such devices, with associated reading and writing heads that are mounted on movable arms. (Related to disk storage.)

disk, moving arm—A type of disk which has a movable arm which contains several heads, each of which covers an area of several tracks of digited information. This is in contrast to a fixed head disk for which the heads are fixed in position, one per track, and the arms are immovable.

disk operating system (DOS)—A more powerful twin of TOS, this is a versatile operating system for IBM System 360 installations having direct-access storage devices. This simple operating system supports almost every peripheral device available for System 360.

disk pack—A set of magnetic disks which have been designed so they can be placed in a processing device for reading and writing. Their design permits them to be interchanged with other disk packs.

disk sorting — A sort program that utilizes disk-type memory for auxiliary storage during sorting.

disk sort/merging—See sort/merging, disk.

disk storage—1. A storage device that uses magnetic recording on flat rotating disks. 2. The storage of data on the surface of magnetic disks. (Related to magnetic disk, and magnetic-disk storage.)

disk, working storage—See storage working.

disorderly, close-down—See close-down, disorderly.

dispatcher—A resident routine called the dispatcher is at the heart of the communication between the computer and its input/output devices. The dispatcher maintains a queue of channel requests for each channel and will honor each in turn as the channel becomes available. In addition, the dispatcher controls the operation of the multiprogrammed symbiont routines, interrupting the user's program temporarily to give control to a symbiont and returning control to the user when the symbiont has released. The dispatcher maintains a pool of buffer areas for the symbionts and a similar pool of drum symbionts are employed (some systems).

dispatcher, translator—The translators are rather large programs that do not reside in memory, but are stored on the system library tape until they are called into memory by the translator (some systems) .

dispatching priority — The priority assigned to an active task in a multiprogramming or multitask environment. An active task is nonreal-time and nonforeground. The dispatch priority establishes precedence for the use of the central processing unit (CPU) when the operating system prepares to return control to the problem program.

dispatching systems—Dispatching systems respond to a demand by assigning resources to meet it, then reporting accordingly. A system that assigns inventory to fill orders is an example. In this case a dispatching system must reduce the recorded balances, prepare the appropriate documents for the warehouses where the items are stocked, and issue reorder documents when inventory levels become too low. The dispatching system also performs such functions as financial accounting, payroll, and management reports on daily operations. The equipment for such a system generally consists of a medium or large computer, magnetic tape transports, magnetic disk files, a card reader-punch, a printer, and perhaps several teletype terminals and a buffer.

disperse—1. The distribution of items among more sets than originally presented. An output item may be distributed to several output sets. 2. A data-processing operation in which input items or fields are distributed or duplicated in more than one output item or field.

dispersing—A designed procedure which results in input data distribution in several, rather than one, output area.

dispersion gate—Same as gate, NAND.

display—Visible representation of data on a console screen in a printed report, graph, or drawing, subject to alteration by a light pen or "stylus."

display adapter unit — The display adapter unit controls the transmission of data, unit control information, unit status information, and the sequencing and synchronizing of the various units in the system. In addition, digital data received from computer storage is formatted for deflection commands for the CRT devices.

display, alphameric-graphic — The display unit provides the system with the means of visually displaying computer-generated information. Alphameric text and graphic images may be projected on the direct-view cathode-ray tube located on the console of the unit. The images appear as a series of dots in the desired pattern. Data is entered manually from one of three sources: the alphameric keyboard of a printer-keyboard, a program-function keyboard, or a handheld light-pen device. The capabilities of the display can be used in the solution of problems encountered in commercial applications, information retrieval, and scientific computing.

display buffer size—The minimum and maximum number of words reserved for display units and used, with automatic refreshing, to present a flicker-free picture.

display category—A group, type, class, or array of data or information presented for visual display on cathode-ray-tubes.

display, character-generation—In addition to automatic line generation, the display hardware can display characters specified by 6-bit codes. Each character is displayed in an average of 15 μsec (some systems).

display, character-mode—This mode provides a rapid means of displaying alphanumeric characters. Three characters or symbols are contained in each variable bit word with provision for a 128-character or larger alphabet. Characters or symbols may be displayed in one or several sizes. The character generator is capable of performing carriage-return functions upon specific character-like commands. Escape from the character mode is accomplished with another similar code.

display characters per frame—The maximum number of whole characters which can be drawn flicker-free at the manufacturer's recommended refresher rate.

display console—*See* console display.

display console plotter—See plotter, display console.

display console visual — *See* console, visual display.

display control—This unit permits up to eight display units to operate in an economical time-sharing configuration. It has a keyboard which makes possible interpretive operations. Its function for a particular job is assigned by the computer program and the keys for that job are identified by removable illuminated overlays (some systems).

display, CRT inquiry—Information is placed into the computer through the alphanumeric keyboard and is simultaneously displayed on its four inch square (or larger screen (CRT). The unit then displays a reply to the inquiry on its screen.

display, data analysis—*See* data analysis display.

display, data-conversion — The incremental display provides a fast, direct method of converting line drawings, photographs and other written data into digital information when used with a photomultiplier system. In such a system the incremental plotter is used as a programmed spot-scanning source of light in combination with a lens system to focus the raster being scanned on the film being read. The photomultiplier gathers the light passing through the film and signals the computer whenever light is sensed. In this manner a digital record of the photograph being scanned is accumulated in the computer memory.

display, digital (DD) —A display of digitally oriented numerals.

display, direct—Cathode-ray tubes that display various alphameric, graphic, or sketch results from a processor for viewing or photographing for records or animation.

display, direct-access channel—This provides automatic collection of data and control information from core memory with a single instruction. This indexible address register contains the memory address of the next display control or data word in memory. Termination of the transfer is controlled by the stop bit which signals the computer upon completion of plotting. The stop bit's location may be determined by examining the contents of the channel register (some systems).

display drum—A magnetic, digital, data buffer, storage drum which stores data that is to be used for display on a visual device.

display, forced—A display made by the system without the operator requesting it.

display, incremental — The precision incremental display is a powerful new general-purpose incremental cathode-ray tube display which permits rapid conversion of digital computer data into graphic and tabular form. Its combined capabilities offer the user an unusual degree of versatility and accuracy.

display, increment-mode—This mode is useful for rapid plotting of curvilinear data output. A single 18-bit word causes the automatic plotting of 4 points at successively adjacent locations on the tube face. Special features of this mode include: (a) Multiple scaling—coding of the scale bits allows the X and Y registers to be incremented by factors at X1, X2, X4, or X8, whenever a point is plotted. (b) Edge flag—whenever the edge of the screen has been violated, the display will stop and inhibit data requested. Escape to the parameter mode automatically occurs. The flag is reset when new data arrives. (c) Intensity bit—Provides the option of visible or hidden incrementing. (d) Escape bit—Provides for automatic return to the parameter mode upon completion of incremental plotting (some computers).

display indicators (NIXIE)—*See* NIXIE display indicators.

display, information-retrieval—*See* retrieval system, fast access.

display, inquiry and subscriber—*See* inquiry and subscriber display.

display, inquiry-terminal — Information is placed into the computer through the alphanumeric keyboard and is simultaneously displayed on the screen. The unit then displays a reply to the inquiry on the screen. Information is displayed many times faster than that produced by an operator by means of a typeout. To reuse the display after the inquiry has been answered requires only a press of the erase button.

display, message control—*See* control message display.

display modes—Each display mode, such as vector, increment, character, point, vector continue, or short vector specifies the manner in which points are to be displayed on the screen.

display, parameter-mode—This mode is used to control the display. It establishes parameter information for each of the other modes. The parameters are changed only when another parameter word is encountered (some computers).

display, point-mode—In this mode, individual points may be established and/or plotted at random locations on the tube face. A point is established by two independent 18-bit words. The first word determines the vertical position, the second word sets up the horizontal position. Once an initial point has been established, subsequent plots may be made by single word changes (some computers).

display, precision CRT — This is a 16-inch random-position, point-plotting cathode-ray tube with magnetic deflection and focusing. It is useful for conversion of digital computer data into graphic and tabular form without the greater flexibility afforded by the ultra-precision CRT display.

display registers, communication—See communication display registers.

display, remote (slave)—A slave unit containing only the analogue portion of the display. Turn-on may be accomplished independently, or by the master-display control.

displays, information recovery and entry— Display consoles are being utilized in conjunction with a D825 data-processing system for a United States Navy application. Computer-generated information is sent to the display consoles under program direction where it is observed by an operator. Based upon the information displayed, the operator may decide to transmit an external message which he accomplishes by operating controls located on the display consoles. The display consoles in this system contain a symbol generator and internal memory in addition to the 17-inch rectangular cathode-rate tube (some systems).

displays, microfilm—See microfilm displays.

displays, monitor—A monitor display is being provided to the Federal Aviation Agency as part of Burroughs AN/FYQ-40 common digitizer for use in the National Airspace System. The common digitizer is designed to process raw video and beacon target information as part of the computerized air-traffic control system. On a cathode ray tube, the monitor display provides a radar-type presentation of the significant steps during target processing and related data for system monitoring under test conditions, and for common digitizer maintenance. The monitor is unique in that it operates in either a random-access plan-position-indicator (RAPPI) mode or a plan-position-indicator (PPI) mode. It provides the ability to monitor the entire system in discrete steps in real time. (Burroughs)

display, subroutining-multilevel — The control state permits the display to jump from accessing one location memory to any other. When it is desired to jump to a display subroutine, the return address is automatically stored in a push-down list.

display, translate—To move, as an image on a screen, from side to side or up and down without rotation of the image.

display tube—A cathode-ray tube used to display information.

display unit—A device that provides a visual representation of data.

display unit, graphic — A communications terminal which can display data on a screen.

display unit, remote (visual)—Remote users who can use a typewriter can now talk to a computer and get answers on the spot. The operator of a display unit simply types in the query and presses the transmit key; the answer appears immediately on the screen. Options cover many diverse applications and there are input interfaces for digital computers, telephone subsets, and other digital sources.

display units, visual—These units provide a dynamic visual presentation of information stored in the computer or in storage files, drums, and tapes. An operator at the display can monitor the progress of his program or solution, and can modify and intervene as necessary. It may be used to immediately display an updated account record as required to respond to an inquiry. Corrections to the record may be made directly on the displayed information, and the corrected record is immediately stored. The unit also can be programmed to present the system operator or programmer, partial results, problem checks, graphs of mathematical results, and other instantaneous computational output. The unit can be used as a computer-operator console; for engineering record-keeping and updating; as a time-shared scientific-computing terminal; for information retrieval; data-acquisition monitoring; data-reduction display; process-control supervision; order entry; inventory inquiry and updating. The major element of one model console is a console with a 12-inch square display screen on which tables, graphs, charts, characters, lines, and curves can be displayed as a series of points. The contents of a page in information—3,848 characters—can be viewed. A built-in electronic marker helps the operator edit messages. Buffer storage is available to hold points, lines and position instructions. A "light pen" can delete or add text, maintain tighter control over programs and choose alternative courses of action (some computers).

display, vector-continue mode—The vector-continue mode is an extension of the vector mode; its word format is the same. This mode is used when it is desirable to draw a vector from any point to the edge of the screen. The vector specified is automatically extended until the edge of the screen is encountered. Upon violation of the screen edge, automatic return is made to the parameter mode. This mode is particularly useful for drawing long, straight lines (for example, grid lines and graph axes) rapidly and efficiently.

display, vector-mode—This mode provides a rapid means for displaying straight lines between two points without specifying any in-between points. A single 18-bit word causes automatic plotting of the vector. Once the display has been programmed to the vector mode, all subsequent data is interpreted as vector-mode data. Data is received in the form of 18-bit words. Each word consists of 8 bits of delta-X information, 8 bits of delta-Y information, an intensify bit, and an escape bit. Delta-X and delta-Y each comprise 7 magnitude bits and 1 sign bit. Since the display area consists of a $1,024 \times 1,024$ point matrix, the maximum length vector which can be drawn with a single instruction is $\pm\frac{1}{8}$ of the display width. There is no limitation for a minimum length vector. Plotting time is $1\frac{1}{2}$ microseconds per individual point (some computers).

dissector — In optical character recognition (OCR), a mechanical or electronic transducer that sequentially detects the level of light in different areas of a completely illuminated sample space.

dissipation, module—The dissipation of the module calculated from the voltage-current product, plus an allowance for transistor dissipation for load current being supplied to other modules.

distance — The number of digit positions which the corresponding digits of two binary words of the same length are different. (Synonymous with Hamming distance.)

distance gate—*Same as* gate, exclusive OR.

distance, Hamming—*See* Hamming distance.

distance signal—*Same as* distance, Hamming.

distortion—An undesired change in waveform between the received signal and the original signal.

distortion, asymmetrical—A distortion affecting a two-condition (or binary) modulation (or restitution) in which all the significant intervals corresponding to one of the two significant conditions have longer or shorter durations than the corresponding theoretical durations of the excitation. If this particular requirement is not met, distortion is present.

distortion, attenuation—Distortion due to variation of loss or gain within a frequency.

distortion, bias—1. Bias distortion or bias of start-stop teletypewriter signals is the uniform shifting of the beginning of all marking pulses from their proper positions in relation to the beginning of the start pulse. 2. Distortion affecting a two-condition (or binary) modulation (or restitution) in which all the significant intervals corresponding to one of the two significant conditions have longer or shorter durations than the corresponding theoretical durations.

distortion, characteristic—1. A fixed distortion which results in either shortened or lengthened impulses. It generally does not change in degree from day to day. 2. Distortions caused by transients which, as a result of the modulation, are present in the transmission channel and depend on its transmission qualities.

distortion, delay/frequency—That form of distortion which occurs when the envelope delay of a circuit or system is not constant over the frequency range required for transmissions.

distortion, end—*See* end distortion.

distortion, fortuitous—An intermittent distortion which results in either shortened or lengthened impulses. It is caused by battery fluctuations, hits on the line, power induction, etc.

distortion, marking-end—End distortion which lengthens the marking impulse by delaying the mark-to-space transition.

distortion, spacing-end—End distortion which lengthens the spacing impulse by advancing the mark-to-space transition.

distribution accounting machine—A machine which sorts amounts into categories and accumulates the totals of each category.

distribution frame—A structure for terminating wires and connecting them together in any desired order.

distribution, time-impulse—A device or circuit for allocating timing pulses or clock pulses to one or more conducting paths or control lines in specified sequence.

distributor—The electronic circuit which acts as an intermediate link between the accumulator and drum storage.

distributor tape transmitter — A device capable of restoring the information punched on a paper tape to a train or sequence of electrical pulses, usually for the purpose of transferring the information to some other storage medium.

distributor, time-pulse—A device or circuit for allocating timing pulses or clock pulses to one or more conducting paths or control lines in specified sequence.

distributor transmitter—The device in a teletypewriter which makes and breaks the teletype line in timed sequence. Modern usage of the term refers to a paper-tape transmitter.

diversity gate—*Same as* gate, exclusive OR.

divide check — An indicator which denotes that an invalid division has been attempted or has occurred.

divided slit scan—A device, in optical character recognition (OCR), which scans an input character at given intervals to obtain its horizontal and vertical components. This scanning device consists of a narrow column of photoelectric cells.

dividend—The quantity that is divided by another quantity; also, the numerator of a fraction.

divider analog—*See* analog divider.

divider, digital—*See* digital divider.

divide time—The period of time required to perform a single division operation with quantities of average length.

division—The parts into which a COBOL program is organized. Identification division provides information to identity the source and object programs. Environment division specifies the equipment to use for translating and running a program. Data division contains entries to define the nature of the data to be processed. Procedure division consists of the processor program to be run with data.

division, data—*See* data division.

division, environment — *See* environment division.

division, identification—The part of COBOL programming in which the programmer gives information to identify the source program and the object program.

division, procedure—The COBOL term for the description of the steps we take in the processing of data into meaningful English.

division subroutine—1. A set of instructions which simulate division by repetitive subtraction or by series expansion. 2. The approximation of reciprocals. 3. A division simulator.

division, time—Interleaving several message channels, which are separated from each other in time, on a single transmission media.

divisor—A quantity by which the dividend is divided; also, the denominator of a fraction.

divisor, trial—An initial approximation in the dividing arithmetic process.

document—1. A form, voucher, or written evidence of a transaction. 2. To instruct, as by citation of references. 3. To substantiate, as by listing of authorities. 4. A medium containing a representation of stored information, such as a sheet of paper, a punched card, etc.

document alignment—The phase of the reading process, in character recognition, in which a transverse or gravitational force is applied to the document to align its reference edge with that of the machine.

documentation—1. The process of collecting, organizing, storing, citing and dispensing of documents or the information recorded in the documents. 2. The group of techniques necessary for the orderly presentation, organization, and communication of recorded specialized knowledge in order to maintain a complete record of reasons for changes in variables. Documentation is necessary not so much to give maximum utility as it is to give an unquestionable historical-reference record.

documentation book—All the material needed to document a computer application, including problem statement, flow charts, coding, and operating instructions.

documentation, empirical — The essence of scientific method, i.e., verifiable documentation from observations, experiments, evidence, past recorded experience—without the use of theory or deduction.

documentation, graphic—A process developed for recording data on graphs and films.

document handling—The process of loading, feeding, transporting, and unloading a cutform document submitted for character recognition.

document, leading edge—The edge which is first encountered during the reading process in character recognition, and whose relative position indicates the direction of travel for the document.

document misregistration — The improper state of appearance of a document, in character recognition, on site in the character

reader, with reference to a real or imaginary horizontal base line.

documentor—A program designed to use data-processing methods in the production and maintenace of program flow charts, text material, and other types of tabular or graphic information.

document reader—See reader, document.

document reference edge—That edge of a source document in character recognition, which provides the basis of all subsequent reading processes.

document retrieval—The system of searching, indexing, and identifying of specific documents which contain the desired data being sought.

document sorter-reader, magnetic—See magnetic document sorter-reader.

document, source — A document originally used by a data processing system and which supplies the basic data to be input to the data processing system.

documents, software—Relating to all the documents and notations associated with the computer; e.g., manuals, circuit diagrams, etc., or programs and routines associated with the computer; e.g., compilers, special languages, library routines.

document, turnaround — A punched card or the like which has been prepared by a computer, so that when it is returned to the computer it serves as evidence of a completed transaction.

document types—The generic designation of varied printing methods in character recognition, the category of which is of paramount consideration to data preparation.

docuterm—A word or phrase descriptive of the subject matter or concept of an item of information that is considered important for later retrieval of information. (Related to aspect card.)

do-nothing instruction—See instruction, dummy.

don't care gate—See gate, don't care.

DOS (disk operating system)—Relates to the tape operating system TOS, this is a versatile operating system for IBM System 360 installations having direct-access storage devices. This simple operating system supports almost every peripheral device available for System 360.

DO statement, range—All FORTRAN statements included in the repetitive execution of a DO loop operation.

dot printer—See printer, wire.

double address—See address, double.

double-bucket — A storage device that provides complete buffering overlap. Usually a magnetic core storage unit. This device processes data with one section of storage while the other section is being loaded.

double entry card—A punched card which contains data for entry into two different accounts, i.e., a card containing both payroll and labor distribution information.

double fallback—See fallback, double.

double length—Pertaining to twice the normal length of a unit of data or a storage device in a given computing system; e.g., a double-length register would have the capacity to store twice as much data as a single-length or normal register; a double-length word would have twice the number of characters or digits as a normal or single-length word.

double-length number—A number having twice as many figures as are normally handled in a particular device. (Synonymous with double-precision number.)

double-length working—For greater precision, oftentimes two or more machine words are used to represent a single number, and this is termed double-length working. *Same as* double precision.

double or reverse calculation—Double or reverse calculation is the calculation, recalculation, and then comparison of the two results to prove accuracy. It is commonly used in payroll and other calculations for which no predetermined control total can be developed. In the recalculation, factors are reversed—the original multiplier becomes the multiplicand and the original multiplicand becomes the multiplier. When processing with unit record equipment, if the recalculation is performed in a separate run, then punching of the result can also be verified.

double precision—Pertaining to a quantity having twice as many digits as are normally carried; e.g., a double-precision number requires two machine words in a fixed-word machine.

double-precision arithmetic—Arithmetic used when more accuracy is necessary than a single word of computer storage will provide. This is accomplished by using two computer words to represent one number.

double-precision hardware — Application problems that require a high degree of precision are easily and quickly solved because of double-precision hardware. By using a word size of 48 bits rather than the ordinary 24, the precision of both fixed and floating-point operations is considerably greater. The double-precision store, load, and add instructions provide swift completion of all double-precision operations.

double-precision number—1. A number having twice as many figures as are normally handled in a particular device. 2. The purpose is to carry more significant digits in a computation to thereby avoid the loss of high or low order positions.

double-precision operation—An operation in which two registers are treated as a 64-bit double-word register containing a single quantity.

double-precision quantity — *Same as* double precision number.

double-pulse recording — A specific method for magnetic recording of bits in which each storage cell comprises two regions magnetized in opposite senses with unmagnetized regions on each side.

double punch—A term which usually refers to more than one numeric punch in any one column of a Hollerith card.

double-punch and blank-column detection—Double-punch and blank-column detection is a feature available on certain machines which perform punching. It is frequently used after punching to check numerical mark-sense fields for any columns which were poorly marked or double-marked. In summary-punch and gang-punch operations, it can be used to recognize any multiple punching or lacing which might occur in numerical fields. Its use does not require a separate pass. This feature also permits some checking of alphabetic fields.

doubler—An internal component which doubles a given digit and is used in the multiplication routine.

double-rail logic—*See* logic, double-rail.

double-word boundary—Any address ending in 000, which is divisible by 8 in the IBM 360 System. A natural boundary for 8-byte double-word items.

double-word command—A double-word that contains detailed information concerning a portion of an input/output operation.

double-word, effective—The double word actually accessed in a double-word operation.

double-word length fixed-point arithmetic—Many arithmetic instructions produce two word results. With fixed-point multiplication, a double-length product is stored in two A registers of control storage for integer and fractional operations. Integer and fractional division is performed upon a double-length dividend with the remainder and the quotient retained in the A registers.

double-word location, effective—The actual storage location pointed to by the effective virtual address of a double-word addressing instruction.

double-word, program status — A double-word that indicates all programmable control conditions of a CPU. The program status double-word is a set of hardware control registers whose contents are collected and stored as a double-word in memory, and whose states can be established by loading a double-word from memory.

double-word register—Two registers used to hold a 64-bit double word (some computers).

down time—The period during which a computer is malfunctioning or not operating correctly due to machine failures. (Contrasted with available time, idle time, or standby time.)

down time, nonscheduled — This is the idle machine time during which the hardware is being repaired because of failures or unforeseen circumstances other than normal servicing or maintenance time. It is usually expressed as a percent of total available time.

down time, scheduled — The determined or required idle time necessary for normal servicing of computer equipment during which such equipment is unavailable for operations. This is usually expressed as a percent of total available time. It is also known as preventive maintenance time.

DPM—The abbreviation for documents per minute, and data-processing machine.

DPMA—Data Processing Management Association.

drift error—That part of the error in analog computers due to drift or change in component values caused by changes in temperature or changes in power supply voltages.

drills, network—A final level of testing in a real-time system in which data from all the sites is transmitted and the entire complex of equipment, personnel, interfaces, and programs are tested.

drive—A device that moves tape past a head. (Synonymous with tape transport.)

drive, data-cell—Data-cell drive provides large bulk storage at low cost. Billions of characters of alphanumeric or digital data can be stored by linking multiple drives. Eight data-cell drives, with up to 6.4 billion digits, can be linked to one control unit.

drive, hypertape—A unit which uses magnetic tape packaged in cartridge form, transfers data at 340,000 alphanumeric characters a second or 680,000 digits a second. A cartridge holds more than 65 million digits. Hypertape drives are designed to read or record information at a rate of 340,000 alphanumeric characters a second or up to 680,000 digits a second. This represents a fast commercially available magnetic-tape system. The drive operates at either of two densities —1,511 or 3,022 bits an inch. Also available is a hypertape drive that operates at 170,000 alphanumeric characters a second, or up to 340,000 digits a second. (IBM)

driven-key—See key driven.

drive pulse—1. A pulsed magnetomotive force applied to a magnetic core. 2. A particular pulse of current in a winding inductively coupled to one or more magnetic cells which produces a pulse of magneto-motive-force.

drive pulse, partial—See pulse, partial-write.

drive, tape—The mechanism that moves magnetic or paper tape past sensing and recording heads; usually associated with data-processing equipment. (Synonymous with tape unit, and clarified by magnetic-tape unit, and paper-tape unit.)

DRO (Destructive Read-Out)—The interrogation of a destructive type of storage system.

drop-dead halt—See halt, dead.

drop-in—An accidental or unwanted appearance of bits.

drop-out—The accidental failure to read or write a necessary character on a magnetic recording surface.

drops, false—The documents spuriously identified as pertinent by an information-retrieval system, but which do not satisfy the search requirements, due to causes such as improper coding, punching spurious or wrong combinations of holes, or improper use of terminology. (Related to noise.)

drum—A circular cylinder with a magnetic surface on which data can be stored by selective magnetization of portions of the curved surface.

drum access, magnetic—Usually individual tracks of a drum can be addressed and data on each track transferred in a sequential manner. It is also possible to address each word on the drum. The individual datum is not read or written until its location appears underneath the drum read/write head, and transfer rates are usually high compared with magnetic tape.

drum buffer—See buffer, drum.

drum, display—See display drum.

drum latency time—The delay or latency time on drums occurs while waiting for a given datum to appear beneath the read-write head and may be minimized by organization procedures, i.e., by programming the next address of the datum to be read or written as a function of the last position of the read/write head, plus the elapsed time for the processing, before the next read/write instruction.

drum, magnetic—A cylinder having a surface coating of magnetic material, which stores binary information by the orientation of magnetic dipoles near or on its surface. Since the drum is rotated at a uniform rate, the information stored is available periodically as a given portion of the surface moves past one or more flux-detecting devices, called heads, located near the surface of the drum.

drum mark—A character used to signify the end of a record on a drum.

drum-memory unit—Fast direct-access storage is supplied by the drum-memory unit. It is particularly useful as an extension of internal main-core memory for greater economy. Average access time in milliseconds permits fast indexing of mass files in other random-access units, particularly the mass-storage unit.

drum parity—See parity, drum.

drum printer—A printing device consisting of a drum embossed with alphabetic and numeric characters. As the drum rotates, a hammer strikes the paper from behind at a time when the desired character(s) on the drum passes the line to be printed. The process continues until the line is finished.

drum, program—A magnetic storage drum which stores a computer program.

drum sorting—A sort program that utilizes magnetic drums for auxiliary storage during sorting.

drum storage—A storage device that uses magnetic recording on a rotating cylinder. A type of addressable storage associated with some computers.

drum, type—See type drum.

DSW—Abbreviation for device status word.

dual-channel controller — This controller increases the sorting and merging powers of the systems by permitting simultaneous tape reading and/or writing. All tapes may be accessed from either channel.

dual-gap rewrite head—A character written on tape is immediately read by a read head so that the accuracy of recorded data might be ensured.

dual operation—Most frequent reference is to the Boolean operation whose result is the negation of the result of another Boolean operation.

dual purpose card — Punched cards which contain printed as well as punched information.

dual recordings—The dual recording of critical data makes it possible to machine-compare the two for verification. It is more commonly used in mark-sense recording operations and those card-punch operations in which it is necessary to verify only one or two fields.

dual storage—See storage, dual.

dual systems—Special configurations that use two computers to receive identical inputs and execute the same routines, with the results of such parallel processing subject to comparison. Exceptional high-reliability requirements are usually involved.

dummy—1. An artificial address, instruction, or record of information inserted solely to fulfill prescribed conditions, such as to achieve a fixed word length or block length, but without itself affecting machine operations except to permit the machine to perform desired operations. 2. A fictitious fact, record, or other item used to test machine operations or to space between pieces of valid data.

dummy address—An artificial address used for illustration or instruction purposes.

dummy instruction—See instruction, dummy.

dump — 1. To accidentally or intentionally withdraw all power from a computer. 2. To record the contents of internal storage at a given instant of time, usually as an aid in detecting program mistakes or errors. 3. To print out or punch out a portion or all of the contents of the computer memory. 4. To transfer all or part of the contents of one section of computer memory into another section, or to some output device.

dump, a-c — The intentional, accidental or conditional removal of all alternating-current power from a system or component. An a-c dump usualy results in the removal of all power, since direct current is usually supplied through a rectifier or converter.

dump, change—A print-out or output recording of the contents of all storage locations in which a change has been made since the previous change dump.

dump check—A check which usually consists of adding all the digits during dumping, and verifying the sum when retransferring.

dump, core—A listing of the contents of a storage device, or selected parts of it. (Synonymous with memory dump and memory print-out.)

dump, d-c — The intentional, accidental, or conditional removal of all direct-current power from a system or component.

dump, dynamic—A dump that is performed periodically during the execution of a program.

dumping, dynamic—A specific feature which prints diagnostic data avoiding interruption in the program which is being tested.

dumping, executive — The facility to obtain printable dumps of the contents of areas of film or core memory in case unexpected errors cause premature termination of supposedly debugged programs. The dumps are recorded on tape for later printing on the high-speed printer.

dumping, periodic (time sharing) — See time sharing, periodic dumping.

dumping storage—A procedure or process for transferring data from one particular storage device to another or from one particular area to another.

dump, memory—1. A listing of the contents of a storage device, or selected parts of it. (Synonymous with core dump and memory print-out.) 2. Routine generated automatically according to a programmer's specification and included in an object program to perform, respectively, program-loading operations and a printout of memory contents upon request.

dump, monitor-control—A memory dump may be specified in the control information for a job. Upon termination of the job, the dump routine is loaded from the system unit and executed. The dump routine overlays the monitor and produces a complete dump of the object program. Upon completion of the dump, the monitor is reloaded to process the next job. Programs terminate normally by returning control to the monitor. A job may be terminated by the operator or the monitor. Once a job has terminated, the monitor automatically initiates the processing of the next job.

If for any reason the resident monitor becomes destroyed and processing is not continuous, the system may be reloaded and initialized by the bootstrap loader.

dump, post-mortem—A listing of the contents of a storage device taken after a routine has been run in order that the final condition of sections of storage may be recorded for debugging purposes.

dump, power—The accidental or intentional removal of all power.

dump, priority error — The dumping into tape, etc., of information and core storage so that the cause of an equipment or program error may be assessed by the analysts.

dump, programmed—The programmed dump is a library subroutine that is called by object programs at run time. The dump may return control to the calling program or to the monitor upon completion. This allows the programmer to take selective dumps, during program execution, for debugging purposes. The dump returns to the calling program upon completion if it is called with the name P DUMP. If it is called with the name DUMP, the dump is taken and control is returned to the monitor to process the next job.

dump, rescue—A rescue dump (R dump) is the recording on magnetic tape of the entire memory, which includes the status of the system at the time the dump is made. R dumps are made so that in the event of power failure, etc., a run can be resumed from the last rescue point (R point) rather than rerunning the entire program. An R dump will consist of CM "CC" followed by eight blocks which contain the contents of memory (some systems).

dump, selective—A dump of one or more specified storage locations.

dump, snapshot—A dynamic, partial print-out during computing occurring at breakpoints and checkpoints, or at selected items in storage.

dump, static—A dump that is performed at a particular point in time with respect to a machine run, frequently at the end of a run.

dump, storage—A listing of the contents of a storage device, or selected parts of it. (Synonymous with memory dump, core dump, and memory print-out.)

duodecimal — Pertaining to the base of 12 numeration system, such as the number of inches in a foot, and the number of hours on a clock.

duodecimal number system — 1. A number system using the equivalent of the decimal number 12 as a base. 2. Preparing the number representation system with a radix of twelve. 3. Pertaining to a characteristic or property involving a selection, choice, or condition in which there are twelve possibilities.

duodecimal numeral—A numeral written in the radix 12 notation, i.e., 10 decimals and two characters.

duoprimed word—A computer word containing a representation of the 6, 7, 8, and 9 rows of information from an 80-column card.

duopurpose card—A Hollerith card containing information recorded on the card as well as the punched equivalent of such data. Such a card often serves as a source document for punching and is contrasted with a transcript card.

dup—An abbreviation for duplication; also, a punched card which is an exact copy of a previous punched card. Improper use of word duplex, but often meant to signify a second set of equipment or computing devices which would substitute for original equipment in case of failure.

duplex—Pertaining to a twin, a pair, or a two-in-one situation; e.g., a channel providing simultaneous transmission in both di-

rections, or a second set of equipment to be used in event of the failure of the primary.

duplex channel—A channel providing simultaneous transmission in both directions.

duplex computer—*See* computer, duplex.

duplex console—A switchover console connecting two or more computers and used to govern which computer is to be on-line.

duplex equipment—An invalid term but one which usually is given to mean a stand-by, reserve, or fail-safe set of equipment or devices to be used in the event of failure of the primary equipment.

duplex, full—A method of operating a communications circuit so that each end can simultaneously transmit and receive.

duplex, full service—A service in which the data communication channel is capable of simultaneous and independent transmission and reception.

duplex, half—Permits one-direction electrical communications between stations. Technical arrangements may permit operation in either direction, but not simultaneously. Therefore, this term is qualified by one of the following suffixes; S/O for send only; R/O for receive only; S/R for send or receive.

duplexing—The scheme of combining a master tape with either a tape or a series of punched cards containing pure data, plus the appropriate switching codes to produce a document. This may be done on a Flexowriter, in conjunction with two tape readers or a tape reader and a card reader, working on a "flip-flop" basis. Duplexing permits substantial reductions in the length of data transmissions in that fixed information and most of the function codes can be stored in the master tape and need never be transmitted over the line.

duplexing, synchro—The scheme of producing a document on a printing device through the synchronous running of a program tape and a master tape or a pure data tape. The operation is completely controlled by function codes in the program tape. A data-processing function.

duplex system—Two computers used in special configuration, one is on-line and the other is standing by ready to be used if a malfunction of the on-line computer occurs. The stand-by computer is often used to complete off-line functions.

duplicate — To reproduce data leaving the original data unchanged.

duplicated record—Images or copies of file records that are located in file modules or frames that are separate from the primary copy. Such duplicate records insure against loss of urgent or critical files or data.

duplicating card punch—*See* punch, gang.

duplicating unit—Automatically reproducing from any card any number of cards containing identical information—may also be performed on the reproducing machine.

duplication—The automatic copying (punching) of repetitive information from a master card or master tape into succeeding tapes or cards.

duplication check—1. A check based on the consistency of two independent performances of the same task. 2. A check in which two independent performances (either concurrently on duplicate equipment or at different times on the same equipment) of the same operation are made to see whether the same result is obtained in both instances.

dyadic operation—An operation on two operands.

dyadic Boolean operation—See Boolean operation, dyadic.

dynamic—Pertaining to a quantity that is affected by time, energy or power, and therefore indicates a relatively transient or unstable condition.

dynamic allocation memory — Each time a subroutine is called using this feature, the unique storage area for that subroutine is assigned to the first storage available. Thus, all subroutines called on the same level will share the same storage area. This results in a significant storage saving in many cases. In addition, a recursive subroutine call is possible because a new storage area is assigned each time a subroutine is entered. This feature together with in-line symbolic coding, provides real-time capability.

dynamic allocator—See allocator, dynamic.

dynamic control—See control, dynamic.

dynamic core allocation—A storage allocation procedure used in multiprogramming for the more efficient utilization of core by shifting units of work from location to location within the core.

dynamic dump—A dump that is performed periodically during the execution of a program.

dynamic dumping—A specific feature which prints diagnostic data, avoiding interruption in the program which is being tested.

dynamic flow diagram — A diagram that shows the operational aspects of a computer program as a function of time. All references to pertinent items, such as tables, index registers, subroutines, etc.

dynamic handling—This corresponds to interpretation in various respects, but generally means a given feature is not handled fully until the generated machine language program is executed.

dynamic instructions—The sequence of machine steps performed by the computer in a real-time or simulated environment.

dynamiciser—A specific logic element which has the capability of converting a space distribution, of simultaneous states representing digits, into a corresponding time sequence.

dynamic loading—The loading of a program module or routine into main memory by reference to it by a loaded executing program.

dynamic loop—See loop, dynamic.

dynamic memory—The storage of data on a device or in a manner that permits the data to move or vary with time, and thus the data is not always instantly available for recovery; e.g., acoustic delay line, magnetic drum, or circulating or recirculating of information in a medium.

dynamic memory relocation—Frees computer user from keeping tract of exactly where information is located in the system's memory. Another important attribute is its ability to keep programs flowing in and out of memory in a highly efficient manner.

dynamic printout—A printout of data which occurs as one of the sequential operations during the machine run.

dynamic program loading — See dynamic loading.

dynamic programming (DP)—The essence of dynamic programming is that an optimum decision must be made at every stage of a multistage problem. When considering only a single stage, there may appear to be a number of different decisions of equal merit. Only when the effect of each decision at every stage on the overall goal is determined can the final choice be made. This integrating of the cumulative effect of a path of decisions through each stage of the network is the real essence of DP.

dynamic programming, cost problem — A method for optimizing a set of decisions which must be made sequentially. Characteristically, each decision must be made in the light of the information embodied in a small number of observables called state variables. The incurred cost for each period is a mathematical function of the current state and decision variables, while future states are functions of these variables. The aim of the decision policy is to minimize the total incurred cost, or equivalently, the average cost per period. The mathematical treatment of such problems involves the theory of functional equations and usually requires a digital computer for implementation.

dynamic program relocation — See program relocation, dynamic.

dynamic relocation—See program relocation, dynamic.

dynamic routine—See subroutine, dynamic.

dynamic scheduling—Scheduling that changes with the different demands that are made on the system rather than being fixed as in conventional applications.

dynamic stop—A specific stop in a loop which consists of a single jump instruction which effects a jump to itself.

dynamic storage—See storage, dynamic.

dynamic storage allocation—Dynamic storage allocation is provided in a separate version of the compiler. Each time a subroutine is called using this feature, the unique storage area for the subroutine is assigned to the first storage available. Thus, all subroutines called on the same level will share the same storage area. This results in a significant storage saving in most cases. In addition, a recursive subroutine call is possible because a new storage area is assigned each time a subroutine is entered. This feature, together with in-line symbolic coding, provides powerful real-time programming capability.

dynamic subroutine—1. A program or routine which the computer changes, adjusts, or completes to carry out the requirements of the data to be developed or processed. 2. A subroutine which involves parameters, such as decimal point position or item size, from which a relatively coded subroutine is derived. The computer itself is expected to ad-

just or generate the subroutine according to the parametric values chosen.

dynamic tape and memory dump routines—These routines, particularly valuable when debugging programs, provide automatic, "on-the-fly" recording of the contents of memory and of magnetic tape files. Calls to these routines may be programmed in advance by use of macroinstructions, or they may be initiated at object time by the operator.

DYNAMO—A digital simulation program developed by Jay Forrester at MIT (Massachusetts Institute of Technology).

E

EAM (Electrical Accounting Machines)—1. Pertaining to data-processing equipment that is predominantly electromechanical, such as key punches, mechanical sorters, collators and tabulators. *See* electrical accounting machine. 2. The set of conventional punchcard equipment including sorters, collators, and tabulators. (Clarified by tabulating equipment.)

early start dates—Used in an optimistic time estimate in which each job is started as early as possible to estimate the duration of the entire task.

EASI (Electrical Accounting for the Security Industry)—This program makes it possible for stock brokers to convert their accounting operations to IBM processing in a short period of time. EASI helps stabilize the broker's costs by absorbing the day-to-day accounting load resulting from sharp fluctuations in trading volumes. (IBM)

EBCDIC—Abbreviation for expanded binary coded decimal interchange code. An 8-bit code used to represent 256 unique letters, numbers, and special characters.

EC—An abbreviation or a notation for error correcting.

ECARS (Electronic Coordinatograph And Readout System)—A land-use evaluation program. An operator electronically traces the boundaries of each land-use parcel and a digital voltmeter translates this analog information into digital coordinates. Additional data obtained includes ward, block number, and land use. The computer printouts summarize the areas in square feet and in acres for each land use on a block-by-block basis for each ward. An overlay of the plot on the original provides a rapid diagnosis of the work done. (Burroughs)

echo—Echo is the effect of a wave, which having derived (for example by reflection) from a primary wave, arrives at either end of the same circuit with sufficient magnitude and delay to be distinctly recognized.

echo attenuation—In a four-wire (or two-wire) circuit equipped with repeaters or

multiplex equipment in which the two directions of transmission can be separated from each other, the attenuation of the echo currents (which return to the input of the circuit under consideration) is determined by the ratio of the transmitted power (P_1) to the echo power received (P_2). It shall be expressed in db.

echo check—1. A check of accuracy of transmission in which the information which was transmitted to an output device is returned to the information source and compared with the original information to ensure accuracy of output. 2. A check which transmits received information back to the source and compares it with the original information.

echo checking—A system of assuring accuracy by reflecting the transmitted information back to the transmitter and comparing the reflected information with that which was transmitted.

echo suppressor—A voice-operated device for connection to a two-way telephone circuit to attenuate echo currents in one direction caused by telephone currents in the other direction.

echo talker—A portion of the transmitted signal returned from a distant point to the transmitting source with sufficient time delay to be received as interference.

ECMA—European Computer Manufacturing Association.

econometrics—The application of mathematical estimation and inference techniques to economic data in order to set the levels of economic parameters and to verify or disprove economic theorems.

E-Conversion—A FORTRAN specification to convert numbers to floating-point for input or output.

ED—The abbreviation for both error detecting and expanded display.

edge, character—*See* character edge.

edge document leading—The edge which is first encountered during the reading process in character recognition, and whose relative position indicates the direction of travel for the document.

edge, document reference—The edge of a document that is used as a reference to specify the location of the printed data.

edge, guide—The edge of a paper tape, magnetic tape, punched card, printed sheet, or other such data containing media that is used for a determination of its transverse position during movement. The edge or a specific data carrier which is used as a reference, i.e., for dimensioning, and which usually controls its position in actual use.

edge, leading card—*See* card, leading edge.

edge, nine—The lower or bottom edge of a card. This edge is most commonly used for entering the equipment first, because of the equipment requirements.

edge-notched card—*See* card, edge-notched.

edge-perforated card—*Same as* card, edge-punched.

edged-punched card—*See* card, edge punched.

edge, stroke—An optical character recognition term relating to an imaginary line that is equidistant at all points from the stroke centerline and that divides the edge irregularities of the printed stroke, in such a way that the unprinted areas on the inside of the center line are approximately equal to the printed areas on the outside of the line.

edge, stroke irregularity — A term used in optical character recognition referring to the deviation of any point on the edge of a character from the stroke edge.

edge, twelve—The upper edge of an 80-column card, or the edge least common to enter the equipment first because of the equipment requirements. Interpreting equipment requires a twelve-edge feed first.

edit—1. To prepare for publication. 2. To rearrange information for machine input or output, i.e., to rearrange, delete, select, or insert any needed data, symbols, or characters. 3. To rearrange data or information. Editing may involve the deletion of unwanted data, the selection of pertinent data, the application of format techniques, the insertion of symbols such as page numbers and typewriter characters, the application of standard processes such as zero suppression, and the testing of data for reasonableness and proper range. Editing may sometimes be distinguished between input edit (arrangement of source data) and output edit (preparation of table formats).

edit capabilities — Edit capabilities permit checking of many characters at a time doing zero suppress, floating dollar sign, asterisk protect, comma and decimal insertions, sign control, and other routines. Editing time in the central processors is reduced.

editing—Flexible editing facilities in the computer program permit the original keyboarding of copy without regard for the eventual format or medium for publication. Once the copy has been punched into paper tape, it can be edited and justified easily and quickly into any required column width and for any specified type font, merely by specifying the format required. Thus, copy for a scientific journal can be punched into paper tape and the tape read and justified for publication of the journal. If later there is a request for a reprint of an article in either the original or in an edited form, the computer can quickly punch a rejustified tape suitable for printing by any of several techniques. Also, if copy initially comes in the form of paper tape from a news service over a press wire, it can be edited, words and sentences cut or inserted, and the whole rejustified very rapidly with only the need to perforate the changes.

editing and modification, text (time sharing)—*See* time sharing, text editing and modification.

editing, post — A procedure or process of editing the output of a prior operation, especially those related to accounting, or programs which might have syntax or construction errors.

editing subroutine—*See* subroutine, editing.

edit, input (card)—The editing of card input is largely a matter of rearranging information into a form suitable for machine processing. Several of the more common considerations of input editing are the recognition of control holes, recognition of negative indicators, and the recognition and translation of over-capacity punching. Each of these considerations is usually approached in the same fashion, that is, through the use of selectors. Wherever possible, as the card is read the punching positions in question are wired to pick up selectors which are later used to direct the program along different paths, or to cause a sign or a value to be stored.

editor—A routine that performs editing operations.

editor, card—A special subroutine relating to the reading of information contained on punched cards with built-in specific capabilities.

editor, linkage—A standard service routine to convert outputs of assemblers or compilers to forms which can be loaded and executed, by combining separately developed object modules or incorporating all or parts of previously processed load modules into a new load module. The linkage editor also replaces, deletes, or inserts control sections, creates overlay facilities, or restores symbolic cross references between various input modules. Usually, linkage editors are run before programs are ready for load in OS, DOS, or TOS operations, i.e., disk and tape operating systems.

editor, print-punch—*See* print-punch editor.

editor, program—*See* program editor.

editor, routine—*Same as* program editor.

editor, symbolic — Permits the editing of source-language programs by adding or deleting lines of text. All modification, reading, punching, etc., is controlled by symbols typed at the keyboard. The editor reads parts or all of a symbolic tape into memory, where it is available for immediate examination, correction, and relisting.

editor, tape—*See* tape editor.

editor, text (QED)—QED is a generalized text editor that allows the on-line user to create and modify symbolic text for any purpose. User capabilities include inserting, deleting, and changing lines of text; a line-edit feature; a symbolic search feature; automatic tabs, which the user can set; and ten string buffers (some systems).

edit, post—To edit the results of a previous computation.

EDP, (electronic data processing)—Data processing performed largely by electronic equipment. (Related to automatic data processing.)

EDP capability (thin film)—The new thin-film memory computer with its wide range of capabilities is readily adaptable to many typical and specialized applications, such as: tactical data systems; command and control systems; digital communications and switching systems; data reduction and analysis; logistics; scientific computation; traffic control; reservation systems; computation analysis; inventory and scheduling systems; intelligence systems; systems simulation; missile and satellite dynamics; process control; and many others. Thin-film memory computers have resulted in microminiaturization of computer components, greater reliability, speeds, and accuracy. Whole circuits etched on film 1/20th of an inch thick replace hundreds of separate diodes (some systems).

EDP center—A complete complex including one or more computers, its peripheral equipment, personnel related to the operation of the center and its functions, and the office space housing the necessary hardware and personnel.

EDP center manager—*See* manager, computer center.

EDPE—Abbreviation for electronic data processing equipment.

EDPM—Electronic data-processing machine.

EDP management science—The field of management science is extending the computer far beyond the automation of routine accounting operations and into the complex decision-making process of management. Through revolutionary computer-programming techniques such as simulation, the objective, scientific approach of management science is providing increased management capability and control.

In addition to the physical or operational processes like inventory management, product planning and control, resource allocation or market forecasting, this also includes the fiscal processes such as bond management, capital investment, risk analysis, profit planning and product pricing.

Manufacturer's broad resources are prepared to meet management's growing demand for this expanded capability and to extend the tradition of "total systems" capability into revolutionary data-processing techniques and applications.

EDPS—Electronic data processing system.

EDSAC—Abbreviation for electronic discrete sequential automatic computer. The EDSAC was the first operational internal-stored-program computer and was completed in 1949 at the Mathematical Laboratory of the University of Cambridge. The EDSAC had a mercury delay-line storage system with a 512-word capacity, an access time of one millisecond, a word length of 34 bits, an addition time of 1.5 milliseconds, and a multiplication time of 4 milliseconds. An important distinguishing feature from EDSAC's predecessor, the EDVAC, was its comprehensive library of subroutines which were stored on paper tape and could be read into the computer as required.

education of a computer—Preparing and assembling programs for a computer so that it can put together programs for many purposes.

edulcorate—1. To improve by eliminating worthless information. 2. To weed out.

EDVAC—Electronic discrete variable automatic computer. Begun in 1945 at the Moore School of the University of Pennsylvania and designed in part by John Von Neumann. EDVAC was to be the first stored-program computer. The EDVAC replaced plugboards and programming switches with an electrically alterable memory for storing both instructions and numbers to be used in calculation. It also was capable of operating on and changing the stored instructions, thus modifying its own program. Because of engineering difficutlies, ECVAC was delayed and the EDSAC was the first internal-stored program computer to become operational.

effective address—1. A modified address. 2. The address actually considered to be used in a particular execution of a computer instruction. 3. An address obtained by the combination of the contents of a specific index register with the address of an instruction. 4. The address used for the execution of an instruction. This may differ from that of the instruction in storage.

effective byte—The byte actually accessed in an operation on a single byte or byte string.

effective byte location—The actual storage location pointed to by the effective virtual address of a byte addressing instruction.

effective data transfer rate—*See* data transfer rate, average.

effective double-word—*The* double word actually accessed in a double-word operation.

effective double-word location—The actual storage location pointed to by the effective virtual address of a double-word addressing instruction.

effective half-word—The half-word actually accessed in a half-word operation.

effective half-word location—The storage location pointed to by the effective virtual address of a half-word addressing instruction.

effective instruction — *See* instruction effective.

effective operand address—An address obtained at the time of execution by the computer to give the actual operand address.

effective speed — Speed (less than rated) which can be sustained over a significant period of time and which reflects the slowing effects of control codes, timing codes, error detection, retransmission, tabbing, hand keying, etc.

effective time—*See* time, effective.

effective transmisson rate — *Same as* data-transfer rate, effective.

effective-transmission speed — The rate at which information is processed by a transmission facility, expressed as the average rate over some significant time interval. This quantity is usually expressed as average characters per unit of time, or average bits per unit of time.

effective virtual address—The virtual address value after only indirect addressing and/or indexing modifications have been accomplished, but before memory mapping is performed.

effective word—The word actually accessed in an operation on a single word.

effective word location—The storage location pointed to by the effective virtual address of a word-addressing instruction.

efficiency, multiprocessing — *See* multiprocessing efficiency.

efficiency, multiprogramming — *See* multiprogramming, efficiency.

eight level—Any teletypewriter code that utilizes eight impulses, in addition to the start and stop impulses, for describing a character.

eighty-column card—*See* card, eighty column.

EITHER-OR operation—*Same as* gate, OR.

electrical accounting machine (EAM)—The set of conventional punch-card equipment including sorters, collectors, and tabulators. (Clarified by tabulating equipment.)

electrical brushes — The small, sensitive brushes in a punched card reader input device which sense the presence or absence of holes in the card. They issue electrical impulses which are converted into the code used by the computer and sent to the memory for processing or storage.

electrical communications—In electrical communications, a conductor with relatively low electrical resistance; e.g. copper wire is the link between sending and receiving points. These points use a translating device (e.g. telephone) to send and receive the intelligence of the signal.

electrical impulses — The signals coming from card or magnetic tape readers, and other similar devices, which are converted into the code used by the computer and sent to the computer memory for processing or storage.

electrically alterable memory — A memory device whose contents can be revised with electrical signals.

electric delay line—A delay line using properties of lumped or distributed capacitive and inductive elements.

electromagnetic communications — The electromagnetic-wave conductor is space itself. The electromagnetic frequencies available today for communications fall into two categories: Light-beam (laser and maser) communication above the ehf frequency band, and nonlightbeam frequency communications in or below ehf band. The latter devices include radio, television, and radar devices covering the frequency spectrum between vlf and ehf bands. More elaborate translators are required than for electrical communications.

electromagnetic delay line — A delay line whose operation is based on the time of propagation of electromagnetic waves through distributed or lumped capacitance and inductance.

electromagnetic relay — An electromagnetic switching device having multiple electrical contacts that are operated by an electrical current through a coil. It is used to complete electrical circuits with an applied control current, and also as a mechanical binary counter.

electromechanical device—A piece of equipment which is partially electronic and partially mechanical in nature. While the central processing unit is a pure electronic device, most random access equipment involves moving parts, and are therefore electromechanical devices.

electronic—Pertaining to that branch of science which deals with the motion, emission, and behavior of currents of free electrons, especially in vacuum, gas, or phototubes and special conductors or semiconductors. This is contrasted with electric which pertains to the flow of electrons in metal conductors.

electronic calculating punch — A card-punch machine which reads a punch card, performs arithmetic and other operations sequentially, and punches the result in a card.

electronic data processing—*See* data processing, electronic.

electronic data-processing equipment (DP) —A machine, or group of interconnected machines, consisting of input, storage, computing, control, and output devices. It uses electronic circuitry in the main computing element to perform arithmetic and/or logical operations automatically by means of internally stored or externally controlled programmed instructions.

electronic data-processing machine—*See* data processing equipment, automatic.

electronic data-processing system—1. A machine system capable of receiving, storing, operating on, and recording data without the intermediate use of tabulating cards, and which also possesses the ability to store internally at least some instructions for data-processing operations, and the means for locating and controlling access to data stored internally. 2. The general term used to define a system for data processing by means of machines utilizing electronic circuitry at electronic speed, as opposed to electro-mechanical equipment.

electronic data-switching center, automatic —*Same as* automatic data-switching center.

electronic differential analyzer — A form of analog computer using interconnected electronic integrators to solve differential equations.

electronic library—A general purpose library system where the user sits at a computer terminal and calls for viewing on his CRT any author, title, or subject in the card catalogue, or any page of any book in the library. At the press of a button any lines or pages can be printed for him to take home. The tremendous potential of the electronic library can be appreciated if one realizes the materials of several libraries may become available to millions of users through the use of computer utilities.

electronic neuron network simualtion—The study and duplication of neuron cells and networks in order to build multiple-purpose systems using analogous electronic components. Computers have been programmed to act as neuron system simulators, and this type of research holds much potential for the future.

electronics—A branch of science dealing with the motion, emission, and behaviour of currents of free electrons and certain ions, especially those in vacuum tubes, gas tubes, semiconductors, and superconductors.

electronic statistical machine—A sorter which can print and add data while sorting.

electronic stylus—A pen-like device which is commonly used in conjunction with a CRT (cathode-ray tube) for inputting or changing information under program control. The electronic stylus is often called a light pen, and works by signalling the computer with an electronic pulse. The computer acts on these signals and can change the configuration plotted across the tube face or perform other operations using the inputted data according to previously programmed instructions.

electronic switch—A circuit element causing a start and stop action or a switching action electronically, usually at high speeds.

electronic tutor—A teaching machine which makes use of instructions in the computer to help each student achieve his educational goals. Each student communicates with the computer via his own terminal. The computer will be programmed to adjust its teaching style automatically to the needs of each student, and each student will progress at his own pace, independently of others. Bright students will move from topic to topic rapidly, while slower students will be carefully tutored and given extra practice to raise them to the desired achievement levels.

electrostatic printer—A device for printing an optical image on paper, in which dark and light areas of the original are represented by electrostatically charged and uncharged areas on the paper. The paper is dusted with particles of finely powdered dry ink and the particles adhere only to the electrically charged areas. The paper with ink particles is then heated, causing the ink to melt and become permanently fixed to the paper.

electrostatic storage—1. The storage of data on a dielectric surface, such as the screen of a cathode ray tube, in the form of the presence or absence of spots bearing electrostatic charges that can persist for a short time after the electrostatic charging force is removed. 2. A storage device so used. 3. A storage device which uses electric charges to represent data.

electrostatic storage tube—A storage device in which information is stored in the form of a pattern of electric charges. This device is generally a cathode-ray tube.

element—A component part.

element, AND—*Same as* gate AND.

element, anticoincidence—*Same as* gate, exclusive OR.

elementary item—In the COBOL system, a data item containing no subordinate items.

element, code—A discrete condition or event in a code, such as a stroke in a printed character.

element, combinational logic — 1. A device having at least one output channel and two or more input channels, all characterized by discrete states, such that the state of each output channel is completely determined by the contemporary states of the input channels. 2. A logic element used in combinational logic.

element, data—A specific item of information appearing in a set of data; e.g., in the following set of data, each item is a data element: the quantity of a supply item issued, a unit rate, an amount, and the balance of stock items on hand.

element, decision—*See* decision element.

element, digit delay—A specific delay element that introduces a delay in a line of signals or pulses of one digit period duration.

element, equivalent-to—*Same as* gate, exclusive NOR.

element, function—*Same as* element, logical.

element, logic—A device that performs a logic function.

element, logical—The smallest building block in a computer or data-processing system, that can be represented by logical operators in an appropriate system of symbolic logic. Typical logical elements that can be represented as operators in a suitable symbolic logic are the AND gate and the OR gate.

element, majority decision — *Same as* gate, majority decision.

element, NAND—*Same as* gate NAND.

element, negation—*Same as* gate, NOT.

element, nonequivalent—*Same as* gate, exclusive OR.

element, NOR—*Same as* gate, NOR.

element NOT—*Same as* gate, NOT.

element, NOT-AND—*Same as* gate, NAND.

element, OR—*Same as* gate, OR.

element, sequential—A device having at least one output channel and one or more input channels, all characterized by discrete states, such that the state of each output channel is determined by the previous states of the input channels.

element, sequential logic—A unit or device which has at least one output channel and one or more input channels, designed so that the state of each output channel is determined by the previous states of the input channels, or by the previous states and the concurrent states of the input channels.

element, start—The first element of a character in certain serial transmissions, used to permit synchronization. In Baudot teletypewriter operation, it is one space bit.

element, stop—The last element of a character in certain serial transmissions, used to ensure recognition of next start element.

element, threshold—A device capable of performing the threshhold logic operation. This operation involves the general case of a special majority decision.

element, unit — Alphabetical signal element having a duration equal to the unit interval of time.

eleven punch—A punch in position 11 of a column. The X punch is often used to control or select, or to indicate a negative number. Also called an 11-punch.

elimination factor—The ratio in information retrieval, obtained by dividing the number of documents that have not been retrieved by the total number of documents contained in the file.

elimination, zero—The elimination of insignificant zeros (those to the left of a quantity in a field or word) during a printing operation.

EL-punch—A special character punched to indicate the end of a line or the end of a paper tape record.

else, OR—*Same as* gate, OR.

else rule—A catch-all rule in decision tables designed to handle the conditions not covered by exact and explicit rules; it is written by leaving all conditions blank. Action then to be taken may be to halt processing, note the conditon, or to correct the situation and continue processing.

embossed plate printer—The data preparation device, in character recognition, which prints through the paper medium by allowing only the raised character to make contact with the printing ribbon.

emergency switch—Switch on most control panels which will disconnect all power from the computer system.

emitter—A device, usually used on punch-card machines, to give timed pulses at regular intervals during the machine cycle.

emitter, character — An electromechanical device used to generate and emit, in some code, pulse groups corresponding to characters.

emitter, digit—*See* digit emitter.

emitter pulse—Relating to a punched card machine, one of the group of pulses that is used to define a particular row within the columns of a card.

emitter, selective digit—*See* digit emitter, selective.

empirical—Pertaining to a statement or formula based on experience or experimental evidence rather than on mathematical or theoretical conclusions.

empirical documentation — *See* documentation, empirical.

empiric function generator — *See* generator, empiric function.

emulate—The ability of one system to imitate another, with the imitating system accepting the same data and programming and achieving the same results as the imitated system, but possibly with a different time of performance.

emulator—Hardware built into a computer causing the system to accept certain software programs and routines and appear as if it were another system, such as 7094 software running on an IBM 360 computer without translation.

enable—Restoration of a suppressed interrupt feature.

enabled—The condition of an interrupt level wherein the level is not inhibited from advancing from the waiting state to the active state, except for priority considerations.

enable pulse—A digit pulse which aids the write pulse, which together are strong enough to switch the magnetic cell.

enabling signal—A means of allowing an operation to take place.

encipher—*Same as* encode.

encode—1. To apply a code, frequently one consisting of binary numbers, to represent individual characters or groups of characters in a message. (Synonymous with encipher.) 2. To substitute letters, numbers, or characters, usually to intentionally hide the meaning of the message except to certain individuals who know the enciphering scheme. (Synonymous with encipher.)

encoded question—A question set up and encoded in a form appropriate for operating, programming or conditioning a searching device.

encoder—A device capable of translating from one method of expression to another method of expression. For instance in translating a message, "add the contents of A to the contents of B," into a series of binary digits. (Contrasted with decoder and clarified by matrix.)

encoder, exception-item—The exception-item encoder offers the final link in banking's total automation chain. Providing "point of entry" encoding before documents enter a bank's paper flow, the unit eliminates costly disruption caused by nonencoded items in a bank's automated system.

encoding strip—On bank checks, the area in which magnetic ink will be deposited to represent characters.

END—A statement used to indicate the physical end of the source program. This statement is used in both FORTRAN and Assembler language.

end-around carry—The bit carried over from the high-order to the low-order position.

end-around shift—*See* shift, circular.

end data symbol—The representation indicating that no more data will follow this symbol.

end distortion—End distortion of start-stop teletypewriter signals is the shifting of the end of all marking pulses from their proper positions in relation to the beginning of the start pulse.

ending file label—The gummed paper containing a description of the file content, which usually appears at the end of each file and then only once.

ending tape label—The gummed label describing the tape contents which follow all other data on the tape.

end instrument—A device that is connected to one terminal of a loop and is capable of converting usable intelligence into electrical signals, or vice versa. It includes all generating, signal-converting and loop-terminating devices employed at the transmitting and/or receiving location.

end, leading—That particular end of a wire, tape, ribbon, line, or document that is processed first.

end logical leading—If the magnetic tape has been recorded in reverse order from that required for decoding, the first end of the tape for the decoding process is termed the logical leading end as contrasted to the regular leading end.

end mark—1. A code or signal that indicates termination of a unit of information. 2. An indicator to signal the end of a word or the end of a unit of data.

end of data—The signal that is read or generated when the final record of a file has been read or written.

end-of-file—1. Automatic procedures to handle tapes when the end of an input or output tape is reached. A reflective spot, called a record mark, is placed on the physical end of the tape to signal the end. 2. Termination or point of completion of a quantity of data.

End of file marks are used to indicate this point. (Synonymous with EOF.)

end-of-file code—*See* code, end-of-fiile.

end-of-file indicator—A device associated with each input and output unit that makes an end of file condition known to the routine and operator controlling the computer.

end-of-file mark—A code that signals the last record of a file has been read.

end-of-file spot—An area used on the tape to signal the end of the file.

end-of-job (EOJ) card control—The EOJ card returns control to the monitor. The monitor automatically processes any jobs remaining in the card reader. Once processing is initiated, intermixed compilations, assemblies, and executions are processed as they are stacked in the card reader. Additionally, a memory dump may be obtained by placing the memory dump program in the job stack. A special termination card terminates the run and places the monitor in an idle state when no more jobs are in the reader.

end of line—A machine code character which indicates the end or termination of a group of records.

end-of-loop code—*See* code, end-of-loop.

end-of-message—The specific set of characters that indicates the termination of a message.

end-of-message character—*See* character end-of-message.

end-of-record word—The last word of a record on tape. It has a unique bit configuration and may be used to define the end of a record in memory.

end-of-tape marker—*See* marker, end of tape.

end-of-tape or end-of-file routines—Such a routine is part of a tape system's program and is executed when the last record on a reel has been read and processed. It should update the control totals found in the tape label or trailer record, balance and record the record count and any other control totals, rewind the tape, and perform any necessary instruction modification.

end of tape warning—A visible magnetic strip on magnetic tape which indicates that the few feet, oftentimes five, of the tape remain available.

end-of-transmission (EOT) recognition—An incoming transmission may end before the associated input buffer area is filled. For example, if an input buffer area for a particular communication line terminal (CLT) is fifty processor words in length and an incoming transmission ends with the fortieth processor word, there will not be an internal interrupt to signal the system to begin processing this segment of data.

endorser—A particular feature now almost standard on most magnetic-ink character readers (MICRs) which is an endorsement record of each bank after the document has been read.

end printing—The conversion of punched information into bold printing across the end of the card simultaneously with gang punching, summary punching, reproducing, or mark-sensed punching. This is similar to interpreting, and makes possible a quick reference to the card.

end, trailing—The last end of a wire, tape, ribbon, or other item that is processed.

engine, difference — A machine capable of computing mathematical tables automatically. It was built in 1812 by Charles Babbage.

engineering improvement time — See time, engineering.

engineering, service — Service engineering most often provides a complete range of support capability for systems engineering and planning, installation and checkout, maintenance and operator training, contractual preventive maintenance, regional service and parts, factory equipment repair, equipment modernization, rehabilitation, and expansion.

In order to provide every user with continued support in the maintenance and operation of his equipment, field engineers maintain close customer liason through courtesy calls, technical assistance by phone, and provision of the latest engineering and new product bulletins. This close contact permits the accumulation and evaluation of reliability data based upon all systems in the field, a significant factor in designing new equipment and improving the dependability and up-time ratios of customer equipment.

engineering time — The total machine down time necessary for routine testing, good or bad, for machine servicing due to breakdowns, or for preventive servicing measures; e.g., block tube changes. This includes all test time, good or bad, following breakdown and subsequent repair or preventive servicing. (Synonymous with servicing time.)

English, ruly — A form of English in which every word has one and only one conceptual meaning and each concept has one and only one word to describe it. This is a hypothetical language based on English that complies uniformly to a definite set of rules, without exceptions.

ENIAC—The electronic numerical integrator and calculator which was developed in World War II at the University of Pennsylvania. This computer is represented by many historians to be the first all electronic computer. It contained over 18,000 vacuum tubes and continued to operate until 1955.

enter key request—See keyboard entry.

entrance—The position where the control sequence begins or transfers into a program or subroutine.

entropy—1. The measure of unavailable energy in a system. 2. The unavailable information in a set of documents. 3. An inactive or static condition (total entropy).

entry—1. An input received from a terminal device. On receipt, an entry is placed by a control program in an entry block whose address is inserted in a list of entries awaiting processing. 2. A notation written in a stub of a row or in a cell of a decision table. Any row must be in the form of either a limited entry or an extended entry. 3. A statement in a programming system. In general each entry is written on one line of a coding form and punched on one card, although some systems permit a single entry to overflow several cards. 4. A member of a list.

entry and inquiry, keyboard — A technique whereby the entry into and the interrogation of the contents of a computer's storage may be initiated at a keyboard.

entry block—A block of main-memory storage assigned on receipt of each entry into a system and associated with that entry throughout its life in the system.

entry conditions—Various languages or specific conventions of computer centers designate unique entry conditions. They are so specified (often scotch-taped to the computer or entry device) and are in effect a special subroutine or addresses of locations of operands, and links or clock signals.

entry data—The writing, reading, or posting to a coding form or to a terminal or processing medium, of information or instructions, i.e., a datum or item which is usually entered on one line, a single entity of processing.

entry instruction—Usually the first instruction to be executed in a subroutine, i.e., it may have several different entry points each of which corresponds to a different function of the subroutine.

entry, keyboard—See keyboard entry.

entry, manual—See keyboard entry.

entry, page—The point, in flowchart symbols, where the flowline continues from a previous page, due to space limitations on the original or previous page.

entry point—1. Points in most subroutines have specific points or places where control can be transferred and re-entered. The entry point usually corresponds to a new or different function to be performed. 2. Usually the first instruction to be executed in a subroutine or as part of the entry conditions for specific computers or installations. Various subroutines may have a number of different entry points corresponding to different programs, subroutines, or their functions. When an instruction of a subroutine designates a place or point for re-entering, it becomes the re-entry point of the major program.

entry, remote job—The inputting of the job information to the main computing system from a remote device. Frequently abbreviated RJE.

entry time—The time when control is transferred from the supervisory to the application program.

entry unit, remote—An input device, frequently a remote terminal, located at a distance from the central computer. Commonly abbreviated REU.

environment division, COBOL — *See* COBOL environment division.

EOF (end-of-file) — Termination or point of completion of a quantity of data. End-of-file marks are used to indicate this point.

epitome—A concise summary of a document.

equality circuit—*Same as* gate, AND.

equality gate—*Same as* gate, exclusive NOR.

equality unit—*Same as* gate, exclusive NOR.

equalization—The process of reducing frequency and/or phase distortion of a circuit by the introduction of networks to compensate for the difference in attenuation and/or time delay at the various frequencies in the transmission band.

equalizer — A modem or peripheral device designed to compensate for undesired levels of signal strength.

equalizer, delay—A corrective network that is designed to make the phase delay or envelope delay of a circuit or system substantially constant over a desired frequency range.

equal-zero indicator—An internal computer-indicator component which signals "on" if the result of an arithmetic computation is zero.

equation, linear — An equation whose left-hand side and right-hand side are both linear functions of the variables. Such an equation can always be put in the form $f(x, y, z, . . .) = C$, where f is a linear function and C is a constant.

equation solver—A calculating device, usually analog, that solves systems of linear simultaneous nondifferential equations or determines the roots of polynomials, or both.

equations, independent—A set of equations none of which can be expressed as a linear combination of the others. With linear equations, the condition for independence is that the matrix (coefficient columns) shall be nonsingular or, equivalently, have rank equal to the number of equations.

equipment, automatic data-processing—*See* data processing equipment, automatic.

equipment, auxiliary—The peripheral equipment or devices not in direct communication with the central processing unit of a computer.

equipment compatibility — The characteristic of computers by which one computer may accept and process data prepared by another computer without conversion or code modification.

equipment complex—An expression to explain an unusually large mixture or group of computing equipment, or a system designed for a specific purpose, i.e., an example would be a large-scale, very fast computer system for tracking missiles.

equipment, conventional — That equipment which is generally considered to be part of the computer system but which is not specifically part of the computer itself. Various card handling devices, tape handlers, disk units, if not built in to the main frame or wired in would be conventional equipment.

equipment, conversion—The equipment that is capable of transposing or transcribing the information from one type of data-processing medium to render it acceptable as input to another type of processing medium.

equipment, data terminal—The modem, device, or unit at either end of a data communication channel, line, station, or link.

equipment, data-transmission—The communications equipment used in direct support of data-processing equipment.

equipment delayed-output—The equipment that removes the data from the system after processing has been completed or while in process.

equipment, duplex—*See* duplex equipment.

equipment, electronic data-processing (EDP)—A machine, or group of interconnected machines, consisting of input, storage, computing, control, and output devices. It uses electronic circuitry in the main computing element to perform arithmetic and/or logical operations automatically by means of internally stored or externally controlled programmed instructions.

equipment failure—A fault in the equipment, excluding all external factors, that prevents the accomplishment of a scheduled job.

equipment, flip-flop—An electronic or electromechanical device that causes automatic alternation between two possible circuit paths. The same term is often applied to any mechanical operation that is analogous to the principles of flip-flop.

equipment, high-performance — Equipment having sufficiently exacting characteristics to permit its use in trunk or line circuits.

equipment, input—1. The equipment used for transferring data and instructions into an automatic data-processing system. 2. The equipment by which an operator transcribes original data and instructions to a medium that may be used in an automatic data-processing system.

equipment, low-performance — Equipment having insufficient characteristics to permit its use in trunk or link circuits. Such equipment may be employed in subscriber line circuits whenever it meets the line circuit requirements.

equipment misuse error—*See* error, equipment misuse.

equipment, off-line — The peripheral equipment or devices not in direct communication with the central processing unit of a computer. (Synonymous with auxiliary equipment.)

equipment, on-line—Descriptive of a system and of the peripheral equipment or devices in a system in which the operation of such equipment is under control of the central processing unit. Its information reflecting current activity is introduced into the data-processing system as soon as it occurs. Thus, directly in-line with the main flow of transaction processing. (Synonymous with in-line processing and on-line processing.)

equipment, on-premise-standby — A duplicate set of computer system devices located nearby, available for performance of operations in the event of equipment failures and as regards time sensitivity functions of requirements.

equipment, output—The equipment used for transferring information out of a computer.

equipment, peripheral — The auxiliary machines that may be placed under the control of the central computer. Examples of this are card readers, card punches, magnetic-tape feeds, and high-speed printers. Peripheral equipment may be used on-line or off-line depending upon computer design, job requirements and economics. (Clarified by automatic data-processing equipment and off-line equipment.)

equipment, peripheral list—The list of peripheral equipment that is available for most computers includes: standard peripheral equipment; magnetic drums; magnetic tape units; punched card units; high-speed printer; paper-tape subsystems; supervisory console auxiliaries; analog-to-digital and digital-analog converters; electronic printers; displays, plotters, and keysets; multiplexers and switching units; real-time units; mass-storage units; off-line systems; and many others.

equipment, remote—Those units or modules of apparatus which perform prescribed functions remote or distant from the main computer.

equipment, remote-control—The formulating and reformulating apparatus used for performing a prescribed function or functions at a distance by electrical means.

equipment, standby—Automatic data-processing equipment that is not in use and that is available in emergencies, such as machine breakdowns or cases of overload.

equipment, tabulating — The machines and equipment using punch cards. The group of equipment is called tabulating equipment because the main function of installations of punch card machines for some 20 years before the first automatic digital computer was to produce tabulations of information resulting from sorting, listing, selecting, and totaling data on punch cards. This class of equipment is commonly called PCM or tab equipment. (Similar to electrical-accounting machine, clarified by tabulator and EAM.)

equipment, terminal—Data source or data sink equipment such as teletypewriters for input terminals and cathode-ray tube screens for output.

equipment, transmission—That large class of equipment, considered peripheral to the computing equipment, which communicates data rather than computing or processing.

equipment, unit—The hardware or apparatus as contrasted to the programs, routines, or methods of use, i.e., the readily detachable parts of the gear are termed equipment units.

equipment, unit record—*See* record equipment, unit.

equipment, working—The basic or primary set of equipment for modules in which more than one set is available and the other sets are standby equipment in the event of a failure of the working equipment.

equivalence — A logical operator having the property that if P is a statement, Q is a statement, R is a statement, . . ., then the equivalence of P, Q, R, . . ., is true if and only if all statements are true or all statements are false, false otherwise.

equivalence element — *Same as* gate, exclusive NOR.

equivalence gate — *Same as* gate, exclusive NOR.

equivalent binary digits—The number of binary digits required to express a number in another base with the same precision; e.g., approximately $3\frac{1}{3}$ binary digits are required to express in binary form each digit of a decimal number. For the case of coded decimal notation, the number of binary digits required is usually 4 times the number of decimal digits.

equivalent, symbolic—A determination of a combination or pattern of meaningful coding, i.e., using punched holes, magnetic spots, etc.

equivalent-to-element — *Same as* gate, exclusive NOR.

equivocation—Is the measure of the difference between the received and transmitted messages over a channel.

erasability—The ease of removing a printed image, in character recognition, without impairing the surface of the medium.

erasable storage—1. A storage medium that can be erased and reused repeatedly, e.g., magnetic-drum storage. 2. A storage device whose data can be altered during the course of a computation, e.g., magnetic tape, drum and cores. 3. An area of storage used for temporary storage.

erase—To replace all the binary digits in a storage device by binary zeros. In a binary computer, erasing is equivalent to clearing. In a coded-decimal computer where the pulse code for decimal zero may contain binary ones, *clearing* leaves decimal zero while *erasing* leaves all-zero pulse codes.

erase character—*See* character, erase.

erase head—A device on a magnetic tape drive whose sole function is to erase previous information prior to writing new information.

eraser, bulk—A device which erases or destroys the magnetic information on a reel or tape without removing the tape from the reel.

error—1. The general term referring to any deviation of a computed or a measured quantity from the theoretically correct or true value. 2. The part of the error due to a particular identifiable cause, e.g., a truncation error, or a rounding error. In a restricted sense, that deviation due to unavoidable random disturbances, or to the use of finite approximations to what is defined by an infinite series. (Contrasted with mistake.) 3. The amount that the computer or measured quantity differs from the theoretically correct or true value. 4. The amount of loss of precision in a quantity; the difference between an accurate quantity and its calculated approximation; *errors* occur in numerical methods; *mistakes* occur in programming, coding, data transcription, and operating; *malfunctions* occur in computers and are due to physical limitations on the properties of materials; the differential margin by which a controlled unit deviates from its target value.

error, absolute—The magnitude of the error disregarding the algebraic sign, or if a vectorial error, disregarding its direction.

error, balancing—*See* balancing error.

error burst—A group of bits that has two successive erroneous bits always separated by less than a given number (X) of correct bits. Note: the last erroneous bit in a burst and the first erroneous bit in the following burst are accordingly separated by X correct bits or more. The number X should be specified when describing an error burst.

error, call—Too many subroutines have been called by the program. A maximum of fifty subroutines may be called by an object program (some computers).

error character—*See* character, error.

error checking and recovery—Parity is computed or checked on all references to central store. If a parity error occurs, the computer will interrupt to the proper location, an alarm will sound, and the appropriate fault lights will be flashed on the operator's console. For all real-time applications, the system will attempt to recover. Once the computer has satisfactorily recovered, the system will continue normal operation (some systems).

error-checking code — *See* code, error-checking.

error code—1. A specific character that may be punched into a card or tape to indicate that a conscious error was made in the associated block of data. Machines reading the error code may be programmed to throw out the entire block automatically. 2. Illegal control code on a binary card.

error, composition—Errors of composition and consistency are detected as soon as the user enters the offending statement. He may immediately substitute a correct statement.

error control, orthotronic—Unprecedented accuracy of information on magnetic tape is insured by orthotronic control which provides unique orthocorrection—the automatic detection and correction of erroneous data. Inefficient manual intervention and correction is virtually eliminated. Basically, orthotronic control can be compared to the accounting technique of "crossfooting," in which a zero balance in rows and columns of figures confirms accuracy and a nonzero balance indicates an error. When information is written on tape, a special checking digit, called a parity bit, is automatically computed and placed at the end of each of the six frames (rows) of data in an information word. (Honeywell)

error-correcting code — *See* code, error-correcting.

error correction, automatic — A technique, usually requiring the use of special codes and/or automatic retransmission, which detects and corrects errors occurring in transmission. The degree of correction depends upon coding and equipment configuration.

error correction, programmer — When an error is detected from the results of a program, the programmer may cause a print-out which traces step-by-step, the operation of the program on actual data, or he may cause a program dump for analysis and correction.

error-correction routine — A series of computer instructions programmed to correct a detected error condition.

error correction (transmission) — Blocks of data containing transmission errors can be retransmitted correctly. Such retransmission is immediate and fully automatic.

error, data—A deviation from correctness in data, usually an error, that occurred prior to processing the data.

error-detecting and feedback system—A system employing an error-detecting code and so arranged that a signal detected as being in error automatically initiates a request for retransmission of the correct signal.

error-detecting code—*See* code, error-detecting.

error-detecting system—A system employing an error detecting code and so arranged that any signal detected as being in error is (a) either deleted from the data delivered to the data sink, in some cases with an indication that such deletion has taken place, or (b) delivered to the data sink, together with an indication that it has been detected as being in error.

error detection, automatic—*See* error correction, automatic.

error detection, remote computing system—Errors of composition and consistency are detected as soon as the user enters the offending statement. He may immediately substitute a correct statement.

Errors of completeness are discovered when the user signifies that his program is complete (by entering the END statement). Some errors (e.g., invalid subscript value, reference to an undefined variable, arithmetic spills, etc.) can, of course, be detected only during execution. In this case, after a display of the error condition and its location, execution is interrupted and the terminal reverts to ready status. The user then has the option of either immediately correcting his error or proceeding with the rest of his program.

For all syntactic errors, the diagnostic message is specific (in that the variable in error is named, or the column where the error occurred is specified) and often tutorial in suggesting the procedure for obtaining correct results.

error-detection routine—A routine used to detect if an error has occurred, usually without special provision to find or indicate its location.

error detection (transmission)—Transmission errors are detected by parity and long (channel) checks.

error diagnostics—An erroneous statement is printed with the erroneous part of the statement clearly marked. The entire statement is processed, even when an error has been detected, whenever possible. Some compilers will continue to the end of the program. Thus, complete error diagnostics may be obtained in one compilation. The errors are listed on the same device as the source-language listing.

error diagnostics, time sharing—See time sharing, error diagnostics.

error dump, priority — The dumping onto tape, etc., by a priority program of information in storage, so that the cause of an equipment or program error interrupt may be assessed by the analysts.

error dynamic—The error, or part of an error, related to frequency, such as the inadequate dynamic response of some computing device or unit. Similar to drift error.

error, equipment-misuse—A logical equipment assignment has been made that doesn't make sense. For example, assigning the binary paper-tape punch as compiler input, or assigning the card reader as the load-and-go unit would be an equipment misuse. The message is given only as a warning. The assignment is made and the job will proceed normally.

error, external—A file mark has been read or end-of-tape has been sensed during a loading operation.

error, illegal control-message — A control message has been read that is not defined. If the message is typed in, it may be retyped. Otherwise, only the compile or assemble phase of the job is processed and a job error is given.

error, inherent—The error in the initial values, especially the error inherited from the previous steps in the step-by-step integration. This error could also be the error introduced by the inability to make exact measurements of physical quantities.

error, inherited—An error in quantities, carried over from a previous operation, that serves as an initial step in a step-by-step set of operations.

error interrupts—Special interrupts are provided in response to certain error conditions within the central computer. These may come as a result of a programming fault (e.g., illegal instruction, arithmetic overflow), a store fault (parity error) or an executive system violation (attempt to leave the locked-in area or violation of guard mode). These faults have special interrupt locations in central store and are used by the executive system to take remedial or terminating action when they are encountered.

error interrupt (time-sharing) — See time sharing, interrupt capability.

error, loading—The error found in the output of the computer which came about as a result of a change in value of the load which was supplied.

error, loading-location misuse—A loading-location specification was made but no load or execute was specified. The loading location specified was not within the available range of memory. The loading location is assigned as the first available location.

error, machine—A deviation from correct data due to an equipment failure.

error, marginal—Such errors irregularly occur in tapes, and most often disappear simply because the writing is done over a slightly different section of tapes.

error, mark-track—A mark-track error indicates that during the course of the previous block transfer a data-parity error was detected, or one or more bits have been picked up or dropped out from either the timing track or the mark track.

error, matching—An error due to inaccuracy in pairing passive components.

error messages—Messages developed by the program to designate a variety of error types.

error messages, complex utility routines (CUR)—The complex utility routine during the course of its operation performs various checks on the validity of its input. Messages are produced which inform the programmer of the nature of the trouble when any of these checks fail. Some errors are forgivable and CUR attempts to continue to run; others are disastrous and result in bypassing the remainder of the operation cards and aborting the run. These errors will indicate, in general, failures in the hardware or bugs in the system itself. In some instances the additional error messages may be produced by cards missing from an element introduced by an ELT control card (some systems).

error, missing — Subroutines called by the program were not found in the library. The names of the missing subroutines are also outputs.

error, module-parity—Parity is checked (reading) or calculated (writing) on each storage-access module. If a parity error is detected, the module will issue a parity-interrupt signal to the processor to which it is currently attached, and rewrite the word in its correct form to assure against subsequent errors when the word is again referenced.

By running random and "worst case" patterns, the storage diagnostic function of the executive can determine whether the failure is purely transient or associated with a marginal or complete outage of the module.

error, no-job definition—The job did not contain a job-definition control card and could not be processed.

error, overflow—A floating-point arithmetic operation resulted in an overflow condition.

error, parity—Indicates that during a course of the previous block transfer of data a parity error was detected, or one or more bits have never been picked up or dropped out from either the timing track or the mark track.

error, potentiometer loading — Relating to devices used in electromechanical analog computers, the error in output voltage which is caused by a connection of a load to the slider of a potentiometer as a voltage divider, a potentiometer scaler, or a potentiometer-multiplier.

error, program—A mistake made in the program code by the programmer, keypuncher, or a machine-language compiler or assembler.

error, propagated—An error occurring in a previous operation that spreads through and influences later operations and results.

error, quiet—These are errors that occur in manual-mechanical systems and are corrected by competent people close to the system before they spread throughout the process or system.

error range—1. The range of all possible values of the error of a particular quantity. 2. The difference between the highest and the lowest of these values.

error, range-of-balance—1. A range of error in which the maximum and minimum possible errors are opposite in sign and equal in magnitude. 2. A range of error in which the average value is zero.

error rate—The total amount of information in error, due to the transmission media, divided by the total amount of information received.

error rate of keying—Ratio of the number of alphabetic signals incorrectly transmitted to the number or alphabetic signals of the message.

error rate, residual—The ratio of the number of bits, unit elements, characters, and blocks incorrectly received but undetected or uncorrected by the error-control equipment, to the total number that are sent.

error relative—A ratio of the error to the value of the quantity which contains the error, as contrasted to absolute error.

error, resolution—An error due to or caused by the inability of a computing unit to demonstrate changes of a variable smaller than a given increment.

error, rounding—The error resulting from rounding off a quantity by deleting the less significant digits and applying some rule of correction to the part retained. For instance, 0.2751 can be rounded to 0.275 with a rounding error of .0001. (Synonymous with round-off error, and contrasted with truncation error.)

error, round-off—The error resulting from deleting the less significant digit or digits of a quantity and applying some rule of correction to the part retained.

error routine—An error routine provides a means of automatically initiating corrective action when errors occur, such as tape read and write, or disk seek, read, and write. It is executed after the programmed check establishes an error. The error routine should cause the operation to be performed at least one more time (in some cases several). If the error persists, processing is interrupted and the condition is signaled on the console. The operator's instruction manual should include procedures for correction and resumption of processing.

errors, altering—Internal machine generated errors resulting from incorrect data transfer within the machine.

errors, catastrophic—When so many errors have occurred that no more useful diagnostic information can be produced, terminate the compilation.

errors, completeness—Errors of completeness are discovered when the user signifies that his program is complete by entering the END statement. Some errors (e.g., invalid subscript value, reference to an undefined variable, arithmetic spills, etc.) can be detected only during execution. In this case, after a display of the error condition and its location, execution is interrupted and the terminal reverts to READY status. The user then either immediately corrects his error or proceeds with the rest of his program.

errors, completeness (remote-computing system)—Errors of completeness are detected after the user has indicated that his program is complete. All such errors are then extracted and immediately displayed at the terminal in a sequential list. When all the errors have been listed, the user can then individually correct or disregard them before initiating the execution of his completed program. Any disregarded errors, when redetected during execution, are considered as execution errors.

errors, composition (remote computing system) — Typographical errors, violations of specified forms of statements and misuse of variable names (e.g., incorrect punctuation, mixed-mode expressions, undeclared arrays, etc.). Errors of composition are detected as soon as the user enters the offending statement. The system rejects the offending statement, and the user can immediately substitute a correct statement.

errors, consistency (remote-computing system)—Most errors of consistency are detected as soon as the user enters the offending statement. (They may be of inconsistent statements or format.) The system rejects the offending statement and the user can immediately substitute a correct statement. However, some errors of consistency are not immediately detected. The errors are handled in the same manner as errors of completeness and should be considered as such.

errors, correctable—CPU will try to correct the error, print an explanatory message and continue the compilation.

error, select—Signifies that a tape transport unit select error has occurred, such as more than one transport in the system has been assigned the same select code or that no transport has been assigned the programmed select code.

error, sequence—A card is out of sequence with an object program.

errors, execution (remote-computing system)—An execution error of a program statement causes an immediate execution interrupt at the point at which the error is encountered. The error is extracted and displayed at the terminal. The user may then correct the error and resume the execution of his program. If the user chooses to ignore the error and continue the execution, he may do so.

For all syntactic errors, the diagnostic message is specific (in that the variable in error is named or the column where the error occurred is specified) and often tutorial in suggesting the procedure for obtaining correct results.

error, single—An erroneous bit, preceded and followed by at least one correct bit.

errors, instrumentation—Where input into a system is directly from instruments such as pressure gauges, limit checks are imposed to prevent instrumentation errors. If these limits are violated, control may be assumed by a violation subroutine for immediate corrective action.

errors, intermittent—The sporadic or intermittent equipment error which is difficult to detect as the fault may not occur when the diagnostics are run.

error size—Occurs when the number of positions to the left of the assumed decimal point exceeds the corresponding positions in the COBOL data-name field.

errors, operator—Errors made by the terminal operator.

errors, precautionary—CPU prints warning message and continues compilation.

errors, scanning—Scanning errors are said to be precluded by an error-scanning format, that uses five rows of bar codes, and several columns of correction codes. This makes defacement or incorrect reading virtually impossible and the control codes also help regenerate partially obliterated data.

errors, semantic (remote computing system)—Semantic errors are concerned with the meaning or intent of the programmer and are his responsibility. However, he is provided with an extensive set of debugging aids that allow him to manipulate portions of a program when in search of errors in logic and analysis.

errors, solid—An error that always occurs when a particular piece of equipment is used.

errors, static—An error that is independent of the time variable, as contrasted with dynamic error, which depends on frequency.

errors, syntactic—Syntactic errors are considered the responsibility of the system and are further categorized as follows:

Composition—Typographical errors, violations of specified form, of statements and misuse of variable names (e.g., incorrect punctuation, mixed-mode expressions, undeclared arrays, etc.).

Consistency—Statements that are correctly composed but conflict with other statements (e.g., conflicting declaratives, illegal statement ending a DO range, failure to follow each transfer statement with a numbered statement, etc.).

Completeness—Programs that are incomplete (e.g., transfers to nonexistent statement numbers, improper DO nesting, illegal transfer into the range of a DO loop, etc.).

errors, tape (read or write)—In reading or writing a tape, quite commonly the machine will detect an error, and one which will quite possibly not appear again if reading or writing is repeated on the same spot. Various recovery routines are used to correct tape errors in most operations.

errors, transient—A one-time nonrepeatable error.

errors, transmission—Such errors are safeguarded by a dual pulse code that effectively transmits the signals and their complements for a double check on accuracy of message.

errors, uncorrectable—If intent of programmer cannot be determined, the CPU prints a diagnostic message, rejects the clause or statement and continues compilation.

error tape—A special tape developed and used for writing out errors in order to correct them by study and analysis after printing.

error, timing—The program was not able to keep pace with the tape transfer rate or a new motion or select command was issued before the previous command was completely executed.

error, truncation—The error resulting from the use of only a finite number of terms of an infinite series, or from the approximation of operations in the infinitesimal calculus by operations in the calculus of finite differences. It is frequently convenient to define truncation error, by exclusion, as any error generated in a computation not due to rounding, initial conditions, or mistakes. A truncation error would thus be that deviation of a computed quantity from the theoretically correct value that would be present even in the hypothetical situation in which no mistakes were made, all given data were exact, no inherited error, and infinitely many digits retained in all calculations. (Contrasted with rounding error.)

error, unbalanced—Those errors or sets of error values in which the maximum and minimum are not opposite in sign and equal in magnitude, as contrasted to balanced errors, i.e., the average of all the error values is not zero.

error, usage—If prior to a job definition of compile or assemble an equipment usage is declared with a usage control, this error is printed. The job will proceed normally.

error, visual representation—*See* visual-error representation.

escape—The departure from one code or language to another code or language, i.e., the withdrawal from existing pattern.

escape character—*See* character, escape.

escape, general—The withdrawal from one of two or more possible alphabets or data sets. Usually the character immediately following the escape character identifies which alphabet is in force.

escape, locking—That escape from one alphabet in which all characters following the escape character will be from the alternative alphabet, much like shifting while typing.

escape, non-locking—A particular escape in which a specified number of characters, following the escape character, are to be from the alternative alphabet, similar to pressing the shift key for one letter on a typewriter.

ESD—Abbreviation for electrostatic storage deflection.

ESI communications—ESI (externally specified index) allows a number of communications networks to operate concurrently on a pair of I/O channels.

ESI communications control—A feature that provides communications control for systems is ESI (externally specified index). ESI makes it possible to handle a substantial number of communications lines through a single computer channel, using buffers in memory. This buffer control permits other transactions to run without interruption. Communications instructions that involve other memory areas interrupt other programs for a minimum period of time, measured in microseconds, because subsequent instructions are in a "ready" position at all times. Real-time circuitry provides tight, accurate operations in rapid succession, handling a vast number of instructions in real-time, communications, and batch-processing modes simultaneously, or with logical priorities.

ESI control—*See* control, ESI.

ESI real time I/O control—The executive system provides full real-time capability, real-time programs being given access to any and all ESI (externally specified index) equipped input/output channels on the highest priority basis. Interrupts from ESI-equipped channels are handled in a manner which provides expeditious transfer of operation control to the real-time programs insuring against the loss of data and providing the required response time. The executive system controls the dynamic acquisition and release of computer system facilities, providing the real-time programs (as well as other programs) with the ability to acquire or release computer facilities to meet the demands of the current operational environment.

ESS—An abbreviation for electronic switching system. A stored program communications system developed by Bell Laboratories.

EUA (Electrical Utilities Applications)—This program is utilized by various electrical utilities to analyze load flow, short circuit, and transient stability in operations and future systems planning. (CEIR)

EULER—An extension of ALGOL -60, including list processing capabilities.

evaluation and review technique program —*See* program evaluation and review technique (Pert).

evaluation, data — The examination and analysis of data to make an assessment of its inherent meaning, probable accuracy relevancy, and its relation to given situations or context.

evaluation, performance — The analysis in terms of initial objectives and estimates, and usually made on-site, of accomplishments using an automatic data-processing system, to provide information on operating experience and to identify required corrective actions.

even-odd check—*See* check digit, parity.

even parity—*See* odd-even check.

even parity check—*See* check, even parity.

event—An occasion or action that causes data to affect the contents of the files of a business, e.g., purchases, shipments, sales, returns, etc.

event chain—The series of actions that result from an initial event. An example is order processing, inventory adjustment, shipping document preparation, etc., resulting from a sale.

event control block—A unique information (control) block designed to control status of operations which are waiting for a special signal, i.e., processing may be halted until one or more events occur. Usually a WAIT macroinstruction is involved.

event, file—A single-file access, either reading or writing. The processing of an action usually requires one or more file events.

evolutionary operations (EVOP)—A statistical technique useful for improving plant operations by slight perturbation of operating conditions repeatedly over a long period of time.

EVOP—Abbreviation for evolutionary operations.

exceed capacity—The generating of a word or number, the magnitude or length of which is too great or too small to be represented by the computer, such as in an attempt to divide by zero.

except gate—A gate developed due to the presence of a pulse in one or more input lines and the absence of a pulse in one or more input lines.

exception-item encoder — See encoder, exception item.

exception-principle system—An information system or data-processing system that reports on situations only when actual results differ from planned results. When results occur within a normal range they are not reported.

exception reporting—A record of departures from the expected or norm. Often times, maximum or minimum limits are the set parameters and the normal range lies within these end numbers or expectations. Reports that have results which exceed these parameters become the basis for an exception reporting output.

exception scheduling routine — When messages or situations occur that require exceptional action, the exception scheduling routine separates them from the normal scheduling loops or routine. The exception action is performed and the system returns to its normal routine.

excess-fifty — A binary representation in which the decimal number n is represented by the binary equivalent of $(n + 50)$.

excess-fifty representation—A binary number system in which any particular number is represented by the binary equivalent of $n + 50$, i.e., -50 is zero, or 0000000, and all numbers above -50 are then positive binary numbers.

excess three code—See code, excess three.

exchange—To interchange the contents of two storage devices or locations.

exchange, automatic—An exchange in which communication between subscribers is effected, without the intervention of an operator, by means of devices set in operation by the originating subscriber's instrument.

exchange buffering—A technique for input/output buffering which prevents or avoids the internal movement of data. Buffers are either filled, empty, or actively in use, by an input/output device. Exchange buffering relates to distinct areas set aside for work and for buffering.

exchange, central-office—The place where a communication common carrier locates the equipment which interconnects incoming subscribers and circuits.

exchange device, remote computing system—The exchange device controls the flow of information between the computer and the terminals. Characters typed at the terminals are sent to the computer one line at a time via the exchange device. The computer returns an answer to the exchange device, which, in turn, sends it to the proper terminal. The exchange device allows each terminal to send or receive data independent of all other terminals.

exchange, dial—An exchange where all subscribers originate their calls by dialing.

exchange, manual—An exchange where calls are employed by an operator.

exchange, memory—See memory exchange.

exchange, message—A device placed between a communication line and a computer in order to take care of certain communication functions and thereby free the computer for other work.

exchange, storage — Same as memory exchange.

exclusive NOR gate — See gate, exclusive NOR.

exclusive OR, logical — Same as gate, exclusive OR.

exclusive segments—See segments, exclusive.

execute—To carry out an instruction or perform a routine. To interpret a machine instruction and perform the indicated operation(s) on the operand(s) specified.

execute phase—1. The part of the computer operating cycle wherein a command in the program register is carried out upon the address indicated. 2. The act of performing a command.

execution — The processes which are performed by computer devices and circuitry which accomplish a particular instruction or design.

execution controls, program — See program execution controls.

execution cycle—That portion of a machine cycle during which the actual execution of the instruction takes place. Some operations (e.g. divide, multiply) may need a large number of these operation cycles to complete the operation, and the normal instruction/operation alternation will be held up during this time. Also called operation cycle.

execution-error detection — Detection concerned with those errors detected during the execution of the user's program. They include errors that are detectable only during program execution (e.g., invalid subscript value, reference to an undefined variable, arithmetic spills, etc.) along with those errors of completeness detected because either (1) they were disregarded by the user when previously detected or (2) they were not detected in the first place because the user did not indicate that his program was completed.

execution errors, remote-computing—*See* errors, execution (remote computing system).

execution, interpretive — Permits retention of all of the information contained in the user's original source statements, thereby making source-language debugging possible. Interpretive execution, plus multiprogramming, make the conversational mode of operation a practical reality.

execution, looping — *See* looping execution.

execution of an instruction—The set of elementary steps carried out by the computer to produce the result specified by the operation code of the instruction.

execution path—The principal course or line of direction taken by a computer in the execution of a routine, directed by the logic of the program and the nature of the data.

execution, program control — *See* program execution control.

execution time—1. The sum total of the amount of time required to complete a given command. 2. The portion of an instruction cycle during which the actual work is performed or operation executed; i.e., the time required to decode and perform an instruction. (Synonymous with instruction time.)

executive capability, mass-storage — *See* storage, mass (executive).

executive command—A command to the executive program to run a subsystem or symbiont.

executive communications—Provides for all communication between the operating programs and the computer operator, and between the executive system and the computer operator. These communications take place via the computer keyboard and the on-line typewriter. This function includes the interpretation of all keyboard inputs addressed to the executive system and the transfer of control to the section of the executive to which the input pertains.

executive-control language — *See* language, executive-control.

executive control logic, multiprogramming— The specific system is a multiprogram processor and, to initiate or preserve a true multiprogramming environment, the executive system must be in complete control of the total system. Therefore, it is necessary that the system contain sufficient control circuitry to effectively and economically maintain this control.

The multiprogramming capabilities of the system are based upon guard mode operation, the setting aside of certain instructions, registers, and storage locations for the exclusive use of the executive system, assuring maximum protection against the interaction of unrelated programs.

executive control, multiprogramming—Multiprogramming permits many jobs into the computer at the same time—routine jobs,

high-priority real-time jobs, or special jobs— without any increase load on the programmer. The system keeps all programs isolated from one another, preventing the unitentional mixing of "apples and oranges." The executive routine keeps the processor constantly computing on work, constantly turning out answers to problems. There is no central processor in the traditional sense of the word. Instead, the separate and combined functions of three modules—processor, memory, and controller—perform the work of the conventional central processor. The system is memory-oriented, not processor-oriented. This means that data by-passes the processor if it isn't needed there, keeping the processor free for productive work.

executive control system—*See* executive system control.

executive control, utility routines — Utility routines are contained as an integral part of the system. These are programs that are useful for data conversion, editing, etc. A description of the individual utility routines provided with the system is given in the individual write-ups of the utility routines. Utility routines are loaded and executed from the master file by an executive control statement. Frequently used object programs may be added to the system as utility routines. These programs may then be called through from the executive master file.

executive deck — A deck of punched cards containing executive programs, routines, and subroutines.

executive diagnostic system — A comprehensive diagnostic system is available within the executive system to aid the check out of user programs. Both allocation time and compilation or assembly time commands are available to trigger snapshot dumps. Postmortem dumps are also available through the executive control statement.

executive dumping—*See* dumping, executive.

executive facilities assignment — Available facilities and their disposition are indicated to the system as system generation time; therefore, the executive system assigns these facilities, as needed and as available, to fulfill the facilities requirements of all runs. The executive system maintains and continually updates inventory tables that reflect what facilities are available for assignment, and which runs are using the currently unavailable facilities.

executive, FORTRAN II—*See* FORTRAN II executive.

executive guard mode — Guard mode prevents programs from executing any of a set of instructions reserved for the executive. It also protects certain locations reserved for executive operations.

executive instruction—Similar to supervisory instruction, this instruction is designed and used to control the operation or execution of other routines or programs.

executive language control — *See* language, executive-control.

executive logging—*See* logging, executive.

executive program—*Same as* executive routine.

executive, real-time—The executive system is also designed to interface with programs which have real-time requirements. The standard communication subsystem, together with efficient scheduling and interrupt processing features of the executive system, provides an environment satisfactory for any real-time program.

executive real-time system — *See* executive system, real-time.

executive resident—The section of the supervisory program that is always located in core. The resident executive is a permanent resident of core.

executive routine—1. The coordinating, directing, or modifying routine that controls the operations of other routines or programs. 2. A routine that controls loading and relocation of routines and in some cases makes use of instructions which are unknown to the general programmer. Effectively, an executive routine is part of the machine itself. (Synonymous with monitor routine, supervisory routine, and supervisory program.)

executive schedule maintenance—The acceptance of job requests from an external medium and the exclusion of these requests in a job request schedule. Executive will reference the job-request schedule to determine the next job to be initiated. Previously submitted requests may be deleted.

executive supervisor—1. The supervisor is the executive-system component that controls the sequencing, setup, and execution of all runs entering the computer. It is designed to control the execution of an unlimited number of programs in a multiprogramming environment, while allowing each program to be unaffected by the coexistence of other programs. 2. The supervisor contains three levels of scheduling—coarse scheduling, dynamic allocation, and CPU dispatching. Runs entering are sorted into information files, and these files are used by the supervisor for run scheduling and processing. Control statements for each run are retrieved and scanned by the control command interpreter to facilitate the selection of runs for setup by the coarse scheduler.

executive system—1. An integrated collection of service routines for supervising the sequencing of programs by a computer. Operating systems may perform debugging, input/output, accounting, compilation, and storage-assignment tasks. (Synonymous with monitor system.) 2. A fully integrated system that provides for concurrent operation of multiple programs, plus input/output, plus real-time control of a complete, on-demand computer network. The executive system also provides for automatic logging, simul-

taneously establishing an automatic and economical computer-accounting system and simplifying its maintenance.

executive system concurrency — *See* concurrency, executive system.

executive system control—Primary control of the executive system is by control information fed to the system by one or more input devices which may be either on-line or at various remote sites. This control information is similar in nature to present control card operations, but allows additional flexibility and standardization.

executive-system function — The executive system has been designed for operation with a minimum of operator intervention. However, it is recognized that some functions in use are beyond the scope of the executive system, while others demand operator concurrence. In addition, certain information must be presented automatically to the operator, while other information must be available to answer operator requests. Insofar as operator functions are required for a large variety of activities, the executive system apportions these functions into several classes, thus equally dividing operator duties in a multioperator installation.

executive system multiprogramming — The system operates in a multiprogram or multiprocessing environment and to initiate and preserve this, the executive routine must be in complete control of the total system. Special hardware features are provided to permit this control.

The multiprogramming and multiprocessing capabilities of the system are based upon guard mode operation, the setting aside of certain instructions, registers, and storage locations for the exclusive use of the executive routine, assuring protection against the interaction of unrelated programs (some systems).

executive system, real-time—The executive system provides full real-time capability, real-time programs being given access to any and all ESI (externally specified index) equipped input/output channels on the highest priority basis. Interrupts from ESI-equipped channels are handled in a manner that provides expeditious transfer of operation control to the real-time programs insuring against the loss of data and providing the required response time. The executive system controls the dynamic acquisition and release of computer system facilities, providing the real-time programs (as well as other programs) with the ability to acquire or release computer facilities to meet the demands of the current operational environment (some systems).

executive system routine—A routine that automatically accomplishes the execution of program runs in compliance with a predetermined computer schedule. In this capacity, the executive routine extracts the programs that are to be executed, positions them in their operating locations, assigns input/output peripheral equipment, provides for the time sharing of several programs running concurrently, and provides special checking features for the job programs.

executive system utilities—Included within the utilities section of the executive system are diagnostic routines, program file manipulation routines, file utility routines, and cooperative routines for aiding the user in performing such functions as reading cards, printing line images on a printer, transferring files from device to device, and carrying out housekeeping junctions required for file-residence on mass-storage devices.

executive termination—The normal or abnormal termination of an operating program and the return of its assigned facilities to an available status. Termination may be initiated by executive program, by the job program, or by the operator.

executive, time-sharing — *See* time sharing, executive.

exerciser, macro—The repeated operation of supervisory programs and other macroinstructions under a variety of conditions to find any program errors.

exit—1. The time or place at which the control sequence ends or transfers out of a particular program or subroutine. 2. A way of momentarily interrupting or leaving a repeated cycle of operations in a program.

exit macroinstruction—1. A supervisory program macroinstruction that is the final instruction in an application program, signifying that processing is complete. The supervisory program takes the needed action such as releasing working storage blocks to return control to other processing. 2. The final macroinstruction in an application program that releases storage — including the message reference block—and resets associative conditions of the transaction if needed.

exit, page—The point in flowchart symbols where the flowline continues to a following page due to space limitation of one page.

exit point—The instruction which transfers control from the main routine to the subroutine.

exjunction gate—*Same as* gate, exclusive OR.

exponent—A number placed at the right and above a symbol in typography to indicate the number of times that symbol is a factor; e.g., 10 to the 4th (10^4) equals $10 \times 10 \times 10 \times 10$, or 10,000.

exponent, biased—In floating point number systems, some systems bias the exponent by a constant so that all exponents become positive, e.g., 10^{-50} becomes 10^0 and 10^{50} becomes 10^{100}.

exponential smoothing—This is a statistical technique for predicting future demands based on current and past demands activity

without storing and saving masses of past history data.

exponentition—A specific mathematical operation denoting increases in the base number by a factor as previously selected.

expression—1. A valid series of constants, variables, and functions that may be connected by operation symbols and punctuated, if required, to cause a desired computation. 2. Any symbol representing a variable or a group of symbols representing a group of variables possibly combined by symbols representing operators in accordance with a set of definitions and rules.

expression, algebraic—*See* algebraic expression.

expression, arithmetic—An expression containing any combination of data-names, numeric literals, and named constants, joined by one or more arithmetic operators in such a way that the expression as a whole can be reduced to a single numeric value.

expression, conditional — In the COBOL language, an expression that has the particular characteristic that taken as a whole, it may be either true or false, in accordance with the various rules.

expression, relational—In the COBOL language, an expression that describes a relationship between two terms. For example, A is less than B.

expressions, conditional — In list processing languages (LISP), conditional expressions are the means used to test conditions and act according to the result of the test.

expressions, logical—*See* logical expressions.

extended area service—An exchange service at a somewhat higher service rate but without toll charges for an area with a community of interest.

extended precision—A real number requiring three words of core storage. The maximum precision of the mantissa is 2,147,483,647.

extended time scale—*See* time scale.

extension character — *See* code extension character.

extension character code — *See* code extension character.

extension register—A 16-bit register treated as an extension of the accumulator register. This register is used to hold the remainder after a division operation and couple to the accumulator to hold the product in a fixed point multiply operation.

extent — Various physical locations in mass storage devices related to volume allocations for use by specific data sets, i.e., extent of data sets.

external clocking—*See* data set clocking.

external data reference time sharing — *See* time sharing, external data reference.

external delay—*See* delay, external.

external device (ED) address—The ED address specifies which external device a particular instruction is referring to. Scores of different external devices can be specified.

external device code—*See* code, external device.

external device communication — *See* communication, external device.

external device control (EXD)—External device action occurs only as a result of a computer external device instruction. The amount of data transferred and the memory locations employed are previously determined by computer. The only other time when the scanner stops scanning for interrupt requests is during an EXD instruction. The EXD instruction uses the same address lines as the scanner on a time sharing basis. Whenever an EXD instruction occurs, the scanner is stopped and switched off the cable lines, and the address from the EDCW (External Device Control Word) is switched onto the lines. The process is reversed at the end of the EXD instruction.

External devices respond with both their busy status and their interrupt request status whenever they recognize their own address. They do not clear out an interrupt request until the interrupt succeeds. The CPU notifies an external device that it has been recognized by sending out an interrupt that has been recognized (some systems).

external device, data flow—The transfer of data between external devices and their associated assembly registers proceeds under the control of the external device. Input/output channels may transfer data simultaneously in multichannel operation. The access to main memory from the in/out channel is made available as needed, subject to channel priority. This is provided by channel priority logic which selects the channel of highest priority requesting transfer, that is, the lowest numbered channel requesting transfer of data. The data rate and channels active are not restricted except that the program must not require data transfer which exceeds a peak word rate considered over all input/output channels.

external-device interrupts—External-device interrupts may occur for any of several reasons. An external device may interrupt when it has completed an operation if it was told to do so by the program when the operation was initiated. An external device may interrupt at a different address to indicate that a failure (parity fail, end of tape, etc.) has occurred. Different devices have different failure conditions and different failure interrupt addresses. An external device may be notifying the program that some specific real-time event has occurred.

external device operands—The program instructs external devices by using the EXD instruction which has the same format as other computer instructions, but may have more than one operand. The last operand of the EXD instruction is the external device control word (EDCW). (Some systems.)

external device, operation code—*See* operation code, external device.

external device response—When an external device recognizes its address and is not busy, it sends a response on the not-busy line to the processor. If no such response is received, the processor will assume that the addressed device is busy. The processor will send a start signal only if a not-busy response is received. If a device is disconnected, it will appear to be busy to the computer.

external devices, instruction—The computer sends instructions to external devices which tell those devices to initiate special operations. After an external device operation has been initiated, all control of events passes to the logic associated with that external device until the operation is completed. During the operation the external device will respond busy to attempts by the processor to initiate further operations. The sequencing of events during this operation derives its timing from the external devices and its logic.

external device start—The ED start signal occurs if the specified external device is not busy, the channel the specified external device is connected to is not busy, and Bit 16 of the EDCW (external device control word) is a "O." The ED start signal is transmitted from the central processor to the specified external device and initiates the specified operation (ESI). (Some systems.)

external device status — External devices respond with both their busy status and their interrupt-request status whenever they recognize their own address. They do not clear out an interrupt request until the interrupt succeeds. The processor notifies an external device that its interrupt has been recognized by sending out an interrupt reset signal.

external error—A file mark has been read or end-of-tape has been sensed during a loading operation.

external, interrupt inhibit—The bit, in the program status double-word, that indicates whether (if 1) or not (if 0) all external interrupts are inhibited.

external interrupts—External interrupts are caused by either an external device requiring attention (such as a signal from a communications device), console switching, or by the timer going to zero.

external interrupt status word — A status word accompanied by an external interrupt signal. This signal informs the computer that the word on the data lines is a status word; the computer, interpreting this signal, automatically loads this word in a reserved address in core memory. If the programmer or operator desires a visual indication of the status word, it must be programmed.

external labels—Labels are normally defined in the same program in which they are used as operands. However, it is possible to define a symbol in one program, use it in a program assembled independently of the first program, and then execute both programs together.

externally specified index operation (ESI)— Each I/O channel has the capability of operating in the externally specified index (ESI) mode. The ESI mode in conjunction with a standard communications subsystem expands the capabilities of an I/O channel to allow up to 128 communications facilities to communicate simultaneously through any I/O channel with some computers. In this mode, each device multiplexed to an I/O channel tells the computer where its associated access-control word is located in central store. The access-control word directs the computer where to store or extract a word of data.

externally stored program—Programs with instruction routines that are set up in wiring boards or plugboards for manual insertion in older models or small-scale processors.

external memory—1. The storage of data on a device that is not an integral part of a computer, but in a form prescribed for use by the computer. 2. A facility or device, not an integral part of a computer, on which data usable by a computer is stored, such as off-line magnetic-tape units or punch-card devices. (Contrasted with internal storage.)

external reference—A distinct reference to a single variable from a range, or an item which is not defined in the particular program, segment, or subroutine. A linkage editor, or a linking load usually integrates various independently written routines which are united before execution. The assembler must be informed that an external symbol is being used to avoid an error condition.

external registers — These registers, which can be referenced by the program, are located in control store as specific addresses. These are the locations (registers) which the programmer references when he desires that some sort of computational function be carried out.

external sense and control lines — See sense and control lines, external.

external signal interrupt—See interrupt, external signal.

external signals—See signals, external.

external sort—The second phase of a multiphase sort program, wherein strings of data are continually merged until one string of sequenced data is formed.

external storage—See storage, external.

external symbol—See symbol, external.

external symbol dictionary (ESD)—Part of a load module which contains the names and address locations within a module of all entry points and specific locations that are accessible by name from outside the module; external symbols also include control section names. The ESD also contains external references, or the names of symbols not defined within this load module.

extract—1. To copy from a set of items all those items which meet a specified criterion. 2. To remove only a given set of digits or characters occupying certain specified locations in a computer word, such as extract the 8, 9, and 10 binary digits of a 44-bit word, as specified by the filter. (Clarified by filter.) 3. To derive a new computer word from part of another word, usually by masking. (Related to unpack.)

extract instruction—An instruction that requests the formation of a new expression from selected parts of given expressions.

extraction—The reading of only selected portions of a record into storage.

extractor—A machine word that specifies which parts of another machine word are to be operated on, thus the criterion for an external command. (Synonymous with mask, and clarified by extract.)

extraneous ink—Ink deposited on a computer printout that is not confined to the printed characters themselves.

extremity, routine — This routine is used when initiating a new tape or when reaching the end-of-reel of a multireel file. This routine need not be included in memory if all tapes are set-up or initiated automatically by the system supervisor and the open or close macros are not used. The importance of this routine is that it performs necessary tape housekeeping, checks on the operator, and provides necessary information concerning the program being run.

F

F—A subscript symbol which designates "final."

face—In optical character recognition (OCR), a character style with given relative dimensions and line thicknesses. (Contrasted with type font.)

face, inner—The face of a magnetic or punched paper tape facing, in contact with

the reading, writing, punching, or sensing head.

face, outer—The face of a magnetic punched paper tape facing away and not in contact with the reading, writing, punching, or sensing head.

facilities, data storage — See data storage facilities.

facilities, macroassembler — *See* assembler, macrofacilities.

facility assignment (executive)—The assignment of memory and external facilities to meet the requirements which are defined symbolically in a job program selected for initiation. Executive maintains a list of all allocatable facilities which is updated to reflect assignment of facilities to newly initiated programs, and to reflect release of facilities by programs during, or at termination of, a run.

facility compare—The ability of a machine to execute set instuctions depending upon the outcome of various possible combinations.

facility, hold — The ability of a computer, when its calculations are interrupted, to keep the current value of all the variables.

facsimile—A commercial method of transmitting images by electrical means developed by American Telephone and Telegraph. The images may be in the form of letters, pictures, diagrams, and maps.

facsimile posting—*See* posting, facsimile.

FACT (Fully Automatic Compiling Technique) — A Honeywell business-data processing compiler that provides for easy and uniform handling of all aspects of data processing, including input editing, sorting, processing of variable-length records, and repórt writing.

fact correlation—A process which is an integral part of linguistic analysis and adaptive learning which uses methods of manipulating and recognizing data elements, items, or codes to examine and determine explicit and implicit relations of data in files, i.e., for fact retrieval rather than document retrieval.

factor—A number used as a multiplier, so chosen that it will cause a set of quantities to fall within a given range of values.

factor blocking—The limit of the data records which can be contained in a given block on tape.

factor, elimination—The ratio in information retrieval, obtained by dividing the number of documents that have not been retrieved by the total number of documents contained in the file.

factor, nonretrieval—The ratio developed by dividing the difference between the number of documents retrieved and the number of relevant documents retrieved, i.e., a measure of the efficiency of the informational retrieval system. A zero would be optimum.

factor, omission—A ratio developed by dividing the number of nonretrieved documents by the total number of relevant documents in the file, i.e., zero would be perfection.

factor, packing—*See* packing density.

factor, pertinency — The ratio obtained by dividing the total number of relevant documents retrieved by the total number of all documents retrieved. The retrieval of the nonrelevant documents is due to several fac-tors, among them the user's poor definition in developing his inquiry, or the system's problems in recognizing the inquiry. The pertinency factor would be 1 if perfect, and demonstrates the systems ability to cope with its users.

factor, scale—*See* scale factor.

factory data collection—*See* data collection stations.

fact retrieval — The automatic recognition, selection, interpretation, and manipulation of words, phrases, sentences, or any data in any form, but particularly in a textural structure, and the relating of these data for conclusions and useful results.

fading—The variation of radio-field intensity caused by changes in the transmission medium.

fading, flat—That type of fading in which all components of the received radio signal simultaneously fluctuate in the same proportion.

fading, selective—Fading which affects the different frequencies within a specified band unequally.

fail, pick-up—A lamp that glows when none of the stations respond to the invitation to send. After 5 seconds a disconnect sequence starts, which extinguishes the lamp.

fail-safe system—A system which continues to process data despite the failure of parts in the system. Usually accompanied by some deterioration in performance.

fail, softly—In case of equipment failure this is a procedure in which the program schedules the system to fall back to a degraded mode of operation, rather than let the system fail completely with no response to the user. Fail softly is also called graceful degradation.

fail soft, time sharing—*See* time sharing, fail soft.

failure, catastrophic—A failure which is total or nearly so, such as: breakdown of the power supply, making all circuits inoperative. Any type of failure which renders the useful performance of the computer to zero.

failure, equipment—A fault in the equipment causing improper behavior or preventing a scheduled task from being accomplished.

failure, incipient—An equipment failure that is about to occur.

failure, induced — An equipment failure caused by the environment around the failed item.

failure logging — An automatic procedure whereby the maintenance section of the monitor, acting on machine-check interrupts (immediately following error detection), records the system state. This log is an aid to the customer engineer in diagnosing intermittent errors.

failure, mean-time-to—The average time the system or a component of the system works without faulting.

failures, mean-time-between — The special limit of the ratio of the operating time of equipment to the number of observed failures as the number of failures approaches infinity.

fallback—A condition in processing when special computer or manual functions must be employed as either complete or partial substitutes for malfunctioning systems. Such procedures could be used anywhere between complete system availability and total system failure.

fallback, double—A procedure to circumvent error that has two procedures, or can contend with two separate equipment failures.

fallback, double failure, mean-time-to—The average time the system or a component of the system works without faulting.

fallback procedure — A procedure to circumvent all equipment faults. The fallback may give degraded service and may include switching to an alternate computer or to different output devices and so on.

fallback, recovery—The restoration of a system to full operation from a fallback mode of operation after the cause of the fallback has been removed.

false add—This is addition without carries; the performance of a logic add.

false code—See character, illegal.

false code check—See check, forbidden combination.

false drop—An unwanted reference which does not pertain to the subject.

false retrievals—Library references that are not pertinent to, but are vaguely related to, the subject of the library search, and are sometimes obtained by automatic search methods.

fan-in—The maximum number of ON gate terms that can be used to drive an input. Generally the terms cannot all be simultaneously true.

fan-out—The number of circuits which can be supplied with input signals from an output terminal of a circuit or unit. The changes of digital circuits depend basically on the number of devices that can drive or be driven by one circuit of a specific type, and the number of elements that one output can drive is related to the power available from the output and the amount of power required for each input.

FAP—(Fortran Assembly Program) —A procedure-oriented software system.

FAST (Flexible Algebraic Scientific Translator —Translates complex statements into basic language, saving the tedious task of absolute programming. FAST offers the ability to write a source program in an algebraic format. The source program is entered by means of punched cards, the translation is made, and the program is executed, all in one computer run. The output is composed of a listing of the program, any error comments, and the result of the program's execution. (NCR)

fast-access information retrieval — See retrieval system, fast access.

fast-access storage—The section of the entire storage from which data may be obtained most rapidly.

faster access memory—Various storage media which obtain or release data faster through the use of two or more differing storage devices or media. For example, magnetic core storage is the faster access memory in equipment where both magnetic core storage and magnetic disk storage are built in.

fast-time scale—The ratio of computer time (interval between two events in a simulation) to the problem time (physical system time), when greater than one, is said to be an extended time scale, or slow-time scale. When the ratio is less than one, it is said to be on a fast-time scale. When the ratio is not constant during a run, it is said to be on a variable-time scale. If the ratio is equal to one, it is a real-time system.

fault—A physical condition that causes a device, a component, or element to fail to perform in a required manner, e.g., a short circuit, a broken wire, an intermittent connection.

fault-location problem—A problem for identification or information regarding faulty equipment. It is designed and used to identify the location or type of fault and is often part of a diagnostic routine.

fault, pattern-sensitive—A fault that appears in response to some particular pattern of data.

fault, permanent—Faults are failures in performance in the manner required or specified. Sporadic faults are intermittent while permanent faults are repetitious, but these may either escape attention when they do not result in failure to perform some particular tasks, or are known and easily correctable.

fault processing, time-sharing — See time sharing, fault processing.

fault, program-sensitive—A fault that appears in response to some particular sequence of program steps.

faults, intermittent—Same as faults sporadic.

faults, sporadic—Faults are failures in performance in the manner required over specified conditions, and sporadic faults are intermittent faults.

fault time—See time, down.

fax—Transmission of pictures, maps, diagrams, etc. by radio waves. The image is scanned at the transmitter and reconstructed at the receiving station. (Synonymous with facsimile.)

F-conversion — One of the three types of FORMAT specification in FORTRAN. F-conversion is used to convert floating-point data for I/O operations.

feasibility study—1. Usually the initial procedures and criteria for determination of suitability, capability, and compatability of computer systems to various firms or organizations. A preliminary systems analysis of potential costs savings and new higher level of operations, decision making, and problem-solving capacity as a result of computer procurement. 2. A study in which a projection of how a proposed system might operate in a particular organization is made to provide the basis for a decision to change the existing system.

feasible solution—A solution to the constraint equations in which all variables satisfy their sign restrictions.

feature, checking — Some computers have various built-in capabilities to automatically check their own performance. This is a feature of the particular machine.

feature, multi-reading—With the utilization of storage, cards are read once only and data is read out of storage on the following cycles, thus avoiding separate cycle reading for each line of print.

feed—1. To supply to a machine the material to be operated upon. 2. A device capable of feeding, as in definition 1.

feedback—1. The use of parts or all of the output of a machine, process, or system, as input for another phase, as when used for self-correcting purpose. Such feedback systems or programs use the process of continual comparisons of output with input to make necessary corrections. The feedback system is considered self-correcting if it is a closed loop. 2. The feeding back of part of the output of a machine, process, or system to the computer as input for another phase especially for the self-correcting or control purposes.

feedback and reports (factory)—Feedback is an all-important aspect of the system. Feedback of factory data is collected and analyzed weekly to control and predict stock requirements. Purchase-order receipts, assembly-labor vouchers, and fabrication-labor vouchers are collected and returned to where they are used to update master open-order records. After the feedback data is checked for validity by the computer, it is compared against master records to adjust inventory balances. The receipt of "first operation vouchers" reduces raw-material balances by the amount applied to parts. Last-operation vouchers add to stock on hand for parts and also reduce open-order quantities. A raw-material status report is printed weekly to show usage and balance on hand. Reports are prepared weekly based on feedback data to show labor by individual, labor by area, and labor by shop order. This data also becomes input to the accounting system. A report on rework, extra work, and scrap losses is prepared by reason code. This data also becomes input to the accounting system.

feedback control—A type of system control obtained when a portion of the output signal is fed back to the input in order to obtain a desired effect.

feedback control signal—That portion of the output signal which is returned to the input in order to achieve a desired effect, such as fast response.

feedback system, error-detecting—See error detecting feedback system.

feed, card—A mechanism that moves cards serially into a machine.

feed holes—See holes, feed.

feed horizontal—That particular attitude in which a card is placed in the hopper and enters and traverses the card track.

feeding—A system used by character readers in character recognition, in which each individual input document is issued to the document transport at a predetermined and constant rate.

feeding, cyclic—A system used by character readers, in which each individual input document is issued to the document transport at a predetermined and constant rate.

feeding, form—The rapid, accurate positioning of document forms on a teleprinter or business machine.

feeding, multicycle — A specific method of processing punched cards, during which several fields of an individual card are read in succession on successive machine cycles, e g., multiread feeding, achieves the result by feeding the same card past the reading station several times.

feeding, multiread—The feeding of punched cards in a manner causing several fields of a single card to be sensed sequentially.

feeding, single-sheet—The feeding of individual sheets of paper rather than roll or fan-folded form.

feed pitch—See pitch, feed.

feed punch, automatic—See punch, automatic feed.

feed reel—A specific reel from which tape is unwound during the processing.

feed, tape—A mechanism that will feed tape to be read or sensed.

feed track—The track of a paper tape which contains the small feed holes for the sprockets.

FEP (IBM 1620 Financial Evaluation Program) — The Financial Evaluation Program provides a computerized method for performing economic evaluations. The program, which is structured on the discounted cash flow method, provides a tool for the realistic evaluation of capital investment and associated investment expenses by considering tax impact, inventory carrying costs and turnover rates, manpower dollars, income, etc. Program flexibility is achieved by using control card input of the constants required in the evaluation. (IBM)

fetch—1. That portion of a computer cycle during which the location of the next instruction is determined, the instruction is

taken from memory and modified, if necessary, then entered into the control register.
2. To obtain a quantity of data from a place of storage.

F-format — A fixed-length logical record format. Sizes of logical records for data management are related to the contents. A data set has F-format logical records if nearly all of the logical records are of identical length. In FORTRAN, the F-format is an input/output specification detail. In PL/1 an F-format is also an I/O format specification similar to FORTRAN.

Fibonacci number—*See* Fibonacci search.

Fibonacci search—A search based on dichotomy and developed in such a way that in each step, the original set or the remaining subset, is subdivided in accordance with successive smaller numbers in the specific Fibonacci series. When the number of items in such a set is not equal to a Fibonacci number, the number of items in the set is assumed to equal the next higher Fibonacci number.

Fibonacci series (sorting)—When the number is equal to the sum of the two preceding numbers, i.e., 1, 2, 3, 5, 8, and so on. Some sort programs distribute strings of data onto work tapes so that the number of strings on successive tapes form a Fibonacci series.

field—1. A set of one or more characters (not necessarily all lying on the same word) which is treated as a whole; a set of one or more columns on a punched card consistently used to record similar information.
2. A specified area of a record used for a particular category of data; e.g., a group of card columns used to represent a wage rate, or a set of bit locations in a computer word used to express the address of the operand.
3. The data which is contained in two or more adjacent core positions and which will be treated as a unit. A flag bit is used to designate the high-order position of the field.

Fieldata—Relates to a family of automatic data processing equipment designed and built to be used in the field by the U.S. Army and militarized, rugged, and mobile. Includes such Fieldata programs as: DYSEAC, FADAC, Basicpac, Compac, and the Mobidic series of systems as applied to control and command plus logistics, intelligence, and fire direction.

field, card—A set of card columns, either fixed as to number and position, or if variable, then identifiable by position relative to other fields. Corresponding fields on successive cards are normally used to store similar information.

field, common—A field accessible to two or more routines.

field, control—*See* control field.

field control (sorting) — A card which is used to specify the parameters for a sort.

field, decrement—A portion of an instruction

word specifically set aside for modifying the contents of a register or storage location.

field, fixed—A given field on punch cards, or a given number of holes along the edge of an edge-punched card set aside for the recording of a given type or classification of information.

field, free — A property of information-processing recording media that permits recording of information without regard to a preassigned or fixed field; e.g., in information-retrieval devices, information may be dispersed in the record in any sequence or location.

field length—The physical extent of a field. On a punch card it refers to the number of columns. On a tape it refers to bit positions.

field mark—A symbol used to indicate the beginning or the end of some set of data, i.e., group, file, record, block. In this case a particular field.

field, multiply—A field used to hold the results of the multiplication operation.

field name—A symbolic name a programmer gives to a specific field of data. During assembly, this field is assigned an absolute address.

field, operand—The portion of an immediate-addressing instruction word that contains the immediate operand value, with negative values represented as two's complements.

field, operating code—The portion of an instruction word that contains the operation code.

field, operation—That particular part of the instruction format which specifies the procedure or process which is to be performed.

field, register address—The portion of an intsruction word that contains a register address.

fields, assembly-language—A language processor that accepts words, statements, and phrases to produce machine instructions. It is more than an assembly program because it has compiler powers. The macroassembler permits segmentation of a large program so that portions may be tested separately. It also provides extensive program analysis to aid in debugging.

field-selected length—The design of a fixed number of characters for each word, element, or field by determining how and what to fill out in shorter data items with zeros and blanks. Initial assignment of an item during the design of punched card, tape, or other input layout.

field selection—The ability of computers to isolate a particular data field within one computer word (or even in two, three, or four words) without isolating the entire word.

field shifting—The adjustment of the address of a field to realign the item of data.

field, signed—A field that has a plus- or minus-character coding over the units position to designate the algebraic sign of the entire number.

field, variable-length—A data field that may have a variable number of characters. This requires item separation to indicate the end of each item.

fifo—First-in first-out. A description of one method used in taking items from a list.

figurative constant—One of several constants which have been "prenamed" and "predefined" in a COBOL processor so that they can be written in the program without having to be described in the data division.

figures shift—A function performed by a teletypewriter machine that causes the machine to shift to upper case for numbers, symbols, etc., when initiated by the figures-shift character.

figures, significant — Digits of a numeral which have specific meanings for particular purposes. Digits which must be kept to preserve a distinct accuracy. Digits which may not be rounded off without losing accuracy or desired precision.

file—1. A collection of related records treated as a unit; e.g., in inventory control, one line of an invoice forms an item, a complete invoice forms a record, and the complete set of such records forms a file. 2. The word file is used in the general sense to mean any collection of informational items similar to one another in purpose, form, and content. Thus, a magnetic-tape master file is a file. The term may also be applied to a punched-paper tape of input items, or if convenient, to a set of cards which is equivalent in nature to a magnetic or a paper tape. File may even be applied to an accumulation of information in the processor memory, if the need arises to refer in a general way to this collection of data.

file, active—A file which is being used in which entries or references are made on a current basis.

file activity ratio—A ratio pertaining to the number of file elements in which changes or transactions are made during a specific updating run or in a given period, to the total number of records or elements in the file. If out of a total of 100 records, 20 are updated in a specific month, the activity ratio is thus 20% for this file.

file address checking program—A program to check addresses when macros instruct to write on the file, to see that the program is not writing on the wrong area.

file addressing — Some data records have a particular key or code which identifies the data. When the program is given this key it can locate and use the data at the particular file address.

file addressing pockets—In a random file, a small area or pocket in which one or more records are kept—an economical method of holding a small number of records.

file addressing, randomizing—The location of a record in a random-access file is lo-cated by means of a key set of characters that identify the file. The key is converted to a random number and the random number is converted to the address where the item may be stored. If the item is not in this pocket, an overflow pocket, chained to the first pocket, will be searched.

file analysis—The examination, study, and resolution of file characteristics to determine similarities, number and type of redundancies, and to check labeling and listing of documents which affect file and data elements contained in files.

file, chained — To conserve searching time and space, some computer files are in chains. Each data item or key in a record in the chain has the address of another record with the same data or key. To retrieve all data which contain the given key, only the first address need be found, since the next address is adjacent to it, and that one is adjacent to the next, etc.

file, change—A list of transactions processed against the master file.

file checks, magnetic tape—Hardware checks for faulty tapes without loss of computer time or manual intervention.

file composition—The filing of records within a storage unit.

file conversion—The transformation of parts of records, customer account records, employee records, and the like from their original documents into magnetic files by the computer.

file, dead—A file that is not in current use but is retained.

file density, trailer record—A process used in cases involving identification numbers which match the disk-file addresses.

file, destination—A CRAM deck or magnetic tape designated to receive the file of information that is output from a computer run.

file, detail—A file of information that is relatively transient. This is contrasted with a master file which contains relatively more permanent information; e.g., in the case of weekly payroll for hourly employees, the detail file will contain employee number, regular time, and overtime, the hours such employee has worked in a given week, and other information changing weekly. The master file will contain the employee's name, number, department, rate of pay, deduction specifications, and other information which regularly stays the same from week to week.

file, end—*See* code, end of file.

file event—A single-file access, either reading or writing. The processing of an action usually requires one or more file events.

file feed — An extension device which increases the punch card capacity of the feed hopper peripheral devices.

file, fixed length—*See* record, fixed length.

file, fixed length record—*See* record, fixed length.

file gap—An interval of space or time to indicate or signal the end of a file.

file identification—The coding required to identify each physical unit of the outputs of electronic data-processing machine runs.

file inactive—A previously active file that, although not currently in use, is expected to be restored to an active status.

file, index—*See* index file.

file index, disk—A table of keyfields identifying the actual disk records in another permanent disk file.

file, inverted—A file containing item labels placed in a single record identified by a label describing the contents of the documents.

file label—A set of alphanumeric characters that uniquely identify the contents of a particular roll of magnetic tape or a portion of a roll of magnetic tape. This file label is written on magnetic tape as a block which contains the file name, reel number, date written, and date expired.

file, magnetic disk—A file storage device which employs a group of flat circular plates with magnetic surfaces, upon which data are stored by selective magnetization of portions of the flat surface.

file, magnetic strip—A file storage device which uses strips of material with surfaces that can be magnetized for the purpose of storing data.

file maintenance—Modification of a file to incorporate changes that do not involve arithmetical operations; for example, insertions, deletions, transfers, and corrections.

file maintenance, graphic—The process designed to update physical representations such as microfilm, film prints, CRT output copies, etc.

file mark—An identification mark for the last record in a file. One of the several labels to indicate end-of-file; i.e., file marks may be followed by trailer label, file mark, and reel mark.

file mark, end of—A code that signals the last record of a file has been read.

file, mass storage—A type of secondary, and usually slower, storage, designed to supply the computer with the required information and data for immediate up-to-date reports on a given program segment.

file, master—The overall file or grouping of records having similar characteristics, but which contain the data which is considered permanent by nature of its contents, such as employee pay data, exemptions claimed, department wage rates, etc.

file, master-program—A tape on which all the programs for a system of runs are recorded.

file, model—The model is an analogue of the processing files. It can be originated, added to (posting), compared with others, held aside, filed for later use, sent somewhere, and so on. Sets of symbols are the simple analogues for these happenings.

file name—Alphanumeric characters assigned to identify a related set of records which constitute a particular file.

file, on-line (central)—The on-line central file may be thought of as a single electronic reservoir, or "data deposit," containing a central-information file index and all major-applications files. The index and the application files are cross-referenced by disk-file memory addresses maintained as integral parts of all records. Under computer control, inquiries may be made directly to any record in the on-line central file. File updating may occur continuously throughout the day. There is no need to accumulate, batch, and sort incoming transactions and other input data for separate application runs.

file operation, magnetic-tape—Magnetic tape is provided for the storage of information to accomplish sequential file updating. It is also used as an interim means of storage in off-line conversion of input to magnetic tape, and when "working tapes" are utilized in operations such as sorting.

file organization—The procedure of organizing various information files; these files are often random-access files to develop maximized use of storage and swift retrieval for processing.

file-organization routine—A specifically designed routine for reading input-data files, and sorting them in random-access locations.

file-oriented programming—I/O coding is simplified with the general file and record control program. Programming is file-oriented rather than device-oriented. Information is requested in device-independent fashion.

file-oriented system—If reference to file storage is the principle or key basis of a system, it is considered to be file-oriented. Auxiliary storage used as fundamental or essential in many commercial systems might be file-oriented, while generally considered incidental in scientific systems.

file, overflow areas—*See* overflow areas, file.

file packing density—The ratio of available file or data storing space to the total amount of data stored in the file.

file preparation—The ordering, sorting, and handling of parts records, customer account records, employee records, and the like from their original or copied documents into a form suitable for transformation via the computer onto magnetic files for storage.

file, problem—All the material needed to document a program to be run on a computer.

file-processing—Modification of a file to incorporate changes that do involve arithmetic operations; for example, receipts, issues, returns, and losses of stock items.

file, program—A flexible, easily updated reference system for the maintenance of the entire software library.

file protection—A device or method that prevents accidental erasure of operative data on magnetic-tape reels.

file reconstruction procedures — The safeguard procedure of protecting against the loss of data should the file be accidentally destroyed by a programmer or operator error, or by an equipment failure. Data must be dumped onto some media such as tape and programs for the reconstruction of the file.

file record compaction — *See* compaction of file records.

file reel—A magnetic tape reel which feeds toward the rewrite head and is also known as the supply reel.

files, batch transaction — Transactions accumulated as a batch ready for processing against the master file.

files, disk—*See* disk files.

file security—The relative privacy or inaccessibility of files from unauthorized users. As computers are used more and more frequently in the future as depositories of many kinds of information, file security will become an important legal issue.

file, sequential—A data file whose keyfields are arranged in a definite sequence. This is contrasted to a random file.

file, source—A CRAM deck or magnetic tape containing the file of information used as input to a computer run.

files, permanent data—*See* data files.

file spot, end of—An area on the used tape to signal the end of the file.

files, protected—Files in a computer system that are accessible only to a specific user. Since most files in a system are protected in this way, one user usually cannot obtain access to the information in another user's files.

files, security of user (time sharing) — *See* time sharing, security of user file.

files, shared—A direct-access device that permits two systems to be linked together. Either system has access to the file.

file storage—A special purpose storage of relatively large capacity, designed to hold a master file.

files, working data—*See* data files.

file, tape—1. A record file consisting of a magnetic or punched-paper tape. 2. A set of magnetic tapes in a tape library.

file, transaction—Transactions accumulated as a batch ready for processing against the master file.

file, tub—An open account file which provides ready accessibility to punched cards or other computer storage documents.

file update, master program — *See* master program, file update.

file, user (time sharing)—*See* time sharing, user file.

file, variable-length record—A file containing a set of records that vary in length.

file, volatile—A temporary or rapidly changing program or file.

file, work—A CRAM deck or magnetic tape used as a buffer or for interim storage

within a run, such as a sort. The final file can be called the destination file.

filing system—An organization or set of plans developed to identify records for efficient retrieval. Filing systems may be sequential, alphabetical, numeric, or coded in various ways.

fill, character—*See* character, fill.

filler—In order to make some data processing items standard, such as a record, a filler is used as some portion of that item. Thus, the standard size is achieved and the filler is not an essential part of the data involved.

fill, memory—*See* memory fill.

fill, storage—The storing of characters in storage areas not used for data storage or the program for a particular machine run.

film—A base which usually contains a layer of magnetic material often less than one micron thick and used for logic or storage elements.

film, magnetic thin — A layer of magnetic material frequently used for logic or storage elements. Magnetic thin films are commonly less than a micron in thickness.

film optical-sensing device — A piece of equipment capable of reading the contents of a film by optical methods; i.e., a system consisting of a light source, sensors, photocells and a film-moving mechanism. The output of the device is digitized and transferred directly to an electronic computer. An example of such a device is the FOSDIC system developed jointly by the Bureau of Census and the National Bureau of Standards.

filmorex system — A system, devised by Jacques Samain, for the electronic selection of microfilm cards. Each card has a microreproduction of the document or abstract and a field of twenty 5-digit code numbers giving the bibliographic reference and the subjects treated.

film reader—*See* reader, film.

film recorder—A mechanism that receives information from a computer and records it in the form of opaque and transparent areas on photographic film.

filter—1. A pattern of characters that is used to control the selection or elimination of portions of another pattern of characters. 2. A device or program that separates data, signal, or material in accordance with specified criteria. 3. A machine word that specifies which parts of another machine word are to be operated on. Also called extractor or mask.

filter, digit—*See* digit filter.

finding — The operation which consists of identifying and then selecting. the operation begins when one object in a group is requested to be found. The selection terminates when the object is found.

fine index—A subsidiary or supplemental index of a pair of indexes used to locate a particular file record. The higher or master index would be often considered the "gross" index.

fine sort—*See* sort, fine.

fire, cross—Interference from one telegraph circuit to another telegraph circuit or into a telephone circuit.

firmware—Logic circuits in read-only memory that may be altered by the software under certain circumstances.

first generation computer — *See* computer, first generation.

first item list—*Same as* indication group.

first-level address—An address that indicates the location where the referenced operand is to be found or stored, with no reference to an index register or B-box.

first-order subroutine—*See* subroutine, first-order.

first-pass sorting (own coding) — Computer instructions created by the programmer, in assembly or absolute form, which are executed by a sort during the first pass of the file after input program has been loaded, but prior to execution of first-pass sequencing instructions.

first remove subroutine—*See* subroutine, first order.

fitting compaction, curve — *See* compaction, curve fitting.

five level—Any teletypewriter code which utilizes five impulses, in addition to the start and stop impulses, for describing a character.

fixed area (FX)—The area on a disk where data files or core image programs may be stored and protected.

fixed block—The number of characters in the block is determined by the logic of the computer.

fixed connector—Used in flowcharting to indicate that only the result indicator can exist after a process completion.

fixed-cycle operation—1. A type of computer performance whereby a fixed amount of time is allocated to an operation. 2. A synchronous or clock-type arrangement in which events occur as a function of measured time within a computer. 3. An operation that is completed in a specified number of regularly timed execution cycles.

fixed data name—The specific reserve term representing a predetermined value.

fixed field—A given field on punch cards, or a given number of holes along the edge of an edge-punched card set aside for the recording of a given type or classification of information.

fixed formats—A state of unchanging description, or a specification of the information content in a particular design or a programmed area.

fixed-form coding—Specific coding instructions with a fixed field assigned to particular labels, operations codes, and operand parts of the instructions.

fixed length—Relates to the number of characters which can be contained in a specific storage location or data element, and which number of characters to be handled as units cannot be changed by programmers. Opposite of variable length, which if placed in fixed length storage locations could result in undesired unused spaces in packing density.

fixed length record—*See* record, fixed length.

fixed-length record file — *See* file, fixed-length record.

fixed-length record system—When a system contains all records with the same number of characters, it is called a fixed-length record system. This is contrasted to systems which have a variable number of characters in a record.

fixed-length word—A computer word which always has a fixed number of characters, i.e., one with 16 alphanumeric characters or 32 binary digits without any variation whatever. Registers, storage locations, gating, etc. are designed to handle a fixed number of digits.

fixed-plus-variable structure — A type of computer design in which the logical organization and physical structure of the central processor are arranged to meet the instantaneous needs of different users. This design is a requirement of communication networks, with their thousands of applications.

fixed point—1. A notation or system of arithmetic in which all numerical quantities are expressed by a predetermined number of digits, with the point implicitly located at some predetermined position. (Contrasted with floating point.) 2. A type of calculation with integers only and without any decimal point or decimal portions.

fixed-point arithmetic—*See* arithmetic, fixed point.

fixed point calculation — *See* calculation, fixed point.

fixed-point computer — *See* computer, fixed point.

fixed-point double-word length arithmetic — *See* arithmetic, fixed-point double-word length.

fixed point, fractional—A particular numeration system (fixed point) in which all quantities are fractions or scaled according to a fixed number of digits, and which has the binary point implicitly located at the left end so that all numerals are less than one. All quantities represented by the computer which lie outside the range of the designed fixed number of digits are thus fractional to it.

fixed-point mathematics—A method of determining the assumed location of the radix point by placing a symbol at the point, or by other rules and/or conventions as predetermined.

fixed-point operation—A calculation of numbers in which the arithmetic point, binary or decimal, is assumed to be or is held at a specific relative position for each number.

fixed-point part—That one of the two elements of the floating-point representation of a number which is not the exponent or power of the base.

fixed-point representation — Positional numeration system which has each number represented by a numeral with a single set of digits and with the radix point fixed with respect to one end of the set of digits, according to established rules, conventions, or design of the system.

fixed-position addressing—This permits selective updating of tape information as in magnetic disk or drum storage devices. Units as small as a single computer word may be stored or recorded on tape without disturbing adjacent information. Data blocks are numbered and completely addressable. Interrecord gaps are eliminated, thereby increasing tape storage capacity.

fixed-product area—The specific area of core storage where the product in a multiply operation is determined. This is also called the product generation area.

fixed-program computer — *See* computer, fixed-program.

fixed radix notation — *See* notation, fixed radix.

fixed radix scale — *Same as* notation, fixed radix.

fixed routine—A routine which cannot be modified during its execution.

fixed-size records—Denumerable file elements each of which has the same number of words, characters, bits, fields, etc.

fixed storage—*See* storage, fixed.

fixed variable—1. A variable in the problem (logical, structural, primal, or dual) fixed at zero level for feasibility. 2. A variable to be bounded away from zero is sometimes "fixed" at its bound in a bounded variable algorithm so that the transformed variable associated with it is then feasible at zero level, thus permitting arbitrary upper and lower bounds.

fixed word—The limitation of equipment as to the constant number of characters which the equipment will handle.

fixed word length—1. A term which refers to computers in which data are treated in units of a fixed number of characters or bits (as contrasted with variable word length). 2. All storage fields must have a predetermined length or capacity (in contrast to a variable word length).

fixed-word-length computer—A computer designed to manipulate information having a fixed number of bit positions. This is contrasted to a variable-word-length computer.

flag—1. A bit of information attached to a character or word to indicate the boundary of a field. 2. An indicator used frequently to tell some later part of a program that some condition occurred earlier. 3. An indicator used to identify the members of several

intermixed sets. (Synonymous with sentinel.) 4. Any of various types of indicators used for identification, e.g., a wordmark. 5. A character that signals the occurrence of some condition, such as the end of a word.

flag operand—The third operand of a symbolic instruction, designating which digits of the object-level instruction will be flagged.

flag, skip—A one bit in this position causes bytes to be skipped until the count equals zero. This is used to ignore portions of an input record (some systems).

FLAP—Program for symbolic mathematics, developed by the U.S. Navy Weapons Lab.

flexibility (modularity)—*See* software flexibility.

flexibility, software—*See* software flexibility.

Flexiwriter—A very common data processing entry device or entry processing system marketed by Friden, Inc., a subsidiary of the Singer Co.

flip-flop register—*See* register, flip-flop.

flip-flop sign control—The control of a specific flip-flop which is used to store the algebraic sign of numbers.

float—To move or shift one or several characters into positions to the right or left as determined by data structure or programming desires; e.g., to float asterisks to the right or left of numerical fields; dollar signs to the rightmost nonspace positions.

floating address—*See* address, floating.

floating-decimal arithmetic — A method of calculating that automatically accounts for the location of the radix point. This is usually accomplished by handling the number as a signed mantissa times the radix raised to an integral exponent; e.g., the decimal number $+88.3$ might be written as $+.883 \times 10^2$; the binary number $-.0011$ as $-.11 \times 2^{-2}$. (Contrasted with fixed-point arithmetic, definition 1.)

floating normalize control — The bit, in the program status doubleword, that indicates whether (if 0) or not (if 1) the result of a floating-point operation is to be normalized.

floating point—1. A form of number representation in which quantities are represented by a number multiplied by the number base raised to a power; e.g., the decimal number 397 can be written as 3.97×10^2, or 0.397×10^3. 2. A notation in which a number x is represented by a pair of numbers y and z (and two integers n and m which are understood parameters in any given representation) with y and z chosen so that $x = y \cdot n^z$ where z is an integer. The quantity z is called the exponent or characteristic; e.g., a decimal number 241,000,000 might be shown as 2.41, 8, since it is equal to 2.41×10^8.

floating-point arithmetic — 1. Arithmetic using a variable location for the decimal or binary point in each number, where the location in each number depends upon the size of the number and its power of 10 or 2; e.g., .025 plus 2.1273×10^2 equals 2.1523 ×

10^2. 2. A method of calculation which automatically accounts for the location of the radix point. This is usually accomplished by handling the number as a signed mantissa times the radix raised to an integral exponent. For example, the decimal number $+.883 \times 10^2$; the binary number $+.0011$ as $+.11 \times 2^{-2}$.

floating-point arithmetic (operation) — In order to add two floating-point numbers, it is first necessary to equalize the exponents of the numbers. This is accomplished by shifting the mantissa of the smaller expression to the right the number of places that equals the difference of the two exponents. For example, in adding the floating-point decimal numbers 0.3×10^4 and 0.27×10^6, 0.3×10^4 is written as 0.003×10^6 and then the two numbers are added which gives the results of 0.273×10^6.

$$\begin{array}{ccc} .3 \ \times 10^4 & & .003 \times 10^6 \\ + \ .27 \times 10^6 & = & + \ .27 \ \times 10^6 \\ \hline & & .273 \times 10^6 \end{array}$$

The same procedure is required for subtraction except that the subtrahend is subtracted from the minuend in the final step of the operation.

$$\begin{array}{ccc} .27 \times 10^6 & & .27 \ \times 10^6 \\ - \ .3 \ \times 10^4 & = & - \ .003 \times 10^6 \\ \hline & & .267 \times 10^6 \end{array}$$

To perform this operation with binary numbers, the exponents are first differenced. Then the mantissa of the number with the smallest exponent is shifted right the specified number of places, that is, the difference between the two exponents. When this is accomplished, the two resulting floating-point expressions are added with a double-precision add instruction, and the exponent of the larger number is affixed to the result. The operation is the same for subtraction except that the sign of the subtrahend is changed before the double precision add is performed. The procedure just outlined is a much simplified analysis of floating point addition and subtraction, but serves to explain the basic principle.

Multiplication and division of the mantissa of the floating point-expression are performed in the same manner as for normal fixed-point numbers. The exponents, however, are added in multiplication, and subtracted in division.

floating point, base—Using the floating point numeration system, the fixed positive integer is the radix of the power.

floating-point calculation—1. Calculation taking into account the changing location of the decimal (if base 10) or binary point (if base 2) and consisting of writing each number by stating separately its sign, its coefficient, and its exponent affecting the base. 2. A calculation made with floating-point arithmetic.

floating point coefficient — See coefficient, floating point.

floating point compaction — See compaction, floating point.

floating point computer—A computer that is designed to represent data as an argument and exponent. An example would be 1234 represented by 0.1234×10^4 in the computer.

floating point mathematics — An automatic method of determining the location of the radix point in values. Such math is usually performed by using a signed mantissa times the radix, raised to an integral number, such as the decimal number 62.4 being equivalent to .624 times 10^2.

floating-point numbers—In many cases, the solution of a problem requires values of numbers that are either too large or too small to be expressed by the computer. The physical size of the number can be reduced by "scaling" or shifting the number to the right or left a predetermined number of places so that the most significant bits of the number may be used. For instance, the decimal number 6,510,000 may be expressed as 0.651×10^7, 0.0651×10^8, 0.00651×10^9, etc. The exponent of the number-system base is the scale factor or the number of places the number is shifted.

floating point operation — A calculation of numbers in which the arithmetic point, binary or decimal, is movable, not necessarily the same for each number.

floating-point package — The floating-point package permits some computers to perform arithmetic operations that many other computers can perform only after the addition of costly optional hardware. Floating-point operations automatically align the binary points of operands, retaining the maximum precision available by discarding leading zeros. In addition to increasing accuracy, floating-point operations relieve the programmer of scaling problems common in fixed-point operations. This is of particular advantage to the inexperienced programmer.

floating-point precision — The maximum number of binary digits used as the mantissa of a single-precision floating-point fraction.

floating point radix—See floating point base.

floating point representation — A system of numeration wherein each numeral is a number which consists of a pair of numerals; one being a coefficient for a fixed positive integer radix raised to a power by an exponent, which is the second number of the pair. An example is 0.0260 represented by 260 −4 or 260×10^{-4}.

floating-point routine—A set of subroutines that cause a computer to execute floating-point arithmetic. These routines may be used to simulate floating-point operations on a computer with no built-in floating-point hardware.

floating point shift—A shift in 4-bit increments, performed on a short-format or long-format floating-point number.

floating-point subroutines—Special routines that handle floating-point numbers as arguments.

floating significance control—The bit, in the program status double-word, that indicates whether (if 0) or not (if 1) the result of a floating-point operation is checked for significance.

floating zero control—The bit, in the program status double-word, that indicates whether (if 0) or not (if 1) the result of a floating-operation is stored, if the characteristic is reduced below zero.

flow—A general term to indicate a sequence of events.

flow, bidirectional—Flow that can extend over the same flow lines in either direction.

flowchart—1. A system-analysis tool that provides a graphical presentation of a procedure. Includes block diagrams, routine sequence diagrams, general flow symbols, and so forth. 2. A chart to represent, for a problem, the flow of data, procedures, growth, equipment, methods, documents, machine instructions, etc. 3. A graphical representation of a sequence of operations by using symbols to represent the operations such as compute, substitute, compare, jump, copy, read, write, etc.

flowchart connector—*See* connector, flowchart.

flowchart, data—*See* data flowchart.

flowchart, operations—A graphic representation of the intercommunicated, interconnected logical steps necessary to solve a particular problem.

flowchart, program—A visual representation of a computer problem in which machine instructions or groups of instructions are designated by symbols.

flowchart, structure — Generalized flowcharts showing input, processing, files, and output without indicating the precise methods of processing.

flowchart symbols—The symbols, such as squares, circles, etc., convey no information and must be labeled. They localize a point of interest but convey only the most general notion of intent. The finished model must include adequate description to explain what the operation does. Liberal use of footnotes is recommended to explain the "why" of operations that are not straight forward.

flowchart systems — Visual representation of the system through which data provided by the source document are converted into final documents.

flowchart technique — Detailed flowcharts showing data and information requirements and the specific methods and calculations for processing the information.

flow control—The time sequence of instruction executions which relate to the maintenance of control of a computer system. Examples are: executive routines, jump instructions, various specific decision programs or instructions.

flow diagram — A chart consisting of various flow diagram symbols such as arrows, rectangular boxes, circles, and other symbols used to represent graphically a procedure or pattern of computation and/or processing of the program.

flow diagram, dynamic — *See* diagram, dynamic flow.

flow direction—The antecedent-to-successor relation, indicated by arrows or other conventions, between operations on flowcharts.

flowline—A line representing a connecting path between symbols on a flowchart.

flow, normal-direction—A flow in a direction from left to right or top to bottom.

flow, parallel—The system of operations designed so that several of them may be conducted simultaneously, such as in house building, the air-conditioning ducting can be completed, while the plumbing is being worked on, while the landscaping is being developed, etc.

flow-process diagram—A graphic representation of the major steps of work in process. The illustrative symbols may represent documents, machines or actions taken during the process. The area of concentration is on where or who does what, rather than how it is to be done. (Synonymous with process chart.)

flow, reverse-direction—A flow in a direction other than left to right or top to bottom.

flow, serial — The system of operations such that each operation is performed singly and not at the same time other tasks are being completed, i.e., the work moves along a single line or channel where each type of operation is performed in succession.

flow tracing—A type of diagnostics and debugging in which the programmer specifies the start and end of those program segments where he wishes to examine the contents of various registers and accumulators. The program will run at machine speed until it encounters the desired segments, and the printing commences and is terminated when the end of the program segment is encountered.

FLPL—An acronym for FORTRAN List Processing Language. It was developed for use in a program for proving theorems in geometry. It is much like LISP, but has no provision for recursion.

flying-head storage retrieval (drum)—The flying-head (air-floating head) technique combines aerodynamic and pneumatic principles. Read/write heads float on a boundary layer of air, generated by the rotation of the drum, at one half of a thousandth of an inch or less from the oxide-coated surface of the drum. The read/write head is suspended in this position by the opposing forces of the boundary layer of air and the head-positioning mechanism.

flying spot—A small, rapidly moving spot of light usually generated by a cathode-ray tube and used to illuminate successive spots of a surface containing dark and light areas.

The varying amount of light reflected is detected by a phototube and used to produce a time succession of electronic signals which effectively describe the surface.

flying-spot scanner — In optical character recognition (OCR), a device employing a moving spot of light to scan a sample space, the intensity of the transmitted or reflected light being sensed by a photoelectric transducer.

FOCUS—An automated credit-union accounting system that provides reports and controls for credit-union management. (IBM)

folder, problem—All the material needed or for use to document a program to be run on a computer.

folder, program—*Same as* problem file.

follower, curve—*See* curve follower.

font—A complete family or assortment of characters of a given size and style.

font, optical—One of the media that can be used as computer input. An optical font is a variety of type which can be sensed by a computer input device and translated into electronic form within the computer.

font reticle—A system of lines forming various character outlines or dimensions in optical character recognition which are placed over the image of an input character and which determines whether that character conforms to the prescribed shape and range of dimensions. Other outlines on the font reticle check for minimum space between lines and characters, and for the maximum size of punctuation marks.

footing control — A summary or total at the end of a control group or for various control groups, i.e., a minor total.

footing, page—The summing of the entries on a particular page, usually appearing at the bottom of each page.

footing, report—The summary of the entire report, which most often appears at the termination and which is also known as final footing.

forbidden character code — *Same as* code illegal.

forbidden code—*See* code, forbidden.

forbidden combination—*Same as* character illegal.

forbidden-combination check—*See* check, forbidden combination.

forbidden digit—*See* character, illegal.

forbidden-digit check — *Same as* check, forbidden-combination.

force—To manually interrupt and intervene in the operation of a routine and to effect an execution of a computer jump instruction.

forced coding—*Same as* programming, minimum access.

forced coding program — *Same as* minimum latency programming.

forced display—*See* display, forced.

foreground—A high priority program, process, or system part which utilizes the computer CPU immediately, or when and where

and as needed, but which still allows less critical or subsidiary programs to be worked on as background tasks during the time when the high priority programs are not being worked. This is the basis of multiprogramming or foreground/background processing.

foreground processing—Top-priority processing most often resulting from real-time entries which usually have precedence, through the use of interrupts, into lower priority or background processing.

foreground program—A program that is initiated via an outside request delaying a background program.

foreground routine—*Same as* foreground program.

foreign-exchange service — That service which connects a customer's telephone to a central-office exchange normally not serving the customer's location.

forest coding—Same as minimum latency programming.

form—A printed or typed document which usually has blank spaces for the insertion of information.

FORMAC—Abbreviation for formula manipulator compiler (IBM).

formal logic—*See* logic, formal.

formal semantics—A language for computer-oriented languages which acts as a compiler-compiler and contains formal semantics.

format—1. A predetermined arrangement of characters, fields, lines, punctuation, page numbers, etc. 2. A defined arrangement of words, totals, characters, stubs, and headings for a desired clear presentation of data or print-out, such as a profit and loss statement in a record.

format, address—*See* address format.

format, character—*See* character format.

format, control—*See* control format.

format-F—A data set has F-format logical records if nearly all of the logical records are of identical length. In FORTRAN, the F-format is an input/output specification detail. In PL/1 an F-format is also a I/O format specification similar to FORTRAN.

format implicit address instructions—*See* instruction format, implicit address.

format, instructon—*See* instruction format.

format, N address instruction — *See* instruction format, N address.

format order—*See* instruction format.

format, packed—A binary-coded decimal format in which two decimal digits are represented within a single byte of storage, accomplished by eliminating the zone bits.

format, symbolic-coding—In writing instructions using the assembly language, the programmer is primarily concerned with three fields: a label field, an operation field, and an operand field. It is possible to relate the symbolic coding to its associated flowchart, if desired, by appending comments to each instruction line or program segment.

format, variable—A changing description of classification for the information content in a particular area.

format, vertical—Pertaining to the vertical arrangement of data, as viewed by an observer of a document.

format, zoned—A binary-coded decimal format in which one decimal digit consists of zone bits and numeric bits, and occupies an entire byte of storage.

form, backus-naur—*Same as* backus normal form.

form, blank—Relates to blank media, i.e., a medium in which data has been recorded only to establish a frame of reference to enable the medium to be used as a data carrier, such as paper tape punched only with feed holes, etc.

form-feed character — *See* character, form feed.

form feeding or form feedout—The rapid, accurate positioning of document forms on a teleprinter or business machine.

form movement time — An elapsed period of time during which a printing cycle produces the printing and movement of hard copy.

form of subscripts (FORTRAN)—A subscript must be in one of the following forms only, where I represents an unsigned nonsubscripted integar variable, and K1 and K2 an unsigned integer constant:

I
K
$I + K1$ or $I - K1$
K1 I
K1 $I + K2$ or K1 $I - K2$

form, pseudoinstruction—Data represented in the same form as an instruction, for convenience when representing small units of data, i.e., predesigned numbers or parameters which are read as instructions although treated as data.

form, quasi-instruction—*Same as* form, pseudoinstruction.

form stop—On a printer, the automatic device that stops the machine when paper has run out.

FORTRAN—1. A programming system, including a language and a processor (compiler), allowing programs to be written in a mathematical-type language. These programs are subsequently translated by a computer (under control of the processor) into machine language. 2. FORmula TRANslator. A compiler language developed by the IBM Corporation, originally conceived for use on scientific problems but now widely adapted for most commercial problems as well. 3. A data-processing language that closely resembles mathematical language. 4. Pertaining to a computer program which translates a FORTRAN-language program into a machine-language program.

FORTRAN II executive—The executive is a routine that accepts and processes information defining the job. This information, called control information, is normally input to the executive on cards, called control cards, or via the console typewriter. The executive verifies the information and sets up a sequence of operations for processing the job. The sequence of operations defines the system routines needed and the order in which they are needed. It also describes the execution of the program. For example, if a job specification is to compile and execute a FORTRAN program, the sequence is: (1) load and execute the FORTRAN compiler, (2) load and execute the system loader to load the compiled program, (3) execute the program, (4) accept control information for the next job. In addition, the executive sets the information specifying a listing of the FORTRAN program and the binary output medium for the object program. The executive is given control upon the termination of each job. If the job terminates abnormally, the executive outputs an error message telling the point at which the job terminated. The remaining sequence of operations for the job is deleted.

FORTRAN IV—FORTRAN IV is a language that is problem oriented. The programmer may think in terms of the problem, rather than thinking in terms of the computer which is used to solve the problem. Initially designed for scientific applications, it has proved quite convenient for many commercial and industrial applications.

FORTRAN IV logical capabilities—FORTRAN IV logical capabilities include: type-declaration statements, logical operators, logical expressions, relational operators, logical assignment statements, and the logical IF statement.

FORTRAN compiler system—The FORTRAN compiler system consists of two basic elements: a source language (FORTRAN IV), whose structure closely resembles the language of mathematics, and a compiler that translates the statements and formulas written in the source language into a machine-language program.

FORTRAN continue—A statement which does not generate machine code. It is useful as the last statement in a DO loop.

FORTRAN function—*See* function, FORTRAN.

FORTRAN language—Programs are written directly as algebraic expressions and arithmetic statements. Various symbols are used to signify equality, addition, subtraction, exponentiation, etc. Additional statements are provided to permit control over how the algebraic expressions and arithmetic statements are to be processed. These include transfer, decision, indexing, and input/output statements.

FORTRAN overflow—In FORTRAN, overflow occurs when the characteristic of a floating-point number exceeds the machine capacity. In assembler language, overflow occurs when a fixed point number is divided by zero, or when an algebraic sum is larger than the accumulator register can hold.

185

FORTRAN, real constants—*See* constants, real (FORTRAN).

FORTRAN, real variables—*See* variables, real (FORTRAN).

FORTRAN statement columns — *See* columns, FORTRAN statement.

FORTRAN subscripts — *See* subscripts (FORTRAN).

forward—Operations involved in interconnecting circuits in order to establish a temporary communication between two or more stations.

forward-backward counter — A device which is capable of adding or subtracting input so that it can count in either an increasing or decreasing direction.

forward break solenoid—An electromechanical device, which when energized, maintains a pressure via a breakpad, forcing magnetic tape against an opposing breakpad, causing a halt in the forward motion of the tape.

forward capstan — A rotating shaft with a minimal tolerance which controls the forward movements of magnetic tapes at uniform speed.

forward scan — An editing operation which makes an output word conform to the control word by comparing positions from right to left and adding punctuation, such as decimals and dollar signs.

forward solenoid—An electromechanical device which, when energized, maintains a pressure via a roller forcing magnetic tape against the forward capstan, which moves the tape in a forward direction.

FOSDIC—Film Optical Sensing Device for Input to Computers. A piece of equipment capable of reading the contents of a film by optical methods; i.e., a system consisting of a light source, lenses, photocells and a film-moving mechanism. The output of the device is digitized and transferred directly to an electronic computer. An example of such a device is the FOSDIC system developed jointly by the Bureau of Census and the National Bureau of Standards.

four address—1. A method of specifying the location of operands and instructions in which the storage location of the two operands and the storage location of the results of the operation are cited, and the storage location of the next instruction to be executed is cited. 2. Having the property that each complete instruction specifies the operation and addresses of four registers.

four-address instruction—A machine instruction usually consisting of the addresses of two operands, the address for storing the result, the address of the next instruction, the command to be executed, and miscellaneous indices. (Synonymous with three-plus-one address instruction.)

four-plus-one address—An address which contains four operand addresses and one control address.

four tape sort—*See* sorting, four tape.

fox message—A standard message that is used for testing teletypewriter circuits and machines because it includes all the alphanumerics on a teletypewriter as well as most of the function characters, such as space, figures shift, letters shift, etc. The message is: The quick brown fox jumped over a lazy dog's back 1234567890 ——— sending. The sending station's identification is inserted in the three blank spaces which precede the word sending.

fractional—The places immediately to the right of an assumed specific point. The decimal 25.678 has three fractional places.

fractional arithmetic units—Arithmetic units operated with the decimal point at the extreme left, thus all numbers having a value of less than one.

fractional fixed point—*See* fixed point, fractional.

fragment—One of the parts of the contents of a document, program, or routine, or the act of rearrangement of contents of documents into smaller series or parts.

fragmentation—The process of loading a program into non-contiguous areas of core memory to achieve maximum utilization of storage space. The memory map feature automatically provides this capability.

fragmenting—The breaking down of a document into a series of terms or descriptors.

frame—The grouping of bits across magnetic tapes as seven which would consist of one from each row that makes up a character frame. Also the group of five, six, seven, or eight punches across punched paper tape.

frame, main—1. The central processor of the computer system. It contains the main storage, arithmetic unit, and special register groups. (Synonymous with CPU and central processing unit.) 2. All that portion of a computer exclusive of the input, output, peripheral and, in some instances, storage units.

frames, data—Data frames are written on some tapes at a density of either 200 or 556 bits per inch. Data block length is not specified. When the end of a block is reached and no more data is transmitted, the tape comes to a stop. After the last block in the file (related group of blocks), the end-of file sentinel (tape mark) is written to indicate the termination of the file.

free field—A property of information-processing recording media which permits recording of information without regard to a preassigned or fixed field; e.g., in information-retrieval devices, information may be dispersed in the record in any sequence or location.

free float, PERT—Certain stops used to halt particular tasks when action will result in an overall delay in the project.

freeze mode—*Same as* hold mode.

freeze point in specifications — A point reached in programming any complex system when the functional specifications of the operational program are frozen.

frequency—In a-c signalling, it refers to the number of complete cycles transmitted per second. Usually expressed in cycles per second (cps); kilocycles per second (kcs), megacycles per second (mcs), etc.

frequency-analysis compaction—*See* compaction, frequency analysis.

frequency, clock—The master frequency of periodic pulses which schedules the operation of the computer. (Clarified by synchronous computer.)

frequency doubling recording—*See* recording, frequency doubling.

frequency, master clock — The time element between pulses of the master clock.

frequency, maximum operating—The maximum repetition or clock rate at which the modules will perform reliably in continuous operation, under worst-case conditions, without special trigger pulse (clock) requirements.

frequency, natural — The frequency of free oscillation of a system.

frequency pulse repetition—*See* pulse repetition rate.

frequency shift—System of telegraph-teletypewriter operation in which the mark signal is one frequency and the space signal a different frequency. Also, the difference between mark and space will vary in different systems, e.g., 170 cps U.S.A., 120 cps Europe.

FSL — An abbreviation for formal semantics language which is a program acting as a compiler-compiler.

full adder—A half adder circuit arrangement which has an additional input of a carry bit or a no bit from a previous position.

full adder, parallel—*See* adder, full (parallel).

full adder, serial—*See* adder, full (serial).

full subtracter, parallel—See subtracter, full (parallel).

full subtracter, serial — *See* subtracter, full (serial).

full-word boundary—In the IBM 360 system, an address which ends in 00 and which is divisible by binary 4, is a natural boundary for a 4-byte machine word.

full-word input/output buffers—Since output data characters are located in the lower half of output data words, while input data characters are found in the upper half of input data words, it is possible to use the same computer word in core storage for both input and output buffers. Since each buffer is controlled by its own buffer-control word, there need be no relationship between the input and output buffers other than that they use the upper and lower halves of the same computer words.

function—1. A special purpose or characteristic action. 2. The relation or association of one item from a set with each item from another set. 3. A means of referring to a type or sequence of calculations within an arithmetic statement.

function address instruction format—*See* address instruction, functional.

functional address instruction — *See* address instruction, functional.

functional design—*See* design, functional.

functional diagram—*See* diagram, functional.

functional element—A combination of logical and delay elements which performs an elementary computer function.

functional generator—A device that produces a given function of an independent variable.

functional interleaving — *See* interleaving, functional.

functional modularity—The addition of modules to a basic data-processing system which broadens the scope or concept of the system as well as adds capacity.

functional multiplier—A device which will take in the changing values of two functions and put out the changing value of their product.

functional requirement—A document most often prepared by systems analysts or operations-research staff people explicitly detailing one of the functions to be performed by the system. Specifications concerning the manner in which the function will be completed often accompany the message. Functional requirements provide a basis for: guiding and assisting people who prepare programs; preparing instruction manuals; obtaining management acceptance of management procedure or policy changes to further integrate a computer "total system."

functional symbols—*See* symbols, functional.

functional unit—A combination of logical and nonlogical elements grouped to perform an elementary computer function such as adding, complementing, or pulse generation.

function buttons—*See* buttons, function.

function codes—*See* codes, function.

function, control—*See* control function.

function digit—A unique computer code digit that describes the arithmetic or logical operation which is to be carried out.

function element—A device that performs a logic function.

function-evaluation routines—A set of commonly used mathematical routines. The initial set of routines will include sine, cosine, tangent, arcsine, arccosine, arctangent, square root, natural logarithm, and exponential. These routines will be written in fixed and floating point.

function, executive-system—The executive system has been designed for operation with a minimum of operator intervention. However, it is recognized that some functions in use are beyond the scope of the executive system, while others demand operator concurrence. In addition certain information must be presented automatically to the operator, while other information must be available to answer operator requests. Insofar as operator functions are required for a large variety of activities, the executive system apportions these functions into five classes, thus equally dividing operator duties in a multioperator installation. These five functional classes are: program status; magnetic-tape activity; visual tape labels; communications activity; cards, printer, and paper-tape activity. The areas above may be associated with as many as five operator consoles or as few as one, depending on the complexity and layout of each installation. Any combination of operator functions may be associated with a physical console operating through the usual console channel or through the standard communication subsystem (some computers).

FUNCTION, FORTRAN—A function is called by a name which usually consists of 4 to 7 alphanumeric characters, the first alphabetic, the last being the letter F. If the value of the function is fixed-point, the first letter of the function name must be an X; the arguments of the function are enclosed in parenthesis.

function objective—That function of the independent variables whose maximum or minimum is sought in an optimization problem.

function part—*Same as* operation part.

function punch—*Same as* control punches.

function, recursive—*See* recursive function.

function register, internal—*See* register, internal-function.

function, search-read—*See* search-read function.

functions, QUIKTRAN—*See* QUIKTRAN functions.

functions, software (time-sharing)—*See* time sharing, software functions.

functions, utility—Auxiliary operations such as tape searching, tape-file copying, media conversion, and dynamic memory and tape dumps.

function switch—A circuit having a fixed number of inputs and outputs designed such that the output information is a function of the input information, each expressed in a certain code, signal configuration, or pattern.

function table—1. A device or routine that can decode multiple inputs into a single output, or encode a single input into multiple outputs. 2. Two or more sets of data so arranged that an entry in one set selects one or more entries in the other sets.

function, transfer—*See* transfer function.

function word, I/O operation—Each channel is capable of operating in three different transfer modes—input, output, or function. The input and output modes are employed when transferring data to or from the central computer. The function mode is the means by which the central computer establishes the initial communication path with a peripheral subsystem. During this mode of transmission, the central computer sends one or more function words to a peripheral subsystem directing the specified units to perform the desired operation.

function words—The function word contains the operating instructions for the peripheral units, its format depending upon the particular subsystem.

function words, communications—The CLT (Communication Line Terminal) identifier is used in many standard communication subsystem function words, (computer generated instructions to the subsystem) . Each pair of input/output CLTs in a standard communication subsystem has a unique seven-bit address (CLT identifier) which enables a central processor to distinguish it from other input/output pairs in the subsystem.

functor—1. A logical element that provides a linkage between variables. 2. A linguistic feature denoting structure rather than lexical meaning. 3. An improper term to be avoided. This term sometimes is used to designate a logic element which performs a specific function or provides a linkage between variables.

future-address patch — *See* patch, future address.

future labels (one-pass assembly only)—Future labels are labels which are referenced by the programmer in the operand field of a statement and have not been defined previously. Since an address cannot be assigned to this reference, the label is put into a symbol table as an unassigned label, accompanied by the address of the command which referenced it (i.e., the last command if it is addressed more than once). Futures with unique increments are entered separately in the symbol table. When it appears as a label in the location field, it becomes a permanent label in the symbol table and all "futures" are removed from the symbols table. Also, a "future patch" is output in the binary output deck to patch, at load time, the locations that referenced the "future." A "future patch" is prepared by the assembler as a control record to the loader. This process is automatic and does not require programmer consideration. Future labels are unique with one-pass assemblers.

G

gain—The ratio between the output signal and the input signal of a device.

game theory — A mathematical process of selecting an optimum strategy in the face of an opponent who has a strategy of his own.

game theory models—The theory of games is a branch of mathematics that aims to analyze various problems of conflict by abstracting common strategic features for study in theoretical "models," — termed "games" because they are patterned on actual games such as bridge and poker. By stressing strategic aspects, that is, aspects controlled by the participants, it goes beyond the classical theory of probability, in which the treatment of games is limited to aspects of pure chance. Zero-sum, two-person games can be solved by linear programming methods.

gang punch—*See* punch, gang.

gang punching, interspersed—The punching of cards with fixed data in one or more cards simultaneously within a larger group of cards.

gap—1. An interval of space or time used as an automatic sentinel to indicate the end of a word, record, or file of data on a tape; e.g., a word gap at the end of a word, a record or item gap at the end of a group of words, and a file gap at the end of a group of records or items. 2. The absence of information for a specified length of time or space on a recording medium as contrasted with marks and sentinels which are the presence of specific information to achieve a similar purpose. (Related to file gap and terminating symbol.) 3. The space between the reading or recording head and the recording medium such as tape, drum, or disk. (Related to gap head.)

gap, block—The space on magnetic tape separating two blocks of data or information.

gap, controlled head—A microscopic gap is maintained between read/write heads and the disk surface — with absolute reliability. A fail-safe head retraction mechanism prevents any contact with the disk. Heads are completely self-adjusting.

gap digits — Digits sometimes included in a machine word for various technical reasons. Such digits are not used to represent data or instructions.

gap, file—An interval of space or time associated with a file to indicate or signal the end of the file.

gap, head—1. The space between the reading or recording head and the recording medium such as tape, drum, or disk. 2. The space or gap intentionally inserted into the magnetic circuit of the head in order to force or direct the recording flux into the recording medium.

gap, interblock—The space on magnetic tape separating two blocks of data or information.

gap, interrecord—An interval of space or time deliberately left between recording portions of data or records. Such spacing is used to prevent errors through loss of data or over-writing and permits tape stop-start operations.

gap, interword — The time period and space permitted between words on a tape, disk, drum, etc. Usually, such space allows for controlling specific or individual words, for switching.

gap, record—An interval of space or time associated with a record to indicate or signal the end of the record.

gap scatter—The deviation from true vertical alignment of the magnetic read-head gaps for the several parallel tracks.

gap, word—*Same as* gap, interword.

garbage—Unwanted and meaningless information carried along in storage.

gate—A combination logic element having at least one input channel. The AND gate, OR gate, etc.

gate, A AND-NOT B—A binary logic coincidence (two-input) circuit for completing the logic operations of A AND-NOT B, i.e., result is true only if statement A is true and statement B is false.

gate, A AND-NOT B or gate B AND-NOT A—A logic operator possessing the property that if A is a statement and B is a statement, the NOT (if A then B) is true if A is true and B is false, and false if A is false and B is true, and false if both statements are true.

gate, add without carry — *Same as* gate, exclusive OR.

gate, A except B—*Same as* gate, A AND-NOT B.

gate A ignore B—A binary logic (two input) coincidence circuit which permits the gate to function as a pass for the A input signal while disregarding the B input signal, i.e., the output is the same as the A input signal regardless of the B input signal.

gate, A ignore B negative — A binary logic (two input) coincidence circuit which permits the logic operation of negative, A ignore B, i.e., the result is true when A is false and false when A is true, the output being independent of B, same as A ignore B whose output is negated.

gate A implies B—*Same as* gate, B OR-NOT A.

gate, A implies B negative—*Same as* gate, A AND-NOT B.

gate, alteration—*Same as* gate, OR.

gate, alternative denial — *Same as* gate, NAND.

gate, amplitude—A transducer which transmits only portions of an input wave lying between two amplitude boundaries. Note: The term is used especially when the two amplitude boundaries are close to each other as compared with the amplitude range of the input.

gate, AND—A signal circuit with two or more input wires in which the output wire gives a signal, if and only if, all input wires receive coincident signals. (Synonymous with AND circuit, and clarified by conjunction.)

gate, AND negative—*Same as* gate, NAND.

gate, AND-NOT—*Same as* gate, A AND-NOT B or gate, B AND-NOT A.

gate, AND positive—*Same as* gate, AND.

gate, anticoincidence—*Same as* gate, exclusive OR.

gate, A OR-NOT B—A binary (two-input) logic coincidence circuit for completing the logic operation of A OR-NOT B, i.e., the result is false only if A is false and B is true.

gate, B AND-NOT A—A binary (two-input) logic coincidence circuit for completing the logic operation of B AND-NOT A, i.e., the result is true only if B is true and A is false.

gate, B EXCEPT A—*Same as* gate, B AND-NOT A.

gate, biconditional—*Same as* gate, exclusive NOR.

gate, B ignore A—A binary (two-input) logic coincidence circuit for completing a function which permits the B input signal to pass and disregard A input signal, i.e., the output signal is the same as B input signal and is independent of the A input signal.

gate, B ignore A negative—A binary (two-input) logic coincidence circuit for completing a function which is identical to the negative A ignore B gate, but with the labels on the input leads reversed, i.e., the result is true if B is false and false if B is true. The result is the negated or reversed value of B and is independent of A.

gate, B implies A negative — *Same as* gate B AND-NOT A.

gate, B OR-NOT A — A binary (two-input) logic coincidence circuit for completing the logic operation of B OR-NOT B; the reverse of A OR-NOT A; the result is false only when A is true and B is false.

gate, buffer—*Same as* gate, OR.

gate, conjunction—*Same as* gate, AND.

gate difference—*Same as* gate, exclusive OR.

gate, disjunction—*Same as* gate, OR.

gate, dispersion—*Same as* gate, NAND.

gate, distance—*Same as* gate, exclusive OR.

gate diversity—*Same as* gate, exclusive OR.

gate, don't care—A gate whose normal operation can be changed or interrupted upon receipt of a control signal. The output is independent of the inputs.

gate, equality—*Same as* gate, exclusive NOR.

gate, equivalence — *Same as* gate, exclusive NOR.

gate, except—A gate which yields an output corresponding to a one, when one or more input lines are true and one or more other input lines are zero or false.

gate, exclusive NOR—A two input (binary) logic circuit designed to perform the logic operation of exclusive-NOR, i.e., if A and B are input statements, the result is true or 1 when both A and B are true or when both A and B are false. The result is false when A and B are different.

gate, exclusive OR — A binary logic coincidence circuit for completing the logic operation of exclusive OR, i.e., the result is true when A is true and B is false, or when A is false and B is true, and the result is false when A and B are both true or when A and B are both false.

gate, exjunction—*Same as* gate, exclusive OR.

gate generator—A circuit or device that produces one or more gate pulses.

gate identity—A specific n-input gate which yields an output signal of a particular kind when all of the n-input signals are alike.

gate, if A then B—*Same as* gate, B OR-NOT A.

gate, if A then NOT-B—*Same as* gate, NAND.

gate, if B then NOT-A—*Same as* gate, NAND.

gate, inclusive NOR—*Same as* gate, NOR.

gate, inclusive OR—*Same as* gate, OR.

gate intersection—*Same as* gate, AND.

gate, join—*Same as* gate, OR.

gate, joint denial—*Same as* gate, NOR.

gate, logic product—*Same as* gate, AND.

gate, logic sum—*Same as* gate, OR.

gate, majority decision—A binary input unit which has the capability of implementing the majority logic operation. The result is true if more than half of the statements are true, and false if half or more of the input statements are false.

gate, match—*Same as* gate, exclusive NOR.

gate, mix—*Same as* gate, OR.

gate, modulo-two sum — *Same as* gate, exclusive OR.

gate, NAND—A logical operator having the property that if P is a statement and Q is a statement, then the NAND of P.Q.R. is true if at least one statement is false and false if all statements are true.

gate, negative (B implies A)—*Same as* gate, B AND NOT A.

gate, negative OR—*Same as* gate, NOR.

gate, neither-NOR—*Same as* gate, NOR.

gate nonconjunction—*Same as* gate, NOR.

gate, nondisjunction—*Same as* gate, NOR.

gate, nonequality — *Same as* gate, exclusive OR.

gate, nonequivalence—*Same as* gate, exclusive OR.

gate, NOR—A gate whose output is energized when, and only when, all inputs are absent.

gate, NOT — A logic element which has only one binary input signal; the variable represented by the output signal is the negation of the variable represented by the input signal, i.e., an element whose output signal is 1 when its input signal is 0 and vice versa.

gate, NOT-AND—*Same as* gate, NAND.

gate, NOT-both—*Same as* gate, NAND.

gate, null—A gate which produces signals representing strings of zeros in a particular system as long as power is applied.

gate, one—*Same as* gate, OR.

gate, OR—An electrical gate or mechanical device which implements the logical OR operator. An output signal occurs whenever there are one or more inputs on a multichannel input. An OR gate performs the function of the logical "inclusive OR operator." (Synonymous with OR circuit and clarified by disjunction.)

gate, partial sum — *Same as* gate, exclusive OR.

gate, positive AND—*Same as* gate, AND.

gate, positive OR—*Same as* gate, OR.

gate pulse — Extended duration signals designed to increase the possibility of coincidence with other pulses. Gate pulses present with other pulses cause circuits or devices to perform intended operations.

gate, rejection—*Same as* gate, NOR.

gate, Sheffer stroke—*Same as* gate, NAND.

gate, sine-junction—*Same as* gate, A AND-NOT B or gate, B AND-NOT A.

gate, subjunction — *Same as* gate, AN AND-NOT B or gate, B AND-NOT A.

gate, symmetric difference — *Same as* gate, exclusive OR.

gate, synchronous—A synchronous gate is a time gate wherein the output intervals are synchronized with an incoming signal.

gate, time—A time gate is a transducer that gives output only during chosen time intervals.

gate, union—*Same as* gate, OR.

gate zero-match—*Same as* gate, NOR.

gathering, data—*See* data collection.

gather-write—A specific operation that creates a single output record from data items which are gathered from nonconsecutive locations in CPY memory. This is accomplished by data-chaining the commands to be executed by the data channel.

gather-write/scatter-read — Gather-write is the ability to place the information from several nonadjacent locations in core storage (for example, several logical records) into a single physical record such as a tape block. Scatter-read is the ability to place the information from a physical record into several nonadjacent locations in core storage.

gating—Gating is the process of selecting those portions of a wave which exist during one or more selected time intervals, or which have magnitudes between selected limits.

gear, integrating — An integrator which has a pair of gears with a variable gear ratio: the input and output variables represent the angles of rotation of shafts; the input transmitting the drive torque from the input shaft to the output shaft, and used in mechanical analog computers.

gear, variable-speed—*Same as* gear, integrating.

general assembly program (GAP)—Allows the programmer to write his own program in symbolic code rather than in the absolute code of the computer. One symbolic code instruction is translated into one computer word—a simple one-for-one ararngement.

general escape—*See* escape, general.

generalized data manipulation — The performance of those data-processing chores common to most users, such as sorting, input/output operations, and report generation.

generalized routine—A routine designed to process a large range of specific jobs within a given type of application.

generalized subroutine—Subroutines that are written for easy and ready use in several various programs with only minor adjustments or adaptations by the programmer or systems analyst.

general program—A program, expressed in computer code, designed to solve a class of problems or specializing on a specific problem when appropriate parametric values are supplied. (Synonymous with general routine.)

general-purpose computer—1. A computer designed to operate on a program of instructions for the purpose of solving many types of data-processing problems rather than being designed to fulfill a single function or type of function. *See* special-purpose computer. 2. A computer designed to solve a wide variety of problems, the exact nature of which may be unknown before the computer was designed. Also called a stored-program computer.

general purpose languages—Combined programming languages which use English words and statements where they are convenient and which serve as mthematical notation for procedures conveniently expressed mathematically. COBOL, FORTRAN, and ALGOL are widely used general-purpose programming languages in both science and business.

general purpose operations programs — *See* programs, general purpose operating.

general purpose simulation program (GPSS) —An IBM discrete system simulation language.

general routine — A program, expressed in computer code, designed to solve a class of problems or specializing on a specific problem when appropriate parametric values are supplied. (Synonymous with generator routine.)

general telephone network, general switched-telephone network — This term refers to facilities provided by the telephone companies in the United States that permit each telephone subscriber to communicate with any other telephone subscriber.

general utility functions—Auxiliary operations such as tape searching, tape-file copying, media conversion, dynamic memory, and tape dumps.

generate—1. To construct a computer program by use of a generator. 2. To develop or produce various required subroutines from parameters of outline skeleton coding.

generated address—See address, calculated.

generated error—The total error accrued by combining the effect of using an exact or imprecise argument with the inexact formula. These errors are compounded by rounding off.

generating program — See program, generating.

generating routine—See routine generating.

generation — Under control of parameters supplied to a generator routine, a technique for producing a complete routine from one which is in skeleton form.

generation, automatic character — See automatic character generation.

generation data group (GDG)—A group, family, or unit of similar data sets which are related to each other because each is a modification of the next most recent data set, i.e., they all have the same name and are distinguished from each other by their generation numbers and their successive dates of creation.

generation, macro—See macrogeneration.

generation, report—See report generation.

generation, synthetic display—Logical and numerical processing to display collected data or calculated data in symbolic form.

generation, systems—See systems generation.

generator—1. A routine designed to create specific routines from specific input parameters or conditions and skeletal coding. 2. In programming, a program that constructs another program from specifically designed sets of instructions by selecting, adjusting, and arranging them in accordance with given specifications.

generator, analytical function — Either an analog device or a specifically programmed digital computer with an operation based on some physical law, such as one used to solve a particular differential equation.

generator, arbitrary-function — A specific function generator (analog) which is not committed by its design function exclusively, so that the function which it generates can be changed at the discretion of the operator.

generator, character-controlled—A generator that takes entries from a library tape and examines the control characters associated with each entry and modifies the library instructions according to direction given by the control characters.

generator, clock-pulse — A specifically designed generator which generates pulses for purposes of special timing or gating in a digital computer, i.e., pulses which are used as inputs to gates to aid in pulse-shaping and timing.

generator clock signal — Same as generator, clock pulse.

generator, compiler—A generating program is a program designed to construct other programs for specific performance or for specific operations, such as a sorting program. A compiler generator then, is a generating program designed to construct compiling programs, which are translating programs for one computer's use when it cannot use a program directly due to a difference in languages.

generator, digit-symbol (display)—Addition of a symbol generator to a visual display greatly increases its capabilities and capacity for character and symbol generation. Some models plot symbols on a 35 matrix (5 dots wide and 7 dots high) in one of several sizes. A total of 220 characters (based upon the average character of 16 points) may be displayed flicker-free. Rate of plotting is increased approximately ten times, by the use of a digit-symbol generator.

generator, empiric function—A computer program or device capable of generating a mathematical function, curve, or set of values from given values, such as test data or laboratory measurements.

generator, function—A specific unit with one or more input and output variables, each output variable being equal to some particular function of the input variable or variables.

generator, function (general purpose)—Same as generator, arbitrary function.

generator, function natural law—See generator analytical function.

generator, gate—Same as generator, clock-pulse.

generator, line (display) — A line generator which receives digital on- or off-line inputs and generates straight lines between any two points on a 512×512 matrix on a cathode-ray tube at a constant writing rate. Dotted, dashed, or blank lines can be generated (some computers).

generator, major-state — One or more major control states are entered to determine and execute an instruction. During any one instruction, a state lasts for one computer cycle. The major state generator determines the machine state during each cycle as a function of the current instruction, the current state, and the condition of the break request signal supplied to an input bus by peripheral equipment.

generator, manual number — A device which accepts manually input data and holds the contents which can be sensed by a computer, controller, and other devices, i.e., used to insert a word manually into computer storage for hold until it is read during the execution of a program.

generator, natural function—Same as generator, analytical-function.

generator, natural law—Same as generator, analytical-function.

generator, number—A set of manual controls on which a computer operator can set a word.

generator, physical law—See generator, analytical function.

generator, pure—A unique generator which is a routine capable of writing another routine. When this is tied to an assembler, the pure generator is usually a section of a program found on a library tape and is called into storage by the assembler, which then writes one or more entries in the routine.

generator, random-number—A special machine routine or hardware designed to produce a random number or series of random numbers according to specified limitations.

generator, report—A technique for producing complete data-processing reports given only a description of the desired content and format of the output reports, and certain information concerning the input file.

generator, report-program — See report program generator.

generator, restorer-pulse—Same as generator, clock-pulse.

generator routine—A designed set of instructions for production of required subroutines.

generator, sort—A sort generator is similar to a compiler in that it will produce an object-sorting program. In other words, it is a program to produce a program. The programmer needs only to indicate the various parameters for his particular sorting job. A sort-generator specifications sheet is furnished for this purpose. The generator itself, as well as the sorting program it produces, is compatible with various executives. Overall compatibility of operating systems is a basic feature of many programs. The sort generator will produce a running program to sort files of any length and also allows for user's own-code intervention on the first and/or last pass of the sort program. This intervention will allow the installation programmer to intervene in the sort process to expand, contract, delete, add, or change records during the first and/or last pass. In many cases this will save an additional run required to edit the data for printout, etc.

generator, sort and merge—This generator uses the features of the systems to produce fast efficient object programs with minimum effort. The generators have options for insertion of programmer coding for manipulation of records or files prior to and following the sort.

generator, time-pulse — Same as generator, clock pulse.

generator, timing pulse—Same as generator, clock pulse.

geodetic system—A computer application system used to reduce the costs of mining and drilling by performing seismographic studies by a computer. Geodesy is the branch of applied mathematics which determines the curvature, shape, and dimensions of the earth. Computers are used for advanced geodetic survey work by mining companies to locate oil and ore deposits.

geometric solution—A graphic method of solving a linear programming problem, by plotting the half-planes determined by the constraints and the lines of constant value for the functional. Its use is restricted to problems with, at most, two structural variables.

geometry—The study of space and of spatial relationships; the investigation of the nature and properties of curves, surfaces and other configurations of points in space.

gibberish—See hash.

gigacycle—A kilomegacycle per second (10^9 cycles per second). (Synonymous with kilomegacycle.)

GIGO (garbage in-garbage out)—Unwanted and meaningless information carried along in storage; a result of undesirable input data or information.

global variable — A variable whose name is known to a main program and all its subroutines.

glossary—A vocabulary with annotations for a particular subject.

go ahead—A polling signal sent from the computer to a terminal, or from one terminal down-line to another, to direct the terminal to begin transmission to the computer.

GP — Abbreviation for generalized programming, general processor, and general purpose.

GPC—Abbreviation for general-purpose computer.

GPS—Abbreviation for general problem solver. A general programming procedure developed for use on the IBM 704 computer by Rand Corporation.

GPSS — A general purpose simulation system developed by IBM.

graceful degradation—See fail softly.

graceful degradation, time sharing—See time sharing, fail soft.

grade, teletype—Represents the lowest type circuit in terms of speed, cost, and accuracy.

grain direction—Important in optical character recognition, it is the arrangement (direction) of the fibers in the paper in relation to the route or manner in which a document travels through the character reader.

grandfather cycle—The period during which magnetic-tape records are retained before reusing so that records can be reconstructed in the event of loss of information stored on a magnetic tape.

grandfather tape—See tape, grandfather.

graph—A sheet of paper onto which have been placed curves, lines, points, and explanatory alphabetic and numerical information representing numerical data.

grapheme—A written or machine code that represents a single semanteme.

graphetic level—An example is a character, either handwritten or printed, usually then capable of being copied, reproduced, transmitted, or manipulated by an ordered set of pulses. This is said to be a representation at a graphetic level.

graph follower—A device that reads data in the form of a graph, usually an optical sensing device.

graphic console — The graphic console provides primary system control. The man-machine-communication components of the graphic console generally are: a 10-inch square CRT display surface, and a position-indicating pencil; 36 program-status lights (with a message overlay) and 36 program control keys; an alphanumeric keyboard; and a card reader. A display is created by having the computer specify the end points of vector to be drawn. 36 program control keys are provided for use in addition to the input pencil. The function of a particular program control key is assigned by the program and can be changed from program to program. Replaceable overlays are used to identify the function of each key for each application. An alphanumeric keyboard, consisting of 36 keys arranged in a 6-by-6 pattern enables the operator to enter data (some systems).

graphic data processing—*See* data processing, graphic.

graphic display unit — A communications terminal which can display data on a screen.

graphic documentation—A process developed for recording data on graphs and films.

graphic file maintenance — The process designed to update physical representation such as microfilm, film prints, CRT output copies, etc.

graphic form—A physical or pictorial representation of data, such as printing plotting output, or CRT engineering drawings.

graphic panel—A master-control panel which pictorially and usually colorfully traces the relationship of control equipment and the process operation. It permits an operator to check at a glance on the operation of a far-flung control system by noting dials, valves, scales, and lights.

graphics — The use of diagrams or other graphical means to obtain operating data and answers. The use of written symbols and visual displays.

graphic solution—A solution obtained with graphs or other pictorial devices, as contrasted with solutions obtained by the manipulation of numbers.

graphic type machine—A machine used to record and reproduce various operations.

gray code—*See* code, cyclic.

grid—In optical character recognition (OCR), two mutually orthogonal sets of parallel lines used for specifying or measuring character images.

grid chart—A representation of the relation between inputs, files, and outputs in matrix form.

grid, control—The electrode of a vacuum tube other than a diode upon which a

signal voltage is impressed in order to regulate the plate current, usually electrode or grid number 1.

gross index—The first of a pair of indexes consulted to locate particular records, etc; the secondary or supplemental index is the fine index.

ground, signal—This conductor establishes the electrical ground reference potential for all interchange circuits except the frame-grounding circuit.

group code—*See* code, group.

group, data control—*See* data control group.

grouped records—*See* record group.

group indicate—The printing of indicative information from only the first record of a group.

group indication—*See* indication, group.

grouping—When a mass of data having common characteristics are arranged into related groups.

grouping of records—The combining of two or more records into one block of information on tape to decrease the wasted time due to tape acceleration and deceleration and to conserve tape space. This is also called blocking of records.

group, link—Consists of those links which employ the same multiplex-terminal equipment.

group mark—A special character used in a write instruction to designate the end of a record in storage.

group printing—The function of a machine which does not print data from every card. Instead, it summarizes the data contained in a group of cards and prints only the summarized total.

group record—*See* record group.

group theory—A study, in the mathematical sense of the rules, for combining groups, sets, and elements; i.e., the theory of combining groups.

guard, memory—*See* memory guard.

guard mode, executive—*See* executive guard mode.

guard mode, real-time—The guard mode is activated only by the instruction load internal function which establishes certain operation parameters. When operative, any attempt to perform a restricted operation will result in an interrupt to an address in central store. Guard mode is terminated by the occurrence of any interrupt.

It is possible for any program to use the prevent-all-interrupts and jump instruction, thereby allowing real-time programs to operate effectively when guard mode is established.

guard signal—1. A signal which allows values to be read or converted only when the values are not in a changing state. 2. An extra output, which is generated when all values are complete, to be used as a guard signal. Used in digital-to-analog or analog-to-digital converters or other converters or digitizers.

guide edge—The edge on which paper and magnetic tape is guided while being fed, if such a method is used.

guide margin — When measuring across a paper tape, it is the distance between the guide edge and the center of the closest track of the tape.

gulp—A small group of bytes, similar to a word or instruction.

H

half-adder — A circuit having two output points, S and C, representing sum and carry, and two input points, A and B, representing addend and augend such that the output is related to the input according to the following table:

INPUT		OUTPUT	
A	B	S	C
0	0	0	0
0	1	1	0
1	0	1	0
1	1	0	1

A and B are arbitrary input pulses, and S and C are sum without carry, and carry, respectively. Two half-adders, properly connected, may be used for performing binary addition and form a full serial adder.

half adder, parallel—See adder, half (parallel).

half adder, serial—See adder, half (serial).

half-adjust—1. A kind of rounding in which the value of the least significant digit of a number determines whether or not a one shall be added to the next higher significant digit, or, in which the two least significant digits determine whether or not a one is to be added to the next higher significant digit. If the least significant digits represent less than one-half, nothing is added to the higher significant digit, if the least significant digits represent one-half or more, then a one is added to the next higher significant digit. 2. To round by one-half of the maximum value of the number base of the counter.

half duplex—A system permitting electrical communications in only one direction between stations. Technical arrangements may permit operation in either direction, but not simultaneously. This term is therefore qualified by one of the following suffixes: S/O for send only; R/O for receive only; S/R for send or receive.

half-duplex channel—A channel capable of transmitting and receiving signals, but in only one direction at a time.

half-duplex circuit—A duplex intercity facility with single loops to the terminals capable of two-way nonsimultaneous operation.

half-duplex operation—Half-duplex or single-telegraph operation refers to communication on a circuit in only one direction at a time, with or without a break feature. The break feature enables the receiving station to interrupt the sending station.

half-duplex service—A type of communication channel that is capable of transmitting and receiving signals, but is not capable for simultaneous and independent transmission and reception.

half subtracter—See subtracter, half.

half-subtracter, parallel—See subtracter, half (parallel).

half subtracter, serial — See subtracter, half (serial).

halftime emitter—A device that emits synchronous pulses midway between the row pulses of a punched card.

half-word—1. A fixed group of bits which can be handled as a unit by the equipment and which is equivalent to two bytes. 2. A group of characters that represent half of a computer word for addressing purposes as a unit in storage.

half-word boundary—In the IBM 360 Computer Series, any address ending in a 0 which is divisible by binary 2 denotes a natural boundary for an item of 2 bytes length. Items of this type must be referenced by an address falling on a boundary of the corresponding type.

half-word, effective — The half-word actually accessed in a half-word operation.

half-word input/output buffer—If for reasons of previous program compatibility or to facilitate systems design it becomes desirable to use the upper half of the computer word for both input data characters and output data characters, this arrangement can be made when the system is ordered. This technique leaves the lower half of the buffer area words free to be used for some entirely unrelated purpose such as the storage of constants.

half-word location, effective — The storage location pointed to by the effective virtual address of a half-word addressing instruction.

halt, dead—A machine halt from which there is no recovery. Such a halt may be deliberately programmed. A drop dead halt may occur through a logical error in programming. Examples in which a drop dead halt occur are division by zero and transfer to a non-existent instruction word.

halt, drop-dead—Same as halt, dead.

halt instruction—A machine instruction that stops the execution of the program.

halt instruction, operational—An instruction that can stop the computer either before or after the halt instruction is obeyed, depending on the governing criterion.

halt, nonprogrammed — An inadvertent machine stoppage, not due to the results of a programmed instruction, such as an automatic interrupt, manual intervention, machine malfunction, power failure, or other cause.

halt, optional—*See* halt instruction, optional.

halt, program—*Same as* program stop.

halt, programmed — A machine stoppage or interruption of machine operations caused deliberately by a program instruction. The halt is automatic with this instruction in the program.

Hamming code—One of the error-correction code systems in use today.

Hamming distance—The number of digit positions by which the corresponding digits of two binary words of the same length are different.

hand-feed punch—*See* punch, hand-feed.

handling, data—*See* data handling.

handling, document—*See* document, handling.

handling, dynamic—Generally means a given feature is not handled fully until the generated machine language program is executed.

handling, interrupt—*See* interrupt handling.

hand punch, portable—A device for punching cards by hand. It does not need electricity and is small enough to be easily carried.

handshaking—In a synchronous transmission scheme, the term is used to describe the process by which predetermined configurations of characters are exchanged by the receiving and transmitting equipment to establish synchronization.

hands-on background — The prior work experience developed by actually operating the hardware and often used as a criteria of programmer capability and knowledge.

hang-up—1. A nonprogrammed stop in a routine. It is usually an unforeseen or unwanted halt in a machine pass. It is most often caused by improper coding of a machine instruction or by the attempted use of a nonexistent or improper operation code. 2. Computer jargon that indicates the failure of a program to operate as planned when terminated for various reasons. 3. An unexplained machine stop. (Slang)

hang-up prevention — The computer logic must be designed or modified so that no sequence of valid or invalid instructions can cause the computer to come to a halt or to go into a nonterminating uninterruptible state. Examples of this latter case are infinitely nested executions or non-terminating indirect addressing.

hard adder—A particular type adder used in incremental computers and which consists of a digital integrator.

hard copy—1. Typewritten or printed characters on paper, produced at the same time

information is copied or converted into machine language, that is not easily read by a human. 2. A printed copy of machine output in a visually readable form; e.g., printed reports, listings, documents, summaries, etc.

hardware—1. The mechanical, magnetic, electrical and electronic devices or components of a computer. 2. The electric, electronic, and mechanical equipment used for processing data consisting of cabinets, racks, tubes, transistors, wires, motors, and such. 3. Any piece of automatic data-processing equipment. (Slang)

hardware check—A provision constructed in hardware for verifying the accuracy of information transmitted, manipulated, or stored by any unit or device in a computer. (Synonymous with built-in check and built-in automatic check, and related to program check.)

hardware, compatible—Components, peripheral equipment, or other devices which can be used on more than one system with little or no adjustment.

hash—1. Considered to be computer or program garbage specifically recorded on tapes to fill or comply with restrictions on conventions of starting procedures, block sizes, and others. 2. Same as garbage.

hash total—*See* control total.

HAYSTAQ — An information storage and retrieval method used in the field of chemistry for documents in connection with patent searching.

head—A device that reads, records or erases information in a storage medium, usually a small electromagnet used to read, write, or erase information on a magnetic drum or tape, or the set of perforating or reading fingers and block assembly for punching or reading holes in paper tape.

head, combined — A small electromagnetic unit used for reading, recording, or erasing information on a magnetic tape, disk, or drum.

header—A file record that contains common, constant, or identifying information for a group of records which are to follow. Also the first part of a message containing all necessary information for directing the message to its destination.

head, erase—A magnetic head used to erase or obliterate the old information prior to writing new information.

header card—A punched card which serves to identify types and characteristics of records maintained on the following cards.

header, record—*See* record header.

header table—*Same as* header record.

head, fixed—Pertaining to the use of stationary, rigidly mounted reading and writing heads on a bulk memory device in contrast to movable heads.

head gap—1. The space between the reading or recording head and the recording medium such as tape, drum or disk. 2. The space or gap intentionally inserted into the magnetic circuit of the head in order to force or direct the recording flux into the recording medium.

head, gap-controlled—A microscopic gap is maintained between read/write heads and the disk surface with absolute reliability. A fail-safe head-retraction mechanism prevents contact with the disk. Heads are completely self adjusting.

heading — A string of characters, usually placed at the beginning of a message, that represents message routing and destination information and that is machine readable.

heading, page — The description of a page context of a report; usually appears at the top of each page.

heading record—A record which contains an identification or description of the output report for which following records are related to and concerned with the body of the report.

heading, report — Description of the report content which is produced, often at the beginning of the report.

head magnetic—Same as head, read/write.

head-per-track—A separate read/write head is fixed over each track of information on the disk surface. The powerful and reliable read/write technique used in high speed magnetic drums has been combined with the low cost, large scale storage capacity of the disk. Electronic switching replaces slow and costly mechanical arm accessing.

head, playback — A head that is used for reading data or a medium, such as tape, disks, drums, cards, or an optical sensor.

head, preread—A read head that may be used to read data on the track of a moving medium such as tape, disk, or drum before the data reaches the read head.

head, read—A head that is used for reading data from a medium, such as tape, disks, drums, or cards.

head, read/write — A small electromagnet used for reading, recording, or erasing polarized spots that represent information on magnetic tape, disk, or drum.

head, record—See read/write head.

head, recording — A head used to transfer data to a storage device such as a drum, disk, tape, or magnetic card.

head stack—A group of recording heads all recording a set of tracks simultaneously, i.e., a recording channel or band. Such heads are usually mounted and used together for other purposes.

head-to-tape contact — The degree to which the surface of the magnetic coating approaches the surface of the record or relay heads during normal operation of a recorder. Good head-to-tape contact minimizes separation loss and is essential in obtaining high resolution.

head, write—A head used to transfer data to a storage device such as a drum, disk, tape, or magnetic card.

HELP—An aid available to inexperienced user personnel. HELP gives users convenient access to a direct self-teaching facility, which accepts questions on the usage of several software subsystems framed in the natural language of the user and provides appropriate answers in English text (some computers).

HELP program, time sharing—See time sharing, HELP program.

hesitation — A temporary halt or temporary suspension of operations in a sequence of operations of a computer in order to perform all or part of the operations from another sequence.

heuristic—1. Procedures or methodology designed to develop a plan or program that will obtain desired results or output as an improvement over current procedures and is satisfactory in relation to the constraints of time, cost, personnel, and the limited use of the result. 2. Pertaining to exploratory methods of problem solving in which solutions are discovered by evaluation of the progress made toward the final result. (Contrast with algorithmic.)

heuristic approach — An approach that encourages further experimentation and investigation. An intuitive trial-and-error method of attacking a problem (as opposed to the algorithmic method).

heuristic problem solving—A series of rules that systematically varies models through formal mutation and regenerative reading.

heuristic program—See program, heuristic.

heuristic programming — See programming, heuristic.

heuristic routine—See program, heuristic.

hexadecimal digit—A digit that is a member of the set of sixteen digits: 0 through 9 and then A, B, C, D, E, or F used in a numerical notation system using a radix of 16. Some systems use letters other than A-F for digits 10-15.

hexadecimal notation—Notation of numbers in the base 16.

hexadecimal number—A number, usually of more than one figure, representing a sum in which the quantity represented by each figure is based on a radix of sixteen.

hexadecimal number system—A number system using the equivalent of the decimal number sixteen as a base.

hierarchy—A specified rank or order of items. A series of items classified by rank or order.

hierarchy, data—See data hierarchy.

high-activity data processing—A condition in which only a comparatively small number of records are updated or referred to frequently.

higher order language—See language, higher order.

high-low bias test—A preventive-maintenance procedure in which certain operating conditions are varied about their normal values in order to detect and locate defective units; e.g., supply voltage or frequency may be varied. (Synonymous with marginal test, and related to check.)

high-low limits — The maximum and minimum values of data expected. These values are used to check the program and results.

high order—Pertaining to the weight or significance assigned to the digits of a number; e.g., in the number 123456, the highest order digit is one; the lowest order digit is six. One may refer to the three high-order bits of a binary word as another example. (Clarified by order.)

high-order digit—*See* digit, high-order.

high-performance equipment — Equipment having sufficiently exacting characteristics to permit their use in trunk or line circuits.

high-positive indicator — An internal computer-indicator component that indicates "on" if the result of an arithmetic operation is positive and not zero (some systems).

high punch—The 12, 11, and zero punch are zone punches; the 12 punch being the highest (vertically) on the standard punched card.

high-speed card reader — *See* reader, high speed.

high-speed carry—A type of carry in which: (1) a carry into a column results in a carry out of that column because the sum without a carry in that column is 9; (2) instead of a normal adding process, a special process is used that takes the carry at high speed to the actual column where it is added. Also called standing-on-nines carry.

high-speed communications station, multiple —*See* multiple station, high speed communications.

high speed core memory—*See* core memory, high speed.

high speed data acquisition (HSDA) — An HSDA system may be thought of as a monitoring and controlling facility that is used to acquire, evaluate, and record data developed during the testing of a system (or assembly, subassembly, or component). The system here refers to anything from an anesthetized rodent in a research laboratory to a Saturn V booster on its test stand.

high speed loop—*See* loop, high speed.

high speed memory—*See* memory, high speed.

high-speed printer—A printer that operates at a speed more compatible with the speed of computation and data processing so that it may operate on-line.

high-speed reader—*See* reader, high speed.

high-speed storage—*See* storage, high-speed.

highway—*See* trunk or bus.

hi-low—Used in exception reporting to relate the maximum and minimum limits beyond which an exception is reported and acted upon.

history run—The printing out of all transactions of a process for reading or recording purposes.

hit—1. A term used in mechanical retrieval systems to represent an answer found by the machine. 2. In file maintenance, the finding of a match between a detail record and a master record.

hit-on-the-fly printer—*See* printer, on-the-fly.

hit-on-the-fly system—A printer where either the paper, the print head, or both are in continual motion.

hit on the line—A momentary open circuit on a teletypewriter loop.

hold—The function of retaining information in one storage device after transferring it to another device, in contrast to clear.

hold, automatic — In an analog computer, attainment of the hold condition automatically through amplitude comparison of a problem variable, or through an overload condition.

hold button, analog—The hold button causes the solution to be temporarily suspended, permitting the user to study the various quantities.

hold facility—The ability of a computer, when its calculations are interrupted, to keep the current value of all the variables.

holding beam—A diffuse beam of electrons for regenerating the charges stored on the dielectric surface of an electrostatic memory tube or cathode-ray storage tube.

hold instruction—*See* instruction, hold.

hold mode—In the hold mode, also called the freeze or interrupt mode, the computing action is stopped and all variables are held at the value they had when the computation was interrupted.

hole, control—*See* control punches.

hole count check—An accuracy checking feature which performs a count of the number of punched holes at the particular read station and compares the total with that of a subsequent reading station total in column by column fashion.

hole, function—*Same as* control punches.

hole, location—*See* holes, feed.

hole pattern—An array of punches, i.e., a configuration of holes in a single column or in a single frame of punched tape.

hole punching, clean — *Same as* chad tape which has punched holes entirely detaching the disk from the paper, leaving the holes completely clean.

holes, code — Data holes in perforated tape that represent the information, in contrast to the feedholes that control movement and positioning.

holes, feed—A series of small holes in perforated paper tape that conveys no intelligence but are solely for the purpose of engaging the feed pawls or sprockets which transport the tape over the sensing pins of various reading devices.

hole site—The area on a punch card or paper tape where a hole may or may not be punched. It can be a form of binary storage in which a hole represents a 1, and the absence of a hole represents a 0.

holes, sprocket—Feed holes punched in a tape to control the tape movement and positioning.

holistic masks—The set of characters which reside within a character reader and which theoretically represent the exact replicas of all possible input characters in the machine's repertory. Only perfect specimens will be accepted.

Hollerith—A widely used system of encoding alphanumeric information onto cards; hence, Hollerith cards is synonymous with punch cards. Such cards were first used in 1890 for the U.S. Census and were named after Herman Hollerith, their originator.

Hollerith card—*See* card, Hollerith.

Hollerith code — An alphanumeric punched-card code invented by Dr. Herman Hollerith in 1889, in which the top three positions in a column are called "zone" punches (12, 11, and 0, or R, X and O, from the top downward), and are combined with the remaining punches, or digit punches (1 through 9) to represent alphabetic, numeric, and special characters. For example, A is a combination of an R (12) and a 1 punch; an L is a combination of an X (11) and a 3 punch, etc.

Hollerith strings—In addition to their use in FORMAT statements, Hollerith strings can also be used as arguments of functions and can be stored with floating-point or fixed-point variable names in an arithmetic assignment statement. A Hollerith string is specified in writing the character count followed by an H, and then the string of characters. A string must have eight characters, or less, when stored with a floating-point variable name; it must have four characters, or less, when stored with a fixed-point variable name. If used as an argument, the string can be any length. When strings are less than the maximum (eight for real, four for integer), they are stored left-justified and blanks are filled in for the missing characters (some computers).

home loop—An operation involving only those input and output units associated with the local terminal.

home record—*See* record, home.

homostasis—The dynamic condition of a system wherein the input and output are balanced precisely thus presenting an appearance of no change; hence, a steady state.

hopper—A device that holds cards and makes them available to a feed mechanism. (Contrasts with stacker and output magazine, and synonymous with input magazine.)

horizontal feed—That particular attitude in which a card is placed in the hopper and enters and traverses the card track—i.e., horizontally rather than vertically or face-up rather than face-down.

horizontal parity check—The comparison of the number of bits tallied and totalled along channels as related to a previously determined quantity.

horizontal raster count—The number of coordinate positions addressable across the width of the cathode-ray tube.

horizontal sorter—A sorter rack which slides backward and forward.

horizontal system—A programming system in which instructions are written horizontally, i.e., across the page.

host computer—A computer that is connected to a stored-program multiplexor and which is the base or independent computer upon which the multiplexor is dependent for certain vital functions as program read-in, etc. In an arrangement of this sort, the multiplexor could have stand-alone capacity in the event the host computer is not always available.

housekeeping — 1. Pertaining to administrative or overhead operations or functions which are necessary in order to maintain control of a situation; e.g., for a computer program, housekeeping involves the setting up of constants and variables to be used in the program. (Synonymous with red tape.) 2. A general term used to describe coding which reserves, restores, and clears memory areas. 3. Those parts of a program that pertain to the setting up or cleaning up of programs in contrast to those parts of the program which are distinctly input and output operations. 4. Operations in a routine that do not contribute directly to the solution of the problem and do not contribute directly to the operation of the computer.

housekeeping operation—A general term for the operation that must be performed for a machine run usually before actual processing begins. Examples of housekeeping operations are: establishing controlling marks, setting up auxiliary storage units, reading in the first record for processing, initializing, set-up verification operations, and file identification.

housekeeping routine — The initial instructions in a program that are executed only one time; e.g., clear storage.

housekeeping runs—Operations required for file maintenance such as sorting, merging, and editing.

HSM—Abbreviation for high-speed memory.

HSP—Abbreviation for high-speed printer.

HSR—Abbreviation for high-speed reader.

hub—A socket on a control panel or plugboard into which an electrical lead or plug wire may be connected in order to carry signals, particularly to distribute the signals over many other wires.

hub, bus—A location on the control panel which permits several entries or exists of pulse signals.

hub, combination — An electrical jack connection which will omit or receive electrical impulses on a control panel.

hunting—A continuous attempt on the part of an automatically controlled system to seek a desired equilibrium condition. The system usually contains a standard, a method of determining deviation from this standard, and a method of influencing the system such that the difference between the standard and the state of the system is brought to zero. (Clarified by servomechanism.)

hybrid computer, hardware-control — The hardware-control program group provides the control and communication between various elements of the hybrid system. The programmer can control analog computer modes and operation of automatic features of the analog device.

hybrid computer, input/output — See input/output, hybrid computer.

hybrid computer, problem-analysis — See analysis, hybrid problem.

hybrid computers—By combining analog computer speed, flexibility, and direct communication capability with digital computer memory, logic, and accuracy, the integrated hybrid computer has introduced a new dimension in engineering, scientific, and business technology . . . the power to attack every aspect of a problem with the computational capability suited to the task. Dynamic simulation and high-speed differential-equation solution may be performed on the analog side; static and algebraic computations may be handled on the digital side. Overall computational economy and efficiency are thereby maximized.

hybrid input/output — The input/output group of programs consists of a system monitor and programs to control operation of analog/digital conversion equipment and special devices such as an oscilloscope display or a digital plotter.

hybrid problem analysis — Programs in the problem analysis group help the hybrid programmer decide which parts of the problem to solve on a digital computer and the mathematical techniques that should be used. For example, multivariable function generation that may be difficult to perform on the analog computer is well-suited to digital solution.

hybrid programming—Routines in the hybrid programming library are designed to help the engineer decide which parts of a problem should be solved in digital domain. They also deal with timing, function-generation integration, and general simulation problems, provide diagnosis of hardware operation, and check whether the analog device is scaled and wired correctly.

hybrid system checkout—These programs implement checkout of system hardware, analog wiring, and the digital program. Normal maintenance checks are performed in conjunction with a standard, wired, analog patchboard. Digital utility programs and analog static check programs are also provided.

hypertape control unit (IBM)—This device attaches to a selector or multiplexor channel of the processor and can control up to eight drives. A feature is available that enables the unit to address many drives when used with a tape-switching unit. Units allow up to 16 hypertape drives to be shared by up to four data channels on the same or separate System/360 processors.

hypertape drives—See drive, hypertape.

hypertape units—High speed tape units which use cartridges which house the supply and take-up reels to permit automatic loading.

hysteresis—1. The lagging in the response of a unit of a system behind an increase or a decrease in the strength of a signal. 2. A phenomenon demonstrated by materials that make their behavior a function of the history of the environment to which they have been subjected.

hysteresis loop—A graph showing the relationship of flux density and the magnetizing force.

I

IAD — Abbreviation for initiation area dicriminator. A unique CRT (cathode-ray tube) combined with a photoelectric cell to discern unmapped or uncorrelated long-range radar data for processing by various specific programs in defense-oriented procedures.

i address—The location of the next instruction to be executed in some brands of equipment based on whether or not a branch operation occurs.

IAL, International Algebraic Language—The forerunner of ALGOL. (Clarified by algorithmic language.)

IAR—Instruction address register which contains the address of the next instruction to be executed.

IBM card—A type of paper card that may have information recorded on it by means of

punched holes, and which may be read by a computer.

IC—The abbreviation for both integrated circuit and instruction counter.

icand—Abbreviation for multiplicand.

icand register—That register which is used in multiplication to hold the multiplicand.

ICC — Abbreviation for International Computation Center. Sponsored by UNESCO in Rome. This computer center makes computer services available to member nations.

ICIP—Abbreviation for International Conference on Information Processing.

I-conversion—A type of FORMAT specification in FORTRAN to convert fixed-point (integer) data for I/O operations.

ICT—The trade name for International Computers and Tabulators, Ltd., a major British equipment manufacturer.

identification—A code number or code name that uniquely identifies a record, block, file or other unit of information.

identification division—The part of COBOL programming in which the programmer gives information to identify the source program and the object program.

identification, file—The coding required to identify each physical unit of the outputs of electronic data-processing machine runs.

identification number — The number, from 0000000 to 9999999, assigned to input data.

identifier—1. A symbol whose purpose is to identify, as to indicate or name a body of data. 2. A key.

identifier, data use—A title or name for the use of the data items for a data element; for instance, an occurrence date such as the employment date of an employee that is used for data base information.

identifier, location — An identification, by label of some kind, assigned to a specific location, for instance, a city, neighborhood, or address, or a specific location in computer storage.

identifier (name)—A special symbol which is used to label or identify data in a programming language. Most often, as in FORTRAN, the choice of characters used as identifiers are subject to various conventional restrictions, such as that of making the first character of an identifier a letter and not a numeral.

identifier words—The identifier word is a full length computer word which is associated with a search or a search-read function. In a search or search-read function, the identifier word is stored in a special register in the channel synchronizer and compared with each word read by the peripheral unit (some systems).

identify—To attach a unique code or code name to a unit of information.

identifying—The procedure that identifies the source of a given information mark and, therefore, of an object or a location. The operation involves selection and translation.

identifying code—A code placed in perforated tape or punched cards to identify the contents, or their origin.

identity unit — An identity unit has several binary input signals and only one binary output signal. The output signal represents 1 only when all the input signals are alike.

idle characters — Control characters interchanged by a synchronized transmitter and receiver to maintain synchronization during nondata periods.

idle time—The time that a computer is available for use, but is not in operation.

IDP, Integrated Data Processing—1. A system that treats as a whole all data-processing requirements to accomplish a sequence of data-processing steps or a number of related data-processing sequences, and that strives to reduce or eliminate duplicating data entry or processing steps. 2. The processing of data

by such a system in which all procedures are in some way tied to the computer.

ier—Short for multiplier.

ier register—That register which holds the multiplier during a multiplication operation.

if-A then B gate—*Same as* gate, B OR-NOT A.

if-A then NOT-B gate—*Same as* gate, NAND.

if-B then NOT-A gate—*Same as* gate, NAND.

IFCS—Abbreviation for International Federation of Computer Sciences.

IFIPS—Abbreviation for International Federation of Information Processing Societies. The predecessor of IFIP.

if statement assembly control—This feature allows for bypassing sections of an object program at assembly time under control of external indications, such as the sense switches.

ignore—1. A typewriter character indicating that no action whatsoever be taken; e.g., in teletype or flexowriter code, a character code consisting of holes punched in every hole position is an ignore character. This convention makes possible erasing any previously punched character. 2. An instruction requiring nonperformance of what normally might be executed; i.e., not to be executed. This instruction should not be confused with a NO OP or Do-Nothing instruction, since these generally refer to an instruction outside themselves.

ignore character—*See* ignore.

ignore character block—*See* character ignore, block.

ignore, instruction—*See* ignore.

illegal character—*See*, character, illegal.

illegal code—*See* code, illegal.

illegal command—*See* character, illegal.

illegal control message error—*See* error, illegal control message.

illegal operation—The process which results when a computer either cannot perform the instruction part or will perform with invalid and undesired results. The limitation is often due to built-in computer constraints.

image—An exact logical duplicate stored in a different medium.

image, card—A representation in storage of the holes punched in a card in such a manner that the holes are represented by one binary digit and the unpunched spaces are represented by the other binary digit.

image core—*See* core, image.

image dissector—In optical character recognition (OCR), a mechanical or electronic transducer that sequentially detects the level of light in different areas of a completely illuminated sample space.

image, library, core—A grouping of computer programs stored on a mass storage device in easily accessible form.

image processor—*See* processor, image.

immediate access—Pertaining to the ability to obtain data from or place data in a storage device or register directly, without serial delay due to other units of data, and usually in a relatively short period of time.

immediate access storage—See storage, immediate access.

immediate address—The designation of an instruction address that is used as data by the instruction of which it is a part.

immediate addressing—See addressing, immediate.

immediate address instruction — See address instruction, immediate.

immediate processing — Same as processing, demand.

imperative operations—An instruction which requires the manipulating of data by the computer.

imperative statements—Action statements of a symbolic program that are converted into actual machine-language instructions.

implementation—The several steps concerned in installing and starting successful operation of computer systems or related machines. The steps begin with feasibility studies, applications studies, equipment selection, systems analysis (present) and design of proposed new system, physical location of equipment, operations analysis, and critical review.

implicit address instruction format—See instruction format, implicit address.

implicit prices—Same as marginal values, shadow prices, dual variable levels, etc.—that is, numbers giving the incremental worth of a relaxation of one unit in the right-hand side of a constraint.

implied addressing — Same as addressing, repetitive.

imprinter—A device which causes the name and account number of a credit card holder to be transferred to the sales slip. Most credit cards show this information in raised, special type that can be automatically read from the sales slip by the computer.

improper character—Same as character, illegal.

improper code—See code, illegal.

improper command—See character illegal.

improper command check — Same as check, forbidden combination.

improvement time, system — See system-improvement time.

impulse noise—A pulse, appearing at the output of a circuit, which was not transmitted from the originating input to the circuit. These pulses usually are induced from circuit functioning or from sources outside the circuit and its associated input/output equipment.

inactive file—See file, inactive.

inactive mode, time sharing—See time sharing, inactive mode.

inadmissible character, automatic checking—See character checking, inadmissable.

incidentals time—Time which is usually alloted to training, demonstrating, or other useful but nonproductive purposes, but not including program development.

incipient failure—An equipment failure that is about to occur.

inclusive NOR gate—Same as gate, NOR.

inclusive OR—The Boolean operator that gives a truth table value of true if either or both of the two variables it connects are true. If neither is true, the value is false.

inclusive OR gate—Same as gate, OR.

inclusive segment—In a program overlay structure two or more different segments can be in the main memory simultaneously, whereas normally all inclusive segments lie on a single path from the root segment to the lowest segment.

incomplete program — See program, incomplete.

incomplete routine—A routine in a library of a programming system that requires parameters to be supplied by a macrostatement or main routine.

iconographic model—A pictorial representation of a system and the functional relations within the system.

increment—1. The quantity by which another is modified. An increment is usually positive; however, a negative quantity when added, is also called an increment. 2. To modify a quantity by adding a smaller quantity.

incremental compaction—See compaction, incremental.

incremental compiler, time sharing—See time sharing, incremental compiler.

incremental computer — A special-purpose computer that is specifically designed to process changes in the variables themselves, e.g., digital differential analyzer.

incremental display—See display, incremental.

incremental integrator—See integrator, incremental.

incremental plotter control — Provides for high-speed plotting of points, continuous curves, points connected by curves, curve-identification symbols, letters, numerals under program control.

incremental representation — Representation of changes in variables rather than the changes of the variables themselves—changes such as increases and decreases as results of equalities or relations expressed in the equations or model.

incremental tape units—Various types of magnetic tape modules which require a tape-flow for the process of reading or writing.

incremental ternary representation—Unique incremental representation by using the value of an increment as rounded to plus one, zero, or minus one. Rate of change maximums are represented as a continuous string of plus ones. Zero is represented by a string of zeros, and negatives by inserting minus ones with the zeros.

increment mode (display)—See display, increment mode.

independent equations—A set of equations none of which can be expressed as a linear combination of the others. With linear equations, the condition for independence is that the matrix (coefficient columns) shall be nonsingular or, equivalently, have rank equal to the number of equations.

independent interrupt processor—*See* interrupt, processor independent.

independent, machine — *See* machine-independent.

independent modularity program — *See* program-independent modularity.

independent sector—A device on certain tabulators which allows the first item of a series of similar data to be printed and inhibits some of the rest of the series.

indepth audit — Detailed examination of all manipulations performed on a single transaction or piece of information.

index—1. A table of computer words or fields containing addresses of records located in file storage. 2. An ordered reference list of the contents of a document, such as names, subjects, etc. 3. A symbol or number used to identify a particular quantity in an array of similar quantities; e.g., the terms of an array represented by x(1), x(2) . . . x(100) have the indexes 1, 2, . . . 100 respectively. 4. Pertaining to an index register.

index addressing, multiple (time-sharing)—*See* time sharing, multiple index addressing.

index, citation—An index or reference list of documents that are mentioned in a specific document or document set. The references are mentioned or quoted in the text. The citation index lists these references.

index, cooperation—An index number constructed by using the product of the drum diameter, in inches, and the line scan advance, in scanning lines per inch. Used in facsimile image transmission.

index, cycle—The number of cycle iterations in digital computer programming. A cycle index register may be used to set the number of cycles desired. Then with each cycle iteration, the register count is reduced by one until the register reaches zero and the series of cycles is complete.

index definition—The number of times a loop operation is to be repeated. This FORTRAN specification can appear in either do, read, or write statements. It is specified by the starting value, the limit value, and the incremental value.

indexed address—An address that is to be modified or has been modified by an index register or similar device. (Synonymous with variable address.)

indexed list — A FORTRAN instruction in read and write statements to form special indexed arrays.

indexed sequential data set — *See* data set, indexed sequential.

index entry—An individual line or item of data contained in an index, such as an entry in a dictionary.

index, etxernally specified (ESI) — *See* externally specified index operation (ESI).

index field value—The contents of the 3-bit index field of an instruction word (bit 12-14), designating one of the current general registers 1-7 as an index register (some systems).

index file—1. A table of keyfields identifying the actual disk records in another permanent disk file. 2. A file of terms in an automatic information retrieval system which is searched by the computer until it finds the index entry which will answer the relevant question. The index entry or the original document can then be printed.

index, fine—A subsidiary or supplemental index of a pair of indexes used to locate a particular file record. The higher or mass index would often be considered the gross index.

index, gross—The first of a pair of indexes consulted to locate particular records, etc. The secondary or supplemental index is the fine index.

indexing—1. The indexing method of random-access file organization in which a part of the file is set aside as an index in order to locate information in other parts of the file. 2. The modification of an instruction by the contents of an index register in order to obtain a new effective address. 3. The storing of copy in electronic form permits rapid and automatic indexing for information-retrieval purposes.

indexing, aspect — A method of indexing single units of information by the joint use of two or more terms, usually of equal rank, with retrieval performed by logical associations among the terms and logical connections to couple the terms, so that all units of information relating to a specific item may be searched out.

indexing, association—A study following two approaches — the automatic generation of word-association maps based on lists of words from the text, and representations based on the number of times words appear in the text.

indexing coordinate — *See* coordinate indexing.

indexing, correlative — *Same as* coordinate indexing.

indexing, cumulative—In a digital computer, the practice of assigning two or more indices to a single address in the instruction word.

indexing, datacode—*Same as* indexing, coordinate.

indexing, manipulative — 1. A system of indexing individual documents by descriptors of equal rank, so that a library can be searched for a combination of one or more descriptors. 2. An indexing technique where the interrelations of terms are shown by coupling individual words. 3. An indexing scheme by which descriptors may be correlated or combined to show any interrelations desired for purposes of more precise information retrieval.

indexing, multiple-aspect—*See* indexing, manipulative.

indexing unit applications — The indexing unit, containing an adder and sensing circuits, is shared by program control and input/output control. Program control uses the indexing unit to advance the P-register, to control repeated sequences, and to perform the indexing operations. The indexing operations include the addition of the modifier to the base address to obtain the effective execution address, the addition of the increment to the modifier, and various tests of the modifier. Input/output control uses the indexing unit to increment (decrement) the data-transfer address and to decrement the word count.

indexing, uniterm—A system of coordinate indexing that utilizes single terms, called uniterms, to define a document uniquely. (Related to uniterm systems.)

indexing, zatacode—*Same as* coordinate indexing.

index, permutation—An index alphabetically listing all of the major, plus minor if desired, words of a title or document so that each word appears once as the first word, followed by the other words rotated in a circular fashion. This is done so that the documents can be retrieved by numerous permutations.

index, permuted-title—*Same as* index permutation.

index point—One of the equally spaced rotational reference positions of the main shaft of card punch machines, labeled according to the row or column to which it corresponds.

index register—1. A register that contains a quantity to be used under direction of the control section of the computer hardware; e.g., for address modification and counting. 2. A device that permits automatic modification or an instruction address without permanently altering the instruction in memory. 3. A register to which an arbitrary integer, usually one, is added (or subtracted) upon the execution of each machine instruction. The register may be reset to zero or to an arbitrary number. Also called cycle counter and B-box.

index register pointer — Index registers may be used as pointers to indicate the current value or the current address in a list structure, or to keep track of the required next item or next location, when ordering items into a list. It may store the current address of the last item added to the list so that a list may be pushed down to add a new item, or the last item added may be pushed up.

index-word—1. A storage position or register the contents of which may be used to modify automatically the effective address of any given instruction. 2. An index based on the selection of words as used in a document, without giving thought to synonyms and more generic concepts related to the term selected.

indicate, group—To select and print indicative information from the initial record of a record group.

indication, group—A device on some tabulators which permits the first item of a series

of same or similar data or information to be printed and also inhibits some of the printing of the rest of the set or series.

indication, negative—It is customary to indicate a negative sign for a card field by the presence of a control punch, which may be located in a part of the card that is distant from the field it controls. Such an example might be a card in which a field in columns 46 to 50 is to be considered negative if there is a 5-punch in column 87. In this case, the 5-punch in column 87 is wired to pick up a selector as the card is being read.

indicator—A device often used as a control unit when it is designed to determine the selection from alternative processes. It can be set into a prescribed state according to the results of a previous process. An example is an overflow indicator. The state of such indicators may be displayed on a control panel for the benefit of programmers and operators.

indicator, branch-on—Branching takes place when appropriate indicators (switches, keys, buttons, etc.), or conditions, have been set to point to a particular group of registers, i.e., a branch may occur dependent upon whether the magnetic tape units are ready to receive a new block of data.

indicator, check—A device that displays or announces that an error has been made, or a checking operation has determined that a failure has occurred.

indicator, check divide—An indicator which denotes that an invalid division has been attempted or has occurred.

indicator, end-of-file — A device associated with each input and output unit that makes an end-of-file condition known to the routine and operator controlling the computer.

indicator, equal-zero—An internal computer indicator component which signals ON if the result of an arithmetic computation is zero.

indicator, high-positive — An internal computer-indicator component that indicates ON if the result of an arithmetic operation is positive and not zero.

indicator, instruction-check—A signaling device that is turned on automatically to alert a machine operator's attention to a machine malfunction, program error, or other malfunction in instructions currently being executed.

indicator, level—In the COBOL system, a symbol or level-number used in a data-division entry to indicate level. For example, FO is a level indicator.

indicator, machine check—A protective device that will be turned on when certain conditions arise within the machine. The machine can be programmed to stop or to run a separate correction routine or to ignore the condition.

indicator, overflow—A signaling device that indicates the occurrence of an overflow; for instance, a number too large to be contained in a given register.

indicator, overflow check—A device that is turned on by incorrect or unplanned for operations in the execution of an arithmetic instruction, particularly when an arithmetic operation produces a number too large for the system to handle.

indicator, read/write check—A device incorporated in certain computers to indicate upon interrogation whether or not an error was made in reading or writing. The machine can be made to stop, try the operation again, or follow a special subroutine, depending upon the result of the interrogation.

indicator, role—A code assigned to a keyboard to indicate the role of the keyword; e.g., a keyword may be a noun, verb, adjective, or adverb; therefore, an indicator is used to identify the specific role of the keyword.

indicator, routing—An identifier, such as a label, that defines the route and destination or addressee of a piece of information such as a message.

indicators—1. The devices that register conditions, such as high or equal conditions resulting from a computation. A sequence of operations within a procedure may be varied according to the position of an indicator. 2. The display device that usually indicates various conditions.

indicators, comparison — Three comparison indicators are: high, low, and equal. They are set on the basis of comparisons of operands in the arithmetic or index registers with operands in memory. The equal indicator is also set and reset by add and subtract instructions. If the result of an addition or subtraction is zero, the equal indicator is set. If the result is not zero, the equal indicator is reset.

indicator, sign check—An error-checking device, indicating no sign or improper signing of a field used for arithmetic processes. The machine can, upon interrogation, be made to stop or enter into a correction routine.

indicators, NIXIE display—See display indicators, NIXIE.

indicators, operator—The independent operator-indicator (console) lights may be used to call the operator's attention to any conditions that the programmer desires. They can be set, cleared, and tested under program control to fulfill the varying requirements of different programs.

indicators, priority—See priority indicators.

indirect address—See address, indirect.

indirect addressing—See addressing, indirect.

indirect control—See control, indirect.

indirect or offline system—See offline or indirect system.

indirect output—See output, indirect.

indirect reference address—See address, indirect reference.

individual line—A subscriber line arranged to serve only one main station, although additional stations may be connected to the line as extensions. An individual line is not arranged for discriminatory ringing with respect to the stations on that line.

induced failure—See failure, induced.

industrial data processing—Data processing designed for industrial purposes, often numerical control (n/c).

industrial process control—Industrial processing applications are as wide and varied as the degrees of control that individual processes may require. Some general process-control application areas are: precious metals production, cement production, environmental control, pilot plants, chemical processes, petroleum refining and many others. The data acquisition and control system provides maximum flexibility in the types of process data that it can accept, and the variety of output signals and data format that a computer may exercise.

inequalities, linear programming — The mathematical problem of minimizing or maximizing a linear function of n variables, subject to n independent restrictions, such as requirements that each variable be non-negative, and also subject to a finite number of other linear constraints. The latter are either equalities or weak inequalities ($\leq$ or $\geq$); strict inequalities of the form $<$ or $>$ are not admissible. An exact solution or other termination to this problem is furnished by the simplex method or one of its variants.

inequality—A proposition (or relation) which relates the magnitudes of two mathematical expressions or functions A and B. Inequalities are four types; A is greater than B ($A>B$); A is less than B ($A<B$); A is greater than or equal to B ($A\geq B$); A is less than or equal to B ($A\leq B$). The first two types are called strict, and the last two are relaxed or weak. The process of identifying a functional argument or range of arguments which makes the proposition true is called solving the inequality, or obtaining a feasible solution to the inequality.

infinite-pad method—A procedure or method of measuring reflectiveness of paper stock used in optical character recognition. A doubling of the number of backing sheets of the same paper, however, does not appreciably change the measured reflectiveness.

infinity—Any number larger than the maximum number that a given computer is able to store in any register.

infix notation—A method of forming one-dimensional expressions (e.g., arithmetic, logical, etc.) by alternating single operands and operators. Any operator performs its indicated function upon its adjacent terms which are defined, subject to the rules of operator precedence and grouping brackets which eliminates ambiguity.

information—1. Knowledge that was not previously known to its receiver. Information can be derived from data only to the extent that the data are accurate, timely, unexpected, and relevant to the subject under consideration. 2. Aggregation of data that are presented in various forms. Sets of symbols that specifically indicate one out of a number of alternatives. 3. The meaning assigned to data by the known conventions used in its representation.

information, administrative—Information of a textual nature, originated and prepared by one person for scrutiny by another.

information bits—Those bits which are generated by the data source and that are not used for error-control by the data transmission system.

information channel—The transmission and intervening equipment involved in the transfer of information in a given direction between two terminals. An information channel includes the modulator and demodulator, and any error-control equipment irrespective of its location, as well as the backward channel when provided.

information, communication — The physical means of connecting one location to another for the purpose of transmitting information.

information efficiency—A ratio of the actual negative entropy to the maximum possible entropy, using the same set of signs.

information-feedback system—An error-control system using message feedback with reception of the erroneous group from the sending station.

information flow analysis—The development of organizing and analyzing techniques to obtain facts and information about the organization, initialization, and flow to the final users of reports throughout the enterprise or organization.

information, machine-sensible — Information in a form that can be read by a specific machine.

information marker, beginning of—A reflective spot on the back of a magnetic tape, 10 feet from the physical beginning of the tape, which is sensed photoelectrically to indicate the point on the tape at which recording may begin.

information messages, input/output—Information messages are listed on the operator message device and the system output device. The operator message device is defined by the available equipment in the system. Normally it is the console typewriter but may be the line printer if no typewriter is available. The system output device may be different than the operator message device. For example, the operator message device may be the console typewriter and the system output device may be the line printer. This gives the operator an indication of the operations being performed and also gives a complete list of the job operations on the system output device for the programmer. Messages are not duplicated when the system output device and operator message device are the same.

information processing — The processing of data representing information and the determination of the meaning of the processed data.

information processing system—A system that receives and delivers information, changing the information in the process.

information rate—The product of the average information content per symbol and the average number of symbols per second.

information recovery and entry displays — See displays, information recovery and entry.

information requirements—The actual or anticipated questions that may be posed to an information system.

information retrieval—1. A method for cataloging vast amounts of data, all related to one field of interest, so that you can call out any or all of this data at any time it's needed with accuracy and speed. 2. A branch of computer science relating to the techniques for storing and searching large or specific quantities of information that may or may not be a real-time system.

information retrieval display — See display, information retrieval.

information retrieval, fast-access — See retrieval system, fast-access.

information-retrieval system — A system for locating and selecting, on demand, certain documents or other graphic records relevant to a given information requirement from a file of such material. Examples of information-retrieval systems are classification, indexing, and machine searching systems.

information, source—An information generator. This output is assumed to be free from error.

information system—The network of all communication methods within an organization. Information may be derived from many sources other than a data-processing unit, such as by telephone, by contact with other people, or by looking at an operation.

information system, management—See management information system.

information system, real-time—See real-time information system.

information theory—The mathematical theory concerned with the information rate, channels, channel width, noise and other factors affecting information transmission. Initially developed for electrical communications, it is now applied to business systems, and other phenomena that deal with information units and flow of information in networks.

information utilities—Data-processing centers are strategically located throughout the United States. These centers offer to management the opportunity of obtaining detailed reports interrelating department activities, with direct phone contact to a computer.

The reports are created from punched paper tape, punched cards, and optical reading of journal tapes. All the necessary data required by the center are prepared as an automatic by-product of a machine operation within a department on the customer's premises. Reports and problem solutions are automatically fed back to the teletype unit or CRT device of the customer.

information word—An ordered set of characters bearing at least one meaning and handled by a computer as a unit, including separating and spacing, that may be contrasted with instruction words. (Related to machine word.)

inherent storage—See storage, inherent.

inherited error—The error in the inital values. Especially the error inherited from the previous steps in the step by step integration. This error could also be the error introduced by the inability to make exact measurements of physical quantities. (Synonymous with inherent error).

inhibit—1. To prevent an event from taking place. 2. To prevent a device or logic element from producing a specified output.

inhibit, counter — The bit, in the program status double-word, that indicates whether (if 1) or not (if 0) all (clock) count zero interrupts are inhibited.

inhibit, external interrupt—The bit, in the program status double-word that indicates whether (if 1) or not (if 0) all external interrupts are inhibited.

inhibiting input—A gate input which, if in its prescribed state, prevents any output which might otherwise occur.

inhibiting signal—A signal that prevents an operation from occurring.

inhibit, input/output interrupt—See interrupt, input/output, inhibit.

inhibition rule—Priority and inhibition rules are usually implemented in the time-sharing hardware to resolve possible conflicts when two interrupts occur simultaneously, or when a second interrupt occurs before a previous one is completely processed.

inhibit pulse—A pulse that tends to prevent a reversal of the magnetic state in a magnetic core by other drive pulses.

initial condition—The value of a variable at the start of computation.

initial error—See error, inherent.

initialize—To originate or establish the basic conditions or startup state. Such procedures might be used to set an initial value for the address of an operand, establish the initial control value for a loop, set all registers to a preset value prior to running, begin a bootstrap operation with a control digit or word, etc.

initialized — The preliminary steps required before execution of iterative cycles to determine efficient start procedures. Usually a single, nonrepetitive operation after a cycle has begun and/or until a full cycle is again begun.

initializer routine—The functions such as error checking performed on a message after

it is entered into a system, but before the application program begins its processing.

initial program loading (IPL) — See program loading, initial.

initiate—The initiate operation is performed by means of a manually controlled jump to the entry point in older type computers, but bootstrap operations cause entry automatically, i.e., the program is then said to be self-triggered.

initiate button—See button, initiate.

initiate key—See button, initiate.

initiation area discriminator—See IAD.

initiator/terminator — A specific program which makes a job step ready to run in some computers and which also performs regular housekeeping tasks after a job has ended. Used in conjunction with job schedulers, which select a job or job part waiting to be executed after allocating and clearing memory space of extraneous data.

ink bleed—In optical character recognition (OCR), the capillary flow of ink beyond the original edges of a printed character.

ink, extraneous—Ink deposited on a computer printout that is not confined to the printed characters themselves.

ink, magnetic—A special ink that contains particles of a magnetic substance whose presence can be detected by magnetic sensors.

ink, reflectance—The reflectance of the special ink which is used in optical character recognition as compared to some particular reference standard.

ink smudge—See ink bleed.

ink squeezout—See ink bleed.

ink uniformity—The degree of light intensity variation over the area of printed characters, specifically within the character edges.

in-line coding—A portion of coding which is stored in the main path of a routine.

inline data processing—See data processing, in-line.

in-line procedures—In COBOL, the set of procedural instructions that are part of the main sequential and controlling flow of the program.

in-line processing—1. The processing of data in a random order not subject to preliminary editing or sorting. 2. A method of processing in which each individual input activity is completely processed, and all pertinent records are updated without previously having been batched or grouped.

in-line subroutine—See subroutine, in-line.

inner face—See face, inner.

in-plant system—A procedure for data handling that might be confined to one building or group of buildings in one locality.

input—1. Information or data transferred or to be transferred from an external storage medium into the internal storage of the computer. 2. Describing the routines with direct input as defined in (1), or the devices from which such information is available to the computer. 3. The device or collective set of devices necessary for input as defined in (1).

input area—*See* input block.

input block—1. A section of internal storage of a computer reserved for the receiving and processing of input information. (Synonymous with input area.) 2. An input buffer. 3. A block of computer words considered as a unit and intended or destined to be transferred from an external source or storage medium to the internal storage of the computer.

input buffer—*Same as* buffered input/output.

input buffer, pooled—*See* pooled input buffer.

input buffer register—That device which accepts data from input units or media such as magnetic tape or disks and which then transfers this data to internal storage.

input, card—*See* card input.

input card edit—*See* edit, input card.

input channel—*See* channel, input.

input (communications) — 1. The current, voltage, power, or driving force applied to a circuit or device. 2. The terminals or other places where current, voltage, power, or driving force may be applied to a circuit or device.

input data—*See* data, input.

input device—The mechanical unit designed to bring data to be processed into a computer, e.g., a card reader, a tape reader, or a keyboard.

input device, optical reader — This device reads printed and typewritten material, and inputs data directly without converting it into punch tape, punch cards, or other intermediate formats. Optical readers recognize all letters of the alphabet, standard punctuation, 0 to 9, and special symbols used in programmed functions. It handles documents and continuous fanfold sheets. This high-speed reader can be used simply as an input device, or it can be used as a complete small system for data processing and storage.

input device, punched card—A machine that reads data from punched cards and makes it available to the other computer components.

input devices—Convert facts into electronic impulses—computer language.

input devices, simulation—This type of simulation is the testing of one set of input equipment by using another set of equipment, specially programmed so that the behavior is similar. Tape input is programmed to appear as terminal input.

input edit (card)—The editing of card input is largely a matter of rearranging information into a form suitable for machine processing. Several of the more common considerations of input editing are the recognition of control holes, recognition of negative indicators, and the recognition and translation of over-capacity punching. Each of these considerations is usually approached in the same fashion, that is, through the use of selectors. Wherever possible, as the card is read, the

punching positions in question are wired to pick up selectors which are later used either to direct the program along different paths or to cause a sign or a value to be stored.

input equipment—1. The equipment used for transferring data and instructions into an automatic data-processing system. 2. The equipment by which an operator transcribes original data and instructions to a medium that may be used in an automatic data-processing system.

input expander, analog—This unit allows a complete analog input system to be configured around the data-adapter unit.

input, inhibiting—A gate input which in its prescribed state prevents any output that might otherwise occur.

input instruction code—*See* code, input, instruction.

input job stream—An input source of documents, usually punched cards or card images, which is the first part of an operating system. The stream contains the beginning-of-job indicators, directions, optional programs, etc.

input limited—The time necessary for the central processing unit to wait for further delivery of input items restricts the speed of the operation.

input loading—The amount of load imposed upon the sources supplying signals to the input.

input magazine—The card-feed magazine in a reader or read-punch unit.

input, manual—The entry of data by hand into a device at the time of processing.

input, on-line—When the input device transmits data directly to, and under the control of, the control processing unit.

input operation, analog — *See* analog input operation.

input/output—1. Commonly called I/O. A general term for equipment used to communicate with a computer. 2. The data involved in such communication. 3. The media carrying the data for input/output. 4. The process of transmitting information from an external source to the computer or from the computer to an external source.

input/output area—*Same as* storage, working.

input-output, buffered—All peripheral equipment contain an input/output buffer register for storage of data to be transferred to the computer so that various devices can be operated simultaneously at their maximum speed. The processor does not wait for a device to complete its cycle before continuing the program.

input/output buffers, full-word — *See* full-word input/output buffers.

input/output cable — Specific cables which have groups of wires which connect various input and output equipment to the mainframe units of the computer.

input/output, central computer—Communication between the central computer and the peripheral units of the same computer systems may be performed over all input/

output channels. Each of the several channels allows bidirectional transfers of data and control signals between the central computer and the peripheral devices. The input/output section acts as an autonomous processor that runs independently of the instruction-execution cycle, scanning the input channels for the presence of input or output word-transfer requests, and transferring data between the channels and central storage.

input/output centralized coordination, time sharing—*See* time sharing, centralized input/output coordination.

input/output channel — *See* channel, input/output.

input/output channel, programmed — Program control of information transfer between the central processor and an external device provides the fastest method of operating on data received from peripheral equipment. The programmed input/output channel allows input directly to the accumulator where the data can be acted on immediately, thus eliminating the need for a memory reference by either the channel or the program. Likewise, output data may be sent directly from the accumulator to an external device.

input/output channels, buffered—*See* input/output section buffered.

input/output channel selection—Permits the computer to designate a particular channel in the terminal.

input/output channels, multiple (time sharing)—*See* time sharing, multiple I/O channels.

input/output communications control system—*See* communications input/output control system.

input/output compiler—*See* compiler input/output.

input/output, concurrent — The acceptance, listing, and processing of all requests for I/O functions from the operating programs. This function of the executive system makes possible the concurrent operation of several programs using the same I/O channels without the danger of one program interfering with another program's I/O functions. Requests for I/O operations are submitted to the executive in the form of a parameter specifying the location of an execution packet which defines the function to be performed. An attempt is made to recover from I/O errors whenever feasible.

input/output control — 1. There are several portions of control which direct interactions between the processing unit and input and output equipment. One is written to control actions with tape, card, and printer equipment. A second control is specifically designed for random processing of records stored on direct access devices. It is a separate control in order to minimize seek times. 2. This program assigns equipment, controls the I/O devices, controls data transfers between memory and the I/O device, and controls the buffering of data for the device.

input/output control center—The input/output control center (IOCC) is connected to the central processor through one of the eight input/output trunks. The IOCC performs all control functions for one card reader/punch, one high-speed printer, and up to four magnetic-tape units. A special buffer in the IOCC enables simultaneous operation of any three of the devices connected to it. The magnetic tapes connected to the IOCC are used independently in input/output conversion operations, while other tape operations are handled by magnetic-tape units connected to a standard tape-control unit. The IOCC affords unique flexibility and added simultaneity and does not in any way limit the number or operation of additional peripheral devices connected in the standard manner to the seven remaining input/output trunks (some computers).

input/output control, extensiveness—Input/output control, includes physical and logical control over I/O records, files and units; buffer control; teleprocessing terminal and message handling; random access I/O control; labeling of files, and error-recovery procedures.

input/output control, interleaving—The I/O control links up to 64 input and output stations by lines to the central processor, calls the stations, and collects and distributes the input/output data. It also controls the interleaving of data during a data interrupt, senses the status of I/O devices and skips instructions based on this status, traps IOT (input output transfer) instructions initiating a program break, and generates real-time signal pulses for use by external peripheral equipment (some computers).

input/output controller—The input/output controller is an independent, wired logic processor which provides: independent data paths between peripheral subsystems and main storage; high-speed communications capability; enhanced systems performance through chained buffer operations; the ability to expand the number of input/output channels available to the system. The data paths of the I/OC provide transfers between peripheral subsystems and main storage independent of the cyclic operation of the central processors.

Operations are initiated from a central processor by sending functional commands to the I/OC via the normal CPU channel interface. The I/OC accepts these commands and then sequences the independent data transfer (UNIVAC).

input/output control module (IOC)—1. The input/output control module (IOC) is a program-controlled macroprocessor for servicing peripherals. It has up to four parts for connections to memory modules. The I/O commands are stored in memory and the

I/O is activated by master-mode processor commands to the IOC through the system controller. The IOC proceeds independently until the I/O process terminates, then communicates this status back to the processor through the system controller. The I/O control module provides control signals, parity checks, time interface, and data transformations for I/O devices. It consists of an instruction register and associated decoding circuitry, a data register, and a manipulation register with associated timing circuits. Each control module is capable of controlling any standard device of the I/O complement. There can be as many simultaneous I/O operations as there are I/O control modules. The I/O exchange automatically connects control modules with any of the I/O devices or command from processor modules. The I/O control modules also provide interface with associate data-processing systems.

input/output control program—The control of the execution of all input and output operations by the supervisory program.

input/output control section — The input/output section functions as a small processor. Programmed input/output instructions load the access-control word locations and establish desired peripheral activity. From this point, I/O control automatically scans the input/output channels, accepting data from the peripheral subsystem at the natural rate of the equipment. When a peripheral subsystem presents or asks for a word of data, its associated access-control register is referenced and I/O control transfers the data word to or from central store, updates the access-control word, and tests for a terminal condition. All of the access-control word indexing and testing is performed in the index section in effectively zero-time, in parallel with normal construction execution and indexing.

input/output control systems (IOCS)—1. Various library routines which a programmer or systems analyst can select to custom-fit an application by means of macro programs or instructions and various facts supplied in the source program for handling input and output for tapes, cards, etc. and printer. A description of machine logic configuration, definition of files, sequencing and interrupts. 2. A group of computer routines designed to automatically control the performance of input/output operations and direct other functions such as error correction, checkpoint, label processing, restart, and others.

input/output control unit—There are several portions of control that direct interactions between the processing unit and input and output equipment. One is written to control actions with tape, card, and printer equipment. A second control is specifically designed for random processing of records stored on direct-access devices. It is a separate control in order to minimize seek times.

input/output device—A unit that accepts new data, sends it into the computer for processing, receives the results, and converts them into a usable form, like payroll checks or bills.

input/output device (communications) — Any subscriber (user) equipment which introduces data into or extracts data from a data-communications system.

input/output device handlers — The input/output device handlers are responsible for controlling the activities of all input/output channels and peripheral equipment.

input/output (I/O) devices—Computer hardware by which data is entered into a computer, or by which the finished computations are recorded for immediate or future use.

input/output exchange, data communications—Throughout the I/O exchange, the communication control unit (DCCU) has full data-communications network control capabilities. Dial TWX, teletype, inquiry typewriter, and other terminal units may be specified.

input/output, hybrid computer—The input/output group of programs consists of a system monitor and programs to control operation of analog digital conversion equipment and special devices such as an oscilloscope display or a digital plotter.

input/output information messages—*See* information messages, input/output.

input/output instructions—Computer instructions which operate input-output devices like card readers, printers, and terminals.

input/output interrupt—*See* interrupt, input/output.

input/output interrupt identification — I/O interruptions are caused by an I/O unit ending an operation or otherwise needing attention. Identifications of the device and channel causing the interruption are stored in the old PSW (program status word); in addition, the status of the device and channel is stored in a fixed location (some computers).

input/output interrupt indicators — Input/output interrupt instructions are used to determine the input/output unit originating an interrupt and the cause of the interrupt by testing the indicators associated with each input/output channel. When the cause of the interrupt has been determined and corrective action, if required, has been taken, the indicators may be reset and the interrupted program resumed. These instructions also provide the facility for setting, resetting, and testing the inhibit input/output interrupt indicator.

input/output interrupt inhibit—*See* interrupt input/output inhibit.

input/output library—Relieves the programmer of having to be familiar with the functional and instructional differences among the peripherals.

input/output limited—Pertaining to a system or condition in which the time for input and output operation exceeds other operations.

input/output limited tapes—A sort program in which the effective transfer rate of tape units determines the elapsed time required to sort.

input/output medium—The vehicle or material designed and used to carry recorded data, i.e., a punched card, magnetic tape, microfilm, etc. The medium is the carrier of data and instructions into a computer.

input/output operation, function word — *See* function word, I/O operation.

input/output operation, normal—*See* operation input/output.

input/output operations, non-data—Processes which relate to input/output operations as differentiated or exclusive of data manipulations, such as tape rewinding.

input/output, peripheral control—The input/output section of the central computer can accommodate a wide range of peripheral subsystems. These include magnetic drum and magnetic tape devices, card punches and readers, printers, document sensing devices, such as check readers and optical readers, and other computer systems. In addition to these standard peripheral subsystems, the central computer can also communicate with many real-time input/output devices. A standard peripheral subsystem, whether it be card, tape or drum, consists of one or more units of the same type, a control unit for the particular type of equipment, and a channel synchronizer. Equally important is the fact that any input/out device can, through its control unit, instantly signal the central processor if it requires a response to an inquiry or if it has completed a task and is ready to begin another. Through the executive routine, all activities, both internal and external to the central processor, are properly correlated, assigned the necessary areas of storage, and carried out in the most advantageous sequence (some systems).

input/output priority and interrupt—It can be used to divert program attention to new input data, the completion of output buffer transfers, or emergency conditions (inquiries, errors) existing on peripherals. Interrupt feature relieves need for much program checking of status of units.

input/output processor (IOP) — A unit that handles normal data input/output control and sequencing.

input/output, programmed—Program control of information transfer between the central processor and an external device provides the fastest method of operating on data received from peripheral equipment. The programmed input/output channel allows input directly to the accumulator where the data can be acted on immediately, thus eliminating the need for a memory reference by either the channel or the program. Likewise, output data may be sent directly from the accumulator to an external device.

input/output, random access—This is an I/O control capability that permits efficient random processing of records stored on a direct-access device. Random access I/O efficiency is achieved by the system in two ways: (1) Seeks are issued in an order which mimimizes the average seek time, rather than in the order in which they were requested. (2) Seeks are overlapped with other processing. Because records must sometimes be processed sequentially (for example, when a report is being written), the ability to call for records sequentially is also available.

input/output, real-time control — All input/output data transfers are automatically controlled by signals emanating from the central processor or from the peripheral subsystems themselves. Any general purpose input/output channel can accommodate a real-time system peripheral device. All I/O channels are buffered. Each input/output device has associated with it a control unit which, once activated by the central processor, carries out the entire operation of the instruction given it while the central processor proceeds with other tasks.

input/output referencing—References to data on tape or disk are made symbolically. Instead of describing the address of a certain disk or tape, the programmer need not keep in mind where data will be coming from.

input/output register—*See* index register.

input/output, remote message — This is an I/O control for obtaining messages from and sending messages to remote terminals. For remote-message control, the I/O control handles the following functions: receipt of messages from remote terminals; sending of messages to remote terminals; automatic dial-up; and code conversion. The user supplies the system with line-control specifications and installation-oriented routines to analyze message headers. Messages received can be stored in processing queues or output-terminal queues. Marcostatements enable the installation program to obtain messages for processing and to send messages. A log of all message traffic may be stored on a secondary storage device.

input/output request — *See* input/output request words.

input/output, request words—Control words for input/output requests that are stored in the message reference block until the I/O is completed.

input/output routines—A set of routines that simplify the programming of input and output functions for standard peripheral equipment.

input/output section, buffered—The buffered input/output permits the processor to continue with computation while input and output communications are proceeding. The transfer of data to or from the central processor is conducted via input/output channels which communicate directly with the magnetic-core memory. Access to the memory is time-shared between the operating program and input/output data transfer. Access also is automatically controlled by the I/O rate of the external device; it is not a programming consideration. Any cycle of the memory time is available for input/output data transfer in preference to its use by the program. The input/output system is provided with program interrupt features so that testing of the condition of the external devices by the running program is not necessary, although possible, if desired.

input/output, simultaneous — Relates to the types of computers which can handle other operations concurrently with input and output operations, most often using buffers which hold input/output data and information as it arrives and on a temporary basis, while other operations are executed by the CPU. Thus, the computer need not wait for data from the very slow I/O units and may instead take it from the faster part of the buffer in massive quantities instead of as it arrives from slower units or terminals.

input/output, storage—A specific storage area in a computer reserved for data or instructions, received by or ready to be transferred from or to, an external (peripheral) input or output device or to another specific section of storage.

input/output switching — By linking certain input or output units to more than one channel, a variety of ways are open to reach the device, even if other units are occupying one or more of the available channels. A single unit can be linked through channel switching to one channel at the start of processing on a job, and then to another channel at the end of processing of the same job.

input/output, symbiont control — There are relatively few input/output limited programs when using the drum, due to the high transfer rate of this unit. For the relatively slower peripherals—tape, card, punch, and printer—a drum buffering system has been designed to effectively disassociate input/output time from central computer time. Small routines, called symbionts, run concurrently with the series of main programs. These symbionts move information back and forth between peripherals and magnetic drum. Main programs desiring communication with these peripherals reference input/output subroutines which themselves fetch or deliver data images from and to the drum. Other symbionts may be concurrently performing typical off-line operations, such as tape to printer, independent of the main program. Symbionts may be initialized by the operator or by a main program. Symbiont operations may be suspended, terminated, or reinitiated at any time.

input/output system subroutines—See system subroutines.

input/output terminal coordination, (time sharing)—See time sharing, terminal input/output coordination.

input/output, time-shared section — *Same as* input/output section, buffered.

input/output traffic control—1. Input/output traffic control directs the time sharing of the main memory by the various peripheral devices and the central processor. This control element makes possible the concurrent performance of central processor computing and up to eight simultaneous input/output operations. For example, the computer can simultaneously read or write tape, read cards, punch cards, store information in a random-access disc storage unit, read information from a random-access drum device, print two separate reports, and compute. 2. The coordination of peripheral simultaneity with internal computation is performed by the central processor element called the input/output traffic control.

input/output trunks—The basic systems are equipped with many input/output trunks, each of which can be connected to a peripheral control. A control which handles both reading and writing (e.g., a magnetic tape control) connects to a pair of trunks. Data are transferred between main memory and a trunk (and thus a peripheral device) via the read/write channel specified in the instruction which initiates the transfer. Additional peripheral devices can be connected to the system simply by adding eight more input/output trunks to the basic configuration. The number of peripheral devices in a system depends only on the number of input/output trunks available.

input/output unit, teletype—A teletype automatic send-receive (ASR) set is included in many standard real-time computers. The ASR set transfers information into the computer from perforated tape or a keyboard, and receives the output information from the computer in the form of perforated tape and/or a typed message.

input pulse, partial select—See pulse, partial write.

input queue, new — A group or a queue of new messages that are in the system and waiting for processing. The main scheduling routine will scan them along with other queues and order them into processing order.

input reference—The reference used to compare the measured variable resulting in a deviation or error signal. Also referred to as set point, or desired value.

input register—See register, input.

input routine — A routine which directs or controls the reading of programs and data into a computer system. Such a routine may be internally stored, wired, or part of a bootstrap operation, and may perform housekeeping or system control operations according to rules.

input section—See input block.

inputs, real-time—Real-time systems are those which have instantaneous input or entry and acceptance, most often determined by the requirements of another independent system, i.e., they are on-line inputs flowing directly to the computer as the activity occurs.

input stacker—The card-feed magazine in a reader, or read-punch unit.

input state—The determination of the condition of that specified set of input channels, i.e., positive, negative, etc.

input station—*See* transacter (input station).

input storage—1. Holds each bundle of facts while it awaits its turn to be processed. This allows successive bundles to be compared to make sure they're in the right order or for other control purposes. 2. Any information that enters a computer for the purpose of being processed or to aid in processing. It is then held until signaled for use by the control program.

input, substantive — The transferral of data from an external storage device to an internal storage device, usually from a mass storage unit and off-line, but not always so.

input, tape—*See* tape input.

input tape, problem — An input tape, either punched paper tape or magnetic tape, that contains problem data for checking out a given computer system.

input unit, manual—A set of manual controls or devices from which operators can set a specific word for input.

input units—Electronic machines that feed or introduce data into the system. Such machines can be paper tape readers, card readers, magnetic document sorter-readers, optical readers, and others.

input work queue—*See* work queue, input.

inquiries, banking—By indexing the account number and the status entry key, the teller may inquire into the status of an account for information relative to the savings balance, available balance, or any unposted items. If mortgages are on-line, inquiry may also be made as to principal balance, escrow balance, delinquency status, or any other information pertinent to the account.

inquiry—A request for information from storage; e.g., a request for the number of available airline seats or a machine statement to initiate a search of library documents.

inquiry and communications systems—Computer systems are now provided with facilities for diversified on-site and long distance inquiry and data-communications networks. Centralized records and data-processing operations can be tied in with information sources at remote locations and will provide instant on-line response to interrogations and input data from a large number of inquiry stations. Communication networks may include standard teletype stations, and electric typewriter stations.

inquiry and subscriber display—The inquiry and subscriber display is a low-cost unit designed to service multiple subscribers requiring real-time access to stored information, or subscriber to subscriber message communication. Under operator control, the display can compose, correct, transmit, and receive formatted alphanumeric text. Operator composed text is automatically assembled and organized for common carrier or direct computer communication links. Operation of the display is independent of the location or type of data source. The display unit makes available the full capabilities of a remote data processor from a subscriber's own location, in his own operational language, when required. For handling restricted data, secure codes and formatting devices are provided to maintain information integrity.

inquiry answer (remote) — In an operating teleprocessing network, several inquiries simultaneously might come into the system from distant cities concerning information that is contained in a disk file. The appropriate records would then be taken from the disk file and the appropriate responses would be prepared and returned to the original cities. Although this appears to be a simple function, it requires design balance to achieve the required variety of terminal speeds and functions. It requires simultaneous operation of many devices operating through a single economical channel. It requires the time-sharing and space-sharing programs that control these devices. It requires the range of disk file capacity and speed. Furthermore, it has to do all these things concurrently with batch job processing.

inquiry application—Transportation reservation and inventory control systems are examples of inquiries which can be handled on an on-line or interrupt basis. Regular running programs are interrupted or halted until an inquiry is completed. Inquiries can also be queued and held up for batches. Inquiries can be introduced by card, tape, direct console, or remote station inquiry. Bank teller processing also is an example of simultaneous inquiry and batch.

inquiry, direct-access — A storage method which allows direct information inquiry from temporary or permanent storage devices.

inquiry display terminal — *See* display, inquiry-terminal.

inquiry, keyboard—Interrogation of program progress, storage contents, or other information by keyboard maneuvering.

inquiry, remote—Inquiry stations when operated on-line permit humans to interrogate the computer files and receive immediate answers to inquiries. In industry they can be located at dozens of remote locations such as office, factory, warehouse, branch locations hundreds of miles away. Such an on-line real-time system permits all levels of industrial management to obtain immediate answers to questions about inventories, work in process, sales, and other facts for effective management.

inquiry station—Device or unit from which an information request is made.

inquiry unit—A device used to "talk" to the computer, usually to get quick answers to random questions like, "How many hammers do we have in stock?" or "When did we last order soap powder and in what quantity?"

in-read, out-read — An optical feature that may be added to certain off-line office machinery permitting on-line operation.

inscribe—The action of reading the data recorded on documents and writing the same data on the same document. The document thus becomes available and suitable for the application of automatic reading by optical character readers or other reading devices.

inscribing — In optical character recognition, the preparation of source documents for automatic reading and which includes both handwritten and printed characters.

inserted subroutine — See subroutine, direct-insert.

insertion, switch — The insertion of information into a computer system by an operator who operates the switches manually.

inside plant—In communication practice, inside plant is that part of the plant within a central office, intermediate station or subscriber's premises that is on the office or station side of the point of connection with the outside plant. Note: The plant in a central office is commonly referred to as central office plant, and the plant on the station premises is referred to as station plant.

installation, computer—See computer installation.

installation date—The date new equipment is ready for use. The commencement of rental normally begins on the day following the date on which the contractor officially notifies the using organization that the equipment is installed and ready for use, subject to the acceptance and standard of performance provisions of the applicable contract.

installation processing control—In an effort to reduce job turn-around time and to minimize time wasted in setup, the scheduling of applications and jobs is automated.

installation tape number — A number permanently assigned to a plastic or metal spool to identify a particular roll of magnetic tape.

installation, terminal — A grouping, at one site, of operable data terminals and related equipment.

installation terminal for data transmission— Installation comprising the data-terminal equipment, the signal-conversion equipment, and any intermediate equipment. Note: In some instances, the data-terminal equipment may be connected directly to a data processing machine or may be a part of it.

installation time—Time spent in testing, installing, error-checking, and diagnosing of such basic electronic but nonprogramming checks, as dry runs, etc. This time does NOT include reliability tests which are defined as supplementary maintenance time.

instantaneous data-transfer rate — See data-transfer rate.

instantaneous storage — Storage, usually in several locations, with an access time which is slight in comparison with operation time.

instantaneous transfer rate—See data transfer rate.

instants, significant (of a modulation or a restitution)—Instants limiting significant intervals of modulation or restitution.

instruction—1. A coded program step that tells the computer what to do for a single operation in a program. 2. A set of characters, together with one or more addresses (or no address), that defines an operation and which, as a unit, causes the computer to operate accordingly on the indicated quantities. 3. A set of identifying characters designed to cause a computer to perform certain operations. A machine instruction to specific functions.

instruction, absolute—A particular computer instruction which specifies completely a specific computer operation and is capable of causing the execution of that operation.

instruction, actual—Same as instruction effective.

instruction address—See address, instruction.

instruction, address functional—See address instruction, functional.

instruction-address registers—Three control-memory registers (instruction-address register 1, instruction-address register 2, and an interrupt register) are used to store the addresses of instructions. Instruction-address register 1 directs the sequential retrieval of instruction characters from their storage locations in main memory. Instruction-address register 2 which exists only in the basic set of control registers can be loaded with the address of another instruction by the programmer. A single program instruction can interchange the contents of the two instruction-address registers, providing a convenient means of branching to and returning from any position in the program. The interrupt register can be loaded with the starting address of a routine to be executed when a program-interrupt condition exists. The controlling program is interrupted automatically upon receipt of a signal from an external device or a program instruction.

instructional constant—A constant written in the form of an instruction but not intended to be executed as an instruction. One form of dummy instruction.

instruction alphanumeric — The name given to instructions that can be used equally well with alphabetic or numeric kinds of fields of data.

instruction area—1. A part of storage allocated to receive and store the group of instructions to be executed. 2. The storage locations used to store the program.

instruction, arithmetic — See arithmetic instruction.

instruction, blank—See instruction, dummy.

instruction, branch—See branch instruction.

instruction, branch-on-zero—If the arithmetic

accumulator is zero, the computer operation will then proceed to an alternate location.

instruction, breakpoint—1. An instruction which will cause a computer to stop or to transfer control in some standard fashion to a supervisory routine which can monitor the progress of the interrupted program. 2. An instruction which, if some specified switch is set, will cause the computer to stop or take other special action.

instruction, breakpoint (conditional)—A conditional jump instruction which, if some specified switch is set, will cause the computer to stop, after which either the routine may be continued as coded or a jump may be forced.

instruction character — *See* character, command.

instruction, character ignore—*Same as* ignore.

instruction check—*See* check, forbidden combination.

instruction-check indicator — *See* check indicator, instruction.

instruction code—The list of symbols, names and definitions of the instructions that are intelligible to a given computer or computing system.

instruction code, input—*See* code input instruction.

instruction codes, mnemonic — *See* codes, mnemonic operation.

instruction complement — A built-in feature designed to provide a number of instructions for each programmer instruction.

instruction, computer—*Same as* machine instruction.

instruction, conditional-break point—A conditional-jump instruction which, if some specified switch is set or situation exists, will cause the computer to stop, after which either the routine may be continued as coded, or a jump may be forced.

instruction, conditional jump—*Same as* branch conditional.

instruction, constant — *Same as* constant instruction.

instruction counter—*Same as* register, control.

instructional cycle—The steps involved in the processing of an instruction.

instruction, decision—*See* branch.

instruction deck—*See* deck, instruction.

instruction digit, unallowable — A character or combination of bits which is not accepted as a valid representatiton by the machine design or by a specific routine. Instruction digits unallowable are commonly detected and used as an indication of machine malfunction.

instruction, discrimination — A more acceptable term for conditional jump instruction or branch instruction. Also called decision instruction. *See* branch.

instruction do-nothing — *See* instruction, dummy.

instruction dummy—1. An artificial instruction or address inserted in a list to serve a purpose other than execution as an instruc-tion. (Related to constant instruction.) 2. A specifically designed artificial instruction to serve a purpose other than its meaningful or purposeful execution, i.e., it is not data. Such an instruction is usually inserted in the sequence for a purpose, but if it is executed no disturbance to the run will occur. It is frequently a no-operation, a do-nothing, or a waste instruction.

instruction, effective—To alter a presumptive or unmodified instruction when using a stored program computer. Such alteration produces a complete instruction, and when it is actually executed it is called an effective instruction or an actual instruction. The modification process uses words or parts of words specifically called modifiers or index words. These are added to or combined with the presumptive or unmodified instruction by means of arithmetical or logical operations.

instruction entry—Usually the first instruction to be executed in a subroutine. It may have several different entry points each of which correspond to a different function of the subroutine.

instruction, execution—The set of elementary steps carried out by the computer to produce the result specified by the operation code.

instruction, executive — Similar to a supervisory instruction, this instruction is designed and used to control the operation or execution of other routines or programs.

instruction, external devices — *See* external devices, instruction.

instruction, extract—An instruction that requests formation of a new expression from selected pairs of given expressions.

instruction format—1. The allocation of bits or characters of a machine instruction to specific functions. 2. Instructions are coded in a two-address, variable-length format. However, one or perhaps both addresses may often be omitted, thereby saving memory space and speeding up instruction execution. 3. The allocation of instructions according to some particular machine or installation conventions or rules. 4. An allocation of characters of various instructions differentiating between the component parts of the instructions, such as, address part, operation part, etc.

instruction format, addressless—*See* addressless instruction format.

instruction format (designators)—The operation of the computer is controlled by a program of instructions stored in memory. Each instruction is read from memory, normally from sequential addresses, and then is transmitted to the program control register for interpretation. Each instruction consists of several parts called designators.

instruction format, functional address—This format contains no operation part because the operation is implicitly specified by address parts.

instruction format, implicit address — This particular format contains no address part because it is used either when no address is required or when it is implicitly shown in some way.

instruction format, N-address—A specific arrangement of component parts of a computer instruction word that references N-storage locations, specifically, a three-address instruction format, etc.

instruction format, N plus one address—An instruction format which contains one, two, three, ..., (N + 1) address parts respectively. The plus-one address being that of the instruction to be executed next.

instruction format, one plus one address— *Same as* address, two.

instruction format, three address — *Same as* address, three.

instruction format, two address—*Same as* address, two.

instruction format, two plus one address— *Same as* address, three.

instruction format, zero-address — *Same as* addressless instruction format.

instruction, four-address—*See* address four.

instruction, functional address—*See* address instruction, functional.

instruction, halt—*See* halt, instruction.

instruction, hold — A computer instruction which caused data called from storage to be also retained in storage after it is called out and transferred to its new location.

instruction, ignore—*See* ignore.

instruction, immediate address—*See* address instruction, immediate.

instruction, internal manipulation — A computer instruction that changes the format or location of data within the computer system.

instruction, jump — A computer instruction causing a jump in the sequence of instructions. *See* branch.

instruction length—In the IBM System/360, data representation is character- or word-oriented as follows:

    byte = 8 bits plus a check bit.
    halfword = 2 bytes.
    word = 4 bytes.
    instruction = 1, 2, 3 halfwords.
    internal code = 8-bit character.

This is an important innovation and replaces the older "bit" connotation; it will be used on all IBM equipment henceforth.

instruction, logic—An instruction causing the execution of an operation defined in symbolic logic statements or operators, such as AND, OR, etc., and to be distinguished from arithmetic instructions, such as add, multiply, and divide.

instruction, logical—An instruction that carries out a logical operation, such as an AND, OR, NOR.

instruction, look up—An instruction designed to allow reference to systematically arranged and stored data.

instruction loop, closed—Indefinite repetition of a group of instructions.

instruction, machine—An instruction that the particular machine can recognize and execute.

instruction, macro—1. An instruction consisting of a sequence of microinstructions that are inserted into the object routine for performing a specific operation. 2. The more powerful instructions that combine several operations in one instruction.

instruction, macro (linkage) — A macroinstruction that provides logical linkage between programs and subroutines and that will save data needed by another program.

instruction, micro—A small, single, short, addshift- or delete-type of command.

instruction mix — Specific computer instructions selected to complete particular problems. The optimum mix of instructions determines the speed and accuracy in most cases, and programmers try to achieve this optimum.

instruction, mnemonic—*See* codes, mnemonic operation.

instruction modification—A change in the operation-code portion of an instruction or command such that if the routine containing the instruction or command is repeated, the computer will perform a different operation.

instruction multiaddress—*See* multiaddress.

instruction, multiple—*See* multiaddress.

instruction, multiple-address—1. An instruction consisting of an operation code and two or more addresses. Usually specified as a two-address, three-address, or four-address instruction. *See* multiple-address code.

instruction, no-address—An instruction specifying an operation that the computer can perform without having to refer to its storage unit.

instruction, nonprint—An instruction that is usually transmitted in a form which prevents the printing of a line or character.

instruction, no-op—1. An instruction that specifically instructs the computer to do nothing but process the next instruction in sequence. 2. A blank instruction. 3. A skip instruction.

instruction, one-address—An instruction consisting of an operation and exactly one address. The instruction code of a single-address computer may include both zero and multiaddress instructions as special cases.

instruction, one-plus-one address — *Same as* address, two.

instruction, operational address—*See* instruction, source destination.

instruction operation codes — *See* codes, instruction operation.

instruction, presumptive—An instruction that will most likely be modified before it is used for the final program.

instruction, pseudo—*See* pseudoinstruction.

instruction, reference — An instruction designed to allow reference to systematically arranged, and stored data.

instruction register—*See* register, instruction.

instruction register, control — A particular register in which the content is the address of the next instruction.

instruction repertory—*See* repertory, instruction.

instruction, repetition—An instruction whose execution is repeated an indicated number of times before the next instruction is processed.

instructions, control—The instructions in this category are used to manipulate data within the main memory and the control memory, to prepare main-memory storage areas for the processing of data fields, and to control the sequential selection and interpretation of instructions in the stored program.

instructions, dynamic—The sequence of machine steps performed by the computer in a real-time or simulated environment.

instruction, short—The use of an index specification in a FORTRAN read or write statement.

instruction, single-address—*Same as* instruction, one-address.

instructions, input/output—Computer instructions which operate input/output devices like card readers, printers, and terminals.

instructions, interpretive—*See* interpretive instructions.

instructions, IOT—Enable the computer to communicate with external devices, send control information, and transfer data. Certain processor commands, such as the clock instructions, are also in the IOT (input/output and transfer) class. The IOT instruction is microcoded to simplify programming for I/O transfers. For example, clearing the AC (accumulator) and loading a device buffer are done in one instruction. The ten bits used for device and mode selection provide 1024 possibilities.

instruction, skip—An instruction having no effect other than directing the processor to proceed to another instruction designated in the storage portion. (Synonymous with skip, and no-op instruction.)

instructions, memory-reference—*See* memory reference instructions.

instructions, microprogrammable — All instructions which do not reference core memory (do not contain a memory address) can be microprogrammed, allowing the programmer to specify several shift, skip, or input/output transfer commands to be performed within one instruction.

instructions, monitored—As shown in the input/output instruction repertoire, instructions calling for input, output, or function transfers may be executed either with or without monitor. When executed with monitor, an internal interrupt will be generated upon completion of the transfer. When an instruction is executed without a monitor the interrupt is inhibited.

instruction, source designation—*Same as* address instruction, functional.

instruction, source-destination — A computer instruction that has no operation part, but rather has the operation implicitly specified by the address parts.

instructions, privileged — Protection against one problem subprogram misusing another problem subprogram's I/O devices is provided by restricting all I/O commands to the supervisor state. A subprogram requests I/O action by issuing a supervisor call instruction. The supervisory subprogram can then analyze this request and take the appropriate action.

instructions, programmed — Special subroutines called programmed instructions, may be used as if they were single commands by employing one of the programmed instructions of the repertoire. This capability allows the programmer to define his own special command, through the use of subroutines, which may be changed by the operating routine if desired.

instructions, return—The specific group of instructions which are sub-routined at the end of a program to provide for the transfer of control from the return subroutine to the main routine.

instructions, shift—Specific instructions which will shift the number either to the left or to the right within an arithmetic register. A shift operation is principally equivalent to multiplying or dividing by the radix of the number base in use, depending upon the direction of the shift. In a decimal computer, a shift of one place to the right is equivalent to dividing by 10, a shift one place to the left is equivalent to multiplying by 10.

instruction statement, machine—*See* machine instruction statements.

instruction, stop—*See* halt instruction.

instruction storage—*Same as* instruction area.

instructions, variable-length — *See* variable length, instructions.

instruction, symbolic — *See* symbolic instruction.

instruction, table-look-up—An instruction designed to allow reference to systematically arranged, and stored data.

instruction tape—*Same as* tape program.

instruction tape, master—A particular magnetic tape which contains most or all of the routines or programs for the basic run or run series. Also a main part of an operating system.

instruction three-address — *Same as* address, three.

instruction, three-plus-one address—*Same as* address four.

instruction time—1. The portion of an instruction cycle when the control unit is analyzing the instruction and setting up to perform the indicated operation. 2. The portion of an instruction cycle when the actual work is performed or operation executed; i.e., the time required to decode and perform an instruction.

instruction transfer — An instruction to a computer that enables the programmer to instruct the computer to choose between alternative subprograms depending upon the conditions determined by the computer during the execution of the program.

instruction, two address—*Same as* address, two.

instruction, two-plus-one address — *Same as* address, three.

instruction, two- three- or four-address—An instruction consisting of an operation and 2, 3, or 4 addresses respectively. The addresses may specify the location of operands, results, or other instructions.

instruction, unconditional-jump — *See* branch unconditional.

instruction, unconditional transfer — *Same as* branch, unconditional.

instruction, unmodified — An instruction which is to be modified in some prescribed way by means of a stored program computer available for a particular purpose; to produce the completed executable instruction.

instruction, waste — *Same as* instruction, dummy.

instruction word—1. A grouping of letters or digits handled by the computer as a distinct unit to signify the provision of definitions of operations to be performed or the description of further data. 2. A part of a word or all of a word which is executed by the computer as an instruction.

instruction, zero-address — An instruction specifying an operation in which the location of the operands are defined by the computer code, so that no address need be given explicitly.

instrumentation errors—Where input into a system is directly from instrumentation such as pressure gauges, etc. Limit checks are imposed to prevent instrumentation errors. If these limits are violated, control may be assumed by a violation subroutine for immediate corrective action.

instrument, end—A device that is connected to one terminal of a loop and is capable of converting usable intelligence into electrical signals or vice versa. It includes all generating, signal-converting and loop-terminating devices employed at the transmitting and/or receiving location.

integer — A complete entity; a whole (not fractional or mixed) number.

integer constants (FORTRAN) — An integer constant is written without a decimal point, using the decimal digits 0, 1, . . ., 9. A preceding + or − sign is optional. An unsigned integer constant is assumed to be positive.

integer programming—A class of optimization problems in which the values of all of the variables are restricted to be integers. Normally, the optimization problem without this integer restriction is a linear program; additional adjectives indicate variations— for example, integer quadratic programming.

integers—The natural or whole numbers; concepts intimately connected with the process of counting or enumeration. Because in-

tegers can be written down in endless series, they are used to indicate order or sequence; i.e., the ordinal aspect of integers. The cardinal aspect of integers concerns how many things are observed or noted and provides a basis of measurement.

integer, single-precision—A fixed-point number that occupies one word of core storage. The value varies depending on the word length of the computer.

integer variables (FORTRAN) — An integer variable consists of a series of not more than six alphameric characters (except special characters), of which the first is I, J, K, L, M, or N (some systems).

integral—In numeric notation, the integral or integer is contained in the places to the left of the assumed point. The decimal 2345.67 has four integral places.

integrand—1. When a unit has two input variables (x and y) and one output variable (z) which is proportional to the integral of (y) — the y is the integrand. 2. A calculus expression, i.e., the math expression or function which is operated upon in the process of integration.

integrated data processing—*See* data processing, integrated.

integrated management information and control system—A management oriented system conceived and designed by management as a singular entity to control an entire organization. Some of the commonly integrated systems are accounting, inventory control, quality control, purchasing, receiving, and financial control. The integrated management information and control system is the prevailing application type of third generation computers and it blends both the administrative and operational applications into a single information system to provide management with timely and meaningful business information.

integrated system—The combination of processes which results in the introduction of data which need not be repeated as further allied or related data is also entered. For example, shipment data may also be the basis for inventory inquiries, invoicing marketing reports, etc.

integrating gear—*See* gear, integrating.

integrator—A device whose output function is a proportional to the integral of the input function with respect to a specified variable; e.g. a watt-hour meter.

integrator, incremental—A digital integrating device with an output signal which is a maximum negative, zero, or a maximum positive value depending on a negative, zero, or positive instantaneous input signal.

integrator, storage—In an analog computer, an integrator used to store a voltage in the hold condition for future use, while the rest of the computer assumes another computer control state.

integrator, summing — An analog computer amplifier which forms the time integral of the weighted sum of the input voltages or currents as an output.

intelligence—The developed capability of a device to perform functions that are normally associated with human intelligence, such as reasoning, learning, and self-improvement. (Related to machine learning.)

intelligence, artificial — The study of computer and related techniques to supplement the intellectual capabilities of man. As man has invented and used tools to increase his physical powers, he now is beginning to use artificial intelligence to increase his mental powers. In a more restricted sense, the study of techniques for more effective use of digital computers by improved programming techniques.

intensity—The density of a black or colored image produced on paper for optical character recognition.

interblock—1. To prevent a machine or device from initiating further operations until the operation in process is completed. 2. To avoid or prevent the operations of one part of a computing system while other parts are operating.

interblock gap—The space on magnetic tape separating two blocks of data or information.

interblock space—That part of a magnetic tape between blocks of information on which nothing is written. Also called inter-record gap.

intercepting trunk—A trunk to which a call for a vacant number, changed number, or a line out of order is connected for action by an operator.

interchangeable card feed—A device which usually converts an 80 column card feed to a 51 column card feed.

interchangeable type bar—A printer type bar which can be removed by the operator to change from one alphabet to another.

intercomputer communication—Data is transmitted from one computer to another so that the data can be reprocessed in order to facilitate handling and increase transmission speed.

interconnecting device—This unit is designed for use with multiple systems where it is desirable to switch peripheral units from one system to another. Any unit which is to be switched between systems must be cable-connected to the interconnector. When switching magnetic files, between systems, it is possible to switch an entire trunk line or up to eight magnetic files with one module. Switching is done automatically by the solenoid-operated switches that are actuated by push buttons located on the console panel of the computer. No cables need to be manually shifted.

interconsole message program — This program provides a means by which the user may request manual operations by the operator and receive acknowledgment. Such an operation would be the mounting/dismounting of user tapes.

intercycle—A step in the sequence of steps made by the main shaft of a punched-card machine. At this time the card feed is stopped, usually due to a control change. In some machines the number of intercycles that are to arise for a control change can be predetermined, in others this determination is made solely by the machine.

interface—1. A common boundary between automatic data-processing systems or parts of a single system. In communications and data systems, it may involve code, format, speed, or other changes as required. 2. A common boundary; e.g., the boundary between two systems or two devices.

interface, communications—The transfer of data between the processor and the standard communication subsystem takes place through input data leads, connected to the processor input channel, and output data leads, connected to the processor output channel. In addition to the data leads, there are several control leads which are used to control the flow of data.

interface computer unit—This specific unit permits attaching a DATANET-30 data communication processor to a General Electric Compatibles/200 information processing system. With this combination, the DATANET-30 is responsible for the communications half of the system, while the GE-200 series system is responsible for the data processing.

interface control module — The compiler is completely modularized into relocatable elements and is handled as any program in the system, thus providing for easy expandability and maintenance. Likewise, the COBOL processor produces as its output relocatable binary elements stored on the drum or mass storage, which are indistinguishable from other elements in the system. Other outputs from the compiler include extensive diagnostic messages, source-language listings, machine-language listings, and special cross-reference listings of name definitions and their references. The machine-language listing consists of side by side procedure-division statements and the corresponding generated symbolic machine code.

interface converter, transmission—The transmission interface converter (XIC) controls information transfer between a system channel and a transmission adapter. The XIC is attached to the selector and/or multiplexor channel, depending on the transmission adapter or adapters.

interface design—For unique user applications such as on-line installations which require specialized input/output equipment, engineering staffs will design the necessary interface units as part of services to their customers. Then, they will fabricate these units for particular systems under close supervision by the same engineers that designed them. These engineers, who are naturally quite familiar with the logic and requirements, are best qualified to do this important work.

interface design, system—*See* system interface design.

interface modules (CLTs)—Modules are provided to interface CLTs with currently available modems in addition to telegraph facilities for which no modem is necessary. Where required, interface modules conform to EIA specifications. The modular concept of the standard communication subsystem permits the addition of new interface modules as new offerings are made available by the common carriers. Jacks are provided on each telegraph interface module which permit a teletypewriter to monitor all data passing through the interface.

interface routines, processor—The processor interface routines provide a simple, standard interface for all processors within the system. Complete facilities are provided for the input of source-language statements and the output of the resulting relocatable binary code.

interference—The presence of undesirable energy in a circuit, caused by electrostatically or electromagnetically coupled external circuits.

interference, adjacent-channel — Adjacent-chanel interference occurs when two modulated carrier channels are placed close together in frequency so that one or both sidebands extend from one channel into the other.

interfix—A technique that allows the relationships of keywords in an item or document to be described so that very specific inquiries can be answered without false retrievals due to crosstalk.

interior label—*See* label, interior.

interlace—To assign successive addresses to physically separated storage locations on a magnetic drum or other rotating storage device in such a way as to reduce average access time.

interlanguage — A modification of common language, suitable for automatic translation by the equipment into machine or computer usable language.

interleave—To insert segments of one program into another program so that the two programs can, in effect, be executed simultaneously; e.g., a technique used in multiprogramming.

interleaving functional—The process of having I/O and computing operations proceed independently of one another but interleaved in their sharing of the memory.

interleaving, input/output control — *See* control module, input/output.

interleaving, memory—Two or more memory banks operating at a fraction of a cycle apart and significantly reducing cycle time and improving memory speed.

interleaving, multiprocessing—*See* multiprocessor interleaving.

interlock—To arrange the control of machines or devices so that their operation is interdependent in order to assure their proper coordination.

interlock circuit—The signal on this circuit originates in the signal converter and shall be in the "on" condition only when all the following conditions are met: (a) That its internal switching circuits are arranged for signaling on a communication facility; (b) That it is not in any abnormal or test condition which disables or impairs any normal function associated with the class of service being used.

interlock (communications)—Any protective feature which helps to prevent interference to normal transmission or processing of data by other operations, such as sending from the keyboard while an automatic transmission is in progress, or to prevent sending more than one character at a time from the keyboard.

interlock time, print—The required time for the printer to accept data from the print storage area and to complete the printing.

interlude—A minor subprogram designed for preliminary computations or data organization, such as, calculating the value of some parameter or clearing parts of the storage. It is usually overwritten after it has served its purpose, as it is usually no longer needed in the program.

intermediate control—The group of various minor controls into a category other than beginning or ending.

intermediate cycle—*See* cycle, intermediate.

intermediate language—*See* language, intermediate.

intermediate memory storage—An electronic scratchpad for holding working figures temporarily until they're needed, and for releasing final figures to the output.

intermediate-pass (own coding) — Computer instructions created by the programmer, in assembly or absolute form, which are executed by a sort during the intermediate passes of the file after the execution of instructions for comparisons of keys, but prior to output of the selected records. May also be executed during the internal sort, but after the selection of records.

intermediate product — *See* product, intermediate.

intermediate storage—*See* storage intermediate.

intermediate total—A total which lies somewhere between a major and a minor total, i.e., a summation developed for some other purpose or in some hierarchy of sums, or due to a termination in a program.

intermittent errors—*See* errors, intermittant.

intermittent faults—*Same as* faults sporadic.

intermix tape — A specific feature of some computer equipment which allows for combinations of different models of tape units to be interconnected to a single computer.

internal and external interrupts—*See* interrupts, internal and external.

internal arithmetic—The computations performed by the arithmetic unit of a computer.

internal checking—The equipment characteristics which are designed for the improvement of accuracy, such as hole counts, parity checks, validity checks, and others.

internal clocking—See clocking, non-data set.

internal code—In the IBM System/360 data representation is character- or word-oriented as follows:

> byte — 8 bits plus a check bit.
> halfword = 2 bytes.
> word = 4 bytes.
> instruction = 1, 2, 3, halfwords.
> internal code = 8-bit character.

This new system of data representation is developed for all IBM/360 computers and is used in all new IBM literature.

internal control systems—Programmed controls built into the system to govern the flow of computer operations.

internal function register—See register, internal function.

internal instruction, manipulation — A computer instruction that changes the format or location of data within the computer system.

internal interrupt — A feature of peripheral equipment using an external device which causes equipment to stop in the normal course of the program and perform some designated subroutine.

internally stored program—See program, internally stored.

internal magnetic recording—Storage of information within the material such as used in magnetic cores.

internal memory—Any one of the internal parts of an automatic data-processing machine capable of retaining data.

internal sort—The sequencing of two or more records within the central computer memory; the first phase of a multipass sort program.

internal storage—See storage, internal.

internal storage locations—Same as storage, working.

International Algebraic Language—The forerunner of ALGOL. (Clarified by algorithmic language.)

interoffice trunk—A direct trunk between local central offices in the same exchange.

interphase, standard—An agreed upon interphase that allows two or more systems to be joined logically and/or associated; for instance, a set of output signal levels from a register that will be input signals to a logic network in a digital computer.

interpolator — A machine which feeds and compares two or more decks of punched cards in order to match or merge them or to check their sequence. The cards which match can be separated from those that do not match, thereby making it possible to select as well as to file cards automatically.

interpret—1. To print on a punched card the graphic symbols of the information punched

in that card. 2. To translate nonmachine language into machine language. 3. To decode. 4. The translation of coded characters into standard letters, numbers, and symbols.

interpreter — 1. A punch-card machine that will take a punch card with no printing on it, read the information in the punched holes, and print a translation in characters in specified rows and columns on the card. 2. An executive routine that, as the computation progresses, translates a stored program expressed in some machine like pseudocode into machine code and performs the indicated operations, by means of subroutines, as they are translated. An interpreter is essentially a closed subroutine that operates successively on an indefinitely long sequence of program parameters, the pseudoinstructions, and operands. It may usually be entered as a closed subroutine and left by a pseudocode exit instruction.

interpreter code—An interim, arbitrarily designed code which must be translated to computer coding in order to function as designed, usually for diagnostic or checking purposes.

interpreter (program)—An essentially closed subroutine (executive) which translates a stored pseudocode program into machine and performs the desired and specified operations. Such an interpreter program usually consists of sequences of pseudoinstructions and operands (program parameters) which are introduced as a closed subroutine and exit by a specific pseudocode instruction.

interpreter routine — An executive routine that, as the computation progresses, translates a stored program expressed in some machinelike pseudocode into machine code and performs the indicated operations, by means of subroutines, as they are translated.

interpreting—Interpreting consists of sensing alphabetical or numerical data punched in a card and printing it on the same card.

interpretive code—A routine that decodes and immediately executes instructions written as pseudocodes. This is contrasted with a compiler which decodes the pseudocodes into a machine-language routine to be executed at a later time. The essential characteristic of an interpretive routine is that a particular pseudocode operation must be decoded each time it is executed.

interpretive execution—Permits retention of all of the information contained in the user's original source statements, thereby making source-language debugging possible. Interpretive execution plus multiprogramming make the conversational mode of operation a practical reality.

interpretive instructions — Various segments of interpreters which automatically reproduce or translate an old program code into a new program code or the interpretation of the old program code on a new machine.

interpretive language—*See* language, interpretive.

interpretive mode — In tracing (debugging) routines when a program is simulated in its execution by using psuedo accumulators and pseudo index registers, branch instructions are inserted at various points to place the machine and program in an interpretative mode for error tracing, and when an error is found, control is transferred back to the main program.

interpretive program—*See* program, interpretive.

interpretive programming — *See* programming, interpretive.

interpretive program translation — *Same as* program interpretive.

interpretive routine—A routine that decodes instructions written as pseudocodes and immediately executes those instructions, as contrasted with a compiler that decodes the pseudocodes and produces a machine-language routine to be executed at a later time.

interpretive tracing—*See* tracing, interpretive.

interrecord gap—1. The unrecorded portion between records on magnetic tape. 2. An interval of space or time, deliberately left between recording portions of data or records. Such spacing is used to prevent errors through loss of data or overwriting, and permits stop-start tape operations.

interrecord gap length — The length of the unused recording area between records written by the unit.

interrogation—A simple inquiry to the system for which a quick reply is expected.

interrogators, video-data—Video-data interrogators, comprised of keyboard and separable associated display, provide a valuable terminal facility for conventional communications lines. Up to eight interrogator units can be serviced by one interrogator control-terminal outside line, using as many as sixteen prerecorded formats, with up to a 480-character display. Transmission rate is up to 180 cps (some computers).

interrupt—1. A break in the normal flow of a system or routine such that the flow can be resumed from that point at a later time. An interrupt is usually caused by a signal from an external source. 2. An interrupt is a special control signal that diverts the attention of the computer from the main program, because of a particular event or set of circumstances, to a specific address which is directly related to the type of interrupt that has occurred. 3. To stop current control sequence; i.e., to jump when affected by signals from on-line peripheral equipment or to skip as triggered by results of programming test techniques.

interrupt, armed—Interrupts may be armed or disarmed. An armed interrupt accepts and holds the interruption signal. A disarmed interrupt ignores the signal. An armed interrupt may be enabled or disabled. An interrupt signal for an enabled condition causes certain hardware processing to occur. A disabled interrupt is held waiting for enablement.

interrupt, automatic—Interruption caused by program instruction as contained in some executive routine; interruption not caused by programmer but due to engineering of devices. Error interrupt.

interrupt, batch-processing—An outstanding feature of any real-time system is its capacity to process real-time and batch-processing applications concurrently. This real-time data-processing innovation is made possible through a unique feature that permits remote external units with information of high precedance to interrupt computer processing. Whenever transaction data for a real-time problem are entered into a remote external unit, the computer's batch-processing program may be interrupted to permit handling the high priority real-time transaction and the sending of processed results back to the external unit.

interrupt capability, time-sharing—*See* time sharing, interrupt capability.

interrupt code — The programmed or arbitrarily selected code which requires translation to computer code in order to result in machine language.

interrupt, contingency—The program is interrupted if any of the following events occur at the operator's console: the operator requests use of the keyboard to type in information; a character has been typed in or out; a type-in has been completed; or the operator requests a program stop. Contingency interrupt also occurs if an arithmetic operation resulted in an overflow, an invalid operation code was specified, or the clock was addressed after clock power was removed.

interrupt control routine—A routine entered when an interrupt occurs that provides for such details as the storage of the working details of the interrupted program, an analysis of the interrupt to decide on the necessary action, and the return of control to the interrupted program.

interrupt, count-pulse — An interrupt level that is triggered by pulses from a clock source. Each pulse of the clock source causes an instruction in a (clock) count pulse interrupt location to be executed, thus modifying the contents of a particular location (byte, halfword, or word) in memory. Each count pulse interrupt level is associated with a count zero interrupt level.

interrupt, count-zero—An interrupt level that is triggered when an associated (clock) counter pulse interrupt has produced a zero result in a clock counter.

interrupt, cycled—The change (by sequence or specific operation cycle) of control to the next or a specific function in a predetermined manner or order.

interrupt, disabled—*See* interrupt, armed.

interrupt, disarmed—*See* interrupt, armed.

interrupt, external inhibit—The bit, in the program status double-word, that indicates whether (if I) or not (if 0) all external interrupts are inhibited.

interrupt, external-signal — This facility allows signals from external equipment to interrupt the program and initiate a subroutine that services the equipment issuing the signal. Operations using this facility speed the transfer of the data and control information between the computer and peripheral equipment by allowing conditions in the equipment to initiate a transfer of program control to a subroutine that enacts a transfer, rather than waiting for the main routine to sample the condition and initiate the subroutine.

interrupt feedback signal—A steady signal, indicating that an interrupt signal has advanced its associated interrupt level to the waiting or active state; the signal is dropped when the interrupt level is reset to the disarmed or the armed state.

interrupt handling—When an interrupt occurs, the control program saves the interrupted program's registers and status, and routes control to routines that handle the interrupt cause. When the interrupt is handled, the original program's registers and status are restored, and control is restored so that the original program continues as if no interrupt had taken place.

interrupt indicators, input/output — *See* input/output interrupt indicators.

interrupt, input/output—Through the use of input/output interrupt, the input/output equipment can be kept running at full capacity with relatively small amounts of central-processor time required for input/output control. The operation of each input/output unit is under the direct control of an associated synchronizer. The performance of a particular input/output operation is initiated by a central-processor instruction which transfers a control word (function specification) to a fixed-memory location associated with the input/output sychronizer concerned. After the microseconds required to execute the initiate instruction, the central processor is free to initiate the operation of other input/output units or to execute other instructions. When the input/output unit is ready to perform the specified operation, its synchronizer accesses and decodes the function specification, which causes the unit to begin executing the specified operation. The synchronizer performs all data transfers, data and equipment checking, and other required control functions (some systems).

interrupt, input/output, inhibit—The bit, in the program status double-word, that indicates whether (if 1) or not (if 0) all internal interrupts of the I/O group are inhibited.

interruption—A brief curtailing or suspension of operations or its sequence of instructions, usually followed by the start of another sequence or a revision to the one stopped. Examples are the stops in priority processing.

interruption, automatic program — *See* automatic program-interruption and time sharing.

interrupt, I/O parity—Each time control is given to the monitor the I/O parity trap is armed and the interrupt location is patched with an instruction. When an I/O parity occurs the computer halts to the instruction at which the parity occurred with the console I/O parity indicator light on.

interrupt logging—The logging or listing of interrupts during program testing, or when a system is being monitored, so that possible program errors caused by interrupts may be classified and corrected.

interrupt log word—The setting of bits into an interrupt log record which indicates the number and type of interrupts that occur during the running of each segment of a program. The output is on a media such as tape for analysis.

interrupt mask—Some of the program interruptions, all external interruptions, and all I/O interruptions can be masked (ignored); when this is done, the external and I/O interruptions are held pending and taken at a later time (governed by the control program).

interrupt, master-control—A signal generated by an input/output device, or by an operator's error, or by request of the processor for more data or program segments, or the like, which permits the master control program to control the computer system.

interrupt monitor, output—*See* output monitor interrupt.

interrupt, not-busy—When an external device recognizes its address and is not busy, it sends a response on the not-busy line to the computer. If no such response is received, the processor will assume that the addressed device is busy. The processor will send a start signal only if a not-busy response is received. If a device is disconnected, it will appear as busy to the computer (some computers).

interrupt, operator—The operator interrupt trap is armed and the fixed interrupt location is patched each time the monitor receives control. When an operator interrupt occurs, control is given to a routine in the monitor. This routine signifies to the operator the type-in is desired by ringing the bell, returning the carriage, and typing.

interrupt oriented—Some programs are not encumbered with instructions that check system components for status or service. Interrupt signals are generated by processors as well as all I/O devices.

interrupt, override — An optional group of power on/off interrupts which have the highest priority and which cannot be disabled or disarmed.

interrupt, parity (memory)—Each time control is given to the monitor the memory parity trap is armed and the interrupt location is patched with an instruction. When a memory parity occurs, the computer halts to the location at which the parity occurred, with the console memory parity indicator light on (some computers).

interrupt (peripheral)—The stop resulting from the signal of readiness for or completion of a task by a peripheral device.

interrupt, power-fail—Only a priority interrupt can interrupt a nonpriority interrupt routine. Power fail is the highest priority interrupt and may interrupt any other program or interrupt routine as long as the power-fail interrupt trap is armed.

interrupt, priority—See priority interrupt.

interrupt priority table — When a computer does not have a fully automatic interrupt handling capability a table is set up that lists the priority sequence of handling and testing interrupts.

interrupt, processing — See processing interrupt.

interrupt processing, time-sharing—See time sharing, interrupt processing.

interrupt, processor-dependent—An example of a processor-dependent interrupt condition is the "presence bit condition" caused by a program being executed on a processor that is executing an operand call which addresses a descriptor with a presence bit of zero.

interrupt, processor-error—If a word accessed in any part of the system is found to contain incorrect check bits, or if an error occurs in the addressing of a memory location, processor-error interrupt occurs.

interrupt, processor-independent—An example of a processor-independent interrupt condition is an I/O finished condition caused by the I/O hardware when an I/O operation has been completed.

interrupt, program—See program interrupt.

interrupt, program-controlled—A one bit in a specific position causes a request for an I/O interrupt as soon as a command with this flag arrives at a channel. This provides the channel with a means of altering the processor program of the progress of chaining during an I/O operation. Among other things, it permits programmed dynamic storage allocation, or the reading of gapless tape, etc.

interrupt, program-error — Program interrupts occur because of programmer errors such as an invalid operation.

interrupt (program signals)—Seventy-four interrupt signals, governing input/output operations and various contingency and error conditions, include internal and external interrupts for every channel. In effect, each interrupt causes a jump from the main program to an associated subroutine. This subroutine may set up input or output transmissions, prepare the computer for error-diagnostic routines, or perform any

other function the programmer may assign to it (some computers).

interrupt, program-switching—The importance of interrupt capability cannot be overstressed. In a serial batch-processing environment, one I/O operation is often used to read in multiple transactions or to write out the results of multiple transactions. However, in a nonscheduled, random-processing environment, many I/O operations are required for each transaction. Since an interrupt is initiated at the completion of each I/O transaction, and since a number of different programs must be switched to handle a transaction, the processor time required to perform a program switch and identify the cause of an interrupt is an important factor in determining the performance of a system.

These interrupts can require considerable housekeeping: contents of registers have to be saved; the stopping point must be noted; resumption of processing must be provided for; and so forth. The computer system performs this interrupt with electronic circuitry.

The cause of the interrupt is identified by hardware, and the processor is automatically switched to the appropriate control routine for servicing in interrupt. If the interrupt resulted from an I/O operation, hardware in the system will designate the I/O unit and the cause. This is the basis of real-time and time/sharing operations.

interrupt (recovery routines)—The act of providing to the operating program the entrances to subroutines which will handle the error interrupts. Upon occurrence of an error interrupt, control is transferred automatically to one of the fixed core-memory addresses. The executive provides jump instructions for these locations. These instructions in turn reference subroutines which will attempt to recover from these errors. Attempts to write into a locked-out area of memory result in program termination when operating under executive control. Recovery routines are permitted for illegal operation code, trace mode, characteristic overflow, characteristic underflow, and divide-fault interrupts. All I/O and other interrupts are handled by other parts of the executive system (some systems).

interrupt routine—A program that performs interrupt action to coordinate the timing I/O with processing.

interrupt routine, tape-driver — See tape driver interrupt routine.

interrupts and control logic—The synchronization of input/output activities and responses to real-time situations is accomplished through interrupts. The interrupt is a control signal that may be received from a peripheral subsystem (external interrupt) or from the control section of the central processor. Each interrupt has a unique fixed address in central store. These interrupt locations are programmed to enter interrupt response subroutines in the executive system.

interrupts, automatic check—Input/output interrupts occur upon successful completion of an input/output operation, if a programmer has specified an input/output operation incorrectly, or if a machine malfunction (such as a parity error) occurrs in the path to or from the input/output device. These interrupts permit an automatic check of the status of the operation and of any errors that may have occurred, and initiation of an error-recovery procedure when practical. In the event of intermittent errors, statistics can be kept and logged out between jobs. This automatic checking as provided by the "interrupt" technique makes for highly efficient and accurate programming.

interrupt, scanner—External devices are continuously scanned for interrupt requests. A scanner counts through the nonpriority external-device addresses sequentially, asking if the addressed device is requesting an interrupt. When an interrupt request is found, the scanner will stop at that address and attempt to interrupt the computer program. This feature (ED interrupt) is the important invention which is the basis for real-time computing time sharing.

interrupt, schemes, time-sharing — *See* time-sharing interrupt schemes.

interrupts, error—Special interrupts are provided in response to certain error conditions within the central computer. These may come as a result of a programming fault (e.g., illegal instruction, arithmetic overflow), a store fault (parity error) or an executive system violation (attempt to leave the locked-in area, or violation of guard mode). These faults have special interrupt locations in central store and are used by the executive system to take remedial or terminating action when they are encountered.

interrupts, external—External interrupts are caused by either an external device requiring attention (such as a signal from a communications device), console switching, or by the timer going to zero.

interrupts, external device (ED)—External device interrupts may occur for any of several reasons. An external device may interrupt when it has completed an operation if it was told to do so by the program when the operation was initiated. An external device may interrupt at a different address to indicate that a failure (parity fail, end of tape, etc.) has occurred. Different devices have different failure conditions and different failure-interrupt addresses. An external device may be notifying the program that some specific real-time event has occurred.

interrupt signal—One of the more powerful control signals governing the input/output operations of the central computer and the peripheral subsystems is the interrupt signal.

This signal is used to demand the immediate attention of the central computer. It causes program control to be switched to a special address connected with the event or circumstances that initiated the interrupt. Interrupts from external sources serve primarily to synchronize the computer program with the status of the subsystem units, and to indicate error conditions occurring within the peripheral subsystems. Internal interrupts synchronize the computer program with the termination of input/output transfers.

interrupts, internal and external—An interrupt is a special control signal which diverts the "attention" of the computer to "consider" an extraordinary event or set of circumstances; that is, it causes program control to be transferred to a special subordinate which corresponds to the "stimulus." Many levels of control can be exercised by the numerous forms of interrupts provided. The interrupts from external sources serve primarily to synchronize the computer program with the readiness of peripheral devices, including other computers, to transmit or receive data. Internal interrupts serve primarily to synchronize the computer program with the termination of input/output transfers and to signal the occurrence of an error. An interrupt causes the next instruction to be procured from a fixed address corresponding to the interrupt source. This fixed address serves as a subroutine entrance by containing a *return jump* instruction.

interrupts, machine—Machine interrupts occur because of a malfunction in the processor. For these interrupts, the control program may call in machine diagnostic routines from the system library. The current program may either be ended with an abnormal end-of-program or restarted after the diagnostic routines have been executed, and the results stored for later analysis.

interrupts, machine-check — Machine-check interrupts are caused by the machine-checking circuits detecting a machine error. The system is automatically switched to a diagnostic procedure.

interrupts, multiprogramming — Some computers are equipped with a set of control signals which are referred to as interrupts. Whenever certain conditions exist, a control signal will direct the central computer to execute the word (instruction) at a specified address in central store. Each interrupt is activated by unique conditions and directs the computer to a correspondingly unique address in central store. The occurrence of an interrupt terminates guard mode, program lockin, and central-store address assignments.

interrupts, nonpriority—Up to 64 nonpriority program interrupts are available on many computers. Each interrupt will lead to a unique interrupt routine associated with the particular interrupt event. At the completion of an interrupt routine, control may be returned to the running program at the point of interruption or transferred to a new program. These interrupts may be used to notify the processor of the completion of some external operation, or the occurrence of some other significant external event. The processor may recognize or ignore these interrupts by setting the external device interrupt to the allow or disallow condition (some computers).

interrupts, optional—See optional priority interrupts.

interrupts, optional multilevel priority—See optional multilevel priority interrupts.

interrupts, optional priority — See optional priority interrupts.

interrupts, processor—See processor interrupt.

interrupts, standard—Various events can lead to a program interrupt. Each interrupt is to a unique fixed memory address which is associated with the event that caused it. Each external device has an interrupt address which is equal to its external-device address. An external device may have more than one interrupt event and each event may have its own interrupt address. Interrupts may occur only at the end of program instructions. It is important to the programmer that each type of interrupt results in transfer of control to a different memory address. This makes it unnecessary for the program to scan interrupt events to see what has happened. A subroutine for each interrupt event may be in memory.

interrupts supervisor — See supervisor interrupts.

interrupts, supervisor-call—Supervisor-call interrupts are caused by the program issuing an instruction to turn over control to the supervisor (the operating system). The exact cause for the call is shown in the old PSW (program status word) (some computers).

interrupts, system-call—System-call interrupts are programmed requests from a processing program to the control program for some action, such as initiation of an I/O operation.

interrupt system—Some processors feature an interrupt system in which an interrupt source, whether internal or external, meets automatic and immediate response. The interrupt source is properly identified, and a change in program sequence to service the interruption is automatically executed.

interrupt, trapped program—Events can cause the program of the computer to be interrupted: (1) memory parity error, (2) add overflow, (3) programmed I/O channel, (4) operator, (5) external device, (6) multilevel priority interrupts, and (7) power failure. An interrupt trap associated with each event may be set under program control to either respond when the event occurs or to ignore it.

interrupt traps—See traps, interrupt.

interrupt trigger signal—A signal that is generated, either internal or external to the CPU, to interrupt the normal sequence of events in the central processor.

intersection — 1. The Boolean operator that gives a truth table value of true only when both of the variables connected by the logical operator are true. 2. A logical operator that has the property that if P is a statement and Q is a statement, when P AND Q are true, both statements are true, and false if either is false or both are false. Truth is normally expressed by the value 1; falsity by 0. 3. The logical operation which makes use of the AND operator or logical product.

intersection gate—Same as gate, AND.

interspersed gang punching — The punching of cards with fixed data in one or more cards simultaneously within a larger group of cards.

interstage punching—A system of punching in which only odd-numbered rows or cards are used. (Contrasted with normal punching.)

intersystem communications—Many users will want to install systems of different sizes to meet a diverse number of data-processing problems. And in many cases it is desirable for the two configurations to be linked so that the flow between the two environments need not be slowed by mechanical transfer. The user of certain configurations will be able to join two configurations together. Any two configurations can share input and output devices or be linked channel to channel. Some configurations can be linked through main or large core storage.

interval, significant—A time interval during which a given significant condition according to the code and the signal to be transmitted is, or should be, transmitted.

intervals, marking, and spacing—In telegraph communication, marking intervals that correspond, according to convention, to one condition or position of the originating transmitting contracts, usually a closed condition; spacing intervals are the intervals which correspond to another condition of the originating transmitting contracts, usually an open condition.

interval timer—With the interval timer, the control program provides the facility to keep track of time of day and to interrupt periodically as required. More than one interval can be controlled at once. For example, a five-second interval between successive polling of a teleprocessing line can be specified, and at the same time a two-minute limit on the duration of a new program undergoing test can be in effect.

interval, time-write — The determination of the interval during machine operation when output data is available for an output operation, i.e., the net time exclusive of transmission which it takes to perform an output operation such as printing or writing on tape.

interval, unit—In a system using an equal-length code, or in a system using an isochronous modulation, the interval of time, such as the theoretical duration of the significant intervals of a telegraph modulation (or restitution), are whole multiples of this interval.

intervention button—*See* button emergency.

intervention switch—*See* button, emergency.

interword gap—*See* gap, interword.

interword space—*Same as* gap, interword.

INTRAFAX—Western Union leases closed-circuit facsimile systems called INTRAFAX to government, military, and industrial users.

introspective program—A self-monitoring program.

inversion—1. The operation of taking the reciprocal of a value; that is, unity divided by the value. 2. In Boolean operations, it is the same as NOT.

invert—To change any logical, mathematical, or two-state value to its direct opposite state.

inverted file—*See* file, inverted.

inverter—*Same as* gate, NOT.

invigilator—This type of equipment is used to discern whether some prescribed condition is present, usually within a predetermined time period. It is often connected to a control unit, as in process control equipment, to give an alarm if the response time of some machinery or process has been exceeded or interrupted.

invoice-total card—Card which provides input data for the accounts receivable system.

I/O—The abbreviation for input/output.

I/O buffer—Permits data-word transfers to and from memory to proceed without main program attention. May be programmed so that when I/O transfer is complete, the computer generates an internal interrupt.

IOC—Abbreviation for input/output controller.

I/O cable—A wire bus or trunk connecting the various input or output devices to the computer.

I/O channels (multiplexing)—The CLTs (Communication Line Terminals) may request access to the central processor via the communication multiplexer in random sequence. The communication multiplexer automatically assigns priorities among CLTs requesting access, and identifies to the central processor the particular CLT granted access. This process is automatic and self-controlled on the UNIVAC System through externally specified indexing (ESI) on each I/O channel.

IOCS—An abbreviation for input/output control system. Specialized program generally related to large scale computer operations.

I/O equipment—Equipment of the peripheral nature which has a primary purpose of feeding input to the computer and taking output from the computer.

I/O interface control module—These microcircuit modules handle all computer inputs and outputs, with the number and type determined by system applications and the peripheral equipment used. There is also provision to directly connect an I/O interface with a memory module, under program control, to allow an efficient method of resolving conflicts in memory access.

I/O parity interrupt—Each time control is given to the monitor, the I/O parity trap is armed and the interrupt location is patched with an instruction. When an I/O parity occurs, the computer halts on the instruction at which the parity occurred with the console I/O parity indicator light on.

IOP (input/output processor)—A unit that handles normal data input/output control and sequencing.

IOR—Abbreviation for input/output register.

I/O referencing symbolic—References to data on tape or disk are made symbolically. Instead of describing the address of a certain disk or tape, the programmer refers to such data with a functional name. This means the programmer need not keep in mind where data will be coming from. He can mount tapes in the most efficient way each day. The control programs set up an input and output assignment table indicating the whereabouts of data files. These tables are used as directories when programs are run.

I/O routines, random-access—Direct, serial, and random processing of drum and disk files are provided by these routines. Macro instructions are available to direct the performance of the input/output functions.

IPC—Abbreviation for industrial process control.

IPL—An abbreviation for information processing language.

(IPL) (initial program loading)—*See* program loading, initial.

IPL-V—Abbreviation for information processing language—five. A list-processing language developed principally by Newell, Simon, and Shaw to manipulate tree structures.

IRL—Abbreviation for information retrieval language.

irregularity-stroke edge—A term used in optical character recognition referring to the deviation of any point on the edge of a character from its stroke edge.

isochronous—Having a regular periodicity.

isochronous modulation (or restitution)—Modulation (or restitution) in which the time interval separating any two significant instants is theoretically equal to the unit interval or to a multiple of it.

ISO (International Standards Organization) code—Codes authorized by the ISO to represent alphabetic, numeric, and special characters.

IT—Internal translator is a programming language translator developed for use on the IBM 650 computer by Carnegie Institute of Technology.

item—1. A field or set of fields holding related data or information that concerns an individual object, event, transaction, or operation. 2. The word is used in a similar sense to the word file and means each of the unit organizations of information of which the file is comprised. 3. Consecutive fields can be combined to form a larger unit of information called an item. Grouping fields to form an item simplifies the manipulation of related data fields, and minimizes the number of instruction executions required to move consecutive fields within the main memory.

item, addition—An item that is to be added at a specific place to an already established file. Addition master item would be the proper term if file is a master file.

item advance—A technique in the grouping of records for operating successively on different records in storage.

item, data—*See* data item.

item design—The set or collection of records or fields to compose an item as delineated, or the sequence in which fields are to be recorded; the type or group of characters to be allocated to each field.

item, elementary—In the COBOL system, a data item containing no subordinate terms.

item, line—An item of data, in data processing, that is on the same level as a given set of items for a given application and which could logically be printed on the same line on a printer page; for instance, stock number, item, quantity, and cost.

item list, first—*Same as* indication group.

item separation symbol — A control symbol which indicates beginning of an item.

item size—1. The magnitude of an item, usually expressed in numbers of words, characters, or blocks. 2. The number of characters in an item.

iterate—To execute successively a series of instructions; for instance, to execute repeatedly a loop in a routine until some condition is satisfied. An example would be to square each value of N from one to ten and accumulate the squared values before exiting the loop and continuing with the program. This is usually done with a series of arithmetic or logical operations on a digital computer.

iteration—1. A single cycle of operations in a solution algorithm made up of a number of such cycles. 2. The technique of repeating a group of computer instructions; one repetition of such a group.

iterative—Describing a procedure or process which repeatedly executes a series of operations until some condition is satisfied. An iterative procedure can be implemented by a loop in a routine.

iterative operation—The standard, usual, or automatic repetition of the solution, for example, of a set of equations with successive or changed combinations of initial conditions, or simply the use of different parameters and the use of the same computing program.

iterative process—A process for calculating a desired result by means of a repeating cycle of operations that comes closer and closer to the desired result; e.g., the arithmetical square root of N may be approximated by an iterative process using additions, subtractions, and divisions only.

Iverson notation—A special set of symbols developed by Dr. Kenneth Iverson to describe the formal structure of computer languages. Used in APL.

J

jack panel—*See* control panel.

Jacquard loom — A loom for weaving cloth which in the early 1800's used the idea of a punched hole in a card to represent a number and control the operation of the loom. In 1886, statistician Dr. Herman Hollerith, while working on the 1880 census, developed the idea that these holes could be sensed by a machine which could sort and manipulate the arithmetic sums represented by the holes. Thus, Dr. Hollerith invented the punched card which is still used as a basic input medium today.

jam—In punch-card machines, a condition in the card feed that interferes with the normal travel of the punch cards through the machine.

jam, card—A pile-up of cards in a machine.

jargon—A vocabulary used by a specific group of people but not generally nor universally accepted in fields other than the one in which it originated. The jargon of the com-

puter industry is colloquially known as computerese.

JCL—Abbreviation for job control language.

jitter—1. Short-time instability of a signal. The instability may be in either amplitude or phase, or both. The term is applied especially to signals reproduced on the screen of a cathode-ray tube. The term "tracking jitters" is used to describe minor variations in the pointing of an automatic-tracking radar. 2. A lack of synchronization caused by mechanical or electrical changes.

job control language — Specifies an environment in which a job is to be run, and optional output desired.

job control, stacked — Under sequential-stacked job control, the jobs are performed in the sequence in which they are received by the system.

job control statement—Individual statements used to direct an operating system in its functions, as contrasted to information needed to process a job but not intended directly for the operating system itself.

job end control card—*See* end-of-job card control.

job flow control—Job flow control includes: I/O transition between jobs and job segments, unit assignments, initial loading and initialization when the computer is first turned on; control between jobs; and control over the type of operation mode, ranging from simple stacked jobs through teleprocessing systems performing concurrent operations.

job input stream—An input source of documents, usually punched cards or card images, which is the first part of an operating system. The stream contains the beginning-of-job indicators, directions, optional programs, etc.

job library—*See* library, job.

job-oriented language — *See* language, job oriented.

job-oriented terminal—1. A terminal designed for a particular application. 2. A terminal specially designed to receive source data in an environment associated with the job to be performed, and capable of transmission to and from the system of which it is a part.

job-processing control—The job processing control is the portion of the control program which starts job operations, assigns input/output units, and performs functions needed to proceed from one job to another.

job processing, master file—The master file contains the programs necessary for job processing. The programs in the master file are sectioned into four categories: (1) input/output drivers (2) system programs (3) utility routines (4) library subroutines.

job-processing monitor—Computer programs are processed by routines contained in the monitor system. The operations that may be performed upon a program are: compilation, assembly, loading, segmenting, execution, and dumping. One or all of these operations may be required to process a program. Other factors, such as inputs and outputs necessary to the program, may be required in order to successfully perform an operation. The information defining the processing of a program plus the operations performed upon the program comprise a job. The operating system processes all programs on a job basis. Job processing is controlled by two system routines: the monitor and the executive. The executive accepts control information for each job. This information is placed in the monitor which controls the sequence of operations performed on the job. The monitor is resident in memory during all operations. The routines necessary for performing the various operations are contained in a master file. The monitor loads and executes each routine as it is needed. Each routine, in turn, returns control to the monitor upon completion. When all operations have been completed for the job, the executive is loaded into memory

to accept control information for the next job. In order to achieve automatic job processing, all computer programs must return to the monitor upon completion (some systems).

job-processing system—The monitor system is composed of a series of individual programs that work together to form a complete operating system. Manuals describe the total monitor system. They also contain a complete description of the primary operating system routines—the monitor program, executive program, system loader, system-preparation routine, and input/output routines. The compiler, assemblers, utility routines, and library subroutines are described in the sense in which they are used as part of the monitor system. The complete description of these routines is provided in separate documents. The words "monitor system," "operating system," and "system" are used interchangeably in manuals and refer to the monitor system (some systems).

job process, termination (monitor)—The programmer specifies monitor system operations with various control statements. These statements may be input via a console typewriter or included with the program on cards, paper tape, or magnetic tape. Programs are processed automatically on a job basis. A job may consist of compilations, assemblies, executions utility requests, editing, and program segmenting. Intermixed jobs are processed in sequence automatically by the monitor system. Programs terminate by returning control to the system. A "job" may be terminated by the operator, or by the monitor system itself. When a job terminates, processing of the next job is automatically initiated.

job-program mode—In the job-program mode, both read/write and jump-storage protection is in effect. Therefore, job programs are limited entirely to those areas assigned by the executive. If the job program reads, writes, or jumps to an out-of-limits address, an interrupt will return control to the executive for remedial action. Read/jump protection allows the executive to stop the program at the point of error, terminate it, and provide diagnostic information to the programmer, thereby minimizing wasted time and smoothing the checkout process. A particular advantage of read/jump protection is that programs of a classified nature can be confidently run together; they are fully protected from audit (inadvertent or otherwise) by other programs.

job-request selection—The use of information contained in the job-request schedule to select the next job to be initiated. Selection is based on the priority and precedence assigned to the job, the sequence relationship of this job to other jobs with the same priority and precedence, and the availability of facilities required by the job.

job schedule—A control program that is used to examine the input work queue and to select the next job to be processed.

job stacking—The monitor system has the facilities for batch processing both FORTRAN compilations and assemblies. Assemblies or compilations, i.e., jobs, can be stacked behind one another. After the operator specifies the operation, assembling or compiling proceeds automatically through one job after another until an end-of-run card is encountered signifying the end of the run (some systems).

job statement control—Individual statements used to direct an operating system in its functions, as contrasted to information needed to process a job, but not intended directly for the operating system itself.

job step—A single unit of work from the user's viewpoint. A job is made up of one or more job steps and a job step is composed of one or more tasks, each task being a single unit of processing.

job stream input—See input, job stream.

joggle—To agitate or jiggle a group or deck of punched cards and bring them into alignment before placing them in the hopper.

join gate—Same as gate, OR.

joint denial gate—Same as gate, NOR.

JOSS (johnniac open-shop system)—A time-sharing language developed by the Rand Corporation to make quick calculations that were too complicated for a calculator.

journal reader, optical—See optical journal reader.

JOVIAL—A language for real-time command and control developed by Systems Development Corp.

JUG—The Joint Users Group is a group of computer users sharing common interests, software, and computers.

jump—See branch.

jump, conditional—See branch conditional.

jump instruction—A computer instruction causing a jump in the sequence of instructions. See branch.

jump instruction, conditional—Same as branch conditional.

jump instruction, conditional transfer—See branch, conditional.

jump instruction, unconditional—See branch, unconditional.

jump operation—The computer departs from the regular sequence of instruction executions and jumps to another routine or program, or even some preceding or forward instructions to alter control, repeat a process or loop, etc.

jump, unconditional—See branch unconditional.

junction hole—Same as control punch.

justification—The act of adjusting, arranging, or shifting digits to the left or right to fit a prescribed pattern.

justified margin—Arrangement of data or type printed on pages in a manner such that the left or right end characters of each horizontal line lie in the same column.

justified, right hand—When a quantity in storage or in a register has no zeroes in the low order (right hand) positions it is considered right hand justified.

justify—1. To adjust exactly, as by spacing; to align a set of characters horizontally (or vertically) to right or left margins. To develop exact format or spacing in words, fields, items, or data as designed by context of exact specifications. 2. To move a data item so that a particular part of the item assumes a particular position relative to some reference point in a storage medium; for instance, to adjust the print on a printed page so that the left, right, or both margins are aligned; also to shift the item in a register to position specifically the most or least signifiicant digit.

justify, right—To format a right margin for the type on a printed page. More difficult and expensive than left justification.

juxtaposition—The positioning or placing of items adjacent to each other or side by side.

K

K—A symbol which is equivalent to the numeral 1000. For example: 32 K would be equivalent to 32,000.

Karnaugh map—A tabular arrangement which facilitates combination and elimination of duplicate logical functions by listing similar logical expressions.

KCS—An abbreviation for 1000 characters per second. The generally accepted measurement of data transmission speed.

key—1. A group of characters usually forming a field, utilized in the identification or location of an item. A marked lever manually operated for copying a character; e.g. type-writer paper-tape perforator, card punch manual keyboard, digitizer or manual word generator. 2. That part of a word, record, file, etc., by which it is identified or controlled. 3. The field by which a file of records is sorted into order; e.g. the key for a file of employee records by a number, department, or letter.

key, activate—Same as button initiate.

key, actual—A data item, in the COBOL language, which can be used for a machine address and which will express the location of a record in a storage medium.

keyboard—A device for the encoding of data

by key depression, which causes the generation of the selected code element.

keyboard, companion — An auxiliary keyboard device which is usually located remotely from the main unit.

keyboard computer — A computer, the input of which employs a keyboard, possibly an electric typewriter.

keyboard display console — *See* console, keyboard display.

keyboard entry — 1. An element of information inserted manually, usually via a set of switches or marked punch levers, called keys, into an automatic data-processing system. 2. A medium for achieving access to, or entrance into, an automatic data-processing system.

keyboard inquiry — Interrogation of program progress, storage contents, or other information by keyboard maneuvering.

keyboard lockout — An interlock feature that prevents sending from the keyboard while the tape transmitter or another station is sending on the same circuit.

keyboard, optical display — *See* optical display keyboard.

keyboard perforator — The unit, containing rows of keys, which causes holes or patterns of holes to occur when keys are depressed. The keys correspond to individual characters, same as keypunch.

keyboard printer — The keyboard printer permits keyboard insertion of transaction data and printed page output of computer responses at speeds related to the common-carrier service available. Either telegraphic or voice grade lines can be utilized. The keyboard and printer can be used separately or in combination.

The keyboard contains a full four-bank set of keys, 10 numeric, 26 alphabetic, 10 special character keys, and a space bar. The printing unit prepares a copy of all transaction data as it is typed on the keyboard. Computer responses are also printed by the printing unit.

keyboard/printer, time-sharing — *See* time sharing, keyboard/printer.

keyboard punch — *See* punch, keyboard.

keyboard send/receive set (KSR) — A combination transmitter and receiver with transmission capability from keyboard only.

keyboard, supervisory — The supervisory console includes the operator's control panel, a keyboard and typeprinter, and a control unit for the keyboard and typeprinter. Optionally, a paper-tape reader and punch may be connected to the computer through the same control unit. Information transfer between the computer and any single device is performed and output channel assigned to the console auxiliaries. Two switches mounted on the control unit permit selection of the paper-tape reader or the keyboard, and the paper-tape punch or the type printer (some computers).

keyboard time-out — Keyboards are equipped with a time-out feature which causes the keyboard to lock if more than 15 seconds elapse between the sending of characters. If a time-out occurs during the typing of a line, any information typed on that line up to that point will be discarded. To avoid this loss of information, the user may press and release shift before the 15-seconds limit has been reached; this action may be repeated as necessary to prevent a time-out. By pressing shift, the user can prevent a time-out without affecting the input information (some units).

key, carriage restore — A button which returns the printer carriage to the start position.

key-driven — Any device for translating information into machine-sensible form, which requires an operator to depress a key for each character, is said to be key-driven.

keying error, rate of — Ratio of number of alphabetic signals incorrectly transmitted to the number of alphabetic signals of the message.

key, initiate — *See* button, initiate.

key, load — A control key, or similar manual device, which is used to input data or instructions into a computer or control system. The instructions are usually made up of computer routines.

key, major — The most significant key in a record.

key, protection — An indicator designed to allow the program access to sections of memory which the program may use, and a denial of access to all other parts of memory, i.e., a memory-protection device with a key which is numbered by the computer. Usually such keys are for most locations in memory, and when a storage key differs from the program protection key, the program can be interrupted and taken over by a supervisory program to handle the problem which arises.

keypunch — 1. A special device to record information in cards or tape by punching holes in the cards or tape to represent letters, digits, and special characters. 2. To operate a device for punching holes in cards or tape.

keypunch and verifier operator — Employees who operate numerical and alphabetical keypunch and verifying machines to transcribe routine or easily identified data from various documents onto punched cards.

keypunch, numeric — A key punch that processes only numeric data.

keypunch operator — This individual converts source documents into machine-acceptable form by keypunching from hand-written or typed forms.

keypunch, printing — A card-printing machine that prints each number or letter on the card as it punches the card.

key, single cycle — A push button on printers, which causes an additional line to be printed despite an end-of-form indication.

231

key, single vertical—A push button on printers which causes an additional line to be printed for indication.

key sorting—The fields in a record which determine, or are used as a basis for determining, the sequence of records in a file.

keys, tape-punch control—These keys control functions such as power on (to punch), feeding tape at beginning and end of reel, tape error, punch on and punch off.

key, stop—A push button on the control panel which causes a halt in the processing, but often only after the completion of an instruction being executed at a given moment.

key, symbolic — In COBOL, contrast with actual key.

key tape load—A specific control push button which causes the first tape unit to read and transfer data into internal storage until the inter-record gap is sensed, at which time the internal storage is read for the first instruction.

key typeout, respond—A particular push button on a console inquiry keyboard which locks the typewriter keyboard and permits the automatic processing to continue.

key-verify—To use the punch-card machine known as a verifier, which has a keyboard to make sure that the information supposed to be punched in a punch card has actually been properly punched. The machine signals when the punched hole and the depressed key disagree.

keyword-in-context index (KWIC)—The keyword-in-context index lists available programs arranged alphabetically by the keywords in the program titles. There is an index entry for each significant keyword in the title. Certain words are not accepted as indexing words but will be printed as part of the title.
A KWIC index is prepared by highlighting each keyword of the title in the context of words on either side of it and aligning the keywords of all titles alphabetically in a vertical column.

keywords—The most informative words in a title or document which describe the content of that document; the significant words.

key, write—A code in the program status double-word that is used in conjunction with a memory lock to determine whether or not a program may write into a specific page of actual addresses.

key, write field—The portion of the program status double-word that contains the write key.

kill, zero—A specific feature of some sorters which determines that only zeros remain in the high order positions of documents while the documents are being sorted in lower order positions, i.e., this permits the machine operator to remove documents that are fully sequenced earlier in the sorting operation.

kilo—A prefix meaning one thousand. Its abbreviation is K; e.g., 8K means 8000. In computer use it may also refer to the power of two closest to a number; e.g., 4K word memory is actually 4096 words.

kilobauds — New and higher capacity data channels. For special applications, some data channels capable of 20 kilobauds have been placed in service.

kilobit—One thousand binary digits.

kilomega—A prefix meaning one billion; e.g., a kilomegacycle means one billion cycles (same as billicycle and gigacycle), and a kilomegabit means one billion bits (same as billibit).

kilomegabit—One thousand million binary digits or one billion binary dibits, such as a one-billion-bit storage device.

kludge—A computer mimic or humorous term indicating the black box or computer. A kludge is slang for, or representation of, an endearment of the pet computer; i.e., "our kludge".

KSR—*See* keyboard send-receive set.

KWIC—Abbreviation for key word in context.

L

label—1. An identification device for introducing a record, groups of records, or an address; a number, symbol, tag, or slip. 2. A name (symbol) which indicates an instruction or data group. Usually this is a mnemonic label for easy recogniton. 3. A set of symbols used to identify or describe an item, record, message, or file. Occasionally it may be the same as the address in storage. 4. A string of alphameric information placed at any location for informational and instructional purposes. 5. To assign a symbol, acronym, or word, as a means of identification, to a body of data, tape, card, deck, block; to create a specialized associated record or filing "handle."

label, file—A set of alphanumeric characters that uniquely identifies the contents of a particular roll of magnetic tape or a portion of magnetic tape. The file label is written on magnetic tape as a block which contains the file name, reel number, data written, and date expired.

label, interior—A label accompanying the data it identifies. As in the case of magnetic tape, the interior labels are usually read by the computer under the control of a program.

label, operational—Tape files are identified, as far as the operator is concerned, by means of an operational label. An operational label may be any combination of letters and digits to a maximum of six characters. Two special characters are also used consisting of the character * and the character—to indicate a scratch tape and an empty (or malfunctioning) tape unit, respectively.

label record—A record used to identify the contents of a file or reel of magnetic tape.

labels, external—Labels are normally defined in the same program in which they are used as operands. However, it is possible to define a symbol in one program, use it in a program assembled independently of the first program, and then execute both programs together. A label is termed an ENTRY point in the program in which it is defined; it is an EXT (external) label in the program in which it is used as an operand.

labels, future—Future labels are labels which are referenced by the programmer in the operand field of a statement and have not been defined previously. Since an address cannot be assigned to this reference the label is put into a symbol table as an unassigned label, accompanied by the address of the command which referenced it.

labels, tab—Those particular labels which are part of a continuous form and thus can feed through a tabulator or printer. After printing, the labels can be detached and affixed to a product, envelope, etc.

label, tape—A tape label consists of two blocks. The first block is an installation tape number which should be assigned on introducing a new reel of tape into the system. This number never changes. The second block identifies the information which will follow on the tape and contains dating information that will be used by special programs to further identify the tape, and to protect information from being destroyed prematurely.

label, track—The installation deck number, card number, and track number that uniquely identifies any CRAM track. The track label is written as the first four slabs of every track of every card of a deck.

laboratory instrument computer—LINC performs several of the functions that external devices or people are normally required to perform. Data recording, analog-to-digital conversion, experiment monitoring, control, and analysis are built-in capabilities of the computer. LINC gives direct assistance to the research worker in many ways.

lace—To punch all rows of a card column.

laced—The condition representing extraneous punching in punch cards or paper tape.

lacing—Extra multiple punching in a card column to signify the end of a special card run. The term is derived from the lace-work appearance of the card.

lag—1. A relative measure of the time delay between two events, states, or mechanisms. 2. The delay between two successive events.

LAMP—Library Additions and Maintenance Program. Honeywell programs that maintain the library of subroutines and mi-

croroutines available through the ARGUS and EASY assembly systems.

language—1. A defined set of characters that is used to form symbols, words, etc., and the rules for combining these into meaningful communications; e.g., English, French, ALGOL, FORTRAN, COBOL, etc. 2. A combination of a vocabulary and rules of syntax.

language, absolute—*Same as* machine language.

language, algebraic—A language which uses symbols and letters, both Greek and English, to express relations, variables, constants, parameters, operators, operands, and mathematical or logical relations. Each algebra has its own set of rules and is designed to delineate situations, relations, operations, and equalities and inequalities.

language, algorithmic—An arithmetic language by which numerical procedures may be precisely presented to a computer in a standard form. The language is intended not only as a means of directly presenting any numerical procedure to any suitable computer for which a compiler exists, but also as a means of communicating numerical procedures among individuals.

The language itself is the result of international cooperation to obtain a standardized algorithmic language. The International Algebraic Language is the forerunner of ALGOL. (Synonymous with ALGOL, and clarified by International Algebraic Language.)

language, artificial—A language specifically designed for ease of communication in a particular area of endeavor, but one that is not yet natural to that area. This is contrasted with a natural language which has evolved through long usage.

language, assembly—The machine-oriented programming language (e.g., EASY, ARGUS) belonging to an assembly system.

language, COBOL common business oriented—*See* COBOL.

language, command—1. The language which is recognized by the executive and utilized to issue control commands to the system. 2. A source language which is usually structured with procedural instructions. Such a language has capabilities of causing the execution of many functions, most of which are basic or used repetitively.

language, common—1. A technique which reduces all information to a form that is intelligible to the units of a data-processing system. 2. A language in machine-sensible form that is common to a group of computers or users of computers. 3. A language or macrocode which can be read or written by many different machines or by various groups of users. 4. A common code used by typewriters, calculators, transmitters, etc.

language, common business-oriented—A specific language by which business data-processing procedures may be precisely described in a standard form. The language is intended not only as a means for directly presenting any business program to any suitable computer for which a compiler exists, but also as a means of communicating such procedures among individuals. (Synonymous with COBOL.)

language, common machine—A machine-sensible information representation which is common to a related group of data-processing machines.

language, common, (OCR)—Universally acceptable language for optical character readers (OCR) approved by most manufacturers and which usually includes commonly accepted character shapes.

language compiler—*See* compiler, programming language.

language computer-dependent—*Same as* language, machine oriented.

language, computer-oriented — A related term for a programming language requiring a low degree of translation. Such programs usually run very efficiently on a related computer but require very extensive translation or compiling on another variety of computer.

language, computer-sensitive—A computer programming language which is dependent totally or in some part upon the type of machine that is to execute programs written in the language.

language, conversational—A language utilizing a near-English character set which facilitates communication between the computer and the user. For example, BASIC is one of the more commonly used conversational languages.

language, conversational algebraic—CAL resembles JOSS. It is primarily aimed at small numerical problems in a highly interactive environment. It relieves the user of all burdens of storage allocation for both programs and data and offers a problem-oriented language for conversational use (some computers).

language converter—A data-processing device designed to change one form of data, i.e., microfilm, strip chart, etc., into another (punch card, paper tape, etc.).

language, executive-control—The executive system offers the user a simple means of directing the execution of the individual activities of a run and to relay operational information concerning the run to the executive. This executive-user interface is a set of control commands, carefully minimized, yet capable of performing all of the desirable or mandatory functions required in a modern executive system. The command language is open ended and easily expanded, so that features and functions may be added as the need arises. The basic format of an executive-control language statement is quite simple, and is amenable to a large number of input devices. Statements are not restricted to card-image format, and may be of variable lengths. Each statement consists

of a heading character, for recognition purposes, followed by a command (which categorizes the statement), followed by a variable number of expressions. The end of a statement-equivalent signal depends on the type of input device.

language, FORTRAN—*See* FORTRAN.

language, higher order—A computer programming language that is less dependent on the limitations of a specific computer; for instance pseudo-languages; problem oriented languages; languages common to most computer systems, such as ALGOL, FORTRAN, and COBOL; and the assembly languages.

language, intermediate—1. A language is a compromise between a machine or absolute language, and a higher order or machine-independent language. An example would be a language for which translators exist to convert from two or more other languages, i.e., it might be a composite language. 2. A language which acts as a bridge in translating from a source language to one of many target languages.

Language, International Algebraic—The forerunner of ALGOL. (Synonymous with IAL, and clarified by algorithmic language.)

language interpretive — A special program writing language which translates and executes each source language expression serially, i.e., before translating and executing the following one, much as an interpreter of languages or speeches might do.

language, job-oriented—Specific types of programming languages which are means of communicating instructions to equipment by using terms distinctly pertinent to the area or type of job which is being processed.

language linear, programming control—The language used to prescribe the course of a linear programming run on a computer. The language consists mainly of verbs (agenda names) which call in a body of code (program or subroutine) embodying the desired algorithm for execution.

language listing, symbolic-assembly—This binary output program of the compiler is optional at compile time. The listing contains the symbolic instructions equivalent to the binary-code output of the compiler. This assembly language output listing is useful as a debugging aid. By including certain pseudo-operation codes in "in-line" assembly language, the assembly language output can be assembled by the assembler (if output is obtained on either cards, paper tape, or magnetic tape). This will allow modification of programs at the assembly language level.

language, machine—1. Information recorded in a form that may be made available to a computer; e.g. punched paper tape may contain information available to a machine, whereas the same information in the form of printed characters on a page is not available to a machine. 2. Information that can be sensed by a machine.

language, machine-independent — A programming language which is not written for application or use with any specific computer system or class of computers. Such languages are usually problem-oriented and widely accepted, such as FORTRAN, COBOL, ALGOL, etc.

language, machine-oriented—1. A language designed for interpretation and use by a machine, without a translation being necessary. 2. A system for expressing information that is intelligible to a specific machine; e.g., a computer or class of computers. Such a language may include instructions that define and direct machine operations, and information to be recorded or acted upon by these machine operations. 3. The set of instructions expressed in the number system basic to a computer, together with symbolic operation codes with absolute addresses, relative addresses, or symbolic addresses. (Synonymous with machine language; clarified by language; related to object language; and contrasted with problem-oriented language.)

language, meta—A formal language which uses special symbols to describe the syntax of computer languages, for example, bacus normal form.

language, native — A communication language or coding between machine units or modules which is peculiar to or usable for a particular class or brand of equipment.

language, natural—A language whose rules reflect and describe current usage rather than prescribed usage.

language, NOMAD — An algebraic compiler adapted from the MAD (Michigan Algorithmic Decoder) language to meet the special needs of the installation. It is a high speed compiler which permits a wide latitude of generality in expressions.

language, object—A language which is the output of an automatic coding routine. Usually object language and machine language are the same; however, a series of steps in an automatic coding system may involve the object language of one step serving as a source language for the next step, and so forth.

language original—See language source.

language, problem—Same as language, problem-oriented.

language, problem-oriented—1. A language designed for convenience of program specification in a general problem area rather than for easy conversion to a machine-instruction code. The components of such a language may bear little resemblance to machine instructions. 2. A machine-independent language where one needs only to state the problem not the how of solution. (Related to program generators, and contrasted with procedure-oriented language.)

language, procedure-oriented — A machine-independent language which describes how the process of solving the problem is to be carried out, e.g., FORTRAN. (Contrasted with problem-oriented language.)

language, program—1. A language, not a machine language, which is used to express computer programs such as assembly, symbolic machine, macroassembly, procedure-oriented, problem-oriented, algebraic, string-manipulation, multipurpose, list processing, etc. 2. A language used by programmers to write computer routines.

language, programming—A specific language used to prepare computer programs.

language, (PL/1) programming — See compiler, programming language.

language, pseudo—See language, artificial.

language, remote computing-system — The language of the remote computing system comprises two types of statements: program statements and operating statements. Program statements, which are upwardly compatible with FORTRAN IV, are used to form the user's program. Operating statements allow the user to communicate with the remote computing system. Operating statements include modification, test, display, and output statements.

languages, general purpose—Combined programming languages which use English words and statements where they are convenient, and which serve as mathematical notation for procedures conveniently expressed mathematically. COBOL, FORTRAN, and ALGOL are widely used general-purpose programming languages in both science and business.

languages, list processing—Specific languages developed by symbol manipulation and used primarily as research tools rather than for production programming. Most have proved valuable in construction of compilers and in simulation of human problem solving.

language, source — The original form in which a program is prepared prior to processing by the machine.

languages, preparation, time sharing—See time sharing, preparation languages.

languages, time sharing—See time sharing languages.

languages, user-oriented (time sharing)—See time sharing, user oriented languages.

language, symbolic — The discipline that treats formal logic by means of a formalized artificial language or symbolic calculus, whose purpose is to avoid the ambiguities and logical inadequacies of natural languages. Advantages of the symbolic method are greater exactness of formulation, and power to deal with complex material.

language, synthetic—A pseudocode or symbolic language. A fabricated language.

language, target—The language into which some other language is to be properly translated.

language translation—The translation of information from one language to another.

language translator—1. A program used to convert a language to equivalent statements in another computer language, usually for a different computer. 2. A routine which aids in the performance of natural language translations such as French to English. 3. Any assembler or compiling program which brings forth same or equivalent output from human-readable statements.

large-capacity core storage—A component that permits one- or two-million increments of directly addressable core storage to be added to a system.

last-pass (own coding) — Computer instructions created by a programmer, in assembly or absolute form, which are executed by a sort during the last pass of the file, after the final merging instructions have been executed but prior to unloading the output record.

latency—1. In a serial storage device, the time required to locate the first bit (or character) in a particular storage location. Access time for such a device includes latency plus the time to read out or write in a complete word. 2. In a serial storage computer, the delay while waiting for information called for from storage to be delivered to the arithmetic unit, e.g. access time minus the word time.

latency code, minimum—*Same as* minimum access code.

latency time—1. The time lag between the completion of instruction staticizing and the initiation of the movement of data from its storage location. 2. The rotational delay time from a disk file or a drum file.

latency time, drum—*See* drum, latency time.

latest start dates, PERT—Used in estimating the completion date of a particular task. Each job is arranged to start as late as possible so that the entire task is completed on the required date.

layout character—*See* character, layout.

layout data—*See* data, layout.

layout, record—*See* record layout.

LDRI—An abbreviation for low data-rate input.

LDT—An abbreviation for logic design translator.

leader—1. A record that precedes a group of detail records, giving information about the group not present in the detail records, e.g., beginning of batch 17. 2. An unused or blank length of tape at the beginning of a reel of tape preceding the start of the recorded data.

leader record—A specific record containing the description of information contained in a classification or group of records, which follow this initial document.

leading control—A title or short definition of a control group of records which appears in front of each such group.

leapfrog test—A program designed to discover computer malfunctions. It is characterized by performing a series of arithmetical or logical operations on one group of storage locations, transferring itself to another group of storage locations, checking the correctness of the transfer, and beginning the series of operations all over again.

learning, computer—That process by which computers modify programs according to their own memory or experience, i.e., changes of logic paths, parameter values. An example is the now famous chess-playing computer. 2. In process-control, an analog computer can alter its parameters by a continuous process according to temperatures or other guage reports it receives. Examples are adoptive autopilots for aircraft, which explore different alternatives.

learning, machine—The capability of a device to improve its performance based on its past performance.

learning program—*See* program, learning.

least significant character—The character in the rightmost position in a number or a word.

least significant digit—The significant digit contributing the smallest quantity to the value of a numeral.

ledgers, magnetic-striped—In certain applications, magnetic-stripe business ledgers extend the capability of the accounting computer. Alphabetic and numeric data such as balances, account numbers, posting-line positions, names, addresses, etc., stored on these stripes on each page are quickly and electronically accessible. Magnetic stripes can be used to read and store 240 digits or 120 alphabetic characters, or a combination of both.

left justified—Data is left justified when the left-hand digit or character (or its sign) occupies the left-hand position of the space allotted for that data.

left justify—To format a left margin for the type on a printed page. Typewriters produce left justified copy.

leg—A course or path taken in a routine from one branch point to the next.

legal retrieval—*See* retrieval, legal.

Leibnitz, Gottfried Wilhelm Von (1646-1716)—An Austrian mathematician and philosopher and inventor of a relatively advanced adding machine called a stepped reckoner, which could add, subtract, multiply, divide and take square roots. He was one of the first to acclaim advantages of the binary over the decimal system for such machines.

length—The number of bits or other characters in a word.

length, block—The total number of records, words, or characters contained in one block.

length, double—Pertaining to twice the normal length of a unit of data or a storage device in a given computing system; e.g., a double-length register would have the capacity to store twice as much data as a single-length or normal register; a double-length word would have twice the number of characters or digits as a normal or single-length word.

length, field—The physical extent of a field. On a punch card it refers to the number of columns. On a tape it refers to bit positions.

length field, selective — *See* field selected length.

length, fixed—*See* fixed length.

length, gap—The dimension of the gap of a head measured from one pole face to the other. In longitudinal recording, the gap length can be defined as the dimension of the gap in the direction of tape travel.

length, instruction—*See* instruction length.

length, interrecord gap—The length of the unused recording area between records written by the unit.

length, record—The number of characters necessary to contain all the information in a record.

length, register—The number of digits, characters, or bits that a register can store.

length, string—The number of records in a string.

length, variable—The number of characters which may be available in a particular storage location or data element. Since it is variable, it is possible that each successive block may have a different, varying, number of words, but the word packing density usually remains constant.

length, word—*See* word length.

letter—One of a set of symbols combined to represent written words.

letter code—In the Baudot code, the function that causes machines to shift to lower case. This code is used to "rubout" errors in tape, as it is made up of intelligence pulses in each of the five channels, and causes receiving machines to print nothing.

letter shift—A function performed by a teleprinter, when initiated by the letters-shift character, that causes the machine to shift from upper case to lower case.

level—A COBOL term indicating the status of one data item relative to another; indicates whether one item includes subsequent ones or whether, as reflected in the numbering scheme which must follow certain rules, data items are independent of each other.

level, activity—The value taken by a structural variable in an intermediate or final solution to a programming problem.

level, addressing—*See* addressing level.

level, average-effectiveness — A percentage figure determined by subtracting the total computer down time from the total performance period hours, and dividing the difference by the total performance period hours. For this computation, equipment down time can be measured by those intervals during the performance period between the time that the contractor or other person having maintenance responsibility is notified of equipment failure, and the time the equipment is returned to the user in proper operating condition.

level, circuit noise—The circuit noise level at any point in a transmission system is the ratio of the circuit noise at that point to some arbitrary amount of a circuit noise chosen as a reference. This ratio is usually expressed in decibels above reference noise, abbreviated dbm, signifying the reading of a circuit noise meter, or in adjusted decibels,

abbreviated dba, signifying circuit noise-meter reading adjusted to represent interfering effect under specified conditions.

level, data—*See* data level.

level, eight — Any teletypewriter code that utilizes eight impulses, in addition to the start and stop impulses, for describing a character.

level, five—Any teletypewriter code that utilizes five impulses, in addition to the start and stop impulses, for describing a character.

level, graphetic—An example is a character, either handwritten or printed, usually then capable of being copied, reproduced, transmitted, or manipulated by an ordered set of pulses. It is said to be a representation at a graphetic level.

level indicator—In the COBOL system, a symbol or level-number used in a data division entry to indicate level. For example, FD is a level indicator.

level-number—A numeric level indicator.

level of addressing—*See* address, indirect.

level-overload—The operating limit of a system, component etc.; that point at which operation ceases to be satisfactory as a result of signal distortion, overheating, damage, etc.

levels, source language—Especially in ALGOL several levels of source languages are noted. Provisions are made for the use of 1. reference level, 2. several publication levels and many hardware levels.

lexeme—The written word, particle, or stem that denotes the meaning.

lexicon—A vocabulary, not necessarily in alphabetic order, with definitions or explanations for all terms.

Liberator—The Honeywell computer systems hardware design concept which makes the basic instruction repertoire of some models equivalent to the instruction repertoires of several other data-processing systems. This allows users of numerous competitive systems to take advantage of the throughput end cost/performance characteristics of some computers without incurring the prohibitive costs of reprogramming. (Honeywell)

librarian—A program that creates, maintains, and makes available the collection of programs, routines and data that make up an operating system. Librarian functions may include system generation and system editing.

librarian, magnetic-tape — Arranges the installation program in acceptable formats on the library tape. While the librarian provides the information needed by the system supervisor to automatically manipulate the running of one program after the other, features within the librarian allow the programmer to control the sequence in which the program will be run.

librarian program — The librarian-program portion of the control function provides maintenance of library programs used as part of the operating system. The library may be stored on a single secondary storage unit, or it may be distributed over several different storage units. In either case, the librarian program keeps this library up to date by adding, deleting, and modifying as required. User-written application programs can be incorporated into the library along with subroutines, the control program itself, compilers, sort/merge, and utility programs.

librarian, system—This individual issues and stores data files and other records of the installation and also maintains a list of all the up-to-date programs.

library—1. A collection of documents for study or reference. 2. An organized collection of standard, checked-out routines. 3. A group of standard, proven routines that may be incorporated into larger routines. 4. The filed collection of available and use-proved computer programs, either printed, kept on tapes, or in random-access file for quick checking, reference, or use with modification. 5. Groups of proven or standard routines, or parts of routines, used to solve problems with or without further modification to adapt to particular individual provisions; most often stored in symbolic coding or compiler programs and subdivided into various volumes according to type of arithmetic or computational technique used.

library allocator—See allocator, library.

library, back-up system—In addition to his own program complex file, the user has available to him a collection of elements in a library. This library is itself a complex and is built up at an installation as is any other complex. If during the allocation process (or for that matter, in nearly any search of the table of contents), a given element or entry point is not found, the library table of contents is searched and the appropriate element is taken from the library. Thus the elements in the library serve to "back up" the user's complex. If, however, the user's complex contains an element whose name is the same as one in the library, or an element which has an externally defined symbol which appears in the library, the user's complex will override the library.

library, COBOL—A COBOL library processor is available to store and retrieve data and procedure division descriptions, and it provides dynamic dumps of specified data areas to facilitate program checkout.

library, direct-access—See direct access library.

library facilities—A basic library of general-purpose software is furnished by manufacturers to perform common jobs; to this the user can add his own often-used programs and routines. Programs in the library can be conveniently assembled into an object program by the use of macroinstructions.

library, input/output—Relieves the programmer of having to be familiar with the functional and instructional differences among the peripherals.

library, job—One or several partitioned data sets used as the primary source of object programs for a definite job and a source of runable programs from which all or most of the necessary programs for a given job will be selected.

library, macro—An assemblage of prepared and specialized, but unparticularized programs, which are located in mass storage and which may be selectively found by an assembler which reads them, particularizes them by replacing general parameters with specific parameters, and incorporates them into programs.

library, object program—See library, program.

library program—An assemblage or organized set of computer programs, routines, or common or specifically designed software, i.e., catalog of program titles, abstracts, etc., reels of magnetic tapes or cabinets of punched cards, tapes containing various programs or routines, source, or object programs classified for intelligence or retrieval, etc.

library programming—A distinct program to form an assemblage or to retrieve from or input to a library, instead of one written for a particular job. It is a program which may be called simply by reference to an index of library program names.

library, routine—1. An ordered set or collection of standard and proven routines and subroutines, usually stored in relative or symbolic coding, by which problems and parts of problems may be solved. (A library may be subdivided into various volumes, such as floating-decimal, double-precision, or complex, according to the type of arithmetic employed by the subroutines.) 2. A checked-out routine which may be incorporated into a larger routine and is maintained in a library as an aid to programmers. 3. A routine for building and maintaining a library of special programs and subroutines. It is capable of inserting, deleting, changing, or replacing routines in the library. With this routine, the library may be altered at will to conform to individual customer requirements.

library, subroutine—A set of standard and proven subroutines which is kept on file for use at any time.

library system, backup—See back-up system, library.

library tapes—Library tapes will have tape labels, skip records, and CMs (control marks) exactly as outlined for data tapes. However, the programs themselves must be stored on magnetic tape according to a particular format. Library tapes may contain two types of intermixed formats—standard format (running programs as set up by the librarian), and debugging format (this includes check data as well as the programs to be checked.) Various CMs are used in this intermixing of formats.

library track—Tracks used to store reference data, such as titles, key words, document numbers, etc., on tapes, drums, disks, or mass storage devices.

LIFT (FORTRAN II to FORTRAN IV translator)—LIFT is a source-language translator that accepts a FORTRAN II source-language program as input, performs a translation, and outputs a source language program acceptable to a FORTRAN IV compiler (not necessarily the UNIVAC FORTRAN IV compiler). There is a need for translation since FORTRAN II is not a proper subset of FORTRAN IV; i.e., that is, there are statement types in FORTRAN II that are not acceptable to FORTRAN IV. LIFT itself written in FORTRAN IV is delivered as a program file element and is thus fully integrated with the executive sytem. There are nine areas of incompatibility between FORTRAN II and FORTRAN IV, and the basic purpose of LIFT is to generate FORTRAN IV source statements to replace the unacceptable FORTRAN II statement.

light-A—A control panel light which monitors the A-register and signals parity check errors.

light-B—A control panel which monitors the B-register and signals parity check errors.

light check—A control panel indicator light which indicates parity errors or arithmetic overflow conditions.

light gun—See light pen.

light, logic—See logic light.

light, NIXIE—See NIXIE light.

light pen (stylus)—1. A visual display unit (CRT) provides a "window into the computer." It can display as a series of points, a message of thousands of characters of information, of tables, charts, graphs and the lines and curve of drawings. The light pen (stylus) available with the display can detect information that has been displayed on the screen and enables the operator to change the information under program control. When this penlike device is pointed at information displayed on the screen, it detects light from the cathode-ray tube (CRT) when a beam passes within its field of view. The pen's response is transmitted to the computer and, in turn, relates the computer action to the section of the image being displayed. In this way, the operation can delete or add text, maintain tighter control over the program, and choose alternative courses of action. 2. An optional device which when used in conjunction with the incremental display, can greatly extend its usefulness. It is a high-speed, photosensitive device with which the operator can cause the computer to change or modify the display on the cathode-ray tube. As the pertinent display information is selected by the operator, the pen signals the computer by generating a pulse. Acting upon this signal, the computer can then instruct other points to be plotted across the tube face in accordance with the pen move-

ments, or exercise specific options previously programmed without the need for separate input devices.

light, punch—A specific light found on most control consoles which indicates that a condition exists in the card punch equipment requiring an operator's attention, i.e., an empty hopper, full stacker, full chip box, mechanism failure, etc.

light, reader—An indicator light usually found on the console which, when it is on, indicates that a condition exists in the card reading equipment which requires the operator's attention. Such faults usually are in the punch area, empty hopper, card jams, validity area, etc.

light, ready—An indicator light on the display panel which, when on, indicates that a piece of equipment is ready for operation.

lights, communication—Located on the keyboard for easy operator visibility, these lights indicate power on (to punch), punch on, low tape supply, and exceed capacity or zero proof warning (some computers).

lights, operator-indicator—The independent operator-inductor lights may be used to call the operator's attention to any conditions that the programmer desires. They can be set, cleared, and tested under program control to fulfill the varying requirements of different programs.

light stability—In optical character recognition (OCR), the resistance to change of color of the image when exposed to radiant energy.

light, storage—The light on a control console panel which indicates that a parity check error has occurred on a character as it was read into storage.

light, tape—A light usually found on the control console which indicates an error during the read or write cycle.

light, thermal—A display signal which is visible to machine operators when internal equipment temperature is higher than a designed level.

limit check—See check, limit.

limited—A word often attached to another word or term to indicate the particular machine activity that needs the most time, e.g., tape-limited, input-limit, computer-limited, etc.

limited, computer—See computer limited.

limited, computer (sorting)—A sort program in which the execution time of the internal instructions determine the elapsed time required to sort.

limited, input—The time that the central processing unit waits for delivery of input items. This restricts the speed of the operation.

limited, input/output—On buffered computers, a section of a routine in which the time required for computation is exceeded by the time required for input/output operations.

limited, output—The speed restriction on a process or on equipment which causes other operations to await the completion of an output operation. This causes other equipment to have idle time.

limited, printer—The restrictions on a process due to the slowness or inadequacy of the printing equipment. Other operations must await the completion of the printing unit.

limited, tape—Just as some computers are limited to the slower speeds of cards for adequate performance, others are bound or limited in performance speeds by the time required for reading, writing, or punching tapes. When computers execute various types of business or large batch data processing, and much of the time is used in moving tapes, the computer or processor must wait and is said to be tape limited.

limiter—A device that reduces the power of an electrical signal when it exceeds a specified value. The amount of reduction or compression increases with an increase of the input power.

limit, priority—The upper bound to the priority list for dispatching or designing a priority rating to various tasks or subtasks, i.e., active, inactive, top priority, lowest priority, or batch processing.

limits, high-low—The maximum and minimum values of data expected. These values are used to check the program and results.

limits, scanning—The action of comparing input variables against either prestored or calculated high and/or low limits to determine if an alarm condition is present.

LINC (Laboratory Instrument Computer)—LINC performs several of the functions that external devices or people are normally required to perform. Data recording, analog-to-digital conversion, experiment monitoring, control, and analysis are built-in capabilities of the computer. LINC gives direct assistance to the research worker in many ways. (DEC)

Lincoln Reckoner—An on-line, time-sharing executive program developed by Lincoln Laboratories.

line adapter communication, teletype—*See* communication line adapter.

linear equation—An equation whose left-hand side and right-hand side are both linear functions of the variables. Such an equation can always be put in the form $f(x, y, z, . . .) = c$, where f is a linear function and c is a constant.

linear programming—1. A technique used in mathematics and operations research to find a best solution for a certain type of problem; e.g., to determine the ratio of quantities to mix, blend, select, etc., for an optimum mixture. Sometimes called optimum programming and mathematical programming. 2. The analysis of problems in which the linear function of a number of variables is to be maximized (or minimized) when those variables are subject to a number of constraints in the form of linear inequalities, or the solution of these problems. 3. A technique

of mathematics and operations research for solving certain kinds of problems involving many variables, where a best value or set of best values is to be found. This technique is not to be confused with computer programming, although problems using the technique may be programmed on a computer. Linear programming is most likely to be feasible when the quantity to be optimized, sometimes called the objective function, can be stated as a mathematical expression in terms of the various activities within the system, and when this expression is simply proportional to the measure of the activities, i.e., is linear, and when all the restrictions are also linear.

linear programming (advertising budgets)—Given a restrictive advertising budget and estimates about the effectiveness of an advertising dollar when applied to a particular medium, linear programming aids in the design of a total advertising program that will maximize advertising effectiveness.

linear-programming-control language—The language used to prescribe the course of a linear-programming run on a computer. The language consists mainly of verbs (agendum names), which call in a body of code (program or subroutine) embodying the desired algorithm for execution.

linear-programming inequalities—The mathematical problem of minimizing or maximizing a linear function of n variables, subject to n independent restrictions, such as requirements that each variable be non-negative, and also subject to a finite number of other linear constraints. The latter are either equalities or weak inequalities ($\leq$ or $\geq$); strict inequalities of the form $<$ or $>$ are not advisable. An exact solution or other termination to this problem is furnished by the simplex method or one of its variants.

linear programming, infeasible or unbounded solutions—A technique for finding the best solution from among all solutions of a system of linear inequalities. The variables are usually processing or scheduling variables in some physical situation; the inequalities are obtained from the physical constraints on these variables; and the criterion for "best solution" is the value of some given linear function of all the variables. As the term is used today, linear programming includes the formulation of the problem in linear-programming terms, algorithms for finding the best solution, and the analysis of the effect of changes in the values of problem parameters. When a solution fails to exist, the system is said to be infeasible or to have no feasible solution. When the best solution is infinite in one or more variables, the system is said to be unbounded.

linear programming (product mix)—Given a set of raw materials with given characteristics and a given set of market prices for finished products, linear programming will indicate how these raw materials should be combined to produce the highest possible profits for the company. Blending of gasoline is an example of this type of application.

linear programming, resource allocation— Linear programming (LP) is a mathematical technique in which the best allocation of limited resources may be determined by manipulation of a series of linear equations. Each factor in the problem is evaluated against all other factors in relation to the long-range goals, yielding optimum paths of action for management consideration.

linear programming (transportation)—Given a large number of warehouses with limited capacities and a large number of distributers with known demands, linear programming enables the design of a shipping schedule that will minimize total costs.

linear selection switch—*Same as* storage, core-rope.

linear unit—A device which follows the rules of mathematical linearity, i.e., in which the change output due to a change in input is proportional to the magnitude of that change and does not depend on the values of the other inputs, i.e., adders, scalars, and integrating amplifiers, whereas multipliers and function generators are often designed as nonlinear.

line-at-a-time printer—*See* printer, line-at-a-time.

line-B—*Same as* index register.

line, character spacing reference—*See* character spacing reference line.

line, code—A single instruction, usually written on one line in a code for a specific computer, to solve a problem. This instruction is usually stored as a whole in the program register of the computer while it is executed, and it may contain one or more addresses of registers or storage locations in the computer where numbers or machine words are to be obtained or sent, and one or more operations to be executed. (Synonymous with program line.)

line, control—*See* control line.

line control unit—A multiplier or line control computer—a special purpose computer for controlling input and output from communication lines when these lines are not directly accessed to the computer.

line, delay—A device capable of retarding a pulse of energy between input and output, based on the properties of materials, circuit parameters, or mechanical devices. Examples of delay lines are material media such as mercury, in which sonic patterns may be propagated in time; lumped-constant electrical lines; coaxial cables; transmission lines; and recirculating magnetic-drum loops. (Related to magnetic delay line.)

line, delay register—*See* register, delay line.

line drivers—*Same as* bus drivers, output.

line, end of—A machine code character which

indicates the end or termination of a group of records.

line-feed code—A function code that causes page teleprinters or similar devices to rotate the platen up one line.

line finder (data processing)—In data processing terminology, an electromechanical device attached to the platen of a printer, which automatically line-feeds it to a predetermined line on a printed form. Similar to vertical tabulation in telegraphic terminology.

line generator—*See* generator, line (display).

line, item—An item of data, in data processing, that is on the same level as a given set of items for a given application and which could logically be printed on the same line on a printed page; for instance, stock number, item, quantity, and cost.

line misregistration—The improper or unacceptable appearance of a line or characters or numerals in optical character recognition, usually so gauged on or with respect to the real or imaginary horizontal baseline.

line noise—Noise originating in a transmission line.

line printer—A printer in which an entire line of characters is composed and determined within the device prior to printing.

line printing—Printing one line of characters across a page; i.e. 100 or more characters simultaneously, as continuous paper advances line by line in one direction past type bars or a type cylinder that contains all characters in all positions.

line skew—A type of line misregistration, in which a string of characters to be read by an optical character reader appears in a uniformly slanted or skewed condition with respect to a real or imaginary baseline.

lines, select—The core memory circuits on various equipment which carry selecting coincident pulses. These pulses select the core position which is to be used in ensuing operation.

line status—The status of a communication line such as receive, transmit, or control.

line terminals, communication—*See* terminals, communication line.

link—1. That part of a subprogram that connects it with the main program. 2. A process to gather or unite two or more separately written, assembled, or compiled programs or routines into various single operational entities, i.e., to complete linkage. Some computer systems have special programs called linkage editors to correct address components into symbols or to perform relocation to avoid overlapping.

linkage—1. Specific instructions that are related to the entry and re-entry of closed subroutines. 2. The interconnections between a main routine and a closed routine; i.e., entry and exit for a closed routine form the main routine.

linkage, communications — Common-carrier equipment provided by such companies as

American Telephone and Telegraph, Western Union, and American Cable and Radio provide high-speed communication facilities for two-way transmission of data between the central computer site and remotely located input/output units. Transactions originating at these remote points are conveyed along linkage wires directly to the computer where they are immediately evaluated and processed. Then the result is returned to the originator and other appropriate distant points. The whole transaction is handled in a matter of seconds.

linkage editor—A standard service routine to convert outputs of assemblers or compilers to forms which can be loaded and executed by combining separately developed object modules, or incorporating all or parts of previously processed load modules into a new load module. The linkage editor also replaces or inserts control sections, creates overlay facilities, or resolves symbolic cross references between various input modules. Usually linkage editors are run before programs are ready for load in OS, DOS, or TOS operations, i.e., disk and tape operating systems.

linkage macroinstruction—See macroinstruction, linkage.

link, communication—The physical means of connecting one location to another for the purpose of transmitting information.

link, data—Equipment that permits the transmission of information in data format.

linked subroutine—Same as subroutine closed.

link group—Consists of those links which employ the same multiplex equipments.

linking loader program—Accepts programs in a form produced by the translators and produces an area of core memory loaded with the program. Upon request, it may also produce a storage map of the loaded programs along with symbol tables. Several programs may be linked together in loading. The loader requests special library tapes to be loaded, and verifies that the program has been completely loaded .

linking, program—See program linking.

link macroinstruction—See macroinstruction, link.

link overflow—See overflow, link.

link, transmission—A section of a channel (or circuit) between: (a) a transmitter station and the following telegraph repeater; (b) two successive telegraph repeaters; (c) a receiving station and the preceding telegraph repeater.

LIPL — Abbreviation for linear information processing language—a version of IPL, a high-order programming language.

LISP (List Processing)—This is an interpretive language, developed for manipulation of symbolic strings of recursive data, i.e., used to develop higher-level languages.

list—1. A string of items written in a meaningful format that designates quantities to be transmitted for input/output. 2. An individual series of similar items, as the names of cities and the current population of each; i.e., a one-dimensional array of numbers. 3. To print every relevant item of input data.

list, assembly—A printed list that is the by-product of an assembly procedure. It lists in logical instruction sequence all details of a routine, showing the coded and symbolic location next to the actual notations established by the assembly procedure. This listing is highly useful in the debugging of a routine.

list, chained—A set of items each of which contains an identifier for the next item in a particular order, but such order does not have any particular relation to the order in which they are stored.

list, command—A sequence of steps, generated by the CPU, pertaining to the performance of an I/O operation.

list, first item—Same as indication group.

list, indexed—A FORTRAN instruction in read and write statements to form special indexed arrays.

listing, assembly-language—This binary-output program of the compiler is optional at compile time. The listing contains the symbolic instructions equivalent to the binary-code output of the compiler. This assembly-output listing is useful as a debugging aid. By including certain pseudo-operation codes in in-line assembly language, the assembly-language output can be assembled by the assembler. (If output is obtained on either cards, paper tape, or magnetic tape.) This will allow modification of programs at the assembly-language level.

listing, proof—See proof listing.

listing, selective—The output printing of data which needs various sets of predetermined criteria.

list, memory-map—The memory map is a listing of all variable names, array names, and constants used by the program with their relative address assignments. The listing will include all subroutines called and the last location when called (some systems).

list, peripheral equipment—See peripheral equipment list.

list, polling—See polling list.

list processing—A specific technique for programming, using list structures to organize storage. Computer storage is organized into many lists or structures of data items, each with a symbolic name, a leader, starting record, and number of entries.

list processing languages—Specific languages developed by symbol manipulation and used primarily as research tools rather than for production programming. Most have proved valuable in construction of compilers and in simulation of problem solving. Other uses have been generalized and verification of mathematical proofs, pattern recognition, information retrieval, algebraic manipulation, heuristic programming, and exploration of new programming languages.

list processing program—A particular type of program called EULER is an extension of ALGOL 60 and has specific list processing capabilities.

list, punch-down—A list of items where the last item entered is the first item of the list, and the relative position of the other items is pushed back one.

list, push-down—*Same as* list punch-down.

list, push-up—A list of items where each item is entered at the end of the list, and the other items maintain their same relative position in the list.

list structure—A specific set of data items combined because each element contains the address of the successor item or element, i.e., a predecessor item or element. Such lists grow in size according to the limits of fixed storage capacity, and it is relatively simple to insert or delete data items anywhere in a list structure.

literal—1. A word, number, or symbol which names, describes, or defines itself and not something else that it might represent. 2. An item of data with its value as stated or listed. Example would be 490, a literal; thus, 490 is its value. 3. An item in a source language whose representation in characters remains unaltered during the operation of the appropriate program, i.e., in the instruction, If $X = 10$ print—STOP, the word STOP is the literal.

literature search—A systematic and exhaustive search for published material on a specific subject, and usually the preparation of abstracts on that material.

load—1. To fill the internal storage of a computer with information from auxiliary or external storage. 2. To enter or add to the internal storage of a computer various information from auxiliary, intermediate, or external storage.

load-and-go—A computer operation and compiling technique in which the pseudo-language is directly converted to machine language and the program run without an output machine-language program being created.

load cards—The punched cards which contain the program instructions and the constant values.

loader, bootstrap—*See* bootstrap loader.

loader, card—*See* card loader.

loader (FORTRAN)—The FORTRAN loader is a two-pass relocating loader that can load separately compiled programs into storage and complete the linkages between them.

loader, program—*See* program loading.

loader program, linking—*See* linking loader program.

loader, system—The system loader loads binary object programs output from compilations and assemblies into computer memory. The system loader is capable of loading binary main programs, binary subprograms, library subroutines, and input/output drivers. The linkage between these programs is performed automatically during loading. The system loader loads input/output drivers from the specified logical equipment for a program and performs all linkages within the monitor. Programs may be loaded from cards, paper tape, or from the master file. Intermixed programs may be loaded in part of each of these devices in one load operation. The loader is resident in upper computer memory and is capable of overlaying itself in part with library subroutines. Common data-storage areas are placed in the loader area to allow complete overlay of the loader. Thus, a program may use all of computer memory. No memory storage is lost because of the size of the loader (some systems).

loading, block—A technique for program loading in which the control or other sections of the program or program segment are loaded into adjacent positions in the main memory.

loading, dynamic program—The loading of a program module or routine into main memory through reference to it by a loaded executing program.

loading error—The error found in the output of the computer which came about as a result of a change in value of the load which was supplied.

loading, input—Amount of load imposed upon the sources supplying signals to the input.

loading, initial program—*See* program loading, initial.

loading-location misuse errors—1. A loading location specification was made but no load or execute was specified. 2. The loading location specified was not within the available range of memory. 3. The loading location is assigned as the first available location.

loading procedure—System, object, and library routines are loaded in a similar manner. A program may have a fixed origin or may be relocatable. Fixed origin programs are loaded into the specified memory address. Programs are relocated by a base address initially set by the executive routine. After the main program has been loaded, any library subroutines or equipment drivers called will then be loaded. When all the necessary routines are in memory, the loader returns to the job processor.

loading, program—*See* program loading.

loading program and allocation—*See* allocation and loading program.

loading routine (bootstrap)—1. A developed routine placed in storage for the purpose of reading into storage another program, routine, or various data. 2. A single subprogram that loads a complete object program.

loading routine, program—The procedure for inserting instructions and the constant values of the program into the computer.

load key—*See* key, load.

load key, tape—*See* key, tape load.

load mode—In load mode, data transmission is such that data delimiters are carried along with the data transmitted, as in contrast with move mode.

load module—A program developed for loading into storage and being executed, the output of which is a linkage editor run. It contains a text section (TXT), an external symbol dictionary (ESD) and a relocation dictionary (RLD).

load on call—When a program is too large to fit into core memory of the central processing unit, sometimes it can be segmented so that some subprograms reside on the disk, to be loaded into core on call.

load point—The preset point at which magnetic tape is initially positioned under the read/write head to start reading or writing

load sharing—Computers placed in tandem (duplexing or triplexing) to share the peak-period load of a system.

LOCAL—An abbreviation for load on call.

local loop—1. A channel that connects a subscriber to a central office exchange. 2. The service provided by the common carrier to connect a customer's location to a central office. This always includes the circuit and some circuit termination equipment, but may also include input/output equipment. Sometimes referred to as subscriber station.

local side—Data-terminal connections to input/output devices.

local store—*See* store, local.

local variable—A variable whose name is known only to the subprogram to which it belongs.

locate—A tape is searched for the first occurrence of specific information.

locate mode—A specific method of communicating with an input/output control system (IOCS) by using a method in which the address of the data involved, but not the data themselves, is transferred between the IOCS routine and the program, thus sparing the programmer from having to incorporate detailed, machine-level I/O logic in every one of his routines, since IOCS in memory communicates with the running program and performs I/O as directed by the program. But, locate-mode operations require that the computer be equipped with index registers or base registers which enable run-time address computation to proceed while individual computer instructions are being interpreted.

location—1. A unit-storage position in the main internal storage that stores one computer word; a storage register. 2. A place in main memory or auxiliary storage where a unit of data may be stored or retrieved.

location, bit—A storage position on a record capable of storing one bit.

location counter—*Same as* register, control.

location, effective byte—The actual storage location pointed to by the effective virtual address of a byte addressing instruction.

location, effective double-word—The actual storage location pointed to by the effective virtual address of a double-word addressing instruction.

locaiton, effective half-word—The storage location pointed to by the effective virtual address of a half-word addressing instruction.

location, effective word—The storage location pointed to by the effective virtual address of a word-addressing instruction.

location hole—*See* holes, feed.

location, identifier—*See* identifier, location.

location, memory—A position in a computer storage device.

location, run—A routine which locates the correct run on a program tape, whether initiated by another routine or manually.

locations, protected—Locations reserved for special purposes, and in which data cannot be stored without undergoing a screening procedure to establish suitability for storage therein.

location, storage—A storage position holding one computer word, usually designated by a specific address or a specific register.

locking, escape—*See* escape, locking.

locking shift character—*See* character, locking shift.

lock, memory write—A p-bit write-protect field optionally provided for each 512-word page of core memory addresses. (some computers)

lockout—A portion of the buffer cycle in which the logic or arithmetic unit must cease operation or neither will be able to communicate with the memory unit.

lockout, keyboard—An interlock feature that prevents sending from the keyboard while the tape transmitter or another station is sending on the same circuit.

lockout switch—Specific manual switches which are provided with drum memory and associated with individual drum memory segments. These provide the contents of such segments with selectable protection from alteration.

lockout, write—In various time-sharing computers, a lockout prevents all programs (usually), from writing to any particular portion of a store, but still allows unimpeded reading of that part of storage by all concurrent programs.

lock-up table—A method of controlling the location to which a jump or transfer is made. It is used especially when there are a large number of alternatives, as in function evaluation in scientific computations.

log—1. A record of everything pertinent to a machine run, including identification of the machine run, record of alteration, switch settings, identification of input and output tapes, copy of manual key-ins, identification of all stops, and a record of action taken on all stops. 2. To print or record one or more values. The values might be the instantaneous values of input variables, or averaged or calculated values.

logarithm—The logarithm of a number is the exponent indicating the power to which it is necessary to raise a given number, called the base, to produce the original number.

logger—A device that automatically records physical processes with respect to time.

loggers, system utilization—A program or a device that collects statistical information about how the system is operating.

logging, executive—The recording of the approximate internal processing times utilized by each program operating concurrently as well as the unused time during which no program can operate pending completion of requested functions. This record will assist the installation scheduler in determining which programs to run in parallel with each other. To facilitate the detection of infinite loops, provision is made to notify the operator of programs which utilize more time than is estimated for them.

logging, failure—An automatic procedure whereby the maintenance section of the monitor, acting on machine-check interrupts (immediately following error detection), records the system state. This log is an aid to the customer engineer in diagnosing intermittent errors.

logging, interrupt—See interrupt logging.

logic—1. The science that deals with the canons and criteria of validity in thought and demonstration; the science of the formal principles of reasoning. 2. The basic principles and applications of truth tables, the relationships of propositions, the interconnection of on-off circuit elements, etc., for mathematical computation in a computer.

logical AND—Same as gate, AND.

logical capabilities, FORTRAN IV—See FORTRAN IV logical capabilities.

logical choice—Making the correct decision where alternates or even a variety of possibilities are open; whether to debit or credit; whether to issue a replacement order; which FWT exemption to apply. The variety of logical choices a computer can make and the speed with which it makes them as an accurate measure of its capability.

logical comparison—The act of comparing A and B. The result of the execution of such an operation is 1, or yes, if A is the same as B, and 0, or no, if A is not the same as B (or vice versa).

logical connectives—The operators or words, such as AND, OR, OR ELSE, IF THEN, NEITHER NOR, and EXCEPT, that make new statements from given statements and also have the property that the truth or falsity of the new statements can be calculated from the truth or falsity of the given statements and the logical meaning of the operator.

logical decision—1. The choice or ability to choose between alternatives. Basically this amounts to an ability to answer yes or no with respect to certain fundamental questions involving equality and relative magnitude; e.g., in an inventory application, it is necessary to determine whether or not there has been an issue of a given stock item. 2. The operation of selecting alternative paths of flow depending on intermediate program data.

logical design—1. The logic of the system, machine, or network. 2. The planning of a computer system prior to its engineering design. 3. Computer design from the viewpoint of data flow within the computer without consideration of the hardware. 4. Design that deals with the logical and mathematical interrelationships that must be implemented by the hardware.

logical diagram—A diagram representing logical elements and their interconnections without construction or engineering details. The graphic representation of the logic elements and their relations in a computer. The graphic presentation of logic processes which are to be performed in a distinct order to achieve a solution.

logical element—The smallest building block in a computer or data processing system that can be represented by logical operators in an appropriate system of symbolic logic. Typical logical elements are the AND gate and the OR gate; they can be represented as operators in a suitable symbolic logic.

logical expressions—Same as logic expressions.

logical flowchart—A detailed solution of the work order in terms of the logic, or built-in operations and characteristics, of a specific machine. Concise symbolic notation is used to represent the information and describe the input, output, arithmetic, and logical operations involved. The chart indicates types of operations by use of a standard set of block symbols. A coding process normally follows the logical flowchart.

logical IF—A FORTRAN IV statement will execute when the logical express is true, or will bypass the statement if it is false.

logical instruction—An instruction that carries out a logical operation, such as AND, OR, NOR.

logical multiply—See AND operator.

logical number—The number assigned to a peripheral unit during autoload or system generation time. This number can be altered whenever convenient, in contrast to a physical unit number.

logical operation—An operation in which a decision affecting the future sequence or instructions is automatically made by the computer. The decision is based upon comparisons between all or some of the characters in an arithmetic register, and their counterparts in any other register on a less than, equal to, or greater than basis; or, between certain characters on arithmetic registers and built-in standards. Also, a shifting operation in which the digits dropped off one end of a word are returned to the other in circular fashion. Operations on a word on a character-by-character basis without regard for other characters as in logical OR operations.

logical operations—The comparing, selecting, making references, matching, sorting, merging, etc. where in essence 1's and O's (corresponding to yes's and no's) constitute the elements being operated on.

logical operator—A mathematical symbol that represents a mathematical process to be performed on an associated operand. In FORTRAN IV, an operation which acts on one or two logical variables or logical expressions. Such operators are AND, the logical product, OR, the logical sum, and NOT, the logical complement.

logical product—*Same as* gate, AND.

logical record—A record whose scope, direction, or length is governed by the specific nature of the information or data which it contains instead of by some feature or limitation of the storage device that holds it. Such records differ in size from the physical records in which they are contained. Physical records might be limited to a 400-character physical record size, (example, an airline standard) but many logical records might require fewer or more than the limit.

logical shift—*See* shift, circular.

logical sum—*See* sum, logical.

logical switch—An electronic device used for directing input cards to one of a number of outputs.

logical symbol—1. A sign used as an operator to denote the particular operation to be performed on the associated variables. 2. A symbol used to graphically represent a logical element.

logical tracing—Tracing as performed only on jump or transfer instructions.

logical unit—A self-contained unit.

logical variable—In FORTRAN IV, a variable which may have only true or false value.

logic analysis—The delineation or determination of the specific steps required to produce the desired output or intelligence information from the given or ascertained input data. The logic studies are completed for many computer processes, programs, or runs.

logic, Boolean—A mathematical analysis of logic. Applications of Boolean logic include information retrieval and circuit-switching designs.

logic card—A grouping of electrical components and wiring circuitry mounted on a board which allows easy withdrawal and replacement from a socket in the equipment. Each such card is related to a basic machine function and on discovery of a bug in that function the card can be replaced.

logic chart—A flow chart of a program or portions of a program showing the major logical steps intended to solve a problem.

logic circuits, silicon transistors—Some logic circuits use silicon semi-conductors exclusively rather than germanium components. Designed to preclude the reduced performance usually inherent with the higher forward voltage drop of silicon devices, these circuits offer such characteristic advantages of silicon over germanium as:

Operation over a much wider temperature range.

Surface passivation for protection against contamination, thus providing longer life.

Much lower-reverse leakage permitting greater fan-in and increased switching efficiency.

logic comparison—*See* comparator.

logic-controlled sequential computer — *See* computer, logic-controlled sequential.

logic decision—A specific decision made in a computing system or environment as a direct result of the internal organization of the system, but one of the binary or yes or no type, and basically relating to questions of equality, inequality, or relative magnitude.

logic design—The specification of the working relations between the parts of a system in terms of symbolic logic and without primary regard for its hardware implementation.

logic diagram—A diagram that represents a logic design or its hardware implementation.

logic, double-rail—Each logic variable in these circuits is represented by a pair of electric lines. Three states can actually be assumed, such as zero, one, and undecided.

logic element—A device that performs a logic function.

logic element, sequential—*See* element, sequential logic.

logic expressions—A logic expression consists of logical constants, variable array elements, function references, and combinations of those operands, separated by logical operators, and parentheses. A logical expression may contain arithmetic expressions, separated by relational operators, and separated by other elements specified by logical operators and parentheses. Logic expressions are most often used in logical IF statements but can also be used in logical assignment statements and as arguments of functions. The logical expression may take on only two values, true or false. When a logical expression appears in a FORTRAN statement it is evaluated according to the rules given below. It will always yield one of the two values, true or false.

logic, formal—An objective study of the structure, form, and design of valid arguments, and disregarding for this purpose the meaning and importance of the terms of the argument itself.

logic instruction—An instruction that executes an operation that is defined in symbolic logic, such as AND, OR, NOR.

logic light—The control-console light which indicates that an error has occurred in an operation.

logic, machine—*See* machine logic.

logic, mathematical—Exact reasoning concerning non-numerical relations by using symbols that are efficient in calculation. (Related to logic.)

logic multiply—A Boolean operation performed on two binary digits so that the result is one, if and only if both digits are one, and zero if either digit, or both, is a zero.

logic, negative—Logic in which the more negative voltage represents the 1 state; the less negative voltage represents the 0 state.

logic, N-level—A particular arrangement or design of gates connected in such a way that no more than N gates are in series in a specific component or frame.

logic operation—1. Nonarithmetic operations that are expressible in terms of the propositional calculus or a two-valued Boolean algebra operating on individual pairs of bits. 2. Sometimes, nonarithmetic operations, such as compare, shift, and jump.

logic product—The result developed from the AND operation as contrasted with product arithmetic.

logic product gate—*Same as* gate, AND.

logic, programmed—The internal logic design which is alterable in accordance with a precompleted program which controls the various electronic interconnections of the gating elements, i.e., the instruction repertory can be electronically changed, or the machine capability can be matched to the problem requirement.

logic shift—A shift which is similar to a cyclic shift and which can affect all positions, i.e., a nonarithmetic shift.

logic, solid-state—Microelectronic circuits are a product of solid logic technology (SLT) and make up many systems basic circuitry. These microminiaturized computer circuits are called logic circuits because they carry and control the electrical impulses that represent information within a computer. These tiny devices operate at speeds ranging from 300 down to 6 billionths-of-a-second. Transistors and diodes mounted on the circuits are only 28 thousandths of an inch thick (some systems).

logic sum—*See* sum, logical.

logic sum gate—*Same as* gate, OR.

logic symbol—1. A symbol used to graphically represent a logic element. 2. A symbol used to represent a logic connective.

logic, symbolic—1. The study of formal logic and mathematics by means of a special written language which seeks to avoid the ambiguity and inadequacy of ordinary language. 2. The mathematical concepts, techniques, and languages as used in definition (1), whatever their particular application or context. (Synonymous with mathematical logic, and related to logic.) 3. Exact reasoning about relations, using symbols that are efficient in calculation. A branch of this subject known as Boolean algebra has been

of considerable assistance in the logical design of computing circuits.

logic, variable—The internal logic design which is alterable in accordance with a completed program which controls the various electronic interconnections of the gating elements.

log-out, time sharing—*See* time sharing, log-out.

log, real-time clock—This built in clock is used for a wide variety of programming-time purposes. It can be used to log the receipt times of a periodic real-time input data. Each input message and its receipt time may be recorded together. This clock is also used in connection with the preparation of statistical and analytical reports dealing with the frequency of certain transactions.

log, remote computing-system—The remote computing system maintains a log of operations that take place between the computer and each terminal. The log contains such information as the number of statements handled, the number and types of errors detected, and the volume of output produced. The information in the log can be used for various purposes. For example, the number of errors may indicate that additional training might be helpful. Similarly, if an individual terminal is busy, it might indicate the need for an additional terminal. If the cost of the system is shared among terminals according to usage, the information in the log can be used for billing purposes.

log word, interrupt—*See* interrupt, log word.

longitudinal check—A system of error control based on the check that some present rules for the formation of the group of bits in the same numerical order in all the character signals in a block are observed.

longitudinal circuit—A circuit formed by one telephone wire (or by two or more telephone wires in parallel) with the return through the earth or through any other conductors except those which are taken with the original wire or wires to form a metallic telephone circuit.

longitudinal parity check—The data line terminal at the transmitting end generates a longitudinal parity character during the transmission of the data characters. This is essentially a count for even parity of all of the bits in each one of the bit levels for all data characters in the message including the start-of-message code but not the end-of-message code. This same count is also being generated for the bits of the data characters entering the data-line terminal of the receiving end.

longitudinal redundance—A condition in which the bits in each track or row of a record do not total an even (or odd) number. The term is usually used to refer to records on magnetic tape, and a system can have either odd or even longitudinal parity.

longitudinal transmission check—An even or odd parity check at fixed intervals during data transmission.

long word—*See* word, long.

look-at table—Finding elements of a table by direct calculation rather than by a comparison search.

look-up—A procedure for obtaining the function value corresponding to an argument from a table of function values.

look-up instruction—An instruction designed to allow reference to systematically arranged, stored data.

look-up table—A collection of data in a form suitable for ready reference, frequently as stored in sequenced machine locations or written in the form of an array of rows and columns for easy entry, and in which an intersection of labeled rows and columns serves to locate a specific piece of data or information.

look-up table, allocator control — *See* table look-up, allocator control.

look-up table instruction — *See* instruction, table look-up.

look-up table techniques—*See* table, look-up techniques.

loom, Jacquard—*See* Jacquard loom.

loop—1. The repeated execution of a series of instructions for a fixed number of times. 2. A coding technique in which a group of instructions is repeated, usually with modified instructions or modified data values. 3. A sequence of instructions that is repeated until a terminal condition prevails. 4. The repetitive execution of a series of instructions caused by having the last instruction in the series return the machine to the first instruction in the same series.

loop box—A register for modifying instructions in a loop.

loop, central processing unit (CPU)—The main routine or a control program and that which is associated with the control of the internal status of the processing unit, in contrast to those control programs of routines developed with terminals and file storage input/output.

loop, central scanning—A loop of instructions which determines which task is to be performed next. After each item of work is completed, control is transferred to the central scanning loop which searches for processing requests in order to determine which is the next item to be processed. The computer may cycle idly in the central scanning loop if no item requires attention, or it may go into a wait state which is interrupted if the need arises.

loop checking—A method of checking the accuracy of transmission of data in which the received data are returned to the sending end for comparison with the original data, which are stored there for this purpose.

loop, closed—A programming technique, system, or device to develop feedback of data

for various control, modification, or checking purposes.

loop, dynamic—A specific loop stop consisting of a single jump instruction which causes a jump to itself. A loop stop is usually designed for operating convenience, such as to indicate an error.

loop, high speed—Magnetic drums and disk storage devices have a section that has a faster access than that provided by a complete revolution of that drum or disk, i.e., a read head and a write head spaced some distance apart on the same track so that data written by one head is read by another head a short time later and sent back to the write head. In consequence, a fixed-length loop of data revolves and may be changed by gating. The delay is similar to that of a delay line.

looping—A computer operation in which a sequence of steps is repeated.

looping execution — The execution of the same set of instructions where for each execution some parameter or sets of parameters have undergone a change. Such change may be a new value for a variable, or addresses of various data may be modified, often through the use of an index register.

loop, nesting—Nesting loops usually contain a loop of instructions which then also contains inner loops, nesting subroutines, outer loops, and rules and procedures relating to in and out procedures for each type.

loop, open—Pertaining to a control system in which there is no self-correcting action for misses of the desired operational condition as there is in a closed loop system.

loop operation—A loop which has an associated set of instructions which restore modified instructions or data to their original or initial values at each entry to the loop, or a sequence of instructions which may be obeyed repetitively.

loop, rapid access—*See* loop, high speed.

loop, recirculating—In drum computers, a small section of memory which has much faster access than the remainder of memory.

loops, outside—Outside loops are most often considered for nested loops when loops within it are entirely contained. The outside loop executes the control parameters that are being held constant while the current loop is being carried through possible values.

loop, stop—A small closed loop usually designed and used for operator convenience, i.e., to indicate an error, improper use, or special result.

loop storage—*See* storage loop.

loop stores, delay—A method of storing information by transmitting bits or no-bits serially through a loop.

loop system, closed—A system in which the computer controls an external program or process without human intervention. An example of a closed-loop process-control system would be a computer connected directly to instrumentation through a digital-to-analog converter to complete the feedback loop.

The computer could then take control directly of the process by setting controllers, activating switches, valves, etc.

loop termination—Many ways exist to terminate loops. For example, when reading data from cards, the cards can simply be let to run out, causing a hang up or stop. More commonly, however, in reading data, the last card contains some particular code number which may be tested and used to terminate the loop. Most often, the first card contains the number of data sets to be read, and this number is put into a counter location, and tested for zero to end the loop.

loss, gap—The loss in output attributable to the finite gap length of the reproduce head. The loss increases as the wavelength decreases, amounting to approximately 4 db when the wavelength is equal to twice the gap length, and subsequently increases rapidly towards a complete extinction of output when the wavelength is approximately equal to 1.15 times the gap length.

loss, transmission—A general term used to denote a decrease in signal power in transmission from one point to another. Transmission loss is usually expressed in transmission units.

low-activity data processing—The processing of a limited number of input transactions against very large master files.

lower curtate—See curtate.

low order—Pertaining to the weight or significance assigned to the digits of a number; e.g., in the number 123456, the low order digit is six. One may refer to the three low-order bits of a binary word as another example. (Clarified by order, definition 3.)

low order digit—A digit that occupies a less significant or lowly weighted position in a numeral.

low-order position—The rightmost position in a number or word.

low-performance equipments—Those equipments having insufficiently exacting characteristics to permit their use in trunk or link circuits. Such equipment may be employed in subscriber line circuits whenever it meets the line-circuit requirements.

low punch—The zero zone punch in a punch-card code.

low speed—Usually, data transmission speed of 600 bps or less.

low-speed storage—A storage modem or device with access time more lengthy in relation to the speeds of arithmetic operations of the central processing unit of the computer and more lengthy when compared to other faster access peripheral units.

LP (linear-programming)—Linear programming (LP) is a mathematical technique whereby the best allocation of limited resources may be determined by manipulation of a series of linear equations. Each factor in the problem is evaluated against all other factors in relation to the long-range goals, thus yielding optimum parts of action for management consideration.

LPM—Lines per minute.

LSC—Abbreviation for least significant character (right-most).

LSD—Abbreviation for least significant digit (right-most).

Luhn scanner—A scanning machine invented by an IBM employee, H. P. Luhn, for photo-electric scanning of punched cards as they are fed through the machine. The scanner has some search capabiliites.

M

MAC—Abbreviation for (a) —multiple access computer, (b) machine aided cognition, (c) memory assisted cognition. Most usually related to the government supported, large computing research and technique implemention being carried out at the Massachusetts Institute of Technology, and initially meaning, multiple access computer.

machinable—See data, machine readable.

machine, accounting—A machine that reads information from one medium (e.g., cards, paper tape, and magnetic tape) and produces lists, tables, and totals on separate forms or continuous paper. (Clarified by tabulating equipment.)

machine address—An absolute, direct, unindexed address expressed as such, or resulting after indexing and other processing has been completed.

machine-available time—Power-on time less maintenance time.

machine check—1. An automatic check. 2. A programmed check of machine functions.

machine-check indicator—A protective device that will be turned on when certain conditions arise within the machine. The machine can be programmed to stop, to run a separate correction routine, or to ignore the condition.

machine-check interrupts — See interrupts, machine check.

machine code—1. The absolute numbers, names, or symbols assigned by the machine designer to any part of the machine. 2. Same as operation code.

machine coding—See coding, machine.

machine cycle—1. The specific time interval in which a computer can perform a given number of operations. 2. The shortest complete process of action that is repeated in order. 3. The minimum length of time in which the foregoing can be performed.

machine, data-processing—A general name for a machine that can store and process numeric and alphabetic information. (Related to analog digital computer and automatic data-processing equipment.)

machine, electrical accounting—The set of conventional punch-card equipment including sorters, collators, and tabulators. (Synonymous with EAM and clarified by tabulating equipment.)

machine, electronic data-processing — See data processing equipment, automatic.

machine error—A deviation from correctness in data resulting from an equipment failure.

machine fault time, no charge—The unproductive time due to computer fault such as nonduplication, transcribing error, input/output malfunction, and machine malfunction resulting in an incomplete run.

machine-independent—An adjective used to indicate that a procedure or a program is conceived, organized, or oriented without specific reference to the operating characteristics of any one data-processing system. Use of this adjective usually implies that the procedure or program is oriented or organized in terms of the logical nature of the problem, rather than in terms of the characteristics of the machine used in solving it.

machine-independent language — See language, machine-independent.

machine-independent solution—Procedures or programs that are organized in terms of the logical nature of the problem rather than in relation to or concerning the various computer equipment used to solve them or process them.

machine instruction—1. A code element, which upon machine recognition, causes a predefined sequence of operations. 2. An instruction that the particular machine can recognize and execute.

machine instruction statements—The direct counterparts of machine instructions. Typical statement consists of tag, mnemonic operation code, one or more operand addresses (or literal operands), and one or more variant characters.

machine-check interruption — Machine-check interruptions are caused by the machine-checking circuits detecting a machine error. The system is automatically switched to a diagnostic procedure.

machine language—1. A set of symbols, characters, or signs, and the rules for combining them, that conveys instructions or information to a computer. 2. A language for writing instructions in a form to be executed by the compiler; the language can be directly interpreted by the control section of the machine. 3. Information or data is expressed in code that can be read directly, used or written by the computer or peripheral machines without further processing.

(*Same as* machine-oriented language and related to object language.)

machine-language code—A system of combinations of binary digits used by a given computer. (Synonymous with machine code, and contrasted with symbolic code.)

machine-language coding—Coding in the form in which instructions are executed by the computer. (Contrasted to relative, symbolic, and other nonmachine-language coding.)

machine learning—Concerns the ability of a device to improve its performance based on its past performance. (Related to artificial intelligence.)

machine-length word — See word, machine.

machine logic—1. Built-in methods of problem approach and function execution; the way a system is designed to do its operations; what those operations are, and the type and form of data it can use internally. 2. The capability of an automatic data-processing machine to make decisions based upon the results of tests performed.

machine, object—The computer on which the object program is to be executed.

machine operator—The person who manipulates the computer controls, places information media into the input devices, removes the output, and performs other related functions.

machine operator, punched-card — Employee who operates all units of conventional punched-card equipment.

machine, (optical) character recognition—The technology of using a machine to sense and encode into a machine language characters that are written or printed to be read by human beings.

machine-oriented language—See language, machine-oriented.

machine-oriented programming system—A system that uses a language that is oriented to the internal language of a specific computer. Systems that are considered to be machine oriented are assembly systems and macrosystems.

machine, pinboard—A machine in which pins are inserted in holes in a panel to call for a function or storage.

machine readable — See data, machine readable.

machine-readable, data—See data, machine-readable.

machine-readable medium — The device or material which is used to convey data to a sensing device or unit such as punched cards, or tapes.

machine recognizable — See data, machine readable.

machine run—The execution of one or several machine routines which are linked to form one operating unit.

machinery, computing — See computing machinery.

machine, scanning—A machine which facilitates the input of data. Two types of scanning machines are the magnetic-ink scanners and the optical scanners.

machine script—*See* data, machine readable.

machine, self-organizing—A class of machine that may be characterized loosely as containing a variable network in which the elements are organized by the machine itself, without external intervention, to meet criteria of successful operation. (Synonymous with self-organizing machine.)

machine sensible — *See* data, machine readable.

machine-sensible information—Information in a form that can be read by a specific machine.

machine, single-address—A machine, whose order codes consist primarily of an operation part and one address (of the operand), is termed a single-address machine. Machines which use codes containing an operation part, the operand address, and the address of the next instruction, have been used and are labeled as modified single-address machines.

machine, source—The computer on which the source program is translated into the object program.

machine-spoiled time—The wasted computer time due to a computer malfunction during production runs, i.e., part of down time.

machines, three-address—Three-address machines will specify not only the address of the two operands, but also the address into which the result is automatically stored; also, variants are common, such as storing more than one instruction code per data word.

machine technicians, card—Employees who wire the punched-card control panels to operate punched-card machines.

machine time, available — 1. Time during which a computer has the power turned on, is not under maintenance, and is known or believed to be operating correctly. 2. The elapsed time when a computer is in operating condition, whether or not it is in use.

machine tool control—A powerful and versatile program for production of tapes for numerically controlled point-to-point and contouring machines.

machine tools, numerically controlled—Computer-controlled machinery used in manufacturing operations. Some numerically controlled machines use paper tape which has been prepared by a specially programmed computer to control the movements of complex machine tools. Computers can control drafting machines, conveyer belts, and many other complicated physical processes.

machine translation—The automatic transmission from one representation to another representation. The translation may involve codes, languages, or other systems of representation. (Related to automatic dictionary.)

machine, Turing—A mathematical abstraction of a device that operates to read from, write on, and move an infinite tape, thereby pro-

viding a model for computerlike procedures. The behavior of a Turing machine is specified by listing an alphabet; i.e., collection of symbols read and written, a set of internal states, and a mapping of an alphabet and internal states which determines what the symbol written and tape motion will be, and also what internal state will follow when the machine is in a given internal state and reads a given symbol.

machine, two-addressed—In contrast to single-address (operand) machines, two address machines will store the result of the binary operation in some assigned register, as well as two operand addresses.

machine, universal-Turing — A Turing machine that can simulate any other Turing machine.

machine word—A unit of information of a standard number of characters which a machine regularly handles in each transfer; e.g., a machine may regularly handle numbers or instructions in units of 36 binary digits; this is then the machine word. Related to word, information.

macro—*See* macroinstruction.

macroassembler facilities — An assembler is available for use in the operating system in assembling object programs from source programs written in a flexible but easy-to-use symbolic language. The assembler language is a versatile, machine-oriented language that can be used for a variety of applications, both commercial and scientific. A number of facilities for assisting the programmer are provided by the assembler. These include macrofacilities as well as facilities for defining constants, for defining data-storage areas, for referring to files and storage locations symbolically, and for using literals.

macroassembly program—A language processor that accepts words, statements, and phrases to produce machine instructions. It's more than an assembly program because it has compiler powers. The macroassembler permits segmentation of a large program so that portions may be tested separately. It also provides extensive program analysis to aid in debugging.

macrocode—A coding system that assembles groups of computer instructions into single code words; the system therefore requires interpretation or translation so that an automatic computer can follow it.

macroexerciser — The repeated operation of supervising programs and other macroinstructions under a variety of conditions to find any program errors.

macroexpansion, conditional — Certain number of lines of coding within a macroinstruction will be included or excluded during expansion, depending upon certain conditions.

macrogeneration—The many-for-one concept or process of generating several machine-language instructions from one macrostatement in source programs.

macroinstruction—1. A machinelike source-language statement that can produce a variable number of machine instructions. 2. A source-language instruction that has the capability of generating more than one machine-language instruction. 3. An instruction that is replaced in a routine by a predetermined sequence of machine instructions. 4. Usually symbolic mnemonic type instructions that programmers can write in a source program to call for special or library routines that perform wanted functions as open, seek, colse, etc. Macroinstructions result in one-for-many instructions and are extensively used.

macroinstruction, debug—A macroinstruction which generates a debugging or program testing capability within a particular program.

macroinstruction exit—A supervising program macroinstruction that is the final instruction in an application program signifying that processing is complete. The supervising program takes the needed action such as releasing working storage blocks to return control to other processing.

macroinstruction link — An operating system (OS/360-IBM) instruction which causes the named program module to be located in an external library and loaded into an available position of storage. Control passes to the named module exactly as though a call macroinstruction had been used. If a copy of the named program module is present in storage, the process is by-passed, and an ordinary call is completed.

macroinstruction linkage — A macroinstruction that provides logical linkage between programs and subroutines and that will save data needed by another program.

macroinstruction, WAIT — In multithread processing, the presentation of a request on one message that causes a delay so that no processing can go on. A WAIT macro shifts control to a supervisory program so that work may continue on other messages. Work on the delayed message will continue only when the cause of the delay is removed.

macrolibrary — An assemblage of prepared and specialized but unparticularized programs which are located in mass storage and which may be selectively found by an assembler which reads them, particularizes them by replacing general parameters with specific parameters, and incorporates them into programs.

macro (macrocode or macroprogram) — A source-language statement, routine, or program that is understandable to a processor or compiler with or without aid of an interpretative routine. Production of many-for-one instructions in machine language; an open-ended sequence of machine instructions, may be linked to consecutive or closed subroutines.

macroparameter — The symbolic or literal that is in the operand part of a macrostatement and which will be substituted into specific instructions in the incomplete routine to develop a complete open subroutine.

macroprogramming—The process of writing machine-procedure statements in terms of macroinstructions.

macros, programmer-defined—Segments of coding, which are used frequently throughout a program, can be defined at the beginning and used and referenced by a mnemonic code with parameters. This increases coding efficiency and readability of the program.

macrostatement number—A number that is associated with a single macrostatement so that the reference may be made to that statement.

macrosystem—A programming system with symbolic capabilities of an assembly system and the added capability of many-for-one or macroinstruction development.

macrotrace—An error detection aid such as core and file dumps, loggings, and simulators. A macrotrace records pertinent information when macroinstructions are being executed; the macrotrace can print out the record of macros or it can record them; and also dump working storage and the needed registers.

MAD—A FORTRAN-like language developed by the University of Michigan.

MADCAP—A language for mathematical problems and set operations.

magazine — A portion of the card handling device which supplies the cards to the processing sections of the machine, i.e., the section or place in which the operator places or stacks the input cards or the blank cards.

magazine, input—The card-feed magazine in a reader or read-punch unit. (Synonymous with input stacker.)

magazine input, card—*See* magazine.

magazine, output—A mechanism that accumulates cards after they have passed through a machine. (Synonymous with output stacker.)

magnetic, all—Relates to the construction and nature of electrical and electronic circuitry components in which all storage, delay, and decision-making elements make particular use of the magnetic properties of the materials.

magnetic card—*See* card, magnetic.

magnetic card storage—*See* card, magnetic.

magnetic cell—*See* cell, magnetic.

magnetic character—A character imprinted with ink having magnetic properties. These characters are unique in that they can be read directly by both humans and machines.

magnetic-character sorter — Some magnetic-character sorters have a document handling rate of more than 2000 items per minute. They will read and sort intermixed documents of various lengths, widths, and thicknesses. The equipment is designed to read and translate the various magnetic-ink type fonts. The magnetic character sorter can operate under control of the processor and is programmed to sort encoded items on a whole number or block basis in any desired order, and with time sharing possible between documents. Magnetic characters are read and transferred directly to the memory of the processor (some systems).

magnetic core—1. A magnetic material, usually toroidal in shape, which is pulsed or polarized by electric currents carried in a wire or wires wound around it. This device is capable of assuming and remaining at one of two conditions of magnetization, thus providing storage, gating, or switching functions. *See* core memory. 2. A small doughnut-shaped ferrite designed and constructed for on or off magnetization and used to store information in the computer. 3. A miniaturized ring of ferromagnetic substance that may be instantaneously magnetized to a negative or positive flux and remains so until changed by further computer operations.

magnetic-core multiplexer—The magnetic-core multiplexer is the equivalent of a multiple-multiposition stepping switch wherein several multibit inputs are commutated to a single output. This device is particularly suited for the handling of digital data. It consists of cores and windings arranged in rows and columns, one magnetic core being designated for each input bit. Due to the size and nature of magnetic-tape cores, the multiplexer may be made extremely rugged and compact, can be of virtually unlimited capacity, and consumes relatively little power

magnetic-core storage—1. A storage device consisting of magnetically permeable binary cells arrayed in a two-dimensional matrix. (A large storage unit contains many such matrices.) Each cell (core) is wire wound and may be polarized in either of two directions for the storage of one binary digit. The direction of a polarization can be sensed by a wire running through the core. 2. The use of planes of magnetic cores; data and information are determined and represented by the positive or negative magnetic state of the core.

magnetic disk—*See* disk, magnetic.

magnetic-disk storage—A storage device or system consisting of magnetically coated disks, on the surface of which information is stored in the form of magnetic spots arranged in a manner to represent binary data. These data are arranged in circular tracks around the disks and are accessible to reading and writing heads on an arm which can be moved mechanically to the desired disk, and then to the desired track on that disk. Data from a given track are read or written sequentially as the disk rotates. (Related to disk storage.)

magnetic document sorter-reader—Magnetic ink character recognition (MICR) was developed through the efforts of the banking profession and the machine manufacturers.

Special properties of the ink used to print the data on the documents can be given small charges of electricity. As a by-product of reading these electrical impulses, the sorter transmits the data to the memory of the computer for processing.

magnetic drum—1. A cylinder with a magnetic surface on which data can be stored by selective magnetization of portions of the curved surface. 2. A rapidly rotating cylinder, the surface of which is coated with a magnetic material on which information may be stored in the form of small polarized spots.

magnetic-drum storage—1. A storage device consisting of a rotating cylindrical drum surfaced with a magnetic coating. Binary data are stored as small magnetized spots arranged in close tracks around the drum. A magnetic reading and writing head is associated with each track so that the desired track can be selected by electric switching. Data from a given track are read or written sequentially as the drum rotates.

magnetic film storage—*See* storage, magnetic film.

magnetic head—A small electromagnet used for reading, recording, or erasing polarized spots on a magnetic surface. Also called R/W head, read head, write head.

magnetic ink—Ink containing particles of magnetic substance which can be detected or read by automatic devices; e.g., the ink used for printing on some bank checks for magnetic ink character recognition. (MICR)

magnetic ink character recognition — *See* MICR.

magnetic ink scanners—Machines which read numbers designed in a special type font and printed in a magnetic (iron oxide) ink.

magnetic memory—Any portion of the memory that uses the magnetic properties of a material to store information.

magnetic optical-character readers—Magnetic character readers can be attached directly to channels for the fast and direct reading into the system of the magnetically inscribed information on checks and other banking transactions. Readers differ mainly in document-reading rates. Some read up to 950 documents per minute; others, as many as 1600 documents per minute. As the documents are read by photoelectric cells, they may be sorted into many classifications. All magnetic inscriptions can be validity-checked.

The documents read may be of intermixed size and thickness, as is typically encountered in check-handling operations. The standard minimum length of the document is 6 inches; shorter documents may be read at appreciably higher rates, but these are not sorted unless a special feature for that purpose is installed. Many other special features are available, including an endorser to print the bank's name.

magnetic read/write head—A small electromagnet used for reading, recording, or erasing, polarized spots on a magnetic surface.

magnetic recording—That special method of recording data by impressing a pattern of magnetization on a thin layer of magnetic material.

magnetic shift register—A register that makes use of magnetic cores as binary storage elements, and in which the pattern of binary digital information can be shifted from one position to the next left or right position.

magnetic storage—A device (or devices) that utilizes the magnetic properties of materials to store information.

magnetic storage, data—See storage, core.

magnetic strip accounting machine—See accounting machine, magnetic strip.

magnetic-striped ledgers—In certain applications, magnetic-striped ledgers extend the capability of the accounting computer. Alphabetic and numeric data, such as balances, account numbers, posting line position, names, addresses, etc., stored on these stripes are quickly and electronically accessible. Magnetic stripes can be used to read and store 240 digits or 120 alphabetic characters, or a combination of both (some systems).

magnetic stripe recording—Relating to magnetic recording, if the magnetic material is deposited in strip form on a document or card, the term magnetic stripe recording is most often used.

magnetic strip file—A file storage device which uses strips of material with surfaces that can be magnetized for the purpose of storing data.

magnetic tape—See tape, magnetic.

magnetic tape, file checks—Hardware checks for faulty tapes without loss of computer time or manual intervention.

magnetic-tape file operation—Magnetic tape is provided for the storage of information to accomplish sequential file updating. It is also used as an interim means of storage in off-line conversion of input to magnetic tape, and when working tapes are utilized in operations such as sorting.

magnetic-tape librarian—Arranges the installation program on the library tape in acceptable formats. While the librarian provides the information needed by the system supervisor to automatically manipulate the running of one program after the other, features within the librarian allow the programmer to control the actual sequence in which the program will be run.

magnetic-tape master file—See tape, master file.

magnetic-tape parity—During writing operations, the processor generates and transmits a parity bit with each character sent to a tape unit. As each character is written, it is automatically read back to verify the write operation. Each character within a record is checked for parity. At the end of

each record, the handler writes a check character which is checked by the processor both for a vertical and an accumulated transverse parity.

magnetic-tape plotting system—1. The magnetic-tape plotting system produces an X-Y plot from data recorded on magnetic tape by a digital computer. Information read from the tape is used to drive a digital incremental plotter, which reproduces the data in either a continuous curve or discrete points. Versatility of the system permits the use of subroutines for generation of any desired symbols, letters, numerals, or scale markings. 2. Most systems are very versatile, reliable, and almost completely automatic. Zero position, scale factor adjustment, curve identification, symbol selection, axis generation, etc., are handled entirely by subroutines within the computer. For this reason, the plotting system may be operated by unskilled personnel. The operator is required only to select the desired plot by means of the automatic SEARCH feature, then initiate the plotting action by pressing either the single- or multiple-plot button. Plots can be produced up to 29½ inches in width and 120 feet in length. Adapters are available for on-line operation for most large computers. They are also designed for off-line operation with virtually any medium or large-scale digital systems. These systems produce completed graphs from data recorded on magnetic tape (some systems).

magnetic-tape reader—A device capable of sensing information recorded on a magnetic tape in the form of a series of magnetized spots.

magnetic-tape sorting—A sort program that utilizes magnetic tapes for auxiliary storage during a sort.

magnetic tape station—A specific tape device which contains a magnetic-tape drive, including reading and writing heads, various controls, etc., for storage or transfer of data.

magnetic-tape storage—A storage device consisting of metal or plastic tape coated with magnetic material. Binary data are stored as small, magnetized spots arranged in column form across the width of the tape. A read/write head is usually associated with each row of magnetized spots so that one column can be read or written at a time as the tape is moved relative to the head.

magnetic-tape switching units—Two tape controls share each other's tape units. A single switching unit allows one group of either half-inch or three-quarter inch units to be switched between two tape controls. Two tape units share the same tape control. An additional function of the tape-switching unit selects one of the two tape units to be attached to a single tape control. All tape units connected to a switching unit are switched simultaneously. If independent switching of more than one group of tape units is desired, switching-unit modules may be added to provide a group-switching capability of up to 64 tape units in groups of four or eight. The size of these independently switched groups depends upon the capability of the tape control (some computers).

magnetic-tape terminal—The magnetic-tape terminal converts the character pulses from serial-bit form to parallel-bit form while checking for odd parity and translating the code to the desired magnetic-tape code for entry into a buffer storage. The longitudinal parity count at the end of the message is verified. The integral part of the magnetic-tape terminal performing this function is called a coupler. The coupler of the magnetic-tape terminal performs a function similar to that of the data line terminal.

magnetic tape unit—The mechanism, normally used with a computer, that handles magnetic tape. It usually consists of a tape transport, reading or sensing and writing or recording heads, and associated electrical and electronic equipments. Most units may provide for tape to be wound and stored on reels; however, some units provide for the tape to be stored loosely in closed bins.

magnetic thin film—See thin-film memory.

magnetic wire—A wire made of or coated with a magnetic material and used for magnetic recording.

magnetostriction—A phenomenon wherein certain materials increase in length in the direction of the magnetic field when subjected to such a field, and restore to their original length when demagnetized.

magnetostrictive delay line—1. A delay line that utilizes the physical principle of magnetostriction. 2. A delay line made of nickel or certain other materials that become shorter when placed in a magnetic field.

magnitude—1. The size or mass. The absolute value of a number. 2. The size of a quantity as distinct from its sign. Thus + 10 and − 10 have the same magnitude.

mag tape—The informal or slang expression for magnetic tape.

main frame—The main part of the computer; i.e., the arithmetic or logic unit. The central processing unit. (CPU)

main memory—Usually the fastest storage device of a computer and the one from which instructions are executed. (Contrasted to auxiliary storage.)

main operation—The primary application or designed procedure which the equipment performs. (Contrasts with by-product.)

main path—The principal course or line of direction taken by a computer in the execution of a routine, directed by the logic of the program and the nature of the data.

main program—Same as program, master control.

main routine—Same as program, master control.

main scheduling routine—See routine, main scheduling.

main storage—Usually the fastest storage device of a computer and the one from which instructions are executed. (Contrasted with auxiliary storage.)

maintenance—1. Tests, measurements, replacements, adjustments, and repairs intended to keep equipment or programs in satisfactory working order. 2. Updating of object program master files, selection of programs to be run, and control of checkout and production operation.

maintenance and operation of programs—Updating of object-program master files; selection of programs to be run, and control of checkout and production operation.

maintenance contracts, preventive—Preventive-maintenance contracts provide either resident field engineers or periodic visit arrangements that are tailored to the user's specific needs. Competent and experienced personnel insure peak performance of all equipment.

maintenance, corrective — When a known fault or malfunction is repaired or corrected using adjustments or replacements after measurements and tests to locate, diagnose, and remove the fault, the service is called corrective maintenance.

maintenance, file—The periodic modification of a file to incorporate changes that occurred during a given period.

maintenance, preventive—The maintenance of a computer system, that attempts to keep equipment in top operating condition and to preclude failures during production runs.

maintenance, program—See program maintenance.

maintenance program chain—An instruction set that will permit the deletion of records from a file.

maintenance, remedial—The maintenance performed by the contractor following equipment failure; therefore, remedial maintenance is performed, as required, on an unscheduled basis.

maintenance routine—That machine time which is specifically devoted to repairs, and usually on some regular pattern or schedule, during which time preventive maintenance activities are also performed.

maintenance, scheduled—Maintenance activities that are performed in accordance with a planned or established schedule or timetable.

maintenance schedule, executive—See schedule maintenance (executive).

maintenance standby time—Time on which the maintenance staff is on duty (and presumably being paid) but during which they are not engaged in scheduled maintenance, installation, repair, or supplementary maintenance, i.e., they may perform other tasks.

maintenance time—The elapsed time during scheduled working hours between the determination of a machine failure and placement of the equipment back into operation.

maintenance time, routine—*Same as* maintenance, routine.

maintenance time, supplementary—This time is designed to modify or change equipment in some major way to improve reliability, but usually without additions of equipment. This time is usually considered part of scheduled engineering time and/or scheduled maintenance time.

major cycle—1. The maximum access time of a recirculating serial-storage element. 2. The time for one rotation of a magnetic drum or pulses in an acoustic delay time. 3. A number of minor cycles.

majority—A logic operator which has the property that if P, Q, and R are statements, the function P, Q, R. . . is true if more than one-half of the statements are true and false if half or less are true, as applied in majority voting logic, which is a form of hardware organization used where reliability is required and involves duplicating all functional elements an odd number of times and supplying each duplicate element with identical parts and comparing the outputs. Majority is concerned when the fact that an output must be generated in identical form by an absolute majority of the redundant units in order to be considered valid.

majority decision element—*Same as* gate, majority decision.

majority decision gate—*See* gate, majority decision.

majority element—Related to a threshhold element or a decision element, if the weights are equal to 1 and the threshhold is equal to (n + 1) /2, the element is called a majority element.

major key—The most significant key in a record.

major-minor sorting—*Same as* sorting, reverse digit method.

major state generator—*See* generator, major state.

major total—The summation or tally of the group of intermediate totals and, therefore, often called the most significant total.

make-break operation—A type of telegraph-circuit operation where the flow of current is interrupted as pulses are transmitted.

malfunction—1. Incorrect function occurring in the equipment. 2. A failure in the operation of the hardware of a computer.

malfunction, program-sensitive—A malfunction that occurs only when some unusual combination of program steps occurs.

malfunction routine—A routine used to locate a malfunction in a computer, or to aid in locating mistakes in a computer program. Thus, in general any routine specifically designed to aid in debugging or troubleshooting. (Related to debugging, definition 2.)

management data—*See* data, management.

management, data base—A systematic approach to storing, updating, and retrieval of information stored as data items usually in the form of records in a file, where many users, or even many remote installations, will use common data banks.

management information—The required data or program results considered the primary prerequisites for decision making with regard to business operations and control.

management information system—1. Specific data-processing system that is designed to furnish management and supervisory personnel with information consisting of data that are desired, and which are fresh or with real-time speed. 2. A communications process in which data are recorded and processed for operational purposes. The problems are isolated for higher-level decision making, and information is fed back to top management to reflect the progress or lack of progress made in achieving major objectives.

management programming system data—A system of progress designed to provide an operator with the capability for querying, augmenting, and manipulating large computer-stored data bases in a natural language.

management science, EDP—The field of management science is extending the computer far beyond the automation of routine accounting operations and into the complex decision-making process of management. Through revolutionary computer programming techniques such as simulation, the objective, scientific approach of management science is providing increased management capability and control. In addition to the physical or operational processes like inventory management, product planning and control, resource allocation or market forecasting, this also includes the fiscal processes such as bond management, capital investment, risk analysis, profit planning, and product pricing. Manufacturer's broad resources are prepared to meet management's growing demand for this expanded capability and to extend the tradition of total systems capability into revolutionary data-processing techniques and applications.

management science operation research—*See* operations research (management science).

management, storage (time-sharing) — *See* time sharing, storage management.

management system, total—*See* system, total management.

manager, computer center—A major function of data processing management, which requires constant attention, is to establish standards and maintain high quality. This means recruiting qualified personnel, training new employees, and updating existing ones. In addition, the manager must develop quantity and quality evaluation systems, develop job descriptions, and constantly review individual and group performance.

manager, operations—This individual is responsible for the operations and scheduled use of data processing equipment.

manager, programming—This individual is responsible for planning, scheduling, and supervising program development and maintenance work.

manager, systems analysis—This individual is responsible for planning, scheduling, and supervising systems analysis and design activities.

manifolding—Relates to the use of many sheets of paper and carbon sheets to produce multiple copies at single printings, i.e., four-part paper suggests an original and three copies.

manipulated variable—In a process that is desired to regulate some condition, a quantity or a condition that is altered by the computer in order to initiate a change in the value of the regulated condition.

manipulation, byte—The ability to manipulate, as individual instructions, groups of bits such as characters. A byte is considered to be eight bits in most cases, and forms either one character or two numerals.

manipulation data—See data, manipulation.

manipulative—See indexing, manipulative.

man-machine digital system—An organization of people, digital computers, and equipment to regulate and control events and achieve system objectives.

mantissa—The fractional part of a logarithm; e.g., in the logarithm 2.5, 2 is the characteristic and 5 is the mantissa.

manual address switches—The external control switches used by the operator to select an address manually for read-off in the storage address display lights or to transfer the contents to a register without disturbing the address contents or area.

manual control—The direction of a computer by means of manually operated switches.

manual entry—The manual insertion of data, usually for remote typewriter units or keyboard modules or terminals. See also keyboard entry.

manual exchange—An exchange where calls are completed by an operator.

manual input—Entry of data into a computer or system by direct manual manipulation of a device.

manual-input unit—See input unit, manual.

manual load key—See key, load.

manual mode—See mode, manual.

manual number generator—See generator, manual number.

manual operation—Processing of data in a system by direct manual techniques.

manual read—An operation in which the computer does the sensing of the contents or settings of manually set switches or registers.

manual-switch storage—See storage, manual-switch.

manual word generator—Same as generator, manual word.

many-to-one—Relates to ratios or measured relations between members of one set and members of another set, in which correspondences are stated that two or more members of one set correspond to one (only) member of another set. When several expressions in a source language are equivalent to one statement in a target language, a many-to-one relation exists.

map—1. To transform information from one form to another. 2. To establish a correspondence between the elements of one set and the elements of another set.

map, Karnaugh — A tabular arrangement which facilitates combination and elimination of duplicate logical functions by listing similar logical expressions.

map, memory—See memory map.

map, memory list—See memory map list.

MAP (Model And Program)—The analyst will find that his planning and thinking are systematized considerably if he prepares a model of the data-processing operation. The term MAP has been chosen to identify the preinstallation techniques and procedures recommend to users of some electronic data-processing systems.

mapping—1. A tranformation from one set to another set. 2. A correspondence.

mapping, memory — An optional mode of computer operation wherein the eight high-order bits of any virtual address greater than 15 are replaced by an alternative value, thus providing for dynamic relocatability of programs (some computers).

mapping mode—The mode of computer operation in which virtual addresses above 15 are transformed through the memory map so that they become references to actual core memory locations (some computers).

maps, status—A status report of programs, and 1/0 operations—usually in tabular form.

map, storage—See storage map.

MARC—Acronym for Machine Readable Cataloging, a Library of Congress project, designed for distribution of catalog data in magnetic-tape form.

margin—1. The difference between the actual operating point and the point where improper operation will occur. 2. Also called range or printing range. In telegraphy, the interval between limits on a scale, usually arbitrary, in which printing is error-free. Incremental and variable derivatives, or rate of change of a function are often used in an exactly synonymous sense. Thus, the composite terms: marginal cost (of production), marginal revenue (from sales), marginal value (of a capacity, of sales, of supplies), etc. The coefficients of a linear programming model are themselves all marginal figures. For example: the cost coefficient of an activity is the marginal cost of performing the activity; the coefficient in a material-balance row is the marginal consumption or production of the material.

marginal check—A preventive-maintenance procedure in which certain operating conditions (e.g. supply voltage or frequency) are varied about their nominal values in order to detect and locate incipient defective parts.

marginal checking—A means of testing circuits for incipient or intermittent failures by varying the voltages applied to the circuit.

marginal cost—The rate of change of cost as a function of quantity.

marginal error—Such errors irregularly occur in tapes, and most often disappear simply because the writing is done over a slightly different section of tapes.

marginal revenue—The rates of change of income as a function of quantity.

marginal test—A preventive-maintenance procedure in which certain operating conditions are varied about their normal values in order to detect and locate incipient defective units, e.g., supply voltage or frequency may be varied. (Synonymous with high-low bias test, and related to check.)

marginal testing—A form of test, usually as part of preventive maintenance or as a fault-finding or correcting operation, to test against safety margins for faults.

marginal tests (voltage and registers)—Built into some computers is a network for marginal test of computer subsections. Two features of the marginal test system make routine checks fast and accurate. The marginal check voltage is continuously variable, and all working registers are displayed simultaneously on the console lights.

margin guide—See guide, margin.

margin, justified—See justified margin.

margin, justify—See justify.

margin-punched card — Same as card, edge-punched.

mark—1.(Communications), an impulse which, in a neutral circuit, causes the loop to be closed; or in a polar circuit, causes the loop current to flow in a direction opposite to that for a space impulse. 2. A sign or symbol used to signify or indicate an event in time or space; e.g., end of word or message mark, a file mark, a drum mark, an end-of-tape mark.

mark, admissible—Specific rules or conventions determine which marks, symbols, and numerals or characters are permitted in various areas of computing for all installations and for various languages.

mark detection—A type of character recognition system which detects from marks placed in areas on paper or cards, called site areas, boxes, or windows, certain intelligence or information. Mark reading results from optical character recognition or mark-sensing systems which seek out the presence or absence of pencil marks or graphite particles, such as on college or school exams, census returns, etc.

mark, drum—A character used to signify the end of a record on a drum.

mark, end—An indicator to signal the end of a word or the end of a unit of data.

marker, beginning-of-information (BIM)—A reflective spot on the back of a magnetic tape, 10 feet from the physical beginning of the tape which is sensed photoelectrically to indicate the point on tape at which recording may begin.

marker, destination-warning—A reflective spot on the back of a magnetic tape, 18 feet from the physical end of the tape, which is sensed photoelectrically to indicate that the physical end of the tape is approaching.

marker, end-of-tape—A special mark, character, long blank, or other coding used to indicate the end of a tape or recording, i.e., oftentimes this is an easy-to-see reflective strip, a transparent section, or a special bit pattern on paper tape.

mark, group—A special character used to designate the end of a record in storage for a write instruction.

mark, hold—The normal no-traffic line condition whereby a steady mark is transmitted.

marking and spacing intervals—In telegraph communication, marking intervals are the intervals which correspond, according to convention, to one condition or position of the originating transmitting contracts, usually a closed condition. Spacing intervals are the intervals that correspond to another condition of the originating transmitting contracts, usually an open condition.

marking bias—Bias distortion that lengthens the marking impulses by advancing the space-to-mark transition.

marking-end distortion—End distortion that lengthens the marking impulse by delaying the mark-to-space transition.

mark matching—A method employed in optical character recognition to correlate or match a specimen character with each of a set of masks representing the characters to be recognized, i.e., the characters are deliberately registered on the reference masks and no allowance is made for character misregistration. Mask types are: holisitic masks (exact), peep-hole masks (more lenient but still exacting), and weighted area masks.

Mark I—An early electromechanical computer, utilizing both mechanical and electrical components to perform computational processes.

mark reading—See reading, mark.

mark, record—A special character used in some computers either to limit the number of characters in a data transfer, or to separate blocked or grouped records in tape.

mark, record-storage—A special character that appears only in the record-storage unit of the card reader to limit the length of the record read into storage.

mark scan—To mark scan is to read a document for a specific mark in a particular location. The mark may be made by a pen or pencil, since the operation is usually based on optical scanning and light reflectance. Mark scanning differs from mark sensing because mark sensing requires an electrographic pencil with conductive ink.

marks, control (CM)—1. A control mark is a one-slab block written on magnetic tape to indicate the type of data that follows, or to indicate the end of useful information. 2. The control mark (any one-slab block) supplies special control features which can be utilized by the programmer. However, several specified CM configurations have been reserved for particular features on data tapes, as FF for end of file.

mark, segment—A special character written on tape to separate one section of a tape file from another.

mark-sense—To mark a position on a punched card by an electrically conductive pencil, for later conversion to machine punching.

mark-sense punch—*See* punch, mark-sense.

mark sensing—1. A technique for detecting special pencil marks entered in special places on a card, and automatically translating the marks into punched holes.

mark, single-quote — A special FORTRAN character used to enclose literal messages.

mark-space multiplier—A specific analog multiplier, in which one input variable is represented as a current or a voltage, and is used to control the mark-to-space ratio of a repetitive rectangular wave and whose amplitude is made proportional to the other variable, which is also represented by a voltage or a current.

mark, storage—The name given to a point location which defines the character space immediately to the left of the most significant character in accumulator storage. An example would be:

a	7	4	6	7	4	8	9

in which the letter "a" would be the storage mark.

mark, tape—The special character that is written on tape to signify the physical end of the recording on tape.

mark, track-error—Indicates that during the course of the previous block transfer a data parity error was detected, or one or more bits have been picked up or dropped out from either the timing track or the mark track.

mark, word—An indicator to signal the beginning or end of a word.

mask—1. A machine word that specifies which parts of another machine word are to be operated on. Also called extractor or filter. 2. Act of replacing characters in the accumulator with characters from a specified storage location that corresponds to the "ones" position in the mask, which is in a specific storage location or register. 3. To extract a selected group of characters from a string of characters.

masking—1. An operation that replaces characters in the accumulator with characters from a specified storage location or register. 2. The process of extracting a non-

word group or field of characters from a word or a string of words. 3. The process of setting internal program controls to prevent transfers which otherwise would occur upon setting of internal machine latches.

mask, interrupt—*See* interrupt mask.

mask register—The mask register functions as a filter in determining which portions of words in masked operations or logical comparisons are tested. In repeated masked-search operations, both the mask register and the repeat counter must be loaded prior to executing the actual search command (some systems).

masks, holistic—*See* holistic masks.

masks, peephole—A set of characters in a character-recognition unit, which resides as a set of strategically placed points and which would theoretically show all input characters as being unique regardless of their style, i.e., for any one character there is only one set of points.

mask words—The mask word modifies both the identifier word and the input word which is called up for a search comparison in a logical AND operation.

mass data—*See* data, mass.

mass data, multiprocessing—*See* multiprocessing mass data.

mass storage—*See* storage, mass.

mass-storage executive capability—*See* storage, mass (executive).

mass storage file—*See* file, mass storage.

mass storage systems—*See* storage system, mass.

master—A file of data considered permanent or semipermanent; i.e., an arrangement or ordering of a series of records; also, a single record from such a file.

master card—A card containing fixed or indicative information for a group of cards. It is usually the first card of that group.

master clock—1. The primary source of timing signals used to control the timing of pulses. 2. The electronic or electric source of standard timing signals, often called "clock pulses," required for sequencing computer operation. This source usually consists of a timing-pulse generator, a cycling unit, and sets of special pulses that occur at given intervals of time. In synchronous computers the basic time frequency employed is usually the frequency of the clock pulses.

master clock frequency — The number of pulses per second produced by the master clock.

master control—1. An application-oriented routine usually applied to the highest level of a subroutine hierarchy. 2. Computer program to control operation of the system, designed to reduce the amount of intervention required of the operator. Master control schedules programs to be processed, initiates segments of programs, controls input/output traffic, informs operator and verifies his actions, and performs corrective action on program errors or system malfunctions.

259

master-control interrupt—Signal generated by an input/output device, or by an operator's error, or by request of the processor, for more data program segments, or the like, which permits the master control program to control the computer system.

master control program—*Same as* program, master control.

master data—A set of data which is altered infrequently and supplies basic data for processing operations. The data content of a master file. Examples include: names, badge numbers, or pay rates in personnel data; or stock number, stock descriptions, or units of measure in stock-control data.

master file—1. A file of relatively more permanent information, which is usually updated periodically. 2. A main reference file of information.

master file inventory — Permanently stored inventory information retained for future use.

master file (job processing)—The master file contains the programs necessary for job processing. The programs in the master file are sectioned into four categories: (1) system programs, (2) input/output drivers, (3) utility routines, (4) library subroutines. System programs are the monitor, executive, recovery dump (R dump), system loader, chain tape preparation routine, FORTRAN compiler, and assist assembler. The monitor is loaded into memory by a bootstrap program. The monitor remains in memory during all job processing. Other system programs necessary for job processing are loaded into memory (some systems).

master file, magnetic tape—*See* tape, master file.

master file, tape—*See* tape, master file.

master instruction tape—A tape on which all the programs for a system of runs are recorded. (Synonymous with MIT.)

master mode—The mode of computer operation in which all legal SIGMA operations are permissible.

master payroll data file—The information bank where data on each employee is kept.

master program—*Same as* program, master control.

master-program file—A tape on which all the programs for a system of runs are recorded.

master program, file-update—Programs from the old master file are deleted, corrected, or left unchanged, and new programs are added from the transaction tape. A new program master file is produced.

master program tape—*See* tape, master.

master record—The basic updated record used in the next file-processing run. A master record is most often a magnetic tape item. Visual copies for possible analysis and alteration are usually developed.

master routine—*Same as* executive routine.

master/slave computer *See* master/slave system.

master/slave mode—This feature guarantees

that one program cannot damage or access another program sharing memory. The unique operating technique in changing from slave to master mode makes multiprogramming not only practical but foolproof.

master/slave modes, time-sharing—*See* time sharing, master slave modes.

master/slave system—A special system or computer configuration for business or scientific use (as production automation) in which one computer, usually of substantial size or capability, rules with complete control over all input/output and schedules and transmits tasks to a slave computer. The latter computer often has a great capacity, and it performs the computations as directed and controlled by the master unit.

master synchronizer—A primary source of timing signals. Often a ring counter synchronized by a crystal-controlled oscillator.

master system tape—This is a monitor program that allows for the centralized control of program operation. It provides a load-and-go operation with one magnetic-tape unit without operator intervention. The operator can specify loading and execution of any program on the master system tape by a simple on-line typewriter directive.

master tape—*See* tape, master.

master timer—*See* master clock.

match—1. A data processing operation similar to a merge, except that instead of producing a sequence of items made up from the input, sequences are matched against each other on the basis of some key. The following is a schematic of a two-item match:

SEQUENCE A	SEQUENCE B
1	1
2	3
3	3
4	4
5	5
6	6
7	7
8	11
9	11
10	13
11	
12	
13	

2. Comparison of keys (records) that are identical. (Synonymous with a hit or strike.)

match gate—*Same as* gate, exclusive NOR.

matching—The matching technique is generally used to verify coding. Individual codes are machine-compared against a group of master codes to select any that are invalid.

matching error—An error due to inaccuracy in pairing passive components.

matching, mark—*See* mark matching.

match-merge—The comparison of two files, usually based on key words designed to place them in the prearranged sequential order of those records which match the arbitrarily selected key words.

mathematical analysis—Includes arithmetic and algebra; deals with numbers, the relationships between numbers, and the operations performed on these relationships.

mathematical check—A check that uses mathematical identities or other properties, occasionally with some degree of discrepancy being acceptable; e.g., checking multiplication by verifying that $A \times B = B \times A$. (Synonymous with arithmetic check.)

mathematical function programs—The several software programs include an extensive collection of basic mathematical subroutines and functions. Collections include all of the standard FORTRAN functions to give the programmer a more complete coverage of the "often used" mathematical routines. Each of these mathematical routines has been carefully developed to offer the programmer maximum accuracy and range with a minimum routine size and executive time. These routines are available to each of the program languages, FORTRAN IV, Assembler, and COBOL.

mathematical logic—1. The mathematical concepts, techniques, and languages as used in symbolic logic whatever their particular application or context. (Related to logic.) 2. Exact reasoning concerning nonnumerical relations by using symbols that are efficient in calculation. Also called symbolic logic.

mathematical model—1. A series or organization of equations that are a mathematical representation of a "real world" problem or process in a skeletonized form, but with precise measurements of the relationships of the variables, parameters, and constants. Each model has some objective function (goal or target) and decision rules (values to be determined) which will solve the problem to develop the answer or range of alternatives. 2. A mathematical representation of a process, device, or concept. 3. A mathematical representation that simulates the behavior of a process, device, or concept.

mathematical operator—A symbol that indicates briefly a mathematical process, which describes the relations and restrictions which exist between the input variables and the output variables of a system.

mathematical parameter—A secondary variable in an application. For example, the analytic geometry description of a line, $y = ax$ plus b can be replaced by the parametric expression $y = a^t x + b$ where t is regarded as a parameter. The constants, a and b, and the dependent variables, x and y, are not considered as parameters.

mathematical power—See power, mathematical.

mathematical program—See program, mathematical.

mathematical programming—Same as linear programming.

mathematical simulation—The use of a model of mathematical equations in which computing elements are used to represent all of the subsystems.

mathematical subroutines—Complete sets of mathematical subroutines including sine, cosine, square root, exponent, log, etc.

mathematics—Involves the definition of symbols of various kinds and describes the operations to be performed, in definite and consistent ways, upon the symbols; a symbolized and extended form of logic to form the patterns of scientific phenomena, the laws obeyed, and the uniformities displayed. Although mathics does not provide these, it expresses and interprets them and helps to deduce their consequences, or to forecast what will happen if they hold. Mathematics points and advises where to look for verification or contradiction of hypotheses.

mathematics, fixed-point — See fixed point mathematics.

mathematics, floating-point — See floating point mathematics.

MATHLAB—A formal algebraic manipulation on-line system.

MATH-PAC—Mathematical and statistical programs for simplifying such scientific and engineering applications as solution of simultaneous linear equations, matrix algebra, multiple linear regression, roots of a polynomial, and least squares polynomial fit. (General Electric)

matrix—1. A rectangular array of numbers subject to mathematical operations, such as addition, multiplication, and inversion, according to specified rules. Any table is a matrix. Also, an array of circuit elements such as diodes, wires, magnetic cores, and relays, arranged and designed to perform a specified function; for example, conversion from one number system to another. 2. In mathematics, an array of quantities in a prescribed form, usually capable of being subject to a mathematical operation, by means of an operator or another matrix, according to prescribed rules.

matrix algebra tableau—The current matrix, with auxiliary rows and/or columns, as it appears at an iterative stage in the standard simplex method computing form of solution.

matrix coefficient—The matrix of left-side coefficients in a system of linear operations. It is to be distinguished from the matrix obtained by appending the right side, which is called the augmented matrix of the system. It may be thought of as including a full set of logical vectors to convert inequality constraints to equations, and in the case of the modified simplex array it also contains the objective function coefficients.

matrix, constraint—In linear programming, the augmented matrix of the constraint equations; it is the matrix formed by the coefficient columns, or left sides, and the column of constants.

matrix, photocell—*See* photocell, matrix.

matrix printer—*See* printer, wire.

matrix printing—The printing of alpha-numerical characters by means of the appropriate selection of pins contained in a rectangular array on the printing head.

matrix, program timing—A unique array of connections which supply timing pulses at regular intervals and in proper sequence to permanently selected groups of lines in the normal execution of operations, i.e., the clock pulses for a clock pulse generator in synchronous digital computers.

matrix, semantic—A graphical device for plotting in a standard conventional form whatever precise elements of meaning have been ascertained from the semantic analysis of a concept.

matrix, storage—*See* storage matrix.

matrix table—A specific set of quantities in a rectangular array according to exacting mathematical rules and designs.

maximal—Highest or greatest.

maximum operating frequency—The maximum repetition or clock rate at which the modules will perform reliably in continuous operations, under worst-case conditions, without special trigger-pulse (clock) requirements.

MAYBE compiler—This was designed and implemented to provide the instructions, commands, and orders for operation of the data channel and various devices. In addition, MAYBE automatically produces the necessary system linkages to process the data channel interrupts and central computer traps. The MAYBE compiler is a macro-generator which feeds symbolic input to the standard assembly program. MAYBE was coded in NOMAD and utilizes standard system I/O routines.

MAYBE language—Some data channels are capable of performing simple iteration loops, full and partial word substitution, and byte testing, as well as driving I/O devices. They cannot, however, add, subtract, shift, or mask.

MCUG—Abbreviation for military computer users group.

MDE—An abbreviation for magnetic decision element.

mean-time-between-failures—The special limit of the ratio of operating time or equipment to the number of observed failures as the number of failures approaches infinity.

mean time to failure—The average time the system or component of the system works without faulting.

mean time to repair—The average time to repair a fault or a component of the system.

measure, data-transmission utilization—The ratio of useful data output of a data-transmission system to the total data input.

measurement, work—*See* work measurement.

mechanical differerential analyzer—A form of analog computer using interconnected mechanical surfaces to solve differential equations; e.g., the Bush differential analyzer, developed by Vannevar Bush at M.I.T., used differential gear boxes to perform addition, and a combination of wheel disk spherical mechanisms to perform integration.

mechanical replacement—An action originated by the contractor and taken by him to substitute one machine for another that is installed at a customer's site. Such action usually is occasioned by the mechanical condition of the equipment being replaced.

mechanical scanner—*See* scanner, mechanical.

mechanical translation—A generic term for language translation by computers or similar equipment.

mechanism, control tape—That part of the printer which controls the printing carriage, to permit desired layout for hard copy printout.

mechanism, decision—*See* decision, mechanism.

mechanism, paper-advance — Two sets of sprocketed tractors—an upper set and a lower set—advance the paper through the printer under program control.

mechanism, tape transport—*See* tape transport.

mechanized data—*See* data, mechanized.

media—1. Magnetic or punched cards, or paper tapes are examples of the various media types devised to carry data or information. 2. The plural form of medium.

media conversion — The program library has a complete set of routines to perform media conversions of all kinds. Media conversion is efficiently done in the multiprogramming mode rather than with off-line equipment or smaller computers.

media conversion, buffer — Small, tightly coded subroutines operating under control of the executive system perform on-line conversion of data between card, printer, punch, and tape equipment concurrently with other programs. Low-speed devices use magnetic drum as a large buffer area between themselves and operating programs. Use of the magnetic drum as a buffer provides increased throughput capability as programs using these drum buffers effectively "read" or "print" information at drum-transfer speeds.

medium — The material on which data are recorded, but generally a term applied to paper tape, punched cards, and magnetic tape rather than disks, drums, or core devices.

medium, empty — Usually printed forms or blank paper tapes, invoices, etc., which are bases or media on which data has been recorded only to develop a frame of reference to determine the feasibility of such instruments to be used later as data carriers.

medium, input/output—The vehicle or material designed and used to carry recorded data, i.e., a punched card, magnetic tape, microfilm, etc. The medium is the carrier of data and instructions to and from a computer. A specific register that contains modifiers of instructions before execution, or a register that controls actions under the direction of the computer or program.

medium, machine readable—*See* data, machine readable.

medium, nonerasable—Paper tapes are examples of nonerasable media used to drive various production machines. It is quite uncommon to use paper tape as an intermediate memory because it is nonerasable.

medium, storage—The material on which data is recorded and which may be paper tape, cards, magnetic tape, strips, or devices such as magnetic drums, disks, etc.

medium, transfer—The material which enables the transfer of ink during printing such as sheets, ribbons, plastic film.

mega—A prefix meaning million.

megabit—One million binary bits.

megacycle—A million cycles per second; 10^6 cycles per second.

member, print—*See* print member.

memories, associative—With associative-memory capability, high-speed memory searches within computers are based on content or subject matter rather than being limited to locating data through specified addresses.

memorize — Typically, meaning to transfer data or information to internal storage.

memory—1. Synonymous with storage. The term memory carries "magic brain" connotations which are considered undesirable; hence, storage is preferred. 2. Any device into which a unit of information can be copied, which will hold this information, and from which the information can be obtained at a later time. (The terms memory and storage are interchangeable.) 3. An organization of storage units, primarily for the retrieval of information and data. Memory types include disk, core, drum, or relay memories. Extremely rapid access-storage elements from which instructions are executed and data operated on are referred to as main memory as contrasted to auxiliary-memory modules.

memory access, quick—*Same as* storage, high speed.

memory, acoustic—A computer memory that uses a sonic delay line.

memory, addressed—Memory sections containing each individual register.

memory address register—1. A register containing the address of the selected word in memory. *See* register. 2. The location in core memory that is selected for data storage or retrieval is determined by the memory address. Some registers can directly address all 4096 words of the standard core memory or of any preselected field of extended core memory.

memory address, virtual—Often interpreted as addressing (1) a particular character relative to the beginning of a page, (2) a particular page relative to the initial point

of that segment, and (3) a particular large memory segment or book. Thus programs can be addressed into noncontiguous areas of memory in relatively small blocks.

memory annex—Small memory unit as a go-between for the input and output units, and the main memory.

memory, bootstrap—The bootstrap memory is a time-saving device built into the main computer. It is programmed to fit the specialized needs of various computer users. The program and words in the bootstrap memory cannot be altered by the computer but can be manually changed when necessary. The purpose of the bootstrap memory is to provide for the automatic reading of new programs into the computer with protection against erasing its vital instructions (some systems).

memory buffer register—*See* register, memory-buffer.

memory capacity—The number of elementary pieces of data that can be contained in a storage device. Frequently defined in terms of characters in a particular code or words of a fixed size that can be so contained.

memory character format—Memory storing techniques of storing one character in each addressable location.

memory, content-addressed—A memory in which the storage locations are identified by their contents rather than their addresses. Enables faster interrogation to retrieve a particular data element.

memory, core—A storage device composed of ferromagnetic cores, or an apertured ferrite plate, through which select lines and sense windings are threaded. *See* memory, thin-film.

memory core, re-entrant routines—*See* re-entrant routines, core memory.

memory, core rope—*Same as* storage, core rope.

memory cycle—An operation consisting of reading from and writing into memory.

memory dump—1. A listing of the contents of a storage device, area, or selected parts of it. 2. *See* storage dump. 3. A process of writing the contents of memory consecutively in such a form that it can be examined for computer or program errors. 4. Routine generated automatically according to a programmer's specification and included in an object program to perform, respectively, program-loading operations and a printout of memory contents upon request.

memory dump (monitor control)—A memory dump may be specified in the control information for a job. Upon termination of the job, the dump routine is loaded from the system unit and executed. The dump routine overlays the monitor and produces a complete dump of the object program. Upon completion of the dump, the monitor is reloaded to process the next job. Programs terminate normally by returning control to the monitor. A job may be terminated by the operator or the monitor. Once a job has terminated, the monitor automatically initiates processing of the next job. If for any reason the resident monitor becomes destroyed and processing is not continuous, the system may be reloaded and initialized by the bootstrap loader.

memory dump routines, dynamic tape— These routines, particularly valuable when debugging programs, provide automatic, on-the-fly recording of the contents of memory and of magnetic tape files. Calls to these routines may be programmed in advance by use of macroinstructions, or they may be initiated at object time by the operator.

memory, dynamic—The storage of data on a device or in a manner that permits the data to move or vary with time, and thus the data is not always available instantly for recovery; e.g., acoustic delay line, magnetic drum, or circulating or recirculating of information in a medium.

memory (dynamic allocation)—Each time a subroutine is called using this feature, the unique storage area for that subroutine is assigned to the first storage available. Thus, all subroutines called on the same level will share the same storage area. This results in a significant storage saving in many cases. In addition, a recursive subroutine call is possible because a new storage area is assigned each time a subroutine is entered. This feature, together with in-line symbolic coding, provides real-time capability.

memory, dynamic relocation—Frees computer user from keeping track of exactly where information is located in the system memory. Another important attribute is its ability to keep programs flowing in and out of memory in a highly effective manner.

memory exchange—1. The interchange of the total contents of two storage devices or locations such as two registers. 2. A switching device capable of controlling and handling the flow or exchange of data between storage units or other elements of a system.

memory, external—A facility or device, not an integral part of a computer, on which data usable by a computer is stored, such as, off-line magnetic-tape units, or punch-card devices. (Contrasted with internal storage.)

memory fill—Placing a pattern of characters in memory registers not in use in a particular problem to stop the computer if the program, through error, seeks instructions taken from forbidden registers.

memory guard—Electronic or program guard inhibiting or preventing access to specific sections of storage devices or areas especially concerning the main or internal memory of the central processor.

memory hierarchy—A set of memories with differing sizes and speeds, and usually having different cost-performance ratios. A hierarchy might consist of a very high speed, small semiconductor memory, a medium-speed core memory, and a large, slow-speed core.

memory, high speed—A unit which is capable of producing information at relatively higher speeds than other peripheral or memory units connected or related to a computer system; also an indication of the lower average access time.

memory, interleaving — See multiprocessor interleaving.

memory, internal—1. The storage of data on a device that is an integral part of a computer. 2. The storage facilities forming an integral physical part of the computer and directly controlled by the computer. In such facilities all data are automatically accessible to the computer; e.g., magnetic core, and magnetic tape on-line. (Contrasted with external storage.) 3. All memory or storage which is automatically accessible to the computer without human intervention.

memory location—A specific position in a computer storage device.

memory locations, scratchpad—See scratchpad memory locations.

memory locations, standard—These are various areas of storage which are reserved for mathematical tables, or for the automatic storage of final contents of registers.

memory-lockout register—Any area in core store may be "locked out" to prevent accidental writing into addresses where information, which it is desired to retain, is stored. A special load memory lockout register (LMLR) instruction is provided to define the desired area(s) in core store which is to be "locked out." This instruction stores the "post-limit codes" in a special 16-bit memory lockout register (MLR) which is divided into four sections: an upper and lower limit for bank 1 and upper and lower limit for bank (some systems).

memory, magnetic—Any portion of the memory that uses the magnetic properties of a material to store information.

memory, main—Usually the fastest storage device of a computer and the one from which instructions are executed. (Contrasted with auxiliary storage.)

memory map—The memory map is a listing of all variables, constants, and statement identifiers in a FORTRAN program and the storage location assigned to each. The memory map allows the programmer to examine values in his program from a memory drum. The memory map is listed during compilation. A memory map is normally given with each program unless control character specified in the job definition or a sense switch is on (some systems).

memory map list—A memory map is provided at compile time on an optional basis. The memory map is a listing of all variable names, array names, and constants used by the program, with their relative address assignments. The listing will include all subroutines called and last location when called.

memory mapping—An optional mode of computer operation wherein the eight high-order bits of any virtual address greater than 15 are replaced by an alternative value, thus providing for dynamic relocatability of programs (some computers).

memory module—A magnetic core module providing storage locations for 4K, 8K, 12K, or 16K, or more words (where K = 1024) .

memory, nonvolatile—A storage medium which retains information when power is removed from the system.

memory Olsen—*Same as* storage, core rope.

memory overlays—The monitor remains resident in lower memory at all times. Object programs are loaded into memory, starting at the end of the monitor. The program loader resides in upper memory. Object programs cannot be loaded into the loader area. This area can be overlaid by common storage. Part of the loader can also be overlaid by library subroutines (some systems).

memory parity interrupt—Each time control is given to the monitor the memory parity trap is armed and the interrupt location is patched with an instruction. When a memory parity occurs, the computer halts at the location at which the parity occurred, with the console memory parity indicator light turning on.

memory, permanent—Storage of information that remains intact when the power is turned off. Also called nonvolatile storage.

memory power—A hierarchy of memories within some large computer systems makes information in core storage available at varying speeds. Control memories operate in as little as 250 billionths-of-a-second. Powerful main memories containing up to 524,000 characters of information range from 2.5 millionths-of-a-second down to one-millionth-of-a-second.

memory print—*See* memory dump.

memory print-out—A listing of the contents of a storage device, or selected parts of it. (Synonymous with memory dump and core dump.)

memory protect—This hardware function provides positive protection to the system executive routine and all other programs. It protects not only against processor execution, but also against I/O data-area destruction. Because it is a hardware function rather than software, it reduces multiprogramming complexities.

memory protection—*Same* as storage protection.

memory protection, time-sharing—*See* time sharing, memory protection.

memory protect, multiprogramming — *See* multiprogramming memory protect.

memory protect no-operation—*See* no-operation, memory protect.

memory, quick-access—*Same as* storage, high speed.

memory, random-access—A storage technique in which the time required to obtain information is independent of the location of the information most recently obtained. This strict definition must be qualified by the observation that we usually mean relatively nonrandom access when compared to magnetic cores for main stores, but are relatively random access when compared to magnetic tapes for file storage. (Contrasted with sequential-access storage.)

memory, rapid—That section of the whole memory from which information may be obtained in the shortest possible time.

memory, rapid-access—*Same as* storage, high speed.

memory, read-only—A memory that cannot be altered in normal use of the computer. Usually, a small memory that contains often-used instructions such as microprograms or system software.

memory-reference instructions—The instructions include arithmetic, logical, data handling, and program control instructions. A memory address is specified as part of a memory-reference instruction. The contents of this memory address are used by the processor in executing the instruction. Bits contain the instruction code and signify that the address is to be indirect. Most memory-reference instructions require two computer cycles. The first cycle fetches the instruction itself. The second cycle fetches the data addressed and executes the instruction. All memory-reference instructions can be executed indirectly.

memory, regenerative—A memory device where contents gradually vanish if not periodically refreshed.

memory register—A register in the storage of the computer, as in contrast with a register in one of the other units of the computer.

memory, scratchpad—A high-speed memory device used to store the location of an interrupted program and to retrieve the latter after the interrupting program has been completed.

memory, secondary—A particular storage which is usually of large capacity, but also with longer access time, and which most often permits the transferring of blocks of data between it and the main storage.

memory section, word select—Many of the significant features of the computer are a result of its fast memory which has been designed to provide a total memory-cycle time of microseconds. This fast memory speed is mainly the result of the "word-select" with diode steering technique that is used for memory addressing. This replaces the more conventional method of X- and Y-axis half-read and half-write currents which is much slower. Another design consideration is the non-destructive readout with a positive automatic-restoration feature that prevents an accidental loss of memory information. (Some computers.)

memory, semiconductor—A memory whose storage medium is a semiconductor circuit. Often used for high-speed buffer memories and for read-only memories. Most memories are magnetic cores.

memory single-level—A memory organization technique using dynamic relocation to combine fast internal memory with slower external mass memory. The combination appears as a single fast internal memory.

memory, slow—That portion of the memory from which information may be obtained automatically, but not at the fastest rate of various sections.

memory, static — A memory device that contains no mechanical moving parts. Also a memory device that contains fixed information.

memory storage—The computer's filing system. It holds standard or current facts such as rate tables, current inventories, balances, etc. and sometimes programming instructions. The memory storage can be internal, that is, a part of the computer itself, such as drums, cores, or thin-film; or, it can be external, such as paper tape, magnetic tape, or punched cards.

memory storage, intermediate—An electronic scratchpad for holding working figures temporarily until they are needed, and for releasing final figures to the output.

memory, thin-film—A storage device made of thin disks of magnetic material deposited on a nonmagnetic base. Its operation is similar to the core memory. *See* core memory.

memory, virtual—A technique that permits the user to treat secondary (disk) storage as an extension of core-memory, thus giving the virtual appearance of a larger core memory. A type of memory with the capability of using a type of algorithm of the paging or segmenting type. In this manner a larger memory is simulated than actually exists in core.

memory, volatile—A storage medium in which information is destroyed when power is removed from the system.

memory, word — A limited characteristic of some equipment, whereby the words are available from the storage and not from individual characters.

memory, word-select — *See* word-select memory.

memory, working — The internal memory which stores information for processing.

memory, write-lock — A 2-bit write-protect field optionally provided for each 512-word page of core memory addresses (some computers).

mercury delay line—A sonic or acoustic delay line in which mercury is used as the medium of sound transmission, with transducers on each end to permit conversion to and from electrical energy. (Related to acoustic delay line.)

mercury memory—Delay lines using mercury as the medium for storage of a circulating train of waves or pulses. Also called mercury storage.

mercury storage—A storage device that utilizes the acoustic properties of mercury to store data. (Related to mercury delay line.)

merge—1. To produce a single sequence of items, ordered according to some rule (that is, arranged in some orderly sequence), from two or more sequences previously ordered according to the same rule, without changing the items in size, structure, or total number. Merging is a special kind of collating. 2. To combine two or more files into one, usually in specified order.

merge, order of—The number of input files to a merge program. Also power of the merge.

merge-sort—The production of a single sequence of items in a specific order as programmed or according to some rules developed without changing the items in structure, size, or total number.

merging sort—*See* sort, merge.

merging, (T − 1)-way—A technique used in a sort program to merge strings of sequenced data. For tape systems that permit backward reading, the effective power of the merge is equal to T − 1.

merging, (T/2)-way—A technique used in a sort program to merge strings of sequenced data. The power of the merge is equal to T/2.

mesh—To combine in an arrangement according to some rule, two or more sequences previously arranged according to the same rule, to obtain a single sequence of items without any change in the number or type of items.

message—1. A finite sequence of letters, digits, symbols, etc. 2. A transmitted series of words or symbols that are designed and intended to convey information. In message switching, a message consists of a header, text, and an end-of-message symbol. 3. A group of words, variable in length, transported as a unit; a transported item of information.

message, automatic—A location in which incoming data from one circuit is transferred to the proper outgoing circuit.

message (communications)—A transmitted series of words or symbols intended to convey information.

message-display console — *See* console, message-display.

message, end of—The specific set of characters that indicates the termination of a message.

message error, illegal control — A control message has been read that it is not defined. If the message is typed it may be retyped. Otherwise, only the compile or assembled phase of the job is processed and a job error is given.

message exchange—A device placed between a communication line and a computer to take care of certain communication functions and thereby free the computer for other work.

message, fox—A standard message which is used for testing teletype circuits and machines because it includes all the alphanumerics on a teletypwriter as well as most of the function characters such as space, figures shift, letters shift, etc. The message is: The quick brown fox jumped over a lazy dog's back 1234567890 – – – sending." The sending station's identification is inserted in the three blank spaces which precede the word sending.

message, multiple-address—A message that is to be delivered to more than one destination.

message program, interconsole—Switches message traffic between the various user-consoles. This program provides a means by which the user may request manual operation by the operator and receive acknowledgment. Such an operation would be the mounting/dismounting of user tapes (some systems).

message queuing—Controls the order in which messages are stored, processed, and transmitted.

message reference block—See block, message reference.

message routing—The function of selecting the route, or alternate route, for a message.

message, semiautomatic (switching center)—A location where an incoming message is displayed to an operator who directs the message to one or more outgoing circuits according to information read from the message.

messages, error — Messages developed by a program to designate a variety of error types.

message, single-address—A message which is to be delivered to only one destination.

message switch—A term for one of the routing points in a store and forward switching system.

message switch and communications, time sharing—See time sharing, message switch and communications.

message switching—1. The technique of receiving a message, storing it until the proper outgoing circuit is available, and then retransmitting it. 2. A system in which data transmissions between stations on different circuits within a network are accomplished by routing the data through a central point.

meta language — A formal language which uses special symbols to describe the syntax of computer languages, for example, bacus normal form.

method, access—See access method.

method, Amble's—An analog computer term relating to a connection devised by O. Amble, such that the output of an integrator contributes through an adder to its own input to solve differential equations of a specific form.

method, infinite-pad — See infinite-pad method.

method, monte-carlo—A trial and error

method of repeated calculations to discover the best solution of a problem. Often used when a great number of variables are present, with interrelationships so extremely complex as to forestall straightforward analytical handling.

methods analyst—Designs systems and supervises their implementation. He also plans, controls, and coordinates conversion to new systems.

method, time-quantum (time sharing) — See time sharing, time quantum method.

MICR code—See code, MICR.

MICR (Magnetic Ink Character Recognition)— A check-encoding system employed by banks for the purpose of automating check handling. Checks are imprinted (using magnetic ink) with characters of a type face and dimensions specified by the American Banking Association. There are fourteen characters—ten numbers (0-9) and four special symbols—which are used to provide amount, identifying, and control information.

microcode—1. A system of coding making use of suboperations not ordinarily accessible in programming; e.g., coding that makes use of parts of multiplication or division operations. 2. A list of small program steps. Combinations of these steps, performed automatically in a prescribed sequence, form a macrooperation like multiply, divide, and square root.

microcoding—A system of coding that uses suboperations not ordinarily accessible in programming.

microfilm computer output (COM)—A microfilm printer that will take output directly from the computer, thus substituting for line printer or tape output.

microfilm displays—The DIGIPRINT system, consisting of a symbol generator, line generator, CRT, and memory, is a low-cost alphanumeric and graphic information-recording system that operates from any digital-data source. Computer generated data consisting of symbol and format commands is converted by the DIGIPRINT system to a CRT display which is photographed with the system's special digitally controlled 16-mm microfilm camera (35-mm option). The camera can also simultaneously photograph an "overlay" that contains basic continuing entries. Up to 10 overlays can be stored. Thus when the recorded information is retrieved, it is "printed" on the forms or maps that were used as overlays. This is a projected microfilm display. The unit is compatible with 63 kc tape drives on a real-time basis.

microinstruction—A small and single add, shift, or delete type of command.

micron — A unit of length equal to one-thousandth of a millimeter, i.e., one-millionth of a meter or 39-millionths of an inch.

microprogram—1. A program of analytic instructions which the programmer intends to construct from the basic subcommands of a digital computer. 2. A sequence of pseudocommands which will be translated by hardware into machine subcommands. 3. A means of building various analytic instructions as needed from the subcommand structure of a computer. 4. A plan for obtaining maximum utilization of the abilities of a digital computer by efficient use of the subcommands of the machine.

microprogrammable instructions — See instructions, microprogrammable.

microprogramming—1. The technique of using a certain special set of computer instructions that consists only of basic elemental operations which the programmer can combine into higher-level instructions as he chooses, and can then program using only the higher-level instructions. 2. Machine-language coding in which the coder builds his own machine instructions from the primitive basic instructions built into the hardware.

microsecond—A millionth part of a second. One second = 1,000,000 microseconds.

MICR scan—The sensing of characters, marks, or codes printed in magnetic ink. The technique was developed by American Bankers' Association and is used on bank checks. The character size, shape, and ink are standardized by the USA Standards Institute.

MIDAS—A digital-simulated analog computing program.

middle punch—Same as eleven punch.

milestone—A task or event that cannot be considered completed until all tasks that feed into it are completed.

millimicrosecond—One thousandth of a millionth of a second. Written symbolically as 10^{-9} seconds.

millisecond—One thousandth of a second (10^{-3} seconds); abbreviated msec. or ms.

MILTRAN—A digital simulation language designed for military applications by Gulton Systems Research Group.

minicard—An Eastman Kodak trademark designating its photographic system for information storage and retrieval.

minimum-access code—A system of coding that minimizes the effect of delays for transfer of data or instructions between storage and other machine components. (Related to optimum code and minimum-latency code.)

minimum-access coding — See coding, minimum access.

minimum-access programming—See programming, minimum access.

minimum-access routine—Same as programming minimum access.

minimum delay coding—Same as coding, minimum-access.

minimum distance code—See code, minimum distance.

minimum-latency code—Same as code, minimum access.

minimum-latency programming — Same as programming minimum access.

minor control—The least significant or lowest category of report grouping of basic detail.

minor control change—When control changes of different levels of significance are used, they can be given distinguishing titles—minor control change, then intermediate, or next major—to establish a hierarchy related to the importance of the data.

minor cycle—The time interval between the appearance of corresponding parts of successive words in a storage device that provides serial access to storage positions.

minuend—The quantity from which another quantity is subtracted or is to be subtracted.

minus zone—The bit positions in a computer code that represent the algebraic minus sign.

MIRFAC — A compiler based on standard mathematical notation and plain English.

MIS—See management information system.

misfeed—When cards, tapes, or other data or storage media fail to pass into or through a device properly. Causes may be damaged, misprogrammed, or missensed input.

misregistration character — The improper state of appearance of a character, in character recognition, with respect to a real or imaginary horizontal base line in a character reader.

misregistration, document — The improper state of appearance of a document, in character recognition, on site in the character reader with reference to a real or imaginary horizontal base line.

misregistration, line—The improper or unacceptable appearance of a line of characters or numerals in optical character recognition, usually guaged with respect to the real or imaginary horizontal baseline.

missing error—Subroutines called by the program were not found in the library. The names of the missing subroutines are also output.

missing unit XX error—A call for a logical XX has been made. The unit was not declared in a usage statement and no driver is in memory to execute the operation.

mistake—A human failing; e.g., faulty arithmetic, use of incorrect formula, or incorrect instructions. Mistakes are sometimes called gross errors to distinguish from rounding and truncation errors. Thus, computers malfunction and humans make mistakes. Computers do not make mistakes and humans do not malfunction, in the strict sense of the word. (Contrasted with error.)

mistake, systems—A human error developed in the creation of instructions, programs, etc.

misuse, error equipment — See error, equipment misuse.

mixed-base notation—A method of expressing a quantity by using two or more characters, where each character is of a different radix.

mixed-base number—A number consisting of two or more characters representing a sum, in which the quantity represented by each character is based on a different radix.

mixed radix—Relates to a numeration system that uses more than one radix, such as the biquinary system.

mixed radix notation—*See* mixed radix number.

mixed-radix number—A number consisting of two or more characters representing a sum, in which the quantity represented by each character is based on a different radix. (Synonymous with mixed-base number.)

mixer, or—*See* OR gate.

mix gate—*Same as* gate, OR.

mix instruction—Specific computer instructions selected to complete particular problems. The optimum mix of instructions determines the speed and accuracy in most cases, and programmers try to achieve this optimum.

ML programmer—That computer programmer who is responsible for writing computer programs in machine language.

mnemonic—Pertaining to or intending to assist the human memory. A mnemonic term is an abbreviation or acronym that is easy to remember.

mnemonic automatic programming—The system features an extensive compiling system which allows for mnemonic expression. Instructions and addresses they refer to can be given alphanumeric names. Compiling in the early stages of program checkout can be accomplished with special aids which include post mortem and register dumping routines. Some of the operators of the system cause several computer instructions to be generated in the final program. A subroutine mechanism facilitates compilation of subroutines in the final program. The compiling system also consists of a high-level language system that allows writing of computer programs using powerful operators that are totally unrelated to machine-code instructions. These operators cause computer instructions to be generated in the final program (some systems).

mnemonic code—A technique to assist the human memory. A mnemonic code resembles the original word and is usually easy to remember; e.g., mpy for multiply and acc for accumulator.

mnemonic instruction—*Same as* codes, mnemonic operation.

mnemonic operation codes—*See* codes, mnemonic operation.

mnemonic symbol—Frequently used symbols for representation of information, selected to assist the memory in recalling meaning, as MPY for multiply.

MOBIDIC—Abbreviation for mobile digital computer, developed by Sylvania Electric Products Company.

MOBILE—A universal, machine-independent, computer language translator.

mod/demod—Abbreviated form for modulating and demodulating units.

mode—1. A method of operation, e.g., the binary mode, the interpretive mode, the alphameric mode, etc. 2. The most frequent value in the statistical sense. 3. The characteristic of a quantity being suitable for integer or for floating-point computation. 4. A method of card reading and punching. There are basically two (a) Hollerith mode; i.e., the normal mode, which reads and punches in this (H) code, and which interprets each column as a six-bit alphanumeric character; and (b) the transcription mode, which interprets each punch as a binary one (1) and each nonpunch as a binary zero (0).

mode, access—Used in COBOL programming, it is the name of a technique to obtain a specific record from, or to place a specific recording in a file contained in a storage device.

mode, alter—A program condition which permits changing or updating data in storage.

mode, analysis—A mode of operation in which special programs monitor the performance of the system for subsequent analysis. Program testing data or statistical data may be automatically recording when the system is running in the analysis mode.

mode, batch-processing—Card systems may have full batch-processing capabilities. Intermixed compilations, assemblies, and executions may be processed in a continuous sequence. The only restriction is that no load-and-go jobs may be processed since no intermediate storage unit is available for binary object programs. For continuous processing, the monitor remains in memory at all times. The compiler, assembler, system loader, (with executive) and utility routines are loaded and executed by the monitor. The monitor itself is loaded into memory by a preset operation. The operations performed upon a program are determined from the absolute binary decks placed in the card reader.

mode, binary—*See* binary mode.

mode, burst—A mode of communications between the processor and I/O devices. When a signal from an I/O device operating through the multiplexor channel indicates burst mode, the receiving unit continues to fetch bits until the unit is finished.

mode, byte—An alternate mode of communications between the processor and I/O devices. Byte mode allows the multiplexor channel to accept data from multiple low-speed devices simultaneously.

mode, card—The status of the computer while cards are being read or punched.

mode, command (remote computing system)—*See* command mode, remote computing system.

mode, compute—Also known as the operate mode, the input signals are connected to the computing units (analog computer), including integrators for the generation of the solution.

mode, conversational—This mode of operation means that real-time man-machine communications are maintained. In this mode the system is used exclusively for servicing remote terminals.

mode, conversational operation — In this mode the system is used exclusively for servicing remote terminals. Real-time man-machine communications are maintained.

mode, freeze—*Same as* hold mode.

mode, hold—*See* hold mode.

mode, inactive (time sharing)—*See* time sharing, inactive mode.

mode, interpretive—In tracing (debugging) routines, when a program is simulated in its execution by using psuedo accumulators and pseudo index registers, branch instructions are inserted at various points to place the machine and program in an interpretative mode for error tracing, and when found, control is transferred back to the main program.

mode, job-program—*See* job program mode.

model—1. Mathematical representation of a process, device, or concept. 2. A general, often pictorial representation of a system being studied.

mode, file—1. The model is an analogue of the processing of files. It can be originated, added to (posting), compared with others, held aside, filed for later use, sent somewhere, and so on. Sets of symbols are the simple analogues for these happenings.

modeling, conceptual—A method of making a model to fit the results of a biological experiment, then conducting another experiment to find out whether the model is right or wrong. The models are created continuously, and are tested and changed in a cyclic manner. The physical sciences have developed through the years in this way, but there has been little use of the approach in biology, mainly because the kind of mathematics that developed is not well suited to biology. But now computers can get around this problem, and the important technique of conceptual modeling is beginning to be used in biology, business, psychology, sociology, etc.

model, mathematical—The general characterization of a process, object, or concept, in terms of mathematics, thus enabling the relatively simple manipulation of variables to be accomplished in order to determine how the process, object, or concept would behave in different situations.

mode, load—In load mode data transmission is such that data delimiters are carried along with the data transmitted, as in contrast with move mode.

mode, locate—A specific method of communicating with an input/output control system (IOCS) by using a method in which the address of the data involved, but not the data themselves, is transferred between the (IOCS) routine and the program. The programmer is spared being forced to incorporate detailed, machine-level I/O logic in every one of his routines, since IOCS in

memory communicates with the running program and performs I/O as directed by the program. But, locate mode operations require that the computer be equipped with index registers or base registers which enable run-time address computation to proceed while individual computer instructions are being interpreted.

model, pilot—A model of a system that is not so complex as a complete model and is used for program testing.

model, process—*Same as* model, process control.

model, process-control—The processor controller rapidly collects the work or processing data that is necessary for the development of a model of the process. The model is developed by using a combination of empirical techniques and observing past methods of running the process. When a more complete and more precise description of the process is required, a model is constructed by using such mathematical techniques as correlation analysis and regression analysis. The process-control program is then tested on the mathematical model prior to its use on the process. Extensive operator information is obtained. In addition, the model represents considerable progress toward complete supervisory control.

models, utility—After the installation has been completed, the utility model of the system continues to be useful. It provides a basis for restudy to improve the system. It provides a basis for system changes necessitated by changing business conditions and new demands by management. The model provides a starting point for studies to extend electronic processes to new areas of application.

The model does not stand entirely unsupported. Diagrams of the organization of input items and magnetic-tape records, of memory-space allocations, index-register assignments, documents to be produced, narrative discussion of the system, and perhaps other types of information are necessary to complete the documentation. The model ties all of these together into a single, unified system, by the use of math and symbols.

model symbols—The symbols such as squares, circles, etc., convey no information and must be labeled. They localize a point of interest, but convey only the most general notion of intent. The finished model must include adequate description with each symbol to explain what the operation does. Liberal use of foot-notes is recommended to explain the "why" of operations which are not straightforward.

MODEM—1. Acronym for MOdulator DEModular unit. 2. A MODEM is a device that converts data from a form which is compatible with data-processing equipment to a form that is compatible with transmission facilities, and vice-versa.

mode, manual—The condition existing when all automatic features are off and the computer is prepared to accept operator instructions directly from the control console.

mode, mapping—The mode of computer operation in which virtual addresses above 15 are transformed through the memory map so that they become references to actual core memory locations (some computers).

mode, master—The mode of computer operation in which all legal SIGMA operations are permissible.

mode, master/slave (multiprogramming) — This feature guarantees that one program cannot damage or access another program sharing memory. The unique operating technique in changing from slave to master mode makes multiprogramming not only practical, but foolproof.

mode, move—The movement of records to be read or written into and out of program-designated storage areas in an input/output control system (IOCS). This is opposite of the locate mode, in which the data records stay in place, and only the addresses of the data areas are used in communication. Index or base registers are not required for move mode operations.

mode, multiplex — See multiplexor channel operation.

mode, noisy—A floating-point arithmetic procedure associated with normalization in which "1" bits, rather than "0" bits, are introduced in the low-order bit position during the left shift.

mode, nonmapping—The mode of computer operation in which virtual addresses are not transformed through a memory map, i.e., the virtual address is used as an actual address.

mode, off-line — Means that the devices are not hooked up together. Perhaps the printer is printing the payroll checks, while the computer is solving a completely unrelated mathematical problem. Both are independent operations.

mode, on-line — Means that all devices are hooked up directly, say with the computer. Although the devices work on different phases of the procedure, all are connected in some way and usually depend on each other for desired results.

mode, operate—Same as mode, compute.

mode, operational—The combination of machine operating modes currently in effect.

mode, point display—See display, point mode.

mode, program (remote-control system)—See program mode (remote control system).

mode, ready (time sharing)—See time sharing, ready mode.

mode, real-time—Real-time is a mode of operation in which data that are necessary to the control and/or execution of a transaction can be processed in time for the transaction to be affected by the results of the processing. Real-time processing is most usually identified with great speed, but speed is rela-

tive. The essence of real time is concurrency —simultaneity. Real-time is refinement in the integration of data processing with communications. Real-time eliminates slow information-gathering procedures, dated reporting techniques and lax communications; insures that facts within the system are as timely as a prevailing situation, as current as the decisions which they must support. Real-time provides answers when answers are needed, delivers data instantly whenever the need for that data arises. Incoming information is edited, updated and made available on demand at every level of responsibility. Imminent departures from established standards are automatically detected, and management is notified in time for action.

mode, real-time guard—See guard mode, real-time.

mode, recording—In the COBOL system, the representation in external media of data associated with a data-processing system.

mode, reset—In analog computing, the integrators are inoperative, and the required initial conditions are applied or reapplied, as contrasted to the operate mode.

modes, communication—Each channel is capable of operating in three different communication modes: input, output, or function. The input and output modes are employed when transferring data to or from the central computer. The function mode is the means by which the central computer establishes the initial communication path with a peripheral subsystem. During this mode of transmission, the central computer sends one or more function words to a peripheral subsystem. These function words direct the units to perform the desired operation (some computers).

modes, display—Each display that is made, such as vector, increment, character, point, vector continue, or short vector, specifies the manner in which points are to be displayed on the screen.

mode, service—An operational mode for the handling of malfunctions or errors in words, etc.

mode, slave — The mode of computer operation in which most of the basic controls affecting the state of the computer are protected from the program.

modes, master/slave, (time-sharing) — See time sharing, master/slave modes.

modes of priority — The organization of the flow of work through a computer. The mode depends upon the sophistication of the system and the machine, and will vary from a normal noninterrupt mode to a system in which there are several depths of interrupt. There also may be different modes in different functions such as the I/O mode.

mode, supervisor — A mode of operation under which certain operations, such as memory-protection modification instructions, and input/output operations, are permitted.

modes, user (time sharing)—*See* time sharing, user modes.

mode, training—The training of terminal operators and the testing of a system in which normal operations are defined and carried on by the operator, in which he is encouraged to enter all types of transactions from normal to exceptional. The randomness and inventiveness of the input operator is used to check the formal test input and any inconsistancies.

mode, trapping—A scheme used mainly in program-diagnostic procedures for certain computers. If the trapping mode flip-flop is set and the program includes any one of certain instructions, the instruction is not performed but the next instruction is taken from location O. Program-counter contents are saved in order to resume the program after executing the diagnostic procedure.

mode, vector—*See* vector mode.

mode, vector continue-display — *See* vector continue mode (display).

modification—The changing of one or more words or parts of words, called modifiers or index words, which are added to the presumptive instruction by means of an arithmetical or a logical operation.

modification, address—*See* address modification.

modification and testing, program preparation—*See* program preparation.

modification instruction — *See* instruction modification.

modification program—The ability of a program to modify itself or to set a switch so that a set of events occurring at one time can effect the action of program at a later time.

modifier—A quantity used to alter the address of an operand; e.g., the cycle index.

modifier register—*Same as* index register.

modifier storage—*Same as* register B.

modify—1. To alter a portion of an instruction so its interpretation and execution will be other than normal. The modification may permanently change the instruction or leave it unchanged and affect only the current execution. The most frequent modification is that of the effective address through use of index registers. 2. To alter a subroutine according to a defined parameter.

modify instruction—An instruction that will most likely be modified before it is used for the final program.

modular—A degree of standardization of computer-system components to allow for combinations and large variety of compatible units.

modularity—1. A condition in the determination of the design of the equipment and programming systems such that the hardware and software components can be readily identified, altered, or augmented without replacements of particular units or sections. 2. Operating system programs conform to specific standards, so that control programs will have an identical interface with all processing programs. These standards are well documented so that user-written programs can follow the same conventions. The user is free to supplement supplied programs to meet special situations. By following the rules indicated in the standards, portions of control or processing programs can be changed or replaced in modular fashion.

modularity, functional—Addition of modules to a basic data-processing system, thus broadening the scope or concept of the system as well as adding capacity.

modularity, processing—Modularity accommodates widely varying off-line data-processing characteristics and workloads. There are several-thousand possible combinations of magnetic core, disk file, and input/output equipment for off-line processing requirements—exclusive of the total modularity of the teller console/communications network, and of the greatly expanded computing power combinations possible in a multiple processor system. The user benefits from the ability to install an initial equipment complement adequate for today's needs, with easy growth potential to cope with future needs as they arise, because the system units are modular, i.e., new units will fit and combine with present "modules" (units).

modularity, program-independent — Defined as the property of a system which allows it to accept changes and adjust processing accordingly to yield maximum utilization of all modules without reprogramming. This system is used in multiprocessing. To achieve this objective, the computer systems incorporate master control programs to exercise an unprecedented degree of automatic control.

modularity, software—The outstanding modularity and resultant flexibility of hardware have their parallels in the programming and operating aids furnished with the systems. Most types of programs in the software library are offered in several versions to run in systems configurations of different sizes and compositions. In particular, it is important to note that software versions written for large systems are designed to take advantage of the increased internal and input/output processing capacities of these systems. In addition, the majority of software programs utilizing punched cards are also implemented for punched paper tape. Furthermore, a comprehensive array of random-access software is often provided, and separate versions of many programs allow their use in either $\frac{1}{2}$ or $\frac{3}{4}$-inch magnetic-tape systems.

module — 1. A segment of core storage. 2. A piece of peripheral equipment with specific capacity for storage (memory). 3. An interchangeable plug-in item containing components. 4. An incremental block of storage or other building block for expanding the computer capacity.

module access, multiple—*See* multiple module access.

module checking—*Same as* module testing.

module dissipation—The dissipation of the module calculated from the voltage-current product, plus an allowance for transistor dissipation for load currents being supplied to other modules.

module, input/output control—*See* input/output control module.

module, load—*See* load module.

module, memory—*See* memory module.

module, object — A program in instruction form which is the output of a compiler and is equipped with control information to aid or modify the linkage editor, i.e., the object module must be operated on by the linkage editor, except in the TSS/360 which permits the module to be loaded and executed directly. The instructions and data of the object module are contained in the text or body of the module.

module, programming — *See* programming module.

module testing—The destructive read-off or use caused by overloading or underloading the computer components, causing failure of substandard units and thereby minimizing nonscheduled downtime.

modulo—A mathematical operation that yields the remainder function of division. Thus 39 modulo 6 = 3.

modulo N check—1. A check that makes use of a check number that is equal to the remainder of the desired number when divided by N; e.g., in a modulo 4 check, the check number will be 0, 1, 2, or 3 and the remainder of A when divided by 4 must equal the reported check number B; otherwise an equipment malfunction has occurred. 2. A method of verification by congruences, e.g., casting out nines. (Related to self-checking number.)

modulo-N count—*See* count, modulo-N.

modulo-N counter—*See* counter, modulo-N.

modulo-N residue — The remainder from a division of a number by another number, i.e., the residue for 58 modulo-8 is 2 since 58 divided by 8 is 7 with a remainder of 2.

modulo-two sum gate—*Same as* gate, exclusive OR.

MOL—An abbreviation for machine oriented language.

monadic Boolean operation—A specific Boolean operation on only a single operand.

monadic operation—An operation on one operand, e.g., negation. (Synonymous with unitary operation.)

monitor—1. To control the operation of several unrelated routines and machine runs so that the computer and computer time are used advantageously. 2. To test, check, or sequence; i.e., supervise the operation of a computer; a master schedule. 3. The specific program to schedule and control the operation of several related or unrelated routines that are part of the schedule of machine runs so that the computer time is efficiently utilized. A monitor program may or may not be designed to operate in real-time.

monitor control dump — *See* dump, monitor-control.

monitor, DAC-1—This system provides: 1. a table which contains the location and size of each subroutine in memory; 2. a table which contains the location and size of all global variables in memory; 3. the basic codes required to retrieve programs and data stored in the auxiliary disk and drum; and 4. a relocation program which, when given data in the form of a subroutine in memory, will relocate the subroutine and assign memory addresses to its variable tables mentioned in 1 and 2.

monitor displays—A monitor display is owned by the Federal Aviation Agency as part of Burroughs AN/FYQ-40 Common Digitizer for use in the National Airspace System. The Common Digitizer is designed to process raw video and beacon target information as part of the computerized air-traffic control system.

The monitor display provides a radar-type presentation of the significant steps during target processing and related data on a cathode-ray tube for system monitoring under test conditions and for Common Digitizer maintenance. The monitor is unique in that it operates in either a random-access plan-position indicator (RAPPI) mode or a plan-position indicator (PPI) mode. It provides the ability to monitor the entire system in discrete steps in real time. (Burroughs)

monitored instructions—As indicated in the input/output instruction repertoire, instructions called for input, output, or function transfers may be executed either with or without a monitor. With a monitor means that upon completion of the transfer, an internal interrupt will be generated. When an instruction is executed without a monitor, the interrupt is inhibited. The programmer generally determines whether an instruction is to be programmed with or without a monitor. In some cases, however, the use of the monitor may be dictated by the particular operation.

monitor, job-processing — *See* job processing monitor.

monitor (job process termination)—The programmer specifies monitor system operations with control statements. These may be input via a console typewriter or included with the program on cards, paper tape, or magnetic tape. Programs are processed automatically on a job basis. A job may consist of compilations, assemblies, executions, utility requests, editing, and program segmenting. Intermixed jobs are automatically processed in sequence by the monitor system. Programs terminate by returning control to the system. A job may be terminated by the operator or the monitor system. When a job terminates, processing of the next job is automatically initiated.

monitor operating system—The monitor exercises primary control of the routines that compose the operating system. It is this operating system which turns the computer into a flexible tool allowing the user to achieve maximum use of the hardware's advanced design features.

monitor, output interrupt—*See* output monitor interrupt.

monitor overlays—*See* overlays, monitor.

monitor program—A specific program developed to indicate the progress and other characteristics of work in various computer systems.

monitor, real-time—The executive system is an operating and programming system designed to monitor the construction and execution of programs, to optimize the utilization of available hardware, and to minimize programmer effort and operator intervention. The executive system, as a monitor, provides for concurrent processing and real-time operation in a classical monitor environment. The executive system is of modular construction, tailored to each user's equipment configuration and applications requirements. Extensions to the system for peripheral devices and application programs may be added, altered, or deleted as required.

monitor, remote-computing system—When the computer is available for batch processing, the computer operator will indicate to a subsystem under the system monitor that files on the auxiliary disk-storage device are to be processed. Under control of the subsystem, the files will be transferred from disk-storage or tape, which is then used as the system-input unit for normal processing under the system monitor. The result of this processing, which is contained on the system output unit, can be handled in either of the following ways: 1. it can be transferred to disk storage for subsequent transmission to a terminal, or 2. it can be printed on an off-line printer and mailed to the terminal.

monitor routine—*See* executive routine.

monitor, sequence—*See* sequence monitor.

monitor system—*Same as* executive system.

monitor system components—The monitor system is composed of a series of individual programs that work together to form a complete operating system. Manuals describe the total monitor system. They also contain a complete description of the primary operating system routines—the monitor program, executive program, system loader, system-preparation routine, and input/output routines. The EXTENDED FORTRAN compiler, assembles, utility routines, and library subroutines are described in the sense in which they are used as part of the monitor system. The complete descriptions of these routines are provided in separate documents. The words "monitor system," "operating system," and "system" are used interchangeably in manuals, and refer to the monitor system.

monitor system, time-sharing—*See* time-sharing monitor system.

monitor tape, system—This is a monitor program that allows for the centralized control of program operation. It provides a load-and-go operation with one magnetic-tape unit without operator intervention. The operator can specify loading and execution of any program on the master system tape by a simple on-line typewriter directive.

monitor, time-sharing—*See* time-sharing monitor.

monitor, typewriter console—*See* typewriter, console monitor.

monitor unit—A device which is supervisory and which is capable of verifying the operation of another device or group in data processing systems, production automation systems, message routing systems, etc. When significant departure from the normal procedures, measurements or guides (criteria) occur, the state of the system is observed, measured, and operators alerted or various departures corrected.

monorobot—A small accounting or data processing system developed by Monroe Calculating Machine Company, Inc., a division of Litton Industries.

monostable—Pertaining to a device that has one stable state.

Monte-Carlo method—1. Any procedure that involves statistical sampling techniques in order to obtain a probabilistic approximation to the solution of a mathematical or physical problem. 2. The branch of linguistic study which deals with the history and functions of derivational forms and inflections.

MO register—Multiple-quotient register.

morpheme—An element of language which relates and connects images or ideas in sentences; i.e., the relation between a noun and a verb.

morphology—The branch of linguistic study that deals with the history and functions of derivational forms and inflections.

mortem, post—*See* post mortem.

most significant character—The character in the left-most position in a number or word.

most significant digit (MSD)—The significant digit contributing the largest quantity to the value of a numeral, i.e., the left-most digit.

motion register—This two-bit register contains a go/stop flip-flop and a forward/reverse flip-flop which control the motion of the selected tape drive. The register is set under program control.

m out of n code—A form of fixed-weight binary code in which m of the n digits are always in the same state.

movable random access—*See* random access, movable.

move mode—*See* mode, move.

move, numeric—*See* numeric move.

moving arm disk—*See* disk moving arm.

M-Q register—A register which is treated as an extension of the accumulator register in multiply and divide operations. *Same as* the extension register.

M-register mask—The mask of M-register holds the mask word used in masked search instructions. It is the responsibility of the programmer to load this address with the mask word before programming masked search instructions. The word format for the M-register is the same as that of the basic data word.

MRT (master relocatable tape)—A Honeywell routine that contains checked-out programs to be scheduled by executive for production operation.

MSC—Most significant character (left-most).

MSD—Most significant digit (left-most).

MT—An abbreviation for mechanical translation, and machine translation.

multiaccess computing — This implies that more than one identical input/output terminal may be directly used with the system. Usually, they are remote, such as teletype or other typewriter-like units, or cathode-ray-tube types in the more modern systems.

multiaddress—1. A type of instruction that specifies the addresses of two or more items which may be the addresses of locations of inputs or outputs of the calculating unit, or the addresses of locations of instructions for the control unit. The term multiaddress is also used in characterizing computers, e.g., two-, three-, or four-address machines. 2. Relates to an instruction that has more than one address part.

multiaddress instruction—*See* multiaddress.

multiaspect—Pertaining to searches or systems that permit more than one aspect or facet of information to be used in combination, one with the other, to effect identifying and selecting operations.

multicomputer—A computing system in which there are many arithmetic and logic units, most often operating in parallel and on the same program, but also possible and probable on several programs. The term also relates to computer systems with several mainframes.

multicomputing, real-time—Real-time command and control situations requiring maximum reliability can combine two or more computers in multicomputer systems. Two or more essentially independent computing systems communicate directly, with access to each other's memory. Capable of tremendous computing power, such systems have the added advantage of reserve equipment. Typical real-time applications demanding this degree of reliability include manned-space vehicle launching, and airport traffic control.

The concept of individual modules for processor, memory, and controller provides multiprocessor and multicomputer systems with multiple functions without undue duplication of hardware.

multicomputing unit—A computer with multiple arithmetic and logic units for simultaneous use and capability.

multicycle feeding — A specific method of processing punched cards during which several fields of an individual card are read in succession on successive machine cycles, e.g., multiread feeding achieves the result by feeding the same card past the reading station several times.

multifile sorting—The automatic sequencing of more than one file, based upon separate parameters for each file, without operator intervention.

multifont optical arena—Basic character reading equipment, having the ability to discern many fonts or formats of characters, usually from hard copy.

multilevel address—*Same as* indirect address.

multilevel subroutining (display) — The control state permits the display to jump from accessing one location in the memory to any other. When it is desired to jump to a display subroutine, the return address is automatically stored in a push-down list.

multipass sort—A sort program designed to sort more data than can be contained within the internal memory of a central computer. Intermediate storage, such as disk, tape, drum, is required.

multiple—A system of wiring so arranged that a circuit, a line, or a group of lines is accessible at a number of points, to any one of which a connection can be made.

multiple access—Reference to a system from which output or input can be received or dispatched from more than one location.

multiple access computer (MAC) — The first large time-sharing system developed in the U.S. at MIT, Massachusetts Institute of Technology.

multiple accumulating registers — Additional little storehouses within the computer that can contain loading, storing, adding, subtracting and comparing factors up to four (computer) words in length.

multiple address—*See* multiaddress.

multiple-address code — *See* code, multiple address.

multiple-address computers — Computers in which the instruction word contains more than one address. For example, the National Bureau of Standards' SWAC is a four-address machine, as is the Raytheon Mfg. Co.'s RAYDAC. In such a machine, three addresses are used, and a fourth gives the location of the next instruction word.

multiple-address instruction—*Same as* multiaddress.

multiple address message—A group of words to be delivered to more than one address, as coded for more rapid, less repetitious communication.

mulitple arithmetic—*See* arithmetic, multiple.

multiple-aspect, indexing—*See* indexing, manipulative.

multiple-computer operation—*See* computer, multiple operation.

multiple connector—A connector to indicate the merging of several lines of flow into one line, or the dispersal of one line to flow into several lines.

multiple graphs — More than one graph plotted, utilizing a set or sets of data. Thus, a set of data may furnish data required for plotting more than one graph.

multiple index addressing, time-sharing—*See* time sharing, multiple index addressing.

multiple I/O channels, time-sharing — *See* time sharing, multiple I/O channels.

multiple-length number — A number having two, three, or more times as many figures as are normally handled in a particular device.

multiple-length numeral—*See* numeral, multiple-length.

multiple-length working—Refers to the use of two or more machine words to represent a number, and to thus increase precision, i.e., the use of double-length procedures, double precision, etc.

multiple module access (MMA)—In a multiprocessor system, an MMA unit is positioned between each storage module and the several processors which may reference it to resolve potential storage-access conflicts. This unit furnishes five priority-ordered processor connection paths. Should an access conflict occur between processors, the MMA will grant storage access to the processor having the relative highest priority attachment to the MMA, then to the next, and so on. Communications between processors and a single storage module can therefore be conducted on an aschronous basis—if the storage module is "busy" servicing one processor, a passive wait cycle is induced in others of lower priority that may be referencing it.

multiple operations — The characteristic of being able to perform two or more computer processes concurrently.

multiple precision—The use of two or more computer words to represent a single numeric quantity or numeral, i.e., with twice as many or more digits as are normally carried in a fixed-length word.

multiple precision arithmetic — A feature of the computer system which allows more than one word to be used to accomodate a quality expressed in more than one word length; this avoids the cutoff of a lesser significant digit.

multiple programming—The programming of a computer by allowing two or more arithmetical or logical operations to be executed simultaneously. (Contrasted with serial programming.)

multiple punch—*See* punch, multiple.

multiple punching—1. The reference to punch cards and more specifically to Hollerith cards. 2. The punching of two or more holes in a column.

multiple regression—An efficient analysis program for determining the mathematical relationships and relative significances of manufacturing parameters associated with a given problem.

multiple station, high-speed communications —A number of high-speed stations can be connected to a CTS (communication terminal station), one at a time over direct distance dialing (DDD) network circuits. Dial-network operation permits data exchange between any two subscriber locations, beginning with a connection procedure (dial) and ending with a disconnect procedure (hang up). Transfers may be initiated by either the CTS or the remote station. If the CTS initiates the transfer, the connection will be made automatically by the central processor through the automatic-calling option available on the CTS. The remote station will automatically answer the call and data transfer can commence. If the remote station initiates the call, the CTS will automatically answer the call utilizing the unattended answering option. Data transfers can then take place in the normal manner. All data transfers over dial high-speed circuits will be at maximum transfer rate. (250 characters per second.)

multiple utility—Allows one to three utility operations to be performed simultaneously. The operations which can be performed are: card-to-tape, tape-to-printer, and tape-to-card. Any combination of utility operations may be initially selected.

multiplex — The process of transferring data from several storage devices operating at relatively low transfer rates to one storage device operating at a high transfer rate in such a manner that the high-speed device is not obliged to "wait" for the low-speed units.

multiplex data terminal—A device that modulates and/or demodulates data between two or more input/output devices and a data transmission link.

multiplexed analog-to-digital converter type —Some multiplexer controls permit up to 64 channels of analog information to be applied singly to the input of the analog-to-digital converter. Channels can be selected in sequence or by individual addresses.

multiplexed operation — A simultaneous operation which shares the use of a common unit of a system in such a way that it can be considered an independent operation.

multiplexer communication—*See* communication multiplexer.

multiplexer, data channel—The multiplexer expands the data-break facilities of the computer to allow large numbers of input/output devices to transfer data directly with the core memory, via the memory buffer register. Simultaneous data-break requests are serviced by the multiplexer according to pre-wired priority.

multiplexer IOP—An input/output processing unit that is capable of performing bidirectional data transfer between core memory and standard-speed peripheral devices, with up to 32 such devices operating concurrently (some computers).

multiplexer[1], magnetic-core—The magnetic-core multiplexer is the equivalent of a multiple-multiposition stepping switch wherein several multibit inputs are commutated to a single output. The device is particularly suited for the handling of digital data. It consists of cores and windings arranged in rows and columns, one magnetic core being designed for each input bit. Due to the size and nature of magnetic tape cores, the multiplexer may be made extremely rugged and compact, can be of virtually unlimited capacity, and consumes relatively little power. Although specifications are given for a typical appliaction, input and output parameters can be tailored to fit almost any situation (some systems).

multiplexer[1], priority communications—The communication multiplexer contains priority logic which enables it to determine, on a priority basis, which CLT (communications line terminal) in the subsystem should be serviced first. Thirteen microseconds elapse from the time the communication multiplexer is freed from its previous CLT, by receiving either an input-acknowledge or an output-acknowledge signal from the central processor, until it is able to make the next input-data request or output-data request. During this 13-microsecond interval, the communication multiplexer must analyze the status of all CLTs in the subsystem, determine which CLT requesting service is connected to the highest number multiplexer position, and perform all of the necessary switching to permit the data transfer (some systems).

multiplexer simulation — A testing program which simulates the multiplexer.

multiplex mode — *See* multiplexer channel operation.

multiplex, multichannel—Use of a common channel in order to make two or more channels, either by splitting of the frequency band transmitted by the common channel into narrower bands, each of which is used to constitute a distinct channel (frequency-division, multiplex), or by allotting this common channel in turn, to constitute different intermittent channels (time-division multiplex).

multiplexor[1]—A specialized computer, with stored program capability, for handling input/output functions of a real-time system.

multiplexor, burst mode—The multiplexor channel can service high-speed devices by operating in burst mode. In burst mode, the

I/O unit keeps control of the multiplexor channel until the I/O unit has completed its operation. Thus when operating in burst mode, a single I/O device captures the complete multiplexor channel data path and does not relinquish it from the time it is selected until the last byte is serviced.

multiplexor[1] channel—These are the configurations which will most effectively be used to control card-read punches, printers, and communications terminals. The multiplexor channel allows attachment of up to eight data-communication units. Up to 31 communications lines can be attached to each of these units, and literally hundreds of terminals can be attached to each of the communications lines. In place of the communications lines, printers, card units, and data terminals can be attached to the multiplexor channel. The multiplexor channel resolves the high speed of the processor with slower input and output equipment by permitting many input or output devices to communicate simultaneously with the processor. The multiplexor channel receives a message from an input unit one character at a time in its usual method of operation. In between these characters, the multiplexor channel sandwiches a character from each of the other units that also want to communicate with the processing unit. There can be up to 248 messages interleaved together on this channel. Operating in this fashion, the channel will transfer up to 40,000 characters a second between the processor and any one peripheral unit. All messages are tagged and are separated and assembled within storage by unit-control words. Only after being assembled is the message actually serviced by the processing unit. Outgoing messages are tagged so that they are directed to the proper peripheral unit. This channel produces a time-sharing effect, so that many terminals are being served although each terminal appears to have the processor to itself (some systems).

multiplexor[1] channel, mode — The multiplexor channel, a completely new concept in data channels, separates the operations of high-speed devices from those of lower-speed devices. Operations on the channel are in two modes: a "multiplex" mode for lower-data rates, and a "burst" mode for the higher.

In the multiplex mode, the single data path of the channel can be time shared by a large number of low-speed I/O devices operating simultaneously; the channel receives and sends data to them on demand. When operating in the burst mode, however, a single I/O device captures the multiplexor channel and does not relinquish it from the time it is selected until the last byte is serviced (some systems).

multiplexor[1] channel operation—Multiplexor channel operation is the key to matching the computer's speed with economic data flow

---

[1]The terms multiplexer and multiplexor are used by different manufacturers to denote the same or similar meaning.

from teleprocessing terminals. It permits simultaneous message flow among as many as 248 lines. The channel accepts a one-character portion of a message from each communication line at a time. It scans from line to line, interrogating all active lines. The interrogation cycle—which takes place in millionths of a second—is repeated until all messages are completed. Inside the computer, messages are properly assembled into separate main storage areas under the control of the multiplexor itself. The processor continues to operate on a batch program until the message is completely composed. At the end of message signal, the channel signals for an interrupt. When the interrupt is recognized as a communications request, the proper teleprocessing program is called to provide the required service. The multiplexor channel can operate like a selector channel in "burst" mode. This limits the channel to one line at a time but increases the data flow to 200,000 characters a second (some systems).

multiplexor[1] terminal unit—Through the use of a multiplexor terminal unit, the system (communications) can connect, via four transmission lines, up to 98 terminal stations to and from the central processor. The processor controls all transmission sequences to and from terminal stations, performs, checks and handles the required visual displays and printers which can also be attached to the processor. They convert signals between the process communication system and the devices in the process. The transmission of data to or from the terminal stations is performed on multidrop transmission channels in half-duplex mode, and is buffered into the processor for greater system efficiency.

multiplex, time-division—A system in which a channel is established by intermittently connecting its terminal equipment to a common channel, generally at regular intervals and by means of an automatic distribution. Outside the times during which these connections are established, the section of the common channel between the distributors can be utilized in order to establish other similar channels in turn.

multiplicand—The quantity that is multiplied by another quantity.

multiplication table—A specific area of storage that holds the groups of numbers to be used during the tabular scanning of the multiplication operation.

multiplication time — The time required to perform a multiplication. For a binary number it will be equal to the total of all the addition times and all the shift time involved in the multiplication.

multiplier—The quantity that is used to multiply another quantity.

multiplier, analog—The analog device which develops the analog product from two or more analog input signals, i.e., the output

variable is proportional to the product of the input variables.

multiplier coefficient unit — *Same as* scaler quantity.

multiplier, digital—*See* digital multiplier.

multiplier factor—In multiplication, when the method of performance makes a distinction between two factors, they are called the multiplier factor and the multiplicand.

multiplier, function — A device causing the generation of a continuously varying analog representation of a product of two continuously varying analog input signals, as particular independent variables, i.e., time or distance change.

multiplier, mark-space — A specific analog multiplier in which one input variable, which is represented as a current or a voltage, is used to control the mark-to-space ratio of a repetitive rectangular wave and whose amplitude is made proportional to the other variable, which is also represented by a voltage or a current.

multiplier-quotient register — A register in which the multiplier for multiplication is placed, and in which the quotient for division is developed.

multiplier unit, digital—*See* digital multiplier unit.

multiply field—A designated field in a character unit used to hold the results of the multiplication operation. The field capacity must exceed by one character the number of characters required in the multiplier and multiplicand fields.

multiplying punch—*Same as* punch, calculating.

multiply, logic—*See* logic multiply.

multiply, logical—1. A logical operator which has the property that if P is a statement and Q is a statement, then P AND Q is true if both statements are true, false if either is false or both are false. Truth is normally expressed by the value 1, falsity by 0. The AND operator is often represented by a centered dot (P·Q), by no sign (PQ), by an inverted "u" or logical product symbol (P∩Q), or by the letter "x" or multiplication symbol (P×Q). Note that the letters AND are capitalized to differentiate between the logical operator AND, and the word *and* in common usage. 2. The logical operator that makes use of the AND operator or logical product. (Synonymous with logical multiply AND, and clarified by conjunction.)

multiply operation—An arithmetic operation in which the operands are factors and the result is the product, as obtained by adding the multiplicand the number of times specified by the multiplier.

multipoint circuit—A circuit interconnecting several that must communicate on a time-shared basis.

multiprecision arithmetic—A form of arithmetic similar to double-precision arithmetic except that two or more words may be used to represent each number.

multipriority—A quip or queue of items waiting for processing. The queue is made up of items of different priorities and in effect is a queue of queues.

multiprocessing—1. The utilization of several computers to logically or functionally divide jobs or processes, and to execute various programs or segments asynchronously and simultaneously. 2. Two or more processors in a system configuration; one processor to control the system, with the others subordinate to it. All processors have direct access to all memory; each can perform computations and request input/output on individual programs stored in system core memory. Devices request memory access and wait until memory is available. They start immediately upon receipt of a memory access, and need not wait for the next clock cycle.

multiprocessing efficiency—Two or more processors are put in the system configuration. One processor is assigned to control the system, with the others subordinate to it. All processors have direct access to all memory; each can perform computations and request input/output on individual programs stored in system core memory. Multiprocessing is more economical. Throughput and reliability are retained without resorting to interconnection of multiple computers with redundant unused circuits.

multiprocessing, executive system—*See* executive system multiprogramming.

multiprocessing mass-data—Multiprocessor systems handle vast masses of general-purpose data. Handling scientific, engineering, and business data with equal ease, such a system tied into coast-to-coast communications network gives a consolidated data-processing operation. Two or more processors, each with direct access to banks of common memory, continuously process a conventional work load, and provide answers to special projects, such as product analysis, market research, site analysis, and operations research. The total system is under executive control of one processor. This results in the most efficient use of the expensive central processor and is the basis for time-sharing of single processors among multiple users, each processor having access to the mass data memories of each other's system.

multiprocessing, sharing—The design of a system permits communications between individual processors by several means. The processors may share a control unit connected to a file device so that information may be communicated through the file. On all models a channel-to-channel adapter may interconnect two system channels. Shared-processor storage enables two interconnected processors to share main storage. Two processors may communicate through shared large-capacity core storage. A direct-control feature can be used to signal directly from one processor to another. This feature would not, in general, be used to transfer any volume of data, but only to set up conditions for an interrupt of the processor receiving the signal.

multiprocessing system—A system that is organized to contain two or more interconnected computers, but which perform functionally or geographically specialized processing tasks.

multiprocessor—A computer with multiple arithmetic and logic units for simultaneous use and capability.

multiprocessor interleaving—Interleaving is a special process of addressing adjacent storage modules in an even/odd fashion. It significantly reduces storage-access conflicts in a multiprocessor system, and thereby increases overall system performance. With interleaving, the modules are divided into even and odd locations (although the addressing structure within the modules themselves remains unchanged). Thus, in a fully-expanded eight module system, modules 0, 2, 4, 6 are referenced for even addresses while modules 1, 3, 5, 7 are referenced for odd addresses.

multiprocessor, overlapping—The processor is capable of determining whether its current operand and next instruction lie in different storage modules. It is also capable, if this situation is present, of retrieving these two words in parallel, at an effective 100% performance increase. Since the I/O controller is not required to reference instructions in main storage except on command transfers, it does not have, nor does it need, the overlapping feature. The overlapping feature permits the separation of the instruction and data of a program into separate physical banks. Furthermore, the basing register of the processor allows either the instruction or data area of a program to be relocated independently—a significant advantage in core compacting to overcome fragmentation.

multiprogramming—A technique for handling numerous routines or programs simultaneously by overlapping or interleaving their execution; i.e., permitting more than one program to time-share machine components.

multiprogramming, degree of—Refers to the number of transactions handled in parallel by the systems involved in a multi-program.

multiprogramming efficiency — The computers use multiprogramming to reduce turn-around time, increase computations per dollar, and increase equipment use. They can process several programs concurrently, with all input/output operations totally overlapped.

The method of multiprogramming minimizes the times when a processor waits for peripherals and vice versa. An object programmer never has to be concerned with anything except his own problem. The mechanics of sophisticated use and operation are handled automatically by the operating supervisor and the hardware.

multiprogramming, executive control — See executive control multiprogramming.

multiprogramming (executive control logic) —See executive control logic, multiprogramming.

multiprogramming, executive-system — See executive system multiprogramming.

multiprogramming (internal function register)—See register, internal function.

multiprogramming interrupts—Some computers are equipped with a set of control signals which are referred to as interrupts. Whenever certain conditions exist, a control signal will direct the central computer to execute the word (instruction) at a specified address in central store. Each interrupt is activated by unique conditions and directs the computer to a correspondingly unique address in central store. The occurrence of an interrupt terminates guard mode, program lockin, and central-store address assignments.

multiprogramming memory protect — This hardware function provides positive protection to the system executive routine and all other programs. It not only protects against processor execution, but also against I/O data area destruction. Because it is a hardware function rather than software, it reduces multiprogramming complexities.

multiprogramming, priority — Priority multiprogramming is oriented toward concurrent operation of several types of applications. Assignment of priority levels is at the discretion of the user. For example, one priority level can be reserved for a program that must provide rapid responses to real-time devices, such as communications control. Another can be reserved for the peripheral control package to accomplish several media conversions —card to tape, tape to printer, etc. The third priority level could then be used to run either a production or a monitor job.

multiprogramming, program competition— One of the major ways in which operational efficiency is achieved in the system is by multiprogramming. Multiprogramming is a process by which several related or unrelated programs or portions of programs are performed concurrently, provided that enough processing, storage, and input/output facilities are available. While one program is awaiting an occurrence, such as the completion of an input/output operation or the end of a time interval, control of the processing unit is directed to another program in accordance with a pre-established order of priority. The competition among several programs for the processing, storage, input/output, and programming facilities of the system helps to ensure that as much of the system as possible is kept busy performing useful work as much of the time as possible. As a result, the total throughput of the system, that is, the total volume of work performed by the system during a given interval of time, is significantly increased.

The design provides facilities for the efficient allocation, scheduling, and dispatching of processing unit control, storage, and input/output among programs being performed concurrently. Facilities are also provided in the design for protecting one program from destruction or interference by another program.

multiprogramming, store protection — Existence in a multiprogram environment requires that each program be protected against all contemporary programs, and in particular, that each program have inviolate storage areas. This is accomplished by independently establishing reserved areas in each store module, and inhibiting a program from reading, writing, or transferring to a location that is not within its reserved areas. Every instruction which references central store has the final address checked to insure that it falls within a permissible area. Store protection is only effective when the guard mode is operative. When an interrupt occurs, the guard mode is terminated and all existing storage is available for executive use. The previously established limits remain loaded and upon executing the load internal function instruction, these limits are once again effective.

multiread feeding—See feeding, multiread.

multireading feature — With the utilization of storage, cards are read only once and data from each field is read out of the storage on the following cycles, thus separate cycle reading for each line of print is unnecessary.

multireel sorting—The automatic sequencing of a file having more than one input tape, without operator intervention.

multisequencing—The simultaneous execution of several parts of a program by separate central processing units.

multistation—Any network of stations capable of communicating with each other, whether on one circuit or through a switching center.

multisystem—Several systems, of the same or different models, may be combined into a multisystem. Various levels of communication among processing units are available. The largest in capacity and slowest in speed is communication via a shared I/O device; for example, a shared disk or drum storage. Faster transmissions are obtained by the direct connection between channels afforded by the channel connector. Finally, storage may be shared between two or more processing units.

multisystem computer—The use of more than one computer in a system because one computer is not big enough or fast enough.

multitask operation — See operation, multitask.

multithread processing—See processing, multithread.

multitone circuit—A telegraph-transmission system in which it is necessary to use two or

MUMPS -- Mash general hospital Utility Multi-Programming System

more channels simultaneously in the same direction for transmitting a signal between the same two points.

multiword operands — With the multiword-operand and field-selection features of the system, fields in any of the three data formats, and ranging in size from one data unit (bit, digit, or character) to four words, can be processed directly with single instructions. With this facility, it is unnecessary to isolate packed fields, to align fields with computer words, or to process each word of a multiword field separately. Therefore, input/output media and memory can be used efficiently by packing fields within words and records. In addition, the need for fewer program steps results in reduced program running times and in conservation of memory (some systems).

Mylar—A DuPont trademark for polyester film often used as a base for magnetically coated or perforated information media.

N

NACPAC (NCR's Applied COBOL PACkages)— NCR's Applied COBOL PACkages are NCR's functional special programs. NACPAC is a concept that makes use of a series of COBOL statements required to perform many of the data-processing functions found in business today. These NACPAC's provide NCR computer users with a series of generalized source programs that can be quickly tailored and compiled into an object program to meet their needs.

N-address instruction format—*See* instruction formal N-address.

name—A term of one or more words to identify one of a general class of items, e.g., to identify a person, machine component, operation code, function, etc.

name, condition—In a source language, programmers often tentatively or conditionally assign names to one or more possible values or ranges of values, which any particular item might represent. An item called "month" may have values 1 through 12, and may be referred to by such condition-names as January, March, etc.

name, data—*See* data name.

name, file—Alphanumeric characters assigned to identify a related set of records which constitute a particular file.

name, program — The brief reference in a program to another program or portion of another program.

name, qualified—A name which is identified by associating it with additional names of things that contain the thing being named, i.e., in COBOL, it is possible to have different items similarly named if they can be distinguished by using qualification, for example, a record called CALENDER, might contain a field subdivided into Month, Day, etc., and the meaning of the instruction can be clarified by using qualified names to refer to subfields.

name, record—In COBOL, the name given to a record within a file and assigned the level number 01. Data names for elements within a record have lower-level numbers, 02, 03, etc.

names—In COBOL, a combination of one to thirty alphanumeric characters containing at least one alpha and no blanks, not starting or ending with a hyphen. Names are used for conditions, data, special procedures or purposes.

name, section—The distinct qualifying term available for a paragraph name.

name, set—An identifier.

name, variable—An alphanumeric name selected by a programmer to represent a specific program variable. Rules for naming variables vary between compilers (FORTRAN, BASIC) and computing equipment.

NAND—A logical operator having the property that if P is a statement, Q is a statement . . . then the NAND of P.Q.R. . . . is true if at least one statement is false, false if all statements are true.

NAND element—*Same as* gate, NAND.

NAND gate—*See* gate, NAND.

NAND operation—*Same as* gate, NAND.

NAND operator—*Same as* gate, NAND.

nanosecond—A billionth of a second. Nanosecond speeds were first introduced to the data-processing industry with a thin-film memory computer.

NASORD—A programming reference to a file not in sequential order.

native language—A communication language or coding between machine units or modules which is peculiar to or usable for a particular class or brand of equipment.

natural language—A language whose rules reflect and describe current usage rather than prescribed usage.

natural law generator—*See* generator, analytical function.

N/C (numerical-control) machines — A punched paper or plastic tape with magnetic spots is used to feed digital instructions to a numerical-control machine, i.e., an automated cutting or forming machine thus guided. Tolerances as fine as 1/10,000 of an inch are achieved on unattended units. Tapes are developed from digital computer programs.

N-cube—A term used in switching theory to indicate two N-1 cubes with corresponding points connected.

N-dimensional cube—*See* N-cube.

NDRO—An abbreviation for nondestructive read out.

NEAT system (National's Electronic Autocoding Technique)—The NEAT system is an automatic system for programming that is used in creating an object program in machine language from a source program written by a programmer. One instruction in the object program is created from one instruction in the source program. Mnemonics and references are used in the source program, as well as macroinstructions that generate subroutines in the object program. It will translate and compile source programs that are written in the COBOL vocabulary.

needle—Used in an edge-punched card system, it is a long wire probing needle which is inserted in the margin of a deck. The deck is then vibrated, causing all cards having a notch cut at the needled hole position to be retained while the others drop out.

negate—1. To perform the NOT logic operation. 2. The conversion of an initially true value to false or vice versa or change signs.

negation—*Same as* NOT operation.

negative A-implies-B gate—*Same as* gate, A AND-NOT B.

negative AND gate—*Same as* gate, NAND.

negative B-implies-A—*Same as* gate, B AND-NOT A.

negative indication—It is customary to indicate a negative sign for a card field by the presence of a control punch which may be located in a part of the card that is distant from the field it controls. Such an example might be a card in which a field in columns 46 to 50 is to be considered negative if there is a 5-punch in column 87. In this case, the 5-punch in column 87 is wired to pick-up a selector as the card is being read.

negative logic—Logic in which the more negative voltage represents the 1 state and the less negative voltage represents the 0 state.

negative OR gate—*Same as* gate, NOR.

negator—*Same as* gate, NOT.

neither-NOR gate—*Same as* gate, NOR.

neither-OR operation—*Same as* gate, NOR.

NELIAC—An abbreviation for Navy Electronics Laboratory International Algol Compiler.

nest—1. To embed a subroutine or block of data into a larger routine or block of data. 2. To evaluate an nth degree polynomial by a particular algorithm which uses N-1 multiply operations and N-1 add operations in succession.

nesting—1. Including a routine or block of data within a larger routine or block of data. 2. The relationship between the statements contained in two perform statements. The statements included in the second or inner perform statement must be wholly included in or excluded from the first, or outer, perform statement. Note special FORTRAN nesting rules for inner loops.

nesting loop—*See* loop, nesting.

nesting storage—*Same as* storage, push down.

nest of subroutines—*See* subroutines, nest of.

NET, DATA—*See* DATANET.

network—1. A series of interconnected points. 2. The interconnection of a number of points by communications facilities.

network, analog—A circuit or circuits that represent(s) physical variables in such a manner as to permit the expression and solution of mathematical relationships between the variables, or to permit the solution directly by electric or electronic means.

network analyzer—1. A simulator for the study of a network, e.g., electrical supply network. 2. An analog computer using electrical circuit elements to represent electrical phenomena to solve problems concerning the behavior of these electrical phenomena.

network awareness—A condition in which the central processor is cognizant of the status of the network.

network, computer—Basically, two or more interconnected computers with advantages for permitting geographical distribution, and thus economy of computer operations. Such a network also permits parallel processing (usually time-sharing), combinations of send-receive communications, multipoint remote entry and output, locally controlled data banks and switching centers, and less requirement for centralized facilities.

network drills—A final level of testing in a real-time system in which data from all the sites is transmitted and the entire complex of equipment, personnel, interfaces, and programs are tested.

network load analysis—A listing of the flow of messages between stations to organize and create station characteristics by volumes of documents, frequency of processing, and special time requirements.

network, Teletype—A system of points interconnected by telegraph channels, which provides hardcopy and/or telegraphic coded (5-channel) punched paper tape, as required, at both sending and receiving points. Typically, up to 20 way-stations share send-receive time on a single circuit and can exchange information without requiring action at a switching center. If two or more circuits are provided, a switching center is required to permit cross-circuit transmission.

Neumann, John Von (1903-1957)—One of the truly great pioneers of the modern computer. In 1947 he devised a procedure for converting the ENIAC externally programmed computer to a stored-program computer. His use of numerals as instruction codes which could be stored electronically just as data numerals were stored, eliminated instruction wiring. His projects toward developing computers capable of reproducing themselves is yet unfinished. He is most often recognized as the true father of modern computing systems.

new input queue—A group or a queue of new messages in the system that are waiting for processing. The main scheduling routine will scan them along with other queues and order them into processing in order.

new-line character—*See* character, new line.

new sync—Allows for a rapid transition from one transmitter to another on multipoint private-line data networks.

next-available-block register — *See* register, next-available block.

nexus—A connection or interconnection. A tie or link.

nine edge—The lower or bottom edge of a Hollerith card. This edge is most commonly used for entering the equipment first because of equipment requirements.

nines compliment — The result achieved by subtracting an original negative number from a counter having the 9 value in each position. A zero value represented by the digit 9 in each position of the counter.

ninety-column card—*See* card, ninety column.

NIXIE display indicators—Some display capabilities concern NIXIE indicator tubes. The tubes are all-electronic, gas filled, cold-cathode indicators that display numerals, letters, or special symbols. These devices are the industry's most widely used electronic readout and are ideal for converting electro-mechanical or electronic signals directly to readable characters. NIXIE tube assemblies and display systems fall into two distinct categories, numeric and alphanumeric. The numeric types are generally used in digital voltmeters, frequency counters, and other devices where digital information of a decimal nature must be displayed. The alphanumeric types are used in schedule boards, arrival-departure displays, computer read-out panels, stock-quotation systems, and in other applications where a minimum of 36 characters (ten numbers and 26 letters) are required. (Burroughs)

NIXIE light—A tube or glowing bulb which has the particular capability of converting a pulse into a visual number. The light or tube is used on various panels, consoles, or other types of visual devices to display decimal numbers indicating register contents, storage locations, or other information for the programmer or operator.

N-level address—An address where N specifies the number of levels of addressing.

N-level logic—*See* logic, N-level.

NMAA — Abbreviation for National Machine Accountants Association.

no-address instruction—An instruction specifying an operation that the computer can perform without having to refer to its storage unit.

no-charge machine fault time — The unproductive time due to computer fault such as the following: nonduplication, transcribing error, input-output malfunction, and machine malfunction resulting in an incomplete run.

no-charge nonmachine fault time — The unproductive time due to no fault of the computer such as the following: necessary dupli-

cation, error in preparation of input data, error in arranging to program deck, error in operating instructions or misinterpretation of instructions, and unscheduled good testing time, and a run during a normal production period when machine malfunction is suspected but is demonstrated not to exist.

node—A point of convergence on a diagram chart or graph. Nodes can be used to designate a state, event, time convergence, or a coincidence of paths or flows.

noise—1. Meaningless extra bits or words that must be ignored or removed from the data at the time the data is used. 2. Errors introduced into data in a system, especially in communication channels. 3. Random variations of one or more characteristics of any entity such as voltage, current, and data. 4. Loosely, any disturbance tending to interfere with the normal operation of a device or system.

noise, broadband (white)—The thermal noise that is uniformally distributed across the frequency spectrum at a wide range of energy levels.

noise characteristics—The most critical consideration in the use of digital circuit modules is noise. In large module assemblies, the spurious signals introduced by noise can cause false operations that, due to their random and transient nature, are extremely difficult to correct. Noise is probably the most frequent source of malfunction in large logic arrays, particularly in a field environment. One error of this type can degrade or destroy the data from a critical test or operation and consequently delay important programs and schedules.

noise factor—The ratio consisting of the difference between the number of documents retrieved and the number of relevant documents retrieved, divided by the number of documents retrieved. A measure of the efficiency of the information retrieval system in which a zero would be optimum.

noise, impulse—A pulse appearing at the output of a circuit that was not transmitted from the originating input to the circuit. These pulses usually are induced from circuit functioning or from sources outside the circuit and its associated input/output equipment.

noise, line—Noise originating in a transmission line.

noise, random—Noise due to the aggregate of a large number of elementary disturbances with random occurrence in time.

noise, reference—The magnitude of circuit noise that will produce a circuit noise-meter reading equal to that produced by 10 watts of electronic power at 1000 cycles per second.

noisy digit—A specific digit that is chosen to be inserted into the units position of a mantissa during left-shifting manipulation associated with the normalizing of various floating-point numbers.

noisy mode—A floating-point arithmetic procedure associated with normalization in which digits other than zero are introduced in the low-order positions during the left shift.

no job definition error—The job did not contain a job definition control card and could not be processed.

NOMAD language—See language, NOMAD.

nonarithmetic shift—A shift in which the digits dropped-off at one end of a word are returned at the other in a circular fashion; e.g., if the register holds eight digits, 23456789, the result of a cyclic shift two columns to the left would be to change the contents of the register to 45678923. (Synonymous with circular shift, end-around shift, logical shift, and ring shift.)

nonconjunction—Same as gate, NAND.

nonconjunction gate—Same as gate, NOR.

nondata I/O operations control — Process which relates to input/output operation as differentiated or exclusive of data manipulation such as tape rewinding.

nondata set clocking—A time base oscillation supplied by the business machine for regulating the bit-rate of transmission.

nondestructive addition — The first operand placed in the arithmetic register is the augend, the next operand is the addend, and the sum replaces the augend. The sum can thus become the augend for a subsequent addition.

nondestructive read — 1. A storage medium that cannot be erased and reused, e.g., punched cards or perforated paper tape. 2. A reading process that does not destroy the data in the source. 3. A reading of the information in a register without changing that information.

nondestructive read-out—A method of sensing the magnetic state of a core without changing its state.

nondestructive storage — A type of storage whose location is regenerated after it is read, since it is desired that the contents be retained at the location after reading. Drums, double cores, punched cards, most magnetic tapes, disks, etc., are examples of nondestructive storage.

nondisjunction gate—Same as gate, NOR.

nonequality gate—Same as gate, exclusive OR.

nonequivalence—See exclusive OR.

nonequivalence element — Same as gate, exclusive OR.

nonequivalence gate—Same as gate, exclusive OR.

nonequivalent element — Same as gate, exclusive OR.

nonerasable medium — Paper tape units are examples of nonerasable media and are used for punching data which may be used to drive various production machines, such as milling machines. It is quite uncommon to use paper tape as an intermediate memory because it is nonerasable in contrast to magnetic tape, which may be erased.

noneraseable storage—See storage, fixed.

nonexistant code—See character, illegal.

nonexistant code check—See check, forbidden combination.

nonlinear control—On-line process control by an analog computer is essentially an extension of conventional control techniques to the next stage of complexity. More input variables can be accommodated and more complex compensation, often nonlinear in nature, can be used to stablize process operation for a wide variety of disturbances.

nonlinear optimization — See optimization, nonlinear.

nonlinear programming — An inclusive term covering all types of constrained optimization problems except those where the objective function and the constraints are all linear. Special types of nonlinear programming for which some theory has been developed are convex programming, concave programming, and quadratic programming.

nonlocking escape—Same as character nonlocking shift.

nonlocking shift character — See character, nonlocking shift.

nonnumeric—Any character or symbol other than a digit.

nonnumerical data processing—See data processing, nonnumerical.

nonnumeric character — Any allowable character except a numeric digit.

nonnumeric coding — See coding, nonnumeric.

nonprint (NP) code—1. The third case of a teleprinter, in which functions may be performed and signals passed without printing or spacing taking place. The nonprint code (NP) code is the function code that triggers this condition. 2. An impulse that inhibits line printing under machine control.

nonprint instruction — See instruction, nonprint.

nonpriority interrupts—Up to 64 nonpriority program interrupts are available on many computers. Each interrupt will lead to a unique interrupt routine associated with the particular interrupt event. At the completion of an interrupt routine, control may be returned to the running program at the point of interruption or transferred to a new program. These interrupts may be used to notify the processor of the completion of some external operation, the failure of some external operation, or the occurrence of some other significant external event. The processor may recognize or ignore these interrupts by setting the external device interrupt to the allow or disallow condition respectively (some computers).

nonprogrammed halt — See halt, nonprogrammed.

nonrealtime processing—Processing historical data such as batch processing. Also used to describe as unsuccessful real time information processing systems.

nonreproducing codes—Codes punched into master tapes that cause functions to be performed, but are not reproduced in the product tape.

nonreturn-to-zero—A method of writing information on a magnetic surface in which the current through the write head winding does not return to zero after the write pulse.

nonscheduled down time—This is the time during which the hardware is being repaired because of failures or unforeseen circumstances. This time does not include normal servicing or maintenance time.

nonscheduled maintenance time—The elapsed time during scheduled working hours between the determination of a machine failure and placement of the equipment back into operation.

nonsequential computer — Requires that the address of the next instruction be contained in the prior instruction. Opposite of sequential computer.

nonvolatile memory — A storage medium which retains information when power is removed from the system.

nonvolatile storage—A storage medium which retains information in the absence of power and which may be made available upon restoration of power, e.g., magnetic tapes, cores, drums, and disks. (Contrasted with volatile storage.)

no operation—An absent or omitted instruction left blank deliberately, often to permit later insertion of data or information without any rewriting, or for the program itself to develop one or more instructions. Oftentimes, a specific instruction which merely advances the instruction content and performs no other function.

no-operation instruction—See no-op instruction.

no-operation, memory protect — A special procedure developed to protect the contents of specific sections of storage from alteration, by inhibiting the execution of any type of memory modification instruction upon detection of the presence of a guard bit associated with the accessed memory location. Such instructions which access protected memory are most often executed as a no-operation or a special violation program interrupt is generated.

no-op instruction—1. An instruction that specifically instructs the computer to do nothing but process the next instruction in sequence. 2. A blank instruction. 3. A skip instruction. 4. A waste instruction. (Synonymous with waste instruction and skip.)

NOR—The Boolean operator that gives a truth table value of true only when both of the variables connected by the logical operator are false, i.e., the negation of inclusive OR.

NOR circuit—A circuit that has an output only when all inputs are down.

NOR element—Same as gate, NOR.

no return point—A first instance in a program in which a rerun is no longer possible, since data may no longer be available.

NOR gate—See gate, NOR.

normal-direction flow — In flowcharts, the normal flow is from left to right and from top to bottom.

normal form, backus — See backus normal form.

normalize—1. In programming, to adjust the exponent and fraction of a floating-point quantity so that the fraction lies in the prescribed normal, standard range. 2. In mathematical operations, to reduce a set of symbols or numbers to a normal or standard form. (Synonymous with standardize.) 3. To alter or position into a regular or standard format as to right- or left-justify.

normalized—A mantissa is normalized if its first digit is not zero.

normalizer—An electronic component of an OCR (optical character reader) which changes or modifies the signal from the scanner to receive a processed rendition of the input character which is more suitable for a detailed or more sophisticated analysis, i.e., essentially a quality improving usage which does not alter the basic character shape. Magnetic ink character normalizers perform a similar function, filling in any voids and cancelling extraneous additions due to erasures, etc.

normally closed contacts—A pair of contacts on a relay that open when the relay is energized.

normally open contacts—A pair of contacts on a relay that close when the relay is energized.

normal orientation — Although most OCRs (optical character readers) can be programmed, and do thus accept a wide variety of character styles and even oddities, they must be normally oriented to direct the reader to perform the scan across the width of the source document. The line elements of the source document appear in parallel with this edge.

normal random number—See random number, normal.

normal range—1. A range of values with specified limits used so that as long as results of a particular plan of action fall within the range, the results are considered satisfactory. This concept is used in exception-principle systems for reporting only results that are not within the normal range. 2. An exception-principle base for reporting only the results that deviate from a specified and defined range called the normal range; results are considered satisfactory if they fall within this definite range.

normal-stage punch—See punch stage normal.

normal stage punching—See punching, normal stage.

normative testing—Standards of performance that are established for the testing of both quantitative and qualitative system performance.

NOR operation—*Same as* gate, NOR.

NOR operator—*Same as* gate, NOR.

NOT—A logical operator having the property that if P is a statement, then the NOT of P is true if P is false, and false if P is true.

NOT-AND element—*Same as* gate, NAND.

NOT-AND gate—*Same as* gate, NAND.

NOT-AND operation—*Same as* gate, NAND.

notation—1. The act, process, or method of representing facts or quantities by a system or set of marks, signs, figures, or characters. 2. A system of such symbols or abbreviations used to express technical facts or quantities, e.g., as mathematical notation. 3. An annotation or note.

notation, base—1. An annotation consisting of a decimal number, in parentheses, written as a subscript suffix to a number, its decimal value indicating the radix of the number; e.g., $11_{(2)}$ indicates the number 11 is in the radix of two, $11_{(8)}$ indicates the number 11 is in the radix of eight. 2. A number written without its radix notation is assumed to be in the radix of ten.

notation binary—*See* number, binary.

notation, binary-coded decimal—A method of representing each figure in a decimal number by a four-figured binary number.

notation, biquinary—A method for expressing a quantity less than ten by using two digits, a 0 and a 5, wherein the first (left) digit is of radix two and the second (right) digit is of radix five.

notation, coded-decimal—A method of representing each figure in a decimal number by a character or a group of characters.

notation, decimal—*See* number, decimal.

notation, fixed radix—A standard positional numeration system designed so that the significance of the successive digit positions are successive integral powers of an integer, referred to as the radix or base. The range for positive radix is from zero to one less than the radix, and negative integral powers of the radix permit the representation of fractions.

notation, infix—A unique notation design for expressing arithmetic and logic statements by alternating single operands and operators. Operators guide or follow particular system conventions for precedence and grouping brackets to avoid ambiguity.

notation, Iverson—A special set of symbols developed by Dr. Kenneth Iverson to describe the formal structure of computer languages. Used in APL.

notation, mixed-base—A method of expressing a quantity by using two or more characters, where each character is of a different radix.

notaton, mixed-radix — *Same as* notation, mixed base.

notation, octal—*See* number, octal.

notation, parentheses-free—A linear or one-dimensional notation system using strings of symbols to indicate various logic, arithmetic, or algebraic expressions but which avoids the use of parentheses, i.e., each string of operands may contain operators and operands.

notation, Polish—*See* Polish notation.

notation, polyvalent—A method for describing salient characteristics in condensed form, using two or more characters, where each character or group of characters represents one of the characteristics.

notation, positional—A method of representing numbers in which the digits are arranged sequentially, each succeeding digit understood as being interpreted as the co-efficient of successive powers of an integer referred to as the base of the number system. For example, in the decimal number system, each succeeding digit is interpreted as successive powers of the base 10.

notation, prefix—*See* prefix notation.

notation, radix—1. An annotation consisting of a decimal number, in parentheses, written as a subscript suffix to a number, its decimal value indicating the radix of the number; e.g., $11_{(2)}$ indicates the number 11 is in the radix of two, $11_{(8)}$ indicates the number 11 is in the radix of eight. 2. A number written without its radix notation is assumed to be in the radix of ten. (Synonymous with base notation.)

notation, sexadecimal—*Same as* number, hexadecimal.

notation, symbolic—A method of representing a storage location by one or more figures.

notation system—*See* numeration system.

notation, ternary—A numeration system designed with a radix of three, i.e., a positional notation arrangement where only three symbols are permitted: zero, one, and two.

notation, two-scale—A number, usually consisting of more than one figure, representing a sum, in which the individual quantity represented by each figure is based on a radix of two. The figures used are 0 and 1.

NOT-both gate—*Same as* gate, NAND.

NOT-BOTH operation—*Same as* gate, NAND.

notched card, edge—*See* card, edge-notched.

NOT circuit—*Same as* gate, NOT.

NOT element—*Same as* gate, NOT.

NOT gate—*See* gate, NOT.

NOT-IF-THEN operation — *Same as* gate, NAND.

NOT operation—A Boolean operation on one operand in which the result has the alternative value of the operand, i.e., if the two possible states of the operand are represented by a zero or a one, the corresponding results are one or a zero. Same as negation, Boolean complementation, or inversion.

NOT operator—*Same as* gate, NOT.

N-plus-one-address instruction—*See* instruction format, N-plus-one-address.

N-tuple—A collection of N elements, usually ordered, e.g., x1, x2 . . . .

nucleus—A part of an operating system which resides in main memory or storage. Control routines are grouped in the resident nucleus and the balance of the operating system (OS) is relegated to auxiliary storage devices as disks, drums, and sometimes, tapes. The nucleus loads parts of the nonresident routines into storage as programmed and as required.

null—1. An absence of information, as contrasted with zero or blank for the presence of no information. 2. Zero. 3. Pertaining to no deflection from a center or end position.

null cycle — The time necessary to cycle through a program without introducing data. This establishes the lower bound for program processing time.

null gate—*See* gate, null.

null string—An empty string.

number—1. A figure or word, or group of figures or words, representing graphically an arithmetical sum; a numeral, as the number 45. (Clarified by number systems.) 2. A numeral by which a thing is designated in a series, as a pulse number. 3. A single member of a series designated by consecutive numerals, as a part number. 4. A character, or a group of characters, uniquely identifying or describing an article, process, condition, document, or class, as a 6SN7 tube. 5. To count; enumerate. 6. To distinguish by a number.

number, ABA—A coding number assigned to banks by the American Bankers Association to assist in check clearing.

number, base—The quantity of characters for use in each of the digital positions of a numbering system. In the more common numbering systems the characters are some or all of the Arabic numerals as follows:

System Name	Characters	Radix
BINARY	(0,1)	2
OCTAL	(0,1,2,3,4,5,6,7)	8
DECIMAL	(0,1,2,3,4,5,6,7,8,9)	10

unless otherwise indicated, the radix of any number is assumed to be 10. For positive identification of a radix 10 number, the radix is written in parentheses as a subscript to the expressed number, i.e., $126_{(10)}$. The radix of any nondecimal number is expressed in similar fashion, e.g., $11_{(2)}$ and $5_{(8)}$.

number, binary—A number, usually consisting of more than one figure, representing a sum, in which the individual quantity represented by each figure is based on a radix of two. The figures used are 0 and 1.

number, binary-coded decimal—A number usually consisting of successive groups of figures, in which each group of four figures is a binary number that represents but does not necessarily equal arithmetically, a particular digit in an associated decimal number; e.g., if the three rightmost figures of a decimal number are 362, the three rightmost figure groups of the binary coded decimal number are 0011 0110 0010.

number, biquinary—A number consisting of a pair of digits representing a sum, in which the left digit is based on the radix two, and the right digit is based on the radix five. The figures 0 or 1 (a 1 represents 5) are used for the left digit, and 0, 1, 2, 3 or 4 are used for the right digit. Example, 13 (5 + 3) is the decimal digit 8. Left digit of each pair of digits has a weight of 0 or 5.

number, biquinary-coded decimal—A number usually consisting of successive pairs of digits, in which each pair is a biquinary number; e.g., if the digits of a decimal number are 3671, the biquinary-coded decimal number would be 03 11 12 01. Left digit (1) of each pair of digits has a weight of 5.

number, call—1. A group of characters identifying a subroutine and containing: (a) information concerning parameters to be inserted in the subroutine, (b) information to be used in generating the subroutine, or (c) information related to the operands. 2. A call word if the quantity of characters in the call number is equal to the length of a computer word.

number, check—A number composed of one or more digits and used to detect equipment malfunctions in data-transfer operations. If a check number consists of only one digit, it is synonymous with check digit. (Related to check digit.)

number, coded decimal—A number consisting of successive characters or a group of characters in which each character or group of characters usually represents a specific figure in an associated decimal number; e.g., if the figures of a decimal number are 45, the coded decimal number might be represented as GQ, or LIZZ, or 0100 0101.

number complements, octal—*See* octal number complements.

number control—This is the quantity of a number (value) which must be the result of a process or problem in order to prove the accuracy.

number control, serial—The control of messages by assigning a number at the time of origination and adding additional numbers as the message passes through specific points.

number, decimal—A number, usually of more than one figure, representing a sum, in which the quantity represented by each figure is based on the radix of ten. The figures used are 0, 1, 2, 3, 4, 5, 6, 7, 8, and 9.

number, designation — Used in truth tables, which are representations of all possible combinations of binary states of a set of variables. A designation numeral thus is the set of digits which represents a particular Boolean expression as a line or a column in such a table.

number, double-length — A specific numeral which contains twice as many digits as ordinary numerals in particular computers and ones which usually require two registers or storage locations. Such numerals are most often used for double-precision computing.

number, double-precision — *See* double-precision number.

number, duodecimal—A number, consisting of successive characters, representing a sum in which the individual quantity represented by each character is based on a radix of twelve. The characters used are 0, 1, 2, 3, 4, 5, 6, 7, 8, 9, T(for ten), and E(for eleven). (Related to number systems.)

number, Fibonacci—A numeral which is part of a unique set for a highly specific search method.

number, floating-point—In many cases, the solution of a problem requires values of numbers that are either too large or too small to be expressed by the computer. The physical size of the number can be reduced by "scaling" or shifting the number to the right or left a predetermined number of places so that the most significant bits of the number may be used. For instance, the decimal number 6510 may be expressed as 0.651×10^7, 0.0651×10^8, 0.00651×10^9, etc. The exponent of the number-system base is the scale factor or the number of places the number is shifted. Some systems are fixed-point arithmetic, and there is no automatic hardware feature for handling the scaling factor or exponent. The programmer is responsible for remembering the scale factors. Also, the possibility of an overflow during intermediate operations must be considered.

number generator—A set of manual controls on which a computer operator can set a word for input.

number generator, manual — *See* generator, manual number.

number generator random — *See* generator, random number.

number, hexadecimal—A specific numeration system which uses the radix of 16, i.e., 16 symbols are used, 0 through 9 plus the characters K, S, N, J, F, and L for digits beyond 9, and each sexadecimal digit thus can be represented by a group of four binary digits, which is called a tetrad.

number, identification — The number from 0000000 to 9999999, assigned to input data.

number, installation-tape—A number permanently assigned to a plastic or metal spool to identify a particular roll of magnetic tape.

number, logical—The number assigned to a peripheral unit during autoload or system generation time. This number can be altered whenever convenient, in contrast to a physical unit number.

number, mixed-base—A number consisting of two or more characters representing a sum, in which the quantity represented by each character is based on a different radix.

number, mixed-radix — *Same as* number, mixed base.

number, multiple-length—A number having two, three, or more times as many figures as are normally handled in a particular device.

number, octal—A number of one or more figures representing a sum, in which the quantity represented by each figure is based on a radix of eight. The figures used are 0, 1, 2, 3, 4, 5, 6, and 7. (Clarified by octal.)

number, operation—1. A number designating the position of an operation, or its equivalent subroutine in the sequence of operations comprising a routine. 2. A number, stated in symbolic code, identifying each step in a program.

number, polyvalent—A number, consisting of several figures, used for description, wherein each figure represents one of the characteristics being described.

number, positional—A method for expressing a quantity using two or more figures, wherein the successive right to left figures are to be interpreted as coefficients of ascending integer powers of the radix.

number, radix—*Same as* number base.

number, random—*See* random number.

number range — The span or dimension or range of values which a number (variable) can assume, and usually expressed within beginning and ending limits or using N, if such limits are unknown.

number, read-around—The number of times a specific spot, digit, or location in electrostatic storage may be consulted before spill over will cause a loss of information stored in surrounding spots. The surrounding information must be restored before the loss occurs.

number, real—An element of a set of all positive and negative numbers, including all types, integers, zeros, mixed, rational, irrational, etc., but not imaginary or complex.

number, reel—A sequence number that identifies a particular reel in a series of reels that make up a file.

number representation system—*See* numeration system.

number, section—A sequence number that identifies a particular section in a series of sections that make up a file.

number, self-checking—A number, with a suffix figure related to the figure(s) of the number, used to check the number after it has been transferred from one medium or device to another. (Related to check bit modulo-N, and error-detecting code.

number, septinary—A number, usually of more than one figure, representing a sum in which the quantity represented by each figure is based on a radix of seven. The figures used are 0, 1, 2, 3, 4, 5, and 6.

number, serial—Numerals usually attached to a device, machine, item, or a sequence or position of an item relative to other items, i.e., numbers representing a label or identifier.

number, sexadecimal—A number, usually of more than one figure, representing a sum, in which the quantity represented by each figure is based on a radix of sixteen. (Synonymous with hexadecimal number.)

number, statement—*See* statement number.

number, symbolic—A numeral used in writing routines for referring to a specific storage location; such numerals are converted to actual storage addresses in the final assembling of the program.

number system binary—*See* number, binary.

number systems—1. A systematic method for representing numerical quantities in which any quantity is represented as the sequence of coefficients of the successive powers of a particular base with an appropriate point. Each succeeding coefficient from right to left is associated with and usually multiplies the next higher power of the base. The first coefficient to the left of the point is associated with the zero power of the base. For example, in decimal notation, 371. 426 represents $(3 \times 10^2) + (7 \times 10^1) + (1 \times 10^0) + (4 \times 10^{-1}) + (2 \times 10^{-2}) + (6 \times 10^{-3})$. 2. The following are names of the number systems with bases 2 through 20:2, binary; 3, ternary; 4, quaternary; 5, quinary; 6, senary; 7 septenary; 8, octal, or octonary; 9, novenary; 10, decimal; 11, undecimal; 12, duodecimal; 13, terdenary; 14, quaterdenary; 15, quindenary; 16, sexadecimal, or hexadecimal; 17, septendecimal; 18, octodenary; 19, novemdenary; 20, vicenary. Also 32, duosexadecimal, or duotricinary; and 60, sexagenary. The binary, octal, decimal, and sexadecimal systems are widely used in computers. (Synonymous with duodecimal number and binary-number system; related to positional representation; and clarified by octal and binary digit.)

number, user—The unique number assigned to each user of a time-shared system enabling him to identify himself to the system when he communicates with it through a remote terminal. (Synonymous with identification number.)

numeral—A digit, or digits normally used to represent a number.

numeral binary—*Same as* number, binary.

numeral, decimal—*Same as* number, decimal.

numeral, designation — Used in truth tables which are representations of all possible combinations of binary states of a set of variables. A designation numeral thus is the set of digits which represents a particular Boolean expression as a line or a column in such a table.

numeral, double-length — *See* number, double-length.

numeral, duodecimal—*Same as* number, duodecimal.

numeral, hexadecimal — *Same as* number, hexadecimal.

numeralization—The use of digits to represent alphabetic data.

numeral, multiple-length — Numeral representation of quantities of items which have two, three, . . . times as many digits than the numeric words usually encountered. Such numerals require two or more registers or storage locations to achieve higher precision calculations.

numeral, octal—*Same as* number, octal.

numeral, self-checking — A unique and very specific numeral containing check digits for even-or odd-parity checking, i.e., a six-bit numeral may have a seventh bit serving as an odd-parity, in which the total number of ones in the numeral must always be odd.

numeral, sexadecimal—*Same as* number, hexadecimal.

numeration system—A system for the representation of numbers, e.g., the decimal system, the roman numeral system, the binary system.

numeric—Composed of numerals; the value of a number as opposed or contrasted to character representation.

numerical analysis—The study of methods of obtaining useful quantitative solutions to problems that have been expressed mathematically, including the study of the errors and bounds on errors in obtaining such solutions.

numerical code — A restrictive type of code which has a character set consisting of digits only.

numerical control—*See* APT.

numerically controlled machine tools — *See* APT.

numeric-alphabetic — *Same as* alphabetic-numeric.

numerical tape—A punched paper or plastic tape used to feed digital instructions to a numerical control (N/C) machine.

numerical word—*See* word, numerical.

numeric character—An allowable digit in a computer system of representing numbers.

numeric code—A system of numerical abbreviations used in the preparation of information for input into a machine, i.e., all information is reduced to numerical quantities.

numeric coding—Coding that uses only digits to represent data and instructions.

numeric control—That field of computer activity which centers around the control of machine tools by mechanical devices; e.g., a computer can control assembly-line tools for machining.

numeric data code—*See* code, numeric.

numeric key punch — A key punch that processes only numeric data.

numeric move—A specific instruction used to transfer the numeric portion bit of an address to another address where the zone bits remain undisturbed. (Contrasts with zone move.)

numeric printer—The numeric printer prints the entire contents of a memory unit or indexed amounts (up to 12 digits) simultaneously, rather than ONE digit at a time. In addition, automatic transaction dates, descriptive codes and memory addresses, when required, print simultaneously with amounts. (Some units.)

numeric punch—*See* punch, numeric.

N-way switch—*See* switch, programmed.

O

object code—The code produced by a compiler or special assembler which can be executed on the target computer.

object computer—The computer which accepts the object program to thus execute the instructions, as contrasted to a computer that might be used to merely compile the object program from the source program.

object configuration—The computer is sometimes used by the compiling program during transformation. It is then called a compiling computer or a source computer. The computer in which the target program is used is thus/or oftentimes the target or object configuration.

objective, design—The planned performance goal based on or chosen prior to the developed operations. The technical estimates of performance requirements, but awaiting confirmation, i.e., standards designed to be met.

objective function—The function of the independent variables whose maximum of minimum is sought in an optimization problem.

object language—1. The machine language developed by the compiler from the source language; the machine language is directly comprehensible to the computer without further refinement or definiton by interpreters, assemblers, or compilers. 2. A result of transforming or translating a source language by any of the many devices or procedures.

object-language program—See object routine.

object machine—The computer on which the object program is to be executed.

object module—See module, object.

object phase—An occasion on which the target program is run is often called run phase, target phase, or object phase. Most often this terminology is used when compiling has taken place.

object program—1. The machine-language program that is the final output of a coding system. 2. The running routine or machine-language routine that has resulted after translation from the source-language program.

object program library—See library program.

object-program preparation—Conversion of programs from one of several easy-to-use source languages, or from certain competitive system languages, to a specific machine code.

object routine—1. The machine-language routine that is the output after translation from the source language. 2. The running routine.

object time—The time at which an object program is executed, as opposed to the time at which a source program is translated into machine language to create an object program.

occurs—In COBOL, describes a sequence of data items of the same format. Subscripting is used to refer or designate a particular item in a procedure statement.

OCR—Optical character recognition.

OCR, common language—See language, common, OCR.

octal—Pertaining to eight; usually describing a number system of base or radix eight; e.g., in octal notation, octal 214 is 2 times 64, plus 1 times 8, plus 4 times 1, and equals decimal 140. Octal 214 in binary-coded octal is represented as 010, 001, 100; octal 214, as a straight binary number is written 10001100. Note that binary-coded octal and straight binary differ only in the use of commas; in the example shown, the left hand zero in the straight binary is dropped. (Clarified by octal number.)

octal, binary-coded—A coding system in which binary numbers are used to represent the octal digits of an octal number.

octal digit—The symbol 0, 1, 2, 3, 4, 5, 6, or 7 used as a digit in the system of notation that uses 8 as the base or radix. (Clarified by number systems.)

octal notation—See octal number.

octal number—A number of one or more figures, representing a sum in which the quantity represented by each figure is based on a radix of eight. The figures used are 0, 1, 2, 3, 4, 5, 6, and 7. (Clarified by octal.)

octal number complements—Octal notation is used in source language and program testing diagnostic printouts. The octal or base 8 number system expresses values as multiples of powers of 8. Octal notation is a fixed-length system of binary notation. The binary number is interpreted octally by grouping the bits into bytes of three, starting from the right, and interpreting each byte into its octal equivalent. Within each byte the bit positions are weighted with the value of 4, 2, and 1, or 2^2, 2^1, and 2^0. If, after grouping the bits in the fashion described, the most significant byte contains less than three bits, as many binary zeros are implied to the left as are required to bring the numbers of bits in that group to three. For example, the binary number 10011101101 is interpreted octally as follows:

(0)10	011	101	101
2	3	5	5

octal number system—A number system which expresses values as multiples of powers of eight. (Clarifiied by octal number complements and octal number.)

octal numeral—Same as octal number.

octet—A sequence of eight binary digits operated on or considered as a unit and usually concerned with an eight-bit byte, i.e., representing one character or two numerals.

octonary—Pertaining to the number representation system with a base of eight.

odd-even check—See check digit, parity.

office automation—Use of an electronic computer or data-processing system to handle routine clerical jobs.

office, central—A common facility that performs the necessary circuit-switching functions required in the operation of communication networks.

off-line—Descriptive of a system and of the peripheral equipment or devices in a system in which the operation of peripheral equipment is not under the control of the central processing unit. (Clarified by off-line equipment.)

off-line equipment — The peripheral equipment or devices not in direct communication with the central processing unit of a computer. (Synonymous with auxiliary equipment.)

off-line mode—A way of computer operation; it means that the devices are not hooked up together. Perhaps the printer is printing the payroll checks, while the computer is solving a completely unrelated mathematical problem. Both are independent operations.

off-line operation—Same as off-line processing.

off-line or indirect system—A remote system in which a mechanical, electronic, or thermal sensing device is used for input and a mechanical, electronic, or thermal controlling device is used for output, but none of these is directly connected to the computer. If there is no human action required in the communications linkage, the system is a direct or on-line system when units are connected to a computer.

off-line output—See output, off-line.

off-line processing—1. Operations performed by auxiliary computer equipment independent of the computer main frame, such as a card to magnetic tape conversion. 2. Processing not directly associated with or required for main program or real-time communication and control. In an off-line mode, human intervention and control is required between data entry and ultimate processing.

offline storage—Storage not under control of the central processing unit.

off-line unit—Input/output device or auxiliary equipment not under direct control of the central processing unit.

offline working—Same as offline operation.

off premise—Standby equipment, usually a back-up or duplicator set of computer equipment at another location. Available for performance of operations under circumstances where the failure of the prime equipment is acute as regards the time sensitivity of the operation being completed.

off-punch—A punch not properly positioned in a column of a card.

offset—An unintentional transfer of ink to

spoil a document's readability, such as from two freshly printed sheets with the back of the one document smearing the face of the other.

offset stacker—A card stacker that can stack cards selectively under machine control so that they protrude from the balance of the deck to give physical identification.

off, sign—The closing instruction to the computer system which terminates communication with the system. On a remote terminal, the user generally signs off by typing the command OFF.

off-time—Time when a computer is not scheduled for use, maintenance, repair, or engineering modifications.

Olsen memory—A specific fixed or permanent storage device which stores coded data in the form of an array of cores and wires, but the wiring holds the information rather than the cores, and these are wound through or bypass the core.

on call, load—See load on call.

on-demand system—A system from which information or service is available at time of request.

one-address—Single address; a system of machine instruction such that each complete instruction explicitly describes one operation and one storage location.

one-address instruction—An instruction consisting of an operation and exactly one address. The instruction code of a single address computer may include both zero and multiaddress instructions as special cases.

one-ahead addressing—Same as addressing repetitive.

one-digit adder—See half-adder.

one-digit subtractor—A unit or device capable of representing the difference between two numbers, usually restricted to permit the subtrahend to have only one nonzero digit.

one-for-one—A phrase often associated with an assembly routine where one source-language instruction is converted to one machine-language instruction.

one-for-one translation—The specific process in which each programming instruction is equal to one machine language instruction.

one gate—Same as gate, OR.

one-level address—Same as direct address.

one-level code—A code using absolute addresses and absolute operation codes; i.e., a code that indicates the exact location where the referenced operand is to be found or stored. (Synonymous with specific code and related to address, absolute.)

one-level subroutine—A program or subroutine which cannot use either subroutines or itself during its execution, i.e., a closed subroutine.

one output—The voltage response obtained from magnetic core in a "1" stage by reading or resetting process.

one output signal—The output of a magnetic

cell in the one condition when a read pulse is supplied.

one-over-one address system—A machine-language system of language that uses two addresses; one of these may be a reference for data.

one-pass operation—Only one pass is made over the source language yielding a binary program. This is true regardless of the input/output configuration. For users without magnetic tape units, this is especially useful. They do not have to reload cards or paper tape for a second pass. However, a two-pass option is included for more comprehensive listings and smaller binary decks.

one-plus-one address—An instruction system having the property that each complete instruction includes an operation and two addresses; one address for the location of a register in the storage containing the item to be operated upon, and one for the location containing the next instruction.

one-plus-one address instruction—An instruction containing two or four addresses one of which specifies explicitly the location of the next instruction to be executed. It is usually used on computers whose storage has a latency factor, e.g., a drum computer.

ones complement—*See* complement, ones.

one-shot operation—*See* operation, single-step.

one-step operation—*See* operation, single step.

one-to-one—A relation between individual members of one set and individual members of another set, i.e., each member of one set has a specific relation to one member of the other set.

one-to-one assembler—*See* assembler, one-to-one.

one-to-one translator — *Same as* assembler, one-to-one.

one-to-partial select ratio—The ratio of a 1 output to a partial select output.

one-way connection—A connection between telegraph sets, one of which is a transmitter and the other a receiver.

one-way reversible telegraph operation — Refers to communication on a circuit in one direction at a time without a break feature.

on-line—Descriptive of a system and peripheral equipment or devices in a system in which the operation of such equipment is under control of the central processing unit. Information reflecting current activity is introduced into the data processing system as soon as it occurs. It is directly in-line with the main flow of the transaction processing. (Clarified by on-line equipment, and synonymous with in-line processing and on-line processing.)

on-line adapter—This unit provides for the interconnection of any configuration of central processors. A single on-line adapter produces a bidirectional, high-speed, memory-to-memory linkage between any two proces-

sors. Data transfer proceeds at a rate of 167,000 characters per second, is monitored under program control, and is initiated by a standard program instruction (some computers).

on-line, central file—*See* file, on line (central).

on-line data processing—*See* on-line processing.

on-line data reduction—The processing of information as rapidly as the information is received by the computing sytem or as rapidly as it is generated by the source.

on-line, debug—*Same as* debug, except the computer is performing on-line functions, utilizing another routine which has previously been checked out.

on-line diagnostics—The running of diagnostics on a system while it is on-line but off-peak to save time and to take corrective action without closing down the system.

on-line disk file—The powerful advanced systems concepts of the computer are fully complemented by the on-line disk file subsystem. With its "head-per-track" design, the disk file provides all-electronic access to any record throughout the file in an average of 20 milliseconds. File organization, programming, and use are simplified because access is entirely by electronic switching with no moving arms, card drops, or the like. Each record segment is equally available regardless of physical location on the disks. Multiple segments can be transferred with a single instruction. Module size is four disks totaling 9.6 million alphanumeric characters of information capacity. Up to 100 of these modules may be used with the computer, effectively extending the memory of the computer system by almost a billion characters. Transfer rate is 100,000 characters per second (some systems).

on-line equipment—Major processing equipment of compatible computer speed that is directly connected to the main processing unit.

on-line implicit calculations — Process variables which cannot be measured directly can be calculated continuously from implicit relationships by relatively simple analog circuits. Calculated quantities, such as composition or the variance of a key variable, are helpful as operator guides or may even be used as inputs to conventional control systems.

on-line input—When the input device transmits data directly to, and under the control of, the control processing unit.

on-line mass storage—*See* storage, mass.

on-line mode—A way of computer operation—means that all devices are hooked up directly, i.e., with the computer (CPU). Although the devices work on different phases of the procedure, all are connected in some way and usually depend on each other for desired results.

on-line operation—*See* on-line processing.

on-line or direct system—A system which has four principal components—a central processor, a communications linkage, a terminal device, and a user. These components interact to carry out a task, but if there is no human action required in the communications linkage, the system is direct or on-line.

on-line plotter—A local or remote digital incremental plotter—in either on-line or off-line operation with a digital computer—provides a high speed plotting system of versatility and reliability. For on-line operation with medium-size computers, a small adapter unit converts the computer output signals to a form suitable for driving a plotter. No modification to the basic computer circuitry is required. Adapters are available for all standard medium-scale digital computers. The plotter can be used for off-line operation with virtually any medium or large-scale computer.

on-line processing—1. The operation of terminals, files, and other auxiliary equipment under direct and absolute control of the central processor to eliminate the need for human intervention at any stage between initial input and computer output. 2. Operations performed by auxiliary computer equipment while it is connected to and a part of the computer, such as magnetic tape units feeding data directly to the central processing unit.

on-line process optimization—An important part of process control is the job of ensuring operating conditions or combinations of conditions for optimum profit. On-line analog computers can be used to adjust one or more process conditions to compensate for uncontrolled variations so that operation is maintained at the optimum level.

on-line, real-time operation (OLRT)—A special system plan and operation in which the input data to the system are given directly from the measuring devices, and the computer results are thereby obtained during the progress of the event. For instance, the data that are received from measurements during a run, with real-time computation of dependent variables during the run, enables the computer to make changes in its output.

on-line storage—Storage under direct control of the central processing unit.

on-line teller system (bank)—If the volume of savings account and mortgage loan activity warrants, these transactions may be handled in real time by the on-line teller system. Teller consoles at each window at each office may be linked to the computer and the on-line central file.

"on-line" teller systems—On-line teller systems have four major elements: (1) a large random access memory tied directly to the computer, used to store account records and auxiliary information; (2) teller consoles, for keyboard entry of transaction information

and computer-controlled printing of replies to passbooks, tickets, and journals; (3) data-communication equipment and telephone lines, linking the teller consoles to the computer; (4) an electronic computer system for control and computation.

on-line typewriter—The on-line typewriter, a standard feature of the computer system, provides monitor control of operating programs. It operates on a character at a time basis under program control, and communicates directly with the accumulator. Data communication is through the programmed input/output channel.

on-line unit—Input/output device or auxiliary equipment under direct control of the computer.

on-line working—*See* on-line processing.

onomasticon—A vocabulary of proper or special names, e.g., a list of titles, chemical compounds, companies, executives, etc.

on-premise stand by equipment—A duplicate set of computer system modules located-nearby, available for performance of operations in the event of equipment failures and as regards time sensitivity functions of requirements.

on, sign—The instruction which commences communication with the computer system. On a remote terminal, the user can generally gain access to the system by typing in his identification number and an appropriate password.

on-the-fly printer—A high-speed line printer using continuously rotating print wheels and fast-acting hammers to print the successive letters contained in one line of text so rapidly that all of the characters in the printed line look as though they were all printed simultaneously.

OP code—A command, usually given in machine language.

open-ended—1. The quality by which the addition of new terms, subject headings, or classifications does not disturb the pre-existing system. 2. Having the capability of being extended or expanded.

open ended system—*See* system, open ended.

open loop—Pertaining to a control system in which there is no self-correcting action for misses of the desired operational condition, as there is in a closed loop system.

open-loop sytem—A system in which the computer does not directly control a process or procedure but instead displays or prints information for the operator to assist in determination of required action. Most real-time systems are basically open-loop systems.

open-routine—A routine that can be inserted directly into a larger routine without a linkage or calling sequence.

open shop—A computing installation at which computer programming, coding, and operating can be performed by any qualified company employee.

open subroutine—1. A separately coded sequence of instructions that is inserted in another instruction sequence directly in low order of the line. 2. A directly inserted subroutine to the main line program specifically where it is required. 3. A subroutine that must be relocated and inserted into the main routine at each place it is used.

operand—1. Any one of the quantities entering into or arising from an operation. An operand may be an argument, a result, a parameter, or an indication of the location of the next instruction. 2. A piece of data upon which an operation is performed. 3. The address or name portion of an operation, e.g., x is the operand of the operation (and x).

operand address—See address operand.

operand address, effective—See address, oprand effective.

operand call—1. A principal method of obtaining values from a PRT (Program Reference Table), using the relative addressing technique, is through use of the operand call syllable. An instruction is referred to as a syllable, and one word accommodates four syllables. Each operand call syllable contains the relative address of the location from which it is to obtain information. 2. The function of the operand call syllable is to obtain an operand and place it in the top of the stack. The method by which this is accomplished varies, according to the kind of data word addressed. When an operand call addresses an operand, the operand is brought to the top of the stack; the processor automatically checks the flag bit and, finding it 0, terminates the operand call operation leaving the operant in the top of the stack (some systems).

operand call syllable—See operand call.

operand field—The portion of an immediate-addressing instruction word that contains the immediate operand value, with negative values represented as twos complements.

operand, flag—The third operand of a symbolic instruction, designating which digits of the object-level instruction will be flagged (some computers).

operands, external-device (EXD)—The program instructs external devices by using the EXD instruction that has the same format as other computer instructions, but may have more than one operand. The last operand of the EXD instruction is the external-device control word (EDCW).

operands, multiword—With the multiword operand, the field-selection features of the system has fields in any of the three data formats, which range in size from one data unit (bit, digit, or character) to four words, and can be processed directly with single instructions. With this facility, it is unnecessary to isolate packed fields, to align fields with computer words, or to process each word of a multiword field separately. Therefore, input/output media and memory can be used efficiently by packing fields within words and records. In addition, the need for

fewer program steps results in reduced program running times and in conservation of memory (some systems).

operate class instructions—These are microcoded instructions used to shift, skip, and complement. Special bits specify which operation the processor is to perform when executing the instruction. Each bit location represents a unique operation. For example, a 1 in bit location 5 is the code to clear the accumulator during the execution of the operate instruction. A number of different operations can be performed simultaneously by coding (selecting) several bits in the same instruction (some systems).

operate mode—Same as the compute mode when the input signals are connected to the computing unit, including integrators, for the generation of the solution as contrasted to the hold, freeze, or interrupt modes.

operating control, concurrent—See concurrent operating control.

operating delay—1. Computer time loss attributable to the mistakes made by system operators or other individuals using the system. 2. During repair time to discover suspected faults, if the investigation shows the equipment to be free of faults, the time lost should count as an operating delay.

operating programs—See programs, operating.

operating ratio—The ratio of the number of hours of correct machine operation to the total hours of scheduled operation. For example if a 168-hour week is scheduled, if 12 hours of preventive maintenance are required and 4.8 hours of unscheduled down time occurs, then the operating ratio is (168-16.8/168). This is equivalent to a 90% operating ratio. (Synonymous with computer efficiency.)

operating system—1. An organized collection of techniques and procedures for operating a computer. 2. A part of a software package (program or routine) defined to simplify housekeeping as input/output procedures, sort-merge generators, data-conversion routines, or tests.

operating system components—The monitor system is composed of a series of individual programs that work together to form a complete operating system. Manuals describe the total monitor system. They also contain a complete description of the primary operating system routine—the monitor program, executive program, system loader, system-preparation routine, and input/output routines. The EXTENDED FORTRAN or other compilers, assemblers, utility routines and library subroutines are described in the sense in which they are used as part of the monitor system. The complete descriptions of these routines are provided in separate documents. The words monitor system, operating system, and system are used interchangeably in manuals and refer to the monitor system (some systems).

operating system, disk (DOS)—A more powerful twin of TOS, this is a versatile operating system for IBM System 360 installations having direct-access storage devices. This simple operating system supports almost every peripheral device available for System 360 or 370.

operating system monitor—*See* monitor, operating system.

operating system supervisor—Operating system consists of a supervisory control program, system programs, and system subroutines. Included are a symbolic assembler and macroprocessor, a FORTRAN or other compiler, and debugging aids. A library of general utility programs is also provided.

operating system, time-sharing—The operating system is a collection of programs remaining permanently in memory to provide overall coordination and control of the total operating system. It performs several functions. First, it permits several users' programs from interfering with other users' programs. Each program is run for a certain length of time, then the monitor switches control to another program in a rotating sequence. Switching is frequent enough so that all programs appear to run simultaneously. Another function of the time-sharing monitor is to process input/output commands.

operation—1. A defined action; the action specified by a single computer instruction or pseudoinstruction; an arithmetical, logical, or transferral unit of a problem, usually executed under the direction of a subroutine. 2. A combination of at least one operator and one operand, e.g., add x. 3. The process of executing a defined action.

operation address instruction—*See* instruction, source-destination.

operational address instruction—A computer instruction having no operation part but rather has the operation implicitly specified by the address parts.

operational, design—*See* design, operational.

operational label—Tape files are identified as far as the operator is concerned by means of an operational label. An operational label may be any combination of letters and digits to a specified maximum. Two special characters are also used consisting of the character "*" and the character "-" to indicate a scratch tape and an empty (or malfunctioning) tape unit, respectively. The assignment of multireel files is accomplished through the use of an operational label. Multireel files are accommodated by associating more than one tape unit with a particular operational label (some systems).

operational mode—The combination of machine operating modes currently in effect.

operational unit—A combination of devices or circuitry which performs a computer process.

operational use time—*See* time, effective.

operational word—A COBOL term used to denote a word which improves readability of the language but need not be on the reserved list.

operation, arithmetical—1. An operation in which numerical quantities form the elements of the calculation e.g., addition, subtraction, multiplication, division. 2. A computer operation in which the ordinary elementary arithmetic operations are performed on numerical quantities. (Contrasted with logical operation.)

operation, asynchronous—The method of processing in which one operation is completed before the next operation is initiated, i.e., initiation and execution are independent on a portion of the equipment while the remainder equipment is free.

operation, attended—In data set applications, individuals are required at both stations to establish the connection and transfer the data sets from talk (voice) mode to data mode.

operation, auxiliary—An operation performed by equipment not under continuous control of the central processor unit.

operation, average calculating—A representative operation which might serve as a base or indication of calculating speeds of various machines, i.e., a number representing, for example, two additions and one multiplication and the time to calculate this, or more commonly accepted, nine additions and one multiplication.

operation, bidirectional—Reading, writing, and searching may be conducted in either direction.

operation, binary—*See* binary operation.

operation, binary arithmetic—*See* arithmetic operation, binary.

operation, binary Boolean—*See* Boolean operation, binary.

operation, bookkeeping—*Same as* housekeeping.

operation, Boolean—*See* Boolean operation.

operation character—*Same as* character command.

operation code—1. The symbols that designate a basic computer operation to be performed. 2. A combination of bits specifying an absolute machine-language operator, or the symbolic representation of the machine-language operator. 3. That part of an instruction that designates the operation of arithmetic, logic, or transfer to be performed.

operation code, augmented—A particular code which is further defined or limited by information found in another position of an instruction, i.e., an instruction word but one which has addresses considered as the operation code.

operation code, external device—Various bits of the EDCW (external device control word) are the operation code that is sent to the external device to specify what operation is to be performed. The operation code is interpreted by the particular device that is addressed. The same operation code may have different meanings to different devices.

operation code field—The portion of an instruction word that contains the operation code.

operation codes—The number of internal machine instructions available.

operation codes, mnemonic—The writing of operation codes in a symbolic notation which is easier to remember than the actual operation codes of the machine.

operation, combination—Relates to the performance of two or more operations simultaneously and as a unit.

operation, complementary—*See* complementary operations.

operation, complete—An operation that includes obtaining the instruction, obtaining all the operands from storage, performing the operation, and returning the results to storage.

operation, computer—*See* computer operation.

operation, concurrent—*See* concurrent operation.

operation control—The control device that directs the arithmetic operation involved in the execution of an instruction in a computing system.

operation-control switch—*See* switch, operation-control.

operation, conversational—*See* conversational mode.

operation cycle—That portion of a machine cycle during which the actual execution of the instruction takes place. Some operations (e.g., divide, multiply) may need a large number of these operation cycles to complete the operation, and the normal instruction/operation alternation will be held up during this time. Also called execution cycle.

operation, dagger—*Same as* gate, NAND.

operation, declarative—*See* declarative operation.

operation, decoded—*See* decoding.

operation decoder—A switching circuit that interprets the operator portion of the machine instruction to be executed, and sets other circuitry for its execution.

operation, double precision—An operation in which two registers are treated as a 64-bit double-word register containing a single quantity (some computers).

operation, dual—Most frequent reference is to the Boolean operation whose result is the negation of the result of another Boolean operation or negation of operand.

operation, dyadic—An operation of two operands.

operation dyadic, Boolean—*See* Boolean operation, dyadic.

operation, EXCEPT—*Same as* gate, NAND.

operation field—That particular part of the instruction format which specifies the procedure or process which is to be performed.

operation, fixed-cycle—A type of computer

performance whereby a fixed amount of time is allocated to an operation; synchronous or clocked-type arrangement within a computer in which events occur as a function of measured time.

operation, fixed-point—*See* fixed-point operation.

operation, floating-point—*See* floating-point operation.

operation, full-duplex—Full-duplex (or duplex) operation refers to communication between two points in both directions simultaneously.

operation, half-duplex—Half-duplex or single-telegraph operation refers to communication on a circuit in only one direction at a time, with or without a break feature. The break feature enables the receiving station to interrupt the sending station.

operation, housekeeping—A general term for the operation that must be performed for a machine run usually before actual processing begins. Examples of housekeeping operations are: establishing controlling marks, setting up auxiliary storage units, reading the first record for processing, initializing, set-up verification operations, and file identification.

operation, illegal—*See* illegal operation.

operation, input/output—1. Each channel is capable of operating in three different transfer modes, input, output, or function. The input and output modes are employed when transferring data to or from the central computer. The function mode is the means by which the central computer establishes the initial communication path with a peripheral subsystem. During this mode of transmission, the central computer sends one or more function words to a peripheral subsystem directing the specified units to perform the desired operation. 2. The input/output section acts as an autonomous processor which runs independently of the instruction-execution cycle, scanning the input channels for the presence of input or output word transfer requests and transferring data between the channels and central storage, controlled by the input/output access-control location associated with the channels.

operation, input/output normal—*See* input/output operation, normal.

operation, iterative—The standard, usual, or automatic repetition of the solution. For example, a set of equations with successive or changed combinations of initial conditions, or simply the use of different parameters and the use of the same computing program.

operation, jump—The computer departs from the regular sequence of instruction executions and jumps to another routine or program, or even some preceding or forward instructions to thus alter control, repeat a process or loop, etc.

operation, logical—1. A logical or Boolean operation on n-state variables which yields a single n-state variable. Operations such as

AND, OR, and NOT on two-state variables which occur in the algebra of logic, i.e., Boolean algebra. 2. The operations of logical shifting, masking, and other nonarithmetic operations of a computer. (Contrasted with arithmetic operation.)

operation, loop—A loop which has an associated set of instructions which restore modified instructions or data to their original or initial values at each entry to the loop, or sequence of instructions which may be obeyed repetitively.

operation, main—The primary application or designed procedure which the equipment performs.

operation, make-break—A type of telegraph-circuit operation where the flow of current is interrupted as pulses are transmitted.

operation mode, conversational—See conversational mode.

operation mode, real-time—Real-time is a mode of operation in which data necessary to the control and/or execution of a transaction can be processed in time for the transaction to be affected by the results of the processing. Real-time processing is most usually identified with great speed but speed is relative. The essence of real time is concurrency—simultaneity. Real-time is refinement in the integration of data-processing with communications. Real-time eliminates slow information-gathering procedures, dated reporting techniques and lax communications; insures that facts within the system are as timely as a prevailing situation, as current as the decisions which they must support. Real-time provides answers when answers are needed, delivers data instantly whenever the need for that data arises. Incoming information is edited, updated, and made available on demand at every level of responsibility. Imminent departures from established standards are automatically detected, and management is notified in time for action.

operation, monadic—An operation on one operand, e.g., negation.

operation, monadic Boolean — See Boolean operation, monadic.

operation, multijob—The simultaneous, concurrent, or interleaved execution of job parts, steps, or segments from more than one job. A type of multiprogramming, when each job or part waits for some external event to occur before it can continue processing: or each job, job part, or step has its own instruction and data areas and may be shared.

operation, multiplexed—A simultaneous operation which shares the use of a common unit of a system in such a way that it can be considered as an independent operation.

operation, multiply—See multiply operation.

operation multitask—A more technical or detailed method for multijobbing or multiprogramming relating to large noninterrelated tasks or task parts, i.e., a single copy of a program module can be used for more than one task. Saving of main memory space and program loading time is developed through sharing of program modules among tasks, usually through the use of artificial languages, and their more refined efficiency.

operation, NAND—Same as gate, NAND.

operation, neither-OR—Same as gate, NOR.

operation, NOR—Same as gate, NOR.

operation, NOT—A Boolean operation on one operand in which the result has the alternative value of the operand, i.e., if the two possible states of the operand are represented by a zero and a one, the corresponding results are one and zero. Same as negation, Boolean complementaion, or inversion.

operation, NOT-AND—Same as gate NAND.

operation, NOT-BOTH—Same as gate, NAND.

operation NOT-IF-THEN — Same as gate, NAND.

operation number—1. A number designating the position of an operation, or its equivalent subroutine in the sequence of operations comprising a routine. 2. A number identifying each step in a program stated in symbolic code.

operation, off-line—See off-line processing.

operation, one-pass—Only one pass is made over the source language yielding a binary program. This is true regardless of the input/output configuration. For users without magnetic tape units, this is especially useful. They do not have to reload cards of paper tape for a second pass. However, a two-pass option is included for more comprehensive listings and smaller binary decks.

operation, one-shot—See operation, single-step.

operation, one-step — See operation, single-step.

operation, on-line—Same as on-line processing.

operation, OR—Same as gate, OR.

operation overhead—Same as housekeeping.

operation, parallel—The simultaneous performance of several actions, usually of a similar nature, through provision of individual similar or identical devices for each such action. Parallel operation is performed to save time over serial operation. Parallel operation usually requires more equipment.

operation part—In an instruction, the part that usually specifies the kind of operation to be performed, but not the location of the operands.

operation, peripheral — See peripheral operation.

operation, polar—A type of circuit operation where the flow of current is reversed as pulses are transmitted. Polar differs from make-break operation in that with polar operation, current always flows when the circuit is closed. Only the direction of current flow is reversed by transmission.

operation protection, nonstop — Ensures against program hang-ups due to infinite indirect address loops or execute instuction loops.

operation, push-to-type — A teletype operation in one direction at a time by using a switch depressed during transmission.

operation ratio—That proportion of the total number of hours during which the equipment is actually operating, including time for operator or programmer errors, to the total number of hours of scheduled equipment operation.

operation, real-time—See real time operation.

operation, real-time (concurrency)—See real-time concurrency operations.

operation, real-time on-line (OLRT)—See on-line real-time operation.

operation, red-tape—Same as housekeeping.

operation register—See register, operation.

operation, repetitive—Operations frequently used in computing such that repeated solutions of the same set of equations, with the same set of initial conditions and parameters, are developed. In CRT (cathode-ray tube) usage, a steady-state solution becomes apparent when displayed on the screen.

operation, representative calculating — See time, representative-computing.

operation, scale—The process of changing a quantity by a specific factor for the purpose of bringing its range within prescribed limits.

operation, scheduled—The periods of time during which the user plans to use specified equipment. Such a designation must be made a given number of hours in advance, provided however, that such scheduled hours of the operation may be modified after that time in the event of an emergency, or in the event that equipment failure creates a need for such rescheduling. Usually the foregoing is further modified in that during the performance period the hours rescheduled as a result of equipment failure usually are not considered as scheduled hours of operation in computing-equipment effectiveness.

operations, analysis—See analysis operations.

operations analysis research — See research operations, analysis.

operation, scatter-write—The process of obtaining various data elements from one location and simultaneously transferring them to several output areas, for contrast.

operations, complementary—See complementary operations.

operations control—Operations control of installation administration and workflow includes instructions from and to the computer operator, adminstrative records, logs of system operation, and the control over library programs.

operations control, non-data — Processes which relate to input/output operations as differentiated or exclusive of data manipulation, such as, tape rewinding.

operations, decoded—See decoding.

operation, sequential—The performance of actions one after the other in time. The actions referred to are of a large scale as opposed to the smaller scale operations referred

to by the term serial operation. For an example of sequential operation, consider Z × (B×C). The two multiplications indicated follow each other sequentially. However, the processing of the individual digits in each multiplication may be either parallel or serial.

operation, serial—The flow of information through a computer in time sequence using only one digit, word, line, or channel at a time. (Contrasted with parallel operation.)

operation, serial digit—Capability of handling digits, one following another, regardless as to whether the bits can be handled in serial or parallel fashion.

operation, serial-parallel — The combined type of serial and parallel operations used, for example, in handling bits in parallel fashion but characters in serial fashion.

operation, serial word—The specific feature of certain handling equipment in which words are read immediately after another in groups.

operations, evolutionary—A statistical technique useful for improving plant operations by slight perturbation of operating conditions repeatedly over a long period of time.

operations flowchart — See flowchart operations.

operation, Sheffer-stroke — Same as gate, NAND.

operations, simultaneous — See simultaneous operations.

operation, simultaneous (scanner selector)—See scanner selector.

operation, simultaneous (subchannels) — See simultaneous operation (subchannel).

operation, single-shot — Same as operation single-step.

operation, single-step—A method of operating an automatic computer manually, in which a single instruction or part of an instruction is performed in response to a single operation of a manual control. This method is generally used for detecting mistakes.

operations manager — See manager, operations.

operations, multiple — The characteristic of being able to perform two or more computer processes concurrently.

operations multitask—Concurrent processing of two or more job steps.

operations research—The use of analytic methods adopted from mathematics for solving operational problems. The objective is to provide management with a more logical basis for making sound predictions and decisions. Among the common scientific techniques used in operations research are the following: linear programming, probability theory, information theory, game theory, monte-carlo method, and queuing theory.

operations research, computerized — Operations research (OR) takes on a new dimension with the computer because it can now be applied to an extent previously prohibitive in time and costs. Most data needed for problem-solving may be quickly accessible and computer-ready as a by-product of such routine computer operations as billing, inventory, or accounts receivable. Capability is another factor. The worth of any OR solution is directly related to the percentage of factors taken into consideration. As a problem becomes more complex, the problem-solving procedure becomes more lengthy and costly using human efforts, or people often economize by over-simplifying the problem and excluding all but the important factors. In so doing, they may arrive at the solutions that are far less than optimal. Using a computer, however, a great number of factors can be handled and manipulated at electronic speeds.

operations research (management science)— The field of management science is extending the computer far beyond the automation of routine accounting operations and into the complex decision-making process of management. Through revolutionary computer-programming techniques such as simulation, the objective, scientific approach of management science is providing increased management capability and control. In addition to the physical or operational processes like inventory management, product planning and control, resource allocation or market forecasting, this also includes the fiscal processes such as bond management, capital investment, risk analysis, profit planning, and product pricing. Manufacturers' broad resources are preparing to meet management's growing demand for this expanded capability and to extend the tradition of "total systems" capability into new revolutionary data-processing techniques and applications.

operations, split-word—*See* split-word operations.

operation, step-by-step—*Same as* operation, single-step.

operation stroke—*Same as* gate, NAND.

operation system, share — The particular process or translation of symbolic instructions into a machine instruction, often abbreviated as SOS.

operation table, Boolean—*See* Boolean operation table.

operation time—The elapsed time required by the equipment in order to execute a specific operation.

operation time, average—That time which is required for a computer to perform specific sets of operations divided by the exact number of operations, such as the average time to perform a single add, multiply, divide, with that sum divided by the total of these operations, or three.

operation time, average calculating—*See* operation time, average.

operation, transfer — 1. An operation that moves information from one storage location or one storage medium to another (e.g., read,

record, copy, transmit, exchange). Transfer is sometimes taken to refer specifically to movement between different media. 2. Storage to movement within the same medium.

operation truetime—*See* operation real-time, on-line.

operation, unary—An operation on one operand, e.g., negative. (Synonymous with monadic operation.)

operation use time—In Federal Government ADP contracts, the time during which the equipment is in operation, exclusive of idle time, standby time, maintenance time, or rerun time due to machine failure, is called the use time. Components not programmed for use in a specific computer run are not considered to be in use even though connected into the computer system.

operation, variable-cycle—A specific operation in which any operation is initiated immediately after the previous cycle is completed, although each cycle time period need not necessarily be of the same length.

operator—1. The what-to-do portion of an operation, e.g., add is the operator of the operation (add x). 2. In the description of a process, that which indicates the action to be performed on operands. 3. The person who actually manipulates the computer controls, places information media into the input devices, removes the output, presses the start button, etc.

operator, AND—*See* AND operator.

operator, complementary — An operator whose result is not of a given operator, for example, NOR and NAND.

operator, computer — Under direct supervision, monitors and controls an electronic computer on established routines. Usually competent in most phases of computer operations to work on his own and only requires some general direction for the balance of the activities.

operator, console—Operates a computer system including entry of variable data through the console keyboard. He initializes and loads programs and monitors programs during execution and records the equipment used.

operator console, visual—*See* display console.

operator control—A central control console provides supervision of computer systems. Through the console, the operator can control the processor and peripheral units . . . observe . . . and monitor processing functions. A console typewriter provides direct communication with the processor memory.

operator control system or section—A portion of the controlling equipment which is readily available to operators for controlling the systems equipment; this is usually a major portion of the console. *See also* operator intervention section.

operator errors—Errors made by the terminal operator.

operator, exclusive OR—A logical operator that has the property that if P and Q are two statements, then the statement P*Q, where the * is the exclusive OR operator, is true if either P or Q, but not both, are true, and false if P and Q are both false or both true, according to the following table, wherein the figure 1 signifies a binary digit or truth.

P	Q	P*Q	
0	0	0	(even)
0	1	1	(odd)
1	0	1	(odd)
1	1	0	(even)

Note that the exclusive OR is the same as the inclusive OR, except that the case with both inputs true yields no output; i.e., P*Q is true if P or Q are true, but not both. Primarily used in compare operations.

operator, inclusive OR — A logical operator which has the property that P or Q is true, if P or Q, or both, are true; when the term OR is used alone, as in OR-gate, the inclusive OR is usually implied.

operator-indicator lights — See indicators, operator.

operator interrupt — The operator-interrupt trap is armed and the fixed-interrupt location is patched each time the monitor receives control. When an operator interrupt occurs, control is given to a routine in the monitor. This routine signifies to the operator the type-in is desired, by ringing the bell, returning the carriage, and typing (some systems).

operator intervention section—That portion of the control equipment in which operators can intervene in normal programming operations on control.

operator, keypunch — Converts source documents into machine-acceptable form by keypunching from hand-written or typed forms.

operator, keypunch and verifier — Persons who operate numerical and alphabetical keypunch and verifying machines to transcribe routine or easily identified data from various documents onto punched cards.

operator, logical — In FORTRAN IV, an operation which acts on one or two logical variables or logical expressions. Such operators are AND (the logical product), OR (the logical sum) and NOT (the logical complement).

operator, machine—The person who manipulates the computer controls, places information media into the input devices, removes the output and performs other related functions.

operator, mathematical—A symbol that indicates briefly a mathematical process which describes the relations and restrictions that exist between the input variables and the output variables of a system.

operator-monitor communication — See communication, operator-monitor.

operator, NAND—Same as gate, NAND.

operator, NOR—Same as gate, NOR.

operator, NOT—Same as gate, NOT.

operator, OR—A logical operator that has the property such that if P or Q are two statements, then the statement that P or Q is true or false varies according to the following table of possible combinations:

P	Q	P or Q
False	True	True
True	False	True
True	True	True
False	False	False

operator oversight—When the unit is on-line, the operator-oversight indicator is set as a result of conditions that require minor operator intervention. It is set only if the standby-location interlock is set or if cards are present in the card path. The punch synchronizer cannot access memory until the condition is corrected, the ABNORMAL CLEAR button-light on the punch control panel is pressed, and the operator-oversight indicator is reset. If a data error occurs during the same cycle as an operator-oversight condition, only the operator-oversight indicator is set. If all three conditions (data error, fault, and operator oversight) occur during the same card cycle, the indicator associated with the condition which first occurs will be set (some systems).

operator part—Same as operation part.

operator, peripheral equipment—Specializes in operating equipment for purposes of converting cards to tape, loading and editing, preparing tape-to-printer reports, or converting paper tape to other media; for advanced installations this type of function is done by the operating system and only one operator is needed to perform all the functions.

operators — The characters that designate mathematical operations, such as +, −, etc.

operators, assembler—The assembler is an assembly program for a symbolic coding language composed of simple, brief, expressions that provide rapid translation from symbolic to a relocatable-object, machine-language code for the computer. The assembly language includes a wide and sophisticated variety of operators that allow the fabrication of desired fields based on information generated at assembly time. The instruction operation codes are assigned mnemonics that describe the hardware function of each instruction. The assembler commands provide the programmer with the ability to generate data words and values based on specific conditions on assembly time.

operator's console—Equipment that provides for manual intervention and for monitoring computer operation.

operator's control panel—The operator's control panel contains all the switches and indicators for the operation of the central processor. Bit-by-bit register display and manual entry into the registers are provided by convenient indicator pushbuttons. The control panel is used primarily for initial set-up prior to a program run or for debugging purposes, rather than to exercise control over a running program. Control of an operating routine is maintained by the use of the on-line typewriter or by sense switches.

operators, machine — Involves loading and unloading, setting up, and control of the equipment in the data processing installation. This may include one or more computers and perhaps a variety of punched card equipment, such as key-punches, sorters, and perhaps some data communications equipment.

operators, postfix—A notation system where the operator appears after the operand, for example, AB + = A + B. It is used in Polish notation.

operator's request control panel—*See* control (panel), operator's request.

operator, store—Storing information in the PRT (Program Reference Table) is done through the use of relative addresses. Storing operations are carried out in the following manner. To store a value in the PRT, a literal (an integer with a value from 0 to 1023) equal to the relative address of the pertinent PRT location must be the top word in the stack. The information to be stored must be the second from top word in the stack. With these conditions existing, a store operator can be executed and the following actions will occur automatically (some systems).

operators, suffix—*Same as* operators, postfix.

op register—That specific register in which the operation code of the instruction set is stored.

optical arena, multifont — Basic character reading equipment having the ability to discern many fonts or formats of characters, usually from hard copy.

optical bar-code reader—This device is available with the data station to read coded information from documents such as premium changes, bills, invoices, and coupons at the rate of hundreds of characters per second. The data station features a high-speed printer, and thus can be used for on-line operations. Card and paper-tape equipment also can be connected to the data station.

optical character reader—This unit reads numerical data printed in widely used type styles on paper or card documents at a rate up to 480 characters per second, and documents at a rate of 400 per minute. The printed data automatically is translated into machine language for direct input to the processor (some systems).

optical character readers, magnetic—*See* readers, optical character (magnetic).

optical character reader, videoscan—A unit that combines OCR (optical character reader) with mark sense and card read. It can read printing and marks in the same pass. It can also read holes in cards.

optical character recognition (OCR) — The identification of graphic characters by use of photosensitive devices.

optical-display keyboard—The display control permits many display units to operate in an economical time-sharing configuration. The keyboard makes possible interpretive operations. Its function for a particular job is assigned by the computer program and the keys for that job are identified by removable illuminated overlays. An operator control panel is used for those processors where the display is used in place of the typewriter control console (some systems).

optical-display plotter—The major element of one plotter unit is a console with a 12-inch-square display screen (a 21-inch cathode-ray tube) on which tables, graphs, charts, alphanumeric characters, or the lines and curves of drawings can be displayed as a series of points. When the full display area is used, 3848 alphanumeric characters—the contents of a page of information—can be viewed. A built-in electronic marker helps the operator edit messages. When the display console is used as a point plotter, it can plot graphs, charts, and drawings with the precision of a square matrix of 1024 points, or more than one million individually addressable points.

Buffer storage for the unit is available in 4096- and 8192-character capacities. These buffer-storage units hold points, lines, and position instructions which may be read from or written at a maximum rate of 238,095 characters a second (some systems).

optical-display terminal—Information is placed into the computer through the alphanumeric keyboard and is simultaneously displayed on its video screen. The unit then displays a reply to the inquiry on its screen. Information is displayed at various rates, such as 600 characters a second, about 40 times faster than that produced for an operator by means of a type-out. Some viewing areas have a 30-line capacity of 40 characters each. To erase the display, once the permissible number of characters has been displayed and the inquiry has been answered, requires only a push of the "erase" button. Most often, the standard 36 alphanumeric characters (A through Z, 0 to 9) plus 23 special characters are available (some systems).

optical document reader—*See* reader, document.

optical font—*See* font, optical.

optical font sensing—*See* font, optical.

optical incremental display — The precision incremental display is a powerful new general purpose incremental cathode-ray tube display which permits rapid conversion of digital-computer data into graphic and tabular form. Its combined capabilities offer the user an unusual degree of versatility and accuracy.

optical journal reader—An optical reader provides input to the computer from the journal tapes (on optical font) that can be output from accounting machines, adding machines, or cash registers. Optical journal readers can be linked to paper-tape punches to convert data on journals into paper-tape format. They can be programmed to reread where read errors occur for HALT, or they can mark for manual entry after the journal has been read.

optical marked-page reader—See reader, marked-page.

optical reader—1. This system is based on the principle that the special shape of each character printed on the input media is capable of being identified by a reading device. For example, the audit-journal from a cash register, if printed in a distinctive optical font, could be used as the input media to a computer. As the optical reader reads each character from the input media, it translates the data into electrical impulses that in turn are transmitted to the computer for processing. 2. Reads printed and typewritten material directly, without converting it into punch-tape, punchcards, or other intermediate formats. It recognizes all letters of the alphabet, standard punctuation, 0 through 9, and special symbols used in programmed functions. It handles documents, and continuous fan-fold sheets.

optical reader input device—See optical reader.

optical scanner—See scanner, visual.

optical scanner, bar-code—An optical-scanning unit that can read documents encoded in a special bar code, at a hundreds character-per-second speed, is an element in the data station. The scanner opens up various systems concepts for such tasks as billing, couponing, retail-item control, and other forms of returnable media. The scanner can read either lithographed or computer-printed bar codes. As it scans, it transfers the encoded data to a buffer for direct transmission or to punched paper tape and printer for pretransmission editing (some systems).

optical scanning—A technique for machine recognition of characters by their images.

optical-sensing device, film—A piece of equipment capable of reading the contents of a film by optical methods, i.e., a system consisting of a light source, sensors, photocells, and a film-moving mechanism. The output of the device is digitized and transferred directly to an electronic computer. An example of such a device is the FOSDIC system.

optical type font—This font was developed as a medium that could be read by both people and machines—a major advance in simplifying the creation of input for data-processing systems. The principle of optical reading is extremely simple. As the salesperson or machine operator records the original entry on an adding machine, accounting machine, or cash register, the information is printed on the journal tape in the stylized font that can be read by the optical reader. The optical reader can operate on-line with the computer for immediate processing of reports. Or, the reader can operate off-line—converting the journal-tape information into punched paper tape.

optima, alternate—Distinct solutions to the same optimization problem.

optimization—A method by which a process is continually adjusted to the best obtainable set of operating conditions.

optimization, linear—Procedures for locating maximum or minimum values of a linear function of variables which are subject to specific linear constraints which may or may not be inequalities.

optimization, nonlinear—A mathematical technique or procedure for the determination of a maximum, minimum, or an attempted optimum value of variables which are subject in the model to predetermined nonlinear constraints, as expressed by sets of inequalities or equations. This is contrasted to linear optimization in which constraints are linear, i.e., in a certain sense, proportional.

optimization, on-line process—See on-line process optimization.

optimization, process—An extensive P-C (processor-controller) program, based on the model of the process directs DAC (Data Aquistion and Control) system. Process data is continuously collected and analyzed for computation of optimum operating instructions. These instructions are given to the process operator via an on-line typwriter (some systems).

optimize—To arrange the instructions or data in storage so that a minimum amount of machine time is spent for access when instructions or data are called out.

optimizer, disk file—To speed transfers between high-speed head-per-track disk files and the central system, the Burroughs 6500 computer uses a block-multiplexing type system allowing blocks containing many bytes to be interleaved in the same way bytes are interleaved in a byte multiplexed system. A hardware device compares entries in a disk access request queue which registers a shaft position, and the smallest difference is selected for the next access.

optimum code—A computer code that is particularly efficient with regard to a particular aspect, e.g., minimum time of execution, minimum or efficient use of storage space, and minimum coding time. (Related to minimum-access code.)

optimum merging patterns—The determination of the sequence in which specific sorted tapes in a file should be processed so as to minimize the total number of merge passes required to create a single file of sequenced records.

optimum programming—See programming, optimum.

optional halt—*See* halt instruction, optional.
optional halt instruction—*See* halt instruction, optional.
optional interrupts—*See* interrupts, optional.
optional multilevel priority interrupts — Interrupt provisions have been made to facilitate the priority requirements of various subroutines. The interrupt requests of these subroutines are handled by the central processor in the sequence of highest priority. If a priority subroutine requests an interrupt, it will have priority over all subroutines of lower priority, even though they have previously requested an interrupt.
optional priority interrupts—Many levels of optional priority interrupts are available on the computer. Any priority interrupt takes precedence over a lower priority interrupt and may interrupt any lower priority program. Each level of priority interrupt may be separately allowed or disallowed by the program, and each leads to a unique interrupt routine. As an option, the several computers may be provided with a programmed input/output channel that sends information to or from the accumulator by programmed instructions. The instructions specify which device is to communicate; thus, the time-sharing of the programmed input/output lines is controlled directly by the program.
optional word — Words introduced in a COBOL program to improve readability.
options—During the execution of any program, including a processor program, options are available to the programmer in the construction, extension, or printing of the results. Updated source code can replace or augment the original code, with listings completely or partially inhibited. Other options control the execution, punching, and timing of the programs.
options, prewired—Optional equipment that is closely related to the processor device, such as the extended arithmetic element, memory extension control, and one of the analog-to-digital converter options, is pre-wired so that the time, effort, and cost involved in adding this option at the factory or in the field is a minimum.
OPUS—Octal Program Updating System. A Honeywell system used to update EASY I program tapes.
O. R. (operations research)—The use of analytic methods adopted from mathematics for solving operational problems. The object is to provide management with a more logical basis for making sound predictions and decisions. Among the common scientific techniques used in operations research are the following: linear programming, probability theory, information theory, game theory, monte-carlo method, and queuing theory.
OR—1. A logical operator having the property that if P is a statement and Q is a statement, then the OR of P.Q. is true if and only if at least one is true; false if all are false. P or Q is often represented by

P+Q, PUQ. 2. *See* inclusive OR and exclusive OR.
OR circuit—A circuit in which the phase or polarity of the output signal results from the inclusive OR function applied to the phase or polarity of the input signals.
order—1. A defined successive arrangement of elements or events. This term is losing favor as a synonym for instructions, due to ambiguity. 2. To sequence or arrange in a series. 3. The weight or significance assigned to a digit position in a number. (Clarified by high order and low order.)
order bloc—A group of computer words or a record being transferred out of the equipment; a section of storage reserve to handle each such outlet.
order, code—*See* code, operation.
order expanded—*See* pseudoinstruction.
order format—*See* instruction format.
ordering—Sorting or sequencing.
ordering bias—*See* bias, ordering.
ordering by merge—A technique of repeated merging, splitting, and remerging can be and is often used to place items into an order.
orderly close-down—*See* close-down, orderly.
order of the merge—The number of input files to a merge program.
order structure—*See* instruction format.
order wire—In communication practice, an order wire is an auxiliary circuit for use in the lineup and maintenance of communication facilities.
ordinary binary—*See* binary.
ordinary life operation system—*See* System for Ordinary Life Operations.
OR element—*Same as* gate, OR.
OR else—*Same as* gate, OR.
organization, central-processor—The central processor may be considered in three main sections: memory, arithmetic and control, and input/output. The memory section provides fast-access storage for data and instructions. In the arithmetic and control section, arithmetic, logical, and shifting operations are performed in the arithmetic portion. The control portion contains logic for controlling and sequencing all of the events that occur in central processor. The input/output section contains the logic for instructing external devices, scanning for external interrupts, and data communication with external devices. In addition, an operator's console provides a convenient means of manual control and information display.
organization, computer service—*See* computer service organization.
organization, data—*See* data organization.
organization file—*See* file organization.
organization, processor—*See* processor organization.
organization, SHARE—*See* SHARE organization.
organizing—Relates to the ability of a system to arrange its internal structure.
OR gate—*See* gate, OR.

OR gate, exclusive—*Same as* gate, exclusive OR.

OR gate, negative—*Same as* gate, NOR.

OR gate, positive—*Same as* gate, OR.

orientation, normal—*See* normal orientation.

orientation range—*See* range (orientation).

oriented, procedure—A programming language that is similar to the language used in the job, and is relatively independent of the data-processing system.

oriented, word—*See* word oriented.

origin—1. The absolute storage address of the beginning of a program or block. 2. In relative coding, the absolute storage address to which addresses in a region are referenced.

original language—*See* language source.

origination—A process to determine the type, nature, and origin of a document.

origination, data—The act of creating a record in a machine-sensible form directly, or as a by-product of a human readable document.

origin counter—*See* counter, origin.

OR mixer—The circuitry which emits an output upon receiving at least one input from any of several alternate sources.

OR operation—*Same as* gate, OR.

OR operator—A logical operator that has the property such that if P or Q are two statements, then the statement that P or Q is true or false varies according to the following table of possible combinations:

P	Q	P or Q
False	True	True
True	False	True
True	True	True
False	False	False

ORSA—Abbreviation for Operations Research Society of America.

orthocode scanning errors—All orthocode formats that use five rows of bar codes and several columns of correction codes that make defacement or incorrect reading virtually impossible, are said to preclude scanning errors. The control codes also help regenerate partially obliterated data.

Orthoscanner—1. An input device designed to read printed documents and to regenerate and read defaced information. It reads orthocode (a series of small vertical bars). 2. This system recognizes characters in the form of a printed code of vertical bars (orthocode). In this form 600 decimal digits can be scanned per second, with a document rejection rate of about one-tenth of one percent. The orthocode contains orthocorrections digits that make possible automatic regeneration of lost data (some systems).

orthotronic control—*See* control, orthotronic.

orthotronic error control—*See* control, orthotronic error.

OS—The abbreviation for operating system.

oscilloscope—An instrument for showing visually the changes in a varying voltage.

outconnector—A flowchart symbol which signifies a place at which a flowline is broken or interrupted for continuation at another location, as contrasted with inconnector.

out device—The unit that translates computer results into usable or final form. *See* input/output device.

outerface—The face of a magnetic punched paper tape facing away and not in contact with the reading, writing, punching, or sensing head.

outline, character—*See* character outline.

out-of-line coding—A portion of coding which is stored away from the main path of a routine.

out of range—A value which does not lie within a specific range of a linear program problem is out of range, or simply a term used to refer to over capacity.

out of service time—*See* time, out of service.

out plant system—A data-transmission system consisting of one or more centrally located terminals and one or more remote terminals.

output—1. Computer results, such as answers to mathematical problems, statistical, analytical or accounting figures, production schedules, etc. 2. Information transferred from the internal storage of a computer to secondary or external storage; information transferred to any device exterior to the computer. 3. Information transferred from internal storage to external storage or to an on-line output device. 4. The state of a sequence of states occurring on a specified output channel. 5. The device or collective set of devices used for taking data out of a device. 6. A channel for expressing a state on a device or logic element.

output area—1. The area of internal storage from which data is transferred to external storage. 2. A specific storage area designated to control and hold information that will be written by an output unit or used in visual scanning. 3. A block of computer words considered as a unit, and intended or desired to be transferred from an internal storage medium to an external designation. 4. A section of internal storage reserved for storing data which is to be transferred out of the computer. 5. A block used as an output buffer.

output, asynchronous (transmission) — *See* asynchronous output (transmission).

output block—A portion of the internal storage reserved primarily for receiving, processing, and transmitting data that is to be transferred out.

output, buffer—*See* buffer, output.

output buffer register—*See* register, output buffer.

output bus drivers—*See* bus drivers, output.

output capability—The number of unit loads that can be driven by the output of a circuit.

output data—Data obtained or obtainable from a device, such as a logic element, or the output channel of a logic element.

output delay—The typical delay of the circuit measured at the 50 percent signal levels, with half of rated d-c load and half of the specified wiring capacity.

output device—The part of a machine that translates the electrical impulses representing data processed by the machine into permanent results such as printed forms, punched cards, and magnetic writing on tape.

output device, paper-tape—Output data comes to this device from the computer. Blank paper tape is placed in the device, which punches the data into the tape. Some computer paper-tape units combine the input and output functions.

output, direct—Printed, visual, or communicated data which results from online output or output equipment, i.e., the final output is produced by equipment directly connected to the computer and directly under computer control as contrasted to printouts from generated tapes, etc., which are processed from stored equipment or off-line.

output edit (printer)—Several important considerations in editing for printout include the alignment of information into proper order for printing, suppression of nonsignificant zeros, insertion of symbols and punctuation, and conversion of a machine minus code to an appropriate printer symbol. Alignment of information may involve rearrangement of fields or possibly only the insertion of spaces between fields. For example, in a straight listing that simply prints out the contents of a number of cards, it is desirable to insert spaces between fields for ease in reading the printed result.

output equipment—The equipment used for transferring information out of a computer.

output indirect—Output which may have come from a computer system originally but which is obtained from off-line equipment or data from off-line origination. Indirect output is usually considered so because it was produced by equipment not directly connected to the computer system.

output, limited—The timing or speed restriction on a process or various pieces of equipment whereby other operations must await the completion of an output operation and thus either restrict or cause other equipment to have idle time.

output magazine—A mechanism that accumulates cards after they have passed through a machine. (Synonymous with output stacker.)

output monitor interrupt—When two or more channels simultaneously request the central computer to process operations occupying the same priority level, access is granted to the lowest numbered channel. When both an input and an output data request are present, priority will alternate. For example, if the input data request has occurred first, priority would be granted in the following manner: process one input data word, alternate and process one output data word, alternate and process one input word, etc. If during the alternating of input/output data requests, a real-time clock incrementation occurs (an operation of higher priority), priority would still alternate but the pattern would differ—process one input data word, alternate, process the real-time clock incrementation, alternate, and process one input data word, alternate and process one output data word, alternate and process one input word, etc. (some systems).

output, off-line—Output which may have come from a computer system originally but which is obtained from off-line equipment, or data from off-line origination. Indirect output is usually considered so because it was produced by equipment not directly connected to the computer system.

output program—*See* program, output.

output power—A characteristic of an amplifier denoting the power it can deliver into its load. The normal power output is the power absorbed by the load of the amplifier under normal operating conditions, and the maximum usable power is that for which the acceptable maximum harmonic distortion of the output signal is reached.

output queue—Messages that are in line or queued which have been produced by the system and are waiting to be scheduled for transmission.

output register buffer—The buffering or transfer device which receives data from internal storage and transfers it to an output media such as magnetic tape.

output routine—That set of instructions which organizes, directs, or controls the handling of output data by starting the output equipment, specifying the output format, speed, monitoring, etc.

output routine, typewriter (TYPOUT)—*See* typewriter output routine (TYPOUT).

output stacker—A mechanism that accumulates cards after they have passed through a machine.

output state—The determination of the condition of that specified set of output channels, i.e., positive, negative, or one or zero, etc.

output storage—*See* output area.

output table—*See* board, plotting.

output, tape punch—*See* tape punch.

output tape(s) sorting—Tapes containing a file in specified sequence as a result of a specified sort/merge process.

output test, processor—An automated processing of the output so that errors may be more easily tracked down.

output unit—The unit which delivers information in acceptable language to a point outside the computer.

output work queue—*See* work queue, output.

output writer—A service program which moves data from the output work queue to a particular output device, a printer, card punch, or terminal. The output writer thus transfers the actual output, oftentimes from an output work queue to an output device, after it has determined the normal rate of speed of the device to be used.

outside loops—*See* loops, outside.

over-capacity—Values which are not in the range of a quantity are said to be out of range or over capacity.

over-capacity, punching — Over-capacity punching is a fairly common method of extending the capacity of a card beyond 90 columns. When this method is employed, certain zero punching positions in the card are assigned the values of a normal vertical-punching column. Thus, through the use of over-capacity punching, a 5-digit card field can actually represent a 6-digit number by using the zero positions to indicate the most significant digit of the value.

overflow—1. In an arithmetic operation, the generation of a quantity beyond the capacity of the register or location which is to receive the result; over capacity; the information contained in an item of information which is in excess of a given amount. 2. The portion of data that exceeds the capacity of the allocated unit of storage. 3. Overflow develops when attempts are made to write longer fields into a field location of a specific length; a 12-digit product will overflow a 10-digit accumulator.

overflow areas, file—In random addressing, the overflow area is an available storage location that is chained to a particular pocket so that when that pocket is full, the generated addresses use the overflow area.

overflow, characteristic—A situation developed in floating-point arithmetic if an attempt is made to develop a characteristic greater than 99 (some systems).

overflow check—Overflow check, a feature associated with arithmetic operations, is a means of immediately recognizing results that exceed the capacity of the counter or accumulator in which they are developed. In order to recognize an overflow and associate it with the proper calculation, the check should be performed immediately after the arithmetic operation. A machine or system which employs this feature can be programmed to detect and signal the condition.

overflow check indicator — A device that is turned on by incorrect, or unplanned for, operations in the execution of an arithmetic instruction, particularly when an arithmetic operation produces a number too large for the system to handle.

overflow error—A floating-point arithmetic operation resulted in an overflow condition.

overflow (FORTRAN)—In FORTRAN, overflow occurs when the characteristic of a floating-point number exceeds the machine capacity (generally $10+38$). In assembler language, overflow occurs when a fixed point number is divided by zero or when an algebraic sum is larger than the accumulator register can hold.

overflow indicator—1. A bistable trigger that changes state when overflow occurs in the register with which it is associated. It may be interrogated and/or restored to the original state. 2. An internal computer-indicator component that is indicated to be "on" if an overflow condition exists due to an arithmetic miscalculation in programming designs.

overflow, link (L)—This one-bit register serves as an extension of the accumulator. The content of this register can be program sampled and program modified. Overflow into the link from the accumulator can be checked by the program to greatly simplify and speed up single- and multiple-precision arithmetic routines.

overflow position—An extra position in the register in which the overflow digit is developed.

overflow, product—*Same as* overflow.

overflow, types—Two types of overflow may occur in computers—add and divide. Overflow may also occur in certain algebraic subtraction operations, such as a negative quantity subtracted from a positive quantity. In reality, of course, this is the same as an additive operation.

overflow (underflow), test conditions — *See* test conditions, overflow (underflow).

overhead operation—*Same as* housekeeping.

overlap—*See* processing overlap.

overlapped channels—*See* channels, overlapped.

overlapped-operations buffer — *See* buffer, overlapped operations.

overlapping—A type, process, or procedure for concurrent operation in which various phases of two consecutive instructions are executed simultaneously, i.e., multiplication can take place while reading from storage is also being completed.

overlapping, multiprocessor—The processor is capable of determining whether its current operand and next instruction lie in different storage modules. It is also capable, if this situation is present, of retrieving these two words in parallel, at an effective 100% performance increase. Since the I/O controller is not required to reference instructions in main storage, except on command transfers, it does not have, nor does it need, the overlapping feature.

overlap, read-punch—Read-punch permits the computer to process simultaneously two separate, related files. Thus, the read-punch can be extremely useful in applications that do not require punching. The overall time required to perform these applications is reduced because collating can be eliminated and faster card throughput results.

overlay—1. The technique of repeatedly using the same blocks of internal storage during different stages of a problem; e.g., when one routine is no longer needed in internal storage, another routine can replace all or part of that storage. 2. The use of one area in storage to successively store more than one different form of storage subroutine or program parts. 3. The utilization of portions of internal storage alternately for two sets of data, information, or instructions which might be needed at different times. 4. A technique for bringing routines into high-speed storage from some other form of storage during processing, so that several routines will occupy the same storage locations at different times. Overlay is used when the total storage requirements for instructions exceed the available main storage.

overlays—Programs or runs too large for memory can be divided into logical segments or overlays. One overlay overlays another, or several segments may be in memory at one time. Overlays are also used when various operations occur infrequently, such as deductions for community chest, union dues, etc. The overlays are called in only when the functions they perform are required. An overlay subroutine is provided to call in these overlays. This subroutine functions in a manner similar to the system supervisor.

overlays, memory-allocation—The monitor remains resident in lower memory at all times. Object programs are loaded into memory starting at the end of the monitor. The program loader resides in upper memory. Object programs cannot be loaded into the loader area. This area can be overlaid by common storage. Part of the loader can also be overlaid by library subroutines.

overlays, monitor—The monitor remains resident in lower memory at all times. Object programs are loaded into memory starting at the end of the monitor. The program loader resides in upper memory. Object programs cannot be loaded into the loader area. This area can be overlaid by common storage. Part of the loader can also be overlaid by library subroutines.

overlays program—*Same as* overlays.

overlays, segments—A segment of a program is defined as that portion of memory which is committed by a single reference to the loader. Usually a segment overlays some other segment and may have within itself other portions which in turn overlay one another, i.e., subsegments. That part of a segment which is actually brought into memory when the loader is referenced is called the fixed part of a segment. Segments are built up from separate relocatable elements, common blocks, or other segments.

overlay supervisor—A specific subroutine which controls the location and execution sequence of parts of computer programs dur-

ing conditions of restricted storage space availability.

overload level—The operating limit of a system, component, etc.; that point at which operation ceases to be satisfactory as a result of signal distortion, overheating, damage, etc.

overloads—When the rate of input into a system is so concentrated that the computer cannot process the flow of messages on a real-time basis.

overload simulator—In order to test a system of under overload conditions, an artificial condition is created that makes the program act as it would during an actual overload or overflow.

overprinting—An optical character reading term designating marks placed in clear bands or areas which are set aside for machine reading after the document has been prepared for machine sensing.

overpunch—1. A punched hole located in one of the three top rows of a punched card and the second punch in one of the nine lower rows, identifies an alphabetic or special character. Also called zone punch. 2. To add holes in a card column that already contains one or more holes. (Synonymous with zone punch, and related to zone bits.)

override interrupt—An optional group of power on/off interrupts which have the highest priority and which cannot be disabled or disarmed.

oversight operator—*See* operator oversight.

own code—*See* code, own.

own coding, intermediate-pass—Computer instructions created by the programmer, in assembly or absolute form, which are executed by a sort during the intermediate passes of the file after the execution of instructions for comparisons of keys, but prior to output of the selected records. May also be executed during the internal sort, but after the selection of records.

own coding, last pass—Computer instructions created by the programmer, in assembly or absolute form, which are executed by a sort during the last pass of the file after the final merging instructions have been executed but prior to unloading the output record.

own coding (sorting)—Special coding provided by the programmer, which is integrated with sort/merge coding.

oxide spots, ferrous—The medium by which information is represented on magnetic tape. These ferrous oxide spots represent information in binary form which is interpreted by the magnetic tape drive and then stored in computer memory for processing.

P

PA—Abbreviation for paper advance.

PABX (Private Automatic Branch Exchange)—A private automatic exchange that provides for the transmission of calls to and from the public telephone network.

pack—1. The combination or consolidation of several short fields into one larger field. 2. To combine two or more units of information into a single physical unit to conserve storage. For example, the fields of an employee's pay number, weekly pay rate, and tax exemptions may be stored in one word, each of these fields being assigned a different location within the word. 3. The procedure which reduces the amount of storage required to hold information by changing the method of coding data or blanks. For example, storing two or more data items into a single word by using a contiguous subfield, or by dividing words into convenient parts, etc.

package, floating point—*See* floating point package.

package, program—*See* program package.

pack, disk—*See* disk pack.

packed decimal—A system means of data representation. Two digits per character can be used to increase speed and capacity in fields where alphabetics and special characters are not being used.

packed format—A binary-coded decimal format in which two decimal digits are represented within a single byte of storage; accomplished by eliminating the zone bits.

packet—*Same as* stacker.

packing—The effect of reducing the time interval between subsequent characters read from tape, caused by a combination of a mechanical skew, gap scatter, jitter, amplitude variation etc. Also called packing bits.

packing density—The determination of the relative number of units of required information or data contained within defined dimensions; e.g., the number of binary digits of polarized spots per linear inch stored on magnetic tapes. Also, the number of useful storage elements per unit of dimension; e.g., the number of bits per inch stored on a drum track.

packing density, file—The ratio of available file or data storage space to the total amount of data stored in the file.

packing factor—*See* packing density.

packing sequence—A procedure for loading the upper half of an accumulator with the first data word, shifting this into the lower half, loading the second datum, shift, etc., so that the three data words are thus packed in sequence.

pad—A process of filling or completing a unit of data such as a word, block, or file, most often with zeros or smaller units of dummy or meaningless characters.

pad character—Character introduced to use up time while a function (usually mechanical) is being accomplished, e.g., carriage return, form eject, etc.

padding—1. A technique used to fill out a block of information with dummy records, words, or characters. 2. Adding characters to a record to enlarge it to a predetermined block length, to make it easier to handle in a specified record-length routine.

P address—Location to which the program branches or to which data is transparent (certain equipment).

pad, scratch—A useful and informal term referring to or designating a unique internal storage area, supposedly reserved for intermediate results, various notations, or working area, quickly erasable storage.

page—A quantity of determination of main-memory capacity and used when allocating memory and for partitioning programs into units or control sections. A page is quite standardized, usually 512 to 4096 bytes or words and/or 8 to 64 lines of source program coding, as used for displaying the coding on CRTs (cathode ray tubes) i.e., in CRTs used in conversational time-sharing a single page of program can be displayed at one time for the programmer or user inspection, the size varying with the size and capacity of the CRT, and not related to the memory page stated above.

page address—The 8-high order bits of a virtual address or an actual address, which represents a page of memory (some computers).

page boundary—The address of the first word or byte within a page of memory, i.e., a memory address expressed as a number having 9 to 12 low-order zeros, the exact number of trailing zeros is related to size of the page used by a specific computer. All programs in a paged-memory system should begin on a page boundary address.

page check—*See* check, page.

page, entry—The point, in flowchart symbols, where the flowline continues from a previous page due to space limitations on the original or previous page.

page, exit—The point, in flowchart symbols, where the flowline continues to a following page due to space limitation on the page on which the flowchart is drawn.

page footing—The summing of the entries on a particular page, usually appearing at the bottom of each page.

page heading—The description of a page context of a report, usually appears at the top of each page.

page, invalid (time-sharing)—*See* time sharing, invalid pages.

page printer—*See* printer, page.

page reader—An optical character reader which can process cut-form documents of differing sizes and which might be able to read information in reel form.

page-turning—1. A technique of providing large single level memory, usually with dynamic memory relocation. 2. A procedure for moving complete pages of information between main memory and auxiliary storage units, to permit several simultaneous programs in execution to share main memory, or to permit cyclic scheduling for time allotments.

page-turning, time-sharing—*See* time sharing, page turning.

page type, time-sharing—*See* time sharing, page type.

paging—The separation of a program and data into fixed blocks, often 1000 words, so that transfers between disk and core can take place in page units rather than as entire programs.

paging, time-sharing—*See* time sharing, paging.

pairs, sorting comparison—The comparison of the keys in two records and placement of the higher value ahead of the smaller value for descending sequences.

panel—*See* control panel.

panel, central control—*See* control panel.

panel, control—*See* control panel.

panel, control console—*See* control panel or console.

panel, graphic—A master control panel that pictorially and usually colorfully traces the relationship of control equipment and the process operation. It permits an operator, at a glance, to check on the operation of a far-flung control system by noting dials, valves, scales, and lights.

panel, jack—A specific control panel which uses electrical connectors, i.e., short wires, plugs, etc., to control the operation of particular devices such as older type punched card machines.

panel, maintenance control—*See* control panel, maintenance.

panel, operator's control—*See* operator's control panel.

panel path—*See* control panel.

panel, programming control—*See* control panel, programming.

panel, wing—A panel which is added on sides of existing panels and which often contains intervention or other type switches. or warning lights.

panic button—*See* button, emergency.

paper-advance mechanism—Two sets of sprocketed tractors—an upper set and a lower set—advance the continuous paper through the printer under program control. While the paper is being printed, the two sets of tractors maintain paper tension.

paper, coordinate—Marginally punched, continuous-form paper, normally used for printout of an XY plotter.

paper, slew—*Same as* paper throw.

paper tape—A strip of paper capable of storing or recording information. Storage may be in the form of punched holes, partially punched holes, carbonization or chemical change of impregnated material, or by imprinting. Some paper tapes, such as punched paper tapes, are capable of being read by the input device of a computer or a transmitting device by sensing the pattern of holes that represent coded information.

paper tape, chadless—A paper tape with the holes partially punched. It is commonly used in teletype operations.

paper tape channels—*See* tape channels, paper.

paper-tape data processing—*See* data processing, paper-tape.

paper-tape output device—Output data comes to this device from the computer. Blank paper tape is placed in the device, and the data is punched into the tape. Some computer paper-tape units combine the input and output functions.

paper tape, perforated—*See* punched tape.

paper tape, punched—*See* tape, punched paper.

paper tape punches—A device which punches paper tape.

paper-tape reader—A device that senses and translates the holes or information on tape into machine code.

paper tape speed—The rate, in characters per second, at which the unit reads or punches paper tape.

paper-tape systems—Systems having paper-tape equipment with no mass storage device have an operating system contained on binary paper-tape reels. The binary reels are of two types—format binary and absolute binary. Format binary programs are loaded by the system loader. Absolute binary programs may be loaded by the monitor or by a "PRESET" operation.

paper tape type—Indicates the unit's function: reader only (RD), punch only (PN), or reader-punch combination (RP).

paper throw—When paper in a printer moves through a distance greater than the normal line spacing without printing, it is called a paper throw or a paper slew, i.e., the speed for throw is usually greater than for single-line feed.

paragraph—A pertinent or allied group of sentences, or those which are related logically and which are smaller or subgroups of pages as described in some computer systems.

parallel—1. The internal handling of data in groups, all elements of a group being handled simultaneously. 2. Objects (programs) considered simultaneously (or nearly so) rather than in sequence or some specific order. 3. Pertaining to simultaneous processing of the individual parts of a whole, such as the bits of a character and the characters of a word, using separate facilities for the various parts. 4. Handled simultaneously in separate facilities. 5. Operation on two or more parts of a word or item simultaneously.

parallel access—1. Simultaneous access to all bits in a storage location comprising a character or word. Equal access time for any bit, character, or word in a storage device. 2. The process of obtaining information from or placing information into storage where the time required for such access is dependent on the simultaneous transfer of all elements of a word from a given storage location. (Synonymous with simultaneous access.)

parallel arithmetic—See arithmetic, parallel.

parallel by bit—Handling all the binary digits (or bits) of a character simultaneously in separate equipment.

parallel by character—The handling of all the characters of a machine word simultaneously in separate lines, channels, or storage cells.

parallel computer—A computer in which the digits or data lines are handled concurrently by separate units of the computer. The units may be interconnected in different ways as determined by the computation to operate in parallel or serially. Mixed serial and parallel machines are frequently called serial or parallel according to the way arithmetic processes are performed. An example of a parallel computer is one which handles decimal digits in parallel, although it might handle the bits which comprise a digit either serially or in parallel. (Contrasted with serial computer.)

parallel data medium—A medium for recording or entering data and as an input/output media for computers such as cards, tapes, paper, and disks. Usually the data carrier is easily transportable.

parallel digital computer—Specific equipment which processes digits in concurrent procedures as contrasted to serial computing.

parallel flow—The system of operations designed so that several of them may be conducted simultaneously, such as in housebuilding, the air-conditioning ducting can be completed, while the plumbing is being worked on, while the landscaping is being developed, etc. This is opposite from serial development where each task must wait until the completion of one before another can begin.

parallel full adder—See adder, full (parallel).

parallel full subtracter—See subtracter, full (parallel).

parallel half adder—See adder half (parallel).

parallel half-subtracter—See half-subtracter, parallel.

parallelism—Concurrent operation of several parts of a computer system. This could be simultaneous processing of multiple programs or simultaneous operation of multiple computers.

parallel operation—The flow of information through the computer or any part of it using two or more lines or channels simultaneously.

parallel processing—The operation of a computer so that programs for more than one run are stored simultaneously in its storage, and executed concurrently. See multiprocessing, concurrent processing, and multiprograming.

parallel programming—See programming, parallel.

parallel reading—When a data card is read row-by-row.

parallel running—1. The checking or testing of newly developed systems by running comparatively in conjunction with previously existing systems. 2. The running of a newly developed system in a data processing area in conjunction with the continued operation of the current system. 3. The final step in the debugging of a system; this step follows a system test.

parallel search storage—Same as associative storage.

parallel-serial—See serial-parallel.

parallel, serial operation—The combined type of serial and parallel operation used, for example, in handling bits in parallel fashion but characters in serial fashion.

parallel storage—1. A storage device wherein characters, words, or digits are dealt with simultaneously. 2. Storage in which all bits, characters, or (especially) words are essentially equally available in space, without time being one of the coordinates.

parallel transfer—1. A method of data transfer in which the characters of an element of information are transferred simultaneously over a set of paths. 2. Simultaneous transfer of all bits (in a storage location) comprising a character or word.

parallel transmission—A system for sending all bits of a particular character simultaneously.

parameter—1. In a subroutine, a quantity which may be given different values when the subroutine is used in different main routines or in different parts of one main routine, but which usually remains unchanged throughout any one such use. 2. A quantity, in a mathematical calculation, that may be assigned any arbitrary value. 3. In generators, the quantity used to designate input/output devices to specify subroutines to be included, or to define the routine to be generated. 5. A constant or a variable in mathematics that remains constant during some calculation. 6. A definable characteristic of an item, device, or system.

parameter, mathematical—See mathematical parameter.

parameter mode (display)—This mode is used to control the display. It establishes parameter information for each of the other modes. The parameters are changed only when another parameter word is encountered. Special features of this mode include: an automatic stop bit—signals the computer when plotting is completed and brings the display to a halt; individual parameter inhibit bits—permit each parameter to be independently established.

parameter, preset—A parameter incorporated into a subroutine during input.

parameter, program—A parameter incorporated into a subroutine during computation. A program parameter very frequently comprises a word stored relative to either the subroutine or the entry point and dealt with by the subroutine during each reference. It may be altered by the routine and/or may vary from one point of entry to another.

parameters, report generation—Manufacturers furnish a program for automatic creation of reports according to user specifications. To use the report generator, the programmer merely prepares a set of parameters defining control fields and report lines. These parameters are used as input to the report generator that produces a symbolic program. The assembled version of this program accepts raw data as input, edits it, and generates the desired reports.

parameters, sorting—The response to the requirement for specifications for a sort/merge generator. Parameters are used to fix input and output formats, computing configuration, location of keys, and so on.

parameter, statement—A parameter statement assigns specified integer values to specified variables at compile time, e.g. parameter $I = 2$ causes the integer 2 to replace I whenever it occurs in the source program. This facilitates the assignment of different values to frequently referenced parameters in different compilations of the same program.

parameter testing—Tests of individual sections or subroutines of a program to assure that specified inputs produce the desired outputs.

parameter word—A word in a subroutine which contains one or more parameters which specify the action of the subroutine, or words which contain the address of such parameters.

parametric programming—A method for investigating the effect on an optimal linear-programming solution of a sequence of proportionate changes in the elements of a single row or column of the matrix. Most commonly, the method is applied to either the objective-function row or the right-side column.

parentheses-free notation—See notation, parentheses-free.

parity—As regards computer operations, parity relates to the maintenance of a sameness of level or count, i.e., keeping the same number of binary ones in a computer word to thus be able to perform a check based on

an even or odd number for all words under examination.

parity bit—1. A redundant bit added to a group of bits so that an inaccurate retrieval of that group of bits is detected. 2. A parity bit is most often used to develop a total of bits, either odd or even, for each character. It is usually associated with the frame for each six-bit character on tape, and parity bits can be placed at intervals to associate them with the seven rows of bits, i.e., six for data and one for parity. 3. The total or summation check in which the binary digits in a single character or word in storage are added to check against a single, previously specified digit; e.g., a check of the test to determine whether the number of ones or zeros is odd or even. 4. A technique in parallel addition wherein some or all of the carries are temporarily stored instead of being allowed to propagate immediately. 5. A binary digit appended to an array of bits to make the sum of all the bits always odd or always even.

parity, block system—A system of using an additional bit to a block of information to detect single bit errors in the block.

parity check—1. A summation check in which the binary digits, in a character or word, are added, and the sum checked against a single, previously computed parity digit; i.e., a check tests whether the number of ones in a word is odd or even. (Synonymous with odd-even check, and related to redundant check and forbidden-combination check.) 2. Use of a redundant and the least significant digit (called the parity digit) carried along as a check of a binary (machine) word. It is 1 if the total number of 1's in the machine word is odd, and 0 if the total number of 1's in the machine word is even, for the even parity check. The digit value is 0 for an odd number of 1's, and 1 for an even number of 1's when the odd parity check is used. See odd-even check.

parity check, character (communications)—During transmission, as the core storage readout is being converted from parallel to serial bit form, the data line terminal at the transmitting end functions to add a parity bit, where necessary, to make each data character odd or even parity. As the data characters are being received, the data line terminal makes a parity check as the conversion from serial to parallel bit form takes place for the storage entry. The parity and synchronizing bits are dropped off at this time. If the wrong parity is detected, an error is signalled by the receiving computer.

parity check digit—See check digit, parity.

parity check, even—See check, even parity.

parity check, horizontal—A parity check applied to the group of certain bits from every character in a block.

parity check, longitudinal (communications)—The data line terminal generates a longitudinal parity count character as the data characters are being transmitted. This is essentially a count for even parity of all bits in each one of the bit levels for all data characters in the message. This same count is also generated for the bits of the data characters entering the data line terminal when it is receiving. The longitudinal parity-count character generated by the magnetic tape terminal at the sending end follows immediately after the end of the block character, to be compared with the longitudinal parity count character generated at the computer.

parity-check, vertical—*Same as* even parity check and similar to odd parity check.

parity-count character (longitudinal)—*Same as* parity check, longitudinal (communications).

parity, drum—A particular use of parity checking in drum storage, i.e., used when transferring data to or from digital computers to magnetic drums.

parity error—*See* error, parity.

parity, even—*See* odd-even check.

parity interrupt, memory — *See* interrupt, parity (memory).

parity, I/O interrupt—*See* interrupt I/O parity.

parity-line circuit—A multistation net in which all stations are on a single circuit. The stations must share the circuit since only one station may transmit at a time.

parity, magnetic-tape—*See* magnetic tape parity.

parity, odd—*See* check digit, parity.

parity or mark-track error — Indicates that during the course of the previous block transfer, a data parity error was detected or one or more bits have been picked up or dropped out from either the timing track or the mark track.

parity, storage—A particular application of parity checking codes or devices when transferring data to or from storage devices such as disk, drum, auxiliary core, etc.

parity, tape—That particular application of parity checking codes or devices when transferring data to or from magnetic or paper tape.

parsing, language theory — The breaking down of the components of a sentence into structural forms.

part—A part of an instruction word that specifies the address of an operand. Loosely, the operator part of an instruction.

part, address—1. A part of an instruction word that specifies the address of the operand. 2. The part of an instruction word that defines the address of a register or location.

part, fixed-point—The segment of the floating-point numeral which expresses the number of times that the number base with exponent is to be multiplied, i.e., in the expression, 8.08×10^8, the 8.08 is the fixed-point part.

part, function—*Same as* operation part.

partial arithmetic, multiple—*See* arithmetic, multiple.

partial carry—*See* carry, partial.

partial drive pulse—*See* pulse, partial write.

partial product—*See* product, partial.

partial-read pulse—Any one of the applied currents that will cause selection of a core for reading.

partial-select input pulse—*Same as* partial write pulse.

partial-select output pulse—*Same as* partial read plus.

partial sum—*See* sum, partial.

partial sum gate—*Same as* gate, exclusive OR.

partial word—A programming device which permits the selection of a portion of a machine word for processing.

partial write pulse—*See* pulse, partial write.

partitioned data set—*See* data set, partitioned.

partitioning — Subdividing one large block into smaller subunits that can be handled more conveniently, e.g., partitioning a matrix.

part, operation—*See* operation part.

part, operator—*Same as* operaiton part.

parts programmer—*See* programmer, parts.

Pascal, Blaise (1623-1662)—A French mathematician and essay writer who built a successful digital calculating machine in 1642. This was the first adding machine to resemble the modern desk calculator.

pass—1. The travel of magnetic tape past a read head, or travel of cards through a card feed; that portion of a program that can be accomplished during the foregoing. 2. A single execution of an instruction group that constitutes a loop. 3. A complete cycle of reading, processing and writing, i.e., a machine run.

pass, band—The difference in cycles/sec between the limiting frequencies of a band in which the attenuation of any frequency, with respect to the central frequency, is less than a specified value (usually half power or three db).

pass, sorting—The processing of each file record once, for the purpose of reducing the number of strings of sequenced records and increasing the number of sequenced records per string.

pass (sorting), intermediate—Any phase of a merging operation which, because of the number of strings or otherwise, does not reduce the file to a single sequenced string.

password—The unique set of digits or characters assigned to a user as part of his identification number in communicating with the computer.

patch—1. A section of coding inserted into a routine (usually by explicitly transferring control from the routine to the patch and back again) to correct a mistake or alter the routine. 2. A special routine linked to the program by unconditional transfers of control; used for checking or correcting programs. 3. To correct or change the coding at a particular location by inserting transfer instructions at that location and by adding the new instructions and the replaced instructions elsewhere.

patch bay—A concentrated assembly of electrical tie points that offers a means of electrical connection between the inputs and outputs of computing elements, multiples, reference voltages, and ground.

patchboard—A removable board containing hundreds of terminals into which patch cords (short wires) are connected, which determine the different programs for the machine. To change the program, the wiring pattern on the patchboard or the patchboard itself must be changed.

patch cord—A handy flexible connector conductor with receptacles or connectors at each end and which is used to interconnect sockets of plugboards.

patch, future-address—The assembler builds a link back list for symbols that have not been defined. These symbols are referred to as "futures" and are handled in the following manner. The link back list is a series of addresses, loaded with each command or data word that link together all references to a particular future symbol. When the symbol is defined, a future patch containing the actual address (p) of the symbol and the address of the last reference (r) is added to that symbol. When the loader recognizes a future patch record, the address portion of location r will be taken as the previous reference, called "r 1." The address p will be placed in the address portion of r. If the address portion of "r 1" is greater than zero, it is taken as the new "r" and this link back process is repeated. When the address portion of "r 1" is equal to zero, the process is terminated. Address p may be absolutely relocatable to the program-loading base or relocatable to the base of common storage in some systems.

patching plug program—A relatively small auxiliary plugboard patched with a specific variation of a portion of a program and designed to be plugged into a relatively larger plugboard patched with the main program.

patch panel—See control panel.

patchplug—A specialized plug of metal or plastic which functions as a patchcord. The patchplug is cordless in contrast to a standard plug which has a wire for jumping or connecting two terminals. A patchplug usually has an insulating handle.

patch-program plugboard—See plugboard, patch program.

patch routine—1. Enables octal changes (or corrections) to be made to specified programs at object program execution time. Changes occur in core memory only and do not affect the object program stored on the run tape. 2. A specific correcting routine

written of a sequence on the program chart and referring to a correct sequence.

path—The logical course or line of direction taken by a computer in the execution of a routine.

path, critical—The longest time path in a project which has to be done as quickly as possible. Because the overall time required to complete the project can not be less than that required along the critical path, it requires the most careful monitoring. Any delay along this path causes the project to be delayed, while minor delays along noncritical paths does not. See PERT.

path, main—The principal course or line of direction taken by a computer in the execution of a routine, directed by the logic of the program and the nature of the data.

pattern, bit—See bit pattern.

pattern compaction, curve—See compaction, curve fitting.

pattern, hole—An array of punches, i.e., a configuration of holes in a single column or in a single frame of punched tape.

pattern recognition—1. The identification, by automatic means, of shapes, forms, or configurations. 2. The recognition of shapes or other patterns by a machine system. The patterns may be either a physical shape or a speech pattern.

pattern-sensitive fault—A fault which is brought forth only as a result to one or certain patterns or sequences of data, i.e., a program for testing for positive, negative, or zero in that order and which could respond incorrectly to minus zero, but would respond properly to all other numbers, or a fault brought on by excessive heat dissipation.

paycheck run—Refers to the processing and actual printing of payroll checks.

PCM—1. Punched card machine—The set of conventional punch card equipment including sorters, collators, and tabulators. (Synonymous with EAM and clarified by tabulating equipment.) 2. Pulse code modulation—Modulation of a pulse train in accordance with a code.

PCMI—An abbreviation for PhotoChromic MicroImage, which is a trademark of National Cash Register Company (NCR), which describes a microimage process developed by NCR which can develop reductions of 140,000 in area, i.e., 1.6 billion words or 7.5 billion characters can be stored on less than 2 square inches of the surface of a film.

peak data transfer—See data transfer rate.

peek-a-boo—A method for checking the presence or absence of punched holes in identical locations on cards by placing one card on top of another card.

peek-a-boo system—See Batten system.

peephole masks—See masks, peephole.

pence coding, single column—A punched card code with relative addresses in the program instructions. See code, relative.

pence conversion equipment—Card equipment capable of punching duodecimal coding, using digits 0 through 11 as a single hole punched in a twelve-position column.

PENCIL—A system for storing, retrieving and manipulating line drawings.

pen, light—An optional device, used in conjunction with the incremental display, that can greatly extend its usefulness. It is a high speed, photosensitive device that can cause the computer to change or modify the display on the cathode-ray tube. As the pertinent display information is selected by the operator, the pen signals the computer by generating a pulse. Acting upon this signal, the computer can then instruct other points to be plotted across the tube face in accordance with the pen movements, or exercise specific options previously programmed without the need for separate input devices.

pen (light) control—A light pen for communication between operator and processor. When this pen-like device is pointed at information displayed on the screen, it detects light from the cathode-ray tube when a beam passes within its field of view. The pen's response is transmitted to the computer, which relates the computer's action to the section of the image being displayed. In this way, the operator can delete or add text, maintain tighter control over the program, and choose alternative courses of action.

perception, artificial—See artificial cognition.

perforated—A more suitable word to use in combination with paper tape than the word punched; e.g., perforated tape includes punched paper tape.

perforated card, margin—See card, edge punched.

perforated card, verge—See card, edge punched.

perforated edge card—Same as card, edge-punched.

perforated paper tape—A strip of paper on which characters are represented by combinations of punched holes.

perforated, tape—See tape, punched paper.

perforation rate—That particular rate at which characters or words are punched in tapes and measured in characters per second.

perforator—An off-line, keyboard-operated device for punching code holes in paper tape.

perforator, keyboard—See keyboard perforator.

perforator, tape—An electronic or manually operated device which punches holes in paper tape.

perforator tape unit—See tape processing unit.

perform—In COBOL, a verb for departing temporarily from the normal sequence of the program to execute some other procedure a specified number of times, and then return to the normal sequence.

performance evaluation—The analysis (in terms of initial objectives and estimates and usually made on site) of accomplishments, using an automatic data-processing system to provide information on operating experience and to identify any required corrective actions.

performance period—A particular time interval in which a device is to operate, i.e., the scheduled hours of operation, but not including various test or preparatory schedules or hours rescheduled due to equipment malperformance.

period, action—The time during which the stored data is read or new data is written in a storage location, specifically in electrostatic storage tubes.

period, digit—The time interval between the occurrence of successive digit signals.

periodic dumping, time sharing—See time sharing, periodic dumping.

period, performance—See performance period.

period, regeneration—The time during which the screen is swept by the electron beam in electrostatic storage tubes for the sole purpose of regenerating or restoring the charge distribution which represents the stored data.

period, retention—The time interval in file maintenance in which records are kept as dead storage before they can be destroyed, i.e., a terminal date is specified which may be fixed or dependent upon some event.

period, scan—See scan period.

peripheral—Operation of input/output and other devices not under direct computer control; most commonly used to designate the transfer of information between magnetic tapes and other media.

peripheral buffers—Magnetic-core buffers outside the main processor memory compensate for speed differences between slower electromechanical input/output devices and processor speeds. Operations are overlapped, with all units operating simultaneously at rated speeds. Buffering eliminates the need for more expensive, multiple I/O channels, and eliminates complex I/O timing considerations from the programming job.

peripheral control, input/output—See input/output peripheral control.

peripheral controls—Peripheral controls regulate the transfer of data between the central processor and peripheral devices. Specifically, they reconcile the mechanical speeds of the peripheral devices with the electronic speed of the computer.

peripheral-control switching unit—A peripheral-control switching unit permits any two processors to share the same peripheral devices. From one to eight peripheral controls can be attached to a switching unit, and consequently, to any one of two central processors. Additional switching-unit modules may be added (up to three) to provide the capability of switching four groups of peripheral controls. Each module and the basic unit may be switched independently. All controls handled by any one switching-unit module are switched simultaneously.

peripheral control unit — An intermediary control device that links a peripheral unit to the central processor, or in the case of off-line operation, to another peripheral unit.

peripheral conversion program—Handles all those jobs normally done by a separate peripheral processor. The priority interrupt system and multiple memory accumulators in the computer eliminate virtually all loss in running time. Such processing is done through the arithmetic processor.

peripheral equipment—1. Various units or machines that are used in combination or conjunction with the computer but are not part of the computer itself, such as typewriters, sorters, tape readers, and others. 2. Operations considered not a part of processing, computing or logic, but instead mainly input and output operations, such as magnetic tape conversion, card punching, printing, reading. *See* auxiliary equipment.

peripheral equipment, list—The list of peripheral equipment that is available for most computers includes: magnetic drums, magnetic-tape units, punched-card units, high-speed printer, paper-tape subsystems, supervisory console auxiliaries, analog-to-digital and digital-to-analog converters, electronic printers, displays, plotters and keysets, multiplex and switching units, real-time units, mass storage units, off-line systems, and many others.

peripheral equipment operator—*See* operator, peripheral equipment.

peripheral interrupt — The stop resulting from the signal of readiness for or completion of a task by a peripheral device.

peripheral operation — Operation of input/output and other devices not under direct computer control; most commonly used to designate the transfer of information between magnetic tapes and other media.

peripheral plotters—*See* plotters, peripheral.

peripheral processing, concurrent — Service functions can be performed on a peripheral computing system that serves as an auxiliary to a larger system, or they can be performed on one system concurrently with other types of processing, such as stacked job processing, in a way that ensures that the data-processing facilities of the system are efficiently employed. When peripheral and stacked job processing are performed concurrently, it is possible to incorporate in the operating system optional features that are designed to enable the operator to mount files for one job while other jobs are being processed.

peripheral processor — For some environments, input and output are best processed by two interconnected computers wherein one computer handles the input/output for the other. The control programs of operating system provide the capability to handle this mode of operation for a configuration of equipment in which a very high-speed, high-storage capacity central processing unit performs calculations upon data supplied by a smaller computer that schedules, buffers, and controls the flow of input data, intermediate results, and output data to and from the larger unit. Usually in this configuration the larger unit is termed the "host" and the smaller one is called "peripheral," but either one may actually be in control of the other's operations and schedule.

peripherals, conversion program—*See* conversion program, peripherals.

peripheral subsystems—A subsystem consists of one or more peripheral units of the same type connected to an available input/output channel. Each subsystem is controlled by a channel synchronizer/control unit that interprets the control signals and instructions issued by the central processor, effects the transfer of data to or from the selected unit and the central processor, indicates to the central processor the status of the available peripheral units, and informs the central processor when errors or faults that affect the operation of the subsystem occurs.

peripheral transfer—A procedure or process for transferring data between two units of peripheral or auxiliary equipment.

peripheral trunks — The basic systems are equipped with many input/output trunks, each of which can be connected to a peripheral control. A control which handles both reading and writing (e.g., a magnetic tape control) connects to a pair of trunks. Data are transferred between main memory and a trunk (and thus a peripheral device) via the read/write channel specified in the instruction which initiates the transfer. Additional peripheral devices can be connected to the system simply by adding eight more input/output trunks to the basic configuration. The number of peripheral devices in a system depends only on the number of input/output trunks available.

permanent data files—*See* data files.

permanent fault—*See* fault, permanent.

permanent memory — Storage information that remains intact when the power is turned off. Also called nonvolatile storage.

permanent storage—*Same as* storage, nonvolatile.

permutated-title, index—*Same as* index, permutation.

permutation—Any of the total number of changes in position or form that are possible in a group.

permutation index—*See* index, permutation.

permuted code cyclic—*See* code, unit distance.

permuted-title index—*Same as* index, permutation.

PERT/COST—A PERT program for providing management with cost control for all phases of a project.

PERT/COST system — A generalized program designed to facilitate planning, scheduling, control, and monitoring of both large- and small-scale research and development projects.

PERT, early start dates—Used in an optimistic time estimate in which each job is started as early as possible to estimate the duration of the entire task.

PERT, free float—Certain stops used to halt particular tasks where no action would have resulted in an overall delay in the project.

pertinency factor—See factor, pertinency.

PERT, latest start dates—Used in estimating the completion date of a particular task. Each job is arranged to start as late as possible so that the entire task is completed on the required date.

PERT (Program Evaluation and Review Technique) network—Use of PERT requires an extensive analysis of an overall project in order to list all the individual activities, or jobs which must be performed in order to meet the total objective. These activities are then arranged in a network that displays the sequential relationship among them. This analysis must be extremely thorough and detailed if it is to be realistic. PERT provides a means of reporting and analysis for project administrators. Information required can be developed and areas which impose the greatest time restrictions on the completion of a product can be high-lighted. Areas with an excess of time for completion, called slack areas, are also high-lighted.

PERT, start dates—Used in estimating the completion date of a particular task. Each job is arranged to start as late as possible so that the entire task is completed on the required date.

PERT/TIME—A PERT program which allows management to plan, schedule, and direct programs and projects, as well as evaluate progress during project execution.

PGEC—Abbreviation for professional group on electronic computers. A technical group devoted to the advancement of computer-related sciences, i.e., programming, engineering, storage devices, etc.

phase, compiling—See compiling phase.

phase, execute—1. The part of the computer operating cycle wherein a command in the program register is carried out upon the address indicated. 2. The act of performing a command.

phase, object—Same as phase, run.

phase recording, redundant—Insures transfer reliability, reduces problem of skew in bi-directional operation. Each tape track is redundantly paired with a second, non-adjacent track. Use of phase (rather than amplitude) recording greatly reduces drop-outs due to variations in amplitude.

phase, run—An occasion on which the target program (after compiling) is run and often called the run phase, the target phase, or the object phase.

phase, shift—The time difference between the input and output signal or between any two synchronized signals of a control unit, system, or circuit.

phase, sorting—An arbitrary segmentation of a sort program. Many sorts are segmented into three phases: initialization phase, internal phase, merge phase.

phase, target—Same as phase, run.

phone, data—A generic term to describe a family of devices available to facilitate data communication.

phoneme—A primitive unit of auditory speech in a given language.

phones, standard data—Standard telephone company data sets (dataphones) at each end of the telephone line convert signals from the RTU (remote terminal unit) and CTU (central terminal unit) into tones for transmission over the line. Conversely, the data set converts tones received from the lines into signals for the terminal units.

phonetic system—The specific equipment which has features for starting and acting upon data from the voice source or having a voice-form output.

photocell light checks—Checks performed on data read from cards passing through a card reader.

photocell matrix—An optical character recognition term which is a device capable of projecting an input onto a fixed two-dimensional array of photocells to develop a simultaneous display of the horizontal and vertical components of the character. The time necessary to scan the character is related to the response time of the photocells.

photoelectric reader—See reader, photoelectric.

photographic storage—1. Photographic copies of data shown on direct-display cathode-ray tubes. 2. High-density storage of data in binary form on photographic disks for quick reference purposes. 3. Facsimile copies of readable documents or of direct output of the processor.

photogravure—A method of printing in which the small cells of the characters contain the ink on a recessed surface. This method is often used in preparing documents for character recognition.

photomultiplier light pen—A fiber optic light pipe and photomultiplier in the light pen allow high-speed detection of information displayed on the various optical displays. Detection of information by the pen can be sampled by the computer to alter the program.

photo-optic memory—A memory that uses an optical medium for storage. For example, a laser might be used to record on photographic film.

phototypesetting—A reproduction process for typed matter from computer outputs to photographic film or paper, and basically using optical character recognition after phototypesetting has been used to perfect or normalize character irregularities off-line. Computer-controlled phototypesetting is also used for computer generated output for clean appearance, rapid processing, and for the use of unusual type characters which ordinary line printers cannot provide, for example to produce phone directories.

physical record—Each punched card is a physical record. Magnetic tapes and disks have physical records bounded at beginnings and ends by interrogated gaps. Physical records on these media are simply the start/stop boundaries while punched paper tape and drums have other special boundaries.

physical simulation—The use of a model of a physical system in which computing elements are used to represent some but not all of the subsystems.

physical system time—*See* time, physical system.

pica—A unit of measure in printing approximating one-sixth of an inch, in horizontal measurement.

pickup—Refers to a memory location from which the processor will obtain specific information.

pick-up fail—A lamp that glows when none of the stations responds to the invitation to send. After 5 seconds a disconnect sequence starts, which extinguishes the lamp.

P.I. codes—Program indicator codes. When two or more programs are used in the same program tape, the use of PI codes permits automatic selection of programs and permits switching from one program to the other.

picosecond—One thousandth of a nanosecond, or 10^{-12} seconds; abbreviated psec.

pictorial—A series of specifications and total layout of columns, blank spaces, margins, headings, stubs, etc., to develop the plan or format for the contemplated reports.

picture—In COBOL, a symbolic description of each data element according to specified rules concerning numerals, alphanumerics, location of decimal points, and length.

piece work programming—The programming technique of using an outside service organization to prepare programs for which payment is arranged by accomplishment, other than on a time-cost basis. Software companies are usually consulted for the above.

pilot—An original or test program, project, or device.

pilot model—A model of a system that is not so complex as a complete model and is used for program testing.

pilot system—The collection of file records and supplementary data obtained from the actual operations of a business over an extended period and used to effect a realistic system for testing by closely simulating the real world environment.

pilot tape—A tape that contains all the data used on a pilot model, and is used for loading the files.

pinboard—A perforated board that accepts manually inserted pins to direct the operation of equipment.

pinboard machine—A machine in which pins are inserted in holes in a panel to call for a function or storage.

pinfeed form—A strip of continuous-form paper that is fed, aligned, and positioned by means of pins or sprockets that fit in holes and is used on writing or printing mechanisms.

pinfeed platen—A cylindrical platen that drives the paper by means of integral rings of pins engaging perforated holes.

ping-pong—The programming technique of using two magnetic-tape units for multiple-reel files and switching automatically between the two units until the complete file is processed.

pitch array—*See* pitch row.

pitch, character—That specific difference from the vertical reference axis of a character to the vertical reference axis of the adjacent character in a line of text or in a printed word.

pitch, feed—The distance between the centers of adjacent feed holes in perforated tape. Feed pitch and row pitch are often the same because there is one row of holes at each feed hole.

pitch-row—The distance measured along punched paper tape between the centers of adjacent holes.

pitch, track—The distance between centers of adjacent tracks on magnetic tapes, disks, drums, cards, or on paper tape, i.e., the distance between centers of holes is measured across the longitudinal axis or traverse to the motion of the recording device or medium.

PL/1 (programming language)—Compilers are provided for use in compiling object programs from source programs written in this programming language. This language has some features that are characteristic of FORTRAN and incorporates some of the best features of other languages, such as string manipulation, data structures, and extensive editing capabilities. Further, it has features not currently available in any language. The language is designed to take advantage of recent developments in computer technology and to provide the programmer with a flexible problem-oriented language for programming problems that can best be solved using a combination of scientific and commercial computing techniques. It is designed to be particularly useful for the increasing number of semicommercial, semi-scientific applications such as information retrieval and command and control applications.

place—In positional notation, a position corresponding to a given power of the base, a given cumulated product, or a digit cycle of a given length. It can usually be specified as the nth character from the right end of the numerical expression.

place, digit—The site of a digit in a numeral in various positional notation systems.

place value—The representation of quantities by a positional value system.

plane digits—A specific array of cells which are arranged in order to affect three dimensions. The plane therefore contains corresponding bits of every word.

plant—The usage in programming is to put or place an instruction which has been formed during the execution of a routine in a storage location, in such a way that it will be obeyed at some later stage in the execution. Thus, plants give the computer the ability to control and execute its own programs by using the ability of the computer to prepare or select instructions or subroutines on the basis of results obtained.

plate embossed, printer—The data preparation device, in character recognition, which prints through the paper medium by allowing only the raised character to make contact with the printing ribbon.

platen — A backing, commonly cylindrical, against which printing mechanisms strike to produce an impression.

platen, pinfeed—See pinfeed platen.

playback head—See head, playback.

plot—To map or diagram. To connect the point-by-point coordinate values.

plotter—1. A visual display or board in which a dependent variable is graphed by an automatically controlled pen or pencil as a function of one or more variables. 2. A device that inscribes a visual display of a dependent variable.

plotter control, incremental — Provides for high-speed plotting of points, continuous curves, points connected by curves, curve identification symbols, letters, and numerals under program control.

plotter, digital incremental — Digital incremental plotters in either on-line or off-line operation with a digital computer provide a high-speed plotting system of high versatility and reliability. For on-line operation with medium size computers, a small adapter unit converts the computer output signals to a form suitable for driving the plotter. No modification to the basic computer circuitry is required. With adapters available for all of the units, the plotter can be used off-line with virtually any medium- or large-scale computer.

plotter, display console—The major element of the unit is a console with a 12-inch square display screen (a 21-inch cathode-ray tube) on which tables, graphs, charts, alphanumerical characters, or the lines and curves of drawings can be displayed as a series of points. When the full display area is used, 3848 alphanumeric characters—the contents of a page of information—can be viewed. A built-in electronic marker helps the operator edit messages. When the display console is used as a point plotter, it can plot graphs, charts, and drawings with the precision of a square matrix of 1024 points, or more than one million individually addressable points. Buffer storage for the unit is available in 4096 and 8192 character capacities. These buffer storage units hold points, lines, and position instructions which may be read from or written at a maximum rate of 238,095 characters a second (some systems).

plotter, on-line—See on-line plotter.

plotters, peripheral — Digital incremental plotters offer varied paper size, speeds, and plotting increments. Since the control unit does not require the use of a computer I/O channel, simultaneous plotting and other I/O channel operations on the same channel are possible.

plotter, XY—A device used in conjunction with a computer to plot coordinate points in the form of a graph.

plotting—The process of placing any type of information on the graph.

plotting, automatic—In many diverse areas of industry and science, a clear graphical representaion of results is essential for rapid interpretation and evaluation of data. From weather mapping to business and stock market reports, from engineering design investigations to insurance actuarial graphs, in research laboratories and in computer laboratories, graphs of X vs Y plots are required for summarizing and presenting information in concise form. This need has been further accentuated by modern high-speed computers. The rapid production of vast quantities of data by these machines requires especially fast and accurate plotting equipment.

plotting board—See board, plotting.

plotting system, magnetic-tape—This system is very versatile, reliable, and almost completely automatic. Zero position, scale-factor adjustment, curve identification, symbol selection, axis generation, etc., are handled entirely by subroutines within the computer. For this reason the plotting system may be operated by unskilled personnel. The operator is required only to select the desired plot by means of the automatic-search feature, then initiate the plotting action by pressing either the single or multiple plot button. These systems produce completed graphs from data recorded on magnetic tape. Information read from the tape is used to drive a digital incremental plotter which reproduces the data in either a continuous curve or discrete points. Versatility of the system permits the use of subroutines for generation of any desired symbols, letters, numerals, or scale markings.

plotting system, tape-format — Each plot is preceded by a block address recognized by the tape system and an identification word recognized by the computer. If more than one record is required for a single plot, the separate records may also be identified by computer ID words. Interrecord codes are used to temporarily halt the plotting action.

plotting table—*See* board, plotting.

plugboard chart—*See* chart, plugboard.

plugboard computer—A computer that has a punchboard input and output, and to which program instructions are delivered by means of interconnecting patch cords on a removable plugboard.

plugboard, detachable—*Same as* patchboard.

plugboard, patch-program—*See* plug, program patching.

plugboard, removable—*Same as* patchboard.

plugging chart—*Same as* chart, plugboard.

plug-in unit— 1. An assembly of electronic components of a standard type, wired together, which can be plugged in or pulled out easily. 2. A self-contained circuit assembly.

plug, patch—*See* patchplug.

plug, program-patching — A relatively small auxiliary plugboard patched with a specific variation of a portion of a program and designed to be plugged into a relatively larger plugboard patched with the main program.

plugs, cordless—On patchcords, if connectors do not include a flexible portion, they are termed cordless plugs.

plus-90 orientation — An optical character recognition term which represents that specific position which indicates line elements on a document.

pocket—In sorters and other like equipment, the stacker assigned for each key position, i.e., a card storage temporary location or pocket for a given key for which totals are developed.

pockets, file addressing—In a random file, a small area or pocket in which one or more records are kept—an economical method of holding a small number of records.

pocket-size reels—Handy to carry, easy to load. Each 3½ inch reel holds up to 3 million bits, the equivalent of 4000 feet of paper tape, assuming 6-bit words are used.

point—In positional notation, the character or implied character that separates the integral part of a numerical expression from the fractional part, e.g., a decimal point or binary point.

point, arithmetic—*See* point, radix.

point, base—*See* point, radix.

point, binary—The radix point in a binary number system; i.e., the dot that marks the position between the integral and fractional, or units and halves, in a binary number.

point, branch—A given condition or instruction at which the computer may either continue on the present logical path, or jump (transfer control of the program) to another or one of several possible paths.

point, check—*See* checkpoint.

point, decimal—*See* decimal point.

point, entry—*See* entry point.

pointer—A table look-up technique that permits each datum (X_1) to be stored with a pointer pointing to a list of associated functions of X_1, as a variant technique to ordered or sequential or even indirect addressing techniques.

pointer, index register—*See* index register pointer.

pointer, register—The portion of the program status double-word that points to a set of 16 general registers to be used as the current register block.

pointer stacker—In nested storage types (push-down), the address of the location at the top of the column is often called the stack pointer and is held in a preassigned register.

point, exit—The instruction that transfers controls from the main routine to the subroutine.

point, fixed—Pertaining to a number system in which the location of a point is fixed with respect to one end of the numerals, according to some convention.

point, floating—Pertaining to a number system in which the location of the point does not remain fixed with respect to one end of the numerals.

point, index—One of the equally spaced rotational reference positions of the main shaft of card punch machines, labeled according to the row or column to which it corresponds.

point, load—A preset point at which magnetic tape is initially positioned under the read/write head to start reading or writing.

point-mode, display — *See* display, point mode.

point of no return—A first instance in a program in which a rerun is no longer possible, since data may no longer be available.

point, radix—The dot that delineates the integer digits from the fractional digits of a number; specifically, the dot that delineates the digital position involving the zero exponent of the radix from the digital position involving the minus-one exponent of the radix. The radix point is often identified by the name of the system, e.g., binary point, octal point, or decimal point. In the writing of any number in any system, if no dot is included the radix point is assumed to follow the rightmost digit. (Synonymous with point.)

point, re-entry—The point at which an instruction or a program is re-entered from a subroutine or main program.

point, rerun—*See* rerun, point.

point, restart—*Same as* restart.

point, restart (sorting)—The point at which a restart (or rerun) can be initiated. Memory registers, and the position of tapes are recorded at this point.

point, set—The specific desired value for the quantity being controlled; usually in a feed back control loop.

point shift, floating—A shift in 4-bit increments, performed on a short-format or long-format floating-point number.

points, rescue—*See* rescue points.

point, summing—Relates to any distinct point at which signals are added algebraically.

point-to-point transmission—Transmission of data between two points.

point, variable—Pertaining to a number system in which the location of the point is indicated by a special character at that location.

polar—When a logical "true" input is represented by an electrical voltage with a polarity opposite to the voltage representing a logical "false" input, the signal is defined as bipolar. If both "true" and "false" inputs are represented by the same voltage polarity, the signal is defined as unipolar.

polar operation—A type of circuit operation where the flow of current is reversed as pulses are transmitted. Polar differs from make-break operation in that with polar operation, current always flows when the circuit is closed. Only the direction of current flow is reversed by transmission.

Polish, Cambridge—Used in the LISP language, the Polish operators = and × are allowed to have more than two operands.

Polish notation—1. A distinct technique or device credited to the Polish logician J. Lukasieqicz for treating algebraic statements as manipulatory strings of symbols followed by manipulatory strings of operations. 2. A specific form of prefix notation.

poll—A flexible, systematic method centrally controlled for permitting stations on a multipoint circuit to transmit without contending for the line.

polling—1. An alternative to contention networks wherein terminals are polled in sequence to see if they have anything to send. Polling prevents any one terminal from an overly long wait. 2. A procedure which relates to the integration in succession of all terminals of a system on a shared communications line to determine which of the terminals requires the services of the mainframe or CPU. The sending device must be ready and the receiving device must be prepared and set to receive, much like a party-line telephone service, and each terminal can demand the attention from the CPU by a signal. Sophisticated computers have automatic polling circuitry, while others require special programming to poll.

polling list—Polling is a means of controlling communication lines by polling or asking the terminals if they have anything to send. The polling list is the device which controls the sequence of polling for every channel.

polling technique, remote—The importance of instantaneous responses to control messages can be best appreciated by this brief description of the on-line system's "polling" technique. The system is controlled through constant polling of teller consoles on each line by the central terminal unit. Polling is a request to each console for a message or for readiness to receive a reply. Because the full-duplex line permits the remote terminal unit to respond instantly to polls (less than $\frac{1}{10}$th of a second), as many as 16 teller consoles can be efficiently serviced on one line. The turn-around delay inherent in a half-duplex line greatly reduces the number of consoles which can be polled and serviced efficiently, thereby requiring more lines.

polymorphic—Relates to the mode of a computer organization or configuration of the major parts or units in such a way that all components at a particular installation are held in a common pool. As each program is selected for execution, a specific set of components is selected from the pool and connected for execution of the program, after which they are returned to the pool, i.e., each configuration of equipment is matched to a program. Thus, many programs can be run concurrently if enough matched sets can be made available from the pool.

polyphase—A unique sorting technique that permits sorting with either an odd or even number of tapes, thus permitting greater system flexibility than conventional methods.

polyphase merging—A technique used in a sort program to merge strings of sequenced data. Given T work tapes, merging is performed at the power of $T-1$. The effective power of the merge varies between $T-1$ and $T/2$, depending on the amount of input data and the number of strings.

polyvalence—The property of being interrelated in several ways.

polyvalent notation—A method for describing salient characteristics, in condensed form, using two or more characters, where each character or group of characters represents one of the characteristics.

polyvalent number—A number, consisting of several figures, used for description, wherein each figure represents one of the characteristics being described. (Similar to polyvalent notation.)

pooled input buffer—A special option is available on input communications buffers. To exercise this option, the ESI (Externally Specified Index) line from the communication multiplexer to the computer is disabled (plugboard connection), thus activating the internally specified index (ISI) mode. ISI is the data-transfer mode used by many standard peripherals. It allows for only one input and/or one output buffer per channel. Under these conditions, the entire word presented by the pooled input buffer would be transferred to memory under the control of the buffer control word associated with the channel. With this approach, the characters from all buffers serviced by the communication multiplexer would be intermixed in the buffer.

port—The entry channel to which a data set is attached. The port is in the central computer, and each user is assigned one port.

portable hand punch—A device for punching

cards by hand. It does not need electricity and is small enough to carry.

position—1. A site on a punched tape or card where holes are to be punched. The position at which the sign of a number is located. 2. An identifiable place in a program, set of instructions, or within a context.

positional notation—1. The procedure used in conventional number systems wherein the value assigned to a particular digit is determined by the symbol used (for example, 3) and by the position of the symbol relative to the radix point (for example, 300.0). 2. A number representation by means of an ordered set of digits, such that the value contributed by each digit depends on its position as well as on the digit value. 3. A method of representing numbers in which the digits are arranged sequentially, each succeeding digit is interpreted as the coefficient of successive powers of an integer referred to as the base of the number system. For example, in the decimal number system each succeeding digit is interpreted as successive coefficient powers of the integer or base 10.

positional number—A method for expressing a quantity, using two or more figures, wherein the successive right to left figures are to be interpreted as coefficients of ascending integer powers of the radix.

positional representation—A number representation or number system in which the significance or value of each digit depends upon its place or position with respect to a radix point. (Related to number system.)

position, code—*See* code position.

position, low-order—The extreme right digit or character position in a number or word.

position, overflow—An extra position in the register in which the overflow digit is developed.

position, pulse—*See* pulse.

position, punch—The row position of a punched hole in a specific column of a punched card. In an 80-column punch card the rows are designated 0 to 9, X or Y; in a 90-column card the rows are designated 0, 1, 3, 5, 7, and 9.

position, sign—The left-hand digit position in a numeric field, or the left-hand character position in an alphanumeric field, in which is stored the sign (minus symbol if negative) of the quantity stored in that field.

positions, print—The maximum number of characters which can be printed on a single line.

positions, punching—The specific areas, i.e., row-column intersects, on a punch card where holes may be punched.

position, units—The furthermost right position or the low order location. In the number 1054, the 4 is in the units position.

positive AND gate—*Same as* gate, AND.

positive OR gate—*Same as* gate, OR.

post—To enter a unit or information on a record.

post edit—To edit the results of a previous computation.

post-edit programs—A test of the application or operational program that is edited, formatted, and sorted into a test result tape.

postfix operators—A notation system where the operator appears after the operand, for example, $AB + = A + B$ as it is used in Polish notation.

posting, facsimile—1. The process of transferring, by a duplicating process, a printed line on a report to a ledger or other recorded sheet. These may be posted from a transaction listing prepared on an accounting machine. 2. A data-processing function.

post mortem—A check routine that prints out information either automatically, or when called for, concerning the contents of all or a specified part of storage after a problem has "died" on the computer. Its purpose is to assist in the location of a program error or a machine malfunction.

post mortem dump—A static dump, used for debugging purposes, that is performed at the end of a machine run.

post-mortem routine—1. A routine that either automatically or on demand prints data concerning registers and storage locations when the routine is stopped in order to assist in locating a mistake in coding. 2. Pertaining to the analysis of an operation after its completion. 3. Specific routine used in diagnostics and debugging operations after an error has been committed and must be located. 4. A service routine useful in analyzing the cause of a failure, such as a routine that dumps out the content of a store after a failure.

postmultiply—To multiply a matrix "A" by some conforming matrix "B," that is, by a matrix "B" that has as many rows as the given matrix "A" has columns ($A \times B$).

postnormalize—To normalize the result of an arithmetic operation.

post-write disturb pulse—*See* pulse post-write disturb.

powder, anti-setoff—Finely powdered limestone or starch applied to paper immediately after printing that allows for a more optically acceptable document in optical character recognition. The powder reduces the unintentional transfer of ink between stacked printed sheets.

power dump—The accidental or intentional removal of all power.

power fail interrupt — *See* interrupt, power fail.

power, mathematical—Relates to the number of times a number or quantity is to be multiplied by itself, i.e., 8^3 is eight cubed, or eight multiplied by itself as, $8 \times 8 \times 8$ or 512.

power, memory — A hierarchy of memories within a system makes information in core storage available at varying speeds. Small local store memories operate in as little as 200 billionths of a second. Control memories operate in as little as 250 billionths of a second. Powerful main memories—containing up to 524,000 characters of information—range from 2.5 millionths of a second down to one millionth of a second.

power of a number—The exponent.

powers card—*See* card, powers.

PPS—An abbreviation for pulses per second.

p-pulse—*See* pulse.

preanalysis—An initial review of the task to be accomplished by the computer in order to increase the efficiency of that task.

precision—The degree of exactness with which a quantity is stated; a relative term often based on the number of significant digits in a measurement. Contrast with accuracy, which refers to the absence of error regardless of precision. For example, a two-digit number is accurate if correctly stated; whereas a five-digit number may be inaccurate, despite having greater precision.

precision CRT display—This is a random-position, point-plotting cathode-ray tube with magnetic deflection and focusing. It is useful for conversion of digital computer data into graphic and tabular form.

precision, double—*See* double precision.

precision floating-point—The maximum number of binary digits used as the mantissa of a single-precision floating-point fraction.

precision, multiple—*See* multiple precision.

precision, single—The number of words or storage positions used to denote a number in a computer. Single-precision arithmetic is the use of one word per number; double precision, two words per number; and so on. For variable word-length computers, precision is the number of digits used to denote a number. The higher the precision, the greater the number of decimal places that can be carried.

precision, triple—The retention of three times as many digits of a quantity as the computer normally handles; e.g., a computer whose basic word consists of ten decimal digits is called upon to handle thirty decimal digit quantities.

precomplier program—A unique program which is designed to detect errors and provide source program correction before the computation of the object, deck, or program.

predefined process—*See* process, predefined.

predicate—To affirm or deny, in mathematical logic, one or more subjects.

pre-edit—To edit input data prior to computation.

pre-edit checking programs—*See* pre-edit programs.

pre-edit programs—A checking of the application or operational program before the test run. A pre-edit run can remove such things as disobedience to established supervisory, core, program segmentation rules, etc.

prefix notation—A method of forming one-dimensional expressions without need for brackets by preceding, with a string or vec-

tor of operators, an operand string or vector that may itself contain operators upon operands.

preliminary proposal review—An on-site review to provide guidance to proponent agencies in the preparation of ADP (automatic data-processing) system proposals.

preliminary review—*See* review, preliminary proposal.

premise, off—Standby equipment, usually a back up or duplicator set of computer equipment at another location. Available for performance of operations under circumstances where the failure of the prime equipment is acute as regards the time sensitivity of the operation being completed.

premultiply—To multiply a matrix "B" by some conforming matrix "A"—that is, by a matrix "A" that has as many columns as the given matrix "B" has rows (A×B).

prenormalize—To normalize the operands of an arithmetic operation before the operation is performed.

preparation aids, program—Program preparation aids convert programs from easy-to-use source languages into computer machine language.

preparation, data—The process of converting data into a medium suitable for input to and processing by the computer.

preparation, file—*See* file preparation.

preparation, object-program—Conversion of programs from one of several easy-to-use source languages, or from certain competitive system languages, to a specific machine code.

preparation, report—*See* report preparation.

preread disturb pulse—*See* pulse, preread disturb.

preread head—*See* head, preread.

prerecorded tracks—A preliminary tape, disk, or drum recorded routine that simplifies programming. Relieves the programmer of the responsibility of furnishing timing, or counting instructions and permits block and word addressability.

preselection—1. A technique for storing data from the next input tape in the computer memory before the data being processed by computer is absorbed. The selection of the next input tape is determined by instruction to the computer. 2. A programming technique in buffered computers in which a block of information is read into the input buffer register from the next input tape to be called upon.

presence, bit—*See* bit, presence.

preset—A preset relates to a variable whose value is established initially for some routine or operation, while to preset is the act of initializing a value of a variable.

preset mode—Card systems may be operated in the preset mode of operation. In this mode of operation the monitor is not resident in memory. Each absolute program is loaded into memory with the preset button on the computer console. The processing of individual jobs is the same as in the batch processing mode, except that the EOJ (end of job) card places the computer in a halt state. To begin processing a new job, the absolute compiler, assembler, loader, or utility program for the job must be preset into memory.

preset parameter—A parameter incorporated into a subroutine during computation. A program parameter frequently comprises a word stored relative to either the subroutine or the entry point, and dealt with by the subroutine during each reference. It may be altered by the routine, or it may vary from one point of entry to another.

presort—The first part of a sort, in which records are arranged into strings that equal or exceed some minimum length.

prestore—1. To store a quantity in an available or convenient location before it is required in a routine. 2. To set an initial value for the address of an operand or a cycle index. 3. To restore.

presumptive address — A number that appears as an address in a computer instruction, but which serves as the base, index, initial or starting point for subsequent addresses to be modified. (Synonymous with reference address.)

presumptive instruction—An instruction that will most likely be modified before it is used for the final program.

prevention, hang-up—See hang-up prevention.

preventive maintenance — 1. A maintenance plan that is designed to prevent failures rather than correct malfunctions. 2. The maintenance of a computer system that attempts to keep equipment in top operating condition and to preclude failures during production runs.

preventive maintenance contracts — Preventive maintenance contracts provide either resident field engineers or periodic-visit arrangements that are tailored to the user's specific needs. Competent and experienced personnel insure peak performance of all equipment.

previewing—An optical character recognition (OCR) term defining a process of trying to gain initial or prior information about characters which appear on an incoming source document. Such intelligence could be the range of ink density, relative position, etc., to be used as an aid to normalization or attempted perfecting of the oncoming reading operations.

prewired options—Optional equipments that are closely related to the processor, such as the extended arithmetic element, memory extension control, and one of the analog-to-digital converted options, are prewired in the basic computer so that the time, effort, and cost involved in adding these options at the factory or in the field is a minimum.

PRF—Abbreviation for pulse repetition rate.

prices, implicit—Same as marginal values, shadow prices, dual-variable levels, etc.—

that is, numbers giving the incremental worth of a relaxation of one unit in the right-hand side of a constraint.

primary equipment—Same as working equipment.

primitive—The most basic or fundamental unit of data, i.e., a single letter digit, element, or machine code as primitive when related to the ultrasophisticated codes or languages now available. Also refers to first or second generation computer equipment.

principle, unit record—Refers to a punched card used to record information about one transaction only in its 80 columns.

print and punch, combined—The simultaneous printing and punching of data onto a punched card.

print control character—See character, print control.

printer—1. A device that expresses coded characters as hard copy. 2. An output device for spelling-out computer results as numbers, words, or symbols. Printers range from electric typewriters to high-speed printers which prepare invoices, checks, statements or documents at 10 lines-per-second and faster.

printer, bar—1. A specific printer which has its type at each print position in a box or magazine. The desired character is selected by moving the box vertically until that character is opposite the printing position. 2. A printing device which utilizes several side-by-side type bars. Printing data involves activating specific bars which move vertically until the characters they contain are properly alligned. Then, the data are printed simultaneously.

printer, chain—A typical high-speed printer with type carried on a moving closed loop chain or belt which is hit-on-the-fly by a component hammer as the type moves across the paper.

printer, character—A device capable of producing hard copy, the printing being accomplished one character at a time.

printer, character-at-a-time—This type of printer is similar to an electric typewriter or teleprinter, or a printing keypunch.

printer, console—An auxiliary output printer used to relay messages to the computer operator.

printer dot—Same as printer, wire.

printer, electrostatic—A device for printing an optical image on paper in which dark and light areas of the original are represented by electrostatically charged and uncharged areas on the paper. The paper is dusted with particles of finely powdered dry ink and the particles adhere only to the electrically charged areas. The paper with ink particles is then heated, causing the ink to melt and become permanently fixed to the paper.

printer, high-speed (HSP)—A printer which operates at a speed more compatible with the speed of computation and data processing so that it may operate on-line. At the present time a printer operating at a speed of 1000 lines per minute and 100 characters per line, is considered high-speed.

printer, keyboard — The keyboard printer permits insertion of transaction data and printed page output of computer responses at speeds related to the common carrier service available. Either telegraphic or voice grade lines can be utilized. The keyboard and printer can be used separately or in combination. The keyboard contains a full four-bank set of keys, 10 numeric, 26 alphabetic, 10 special character keys, and a space bar. The printing unit prepares a copy of all transaction data as it is typed by the printing unit. The keyboard printer may be supplied with special features which make it an extremely versatile input/output device. For example, the unit can be used to prepare multilith masters, multiple interleaved carbon sets, horizontal and vertical tabulation, as well as a large variety of printed page requirements. It may be used to print payroll checks and a variety of order and invoice forms, and can be programmed to extract selected portions of a transmitted message at various locations.

printer/keyboard time-sharing — *See* time sharing, keyboard/printer.

printer limited — Often, the timing restrictions on a process due to the slowness or inadequacy of the printing equipment, whereby other operations must await the completion of the printing unit.

printer, line — A device capable of simultaneously printing one line of characters across a page (100 or more characters) as continuous paper advances line by line in one direction past type bars or a type cylinder that contains all characters in all positions.

printer, line-at-a-time — A device capable of printing 100 or more characters simultaneously as continuous paper advances line-by-line in one direction past type bars or a drum printer that contains all print characters in all positions.

printer, matrix — *Same as* printer, wire.

printer, numeric — The numeric printer prints the entire contents of a memory unit or indexed amounts (up to 12 digits) simultaneously, rather than one digit at a time. In addition, automatic transaction dates, descriptive codes, and memory addresses, when required, print simultaneously with the indexed amounts. (Some units.)

printer, on-the-fly — A high-speed line printer using continuously rotating print wheels and fast-acting hammers to print the successive letters contained in one line of text so rapidly that all of the characters in the printed line look as though they were all printed simultaneously.

printer, output edit — Several important considerations in editing for printout include the alignment of information into proper order for printing, suppression of nonsignificant zeros, insertion of symbols and

punctuation, and conversion of a machine code to an appropriate printer symbol. Alignment of information may involve rearrangement of fields or possibly only the insertion of spaces between fields. For example, in a straight listing that simply prints out the contents of a number of cards, it is desirable to insert spaces between fields for ease in reading the printed result.

printer, page — A unique printer which composes a full page of characters before printing this full page during a cycle of operations. Such types are xerographic printers, CRT (cathode-ray tube) printers, photographic devices.

printer, serial — A device capable of printing characters, one at a time across a page. Many variations in serial printers exist, e.g., typewriter; stylus or matrix serial printer; and high-speed, multiple-line stylus or matrix serial printer.

printer, skip — A skip function may be signaled on any step. When skip is signaled on a step that also impulses print, the skip function is effective after the line has been printed. If skip is signaled on any other step, the skipping action is initiated immediately.

printer skipping — The rate at which the unit advances a form through the carriage without printing.

printer spacing chart — A form for developing a layout and spacing, or general design of printed output, as well as the preparation of the carriage control tape.

printer speed — The rate at which the unit operates when actually printing data, ranging from the slowest to the fastest speed of the unit.

printer, stick — An antiquated printer consisting of a stick which prints one character at a time as the stick moves from left to right.

printer, stylus — *See* printer, wire.

printer type bar — A narrow box or magazine contains the type bars and when a particular character is selected a vertical movement of the box proceeds until the selected character is opposite the printing position. Each bar contains the entire alphabet and may be interchangeable or fixed.

printer type bar, interchangeable — A printer type bar which can be removed by the operator to change from one alphabet to another.

printer, wheel — A printer which has the type face mounted or engraved on the outside of a rim of a disk or a wheel, i.e., a wheel exists for each line of print and is keyed to a shaft which is rotated at high speed. Printing is accomplished by a hammer pressing the paper against the ribbon.

printer, wire — A high-speed printer that prints characterlike configurations of dots through the proper selection of wire-ends from a matrix of wire-ends, rather than conventional characters through the selection of type faces. (Synonymous with matrix printer.)

printer, xerographic—A device for printing an optical image on paper in which dark and light areas of the original are represented by electrostatically charged and uncharged areas on the paper. The paper is dusted with particles of finely powdered dry ink and the particles adhere only to the electrically charged areas. The paper with ink particles is then heated, causing the ink to melt and become permanently fixed to the paper.

printing control—A specific list of control group identifications or particulars through a procedure which omits listing of detail records.

printing counter—This counter on the magnetic-tape terminal advances by one for each tape block transmitted or received. At the end of transmission, the total number of tape blocks for the run is printed automatically. During a run upon the detection of an error block when receiving, the number of that tape block is printed.

printing, data-protection—Operation of the printers is checked automatically to ensure that they respond correctly to control-unit printing signals. If this check fails, an indicator, which can be tested by a programmed instruction, is automatically set.

printing, detail—A card to hard-copy operation. A data processing function for preparing documents from series of punched cards. Automatic addition, or cross-subtraction may be combined in the same operation.

printing, end—The conversion of punched information into bold printing across the end of the card simultaneously with gang punching, summary punching, reproducing, or mark-sensed punching. This is similar to interpreting, and makes possible quick reference to the card.

printing, key punch—A card-printing machine that prints each number or letter on the card as it punches the card.

printing, line—The printing of an entire line of characters at once.

printing matrix—*Same as* printer, wire.

printing unit—This machine lists individual cards, adds or subtracts, and prints the totals and/or grand totals of a card-group. It also prints totals and/or grand totals only without listing the individual cards. It operates at the rate of 100 cards-per-minute . . . and faster.

print interlock time—The required time for the printer to accept data from the print storage area and to complete the printing of its output.

print member—The particular part or component of a printer which is the element developing the form of the printed character, such as the print bar, type bar, or wheel.

printout—Sometimes an instruction to cause the printing of data in storage or from other external storage media into hard copy.

print-out, dynamic—A sequential operation of printing as part of a computer run and during the run instead of at the end of the run.

print-out, memory—A listing of the contents of a storage device, or selected parts of it. (Synonymous with memory dump and core dump.)

print-out, static—The printing of data after the run instead of as part of the run, which is called a dynamic print-out.

print positions—The maximum number of characters which can be printed on a single line.

print-punch editor—A subroutine controlling the printing and the punching of cards and editing operations, such as the translating of straight binary codes to binary coded decimal or Hollerith codes.

print restore (PR) code—The function that causes a printer to resume printing when it has been in nonprint case. The PR code triggers this function.

print timing dial—The control knob on the printer which is an adjustment of the printing quality.

print wheel—A single element providing the character set at one printing position of a wheel printer.

print-wheel assembly—An assembly of print wheels keyed and fastened to a shaft which is rotated at a high speed with a print wheel at each print position. A hammer forces the ribbon against the paper at the instant the desired character to be printed at a position is aligned with the line of the print.

priority—1. The sequence in which various entries and tasks will be processed by the analysis of action codes and other priority-real-time systems, as controlled by program level indicators. 2. The positioning of various routines as input/output ahead or taking precedence over the normal control sequence of the basic routine. (Clarified by priority circuits.)

priority circuits—*See* circuits, priority.

priority, dispatching—*See* dispatching priority.

priority error dump—*See* dump, priority error.

priority indicators—1. Groups of characters used in the header of a message to define the order of transmitting messages over a communication channel. 2. Information that is used to order a queue.

priority interrupt—Priority interrupt levels must be assigned using the interaction of functions with each other as a primary basis. The on-line systems designer must ensure all possible interrupts are operating compatibly when worst-case conditions occur. Debugging can become a "horrendous" task; consequently these problems must be solved during the design of the system, not during program and hardware checkout. It may be necessary to reassign the priority levels of key interrupts dynamically under program control. Hardware solutions to this have ranged from large banks of flip-flops to core switching matrices. At least two advances are required in the priority interrupt area to make effective use of the higher performance hardware being developed for on-line systems use. They are time-related priority assignments and externally weighted priority. Adequate solutions have not been found to meet all foreseen requirements, although designers are learning to make use of what is available to make the computer react to the on-line environment.

priority interrupt input/output—*See* input/ output priority and interrupt.

priority interrupts, multilevel — Interrupt provisions have been made to facilitate the priority requirements of various subroutines. The interrupt requests of these subroutines are handled by the central processor in the sequence of the highest priority. If a priority subroutine requests an interrupt, it will have priority over all subroutines of lower priority, even though they have previously requested an interrupt.

priority interrupts, optional—Many levels of optional priority interrupts are available on the computer. Any priority interrupt takes precedence over a lower priority program. Each level of priority interrupt may be separately allowed or disallowed by the program and each leads to a unique interrupt routine. As an option, the several computers may be provided with a programmed input/output channel that sends information to or from the accumulator by programmed instructions. The instructions specify which device is to communicate; thus, the time-sharing of the programmed input/output lines is controlled directly by the program.

priority interrupt table—When a computer does not have a fully automatic interrupt handling capability, a table is set up that lists the priority sequence of handling and testing interrupts.

priority limit—The upper bound to the priority list for dispatching or designing a priority rating to various tasks or subtasks, i.e., active, inactive, top priority, lowest priority, or batch processing.

priority, modes of—*See* modes of priority.

priority (multiplexing)—Some specific standard communications subsystems have been designed to handle a multiplicity of different speed communications facilities in the most efficient manner possible. The communication multiplexer contains priority logic which permits high-speed facilities to be serviced more frequently than low-speed facilities on a completely random basis.

priority, multiprogramming—This priority is oriented toward the concurrent operation of several types of applications. Assignment of priority levels is at the discretion of the user. For example, one priority level can be reserved for a program that must provide rapid responses to real-time devices, such as communications control. Another can be

reserved for the peripheral control package to accomplish several media conversions—card to tape, tape to printer, etc. The third priority level could then be used to run either a production or monitor job.

priority ordered interrupts—Some time-sharing computers can have over 200 priority ordered interrupts for external lines. This extensive interrupt capability allows a terminal to be attached to more than one interrupt line. If the attached interrupts cover a range of priorities, by selectively arming and disarming the external interrupt lines, the executive program can change the relative priority of a terminal's attention requests, allowing different classes of service or response to be given to the terminal.

priority processing—*See* processing, priority.

priority routine—In an interrupt, the leaving of one program by the processor to work on the program connected with the interrupt or the priority routine.

priority rules—Priority and inhibition rules are usually implemented in the time-sharing hardware to resolve possible conflicts when two interrupts occur simultaneously or when a second interrupt occurs before a previous one is completely processed.

priority selection—The use of information contained in the job request schedule to select the next job to be initiated. Selection is based on the priority and precedence assigned to the job, the sequence relationship of this job to other jobs with the same priority and precedence, and the availability of facilities required by the job.

priority structure — The organization of a system for processing. The priority structure of the system depends not upon the number of instructions but upon the complexity of the programs. The structure can range from systems with no priority to multicomplex organizations with multilayers of interrupts and multilevels of priority.

privileged instructions — Protection against one problem subprogram misusing another problem subprogram's I/O devices is provided by restricting all I/O commands to the supervisor state. A subprogram requests I/O action by issuing a supervisor call instruction. The supervisory subprogram can then analyze this request and take the appropriate action.

problem—A set of circumstances, situations, or states which develop when some unknown information is to be discovered, i.e., a solution is sought from some known information and a procedure is understood to acquire the unknown.

problem analysis, hybrid computer — Programs in the problem-analysis group help the hybrid programmer decide which parts of the problem to solve on a digital computer, and the mathematical technique that should be used. For example, multivariable function generation that may be difficult to perform on the analog computer is well-suited to digital solution.

problem, benchmark—A routine used to determine the speed performance of a computer. One method is to use one-tenth of the time required to perform nine complete additions and one complete multiplication. A complete addition or a complete multiplication time includes the time required to procure two operands from storage, perform the operation and store the result, and the time required to select and execute the required number of instructions.

problem, check—A problem chosen to determine whether the computer or a program is operating correctly.

problem definition—The art of compiling logic in the form of general flow charts and logic diagrams that clearly explain and present the problem to the programmer in such a way that all requirements involved in the run are presented.

problem description—A statement of a problem and possibly a description of the method of its solution, or the solution itself. The transformations of data and the relationship of procedures, data, constraints, environments, etc. may also be included.

problem, fault-location — *See* fault-location problem.

problem file—All the material needed or for use to document a program to be run on a computer.

problem folder—*Same as* problem file.

problem input tape—An input tape, either punched paper tape or magnetic tape, that contains problem data for checking out a given computer system.

problem language—*Same as* language, problem-oriented.

problem-oriented language—1. A source language oriented to the description of a particular class of problems. 2. A specific language designed for solutions to problems of a particular class of problems. COBOL AND FORTRAN programs are designed for various classes of problems whether scientific or commercial types, and although they require elaborate and extensive translation and compilation, they are relatively simply developed and quite easily understood even by the novice computer personnel.

problem-solving heuristic—A series of rules that systematically vary models through formal mutations and regenerative recording.

problem, test—A problem chosen to determine whether the computer or a program is operating correctly.

problem time—Often called physical system time, it is the time interval between corresponding events in the physical system being simulated.

problem, trouble-location — A test problem whose incorrect solution supplies information on the location of faulty equipment. It is used after a check problem has shown that a fault exists.

problem, trouble-shooter—The unique program for or designed as a series of test computations whose incorrect answers will isolate a fault. This type of procedure is used most often after a check problem shows that a fault exists.

procedural and exception tests—Procedural and exception tests are designed to check machine control and operation before processing. They consist of test data (generally punched into cards) covering all or most conditions which can arise during the run, as well as a control panel and/or program which will process the test data and check out machine components. The control panel is inserted, or the program loaded, or both; the test data is then read into the machine and processed. The results are compared against predetermined ones. If they are satisfactory, actual processing can begin. In some installations these tests are made only at the beginning of each working day; in others they are made before specific runs.

procedural testing—Tests of alternative human responses in system operations. This is distinguished from hardware or software tests.

procedure — A precise step-by-step method for effecting a solution to a problem.

procedure analysis—The analysis of a business activity to determine precisely what must be accomplished and how.

procedure, bypass—*See* bypass procedure.

procedure control—A basic key to achievement of high operating efficiency in a computing or data-processing installation is a good control procedure. This procedure must include many functions: administrative control of job schedules, workflow, and computer usage records; control over data and program libraries; control over computer operations; and control over the flow of programs and data within the computer system during job runs.

procedure descriptor—The procedure descriptor is a program descriptor uniquely marked as a descriptor that will cause subroutine entry when addressed by an operand call syllable.

procedure division—A routine in COBOL that describes the procedures to be used in processing the data described in the data division; it contains all the necessary steps to solve a given problem. Procedures are written as sentences which are combined to form named paragraphs. Likewise, paragraphs may be combined to form sections. Paragraph and section names are assigned by the programmer so that control may be transferred from one section or paragraph to another.

procedure, fallback—*See* fallback procedure.

procedure, loading—System, object, and library routines are loaded in a similar manner. A program may have a fixed origin or may be relocatable. Fixed origin programs are loaded into the specified memory address.

Programs are relocated by a base address initially set by the executive routine. After the main program has been loaded, any library subroutines or equipment drivers called will then be loaded. With all the necessary routines in memory, the loader returns to the job processor.

procedure name—The brief reference in a program to another program or portion of another program.

procedure-oriented—A programming language that is similar to the language used in the job, and is relatively independent of the data-processing system.

procedure-oriented language—A source language oriented to the description of procedural steps in machine computing.

procedures, in-line—A COBOL TERM for procedural instructions which are part of the main sequential and controlling instructions of the program.

proceed-to-select signal—See signal, proceed-to-select.

process—A generic term that may include compute, assemble, compile, interpret, generate, etc.

process, batch—See batch process.

process chart—Same as flowchart.

process code CC—When the terminal is in the program mode, the user can execute a single statement that he does not want included in the active program. By typing process code CC in columns 1 and 2 and an arithmetic assignment statement or an output statement in columns 7 through 72, the user indicates to the system that the statement is to be executed immediately, but not retained as part of the program (some computers).

process codes, remote computing system—Some types of program statements are also useful for manipulating the values of a user's program. When the terminal is in the program mode, the user may insert special characters, called "process codes," into the first two columns so that these statements can be used as commands. For example, CC preceding a statement has the following effect: the statement is immediately executed with all the effects of normal execution, but no new variable names are created; the statement is then discarded and does not become a part of the program. Thus, the user may insert values into parameters at any time, thereby creating completely new testing situations (some computers).

process communication system—1. A communication terminal for on-line data transmission between remote process input/output stations and a central computer. It provides real-time control of natural gas and oil pipe lines, petroleum refineries, iron and steel works, or batch-process manufacturing operations. 2. In these systems, multiplexor terminal stations are designed to handle a user's standard control system input/output devices and transducers. These stations convert the signals between process communica-

tions systems and the devices in the process. The transmission of data to or from the terminal stations is performed on multidrop transmission channels in half-duplex mode at high speeds. The transmission is buffered into the processor for greater system efficiency.

process control—1. Pertaining to systems whose purpose is to provide automation or continuous operations. This is contrasted with numerical control that provides automation of discrete operations (e.g. machines). 2. Automatic control of continuous-manufacturing industrial processes by using, for example, hybrid computers.

process control, industrial—See industrial process control.

process-control model—See process model.

process-control system—A system whose primary purpose is to provide automation of continuous operations.

processing, automatic data—Data processing performed by a system of electronic or electrical machines so interconnected and interacting as to reduce to a minimum the need for human assistance or intervention. (Related to automatic data-processing system.)

processing, background—Work which has a low-priority and is handled by the computer when higher priority or real-time entries are not occurring. Batch processing such as inventory control, payroll, housekeeping, etc., are often treated as background processing but can be interrupted on orders from terminals or inquiries from other units.

processing, batch—A technique by which items to be processed must be coded and collected into groups prior to processing.

processing, batch data—See batch processing.

processing, business-data—Data processing for business purposes, e.g., recording and summarizing the financial transactions of a business.

processing capacity—Often the maximum limitation of places of a number which can be processed at any one time. An example is a 12 place number.

processing, centralized data—Data processing performed at a single, central location on data obtained from several geographical locations or managerial levels. Decentralized data processing involves processing at various managerial levels or geographical points throughout the organization.

processing, central terminal unit (CTU)—The central terminal unit at the processing center receives incoming transaction messages at random intervals, stores them until the central processor is ready to process them, and returns the processed replies to the teller consoles that originated the transactions. The storing of the transactions is a buffering function that compensates for the peak loads that result from the random input of transactions.

processing, concurrent—See concurrent processing.

processing, continuous—The technique of constantly processing input items. This is sometimes referred to as on-line or real-time processing and is contrasted to batch processing.

processing control (installation)—In an effort to reduce job turnaround time and to minimize time wasted in setup, the scheduling of applications and jobs is automated.

processing control sequence—The control program initializes job operations, assigns input/output units, and performs the functions needed for automatic transition from one job to another, whether concurrent operations are under way or not. When the computing system is restarted after being turned off for some period of time, the control program is initially loaded, establishes initial control over all I/O units, and starts processing-program operation according to the schedule established by the user.

processing, conversational—The user is said to be communicating with the system in a conversational manner when each statement he enters through the terminal is processed (translated, verified, and, if desired, executed) immediately. The system then sends a reply to the terminal. The information contained in the reply varies. For example, it might be a message indicating that the previous statement contained an error. Operations in the conversational manner must be in either of two possible modes—the program mode, or the command mode (some computers).

processing, data—See data processing.

processing, deferred—Processing which can be delayed or is considered low priority, and is completed when computer time is at nonpeak periods.

processing, demand—The processing of data as quickly as it becomes available or ready. This is real-time and thus avoids the need for storage of any appreciable amount of unprocessed data.

processing, demand (time sharing) — See time-sharing, demand processing.

processing, direct-address—Reading or writing of data from a sector whose address is given.

processing, electronic data—Data processing performed largely by electronic equipment. (Related to automatic data processing.)

processing, fault (time-sharing)—See time sharing, fault processing.

processing, file—See file processing.

processing, industrial data—Data processing designed for industrial purposes, often numerical control.

processing, information—A less restrictive term than data processing, encompassing the totality of scientific and business operations performed by a computer.

processing, in-line—Same as on-line processing.

processing, integrated data (IDP)—1. A system that treats as a whole, all data-processing requirements to accomplish a sequence of data-processing steps, or a number of related data-processing sequences, and that strives to reduce or eliminate duplicating data entry or processing steps. 2. The processing of data by such a system in which all operations are in some way connected or associated with a computer.

processing, interrupt — An outstanding feature of the real-time system is its capacity to process real-time and batch-processing applications concurrently. This impressive real-time data-processing innovation is made possible through a unique feature that permits remote external units with information of high precedence to interrupt computer processing. Whenever transaction data for a real-time problem is entered into a remote external unit, the computer's batch-processing program may be interrupted to permit handling the high priority real-time transaction and the sending of processed results back to the external unit.

processing (LISP)—See LISP.

processing list—See list processing.

processing machine, data—A general name for a machine that can store and process numeric and alphabetic information. (Related to analog digital computer and automatic data-processing equipment.)

processing mode, batch—See batch processing mode.

processing modularity—See modularity, processing.

processing multithread—A sequence of events in programs required for the computer processing of a message known as a thread. In single-thread processing all work is completed before work is begun on a new message. In multithread processing, message threads are handled in parallel.

processing, off-line—See off line processing.

processing, on-line—See on-line processing.

processing, overlap—Processor operations performed at the same time by using different parts of the circuitry, for example, read-process-write, or any two of these.

processing, parallel—The operation of a computer so that programs for more than one run are stored simultaneously in its storage, and executed concurrently.

processing, priority—A type of time-sharing or facility-sharing in which the programs to be run are selected by priority rules or criteria.

processing programs—Processing programs actually accomplish work such as updating inventory records, preparing reports and compiling new programs. They include both support programs and application programs. The application programs will be written making use of FORTRAN, COBOL, and other macrostatements of the assembly program wherever possible.

processing, random—Transfer of an item between core memory and a drum or disk location. The address of the item is determined by mathematical transformation of its key.

processing, random-access (central file)—See random access processing (central file).

processing ratio—The end result in the calculation of the time the equipment is being properly used, including lost time because of human error and the total available time.

processing, real-time — See real-time processing.

processing, real-time (bank)—See real-time processing (bank).

processing, remote—See remote message processing.

processing, scientific—The processing of data involved with solving mathematical functions or equations.

processing, sequential—The requirements for real-time action are known frequently to occur in peaks and valleys. In many businesses these requirements tend to increase from early morning through the middle of the day and to taper off from then on. In other businesses the occurrence of these demands may be sporadic. The real-time system is so designed that it will, as its facilities are freed from the dynamic demands of real-time processing, load them up with the ordinary day to day backlog of less urgent work of the familiar batch processing type—typically, the sequential processing of sequentially ordered files such as accounts receivable, payable, or payrolls.

processing, serial—Reading or writing of an item following the item currently being processed.

processing, short-card—Short cards used as store sales checks, gasoline sales checks, account-receivable transmittal advices, and so forth, can be processed with full-size name and address cards or balance cards. The short cards are fed by the processor equipped with a short-card feed; the full size cards by the read punch. Reproduction of short cards into standard size cards is not necessary.

processing, single thread — The complete processing of all programs and events of one message before starting in another message. See processing, multithread.

processing, specialized — Various types of automatic data processing have become distinct enough to be designated by proper names. Among these are: Business Data Processing, Automated Production Management, Administrative Data Processing, and many others.

processing system, job—See job processing system.

processing unit—A part of a computing system which is the primary arithmetic and logical performing modules.

process, input/output (IOP)—A unit that handles normal data input/output control and sequencing.

process, iterative—A process for calculating a desired result by means of a repeating cycle of operations that comes closer and closer to the desired result; e.g., the arithmetical square root of N may be approximated by an iterative process using only additions, subtractions, and divisions.

process, limited—The speed of the central processing unit controls the processing time and not the input/output speeds or capability.

process, limited (sorting)—A sort program in which the execution time of the internal instructions determines the elapsed time required to sort.

process model—The processor controller rapidly collects the process data that is necessary for the development of a model or the process. The model is developed by using a combination of empirical techniques and observing past methods of running the process. When a more complete and more precise description of the process is required, a model is constructed by using such mathematical techniques as correlation analysis and regression analysis. The process control program is then tested on the mathematical model prior to its use on the process. Extensive operator guide information is obtained. In addition, the model represents considerable progress toward complete supervisory control.

process optimization—An extensive process-controller program, based on the model of the process, directs the DAC (data aquisition and control) system. Process data is continuously collected and analyzed for computation of optimum operating instructions. These instructions are given to the process operator via an on-line typewriter.

process optimization, on-line—An important part of process control is the job of ensuring operating conditions or combinations of conditions for optimum profit. On-line analog computers can be used to adjust one or more process conditions to compensate for uncontrolled variations so that operation is maintained at the optimum level.

processor—1. A device capable of receiving data, manipulating it, supplying results usually of an internally stored program. 2. A program used in compiling a source program that will produce, when completed, an execution of the objective function of the program or process. 3. A generic term that includes assembly, compiling and generation. 4. A shorter term for automatic data processor or arithmetic unit.

processor, attached support ASP—The utilization of multiple computers, usually two, connected via channel-to-channel adaptors, to increase the efficiency in processing many short duration jobs.

processor, central—See processor unit, central (CPU).

processor, COBOL—See COBOL processor.

processor-controller applications—Processor-controller (P-C) can be used for editing, supervisory control, direct control, or data analysis. A control and data path provides for the attachment of the system where more powerful supervision is required. For example, the aspects of an application with the controlling operations exercised by an analog computer. This multiprocessor system capability enables the handling of real-time applications of any size or complexity.

processor controller, supervisory control—*See* supervisory control, process controller.

processor, cycle time — *See* cycle time processor.

processor, data—*See* data processor.

processor-dependent interrupt—*See* interrupt, processor-dependant.

processor design, real-time—A current typical design is described as follows: sixty two basic instructions which may be modified to provide unprecedented programming versatility; magnetic-core storage capacity of 16,000 to 32,000 computer words of 30 bits each; 10 millionths of a second average instruction time; the ability to accomodate any standard communication code or effective use of random-access drum storage as well as magnetic tapes; plus the ability under automatic executive-program control to perform all of its functions including control of or response to central or remote input/output devices in a time scale proportional to the need for action; and precision electronic clocks for use in compiling statistics for analysis and improvement of computer utilization, for initiation of action at specific times during the day, and for checking the proper execution of operations. In addition to all of this, the central processor may be connected to a satellite computer or to another entire system complex. (UNIVAC)

processor-error interrupt — Processor-error interrupt occurs if a word accessed in any part of the system is found to contain incorrect check bits, or if an error occurs in the addressing of a memory location.

processor, image—The image processor provides the input and output of data in graphic form. Some units contain two photographic-film transport units which are similar in operation but which differ in the function that they perform. For convenience, they are designated as transport A and transport B. Transport A exposes film from the high-resolution recording cathode-ray tube, exposes processes, and scans processed film for computer input at the read station using a high-resolution scanning CRT and it projects the processed film from the read station to a 20 × 22-inch read-projection screen located at the front of the unit. Transport B exposes film from the record CRT, processes, and projects exposed film. The large screen projector permits the operator to study the output image off line from the computer. The image is larger and of higher quality than can be obtained on the graphic console and the image can be studied and compared with drawings or other graphic console images.

processor interface—The transfer of data between the processor and the standard communication subsystem takes place through input data leads, connected to the processor input channel, and output data leads, connected to the processor output channel. In addition to the data leads, there are several control leads that are used to control the flow of data.

processor interface routines—The processor interface routines, provide a simple, standard interface for all processors within the system. Complete facilities are provided for the input of source-language statements and the output of the resulting relocatable binary code.

processor interrupt—As the computer is sequencing through a set of instructions, there are definite times when it is desirable to interrupt the program for such things as handling a machine error, an I/O device, a supervisor call, or a program exception such as an arithmetic overflow. Electronic circuitry instead of complex programming recognizes and handles these interrupts. This results in the most efficient utilization of the processor. Interrupts are automatic procedures that alert the system to conditions arising that may affect the sequence of instructions being executed. To make possible the operation of a system in a nonstop environment, and to increase the efficiency of I/O equipment, the system must have the ability to switch to the appropriate routine when a supervisory call or exceptional condition arises, and then resume the processing that has been interrupted. Records of the complete status of the system are automatically stored as soon as an interrupt occurs, together with an identification of the cause of the interrupt.

processor, interrupt dependent—An example of a processor-dependent interrupt condition is the presence bit condition caused by a program being executed on a processor that is executing an operand call. This addresses a descriptor with a presence bit of zero (some computers).

processor, interrupt independent—An example of a processor-independent interrupt condition is an I/O finished condition caused by the I/O hardware when an I/O operation has been completed (some computers).

processor organization—The computer can be divided into three main sections: arithmetic and control, input/output, and memory. The arithmetic and control section carries out the directives of the program. The calculations, routing of information, and control of the other sections occur in this part of the central processor. All information going into and coming out of the central processor is handled by the input/

output section. It also controls the operation of all peripheral equipment. The memory section is the heart of the central processor; it provides temporary storage for data and instructions. Because of its importance, the total cycle time of the memory is the main determining factor in the overall speed of the processor.

processor organization, central—*See* central processor organization.

processor, output test—In a complex system an automated processing of the output so that errors may be more easily tracked down.

processor, peripheral—For some environments, input and output are best processed by two interconnected computers wherein one computer handles the input/output for the other. The control programs of the operating system provide the capability to handle this mode of operation for a configuration of equipment in which a very high-speed, high-storage capacity central processing unit performs calculations upon data supplied by a smaller computer that schedules, buffers, and controls the flow of input data, intermediate results, and output data to and from the larger unit. Usually in this configuration the larger unit is termed the host and the smaller one is called peripheral, but either one may actually be in control of the other's operations and schedule.

processor program—*See* program, processor.

processor, radar video—The radar video processor, designed and built by Burroughs for the Federal Aviation Agency's new electronic air traffic control system, provides a three-dimension radar picture of all aircraft under surveillance. This highly sophisticated radar video system has successfully completed FAA evaluation tests.

processor, satellite—A smaller processor used to support a large processor to increase its productivity. The smaller processor is used for card to tape conversion, off-line printing, and communication interface.

processors, auxiliary—Contained within the executive system is a set of auxiliary processors for performing functions complementing those of the source language processors such as FORTRAN. This set of processors includes the collector for linking relocatable subprograms, the procedure-definition processor for inserting and modifying procedure definitions in a library, the COBOL library processor for manipulation of COBOL library elements, and the data-definition processor for introducing data descriptions.

processor storage relocation—The processor must have the ability to relocate programs in storage during normal processing, since many different types of transactions may necessitate bringing a program from file storage into a location in core storage for which the program was not assembled.

processor transfer time—Once the communication multiplexer has performed the

necessary priority analysis and activated its input data request or output data request lead, some finite period of time elapses while the actual transfer of data takes place and before the central processor activates its input acknowledge or output acknowledge lead. This time interval is independent of the standard communication subsystem and depends solely on the internal cycle time and channel transfer rate of the central processor to which the subsystem is attached.

processor unit, central (CPU)—The principal unit of the computer that controls the processing routines, performs the arithmetic functions, and maintains a quickly accessible memory. It also often contains the console.

processor verbs—Verbs which specify to the processor the procedures by which a source program is to be translated into an object program. Such verbs do not cause action at object time.

process, predefined—A type of identified process which is defined and delineated in another location in greater detail than the subject one.

process, read/write—To read in one block of data while simultaneously processing the previous block and writing out the results of the preceding processed block.

process, recursive—In data processing, a method of computing values of functions in which each stage of processing contains all subsequent stages, i.e., the first stage is not completed until all other stages have been completed.

process study—The processor-controller rapidly collects the process data that is necessary for the development of a model of the process. The model is developed by using a combination of empirical techniques and observing past methods of running the process. When a more complete and more precise description of the process is required, a model is constructed by using such mathematical techniques as correlation analysis and regression analysis. The process-control program is then tested on the mathematical model prior to its use on the process. Extensive operator guide information is obtained. In addition, the model represents considerable progress toward complete supervisory control.

process time—The time for translating a source program into an object program through the action of a processor program and the computer.

product—The quantity that results from multiplying two quantities.

product area—Some computers have an area in main storage to store results of multiplication operations specifically.

product, intermediate—When multiplying the multiplicand by just one of the digits of the multiplier, the result is a partial product, i.e., a series of first partial product, etc. The partial sums then are simply shifted and added to obtain the final or total product, which is then called *product*.

production control—As applied by computers, a data acquisition system from the floor of a product in line or process for the speed up and simplification of the flow of production information for management.

production, language theory—In formal language theory (BNF), the translation of an input string to an output string.

production routine—That routine which produces the results of the problem or program as it was designed, as contrasted with the routines which are designed for support, housekeeping, or to complile, assemble, translate, etc.

production run—A run that fulfills the program objective. It occurs after the projected program has been successfully checked out.

production run tape—A principal method of obtaining values from a PRT (production run tape), using the relative addressing technique, is through use of the operand call syllable. An instruction is referred to as a syllable, and one word accomodates four syllables. Each operand call syllable contains the relative address of the location from which it is to obtain information.

production time—That time which is used to accomplish designed, desired, or useful work and during which the computer is running properly, satisfactorily—without faults, malfunctions, or important errors, i.e., not idle or using development or incidentals.

productive time—That time which is spent in processing work without the occurrence of faults or errors.

product, logical—*Same* as gate, AND.

product overflow—*Same as* overflow.

product, partial—A particular result developed by multiplying the multiplicand by one of the digits of the multiplier, i.e., there are as many partial products in a multiplication operation as there are significant digits in a multiplier, as partial sums are shifted and added to obtain the final product.

PROF (Pupil Registering and Operational Filing)—In order to enable secondary schools to apply the power of computers to their specific requirements, Honeywell has developed a series of education-support, computer programs called PROF. One of the most significant parts of PROF is the course-scheduling and pupil-assignment subsystem. PROF also incorporates grade recording, attendance accounting, testing, educational research, instruction in computer usage, and financial accounting. Information on these applications is available. (Honeywell)

program—1. A plan for the automatic solution of a problem. A complete program includes plans for the transcription of data, coding for the computer, and plans for the absorption of the result into the system. The list of coded instructions is called

a routine. 2. A set of instructions or steps that tells the computer exactly how to handle a complete problem—payroll, production scheduling, or other applications. Most programs include alternate steps or routines to take care of variations. Generally, program steps form a complete cycle. Each incoming bundle of facts (unit of information) sets off the whole cycle from start to finish, the succeeding unit sets it off again, and so forth. 3. To plan a computation or process from the asking of a question to the delivery of the results, including the integration of an operation into an existing system. Thus, programming consists of planning and coding, including numerical analysis, specification of printing formats, and any other functions necessary to the integration of a computer into a system. 4. To plan the method of attack for a defined problem. 5. To plan the whole operation from input to output and set the control section to handle it.

program-address counter—A register in which the address of the current instruction is recorded. (Synonymous with instruction counter.)

program allocation and loading—Relocatable binary elements produced by compilation are linked together for execution or for future use by an allocation program that is resident in the system at all times. An extensive selection of subroutines is directly available from the system library, enabling the allocator to incorporate them dynamically as the compiled elements are being constructed into a program. The relocatable element is the common denominator output of processors, allowing applications to be programmed in several different languages, compiled, and properly linked at execution time (some computers).

program analyzer—*See* analyzer.

program, assembler—*See* assembly routine.

program, assembly—*Same as* assembly routine.

program, automatic recovery—A program enabling a system to remain functioning when a piece of equipment has failed. The automatic recovery program often activates duplex circuitry, a standby computer, or switches to a mode of degraded operation.

program, background—This program is of lower priority than the foreground or main program and is at halt or standby while the main program runs.

program, bootleg—A conventional routine or stop-gap program used to begin, capture, and process data in a specifically prescribed manner. Usually to start or initiate the reading of a program by means of its own action.

program bootstrap, input—*See* bootstrap, input program.

program card—A prepunched card that serves to instruct the machine in the steps or operations it is to perform.

program, chain additions—A specific set of instructions which adds new records to individual files.

program check—1. A system of determining the correct program and machine functioning either by running a sample problem with similar programming and a known answer, or by using mathematical or logic checks such as comparing A times B with B times A. 2. A check system built into the program or computers that do not have automatic checking. This check system is normally concerned with programs run on computers that are not internally self-checking. (Synonymous with routine check, and related to automatic check.)

program checking—See checking, program.

program checkout—A standard runthrough of a program on a computer to determine if all designs and results of a program are as anticipated.

program, coded—A program that has been expressed in the code or language of a specific machine or programming system.

program compatibility—A distinctive feature of most programming aids and the objective programs that they produce is operational compatibility. This property enables the operating system to integrate all elements.

program compilation—Programs written in the languages of ALGOL, COBOL, FORTRAN IV, or the other assembly languages are compiled at several thousand statements per minute without sacrificing object code efficiency.

program, compiler—Same as compiler.

program, computer—See computer program.

program, control—1. A sequence of instructions that prescribe the series of steps to be taken by a system, a computer, or any other device. 2. Descriptive of a system in which a computer is used to direct an operation or process and automatically to hold or to make changes in the operation or process on the basis of a prescribed sequence of events.

program, control command—A program that handles all commands addressed to the system from the user-consoles. These commands would include requests to log in or out, a request to use the edit program, requests to have a program placed on the run queue, requests to load a program, etc.

program controlled interrupt—See interrupt, program controlled.

program-controlled sequential computer—See computer, logic-controlled sequential.

program debugging—See debugging program.

program development time—That time used by computers to test or debug programs, or to perform trials of new procedures, processes, or techniques, i.e., part of uptime (effective) but not part of production or incidentals time, which both have specific definitions.

program, diagnostics—A program used by the supervisory program or the computer operator to check malfunctions and to locate faulty components.

program documentation—This is a vital part of programming. Documentation is required so that programs can be modified, so that people can be trained, and so that machine operators know how to run programs and diagnose the problems if they occur.

program drum—A revolving cylinder on which the program card is mounted.

program, editor—A program that provides a means for manipulating the text of a named file on a microtape or in the user area of the drum. This program may be used for the creation of the text, or for later use as data or as a program to be translated by the FORTRAN compiler, etc. The commands provided by the editor allow text to be created, deleted, or moved about.

program error—A mistake made in the program code by the programmer, keypuncher, or a machine-language compiler or assembler.

program-error interrupt—Program interrupts occur because of programmer errors such as an invalid operation code, an attempt to violate storage protection, and exceptional results of a calculation. When a program interrupt occurs, control may be passed to an error routine in the current program segment, or the program may be ended with an abnormal end-of-program indication.

program evaluation and review technique (PERT)—Use of PERT requires an extensive analysis of an overall project, in order to list all the individual activities or jobs which must be performed in order to meet the total objective. These activities are then arranged in a network that displays the sequential relationships among them. This analysis must be extremely thorough and detailed if it is to be realistic, and it will require application of all the talents and experience available to the organization. PERT provides a means of reporting an analysis for project administrators. Information required can be developed and areas that impose the greatest time restrictions on the completion of a product can be highlighted. Areas with an excess of time for completion, called slack areas, are also highlighted.

program execution control—A part of the basic control function is performed by the program execution control. When an interruption occurs, it is the program execution control which determines the nature of the interruption and the appropriate action to be taken. The program execution control determines relative priority of programs ready to run, and loads other programs into storage (some computers).

program execution controls sequence—During the execution of a series of instructions, each one follows the one preceding it in storage, except for (I) the execution of a branch instruction which specifies where the next instruction is to be found, and (2) an interrupt which breaks into the operation sequence and substitutes a different starting point for a new series of instructions that may have no relationship to the first series.

program, externally stored — A program which is stored in one of many input devices or media and which must be read from the medium or device by connection and interrogation or interpretation, i.e., programs on tapes, cards, disks, etc., rather than wired or internally stored types.

program file—A flexible, easily updated reference system for the maintenance of the entire software library.

program, flowchart—*See* flowchart program.

program, general—A program expressed in computer code designed to solve a class of problems, or specializing on a specific problem when appropriate parametric values are supplied. (Synonymous with general routine.)

program, generating — A designed program for construction of other programs, i.e., for performing particular types of operations such as sorting programs, output programs, etc. The generating program can select among various broad methods for performing a task and adjust those details of the selected method to provide a program with specific characteristics, which then are matched to the characteristics of the data to be handled by the generated program. It may include an assembly program.

program generator, report—*See* report program generator.

program halt—*Same as* program stop.

program, HELP (time sharing)—*See* time sharing HELP program.

program, heuristic—1. A routine by which the computer attacks a problem not by a direct algorithmic procedure, but by a trial and error approach frequently involving the act of learning. 2. A set of computer instructions that simulates the behavior of human operators in approaching a similar problem.

program, incomplete—A specific program not complete in itself and usually a specification of a process to be performed on data. It may be used at more than one point in any particular program, or it might be made available for inclusion in other programs, i.e., a subroutine. Often called subprogram, incomplete program, etc.

program-independent modularity — Defined as the property of a system which allows it to accept changes and adust processing accordingly to yield maximum utilization on all modules without reprogramming. This system is used in multiprocessing. To achieve this objective, the computer system incorporates master control programs to exercise an unprecendented degree of automatic control.

program, internally stored—A program which is stored or contained within the computer,

such as in the same area in which the data is stored or in some high speed on-line auxiliary core storage, i.e., immediately accessible to the control and arithmetic or CPU units.

program, interpreter—An essentially closed subroutine (executive) which translates a stored pseudocode program into a machine and performs the desired and specified operation. Such an interpreter program usually consists of sequences of pseudo instructions and operands (program parameters) which are introduced as a closed subroutine and exist by a specific pseudocode instruction.

program, interpretive—A specialized program which relates and handles the execution of a program by translating each instruction of the source language into a sequence of computer instructions and allows these to be executed before translating the next instruction, i.e., the translation of an instruction is performed each time the instruction is to be obeyed. If the interpretative program allows for programs written for one type of a computer to be run on a different type, it is often called a simulator program.

program, interpretive trace — A trace or diagnostic program used for performing a desired check on another program may include instructions as its output, and intermediate results of those instructions can be arranged in the order in which the instructions are executed. When such a trace program is an interpretive type, it is called an interpretive trace program.

program, interrupt—An important function of the control unit is to detect special conditions in the system that require programmed or operator action outside of the program in progress. When any of these conditions is detected, the program in progress is interrupted automatically. To provide for subsequent re-entry into the interrupted program, the point where the interrupt occurs is recorded in a fixed-memory location. Program control is then transferred to another fixed location, where a routine is initiated to process the condition causing the interrupt. There are six fixed-memory locations; the two used when an interrupt occurs are selected by the control unit according to the class of special condition detected; input/output, contingency, or processor error. A set of indicators is also associated with each class of interrupt; these indicators specify the condition or conditions that caused the interrupt (some systems).

program interrupt, automatic—*See* interruption, automatic program.

program interrupts, addressing — Various events can lead to a program interrupt. Each interrupt is to a unique fixed memory address that is associated with the event that caused it. Addresses are reserved for these interrupts. Each external device has an interrupt address that is equal to its external device address. An external device may have more than one interrupt event and each event may have its own interrupt address. Interrupts may occur only at the end of program instructions. It is important to the programmer that each type of interrupt results in transfer of control to a different memory address. This makes it unnecessary for the program to scan interrupt events to see what has happened. A subroutine for each interrupt event may be in the memory. (Some systems.)

program-interrupt signal—*Same as* interrupt, external-signal.

program interrupt (trapped)—Six events can cause the program of the computer to be interrupted: (1) busy, (2) add overflow, (3) divide overflow, (4) operator, (5) external device, and (6) index overflow. An interrupt trap associated with each event may be set under program control to either respond when the event occurs or to ignore it. Many addresses in memory are reserved for external device interrupt. Each interrupt occurs at its own address so it can lead to its own unique subroutine. Upon completion of the subroutine, control can be returned to the original program at the point of interruption (some computers).

program, introspective — A self-monitoring program.

program language—*See* language, program.

program, learning—The unique program designed to alter itself by making changes based on the experience of the program and results unknown until portions of the program have been run. For example, a program designed to increase efficiency and provide instructions for program modification or a predestined basis, concerning various analysis techniques built into the program itself resulting in corrective action or alternations of program instruction based on various criteron established within the program.

program, librarian — The librarian program portion of the control function provides for maintenance of library programs used as part of the operating system. The library may be stored on a single secondary storage unit or it may be distributed over several different storage units. In either case the librarian program keeps this library up to date by adding, deleting and modifying as required. User-written application programs can be incorporated into the library along with subroutines, the control program itself, compilers, sort/merge, and utility programs.

program library—*Same as* library, program.

program line—A single instruction usually written on a standard coding format stored as a single entity.

program linking—If a program is too large to be stored in memory, the programmer can divide it into "links" by means of a FORTRAN link statement. At run time, routines in the monitor system automatically handle the execution of the segments of the linked program (some computers).

program, list processing—A particular type of program called EULER is an extension of ALGOL 60 and has specific list processing capabilities. Several others also exist.

program loading—During the execution of a processing program, and as a result of many different actions of the control programs, additional programs or program segments may be brought into main storage. The loader alters all necessary addresses in the object program to allow loading at an address of main storage assigned by the control program. The loader has the capability to load separately assembled program segments as if they were a single program, to call in segments from the system program library and combine them with other programs, to link one program segment with another through the use of symbolic references, and to enable different program segments to refer to common data areas. The loader can also perform program overlays, and enable patching of object programs.

program loading, dynamic—The loading of a program module or routine into main memory by reference to it by a loaded executing program.

program loading, initial—An initiation process which brings a program or operating system into a computer with the data records which participate in the process. A routine such as the above is established in memory, making it possible to load and execute any other desired program—a first record loading, the second, etc.

program loading routine—The procedure for inserting instructions and the constant values of the program into the computer.

program, macroassembly—A language processor that accepts words, statements and phrases to produce machine instructions. It is more than an assembly program because it has compiler powers. The macroassembler permits segmentation of a large program so that portions may be tested separately. It also provides extensive programming analysis to aid debugging.

program main—*Same as* program, master control.

program maintenance—A specific computer program most often consisting of various diagnostic routines, checking or test routines, and other types designed to complete the removal or reduction of malfunctions, mistakes, and errors and to thus repair or maintain programs and routines.

program, master control—The master control program:

1. Controls all phases of a job set-up; directs program compiling and debugging, allocates memory, assigns input-output activity, schedules and interweaves multiple programs for simultaneous processing.

2. Directs all equipment functions and the flow of all data; provides for comprehensive automatic error detection and correction.
3. Directs the operator with printed instructions.
4. Adjusts system operation to changes in system environment.

Thus, the program-independent modularity of the computer, combined with the automatic schedule and control features of the master control system, provides true multiprocessing ability of the system. A good example of this is shown by the ability of a system to perform four read/write operations simultaneously with the program executions on two processors (some systems).

program master file update—Programs from the old master file are deleted, corrected, or left unchanged and new programs are added from the transaction tape. Updating can include changing of program job assignments. A new program master file is produced.

program, mathematical—Considered by many to be the same as linear programming but not committed to be so defined because of sophisticated uses of research-type operations used as decision tools by modern management science enthusiasts.

programmed card—See card, programmed.

programmed check—A check procedure designed by the programmer and implemented specifically as a part of his program. (Contrasted with automatic check.)

programmed data transfer—See data transfer programmed.

programmed dump—See dump, programmed.

programmed halt—See halt, programmed.

programmed input/output channel—Program control of information transfer between the central processor and an external device provides the fastest method of operating on data received from peripheral equipment. The programmed input/output channel allows input directly to the accumulator where the data can be acted on immediately, eliminating the need for a memory reference by either the channel or the program. Likewise, output data may be sent directly from the accumulator to an external device.

programmed instructions—Special subroutines may be used as if they were single commands by employing one of the progammed instructions of the system repertoire. This capability allows the programmer to define his own special commands through the use of subroutines which may be changed by the operating routine if desired. The number of instructions required in a typical program is reduced because each subroutine may be called by a single instruction instead of 2 or 3. Programmed instructions also provide, with standard recommended subroutines, complete instruction compatibility.

programmed logic—See logic, programmed.

programmed operators system (SYSPOP)—A

function which makes monitor mode service routines available to USER mode programs without loss of system control or use of user memory space.

programmed switch—See switch, programmed.

programmed tools, automatically (APT)—See APT.

programmer—1. One who prepares programs for a computer. 2. A person who prepares instruction sequences without necessarily converting them into the detailed codes. 3. A person who prepares problem solving procedures and flow charts and who may also write and debug routines.

programmer analyst—See analyst, programmer.

programmer defined macros — See macros, programmer-defined.

programmer, design—This individual designs and tests the program logic, and selects the subroutines and other software aids for use in the program.

programmer, maintenance—This individual codes and tests revisions to the production programs needed to maintain operations. He must also be able to debug these programs.

programmer, parts — A programmer specifically trained in the technique of translating physical machining of a part to a series of program steps.

programmer, senior—Develops and prepares machine-logic flowcharts for the solution of business, engineering and/or scientific problems through the use of electronic data-processing equipment.

programmer, systems — This individual is primarily concerned with writing either operating systems (computer internal control programs) or languages for computers. System programmers produce these control programs and/or monitors that operate central processing and peripheral equipment. They write test programs that detect errors and malfunctions. They design utility programs to control formats of output and do sorting and merging of files. It is they who are primarily responsible for the efficicency of many computer systems.

programming—1. The process of creating a program. 2. The art of reducing the plan for the solution of a problem to machine-sensible instructions.

programming, applications — Applications programs range from sorting, payroll processing, and billing, to linear programming, matrix manipulation, and simulation. Whenever applications programs can be sufficiently generalized, the computing system provides and maintains them. Among the standard applications programs available are: (1) linear programming; (2) APT III; (3) PERT/COST; (4) mathematical subroutines.

programming, audit—A program designed to enable use of the computer as an auditing tool.

programming, automatic—A computer process which helps to prepare various programs.

Such capability includes various translators as compilers, generators, assemblers, and coders. Other types of automatic programming capabilities might be integration of subroutines into master programs or interpretation of instructions, e.g., much research is in process to make computers fully automatic program generators or developers by assembling or locating programs by simple statements of problems.

programming automatic, mnemonic — *See* mnemonic automatic programming.

programming competition, multiprogramming—*See* multiprogramming, program competition.

programming, conversational — A technique used in instructing the computer to perform its operations, whereby common vocabulary can be utilized by the user to describe his procedures most accurately. If a statement cannot be understood by the computer, it asks the user for a clarified instruction. This conversational procedure continues until the user has selected the series of statements in the proper sequence which will solve his problem. Conversational programming saves the user the inconvenience of having to study other programming languages extensively before he can solve his problem.

programming, convex — An operations research term for the development of nonlinear programming procedures in which the function to be optimized and the constraints are convex or concave functions of the independent variables, i.e., not related to programming in a computer sense.

programming, dynamic—The essence of dynamic programming is that an optimum decision must be made at every stage of a multistage problem. When considering only a single stage, there may appear to be a number of different decisions of equal merit. Only when the effect of each decision at every stage on the overall goal is determined can the final choice be made. This integrating of the cumulative effect of a path of decisions through each stage of the network is the real essence of DP (dynamic programming).

programming, dynamic (cost problem) — A method for optimizing a set of decisions that must be made sequentially. Characteristically, each decision must be made in the light of the information embodied in a small number of observables called state variables. The incurred cost for each period is a mathematical function of the current state and decision variables, while future states are functions of these variables. The aim of the decision policy is to minimize the total incurred cost, or equivalently the average cost per period. The mathematical treatment of such problems involves the theory of functional equations, and usually requires a digital computer for implementation.

programming, file-oriented—I/O coding is simplified with the general file and record control program. Programming is file-oriented rather than device-oriented. Information is requested in a device-independent fashion.

programming, heuristic—Most programming is algorithmic, that is, one sets out the various conditions in advance and the computer follows a preset path through the program depending on the input data received. Under a heuristic programming procedure, the computer searches through a number of possible solutions at each stage of the program, it evaluates a good solution for this stage, and then proceeds to the next stage. Essentially, heuristic programming is similar to the problem solving techniques by trial and error methods which we use in everyday life.

programming, hybrid—Routines in the hybrid programming library are designed to help the engineer decide which parts of the problem should be solved in a digital domain. They also deal with timing, function generations, integration, and the general simulation problems provide a diagnosis of the hardware operation, and check whether the analogue device is scaled or wired correctly.

programming, integer—A class of optimization problems in which the values of all the variables are restricted to be integers. Normally, the optimization problem without this integer restriction is a linear program; additional adjectives indicate variations—for example, integer quadratic programming.

programming, interpretive — The writing of programs in a pseudomachine language that is precisely converted by the computer into actual machine-language instructions before being performed by the computer.

programming language—A specific language used to prepare computer programs.

programming language, automatic (APL)—A device, technique, or language which permits the computer to aid in doing part of the coding and programming.

Programming Language/1 compiler—Compilers can be included in operating systems for use in compiling object programs from source programs written in Programming Language/1 which has some features that are characteristic of FORTRAN, and which also incorporates some of the best features of other languages such as string manipulation, data structures, dynamic-storage allocation, asynchronous operation, and extensive editing capabilities.

Programming Language/1 (PL/1) — A compiler is provided in the special support system for use in compiling object programs from source programs written in this programming language. This language has some features that are characteristic of string manipulation, data structure, and extensive editing capabilities. Further, it has features not currently available in any language.

The language is designed to take advantage of recent developments in computer technology and to provide the programmer with a flexible problem-oriented language for programming problems that can best be solved using a combination of scientific and commercial computing techniques. It is designed to be particularly useful for the increasing number of semicommercial, semiscientific applications such as information retrieval and command and control applications.

programming, linear—A technique of mathematics and operations research for solving certain kinds of problems involving many variables where a best value or set of best values is to be found. This technique is not to be confused with computer programming, although problems using the technique may be programmed on a computer. Linear programming is most likely to be feasible when the quantity to be optimized, sometimes called the objective function, can be stated as a mathematical expression in terms of the various activities within the system. When this expression is simply proportional to the measure of the activities, and all the restrictions are also linear, it is a linear program.

programming manager — This individual is responsible for planning, scheduling, and supervising program development and maintenance work.

programming, mathematical—Techniques of finding an optimum value of a function of many variables when these variables are subject to restrictions in the form of equations or inequalities. The term is usually restricted to problems so complex that they require a digital computer for their solution. Special types of programming are linear programming, quadratic programming, and nonlinear programming.

programming, micro—The programmer technique of using a certain special set of instructions for an automatic computer that consists only of basic elemental operations, and combining them into higher-level instructions. He may then program using only the higher level instructions; e.g., if a computer has only basic instructions for adding, subtracting, and multiplying, the instruction for dividing would be defined by microprogramming.

programming, minimum-access — Programming in such a way that minimum waiting time is required to obtain information out of storage. (Synonymous with minimum-latency programming, and contrasted with random-access programming.)

programming, minimum latency — *Same as* programming, minimum access.

programming module—Specific name for a set of programming instructions which is treated as a unit by an assembler, compiler, loader, or translator.

programming, multiple — The programming of a computer by allowing two or more arithmetical or logical operations to be executed simultaneously. (Contrasted with serial programming.)

programming, nonlinear—An inclusive term covering all types of constrained optimization problems except those where the objective function and the constraints are all linear. Special types of nonlinear programming for which some theory has been developed are convex programming, concave programming, and quadratic programming.

programming, optimum—Programming in order to maximize efficiency with respect to some criteria, e.g., least-storage usage, least time-share of peripheral equipment, or least use of time between operations.

programming, parallel—The feature of programming which provides for two or more results when concurrent operations are to be performed simultaneously. Contrast with serial programming.

programming, parametric—A method for investigating the effect on an optimal linear-programming solution of a sequence of proportionate changes in the elements of a single row or column of the matrix. Most commonly, the method is applied to either the objective function row or the right hand column.

programming, piece work — The programming technique of using an outside service organization to prepare programs for which payment is arranged by accomplishment, other than on a time-cost basis. Software companies are usually consulted for the above.

programming, quadratic—A program of an objective quadratic function stated in maxims that are subject to linear constraints. This is one of the few convex programming problems, aside from linear programming, which have solution algorithms that terminate in a finite number of steps.

programming, random-access—Programming without regard to the time required for access to the storage positions called for in the program.

programming, sequential—Programming of a special type in which only one logic or arithmetic operation is performed at a time, i.e., all programming is sequential, one step after another, unless a specific modifier labels it otherwise, such as time-sharing, interleaving, etc.

programming, serial—The programming of a computer by which only one arithmetical or logical operation can be executed at one time, e.g. a sequential operation. (Contrasted with multiple programming.)

programming, stochastic—A generalization of linear programming in which any of the unit costs, the coefficients in the constraint equations, and the right hand sides are random variables subject to known distributions. The aim of such programming is to choose levels for the variables which will minimize the expected (rather than the actual) cost.

programming, symbolic—The use of arbitrary symbols to represent addresses in order to facilitate programming.

339

programming system—An assemblage of programs, programming languages, routines and subroutines for use in specific computing systems, i.e., such are the bases for operating systems of data processing and computing.

programming system, machine-oriented — A system that uses a language that is oriented to the internal language of a specific computer. Systems that are considered to be machine-oriented are assembly systems and macrosystems.

program mode (remote control system)—1. When a program is active at a given terminal, that terminal is in the program mode. In this mode, the user enters program statements that make up the substance of his program, and he operates on the program (i.e., modifies, tests, executes, and debugs it) by using operating statements. While the terminal is in the program mode, the user can also enter single statements that are executed immediately, but are not retained in storage. 2. When a program is active at a given terminal, that terminal is in the program mode.

program, modification—The ability of a program to modify itself or to set a switch so that a set of events occuring at one time can affect the action of program at a later time. *See also* executive routine and system, monitor-operating.

program, monitor—A specific program developed to indicate the progress and other characteristics of work in various computer systems.

program, object—The program that is the output of an automatic-coding system. Often the object program is a machine-language program ready for execution, but it may well be in an intermediate language. (Synonymous with target program, and contrasted with source program.)

program, object-language — *See* object routine.

program, output—A program which organizes the output procedures of computers, i.e., which start the output equipment, present data to them at suitable intervals of time, specifies formats, etc.

program, overlays — Programs or runs too large for memory can be divided into logical segments or overlays. (One program overlays another or several segments may be in memory at the same time.) Overlays are also used when various operations occur infrequently such as deduction for Community Chest, union dues, etc. The overlays are called in only when the functions they perform are required. An overlay subroutine is provided to call in these overlays. This subroutine functions in a manner similar to the system supervisor.

program package—A group or collection of logicaly related operational program segments, i.e., all those having to do with the processing of a certain type of inquiry.

program parameter—1. A parameter incorporated into a subroutine during computation. A program parameter frequently comprises a word stored relative to either the subroutine or the entry point and dealt with by the subroutine during each reference. It may be altered by the routine and/or may vary from one point of entry to another. 2. The arbitrarily selected or given outer limits of the data being processed; often constraining the results of programming itself.

program, partial—A specific program not complete in itself and usually a specification of a process to be performed on data. It may be used at more than one point in any particular program, or it might be made available for inclusion in other programs, i.e., a subroutine, and that which is often called subprogram, incomplete program, etc.

program patching plug — A relatively small auxiliary plugboard patched with a specific variation of a portion of a program and designed to be plugged into a relatively larger plugboard patched with the main program.

program post-edit—A test of the application or operational program that is edited, formatted, and sorted into a test result tape.

program, precompiler — A unique program which is designed to detect errors and provide source program correction before the computation of the object, deck, or program.

program preparation aids — These convert programs from easy-to-use source languages into machine language.

program preparation, modification and testing—Most of the general purpose time-sharing systems have provisions for and even seem to be oriented to the preparation and testing of computer programs. It would seem that the composition of programs at an on-line terminal is uneconomical for large programs due to the slow input rate. These programs should be submitted for initial compilation in the usual batch mode way. After the intial compilation, it becomes desirable to allow a programmer to interact directly with the computer in the modification and testing of the program. After programmers become adapted to the on-line way of debugging and have gained experience in interactive techniques the elapsed time required to get a program into operational status should be greatly reduced.

program preparation (object)—Conversion of programs from one of several easy-to-use source languages, or from certain competitive system languages, to a machine code.

program processor — A programming aid which reads symbolic instructions and then compares and converts them into a suitable computer language.

program, random number—*See* random number program.

program read-in—The procedure and means of developing, by either hardware or software techniques, the programs that do not normally reside in main memory and that must be read in from auxiliary storage when required for processing. These techniques are required in any system that cannot retain all computer instructions in main memory at one time.

program, recycling—An organized arrangement for recycling programs through a computer when alterations have been made in one program that may change or have an effect on other programs.

program reference table (PRT)—Every program for some computers has a PRT. The PRT contains the locations reserved for program variables, data descriptions that give information about data arrays, and other program information.

When a program references a word in its PRT, the relative address of the word is used, never the absolute address. The relative address of any particular location is based on its position relative to the beginning of the PRT. The first PRT word is word zero. This method of addressing is used because it does not rely on actual addresses that exist at run time.

program register—*See* register, program.

program, relocatable — A special routine whose instructions are written in a special manner so that it can be located and executed in many areas of the memory. Some modification before execution may be involved to the instructions originally coded relative to a fixed starting place in the memory. Relocatable programs allow for the highly flexible real-time use of the main memory.

program relocation—The execution of a program in a location that is different from the location for which the program was originally assembled.

program relocation, dynamic — The moving of a partially executed program to a different location in main memory without detrimentally affecting the ability to complete normal processing.

program runs—A run is the same as a program except that a program refers to the writing or coding of the job, whereas the run refers to the actual running of the program. Consequently, programs and runs are synonymous except to denote the time and action being performed.

programs, applications—Problem-solving programs are given maximum operating efficiency when functioning under an operating system. Standard functions, such as I/O control, are furnished the user so that he need only program the data-handling portion of his job. In addition, operating systems provide a standardized operating procedure for all application programs.

program scheduler—Called at regular intervals to decide which program in memory is to be run. A running program is temporarily terminated each time its allotted

time has run out, or when it requires input/output operations with a device that is busy. A program may be terminated temporarily by user intervention to the scheduler, or it may suspend its own operation. Temporary termination does not remove the program from memory. A program may be dumped on backing storage and permanently discontinued by calling the scheduler and allocator.

programs, compaction—A series of techniques used for the reduction of space, bandwidth, cost, transmission, generating time, and storage of data. These techniques are designed to perform elimination of repetition and removal of irrelevancies.

programs, control—*See* control programs.

programs, conversion—Conversion programs enable users of several competitive systems to take advantage of the improved throughput and cost-performance characteristics of these computers without incurring the prohibitive reprogramming costs.

program segment—Various computer instructions set in groups of an artificially fixed size to fit into standard-sized areas of main storage in order to facilitate memory allocation and program read-in.

program segmenting—Programs that do not fit into memory may be segmented by use of the source-language linking statements. This allows sections of the program to be loaded and executed independently. Common storage is used by each link for passing data.

program segment size—Programs are usually divided into segments, and in most systems the infrequently used segments which may well be the greater part of the program are kept in file rather than core. The question of variable or fixed segment size is determined by the complexity of the program, the response or read-in time and the frequency of use.

program selection—To change from one job to another, the operator simply changes the program selector switch. There are no control bars, wired panels or control tapes to change. Switching from one job to another is a matter of seconds not minutes.

program, self-modification—The ability of a program to justify itself or to set a switch so that a set of events occurring at one time can affect the action of program at a later time.

program, self-triggered—The initial operation is performed by means of a manually controlled jump to the entry point in older computers, but bootstrap operations cause entry automatically, i.e., the program is said to be self-triggered.

program-sensitive error — An error arising from the unforeseen behavior of some circuits when a comparatively unusual combination of program steps occurs during a run.

program-sensitive fault—A fault that appears

in response to some particular sequence of program steps.

program-sensitive malfunction — A malfunction that occurs only during some unusual combination of program steps.

program sequencing (librarian)—This group of instructions tells the librarian the sequence in which the programs are to be put on the library tape. In other words, which program is to be first, second, third, etc. (1) Select—This instruction is used: when the input media is on two or more handlers; when the input media is any combination of punched cards, paper tape, or magnetic tape; or when the input media is on two or more input units. Each time the input media or unit changes it will be necessary to issue a new select instruction. If the input does not change, the original select instruction is sufficient. (2) Copy—This instruction performs a straight copy function. It will not make changes to the program(s) copied. The programs to be copied are indicated in the operand column. The copy instruction should only be used to copy from one library tape to create another library tape. This instruction cannot be used if the input is a tape, punched cards, or paper tape. (Some systems.)

program, service — A particular program which is designed to indicate a progress of work, i.e., one which provides a service to another program, an input program, a monitor program, an output program.

programs, generalized data-manipulation— Generalized data-manipulation programs perform common data-processing chores such as sorting, input/output operations, and report generation.

programs, general-purpose operating—Plans or instructions for controlling input/output operations, remote data transmission, and multiple users which can be used and reused to control these operations. Since these control programs are generally applicable to all users, they are usually prepared by computer manufacturers and offered as part of the free service. They are called by various names such as input/output control system, operating system, or executive system.

program signals, interrupt — See interrupt (program signals).

program simulation, supervisory—When the supervisory program is not available, this refers to the use of a replacement program that initiates the supervisory program.

program, simulator—An interpretative program that allows programs written for one type of a computer to be run on a different type of computer.

programs, manufacturer—Utility routines, assemblers, application package programs, and a large array of other programs, subroutines and programming aids developed and proved in use for customers, are available for direct use.

programs, mathematical function—See mathematical function programs.

program, snapshot—See snapshot program.

programs, operating — Operating programs direct the loading, segmentation, library search, space and time sharing of memory for a group of programs running both sequentially and concurrently.

program, sort/merge—See sort/merge program.

program, source—A computer program written in a language designed for ease of expression of a class of problems or procedures, by humans, e.g., symbolic or algebraic. A generator, assembler, translator or compiler routine is used to perform the mechanics of translating the source program into an object program in machine language. (Contrasted with object program.)

programs, packaged—These are various programs or routines which have been written by various indiivduals or organizations that are available from computer manufacturers of software companies.

program, specific—A program which can only be used to solve a particular problem, i.e., one which is thoroughly unique to that problem and not reusable with any other.

program specification—The precise and ordered definitions of logic and scope of processing functions that are performed by particular programs or program segments.

programs, post-edit—A test of the application or operational program that is edited, formulated, and sorted into a test result tape.

programs pre-edit—A checking of the application or operational program before the test run. A pre-edit run can remove such things as disobedience to established supervisory, core, or program segmentation rules, etc.

programs, processing — Complementing the control programs and functioning under them are those programs necessary to handle users' specific data processing needs. These programs, known collectively as processing programs, include application programs both manufacturer and user-written, compilers, report program generator, sort/merge, and utility programs. Although they rely upon the control programs for such functions as job scheduling, loading, and I/O control, processing programs function independently of one another, each performing a specific job or segment.

programs, psuedo applications—An operational program that is written to test the supervisory program.

programs, standard procedures — Suggested programming methods set by the manufacturer.

programs, support—Those programs which support or aid the supervisory programs and the application programs and include diagnostics, testing, data generators, etc.

programs, systems—These are the programs designed to implement system functions that may be requested from the user console. This is in contrast to system subroutines that may be called by system programs or other programs. System programs are normally provided by manufacturers, but they may be developed by the programmer. The programs contain a termination mode to return the communication link to the system program.

program, standard—Such a program meets certain specific criteria such as one written in a standard FORTRAN, COBOL, or ALGOL language and which brings forth an approved solution to a problem, such as a square root problem, or a standardized payroll problem which is very commonly used on thousands of machines.

program, star—A handwritten program independently designed by a programmer and checked so that no mistakes or bugs are contained, i.e., the star program should run correctly the first time, excepting machine malfunctions.

program statements—The user's program is made up of program statements. When entered from a terminal, these statements are always retained in storage as part of the active program. If the user has a statement in his program that refers to an executable program statement within the program, he should assign a statement number to the statement referred to.

program status double-word—See double-word, program status.

programs status word (PSW)—The PSW is stored at a fixed location, the address of which depends on the type of interruption. The system then automatically fetches a new PSW from a different fixed location, the address of which is also dependent on the type of interruption. Each class of interruption has two fixed locations in main storage—one to receive the old PSW when the interruption occurs, and the other to supply the new PSW that governs the servicing of that class of interruption. After the interruption has been serviced, a single instruction uses the stored PSW to reset the processing unit to the status it had before the interruption (some computers).

program step—1. A phase of one instruction or command in a sequence of instructions; thus, a single operation. 2. An increment, usually one instruction, of a program.

program stop—A stop instruction built into the program that will automatically stop the machine under certain conditions, or upon reaching the end of the processing, or completing the solution of a problem.

program storage—A portion of the internal storage reserved for the storage of programs, routines, and subroutines. In many systems protection devices are used to prevent inadvertent alternation of the contents of the program storage. (Contrasted with working storage.)

program, storage print—A program that produces a printout of storage and registers to aid the user in locating the reason(s) for a program malfunction.

program, stored—A series of instructions in storage to direct the step-by-step operation of the machine.

program, subject—Same as program source.

program, supervisory—Same as executive routine.

program switching—On a single transaction the control program initiates several switches among the various programs; therefore, the processor must be designed to accomplish very rapid program switching.

program-switching interrupt—See interrupt, program-switching.

program system testing—Test and checkout of complete programs as opposed to parameter or assembly testing.

program tape—See tape program.

program tape or drum—A tape or drum used to store a complete routine for future input. In the event that the length of the routine exceeds the available internal storage capacity, it will be read in and operated on by the computer, one segment at a time.

program, tape-to-card—Transfers binary or EBCDIC data from cards to magnetic tape.

program, tape-to-printer—Transfers data from magnetic tape to printer.

program, target—The program that is the output of an automatic coding system. Often the target program is a machine-language program ready for execution, but it may well be in an intermediate language. (Synonymous with object routine, and contrasted with source program.)

program test—A system of checking before running any problem, in which a sample problem of the same type with a known answer is run.

program tester—A program tester is available that enables a program or part of a program to be loaded and dynamically and selectively tested in accordance with simple and concise specifications expressed in terms of symbols and definitions used in the original source program. A variety of testing and monitoring facilities are provided by the program tester including file and storage display facilities designed to simplify the analysis of programming errors.

program testing—This is completed to discover whether the program is successful in meeting the defined systems requirements.

program testing time—The machine time expended for program testing, debugging, and volume and compatibility testing.

program, test supervisor—A supervisory program that is used only for testing.

program test tape—That specific tape which contains both program instructions and pre-approved test data or coding to be used for analysis diagnostics, or checkout runs.

program timing matrix—See matrix, program timing.

program, trace—A particular type of diagnostic program for the performance of checks on other programs for demonstrating such operations. The output of a trace program may include instructions of the program which is being checked and intermediate results of those instructions arranged in the order in which the instructions are executed.

program, trace-interpretive — A trace or diagnostic program used for performing a desired check on another program may include instructions as its output, and intermediate results of those instructions can be arranged in the order in which the instructions are executed. When such a trace program is an interpretive type, it is called an interpretive trace program.

program translating—A particular program (often called a translater) which translates from one language into another, i.e., from one programming language into another programming lnaguage.

program translation, interpretive—See program, interpretive.

program, translator—This program uses the source language program as input and produces from it a programming machine language. Like any other machine program, this may either be run immediately or stored for later use.

program, utility—A standard routine used to assist in the operation of the computer, e.g., a conversion routine, a sorting routine, a printout routine, or a tracing routine.

program verbs—Verbs which cause the processor to generate machine instructions that will be executed by the object program.

progression code, continuous—Same as code, unit distance.

progressive code continuous—Same as code, unit-distance.

PROMOCOM—A project monitoring and control program employing the G-E critical path method; it allows reporting of projected progress and project status for efficient management control.

PRONTO—A simple, easy-to-use program for point-to-point work only. Built-in macros for such operations as drilling, boring, tapping, and counterboring; flexibility in calling for a variety of operations on individual holes; and a smaller hardware requirement make PRONTO a possible alternative approach where requirements and facilities are smaller. (General Electric)

proof factor in multiplication—This factor is a group-type control and is used to verify a number of calculations in one operation. In using this technique, it is necessary that the proof factor be larger than any one of the multipliers with which it is used. During each multiplication, the multiplicand is multiplied once by the multiplier and again by a factor which is the difference between the multiplier and the proof factor. A total of these products and a total of the multiplicands are accumulated for the run or group. At the end, the total of multiplicands is multiplied by the proof factor and the result is compared against the final total of the products.

proof listing—A specific report prepared by a processor, that indicates the coding as it was originally devised and written plus the comments that have been written, and the machine language that has been produced. In accounting, it is an itemized list of the transactions and their detail together with the control totals, sequence checks, or other data for proofing and audit trial.

proof total—One of a number of check totals which can be correlated in some manner for consistency or reconciliation in a range, set, or distinct calculation.

proof, zero—See zero proof.

propagated error—An error occurring in one operation, that spreads through and influences later operations and results.

propagation time—This is the time required for an electrical impulse to travel from one point to the other.

property—A characteristic quality.

property detector—See detector, property.

property sort—See sort, property.

proportional band—The range of values of a condition being regulated that will cause the controller to operate over its full range. Usually expressed by engineers in terms of percentage of instrument full scale range.

proportional control—A method of control in which the intensity of action varies linearly as the condition being regulated deviates from the condition prescribed.

PROSPORO—A fill-in-the-blanks process control system developed by IBM and Humble Oil Co.

protected files—See files, protected.

protected location — A storage location reserved for special purposes in which data cannot be stored without undergoing a screening procedure to establish suitability for storage therein.

protection, character — See character protection.

protection, file—A device or method that prevents accidental erasure of operative data on magnetic-tape reels.

protection key—See key, protection.

protection, memory—Same as storage protection.

protection, memory (time sharing)—See time sharing, memory protection.

protection, nonstop operation — Ensures against program hang-ups due to infinite indirect address loops or execute instruction loops.

protection, read/jump—Read/jump protection allows the executive to stop the program at the point of error, terminate it, and provide diagnostic information to the programmer, thereby minimizing wasted time and smoothing the checkout process. A particular advantage of read/jump protection is that programs of a classified nature can be confidently run together; they are fully protected from audit (inadvertant or otherwise) by other programs.

protection, storage—*See* storage protection.

proving time—The time which is used for the testing of the machine or system to ensure that no faults exist or malfunctions are present, by using special diagnostic routines of circuit testing or to discern status or conditions of components. Such time could be included in fault time after the repair of the fault and in scheduled maintenance time.

PRT (production run tape)—A tape containing checked-out and scheduled production running on various computers.

pseudo application programs — An operational program that is written to test supervisory programs.

pseudocode—1. An arbitrary code, independent of the hardware of a computer, that must be translated into computer code. 2. Computer instructions written in mnemonic or symbolic language by the programmer. These instructions do not necessarily represent operations built into the computer. They must be translated into machine language and have absolute addresses assigned them before they can become a finished and assembled program that the computer can use to process data.

pseudo file address—The use of a false address by the application program to obtain a record from file. The pseudo address is converted by the supervisory program into an actual machine address. The actual machine address may change as different file units are used in duplexing and fall-backs.

pseudoinstruction—1. A symbolic representation in a compiler or interpreter. 2. A group of characters having the same general form as a computer instruction, but never executed by the computer as an actual instruction. 3. An instruction written in an assembly language designating a predetermined and limited group of computer instructions for performing a particular task.

psuedolanguage—An artificial language which is uniquely constructed to perform a distinct task, i.e., a special set of rules is devised with particular meanings assigned to chosen expressions. Some types of programs are quite easily written in pseudolanguage, especially various problem or procedure-oriented types, and most of these have some English-type statements in either semantics, syntax, logic, or mnemonics.

psuedo-offline working — *Same as* working, psuedo-offline.

psuedo-op—*Same as* pseudoinstruction.

pseudo-operation—An operation that is not part of the computer's operation repertoire as realized by hardware; hence an extension of the set of machine operations.

pseudorandom—This relates to the desire for satisfaction of one or more criteria for statistical randomness, which is briefly defined as equal probability of occurrence of given digits or events occurring in an equal number of times in large numbers of digits or events. The randomness is produced by definite calculation processes. Pseudorandomness is not full random status, but often partial or close, and designed and known to be such.

pseudorandom number sequence—A sequence of numbers, determined by some defined arithmetic process, that is satisfactorily random for a given purpose such as by satisfying one or more of the standard statistical test for randomness. Such a sequence may approximate any one of several distributions, e.g., uniform distribution or a normal (Gaussian) distribution.

PTS (Program Test System)—A specific system that automatically checks out programs, producing diagnostic information where necessary to aid in production run organization.

PTT/8—An 8-level channel paper tape transmission code.

PTT (Program Test Tape)—A specific tape that contains programs and test data to be tested during a checkout run.

pulse—1. A pulse developed at a particular instant in time relative to a specific reference pulse, which may be a major or minor cycle pulse, and one which is often used to mark, clock, or control a particular binary digit position in a computer word. 2. One of a group of pulses which are used to define particular digit periods within a word period.

pulse amplitude—Maximum instantaneous value of a pulse.

pulse, clock—A pulse positioned next to recorded characters on tapes, drums, disks, etc., to control the timing of read circuits, count characters, or develop and perform related type functions which a clock pulse would perform.

pulse code—1. A code in which sets of pulses have been assigned particular meanings. 2. The binary representations of characters.

pulse commutator—A pulse developed at a particular instant in time relative to a specific reference pulse, which may be a major or minor cycle pulse, and one which is often used to mark, clock, or control a particular binary digit position in a computer word.

pulse decay time—That specific time which is required for the trailing edge of a pulse to decline and which is measured as the time required to drop from 90% of full amplitude to 10%.

pulse, digit — A particular drive pulse corresponding to a one digit position in some or all the words in a storage unit. In some techniques it may always be an inhibit pulse or always an enable pulse which are more acceptable names for the general term.

pulse-double recording — A specific method for magnetic recording of bits in which each storage cell comprises two regions magnetized in opposite senses with unmagnetized regions on each side.

pulse duration—See pulse length.

pulse (electric)—A momentary and significant rise or fall in voltage level. A pulse provides the primary means for the transmission of data into a computer. The presence or absence of a pulse during a particular time period is interpreted as binary information.

pulse emitter—Relating to a punched card machine, one of the group of pulses that is used to define a particular row within the columns of a card.

pulse enable—A digit pulse which aids the write pulse, so when they are together they are strong enough to switch the magnetic cell.

pulse, full drive—See pulse, full read.

pulse, full read—In coincident-current selection, the resultant of the partical drive pulses which, when applied together, cause the selection of, for example, full read pulse, or full write pulse.

pulse, gate—A pulse that enables a gate circuit to pass a signal; usually, the gate pulse is of longer duration than the signal, to make sure that a coincidence in time occurs.

pulse generator, clock—See generator clock-pulse.

pulse generator, restorer—Same as generator, clock-pulse.

pulse generator timing—Same as generator, clock pulse.

pulse inhibit—A specific pulse which prevents an action which might otherwise occur if such a pulse were not present, i.e., close a gate, prevent reading, etc.

pulse length—Nominal duration of a standard pulse which is the time interval between the half amplitude points of the rise and decay points of the curve. For pulses of other shapes, the points on the curve must be stated. Time interval between the points on the leading and trailing edges at which the instantaneous value bears a specified relation to the pulse amplitude. Note: Frequently the specified relation is taken as 50%.

pulse, marking (teletypewriter)—A marking pulse or "mark" is the signal pulse which, in d-c neutral operation, corresponds to a "circuit closed" or "current on" condition.

pulse, P—See pulse.

pulse, partial drive—Same as pulse, partial write.

pulse, partial select input—Same as pulse, partial-write.

pulse, partial-write—In coincident-current, magnetic-core storage devices, one of two or more pulses that are required to affect the selection or the switching of a core, when entering or storing data.

pulse, position—See pulse.

pulse, post-write disturb—In a coincident-current, magnetic-core storage device, a pulse applied after a write pulse to put all

cores in the disturbed state, as contrasted with pulse, preread disturb.

pulse, preread disturb—In a coincident-current, magnetic core storage device, a pulse applied before a read pulse to ensure that the core about to be read is in the disturbed state, as contrasted with pulse, post-write disturb.

pulse rate—The time interval of periodic pulses which are integrated with the control of the computer or the entire system.

pulse, read—In coincident-current core storage devices, a specific pulse or the sum of several pulses (simultaneous) which are capable of switching a core, or producing a change in its residual flux density so as to produce an output signal on the read winding provided for this purpose.

pulse regeneration—A pulse regeneration is the process of restoring a series of pulses to the original timing, form, and relative magnitude.

pulse repetition rate—The number of electric pulses per unit of time experienced by a point in a computer; usually the maximum, normal or standard pulse rate.

pulse, reset—A pulse designed and used to position a binary storage cell, i.e., a flip-flop, or a magnetic core, back to its original reset state.

pulse rise time—That specific time which is required for the leading edge or a pulse to rise, i.e., for the amplitude to reach a specified value, such time being measured as the time required to rise from 10% to 90% of full amplitude.

pulse, set—A pulse designed and used to position a binary storage address, i.e., a flip-flop or magnetic core, into a specified state or original condition or state.

pulse shaping—Same as pulse regeneration.

pulse, shift—A pulse which causes the characters in a register to shift.

pulse spacing (teletypewriter)—A spacing pulse or "space" is the signal pulse which, in d-c neutral operation, corresponds to a "circuit open" or "no current" condition.

pulse, sprocket—1. A pulse generated by a magnetized spot which accompanies every character recorded on magnetic tape. This pulse is used during read operations to regulate the timing of the read circuits and also to provide a count on the number of characters read from tape. 2. A pulse generated by the sprocket or driving hole in paper tape which serves as the timing pulse for reading or punching the paper tape.

pulse standardization—Same as pulse regeneration.

pulses, transmission—Electrical impulses which can be transmitted and received through communication lines. Transmission pulses may be either voice or data communications in nature. In the latter case, computer interface equipment converts incoming pulses into the proper binary code and delivers the data to storage.

pulse string—A particular group of pulses which happen in time sequence at a point in a circuit, i.e., an amplitude vs time plot of the pulses appears as though the pulse group occurs in space sequence or along a line, thus the terms pulse string or pulse train.

pulse, teletypewrite marking—A unique signal pulse which corresponds to a circuit-closed or a current-on state, in dc or neutral teletype operation.

pulse, timing—*See* pulse, clock.

pulse width—*See* pulse length.

pulse, write—That drive pulse (or the sum of several simultaneous drive pulses) which under suitable conditions can write into a magnetic cell or set a cell, i.e., usually to a one condition.

punch—*See* punch, automatic feed.

punch, automatic feed—A card punch having a hopper, a card track and a stacker. The movement of cards through the punch is automatic.

punch, automatic tape—A peripheral device which punches holes which represent patterns of characters on tapes with automatic movement of tape with each character punched. Such characters arrive at the punch in coded electrical signals, and the program of the punch arranges them into rows of holes.

punch calculating—A type of punched card device which reads data from cards and performs various arithmetic or logic operations as well. The results are then punched on another card, or if desired, on the same card.

punch, calculating electronic—A card-handling machine that reads a punched card, performs a number of sequential operations, and punches the result on a card.

punch, card—A machine that punches cards in designated locations to store data which can be conveyed to other machines or devices by reading or sensing the holes. (Synonymous with card-punch unit.)

punch card—A heavy stiff paper of constant size and shape, suitable for punching in a pattern that has meaning, and for being handled mechanically. The punched holes are sensed electrically by wire brushes, mechanically by metal fingers, or photoelectricaly by photocells. (Related to eighty-column card and ninety-column card.)

punch-card control units—These units contain all logic, control and power electronics to make compatible card formats.

punch, control function—*Same as* punch.

punch designation—*Same as* control punches.

punch, duplicating card—A unit with an automatic-feed punch which has in its card track a sensing station which each punched card passes after being punched. At the same time, the following card is passing under the punch knives and the sensing station causes common data to be duplicated from each card to the following one.

punched card—1. A card which may be punched with holes to represent letters, digits or characters. 2. A card punched with a pattern of holes to represent data.

punched card, border—*See* card, edge-notched.

punched card, ducol—*See* card, ducol punched.

punched-card duplicating—Automatic punching of repetitive information from a master card into a group of succeeding detail cards. Common information punched into the first card of each group is automatically punched into all remaining cards of a particular group.

punched-card field—A set of columns fixed as to number and position into which the same items or items of data are regularly entered.

punched-card input device—A machine that reads data from punched cards and makes it available to the other computer components.

punched-card machine operator—Employee who operates all units of conventional punched-card equipment.

punched card, margin—*Same as* card, edge-punched.

punched card output device—The device which punches the data onto punched cards.

punched-card reader—*See* reader, card.

punched card, sorter—Sequential ordering of punched cards.

punched paper tape—*See* tape, punched paper.

punched paper tape channels—The parallel tracks along the length of the tape.

punched tape—1. Tape, usually paper, upon which data may be stored in the form of punched holes. Hole locations are arranged in columns across the width of the tape. There are usually 5 to 8 positions (channels) per column, with data represented by a binary-coded alphanumerical decimal system. All holes in a column are sensed simultaneously in a manner similar to that for punched cards. 2. Paper tape punched in 'a pattern of holes so as to convey information. Mylar and other plastic tapes are used instead of paper tapes for more permanent purposes and when such tapes are frequently used and reused.

punched tape code—*See* code, punched tape.

punched tape machine—Any tape punch that automatically converts coded electrical signals into perforations in tape.

punch EL—A special punch to indicate end of line or the end of a paper tape record.

punch, eleven (11)—A punch in position 11 of a column. This is the X punch often used to control or select, or to indicate a negative number as if it were a minus sign. Also called an 11-punch.

punches, control—*See* control punches.

punch, gang—1. A process for duplicating cards and card data, or punching cards in any format. Also called reproduce. 2. To punch all or part of the information from one punched card onto succeeding cards.

punch, hand-feed—A manual card punch with a simple keyboard which operates to punch cards fed into it by hand and one at-a-time.

punch, high—The 12, 11, and zero punches are zone punches, the 12 punch being the highest (vertically) on the standard punched card.

punching, card—The basic method for converting source data into punched cards. The operator reads the source document and converts the information into punched holes.

punching, control—Punches which determine how the data on a punched card is to be treated with a machine, or which functions the machine is about to or is capable of performing.

punching double—*Same as* punching multiple.

punching, interstage—A system of punching in which only odd numbered rows of cards are used. (Contrasted with normal-stage punching.)

punching, multiple—1. The reference to punch cards and more specifically to Hollerith cards. 2. The punching of two or more holes in a column.

punching normal stage—In a punching system for punched cards with 24 rows, each column is treated as though it were two separate columns, one digit being represented by holes in the even numbered rows, and the other by those in the odd-numbered rows. A punched card with 80 columns of 24 rows is thus used as though it were a punched card with 160 columns of 12 rows.

punching, over-capacity — Over-capacity punching is a fairly common method of extending the capacity of a card beyond 90 columns. When this method is employed, certain zero-punching positions in the card are assigned the values of a normal vertical-punching column. Thus, through the use of over-capacity punching, a 5-digit card field can actually represent a 6-digit number by using the zero positions to indicate the most significant digit of the value.

punching positions—The specified areas, i.e., the row-column intersects, on a punch card where holes may be punched.

punching, rate of — The number of cards, characters, blocks, fields or words of information placed in the form of holes on cards, or tape per unit of time.

punchings, designation—The same as control holes or function holes. They are punchings which determine how the data on a punched card are to be treated within the machine, such as which functions the machine is to perform and when.

punching station—The area of a keypunch machine where a card is aligned to be punched.

punching, summary—The automatic conversion into punched-hole form of information developed by the accounting machine.

punch, interstage—A punching system in which only odd numbered rows or cards are used.

punch, keyboard—A particular punch unit which has a bank of keys and a manual depression of such keys marked with a specific character causes the data or information carrier to move to the next card column or paper tape row. Punching can be achieved on some units by depressing more than one key. Such units can punch paper tape feed holes as well as code holes.

punch knife—That part of the card punch which makes the hole in the card.

punch light—A specific light found on most control consoles which indicates that a condition exists in the card punch equipment that requires an operator's attention, i.e., an empty hopper, full stacker, full chip box, mechanism failure, etc.

punch, low—The zero zone punch in a punch code.

punch, mark-sense—The punching of holes in a card with an automatic process but based on electrically conductive marks, i.e., using magnetic ink, carbon, etc., thus producing cards at the source and sending them to a control place for processing.

punch, middle—*Same as* eleven punch, also known as the X punch, located next to the top row on an 80 column card; used for the J through R of the alphabet and for special characters.

punch, multiple—To punch two or more holes in a single column of a card thus permitting the representation of a larger number of different characters.

punch, multiplying—*Same as* punch, calculating.

punch, numeric—To punch holes in card columns such that only a single hole in rows one through nine is punched in the given column being analyzed or considered.

punch, portable hand—A device for punching cards by hand; does not need electricity and is small enough to carry.

punch position—1. A site of a punched tape or card where holes are to be punched. 2. In the case of 80-column punch cards, the position of a punch in a row on the card.

punch-print editor—*See* print-punch editor.

punch reproducer—*See* punch, gang.

punch, reproducing—*Same as* card reproducer.

punch single—Relates to a system of punched card coding in which any one of various numeric values zero to 11 can be represented by one hole punched in a specified position or row in a column, as contrasted with double punching.

punch, spot—A hand-operated device, resembling a pair of pliers, for selectively punching holes in punch cards.

punch stage, normal—The punching of holes in a punch card only in the even numbered rows in each card.

punch, summary — A card-handling machine may be electrically connected to another machine, e.g., tabulator. The card punch will punch out on a card the information produced, calculated, or summarized by the other machine (tabulator).

punch tape — A tape, usually paper, upon which data may be stored in the form of punched holes. Hole locations are arranged in columns across the width of the tape. There are usually 5 to 8 positions, channels, per column, with data represented by a binary coded decimal system. All holes in a column are sensed simultaneously in a manner similar to that for punch cards. (Synonymous with perforated tape.)

punch-tape code — A code used to represent data on punch tape.

punch, twelve (12) — A punch in position 12 of a column. It is often used for additional control or selection, or to indicate a positive number as if it were a plus sign.

punch verifier — The punch verifier punches and checks 80-column cards under direction of the program. A card is sent through the unit; information generated by the program is punched into the card at the punch station. The card is moved to the wait station, and then is moved to the third read station where it is verified. The verification is accomplished by reading the card and comparing the results hole by hole with the card image which is retained in the control unit until the checking is complete. When this has been completed, the card is placed in the normal output stacker or the stacker selected by the program.

punch, X — 1. A punch in the X or 11 row of an 80-column card. 2. A punch in position 11 of a column. The X punch is often used to control or select, or to indicate a negative number as if it were a minus sign. Also called an 11-punch. (Synonymous with eleven (11) punch.)

punch, Y — 1. A punch in the Y or 12 row of an 80-column card, i.e., the top row of the card. 2. A punch in position 12 of a column.

It is often used for additional control or selection, or to indicate a positive number as if it were a plus sign. (Synonymous with twelve (12) punch.)

punch, zone — To add holes in a card column that already contains one or more holes.

punctuation bits — The use of a variable-length data format requires that there be a method of indicating the actual length of a unit of information. This requirement is fulfilled by two punctuation bits associated with each memory location. These bits can constitute a word mark, used to define the length of a field, an item mark, used to define the length of an item; or a record mark, used to define the length of a record. In addition to defining the lengths of data fields, word marks are also used to define the lengths of instructions in memory.

pure generator — *See* generator, pure.

purification, data — The reduction of the number of errors as much as possible prior to using data in an automatic data-processing system.

push-button switching — A switching system in a reperforator that permits the selection of the outgoing channel by an operator.

push-down — A last-in, first-out method of queuing in which the last item attached to the queue is the first to be withdrawn.

push-down list — A list of items where the last item entered is the first item of the list, and the relative position of the other items is pushed back one.

push down storage — *See* storage, push down.

push-to-type operation — A teletype operation in one direction at a time by using a switch depressed during transmission.

push-up list — A list of items where the first item is entered at the end of the list, and the other items maintain their same relative positions in the list.

push-up storage — *See* storage, push-up.

putaway — Refers to a memory location in which the processor will store specific information.

Q

Q address — A source location in internal storage in some types of equipment from which data is transferred.

(QED) text editor — QED is a generalized text editor that allows the on-line user to create and modify symbolic text for any purpose. User capabilities include: inserting, deleting, and changing lines of text; a line-edit feature; a powerful symbolic search feature; automatic tabs, which the user can set; and ten string buffers (some systems) .

Q test — A comparison test of two or more

units of quantitative data for their equality or nonequality.

quad — An assembly of four separately insulated conductors, twisted together in such a manner as to provide two pairs.

quadratic programming — Maximization, subject to linear constraints, of an objective function that is a quadratic function. This is one of the few convex programming problems, aside from linear programming, that have solution algorithms that terminate in a finite number of steps.

quadrature—Quadrature expresses the phase relationship between two periodic quantities of the same period when the phase difference between them is one fourth of a period.

quadripuntal — Pertaining to four punches, specifically having four random punches on a punch card. This term is used in determinative documentation.

quadruplex system—A system of Morse telegraphy arranged for the simultaneous independent transmission of two messages in each direction over a single circuit.

qualification—In COBOL, the technique of making a name unique by adding IN or OF and another name, according to defined rules and procedures.

qualified name—See name, qualified.

qualifier—A name used to qualify another name with an action similar to an adjective in English grammar, i.e., to give additional information about a name or to distinguish the named thing from other things having the same name.

quantification—An act of quantifying or giving numerical value to the measurement of an item, i.e., to attempt to give discrete values to human characteristics using statistical terms, numerical indicators, or weights.

quantity—1. A constant, variable, function name, or expression. 2. A positive or negative real number in the mathematical sense. The term quantity is preferred to the term number in referring to numerical data; the term number is used in the sense of natural number and reserved for "the number of digits," the "number of operations," etc.

quantity, double-precision—A quantity having twice as many digits as are normally in a specific computer.

quantity scaler—See scaler, quantity.

quantity, variable—A quantity that may assume a succession of values.

quantity, vector—A quantity which has both magnitude and direction such as field intensity, velocity, etc., as contrasted with scaler quantities.

quantization—The subdivision of the range of values of a variable into a finite number of nonoverlapping subranges.

quantization distortion—In communication, quantization is a process in which the range of values of a wave is divided into a finite number of smaller subranges, each of which is represented by an assigned (or quantized) value within modifying various forms of modulation; for example, quantized pulse-amplitude modulation.

quantize—To subdivide the range of values of a variable into a finite number of non-overlapping subranges or intervals, each of which is represented by an assigned value within the subrange; e.g., to represent a person's age as a number of whole years.

quantizer—A device that converts an analog measurement into digital form.

quantum — The subranges resulting from quantization.

quasi-instruction—See pseudoinstruction.

quasi-instruction form—Same as form, pseudoinstruction.

queries, time sharing—Many organizations have problems requiring retrieval from data or document libraries. Remote terminals are being used to browse through the data file searching for material fulfilling the requirements.

query—A specific request for data, instructions, characteristics of states of switches, position in a queue, etc., while the equipment is computing or processing.

query station—A specific unit of equipment which introduces requests or queries for data, states of processing, information, etc., while the equipment is computing or processing or communicating.

question, automated answering (time sharing)—See time sharing, automated question answering.

question, encoded—A question set up and encoded in a form appropriate for operating, programming or conditoning a searching device.

queue—A line or group of items waiting for the attention of the processor—usually in core and chained together by address words.

queue, input work—See work queue, input.

queue, multipriority—See multipriority.

queue, new input—A group or a queue of new messages that are the system and are waiting for processing. The main scheduling routine will scan them along with other queues and order them into processing in order.

queue, output—Messages that are in line or queued which have been produced by the system and are waiting to be scheduled for transmission.

queue, output work—See work queue, output.

queue, push-down—A first-out method of queuing in which the last item attached to the queue is the first to be withdrawn.

queue, sequential — The first-in, first-out method of queuing items waiting for the processor.

queue, work-in-process—Items that have had some processing and are queued by and for the computer to complete the needed processing.

queuing—A study of the patterns involved and the time required for discrete units to move through channels; e.g., the elapsed time for auto traffic at a toll booth or employees in a cafeteria line.

queuing analysis—The study of the nature and time concerning the discrete units necessary to move through channels; e.g., the time and length of queue at service centers of grocery check-out stands, harbors, airports, etc. Queuing analysis is employed to determine lengths of lines and order, time, discipline of service.

queuing, message — Controls the order in which messages are stored, processed, and transmitted.

queing theory—A form of probability theory useful in studying delays or line-ups at servicing points.

queuing-theory problems—When a flow of goods (or customers) is bottlenecked at a particular servicing point, losses accumulate in the form of lost business, idle equipment, and unused labor. Minimizing such costs involved in waiting lines, or queues, is the object of queuing theory, an OR (operations research) technique for the most efficient handling of a line at a particular point of service.

quibinary code—A binary-coded decimal code for representing decimal numbers in which each decimal digit is represented by seven binary digits that are coefficients of 8, 6, 4, 2, 0, 1, 0, respectively.

quick-access reports—Single-record inquiries, or interim reports, may be produced in seconds or minutes on a demand basis. Exception reports may be prepared automatically for a single activity requiring management attention.

quick-access storage—*Same as* storage, high speed.

quiescent carrier telephony — That form of carrier telephony in which the carrier is suppressed whenever there are no modulating signals to be transmitted.

quiesing—The process of completing a multiprogrammed computer to a stop by denying it new or continuing tasks.

QUIKTRAN—Through the drastic reduction of turnaround time developed through real-time and time-sharing, the user and system form a problem-solving team. The user sees only his terminal and is unaware of others using the processing facilities concurrently. Using the powerful facilities for substitution and deletion, the scientist can rapidly exercise his judgment and experience in the formulation and testing of a problem. QUIKTRAN is a subset of FORTRAN including built-in functions augmented by powerful and versatile and operating statements for complete control maintenance. Special codes for easy parameter insertion and changes, such as assigning new values to variables, and for deletion and replacement plus cross-referencing and selective output make this an outstanding innovation to computer science

QUIKTRAN communications — A communications system with printer-keyboard is used as the terminal device at the user's location. A card reader/punch may be added if needed. The terminal is linked by telephone lines to a communications control system at the computer center.

QUIKTRAN communications control—A communications control system is used for communication processing and message control. It continuously monitors incoming lines and relays programming statements from each line to the computer.

QUIKTRAN data-processing system — The data-processing system, under control of the QUIKTRAN program stored in its memory, compiles, checks or executes each statement according to instructions from the sending location. Lengthy jobs, that must be processed in their entirety rather than statement-by-statement, can be placed temporarily in disk storage until the computer is free to handle them.

QUIKTRAN functions—Uses FORTRANlike language and includes built-in functions augmented by powerful and versatile operating statements that permit the user to operate upon and maintain complete control over his program. Special codes are used for easy parameter insertion and changes, such as assigning new values to variables. The language has the facility to start execution at any point and provides for easy insertion, deletion, or replacement of program statements. Other provisions include cross-reference listing of program statement names and labels, detection of incomplete executions, and selective output. More than thirty control statements are used for programming. Five types of operating statements are: modification, control, test, display and input/output.

QUIKTRAN source language—All communications between man and machines are expressed in the same problem-oriented language. Diagnostic error messages and debugging information are printed in QUIKTRAN, the source language. Therefore, there is no need for the user to learn machine or assembly language.

QUIKTRAN structure—The operative and diagnostic structure of QUIKTRAN is reflected in its collection of operating statements used to build, manipulate, test and debug programs. Control statements control the user's terminal and his program. Modification statements alter and modify the user's formulas or program. Test statements test and debug the user's program. Display statements selectively display intermediate or final results. Input/output statements select the input or output unit . . . and also are used to specify or change output formats. The QUIKTRAN capability makes it simple for the user to execute a single statement or sequence of statements. The user can add, delete or change statements as desired, list his program to clarify the most recent version, or interrupt execution at any time.

QUIKTRAN subsystems—The computer system is divided into subsystems as follows: The scheduler controls operations and maintains consistent response times at all terminals; the translator transforms the source language into an efficient equivalent internal form; the interpreter performs the execution; the process control program coordinates the activities of the translator and the interpreter; the input/output control system performs all I/O functions; the exchange program runs the communications control system. A disk storage is available for user-library storage; a drum storage acts as a temporary working storage for the users' programs, and a magnetic-tape unit is used for logging transactions and for maintaining normal computer capabilities.

QUIKTRAN, time sharing — One key to this approach to remote computing—man/machine interaction of statement and instantaneous response—is QUIKTRAN, a programming system for the remote computing system. QUIKTRAN makes computer time-sharing a practical reality. Through the use of this unique programming system, hundreds of users at remote locations can utilize concurrently the centrally located computer for problem solution and program testing.

Written in the familiar FORTRANlike language, QUIKTRAN contains versatile operating, testing and debugging statements which provide the user with easily learned means for solving problems and developing programs on a statement-by-statement basis. The time-sharing environment of this remote system permits the user to make immediate changes or alterations to these statements. As a result of this man/machine interaction, the scientist, engineer or businessman can rapidly exercise his judgment and experience in the formulation and testing of solutions of problems.

quinary — Number representation system in which each decimal digit N is represented by the digit pair AB, where $N = 5A + B$, and where $A = 0$ or 1 and $B = 0, 1, 2, 3$, or 4, e.g., decimal 7 is represented by biquinary 12. This system is sometimes called a mixed-radix system having the radices 2 and 5.

quote mark, single—A special Fortran character used to enclose literal messages.

quotient—The quantity that results from dividing one number by the other.

quotient-multiplier register—*See* multiplier-quotient register.

R

radial transfer—A procedure or process for transferring data between peripheral equipment and the internal memory of the machine.

radio communication — Any telecommunication by means of radio waves.

radio link—The channel provided by means of a radio transmitter and a radio receiver.

radix—*See* number base.

radix complement—*Same as* complement.

radix complement, diminished — *Same as* complement, radix-minus-one.

radix floating point—*See* floating point base.

radix-minus-1 complement — A complement on N-1 is obtained by subtracting each digit of the given quantity from N-1 (where N = radix); e.g., the ones complement of binary 11010 is 00101; the nines complement of decimal 456 is 543.

radix mixed—Relates to a numeration system that uses more than one radix, such as the bioprimary system.

radix notation—*See* notation base.

radix number—*See* number base.

radix point—The dot that marks the separation between the integral and fractional parts of a number. In the decimal number system, the decimal point; in the binary number system, the binary point.

radix scale—*Same as* notation base.

rail logic, double—*See* logic, double rail.

Rajchman selection switch—*Same as* storage, core rope.

RAM (random-access memory)—*See* memory, random access.

RAMAC—Random-access method of accounting and control, a data file that consists of a number of rotating disks stacked one on top of another.

random access—1. Access to storage under conditions in which the next location from which data are to be obtained is in no way dependent on the location of the previously obtained data. 2. Pertaining to the process of obtaining data from, or placing data into, storage when there is no sequential relation governing the access time to successive storage locations. 3. A quality of memory device that allows data to be written in, or read from, the memory through direct locating rather than locating through reference to other data in the memory. No search is required; the machine can proceed directly to the desired memory location.

random-access auxiliary storage, time sharing—*See* time sharing, random access auxiliary storage.

random-access disk file—*See* disk file, random-access.

random-access input/output—This is an I/O control capability that permits efficient random processing of records stored on a direct-access device. Random-access I/O efficiency is achieved by the system in two ways: (1) Seeks are issued in an order that minimizes the average seek time, rather than in the order in which they were requested. (2) Seeks are overlapped with other processing. Because records must sometimes be processed sequentially (for example, when a report is being written), the ability to call for records sequentially is also available.

random-access I/O routines — Direct, serial, and random processing of drum and disk files are provided by these routines. Macro-instructions are available to direct the performance of the input/output functions.

random-access memory — *See* memory, random-access.

random-access memory (RAM) (Bank) — Provides storage of on-line account records containing all information — account balance, available balance, unposted dividends and previous no-book transactions, account holds, etc.—required for complete processing of transactions and inquiries, as well as for updating of passbooks.

random access, movable—Describes a feature of a storage device like disk packs, tape strips, or card strips which can be physically removed and replaced by another, thereby allowing for a theoretically unlimited storage capacity.

random-access processing (central file) — Application records stored in the on-line central file may be updated quickly because transactions may be processed as soon as they arrive at the bank's processing center, in any sequence or mix of transaction types.

random-access programming — Programming without regard to the time required for access to the storage positions called for in the program. (Contrasted with minimum-access programming.)

random-access software — A comprehensive array of programming and operating aids that includes a loader/monitor, a program for updating program files, a special sort, input/output routines, and utility routines.

random-access sorts—Separate programs are furnished by manufacturers to sort data stored on random-access disks and drums. These programs strip off the item keys of data stored on a random-access device, sort the keys, and then store on the disk or drum a table containing the keys and the addresses of the corresponding file items. Items may be brought in from the disk or drum in the order of the sorted keys by using macroinstructions.

random-access storage—1. A storage medium in which the time required to obtain information is statistically independent of the location of the information most recently obtained. 2. A type of storage in which access can be made directly to any storage regardless of its position, either absolute or relative to the previously referenced information.

random access system—A particular method of filing data in a manner which approximates equal time to the processing of the data, i.e., usually that type of core storage or auxiliary storage which is ultrafast.

randomize—The procedure for making numbers, data, or events random, i.e., without bias as to the selection of each number or event by assigning pseudorandom codes or characters to particular locations in storage.

randomizing, file addressing — *See* file addressing, randomizing.

randomizing scheme—Plans for the distribution of file records among several file storage modules designed so that the accesses to these records will be distributed equally and the waiting times for file information will be set evenly.

random noise—Noise due to the aggregate of a large number of elementary disturbances with random occurrence in time.

random number—1. A set of digits constructed of such a sequence that each successive digit is equally likely to be any of N digits to the base n of the number. 2. A number formed by a set of digits selected from a random table or sequence of digits. 3. A number formed by a set of digits selected from an orderless sequence of digits.

random-number generator — A special machine routine or hardware unit designed to produce a random number or a series of random numbers according to specified limitations.

random number, normal—A number selected by pure chance from a set of numbers distinctly characterized, in which each number has an equal chance of being selected. The distribution of numbers in the set follows a normal or Gaussian distribution.

random number program—A program to develop and store a given quantity of uniform random numbers. Also called a random number generator.

random-number sequence—A unpredictable array of numbers produced by chance, and satisfying one or more of the tests for randomness.

random number, uniform—A set of digits constructed in such a sequence that each successive digit is equally likely to be any of n digits to the base of the number.

random processing—1. Information and data records are processed in the particular order specified by the control system and not in the order in which they are stored. 2. Transfer of an item between core memory and a drum or disk location whose address is determined by mathematical transformation of the item's key.

random sequence—A sequence that is not arranged by ascending or descending keys, as in alphanumeric or numeric sequences, but is instead arranged in an organized fashion in bulk storage, by locations determined by calculations performed on keys to develop addresses. The calculations are repeated in order to acquire the address and locate the item desired.

random sequential access—*See* access, random sequential.

random walk—A statistical term which relates to the movement of a body to its next position, in such a way that it is likely to move in any direction with equal probability by a specified fixed distance from its current position, i.e., numbers can be involved which correspond to the distances. Mathematics techniques such as Monte Carlo are used in developing random walks.

range—1. All the values that a function or word may have. 2. The difference between the highest and lowest of these values.

range, balanced error — An error range in which the highest and lowest error values are opposite in sign and equal in magnitude.

range check—See check, range.

range, dynamic — The dynamic range of a transmission system is the difference in decibels between the noise level of the system and its overload level.

range, error—1. The range of all possible values of the error of a particular quantity. 2. The difference between the highest and the lowest of these values. 3. The binary program with its associated subroutines will not fit into the available core memory. The names of any missing subroutines are listed following this message.

range limit or limit priority — The upper bound to the priority list for dispatching or designing a priority rating to various tasks or subtasks, i.e., active, inactive, top priority, lowest priority, or batch processing.

range (orientation)—In printing telegraphy, range is that fraction of a perfect signal element through which the time of selection may be varied so as to occur earlier or later than the normal time of selection, without causing errors while signals are being received. The range of a printing telegraph receiving device is commonly measured in percent of a perfect signal element by adjusting the indictor.

range, out of—A value which does not lie within a specific range of a linear program is out of range, or simply a term used to refer to over capacity.

range, proportional—The band, range, or set of values of a specific condition which is being controlled and which will cause the controller to operate over its full linear range. A proportional range is most often expressed by engineers or design teams in terms of percentage of full scale of the associated instrument.

rank—To arrange in an ascending or descending series according to importance.

rapid access—Rapid access is often synonymous with random access and is contrasted with sequential access, i.e., dependency upon access of preceding data.

rapid access loop—See loop, high speed.

rapid-access memory—In computers having memories with different access times, the section that has much faster access than the remainder of the memory.

rapid access storage—Same as storage, high speed.

rapid memory — That section of the whole memory from which information may be obtained in the shortest possible time.

rate, action—A type of control action in which the rate of correction is made proportional to how fast the condition is going awry. This is also called derivative action.

rate, bit—The rate at which binary digits, or pulses representing them, pass a given point on a communications line or channel. (Clarified by baud and channel capacity.)

rate, clock—The time rate at which pulses are emitted from the clock. The clock rate determines the rate at which logical or arithmetic gating is performed with a synchronous computer.

rate, data signalling—See data signalling rate.

rate, effective data transfer—See data transfer rate, average.

rate, error—The total amount of information in error, due to the transmission media, divided by the total amount of information received.

rate, instantaneous data-transfer—See data-transfer rate.

rate, modulation—Reciprocal of the unit interval measured in seconds. (This rate is expressed in bauds.)

rate of error, keying—Ratio of numbers of alphabetic signals incorrectly transmitted to the number of alphabetic signals in the message.

rate, perforation—See perforation rate.

rate pulse — The time interval of periodic pulses which are integrated with the control of the computer or the entire system.

rate, pulse-repetition—The number of electric pulses per unit of time experienced by a point in a computer; usually the maximum, normal, or standard pulse rate.

rate, punching—The number of cards, characters, blocks, fields or words of information placed in the form of holes distributed on cards, or paper tape, per unit of time.

rate, read—See read, rate.

rate, reading — The number of characters, words, fields, blocks or cards sensed by a sensing device, per unit of time.

rate, reset—The number of corrections per unit of time made by the control system.

rate, residual-error—The ratio of the number of bits, unit elements, characters and blocks incorrectly received but undetected or uncorrected by the error-control equipment, to the total number of bits, unit elements, characters, blocks that are sent.

rate, sampling—The time developed during the sampling of physical quantities for measurement, i.e., to obtain data to feed into a computing system so that the results of the computations can be made available to complete a specific task or purpose. Some examples are on-line processing for controlling weather data, timesharing of equipment, future positions for missile guidance, etc.

rate, scan—A frequency at which data is compared or read to various predetermined sense of criteria, for the purpose of seeking certain data.

rate, signalling—The rate at which signals are transmitted.

rates, reading—*See* reading rates.

rate, storage data transfer—*See* data transfer rate, average.

rate, transmission — *Same as* data transfer rate.

rate, undetected-error—*Same as* rate, residual-error.

ratio, availability—The ratio of total service time to the total of fault time, regular maintenance time, supplementary time, and serviceable time.

ratio, break-make—The ratio of the break period to the make period.

ratio control—That specific limitation in the relation between two quantities as expressed in direct or percentage comparison.

ratio, file activity—*See* file activity ratio.

ratio, operating—The ratio of the number of hours of correct machine operation to the total hours of scheduled operation; e.g., on a 168-hour week scheduled operation, if 12 hours of preventive maintenance are required and 4.8 hours of unscheduled down time occurs, then the operating ratio is (168-16.8)/168, which is equivalent to a 90% operating ratio. (Synonymous with computer efficiency.)

ratio, processing—The end result in calculating the time equipment is being used properly, including lost time because of human error and the total available time.

ratio, read-around—The number of times a specific spot, digit, or location in electrostatic storage may be consulted before the spillover of electrons will cause a loss of data stored in the surrounding spots.

ratio, read time-working—*See* time scale, extended.

ratio, recall—*See* recall ratio.

ratio, reflectance—*See* reflectance ratio.

ratio, relevance—*See* relevance ratio.

ratio, serviceability—*See* serviceability ratio.

ratio, signal-to-noise — The ratio of the amount of signals conveying information to the amount of signals not conveying information.

ratio, variable time—*Same as* time scale, extended.

raw data—Data that has not been processed; it may or may not be in machine-sensible form.

read—1. The process of introducing data into a component or part of an automatic data-processing machine. 2. To copy, usually from one form of storage to another, particularly from external or secondary storage to internal storage. 3. To sense the meaning by arrangements of hardware. 4. To accept or copy information or data from input devices or a memory register, i.e., to read out; to position or deposit information into a storage or output medium, or a register, i.e., to read in. 5. To transcribe information from an input device to internal or auxiliary storage.

readable, machine—*See* data, machine readable.

read amplifier—A set of circuitry which increases the level of current received from the read head or various other sensing devices.

read-around number—The number of times a specific spot, digit, or location in electrostatic storage may be consulted before spill over of electrons will cause a loss of information stored in surrounding spots.

read-around ratio — In electrostatic storage tubes, the number of times that information can be recorded successively as an electrostatic charge on a single spot in the array before the charge on surrounding spots must be restored to prevent loss of this storage area. Also called read-round.

read, backward—A feature available on some magnetic-tape systems whereby the magnetic-tape units can transfer data to a computer storage while moving in a reverse direction. Normally used, if available, during the external sort phase to reduce rewind time.

read, destructive—The sensing of data using a process which inherently destroys (erases) the record of the data which has been read. In some core storage, reading is destructive, but such data is usually regenerated after each readout. In tapes, drums, disks, etc., reading is usually accomplished without destruction.

reader—Any device, which has the capability of sensing, detecting, or converting data, i.e., transferring to another form or medium.

reader, badge—A device for the automatic collection of data. The badge reader is usually activated by the insertion of a specially shaped badge or card.

reader, card—1. This peripheral unit converts holes punched in cards into electrical impulses, and transmits the data to the memory of the computer for processing. 2. A mechanism that permits the sensing of information punched on cards, by means of wire brushes or metal feelers. 3. An input device consisting of a mechanical punch card reader and related electronic circuitry that transcribes data from punch cards to working storage or magnetic tape. (Synonymous with card-reader unit.)

reader, character—A specialized device that can convert data (represented in one of the type fonts or scripts readable by human beings) directly into machine language. Such a reader may operate optically; or, if the characters are printed in magnetic ink, the device may operate magnetically or optically.

reader, document—An input device which can read documents as a human would, so that data can be directly and easily put into the computer for procesisng. Although document readers cannot read human script as yet, they can read a large variety of hand-printed and typed documents; for example, bank checks with the account numbers in magnetic ink and specially formed numbers made by the raised letters on credit cards.

reader, film—A unit of peripheral equipment which projects film to permit reading by clients or customers of the data stored on the film, such as microfilm or microfiche, or a device which converts patterns of opaque and transparent spots on a photofilm to electrical pulses which correspond to the patterns.

reader, high-speed (HSR)—A reading device capable of being connected to a computer so as to operate on-line without seriously holding up the computer. A card reader reading more than 1000 cards per minute would be called a high-speed reader. A reader that reads punched paper tape at a rate greater than 500 characters per second could also be called a high-speed reader.

reader light—*See* light, reader.

reader, magnetic-tape—A device capable of restoring information recorded on a magnetic tape to a train or sequence of electrical pulses, usually for the purpose of transferring the information to some other storage medium.

reader, marked-page—Optical marked-page readers can be attached to a system for direct reading of marks made by an ordinary lead pencil in specified positions (like the marks made for an electronic test scoring) on 8½ x 11-inch sheets of paper. The sheeets can be read at a maximum rate of 2000 per hour, or one each 1.8 seconds. The reader is normally attached to the multiplexor channel and operation is in the multiplex mode. Applications for the reader are in payroll, order entry, accounts payable, inventory control, sales analysis, general ledger work, and many other phases of business, government, and institution (some units).

reader, optical—1. This system is based on the principle that the special shape of each character printed on theh input media is capable of being identified by a reading device. For example, the audit-journal from a cash register, if printed in a distinctive optical font, could be used as the input media to a computer. As the optical reader reads each character from the input media, it translates the data into electrical impulses that in turn are transmitted to the computer for processing. 2. Reads printed and typewritten material directly, without converting it into punch-paper, punch cards, or other intermediate formats. It recognizes all letters of the alphabet, standard punctuation, zero through nine, and special symbols used in programmed functions. It handles documents, and continuous fan fold sheets.

reader, optical bar-code—This device is available with the data station to read code information from documents such as premium changes, bills, invoices, and coupons at the rate of hundreds of characters per second. The data station features a high-speed printer, and thus can be used for on-line operations. Card and paper-tape equip-

ment also can be connected to the data station.

reader, optical document—*See* reader, document.

reader, page—An optical character reader which can process cut-form documents of differing sizes and which might be able to read information in hand-written form.

reader, paper-tape—A device capable of restoring the information punched on a paper tape to a train or sequence of electrical pulses, usually for the purpose of transferring the information to some other storage medium.

reader, photoelectric—A unit of peripheral equipment which has the capability of converting data in the form of patterns of holes in storage media as tapes or cards, into electric pulse patterns by means of photosensitive diodes and transistors, i.e., a reader used for rapid input to a computer and one which usually can also drive a printer, plotter, etc.

reader/punch, card—*See* card reader/punch.

readers, optical-character (magnetic)—Magnetic character readers can be attached directly to channels for the fast and direct reading into the system of the magnetically inscribed information on checks and other banking transactions. Readers differ mainly in document-reading rates; some read up to 950 documents per minute, others as many as 1,600 documents per minute. As the documents are read, they may be sorted into many classifications. All magnetic inscriptions can be checked for validity. The documents read may be of intermixed size and thickness, as typically encountered in check-handling operations. The standard minimum length is 6 inches; shorter documents may be read at appreciably higher rates, but these are not sorted unless a special feature for that purpose is installed. Many other special features are available.

reader-sorter—A unit of punch card equipment which senses and transmits input while sorting documents.

read-gather, write-scatter—*See* gather-write/scatter-read.

read head—A head that is used for reading data or a medium, such as tape, disks, drums, cards, or an optical sensor.

read-in—To sense information contained in some source and transmit this information to an internal storage.

readiness review—An on-site examination of the adequacy of preparations for the effective utilization of a new computer installation, and to indicate any necessary corrective actions.

reading access time—The elapsed time before data may be read or used in the computer during the equipment read cycle.

reading, destructive—A reading process that destroys the source data.

reading, mark—A form of mark detection using a photoelectric device to locate and verify information as coded or marked in special boxes or windows on preprepared forms. The unit, a scanner, reads by detecting the reflected light from the document.

reading, nondestructive — A reading process that does not destroy the data in the source.

reading, parallel—When a data card is read row-by-row.

reading, rate of — Number of characters, words, fields, blocks or cards sensed by an input sensing device per unit of time.

reading rates—The designation of the volume unit of reading punched cards, characters, words, and fields or blocks of data which are sensed by a sensing device. This rate is usually expressed as a unit of time.

reading station—1. The keypunch area where a data card is aligned to be read by a sensing mechanism. 2. A specific location in the reading device in which data is obtained from media, such as punched cards or magnetic tape.

read-in program—*See* program, read-in.

read-in, read-out—An optical feature that may be added to certain off-line office machinery permitting on-line operation.

read/jump protection—*See* protection, read/jump.

read, manual—An operation in which the computer does the sensing of the contents or settings of manually set switches or registers.

read, nondestructive—A reading of the information in a register without changing that information.

read-only memory—*Same as* read-only storage.

read-only storage — A storage device that stores data not alterable by computer instructions, e.g., magnetic-core storage with a lockout feature, or punched paper tape. (Synonymous with nonerasable storage and permanent storage.)

read operation, scatter—A specific process of obtaining groups of data elements and transferring the elements into different locations from the computer core memory simultaneously.

read-out—1. The act of removing and recording information from a computer or an auxiliary storage. 2. The information that is removed from computer storage and recorded in a form that the operator can interpret directly. 3. To sense information contained in the internal storage of computer and transmit this information to an external storage unit.

readout, destructive—The act of retrieving information from memory by using a process which erases the contents of the cells. With a nondestructive readout, the contents are not erased.

read-out device—A device that records the computer output either as a curve or as a group of printed numbers or letters.

read-process-write—The process of reading in one block of data, while simultaneously processing the preceding block and writing out the results of the previously processed block and writing out the results of the previously processed block. Some special processors can perform concurrently on any two or three of these operations, others are limited to read/write.

read, pulse—*See* pulse, read.

read-punch overlap—The read-punch adds to the outstanding versatility of the computer, the ability to read two related card files simultaneously and punch into one of the files. Reports requiring separate collating, gang punching, segregating, calculating, and printing operations can be performed in one pass through the computer equipped with a read-punch. In addition to the time saved by eliminating these auxiliary operations, computer throughput rates are increased by the two-file operation because the read-punch functions overlap the processor functions.

read-punch unit—An input/output unit of a computing system that punches computer results into cards, reads input information into the system, and segregates output cards. The read-punch unit generally consists of a card feed, a read station, a punch station, another read station, and two output card stackers.

read rate—The particular rate which measures the number of units of data that are sensed by a device in a unit of time, usually expressed as bits, words, or pages per second or minute.

read release—A feature of some equipment which permits more computer processing time by releasing the read mechanism.

read reverse—The unit can read tape under program control in either direction.

read-scatter—The ability of a computer to distribute or scatter data into several memory areas as it is being entered into the system on magnetic tape.

read time—1. The time it takes a computer to locate data or an instruction word in its storage section and transfer it to its arithmetic unit where the required computations are performed. 2. The time it takes to transfer information that has been operated on by the arithmetic unit to a location in storage. (Synonymous with read time, and related to write time and word time.)

read while writing—The reading of a record or group of records into storage from a tape at the same time another record or group of records is written from storage onto tape.

read/write channels—The data path between the main memory and a peripheral device that is completed by a programmer-assigned read/write channel. This channel is not a fixed connection to any one unit but is rather a floating link that can be used by any device. As opposed to the conventional method of complex and costly high-speed and low-speed transmission lines, the read/

write channel can be assigned to any device regardless of speed or mode of data transfer.

read/write check—*See* check, read/write.

read/write check indicator—A device incorporated in certain computers to indicate upon interrogation whether or not an error was made in reading or writing. The machine can be made to stop, retry the operation, or follow a special subroutine depending upon the result of the interrogation.

read/write counters—Data is transferred between the main memory and peripheral devices via read/write channels. Associated with each channel are two read/write counters. These counters store the starting and current addresses of the data being transferred by the read/write channel.

read/write head — A small electromagnetic unit used for reading, recording, or erasing polarized spots that represent information on a magnetic tape, disk, or drum.

read/write indicator check — *See* indicator, read/write check.

read/write scatter—An operation performed under program control, that reads a block of data from tape and breaks it up into processable elements. After processing, data is recombined and written on the tape as a block.

ready light—An indicator light on the display panel which, when on, indicates the equipment is ready for operation.

ready mode, time sharing—*See* time sharing, ready mode.

ready-read card—*See* card, ready-read.

real constants—A real constant is written with a decimal point, using the decimal digits 0, 1, . . ., 9. A preceding + or − sign is optional. An unsigned real constant is assumed to be positive. An integer exponent preceded by an E may follow a real constant. The exponent may have a preceding + or − sign. An unsigned exponent is assumed to be positive.

real number—An element of a set of all positive and negative numbers, including all types: integers, zeros, mixed, rational, irrational, etc., but not imaginary or complex.

real time—*See* time, real.

real-time address—*Same as* address, immediate.

real-time addressing — *Same as* addressing, immediate.

real-time application — Real-time processing is accomplished on a time-current basis. It handles the flow of data from widespread manufacturing inventories and production lines such as the shifting pattern of transportation schedules, or the scattered operations of the utility industry. For example, in airlines reservation control, the real-time system provides an instantaneous picture of seat availability, cancellations, sales, and flight data for the whole airline. The airline agent simply presses buttons.

real-time applications, externally specified index (ESI)—The computer sytem is ideally

suited for real-time and communications based applications because of its extremely fast interrupt response time, autonomous I/O transfer logic and rapid-access mass storage drums. A feature called ESI (externally specified index) enables the computer system to become a central message-switching center for a variety of remote devices through a standard communication subsystem. The ESI feature provides for automatic routing of messages to and from main store without disturbing the program sequence of the central processor. When a full or empty buffer is detected, an ESI interrupt is generated for immediate program response.

All system operations are coordinated and controlled by a versatile executive system having full real-time and multiprogramming capabilities, but possessing the classic simplicity of a monitor system.

real-time, batch processing—The requirements for real-time action are known frequently to occur in peaks and valleys. In many businesses these requirements tend to increase from early morning through the middle of the day and to taper off from then on. In other businesses the occurrence of these demands may be sporadic. The real-time system is so designed that it will automatically, as its facilities are freed from the dynamic demands of real-time processing, load them up with the ordinary day to day backlog of less urgent work of the familiar batch-processing type—typically, the sequential processing of sequentially ordered files such as accounts receivable, payable, or payrolls.

real-time buffer (single character)—Each buffer permits teletype communication with many remote locations. Since the buffer operates on one character at a time, many teletypes may be communicating with the processor simultaneously at full speed in either direction through the same buffer.

real-time central-processor capability—The real-time system provides the user with the following typical capabilities: ninety-four basic instructions that may be modified to provide unprecedented programming versatility; magnetic core storage capacity of 4,096 to 65,536 computer words of 18 bits each, plus a parity bit; 4 millionths of a second average instruction execution time; the ability to accommodate any standard communication code or speed; the ability to execute programs concurrently to make effective use of random-access drum storage as well as magnetic tapes. Under automatic executive program control, the real-time system performs all of its functions including control of or response to central or remote input/output devices in a time scale proportional to the need for action; precision electronic clocks for use in compiling statistics for analysis and improvement of computer utilization, for initiation of action at specific times during the day, and for checking the proper execution of operations. In addition to all of this, the central processor may act as a satellite computer to a large scale system (some systems).

real-time channel—The various units of equipment that provide interface between the end of communication and the computer memory. Such a channel performs the identical basic function as a multiplexor but has more limited storage capability and does not have stored-program capacity.

real-time clock—A real-time clock develops readable digits or periodic signals for the computer to allow computation of elapsed time between events, and to initiate the performance of time-initiated processing.

real-time clock-count word—The contents of this 36 bit address are decremented by 1 approximately every millisecond. Decrementation is performed by the index adder circuitry. When the clock count word has been reduced to zero, an internal interrupt is generated; the program then executes the instruction programmed at the real-time clock-interrupt address (some systems).

real-time clock logs—This built-in clock is used for a wide variety of programming-time purposes. It can be used to log the receipt times of a periodic real-time input data. Each input message and its receipt time may be recorded together. This clock is also used in connection with the preparation of statistical and analytical reports dealing with the frequency of certain transactions.

real-time clock, time-sharing—See time-sharing, real-time clock.

real-time, concurrency—Real-time is a mode of operation in which data, necessary to the control and/or execution of a transaction, can be processed in time for the transaction to be affected by the results of the processing. Real-time processing is most usually identified with great speed, but speed is relative. The essence of real-time is concurrency—simultaneity. Real-time is a refinement in the integration of data-processing with communications. Real-time eliminates slow procedures for gathering information, dated reporting techniques and lax communications; insures that facts within the system are as timely as a prevailing situation, as current as the decisions that they must support. Real-time provides answers when answers are needed, delivers data instantly whenever the need for that data arises. Incoming information is edited, updated, and made available on demand at every level of responsibility. Imminent departures from established standards are automatically detected, and management notified in time for action.

real-time concurrency operations — The great point is that the real-time system is at no moment necessarily committed to real-time operations or to batch processing operations exclusively. Both may proceed con-currently and several kinds of each may proceed concurrently under the control of an internally stored executive program. But the real time operations always have priority and the system will assign its facilities as these priorities require, relinquishing them to other activities, such as engineering calculations or normal business processing tasks, as soon as they no longer need to keep pace with real time events. In this way maximum use may be made of the components of any desired configuration of the real-time system; and the advantages of its enormous storage capacity, speed, flexibility, and communications capabilities may be obtained at a low cost per unit of work accomplished. To sum up, it should be said that experience indicates that the real-time system will quite probably outperform, by a wide margin, any other system of its kind in a wide range of applications.

real-time control, input/output—All input/output data transfers are automatically controlled by signals emanating from the central processor or from the peripheral subsystems themselves. Any general purpose input/output channel can accommodate a real-time system peripheral device. All I/O channels are buffered. Each input/output device has associated with it a control unit that, once activated by the central processor, carries out the entire operation of the instruction given it while the central processor proceeds with other tasks.

real-time control processor design—A typical design may have the following characteristics: sixty two basic instructions which may be modified to provide new programming versatility; magnetic core storage capacity of 16,000 to 32,000 computer words of 30 bits each; 10 millionths of a second average instruction execution time; the ability to accommodate any standard communication code or speed; the ability to carry out several programs concurrently, to make most effective use of random access drum storage as well as magnetic tapes; plus the ability under automatic executive program control to perform all of its functions including control of or response to central or remote input/output devices in a time scale proportional to the need for action; and precision electronic clocks for use in compiling statistics for analysis and improvement of computer utilization, for initiation of action at specific times, during the day, and for checking the proper execution of operations. In addition to all of this, the central processor may be connected to a satellite computer (some systems) .

real-time control system—A computer system that processes the data and makes the necessary decisions in real time. For example, the automatic control of manufacturing processes by a computer in an oil refinery.

real-time data reduction—See data reduction, real-time.

real-time, executive—The executive system is designed to interface with programs that have real-time requirements. The standard communication subsystem, together with the efficient scheduling and the interrupt processing features of the executive system, provides an environment satisfactory for any real time program.

real-time, externally specified index (ESI)—The executive system provides full real-time capability, real-time programs being given access to any and all ESI (externally specified index) equipped input/output channels on the highest priority basis. Interrupts from ESI-equipped channels are handled in a manner which provides expeditious transfer of operation control to the real-time programs insuring against the loss of data and providing the required response time. The executive system controls the dynamic acquisition and release of computer system facilities, providing the real-time programs (as well as other programs) with the ability to acquire or release computer facilities to meet the demands of the current operational environment (some systems).

real-time information system—A real-time information system is a system that can provide information about the process it is describing fast enough for the process to be continuously controlled by an operator using this information (for example, a scientist controling the path of a space rocket).

real-time inputs—*See* inputs, real-time.

real-time mode—*Same as* real-time concurrency.

real-time monitor—The executive system is an operating and programming system designed to monitor the construction and execution of programs, to optimize the utilization of available hardware, and to minimize programmer effort and operator intervention. The executive system, as a monitor, provides for concurrent processing and real-time operation in a classical monitor environment. The executive system is of modular construction, tailored to each user's equipment configuration and applications requirements. Extensions to the system for peripheral devices and application programs may be added, altered, or deleted as required.

real-time multicomputing—Real-time command and control situations requiring maximum reliability utilize two or more computers in multicomputer systems. Two or more essentially independent computing systems communicate directly, with access to each other's memory. Capable of tremendous computing power, such systems have the added advantage of reserve equipment. Typical real-time applications demanding this degree of reliability include manned space-vehicle launching and airport traffic control. The concept of individual modules for processor, memory, and controller provides multiprocessor and

muliticomputer systems with multiple functions without duplication of hardware.

real-time, on-line operation (OLRT) — The processing of data in synchronism with a physical process, in such a fashion that the results of the data-processing are useful to the physical operation.

real-time operation—1. A data-processing system synchronized with a physical process so that the results of the data processing are useful to the physical operation. 2. Concurrent operations for data processing (computing) and physical processing in such a way that the results of the computing operations are available whenever needed by the physical processing operations, and vice versa. 3. Paralleling data processing with a physical process so that the results of the data processing are immediately useful to the physical operation. 4. Operations performed in a computer simultaneously with a physical process so that the answers obtained are useful in controlling the process.

real-time processing—1. The processing of information or data in a sufficiently rapid manner so that the results of the processing are available in time to influence the process being monitored or controlled. 2. A real-time system is a combined data processing and communications system that involves the direct communication of transaction data between remote locations and a central computer, via communication lines, and allows the data to be processed while the business transaction is actually taking place. A real-time system may be thought of as a communications-oriented data-processing system that is capable of performing batch-processing functions while concurrently processing inquiries or messages, and generating responses in a time interval directly related to the requirements of the batch process.

real-time processing (bank)—If the volume of savings account and mortgage-loan activity warrants, these transactions may be handled in real-time by the on-line teller system. Teller consoles at each window at each office may be linked to the computer and the on-line central file.

real-time processing communication—A real-time system is a combined data processor and communicator of transaction data between remote locations and a certain computer, via communication lines, and allows the data to be processed while the business transaction is actually taking place. A real-time system may be thought of as a communications-oriented data-processing system which is capable of performing batch-processing functions while concurrently processing inquiries or messages, and generating responses in a time interval directly related to the operational requirements of the system.

real-time processing, inventory—The remotely located sales offices are supplied with an inquiry/answer device capable of communicating directly with the computer itself. To place an order, the required information is entered into the system by the input device. Since the device is connected directly to the computer, complete information, including the availability and status of the item ordered, is confirmed in seconds. If the items are available, the invoice is printed automatically, along with associated shipping information, at the sales office, indicating to the salesman that the order has been filled as requested. If any particular item on the order depleted the inventory to the recorder point, the computer automatically sends a message to the recorder source, connected directly to the computer, requesting an updating in inventory. All these operations are accomplished in a matter of seconds.

real-time relative addressing—Relative addressing is a feature of great significance in multiprogramming, time-sharing, and real-time operations, for it allows storage assignments to be changed dynamically to provide contiguous storage for operation of another program, and permits programs to dynamically request additional main storage according to processing needs. An additional advantage is that system programs stored on mass storage may be brought in for operation in any available area without complicated relocation algorithms. Relative addressing is provided for through basing registers contained within the processor. A separate register controls the basing of the program instruction and the data bank, and a third register controls the selections of the appropriate basing register.

real-time, remote inquiry—On-line inquiry stations permit users to interrogate the computer files and receive immediate answers to their inquiries. In industry, the stations can be located at dozens of remote locations such as office, factory, warehouse, and remote branch locations. Such a system permits all levels of industrial management to obtain immediate answers to questions about inventories, work-in-process, sales, etc.

real-time satellite computer—A satellite computer in the real-time system relieves the larger computer system of time consuming input and output functions as well as performing preprocessing and postprocessing functions such as validity editing and formatting for print.

real-time simulation—A particular operation of a simulator or simulation program, such that the instants of occurrence of many basic events in the simulator occur at the same times as they would in the system being simulated.

real-time system—The processing of information or data in a sufficiently rapid manner so that the results of the processing are available in time to influence the process being monitored or controlled.

real-time system characteristics—The system itself can communicate directly with central site or remote locations—points of sale or other customer contract, production or transportation facilities, warehouses, domestic or foreign branches or affiliates. The system can store large masses of information and almost instantly retrieve and deliver in useful form any item or group of items—data required for customer service, for the most advantageous stocking and distribution of materials or products, or for use by central or local management. Under automatic executive-program control the system can concurrently execute several programs—the saving in processing time and, therefore, in cost, is very large. The system operates in real time—that is, it responds to the need for action in a period of time proportional to the urgency of the need—first things are done first. The system can be depended on to provide the information necessary to base this minute's or this hour's decisions on information up to date as of the minute or the hour—the value of information diminishes rapidly with the passage of time—this system, because the data it provides reflects the present facts, makes it possible to avoid many difficulties and to seize many opportunities which would otherwise be lost.

real-time system, executive—The real-time executive system controls, sequences, and provides for the efficient allocation of facilities for operating the real-time system. Normally, the real-time executive system controls a real-time program operating concurrently with one or more batch programs. The real-time executive system eliminates the need for the programmer to plan concurrently. It maintains and restores the operational environment of each program so that as far as the programmer is concerned, his program operates as if it were the only one being run in the system. The real-time executive system also provides a number of basic subroutines that assist in matters of console control, rerun, the loading of segments or overlays, and input/output control for the various subsystems (some systems).

real-time working—The use of the computer as an element of a processing system in which the times of occurrence of data transmission are controlled by other portions of the system, or by physical events outside the system, and cannot be modified for convenience in computer programming. Such an operation either proceeds at the same speed as the events being simulated or at a sufficient speed to analyze or control external events happening concurrently.

real-time working ratio—*See* time scale, extended.

real variables (FORTRAN)—A real variable consists of a series of not more than six alphanumeric characters (except special characters) of which the first is alphabetic but can not be one of the integer indicators, i.e., I, J, K, L, M, or N.

reasonableness tests—These tests provide a means of detecting a gross error in calculation or, while posting to an account, a balance that exceeds a predetermined limit. Typical examples include payroll calculations and credit-limit checks in accounts receivable. In some cases both an upper and a lower limit are established; each result is then machine-compared against both limits to make certain that it falls between the two.

recall ratio—In information retrieval systems, the ratio of the number of pertinent documents retrieved by a single query to the total number of pertinent documents in the total collection, as determined by the query criteria.

receive only—The description of a teletype device which has only printer capabilities. Such a machine can receive information from the computer but cannot send it.

receive-only service—Service in which the data-communication channel is capable of receiving signals, but is not equipped to transmit signals.

receiver—Also called the card stacker, it is that part of the machine in which punched cards are deposited after passing through the machine.

receiver signal—Equipment controlled by signalling currents transmitted over the line and used generally to send out new signals.

receive/send keyboard set (KSR) — A combination transmitter and receiver with transmission capability from keyboard only.

receiving margin—Sometimes referred to as range or operating range. The usable range over which the range finder may be adjusted. The normal range for a properly adjusted machine is approximately 75 points on a 120 point scale.

reciprocal — The mathematical expression establishing the relation of a number which exists when that number is divided into a single unit or one, i.e., the process of multiplying by the reciprocal of the number is equivalent to dividing by that number.

recirculating loop—In drum computers, a small section of memory that has much faster access than the remainder of memory.

reckoner, Lincoln — An on-line, time-sharing executive program developed by Lincoln Laboratories.

recognition, character—The technology of using a machine to sense and encode into a machine language characters that are written or printed to be read by human beings.

recognition, magnetic ink—See MICR.

recognition, pattern—The recognition of shapes or other patterns by a machine system. Patterns may be such as physical shapes or speech patterns.

recognizable machine — See data, machine readable.

recognizer, syntax—A subroutine which recognizes the phase class in an artificial language, normally expressed in backus normal form (BNF), formal language theory.

recomplementation—An internal procedure that performs nines or tens complementation, as required, on the result of an arithmetic operation.

record—1. A set of one or more consecutive fields on a related subject, as an employee's payroll record. Although a record need not be a block in length, such an arrangement is often useful. 2. A listing of information, usually in printed or printable form; one output of a compile consisting of a list of the operations and their positions in the final specific routine and containing information describing the segmentation and storage allocation of the routine. 3. To make a transcription of data by a systematic alteration of the condition, property, or configuration of a physical medium, e.g., placing information on magnetic tapes or a drum by means of magnetized spots. 4. A group of related facts or fields of information treated as a unit, thus a listing of information usually in printed or printable form. 5. To put data into a storage device. 6. To group related facts or fields of information treated as a unit.

record, addition—A record that results in the creation of a new record in the updated master file.

record block—A specific storage area of fixed size which is usually in a main memory or file storage; it is organized into such standard blocks to allow more flexibility in storage allocation and control. (Synonymous with physical record.)

record, chained — Physical records, located randomly in main or auxiliary memory modules, that are linked or chained by means of a control field in each record which contains the address of the next record in the series or chains. Long waiting lists or files can be connected or chained in this way.

record check time—The elapsed time which is required to verify a record transfer on tape. The volume of time or duration that is based on tape speed or distance between the rewrite heads.

record control schedule — A type of master record or schedule designating all activities involved regarding disposition of business records, i.e., transfers, retention, etc.

record, data—A record containing data to be processed by a program.

record, deletion—A new record added to a file, or removing and replacing an existing record in a file as contrasted with record, addition.

record description—In COBOL, a record is described in terms of the data elements it contains. For each element in a record, a character picture is used to specify its level, name, and format.

record, detail—The specific listing of data which is a unit part of a major classification of larger segments or a total classification of data.

record, duplicated—Images or copies of file records that are located in the file modules, or frames that are separate from the primary copy. Such duplicate records ensure against loss of urgent or critical files or data.

record equipment, unit — This is the basic hardware which uses punched cards as the media for individual records. Standard punched card equipment of this type: sorters, tabulators, collators, etc. Also known as electronic accounting machine equipment or EAM or TAB equipment.

recorder, digital — A peripheral device that records data as discrete, numerically defined points.

recorder, film—A unit of equipment which has the capability of making records or placing data on film by using light, dark, opaque, or transparent spots on photographic roll film or some of the latest digital type of photography of shadow or depths of gray. Such data may be digital output from a computer or from a sensor. Some types use a light beam passing through the film to a photocell to read data.

record file, fixed length — See record, fixed length.

record file, variable-length—A file containing a set of records that vary in length.

record, fixed-length—A record in which the number of characters is fixed. The restriction may be deliberate to simplify and speed processing, or it may be caused by the limitations of the equipment used.

record gap—1. The space between records on a tape, usually produced by tape acceleration or deceleration during the writing stage of processing. 2. A gap used to indicate the end of a record.

record group—Several records, which when placed together associate or identify with a single key which is located in one of the records. Grouping is efficient in time and space-saving on magnetic tapes.

record head—A head used to transfer data to a storage device, such as a drum, disk, tape, or magnetic card.

record header—A specific record containing the description of information contained in a classification or group of records, which follow this initial document. Also known as header table.

record heading—A record which contains an identification or description of the output report to which following records are related and which is concerned with the body of the report.

record, home—Usually the first record in a chain of records, i.e., the home record is used with the chaining method of file development or organization.

recording—The operation by which an input device facilitates the presentation of source data to be processed.

recording density—The number of bits per a given unit length of a linear track in a recording medium.

recording density, tape — See tape recording density.

recording double-pulse — A specific method for magnetic recording of bits, in which each storage cell comprises two regions, magnetized in opposite senses with unmagnetized regions on each side.

recording-frequency doubling—Magnetic recording of bits by a specific method in which each storage cell comprises two magnetized regions with unmagnetized regions on each side. The magnetized regions are magnetized in opposite senses to represent zero and in the same sense to represent one. The sense of the magnetization is changed in passing from one cell to the next.

recording head—A head used to transfer data to a storage device, such as a drum, disk, tape, or magnetic card.

recording, magnetic—That special method of recording data by impressing a pattern of magnetization on a thin layer of magnetic material, usually on a non-magnetic base, such as a disk, drum, tape, etc.

recording mode—In the COBOL system, the representation in external media of data associated with a data-processing system.

recording phase, redundant—See redundant phase recording.

recordings, dual — The dual recording of critical data makes it possible to machine-compare the two for verification. It is more commonly used in mark-sense recording operations and those card-punch operations in which it is necessary to verify only one or two fields.

recording, source—The recording of data in machine-readable documents, such as punched cards, punched paper tape, magnetic tapes, etc. Once in this form, the data may be transmitted, processed, or reused without manual processing.

record, label—A record used to identify the contents of a file or reel of magnetic tape.

record layout—A record must be organized or arranged in sequence as to occurrence of items and the size, distribution, etc., i.e., as the two-dimensional format of a printed page.

record length—1. In a computer, the number of characters necessary to contain all the information in a record. 2. An arbitrarily chosen number of characters that comprise the records in a given program. To secure this record length, it is sometimes necessary to pad the records. (Clarified by padding.)

record length or word—The number of characters, digits or words which comprise a data set of fixed or variable size.

record, logical—A record that contains pertinent information about a common subject. The most basic subdivision of a record is called a field.

record mark—A special character used in some computers either to limit the number of characters in a data transfer, or to separate blocked or grouped records in tape.

record, master — The basic updated record used in the next file-processing run. A master record is most often a magnetic tape item. Visual copies for possible analysis and alteration are usually developed.

record name—In COBOL, the name given to a record within a file and assigned the level number 01. Data names for elements within a record have lower-level numbers, 02, 03, etc.

record, physical—Punched cards are each a physical record, and magnetic tapes and disks have physical records as bounded by interrecord gaps.

record ready—A signal from a file-access mechanism to the computer that a record whose address was previously provided by a seek command has now been located and may be read into memory.

record, reference—An output of a compiler that lists the operations and their positions in the final specific routine, and contains information describing the segmentation and storage allocation of the routine.

records—Any unit of information that is to be transferred between the main memory and a peripheral device is defined as a record. Records can be of any length.

record, semifixed length—A particular fixed-length record which has a length subject to change at the choice of the system analyst or programmer, although such lengths usually remain fixed for a given problem, run, specific operation, or routine.

records, grouped—A set of records sharing the same label, tag, or key.

records, grouping of—The combining of two or more records into one block of information on tape, to decrease the wasted time due to tape acceleration and deceleration and to conserve tape space. This is also called blocking of records.

records management—A specific program designed to provide economy and efficiency in the creation, organization, maintenance, use, and disposition of records. Thus, needless records will not be created or kept and only the valuable records will be preserved.

record sorting—The basic element of a file such that the sorting of file constitutes the reordering of file records; also referred to as item.

record-storage mark—A special character that appears only in the record-storage unit of the card reader to limit the length of the record read into processor storage.

record, strip—A recording method in which information is stored vertically with strips visible for information location.

records, variable-length (sorting)—Denumerable file elements for which the number of words, characters, bits, fields, etc., is not constant.

record system, fixed-length—See fixed-length record system.

record, trailer—A record that follows a group of records and contains pertinent data related to the group of records.

record, transaction — Specific information which modifies information in a file.

record, unit—1. A separate record that is similar in form and content to other records, e.g., a summary of a particular employee's earnings to date. 2. Sometimes refers to a piece of nontape auxiliary equipment, e.g., card reader, printer, or console typewriter.

record, variable length—A record which has a loose or unfixed number of constituent parts, i.e., blocks, words, etc., are subject to particular installation or chief programmer rules, constraints, conventions, or by the equipment design.

recovery fallback—The restoration of a system to full operation from a fallback mode of operation after the cause of the fallback has been removed.

recovery interrupt—See interrupt (recovery routines).

recovery program, automatic — The process in a system built on providing a high degree of reliability, where a diagnostic routine locates the trouble and the automatic recovery program shifts to duplexed or standby equipment, or to a fallback mode of operation.

recovery routine—Most commonly in tape operations a reading or writing error will occur. Usually the record is reread or rewritten several times before any appropriate action is taken. If the error does not disappear, the program is halted, but preferably a record should be made of the error and the program continued, as devised by scores of special recovery routines.

recursion—The continued repetition of the same operation or group of operations.

recursive—Pertaining to a process that is inherently repetitive. The result of each repetition is usually dependent upon the result of the previous repetition.

recursive function—A mathematical function which is defined in terms of itself. I.e., an operation which takes advantage of the recursive definition of the function, resulting in either repetition of the calculations using the same function, or using the same function with a slight modification.

recursive process — In data processing, a method of computing values of functions in which each stage of processing contains all subsequent stages, i.e., the first stage is not completed until all other stages have been completed.

recycling of programs — An organized arrangement for recycling programs through a computer when alternates have been made in one program that may change or have an effect on other programs.

redact—To edit or revise input data.

redaction—A new or revised edition of input data.

redefine—In COBOL, to reuse the same storage area for different data items during program execution by means of appropriate instructions in the data program.

red tape—1. Pertaining to administrative or overhead operations or functions that are necessary in order to maintain control of a situation; e.g., for a computer program, housekeeping involves the setting up of constants and variables to be used in a program. 2. A general term that reserves, restores, and clears the memory areas.

red-tape operation—1. A computer operation that does not directly contribute to the solution; i.e., arithmetical, logical, and transfer operations used in modifying the address section of other instructions, in the counting cycles, and in the rearrangement data. 2. Those internal operations that are necessary to process the data, but do not contribute to any final solution.

reduction, data—The transformation of raw data into a more useful form, e.g., smoothing to reduce extraneous noise.

reduction, data, real time—*See* data reduction, real time.

redundance, longitudinal — A condition in which the bits in each track or row of a record do not total an even (or odd) number. The term is usually used to refer to records on magnetic tape, and a system can have either odd or even longitudinal parity.

redundance, vertical—An error condition that exists when a character fails a parity check, i.e., has an even number of bits in an odd-parity system, or vice versa.

redundancy—1. In the transmission of information, redundancy is the fraction of the gross-information content of a message that can be eliminated without the loss of the essential information. Numerically, it is one minus the ratio of the net information content to the gross information content, expressed in percent. 2. An extra piece of information used to assist in determining the accuracy of moved digits or words in a computer. (Clarified by redundant check.)

redundancy check—A checking technique based on the presence of extra (redundant) information which is used only for checking purposes. Parity checking, check digits, control totals, and hash totals are all examples of redundancy checks.

redundant character—A character specifically added to a group of characters to insure conformity with certain rules that can be used to detect a computer malfunction.

redundant check—The use of extra bits in machine words for the purpose of detecting malfunctions and mistakes.

redundant checking — *See* checking, redundant.

redundant code—A code using more signal elements than necessary to represent the intrinsic-processing information.

redundant phase recording—Ensures transfer reliability, reduces problem of skew in bi-directional operation. Each tape track is redundantly paired with a second, non-adjacent track. Use of phase (rather than amplitude) recording reduces the drop-outs due to variations in amplitude.

reel—A spool of tape; generally refers to magnetic tape.

reel, feed—A specific reel from which tape is unwound during the processing.

reel number—A sequence number that identifies a particular reel in a file of reels.

reels, pocket-size—Handy to carry, easy to load. Each 3½-inch reel holds up to 3 million bits, the equivalent of 4000 feet of paper tape, assuming 6-bit words are used.

reel, take-up—A specific reel on which tape is wound or may be wound during processing.

re-entrant—That property of a program that enables it to be interrupted at any point by another user, and then resumed from the point of interruption. Re-entrant programs are often found in multiprogramming and time-sharing systems, where there is a requirement for a common store of so-called public routines that can be called by any user at any time. The process is controlled by a monitor that preserves the routine's environment (registers, working storage, control indicators, etc.) when it is interrupted and restores that environment when the routine is resumed for its initial use.

re-entrant routines, core memory — To ease the constraints of the limited size of core memory, a type of coding of routines has been developed which permits a routine to be concurrently used by many users. Memory is conserved by coding all frequently used general purpose or common routines in this manner. Then only a single copy of each must be kept in core memory, regardless of how many users require the routine. The coding techniques employed for re-entrant routines are twofold. First, the routine must make no modification of itself. All temporary storage must be in a block of memory supplied by the calling program. Second, the routine as it is executed will put up and clear busy signals, preventing the entry by another user of portions of the routine until sequencing through these portions by a previous user has been completed.

re-entry point—The point at which an instruction or a program is re-entered from a subroutine or main program is called the re-entry point.

reference—An indication of where to find specific information, e.g., by reference to a document, an author, an instruction, etc.

reference address—1. Addresses that are used in converting related addresses to machine-language addresses. 2. An address used as a reference for a group of related addresses.

reference address, indirect—*See* address, indirect reference.

reference axis—A line drawn across the plotting grid at the location of a selected value such as at the zero of an axis.

reference block, message—*See* block, message reference.

reference debugging aids — *See* debugging aids, reference.

reference, direct address—*See* address, direct reference.

reference, external—*See* external reference.

reference instruction — An instruction designed to allow reference to systematically arranged or stored data.

reference line, character-spacing—*See* character-spacing reference line.

reference programming, library—A distinct program to form an assemblage, or to retrieve from or input to a library, instead of one written for a particular job. It is a program which may be called simply by reference to an index of library program names.

reference record—An output of a computer that lists the operations and their positions in the final specific routine. The output also contains information describing the segmentation and storage allocation of the final routine.

reference table, program — That section of storage used as an index for operations, subroutines, and variables.

reference time—An instant near the beginning of a switching routine, chosen as an origin for time measurements. It is the instant when the drive pulse reaches a specific fraction of its instantaneous value. The drive pulse is also called magnetic cell response pulse, and integrated voltage pulse.

referencing, input/output—References to data on tape or disk are made symbolically. Instead of describing the address of a certain disk or tape, the programmer refers to such data with a functional name. This means the programmer need not keep in mind where data will be coming from.

reflectance—In OCR (optical character recognition) the diffuse reflectivity of ink-free areas of the substrate on which the printing exists.

reflectance, background—An optical character recognition term related to the reflectance of the background of a document surface within the area reserved for printing (clear band), as compared to a reference standard.

reflectance ink—*See* ink, reflectance.

reflectance ratio—The reciprocal of the ratio of the intensity of the light reflected from the image area of a picture to the intensity of light reflected from the background or light area.

reflectance, spectral—The determined reflectance related or caused by a specific wavelength of incident light from a specified surface.

reflected binary—*See* binary, reflected.

reflected-binary code—Any binary code in which sequential numbers are represented by binary expressions, each of which differs from the preceding expression in one place only. (Synonymous with reflected code and cyclic code.)

reflected code—Any binary code that changes by only one bit when going from one number to the number immediately following. (Synonymous with reflected-binary code and cyclic code.)

reflection, coefficient—The ratio of incident to reflected light intensity at a point on a surface.

reflective spot—An evident mark which indicates the beginning or end of a tape.

refresher rate, display—The manufacturer's recommended number of frames per second for regenerating the display.

regenerate—The restoring of information that is electrostatically stored in a cell, on the screen of a cathode-ray tube in order to counteract fading and other disturbances that are prevalent with this type of information.

regeneration—1. The process of returning a part of the output signal of an amplifier to its input circuit in such a manner that it reinforces the excitation and thereby increases the total amplification. 2. Periodic restoration of stored information. 3. The inclusion of logic in a system design to permit the generation of data (when required) from basic formulae as opposed to storage of large volumes of static data.

regeneration period—*See* period, regeneration.

regeneration pulse—*See* pulse, regeneration.

regenerative memory — A memory device whose contents gradually vanish if not periodically refreshed.

regenerative repeater—A repeater in which retransmitted signals are practically free from distortion.

regenerative storage—*See* storage, regenerative.

regenerative track—*Same as* loop, high speed.

REGENT—A problem-oriented programming system and report-program generator that is designed to reduce substantially the time and effort necessary to translate general-data processing and reporting requirements into detailed computer instructions. It demands little knowledge of computer coding or instructions other than the basic rules of writing in the simplest form of the PAL assembly language. Essentially, the REGENT report-program generator is a program which, on the basis of a series of statements provided to it, produces another program which will produce a report or other output of the desired kind. These statements are written on the standard PAL coding form and then keypunched into cards. (UNIVAC)

region—1. In relative coding, a group of location addresses that are all relative to the same specific reference address. 2. A group of machine addresses that refer to a base address.

regional address—An address of a machine instruction within a series of consecutive addresses; e.g., R18 and R19 are specific addresses in an "R" region of "N" consecutive addresses, where all addresses must be named.

register—1. A device for the temporary storage of one or more words to facilitate arithmetical, logical, or transferral operations. Examples are the accumulator, address, index, instruction, and M-Q registers. 2. The hardware for storing one or more computer words. Registers are usually zero-access storage devices. 3. A term to designate a specific computer unit for storing a group of bits or characters.

register-A—*Same as* register, arithmetic.

register, accumulator—That part of the arithmetic unit in which the results of an operation remain; into which numbers are brought from storage, and from which numbers may be taken for storage.

register, address—A register that stores an address.

register, addressable—That specific temporary storage unit or device as represented by particular storage location numbers.

register address field—The portion of an instruction word that contains a register address.

register address, general — A value in the range 0 through 15 that designates a register in the current register block, whether by means of the R field of the instruction word or by means of an effective virtual address (some computers).

register, arithmetic—That particular register in the logic unit which holds the operands required for a specific operation. i.e., it can hold the addend for addition, the multiplier for multiplication, or particular words to be compared or shifted, etc.

register, B—*Same as* index register.

register, base—*Same as* index register.

register, block—An address register of available blocks of storage that are chained together for use by the line control computer, for the allocation of incoming information.

register, boundary—A special register used in a multiprogrammed system to designate the upper and lower addresses of each user's program block in the core memory.

register, buffer output — The buffering or transfer device which receives data from internal storage and transfers it to an output media such as magnetic tape.

register capacity—The upper and lower limits of the numbers that may be processed in a register.

register, check—A register used to store information temporarily where it may be checked with the result of a succeeding transfer of this information.

register, circulating—1. A shift register in which the stored information is moved right or left, and the information from one end is reinserted at the other end. In the case of one-character right shift, the rightmost character reappears as the new leftmost character and every other character is shifted one position to the right. 2. A register in which the process, as in the preceding statement, is continuously occurring. This can be used as a delaying mechanism.

register, console display—There are binary displays on many computer operator's consoles. One display bit indicates the memory word parity; other display bits may indicate: (1) the next instruction, (2) the contents of any memory location, (3) the contents of the accumulator, (4) the contents of index registers, (5) the status of the traps. When the computer halts, the display register will indicate the next instruction word, while a register will contain the address of the halt instruction that stopped the computer. To display anything else, the appropriate push-button display switch must be pressed. When the DISPLAY M (memory button) is pressed, the contents of the memory location specified by a register will be displayed. When either the DISPLAY or other buttons are pressed; the contents of other registers or the condition of the traps are displayed. The display register is also used as an entry register. Buttons are provided which may clear all or various parts of the display register. The contents of the display register may be entered in any memory location. Pushing any of the ENTRY buttons will accomplish entry of the display register contents into the appropriate memory location or register.

register, control—1. A register which holds the identification of the instruction word to be executed next in time sequence, following the current operation. The register is often a counter that is incremented to the address of the next sequential-storage location, unless a transfer or other special instruction is specified by the program. (Synonymous with program counter, and contrasted with program register.) 2. The accumulator, register, or storage unit that stores the current instruction governing a computer operation; an instruction register.

register, current-instruction—The control-section register that contains the instruction currently being executed after it is brought to the control section from memory. Also called instruction register.

register, delay line—A unique register incorporating a delay line plus a means for a signal regeneration, and a feedback channel. Thus, the storage of data in serial representation is achieved through continual circulation.

register, designation—A register into which data is being placed.

register display, communication — The contents of the x-y position registers and the display-address counter can be read into the accumulator via IOT (input/output transfer) instructions. Likewise, the display used for starting the display or setting up certain control conditions. All of the features tend to make programming for a given application easier. The programmer not only has a powerful computer to generate the display, to control interfaces to external-data sources, or to handle real-time requests, but he also has a powerful display that can operate with a high degree of independence from the computer.

register, double-word—Two registers used to holds a 64-bit double-word (some computers).

register, E—A register treated as an extension of the accumulator register and/or the quotient register. This register is used to perform arithmetic requiring double-words.

register, extension—See register, E.

register, flip flop—Chain-like connections of flip-flops used to store binary digits which are stored in parallel or, if desired, serially, wherein data may be fed from one end and shifted bit-by-bit. If chained in parallel, all flip-flops can be set to the desired state simultaneously.

register, icand—That register which is used in multiplication to hold the multiplicand.

register, ier—That register which holds the multiplier during a multiplication operation.

register, index—See index register.

register, input—A specific register which receives data from input devices to hold only long enough to complete transfer to internal storage, i.e., to an arithmetic register, etc., as directed by the program.

register input-buffer—That device which accepts data from input units or media such as magnetic tape or disks and which transfers this data to internal storage.

register input/output—Same as index register.

register, instruction—A temporary storage device which retains the instruction code of the instruction currently being executed. Also, known as instruction counter. The arrangement of information; an item of data which is discernible as the equivalent to a command to perform a certain operation; the sequence of operations for equivalent or programming sequences.

register, internal-function—The internal-function register (IFR) is a one-word representation of various states and conditions germane to the currently running program. The information in this register is continuously updated by hardware during the execution of a program. Whenever an interrupt occurs, the contents of the IFR are stored in a temporary register where they are available to the executive system and are used to re-establish program conditions at the time of interrupt (some systems).

register length—The number of digits, characters, or bits that a register can store.

register, magnetic-shift—A register that makes use of magnetic cores as binary-storage elements, and in which the pattern of binary digital information can be shifted from one position to the next left or right position.

register, mask—The mask register functions as a filter in determining which portions of words in masked operations or logical comparisons are to be tested. In repeated masked-search operations, both the mask register and the repeat counter must be loaded prior to executing the actual search command (some systems).

register, memory—A register in the storage of the computer, in contrast with a register in one of the other units of the computer.

register, memory-address (MA)—The location in core memory which is selected for data storage or retrieval is determined by the MA. This register can directly address all words of the standard core memory or in any preselected field of extended core memory.

register, memory-buffer (MB)—The MB serves as a buffer register for all information passing between the processor and the core memory, and serves as a buffer directly between core memory and peripheral equipment during data break information transfers. The MB is also used as a distributor-shift register for the analog-to-digital converter.

register, memory-lockout—See memory-lockout register.

register, modifier—Same as index register.

register, motion—This 2-bit register contains a go/stop flip-flop and a forward/reverse flip-flop that control the motion of the selected tape drive. The register is set under program control.

register, MQ—Multiple-quotient register.

register, multiplier-quotient—A specific register in the arithmetic or logic portion of a computer in which the multiplier for multiplication is placed and in which the quotient for division is formed.

register, next available block—An address register of available blocks of core storage that are chained together for use by the line control computer for the allocation of incoming information.

register, op—That specific register in which the operation code of the instruction set is stored.

register, operation—1. A register in which an operation is stored and analyzed in order to set conditions for the execution cycle. 2. A temporary storage device which retains the operation number while that number is being analyzed. 3. A register which stores the operation code of the instruction or program in process.

register, output buffer—The buffering or transfer device which receives data from internal storage and transfers it to an output media such as magnetic tape.

register, payroll — A payroll system which records the employees and the amount due each of them.

register pointer—The portion of the program status double-word that points to a set of 16 general registers to be used as the current register block.

register, program—1. Register in the control unit that stores the current instruction of the program and controls computer operation during the execution of the program. 2. A temporary storage device or area which retains the instruction code of the instruction being executed.

register, R—The register that holds the ten low-order digits.

register, return code—A particular register which is used to store data which controls the execution of follow-on or subsequent programs.

registers, access-control—The actual word-by-word transmission (regardless of the communication mode) over a given channel is governed by the access-control registers in magnetic-film storage. Two of these registers, one for input and one for output, are assigned to each of the sixteen channels (some computers).

register, sequence—Controls the sequence of the instructions.

register, sequence control—A hardware register which is used by the computer to remember the location of the next instruction to be processed in the normal sequence, but subject to branching, execute instructions, and interruptions.

registers, general—Very fast registers which can be used for any purpose (usually as scratchpad). More recently they are used in place of special registers such as the accumulator.

register, shift—A register in which the characters may be shifted one or more positions to the right or left. In a right shift, the rightmost character is lost. In a left shift, the leftmost character is lost.

register, standby—A register in which accepted or verified information can be stored so as to be available for a rerun in case the processing of the information is spoiled by a mistake in the program, or a malfunction in the computer.

register, stepping—*Same as* register, shift.

register, storage—A register in the storage of the computer, in contrast with a register in one of the other units of the computer. (Synonymous with memory register.)

register, storage limits (SLR)—To prevent an inadvertant program reference to out-of-range storage addresses, the processor provides a hardware storage protection feature called the storage limits register (SLR). The SLR can be loaded by the executive system to establish allowable operating areas for each program. These areas are termed the program I (instruction) and D (data) areas. When control is given to a particular program, the executive loads the SLR with the

appropriate I and D boundaries (some systems).

register, tally—A specific register which holds information such as the tally, count, or total of particular happenings.

register, time delay — *Same as* delay line storage.

registration—The accuracy of the positioning of punched holes in a card.

regression, multiple — An efficient analysis program for determining the mathematical relations and relative significances of manufacturing parameters associated with a given problem.

regular binary—*See* binary.

regulation—A specific statement which can be considered a law or convention of a particular computer system and usually one which rules as to the place, time, and even manner of assigned duties or responsibilities of that computer installation.

reimbursed time—The machine time which is loaned or rented to another office, agency, or organization either on a reimbursable or reciprocal basis.

rejection gate—*Same as* gate, NOR.

REL—A symbol and list structure adaptive system developed by California Institute of Technology.

relational expression—In the COBOL language, an expression that describes a relationship between two terms; for example, A is less than B.

relationship, analytic—The relationship that exists between concepts and corresponding terms, by virtue of their defiintion and inherent scope of meaning.

relationship, synthetic—A relation existing between concepts that pertains to an empirical observation. Such relationships are involved not in defining concepts or terms, but in reporting the results of observations and experiments.

relative address—1. An address of a machine instruction that is referenced to an origin; e.g. R + 15 is a specific address relative to R, where R is the origin; the other R + machine addresses do not need to be named. 2. A label used to identify a word in a routine or subroutine with respect to its relative position in that routine or subroutine. A relative address is translated into an absolute address by addition of some specific address for the subroutine within the main routine.

relative addressing—*See* addressing, relative.

relative addressing, real-time—*Same as* relative addressing, time-sharing.

relative addressing, time-sharing—Relative addressing is a feature of great significance in multiprogramming, time-sharing, and real time operations. It allows storage assignments to be changed dynamically to provide contiguous storage for operation of another program, and permits programs to dynamically request additional main storage according to processing needs. An additional advantage is that systems programs stored on mass storage may be brought in for operation in any available area without complicated relocation algorithms. Relative addressing is provided for through basing registers contained within the processor. A separate register controls the basing of the program instruction and data bank, and a third register controls the selection of the appropriate basing register.

relative code—A code in which all addresses are specified or written with respect to an arbitrarily selected position, or in which all addresses are represented symbolically in machine language.

relative coding—1. Coding in which all addresses refer to an arbitrarily selection position. 2. Coding using relative addresses.

relative error—A ratio of the error to the value of the quantity which contains the error, as contrasted to absolute error.

relative transmission level—The relative transmission level at any point in a transmission system is the ratio of the test-tone power at that point to the test-tone power at some point in the system chosen as a reference point. The ratio shall be expressed in db. The transmission level at the transmitting switch-board is frequently taken as zero level reference point.

relativization—A means by which the next written instruction address and operand address are given relative addresses. The relative address is translated automatically to an obsolute address during execution of the program.

relay—An electromagnetic switching device, having multiple electrical contacts, energized by electrical current through its coil. It is used to complete electrical circuits.

relay center—A location where an incoming message is automatically directed to one or more outgoing circuits according to intelligence contained in the message. (Clarified by switching center.)

relay, tape—A method used, (using perforated tape as the intermediate storage), for relaying messages between the transmitting and receiving stations.

release-guard signal — *See* signal, release guard.

release read—A feature of some equipment which permits more computer processing time by releasing the read mechanism.

relevance ratio — An information retrieval term expressing the ratio of the number of pertinent documents retrieved by a particular query to the total number of documents retrieved by the query criteria, as contrasted with recall ratio.

reliability—1. A measure of the ability to function without failure. 2. The amount of credence placed in the result. 3. A word to indicate a measurement trustworthiness and dependability, and frequently used to imply a reliability factor or coefficient.

reliability, channel—The percentage of time

the channels meet the established abitrary standards.

reliability, circuit—The percentage of time the circuit meets arbitrary standards set by the user.

reliability data—*See* reliability.

relocatability of programs and data, time-sharing—*See* time-sharing, relocatability of programs and data.

relocatable program—A special routine whose instructions are written in a special manner so that it can be located and executed in many areas of the memory. Some modification before execution may be involved to the instructions originally coded relative to a fixed starting place in the memory. Relocatable programs allow for the highly flexible real-time use of the main memory.

relocatable subroutine—A subroutine that can be located physically and independently in the memory—its object-time location is determined by the processor.

relocate—1. To modify the instructions of a routine in such a way that the routine can be moved to another location and then executed at that location. 2. To modify the addresses relative to a fixed point or origin.

relocation, base address—The ability to augment memory references by the contents of a specific base register, alterable only in the supervisor mode.

relocation dictionary—*See* dictionary, relocation.

relocation, dynamic-memory—Frees programmer from keeping track of exactly where certain information is located in the system's memory. Another important attribute is its ability to keep programs flowing in and out of the memory in a highly efficient manner.

relocation, dynamic page—The segmentation of internal storage into blocks whose addressing is automatically controlled by a memory-protected set of addressable registers.

relocation, program—The execution of a program or location which is different than the location from which the program was originally assembled.

remark—Part of a statement providing an explanation of the use or function. This is contrasted to a comment which is a separate statement.

remedial maintenance—*See* maintenance, remedial.

remember—That instruction referring to nondestructive readout.

remote batch—*See* batch, remote.

remote batch access — *See* access, remote batch.

remote-batch computing—When the computer is available for batch processing, the computer operator will indicate to a subsystem under the system monitor what files on the auxiliary disk storage device are to be processed. Under control of the sub-system, the files will be transferred from disk storage to tape, which is then used as the system input unit (S.SIN1) for normal processing under the system monitor. The result of this processing, which is contained on the system output unit (S.SOU1), can be handled in either of the following ways: (1) it can be transferred to disk storage for subsequent transmission to a terminal, or (2) it can be printed on an off-line printer and mailed to the terminal. (IBM)

remote calculator—*See* calculator, remote.

remote computer—A system which has four principal components—a central processor, a communications linkage, a terminal device, and a user. These components interact to carry out a task.

remote-computing monitor system—*See* monitor, remote computing system.

remote-computing system completeness errors—*See* errors, completeness (remote computing system).

remote-computing system consistency errors—Most errors of consistency are detected as soon as the user enters the offending statement. The system rejects the offending statement and the user can immediately substitute a correct statement. However, some errors of consistency (e.g., illegal branch into the range of a DO) are not immediately detected. These errors are handled in the same manner as errors of completeness and should be considered as such.

remote computing-system error detection—Those errors detected during the execution of the user's program. They include errors that are detectable only during program execution (e.g., invalid subscript value, reference to an undefined variable, arithmetic spills, etc.) along with those errors of completeness detected because either (1) they were disregarded by the user when previously detected or (2) they were not detected in the first place because the user did not indicate that his program was complete.

remote computing system, exchange device—The exchange device controls the flow of information between the computer and the terminals. Characters typed at the terminals are formed into statements within the exchange device and then are sent to the computer, one statement at a time. The computer returns an answer to the exchange device, which, in turn, sends it to the proper terminal. An exchange device allows each terminal to send or receive data independent of all other terminals.

Programs are permanently stored in disk storage. When the user indicates that a program he has constructed is to be saved, the remote computing system places it in disk storage. Thereafter, the program will be available to the user whenever needed.

remote computing system execution errors

—*See* errors, execution (remote computing system).

remote computing-system language—The language of the remote computing system comprises two types of statements—program statements and operating statements. Program statements that are upwardly compatible with Fortran IV are used to form the user's program. Operating statements allow the user to communicate with the remote computing system. Operating statements include modification, test, display, and output statements. The statements that are available for use in constructing a program are described under program statements. Statements that are available for changing, testing, and executing programs are described as operating statements.

remote computing-system log—The remote computing system maintains a log of operations that take place between the computer and each terminal. The log contains information as the number of statements handled, the number and types of errors detected, and the volume of output produced. The information in the log can be used for various purposes. For example, the number of errors might indicate that additional training might be helpful. Similarly, if an individual terminal is always busy, it might indicate the need for an additional terminal. If the cost of the system is shared among terminals according to usage, the information in the log can be used for billing purposes.

remote computing system process codes — *See* codes, process (remote computing system).

remote-control equipment — *See* equipment, remote-control.

remote control system, program mode—*See* program mode (remote control system).

remote-control system (semantic errors)—Semantic errors are concerned with the meaning or intent of the programmer and are his responsibility. However, he is provided with an extensive set of debugging aids that allow him to manipulate portions of a program when in search of errors in logic and analysis.

remote data-station console—The consoles are equipped with specialized devices that perform three basic functions—document reading, information printing, and data transmission and reception. Document reading is done by an optical scanner that reads the information, printed in a special bar-code, by means of a beam of light. A teleprinter terminal is used to simultaneously print information and punch it onto paper tape for data transmission to the primary counter. A communications device to send and receive data is also part of the console. The console provides each office with its own data-collection system, which (via conventional lines) can be directly linked to the centralized computer to provide an integrated information-processing system. Principal users of the unit are retail firms, educational systems, government agencies, manufacturing firms, insurance companies and other geographically dispersed organizations, such as branches, warehouses, remote plants, etc. Transmission errors are detected by parity and channel checking, and corrected by automatic transmission of the data (some systems).

remote data stations—Remote data stations can be installed by any normal office environment without special cooling or electrical requirements. They can be linked as single remote units, or as multiple stations, to one or more computers, using conventional voice-grade telephone lines.

remote data terminal—The remote data terminal provides the capability of sending 80 or 90 column cards, keyboard information, and paper tape from a remote location to a central processor, as well as the capability of punching 80 or 90 column cards, punching paper tape, and printing information received from a central processor. Also it can provide visual input and output.

remote debugging—The use of remote terminals in a mode suitable for testing of programs, most frequently found in systems devoted to scientific or engineering computation.

remote device — An input/output unit, or other piece of equipment, which is removed from the computer center but connected by a communication line. In a typical on-line, real-time communications system the remote device is usually a teletypewriter, an audio answer back device, or a CRT visual display unit.

remote display, slave—A slave unit containing only the analogue portion of the display. Turn-on may be accomplished independently, or by the master-display control.

remote display unit, visual—*See* display unit, remote (visual).

remote entry unit—*See* entry unit, remote.

remote inquiry—*See* inquiry, remote.

remote inquiry (real time)—On-line inquiry stations permit users to interrogate the computer files and receive immediate answers to their inquiries. In industry, the stations can be located at dozens of remote locations such as office, factory, warehouse, and remote branch locations. Such a system permits all levels of industrial management to obtain immediate answers to questions about inventories, work-in-process, sales and other facts.

remote job entry—*See* entry, remote job.

remote message, input/output (I/O)—This is an I/O control for obtaining messages from, and sending messages to, remote terminals. For remote message control, the I/O control handles the following functions: receipt of messages from remote terminals, sending of messages to remote terminals, automatic

dial-up, and code conversion. The user supplies the system with line-control specifications and installation-oriented routines to analyze message headers.

Messages received can be stored in processing queues or output-terminal queues. Macrostatements enable the installation program to obtain messages for processing and to send messages. A log of all message traffic may be stored in a secondary storage device.

remote message processing—The operating system can be used to process messages received from remote locations by way of communication lines and telecommunication equipment. Remote message processing is, in effect, an extension of the full power of the data processing and programming facilities of the computer to remote locations. A message received from a remote location may be in the nature of a request to the system for a particular service, and may or may not be accompanied by data. The requested service may be simply the routing of a message to another remote location or it may be the processing of a job or transaction similar to jobs and transactions that are received locally. By extending the services of the system, via communication lines, directly to the user, the turnaround or response time of the system is reduced from hours to seconds. Consequently, the system can directly participate in and control various commercial and scientific activities as they are being carried on. For example, the system may be used to centrally control a geographically dispersed banking activity. In such a system, master files containing account records for thousands of depositors are stored in direct-access storage. By entering pertinent data into the system, tellers at widely separated locations can check balances, update passbook records, and handle other similar transactions, all within a few seconds.

remote polling technique—*See* polling technique, remote.

remote processing—*Same as* remote message processing.

remote station—*See* station, remote.

remote subsets—Input and output devices located at points other than the central computer site. Information is indexed on the subset and transmitted by wire to the computer. When the information has been processed by the central-site computer, it is returned over the common-carrier lines to the subset that reproduces the final results at the remote location—all in seconds or minutes.

remote terminal unit (bank)—The teller consoles in each office communicate with the processing center (over telephone lines) through the remote terminal unit that converts information for transmission to, and information received from, the processing center. The remote terminal unit always knows the input/output status of the teller console; provides temporary storage of information received for, and from, the teller console; maintains constant contact with the processing center through control messages and replies; initiates message and reply transmission; and checks the accuracy of data received from the teller console and processing center, as well as adding checking data to all messages it transmits.

removable plugboard—*Same as* patchboard.

removable random access — *See* access, removable random.

remove subroutine, first — *See* subroutine, first order.

repair delay time—That particular time during which the maintenance personnel are on duty, but the repair is not being completed, most often due to lack of parts, advice, or assistance.

repair, mean time to—The average time to repair a fault or a component of the system.

repair time—That time which is devoted or used to diagnose, clear, or repair machines or systems, including fault location, detection, correction, and consequent tests. This is part of down time, including proving time after a repair is made; also if the case exists, repair delay time, machine spoiled work time, and scheduled engineering time.

repeat counter—The repeat counter is used to control repeated operations such as block transfer and repeated search commands. To execute a repeated instruction "k" times, the repeat counter must be loaded with "k" prior to the execution of the instruction. A repeated sequence may be suspended to process an interrupt, with circuitry providing for the completion of the repeated sequence after the interrupt has been processed.

repeater—A device used to amplify and/or reshape signals.

repeater, regenerative—A repeater in which signals retransmitted are practically free from distortion.

repeater station—1. Station at which a repeater is located for the purpose of building up and equalizing the strength of a telephone or telegraph signal in a long line. 2. Intermediate station in a microwave system which is arranged to receive a signal from an adjacent station and amplify and retransmit to another adjacent station. Usually performs the function in both directions simultaneously.

reperforator—1. The contraction of the words receiving and perforator. 2. Any tape punch that automatically converts coded electrical signals into perforations in tape. 3. A tape punch that operates without direct human control.

reperforator transmitter — A receiver-transmitter consisting of a reperforator and a tape distributor, where each unit is independent of the other unit. It is used as a relaying device and is especially suitable for

transforming the incoming speed to a different outgoing speed.

repertoire, instruction—An instruction repertoire includes fixed and floating point, integer and fractional arithmetic. Provision is also usually made for partial word transfers, partial compares, repeated search operations and masking. Special add and subtract instructions perform parallel addition or subtraction of two or three fields within a single data word. To provide fast programming of double precision arithmetic, special features can be incorporated into the arithmetic section. The basic function codes in the instruction repertoire of the system can provide unlimited programming versatility. Much of the real programming power of the computer lies in the unique format of the instruction word. Of the 30 bit positions in the instruction word, nine serve as special purpose designators. When these designators are used in combination with the function codes, the computer can perform more than 25,000 individual programming operations (some systems).

repertory—The many sets of operations that can be represented in a given operation code.

repertory code—*Same as* code, instruction.

repertory instruction—1. The set of instructions that a computing or data-processing system is capable of performing. 2. The set of instructions that an automatic coding system assembles.

repetition instruction—An instruction that causes one or more instructions to be executed an indicated number of times.

repetitive addressing — *Same as* addressing, one ahead.

repetitive operation—Operations frequently used in computing, such that repeated solutions of the same set of equations with the same set of initial conditions and parameters are developed. In CRT (cathode-ray tube) usage, a steady-state solution becomes apparent when displayed on the screen.

replacement — The substitution of various types of equipment for other units which perform the same or similar operations.

replacement, mechanical—The computer contractor substitutes another unit for customer's original machine. Such action usually is warranted by the poor mechanical condition of the original equipment.

replacement-selection technique — A technique used in the internal portion of a sort program. The results of the comparisons between groups of records are stored for later use.

replica reproduction—Facsimile copies of documents produced by copiers or photocopiers.

report delay—*See* delay.

report footing—The summary of the entire report, which most often appears at the termination and which is also known as final footing.

report generation—1. A technique for producing complete machine reports from information that describes the input file and the format and content of the output report. 2. Production of complete output reports from only a specification of the desired content and arrangement, and from input-file specifications.

report generator—A software program that can direct the production of output reports if the computer is provided with format and specifications, input file detail, sorted input data, inout/output procedure rules and other information.

report heading — Description of the report content which is produced, usually at the beginning of the report.

reporting, exception—A record of departures from the expected or norm. Often times, maximum or minimum limits are the set parameters and the normal range lies within these end numbers or expectations. Reports that have results which exceed these parameters become the basis for an exception reporting output.

reporting period—The length of time covered by a report.

report interval—The measure of the length of the time between the preparation of two issues of a corresponding report. The interval may be variable in length when events, rather than the passage of time, trigger the preparation of reports, as in inventory-control routines when "order points" are reached.

report preparation—During report preparation, the primary control objective is proving that all items (accounts or transactions, etc.) are included in the processing and that arithmetic is performed accurately. It can be assumed that the data itself is correct, since punching summary and posting operations should be proved when they occur.

To insure the inclusion of all items in the report, a final control total is developed during processing and balanced at the end of the run to a predetermined one. In cycle-billing operations, the control may be an account number hash total of these accounts which are in the cycle; for other reporting operations it may be a control total based upon an amount, a quantity, or another code field.

report program generator—The report program generator provides a convenient programming method for producing a wide variety of reports. The generator may range from a listing of a card deck or magnetic-tape reel to precisely arranged, calculated, and edited tabulation of data from several input sources.

report, progress—A current status report of a specific activity or group of activities in the form of a summary of results, i.e., of a run at a point, etc.

reports and feedback, factory—See feedback and reports (factory).

reports, difference—A report noting resulting changes from an original computer program and a program change.

reports, interim—Single-record inquiries, or interim reports, may be produced in seconds or minutes on a demand basis. Exception reports may be prepared automatically to signal activity requiring management attention.

reports, single quick-access—Same as reports, interim.

representation—A combination of one or more characters to represent a unit.

representation, analog—A representation that does not have discrete values but is continuously variable.

representation, binary incremental—See binary incremental representation.

representation, calculating operation — See time, representative computing.

reperesentation, deleted—See deleted representation.

representation, digital—See digital representation.

representation, excess fifty—See excess fifty.

representation, fixed-point—See fixed-point representation.

representation, floating point—See floating point representation.

representation, incremental — See incremental representation.

representation, incremental ternary—See incremental ternary representation.

representation, number — Any system designed to represent the numbers with an agreed upon set of rules.

representation, positional—A number representation or number system in which the significance or value of each digit depends upon its place or position with respect to a radix point. (Related to number system).

representation system, numeration — See numeration system.

representation, variable point—See variable point representation.

representative calculating time—A method of evaluating the speed performance of a computer. This method is based on one-tenth of the time required to perform nine complete additions and one complete multiplication. A complete addition or a complete multiplication time includes the time required to procure two operands from high-speed storage, perform the operation, and store the result, and the time required to select and execute the required number of operand instructions.

reproduce—To prepare a duplicate of the stored information, especially for punched cards, punched paper tape or magnetic tape.

reproducer—1. A machine for duplicating cards and card data, or for punching cards in any format. Also called gang punch. 2. A device that will duplicate on one card, all or part of the information contained on another card.

reproducer, accumulating—A piece of equipment that reproduces punched cards and has limited additional capabilities of adding, subtracting, and summary punching.

reproducer, card—A device that reproduces a punch card by punching another similar card.

reproducer, tape — A particular machine which is used to either copy or edit paper tape or to do both.

reproducing brushes—Reading brushes transfer the data from a card to punches so that an exact duplicate of the card is punched.

reproducing punch—*See* reproducer.

reproducing unit—A unit that punches a new set, or file of cards, from an original set of cards. The new cards can be an exact reproduction or they can be modified according to requirements. In this reproducing process, additional data can be punched or card columns can be eliminated or transposed, as required.

reproduction codes—Function codes in a master tape that are carried through the data operations and also appear in the produced tape. (Clarified by nonreproducing codes.)

reproduction replica—Facsimile copies of documents produced by copiers or photocopiers.

request control panel, operator—*See* control panel, operator's request.

request enter key—*See* keyboard entry.

request-repeat system—A system employing an error-detecting code and so arranged that a signal detected as being in error automatically initiates a request for retransmission of the signal that was detected as being in error.

request-send—*See* circuit send-request.

request words for input/output — Control words for input/output requests that are stored in the message reference block until the I/O is completed.

requirement, functional—*See* functional requirements.

requirements, information—The actual or anticipated questions that may be requested of an information system.

rerun—1. To repeat all or part of a program on a computer. 2. A repeat of a machine run, usually because of a connection, an interrupt, or a false start.

rerun point—1. That stage of a computer run at which all information pertinent to the running of the routine is available either to the routine itself or to a rerun in order that a new run may be reconstituted. 2. One of a set of planned-for points in a program used so that if an error is detected between two such points, to rerun the problem it is only necessary to go back to the last rerun point. Rerun points are often three to five minutes apart, so that little time is required for a rerun. All information pertinent to a rerun is available in standby storage during the whole time from one rerun point to the next. 3. The initialization

of a restart after the discovery of an error or computer stoppage.

rerun routine—A routine designed to be used after a computer malfunction or a coding or operating mistake to reconstitute a new routine from the last previous rerun point. (Synonymous with rollback routine.)

rescue dump—A rescue dump (R dump) is the recording on magnetic tape of the entire contents of the memory, which includes the status of the computer system at the time the dump is made. R dumps are made so that in the event of power failure, etc., a run can be resumed from the last rescue point (R point) rather than rerunning the entire program.

rescue points—For many applications it is very desirable, indeed essential, to create rescue points (R points) from which it is known that the program can be resumed in a proper manner. If a processing mishap does occur after creating a rescue point, the operator can restart his run at any rescue point by use of the restart routine. For long runs, the liberal use of rescue points will mean that the run is, in essence, segmented. A mishap will affect only one segment and all the valid processing that preceded the establishing of the latest point is saved and need not be reprocessed.

research, analytic aid (time sharing) — *See* time sharing, analytic aid to research.

research, operations (analysis) — The vast area of computation devices and techniques which concerns itself with mathematical tools directed toward the solution of sets of problems concerned with optimizing the management function and math models of business (conflicting interest) situations. Its task is to analytically resolve control variables to optimal decisions. Some complex models are expressed and solved with the simplex method, matrix algebra and the computer. Among the OR computational techniques are: linear programming, game theory, econometrics, input/output, queue analysis (waiting lines), simulation, critical-path method (CPM), Project Evaluation and Review Techniques (PERT) and others.

reserve—*Same as* allocate.

reserved words—The words which are set aside in COBOL language which cannot be used as data names, file names, or procedure names, and are of three types; connected, optional words, and key words.

reset—1. To return a device to zero or to an initial or arbitrarily selected condition. 2. To restore a storage device to a prescribed initial state, not necessarily that denoting zeros. 3. To place a binary cell into the zero state.

reset cycle—The return of a cycle index to its initial or some preselected condition.

reset mode—In analog computing, the integrators are inoperative and the required initial conditions are applied or reapplied, as contrasted to the operate mode when the input signals are connected to the computing units including integrators, for the generation of the solution.

reset pulse—*See* pulse, reset.

reset rate—The number of corrections, per unit of time, made by the control system.

reset-to-n—The procedure to set a device as a register, counter, etc., for storing or displaying a particular value, say n, by returning a counting device to its initial state, thus representing n, i.e., some number as it was predetermined or desired.

resident, core memory—The term resident is used to denote a part of the executive which resides in core memory at all times. Examples of resident routines are the dispatcher, the real-time clock routine, and the internal-error processing routines. Nonresident routines are taken from the library.

resident, executive—The section of the supervisory program that is always located in core. The resident executive is a permanent resident of core.

residual error—The difference between an optimum result derived from experience or experiment and a supposedly exact result derived from theory.

residue check—*Same as* check, modulo-N.

residue, modulo-N—*See* modulo-N check.

resolution error—*See* error, resolution.

resolver—A small section of storage, particularly in drum, tape or disk storage units, that has much faster access than the remainder of the storage.

resource-sharing—The sharing of one central processor by several users and several peripheral devices. Principally used in connection with the sharing of time and memory.

resources, scheduling (time sharing) — *See* time sharing, scheduling resources.

respond-typeout key—A particular push button on a console inquiry key board which locks the typewriter keyboard and permits the automatic processing to continue.

response—The response of a device or system is an explicit quantitative expression of the output as a function of the input. The response characteristic, often presented graphically, gives the response as a function of some independent variable, such as frequency.

response, external device—*See* external device response.

response, fast—This is dependent on the situation. A fast response in a desk calculator would be a 30-second answer; in computer-assisted instruction, it would be a response time of up to 10 seconds; in inputting information, it would be a response of less than 1 second.

response, frequency—A measure of the ability of a device to take into account, follow, or act upon a varying condition; e.g., as applied to amplifiers, the frequencies at which the gain has fallen to the one-half power point or to 0.707 of the voltage gain, either at the high or low end of the frequency spectrum. When applied to a mechanical controller, the maximum rate at which changes in condition can be followed and acted upon, since it is implied that the controller can follow slow changes.

response operation, audio—A typical audio unit provides composed audio responses to digital inquiries sent from telephones linked to the computer system. The calling party enters a request by dialing digits which are immediately transmitted to the unit and then sped to the processor. The computer processes the data, composes a coded response, and returns the message to the audio unit. The unit interprets the coded reply, selects the proper words from its stored vocabulary, and tells the inquirer what he wants to know (some systems).

response signal, partial disturbed—The output signal from a core subjected to a partial read pulse after it has been set to a one or zero condition, there having been one or more intervening partial drive pulses.

response time—The amount of time which elapses between generation of an inquiry at a terminal and the receipt of a response at the terminal. Response time would be: transmission time to the computer, processing time at the computer, access time to obtain any file records needed to answer the inquiry, and transmission time back to the terminal.

response unit, audio — *See* audio response unit.

restart—1. One of a set of preselected points located in a program such that if an error is detected between two points, the problem may be rerun by returning to the last such point instead of returning to the start of the problem. 2. To return to a previous point in a program and resume operation from that point.

restart checkpoint and procedures — *See* check-point and restart procedures.

restart point—*Same as* rerun point.

restart point (sorting)—*Same as* restart sorting.

restart routine—*Same as* rerun routine.

restart, sorting—The return to a previous point in the program where processing may begin. The previous point may be the beginning of the program or it may be a checkpoint.

restitution—A series of significant conditions resulting from decisions based on demodulated telegraph signals.

restore—1. To return a variable address or other computer word to its initial or pre-selected value. 2. To return a register, trigger, error-condition signal, etc., to zero or to a specific initial condition.

restore pulse generator—*Same as* generator, clock pulse.

restorer, direct-current—A method of restoring the d-c or low-frequency components to a transmitted signal.

restore, tape-skip—A function that permits certain portions of tape to be idled through a tape reader without being acted upon. This function is initiated by depressing the tape-skip key. Skipping continues until the reader finds a tape-skip restore character in the tape. This character must have been included in the original programming.

result, address—That address into which the results of an arithmetic process are transferred.

retention period—*See* period, retention.

reticle, font—*See* font, reticle.

retrieval—1. The recovery of research material. 2. The act of finding stored material.

retrieval, coordinate—*Same as* concept coordination.

retrieval data—*See* data retrieval.

retrieval, document—*See* document retrieval.

retrieval, fact—*See* fact retrieval.

retrieval, information—The recovering of desired information or data from a collection of documents or other graphic records.

retrieval, legal—A language developed at the University of Pittsburgh to retrieve legal information such as citations, references, specific literature, court decisions, and which has a rather elaborate indexing system. The service is offered to lawyers and provides assistance concerning Pennsylvania state laws. An expansion of this program into other areas appears imminent with more elaborate use of KWIC indexing programs.

retrievals, false—The library references that are not pertinent to, but are vaguely related to, the subject of the library search and are sometimes obtained by automatic search methods.

retrieval system, fast-access — A fast-access information-retrieval system has been designed and manufactured to file, store, and locate reservation and flight information for airlines. The basic units of the system are a data processor and a fast-access disk-file memory. The processor contains parallel input/output channels which interface with the disk file, standard peripheral equipment, and common carrier communications terminals via a communication scan unit in the processor. Subscribers with appropriate inquiry units have access to the system via ordinary communication links. Each input/output channel of the processor operates independently of the processor, as does the scan unit. Displays for this type of system contain a refresh memory, symbol generator, timing and control, keyboard logic, and dataphone buffer as integral parts of the display. Only the interconnections to standard communication terminals are required to complete the hookup (some systems) .

retrieval system, information—*See* information-retrieval system.

retrieve—To find and select specific information in the record of a file storage.

retrieving—Searching of storage to locate the data required, and selecting or removing the required data from storage.

retrofit—The adjusting of existing systems or programs for the purpose of fitting in or accommodating a new part and performing all other changes necessary in related systems or programs.

retrofit testing—Testing to assure system operation after replacing some equipment or programs.

return—1. The mechanism providing for a return to a previous point in the usual sense. In particular, a set of instructions at the end of a subroutine that permit the system control to be returned to the proper point in the main routine. 2. To go back to a specific, planned point in a program, usually when an error is detected, for the purpose of rerunning the program. Rerun points are usually three to five minutes apart to avoid long periods of lost computer time. Information pertinent to a rerun is available in standby registers from point to point.

return, carriage—The operation that causes the next character to be printed at the left margin of printout.

return instructions—The specific group of instructions which are subroutined at the end of a program to provide for the transfer of control from the return subroutine to the main routine.

return point (sorting)—*Same as* restart, sorting.

return-to-zero (RZ)—A method of writing information on a magnetic surface in which the current through the write-head winding is returned to zero after the write pulse.

reverse capstan—A rotating shaft with minimal tolerances which controls the reverse or rewind movement of magnetic tape at uniform speed.

reverse-code dictionary—An alphabetic or numeric-alphabet arrangement of codes associated with their corresponding English words or terms. (Related to dictionary code.)

reverse-digit sorting method — *See* sorting, reverse-digit method.

reverse-direction flow—A flow in a direction other than left to right or top to bottom.

reverse, read—The unit can read tape in either direction under program control.

reverser sign—*See* sign changer.

reverse solenoid—That electrical-mechanical device which provides pressure via a roller to force magnetic tape against the reverse capstan and move the tape in a reverse direction.

reversible, counter—*See* counter reversible.

review, preliminary-proposal—An on-site review to provide guidance to proponent agencies in the preparation of ADP system proposals.

review, readiness—An on-site examination of the adequacy of preparations for the effective utilization of a new computer installation, and to indicate any necessary corrective actions.

revolver—*Same as* loop, high speed.

revolver track—*Same as* loop, high speed.

rewind—The process of returning a film or magnetic tape to its initial data point.

rewind time—The measurement of elapsed time required to transfer tape to the supply reel.

rewind time (sorting) — Elapsed time consumed by a sort/merge program for restoring intermediate and final tape files to original position.

rewrite—The process of restoring the information in the storage device to its prior-to-reading state.

re-write dual gap head—A character written on tape is immediately read by a read head so that the accuracy of recorded data might be ensured.

RF—Abbreviation for report footing.

RH—Abbreviation for report heading.

right hand justified—*See* justified, right hand.

right justified—Data are right justified when the right-hand digit or character occupies its allotted right-hand position.

right justify—*See* justify, right.

ring counter—A loop of interconnected bi-stable elements such that one and only one is in a specified state at any given time and such that, as input signals are counted, the position of the element in the specified state moves in an ordered sequence around the loop.

ring shift—*See* shift, circular.

ripple-through carry — *Same as* carry, high speed.

rise time—The time required for the leading edge of a pulse to rise from one-tenth of its final value to nine-tenths of its final value. Rise time is proportional to the time constant of the circuit.

RJE—The abbreviation for remote job entry.

RLD—Abbreviation for relocation dictionary. *See* dictionary, relocation.

role indicator—A code assigned to an individual word, indicating the nature or particular function that this specific word is to play in any textual occurrence.

rollback—A system that will restart the running program after a system failure. Snapshots of data and programs are stored at periodic intervals and the system rolls back to restart at the last recorded snapshot.

rollback routine—*Same as* rerun routine.

roll-in—Return to a main or internal storage unit of data which had previously been transferred from main or internal memory units to various external or auxiliary units.

roll-out—A process, often used in diagnostic routines, in which a register or counter is read out by the following process: add 1 to the digits in each column simultaneously; do this n times, where n is the radix of the number in the register; when the result in each column changes from n-1 to 0, issue a signal.

rope storage—*Same as* storage, core rope.

ROPP—Abbreviation for receive only page printer. A teleprinter unit with printer only for stations which do not generate messages.

RO (Receive Only)—A receive only printer.

rotor — Phonetic term for ROTR (Receive Only Typing Reperforator).

ROTR—Abbreviation for receive-only typing reperforator. A teletypewriter receiver which produces perforated tape with characters along the edge of the tape.

round—To adjust the least significant digits retained in truncation to partially reflect the dropped portion; e.g., when rounded to the digits, the decimal number 2.7561 becomes 2.76.

rounding—Often less important or less significant digits are dropped for development of increased accuracy by adding the more significant digits that are retained. The rounding rule of adding 5 in the left-most position to be dropped would then round 2.3456 to 2.346 for rounding to three decimals.

rounding error — The error resulting from dropping certain less significant digits and some adjustment is applied to the more significant retained. Also called round-off error. A common round-off rule is to take the quantity to the nearest digit.

round-off—1. To change a more precise quantity to a less precise one, according to some rule. 2. An arbitrary but consistent rule for the limitation of cumulative errors arising from truncation through this lesser decrease of precision.

round-off error — The error resulting from rounding off a quantity by deleting the less significant digits and applying some rule of correction to the part retained; e.g., 0.2751 can be rounded to 0.275 with a rounding error of .0001. (Contrasted with error truncation.)

route—1. The route followed, or to be followed, for the transmission of a telegram or the establishment of a connection. 2. The means of transmission (wire, cable radio) used, or to be used, for the transmission of a telegram or the establishment of a connection.

routine—1. A sequence of machine instructions that carry out a well-defined function. 2. A set of coded instructions arranged in proper sequence to direct the computer to perform a desired operation or series of operations.

routine, algorithmic — *See* algorithmic routine.

routine, alternate — Assignment of a secondary communications path to a destination if the primary path is unavailable.

routine, assembly—*See* assembly routine.

routine, automatic—A routine that is executed independently of manual operations, but only if certain conditions occur within a program or record, or during some other process.

routine, auxiliary—A routine designed to assist in the operation of the computer and in debugging other routines.

routine, check—A check system built into the program or computers that do not have automatic checking. This check system is normally concerned with programs run on computers that are not internally self-checking. (Related to automatic check.)

routine, checkpoint—*See* checkpoint routine.

routine, closed—A routine that is not inserted as a block of instructions within a main routine, but is entered by basic linkage from the main routine.

routine, compile — A computer instruction that is also called a compile, compiler, compiling routine, and a compilation. An executive routine that, before the desired computation is started, translates a program expressed in pseudocode into machine code (or into another pseudocode for further translation by an interpreter). In accomplishing the translation, the compiler may be required to adapt or to specialize the instructions.

routine, compiling — An executive routine that, before the desired computation is started, translates a program expressed in pseudocode into machine code (or into another pseudocode for further translation by an interpreter). In accomplishing the translation, the compiler is required to decode, convert, select, generate, allocate, adapt, orient, incorporate, or record.

routine, complete—A routine that does not require modification before it is used. Such routines are usually in company or manufacturer libraries.

routine, condensing—A routine used to convert the machine language, i.e., the one-instruction per card output format, from an assembly program or system into several instructions per card.

routine, control—*Same as* executive routine.

routine, conversion—A flexible and generalized program which can be used by a programmer to change the presentation of data from one form to another, such as changing from card to disk.

routine, dating — A routine that computes and/or stores, where needed, a date such as current date, expiration date of a tape, etc.

routine, debugging-aid — A routine to aid programmers in the debugging of their routines. Some typical routines are: storage, print-out, tape print-out, and drum print-out.

routine, diagnostic—1. A routine used to locate a malfunction in a computer, or to aid in locating the mistakes in a computer program. Thus, in general any routine specifically designed to aid in debugging or troubleshooting. (Synonymous with malfunction routine, and related to debugging.) 2. A specific routine designed to locate either a malfunction in the computer or a mistake in coding.

routine, direct-insert—*Same as* subroutine, direct insert.

routine, dynamic—*Same as* subroutine, dynamic.

routine, editor—*Same as* program, editor.

routine, error—*See* error routine.

routine, error-correction—A series of computer instructions programmed to correct a detected error.

routine, error-detection—A routine used to detect whether or not an error has occurred, usually without a special provision to find or indicate its location.

routine, executive—*See* executive routine.

routine, executive system—*See* executive system routine.

routine, extremity — This routine is used when initiating a new tape or when reaching the end-of-reel of a multireel file. This routine need not be included in memory if all tapes are set-up or initiated automatically by the system supervisor and the open or close macros are not used. The importance of this routine is that it performs necessary tape housekeeping, checks on the operator, and provides necessary information concerning the program being run.

routine, file-organization—A specifically designed routine for reading input-data files, and sorting them in random-access locations.

routine, fixed — A routine which cannot be modified during its computer execution.

routine, floating-point—A set of coded instructions arranged in proper sequence to direct the computer to perform a specific set of operations that will permit floating-point operation; e.g., enable the use of a fixed-point machine to handle information on a floating-point basis from an external point of view. Floating-point routines are usually used in computers that do not have built-in floating-point circuitry, in which case floating-point operation must be programmed.

routine, general — A routine expressed in computer coding designed to solve a class of problems specializing to a specific problem when appropriate parametric values are supplied.

routine, generating — A compiling routine that is capable of handling less fully defined situations.

routine, generator—*See* generator routine.

routine, heuristic—A routine by which the computer attacks a problem not by a direct algorithmic procedure, but by a trial and error approach frequently involving the act of learning. (Synonymous with heuristic program.)

routine, housekeeping—The initial instructions in a program that are executed only one time, e.g., clear storage.

routine, incomplete—A routine in a library programming system that requires parameters to be supplied by a macrostatement or main routine.

routine, initializer—The functions such as error checking performed on a message after it is entered into a system, but before the application program begins processing.

routine, input—See input routine.

routine, interpreter — An executive routine which translates a stored machinelike pseudocode into a machine code and performs the operations indicated by subroutines during computation.

routine, interpretive—1. An interpretive routine is essentially a closed subroutine that operates successively on an indefinitely long sequence of program parameters. It may usually be entered as a closed subroutine and executed by a pseudocoded exit instruction. 2. A routine that decodes and immediately executes instructions written as pseudocodes. This is contrasted with a compiler that decodes the pseudocodes into a machine-language routine to be executed at a later time. The essential characteristic of an interpretive routine is that a particular pseudocode operation must be decoded each time it is executed. (Synonymous with interpretive code.)

routine, interrupt—A program that performs interrupt action to coordinate the timing I/O with processing.

routine interrupt (tapedriver) — See tape driver interrupt routine.

routine, library—See library, routine.

routine, loading — That set of instructions which brings other data and instructions into storage and which is frequently built into various computer models.

routine, main scheduling—The control by the supervisory program of the work load of a processor. The loop of instructions that determines the next job to be done. Control is transferred to a control sequencing loop which scans requests for work and makes a determination of the work to be done. If there is no work, the computer cycles idly or goes into a wait mode.

routine maintenance time—Same as maintenance routine.

routine, malfunction—A routine used to locate a malfunction in a computer, or to aid in locating mistakes in a computer program. In general, any routine specifically designed to aid in debugging or troubleshooting. (Related to debugging.)

routine, minimum-access—A routine so coded that by judicious arrangement of data and instructions in storage, the actual access time is less than the expected random-access time. Such a routine is used with serial storage systems. (Synonymous with minimum-latency routine.)

routine, minimum-latency—See routine, minimum-access.

routine, monitor—Same as executive routine.

routine, object—The program that is the output of an automatic coding system. Often the object program is a machine-language program ready for execution, but it may well be in an intermediate language. (Synonymous with target program, and contrasted with source program.)

routine, open—A routine that can be inserted directly into a larger routine without a linkage or calling sequence.

routine, output—See output routine.

routine, patch—A specific correcting routine written of a sequence on the program chart and referring to a correct sequence.

routine, post-mortem — 1. A routine that either automatically or on demand prints data concerning contents of registers and storage locations, after the routine stops, in order to assist in locating errors or mistakes in coding. 2. A service routine useful in analyzing the cause of a failure, such as a routine that dumps out the content of a store after a failure. (Related to post mortem.)

routine, priority—See priority routine.

routine, production—See production routines.

routine program—The procedure for inserting instructions and the constant values of the program into the computer.

routine, program loading — The procedure for inserting instructions and the constant values of the program into the computer.

routine, recovery—See recovery routine.

routine, relocatable — A specific routine designed and stored such that it may be moved quickly and conveniently to other locations.

routine, rerun—A routine designed to be used in the wake of a computer malfunction or a coding or operating mistake to reconstitute a routine from the last previous rerun point. (Synonymous with rollback routine.)

routine, restart—Same as routine rerun.

routine, rollback—Same as routine rerun.

routine, selective tracing—A tracing routine designed to permit only specific instructions to be selected and evaluated, i.e., as I/O instructions.

routine, sequence-checking—A routine that checks every instruction executed, printing certain data; e.g., to print-out the coded instruction with addresses, and the contents of each of several registers, or it may be designed to print-out only selected data, such as transfer instructions and the quantity actually transferred. The automonitor routine on some computers is an example of a sequence-checking routine.

routine, service—1. A broad class of routines that are standardized at a particular installation for the purpose of assisting in maintenance and operation of the computer as well as the preparation of programs, as opposed to routines for the actual solution of production problems. This class includes monitoring or supervisory routines, assemblers, compilers, diagnostics for computer malfunctions, simulation of peripheral equipment, general diagnostics and input data. The distinguishing quality of service routines is that they are generally standardized so as to meet the servicing needs at a particular installation, independent of any specific production-type routine requiring such services. 2. A routine designed to assist in the actual operation of the computer. Memory print-out, memory punch-out, and the clear memory routines are examples of service routines.

routines, function-evaluation—A set of commonly used mathematical routines. The initial set of routines will include sine, cosine, tangent, arcsine, arccosine, arctangent, square root, natural logarithm, and exponential. These routines will be written in fixed and floating point.

routines, input/output random-access — *See* random access I/O routines.

routine source—*Same as* program source.

routine, specific — A routine expressed in computer coding designed to solve a particular mathematical, logical, or data-handling problem in which each address refers to explicitly stated registers and locations.

routine, static — A subroutine that involves no parameters other than the addresses of the operands.

routine, storage—1. A part of storage allocated to receive and store the group of instructions to be executed. 2. The storage locations used to store the program.

routine, stored—*Same as* program, stored.

routine, supervisory—*See* executive routine.

routine, target—*Same as* object program.

routine, test — A routine designed to show whether a computer is functioning properly or not.

routine, trace—A routine used to observe how the object program operates while it is being executed.

routine, tracing—A diagnostic routine used to provide a time history of one or more machine registers and controls during the execution of the object routine. A complete tracing routine would reveal the status of all registers and locations affected by each instruction each time the instruction is executed. Since such a trace is prohibitive in machine time, traces which provide information only following the execution of certain types of instructions are more frequently used. Furthermore, a tracing routine may be under control of the processor, or may be called in by means of a trapping feature. (Related to trap.)

routine, translating—*Same as* translator.

routine, translator—A routine that compiles (translator) a source program expressed in problem oriented language into an object program in machine code.

routine, typewriter output (TYPOUT) — The typewriter output routine (TYPOUT), is contained in the monitor routine and develops the output messages to the operator. TYPOUT is used by the monitor, the system loader, and library subroutines for diagnosing errors. It may be used by any program to output messages since it is in memory with the monitor. The output device used by TYPOUT is the operator message device—normally a console typewriter, but it may be a line printer. TYPOUT also develops an output message for the system-output device (SO) if it is different from the operator-message device.

routine, utility—1. Subroutines for handling machine operations necessary to data processing but not contributing directly to the required output; such routines might be copying, loading and organizing disks, printing, etc. 2. A standard routine used to assist in the operation of the computer, e.g., a conversion routine, a sorting routine, a printout routine, or a tracing routine. (Synonymous with utility program.)

routine, working—That routine which produces the results of the problem or program as it was designed, as contrasted with the routines which are designed for support, housekeeping, or to compile, assemble, translate, etc.

routing—The assignment of a communications path for the delivery of a message.

routing, alternate—Assignment of a secondary communications path to a destination if the primary path is unavailable.

routing indicator—An address, or group of characters, in the message header that defines the final circuit or terminal.

routing, message — The function performed at a central message processor of selecting the route, or alternate route if required, for delivery of a message.

row—The horizontal vector of a matrix. *See* card row.

row, binary—1. Pertaining to the binary representation of data or punched cards in which adjacent positions in a row correspond to adjacent bits of the data; for example, each row in an 80-column card may be used to represent 80 consecutive bits or two 40-bit words. 2. A method of representing binary numbers on a card where successive bits are represented by the presence or absence of punches in a successive position in a row as opposed to a series of columns.

row binary card—A card in which the rows are contiguous components of a binary vector. (Contrast with column binary card.)

row, check—A particular check on input from a punched tape may be developed by treating each row as if it represented a symbol, i.e., the check symbol is represented by a check row (or rows) punched on the tape.

row pitch—The distance measured along a paper tape between the centers of adjacent holes.

R register—*See* register, R.

RT (reperforator transmitter) — A receiver-transmitter consisting of a reperforator and a tape distributor, where each unit is independent of the other unit. It is used as a relaying device and is especially suitable for transforming the incoming speed to a different outgoing speed.

rule, else—A catch-all rule in decision tables designed to handle the conditions not covered by exact and explicit rules; it is written by leaving all conditions blank. Action then to be taken may be to halt processing, to note the condition, or to correct the situation and continue processing.

rules, data—The unique group of conditions surrounding data elements, sets, and files, and the action to be taken when the conditions are satisfied. The rules are usually expressed in tabular form, rather than narrative, to ensure complete, consistent, and accurate documentation of the processing methodology, and at the same time to provide flexibility for change.

rules, decision — The programmed criteria which an on-line, real-time system uses to make operating decisions. It is important to periodically review the decision rules which are being used by a system because the nature of the problems to be solved changes over time and because new situations may have arisen which were not at first anticipated.

rules, decision (time-sharing)—*See* time sharing, decision rules.

rules, inhibition—*See* inhibition rules.

rules, priority—*See* priority rules.

rules, syntax—The rules governing sentence structure in a language or statement structure in a language, such as that of a compiler program.

ruly English — An English in which every word has one and only one conceptual meaning, and each concept has only a single word to describe it. Used by the U. S. Patent Office to develop their index codes.

run—1. The act of processing a batch of transactions while under the control of one or more programs, and against all the files that are affected to produce the required output. 2. One performance of a program on a computer. 3. Performance of one routine, or several routines automatically linked so that they form an operating unit, during which manual manipulations are not required of the computer operator.

run book—All materials needed to document a computer application, including problem statement, flow charts, coding, and operating instructions.

run chart—A flowchart of one or more computer runs in terms of input and output.

run diagram—A graphic representation of the files, transactions, information, and data that are to be handled together under the program control to produce the newly updated files, list of changes, or specific reports.

run duration—On the occasion on which, after compiling, the target program is run during the run phase or target phase, the duration or the run is called the run duration, and the compiling is called the compiling duration.

run, history—The printing out of all transactions of a process for reading or recording purposes.

run, location—A routine which locates the correct run on a program tape, whether initiated by another routine or manually.

run, machine—The execution of one or several machine routines that are linked to form one operating unit.

running accumulator—*Same as* storage, pushdown.

running mode, time sharing—*See* time sharing, running mode.

running open—A term used to describe a machine connected to an open line or a line without a battery. A teleprinter under such a condition appears to be running, as the typehammer continually strikes the type box but does not move across the page.

running, parallel—1. A test run in which a newly developed program is processed along with the current program in the computer. 2. The final step in the debugging of a system; this step follows a system test.

run phase—An occasion on which the target program (after compiling) is run is often called the run phase or the target phase or the object phase.

run, production tape—A principal method of obtaining values from PRT (production run tape) , using the relative addressing technique, is through use of the operand call syllable. An instruction is referred to as a syllable, and one word accommodates four syllables. Each operand-call syllable contains the relative address of the location from which it is to obtain information.

run schedule—A specific listing of work to be performed under time required to perform such work.

runs, housekeeping—The activities of sorting, editing, or merging runs needed for the file maintenance—the nonproduction runs. In a special sense, the set-up and clean-up parts of programs in contrast to actual production processing.

runs, program—A run is the same as a program except that a program refers to the writing or coding of the job, whereas the run refers to the actual running of the program. Consequently, programs and runs are synonymous except to denote the time and action being performed.

run, test—A diagnostic run of the program, using manufactured data. The results of this run are checked against the correct answers for this problem.

run, trial—The procedure for using equipment with a sample card deck or part of data which is used on the actual run designed to promote the check for accuracy of methods.

RWD—A shortened program term of designated added instruction to rewind a reel of tape.

R/W (read/write) head — A small electromagnet used for reading, recording, or erasing polarized spots on a magnetic surface. Also called magnetic head, read head, and write head.

S

SABE—Abbreviation for Society for Automation in Business Education.

sampling—1. Obtaining a value of a variable at regular or intermittent intervals. 2. A procedure of systems analysis in which traffic volumes, file activity, and other transfers are estimated on the basis of representative samples taken. 3. A method of communication line control in which messages on a circuit are sampled by a computer that selects only those for which computer processing is required. 4. Sampling provides a random method of checking and control. In using it, a transaction or item is selected and the processing that it undergoes is checked in detail. This provides an indication of accurate and complete processing.

sampling, analog—The process by which the computer selects individual hybrid input signals from the process, converts them to an equivalent binary form, and stores the data in memory.

sampling rate—The rate at which measurements of physical quantities are made, e.g., if it is desired to calculate the velocity of a missile and its position is measured each millisecond, then the sampling rate is 1,000 measurements per second.

satellite computer, real-time—As a satellite computer the real-time system relieves the larger system of time consuming input and output functions as well as performing preprocessing and postprocessing functions, such as validity editing and formatting for print.

satellite processor—The usually small processor designed especially and primarily for card-to-tape conversion, printing of tape contents, and other selected, high-volume operations; frequently used to support and add to the capacity of a large processor to further increase its productivity.

saturating integrator—*Same as* integrator, incremental.

saturation testing—The testing of a program by pushing through a great many messages in an attempt to find errors.

scale—1. A rulerlike drawing placed on the graph to aid in the determination of values within the plotting grid. 2. A range of values frequently dictated by the computer wordlength or routine at hand. 3. To alter the units in which the variables are expressed, in order to bring all quantities within a

given range. 4. To change the units in which a variable is expressed so as to bring it within the capacity of the machine or the program at hand.

scale, binary—*See* binary scale.

scale coefficient—*Same as* scale factor.

scale factor—1. A number used as a multiplier or divisor that is chosen because it will cause a set of quantities occuring in a problem to fall within an acceptable range of values. 2. The coefficient necessary to convert a scale or instrument reading to the value of a quantity being measured.

scale factor, time—*Same as* time scale.

scale, fixed radix — A standard positional numeration system designed so that the significance of the successive digit positions are successive integral powers of an integer, referred to as the radix or base. The range for positive radix is from zero to one less than the radix, and the negative integral powers of the radix permit the representation of fractions.

scale, label—Numerical labels placed next to the scale to indicate the value of the scale at that point.

scale operation—*See* operation, scale.

scaler—A specific unit with an output variable which equals the input variable multiplied by some constant.

scale radix—*Same as* radix notation.

scaler, quantity — A specific quantity which has magnitude but not direction, i.e., the magnitude of a vector quantity, as contrasted to vector cells of multiple values. Scalers are single, such as volume, size, temperature, etc., while vector quantities, such as wind velocity, have both magnitude and direction.

scale, time—*See* time scale.

scale, variable time—*See* time scale.

scaling—1. The conversion of a standard signal into the corresponding engineering units. 2. Use of a factor to multiply the results obtained in a problem so that the results will be within a range that can be expressed by the machine.

scaling, analog—The scaling of a problem involves consideration of the limited range of values obtainable on the computer. For example, reference levels of -100 to $+100$ volts may be available, but higher or lower voltages are not attainable. If the output of an amplifier were driven beyond these values, the amplifier would saturate; its output would become distorted, and meters and servomechanisms would go off-scale. Therefore, it is necessary to restrict the variable so that all points within the computer are within the prescribed limits. In general, the various circuits and devices are protected against damage from an overload, so that no actual harm will result. In addition, there are usually warning lights to indicate an overload.

scan—1. To examine stored information for a specific purpose as for content or for arrangement. 2. To examine the status of communication lines or other input/output channels to determine whether data is being received or transmitted.

scan, divided slit—A device, in optical character recognition (OCR), which scans an input character at given intervals to obtain its horizontal and vertical components. This scanning device consists of a narrow column of photoelectric cells.

scan, forward—An editing operation which makes an output word conform to the control word by comparing positions from right to left and adding punctuation, such as decimals and dollar signs.

scan, mark—*See* mark scan.

scan, MICR—*See* MICR scan.

scanner—1. An instrument which automatically samples or interrogates the state of various processes, files, conditions, or physical states and initiates action in accordance with the information obtained. 2. A scanner instrument sequentially checks each of the sites on a particular leased line for traffic. Another scanner at the control center can sequentially check several lines to determine whether a message is present or not.

scanner, bar-code—An optical scanning unit that can read documents encoded in a special bar code representing digits at a 50 character-per-second speed, is an element in the data-system. The scanner opens up various systems concepts for such tasks as billing, couponing, retail item control, and other forms of returnable media.

The scanner can read either lithographed or computer-printed bar codes (vertical or horizontal bars or lines) at speeds of 30 to 45 documents per minute. As it scans, it transfers the encoded data to a buffer for direct transmission or to punched paper tape and printer for pretransmission editing (some systems).

scanner, flying-spot—An optical character reading device which uses a moving spot of light to scan a sample space or area by applying a photoelectric transducer to sense the intensity of the transmitted or reflected light, which varies in accordance with the data being sent, i.e., differing reflectances and intensities.

scanner, interrupt—External devices are continuously scanned for interrupt requests. A scanner in the computer counts through the nonpriority external device addresses sequentially, each time asking if the addressed device is requesting an interrupt. When an interrupt request is found, the scanner will stop at that address and attempt to interrupt the computer program.

scanner, Luhn—A scanning machine invented by an IBM employee, S. P. Luhn, for photoelectrical scanning of punched cards as they are fed through the machine and with some search capabilities.

scanner magnetic ink—A machine which reads numbers designed in a special type font and printed in a magnetic (iron oxide) ink.

scanner mechanical—An optical character recognition device which projects an input character into a rotating disk which has a series of small uniformly spaced apertures on its outer edge. A light passing through the apertures is collected by a photoelectric cell which results in an analog waveform.

scanner selector—In cases where more than one communication multiplexer is used on a single input/output computer channel, a scanner selector must be employed to control the simultaneous operation of the multiplexers. A maximum of four multiplexers may be connected to one scanner selector.

scanner, visual—1. A device that scans optically and usually generates an analog or digital signal. 2. A device that optically scans printed or written data and generates their digital representations.

scanning—The action of comparing input variables to determine a particular action.

scanning errors, orthocode—An orthocode format that uses five rows of bar codes and several columns of correction codes that make defacement or incorrect reading virtually impossible, is said to preclude scanning errors. The control codes also help regenerate partially obliterated data. (Honeywell)

scanning limits—The action of comparing input variables against either prestored or calculated high and/or low limits to determine if an alarm condition is present.

scanning loop, central—*See* loop, central scanning.

scanning machine—A machine which automatically reads printed data and converts it into machine language. There are two basic types—optical scanners and magnetic ink scanners.

scanning, optical—A technique for machine recognition of characters.

scanning rate (or speed)—The speed at which a computer can select, convert, and compare an analog input variable to its high and/or low limits.

scan period—The time during which the screen is swept by the electron beam in electrostatic storage tubes for the sole purpose of regenerating or restoring the charge distribution which represents the stored data.

scan rate—The rate at which a control computer periodically checks a controlled quantity.

scan, reverse—The specific editing operation which supresses zeros, i.e., replaces zeros with blanks, and thus eliminates the zeros, and the zero suppression word mark.

scan, slit-divided—A device, in optical character recognition (OCR), which scans an input character at given intervals to obtain its horizontal and vertical components. This scanning device consists of a narrow column of photoelectric cells.

scatter gap—The alignment deviation (of magnetic recording head gaps) for groups of heads for several racks of a magnetic tape handler.

scatter/gather by record—A power of the central processors that enhances sorting and merging capabilities. It permits tighter packing of data on tape, and saves tape time. But the feature is not limited to tapes; it works with all subsystems.

scatter loading—The process of loading a program into main memory, such that each section or segment of the program occupies a single, connected memory area, but the several sections of the program need not be adjacent to each other.

scatter read—The ability of a computer to distribute or scatter data into several memory areas as it is being entered into the system on magnetic tape.

scatter-read/gather-write — Gather-write is the ability to place the information from several nonadjacent locations in core storage (for example, several logical records) into a single physical record such as a tape block. Scatter-read is the ability to place the information from a physical record into several nonadjacent locations in core storage.

scatter read operation—*See* read operation, scatter.

scatter read/write—An operation performed under program control that reads a block of data from tape and breaks it up into processable elements. After processing, data is recombined and written on tape as a block.

scatter write operation—The process of obtaining various data elements from one location and simultaneously transferring them to several output areas.

scheduled down time—The determined or required idle time necessary for normal servicing of computer equipment during which such equipment is unavailable for operations. This is usually expressed as a percent of total available time. It is also known as preventive maintenance time.

scheduled engineering time—*See* time, scheduled engineering.

scheduled maintenance — *See* maintenance, scheduled.

scheduled maintenance time — *See* time, scheduled maintenance.

scheduled operation — The periods of time during which the user plans to use specified equipment. Such a notice must be made a given number of hours in advance. The scheduled hours of operation may be modified in the event of an emergency. The hours rescheduled as a result of equipment failure usually are not considered as scheduled hours of operation in computing equipment effectiveness.

schedule job—A control program that is used to examine the input work queue and to select the next job to be processed.

schedule maintenance (executive)—The acceptance of job requests from an external medium and the inclusion of these requests in a job request schedule. The executive will reference the job request schedule to determine the next job to be initiated. Previously submitted requests may be deleted.

scheduler—A special system of the executive software section. The scheduler controls the time when the execution of the program will be performed.

scheduler, program—The scheduler is called at regular intervals to decide which program in memory is to be run. A running program is temporarily terminated each time its alloted time has run out, or when it requires input/output operations with a device that is busy. A program may be terminated temporarily by user intervention to the scheduler, or it may suspend its own operation. Temporary termination does not remove the program from memory. A program may be dumped and permanently discontinued by calling the scheduler and allocator.

schedule, rung—A specific listing of work to be performed under time required to perform such work.

scheduler, work process—Schedules the operating time of the over-all electronic data processing activity in order to ensure that the data-processing ecuipment is effectively and efficiently utilized.

scheduling algorithm—A set of rules that is included in the scheduling routine of the executive program. The scheduling algorithm determines the length of a user's quantum and the frequency with which this quantum is repeated.

scheduling, dynamic — Scheduling that changes with the different demands that are made on the system rather than being fixed as in conventional applications.

scheduling resources, time sharing—*See* time sharing, scheduling resources.

scheduling routine, main—*See* routine, main scheduling.

scheduling rules, time sharing — *See* time sharing, scheduling rules.

scheduling user tasks, time sharing—*See* time sharing, scheduling user tasks.

scheme, randomizing — *See* randomizing scheme.

schemes, interrupt (time sharing)—*See* time sharing, interrupt schemes.

science, management—The field of management science is extending the computer far beyond the automation of routine accounting operation and into the complex decision-making process of management. Through revolutionary-computer programming techniques such as simulation, the objective, scientific approach of management science is providing increased management capability and control. In addition to the physical or operational processes like inventory management, product planning and control, resource allocation or market forecasting, this also includes the fiscal processes such as bond management, capital investment, risk analysis, profit planning and product pricing. Manufacturer's broad resources are preparing to meet management's growing demand for this expanded capability and to extend the tradition of total systems capability into new revolutionary data-processing techniques and applications.

scientific application — Various uses of the computer which are classified as nonbusiness and related to various scientific or research problem solving questions or programs. Such programs are relatively characterized by a low volume of input and distinctly lack volumes of processing and, again, a low volume of output.

scientific computer—Scientific problems are characterized by a minimum of input, a maximum of compute, and a maximum of iteration. Management science applications have these attributes, plus the massive data loads of the normal commercial applications. The requirements for a computer to handle these special applications are a very large memory, extremely high-speed arithmetics, and a very large variety of floating-point arithmetic commands.

scientific data processing—The processing of data involved with solving mathematical functions or equations.

scientific notation—A notion in which quantities are expressed as a fractional part (mantissa) and a power of ten (characteristic).

scientific subroutines—1. An extensive library of subroutines complementing the capabilities of the FORTRAN compilers. This library includes standard FORTRAN routines —such as square root, exponential, trigonometric, an logarithmic functions—as well as matrix, statistical and other routines. Scientific hardware, though not required by these subroutines, increases their operating speed. 2. Computer systems have available to them several subroutines which perform standard mathematical operations. These operations include fixed-point multiplication and division; floating-point addition, subtraction, multiplication, and division; square-root extraction; matrix and statistical functions; and calculation of logarithmic and trigonometric functions.

scientific system — A particular system de-

voted principally to computation, in contrast to a commercial or data-processing system on which the main emphasis is on file updating rather than performance of calculations.

SCOPE (System to Coordinate the Operation of Peripheral Equipment)—1. A group of Honeywell routines that optimize the use of peripheral devices (on H-200, H-800, H-1800 and other computers) during parallel operation. Card readers, card punches, high-speed readers are controlled for simultaneous operation at full speed. 2. A group of independent routines which control the automatic transfer of data between pairs of peripheral devices, such as magnetic tape to punched card, or paper tape to magnetic tape. "Own-coding" routines may be included to perform such functions as editing and unblocking of records. (Honeywell)

scramble time—*See* time, scramble.

scratchpad memory — A high-speed memory device used to store the location of an interrupted program, and to retrieve the latter after the interrupting program has been completed.

scratchpad memory locations—The scratchpad memory contains individually addressable scratchpad storage locations each of which can store the address of a main-memory location. Scratchpad locations may be used for temporary storage or for indirect addressing of main memory. Only one character is necessary in an instruction address to reference a scratchpad location. This address is interpreted as a reference to the main-memory location whose address is stored in the referenced scratchpad location. Memory space is conserved by this method of addressing, since only one character is used in the address portion of the instruction. Operating time is also reduced, due to the extremely fast access time of the scratched memory (some systems) .

scratchpad storage — *Same as* scratchpad memory.

scratch tape (sorting)—Tape (s) used to store intermediate-pass data during a sort program.

screen—1. The surface in an electrostatic cathode-ray storage tube where electrostatic charges are stored, and by means of which information is displayed or stored temporarily. 2. To make a preliminary selection from a set of entities, the selection criteria being based on a given set of rules or conditions.

script, machine—*See* data, machine readable.

SDA, (source-data automation)—The many methods of recording information in coded forms on paper tapes, punched cards, or tags that can be used over and over again to produce many other records without rewriting.

SDI—Abbreviation for selective dissemination of information. Related to a particular literature search notification and hard copy supply system and which thus serves clients with internal or external reports, articles, or other documents, i.e., any system for selectively distributing information in accordance with given profiles.

search — A systematic examination of the available information in a specific field of interest.

search, area—An area search relates to information retrieval by examining a collection of data or documents, but specifically those within a particular subset according to some criteria determination, i.e., belonging to some class, category, geographical area, location, etc.

search, binary—A technique for finding a particular item in an ordered set of items by repeatedly dividing in half the portion of the ordered set containing the sought-for item until only the sought-for item remains.

search, chain—See chain search.

search, chaining—See chain search.

search, conjunctive — A search defined in terms of a logical produce, i.e., conjunctive form, in contrast to a disjunctive form, or logical sum.

search cycle—The sequence of events or the time interval needed for the occurrence of a fixed number of events required to complete a single search operation, such as carrying out a comparison.

search, dichotomizing—A search in which the series of items is divided into two parts, one of which is rejected, and the process is repeated on the unrejected part until the item with the desired property is found. This process usually depends upon the presence of a known sequence in the series of items.

search, disjunctive—A search defined in terms of a logical sum, i.e., disjunctive form, in contrast to a conjunctive form or logical product.

search Fibonacci—See Fibonacci search.

searching storage—Same as storage, content addressed.

search, literature—A particularized search of published items of information which is usually made in order to become aware of unique characteristics of certain subjects prior to developing full research on the subject.

search-read function—In a search or search-read function, the identifier word (a full length computer word) is stored in a special register in the channel synchronizer and compared with each word read by the peripheral unit.

search time—Time required to locate a particular field of data in storage. Searching requires a comparison of each field with a predetermined standard until an identity is obtained. A contrast with access time, which is based upon locating data by means of the address of its storage location.

secondary storage—Same as storage, external.

second generation computer—See computer, second generation.

second-level address—Same as indirect address.

second, millimicro—Same as nanosecond. One billionth of a second.

second order subroutine—See subroutine, second order.

second remove subroutine — See subroutine, second order.

section—In the COBOL system, a sequence of one or more paragraphs designed in accordance with COBOL rules. Also defined as one of the portions of the program.

section, arithmetic—The portion of the hardware of a computer in which arithmetic and logical operations are performed. The arithmetic unit generally consists of an accumulator, some special registers (for the storage of operands and results) and shifting and sequencing circuitry. (Synonymous with ALU.)

section, input—Same as input block.

section name—The distinct qualifying term available for a paragraph name.

section number—A number that identifies a particular section in a series of sections that make up a file.

section, operator intervention—That portion of the control equipment through which operators can intervene in normal programming operations.

section text—Part of a load module which has computer instructions in final form and data defined with specified initial values.

sector—Similar to a binary word except it may include characters or bits not allotted to the programmer. Example: A word can be 27 bits, plus sign. However, the sector can contain 32 bits—the remaining 4 bits may be used by the logic in the computer for spacing, etc.

sector, independent — A device on certain tabulators which allows the first item of a series of similar data to be printed, and inhibits some or all printing of the rest of the series.

sectors—The smallest addressable portion of an auxiliary storage track or band.

security, file—See file security.

security of user files, time sharing—See time sharing, security of user files.

seek—1. A term applied to the process of obtaining specific records from a random-access file. The number of seeks is the number of file items inspected before the desired item is found. 2. To look for data according to information given regarding that data; occasionally used interchangeably and erroneously for search, scan, and screen.

seek time—The time required to make the auxiliary storage unit ready to access a specified location by selection or positioning. The range is from the minimum time for the best possible case to the maximum time for the worst possible case.

segment—1. In a routine too long to fit into internal storage, a part short enough to be stored in the internal storage. These parts contain the addresses of succeeding parts of the routine. Routines that exceed internal storage capacity may be automatically divided into segments by a compiler. 2. The process of dividing a routine into an integral number of subroutines with each part capable of being completely stored in the internal storage and containing the instructions to jump to other segments. 3. To store part of a program or routine separately, usually in external or intermediate storage areas and devices to be brought in as needed to high-speed storage.

segmentation — A programmer-defined and monitor-implemented technique of dividing a program into essentially self-contained segments so that only certain parts need be in memory at any instant. Segmentation may be performed to allow several programs to be in memory at the same time or to allow a program to be operated that is too large for the available memory space.

segmentation and control, automatic—Automatic segmentation and control permits the computer to efficiently handle programs that exceed the core-memory capacity of a particular system configuration. Without re-programming, the computer automatically adapts its operational procedures to allow the processing of any program on any system configuration. Segments of all programs concurrently being executed are "fitted" into available memory space for execution. Thus, the user is not forced to install a system of maximum memory capacity to accommodate one long program; he need not purchase more equipment than he normally needs for efficient operation.

segmentation, COBOL—COBOL programs can be segmented by use of priority numbers on each section.

segment, inclusive — In a program overlay structure, two or more different segments can be in the main memory simultaneously, whereas normally all inclusive segments lie on a single path from the root segment to the lowest segment.

segmenting—The act of dividing information into unique sections which can be handled as a unit.

segmenting, program—See program segmenting.

segment mark—A special character written on tape to separate each section of a tape file.

segment, program—See program segment.

segments exclusive—Relating to an overlay program structure that is not resident in main memory simultaneously with other parts. Very large programs are often segmented into overlays, and such segments are called into memory from auxilliary storage and thus main memory capacity is not over-

strained. Overlay segments are ordered as first-level, second-level, etc.

segment size, program—See program segment size.

segments, overlays—See overlays segments.

segregating unit—A segregating unit pulls or separates individual cards from a group. This machine is equipped with two feeding magazines and four receivers that interfile or segregate the cards in various sequences—at the rate of hundreds of cards per minute from each feeding magazine.

select—1. To choose one of several alternate subroutines from a file of subroutines. 2. To activate the control and data channels to and from an I/O (input/output) unit, preparatory to "reading from" or "writing on" the selected device. 3. To take the alternative A if the report on a condition is of one state, and alternate B if the report on the condition is of another state.

selectable-length word—See word selectable-length.

select, data—A special selection operation in which one set of items is taken for printing or punching from several sets presented on tape.

selected-length field — See field, selected-length.

select-error—Signifies that a tape-transport unit "select-error" has occurred; e.g., that more than one transport in the system has been assigned to the same select code or that no transport has been assigned the programmed select code.

selecting—A data-processing function of pulling from a mass of data certain items that require special attention. Typical selections are: items containing specific digits, items for a specific date, items higher than a specific number, items below a specific number, items below two specific numbers, etc.

selecting data—The process of extracting pertinent or specific information from a large body of data or the removal of certain records from the file.

select input pulse, partial—See pulse, partial write.

selection check—A check (usually an automatic check) to verify that the correct register, or other device, is selected in the interpretation of an instruction.

selection control—See control selection.

selection, job-request—See job request selection.

selection, priority—Same as job request selection.

selection, program—To change from one job to another, the operator simply turns the program-selector knob. There are no control bars, wired panels, or control tapes to change. Switching from one job to another is a matter of seconds, not minutes.

selection ratio—The ratio of the least magnetomotive force used to select a cell or core, to the maximum magnetomotive force used, which is not intended to select a cell or core.

selection-replacement technique — A technique used in the internal portion of a sort program. The results of the comparisons between groups of records are stored for later use.

selection switch, Rajchman—*Same as* storage, core-rope.

selective assembly—Run tapes that contain specific programs selected by the programmer from both an input deck of new programs and a tape file of previously processed symbolic programs.

selective calling—1. The ability of a transmitting station to specify which of several stations is to receive a message. 2. A form of teletypewriter communications system. One loop may include several machines, but with selective calling, only the machine selected will respond. The device that controls the individual machines in response to a selective call (call-directing characters) is called a stunt box.

selective digit emitter—*See* digit emitter, selective.

selective dump—A dump of a selected area of internal storage.

selective listing—The output printing of data which needs various sets of predetermined criteria.

selective trace—A tracing routine that uses only specified criteria. Typical criteria are: instruction type (arithmetic jump), instruction location (specific region), and data location (specific region).

selectivity, adjacent-channel—Characteristic of a receiver which governs its ability to reject symbols or channels adjacent to that of the desired signals.

select lines—In a core-memory array, the leads that pass through magnetic cores and carry the selecting currents.

selector—1. A device for directing electrical input pulses onto one of two output lines, depending upon the presence or absence of a predetermined accompanying control pulse. 2. A mechanism that reports a condition and causes a card or an operation to be selected accordingly.

selector channel—Selector channels are used where high-speed devices are to be attached to a system. A single channel can operate only one I/O (input/output) device at a time. Two or more channels connected to any computer system provide the ability to read, write, and compute from multiple input/output devices.

selector digit—*See* digit selector.

selectors — Automatic switches that provide tremendous flexibility in system processing. They allow a computer to consider a variety of values and operations at any time during a program and to pick out the appropriate one, based on input coding or processed results up to that point. They permit the computer to reuse earlier steps in a program with new factors and functions. *See* logical choice.

selector, scanner—*See* scanner selector.

select switch, tape—*See* switch, tape select.

self-adapting—Pertaining to the ability of a computer system to change its performance characteristics in response to its environment.

self-checking code—A code in which errors produce forbidden combinations. A single-error detecting code produces a forbidden combination if a digit gains or loses a single bit. A double-error detecting code produces a forbidden combination if a digit gains or loses either one or two bits and so forth. (Related to self-checking number and error-detecting code.)

self-checking number—A number with a suffix figure related to the figure(s) of the number, used to check the number after it has been transferred from one medium or device to another. (Related to check bit, modulo-N check, and error-detecting code.)

self-checking numeral — *See* numeral, self-checking.

self-complementing code—A machine language in which the code of the complement of a digit is the complement of the code of the digit.

self-demarcating—*See* code, self-demarcating.

self-demarking code — 1. A code in which the symbols are so arranged and selected that the generation of false combinations by interaction of segments from two succesive codes is prevented. 2. *Same as* error-detecting code.

self-learning—A special capability of a device or machine such that it can improve its capability in decision-making as programmed with instructions and based on information received, new instructions received, results of calculations, or environmental change, i.e., error histories and historical performance can and does relate to improving techniques.

self-modification program—*See* program, self modification.

self-organization—The capability of a machine to automatically organize a program into a logical sequence order or efficient steps of execution.

self-organizing — Having the capability of classification or internal rearrangement, depending on the environment, in accordance with given instructions or a set of rules.

self-organizing machine—A class of machines that may be characterized loosely as containing a variable network in which the elements are organized by the machine itself, without external intervention, to meet the criteria of successful operation.

self-organizing system — A system that is capable of internal reconfiguration in response to externally occurring events.

self-relative addressing—In relative addressing, if the number added corresponds to the address of the instruction under consideration, the term is usually, self-relative addressing.

self-repairing—An unusual characteristic or capability of some machines to detect, locate, repair, remove, or change (sidetrack), various types of malfunctions (or parts) during its operations and without human intervention other than supplementing such repairs as making components or parts available for automatic insertion, connections, etc.

semanteme—An element of language that expresses a definite image or idea, e.g., the word tree. (Contrasted with morpheme, an element of language that conveys relations between nouns, verbs, etc.)

semantic errors—Semantic errors are concerned with the meaning or intent of the programmer and are definitely his responsibility. Consequently, he is provided with an extensive set of debugging aids for manipulating and referencing a program when in search of errors in the logic and analysis.

semantic matrix—A graphical device for plotting the precise elements of meaning that have been ascertained from the semantic analysis of a concept in a standard conventional form.

semantic remote-control system errors—*See* remote control system (semantic errors).

semantics—The study of meanings; the significance and connotation of words.

semantics, formal—A language for computer-oriented languages which acts as a compiler-compiler and contains formal semantics.

semantics, language theory—The meaning of a sentence as contrasted to syntax, which is the structure of a sentence.

semiautomatic message-switching center—A center at which an operator routes messages according to information contained in them.

semiautomatic-switching center—A point at which messages are routed by an operator according to the message content.

semifixed length record—*See* record, semifixed length.

send-only service—Service in which the data-communication channel is capable of transmitting signals, but is not equipped to receive signals.

send-receive, automatic—A combination teletypewriter transmitter and receiver with transmission capability from either keyboard or paper tape. Most often used in a half-duplex circuit.

send-request circuit—*See* circuit, send-request.

sense—1. To examine data particularly relative to a set of criteria. 2. To determine the present arrangement of some element of hardware, especially a manually set switch. 3. To detect special signals. 4. To read holes in paper or cards and magnetic spots on tape, drums, etc.

sense and control lines, external—These lines can be used to inform the central

processor of the condition of any two-level possibility such as: switch on or off: temperature normal or abnormal, voltage in regulation or out, etc. The same lines may be used for control purposes, each capable of providing a two-level control signal to any external device. Typical applications include: turn indicating lights on or off at remote areas, control of relays in special equipment, initiation of analog sequences, etc.

sense light—A light that may be turned on or off and may be interrogated by the computer to cause a program branch.

sense, mark—To mark a position on a punched card by an electrically conductive pencil, for later conversion to machine punching.

sense switch—1. A switch on the console of a computer that may be set up or down. Statements may be included in a program to test the condition of these switches and to vary program execution based on these settings. 2. *See* alteration switch.

sensible, machine—*See* machine sensible.

sensing, automatic display flags—Control state or mode permits the visual display to jump, conditioned on the states of its own flags (light pen flag, edge flag, stop flag, etc.). This reduces the number of program interrupts.

sensing, mark—A technique for detecting special pencil marks entered in special places on a punch card, and automatically translating the marks into punched holes.

sensing signal—A specific signal which is often translated at the start of a message for the purpose of initiating circuit operation at the receiving end of a circuit.

sensing station—*See* station, sensing.

sensitive-language, computer—*See* language, computer-sensitive.

sensitivity—The degree of response of an instrument or control unit to change in the incoming signal.

sensor—A device that permits a computer to obtain analog information concerning temperatures, flows, pressure, and so forth.

sensors, dialectric—A method used in reading data from paper tape by a special sensor.

sentence—In COBOL, a sequence of one or more statements specifying one or more operations, according to certain rules, and terminated by a period.

sentinel—A symbol to mark a unit of information, e.g., the end of an item, field, block, tape, file, etc.

separating character—*See* character, separating.

separation symbol, item—A control symbol which indicates beginning of an item.

separator—A flag that separates and organizes items of data.

separator, word—A character in machine coding that segregates fields.

SEPOL—Soil-Engineering Problem-Oriented Language.

septenary number — A number, usually of more than one figure, representing a sum, in which the quantity represented by each figure is based on a radix of seven. The figures used are: 0, 1, 2, 3, 4, 5, and 6.

sequence — 1. To put a set of symbols into an arbitrarily defined order; i.e., to select A if A is greater than or equal to B, or select B if A is less than B. 2. In sorting, the planned ordering of items in a data element according to the processor-collation table. 3. An arbitrarily defined order of a set of symbols; i.e., an orderly progression of items of information or of operations in accordance with some rule.

sequence break (sorting) — That point in a file between the end of one string and start of another.

sequence, calling — A specified arrangement of instructions and data necessary to set up and call a given subroutine.

sequence check — A data-processing operation designed to check the sequence of the items in a file.

sequence checking — A sequence check is used to prove that a set of data is arranged in either ascending or descending order before it is processed. It is generally a mechanized operation performed in a separate machine run or simultaneously with another operation run.

sequence-checking routine — A routine that checks every instruction executed, and prints out certain data; e.g., to print out the coded instructions with addresses, and the contents of each of several registers, or it may be designed to print out only selected data, such as transfer instructions and the quantity actually transferred.

sequence, collating — A sequence of characters as arranged in the order of their relative precedence. The collating sequence of a particular computer is determined as part of its design; each character acceptable to the computer has a preassigned place in this sequence. A collating sequence is used primarily in comparing operations.

sequence (consecutive) computer — *Same as* computer, sequential.

sequence, control — The normal order of selection of instructions for execution. In some computers one of the addresses in each instruction specifies the control sequence. In most computers, the sequence is consecutive except where a transfer occurs.

sequence control register — *See* register, sequence control.

sequence control tape — A tape that contains the sequence of instructions required for solving a problem.

sequence counter — *Same as* register, sequence control.

sequence error — A card is out of sequence within an object program.

sequence monitor — Computer monitoring of the step-by-step actions that should be taken by the operator during a startup and/or shutdown of a power unit. As a minimum, the computer would check that certain milestones had been reached in the operation of the unit. The maximum coverage would have the computer check that each required step is performed, that the correct sequence is followed, and that every checked point falls within its prescribed limits. Should an incorrect action or result occur, the computer would record the fault and notify the operator.

sequence packing — A procedure for loading the upper half of an accumulator with the first data word, shifting this into the lower half, loading the second datum, shifting, etc., so that the three data words are thus packed in sequence.

sequence, pseudorandom number — A sequence of numbers, determined by some defined arithmetic process that is satisfactorily random for a given purpose, such as satisfying one or more of the standard statistical tests for randomness. Such a sequence may approximate any one of several statistical distributions, e.g., uniform distribution or a normal (Gaussian) distribution.

sequence, queue (any) — A collection of items in the system which are waiting for the attention of the processors. The any-sequence queue is organized so that items may be removed from the collection without regard to the sequence in which they entered it.

sequencer — A machine which puts items of information into a particular order; e.g., it will determine whether A is greater than, equal to, or less than B and sort or order accordingly.

sequence, random — A sequence that is not arranged by ascending or descending keys, as in alphameric or numeric sequences, but is instead arranged in an organized fashion in bulk storage by locations determined by calculations performed on keys to develop addresses. The calculations are repeated in order to acquire the address and locate the item desired.

sequence, random-number — An unpredictable array of numbers produced by change, and satisfying one or more of the tests for randomness.

sequence register — 1. A counter in a computer that is pulsed or reset following the execution of an instruction, to form the new memory address that locates the next instruction. 2. A special register that, when activated, designates the address of the next instruction to be performed by the computer.

sequence timer — A succession of time-delay circuits arranged so that completion of the delay in one circuit initiates a delay in the following circuit.

sequencing — The act which puts into order various data as to rank, time, or other predetermined order classification.

sequencing, automatic — The ability of equipment to put information in order or in a connected series without human intervention.

sequencing by merging—A technique of repeated merging, splitting, and remerging can be and is often used to place items into an organized arrangement.

sequencing criteria (sorting)—The fields in a record which determine, or are used as a basis for determining, the sequence of records in a file.

sequencing key (sorting)—The field in a record which determines, or is used as a basis for determining, the sequence of records in a file.

sequencing, time—Switching signals generated by a program purely as a function of accurately measured elapsed time.

sequential-access storage—A storage technique in which the stored items of information become available only in a one after the other sequence, whether or not all the information or only some of it is desired, e.g., magnetic-tape storage. (Related to serial storage, and contrasted with random-access storage.)

sequential collating—Sequencing a group of records by comparing the key of one record with another record until equality, greater than, or less than, is determined.

sequential computer—The equipment which performs complete operating system activity, but which is designed so the instructions are normally followed in a specific sequence.

sequential control—1. The manner of control of a computer in which instructions to it are set up in a sequence and are fed in that sequence to the computer during solution of a problem. 2. A mode of computer operation in which instructions are executed in consecutive order, unless otherwise specified by a jump.

sequential data set, indexed—*See* data set, indexed sequential.

sequential element—A device having at least one output channel and one or more input channels, all characterized by discrete states, such that the state of each output channel is determined by the previous states of the input channels.

sequential file—*See* file, sequential.

sequential logic element—*See* element, sequential logic.

sequential operation—Pertaining to the performance of operations one after the other.

sequential operation, automatic—To develop a series or family of solutions from a set of equations, various initial conditions are recalculated with other parameters.

sequential processing—The procedure of processing information or data records in the same order in which they happen.

sequential programming—*See* programming, sequential.

sequential queue—The first-in-first-out method of queuing items waiting for the processor.

sequential testing—A series of tests performed in a predetermined order and requiring repeated observations.

serial—1. The internal handling of data in sequential fashion. (Contrasts with parallel.) 2. To handle one after the other in a single facility, such as transfer or store in a digit-by-digit time sequence. 3. Pertaining to the time-sequencing of two or more processes. 4. Pertaining to the time-sequencing of two or more similar or identical processes, using the same facilities for the successive processes. 5. Pertaining to the time-sequential processing of the individual parts of a whole, such as the bits of a character, the characters of a word, etc., using the same facilities for successive parts.

serial access—Sequential access to elements of data (bits, characters, or words) within all or part of a storage device. For example, storage in which words, within a group of words (as on a track of a magnetic drum), appear one after the other in time sequence is said to be serial by word. Access may still be parallel by character or by bit, despite being serial by word.

serial addition—*See* addition, serial.

serial arithmetic—*See* arithmetic, serial.

serial-by-bit—This equipment has features which permit it to handle bits of a character in a fashion of one immediately following another. Characters may be handled either serially or in parallel.

serial-by-character—*See* serial-by-bit.

serial computer—A computer in which digits or data lines are handled sequentially by separate units of the computer. Mixed serial and parallel machines are frequently called serial or parallel according to the way arithmetic processes are performed. An example of a serial computer is one which handles decimal digits serially although it might handle the bits which comprise a digit either serially or in parallel. (Contrasted with parallel computer.)

serial digital computer—A machine in which the digits are handled in a serial manner, especially in the arithmetic unit.

serial digit operation—*See* digit operation, serial.

serial flow—The system of operations such that each operation is performed singly and not at the same time other tasks are being completed, i.e., the work moves along a single line or channel where one type of operation is performed in succession or at each station and none are performed at the same time or simultaneously with other tasks. Opposite from flow, parallel.

serial full adder—*See* adder, full (serial).

serial half adder—*See* adder, half (serial).

serial half subtracter—As regards half subtracters, when serial representation is used, a serial half subtracter may be formed from a two-input subtracter with a digit delay element connected between the borrow output and the subtrahend input.

serialize—To change from parallel-by-bit to serial-by-bit.

serial number control — *See* control, serial number.

serial numbering—The serial numbering of orders, invoices, checks, etc., provides control while the data is in transit. Each item or document in the series or group is assigned a successive number; an indication of the beginning and ending of numbers accompanies the group.

serial operation—1. A type of information transfer within a digital computer whereby all digits of a word are handled sequentially rather than simultaneously. 2. Sequential performance of arithmetic or data transmission on one character at a time.

serial-parallel—1. A combination of serial and parallel; e.g., serial by character, parallel by bits comprising the character. 2. Descriptive of a device that converts a serial input into a parallel output.

serial printer — The specific output device which prints one character at a time, such as typewriters, and some types of printers.

serial processing—Reading or writing of the item following the one currently being processed.

serial programming—The programming of a computer by which only one arithmetical or logical operation can be executed at one time; e.g., a sequential operation. (Contrasted with multiple programming.)

serial storage—*See* storage, serial.

serial transfer—In a serial transfer, the bits stored in a string of flip-flops are caused to move along the string from one flip-flop to the next, toward one end of the string, so that all of the bits eventually pass through the end flip-flop. This process is generally called shifting, and a string of flip-flops connected in this manner make up a shift register. The bits shifted out of one register can be shifted into another similar register, thereby shifting the contents from one register to another.

serial transmission — To move data in sequence, one bit at a time, as contrasted with parallel transmission.

serial word operation—Th specific feature of certain handling equipment in which words are read one after another, in groups.

series, Fibonacci—*See* Fibonacci series.

series, time—The discrete or continuous sequence of quantitative data assigned to specific moments in time, and usually studied with respect to their distribution in time.

serviceability, ratio—It is that ratio of the serviceable time to the sum of the serviceable and the fault time, or of the availability ratio, which is the sum of the serviceable time, fault time, routine maintenance time, and the supplementary maintenance time.

service bits—Those overhead bits that are not check bits, e.g., request for repetition, numbering sequence, etc.

service bureau—The data processing organization which offers leased time on computers or other peripheral equipment; sells manpower on an hourly basis to businesses or organizations.

service engineering — Service engineering provides a complete world-wide range of support capability for systems engineering and planning; installation and checkout; maintenance and operator training; contractual preventive maintenance; regional service and parts; factory equipment repair; and equipment modernization, rehabilitation, and expansion. In order to provide every user with continued support in the maintenance and operation of his equipment, field engineers maintain close customer liaison through courtesy calls, technical assistance by phone, and provision of the latest engineering and new product bulletins. This close contact permits the accumulation and evaluation of reliability data based upon all systems in the field, a significant factor in designing new equipment and improving the dependability and up-time ratios of customer equipment.

service, full-duplex—A service in which the data-communication channel is capable of simultaneous and independent transmission and reception.

service, half-duplex—A type of communication channel which is capable of transmitting and receiving signals, but is not capable for simultaneous and independent transmission and reception.

service, mode—An operational mode for the handling of malfunctions or errors in words, etc.

service organization, computer — *See* computer service organization.

service program—*See* program, service.

service, receive-only—Service in which the data-communication channel is capable of receiving signals, but is not equipped to transmit signals.

service routine—A program or routine to assist in the operation or maintenance of a computer system.

service routines— A set of routines for performing on-line, concurrently with other programs, input and output operations such as tape to printer, card to tape, etc.

service, send-only—Service in which the data-communication channel is capable of transmitting signals, but is not equipped to receive signals.

services, setup—The action or services performed on a message before it meets the application program. Services include error checking, analyzing the action code, etc.

service, teletypewriter-exchange—A form of teletypewriter in which suitably arranged teletypewriter stations are provided with lines to a central office where connections may be established between any such stations and any other similar station in the same city, or in other cities under control of the subscriber.

service, teletypewriter private-line—A form of teletypewriter service differing from exchange service in that it is limited to service between certain specified stations. The service may be contracted for on a full-time or part-time basis.

servicing time—*Same as* engineering time.

servomechanism—1. A device for controlling a system using a measurable variable. 2. A device to monitor an operation as it proceeds, and to make necessary adjustments to keep the operation under control. A furnace thermostat is an example of a servomechanism. 3. A feedback-control system in which at least one of the system signals represents mechanical motion. 4. A closed-loop system in which the error or deviation from a desired or present condition is reduced to zero, and in which mechanical position is usually the controlled variable. 5. Any feedback-control system.

servomultiplier—An analog computer device or unit which has a position control and a capability of multiplying each of several different variables by a single variable, represented by analog voltages. The multiplier is used as an input signal to a mechanism that turns shafts.

servo swap—*Same as* swap, tape-servo.

set—1. To place a storage device in a prescribed state. 2. To place a binary cell in the one state. 3. A collection of elements having some feature in common or which bear a certain relation to one another; e.g., all even numbers, geometrical figures, terms in a series, a group of irrational numbers, all positive even integers less than 100, may be a set or a subset.

set, alphanumeric character—Special character set of letters and digits plus other special characters, including punctuation marks.

set, character—An agreed set of representations, called characters, from which selections are made to denote and distinguish data. Each character differs from all others, and the total number of characters in a given set is fixed; e.g., a set may include the numerals 0 to 9, the letters A to Z, punctuation marks, and a blank or space. (Clarified by alphabet.)

set, code—*See* code set.

set, instruction—1. The set of instructions that a computing or data-processing system is capable of performing. 2. The set of instructions that an automatic coding system assembles.

set name—An identifier.

set of data—The x values and y values representing points which will be drawn as a set of curves on the graph. Thus, a set of data consists of the multiple x values and associated y values required to define the curve.

set point—The specific desired value for the quantity being controlled, usually in a feed back control loop.

set pulse—*See* pulse, set.

394

sets, data—*See* data sets.

set theory—The study of the use and application of groups or sets.

settings, trap—*See* trap settings.

set up—The preparation of pieces of equipment for operation, i.e., placing paper in printers, adjusting paper feeds for tape units, etc.

set up, single—*Same as* single step.

set-up time—The portion of the elapsed time between machine operations that is devoted to such tasks as changing reels of tape, and moving cards, tapes, and supplies to and from the equipment.

several-for-one—A transaction which often is considered to mean the creation of a number of machine instructions from one program instruction. This is an indication of the various types of software.

sexadecimal—Pertaining to a characteristic or property involving a selection, choice, or condition in which there are sixteen possibilities.

sexadecimal notation—*See* notation, sexadecimal.

sexadecimal number—*See* number, sexadecimal.

sexadecimal numeral—*See* numeral, sexadecimal.

shaping pulse—*Same as* pulse regeneration.

shaping signal—*Same as* pulse regeneration.

share—To use a device for two or more interleaved purposes.

shared files—A direct-access device that permits two systems to be linked together. Either system has access to the file.

shared-files system—A special file system configuration in which two computers have access to the same file-storage device, though not necessarily at the same time.

shared storage—The ability to share core storage between two computers. This means that either machine can insert information into storage, and either machine can access the data and use it.

share operation system—The particular process or translation of symbolic instructions into a machine instruction. Often abbreviated as SOS.

SHARE organization—The SHARE organization coordinates the effective use of IBM data-processing systems through exchange of programming and application information, thereby seeking to reduce redundant programming effort. Programs written by SHARE members provide meaningful solutions to many data processing problems encountered in using IBM 704, 709, 7040/44, 7090, and 7094 data processing systems and future versions of these systems and the 360 systems.

sharing, load—Computer placed in tandem (duplexing or triplexing) to share the peak-period load of a system.

sharing, multiprocessing—*See* multiprocessing, sharing.

sheet, coding—A form upon which computer instructions are written prior to being punched into cards.

Sheffer stroke function—The Boolean operator that gives a truth table value of true only when both of the variables connected by the logical operator are not true.

Sheffer stroke gate—*Same as* gate, NAND.

shift—1. A movement of bits, digits, or characters to the left or right. 2. The movement of a character or group of characters to the left or right of a given point of reference in a memory or arithmetic unit. Also, a portion of a 24-hour period during which ADP equipment is operated. 3. To multiply or divide a quantity by a power of the number base. 4. To move the characters of a unit of information column-wise right or left. For a number, this is equivalent to multiplying or dividing by a power of the base number.

shift, arithmetic—To multiply or divide a quantity by a power of the number base; e.g., if binary 1101, which represents decimal 13, is arithmetically shifted twice to the left, the result is 110100, which represents 52, which is also obtained by multiplying (13 by 2)twice; on the other hand, if the decimal 13 were to be shifted to the left twice, the result would be the same as multiplying by 10 twice, or 1300. (Related to shift and cyclic shift.)

shift, carrier—Difference between the steady state, mark, and space frequencies in a data-carrier system using frequency-shift modulation.

shift, case—The changeover of the translating mechanism of a telegraph receiving machine from letters case to figures case or vice versa. This shift is normally performed in telegraph apparatus by preceding the transmission of letters-case characters or functions by a figures-shift signal.

shift character, nonlocking — *See* character, nonlocking shift.

shift, circular—A shift in which the digits dropped-off at one end of a word are returned at the other in a circular fashion; e.g., if a register holds eight digits, 23456789, the result of a cyclic shift two columns to the left would be to change the contents of the register to 45678923. (Synonymous with end-around shift, logical shift, nonarithmetic shift, ring shift, and cyclic shift.)

shift, cyclic—*Same as* shift circular.

shift, end-around—*Same as* shift circular.

shift, figures—A function performed by a teletypewriter machine, when initiated by the figures-shift character, that causes the machine to shift to upper case for numbers, symbols, etc.

shift, floating point—A shift in 4-bit increments, performed on a short-format or long-format floating-point number.

shift, frequency—A system of telegraph-teletypewriter operation in which the mark signal is one frequency and the space signal is a different frequency.

shift-in character—*See* character, locking shift.

shifting — The arithmetic process during which each movement of value to the left multiplies its value by the radix in use, and each movement to the right divides the number by the radix. Shifting may also feed a process for other radix points.

shift, letters—A function performed by a teleprinter, when initiated by the letters-shift character, which causes the machine to shift from upper case to lower case.

shift locking character—*See* character, locking shift.

shift, logic—*Same as* shift, circular.

shift, logical—*Same as* shift circular.

shift, nonarithmetic—Same as shift circular.

shift out—To move information within a register toward one end so that as the information leaves this same end, zeros enter at the opposite end.

shift-out character — *See* character, locking shift.

shift, phase—The time difference between the input and output signal or between any two synchronized signals of a control unit, system, or circuit.

shift pulse—A pulse which causes the characters in a register to shift.

shift register—1. A register that shifts every bit stored in it one place to the left upon the application of a shift pulse. Used to perform multiplication and to convert serial data to parallel data, or vice versa. 2. A register in which the stored data can be moved to the right or left.

shift register, magnetic—*See* register, magnetic shift.

shift, ring—*Same as* circular shift.

shop, closed—The operation of a computer facility where programming service to the user is the responsibility of a group of specialists, thereby effectively separating the programming from that of computer implementation. The programmers are not allowed in the computer room to run or oversee the running of their programs. (Contrasted with open shop.)

shop, open—The operation of a computer facility where computer programming, coding, and operating can be performed by any qualified employee of the organization, not necessarily by the personnel of the computing center itself and where the programmer may assist in, or oversee the running of, his program on the computer. (Contrasted with closed shop.)

short-card processing—Short cards are used as store-sales checks, gasoline sales checks, account receivable transmittal advices, and so forth. Short cards can be processed with full-size name and address cards of account balance cards. The short cards are fed by a processor equipped with a short card feed; the full size cards by a read-punch unit.

Reproduction of short cards into standard-size cards is not necessary.

shortest word—A word of the shortest length a computer can use, and which is most often half of the full length word.

short instruction—The use of an index specification in a FORTRAN READ or WRITE statement.

short-term storage—Used to refer to data stored in core memory for a short period of time.

short word—A fixed word of lesser length that is capable of handling words of two different lengths. In many computers this is referred to as a half-word because the length is exactly the half-length of a full word.

SICOM—SICOM is a general-purpose interpretive system utilizing floating-point arithmetic. Using SICOM, the computer operates as a decimal floating-point machine with a 10-decimal digit (plus exponent) word length. Many arithmetic and trigonometic subroutines are included in the SICOM library. (CDC)

side circuit—One of two physical circuits in a phantom group.

sideways sum—See sum, sideways.

sight check—1. The determination by visual means whether or not a particular punch is present in all cards of a deck; to check keypunching by reading the tabulation printout of card data. 2. To verify the sorting or punching of punched cards by looking through the pattern of punched holes.

sign—1. In arithmetic, a symbol that distinguishes negative quantities from positive ones. 2. An indication of whether a quantity is greater than zero, or less than zero. The signs often are the marks + and −, respectively; other arbitrarily selected symbols may be used, such as a 0 and 1, or 0 and 9. These symbols must be interpreted by a person or the machine. 3. A binary indicator that positions the magnitude of a number relative to zero.

signal—The event, phenomenon, or electrical quantity, that conveys information from one point to another.

signal, carry-complete—A signal generated by a digital parallel adder, indicating that all carries from an adding operation have been generated and propagated and the addition operation is completed.

signal, clock—Same as pulse, clock.

signal conditioning—1. Any manipulation of transducer or transmitter outputs to make them suitable for input to the computer peripheral equipment. 2. Operations such as linearizing and square-root extraction performed within the computer. 3. To process the form or mode of a signal so as to make it intelligible to, or compatible with, a given device, including such manipulation as pulse shaping, pulse clipping, digitizing, and linearizing.

signal, correcting—In synchronous systems, a special signal that may be sent recurrently for correction of data.

signal distance—The number of digit positions in which the corresponding digits of two binary words of the same length are different. (Synonymous with Hamming distance.)

signal-enabling—A means of allowing an operation to take place.

signal, feedback-control—The portion of the output signal that is returned to the input in order to achieve a desired effect, such as fast response.

signal, ground—A conductor establishing electrical ground reference potential for all transmitting circuits in a communications network.

signal, guard—1. A signal which allows values to be read or converted only when the values are not in a state of changing, i.e., to avoid errors or ambiguity. 2. An extra output which is generated when all values are complete to be used as a guard signal. Used in digital-analog or analog-digital converters or other converters or digitizers.

signaling, binary—A communications mode in which information is developed by the presence and absence, or the plus and minus variations, of only one parameter of the signal.

signaling, closed-circuit—That type of signaling in which there is current in the idle condition, and a signal is initiated by increasing or decreasing the current.

signaling, data rate—Relating to data transmission, an expression in bits per second relating to data transmission capacity of a particular channel.

signaling, d-c—A transmission method which utilizes direct current.

signal inhibiting—A means of preventing an operation from happening.

signal, interrupt—See interrupt signal.

signal, interrupt feedback — See interrupt feedback signal.

signal, interrupt trigger—See interrupt trigger signal.

signal level—An optical character recognition term which relates to the amplitude of the electronic response which occurs from the contrast ratio between the area of a printed character and the area of a document background.

signal, normalization—Same as pulse regeneration.

signal, one output—The output of a magnetic cell in the one condition when a read pulse is supplied.

signal, proceed-to-select—The signal returned from distant automatic equipment over the backward signaling path, in response to a calling signal, to indicate that selecting information can be transmitted. Note: In certain signaling systems, this signal can be one and the same as the "call-confirmation signal."

signal, program-interrupt—*See* interrupt, external-signal.

signal, pulsing—Signals which are transmitted in the forward direction and carry the selective information to route the call in the desired direction.

signal, read output—*Same as* read out.

signal, regeneration—*Same as* pulse regeneration.

signal, release-guard—A signal sent back in response to the clear-forward signal to indicate that the circuit has become free at its incoming end. This signal is provided to protect the circuit at its outgoing end against subsequent seizing before the release operation, controlled by the clear-forward signal, has been completed at the incoming end.

signal, reshaping—*Same as* pulse regeneration.

signals, control—Various control signals are provided to control, and to ensure to orderly flow of information words between the central computer and the peripheral subsystems. These signals do not transmit data, but are used to command and identify the transfer of information words at the proper times and in the proper sequence. These control signals travel over the control lines of the input/output channel.

signals, correction from—A system of correction in which the maintenance of synchronous equipment is controlled, not by a special correcting signal, but by the position of the characteristic instants of restitution of telegraph signals comprising the text.

signal, seizing—In semiautomatic or automatic working, a signal transmitted at the commencement of a call to initiate circuit operation at the incoming end of the circuit.

signals, external—External signals are given to the operator to indicate conditions which result in no output. Some conditions that produce warning signals are as follows: Equipment Off—If an I/O (input/output) operation is requested from the equipment and the equipment is not turned on or otherwise not available, the bell on the typewriter is rung. The bell continues ringing until the equipment is turned on by the operator. If the system has no typewriter, the flag-indicator lights on the console are blinked. Memory parity—If a memory parity error occurs, the computer is placed in a halt condition and the console memory parity light is turned on. The sequence register contains "the address-plus-one" of the instruction that caused the parity fail. I/O parity—If an I/O parity error occurs, the computer is placed in a halt condition and the console I/O parity light is turned on. The sequence register contains the address of the instruction prior to which the parity fail occurred.

signal shaping—*Same as* pulse regeneration.

signal standardization — *See* pulse regeneration.

signal, start-dialing—In semiautomatic or automatic working, a signal transmitted from the incoming end of a circuit, following the receipt of a seizing signal, to indicate that the necessary circuit conditions have been established for receiving the numerical routine information.

signal, start (in a start-stop system)—Signal servicing to prepare the receiving mechanism for the reception and registration of a character, or for the control of a function.

signals, timing — Electrical pulses sent throughout the machine at regular intervals to ensure absolute synchronization.

signal, stop (in a start-stop system)—Signal serving to bring the receiving mechanism to rest in preparation for the reception of the next telegraph signal.

signal strength—A measure of the amplitude of the signal obtained from reading devices such as photocells, magnetic tape read heads, etc.

sign bit—A binary digit used to designate the algebric sign of a quantity, plus or minus.

sign changer—As regards scalers, when the constant which is used as a multiplier, has the value of −1, the scaler may be called a sign changer, an inverter, or a sign reverser.

sign check—It is possible to detect a change in sign during arithmetic operations and either stop the machine or signal for subsequent review. In pay roll applications, the sign check is used to indicate the condition in which deductions exceed gross pay. This sign is also used in accounts receivable, accounts payable, inventory, and general ledger applications. The sign check can be used to recognize any balance that becomes negative.

sign-check indicator—A device that detects and signals the occurrence of an error in the sign of a number or of a field.

sign digit—*Same as* sign bit.

signed field—A field that has a plus or minus character coding over the units position to designate the algebraic sign of the entire number.

signed-magnitude arithmetic—In a signed-magnitude computer; all the arithmetic operations are accomplished by the process of addition and subtraction of magnitudes. Since multiplication and division can be broken down into a series of additions and subtractions, respectively, signed-magnitude computers will perform these operations as well. Operations with signed-magnitude numbers are identical with the algebraic addition using a pencil and paper.

signed-magnitude computer — *See* computer, signed magnitude.

sign, flip-flop—The specific flip-flop used to store the algebraic sign of numbers.

significance—1. Circumstances or solutions discerned to be unlikely to arise out of chance factors alone. 2. The number of digits of a number that have meaning and are not for decimal point positioning only. 3. The arbitrary rank, priority, or order of relative magnitude assigned to a given position or column in a number; the significant digits of a number are a set of digits, usually from consecutive columns, beginning with the most significant digit different from zero and ending with the least significant digit whose value is known are assumed relevant; e.g., 2300.0 has five significant digits, whereas 2300 probably has two significant digits.

significant character, least—The character in the right-most position in a number or a word.

significant character, most—The character in the left-most position in a number or word.

significant conditions of a modulation—Distinct conditions, assumed by the appropriate device of the sending apparatus, which serve to characterize the variety of the elements of the alphabetic telegraph signals to be transmitted.

significant conditions of a restitution—Distinct conditions, assumed by the appropriate device of the receiving apparatus, which serve to characterize the variety of the elements of the alphabetic telegraph signals received.

significant digit—See digit, significant.

significant digit arithmetic—See arithmetic, significant digit.

significant digit, least—See digit, least significant.

significant figures—See figures, significant.

significant interval—A time interval during which a given significant condition according to the code and the signal to be transmitted is, or should be, transmitted.

sign off—The closing instruction to the computer system which terminates communication with the system. On a remote terminal, the user generally signs off by typing the command OFF or SIGN OFF.

sign on—The instruction which commences communication with the computer system. On a remote terminal, the user can generally receive access to the system by typing in his identification number and an appropriate password.

sign position—1. The left-hand digit position in a numeric field, or the left-hand character position in an alphanumeric field, in which is stored the sign (minus symbol if negative) of the quantity stored in that field. 2. The position at which the sign of a number is located.

sign reverser—See sign changer.

sign, special—Same as character, special.

simplex—A circuit capable of one-way operations only. The term is seldom used today because no such circuit is offered by the common carriers. Terminal equipment may limit transmission to one direction only, but the circuit used will be half-duplex.

simplex channel—A channel that permits transmission in one direction only.

simplex system—A system configuration that does not include standby equipment.

simulate—To represent the functioning of one system by another; e.g., to represent one computer by another, to represent a physical system by the execution of a computer program, or to represent a biological system by a mathematical model.

simulated real-time, on-line operation—The processing of data in synchronism with a physical process in such a manner that the results of the data processing are useful to the physical operation.

simulating the multiplexor—A testing program which simulates the multiplexor.

simulation—1. The experimental technique of an operating system by means of mathematical or physical models that operate on real world or specifically devised problems in a time-sequential method similar to the system itself. 2. A pseudoexperimental analysis of an operating system by means of mathematical or physical models that operate in a time-sequential manner similar to the system itself. 3. Many problems cannot be solved analytically, but adequate criteria for success can be deduced from trial-and-error processes in which the model of the system is dynamically studied. For example, to determine the best operating conditions for a pilot manufacturing plant, one could build a mathematical model of the plant to "try out" the multitude of variables, parameters, i.e., conditions and circumstances, by simulating dynamic operations—all this "before" deciding on size, structure, locations and variations of the plant. 4. The representation of physical systems and phenomena by computers, models or other equipment; e.g., an imitative type of data processing in which an automatic computer is used as a model of some entity, e.g., a chemical process. When information enters the computer to represent the factors of process, the computer produces information that represents the results of the process, and the processing done by the computer represents the process itself. 5. In a computer programming, the technique of setting up a routine for one computer to make it operative as nearly as possible like some other computer.

simulation (advantages)—Simulation is often relegated to undeserved second choice because the sheer complexity of some problems makes mathematical formulation prohibitive (if not impossible). Even when a problem can be solved by mathematical analysis, it may be more economical to solve it by simulation. Whereas analysis sets out to provide a general solution to all problems of the type being considered, simulation manipulates only the data relevant to the problem in question and thus simulation often offers a much simpler and cheaper solution.

simulation, design and monitoring — The building of a model of a system in the form of a computer program by the use of special languages. The models of a system can be adjusted easily and the system that is being designed can be tested to show the effect of any change.

simulation input devices—*See* input devices. simulation.

simulation, man-machine—The scope of simulation, clearly includes models of systems in which human beings participate (operational or behavioral models). However, the possibility also exists of incorporating people within the model. In other words, the model is no longer completely computer-based but requires the active participation of a man.

simulation, mathematical — The use of a model of mathematical equations in which computing elements are used to represent all of the subsystems.

simulation monitoring and design — The building of a model of a system in the form of a computer program by the use of special languages. The models of a system can be adjusted easily and the system that is being designed can be tested to show the effect of any change.

simulation, physical—The use of a model of a physical system in which computing elements are used to represent some, but not all, of the subsystems.

simulation, real-time—*See* real-time simulation.

simulation, representative—A model of a system in which the components, processes, and interactions of the model bear a clear relation to the system under study. This tends to rule out highly abstract, mathematical models.

simulation, static vs. dynamic—In a dynamic system the activity is time-dependent. This activity may be further classified as stable or unstable (under given conditions). One may choose to study steady-state or transient behavior of a dynamic system.

simulation, supervisory programs—When the supervisory program is not available, the use of a replacement program that imitates the supervisory program.

simulator—1. A specific program or routine corresponding to a mathematical model or developed representation of a physical model. 2. A program or routine corresponding to a mathematical model or representing a physical model. 3. A routine that runs on one computer and imitates the operations of another computer. 4. A computer or model that represents a system of phenomenon that mirrors or maps the effects of various changes in the original, enabling the original to be studied, analyzed, and understood by means of the behavior of the model.

simulator, overload—In order to test a system under overload conditions, an artificial condition is created that makes the program act as it would during an actual overload or overflow.

simulator program—*See* program simulator.

simulator, table—*See* table simulator.

simultaneity—The simultaneous operation of peripheral devices is automatically monitored by traffic control hardware, so that peripheral demands are guaranteed immediate response. Complex software monitoring is rendered unnecessary due to this advanced design feature.

simultaneity, input/output—The read-punch unit functions do not interlock the processor; therefore, both reading and punching can overflow printing, processing, and reading by the processor.

simultaneity, tape-processing—*See* tape-processing simultaneity.

simultaneous access—The process of obtaining information from or placing information into storage where the time required for such access is dependent on the simultaneous transfer of all elements of a word from a given storage location.

simultaneous computer—*See* computer, simultaneous.

simultaneous input/output — *See* input/output, simultaneous.

simultaneous-operation computer — *Same as* computer, simultaneous.

simultaneous operations—The input and output channels for the computer are designed for maximum performance and flexibility. Any channel may control any input or output device within its speed range. This universal ability to attach any device is a major achievement of combined computer and I/O design.

All I/O operations may be performed simultaneously with program processing by the computer data channels. An especially powerful feature of these channels is the ability of the system to execute a complete sequence of I/O instructions—a small program independent of the main program. This capability, together with special features in the I/O control units, permits the channel to perform such outstanding operations as the searching of a disk file independently from the main computer program. The processing program is not interrupted until the complete I/O sequence is finished or unless an error condition occurs.

simultaneous operation (scanner selector)— In cases where more than one communication multiplexer is used on a single input/output computer channel, a scanner selector must be employed to control the simultaneous operation of the multiplexers. A maximum of four multiplexers may be connected to one scanner selector (some systems).

simultaneous operation (subchannels)—A multiplexor channel provides many subchannels, each of which operates with the identical channel logic of the selector channels. It makes possible the operation of many low-speed units, such as card readers, punches, printers, and remote terminals, concurrently with selector channel I/O operations and program processing. All subchannels also operate simultaneously with each other, time-sharing the multiplexor channel. The multiplexor channel thus provides an economical and efficient method of attaching a large number of devices (some systems).

simultaneous working—*See* simultaneous operations.

sine-junction gate—*Same as* gate, A AND-NOT B or gate, B AND-NOT A.

single address—A system of machine instruction such that each complete instruction explicitly describes one operation and involves one storage location. (Related to one-address instruction.)

single address code—*See* code, single address.

single-address instruction—An instruction having one operand address. (Contrast with multiple-address instruction.)

single-address machine—*See* machine, single address.

single-address message—A message to be delivered to only one destination.

single character, real-time buffer—*See* real time buffer (single character).

single circuit—A telegraph circuit capable of nonsimultaneous two-way communications. *See* half-duplex circuit.

single cycle key—A push button on printers, which when depressed, causes an additional line to be printed despite an end-of-form indication.

single error—An erroneous bit, preceded and followed by at least one correct bit.

single-level address—*Same as* address, direct.

single level memory—*See* memory, single level.

single precision—The number of words, or storage positions, used to denote a number in a computer. Single-precision arithmetic is the use of one word per number; double-precision arithmetic, two words per number, and so on. For variable word-length computers, precision is the number of digits used to denote a number. The higher the precision, the greater the number of decimal places that can be carried.

single precision integer—*See* integer, single precision.

single punch—*See* punch, single.

single (quick-access) reports — *See* reports, single quick-access.

single quote mark — A special FORTRAN character used to enclose literal messages.

single setup—Pertaining to a method of operating a computer, in which each step is performed in response to a single manual operation.

single-sheet feeding—The feeding of individual sheets of paper rather than roll or fan-folded form.

single-shot operation — *Same as* operation, single-step.

single-station, broadband — A single broadband station can be connected to a communication terminal system (CTS) by a leased Telpak A line. Leased Telpak A line operation permits continuous data exchange between two fixed locations. Data transfer can be initated by either device providing the remote hardware can handle such an operation. The data format will be such that character parity, start and end of message limits, message parity and character synchronization will be established. The CTS will be prepared to receive data at all times.

These modes of operation reflect the influence of presently available communications tariff offerings. The CTS design and packaging philosophy will allow for future higher speed operation (up to 100,000 bits/sec) and also for operation with communications hardware using more advanced techniques.

single step—Pertaining to a method of operating a computer in which each step is performed in response to a single manual operation.

single-step operation—A method of operating an automatic computer manually in which a single instruction or part of an instruction is performed in response to a single operation of a manual control. This method is generally used for detecting mistakes.

single thread processing — *See* processing, single thread.

single vertical key—A push button on a printer which produces an additional printed line for indication.

sink, data—Relating to a data transmission system, data sink often refers to equipment which accepts data.

site, bit—A location on magnetic recording media where a "bit" of information is stored.

site, hole—*See* hole site.

size, address—The maximum number of binary digits in an instruction used in directly addressing memory.

size, character—The number of binary digits in a single character in the storage device.

size, error—Occurs when the number of positions to the left of the assumed decimal point exceeds the corresponding positions in the COBOL data-name field.

size, item—1. The magnitude of an item, usually expressed in numbers of fields, words, characters or blocks. 2. The number of BCD or alphanumeric characters in an item.

skeletal code—The framework of a routine that is formed by a generalized routine using input parameters.

sketchpad — A tool for engineers developed by Massachusetts Institute of Technology. The user draws with a light pen on a computer display scope. If he sketches a rough circle, it becomes perfect. He may erase, or he may magnify and reduce at a ratio of 2000 to 1. He may also sketch a part in perspective, then rotate the sketch to see the top, side, or bottom views of the sketched part.

skew character—*See* character skew.

skew line—A type of line misregistration in which a string of characters to be read by an optical character reader appears in a uniformily slanted or skewed condition with respect to a real or imaginary baseline.

skip—An instruction to proceed to the next instruction; a "blank" instruction.

skip code—A functional code which instructs the machine to skip certain predetermined fields in memory.

skip flag—A one bit in this position causes bytes to be skipped until the count equals zero. This skip instruction permits the computer to ignore portions of the input record to the memory.

skip instruction—An instruction having no effect other than directing the processor to proceed to another instruction designated in the storage portion.

skip (printer)—A skip function may be signaled on any step. When a skip is signaled on a step that also impulses a printout, the skip function is effective after the line has been printed. If skip is signaled on any other step, the skipping action is initiated immediately.

skip, tape—A machine instruction to forward space and erase a portion of a tape when a defect on the tape surface causes a write error to persist.

skip test—A specific type of microinstruction designed and utilized for conditional operations based on the state of readiness of various devices or the conditions of a register.

slab—The basic subunit of information for processing on the NCR 315. A slab consists of 12 bits which may be treated as two groups of 6 (alphanumeric information called alpha), or as three groups of 4 (numeric information called digit).

The term slab is a contraction of "syllable." A set of one to eight slabs make up a word.

slave application—*See* computer, slave.

slave computer—*See* computer, slave.

slave mode—The mode of computer operation in which most of the basic controls affecting the state of the computer are protected from the program.

slave system—A particular system which is connected to another system and in which the commanding or master system discharges commands and orders which are thus imitated by the slave system.

slew, paper—*Same as* paper throw.

slice, time—*See* time slicing.

slit scan, divided—*See* scan, divided slit.

slot—On a magnetic drum, all the cells under a set of read/write heads at one instant of time.

slow memory—Those portions of the memory

with a relatively slow-access rate from which information may be obtained automatically.

SMS—Abbreviation for Standard Modular System. A system of computer component packaging and subassembly procedures developed by IBM.

smudge—In OCR (optical character recognition), the displacement of ink under shear beyond the original edges of a printed character.

smudge resistance—Manufacturers have designed ink to avoid the inadvertent smudging of a printed image in normal use.

snapshot debugging — *See* debugging, snapshot.

snapshot dump—A selective dynamic dump performed at various points in a machine run. (Clarified by snapshot.)

snapshot program—When a trace program is an interpretive program, it is called an interpretive trace program, and when a trace program gives output only on selected instructions or for a selected set or single condition it is called a snapshot program.

SNOBOL—A strong-manipulation and pattern-recognition language, developed by Bell Laboratories.

soft adder—*See* adder, soft.

softly, fail—*See* fail softly.

software—1. The internal programs or routines professionally prepared to simplify programming and computer operations. These routines permit the programmer to use his own language (English) or mathematics (Algebra) in communicating with the computer. 2. Various programming aids that are frequently supplied by the manufacturers to facilitate the purchaser's efficient operation of the equipment. Such software items include various assemblers, generators, subroutine libraries, compilers, operating systems, and industry-application programs.

software, common — Programs or routines which usually have common and multiple applications for many systems, i.e., report generators, sort routines, conversion programs which can be used for several routines in language common to many computers.

software, communication — *See* communication software.

software, compatible—Languages which can be used on more than one computer system.

software documents — *See* documents, software.

software flexability—*See* modularity, software.

software functions, time sharing—*See* time sharing, software functions.

software modularity — *See* modularity, software.

software, random access—*See* random access software.

software requirements, time sharing — *See* time sharing, software requirements.

solenoid, forward—An electromechanical device which, when energized, maintains pressure via a roller, forcing magnetic tape against the forward capstan, which moves the tape in a forward direction.

solenoid, reverse—That electrical mechanical device, which apart from being energized, performs a maintenance of pressure via a roller, forcing magnetic tape against the reverse capstan which moves the tape in reverse direction.

solid errors—An error that always occurs when a particular piece of equipment is used.

solid-logic technology (SLT) — Microelectric circuits, the product of solid-logic technology, are the basic components of some systems. Called logic circuits because they carry and control the electrical impules that represent information within a computer, these tiny devices operate at speeds ranging from 300 down to six billionths of a second. Transistors and diodes mounted on the circuits are as small as 28 thousandths of an inch square and are protected by a film of glass 60 millionths of an inch thick.

solid-state circuitry—The solid-state components in circuits of computers.

solid-state component—A component whose operation depends on the control of electric or magnetic phenomena in solids, e.g., a transistor, crystal diode, or ferrite cores.

solid-state computer—1. A computer built primarily from solid-state electronic circuit elements. 2. A computer using semiconductor devices.

solid-state design—The solid-state components and circuitry of the real-time computer system offer numerous advantages including standardized production of components and the reduction of maintenance procedures. In addition to ease of maintenance, solid-state circuits also impart a high degree of operating reliability to the computer and reduce the power, cooling, and space requirements of the system at the same time.

solid-state devices — The electronic components that convey or control electrons within solid materials, e.g., transistors, germanium diodes, and magnetic cores. Thus, vacuum and gas tubes are not included.

solid-state logic—*Same as* solid-logic technology.

solution check—A solution to a problem obtained by independent means to verify a computer solution.

solution, feasible — A solution to the constraint equations in which all variables satisfy their restrictions (linear programming).

solution, geometric—*See* geometric solution.

solution, graphic—A solution obtained with graphs or other pictorial devices. (As contrasted with solutions obtained by the manipulation of numbers.)

solution, machine independent—A solution procedure developed in terms of a logical solution to a problem rather than in terms of a particular mechanized processing system.

solver, equation—A calculating device, usually analog, that solves systems of linear simultaneous nondifferential equations or determines the roots of polynomials, or both.

sonic delay line—A delay line using a medium (such as mercury or quartz) providing acoustic delay. (Related to mercury delay line.)

sophisticated vocabulary—An advanced and elaborate set of instructions. Some computers can perform only the more common mathematical calculations such as addition, multiplication, and subtraction. A computer with a sophisticated vocabulary can go beyond this and perform operations such as linearize, extract square root, and select highest number.

sort—1. To break down or distribute into groups according to a given set of rules, usually to make a numerical, alphabetic, or alphameric sort. 2. To arrange items of information according to rules dependent upon a key or field contained in the items. 3. A systems program which arranges a file of items in a logical sequence according to a designated key word contained within each item (e.g., the arranging of items according to date, code number, etc.).

sort and merge generator—*See* generator, sort and merge.

sort, ascending—A sort in which the final sequence of records is such that successive keys compare greater than, or equal to.

sort, block—A sort of one or more of the most significant characters of a key to serve as a means of making workable-size groups from a large volume of records.

sort, bubble—A sorting technique which exchanges a pair of numbers if they are out of order.

sort, descending—A sort in which the final sequence of records is such that the successive keys compare less than, or equal to.

sort, diigtal—*See* digital sort.

sorter-comparator—A unit of punch card equipment which has the capability of sorting and selecting particular cards, sequence checking them, and making comparisons between stored data and those new items.

sorter, magnetic-character—The magnetic-character sorter has a document-handling rate of thousands of items per minute. It will read and sort intermixed documents of various lengths, widths, and thicknesses. The equipment is designed to read and translate the various magnetic-ink type fonts. The magnetic-character sorter can operate under control of the processor and is programmed to sort encoded items on a whole number or block basis in any desired order and with possible time-sharing between documents. Magnetic characters are read and transferred directly to the memory of the processor.

sort, external—The second phase of a multipass sort program, wherein strings of data are continually merged until one string of sequenced data is formed.

sort, fine—Usually off-line detail sorting by the sorter especially used in banks; for example, fine sorting could be the function of arranging checks and deposits into customer account number order.

sort, four-tape—*See* sorting, four-tape.

sort, generalized—A sort program which will accept the introduction of parameters at run time and which does not generate a program.

sort, generated—A production program which was produced by a sort generator.

sort generator—*See* generator, sort.

sorting—The process of arranging data into some desired order according to rules dependent upon a key or field contained by each item.

sorting, balanced—A technique used in a sort program to merge strings of sequenced data.

sorting, checkpoint—*Same as* sorting, restart.

sorting, collating—A sort which uses a technique of continuous merging of data until one sequence is developed.

sorting, comparison-of-pairs—The comparison of the keys in two records and placement of the higher value of the smaller value for descending sequences.

sorting, computer limited—A sort program in which the executive time of the internal instructions determines the elapsed time required to sort.

sorting, control card—A card which is used to specify the parameters for a sort.

sorting, control field—A continuous group of characters within a record which form all or part of the control word.

sorting devices (control)—The use of the card-counting device during sorting will indicate any missing cards if the operator has a card count to which he can balance. The accuracy of sorting or merging can be verified by a sequence check on the collator or a visual sequence check of the data when a report is printed. Control of magnetic-tape sorting is accomplished by the stored program; in each pass the sum of the control totals from incoming tapes is balanced against the sum of those developed for the outgoing tape or tapes. On the final pass, sequence is verified.

sorting, digital—To sort first the keys on the least significant digit, and then to re-sort on next higher-order digit until the items are sorted on the most significant digit. A punched card technique.

sorting, disk—A sort program that utilizes disk-type memory for auxiliary storage during sorting.

sorting, drum—A sort program that utilizes magnetic drums for auxiliary storage during sorting.

sorting, Fibonacci series—When the current number is equal to the sum of the two preceding numbers, i.e., 1, 2, 3, 5, 8, and so on. Some sort programs distribute strings of data onto work tapes so that the number of strings on successive tapes form a Fibonacci series.

sorting, first-pass (own coding)—Computer instructions created by the programmer, in assembly or absolute form, which are executed by a sort during the first pass of the file after input program has been loaded but prior to execution of first-pass sequencing instructions.

sorting four-tape—Merge sorting in which input data are supplied on two tapes and are sorted into incomplete sequences alternately on two output tapes. The output tapes are used for input on the succeeding pass, resulting in longer and longer sequences after each pass until the data are all in one sequence on one output tape.

sorting, input tape(s)—Tape(s) containing a file in arbitary sequence to be introduced into a sort/usage program.

sorting, insertion method—A method of internal sorting where records are moved to permit the insertion of records.

sorting, intermediate pass—Any phase of a merging operation which, because of the number of strings or otherwise, does not reduce the file to a single sequenced string.

sorting, item—The basic element of a file such that the sorting of the file constitutes the reordering of file records.

sorting, key—The fields in a record which determine, or are used as a basis for determining, the sequence of records in a file.

sorting, magnetic-tape—A sort program that utilizes magnetic tapes for auxiliary storage during a sort.

sorting, merge—To produce a single sequence of items, ordered according to some rule, from two or more previously unordered sequences, without changing the items in size, structure, or total number. Although more than one pass may be required for a complete sorting, items are selected during each pass on the basis of the entire key.

sorting, multifile—The automatic sequencing of more than one file, based upon separate parameters for each file, without operator intervention.

sorting, multireel—The automatic sequencing of a file having more than one input tape, without operator intervention.

sorting, own coding—Special coding provided by the programmer, which is intergrated with sort/merge coding.

sorting, pass—The processing of each file record for the purpose of reducing the number of strings of sequenced records and increasing the number of sequenced records per string.

sorting, phase—An arbitrary segmentation of a sort program. Many sorts are segmented into three phases; initialization phase, internal phase, and merge phase.

sorting, process-limited—A sort program in which the exception time of the internal instructions determines the elapsed time required to sort.

sorting, restart—The return to a previous point in the program where processing may begin. The previous point may be the beginning of the program or it may be a checkpoint.

sorting, return point—*Same as* sorting, restart.

sorting, reverse-digit method—Sorting which begins with the units position of a given field and proceeds one column at a time (from right to left) until the field is completely sorted.

sorting, rewind time—Elapsed time consumed by a sort/merge program for restoring intermediate and final tape to original position.

sorting, scratch tape—Tape(s) used to store intermediate-pass data during a sort program.

sorting, sequencing criteria—*Same as* sorting, sequencing key.

sorting, sequencing key—The field in a record which determines, or is used as a basis for determining, the sequence of records in a file.

sorting, string—A group of sequential records, normally stored in auxiliary computer storage, i.e., disk, tape, or drum.

sorting, tape-limited—Also input/output limited. A sort program in which the effective transfer rate of tape units determines the elapsed time required to sort.

sorting, twin drum—In a multidrum computer configuration, the use of two drums for storing a file of data. The elapsed time required to sort is significantly reduced by alternating the moving of one drum head with the reading and writing of data from another drum.

sorting, variable-length records—Denumerable file elements for which the number of words, characters, bits, fields, etc., is not constant.

sorting, von Neuman—A technique used in a sort program to merge strings of sequenced data. The power of the merge is equal to T/2.

sorting, work tape(s)—Tape(s) used to store intermediate-pass data during a sort program.

sorting, Xmas-tree—A technique used in the internal portion of a sort program. The results of the comparisons between groups of records are stored for later use.

sort, internal—The sequencing of two or more records within the central computer memory; the first phase of a multipass sort program.

sort/merge—A set of routines to arrange random items in an ordered sequence. These routines can also be used to combine two or more ordered sequences into a single file.

sort/merge generator—Custom programs for sorting files of data.

sort/merge program—The sort/merge program is designed to satisfy the sorting and merging requirements of tape or random storage-oriented installations. It is a generalized program that can produce many different sorting or merging programs in accordance with control information specified by the user.

sort/merging, disk—Sort/merging of data on disks may often be programmed to avoid excessive positioning or waiting time until the disk rotates to a desired position. This is accomplished by placing the blocks of data so that after reading data block N, and the processing of data block N, the reading (or writing) of block N + 1 will take place just at that point to which the disk has rotated or head has moved.

sort, multipass—A sort program which is designed to sort more data than can be contained within the internal memory of a central computer. Intermediate storage, such as disk, tape, drum, is required.

sort, property—A sort completed by selecting from groups of items which have particular characteristics which meet selected criteria and according to certain keys, such that the priority or ordering of the sort relates to a specific property of the key, i.e., sorting by countries, then by states, then by counties, then by cities, and each according to population sizes within their individual groups.

sort, radix—A sort which uses a technique similar to sorting on tabulation machines (e.g. IBM sorter). The elapsed time is directly proportional to the number of characters in the sequencing key and the volume of data.

sorts, random-access—Separate programs are furnished by manufacturers to sort data stored on random-access disks and drums. These programs strip off the memory-item keys of data stored on a random-access storage unit, sort the keys, and then store on the disk or drum a table containing the keys and the addresses of the corresponding file items. Items may be brought in to memory from the disk or drum in the order of the sorted keys by using the macroinstructions.

sorts, tape—These are generalized programs that adapt themselves, as directed by programmer-specified parameters, to operate in a particular configuration and to sort data in a particular format. Many of these programs take advantage of the polyphase-sorting technique developed by Honeywell. Tailored for use in small card-oriented systems is a sort program that requires only three tape units and receives its specialization parameters by card. This program sorts fixed-length records on up to seven keys, and provides facilities for self-coding.

source address instruction—*Same as* address instruction, functional.

source computer—The computer that is utilized to prepare problems as input for other computer operations.

source data—*See* data source.

source-data automation (SDA)—The many methods of recording information in coded forms on paper tapes, punched cards, or tags that can be used over and over again to produce many other records without rewriting.

source-destination instruction — *See* instruction, source-destination.

source document—*See* document, source.

source file—A CRAM (Card Random-Access Memory) deck, disk, drum, or magnetic tape containing the file of information used as input to a computer run.

source language—1. The language used to specify computer processing; translated into object language by an assembler or compiler. 2. A compiler language such as FORTran from which machine-language instructions are developed by the use of translation routines or compilers. 3. The language in which the input to the FORTRAN processor is written.

source-language debugging—Debugging information is requested by the user and displayed by the system in a form consistent with the source programming language.

source language, QUIKTRAN—*See* QUIKTRAN source language.

source machine—The computer on which the source program is translated into the object program.

source program—A program coded in other than machine language that must be translated into machine language before use.

source recording—*See* recording source.

source routine—*Same as* program, source.

SPA—Abbreviation for Systems and Procedures Association, an organization of management personnel.

space—Refers to a blank space in a printed line or to vertical line spacing of a printer.

space code—Similar to skip code, but restricted to one space at a time.

space, dead—A specific range of values in which the incoming signal can be altered without also changing the outgoing response. (Synonymous with dead zone, and similar to neutral zone.)

space, interblock—*Same as* gap, interrecord.

space, interword—*Same as* gap, interword.

space suppression—The withholding of the movement of platen and/or paper for a line of printing.

space, switching—*Same as* gap, interword.

space-to-mark transition—The transition, or switching, from a spacing impulse to a marking impulse.

space, word—The actual area or space occupied by a word in serial digital devices such as drums, disks, tapes, and serial lines.

space, working—A portion of the internal storage reserved for the data upon which operations are being performed. (Synonymous with temporary storage, and contrasted with program storage.)

spacing—The condition that exists on a telegraph circuit during transmission when a bit of intelligence corresponding to a "no" is being sent.

spacing bias—Bias distortion which lengthens the spacing impulse by delaying the space-to-mark transition.

spacing chart printer—*See* printer, spacing chart.

spacing-end distortion—End distortion which lengthens the spacing impulse by advancing the mark-to-space transition.

spacing pulse (teletypewriter)—A spacing pulse or "space" is the signal pulse which, in d-c neutral operation, corresponds to a "circuit open" or "no current" condition.

spacing, reference line character—*See* character spacing reference line.

SPAR (Selection Program for ADMIRAL Runs)—Honeywell's three-phase utility system that updates ADMIRAL (Automatic and Dynamic Monitor with Immediate Relocation, Allocation and Loading) and object program areas of an ADMIRAL Run Type (ART) by selecting or deleting programs from a symbolic program tape (SPT).

special character—A character other than a digit or letter, e.g., $* + - \$ =$.

special-instruction repertoire—*See* repertory, instruction.

specialized data processing—*See* data processing, specialized.

specialized processing—*See* data processing, specialized.

special-purpose computer—A computer designed to solve a specific class or narrow range of problems.

special sign—*Same as* character, special.

specific address—An address that indicates the exact storage location where the referenced operand is to be found or stored in the actual machine-code address-numbering system. (Related to absolute code.)

specific addressed location—*See* addressed location, specific.

specific addressing—*See* addressing, specific.

specification—1. For programming, a precise definition of the records and programs needed to carry out a particular processing function. 2. As an equipment concept, a technical or engineering description of the hardware.

specification, program—The precise and ordered definitions of logic, and scope of processing functions, that are performed by particular program or program segments.

specification statement—*See* statements, specification.

specific code—*See* code, absolute.

specific coding—*Same as* addressing, specific.

specific program—A program for solving a specific problem only.

specific routine—A routine to solve a particular mathematical, logical, or data-handling problem in which each address refers to explicitly stated registers and locations.

specific symbol—*Same as* character, special.

speed, card unit—The rate, in cards per minute, at which cards may be read or punched by the unit.

speed, effective-transmission—The rate at which information is processed by a transmission facility, expressed as the average rate over some significant time interval. This quantity is usually expressed as average characters per unit of time, or average bits per unit of time.

speed, paper tape—The rate, in characters per second, at which the unit reads or punches paper tape.

speed, printer—The rate at which the unit operates when actually printing data, ranging from the slowest to the fastest speed of the unit.

speed, tape—The rate at which the tape moves past the recording head during a data transfer.

speed telegraph—Reciprocal of the unit interval measured in seconds. (This rate is usually expressed in bauds.)

speed, transmission—The number of information elements sent per unit time, usually expressed as bits, characters, items, word groups, or records per second or per minute.

spelling—The order of signs as they appear within printed or written words.

split—The formation of two ordered files from one regular file, as contrasted with merged, i.e., usually unordered.

split catalog—A library catalog in which the different varieties of entry are filed separately, e.g., subject entry, author entry, title entry.

split, column—A device designed and used on some punched card machines to sense a column in two parts during reading, i.e., punch positions can then be permitted in a single column and treated separately from other punches in the same column.

split-word operations—Either addition or subtraction can be performed on whole words, half words, or third words simultaneously, but there is never any interaction between the partial words. The right halves of two operands, for example, are added and the sum is stored in the right half of the selected accumulator. At the same time, the left halves of the same two operands are added and the result is stored in the left half of the same accumulator. Again, there is no carry interaction between the halves. (The same holds true for whole and third words.) Thus, split-word arithmetic increases computer speed and saves storage space due to shorter operands.

spool—1. The mounting for a magnetic, paper, or plastic tape. 2. A tape reel.

sporadic fault—*See* fault, sporadic.

spot, carbon—Carbon paper carbonized on some areas only so that certain entries will not be reproduced on the copy.

spot, flying—A small, rapidly moving spot of light, usually generated by a cathode-ray tube and used to illuminate successive spots of a surface containing dark and light areas. The varying amount of light reflected is detected by a phototube and used to produce a time succession of electronic signals that effectively describe the surface.

spot punch—A hand-operated device, resembling a pair of pliers, for selectively punching holes in punch cards.

spot, reflective—An evident mark which indicates the initial beginning or end of tape.

spread—The time interval, at either side of an ideal instant of modulation or restitution of a modulated carrier signal, in which occurs the actual significant instants of the modulation or restitution.

sprocket holes—Feed holes punched in a tape to control the movement and positioning of the tape.

sprocket pulse—1. A pulse generated by a magnetized spot which accompanies every character recorded on magnetic tape. This pulse is used during read operations to regulate the timing of the read circuits and also to provide a count on the number of characters read from tape. 2. A pulse generated by the sprocket or driving hole in paper tape that serves as the timing pulse for reading or punching the paper tape.

SPS—Abbreviation for symbolic programming systems. A programming language in which terms may represent quantities and locations.

SPT (symbolic program tape)—A Honeywell tape that contains a file of programs, each of which is in the original assembly language and also the machine language. From this tape, programs can be selected for either checkout or production runs.

squeal—As related to magnetic tape, subaudible tape vibrations, primarily in the longitudinal mode, caused by frictional excitation at heads and guides.

squeezeout—In optical character recognition (OCR), the displacement of ink from the center to the edges of a character during printing, resulting in a character with "darker" outlines than the center.

stability—In optical character recognition (OCR), the resistance to change of color of the image when exposed to radiant energy.

stability, computational—That particular degree to which a computational process becomes or remains valid and reliable when subjected to various conditions which tend to produce errors or malfunctions.

stability, light—The ability of an image to hold its spectral appearance when exposed to light or radiant energy in optical character reading equipment.

stack—That portion of a computer memory and/or registers used to temporarily hold information.

stacked graph—A graph with two or three x scales and the same number of y scales plotted in such a way that there are discrete plotting grids placed one above the other.

stacked job control—See job control, stacked.

stacker—An output device that accumulates punched cards in a deck. (Contrasted with card hopper.)

stacker, card—1. A receptacle that accumulates cards after they have passed through a machine. 2. A hopper.

stacker, input—The card-feed magazine in a reader, or read-punch unit.

stacker, offset—A card receptacle or container in which various cards can be made to protrude from the machine control so that physical identification with adequate speed is possible on the manned system.

stacker, output—A mechanism that accumulates cards after they have passed through a machine.

stackers, radial—The many receptacles which hold supplies of cards which have been processed.

stack head—See head stack.

stacking, job—See job stacking.

stack pointer—In nested storage types (push-down), the address of the location at the top of the column is often called the stack pointer and is held in a pre-assigned register.

stack, push-down—A reserved area of memory into which operands are pushed and from which operands are pulled on a last-in, first-out basis.

stack, storage—See storage stack.

stage punching, normal—See punching, normal stage.

STAMP (Systems Tape Addition and Maintenance Program)—A Honeywell program that simplifies making up the file of systems programs on the symbolic program tape or master relocatable tape; it reduces significantly the time and effort in updating, correcting, and maintaining the systems programs on these tapes.

stand-alone capability—A multiplexor designed to function independently of a host or master computer, either some of the time or all of the time.

standard—1. An accepted criterion or an established measure for performance, practice, design, terminology, size, etc. 2. A rule or test by which something is judged. 3. The accepted, approved, or established criteria or requirements for controlling the technical performance and practices of programmers and others responsible for system organization and integration. Standards must necessarily be precisely developed and written, thoughtfully reviewed, and widely distributed in order to be of maximum effectiveness and acceptability.

standard communication subsystem—A central processor exchanges data simultaneously with a number of remote locations over a standard common-carrier communications facility. The communication subsystem consists of a multiplexor or multiplexors, each of which allows simplex communica-

tion circuits to share a computer I/O channel, and communication line terminal units. These units properly terminate the communication circuits and translate the data from these circuits to a form compatible with the central processor.

standard graph—A graph plotted with one x scale and one or two associated y scales forming a single plotting grid.

standard interphase—See interphase, standard.

standard interrupts—Various events can lead to a program interrupt. Each interrupt is to a unique fixed-memory address that is associated with the event that caused it. Addresses are reserved for these interrupts. Each external device has an interrupt address. An external device may have more than one interrupt event and each event may have its own interrupt address. Interrupts may occur only at the end of program instructions.

standardization—The establishment of specific procedural methods for the processing of data.

standardization, pulse—Same as pulse regeneration.

standardization, signal—See pulse regeneration.

standardize—1. To cause conformity with established standards. 2. To establish standards. 3. To change a floating-point result so that the exponent and mantissa lie in a range that can vary according to the computer's design (mantissas represented by numbers between 1 and 9.99, e.g., 6.28×10^{18}, or numbers between 0 and .999, e.g., $.628 \times 10^{19}$). To replace any given floating-point representation of a number with its representation in standard form. That is, to adjust the exponent and fixed point so that the new fixed-point part lies within a prescribed standard range.

standard memory locations—See memory locations, standard.

standard procedures, program—Suggested programming methods set by the manufacturer.

standard program—See program, standard.

standards, systems—System standards are either of the following: (1) the minimum required electrical performance characteristics of communication circuits that are based on the measured performance of existing developed circuits under the same operating conditions for which the new circuits were designed, (2) the specified characteristics necessary in order to permit interoperation of the system. (For example, the values for center frequencies for telegraph channels, test tone, etc.)

standard subroutine—A subroutine that is applicable to a class of problems.

standard, system—See system standard.

standard, working—A specified combination of a transmitting and receiving system, or subscriber's lines and feeding circuits (or equivalent systems), connected by means of a distortionless variable attenuator, and employed under specified conditions to determine by comparison the transmission quality of other telephone systems or parts of systems.

standby application—An application in which two or more computers are tied together as part of a single overall system and which, as in the case of an inquiry application, stand ready for immediate activation and appropriate action.

standby block—1. Locations always set aside in storage for communication with buffers in order to make more efficient use of such buffers. 2. An extra or reserve block of information stored in the internal computer memory so that the central computer need not wait for an input device to feed in, or an output device to take out, information.

standby computer—The computer that is used in a dual or duplex system and is waiting to take over the real-time processing burden whenever the need arises.

standby equipment—Automatic data-processing equipment that is not in use and that is available in emergencies, such as machine breakdowns or cases of overload.

standby register—A register in which accepted or verified information can be stored so as to be available for a rerun in case the processing of the information is spoiled by a mistake in the program, or by a malfunction in the computer.

standby time—1. The elapsed time between inquiries when the equipment is operating on an inquiry application. 2. The time during which two or more computers are tied together and available to answer inquiries or process intermittent actions on stored data.

standby time unattached—*Same as* standby unattended time.

standby unattended time—The time in which the machine is in an unknown condition and not in use working on problems. This includes time in which the machine is known to be defective and work is not being done to restore it to operating condition. It also includes breakdowns that render it unavailable due to outside conditions such as power shortages.

standing-on-nines carry—A carry out of a digit position generated by a carry into the digit position; the normal adding circuit is by-passed.

star program—*See* program, star.

start button—*Same as* button, initiate.

start dates, PERT—*See* PERT, start dates.

start, external device—*See* external device start.

starting-dialing signal—In semiautomatic or automatic working, a signal transmitted from the incoming end of a circuit, following the receipt of a seizing signal, to indicate that the necessary circuit conditions have been established for receiving the numerical routine information.

start key—The push button on the control panel which initiates or resumes the operations of the equipment after an automatic or programmed stop.

start signal—*See* start-stop system.

start-stop system—A system in which each group of code elements corresponding to an alphabetical signal is preceded by a start signal which serves to prepare the receiving mechanism for the reception and registration of a character, and is followed by a stop signal which serves to bring the receiving mechanism to rest in preparation for the reception of the next character.

start-stop system, stepped—A start-stop system in which the start signals occur at regular intervals.

start-stop time — *Same as* acceleration time, deceleration time.

start-stop transmission—Asynchronous transmission in which each group of code elements corresponding to a character signal is preceded by a start signal which serves to prepare the receiving mechanism for the reception and registration of a character, and is followed by a stop signal which serves to bring the receiving mechanism to rest in preparation for the reception of the next character.

start time—1. The time between the "interpretation" of the tape instructions to read or write and the "transfer" of information to or from the tape into storage, or from storage into tape.) (Synonymous with acceleration time.) 2. The time interval for a magnetic tape to accelerate from dead reset to full reading or writing speed. (Compares with stop time.)

start time, punch—That particular measurement of the elapsed time at the beginning of a card punch cycle before actual card punching can begin.

start time read—The determination or measurement of the elapsed time at the beginning of a card-read cycle before actual card reading begins.

state—A computing term relating to the condition of all the units or elements of the system, i.e., the storage data, digits in registers, settings on switches, etc., including the question, what is their state?

state, input—*See* input state.

statement—1. In computer programming, a meaningful expression or a generalized instruction in a source language. 2. An instruction (macro) to the computer to perform some sequence of operations.

statement, arithmetic—A type of FORTRAN statement that specifies a numerical computation.

statement, data definition—Control card used to describe a data set that is to be used by a job step in IBM OS/360.

statement, declarative—Instructions in symbolic coding, or systems used to define and designate areas, constants, and symbols.

statement, job control—*See* job control statement.

statement number—A number that is associated with a single macrostatement so that the reference may be made to that statement in terms of its number.

statement number columns—Usually columns 1-5 are reserved on punched cards for statement numbers, especially in FORTRAN programming.

statement, parameter—A parameter statement assigns specified integer values to specified variables at compile time, e.g., parameter $I = 2$ causes the integer 2 to replace I whenever it occurs in the source program.

statement range, DO—All FORTRAN statements included in the repetitive execution of a DO loop operation.

statements, control—*See* control statements.

statements, data-formatting—This type of statement instructs the assembly program to set up certain constants and to designate reserved memory areas and also to punctuate the memory to indicate field boundaries.

statements, imperative—Action statements of a symbolic program that are converted into actual machine-language instructions.

statements, program (communications)—A user's program is made up of program statements. When entered from a terminal, these statements are always retained in storage as part of the active program. If the user has an executable program statement within the program, he should assign a statement number to the statement referred to. Numbers 1 through 999 may be used as statement numbers, with no two statements having the same number. The statements acceptable to the remote-computing system are described in tables which give each statement in general form, its purpose, and one or more examples of its use.

statements, specification—These are nonexecutable FORTRAN compiler information required to define variables, allocate storage, and define subprograms to be used. The statements are type statements: REAL, INTEGER, EXTERNAL, DIMENSION, COMMON, EQUIVALENCE, DATA, and DEFINE FILE statements.

statements, type—Statements in FORTRAN used to overide the normal mode of assigning variable names and to reserving arrays.

statement, trace—*See* trace statement.

state, output—The determination of the condition of that specified set of output channels, i.e., positive or negative, one or zero, etc.

static check—*See* check, static.

static dump—A dump that is performed at a particular point in time with respect to a machine run, frequently at the end of a run.

static handling—Such handling is done completely by the compiler program.

staticize—1. To convert serial or time-dependent parallel data into static time form. 2. Occasionally, to retrieve an instruction and its operands from storage prior to its execution.

staticizer—1. A storage device for converting time-sequential information into static time parallel information. 2. A type of buffer.

static memory—*See* memory, static.

static print-out—*See* print-out, static.

static storage—*See* storage, static.

static subroutine—A subroutine that involves no parameters other than the addresses of the operands.

station—A device containing a tape drive, together with reading and writing heads and associated controls. (Synonymous with tape station.)

station, brush—*See* brush station.

station, called—In communications switching, a called station is the one which receives the request from a calling station.

station, calling—In communications switching, the calling station directs the operations of selecting, polling, etc.

station, control—A switching network station directing operations such as polling, alerting, recovering, selecting tape sequence, and control.

station, input—*See* input station.

station, inquiry—*See* inquiry station.

station, magnetic tape—*See* magnetic tape unit.

station, master—In a switching network this is a station which sends data to a slave station.

station, net-control—A station on a network which coordinates the use of the network (or circuit) by all of the stations on the net.

station, punching—The area of a keypunch machine where a card is punched.

station, reading—*See* reading station.

station, remote—Usually input/output devices which are not at the immediate site of the computer and which permit additional input queries for data or information.

station, repeater—1. A station at which a repeater is located for the purpose of building up and equalizing the strength of a telephone or telegraph signal in a long line. 2. An intermediate station in a microwave system which is arranged to receive a signal from an adjacent station and amplify and retransmit to another adjacent station. It usually performs the functions in both directions simultaneously.

station, sensing—That position on a card track where data on a card is read, i.e., a brush station where wires make contact through the holes to indicate the presence of a hole in tapes and cards.

station, subscriber—The service provided by the common carrier to connect a customer's location to a central office. This always includes the circuit and some circuit-termination equipment, but may also include input/output equipment. Sometimes referred to as "local loop."

station, tape unit—*See* magnetic tape unit.

station, way—A telegraph term for one of the stations on a multipoint circuit.

statistical analysis—One of the four main techniques of operations research. Data gathering, arranging, sorting, sequencing, and evaluating are all common statistical analyses. Statistical analysis combines mathematical techniques and computer technology to handle a wide range of business and scientific problems wherever large amounts of information or data must be evaluated and analyzed.

STAT PACK (Statistical Routines)—In addition to the mathematical routines available via Math Pack, UNIVAC has implemented a complete set of statistical users. STAT PACK includes routines for parameters (such as chi-squared tests), analysis of variance, regression and correlation analysis, factor analysis, time-series analysis, multi-variant analysis, and distribution functions. (UNIVAC)

status, external-device (ED)—An external device that responds with both its busy signal and interrupt-request signal whenever it recognizes it own address. The unit does not clear out an interrupt request until the interrupt succeeds. The processor notifies the external device that its interrupt has been recognized by sending out an interrupt-reset signal.

status, program (double-word)—*See* double-word, program status.

status routine, channel—*See* channel status routine.

status table, subroutine—*See* table, subroutine.

status word—Information necessary to resume processing following the handling of an interruption of operations.

status word CANCL—This status word indicates that the remote computing system has deleted some information.

status word (communications)—The status word is sent to the central processor in the same manner as the input data word, except that an external interrupt signal is generated after the channel synchronizer has placed the word on the input data lines. In this way, the central processor can distinguish status words from input data words.

status word ERROR—This status word indicates that the remote computing system has detected an error.

status word, external-interrupt—A status word is accompanied by an external-interrupt signal. This signal informs the computer that the word on the data lines is a status word; the computer, interpreting this signal, automatically loads this word in a reserved address in core memory. If the programmer or operator desires a visual indi-

cation of the status word, it must be programmed.

status word, programs—*See* program status word.

status word READY—This status word indicates that the remote computing system is waiting for a statement entry from the terminal.

status words—1. These words either indicate something about the status of the system or indicate that the system is making response to, or diagnosis of, a statement that has been entered. The majority of status words are responses to program-debugging statements and are described under the corresponding debugging statement. 2. The status word contains control information generated by the peripheral control unit and the channel synchronizer. The status word is transmitted to the central processor over the data lines.

step—1. One instruction in a computer routine. 2. To cause a computer to execute one instruction.

step-by-step operation—*See* single step.

step change—The change from one value to another in a single increment and in negligible time.

step counter—A counter used in the arithmetical unit to count the steps in multiplication, division, and shift operation.

step, job—A single unit of work from the user's viewpoint. A job is made up of one or more job steps. A job step is composed of one or more tasks, each task being a single unit of processing.

stepped start-stop system—A start-stop system in which the start signals occur at regular intervals.

stepping register—*Same as* register, shift.

step, program—A phase of one instruction or command in a sequence of instructions. Thus, a single operation.

STET (Specialized Technique for Efficient Typesetting)—A package of precoded subroutines and systems charts covering justification and hyphenation of copy. Exceptional flexibility in editing and control of format is provided. Productivity is increased over manual methods of typesetting by eliminating the decision time for hyphenation, the rubout time for loose and tight lines, and the extra keystrokes for typesetting codes. Straight copy, tabular copy (such as stock exchange tables), and advertising matter may be set in the simplest manner, resulting in faster copy preparation. (Honeywell)

stochastic—A term that refers to trial-and-error procedures as contrasted with the fixed step-by-step procedures of algorithms; results defined in probability terms.

stochastic programming—A generalization of linear programming in which any of the unit costs, the coefficients in the constraint equations, and the right hand sides are random variables subject to known distributions. The aim of such programming is to choose levels for the variables which will minimize the expected (rather than the actual) cost.

stock report, inventory—A report showing the current amount of inventory on hand for each item carried in inventory.

stop, automatic—An automatic halting of a computer-processing operation as the result of an error detected by built-in checking devices.

stop code—A code read in the reader of tape-operated equipment (other than tape-to-card converters), that stops the reader and suspends machine operations. On some machines (like the flexowriter) it is normally nonreproducing; on teletype it is usually reproducing.

stop, coded—A stop instruction built into the routine.

stop control, analog—The stop control terminates the solution, enabling the final values to be observed.

stop, dynamic—A specific stop in a loop which consists of a single jump instruction which effects a jump to itself.

stop element—The last element of a character in certain serial transmissions, used to ensure recognition of the next start element.

stop, form—The automatic device on a printer that stops the machine when the paper has run out.

stop instruction—A machine operation or routine that requires manual action other than the use of the start key to continue processing.

stop key—A push button on the control panel which can halt the processing. This often happens only after the completion of an instruction being executed at a given moment.

stop loop—A small closed loop usually designed and used for operator convenience, i.e., to indicate an error, improper use, or special result.

stopper—The highest memory location in any given system.

stop, program—A stop instruction built into the program that will automatically stop the machine under certain conditions, or upon reaching the end of the processing, or completing the solution of a problem.

stop signal (in a start-stop system)—Signal serving to bring the receiving mechanism to rest in preparation for the reception of the next telegraph signal.

stop time—The time that elapses between completion of reading or writing of a tape record and the time when the tape stops moving.

storage—1. A general term for any device capable of retaining information. 2. Portions of electronic data-processing equipment capable of retaining data for later use. 3. A device capable of receiving data, retaining them for an indefinite period of time, and supplying them upon command. 4. Any device into which units of informa-

tion can be copied, which will hold this information, and from which the information can be obtained at a later time. Devices, such as plugboards, which hold information in the form of arrangements of physical elements, hardware, or equipment; the erasable storage in any given computer.

storage access, auxiliary—Those storage units of relatively larger capacity than the working (scratchpad or internal) storage, but of longer access time, and whose transfer capability is usually in blocks between storage units,

storage access, cyclic—A storage unit in which access to any given location is only possible at specific, equally-spaced times, such as from magnetic drums, delay lines, etc.

storage, acoustic—Normally considered acoustic stores.

storage address display lights—The various indicator lights on the control panel to specify the bit pattern in a selected address.

storage allocation—1. The assignment of blocks of data to specified blocks of storage. 2. The process of allocating storage.

storage allocation, dynamic—Each time a subroutine is called, using this feature the unique storage area for the subroutine is assigned to the first storage available. Thus, all subroutines called on the same level will share the same storage area. This results in a significant storage saving in many cases. In addition, a recursive subroutine call is possible because a new storage area is assigned each time a subroutine is entered.

storage, annex—Same as associative, storage.

storage area—A specifically designated location in various types of storage units, i.e., for programs, constants, input/output buffer storage, etc.

storage area, disk—See storage, working.

storage, automatic—Same as storage, computer.

storage, auxiliary—Same as storage, external.

storage, backing—Same as storage, auxiliary.

storage block—A portion or section of storage usually within a storage area. A storage block is considered a single element for holding a specific or fixed number of words.

storage, buffer—See buffer storage.

storage, built-in—Same as storage, internal.

storage, bulk—See storage, external.

storage capacity—1. Number of units of data that may be stored in a given storage device at one time. It is variously expressed in terms of bits, characters, or words. 2. The amount of data that can be retained in the storage or memory unit of a computer, often expressed as the number of words that can be retained.

storage, cathode-ray tube—Storage is accomplished by beams of electrons accessing storage cells and operating on them. This does not include storage tubes used for display purposes which are cathode-ray tubes of special designs for continuously holding images on the screen.

storage cell—An elementary unit of storage, e.g., binary cell, decimal cell.

storage cells—The actual areas of a magnetic surface that are separately and distinctly magnetized by the storage information.

storage, changeable—Data are not destroyed (nondestructive) in this peripheral or storage device in the process of changing medium to disks, paper tape magazines, or tape reels. The parts of this storage device which contain the data can be removed and replaced by other parts containing different data.

storage charge—The expense per unit of storage on a peripheral device like disks, drums, or tape. The storage charge is usually levied by time-sharing service companies on a monthly basis and usually involves the data which the customer desires to be saved on a fairly permanent basis.

storage, circulating—A device or unit that stores information in a train or pattern of pulses, where the pattern of pulses issuing at the final end are sensed, amplified, reshaped and reinserted into the device at the beginning end.

storage, common—Since COBOL programs can be chained (an executive function), intermediate data results can be maintained between programs using the common storage provision of COBOL.

storage compacting—Certain hardware features make feasible the dynamic relocation of programs residing in the central storage —a necessity in order to provide an effective multiprogramming environment. At program termination, the storage assigned is returned to the pool of the available central storage. Storage compacting is initiated if, and only if, a requirement exists for contiguous storage, and compacting can meet this requirement. Compacting is never performed unnecessarily, as the storage-contents control routine always attempts to fit the programs into the gaps in the in-use store, if possible.

storage, computer—Often called computer or automatic storage, it is a designed part of the automatic data processing system or hardware and may be controlled automatically and without the need for human intervention.

storage concept, add to—The process which immediately enters the final sum of the accumulator into the computer memory.

storage, constant—A part of storage designated to store the invariable quantities required for processing.

storage, content-addressed—1. A storage device in which storage locations are identified by their contents, not by names or positions. 2. A memory mechanism which interrogates the computer memory for content rather than memory location. Normally, a computer memory is accessed by address loca-

tion such as 04267 rather than by content, such as "Print Total Balance of J. J. Jones."

storage, coordinate—A storage unit whose elements are arranged in a matrix so that access to any location requires the use of two or more coordinates, i.e., a cathode-ray tube store and a core store using coincident-current selection.

storage, core—The fundamental and most important storage of the central processing unit and usually of magnetic cores, each core of which is capable of storing one binary digit and which are uniquely arranged in matrix arrays on digit planes or worked strings. Almost all core storage is high speed, random access, and expandable with high speed auxilliary units or extra cores.

storage, core-rope—A unique memory device invented by Olsen of the Lincoln Laboratory of the Massachusetts Institute of Technology. Information is stored in the form of an array of cores and wires, the wires being wound in one direction or the other through the core. The pattern which results resembles a rope and permits a selection of a single core for a given pattern or pulse. The information is stored in the wiring rather than in the core itself, the core acting much as a switch. *Same as* core-rope storage, linear selection switch, rope memory, rope storage, and Olsen memory.

storage cycle—1. A periodic sequence of events occurring when information is transferred to or from the storage device of a computer. 2. Storing, sensing, and regeneration form parts of the storage sequence.

storage cycle time (in microseconds)—For core storage, the total time to read and restore one storage word. For drum or other serial storage the total time for one revolution.

storage, cyclic—*Same as* storage, circulating.

storage data, carrier—This type of storage usually requires some action by an operator such as selection and loading before automatic control becomes operable.

storage data, magnetic—A storage device in which binary data are represented by the direction of magnetization in each unit of an array of magnetic material, usually in the shape of toroidal rings, but also in other forms such as wraps on bobbins.

storage, dedicated—The allocation of, reservation of, or obligation of, set-aside, earmarked, or assigned areas of storage which are committed to some specific purpose, user, or problem, i.e., exclusively reserved space on a disk storage unit for an accounting procedure, problem, or data set.

storage, delay-line—A storage technique in which data are stored by allowing them to travel through some medium such as mercury (acoustic storage).

storage density—The number of characters stored per unit length or area of storage medium (for example, number of characters per inch of magnetic tape).

storage, destructive—Some storage devices are designed so that contents at a location need to be regenerated after being read, if they are to be retained. CRT (cathode-ray tube) storage and some cores are of the destructive type, and regeneration is most often automatic when retention is desired.

storage device—A device in which data can be inserted, retained and then retrieved for later use.

storage, di-cap—A device capable of holding data in the form of an array of charged capacitors, or condensers, and using diodes for controlling information flow.

storage, direct-access—A type of storage device wherein access to the next position from which information is to be obtained is in no way dependent on the position from which information was previously obtained.

storage, disk—The storage of data on the surface of magnetic disks. (Related to magnetic disk and magnetic-disk storage.)

storage drum—A random-access storage device for approximately four million alphanumeric characters or up to eight million digits, which can be retrieved at a rate of 1.2 million characters a second. Many units, providing on-line storage for millions of alphanumeric characters, can be linked to a processor (some systems) .

storage, dual—These storage devices permit storage of logic of a particular programmer's own design as well as specific instructions and data, i.e., the programmer's instruction code is utilized to write a program of instructions.

storage dump—1. To copy, or the process of copying, the contents of all or part of a storage, usually from an internal storage into an external storage. 2. A printout of the contents of all or part of a particular storage device. 3. The data resulting from the process, as in 1. (Synonymous with memory dump, memory printout, and dump.)

storage, dynamic—Refers to mobility of stored data in time and space. Acoustic delay lines, in which stored data are constantly in motion relative to storage medium and require continuous regeneration, are an example of a dynamic storage device. Magnetic-core storage, in which the stored data are fixed in time and space, is an example of a static storage device.

storage, electrostatic—1. The storage of data on a dielectric surface, such as the screen of a cathode-ray tube, in the form of the presence or absence of spots bearing electrostatic charges; these spots can persist for a short time after the removal of the electrostatic charging force. 2. A storage device used as in the foregoing description.

storage, erasable—1. A storage device whose data can be altered during the course of a computation, e.g., magnetic tape, drum, and cores. 2. An area of storage used for

temporary storage. 3. Media that may hold information that can be changed. The media can be reused, e.g., magnetic tape, drum, or core.

storage exchange—1. The interchange of the total contents of two storage devices or locations, such as two registers. 2. A switching device capable of controlling and handling the flow or exchange of data between storage units or other elements of a system.

storage, external—1. Storage facilities divorced from the computer itself but holding information in the form prescribed for the computer, e.g., magnetic tapes, magnetic wire, punched cards, etc. 2. The storage is the source of operating data. It may be under the control of the computer, but data to be operated upon must be transferred to secondary or internal storage before operations commence, and they are returned to external storage only after operations are completed. External storage devices usually have larger capacities and lower access speeds than internal secondary storage.

storage facilities, data—See data storage facilities.

storage-fast—High-speed input or access storage, usually in a hierarchy of storage units and related relatively. An imprecise term.

storage, fast-access—The section of the entire storage from which data may be obtained most rapidly.

storage-file—A specific purpose type of storage designed to contain a master file, usually relatively large and uniformly accessible.

storage fill—The storing of characters in storage areas not used for data storage or the program for a particular machine run.

storage, fixed—A storage device that stores data not alterable by computer instructions, e.g., magnetic core storage with a lockout feature, and punched paper tape. (Synonymous with permanent storage and nonerasable storage.)

storage flip-flop—A bistable storage device which stores binary data as states of flip-flop elements.

storage, high-speed—A specific storage device which has relatively short access time, as compared to main memory of the CPU, i.e., at least significantly shorter than other devices in the same computer system, such as disk-tape storage.

storage-immediate access—Storage, usually in several locations, which has access time that is slight in comparison with operation time, i.e., very fast or real-time capabilities.

storage inherent—Often called computer or automatic storage, it is a designed part of the automatic data processing system or hardware, and may be controlled automatically and without human intervention.

storage input—See input storage.

storage input/output—A specific storage area in a computer reserved for data or instructions received by, or ready to be transferred from or to, an external (peripheral) input or output device or to another specific section of storage.

storage inquiry, direct access—A process through which information can be directly requested from temporary or permanent storage devices.

storage instantaneous—Storage, usually in several locations, having access time which is slight in comparison with operation time, i.e., very fast or real-time capabilities.

storage, instruction—*Same as* instruction area.

storage integrator—In an analog computer, an integrator used to store a voltage in the hold condition for future use while the rest of the computer assumes another computer control state.

storage, intermediate—A kind of an electronic scratchpad. As input is turned into output, it usually goes through a series of changes. An intermediate memory storage holds each of the successive changes just as long as it is needed. It can hold data picked up or developed in one program cycle for use in succeeding program cycles. It can accumulate data from cycle to cycle.

storage, internal—1. The storage of data on a device that is an integral part of a computer. 2. The storage facilities forming an integral physical part of the computer and directly controlled by the computer. In such facilities all data are automatically accessible to the computer, e.g., magnetic core, and magnetic tape on-line. (Synonymous with internal memory and contrasted with external storage.)

storage, large-capacity core—A component that permits one or two million increments of directly addressable core storage to be added to a system. The address structure allows a maximum of 16 million bytes of core storage. These units are not I/O (input/output) units. This low cost auxiliary bulk storage may be used as an extension of main storage or as intermediate storage between main storage and I/O devices.

storage light—The light on a control console panel which indicates that a parity check error has occurred on a character as it was read into storage.

storage limits register (SLR)—To prevent inadvertant program reference to out-of-range storage addresses, the processor provides a hardware storage protection feature called the storage limits register (SLR). The SLR can be loaded by the executive system to establish allowable operating areas for each program. These areas are termed the program I (instruction) and D (data) areas. When control is given to a particular program, the executive loads the SLR with the appropriate I and D boundaries. (UNIVAC)

storage list, available—The queuing or chaining of uncommitted core blocks together for allocation by the supervisory program.

storage list, uncommitted—Blocks of storage that are chained together which are not allocated at any specific moment.

storage location—1. A storage position holding one machine word and usually having a specific address. 2. The character position used to address a data field in a character-addressable machine.

storage locations, buffer—*See* buffer storage locations.

storage locations, internal—*Same as* storage working.

storage, loop—A particular storage device which uses continuous closed loops of magnetic tape with read/write heads as a storage medium. Such tapes are read forward or backward to increase speed and efficiency of access, and a significant number of such ready for read/write loops compose a tape bin.

storage, magnetic—A storage device that utilizes the magnetic properties of materials to store data, e.g., magnetic cores, tapes, and films.

storage, magnetic card—A magnetic storage type in which the storage medium is the surface of plastic flexible cards, which are operated upon individually. NCR calls their cards CRAM cards, meaning card random access memory.

storage magnetic core—*See* magnetic core storage.

storage, magnetic data—*See* storage, core.

storage, magnetic-disk—A storage device or system consisting of disks, on whose surface information is stored in the form of magnetic spots arranged in a manner to represent binary data. These data are arranged in circular tracks around the disks and are accessible to reading and writing heads on an arm that can be moved mechanically to the desired disk and then to the desired track on that disk. Data from a given track are read or written sequentially as the disk rotates.

storage, magnetic-drum—The storage of data on the surface of magnetic drums. (Related to magnetic drum.)

storage, magnetic-film—1. The magnetic film storage of the computer provides high-speed internal storage. By using this thin-film storage area as an auxiliary temporary storage medium, faster computation can be obtained. In a typical installation, any one of the addresses in control store can be accessed in 167 nanoseconds and have a complete cycle time of 667 nanoseconds. Because of this high speed, thin-film is the most frequently used portion of the computer's internal storage area; it may be referenced three times in the same time that it takes to make one reference to the core-storage area. The high access and internal switching times of thin-film store make it ideal for use as temporary storage of operands while the actual computation of data is taking place. (UNIVAC)

storage, magnetic-tape—A storage device in which data is stored in the form of magnetic spots on iron oxide or coated plastic tape. Binary data are stored as small magnetized spots arranged in column form across the width of the tape. A read/write head is usually associated with each column of magnetized spots so that all columns can be read or written at a time as the tape traverses the head.

storage, main—Usually the fastest storage device of a computer and the one from which instructions are executed. (Contrasted with auxiliary storage.)

storage management, time sharing—See time sharing, storage management.

storage, manual-switch—Storage is in the form of arrays of manually set switches, and data may be entered by manually placing the switch in certain positions which either represent data or control data flow.

storage map—Pictorial aid that the programmer uses to estimate the proportion of storage capacity to be allocated to data.

storage mark—The name given to a point location that defines the character space immediately to the left of the most significant character in accumulator storage. An example would be:

a	7	4	6	7	4	8	9

in which the letter "a" would be the storage mark.

storage mark, record—A unique or specific symbol on the machine equipment which indicates the length of the record being read into storage from a card reader.

storage, mass—The type of memory device now available in many designs and media forms which is capable of retaining and communicating vast amounts of data, often in the trillion bit range.

storage, mass (executive)—The executive system is designed to provide installations with an effective and efficient utilization of the mass storage devices available. The result is an ability to relieve operators and programmers of responsibilities in maintaining and physically handling cards, magnetic tapes, etc., thus, eliminating many of the errors that heretofore inherently accompanied the use of large-scale software systems. At the same time, the overall efficiency of operating is considerably improved. Provisions are made for the maintenance of permanent data files and program files on the mass storage devices, with full facilities for modification and manipulation of these files. Security measures are invoked by the executive system to ensure that files are not subjected to unauthorized use. Provisions are also made within the executive system for automatic relocation of files of low usage-frequency to magnetic tape, as unused mass storage space approaches exhaustion. When the use of files related in such a manner is requested, they are retrieved and restored, under control of the executive system, with no inconvenience to the user.

storage, matrix—A storage unit whose elements are arranged in a matrix so that access to one location requires the use of two or more coordinates, i.e., a cathode-ray tube store and a core store using coincident-current selection.

storage medium—The material on which data is recorded and which may be paper tape, cards, magnetic tape, strips, cards, or devices such as magnetic drums, etc.

storage, mercury—The storage of data in a mercury delay line. (Related to mercury delay line.)

storage, modifier—Storage where a set of locations is used primarily to hold modifiers.

storage, nesting—See storage, push-down.

storage, nondestructive—A type of storage whose location is regenerated after it is read, since it is desired and designed into the unit that the contents are to be retained at the location after reading. Drums, double cores, punched cards, most magnetic tapes, disks, etc., are examples of nondestructive storage.

storage, nonerasable—See storage, fixed.

storage, nonvolatile—Storage media that retains information in the absence of power and which may be made available upon restoration of power, e.g., magnetic tapes, drums, or cores.

storage, off-line—Storage not under control of the central processing unit.

storage, on-line—A storage device under direct control of the central processing unit.

storage, on-line mass—See storage, mass.

storage output—See output area.

storage, parallel—1. Storage in which all bits, or characters, or (especially) words are essentially equally available in space, without time being one of the coordinates. Parallel storage contrasts with serial storage. When words are in parallel, the storage is said to be parallel by words; when characters within words (or binary digits within words or characters) are dealt with simultaneously, not one after the other, the storage is parallel by characters (or parallel by bit respectively). 2. A storage device wherein characters, words, or digits are dealt with simultaneously. (Contrasted with serial storage.)

storage, parallel-search—A storage device in which storage locations are identified by their contents. (Synonymous with content-addressed storage and associative storage.)

storage parity—See parity, storage.

storage permanent—Same as storage, nonvolatile.

storage, photographic—Any storage scheme utilizing photographic processes. This includes various microimage systems, computer-output microfilm, and binary data storage on photographic mediums.

storage, primary—*Same as* storage, main.

storage print, program—A program that produces a printout of storage and registers to aid the user in locating the reason(s) for a program malfunction.

storage, program—A portion of the internal storage reserved for the storage of programs, routines, and subroutines. In many systems protection devices are used to prevent inadvertent alteration of the contents of the program storage. (Contrasted with working storage.)

storage protect—This hardware function provides positive protection to the system executive routine and all other programs. It not only protects against processor execution, but also against I/O (input/output) data area destruction. Because it is a hardware function rather than software, it reduces multiprogramming complexities.

storage protection—1. Continued existence of a stored program requires protection from all contemporary programs and, in particular, that each stored program have inviolate storage areas. This is accomplished by independently establishing reserved areas in each storage module and inhibiting a program of reading, writing, or transferring to a location that is not within its reserved areas. Every instruction that references the central store has the final address checked to ensure that it falls within a permissible area. 2. Allows several programs to reside in core storage at the same time while one is being executed. It also allows transfer of data from peripheral equipment to memory while other programs already are in memory. Storage protection eliminates danger that one program would inadvertently be placed over, and thereby destroy, another program.

storage, push-down—A storage which works as though it comprised a number of registers arranged in a column, with only the register at the top of the column connected to the rest of the storage. Each word in turn, enters the top register and is then "pushed down" the column from register to register to make room for the next words to arrive. As the words are transferred out of the storage units (out of the top register), other data in storage moves back up the column from register to register to fill the top register.

storage, push-up—Special storage which operates so as to maintain a pushdown list so that the next item of data to be retrieved is the oldest item on the list, i.e., it is pushed up in a type of queue arrangement wherein the word at the top came from the bottom in steps and has been in the longest and will go out first.

storage, quick-access—*Same as* storage, high speed.

storage, random-access—A storage technique in which the time required to obtain information is independent of the location of the information most recently obtained. This strict definition must be qualified by the observation that we usually mean relatively random. Thus, magnetic drums are relatively nonrandom access when compared to magnetic cores for main storage, but are relatively random access when compared to magnetic tapes for file storage. (Synonymous with random-access memory and contrasted with sequential-access storage.)

storage, rapid access—*Same as* storage, high speed.

storage, read-only—*Same as* storage, fixed.

storage, recording—1. A process providing for the preservation, in any form, of telegraph signals, or the elements of a telegraph signal. 2. The result of this process.

storage, regenerative—*See* storage, circulating.

storage register—A register in the storage of the computer, in contrast with a register in one of the other units of the computer. (Synonymous with memory register.)

storage registers, associative—*Same as* associative storage. Those registers which are not identified by their name or position but which are known and addressed by their content.

storage resolver—A small section of storage, particularly in drum tape or disk storage units, that has much faster access than the remainder of the storage.

storage retrieval, flying-head—Exceptional information-retrieval speed is developed by use of flying-head mechanisms on various drum units. The flying-head (air-floating head) technique combines aerodynamic and pneumatic principles. Read/write heads float on a boundary layer of air generated by the rotation of the drum, at one half of a thousandth of an inch or less from the oxide-coated surface of the drum. The read/write head is suspended in this position by the opposing forces of the boundary layer of air and the head-positioning mechanism.

storage, routine—*Same as* instruction area.

storage, scratchpad—High-speed memory device used to store the location of an interrupted program and to retrieve the latter after the interrupting program has been completed.

storage, searching—*Same as* storage, content addressed.

storage, secondary—*Same as* storage, external.

storage, sequential-access—A storage technique in which the items of information stored become available only in a one after the other sequence, whether or not all the information or only some of it is desired, e.g., magnetic-tape storage. (Related to serial storage, and contrasted with random-access storage.)

storage, serial—1. Storage in which time is one of the coordinates used to locate any given bit, character, or (especially) word.

Storage, in which words within given groups of several words appear one after the other in time sequence, and in which access time, therefore, includes a variable latency or waiting time of zero to many word-times, is said to be serial by word. Storage in which the individual bits comprising a word appear in time sequence is serial by bit. Storage for coded-decimal or other nonbinary numbers in which the characters appear in time sequence is serial by character; e.g., magnetic drums are usually serial by word but may be serial by bit or parallel by bit. or serial by character and parallel by bit, etc. 2. A storage technique in which time is one of the factors used to locate any given bit, character, word, or groups of words appearing one after the other in time sequence, and in which access time includes a variable latency or waiting time of from zero to many word times. (Related to sequential-access storage, and contrasted with random-access storage.)

storage, shared—The ability to share core storage between two computers. This means that either machine can insert information into the storage and either machine can have access to the data and use it.

storage stack—A group of storage elements connected together in some fashion, i.e., a stack of data could be operated on a first-in, first-out basis.

storage, static—Storage of information that is fixed in space and available at any time, e.g., flip-flop, electrostatic, or coincident-current magnetic-core storage.

storage switch, manual—*See* storage, manual switch.

storage system, mass—Mass storage systems contain a mass-storage device such as a magnetic-tape unit. Other mass-storage devices may be used such as a CRAM (Card Random Access Memory) unit, disk unit, or cartridge-tape unit. The operating system is basically the same with minor exceptions. The magnetic-tape unit is used as the system unit, which contains the master file of operating-system routines, input/output drivers, utility routines, and library subroutines. The first program on the system unit is a bootstrap loader. This loader loads the monitor and initalizes system operations. The bootstrap loader is brought into memory with the "preset" button on the computer console.

Full job stacking and load and go capabilities are available in mass-storage systems. The monitor automatically controls job processing by utilizing the routines contained on the system unit. Control information for each job is taken from the system input unit. In the operator mode of operation this unit is a typewriter.

storage, tape-loop—*See* storage loop.

storage tape, magnetic—A tape or ribbon or any material impregnated or coated with magnetic material on which information may be placed in the form of magnetically polarized spots.

storage, temporary—Internal-storage locations reserved for intermediate and partial results.

storage, thin film—*See* thin film memory.

storage tube, charge—An early computer memory device that stored a single charge in a tube. The presence or absence of a charge in the tube was the equivalent of a binary digit.

storage, uniformly accessible—That particular storage which is designed to reduce the effect of variation of access time for an arbitrary sequence of addresses.

storage unit—Any of several registers in the memory or storage of the computer.

storage, variable field—An indefinite limit of length for the storage field.

storage, volatile—Storage media such that if applied power is cut off, the stored information is lost e.g., acoustic delay lines, electrostatic tubes.

storage, Williams-tube—A cathode-ray tube used as an electrostatic storage device and of the type designed by F. C. Williams, University of Manchester, England.

storage, working—1. A portion of internal storage reserved for intermediate results. 2. The portion of the internal storage reserved for the data of a current program, and for intermediate and partial results. 3. The area on a disk used to hold dynamic or working data. This is contrasted to reserved area containing permanent information such as compilers, track and sector information, etc., and user area for semipermanent storage.

storage, zero-access—1. The storage for which the latency (waiting time) is small. Though once widely used, this term is becoming less acceptable, since it constitutes a misnomer. 2. Storage for which the waiting time is negligible at all times.

store—1. To transfer an element of information to a device from which the unaltered information can be obtained at a later time. 2. To retain data in a device from which it can be obtained at a later time. 3. The British term for storage. 4. To put in storage. 5. To place information in a location in storage so that it may be retrieved for later use.

store-and-forward—A type of message-switching system.

store-and-forward switching center—A message-switching center in which the message is accepted from the sender whenever he offers it, held in a physical store, and forwarded to the receiver whenever he is able to accept it.

store, B—*Same as* register, B.

store, computer—*Same as* storage.

stored program—*See* program, stored.

stored-program computer—1. A computer that can alter its own instructions in storage as though they were data and subsequently execute the altered instructions. 2. A computer in which the instructions that specify the operations to be performed are stored in the form of coded information in main memory, along with the data currently being operated upon, making possible simple repetition of operations and modification by the computer of its own instructions.

stored routine—A series of instructions in storage to direct the step-by-step operation of the machine. (Synonymous with stored program.)

store, local—Local store is used by IBM System/360 for several things. Here indexing registers are maintained for keeping track of addresses and for storing results of intermediate arithmetic. Local store also provides a place for control words of the programs residing in core storage. One might almost call this the computer's scratchpad, although most computers have too little capacity to carry out the function with full effectiveness. As a consequence, registers are often loaded and unloaded into the main memory to make room for intermediate steps. The loading and unloading take time and are unproductive.

store operators—Storing information in the PRT (Program Reference Table) is done through the use of relative addresses. Storing operations are carried out in the following manner. To store a value in the PRT, a literal (i.e., an integer with a value from 0 to 1023) equal to the relative address of the pertinent PRT location must be the top word in the stack. The information to be stored must be the second from top word in the stack. With these conditions existing, a store operator can be executed and the following actions will occur automatically (some systems).

store protection, multiprogramming—*See* multiprogramming, store protection.

storing associative—*Same as* storage, content addressed.

straight binary—*See* binary, straight.

straight-line code—The repetition by explicit instructions for each repetition, of a sequence of instructions, with or without address modification. Generally, straight-line coding will require less execution time and more space than equivalent loop coding. If the number of repetitions is large, this type of coding is tedious unless a generator is used. The feasibility of straight-line coding is limited by the space required as well as by the difficulty of coding a variable number of repetitions.

straight-line coding—Coding in which loops are avoided by the repetition of parts of the coding when required.

stream, bit—A term commonly used in conjunction with a transmission method in which character separation is accomplished by the terminal equipment, and the bits are transmitted over the circuit in a consecutive line of bits.

stream bit transmission—The method of transmitting characters at fixed time intervals. No stop-start elements are used, and the bits making up the characters follow each other without pause.

stream, input job—An input source of documents, usually punched cards or card images, which is the first part of an operating system. The stream contains the beginning of job indicators, directions optional programs, etc.

STRESS—Structural Engineering System Solver.

string—1. A connected sequence of characters, words, or other elements. 2. A set of records arranged in an ascending or a descending sequence according to the increasing or decreasing magnitude of their keys.

string, alphabetic—A sequence of letters from the same alphabet, i.e., a character string.

string, bit—*See* bit string.

string break—The point at which a sort can find no more records with sufficiently high control keys to fit on the current output string.

string, character—*See* character string.

string file—Tape, wire, or string used to arrange documents for convenient reference and use.

string length—The number of records in a string.

string manipulation—A technique for manipulating strings of characters.

string of bits—*See* bits, string of.

string process system (SPS)—This consists of a package of subroutines that perform basic operations on strings of characters. SPS is used by the executive and many computer subsystems. It performs string reading and writing, hash-code string look-up, and string comparisons (some computers).

strings, Hollerith—*See* Hollerith strings.

string sorting—A group of sequenced records, normally stored in auxiliary computer storage, i.e., disk, tape, or drum.

string, symbol—*See* symbol string.

strip, encoding—On bank checks, the area in which magnetic ink will be deposited to represent characters.

stripe recording, magnetic—If the magnetic material is deposited in strip form on a document or card, the term magnetic stripe recording is often used.

strip file, magnetic—*See* file, magnetic strip.

strip, magnetic-file—A file storage device which uses strips of material with surfaces that can be magnitized for the purpose of storing data.

strip, magnetic-tape—On each magnetic-tape strip is listed hundreds of individual records. As a specific record is needed, a computer signal similar to the combination to a safe causes the proper strip to drop from the deck. The strip then whips around the fast-moving drum that, at eye-blinking speeds, searches for the current record, reads or writes on it, and transmits its data to the computer for further processing.

strip record—*See* record, strip.

strips, tape—*See* tape strips.

strobe pulse—A pulse to gate the output of a core-memory sense amplifier into a trigger in a register. Also called sample pulse.

stroke—A line segment, point, or other mark used in the formation of characters.

stroke, character—*See* character stroke.

stroke edge—*See* edge stroke.

stroke edge irregularity—*See* edge, stroke irregularity.

stroke gate, Sheffer—*Same as* gate, NAND.

stroke, Sheffer—*Same as* NAND.

structure, block—A technique allowing program segmentation into blocks of information or sub-routines of a total program.

structure flowcharts—*See* flowchart structure.

structure, list—*See* list, structure.

structure, order—*See* instruction format.

structure, priority—The organization of a system for processing. The priority structure of the system depends not upon the number of instructions, but upon the complexity of the programs. The structure can range from systems with no priority to multicomplex organizations with multilayers of interrupts and multilevels of priority.

structure, system—*See* system structure.

structure tables—*See* tables, structure.

study, application—The detailed process of determining a computer system or set of procedures for using a given computer for definite functions or operations, and establishing the specifications to be used as the basis for the selection of computer equipment.

study, process—*See* process study.

study, systems—*See* systems study.

stunt box—A device to control nonprinting functions of a teletype terminal.

style—A construction, without any size restiction, that is used in optical character recognition. Different sizes of the given character style are proportional in all respects.

stylus, electronic—*Same as* light pen.

stylus, light (pen)—When this pen-like device is pointed at information displayed on the screen, it detects light from the cathode-ray tube when a beam passes within its field of view. The pen's response is transmitted to the computer which relates the computer's action to the section of the image being displayed. In this way, the operator can delete or add text, maintain tighter control over the program, and choose alternative courses of action.

stylus printer—*See* printer, wire.

subalphabet—A subset of an alphabet, i.e., any group of less than 26 letters.

subchannel, sharing—A multiplexor channel allows the attachment of up to eight control units. Each control unit is attached logically to one or more subchannels. For example, the transmission-control unit attaches logically to up to 31 subchannels. Various numbers of subchannels are available in the multiplexor channels. Some subchannels can be shared by multiple units attached to a single control unit, for example, magnetic-tape units attached to a single tape-control unit. Subchannels, programmed as separate channels, can operate concurrently, but only one device on a subchannel can be in operation at a given time. In the multiplex mode, there is some overlap of processing with I/O (input/output) operations. In the burst mode, there is some overlap between processing and I/O operations. (IBM)

subchannels, multiplexor—The multiplexor permits simultaneous operation of attached low-speed devices through a time-sharing (byte-interleaved mode) principle. Each device sends an identifier to the channel each time it requests service. The multiplexor channel, using this identifier, updates the correct control counts, etc., and stores the data in the correct locations.

subcomponents, system (time sharing)—*See* time sharing, system subcomponents.

subject program—*Same as* program, source.

subjob—A routine or machine run. A program may be broken into several subjobs or tasks to utilize more effectively computer CPU.

subjunction gate—*Same as* gate, AND-NOT B or gate, B AND-NOT A.

suboptimization—The process of fulfilling or optimizing some chosen objective that is an integral part of a broader objective. Usually the broad-level objective and lower-level objective are different.

suboptimization, pricing—When using a multiple-pricing alogrithm, suboptimization enters the first variable into the basic program which gives by itself the greatest improvement in the objective; the next variable entered gives the greatest additional improvement, and so on. This technique tends to prevent the first entering variable from being removed by the second, etc.

subprogram—1. A part of a larger program that can be compiled independently. 2. Part of a program. *See* program. 3. *See* routine.

subroutine—1. The system or sequence of machine instructions that complete the carefully defined function or program. 2. The set of instructions in machine code to direct the computer to carry out a well-defined mathematical or logical operation; a part of a routine. A subroutine is often written with symbolic relative addresses even when the routine to which it belongs is not written in symbolic addresses. 3. A sequence of instructions to tell the computer to perform a specific task. For example, calculating an employee's social security deduction. Extensive libraries of subroutines are delivered with every computer system—a time and money savings for the user. 4. A program that defines desired operations and which may be included in another program to produce the desired operations. 5. A routine which is

arranged so that control may be transferred to it from a master routine and so that, at the conclusion of the subroutine, control reverts to the master routine. Such a subroutine is usually called a closed subroutine.
6. A single routine may simultaneously be both a subroutine with respect to another routine and a master routine with respect to a third. Usually control is transferred to a single subroutine from more than one place in the master routine and the reason for using the subroutine is to avoid having to repeat the same sequence of instructions in different places in the master routine. (Clarified by routine.)

subroutine analyzer—*Same as* analyzer.

subroutine calls—The linkage between a call to a subroutine and the actual entry to the subroutine is made in a manner similar to future patching. All calls to a particular subroutine are linked in the same way. When a call to a subroutine is indicated to the loader, the address where it was last called and the name of the subroutine are entered in a subroutine call table (SCT). A subroutine should not be loaded twice, therefore a check is made to determine if it has been previously called or loaded. If a subroutine is called which is already in the table, the first call in the new program is linked to the last call specified in the new subroutine call record. When a subroutine is loaded, its name and entry address are entered in the SCT and any previous calls are patched and directed to the subroutine entry point with use of the link-back process.

subroutine, closed—A frequently used subroutine which can be stored in one place and then connected to a routine using various linkages or calling sequences or commands, at one or more locations, i.e., when it is stored separately from the main routine, jump instructions from program control will fetch or call the beginning of this subroutine, and at its end, another transfer instruction will return it.

subroutine, dating—A specific subroutine which computes and stores associated dates and times and is programmed for file updating relating to work with computer runs of various types, but usually time-sensitive.

subroutine, direct-insert—A subroutine inserted directly into the linear operational sequence rather than by a jump. Such a subroutine must be recopied at each point that it is needed in a routine.

subroutine, division—*See* division subroutine.

subroutine, dynamic—A subroutine which involves parameters, such as decimal-point position or item size, from which a relatively coded subroutine is derived. The computer itself is expected to adjust or generate the subroutine according to the parametric values chosen.

subroutine, editing—This subroutine has pa-

rameters whose values are selected prior to execution and are used for performing various operations, usually on input and output data and before main program operations.

subroutine, first-order—This subroutine is entered directly from the main routine or program and subsequently returned to it.

subroutine, first remove—*Same as* subroutine, first order.

subroutine, generalized—Subroutines that are written for easy and ready use in various programs with only minor adjustments by the programmer.

subroutine, in-line—A subroutine inserted directly into the linear operational sequence. Such a subroutine must be recopied at each point that it is needed in a routine.

subroutine library—A set of standard and proven subroutines which is kept on file for use at any time.

subroutine, linked—*See* subroutine closed.

subroutine, one-level—A program which cannot use other subroutines or itself during its execution, i.e., a closed subroutine.

subroutine, open—*Same as* direct-insert subroutine.

subroutine, relocatable—A subroutine that can be located physically and independently in the memory. Its object-time location is determined by the processor.

subroutines, arithmetic — Often includes all the arithmetic subroutines required for FORTRAN, such as sine, cosine, $\log_e$, $\log_{10}$, exponent, tangent, arctangent, and square root.

subroutine, second order—This subroutine is entered from a first order subroutine and returned to it or to the main routine, whereas, the first order subroutine is entered directly from the main program.

subroutine, second remove—*Same as* subroutine second order.

subroutines floating-point—Special routines that handle floating point numbers as arguments.

subroutines, I/O (input/output) system—I/O format control that provides for the various format statements used in the FORTRAN language. These subroutines are also available to other programs and may be called from the systems library tape.

subroutines, mathematical—These subroutines provide complete sets of mathematical subroutines including sine, cosine, sq. root, exponent, log, etc.

subroutines, nest of—The process of sublevels for subroutines, wherein one subroutine will transfer control to another subroutine and so on with ultimate control climbing back through the array of subroutines to the subroutine which first transferred control.

subroutines, scientific—Several subroutines that perform standard mathematical operations are available in computer systems. These operations include fixed-point multiplication and division; floating-point addition, subtraction, multiplication, and division; square-root extraction; matrix and statistical functions; and calculation of logarithmic and trigonometric functions.

subroutine, standard—A subroutine that is applicable to a class of problems.

subroutine, static—A subroutine that involves no parameters other than the addresses of the operands.

subroutine status table—*See* subroutine table.

subroutines, violation—When the input does not conform to preset criteria or limits, a violation subroutine takes over.

subroutine table—The routine for maintaining a listing of the subroutines in core and for bringing from file the subroutines as needed by the application program.

subroutine, test—A routine designed to show whether a computer is functioning properly.

subroutining, multilevel (display)—The control state permits the display to jump from accessing one location in the memory to any other. When it is desired to jump to a display subroutine, the return address is automatically stored in a push-down list.

subscriber and inquiry display—*See* display inquiry and subscriber.

subscriber station—The service provided by the common carrier to connect a customer's location to a central office. This always includes the circuit and some circuit-termination equipment, but may also include input/output equipment. Sometimes referred to as local shop.

subscript—1. A letter or symbol in typography written below a set name to identify a particular element or elements of that set. 2. An indexing notation. 3. An integer used to specify a particular item in a list or table according to COBOL rules, and consisting of a numeric data literal-name. 4. A notation used to specify a particular member of an array where each member is referenced only in terms of the array name.

subscripted variable—A variable followed by one or more subscripts enclosed in parentheses.

subscripts (FORTRAN)—An array is a group of quantities. It is often advantageous to be able to refer to this group by one name and to refer to each individual quantity in this group in terms of its place in the group. For example, suppose it is desired to refer to the second quantity in a group, in ordinary mathematical notation this would be (the variable) $NEXT_2$. The quantity 2 is called a subscript. In FORTRAN, it is expressed NEXT(2), and if the array consists of 15, 12, 18, 42, 19, then the second (position) value or subscripted NEXT(2) would have the value 12.

subsegment—1. A segment of a program is defined as that portion of memory which is committed by a single reference to the loader. Usually a segment overlays some other segment and may have within itself other portions which in turn overlay one another, i.e., subsegments. 2. That part of a segment which is actually brought into memory when the loader is referenced is called the fixed part of a segment. Segments are built up from separate relocatable elements, common blocks, or other segments.

subsegment tables—For each segment which itself has subsegments, a table is automatically associated with its fixed part. This table contains a seven-word entry for each of the subsegments. The entry holds information for the loader that describes the action necessary to load the corresponding subsegment and the limits of memory in each bank that is used by the segment. It also contains some pointer addresses to allow the diagnostic system to analyze the current state of a program. Using the information in this entry, it is possible to maintain up-to-date indications as to which segments are currently intact in memory and which were destroyed by the loading of some other segment.

subsequent counter—*See* counter, subsequence.

subset—1. A set contained within a set. 2. A subscriber apparatus in a communications network. 3. A contraction of the words "subscriber set" which has been used for many years to refer to the device which is installed on a subscriber's premises. 4. A modulation/demodulation device designed to make business-machine signals compatible with the communications facilities and vice versa. A data subset accepts digital information, converts it into a suitable form for transmission over the telephone circuits, and then reconverts the data to its original form at the receiving end.

subset, character—A smaller set of certain characters from a larger or universal set, all with specified common features.

subsets, remote—*See* remote subsets.

substantive input—The transferral of data from an external storage device to an internal storage device, usually from a mass storage unit and off-line, but not always so.

substep—A part of a step.

substitute—To replace an element of information by some other element of information.

subsystem control communication—*See* communication subsystem control.

subsystems—When the main program requires that the central processor employ a subsystem, the central processor issues control signals which select the proper subsystem and initiate the desired action. Once this is done the execution of the main program automatically continues until the subsystem has completed the required action. At this point the subsystem signals the central processor that the action is complete and the central processor now deals with the results of the action taken, for example, the processing of data transferred from the subsystem.

In similar manner a subsystem signals the central processor its state of readiness to require action on the part of the central processor, such as response to an inquiry, and it also signals the central processor when its requirements have been met. These characteristics not only provide almost instantaneous availability of the services of the subsystems to the central processor, and those of the central processor to the subsystems, but they also reduce to at most a few thousandths of a second those central processor delays ordinarily associated with drum-latency periods, magnetic-tape reading or writing, or the employment of printing, punched card, or communications subsystems.

subsystems, communications—To allow its central processors to function most effectively as real time systems, computers are designed with standard communication subsystems. Some recent additions to the family of subsystems enable a central processor to exchange data simultaneously with a number of remote locations over standard common-carrier communications facilities. The subsystem consists of a multiplexer or multiplexers, each of which allows simplex communication circuits to share a computer I/O channel, and communication-line terminal units which properly terminate the communication circuits and translate the data from these circuits to a form compatible with the central processor.

subsystems, peripheral—*See* subsystems.

subsystems, QUIKTRAN—The computer system is divided into subsystems as follows: the scheduler controls and maintains system operations and provides rapid and consistent response times at all terminals; the translator transforms the source language into an efficient equivalent internal form; the interpreter performs the execution; the process-control program coordinates the activities of the translator and the interpreter; the input/output control system performs all I/O functions; and the exchange program runs the communications-control system. A disk storage is available for user library storage, a drum storage acts as a temporary working storage for users' program, and a magnetic-tape unit is used for logging transactions and for maintaining normal computer capabilities.

subtracter—A particular unit capable of forming the representation of the difference between two numbers represented by signals applied to its inputs.

subtracter digital—A unit with the capability of developing the representation of the difference between two numbers represented by signals applied to its inputs.

subtracter full (parallel)—As regards digital subtracters (full), when parallel representation is involved, a parallel full subtracter

may be formed from as many three-input subtracters as there are digits in the input words, with the borrow output of each connected to the borrow input of the three-input subtracter corresponding to the digit position of next higher significance.

subtracter, full (serial)—As regards digital subtracters, when serial representation is used, a serial full subtracter may be formed from a three input subtracter with a digit delay element connected between the borrow output and the borrow input.

subtracter half—A unit or device capable of representing the difference between two numbers, usually restricted to permitting the subtrahend to have only one nonzero digit.

subtracter, half (parallel)—A special half subtracter resulting from as many half subtracters as permitted digits in the input numerals, but with the borrow output of each half subtracter connected to the subtrahend input of the half subtracter matching the next higher significant digit position, i.e., forming a full parallel subtracter.

subtracter, half (serial)—When serial representation is used, a serial half subtracter may be formed from a two-input subtracter with a digit delay element connected between the borrow output and the subtrahend input.

subtracter, one digit—*Same as* subtracter, half.

subtracter, two-input—*Same as* subtracter, half.

subtract time—A determination of the elapsed time required for one subtraction operation, but excluding the time required to obtain and return the quantities from storage.

subtrahend—1. The number or quantity that is subtracted from another number, called the minuend, giving a result usually called the difference, or sometimes called the remainder. 2. The quantity that is subtracted from another quantity.

suffix—A label often used in the description of an item by a programming language in order to select that item from a table in which it occurs.

sum—The quantity that results from adding two quantities.

sum, check digit—A check digit produced by a sum check.

sum, logical—A result, similar to an arithmetic sum, obtained in the process of ordinary addition, except that the rules are such that a result of one is obtained when either one or both input variables is a one, and an output of zero is obtained when the input variables are both zero. The logical sum is the name given the result produced by the inclusive OR operator.

summarizing—For control of operations in which data is summarized and then recorded in summary form, a final total of a key field or fields can be accumulated from the summarized data and balanced to one accumulated from the detail data. In card-to-card and tape-to-tape runs, the stored program should develop the necessary final totals of the summary data when it is recorded on the output tape; it should also balance it at the end of the run to a control total read from a control card or the tape label.

summary—A report that is lacking in details.

summary punch—A punched-card machine that may be attached by cable to another machine (for example, a tabulator), and that will punch out on a card the information produced, calculated, or summarized by the other machine.

summary punching—The automatic conversion into punched-hole form of information developed by the accounting machine.

summary punching unit—Summary punching is the punching of specific group information contained in numerous detail cards into one summary card. The summary card punch, synchronized with a tabulator, automatically punches summary cards for those designated classifications, either total groups or grand total groups, summarized on the tabulator. It automaticaly produces a punched card for each group total printed by the tabulator.

summation check—*See* check, summation.

summer—In analog representation, a unit with two or more input variables and one output variable which is equal to the sum, or a weighted sum, of the input variables.

summing point—*See* point, summing.

sum, partial—A particular result obtained from the addition of two or more numbers without considering carries, i.e., in binary numeration systems, the partial sum is the same result as is obtained from the exclusive OR operation.

sum, sideways—Relates to a specific sum which is developed by adding digits without regard to position, i.e., sideways sums are brought forward by attaching various weights to the different digit positions and most often forms check digits through odd or even parity techniques.

superimposed circuit—An additional channel obtained from one or more circuits, normally provided for other channels, in such a manner that all the channels can be used simultaneously without mutual interference.

superimpose (SI)—Moves data from one location to another, superimposing bits or characters on the contents of specified locations.

superscript—In mathematical and model-building notation, a symbol written above and to the right of the base symbol to indicate a specified function or differentiation from some other similar or same base letter or character. Also the power to which a number is to be raised is placed in the superscript location, and most often to indicate a cell of a matrix or a derivation, or

a unit of a particular set, if the character indicates the universal set.

supervisor—An executive routine, e.g., a supervisor routine is an executive routine.

supervisor, computer—This individual is responsible for the operation and scheduled use of computer and peripheral devices.

supervisor, executive—The supervisor routine is the executive-system program component that controls the sequencing, setup, and execution of all runs entering the computers. It is designed to control the execution of an unlimited number of programs in a multiprogramming environment, while preventing each program from being affected by the coexistence of other programs. The supervisor contains three levels of scheduling; coarse scheduling, dynamic allocation, and central processor unit dispatching. Runs entering are sorted into information files, and these files are used by the supervisor for run scheduling and processing. Control statements for each run are retrieved and scanned by the control-command interpreter to facilitate the selection of runs for setup by the coarse scheduler.

supervisor interrupts—Supervisor call interruptions are caused by the program issuing an instruction to turn over control to the supervisor (a type of master-control program). The exact reason for the call is shown in the PSW (program status word).

supervisor mode—A mode of operation under which only certain operations, such as memory-protection modification instructions and input/output operations, are permitted.

supervisor, overlay—*See* overlay supervisor.

supervisor program test—A supervisory program that is used for nothing else, except testing.

supervisor, system—*See* system supervisor.

supervisor system, magnetic-tape—*See* system supervisor, magnetic tape.

supervisory console — The supervisory console includes the operator's control panel, a keyboard and type-printer, and a control unit for the keyboard and type-printer. Optionally, a paper-tape reader and punch may be connected through the same control unit. The transfer of information between the computer and any of these devices is performed on a character basis over the input and output channels assigned to the console auxiliaries. Two switches mounted on the control unit permit selection of the paper-tape reader or the keyboard and the paper-tape punch or the type-printer (some systems) .

supervisory control—A control system that furnishes intelligence, usually to a centralized location, to be used by an operator to supervise the control of a process or operation.

supervisory control, operating system—The operating-system software consists of a supervisory control program, system programs, and system subroutines. Included are a symbolic assembler and macroprocessor, a language compiler, and debugging aids. A library of general utility programs is also provided as well as other software packages.

supervisory control, processor controller (P-C)—The P-C communicates the messages and the commands to the operator and, if desired, directly to the process equipment and instrumentation. The sensors that measure process conditions are continuously monitored by the P-C. The P-C program analyzes this information and then generates the required output information. Messages from the P-C to the operator may be displayed by several methods in the operator's working area. These messages guide the operator in adjusting the status of instruments located at the point of control.

supervisory program—*Same as* executive routine.

supervisory programs simulation—*See* simulation, supervisory programs.

supervisory routine—*Same as* executive routine.

supervisory system—All of the supervisory programs used by one given system.

supplementary maintenance time—*See* maintenance time, supplementary.

support processor, attached—The utilization of multiple computers, usually two, connected via channel-to-channel adaptors, to increase the efficiency in processing many short duration jobs.

support programs—Those programs which support or aid the supervisory programs and the application programs, and include diagnostics, testing, data generators, tec.

support systems—1. Programming systems that are used to develop or support the normal translation functions of any of the machine, procedural, or problem-oriented languages. 2. A collection of computer programs to aid the production and checkout of a system. 3. The combination of the skills, techniques, and equipment to operate and maintain a system.

suppression—An optional function in either on-line or off-line printing devices that permits them to ignore certain input characters or groups of characters. *See* nonprint code.

suppression, space—*See* space suppression.

suppression, zero—The elimination of the zeros to the left of the significant digits, usually before printing.

suppressor, echo—A voice-operated device for connection to a two-way telephone circuit to attenuate echo currents in one direction caused by telephone currents in the other direction.

surface recording—Storage of information on the ferric-oxide coating on magnetic tape, magnetic drums, etc.

swapping pulse—*Same as* pulse regeneration.

swapping tape—*See* swap, tape servo.

swap servo—*Same as* swap, tape-servo.

swap, tape-servo—A process of multiple or simultaneous operations of magnetic tapes, i.e., mounting the first tapes on each of two handlers, running the first and then the second, while the first is being rewound, removed, and replaced by a third tape. Then, running the third while the second is being rewound, removed, and replaced by a fourth, etc. This saves mainframe time by using two extra tape handlers efficiently.

swap time—The time required to transfer a program from external memory to high-speed internal memory and vice versa.

swing, frequency—Pertaining to a modulated wave, the variation due to modulation, of the instantaneous frequency above and below the carrier frequency.

switch—1. A point in a program from which a program may proceed to one of several possible courses of action, depending on conditions established by the programmer; conditional statements are often used to establish switches of this kind; a branch point. 2. A mechanical, electromechanical, or electronic device, built into a unit of equipment, that can be interrogated in order to select a course of action. 3. A symbol used to indicate a branchpoint, or a set of instructions to condition a branch. 4. A part of a device within the processor that stores an indication of various conditions encountered during processing; the standard FORTRAN "IF" is the statement requesting the comparison of less than, equal to, and greater than. The switch contents are frequently tested by such comparing techniques or by conditional jump instructions to execute appropriate routines in the program. 5. A device that can alter flow. Switches may be activated manually or under program control.

switch, breakpoint—A manually operated switch that controls conditional operation at breakpoints, used primarily in debugging.

switch-control computer—A computer designed to handle data transmission to and from remote computers and terminals.

switch, diamond—*Same as* storage, core-rope.

switched-message network—A service offered by the common carrier in which a customer may communicate with any other customer receiving the same service. Examples are TELEX and TWX.

switch, electronic—A circuit element causing a start and stop action or a switching action electronically, usually at high speeds.

switches, manual address—The external control switches used by the operator to select manually an address for read off in the storage address display lights, or to transfer the contents to a register without disturbing the address contents or area.

switch, function—A circuit having a fixed number of inputs and outputs designed so that the output information is a function of the input information. Each circuit expresses a certain code, signal configuration, or pattern.

switching—The process of using interconnecting circuits in order to establish a temporary communication between two or more stations.

switching, blank—A specific range of values in which the incoming signal can be altered without also changing the outgoing response. (Synonymous with dead space and dead zone, and similar to neutral zone.)

switching center—1. A location at which incoming data from one circuit is transferred to the proper outgoing circuit. 2. A location where an incoming message is automatically or manually directed to one or more outgoing circuits, according to the intelligence contained in the message.

switching center, automatic message—A location where an incoming message is automatically directed to one or more outgoing circuits according to intelligence contained in the message.

switching center, semiautomatic message—A location where an incoming message is displayed to an operator who directs the message to one or more outgoing circuits according to information read from the message.

switching center, torn-tape — A location where operators tear off the incoming printed and punched paper tape and transfer it manually to the proper outgoing circuit.

switching, circuit or line—A switching technique where the connection is made between the calling party and the called party prior to the start of a communication (for example, telephone switching).

switching coefficient—The derivative of the applied magnetizing force with respect to the reciprocal of the resultant switching time.

switching, compute-limited—Provides for the transfer of operational control among two or more independent programs being operated concurrently. This function makes possible the operation of compute-limited programs concurrently with I/O (input/output)-limited programs. Operational control is transferred to a compute-limited program whenever the I/O-limited programs must wait, pending completion of requested I/O functions. This function of the executive program allows an installation to make maximum use of its total computer facility.

switching, cross-channel—This optional feature permits direct-program access to attached input/output devices through two channels.

switching, message—The technique of receiving a message, storing it until the proper outgoing circuit is available, and then retransmitting it.

switching, program—On a single transaction the control program initiates several switches among the various programs, therefore, the

processor must be designed to accomplish very rapid program switching.

switching, push-button — A reperforator switching system which permits the selection of the outgoing channel by an operator.

switching space—*Same as* gap, interword.

switching, store and forward—*Same as* message switching.

switching theory—A particular branch of theory relating to combinational logic, its operation, behavior, and consequences, i.e., concerning such devices as computer Turing machines, logic elements, and switch networks.

switching unit, communication—This unit, like the magnetic-tape switching unit, can also perform two switching functions. Two processors share the same lines. The communication switching unit allows any two processors to share a group (one to eight) of communication lines. One processor shares different lines. Additionally, a switching unit enables one processor to switch between different groups of communication lines. Additional expansion features can provide a group-switching capability of up to 63 lines (some systems).

switching unit, peripheral-control—*See* peripheral-control switching unit.

switching units, magnetic-tape — The unit consists of two controls that share each other's tape units. A single switching unit allows one group of either half-inch or three-quarter inch units to be switched between two tape controls. An additional function of the tape switching unit selects one of the two tape units to be attached to a single tape control. All tape units connected to a switching unit are switched simultaneously. If independent switching of more than one group of tape units is desired, switching-unit modules may be added to provide a group switching capability of up to 64 tape units in groups of four or eight. The size of these independently switched groups depends upon the capability of the tape control (some systems).

switch, insertion—The insertion of information into a computer system by an operator who operates the switches manually.

switch, linear selection—*Same as* storage, core-rope.

switch, logical—An electronic device used for directing input cards to one of a number of outputs.

switch, manual—The hand operated device designed to cause alternate actions. Contrasted with the electronic switch.

switch, manual storage—*See* storage, manual switch.

switch, N-way—*See* switch, programmed.

switch, operation-control—A particular type matrix switch that selects the input lines of a matrix. The output of the matrix controls the logic elements which execute specific operations.

switchover—The act of transferring the real-time processing work load from one specific or multiplexor program to another in a duplex system. Switchover must be initiated manually in some systems; in many others, it can be accomplished automatically.

switch, programmed—A particular instruction which may be in the form of a numeral and may be placed in a routine to allow the computer to select one of a number of alternative paths in its program, i.e., switch settings on the console equipment can be inspected by operators or the computer and results in changes or branches in the main program.

switch, Rajchman selection—*Same as* storage, core-rope.

switch register (SR)—Twelve toggle switches on the operator console provide a means of manually establishing a word to be set into the computer. The content of the SR can be transferred into the machine as an address by pressing the load-address key, or can be stored in core memory at the address contained in the machine by pressing the deposit key. The content of the SR can also be loaded into the AC (accumulator) under program control to allow program modification by programmed evaluation of the word manually set into the SR (some systems).

switch, sense—The sense switches on the operator's console provide manual control of program branching. Testing of the sense-switch settings occurs when the sense-switch instruction is given.

switch setting, branch-on—*See* branch-on switch setting.

switch, storage—*See* storage, manual-switch.

switch, tape-feed—This causes the reperforator to meter a predetermined length of blank tape.

switch, tape select—A particular control rotary switch which has the capability of selecting either a neutral mode during automatic operation or the use of one of the on-line tape units.

switch, toggle—1. A manually operated electric switch, with a small projecting knob or arm that may be placed in either of two positions, "on" or "off," and will remain in that position until changed. 2. An electronically operated circuit that holds either of two states until changed.

syllable—A term used to describe groups of characters or portions of machine words, such as a byte, slab, catena, are used.

symbiont control—Symbionts, besides being routines from main programs, may be concurrently performing typical off-line operations, such as tape-to-printer, independent of the main program. Symbionts may be initialized by the operator, or by a main program. Symbiont operations may be suspended, terminated, or reinitiated at any time.

symbiont control with I/O (input/output)—

There are relatively few input/output limited programs when using the magnetic drum, due to the high transfer rate of this unit. For the relatively slower peripherals —tape, card, punch, and printer—a drum buffering system has been designed to effectively disassociate input/output time from central computer time. Small routines, called symbionts, run concurrently with the series of main programs. These symbionts move information back and forth between peripherals and magnetic drum. Main programs desiring communication with these peripherals reference input/output subroutines which themselves fetch or deliver data images to and from the drum. Other symbionts may be concurrently performing typical off-line operations, such as tape-to-printer, independent of the main program. Symbionts may be initialized by the operator, or by a main program. Symbiont operations may be suspended, terminated, or reinitiated at any time. (Clarified by symbionts.)

symbionts—Small routines, called symbionts, run concurrently with the series of main programs. These symbionts move information back and forth between the peripherals and magnetic drum. Main programs desiring communication with these peripherals reference input/output subroutines that transfer data images between the drum and peripherals.

symbol—A substitute or representation of characteristics, relationships, or transformations of ideas or things.

symbol, abstract—A specific symbol whose shape or pattern is not indicative of its meaning or use, and which almost always requires definition for each particular application.

symbol, breakpoint—A symbol that may be optionally included in an instruction (as an indication, tag, or flag) to designate it as a breakpoint.

symbol, check—*See* check symbol.

symbol dictionary, external—*See* external symbol dictionary.

symbol, external—A symbol for a location name which appears in the external symbol dictionary of a program. The program must permit the named location to be referred to by other programs. Since in most programming, separately written subroutines must be united before execution by a linkage loader or editor, they must not occupy overlapping regions of memory, but instead must occupy adjacent areas. Thus, the programs must refer to a data item or instruction in other programs by external symbols.

symbol, flowchart—Symbols used to represent operations, data, and equipment in data processing problems.

symbolic address—A label assigned to a specific word in a routine for the convenience of the programmer. The symbol used is independent of the location of a word within a routine. It identifies the field of data to be operated on or the operation to be used, rather than its storage location.

symbolic addressing—*See* addressing, symbolic.

symbolic assembler — Lets the programmer code instructions in a symbolic language. The assembler allows mnemonic symbols to be used for instruction codes and addresses. Constant and variable storage registers can be automatically assigned. The assembler produces a binary object tape and lists a symbol table with memory allocations and useful diagnostic messages.

symbolic assembly-language listing — The listing contains the symbolic instructions equivalent to the binary code output of the compiler. This assembly-language output listing is useful as a debugging aid. By including certain pseudo operation codes in "in-line" assembly language, the assembly language output can be assembled by the assembler routine. (If output is obtained on either cards, paper tape, or magnetic tape.) This will allow modification of programs at the assembly language level.

symbolic assembly system—A program system developed in two parts: a symbolic-language program and a computer program (processor). The processor translates a source program developed in symbolic language to a machine object program.

symbolic code—This code expresses programs in source language; i.e., by referring to storage locations and machine operations by symbolic names and addresses that are independent of their hardware determined names and addresses. (Synonymous with pseudocode and contrasted with machine-language code.)

symbolic coding—1. Coding in which the instructions are written in nonmachine language; i.e., coding using symbolic notation for operators and operands. 2. Writing programs in any language other than absolute machine language. 3. In digital computer programming, any coding system using symbolic code rather than the machine code.

symbolic-coding format—In writing instructions using the assembly language, the programmer is primarily concerned with three memory fields: a label field, an operation field, and an operand field. It is possible to relate the symbolic coding to its associated flowchart, if desired, by appending comments to each instruction line or program segment. All of the memory fields are in free form, providing the greatest convenience possible for the programmer. Consequently, the programmer is not hampered by the necessity to consider fixed form boundaries in the design of his symbolic coding.

symbolic conversion program—Represented by the abbreviation SCP. A one-to-one compiler for symbolic addresses and operation

codes designed for systems of the International Telephone and Telegraph Co. (ITT).

symbolic debugging — Symbolic commands (or marcoinstructions) are utilized to assist in the debugging procedure.

symbolic deck—A deck of punched cards containing programs written in symbolic language as opposed to programs written in binary language.

symbolic editor — Permits the editing of source-language programs by adding or deleting lines of text. All modification, reading, punching, etc., is controlled by symbols typed at the keyboard. The editor reads parts or all of a symbolic tape into memory where it is available for immediate examination, correction, and relisting.

symbolic input/output referencing — References to data on tape or disk are made symbolically. Instead of describing the address of a certain disk or tape, the programmer refers to such data with a functional name. This means the programmer need not keep in mind where data will be coming from. It also means that there is a good deal of flexibility for the machine operator. He can mount tapes in the most efficient way each day. The control programs set up an input and output assignment table indicating the whereabouts of data files. These tables are used as directories when programs are run.

This flexibility helps the operator schedule work so that jobs can be loaded, tapes mounted and disk packs attached before a job is called by the control program.

symbolic instruction—An instruction in an assembly language directly translatable into a machine code. An instruction using symbols to represent or express the operator part and the address parts.

symbolic key—In COBOL, contrast with actual key.

symbolic language — The discipline that treats formal logic by means of a formalized artificial language or symbolic calculus whose purpose is to avoid the ambiguities and logical inadequacies of natural languages. Advantages of the symbolic method are greater exactness of formulation, and power to deal with complex material.

symbolic logic—1. The study of formal logic and mathematics by means of a special written language that seeks to avoid the ambiguity and inadequacy of ordinary language. 2. The mathematical concepts, techniques and languages as used in the foregoing definition, whatever their particular application or context. (Synonymous with mathematical logic, and related to logic.)

symbolic manipulation—Because data are not usually numerical, the formal use of a symbol manipulation has resulted in specific list-processing languages. The first real list processing language or information processing language was developed by Newell, Shaw, and Simon in 1957.

symbolic notation—A method of representing a storage location by one or more figures.

symbolic number—A numeral, used in writing routines, for referring to a specific storage location; such numerals are converted to actual storage addresses in the final assembling of the program.

symbolic programming—The use of arbitrary symbols to represent addresses in order to facilitate programming.

symbol, item separation—A control symbol which indicates beginning of an item.

symbol, logic—1. A symbol used to represent a logic element graphically. 2. A symbol used to represent a logic connective.

symbol, logical—A sign used as an operator to denote the particular operation to be performed on the associated variables.

symbol, logical element—That circuitry which provides an output resulting from the input of two variables.

symbol, mnemonic—Frequently used symbols for representation of information and so selected to assist the programmer's memory in recalling meaning, as MPY for multiply.

symbols, atomic—In list processing languages, atomic symbols are sometimes referred to as atoms when using list processing languages and may either be numeric or nonnumeric. The external representation of a nonnumeric atomic symbol is a string of letters or digits starting with a letter such as AB5,W or epsilon.

symbols, flowchart—The symbols, such as squares and circles, convey no information and must be labeled. They localize a point of interest, but convey only the most general notion of intent. The finished model must include adequate description with each symbol to explain its operation. Liberal use of footnotes is recommended to explain the "why" of operations that are not straightforward in meaning.

symbols, functional—A block diagram term representing the functional design, i.e., the practical specification of the working relations between all parts of a system.

symbols, model—The symbols such as squares, circles, etc., convey no information and must be labeled. They localize a point of interest, but convey only the most general notion of intent. The finished model must include adequate description with each symbol to explain what the operation does. Liberal use of footnotes is recommended to explain the why of operations which are not straightforward.

symbol, specific—*Same as* character, special.

symbols, standard language — Prescribed graphical shapes used to represent special meanings or functions in any computer program.

symbol string—A concatenation of items or characters, i.e., a one dimensional array of such items ordered only by reference to the relations between adjacent members.

symbol table—*See* table, symbol.

symbol table control — Symbols that have been defined and used, but are no longer required, may be deleted from the symbol table. This allows room for new symbols. Thus, a very large program can be assembled with a relatively small symbol storage area.

symbol, terminating—A symbol on the tape indicating the end of a block of information. (Related to gap.)

symmetric difference gate—*Same as* gate, exclusive OR.

symmetric linear programming—A fast, efficient mathematical technique for solving distribution and allocation problems in manufacturing operations.

symmetric list processor—A high-level list processing language.

synch—Signal that identifies the start of a block.

synchro-duplexing—The scheme of producing a document on a printing device through the synchronous running of a program tape and a master tape or a pure data tape. The operation is completely controlled by function codes in the program tape. A data-processing function.

synchronization—In the COBOL system, the alignment of data with respect to the left or right boundaries of machine words. (Compare with justification.)

synchronizer—A storage device used to compensate for a difference in the rate of flow of information or the time of occurrence of events when transmitting information between two devices.

synchronizer, channel—The channel-synchronizer signals provide for orderly transfer of the digital information. These signals do not transmit data, but are used to command and identify the transfer of data words, function words, etc., at proper times and in proper sequence.

synchronizer, master—*Same as* master clock.

synchronizer, tape—A tape device which controls the exchange of data between the central processor (CPU) and the various tape units, i.e., a buffer for programmed control of the events.

synchronizing pilot—A reference signal for the purpose of maintaining the synchronization of the oscillators of a carrier system. The signal is also used to compare the frequencies and phases of the currents generated by these oscillators.

synchronous—A term applied to a computer in which the performance of a sequence of operations is controlled by equally spaced clock signals or pulses.

synchronous clock—Even in the case of static circuitry, a clock frequency is generally used to keep the various events in the computer in step and running at the proper rate. This action results in synchronous operation, as contrasted with asynchronous operation.

synchronous computer—A computer in which each event or the performance of each operation starts as a result of a signal generated by a clock. (Contrasted with asynchronous computer, and clarified by clock frequency.)

synchronous data transmission—In this type of data transmission, each character consists of 5, 6, 7, or 8 information bits depending on the code structure. There are no start and stop bits. Timing is derived through synchronizing characters at the beginning of each message or block of data.

synchronous gate—A synchronous gate is a time gate wherein the output intervals are synchronized with an incoming signal.

synchronous system (communications)—A system in which the sending and receiving instruments are operating at approximately the same frequency, and the phase is maintained by means of feedback.

syndetic—1. Having connections or interconnections. 2. Pertaining to a document or catalog with cross references.

synergic—The combination of every organ of a system, e.g., a coordinated system.

syntactic errors, remote computing system—Syntactic errors are considered the responsibility of the system and are further categorized as follows:

Composition—Typographical errors, violations of specified forms of statements and misuse of variable names (e.g., incorrect punctuation, mixed-mode expressions, undeclared arrays, etc.).

Consistency—Statements that are correctly composed but conflict with other statements (e.g., conflicting declaratives, illegal statement ending a DO (FORTRAN) range, failure to follow each transfer statement with a numbered statement, etc.).

Completeness—Programs that are incomplete (e.g., transfers to nonexistent statement numbers, improper DO nesting, illegal transfer into the range of a DO loop, etc.).

syntax—The rules governing sentence structure in a language, or statement structure in a language such as that of a compiler program.

syntax-directed compiler—A compiler based on the syntactical relation of the character string.

syntax recognizer—A subroutine which recognizes the phase class in an artificial language, normally expressed in backus normal form (BNF), formal language theory.

synthesis—The combining of parts in order to form a whole; e.g., to develop at a circuit, computer, or program from performance requirements. This can be contrasted with analysis of a given performance circuit or program.

synthesis, systems—Procedural planning to solve problems. This involves: analysis of the problem, preparation of a flow chart, detailed preparation, development of subroutines, location of storage locations, specification of input and output formats, and

the incorporation of a computer run into a complete data processing system.

synthetic address—*Same as* address, calculated.

synthetic-display generation—Logical and numerical processing to display-collected data or calculated data in symbolic form.

synthetic language—A pseudocode or symbolic language. A fabricated language.

synthetic relationship—A relation existing between a concept that pertains to an empirical observation. Such relationships are not involved in defining concepts or terms, but in reporting the results of observations and experiments.

SYSPOP—Abbreviation for system programmed operators.

system—1. An assembly of components united by some form of regulated interaction to form an organized whole. 2. A collection of operations and procedures, men, and machines, by which business activity is carried on. 3. Any purposeful organization of resources or elements. 4. A collection of operations and procedures united to accomplish a specific objective. 5. A devised and designed regular or special method or plan or methodology or procedure. The organization of hardware, software, and people for cooperative operation to complete a set of tasks for desired purposes. 6. Any regular or special method or plan of procedure.

system, accuracy-control—An error-detection and correction system.

system, addressing—*See* addressing system.

system, assembly—1. An automatic programming software system that includes a programming language and a number of machine-language programs. These programs aid the programmer by performing different programming functions such as checkout, updating, etc. 2. An assembly system comprises two elements, a symbolic language and an assembly program that translates the source programs written in the symbolic language into machine language.

systematic error checkng code—*See* code, systematic error checking.

systematic inaccuracies—Inaccuracies due to limitations in equipment design.

system, automatic data-processing—The term descriptive of an interacting assembly of procedures, processes, methods, personnel, and automatic data-processing equipment to perform a complex series of data-processing operations.

system, back-up—Such systems combine error-detection and correction techniques that spot and correct computer and transmission errors.

system, BASIC—*See* BASIC.

system, Batten—*See* Batten system.

system, binary notation—*See* binary number.

system, binary number—*See* binary number.

system, binary-weighted error-detection—This system is based upon the concept of assigning binary one values to all marking pulses of each code combination.

system, biquinary—*See* number, biquinary.

system call interrupts—*See* interrupts, system call.

system characteristics, real-time—*See* real-time systems characteristics.

system chart — A flowchart of an overall procedure or system showing the flow of information and/or documents.

system check—A check on the overall performance of the system, usually not made by built-in computer check circuits, e.g., control totals, hash totals, and record counts.

system, checkout, hybrid-computer—*See* hybrid system checkout.

system commands—A typical executive accepts and interprets a collection of system commands by a user allowing him to: log in and out; save and restore program and data files, compile and execute a program; interrupt and terminate a running program; edit, manipulate, and list program and data files; request status of system and user programs; and specify systems subcomponent desired.

system commands interpretation, time sharing—*See* time sharing, system commands interpretation.

system commands, time sharing—*See* time sharing, system commands.

system communications—*See* communications system.

system communications processing—The transmission of data to the central computer for processing from a remote terminal as opposed to a terminal connected directly to the central computer.

system constants—System constants are permanent locations contained in the monitor (control unit). These locations contain data used by system programs. Some constants contain data that may be used by certain programs.

system, control—A system of the closed-loop type in which the computer is used to govern external processes.

system controller — The system controller regulates and coordinates all communications between major computer-system components (processor, memory, input/output controller, and real-time devices). The independent operation of these two functions provides a means of expansion, and provides for the maximum utilization of the components.

system control panel—Manual control operations are held to a minimum by the system design and operating system. The result is fewer operator errors. The system control panel is divided into three major sections: operator control section—contains only those controls required by the operator when the processor is operating under full supervisory control; operator intervention section—contains additional controls required for the operator to intervene in normal program-

ming operation; customer engineering section—contains controls intended only for customer engineering use in diagnostics and maintenance.

system, Cordonnier—*Same as* Batten system.

system data-acquisition—*See* data acquisition system.

system, data-processing—A network of machine components for accepting information, processing it according to a plan, and producing the desired results.

system, data-processing machine—An interconnected assembly of data-processing machines that are regulated to solve a problem or problems.

system, decimal numbering—1. A system of reckoning by 10 or the powers of 10 using the digits 0 through 9 to express numerical quantities. 2. A system of numerals using digits 0 through 9 and thus having a base, or radix, of 10.

system design problem—When the desired properties of a system are specified, and the problem is to design a document which describes the optimum (or close to optimum) realization of these properties. This is almost entirely an information-handling process.

system diagnosis, continuous (time sharing)—*See* time sharing, continuous system diagnosis.

system, diagnostic—A program resembling the operational program rather than a systematic logical pattern program which will detect overall system malfunctions rather than isolate or locate faulty components.

system, direct or on-line—*See* on-line or direct system.

system, disk operating—*See* disk operating system.

system, duplex—Two computers used in special configuration, one is on-line and the other is standing by ready to be used if a malfunction of the on-line computer occurs. The stand-by computer is often used to complete off-line functions.

system, electronic data-processing—The general term used to define a system for data processing by means of machines utilizing electronic circuitry as opposed to electromechanical equipment.

system engineering—The analysis and implementation of the procedures and plans adopted involving all the elements in an industrial process, business problem, or control situation.

system, error-correcting telegraph—A system employing an error-detecting code that will cause any false signal to initiate a repetition of the transmission of the incorrectly received character.

system, error-detecting—*See* error-detecting system.

system, error-detecting and feedback — A system employing an error-detecting code and so arranged that a signal detected as being in error will automatically initiate a request for the retransmission of the incorrectly received signal.

system, error-detection—A system employing an error-detecting code and so arranged that any signal detected as being in error is deleted from the data delivered to the data link (in some cases with an indication that such a deletion has taken place), or delivered to the data link, along with an indication that it has been detected as being in error.

system, exception principle—An information system or data-processing system that reports on situations only when the actual results differ from the planned results. When the results occur within a normal range, they are not reported.

system, executive—*See* executive system.

system, executive-control — Primary control of the executive system is by control information fed to the system by one or more input devices that may be either on-line or at various remote sites. This control information is similar in nature to present control-card operations, but allows additional flexibility and standardization.

system fail-safe—A system which continues to process data despite the failure of parts in the system. Usually accompanied by some deterioration in performance.

system, file-oriented—*See* file oriented system.

system, filmorex—A system for the electronic selection of microfilm cards devised by Jacques Samain. Each card has a micro-reproduction of the document or abstract and a field of twenty 5-digit code numbers giving a bibliographic reference and the subjects treated. Retrieval of a certain document or abstract is initiated by a 5-digit code.

system, fixed-length record—*See* fixed-length record system.

System for Ordinary Life Operations (SOLO) —Solo is a dynamic, total system approach—modular in design—tailored to the general needs of all life insurance companies, yet effectively adaptable to the individual company. SOLO organizes the required information for new policy issue—usually one of the most expensive processes of the life insurance operation—into an economical operation. And it also solves the problems involved in a life insurance company's every-day record keeping. SOLO, with its wide range of capabilities, can process automatic internal changes—including premium billing, loan interest, coupon/dividend funds, policy face amount changes—as well as changes due to conditions outside the computer system, such as benefits to be added or deleted, inquiry as to policy status, loan payment, or loan request. (Honeywell)

system, FORTRAN-compiler—FORTRAN compiler system consists of two basic elements—a source language (FORTRAN) whose structure closely resembles the language of mathematics, and a compiler that translates the statements and formulas written in the source language into a machine-language program.

system, horizontal—A programming system in which instructions are written horizontally, i.e., across the page.

system-improvement time—1. The machine down time needed for the installation and testing of new components, large or small, and machine down time necessary for modification of existing components. This includes all programming tests to check out the modified machine. 2. All machine down time needed for the installation and testing of new components and modification of existing components.

system, indirect or off-line—*See* off-line or direct system.

system, information — The network of all communication methods within an organization. Information may be derived from many sources other than a data-processing unit, such as by telephone, by contact with other people, or by studying an operation.

system, information-feedback — An error-control system using message feedback when an erroneous group is received from the sending station.

system, information processing—A system that receives and delivers information, changing the information in the process.

system, information-retrieval—A system for locating and selecting on demand, certain documents or other graphic records relevant to a given information requirement, from a file of such material. Examples of information-retrieval systems are classification, indexing, and machine-searching systems.

system, information transmission—A system which receives and delivers information without changing it.

system, inplant—A data-handling system confined to one building or a number of buildings in one locality.

system, integrated—*See* integrated system.

system interface design — For unique user applications, such as on-line installations that require specialized input/output equipment, liason engineering staffs design the necessary interface units as part of the services to the customers. Then, the manufacturer will fabricate these units, at a normal product cost, for the particular system under close supervision by the same engineers that designed them. These engineers, who are naturally quite familiar with the logic and requirements are best qualified to do this important work.

system interrupts—System call interrupts are programmed requests from a processing program to the control program for some action, such as initiation of an input/output operation.

system librarian—This individual issues and stores data files and other records of the installation and also maintains a list of all the up-to-date programs.

system loader—*See* loader, system.

system, macro—A programming system with symbolic capabilities of an assembly system and the added capability of many-for-one or macroinstruction development.

system, macroinstruction — Various macroinstructions control the translation procedure and do not necessarily develop usable machine-language programs or instructions.

system, management-information — A communications process in which data are recorded and processed for operational purposes. The problems are isolated for higher-level decision making, and information is fed back to top management to reflect the progress or lack of progress made in achieving major objectives.

system, monitor—*Same as* executive system.

system, monitor-operating — The monitor (control unit) exercises primary control of the routines that compose the operating system. It is this operating system that turns the computer into a flexible tool—allows the user to achieve maximum use of the hardware's advanced design features.

system monitor, remote-computing—*See* monitor, remote-computing system.

system monitor tape—*See* monitor tape, system.

system, multicomputer—The use of more than one computer in a system.

system, multiprocessing—A system that is organized to contain two or more interconnected computers, but which performs functionally or geographically specialized processing tasks.

system, notation—*See* numeration system.

system, number—*See* number system.

system, numeration—*See* numeration system.

system numeration, representation—*See* numeration system.

system, numerical—*See* numeration system.

system, octal—*See* octal.

system, octal number—*See* octal number system.

system, on-demand — A system from which timely information or service is available on request.

system, open-ended —An optical character recognition term that denotes a system in which the input data is taken from sources other than the computer with which the character reader is associated or data which is part of the system.

system, operating—*Same as* executive system.

system or section, operator control—A portion of the controlling equipment which is readily available to operators for controlling the systems equipment; this is usually a major portion of the console.

system, out-plant — A data-transmission system consisting of one or more centrally located terminals and one or more remote terminals.

system, peek-a-boo—*Same as* Batten system.

system, PERT/COST—A generalized program designed to facilitate planning, scheduling, control, and monitoring of both large and small scale research and development projects.

system, phonetic—The specific equipment which has features for starting and acting upon data from the voice source.

system, polymolphic—A specific or particular system which can take on various forms ideally suited to the problems at hand, usually by altering, under its own control its interconnections and the functions of its component parts, i.e., it may occur with respect to logic construction or organization and a master unit controls a variety of jobs executed simultaneously and automatically.

system, process control—A system whose primary purpose is to provide automation of continuous operations.

system programmed operators (SYSPOP)—A function which makes monitor mode service routines available to USER mode programs without loss of system control or use of user memory space.

system, programming—An assemblage of programs, programming languages, routines, and subroutines for use in specific computing systems, i.e., the basis for operating systems or total systems of data processing and computing.

system, quadruplex—A system of Morse telegraphy arranged for the simultaneous independent transmission of two messages in each direction over a single circuit.

system, real-time—See real-time processing.

system reliability — The probability that a system will accurately perform its specified task under stated tactical and environmental conditions.

system reliability, time sharing—*See* time sharing, system reliability.

system, request-repeat—A system employing an error-detecting code and so arranged that a signal detected as being in error automatically initiates a request for retransmission of the signal detected as being in error.

system, rollback—*See* rollback.

systems analysis—1. The analysis of a business activity to determine precisely what must be accomplished and how to accomplish it. 2. The organized, step-by-step study and analysis of the detailed procedure for collection, manipulation, and evaluation of information about an organization with the goal of improving control over its total operation or segments of it. 3. The examination of an activity, procedure, method, technique, or a business to determine what must be accomplished and the best method of accomplishing the necessary operations.

systems analyst—*See* analyst, systems.

systems and procedure—Organization of *all* the manual and machine data processing operations required to produce information about one particular activity.

systems approach—Looking at the over-all situation rather than the narrow implications of the task at hand; particularly, looking for interrelationships between the task at hand and other functions which relate to it.

systems, card—*See* card systems.

system, scientific—A particular system devoted principally to computation, in contrast to a commercial or data-processing system on which the main emphasis is on file updating rather than performance of calculations.

systems compatibility—In complex systems applications, modules are completely compatible electrically, logically, and mechanically with other systems components, that include digital computers, a complete line of input/output devices, and analog interface equipment.

systems consultant—This individual supplies technical assistance and direction with specific emphasis on problem identification, organization analysis, conversion planning, forms control and analysis, and reports control.

systems design—The formulation and graphic description of the nature and content of input, files, procedures, and output in order to display the necessary connection processes and procedures.

system, self-organizing—A system that is capable of internal reconfiguration in response to externally occurring events.

systems flowchart—*See* flowchart, systems.

systems generation—In some computers, a systems disk must be generated by the user who specifies the configuration, file protected area, error handling, etc.

system, shared-files—A special file system configuration in which two computers have access to the same file-storage device, though not necessarily at the same time.

system, share operation—The particular process or translation of symbolic instructions into a machine instruction. Often abbreviated as SOS.

systems, hybrid—There have been a number of efforts to utilize the best properties of both digital and analog computers by building hybrid systems. In the hybrid system, a digital computer is used for control purposes and provides the program, while analog components are used to obtain the more lengthy solutions.

system, simplex—A system configuration that does not include standby equipment.

system simulation—An assemblage of interacting components and processes. The interactions are largely internal to the system, although links to an external environment will be recognized.

systems, inquiry and communications—Computer systems are now provided with facilities for diversified on-site and long-distance inquiry and data-communications networks. Centralized records and data-processing operations can be tied in with information sources at remote locations, and will provide instant, on-line response to interrogations and input data from a large number of inquiry stations. Communication networks include standard teletype stations, and electric typewriter stations.

system, slave—*See* slave system.

system, software, time sharing—*See* time sharing, software requirements.

systems, open-loop—A system in which the computer does not directly control a process or procedure but instead displays or prints information for the operator to assist in determination of required action. Most real-time systems are basically open-loop systems.

systems, paper-tape—Systems having paper-tape equipment with no mass-storage device have a storage system contained on binary paper-tape reels. The binary reels are of two types: formatted binary, and absolute binary. Formatted binary programs are loaded by the system loader. Absolute binary programs are loaded by the monitor.

systems, procedure (and)—Organization of all the manual and machine data processing operations required to produce information about one particular activity.

systems programmer—*See* programmer, systems.

systems, programs—*See* programs systems.

systems study—The detailed process by which a set of procedures is determined in order to use a computer for definite functions or operations. Also, specifications are established to be used as a basis for the selection of equipment suitable for the specific needs.

systems synthesis—*See* synthesis systems.

system standard—A specified characteristic often necessary to permit system operation such as test tones, or character patterns, or in communications, a specific electrical performance predetermined design based on measured and known performance of circuits under test operating conditions.

system, start-stop—A system in which each group of code elements corresponding to an alphabetical signal is preceded by a start signal which serves to prepare the receiving mechanism for the reception and registration of a character, and is followed by a stop signal which serves to bring the receiving mechanism to rest in preparation for the reception of the next character.

system, stepped start-stop—A start-stop system in which the start signals occur at regular intervals.

systems test—1. The running of the whole system against test data. 2. A complete simulation of the actual running system for purposes of testing out the adequacy of the system. 3. A test of an entire interconnected set of components for the purpose of determining proper functioning and interconnection. 4. The running of the whole system of runs making up a data processing application against test data.

system, string process (SPS)—*See* string, process system.

system structure—The consideration of the specific nature of a chain of command and its origin, sequence, and type of data collected. The form and destination of the results, and the procedures used to control these operations.

system subcomponents, time sharing—*See* time sharing, system subcomponents.

system subroutines—I/O (input/output) format control that provides for the various format statements used in the FORTRAN language. These subroutines are also available to other programs and may be called from the systems library tape.

system supervisor—The system supervisor is designed to allow an installation to proceed automatically from run to run with little or no computer time loss because of setting up the "next program." It is also designed to accomplish as many of the set-up and control functions as is possible prior to reading in the actual program. It is assumed that the programs are located on tape in the exact order that they are to be run. This order can be superseded by the operator. Each program on completion should transfer control to the "finish" entry point of the control program. This program will read in the next system supervisor from the library tape. Control is then transferred to the supervisor.

system supervisor, magnetic-tape — Even though the magnetic-tape system supervisor is not a part of the librarian program, it works in such close conjunction with the librarian that the following brief description of the magnetic-tape system supervisor is included. The system supervisor for magnetic tape will automatically select, set-up, and process each day's individual installation program as though it were a single, logical process or run. It will automatically include weekly, monthly, quarterly, or periodic operations or programs on the day that they are to be run and will ignore them on all other days (holidays included). The system supervisor will also provide a step by step log of the entire day's operation. All of this is accomplished without operator intervention (some systems).

system, supervisory — All of the supervisory programs used by one system.

system, support — A collection of computer programs to aid the production and check-out of a system. The combination of the skills, techniques, and equipment to operate and maintain a system.

system, synchronous (communications)—A system in which the sending and receiving instruments are operating continuously at substantially the same frequency and are maintained, by means of correction if necessary, in a desired phase relationship.

system, tandem—A special system configuration in which the data proceeds through one central processor into another processor. This is the system of multiplexors and master/slave arrangements.

system, tape addition and maintenance program (STAMP) —A Honeywell program that simplifies making up the file of systems programs on the symbolic program tape or master relocatable tape; it reduces significantly the time and effort in updating, correcting, and maintaining the systems programs on these tapes.

system testing program—Test and checkout of complete programs as opposed to parameter or assembly testing.

system, time-shared—A specific system in which available central-computer time is shared among several jobs, as directed by a scheduling plan or formula.

system, time-sharing (monitor)—*See* monitor system, time-sharing.

system total—*See* total system.

system, total management—A management oriented system conceived and designed by management as a singular entity to control the entire organization. Some of the systems which are integrated to form the total management system are accounting, inventory control, quality control, purchasing, receiving, and financial control. The total management system is an integrated management information and control system, and it is the prevailing application type of third generation computers. It blends both the adminstrative and operational applications into a single information system which provides management with timely and meaningful business information.

system, uniterm — An information-retrieval system that uses uniterm cards. Cards representing words of interest in a search are selected and compared visually. If identical numbers are found to appear on the uniterm card undergoing comparison these numbers represent documents to be examined in connection with the search. (Related to aspect card and uniterm indexing.)

system, upset-duplex—A direct-current telegraph system in which a station between any two duplex equipments may transmit signals by opening and closing the line circuit, thereby causing the signals to be received by upsetting the duplex balance.

system, utility—A system or program that is developed to perform miscellaneous or utility functions such as card-to-tape, tape-to-printer, and other peripheral operations or suboperations.

system utilization loggers—A program or a device that collects statistical information about how the system is operating.

system, zatacode—*Same as* coordinate indexing.

T

tab—1. A label, marker, or indicator used at one or both ends of a medium, such as tapes, to permit quick awareness of its message. 2. A slang term or abbreviation for tabulating equipment.

table—A collection of data in a form suitable for ready reference. It is frequently stored in sequenced machine locations or written in the form of an array of rows and columns for easy entry, in which an intersection of labeled rows and columns serves to locate a specific piece of data or information.

table, addition—The area or core storage that holds a table of numbers to be used during the table-scan concept of addition.

tableau, matrix-algebra — The current matrix, with auxiliary rows and/or columns, as it appears at an interactive stage in the standard-simplex method solution.

table, block—A distinct portion or subset of a table of data or instructions, usually specifically identified for convenient access.

table, Boolean operation—See Boolean operation table.

table, decision—A tabulation or array of possible courses of action, selections, or alternatives which can be possible and thus considered in the analysis of various problems, i.e., a graphic aid to problem description, flow and potential results, much as the purpose of a flowchart.

table, function—1. The two or more sets of information so arranged that an entry in one set selects one or more entries in the remaining sets. 2. A dictionary. 3. A device constructed of hardware, or a subroutine, which can either decode multiple inputs into a single output or encode a single input into multiple outputs. 4. A tabulation of the values of a function for a set of values of the variable.

table lock-up—A method of controlling the location to which a jump or transfer is made. It is used especially when there are a large number of alternatives, as in function evaluation in scientific computations.

table look-at—Finding elements of a table by direct calculation rather than by a comparison search.

table look-up, allocator control—The allocator is a system routine that collects subprograms and interconnects them. Cross-references between these subprograms are resolved and relative locations are assigned. Depending on how the allocator is called, it may go on to produce an absolute program that is put away on drum. Finally this absolute program may be loaded into core and run. The allocator will also, unless requested otherwise, construct a group of tables that serves as one of the inputs to the diagnostic system. If desired, the allocator can work with the output of the memory allocation-processor in order to provide a more flexible computer system. In the absence of a map, the allocator assumes that all subprograms and common blocks will simultaneously occupy a core.

table look-up (TLU)—1. The process of extracting from a table the additional information associated with a particular field in the table. 2. To obtain a function value corresponding to an argument, stated or implied, from a table of function values stored in the computer. Also, the operation of obtaining a value from a table.

table look-up instruction—An instruction designed to allow reference to systematically arranged, stored data.

table look-up techniques — 1. If particular variables are associated with a table of functions, e.g., X_1 links with F_1, G_1, . . ., and if the values of X_1 are equally spaced, locations of associated functions can be conveniently generated by some simple linear relation. 2. If arguments are not equally spaced, the addresses of each X_1 and others can be separated with an appropriate constant. Compare-type order codes can be invoked to locate and the addresses of the associated function can be computed. 3. Each datum X_1 can be stored with a pointer pointing to a list of associated functions of X_1. 4. Indirect addressing may be used to jump from an ordered sequential storage of arguments to nonsequential, nonordered stores of associated functions (some systems).

table, multiplication—A specific area of storage that holds the groups of numbers to be used during the tabular scanning of the multiplication operation.

table, output—See board, plotting.

table, plotting—Same as board, plotting.

table, program reference—That section of storage used as an index for operations, subroutines, and variables.

table simulator—A specific computer program which has the capability of computing the values in a table rather than simply looking them up as stored.

tables structure—These tables allow complex decision logic to be represented in tabular form. They are easy to prepare, read, and teach to others. Structure tables solved automatically offer levels of accuracy unequalled in manual systems—first, because structure table errors are reported in the same language in which the table was written and therefore can be corrected at that level; and second, the inherent accuracy of the computer lends its full power to the solution of the structure tables.

The multiplexor channel has the effect of subdividing the data path into many subchannels. To the programmer, each subchannel is a separate channel, and can be programmed as such. A different device may be started on each subchannel and controlled by its own list of channel commands. Card readers, punches, printers, terminals, etc., are examples of devices that can operate in the multiplexing mode. The polling of terminals is initiated by the processor, but continues independently of the processor under control of the multiplexor channel.

The multiplexor channel can also service high-speed devices by operating in burst mode. In burst mode, the I/O (input/output) unit keeps control of the multiplexor channel until the I/O unit has completed its operation. Thus when operating in burst mode, a single I/O device captures the complete multiplexor-channel data path and does not relinquish it from the time it is selected until the last byte is serviced. Tape units, disk, drum, and data-cell storage are examples of I/O devices that operate in a burst mode. (IBM)

table, subroutine—The routine for maintaining a listing of the subroutines in core and for bringing from file the subroutines as needed by the application program.

table, symbol—A mapping for a set of symbols to another set of symbols or numbers. In programming, the assembler builds a table of labels used in an assembler language program and assigns to those labels a set of relative or absolute core locations.

table, symbol control—Symbols that have been defined and used, but are no longer required, may be deleted from the symbol table. This allows room for new symbols. Thus, a very large program can be assembled with a relatively small symbol storage area.

table, transfer—*See* transfer vector.

table, truth—A representation of a switching function, or truth function, in which every possible configuration of argument values 0-1, or true-false is listed, and beside each is given the associated function value 0-1 or true-false. The number of configurations is 2^n, where "n" is the number of arguments, unless the function is incompletely specified, i.e., don't care conditions. An example of a truth table for the AND-function and the OR-function (inclusive) is:

Variable		AND Function	OR
A	B	AB	A+B
0	0	0	0
0	1	0	1
1	0	0	1
1	1	1	1

TABSIM (TABulator SIMulator)—A simulator program that speeds the conversion of tabulating-equipment tasks to computer processing. They are load-and-go type packages

that permit users to run tab jobs on computers. (Honeywell)

TABSOL (TABular Systems Oriented Language)—A tabular structure language for convenient solutions to problems involving multiple sequential decisions; particularly useful in manufacturing planning, engineering design, and inventory control. (General Electric)

tabular language—A composition of decision tables that become the problem-oriented language used in computation.

tabulate—The process of accumulating groups (families) of separate totals simultaneously. Each total is usually controlled by its individual key; as each key in turn changes causing a total break, the total of this group is printed and added into the next higher level of totals.

tabulating equipment (electronic accounting machine)—The machines and equipment using punched cards. This group of equipment is called tabulating equipment because the main function of punch card machines (for some 20 years before the introduction of the first automatic digital computer) was to produce tabulations of information resulting from sorting, listing, selecting, and totaling data on punch cards. This class of equipment is commonly called PCM (punched-card machines) or tab equipment. (Similar to electrical-accounting machine, and clarified by tabulator.)

tabulating system (electronic-accounting machine)—Any group of machines capable of entering, converting, receiving, classifying, computing, and recording data by means of tabulating cards, and in which tabulating cards are used for storage of data and communicating within the system.

tabulation character—*See* character, tabulation.

tabulator—1. A punched-card machine that takes in punched cards and instructions and produces lists, totals, and tabulations of the information on seperate forms or on one continuous paper. 2. An item of peripheral equipment that reads information from one medium, e.g., cards, paper tape, magnetic tape, etc. and produces lists, tables, and totals on separate forms or continuous paper. 3. A machine that copies specified fields of information, usually from punched cards or tapes, and types or prints the information on continuous paper or special forms.

tabulator list, first item—On some tabulators, the first item of a series of similar data to be printed, which inhibits some or all printing for the rest of the series. Also called group indication and independent sector.

tabulator simulator—*See* TABSIM.

tag—1. A unit of information, whose composition differs from that of other members of the set so that it can be used as a marker or label. A tag bit is an instruction word that is also called a sentinel or a flag. 2.

A specific identifier such as a label, an index, etc.

tag converting unit—The automatic reproduction of information from perforated price tags to punched cards. This machine provides cards for the tabulation of detailed and up-to-date merchandise reports, including size, color, priceline, fabric, and style.

takedown—Those actions performed at the end of an equipment-operating cycle to prepare the equipment for the next set up; e.g. removal of tapes from the tape handlers at the end of a computer run according to a takedown procedure.

takedown time—The time required to take down a piece of equipment.

take-up reel—A specific reel on which tape is wound or may be wound during processing.

talk, cross—Cross talk occurs when signals on one telephone circuit appear on another circuit as interference. The circuit which is the source of the signals is known as the disturbing circuit, and that on which the signals are heard is the disturbed circuit.

talker, echo—A portion of the transmitted signal returned from a distant point to the transmitting source with sufficient time delay to be received as interference.

tally—To add or subtract a digit "1" from a quantity, usually the contents of a register.

tandem system—A special system configuration in which the data proceeds through one central processor into another processor. This is the system of multiplexors and master/slave arrangements.

tape—1. A linear medium for storing information that can be used as input or output to a computer, e.g., magnetic tape. 2. Magnetic, punched paper, sometimes other types of tape as paper loops, etc. used to control vertical formatting of printers, or plastic tapes used to control automatic typewriters. 3. A strip of material that may be punched, coated, or impregnated with magnetic or optically sensitive substances, and used for data input, storage, or output. The data is stored serially in several channels across the tape, transversely to the reading or writing motion.

tape, advance-feed—Perforated paper tape that has the leading edge of the feed holes directly in line with the leading edges of the intelligence holes. This characteristic makes it possible to readily identify and differentiate between the front end and the tail end of an uninterpreted tape. While some applications still use advance-feed tape, most new ones no longer use it. See center-feed tape.

tape alternation—A selection, usually controlled automatically by a program, of first one tape unit and then another, normally during input or output operations, that permits successive reels of a file to be mounted and removed without interrupting the program.

tape, beginning control—A special perforation, reflective spot, or transparent portion of the first part of a magnetic tape to indicate its start.

tape bootstrap routine—The load tape has as its first block a bootstrap routine that serves to bring in the remainder of the resident and various other parts of the system. The bootstrap routine also provides a simple card-load routine, a panic dump, and a method of patching the resident system prior to writing it to drum.

tape bound—Same as tape limited.

tape, carriage control—This tape contains the control codes related to the movement of the carriage of the printer, and thus controls the vertical and horizontal positioning of the carriage as well as the paper feed unit.

tape, center-feed—Perforated paper tape that has the feed holes centered directly in line with the centers of the intelligence holes. The most common method in use today.

tape, chadded paper—A paper tape with the holes fully punched.

tape, chadless paper—A paper tape with the holes partially punched. It is commonly used in teletype operations.

tape, change—A paper tape or magnetic tape carrying information that is to be used to up-date filed information on a master tape. (Synonymous with transaction tape.)

tape channels, paper—The presence of a hole in the tape indicates the presence of a code bit. The holes are punched in channels parallel to the edge of the tape, and paper tape of 5, 6, 7, 8 information channels is in use at present. An 8-channel tape (with an additional sprocket channel for guiding the tape or for code synchronization) will commonly be of 1-in. width with codes spaced at 10 per inch along the tape.

tape channels, punched paper—The parallel tracks along the length of the tape.

tape character—Information consisting of bits stored across the several longitudinal channels of a tape.

tape character check—See character check, tape.

tape coil, blank paper—A coil of paper tape that has to be punched with the feed holes and can be punched with a pattern of holes that represent data.

tape coil, paper—The roll of paper tape as coiled and ready for use at the punch station, but one which may be blank or punched in preparation for working.

tape comparator—A unique machine which automatically compares two tapes which are expected to be identical. The comparison is row by row and the machine stops when a discrepancy occurs.

tape compiler, BPS FORTRAN—This compiler is a seven-phase program which translates programs written in the IBM system/360 FORTRAN IV language into relocatable object programs. A source program listing along with error indicators and a storage map of the variables, external references, and constants is provided on request.

tape, control—A paper or plastic tape used to control the carriage operation of some printing output devices.

tape-controlled carriage—An automatic paper-feeding carriage controlled by a punched paper tape.

tape, control unit—The unit, including associated buffering, for controlling the operation of the magnetic tape transport.

tape, cycling—An updating procedure which creates a new tape file.

tape drive—The mechanism that moves magnetic or paper tape past sensing and recording heads and is usually associated with data-processing equipment. (Synonymous to tape transport and feed tape, and related to tape unit, magnetic-tape unit, and paper-tape unit.)

tape-driver interrupt routine—In the interrupt routine, the driver determines whether a fail condition has occurred on the addressed unit. A fail condition is recognized when the unit is at the end of the tape, at a file mark, or if a parity fail has occurred. If no fail has occurred and the operation requested requires a series of commands, i.e., "special rewind," "ready to file," etc., the driver will give the next command and exit to the interrupt point.

tape dump—The transfer of complete contents of information recorded on tape to the computer or another storage medium.

tape editor—The symbolic tape editor program is used to edit, correct, and update symbolic program tapes using the computer and the teletype unit. With the editor in the core memory, the user reads in portions of his symbolic tape, removes, changes, or adds instructions or operands, and gets back a corrected symbolic tape. The user can work through the program instruction by instruction, spot-check it, or concentrate on new sections.

tape erasure—A process by which a signal recorded on a tape is removed and the tape made ready for re-recording. Erasure may by accomplished in the two ways; in ac erasure, the tape is demagnetized by an alternating field which is reduced in amplitude from an initially high value; in dc erasure the tape is saturated by applying a primarily undirectional field.

tape error—A special tape developed and used for writing out errors in order to correct them by study and analysis after printing.

tape feed—A mechanism that will feed tape to be read or sensed by the machine.

tape-feed switch—The switch actuates the reperforator to meter a predetermined length of tape.

tape file—1. A record file consisting of a

magnetic or punched-paper tape. 2. A set of magnetic tapes in a tape library.

tape file checks, magnetic—Hardware checks for faulty tapes without loss of computer time or manual intervention.

tape, fully perforated (chad tape)—Perforated paper tape in which the perforations are complete—that is, in which the punch makes a complete hole in the tape (as opposed to chadless tape, where the hole is not completely punched out).

tape, grandfather—A magnetic tape which contains basic or initial information, which is used on a second tape, and this second tape is the one which is updated according to the latest transactions or changes. When this second tape is copied, it becomes the new grandfather tape, and a series of grandfather tapes is the historical record or statistical base for further manipulation, analysis, or an audit trial. They are also backup tapes in case of accidental erasure or loss of latest developed tapes.

tape input—A method of introducing data to an input device by the use of plastic or metallic magnetic tape, perforated paper tape, or fabric tape loops; the mechnical method by which data is read from tape and fed into a machine.

tape input/output control (TIPTOP)—The tape input/output control provides machine code, as directed by macroinstructions, to perform the following functions: reading and writing tape records, opening and closing files, blocking and unblocking items within records, and detection of automatic correction of errors. (Honeywell)

tape, instruction—*Same as* tape, program.

tape, intermix—A specific feature of some computer equipment which allows for combinations of different models of tape units to be interconnected to a single computer.

tape labels—1. A tape label appears on each reel of magnetic tape in the form of a leader and/or a trailer record; its contents will be determined to some extent by the application and the type of data found on the tape. The leader record appears as the first and the trailer record as the last on the tape. Together they provide the means for machine-performed accounting control of tape operations. Types of information which may be included in a tape label are: a name or code for the tape which identifies the application and tape data type, reel number or sequence number if there is more than one, frequency of use, record format, date of preparation or date last used, purge date, operation in which the tape was written (generally a code), name of individual chiefly responsible, output number if there are several tapes, record count, control totals, any instructions to be typed out to the operator as well as an end-of-reel or end-of-file code. 2. Every tape in the system should be identified by a tape label. The tape label consists of two blocks which should be assigned upon introduction. The first is an installation tape number which should be assigned upon introducing a new reel of tape into the system. This number never changes. The second identifies the information that will follow on the tape and contains dating information that will be used by special programs to further identify the tape, and to protect the information from being destroyed prematurely.

tape leader—Section at the beginning of a reel of magnetic or punched tape which is often left blank to allow for initial threading or to contain some sort of marker or code to indicate the nature of the data stored on the tape. Holes, notches, some special magnetization, etc., are used for such purposes.

tape, library—*See* library tapes.

tape-limited—Just as some computers are limited to the slower speeds of cards for adequate performance, others are bound or limited in performance speeds by the time required for reading, writing, or punching tapes. When computers execute various types of business or large batch data processing and much of the time is used in moving tapes, then the computer or processor must wait and is said to be tape-limited.

tape limited (sorting)—A sort program in which the effective transfer rate of tape units determines the elapsed time required to sort.

tape loadpoint—The initial position of the magnetic tape under the heads, at which point magtape reading or writing can begin.

tape-loop storage—*See* storage loop.

tape, mag—The informal or slang expression for magnetic tape.

tape, magnetic—A tape or ribbon or any material impregnated or coated with magnetic material on which information may be placed in the form of magnetically polarized spots.

tape mark—The special character that is written on a tape to signify the physical end of the recording on tape.

tape marker beginning (BIM)—A special perforated reflective spot or a transparent portion of the first part of a magnetic tape to indicate its start.

tape, master—Usually a magnetic tape containing the main program or the data master file, which is updated by data contained in a change tape.

tape, master-file—The word "file" is used in a general sense to mean any collection of informational items similar to one another in purpose, form, and content. Thus a magnetic tape master file is a file; the term may also be applied to a punched paper tape of input items, or if convenient, to a set of cards that is equivalent in nature to either the magnetic or paper tape. File may even be applied to an accumulation of information in the processor memory if the

need arises to refer in a general way to this collection of data.

tape, master-instruction (MIT)—A tape on which all the programs for a system of runs are recorded.

tape master program—*See* tape master.

tape, master-system—This is a monitor (control unit) program that allows for centralized control of program operation. It provides a load-and-go operation, without operator intervention, with one tape unit. The operator can specify loading and execution of any program on the master-system tape by a simple on-line typewriter directive.

tape, Mylar—A specific data processing tape manufactured by E.I. Dupont Nemours Co., made of polyester film with a magnetic oxide coat.

tape, numerical—A punched paper or plastic tape with magnetic spots is used to feed digital instructions to a numerical control (N/C) machine, i.e., an automated cutting or forming machine thus guided. Tolerances as fine as 1/10,000 of an inch are achieved on unattended units. Tapes are developed for digital-computer programs.

tape or drum program—A tape or drum used to store a complete routine for future input. In the event that the length of the routine exceeds the available internal storage capacity, it will be read in and operated on by the computer, one segment at a time.

tape, paper—A strip of paper capable of storing or recording information. Storage may be in the form of punched holes, partially punched holes, carbonization or chemical change of impregnated material, or by imprinting. Some paper tapes, such as punched paper tapes, are capable of being read by the input device of a computer or a transmitting device by sensing the pattern of holes that represent coded information.

tape parity—*See* parity, tape.

tape, perforated—*See* tape, punched paper.

tape perforating—The recording of data in paper tape by means of punched holes. This is generally done by a card-to-tape converter which automatically senses the information from punched cards and perforates a 5-channel or 8-channel tape used in telegraphic transmission and other common-language applications.

tape perforator—An off-line, keyboard-operated device for punching code holes in paper tape.

tape, pilot—A tape that contains all the data used on a pilot model. It is often used for loading the files.

tape plotting system—The magnetic tape plotting system is extremely versatile, reliable, and almost completely automatic. Zero position, scale factor adjustment, curve identification, symbol selection, axis generation, etc., are handled entirely by subroutines within the computer. For this reason, the plotting system may be operated by unskilled personnel. The operator is required only to select the desired plot by means of the automatic-search feature, then initiate the plotting action by pressing either the "Single-Plot" or "Multiple-Plot" button (some systems).

tape, problem input—An input tape, either punched-paper tape or magnetic tape, that contains problem data for checking out a given computer system.

tape-processing simultaneity—A feature of some computers is tape processing simultaneity. All tape units are capable of transferring data simultaneously with other central processor operations. The ability to perform tape operations simultaneously is further enhanced by the fact that the central processor is involved in a tape read or write operation during only two microseconds per character transferred. Thus, the majority of a tape-processing interval is available to the central processor to perform computations or direct other peripheral operations.

tape-processing unit—Tape processing includes the functions of recording, transcribing, transmitting, receiving and converting data recorded in perforated paper tape. Data recorded in paper tape can be processed to: produce punched cards by automatic conversion, provide input for electric computers, provide automatic wire transmission of all or selected data, type subsequent related records and documents, and provide master tapes, or cards, for use in repetitive data operations.

tape, program—A tape that contains the sequence of instructions required for solving a problem.

tape, punch—A tape, usually paper, upon which data may be sorted in the form of punched holes. Hole locations are arranged in rows across the width of the tape. There are usually 5 or 8 channels per row, with data represented by a binary-coded decimal system. All holes in a column are sensed simultaneously in a manner similar to that for punch cards. (Synonymous with perforated tape.)

tape-punch, automatic—*See* punch, automatic tape.

tape, punch code—A code used to represent data on punch tape.

tape-punch control keys—These keys are located for convenient use by the operator. They control functions such as power on feeding tape at beginning and end of reel, tape error, and punch on and off.

tape, punched paper—1. Paper or plastic material from 300 to 1000 feet long into which data is recorded in the form of small round holes punched into prescribed positions. 2. Another input and/or output medium, used primarily in systems where information is received over wire communication circuits.

tape reader—1. A device capable of sensing information punched on a paper tape in the

form of a series of holes. 2. A device capable of sensing information recorded on a magnetic tape in the form of a series of magnetized spots.

tape recording density—The number of recording densities are 200 characters per inch, 556 per inch, 800 per inch, or even higher in the newest "packed" tapes. Blocks or records are usually separated by blank gaps on tapes, most commonly of ¾ in.

tape reproducer—A particular machine which is used either to copy or edit paper tape or to do both.

tape scratch (sorting)—Tape(s) used to store intermediate-pass data during a sort program.

tape, sequence control—A tape that contains the sequence of instructions required for solving a problem.

tape-servo swap—*See* swap, tape-servo.

tape skew—The deviation of a tape from a linear path when transported across the heads, causing a time displacement between signals recorded on different tracks and amplitude differences between the outputs from individual tracks owing to variations in azimuth alignment.

tape skip—A machine instruction to space forward and erase a portion of tape when a defect on the tape surface causes a persistent write error.

tape skip, tape-skip restore—A function that permits certain portions of the tape to be idled through a tape read head without being read. This function is initiated by depressing the tape-skip key. Skipping continues until the read head finds a tape-skip restore character in the tape. This character must be included in the original programming.

tapes, library—Library tapes will have tape labels, skip records and control marks. However, the programs must be stored on magnetic tape according to a particular format. Library tapes may contain two types of intermixed formats—standard-format (running programs as set up by a librarian), and debugging-format (this includes check data as well as the programs to be checked).

tape sort and collate programs—Generalized programs that adapt themselves, as directed by programmer-specified parameters, to operate in a particular configuration—sort and collate data into a particular format.

tape sort, four—*See* sorting, four tape.

tape speed—The speed at which tapes are transported from feed to take-up reels during normal recording or reproduction.

tape station—*Same as* tape unit.

tape storage, magnetic—*See* storage, magnetic-tape.

tape strips—A material used in random access storage devices that have removable or replaceable storage, in contrast to fixed storage. Card strips and disk packs, as well as tape strips, are used to store information, but they can be removed and replaced by other strips or packs, thereby allowing for a theoretically unlimited storage capacity.

tape synchronizer—*See* synchronizer, tape.

tape, test input—A method of testing and simulation, wherein a test input tape is prepared from an input message tape, which is then read by the test supervisory program in a manner as if it had actually arrived from regular input devices.

tape-to-card—Pertaining to usually off-line equipment or methods that transfer information directly from tape to cards.

tape-to-card program—Transfers binary or EBCDIC data from cards to magnetic tape.

tape-to-head speed—The relative speed of tape and head during normal recording or replay. The tape-to-head speed coincides with the tape speed in conventional longitudinal recording, but is considerably greater than the tape speed in systems where the heads are scanned across or along the tape.

tape-to-printer program—Transfers data from magnetic tape to printer.

tape-to-tape converter—A device for changing from one form of input/output medium or code to another; i.e., magnetic tape to paper tape (or vice versa), or eight-channel code to five-channel code, etc.

tape trailer—A special strip or tape length at the end of tape reels, usually containing a type of end-of-tape marker, i.e., a hole, long blank, special magnetic spots, etc.

tape, transaction—Information on a paper tape or magnetic tape that is to be used to update filed information on a master tape.

tape transmitter, automatic—A peripheral unit which senses data on paper, magnetic, or mylar tape and which holds, feeds, controls, and reels the tape. They are used basically for computer input units, and often used to drive printers, plotters, card punches, or transmission modems.

tape transmitter distributor—*Same as* tape reader.

tape transport—The mechanism that moves magnetic or paper tape past sensing and recording heads. This mechanism is usually associated with data-processing equipment. (Synonymous with drive tape and tape feed; related to tape unit, magnetic-tape unit, and paper-tape unit.)

tape unit—1. A device for reading data from magnetic tape or writing new data on tape. The device also rewinds completed tape. Some units read in either direction, although they write only in the forward direction. 2. The mechanism for reading or writing a magnetic tape. 3. A device consisting of a tape transport, controls, a set of reels, and a length of tape that is capable of recording and reading information on and from the tape, at the request of the computer. (Clarified by tape transport, magnetic-tape unit, and paper-tape unit.)

tape unit perforator—*See* tape processing unit.

tape units, incremental—Various types of

magnetic tape modules which require a tape flow "halt" for the process of reading or writing. *See also* variable speed tape units.

tape verifier—A device designed for checking the accuracy of punched tape by comparing previously punched tape with a second manual punching of the same data, with the machine signalling discrepancies.

tape, work (sorting)—Tape(s) used to store intermediate-pass data during a sort program.

target computer—*Same as* object computer.

target configuration—*Same as* object configuration.

target language—The language into which some other language is to be translated.

target phase—An occasion on which the target program is run is often called the run phase or the target phase or the object phase, i.e., most often target phase terminology is used when compiling has taken place.

target program—*Same as* object program.

target routine—*Same as* object program.

task—A routine or machine run. A program may be broken into several subjobs or tasks to utilize more effectively computer CPU time.

technique—1. The detailed procedures essential to the expert execution of an art or science. 2. The method used to collect, process, convert, transfer, and retrieve data to prepare reports.

technique, advance item—A programming technique which groups records in specific arrangements disregarding location aspects of the data.

technique, flowchart—*See* flowchart technique.

technology, solid-logic—Microelectronic circuits, the product of solid-logic technology, make up some system's basic components. Called logic circuits because they carry and control the electrical impulses that represent information within a computer, these tiny devices operate at speeds ranging from 300 down to six billionths-of-a-second.

telecommunication—The transmission or reception of signals, writing, sounds, or intelligence of any nature by wire, radio, light beam, or any other electromagnetic means.

teledata—A device that introduces parity bits to punched paper type for transmission. The receiving unit checks parity for code accuracy and repunched paper tape with valid data.

telefile—An early on-line banking system developed for Howard Savings Institution of Newark, New Jersey.

telegraph channel—The transmission media and intervening apparatus involved in the transmission of telegraph signals in a given direction between two terminal sets, or more generally, between two intermediate telegraph installations. A means of one-way transmission of telegraph signals. Separate telegraph channels can have common constituent parts; e.g., side and phantom circuits or share a common path as in the case of a multiplex. A channel between two terminal sets can be referred to as a complete telegraph channel. A transmitter with a storage of signals is considered a terminal set and terminates a complete channel. A complete channel may include regenerative repeaters (without storage capacity). A telegraph channel is characterized by the number of the significant conditions and by the modulation rate it is designed to transmit; for example, a fifty-band channel for a two-condition modulation.

telegraph, error rate of (communication)— Ratio of the number of alphabetic signals of a message incorrectly received (after automatic translation) to the number of alphabetic signals of the message, the keying being correct. Note: A telegraph communication may have a different error rate for the two directions of transmission. The notation of error rate could be applied to any operation taking place in a telegraph communication (e.g., keying, translation, etc.). The statement of error rate will be accompanied by that of the time interval, generally limited, during which the observation was made. For a communication established for a sufficiently long time, the probability of exceeding an assigned value of error rate could be considered.

telegraph, voice-frequency carrier (V.F.C.T.) —A telegraph-transmission system which provides several narrow-band individual channels in the voice-frequency range.

telemeter—1. An electric telemeter is the formulating and reformulation apparatus for indicating and/or recording the value of a measured quantity by electrical means at a remote station. 2. To transmit digital and/or analog data by radio waves; e.g. data can be telemetered from a missile and recorded at a ground station.

telemetering—The transmission, by electromagnetic means, of a measurement over long distances.

telemetry systems, adapter unit—A data-adapter unit provides the system with greatly expanded input/output device capability. It provides direct connection for a variety of remote and local external devices, e.g., teletypewriter terminals, telemetry terminals, test instrumentation and data-acquisition equipment. The unit attaches to a selector channel or multiplexor channel. A selector channel handles high-speed input/output devices. It is overlapped with other selector channels and a multiplexor channel, in a processor's input/output control element, to provide simultaneous operations. When a selector channel is used, only one device at a time can read data into that channel, although as many as eight input/output control units can be connected to it. A multiplexor channel can handle

many low- or medium-speed devices simultaneously on a character-by-character basis, or a single device in a burst of characters. The maximum data-rate capability of the unit is generally specified by the particular transmission interface adapter used, the input/output channel capacity, and the overall systems configuration (some systems).

telephone communication units—The data sets as used with the many data communications systems provide half-duplex capability. They are used for sending and receiving but not for both operations simultaneously. The data set at the transmitting end takes the character pulses from the data-line terminal and converts them to modulated information-bearing signals that can be transmitted over the telephone line. The data set at the receiving end converts the signals from the telephone line back to the same character pulses as those delivered by the transmitting data-line terminal and delivers these pulses to the receiving data-line terminal. A data set conditions itself in the receiving mode unless instructed to be in the transmitting mode. The turn-around of the data set at the transmitting end is performed by the "request to transmit step" in the program of the computer at the sending end. It may be used with either the private line or the exchange telephone facilities.

telephone company data set—1. A standard telephone company data set is required at each end of the telephone line. In each office, the data set connects the RTU (remote terminal unit) to the telephone line, and converts the RTU's signals into tones for transmission over the line. The same data set also converts reply tones received from the processing center into signals for the RTU. 2. Most data sets can be equipped for unattended operation. This means that the data set will automatically answer any incoming calls that are directed to it. The data set, however, has no way of recognizing the termination of a transmission, and for this reason, the signal to disconnect must come from the associated CLT (Communications Line Terminal). Similarly, when the central processor dials a remote location, the CLT must signal its associated data set to disconnect after the transmission is completed. Automatic calling units, supplied by the telephone company, must be disconnected from their associated transmission lines between every call. The CLT dialing must signal the automatic calling unit to disconnect after a connection has been established. The ability to hang up or disconnect is provided by the unattended operation feature. This feature is provided on output CLTs only; however, the function of hanging up after input-data transmission can be performed by an output CLT.

telephone line, teller system — The telephone lines specified for the on-line teller system are private lines, leased from the telephone company, of the same type used for voice transmission. The lines are full-duplex, permitting instantaneous response to control signals. The system is controlled through constant polling of teller consoles on each line by the central terminal unit. Polling is a request to each console for a message, or for readiness to receive a reply. Because the full-duplex line permits the RTU (remote terminal unit) to respond instantly to polls, many teller consoles can be efficiently serviced on one line. The full-duplex line was chosen for the on-line teller system for maximum economy and efficiency of operation. It eliminates the turn-around delay inherent in a half-duplex line, greatly increases the number of consoles that can be polled and serviced efficiently, and requires fewer lines (some systems).

teleprinter—1. Descriptive name for telegraphic terminals. 2. Generally an electric typewriter that can be operated manually or electrically by reading a reperforating paper tape. 3. The typewriter usually connected to a leased or dial-switched telegraph-grade circuit for transmitting text or data messages in a readable form. 4. An input/output terminal device, normally used on low-speed circuits, that includes at least a page printer.

teleprinter grade service—This term originally referred to a service provided by the common carriers which included a communication circuit of narrow bandwidth that was capable of speeds no greater than 180 bauds per second, and furnished a compatible d-c signal to the terminal input/output device directly. This definition is no longer completely valid because much of the low-speed data transmission is accomplished over circuits utilizing a-c signaling so a dataset must be provided between the circuit and the terminal equipment. The term now is used primarily to distinguish this type of service from voice-grade service in reference to regulatory agencies' tariffs.

teleprocessing—An IBM registered term denoting systems that transmit data from one point to another in the course of processing.

teleprocessing network—In an operating teleprocessing network, several inquiries simultaneously might come into the system from distant cities concerning information that is contained in the disk file. The appropriate records are then taken from the disk file and the appropriate responses would be prepared and returned to the originating cities. Although this appears to be a simple function, the network requires design balance to achieve the required variety of terminal speeds and functions. The network requires: simultaneous operation of many devices operating through a single economical channel, the time-sharing and space-sharing programs that control these devices, and disk-file capacity and speed.

Furthermore, it has to do all of these things concurrently with batch-job processing. The system has the data communications facilities to handle these functions as an integral part of its processing units. Special provision is made for code conversion within the processing units (some systems).

teleprocessing terminal—A teleprocessing terminal is used for on-line data transmission between remote process locations and a central computer system. Connection to the computer system is made by a data adapter unit or a transmission control. This system facilitates the control of natural gas and petroleum pipe lines, utility distribution systems, and the collection of process data in petroleum refineries, chemical plants, paper mills, iron and steel works, batch processes in manufacturing, and many other applications.

teletype—Trademark of the Teletype Corporation. A system for transmitting messages over a distance. This system employs keyboard or paper-tape transmitting devices and print-out receiving units.

teletype code—*Same as* code, Baudot.

teletype grade—Represents the lowest-type communication circuit in terms of speed, cost, and accuracy.

teletype input/output device—A teletype automatic send-receive (ASR) set is included in many standard computers. The ASR set transfers information into the computer from perforated tape or a keyboard, and supplies output information from the computer in the form of perforated tape and/or a typed message. The teletype rate is in characters per second in either direction.

teletypewrite marking pulse—*See* pulse, teletypewrite marking.

teletypewriter—Trade name used by AT&T to refer to the telegraph-terminal equipment.

teletypewriter exchange service (TWX)—A switching network providing interconnection for AT&T now Western Union teletypewriter subscribers.

Telex (TEX)—An automatic teletype-exchange service provided by Western Union and extending into Canada via Canadian Pacific railroad facilities. Subscribers can dial each other for direct two-way telemeter communications.

teller consoles (bank)—Accepts teller-indexed transaction messages for transmission to the computer and prints the processed replies (received from the computer) on to customer passbooks, transaction tickets, and the transaction journal. 2. Accepts keyboard-indexed messages for transmission to the processing center and prints processed replies received from the center to passbooks, tickets, and transaction journal.

teller systems, on-line—No matter what the application, all "on-line" computer systems have one common trait; they permit direct access to a computer, including the per-

443

tinent records stored in its electronic memory. This direct access may come from one or many inquiry stations of various types, which may be located either close by the computer or miles away, connected to the computer over various communication devices such as telephone or telegraph lines. In on-line teller systems, all tellers are in direct communication with, and are under complete control of, a computer that is connected, via communications lines, to each teller console. On-line teller systems have four major elements: a large random-access memory tied directly to the computer, used to store account records and auxiliary information; teller consoles for keyboard entry of transaction information and computer-controlled printing of replies to passbooks, tickets, and journals; data-communication equipment and telephone lines, linking the teller consoles to the computer; and an electronic computer system for control and computation.

telpak—1. A name used by AT&T to designate its service for leasing wide band channels. 2. Broad-band communication channels for transmitting data from magnetic tape to magnetic tape or directly between computers at rates greater than 60,000 characters a second.

temporary storage—Internal-storage locations reserved for intermediate or partial results.

tens complement—The radix complement of a numeral whose radix is ten. The tens complement is obtained by subtracting each digit of a number from 9, and adding 1 to the least significant of the resultant number. For example, the tens complement of 2456 is 7544.

teracycle—A million megacycles per second (10^{12} cycles per second).

terminal—A point at which information can enter or leave a communication network. An input/output device designed to receive data in an environment associated with the job to be performed, and capable of transmitting entries to, and obtaining output from, the system of which it is a part.

terminal, control (CTU)—This unit supervises communication between the consoles and the processing center. It receives incoming messages at random intervals, stores them until the central processor is ready to process them, and returns the processed replies to the remote consoles which originated the transactions.

terminal console devices —See console devices, terminal.

terminal, data—A device that modulates and/or demodulates data between one input/output device and a data-transmission link.

terminal, data-communication—A data station is an all-purpose remote-communication terminal that can be used for a broad range of applications. These applications involve

direct on-line data transmission to and from company-branch offices or warehouses, and remote locations throughout a plant. When not being used for actual on-line transmission (remote mode), the data station can be used for off-line (local mode) data preparation and editing.

terminal-digit posting—The arranging and recording of serial numbers of documents on the basis of the final configuration of the digits of the serial number.

terminal equipment—Data source or data sink equipment such as teletypewriters for input terminals and CRT (cathode-ray-tube) screens for output.

terminal equipment, data—See data terminal equipment.

terminal inquiry, display—See display, inquiry terminal.

terminal installation—A grouping, at one site, of operable data terminals and related equipment.

terminal installation for data transmission—Installation comprising the data-terminal equipment, the signal-conversion equipment, and any intermediate equipment. Note: In some instances, the data-terminal equipment may be connected directly to a data-processing machine or may be a part of it.

terminal interchange—A buffering device at a location remote from the processing center. Such a device provides temporary storage for messages originating at the terminals that it serves and at the processing center.

terminal, job-oriented—A terminal specially designed to receive the job-source data in the environment of the job. The terminal also is capable of transmission to and from its computer system.

terminal, magnetic-tape—The magnetic-tape terminal converts the character pulses from serial-bit form to parallel-bit form, while checking for odd parity and translating the code to the desired magnetic-tape code for entry into a buffer storage. The longitudinal parity count at the end of the message is verified. The integral part of the magnetic-tape terminal performing this function is called a coupler. The coupler of the magnetic-tape terminal performs a function similar to that of the data-line terminal.

terminal module, controller communications —See communications terminal module controller.

terminal modules, communications (CTMS)—See communications terminal modules.

terminal, multiplex-data—A device that modulates and/or demodulates data between two or more input/output devices and a data-transmission link.

terminal, optical display—See optical display terminal.

terminals, communication line (CLT)—There are three basic kinds of input and output CLTs: low speed (up to 300 bps), medium speed (up to 1600 bps) and high speed (2000-4800 bps). Each is easily adjusted to the speed and other characteristics of the line with which it is to operate. Each CLT requires one position, either input or output, of the communication multiplexer. The CLT-Dialing is an output CLT which is employed to enable the central processor automatically to establish communications with remote points via the common carrier's switching network. Each CLT-Dialing requires one output position of a communication multiplexer. Since CLT-Dialing does not transmit data, it is always used in conjunction with an output CLT, an input CLT, or, for two-way communications. (UNIVAC)

terminal, teleprocessing—*See* teleprocessing terminal.

terminal unit—A part of the equipment in a communication channel that may be used for either input or output to the channel.

terminal unit, central (CTU)—The central terminal unit (CTU) at the processing center receives transaction messages at random intervals, stores them until the computer is ready to process them, and returns the processed replies to the remote consoles that originated the transactions. Besides the storage of messages and replies, the principal function of the CTU is to supervise all communication between the remote consoles and the processing center. The CTU polls all remote consoles constantly to determine their readiness to send transaction messages and receive processed replies, checks the accuracy of messages transmitted, transmits replies to appropriate remote consoles, and adds checking data to all replies transmitted.

terminal unit, multiplexor—Through the use of a multiplexor terminal unit, the communications system can connect, via four transmission lines, up to 98 terminal stations to and from the central processor. The terminal multiplexor processor controls all transmission sequences to and from the central processor and the terminal stations, and also performs, checks, and handles the required calculations. Input/output devices such as storage files, magnetic tapes, visual displays and printers also can be attached to the terminal multiplexor processor. These multiplexor-terminal stations are designed to handle standard-control system input/output devices and transducers. The transmission of data to or from the terminal stations is performed on multidrop transmission channels in half-duplex mode at high speeds; it is buffered into the processor for greater system efficiency (some systems).

terminating symbol—A symbol on the tape indicating the end of a block of information. (Related to gap.)

termination, executive—The normal or abnormal termination of an operating program and the return of its assigned facilities to an available status. Termination may be initiated by executive program, by the job program, or by the operator.

termination, job process monitor—The programmer specifies monitor system operation with various control statements. These statements may be input via a console typewriter or included with the program on cards, paper tape, or magnetic tape.

termination, loop—*See* loop termination.

terminator/initiator—A specific program which makes a job step ready to run in some computers and which also performs regular housekeeping tasks after a job has ended. Used in conjunction with job schedulers which select a job or jobs part waiting to be executed after allocating and clearing memory space of extraneous data.

ternary—1. Pertaining to a characteristic or property involving a selection, choice, or condition in which there are three possibilities. 2. Pertaining to the number-representation system with a radix of three. 3. Having the capability of assuming three distinct states.

ternary code—A code in which only three states are considered.

ternary representation incremental—*See* incremental ternary representation.

test—To examine, particularly relative to a criterion; to determine the present arrangement of some element of computer hardware, e.g., a manually set switch.

test, branch instruction—*See* branch instruction test.

test case—Verfication for accuracy or completeness by using a sample of the input data as a testing or checking exercise.

test, compatability—Specific tests run to check acceptability of both software and hardware as a system, i.e., to test component workability.

test conditions overflow (underflow)—Often tests are made for conditions called underflow and overflow which occur when a result too large or too small for the arithmetic register has been generated, i.e., once an underflow or an overflow occurs, the appropriate indicator can remain "set" until it is tested. After the test, it is conventional for the overflow or underflow condition to be restored to normal.

test, crippled-leapfrog—A variation of the leapfrog test, modified so that it repeats its tests from a single set of storage locations rather than a changing set of locations. (Related to leapfrog test.)

test data—A set of data developed specifically to test the adequacy of a computer run or system. The data may be actual data that has been taken from previous operations, or artificial data created for this purpose.

test, destructive—A test of equipment capability in which results prove to be a cause of permanent degradation due to the type of performance exacted from the equipment tested; for example, the application of excess power, voltages, heat, etc., to cause eventually the circuits or elements to burn, shatter, burst, or otherwise be destroyed.

test, diagnostic—The running of a machine program or a routine for the purpose of discovering a failure or a potential failure of a machine element, and to determine its location or its potential location.

test, high-low-bias—A preventive maintenance procedure in which certain operating conditions are varied about their normal values in order to detect and locate incipient defective units, e.g., supply voltage or frequency may be varied. (Synonymous with marginal test, and related to check.)

testing—The method for examining to determine the real character or specific aspects of an item, program, or system. Acceptance testing for equipment determines capacity, capability, and reliability. Program testing determines whether programs do what they are supposed to do when used with the test, simulated, or live data.

testing, bias—*See* testing, marginal.

testing, cross-sectional—A series of tests to get a representative sampling of system performance. These tests are usually one-pass tests such as an acceptance test.

testing, degradation—Measurement of the performance of a system at the extreme operating limits. Tests are performed to determine the gradual change in performance characteristics.

testing, longitudinal—Iterative tests which compare earlier performance with later performance.

testing, loop—That particular procedure developed to determine whether or not further loop operations are required.

testing, marginal—A form of test usually as part of preventive maintainance or as a fault-finder or correcting operation, to test against safety margins for faults.

testing, normative—Standards of performance that are established for the testing of both quantitative and qualitative system performance.

testing, parameter—*See* parameter testing.

testing, procedural—Tests of alternative human responses in system operations. This is distinguished from hardware or software tests.

testing, program—This is completed to discover whether the program is successful in meeting the defined systems requirements.

testing, program system—Test and checkout of complete programs as opposed to parameter or assembly testing.

testing, retrofit—Testing to assure system operation after replacing some equipment or programs.

testing, saturation—The testing of a program by pushing through a great many messages in an attempt to find errors that happen infrequently.

testing, sequential—A series of tests performed in a predetermined order and requiring repeated observations.

testing time—The time which is used for the testing of the machine or system to ensure

that no faults exist or malfunctions are present by using special diagnostic routines for circuit testing or to discern status or conditions of components. Usually such time could be included in fault time after the repair of the fault and included in scheduled maintenance time.

testing time, program—*See* program testing time.

test input tape—*See* tape, test input.

test instructions (debugging)—Most good compiler systems are designed to automatically remove various temporary tracing (debugging) instructions after tests are automatically made to ensure accuracy and precision.

test, leapfrog—A program designed to discover computer malfunction, characterized by the property that it performs a series of arithmetical or logical operations on one group of storage locations, transfers itself to another group of storage locations, checks the correctness of the transfer, then begins the next series of operations again. Eventually, all storage positions will have been occupied and the test will be repeated. (Related to crippled-leapfrog test.)

test, marginal—*Same as* high-low bias test.

test, marginal (voltage and registers)—Built into some computers is a network for marginal test of computer subsections. Two features of the marginal test system make routine checks fast and accurate: the marginal check voltage is continuously variable, and all working registers are displayed simultaneously on the console lights.

test, output processor—In a complex system, an automated processing of the output so that errors may be more easily tracked down.

test problem—A problem chosen to determine whether the computer or a program is operating correctly.

test processor, output—*See* test, output processor.

test, program—A check system in which a sample problem with a known answer is run before processing a problem.

test routine—A routine designed to show whether a computer is functioning properly.

test run—A diagnostic run of the program, using manufactured data. The results of this run are checked against the correct answers for this problem.

test set, tape—A peripheral device or unit designed to locate defects in magnetic tape before use, such as oxide emissions, unevenness, bubbles, etc.

tests, procedural and exception—Procedure and exception tests are designed to check machine control and operation before processing. They consist of test data (generally punched into cards) covering all or most conditions which can arise during the run, as well as a control panel and/or program which will reprocess the test data and check out machine components. The control panel is inserted, or the program loaded, or both.

The test data is then read into the machine and processed. The results are compared against predetermined ones. If they are satisfactory, actual processing can begin. In some installations, these tests are made only at the beginning of each working day; in others they are made before specific runs.

tests, reasonableness—These tests provide a means of detecting a gross error in calculation or, while posting to an account, a balance that exceeds a predetermined limit. Typical examples include payroll calculations and credit limit checks in accounts receivable. In some cases, both an upper and lower limit are established; each result is then machine-compared against both limits to make certain that it falls between the two.

test, supervisor program—A supervisory program that is used only for testing.

test, system—1. The running of the whole system against test data with a verified solution. 2. A complete simulation of the actual running system for purposes of testing out the adequacy of the system. 3. A test of an entire interconnected set of components for the purpose of determining proper functioning and interconnection.

test tape program—That specific tape which contains both program instructions and pre-approved test data or coding to be used for analysis diagnostics, or checkout runs.

test, volume—The processing of a volume of actual data to check for program malfunctions.

tetrad—A group of four, especially a group of four pulses used to express a digit in the scale of 10 or 16.

text—That part of a message that contains the information to be conveyed.

text editing and modification, time sharing—See time sharing, text editing and modification.

text editor (QED)—See editor, text (QED).

text section—Part of a load module which has computer instructions in final form and data defined and with specified initial values.

theory, communication—A branch of mathematics that is concerned with the properties of transmitted messages. The messages are subject to certain probabilities of transmission failure, distortion, and noise.

theory, game—A mathematical process of selecting an optimum strategy in the face of an opponent's strategy.

theory group—See group theory.

theory, information—See information theory.

theory, probability—A measure of the likelihood of the occurrence of a chance event that is used to predict behavior of a group,

theory, queuing—A form of probability theory useful in studying delays or line-ups at servicing points.

theory, switching—A particular branch of theory relating to combinational logic, its operation, behavior, and consequences, i.e., concerning such devices as computers, Tur-

ing machines, logic elements, and switch networks.

thesaurus—1. An assemblage of alphabetized items (or grouped in some other concept or meaningful collection) providing the user with very close or direct synonyms or meanings, close to the term so alphabetized and used as an aid to writers, poets, programmers. 2. In computing, a collection of words or terms used to index, classify, or sort, and then store and retrieve information in a data store or bank, i.e., main terms serve as labels, keywords, or descriptors, and when such references are cited along with the thesaurus, a very useful index is developed.

thin film—An ultra high-speed storage device consisting of a molecular deposit of material on a suitable plate, usually silicon or glass. Common sizes are 1/20th of an inch square that may contain entire etched circuits replacing thousands of transistors, etc.

thin film (control store)—The magnetic-film storage of the computer provides high-speed internal storage. By using this thin-film storage area as an auxiliary, temporary storage medium, faster computation can be obtained. Thin film permits whole circuits (many of them) to be etched on chips as small as 1/20 of an inch square. This saves space and increases reliability.

Any one of the addresses in control store can be accessed in 167 nanoseconds and have a complete cycle time of 667 nanoseconds. Because of this high speed, thin film is a very frequently used portion of the computer's internal storage area; it may be referenced three times in the same time that it takes to make one reference to the core storage area. The high access and internal switching times of thin-film store make it ideal for use as temporary storage of operands while the actual computation of data is taking place. Special address assignments for arithmetic registers, index registers and other purposes are provided. These special addresses have dual accessibility in most instructions, that is, they can be referenced directly by the base operand (U) address of an instruction word or by a special (A) designator within the word (some systems) .

thin film, magnetic—See thin film memory.

thin-film magnetic modules—The thin-film magnetic module is made by the deposition of magnetic alloys, in a vacuum and under the influence of a high magnetic field, on planes of glass so thin that the direction of their magnetic fields can be switched within several billionths of a second (nanoseconds). This feature allows information to be stored or retrieved at extremely high speeds. The immediate benefits derived from this include savings in processing time, reduced power requirements, and miniaturized storage units.

thin-film memory—1. A method of computer storage that utilizes a film (only a few millionths of an inch thick) of metallic vapor that has been deposited on a thin glass plate. The film can be polarized in a billionth of a second (a nanosecond) for fast-memory access. 2. A storage device made of thin disks of magnetic material deposited on a nonmagnetic base. Its operation is similar to the core memory.

third-level address—*See* address, third-level.

thirty-nine feature code—*See* code, thirty-nine feature.

THOR (Tape Handling Option Routine)—1. A set of general tape-handling and correction routines performing the functions of compare and print, locate, correct and copy, and many others. 2. A Honeywell utility program that positions, copies, corrects or edits tape; it can also locate data on tape, compare the contents of two tapes for discrepancies, and perform general tape maintenance. Used with Honeywell 200, 800 and other computers.

three address—A method of specifying the location of operands and instructions in which the storage location of the two operands and the storage location of the results of the operations are cited; e.g., addend, augend, and sum addresses all specified in one instruction word.

three address code—*See* address, three.

three address instruction—*See* instruction, three address.

three, excess (code)—*See* code, excess three.

three input adder—*Same as* adder.

three plus one address—A method of specifying the location of operands and instructions in which the storage location of the two operands, results of the operations, and the next instruction to be executed are specified.

three plus one address instruction—A machine instruction usually consisting of the addresses of two operands, the address for storing the result, the address of the next instruction, the command to be executed, and miscellaneous indices.

three plus one instruction—A specific instruction which contains four addresses, one of which specifies the location of the next instruction which is to be performed.

threshold—A logical operator having the property that if P is a statement, Q is a statement, R is a statement . . . ., then the threshold of P, Q, R, ... , is true if and only if at least N statements are true, false if less than N statements are true, where N is a specified nonnegative integer called the threshold condition

threshold element—A device that performs the logic-threshold operation, in which the truth of each input statement (or weight) completes the output determination of the threshold state.

throughput—The productivity based on all facets of an operation, e.g., a computer with a capability of simultaneous operations of

read/write/compute would have a high-throughput rating.

throughput, simultaneous—Computer functioning at the same time input and output data is being transferred.

throw-away characters—*See* characters, throw-away.

throw, paper—*See* paper throw.

ticket, batch—A control document used to identify groups of source documents, often with group totals.

tie-line—A leased-communication channel or circuit between two or more PBXs.

time, acceleration—The time between the interpretation of instructions to read or write on tape and the transfer of information from the tape into storage, or from storage into tape, as the case may be. (Synonymous with start time.)

time, access—1. The time it takes a computer to locate data or an instruction word in its storage section and transfer it to its arithmetic unit where the required computations are performed. 2. The time it takes to transfer information that has been operated on from the arithmetic unit to the location in storage where the information is to be stored.

time, actual—*Same as* time, real.

time, add—The time necessary to perform the actual addition of two quantities, but not including the time necessary to either obtain the quantities from storage or to store the sum or result, i.e., usually the time to add two words of fixed word length.

time, add-subtract—The time required to perform an addition or subtraction, exclusive of the time required to obtain the quantities from storage and put the sum or difference back into storage.

time, available—1. The number of hours a computer is available for use. 2. The time during which a computer has the power turned on, is not under maintenance, and is known or believed to be operating correctly. (Synonymous with available machine time.)

time, available-machine—The time during which a computer has the power turned on, is not under maintenance, and is known or believed to be operating correctly.

time, average operation—*See* operation time, average.

time, carry—1. The time required for transferring a carry digit to the next higher column and adding it there. 2. The time required for transferring all the carry digits to their respective next higher column and adding them.

time, clock (real time)—This built-in clock is used for a wide variety of program-timing purposes. It can be used to log the receipt times of a periodic real-time input data. Each input message and its receipt time may be recorded together. This clock is also used in connection with the preparation of statistical and analytical reports dealing with the frequency of certain transactions.

time, code-checking—The time spent checking out a problem on the machine making sure that the problem is set up correctly, and that the code is correct.

time comparator, word—That circuitry which compares the word time counter with the specified word time at the moment of a coincident pulse. This is done in order to verify that the correct word is being read.

time conversion—The length of time required to read out all the digits in a given coded word.

time, current—*See* time, real.

time, cycle—The interval between the call for, and the delivery of, information from a storage unit or device.

time, data—The unit of measurement relating to the time necessary to fulfill a single instruction.

time, dead—Any definite delay deliberately placed between two related actions in order to avoid overlap that might cause an entirely different event such as a control decision, switching event, or similar action to take place.

time, debateble—When there is no proof as to what difficulty has caused a delay, such time is labeled debatable time, and a search for evidence ensues to determine if a program mistake, operating mistake, or perhaps a transient fault has occurred.

time, decay—The time in which a voltage or current pulse will decrease from nine-tenths to one-tenth of its maximum value.

time, deceleration—The time that elapses between completion of reading or writing of a tape record and the time when the tape stops moving. (Synonymous with stop time.)

time, delay—The amount of elapsed time between the end of one event and the beginning of the next sequential event.

time, delay register—*See* register, time delay.

time, departure—The time at which control is returned to the supervisory program when a segment of an application program is completed.

time-derived channel—Any channel obtained by the time-division multiplexing of a channel.

time division—A communication process in which several messages time-share a single transmission channel.

time-division multiplex—A sequential switching system that connects the terminal equipment to a common channel. Outside the times during which these connections are established, the section of the common channel between the multiplex distributors can be utilized to establish other terminal connections.

time, down—The period during which a computer is malfunctioning or not operating correctly due to mechanical or electronic failure, as opposed to available, idle time,

or stand-by time, during which the computer is functional.

time, effective—That specific time in which equipment is in actual use, such as production time, incidental time, development time (program), etc.

time, engineering—The total machine down time necessary for routine testing, for machine servicing, due to breakdowns, or for preventive servicing measures, e.g., block-tube changes. This includes all test time, following a breakdown and the subsequent repair or preventive servicing. (Synonymous with servicing time.)

time, entry—The time when control is transferred from the supervisory to the application program.

time, execution—The portion of an instructive cycle during which the actual work is performed or operation executed, i.e., the time required to decode and perform an instruction. (Synonymous with instruction time.)

time, fault—*Same as* time, down.

time frame—The limits of time needed for a particular situation or event.

time, from movement—An elapsed period of time during which a printing cycle produces the printing and movement of hard copy.

time, idle—1. The period between the end of one programmed computer run and the commencement of a subsequent programmed run. 2. The time normally used to assemble cards, paper, tape reels, and control panels required for the next computer operation. 3. The time between operations when no work is scheduled.

time, incidentals—Time used for training, demonstrations, or other useful purposes, but not production or program time.

time, ineffective—Time in which the equipment is not working due to operating delays or idle time.

time, installation—Time spent in testing, installing, error-checking, diagnosing of basic electronic but nonprogramming checks, such as dry runs, etc. This time does not include reliability tests which are defined as supplementary maintenance time.

time, instruction—The portion of an instruction cycle during which the control unit is analyzing the instruction and setting up to perform the indicated operation.

time, latency—The delay while waiting for the information called for from the memory to be delivered to the arithmetical unit. More specifically, in a serial-storage system, the access time minus the word time.

time, machine spoiled—The wasted computer time due to a computer malfunction during production runs, i.e., part of downtime.

time, maintenance routine—*See* time scheduled maintenance.

time, maintenance standby—Time in which the maintenance staff is on duty but during which they are not engaged in scheduled maintenance, installation, repair, or supplementary maintenance, i.e., they may perform other tasks.

time, multiplication—The time required to perform a multiplication. For a binary number it will be equal to the total of all the additions and all the shift time involved in the multiplication.

time, no charge—That period of time for which there is no rental charge or cost for the equipment, generally as a result of a machine malfunction and the manufacturer's warranty.

time, no-charge machine fault—The unproductive time due to computer fault such as the following: nonduplication, transcribing error, input/output malfunction and machine malfunction resulting in an incomplete run.

time, noncharge nonmachine fault—The unproductive time due to no fault of the computer such as the following: good duplication, error in preparation of input data, error in arranging the program deck, error in operating instructions or misinterpretation of instructions, and unscheduled good testing time, and a run during a normal production period when a machine malfunction is suspected but is demonstrated not to exist.

time, nonscheduled maintenance—The elapsed time during scheduled working hours between the determination of a machine failure and placement of the equipment back into operation.

time, object—The time at which an object program is executed, as opposed to the time at which a source program is translated into machine language to create an object program.

time-of-day clock—Records time in hours, minutes, seconds, over 24-hour range—from 0.1 second to 23:59:9; sends time to central processor upon command.

time, off—Time when the machine is off, i.e., not in use or intended to be, i.e., work is not being performed by it or on it.

time, operational—The elapsed time required by the equipment in order to execute a specific operation.

time, operation-use—1. In federal government ADP contracts the time during which the equipment is in operation, exclusive of idle time, standby time, maintenance time, or rerun time due to a machine failure. Components not programmed for use in a specific computer run are not considered to be in use even though connected into the computer system. 2. The time during which equipment is in actual operation and is not synonymous with power-on time.

time-out, keyboard—See keyboard, time-out.

time, out of service—Such time periods may be: fault time, awaiting repair time, repair delay time, repair time, machine spoiled work-time, but not generally debatable time, external delays or unused time.

time-out printing—Same as keyboard time-out.

time, physical system—The ratio of computer time (time interval between two events in a simulation) to the problem time, i.e., the physical system time. When greater than one, it is said to be an extended time scale, or slow-time scale; when less than one, it is said to be on a fast time scale, and when it is constant during a run, it is said to be on a variable time scale. If the ratio is equal to one, it is on real-time.

time, preventive maintenance—This is usually scheduled maintenance time or supplementary maintenance time.

time, problem—Often called physical system time, it is the time interval between corresponding events in the physical system being simulated.

time, process—See process time.

time, production—See production time.

time, productive—That time which is spent in processing work without the occurrence of faults or errors.

time, program development—See program development time.

time, program-testing—The machine time expended for program testing, debugging, and volume and compatibility testing.

time, proving—See proving time.

time, pulse decay—See pulse decay time.

time-pulse distribution—A device or circuit for allocating timing pulses or clock pulses to one or more conducting paths or control lines in specified sequence.

time, pulse rise—See pulse rise time.

time quantum method, time sharing—See time sharing, time quantum method.

timer—A timer provides the system with the ability to read elapsed time in split-second increments and to inform the system when a specified period of time has passed.

time ratio, variable—See time scale, extended.

timer clock—This clock device cycles a value contained in a full word of the main storage location. It can be used for job accounting by measuring the duration of time for each job, for an interrupt to prevent a runaway job from gaining control of the system, for time-of-day recording, and for polling a communication network on a regular basis—for example, every minute, every half hour, etc. The full cycle of a typical timer is 15.5 hours.

time, read—1. The time it takes a computer to locate data or an instruction word in its storage section and transfer it to its arithmetic unit where the required computations are performed. 2. The time it takes to transfer information which has been operated on from the arithmetic unit to the location in storage where the information is to be stored.

time, real—Relating to the performance of computing during the specific time in which the related process, event, problem, or communication is taking place, i.e., the computing must be fast enough, during the process of the happening of the event for the results of this computing to influence the related process or result.

time, record-check—*See* record-check time.

time, reference—An instant near the beginning of a switching routine, chosen as an origin for time measurements. It is the instant when the drive pulse reaches a specific fraction of its instantaneous value.

time, reimbursed—The machine time that is loaned or rented to another office agency or organization either on a reimbursable or reciprocal basis.

time, repair—*See* repair time.

time, repair delay—*See* repair delay time.

time, representative-computing—A method of evaluating the speed performance of a computer. One method is to use one-tenth of the time required to perform nine complete additions and one complete multiplication. A complete addition or a complete multiplication time includes the time required to procure two operands from high-speed storage, perform the operation, store the result, and the time required to select and execute the required number of instructions to do this.

time, response—The amount of time which elapses between generation of an inquiry at a terminal and the receipt of a response at the terminal. Response time would be: transmission time to the computer, processing time at the computer, access time to obtain any file records needed to answer the inquiry, and transmission time back to the terminal.

time, rewind—The measurement of elapsed time required to transfer tape to the supply reel.

time, rewind (sorting)—Elapsed time consumed by a sort/merge program for restoring intermediate and final tape files to original position.

timer, interval—With the interval timer, the control program provides the facility to keep track of the time of day, and to interrupt periodically as required. More than one interval can be controlled at once. For example, a five-second interval between successive polling of a teleprocessing line can be specified, and at the same time a two-minute limit on the duration of a new program undergoing test can be in effect.

time, rise—*See* pulse, rise time.

timer, master—*Same as* master clock.

timer, sequence—A succession of time-delay circuits arranged so that completion of the delay in one circuit initiates a delay in the following circuit.

timer, watchdog—A timer set by the program to prevent the system from looping endlessly or becoming idle because of program errors or equipment faults.

time scale—A time scale relates to a correspondence between the time required for a process or event set to occur or be completed and the solution time required to, for example, control or analyze the process. In computing, when the machine solution time is greater than the actual physical time of processing, the time scale is considered to be greater than one, and the computation is said to be on extended-time scale or slow-time scale. Time scale is less than one if the opposite occurs, or at unity if computations proceed in the same time period with the actual process, which is then real-time.

time scale, extended—*See* time scale.

time-scale factor—*See* time scale.

time scale, variable—*See* time scale.

time, scheduled engineering—That particular time in which a system is scheduled to be out of service due to servicing schedules for engineering improvements and maintenance, i.e., it can be scheduled on a regular basis relative to the running schedules and work loads and is considered out-of service time but not down time, because the machine is not necessarily malfunctioning.

time, scheduled maintenance—That machine time which is specifically devoted to repairs, and usually on some regular pattern or schedule, during which time preventive maintenance activities are also performed.

time, scramble—Specific computer time set aside for use by programmers who have programs ready to run and which are short, urgent, and one-shot types, i.e., particular system rules or conventions schedule scramble time, as at some universities, Saturday night after midnight.

time, search—The time required to locate a particular field of data in storage. Searching requires a comparison of each field with a predetermined standard until an identity is obtained. This is contrasted with access time that is based upon locating data by means of the address of its storage location.

time, seek—The time required to make the auxiliary storage unit ready to access a specified location by selection or positioning. The range is from the minimum time for the best possible case to the maximum time for the worst possible case.

time sequencing—Switching signals generated by a program purely as a function of accurately measured elapsed time.

time series—The discrete or continuous sequence of quantitative data assigned to specific moments in time, usually studied with respect to their distribution in time.

time, serviceable—1. The time during which equipment is either producing work or is available for productive work. (Contrasted with down time.) 2. That time which is available for use of any type and which is known to be time when the system is functioning properly, which thus includes production, program development, incidentals, delay idle, or even unused time.

time, servicing—*Same as* engineering time.

time, set-up—The portion of the elapsed time

between machine operations that is devoted to such tasks as changing reels of tape, and moving cards, tapes, and supplies to and from the equipment.

time share—The use of a device for two or more purposes during the same overall time interval, accomplished by interspersing the computer component actions in time.

time-shared input/output—*See* input/output section, buffered.

time-shared system—A specific system in which available central-computer time is shared among several jobs as directed by a scheduling plan or formula.

time sharing—1. The apportionment of intervals of time availability of various items of equipment to complete the performance of several tasks by interlacing. (Contrasted with multiprogramming.) 2. The use of a device for two or more purposes during the same overall time interval, accomplished by interspersing the computer component actions in time. 3. A multiple communications control unit (MCCU) attached to the computer allows many consoles to "time-share" the central processing unit simultaneously during transmission and receiving periods. Time sharing is a computing technique in which numerous terminal devices can utilize a central computer concurrently for input, processing and output functions.

time sharing accounting—The executive must provide for the recognition and log-in of users. It must keep detailed records as required by the administrators of the system on the amount of central processor time, the amount of storage, and the usage of peripherals to be charged to each other. Other statistics as required may be maintained on idle time, error conditions, and the like.

time sharing allocation of hardware resources—User and system programs and data reside on auxiliary random access storage devices with possible back up copies on a slower serial access medium such as magnetic tape. The system executive decides where information is to be stored and maintains necessary directories to permit retrieval. Programs and data must be brought into core memory for execution or modification. The executive assigns and transfers information between auxiliary and core memory as needed. The executive must also manage the assignment of serial access devices and peripheral devices to prevent conflict between concurrent user programs seeking use of peripheral devices. For example, a line printer cannot be used concurrently by several users.

time sharing allocator (dynamic)—*See* allocator, dynamic.

time sharing, analytic aid to research—Besides the calculation capabilities aiding research workers, interactive computer systems allow the research scientist to experiment and arrive at a solution to a problem by trial-and-error techniques. The insight provided by direct interaction in the carrying out of solution steps furnishes clues to the next steps to try. These techniques have been applied to research in bio-medicine, linguistics, physics, and mathematics.

time sharing and automatic program interruption—In order to provide maximum time sharing and efficiency in operation, most of the peripheral components of the computer systems have an automatic interrupt feature. The magnetic character sorter-readers, high-speed line printers, card readers, card punches, inquiry units, and magnetic-card random-access units all possess this interrupt feature. Also, each of these units is capable of independent operation after being activated by the processor. Under permissive control these units may interrupt, be reactivated, and continue their operation independently while the processor returns to the primary program. Thus, the computer can coordinate the operation of a number of peripheral units, each performing input, output, or file operations at its own independent rate of speed.

time sharing, automated question answering—It is desirable in a remote computer system to relieve the user of the need for digging through a set of manuals, by providing him with a facility for answering his questions from a bank of prestored questions. A good example of a question answering facility is found in the HELP subsystem of the SDS-940 XEROX time sharing system.

time sharing, base registers—IBM's System 360 has multiple indexed addressing. Many 360 instructions may have two index registers specified. One of these registers acts as a base register containing the base address of a program or data segment. The other register is used for normal indexing. By convention, the first instruction executed in a program segment loads one of the general registers with its location plus 1. This automatically provides the base address for the segment regardless of its location. All reference by instructions within the segment to other addresses within the segment are via the base register and thus the program may operate at any position in core memory. External data references are dealt with in a similar manner using another register for the base address of the data segment.

time sharing, centralized input/output coordination—If the executive is to maintain control of the system, input/output operations must be forbidden to all users and to all system components except the executive. The executive must provide substitutes for these forbidden operations by means of a centralized input/output package. This package accepts requests for input or output, queues these requests, and schedules the input/output capabilities of the hardware in filling the requests.

time sharing, command mode—A user is in

"command" mode when there is no current task to be performed. Any console actions by a user in the command mode are interpreted by the executive as task requests (system commands). Receipt of a valid task request changes a user status to "ready" or to "waiting to be loaded." If an excessive time interval elapses without a task request, the system logs-out the user, returning him to an inactive status.

time sharing, console to console consulting—Even though a remote system may be well documented, may have excellent diagnostic messages, and even may have a question-answering program, there will still be times when a user cannot resolve a problem without consulting with an expert on the system. It is helpful at such times if the system permits message exchange between consoles and provides a system control officer to answer questions and provide advice to users with special problems. Console to console discussions are also desirable.

time sharing, continuous system diagnosis—Another useful technique which can be included in a time-sharing system is to carry out continuous system diagnosis. A collection of diagnostic tasks are permanently placed in the task queue with only a low priority assigned to them. Whenever the queue of user "ready" tasks is empty, the system selects and runs one of these test programs, sending the results to a special monitor console.

time sharing, conversational compilers—General purpose systems usually provide languages and procedures by means of which a user may construct a program, modify it, test it, and, in some cases, add it to the file of system subcomponents. Most of the program preparation languages developed for time-sharing systems are dialects of existing languages. Processors for the languages vary from those borrowed with only slight modification from batch mode processing to conversational mode compilers designed especially for on-line use.

time sharing, conversational guidance—Most time shared systems operate part of the time in a conversational or dialog mode. Here the user takes some action and the system responds. Then the system requests input or takes other action and the user responds. In this alternating stimulus-response mode, the system can and should provide guidance to the user on the form and content of the user response.

time sharing, data base management and reporting—Most of the business data processing falls into this category. The range is from rather routine processing provided for small businesses who cannot afford their own computer to large dedicated systems operating in real-time, such as stock exchange systems.

time sharing, decision rules—*See* time sharing, page turning.

time sharing, demand processing—Comple-

menting the batch-processing capabilities of the executive system are its time-sharing capabilities, i.e., the simultaneous accommodations by the executive systems, of requests and demands from users at numerous remote inquiry terminals, operating in a demand (or conversational) mode. All facilities available to the batch-processing user are also available in the demand mode; the primary difference is that the executive system utilizes its knowledge of the existence of such demand devices to permit the user additional flexibility in the statement of and control of individual runs. The demand user may communicate directly with the executive, a worker program, or he may communicate with a conversational processor.

time sharing, education—Because of the reinforcement effect on a learner of the immediate response of an interactive system, time-shared systems are receiving considerable attention in teaching (learning would be more precise). Experiments are being conducted with all levels of students from first-graders to advanced graduate students.

time sharing, error diagnostics—It is highly desirable in a remote system that a user's actions be closely monitored by the system, with errors in procedure or entry called to the user's attention as soon after commission as possible. The error message sent to an offending user should be provided whenever possible.

time-sharing executive—A typical executive processes all users' requests (executive commands) and allows users to call for, operate, and modify object programs using all available system services. It provides complete bookkeeping facilities for file storage in, and retrieval from, secondary memory. It includes facilities for collecting accounting data.

time sharing, external data reference—*Same as* time sharing, base registers.

time sharing, fail soft—A concept that has been proposed for remote computer systems but that thus far has not been widely implemented is the principle of "graceful degradation" or "fail-soft." This concept implies a system which can reorganize itself to isolate and cut off the offending equipment while continuing to operate. The capacity and efficiency of the system decreases, but service to users continues in the best manner with the remaining equipment.

time sharing, fault processing—The executive program of a time-shared system must be in control or able to regain control at all times. User actions or executing user programs may generate unpredictable interrupt and fault conditions. The executive must process all such conditions if it is to maintain control of the system. Clock interrupts must be set up before control is given temporarily to a user program. Interrupts on completion of input/output transmission affect the ready status of deferred tasks. Interrupts from user consoles indicate user actions and request for attention.

time-sharing, FORTRAN—The General Electric Missiles and Space Division at Valley Forge, Pennsylvania has implemented a time-sharing version of FORTRAN, which is available through the commercial GE Time-Sharing service. This is an extension of FORTRAN II with certain features of FORTRAN IV. Other modifications to allow operation in a time-sharing environment have also been made.

time sharing, graceful degradation—*See* time sharing, fail soft.

time sharing, HELP program—HELP is a question-answering program that accepts queries in natural language and responds with appropriate answers from one of several data bases associated with the system components of the XDS Time-Sharing System. When a user does not know how to employ a particular service or if he runs into difficulties while using a service program, he merely types the word HELP to invoke the question-answering program. HELP places very few constraints on the user. (1) No rigid structure is imposed. (2) Unrestricted grammer and phrasing are accepted. (3) Character and the line delete (similar to strike-overs) facilitate input. (4) Reasonable misspelling is understood.

time sharing, inactive mode—A user in the inactive mode is not concurrently logged-in. The only console action allowed for an inactive user is log-in. Log-in, when successfully completed, changes the user mode to "command." A user returns to the inactive mode when he is logged-out either by himself or by the system.

time sharing incremental compiler—A new concept in conversational compilers is the incremental compile technique developed by XEROX Data Systems and Tymshare. Each statement input is considered to be a separate entity. It is checked for syntax correctness and a code module generated. At any time, a user can string these modules together in any way he desires, reordering as needed. He may cause some collection of these to be compiled, executed, deleted, and so forth. With this capability, a user can build and test a program incrementally and then restructure it as required.

time sharing, interrupt capability—A time-shared computer should have a sophisticated interrupt capability with interrupts occurring on internal faults: input/output transmission errors or completion, invalid instructions or operand addresses, and the like. Handling of communications with remote terminals can be handled on a polling basis. However, interrupts from a terminal when a message has been transmitted eliminates the necessity for the computer to continuously cycle through all communication lines seeking messages.

time sharing, interrupt processing—Interrupt processing varies in detail from computer to computer. The following functions are usually performed. (1) Normal program sequencing is stopped usually at some convenient and appropriate point in the instruction cycle. (2) The interrupt conditions are recorded in dedicated memory cells (location may depend on interrupt class). Recorded conditions include: program counter setting at time of interrupt, class of interrupt, type within class, channel or device number, and the like. (3) The next instruction to be executed is taken from a dedicated memory cell (the location may depend on interrupt class).

time sharing, interrupt schemes—One of the features of computers of the third or late second generations is a sophisticated interrupt scheme. An interruption is the cessation of normal sequencing and branching under program control when an internal fault (such as, arithmetic overflow) or an event external to the running program occurs. Interrupts may be categorized in five classes: (1) input/output or channel, (2) external, (3) machine malfunction, (4) program fault, (5) supervisory call (on master/slave mode computers).

time sharing, invalid pages—*Same as* time sharing, page type.

time-sharing keyboard/printer—This unit can be arranged for split operation for each user station. Printer should be independent of keyboard and operated on a full-duplex circuit. Proper provision must be made for tying into the computer's communication system, either locally or remotely through private lines or the switched network.

time sharing, languages—There are two types of languages which seem to be suitable for standardization — conversational calculation and text editing. Most of the conversational languages available on present time-shared systems have been modeled after FORTRAN or JOSS. However, added gimmicks, committed capabilities, and differing formats make each version incompatable with any other. A standard language, probably exactly like JOSS, would seem to be desirable.

time sharing, log-out—A user with a task in the ready or running modes has only limited console actions which he may take. These are certain reserved functions, such as "cancel the last task," "interrupt the last task," and "log-out."

time sharing, master/slave modes—Even with memory protection, it is still possible for a user program to wrest control from the system or to otherwise disrupt system operations unless the user program is forbidden the use of certain privileged operations. These operations include input/output, setting the clock, setting the memory protection bounds, and similar instructions affecting control of the computer. The usual solution is to have two modes of operation for the computer — master and slave. Privileged instructions can be executed only in the master mode. With such a hardware feature, the executive program of the system is the only program allowed to operate in master mode. User programs are forced to operate in slave mode and thus must remain under control.

time sharing, memory protection—During the execution of a user prepared program, the resident portion of the system, the executive plus utility subroutines, is also present in core memory. In addition, the programs and data of other users may also be coexistent in memory. Hardware features are required which will trap any instruction of an executing program which has an effective address, out of the bounds of the executing program and its data. Otherwise, inadvertent or deliberate obliteration of the executive can occur, which causes the system to become uncontrollable. Time-sharing systems have been implemented on computers without memory protection features. However, other means were used to protect the system from users and users from each other.

time sharing, message switching communications—Remote computer use is an important factor in the modernization of communications facilities. Many dedicated systems are being established within large firms for handling messages. Reservation systems for airlines and hotels are primarily message handling systems.

time-sharing monitor—Generally a time-sharing monitor provides all I/O service to user programs; selective communications service for interactive message processing (selective end-of-message processing control characteristics) ; error processing and recovery; multiprocessing "forks"; multilevel, nested intervention (break) capability; memory allocation and control; interstation communication; and scheduling of user program operations. The monitor permits the user to create control programs and dependent programs. A dependent program may also be a control program for a lower level dependent program. This hierarchy of dependency may be extended to various depths. The highest level control program is usually the time-sharing executive.

time-sharing monitor system—The monitor system is a collection of programs remaining permanently in memory to provide overall coordination and control of the total operating system. It performs several functions. First, it permits several users' programs to be loaded into core memory simultaneously. The monitor makes use of the time-sharing hardware to prevent one user's program from interferring with other users' programs. Each program is run for a certain length of time; then the monitor switches control to another program in a rotating sequence. Switching is frequent enough so that

all programs appear to run simultaneously. Another function of the time-sharing monitor is to process input/output commands. The input/output service routines preprocess data so that all devices appear identical to the user's program, thus simplifying coding. The monitor makes use of the program interrupt system to overlap input/output operations with computation. If a user's program must wait for completion of an input or output operation, the monitor automatically switches to another user's program. A program may be terminated temporarily by user intervention, or it may suspend its own operation. Temporary termination does not remove the program from memory. A program may be dumped on backing storage and discontinued under user control.

time sharing, multiple index addressing—The problem of relocating a program, that is the modification of instruction addresses to allow the program to operate from the positions in core memory to which it has been assigned, is a critical one in time sharing. Core memory is shared among many users and no user can preplan the execution location of his programs. Moreover, user programs must be swapped in and out of core constantly. It is desirable that programs be easily movable from one core area to another with minimum address modification.

time sharing, multiple I/O channels—A time-sharing computer must be able to service numerous communication lines connecting it to the user terminals. This requires multiple input/output channels operating asynchronously with the data processing. An alternate and better solution is to have a separate computer or processor serving as an input/output coordinator or concentrator. This processor services the individual terminals and accumulates character by character until an entire message is transmitted. Then the main processor is interrupted and the entire message transmitted. The input/output coordinating computer is especially designed for servicing communications networks and has multiple I/O channels attached to it.

time sharing, multiplexor channel — The channel permits simultaneous operation of attached low-speed devices through a time-sharing (byte-interleaved mode) principle. Each device sends an identifier to the channel each time it requests service. The multiplexor channel, using this identifier, updates the correct control counts, etc., and stores the data in the correct location. The multiplexor channel has the effect of subdividing the data path into many subchannels. To the programmer, each subchannel is a separate channel, and can be programmed as such. A different device may be started on each subchannel and controlled by its own list of channel commands. Card readers, punches, printers, terminals, etc., are examples of devices that can operate in the multiplexing mode. The polling of terminals is initiated by the processor, but continues independently of the processor under control of the multiplexor channel (some systems) .

time sharing, not in core, type code—*See* time sharing, page turning.

time-sharing operating system—*See* operating system, time-sharing.

time sharing, page turning—An extension of page type permits a user to have a very large virtual memory even though the core space available to him may be restricted. An additional type code "not in core" must be recognized. User pages which cannot be loaded into core due to space limitations are marked with this type code. Reference to a page "not in core" causes interrupts and allows the executive to regain control. The executive then loads the needed page from auxiliary storage into core. The page table is adjusted and the instruction executed again. This time the proper address is formed. The technique is referred to as "page turning." The allocation routine of the executive must have decision rules supplied, to allow it to make room for the page to be loaded by dumping a page from core onto the disk.

time sharing, page type—Memory protection is accomplished by adding a specific element to the page type. The value of the page type can be used to signal "read-only," "read/write," or "invalid." The system executive can set the value for each physical page of core memory and allow or deny access to it by a user program. Reference to "invalid" pages or attempts to write a "read-only" page cause fault interrupts.

time sharing, paging—A technique used in third generation computers to solve storage management problems is "paging." A page is a fixed size segment of storage, usually 512 or 1024 addressable units. When the central processor is in paging mode, it treats each address as a two-part item. One portion (the least significant 9 or 10 bits) is an absolute address relative to a page boundary. This portion is usually called the displacement. The other portion (the remaining bits of the address) is considered to be a page number or identifier. A table of identifiers vs. current page locations is searched and the location corresponding to the matched page identifier is added to the displacement to form an absolute address. The problem of relocatability is reduced since all addresses are stated relative to page boundaries. Pages of data and programs may be loaded or moved into physical pages and relocation accomplished simply by adjusting the page table.

time sharing, periodic dumping—Provisions should be included in a time-shared system for periodic dumping of system and user files onto a back-up medium, such as a magnetic tape. This function, which can be carried out during off-peak hours, guards against catastrophic system failures which destroy current working files.

time sharing, preparation languages—General purpose systems usually provide languages and procedures by means of which a user may construct a program, modify it, test it, and, in some cases, add it to the file of system subcomponents. Most of the program preparation languages developed for time-sharing systems are dialects of existing languages. Processors for the languages vary from those borrowed with only slight modification from batch mode processing to conversational mode compilers designed especially for on-line use.

time sharing, processing interrupt—Interrupt processing varies in detail from computer to computer. The following functions are usually performed: (1) normal program sequencing is stopped, usually at some convenient and appropriate point in the instruction cycle; (2) the interrupt conditions are recorded in dedicated memory cells (location may depend on interrupt class) ; recorded conditions include program counter setting at time of interrupt, class of interrupt, type within class, channel or device number, and the like; (3) the next instruction to be executed is taken from a dedicated memory cell (the location may depend on interrupt class).

time sharing programs and data, relocatability—*Same as* time sharing, relocatability of programs and data.

time sharing, QUIKTRAN—*See* QUIKTRAN, time sharing.

time sharing, random access auxiliary storage—The programs and data that are in waiting or inactive status are usually kept in a random-access auxiliary storage, such as drum or disk. The experience with most systems is that the transfer rate between primary and auxiliary storage is the largest factor in determining response times and that the quantity of drum or disk storage is the most limiting factor on the number of users permitted on a system.

time sharing, ready mode—A user task in ready status can be executed or resumed. Usually a separate queue of ready tasks is maintained by the executive. Whenever a processor is available, the executive activates the task at the head of the ready queue changing its status to "running."

time sharing, real time—A process is providing data on a critical real-time basis and requires that immediate processing and response be made if the process is to continue.

time sharing, real-time clock—A real-time clock is capable of being set to interrupt a running program at the end of a specified time. The minimum clock interval must be less than the basic quantum of time during which a user program is to be allowed to run. This clock, under the control of the executive, provides the best, and in some cases, the only means for the executive to regain control of the computer after a user program has exhausted its time allotment.

time sharing, relative addressing—Relative addressing is a feature of great significance in multiprogramming, time sharing, and real-time operations, for it allows storage assignments to be changed dynamically to provide contiguous storage for operation of another program, and permits programs to dynamically request additional main storage according to processing needs. An additional advantage is that systems programs stored on mass storage may be brought in for operation in any available area without complicated relocation algorithms. Relative addressing is provided for through basing registers contained within the processor. A separate register controls the basing of the program instruction and data bank, and a third register controls the selections of the appropriate basing register.

time sharing, relocatability of programs and data—It is desirable that program and data segments be allocatable dynamically in a time-shared system. This avoids the constraint of dedicating a fixed portion of core memory to a user program and allows flexibility in intermixing programs in a multiuser environment. However, when executed, a program must have the operand addresses of its instructions modified to reflect the current assigned locations of the program and the data segments referenced by it. Hardware features which minimize the effort required to relocate a program or data segments by providing automatic address adjustment increase the efficiency of a time-shared system.

time sharing, running mode—A user task is in the running mode when it is in control of a processor and is executing. A task leaves the running mode either voluntarily or involuntarily in accordance with the scheduling rules of the executive. Reasons for leaving the running mode may include: (1) request for input/output, (2) request for console response, (3) suspension on expiration of time quantum, (4) termination.

time sharing, scheduling resourses—*See* time sharing, scheduling user tasks.

time sharing, scheduling rules—Scheduling rules specify for a time-shared system: (1) the types of status or mode queue to be maintained, (2) the actions which cause a task (or user) to change modes and/or queues, (3) the time intervals which may elapse before one of the actions is taken, (4) the manner in which a task is placed on or taken from a queue.

time sharing, scheduling user tasks—In a time-shared system, many users contend simultaneously for use of a central processor's resources or processors. The executive must establish and maintain a list of tasks to be performed for each user and then schedule the available processors to the various tasks in such a manner that the response rate to each user is as fast as possible. Scheduling must be performed not only for the central arithmetic and data processing units, but also for disk and drum storage, and for peripheral and serial device operations.

time sharing, scientific and engineering calculation—Most time-shared sytems provide conversational calculation facilities allowing research scientists, engineers, and technicians to use the computer as a large slide-rule.

time sharing, security of user files—Each user is assigned a password composed of a string of randomly chosen characters. This password is known only to the user and to the system. At log-in the user must give his identification (name and/or account number) together with his password. The system verifies that the two match. The system may keep a table giving the authority level of the user and allow him access only to files appropriate to his level. Or a double lock may be provided by allowing the user who creates and establishes a file to specify two passwords for the file. One password authorizes reading of the file, the other authorizes modification of the entries of the file. A user specifying use of a file must know one or both of these passwords and input these to the system before being granted access to the protected data.

time sharing, software functions—Software functions required in a time-shared system include: (1) allocation of hardware resources, (2) scheduling of user tasks, (3) interrupt and fault processing, (4) terminal input/output coordination, (5) centralized input/output supervision, (6) accounting, (7) interpretation and execution of system commands, (8) management of subcomponents of system, (9) management of user files, (10) miscellaneous utility functions. These functions are referred to as executive, supervisory, or monitor functions. In some time-shared systems, certain of these functions may be omitted or may be present only in a very limited way.

time sharing, software requirements—Software in a time-shared system may be divided into three categories: 1. The system proper. This is a collection of programs which controls the time-shared system, provides general services to the user, and fulfills user requests. The programs include the executive package, which is not directly callable by a user, and a utility package which is directly usable. 2. The system subcomponents. These are application packages not necessarily vital to the system's operations. These programs provide specific services to the user. An example of a system subcomponent is a FORTRAN compiler. 3. The user program. These are programs prepared by the user for his private purposes or in some cases for availability to some or all other users.

time sharing, storage compacting—Certain hardware features make feasible the dynamic relocation of programs residing in central storage—a necessity in order to provide an effective multiprogramming environment. At program termination, the assigned storage is returned to the pool of available central storage. Storage compacting is initiated if, and only if, a requirement exists for contiguous storage, and compacting can meet this requirement. Compacting is never performed unnecessarily, as the storage-contents control continuously routine attempts to fit programs into gaps in the in-use store.

time sharing, storage management—Two of the problems in the time-shared management of storage — the protection of user files and the reduction of constraints on the size of user programs due to limited core space — are common to all time-shared systems and have received considerable attention in software development.

time sharing, system commands—The design of most time-shared systems centers around an executive monitor. This executive accepts, interprets, and schedules tasks requests from the user. A collection of commands are usually provided by which the user instructs the system what task he desires to have performed. The specific commands available and the form in which they are phrased vary widely from system to system, but usually include the following categories: (1) commands governing entry into and exit from the system, (2) commands requesting the establishment of certain system modes, (3) commands controlling allocation of memory, (4) commands modifying scheduling rules or establishing priorities, etc.

time sharing, system commands interpretation—A user communicates with the time-sharing executive via system commands. These commands request the executive to perform one of the system functions, to call a system subcomponent, or to execute a user program. The executive accepts the system command, interprets it, and sets up a task on the user's list to be executed in accordance with the scheduling rules.

time sharing, system reliability—Although reliability of the hardware and software of a computer installation is always an important issue, in a time-shared system it is critical. Malfunction of a computer component in a batch-mode system disrupts only a few users. In a time-shared system, many users may be disturbed. Provisions must be included in a time-shared system to minimize the inconvenience and possible loss of information caused by system failure.

time sharing, system software—*See* time sharing, software requirements.

time sharing, system subcomponents—Time-shared system subcomponents are different form user files only in their availability. System subcomponents may be used by all users, but may not be modified by anybody

except those specially designated as system users. The executive merely maintains records on the location and attributes of the files of data and programs, stores and retrieves them as requested, and if the file is executable binary code, it loads, relocates as required, and executes the file as requested.

time sharing, terminal input/output coordination—If input from a user console is one character at a time, the console coordination program must accumulate these in a message buffer until a "break" or "end-of-message" character is received. Then the executive is interrupted so that it may process the message.

time sharing, text editing and modification—Many time-shared systems provide a text handling component. This facility is used by authors composing reports, by production groups preparing manuals, by secretaries handling correspondence, and in one large system in the preparation of land title reports. Experiments are being conducted coupling this capability with direct typesetting and computer-controlled document reproduction.

time sharing, time-quantum method—Scheduling rules are highly dependent upon the objectives, constraints, and usage of the system. Usually, a time quantum or interval is allotted to a running task. If the task does not terminate or otherwise relinquish control prior to the expiration of this time quantum, the executive regains control, suspends the task, and places it on the ready queue, usually at the bottom. If the only functions which can be requested by a user are system functions (that is, no user prepared programs are permitted), the time quantum method may not be necessary, since the system functions can be constructed to relinquish control at or before specified time intervals.

time sharing, time slices—Time quanta of a few hundred milliseconds are usually chosen. It has been shown in the second time-shared system that the smaller the time quantum the better average response time, if all user tasks are highly interactive. However, very small time slices badly penalize programs requiring a large amount of computation between console interactions. To work out of this dilemma, some systems have two ready queues; one with a small time interval for highly interactive programs, another with a large time interval for lone computation problems. This compromise technique reduces the amount of swapping and overhead on the longer running programs caused by frequent interruptions, but provides rapid response for highly interactive programs.

time sharing, type code ("not in core")—*See* time sharing, not in core, type code.

time sharing, user—The experience of many of the operational time-shared systems has been that special consideration must be given to the current level of experience of the user with the system in proving conversation and guidance to him. The first time a user makes a mistake and the system responds with a lengthy explanation of the error and suggestions on how to correct it, the user is impressed. Several occurrences of the same long-winded message start to annoy him. When it occurs the tenth or twentieth time, he is insulted and frustrated and feels that the computer is insensitive to the fact that by now he is aware of all the details of the error message.

time sharing, user file—Time-shared system subcomponents are different from user files only in their availability. System subcomponents may be used by all users but may not be modified by any except those specifically designated as system users. The executive merely maintains records on the location and attributes of the files of data and programs, stores and retrieves these as requested, and if the file is executable binary code, it loads, relocates as required, and executes the file as requested.

time sharing, user modes—At any given time, a user is in one of the following execution modes: (1) inactive; (2) command; (3) ready; (4) running; (5) waiting - (a) for I/O completion, (b) for console action, (c) for task completion, (d) to be loaded.

time sharing, user-oriented languages—The design of languages to be used at remote terminals is more critical than in batch-mode systems. One of the aims of time sharing is to increase the accessibility of computers to nonprogramming problem solvers. One would therefore expect to have a higher percentage of lay users in a time-shared system. Language forms, syntax, and special words should be tailored to these users lacking in computer expertise. While this seems to have been done in the numeric calculation languages so far developed, it is not always the case in other nonnumeric areas.

time sharing, waiting mode—Tasks in "waiting" mode are voluntarily suspended until some operation is complete. Upon completion of the awaited operation, the waiting task is returned to the ready mode (or in some systems to the running mode).

time slices, time-sharing—See time-sharing time slices.

time slicing—Same as time sharing.

time, standby—1. The elapsed time between inquiries when the equipment is operating on an inquiry application. 2. The time during which two or more computers are tied together and are available to answer inquiries or to process intermittent actions on stored data.

time, standby maintenance—See time, maintenance standby.

time, standby unattached—Time in which the machine is in an unknown condition and is not processing a problem. Includes

time in which machine is known to be defective and work is not being done to restore it to operating condition. Includes breakdowns that render it unavailable due to outside conditions (power outages, etc).

time, start—The time between the interpretation of instructions to read or write on tape and the transfer of information to or from the tape into storage, or from storage into tape, as the case may be.

time, stop—The time that elapses between the completion of a reading or writing of a tape record and the time when the tape stops moving.

time, subtract—A determination of the elapsed time required for one subtraction operation, but excluding the time required to obtain and return the quantities from storage.

time, supplementary maintenance—This time is designed to modify or change equipment in some sort of major way to improve reliability, but usually without additions of equipment. This time is usually considered part of scheduled engineering time and/or scheduled maintenance time.

time, swap—The time required to transfer a program from external memory to high-speed internal memory and vice versa.

time, switching—1. The time interval between the reference time, or time at which the leading edge of switching or driving pulse occurs, and the last instant at which the instantaneous voltage response of a magnetic cell reaches a stated fraction of its peak value. 2. The time interval between the reference time and the first instant at which the instantaneous integrated voltage response reaches a stated fraction of its peak value.

time, system-improvement—All the machine down time needed for the installation and testing of new components, large or small, and machine down time necessary for modification of existing components. Includes all programmed tests following the above actions to prove the machine is operating properly.

time, takedown—The time required to take down a piece of equipment.

time, testing—See testing time.

time-to-digital conversion—The process of converting an interval into a digital number.

time, training—The machine time expended in training employees in the use of the equipment, including such activities as mounting, console operation, converter operation, printing operation and related activities, and time spent in conducting required demonstrations.

time transfer—That specific time interval between the instant the transfer of data to or from a storage commences and the instant it is completed.

time, true—Same as time, real.

time, turn-around—The time required to reverse the direction of a transmission in a communication channel.

time, unattended—This is time during which the equipment is in an unknown condition and during which it is not in use. This also includes most often time during breakdown.

time, unused—That time which is available for machine operations, but which is left unused and most often unattended by any computer system personnel, i.e., since seven twenty-four hour periods per week total 168 hours, total time is the addition of attended time and unused time, i.e., just reset time.

time, up—The time during which equipment is either producing work or is available for productive work. (Contrasted with down time.)

time utilization—The arrangement of a program which allows processing to continue while records necessary for processing are being located in file and read into core and working storage.

time waiting—Same as latency, the time interval between the instant the control unit signals the details, addresses, etc., of a transfer of data to or from the storage unit and the instant the transfer commences.

time, word—1. The amount of time required to move one word past a given point. The term is used especially in reference to words stored serially. 2. The time required to transport one word from one storage device to another. (Related to access time.)

time, write—The amount of time it takes to record information. (Related to access time.)

timing error—The program was not able to keep pace with the tape-transfer rate, or a new motion or select command was issued before the previous command was completely executed.

timing matrix, program—See matrix program timing.

timing pulse—See pulse, timing.

timing-pulse distributor—A circuit driven by pulses from the master clock, it operates in conjunction with the operation decoder to generate timed pulses by other machine circuits to perform the various operations. Also called the waveform generator.

timing signals—Electrical pulses sent throughout the machine at regular intervals to ensure absolute synchronization.

timing track—See track, timing.

TIPTOP (Tape Input/Tape Output)—TIPTOP relieves the programmer of writing detailed coding for common magnetic-tape input and output routines. The programmer writes a few simple macrostatements (instead of many detailed instructions), causing the necessary coding to be generated automatically. (Honeywell)

title index, permutated—Same as index, permutation.

TLU (table look up)—To obtain a function value corresponding to an argument, stated or implied, from a table of function values

stored in the computer. Also, the operation of obtaining a value from a table.

toggle—1. Same as flip-flop. 2. Pertaining to any device having two stable states. 3. Pertaining to flip-flop, see-saw, or bistable action. 4. A circuit or device containing active elements, capable of assuming either one or two stable states at a given time.

toggle switch—1. A manually operated electric switch, with a small projecting knob or arm that may be placed in either of two positions, on or off, and will remain in that position until changed. 2. An electronically operated circuit that holds either of two states until changed.

token—A distinguishable unit in a sequence of characters.

torn-tape switching center—1. A location where operators tear off incoming printed and punched paper tape and transfer it manually to the proper outgoing circuit. 2. A center at which messages are produced in a physical form and then retransmitted to the proper destination.

total, batch—The sum of certain quantities, pertaining to batches of unit records, used to verify accuracy of operations on a particular batch of records; e.g., in a payroll calculation, the batches might be departments, and batch totals would be number of employees in the department, total hours worked in the department, total pay for the department. Batches, however, may be arbitrary, such as orders received from 9 a.m. to 11 a.m. on a certain day.

total, check—See check total.

total, control—See control total.

total, gibberish—Same as hash total.

total, hash—See hash total.

total, intermediate—A total which lies somewhere between a major and a minor total, i.e., a summation developed for some other purpose, or in some hierarchy of sums, or due to a termination in a program.

total, major—The summation or tally of the group of intermediate totals and, therefore, often called the most significant total.

total management system—See system, total management.

total, minor—The sum of the least significant type of grouping are sales by individual sales men; grouped minor totals of such sales are categorized within the state and contrasted with intermediate totals such as sales by regions, or major totals such as total sales for a company.

total, proof—One of a number of check totals which can be correlated in some manner for consistency or reconciliation in a range, set or distinct calculation.

total system—Often called the integrated system, it is a plan to place all important and significant operational components of an organization under the complete or partial control of computers. Real-time system configurations, and their immediacy of data collection, processing, and generation are convenient to this total-system concept.

total transfer—Total transfer is used during report preparation when more than one class of totals (minor, intermediate and major) are accumulated. If the cards are in sequence, it ensures that minor and intermediate totals are correct if the major total is correct. In performing total transfer, only the minor total is accumulated directly from the card field; the intermediate total is an accumulation of minor totals and the major total an accumulation of intermediate totals.

trace—An interpretive diagnostic technique that provides an analysis of each executed instruction and writes it on an output device as each instruction is executed.

trace flow—A debugging device which prints out contents of various registers and memory location in a particular program segment specified by the user.

trace, macro—*See* macrotrace.

trace program—*See* program, trace.

trace program, interpretive—*See* program, interpretive trace.

trace routine—An executive routine that develops a sequence record of the execution of programs to be checked or traced.

trace, selective—A tracing routine wherein only instructions satisfying certain specified criteria are subject to tracing. The following criteria are typical examples. (a) Instruction type—arithmetic jump. (b) Instruction location—a specific region. (c) Data location—a specific region. For case (a), where tracing is performed on a transfer or a jump instruction, the term logical trace is sometimes used.

trace statement—A trace statement provides for the tracing of certain variables or segments of a program. The trace is used at the source-language level and can be used in two different ways. The first way will generate a list of a specified set of variables and their values each time one of the variables is defined. The second will generate a list of the values of all variables appearing on the left side of an assignment statement. IF expressions are evaluated, and the statement numbers of all statements are executed in a particular segment of a program. Values listed include the name of the variable or a designation specifying the listed value as an IF expression result or statement number. The trace facility means the FORTRAN programmer can debug at the source-language level without having to resort to octal-memory dumps or console debugging.

tracing—1. An interpretive diagnostic technique to record on an output device during the execution of each instruction and its results. 2. Provides a record of each processed instruction by the recording of all instructions, operands, and results for analysis of computer run.

tracing, flow—A type of diagnostics and debugging in which the programmer specifies the start and end of those program segments where he wishes to examine the contents of various registers and accumulators. The program will run at machine speed until it encounters the desired segments, and the printing commences and is terminated when the end of the program segment is encountered. It is also possible to then include "snapshot" traces which indicate the contents not only of the various accumulators and registers, but also of specified memory locations.

tracing, interpretive—Such routines interpret rather than execute directly each instruction in either source language or machine code. The program is simulated in its execution by using accumulators and pseudo index registers which are not identical to the accumulators and registers used by the tracing program, thus control does not pass from the tracing program to the program which is being traced when a branch instruction is encountered.

tracing, logical—Tracing which is performed only on specific jump or transfer instructions and for specific purposes.

tracing routine—A routine that supplies automatic tracing.

tracing, selective—Specific tracing on particular data most often related to some highly specific instructions such as transfer instructions only, or for specified locations, registers, storage units, areas, etc.

tracing structure, built-in—Various debugging, diagnostic, or error-tracing routines are built-in parts of programs, i.e., instructions to output partial results during any program execution cycle. Such instructions may be of a temporary nature and can be easily removed using various series of test instructions.

track—1. A sequence of binary cells arranged so that data may be read or written from one cell at a time in serial fashion; for example, a track on a magnetic drum is a path one-bit wide around the circumference of the drum. 2. The portion of a moving-storage medium, such as a drum, tape, disk, that is accessible to a given reading station.

track, card—*See* card track.

track, clock—*Same as* track, timing.

track, CRAM—A lane on a CRAM card for the writing of a block of information. (NCR)

track density—The number of adjacent tracks per a given unit of distance measured in a direction perpendicular to the direction of individual tracks. The inverse of track pitch.

track, feed—The track of a paper tape which contains the small feed holes for the sprockets.

tracking cross—A crosslike array of bright dots on the display, used for locating points and lines or for drawing curves.

track label—The installation deck number, card number, and track number that uniquely identifies any CRAM track. The track label is written as the first four slabs of every track of every card of a deck.

track, library—Tracks used to store reference data, such as titles, key words, document numbers, etc., on tapes, drums, disks, or mass storage devices.

track, magnetic—That part of a moving magnetic medium which is influenced by a magnetic head, i.e., the ring-shaped portion of the surface of a magnetic drum storage as connected with one physical position of one magnetic head.

track pitch—See pitch track.

track regenerative—Same as loop, high speed.

tracks, density—The number of bits which may be written in a single postion across the width of the tape, including parity bits.

tracks, prerecorded—A preliminary tape-, disk, or drum-recorded routine that simplifies programming. Relieves the programmer of the responsibility of furnishing timing or counting instructions and permits block and word addressability.

track, timing—A specific track on magnetic tape, magnetic disks, drums, etc., on which a long string of pulses is recorded developing a clock signal to thus recognize rows of data by counting or by the positioning of the pulses or marks in the track.

traffic control, input/output—See input/output traffic control.

trail, audit—See audit trail.

trailer—1. A record that follows a group of detail records and gives information about a group not present in the detail records. 2. A record that follows a header.

trailer label—The end-of-tape file record that lists summary information concerning that file.

trailer record—A record that follows a group of records and contains pertinent data related to the group of records.

trailer, tape—See tape trailer.

training mode—See mode, training.

training specialist—This individual develops and conducts educational programs dealing in data processing and guides the technical training of new employees.

training time—See time, training.

transacter (input stations)—The transacter (input stations) can be linked with a computer system to provide real-time processing of manufacturing data. Input stations located at widely scattered points throughout the factory, can feed fixed and variable manufacturing data directly to the processor. The data can be processed immediately to provide management with up to the minute information concerning all phases of operation within the plant. The ability to have data fed into the computer as the transaction occurs, enables vital facts to be generated in time to be used most effectively by all levels of industrial management. (NCR)

transaction—A collection or grouping of several related actions entered by a terminal operator as in an airline reservation system

where the sale of a space on one flight is an action, and the sale of an itinerary or schedule including several alternate flights for the same passenger would be a transaction.

transaction data—Data describing a specific event in a data-processing application area, such as job number, quantity, price, tec.

transaction file—Transactions accumulated as a batch ready for processing against the master file.

transaction record—Specific information which modifies information in a file.

transaction recorder, automatic—1. Routines or systems are developed for recording several facts about each transaction with minimum manual input. Worker and job identification are picked up from plates or individual cards, start-stop times are checked by clock notations, completions are developed by recording dials at inquiry stations throughout plants. 2. This data capture method is used in mechanical payroll systems using badge readers and a digital clock for capturing employee working hours.

transaction tape—A paper tape or magnetic tape carrying information that is to be used to up-date filed information. This filed information is often on a master tape.

transceiver—1. Equipment for card-to-card transmission by way of telephone or telegraph wires. 2. A device that transmits and receives data from a punched card to a punched card. It is essentially a conversion device which at the sending end reads the card and transmits the data over the wire. At the receiving end it punches the data into a card.

transceiver, card—See card transceiver.

transcribe—To copy, with or without translating, from one external storage medium to another.

transcriber—The equipment associated with a computer for the purpose of transferring the input or output data from a record of information in a given language to the computer medium and language, or from a computer to a record of information.

transcript card—That specific card which is keypunched from a source document other than the card itself.

transcription break—A flowchart symbol or device that shows the relationship between two files. The symbol is directional and suggests the flow of information from one file to the file that is affected by the information. The operation symbol should be on the history lines of the file that is affected.

transducer—A device that converts energy from one form to another; e.g., a quartz crystal imbedded in mercury can change electrical energy to sound energy as is done in sonic delay lines in computer-storage systems.

transducer, syntax—A subroutine which recognizes the phase class in an artificial language, normally expressed in Backus normal form.

transfer—1. To transfer control by means of an instruction or signal that specifies the location of the next instruction and directs the computer to that instruction; to jump. A transfer is used to alter the normal sequence control of the computer. 2. To transfer data; to copy, exchange, read, record, store, transmit, transport, or write data. 3. To terminate one sequence of instructions and begin another sequence.

transfer, average data rate—*See* data transfer rate, average.

transfer, block—The conveyance of a group of consecutive words from one place to another.

transfer card—*See* transfer of control card.

transfer character—*See* character, transfer.

transfer check—A check on the accuracy of a data transfer.

transfer command—A particular order or instruction which changes control from one part of the program to another part by indicating a remote instruction.

transfer, conditional—*See* branch, conditional.

transfer control—*Same as* transfer, definition 2.

transfer control, unconditional—*Same as* branch unconditional.

transfer, cyclic—This optional channel provides continuous cyclic word communication with from one to four equal-length blocks of memory. The blocks are contiguous and contain from one to 4,096 words. Both input and output modes are accommodated. The cyclic feature of this channel is beneficial in such applications as telemetry or other high-speed repetitive operations because once initiated, this channel continues to function without the need of a program instruction to start each cycle (some computers).

transfer, data-break—Individual words or blocks of data can be transferred between a peripheral device and the computer core memory, via the MB (memory buffer), at very rapid rate. A data break is entered upon receiving a break-request signal and a transfer-direction signal from the device. When the request is made the computer completes the current instruction, then enters the break state to enact the transfers. Transfers are performed during every computer cycle until the break-request signal is removed by the device. The core-memory address of each transfer is specified by the peripheral device (some computers).

transfer, data rate—*See* data transfer rate.

transfer function—1. A mathematical expression, frequently used by control engineers, that expresses the relationship between the outgoing and the incoming signals of a process or control element. The transfer function is useful in studies of control problems. 2. A mathematical expression or expressions that describe(s) the relationship between physical conditions at two different points in time or space in a given

system, and also describes the role played by the intervening time or space.

transfer instruction—*Same as* branch instruction.

transfer instruction, conditional—*See* branch, conditional.

transfer instruction, unconditional—*See* branch, unconditional.

transfer medium—The material which enables the transfer of ink during printing, i.e., sheets, ribbons, plastic film.

transfer of control—*Same as* branch.

transfer-of-control card—A card, used in the loading of a deck of program cards, that causes the termination of loading and initiates the execution of the program. (Synonymous with transfer card.)

transfer operation—An operation that moves information from one storage location or one storage medium to another; e.g., read, record, copy, transmit, or exchange. Transfer is sometimes taken to refer specifically to movement between different storage media.

transfer, parallel—In a parallel transfer, all the bits stored in one string of flip-flops are transferred simultaneously to another string, using one wire (or a pair of wires) for each flip-flop.

transfer peak—*See* data transfer rate.

transfer, peripheral—A procedure or process for transferring data between two units of peripheral or auxiliary equipment.

transfer, radial—A procedure or process for transferring data between peripheral equipment and the internal memory of the machine.

transfer rate, character—The speed at which data may be read from or written to the unit, exclusive of seek or latency delays.

transfer rate, data—The speed at which data may be read from or written to the device, from the lowest to the highest speed and density available.

transfer rate instantaneous—*See* data transfer rate.

transfer rate, maximum—The maximum number of binary digits per second which can be accommodated on the channel. For a duplex channel (input/output) the transfer rate is usually shown for one direction only.

transfer register data—The temporary store or device which eases the communication or movement of data within the computer. Often called memory data register (mdr).

transfers, automatic-word—An instruction that uses the data-break facility to allow concurrent-information processing and data acquisition during block transfers.

transfer, serial—A system of data transfer in which the characters of an element of information are transferred in sequence over a single path in consecutive time positions.

transfer table—A table that contains a list of transfer instructions of all the programs that are in core, which enables transfers of control to be made from one to another program.

463

transfer time—That specific time interval between the instant the transfer of data to or from a storage commences and the instant it is completed.

transfer unconditional—*Same as* branch unconditional.

transfer vector—*See* transfer table.

transfer, word—Transmission is of entire words (often 24 bits in parallel). The 24 bits are transferred between the computer and the external device at one time. This means that no breakdown of words into characters on output, or assembling of characters into words on input, takes place.

transfluxor—A magnetic-memory element in which the magnetic field varies appreciably across the core to give a nondestructive readout. The magnetic core has two or more openings. Storage of a binary bit is controlled by the flux in the various legs of the magnetic circuit.

transform—To change the structure or composition of information without altering its meaning or value; to normalize, edit, or substitute.

transient—1. A physical disturbance intermediate to two steady-state conditions. 2. Pertaining to rapid change. 3. A build-up or breakdown in the intensity of a phenomenon until a steady-state condition is reached. The time rate of change of energy is finite and some form of energy storage is usually involved.

transient error—Some errors arise which are not because of any inherent defect in tapes, machines, or programs, but because of the presence of some dust, which will disappear when the tape is physically moved again. Such errors are termed to be transient.

transition—The change from one circuit condition to the other; that is, the change from mark to space or from space to mark.

transition card—1. A card, used in the loading of a deck of program cards, that causes the termination of loading and initiates the execution of the program. (Synonymous with transfer-of-control card and transfer card.) 2. A card that signals the computer that the reading in of a program has ended and the carrying out of the program has started.

transition, mark-to-space—The transition, or switching, from a marking impulse to a spacing impulse.

transition, space-to-mark—The transition, or switching, from a spacing impulse to a marking impulse.

translate—To change information from one language to another without significantly affecting the meaning, e.g., problem statements in pseudocode, data, or coding to machine.

translate (display)—To move, as an image on a screen, from side to side or up and down without rotation of the image.

translating program—A particular program (often called a translator) which translates from one language into another.

translating routine—A program whose input is a sequence of statements in some language and whose output is an equivalent sequence of statements in another language.

translation—The operation that re-establishes the text of a message from the restored signals and includes printing of the text.

translation, algorithm—A specific, effective, essentially computational method for obtaining a translation from one language to another.

translation, error rate of (communication)—Ratio of the number of alphabetic characters incorrectly translated to the number of alphabetic characters in the undistorted and restored message at the input of the receiving apparatus.

translation, frequency—The transfer, en block, of the signals occupying a definite frequency band, from one position in the frequency spectrum to another so that the arithmetic frequency difference of the signals is unaltered.

translation, language—The translation of information from one language to another.

translation, machine—The automatic translation from one representation to another representation. The translation may involve codes, languages, or other systems of representation. (Related to automatic dictionary.)

translation, mechanical—A generic term for language translation by computers or similar equipment.

translation one-for-one—The specific process in which each programming instruction is equal to one machine language instruction.

translation program, interpretive—*Same as* program, interpretive.

translator—1. A program whose input is a sequence of statements in some language and whose output is an equivalent sequence of statements in another language. (Synonymous with translating routine.) 2. A translating device.

translator dispatcher—A device used to load the FORTRAN, MACRO-6, or other translators which are rather large programs that do not reside in memory, but are stored on the system library tape until they are called into memory by the translator. (DEC)

translator, language—*See* language translator.

translator, one-to-one—*Same as* assembler, one-to-one.

translator program—This program uses the source language program as input and produces from it a programming machine language. Like any other machine program this may either be run immediately or stored for later use.

translator, routine—A routine that compiles (translates) a source program expressed in problem-oriented language into an object program in machine code.

transliterate—To represent the characters or words of one language by corresponding characters or words of another language.

transmission—The electrical transfer of a signal, message, or other form of intelligence from one location to another.

transmission adapter — The transmission adapter (XA) provides for the connection of remote and local devices to the data adapter as well as the necessary controls to move data to or from the processing unit via the XIC (transmission interface connector). A number of data adapters are available to allow attachment of various remote devices through their communication facility as well as the attachment of various local devices (some systems).

transmission, asynchronous—The transmission process such that between any two significant instants in the same group (block or character), there is always an integral number of unit intervals. Between two significant instants located in different groups, there is not always an integral number of unit intervals.

transmission codes, fixed ratio—Error detection codes that use a fixed ratio of one bit to the total number of bits.

transmission codes, recurrent—Codes in which check symbols are used to detect against the burst type of error.

transmission codes, spiral parity checking—A method used to detect single bit errors. Each check character is obtained by shifting the level for each successive checking character.

transmission control—1. The system services many locations, some on common communication lines and some on separate lines. It supplies the equipment and programming required to handle the multiple inputs arriving in unscheduled fashion into the computer. 2. Control can communicate directly with various types of communication terminals. Examples of such terminals include the data-collection system, the data-communication systems, the process-communication system and telegraph terminals, including terminals using the new American Standard Code for information interchange.

Terminal attachments to the control can be made via common carrier-leased private telegraph, voice- or subvoice-grade lines. Accommodations also include attachment, via privately owned voice-grade communication lines and common carrier-switched voice and data networks. Multiple terminals can be attached to each communication line. However, the limiting number of terminals per line is determined by the addressing capability of that particular terminal. Each communication line is under the channel control.

transmission, data — The sending of data from one place to another, or from one part to another part of the system.

transmission, data trap—*See* data transmission trap.

transmission, effective speed of—The rate at which information is processed by a trans-

mission facility, expressed as the average characters per unit time or average bits per unit time.

transmission equipment—That large class of equipment considered peripheral to the computing equipment itself which communicates data rather than computing or processing.

transmission interface converter—The transmission interface converter controls information transfer between a transmission channel and a transmission adapter.

transmission level—The expression in transmission units of the ratio P/P_0, where P represents the power at the point in question, and P_0 the power at the point chosen as the origin of the transmission system.

transmission link—A section of a channel (or circuit) between: (1) a transmitter station and the following telegraph repeater, (2) two successive telegraph repeaters, (3) a receiving station and the proceeding telegraph repeater.

transmission output, asychronous—Timing on asynchronous output-data transfers is not time critical. Since each output-data character is preceded by a start bit and followed by a stop bit, the time interval between characters will appear to the transmission facilities as nothing more than an extra-long stop bit. Although no information is lost if a data character is not transferred from the central processor to the asychronous output CLT within the "character availability interval," a failure to do so will result in a reduced transmission rate.

transmission, parallel—A system for sending all bits of a particular character simultaneously.

transmission, point-to-point — Transmission of data between two points.

transmission ratio, utilization—The data transmission ratio of useful or acceptable data output to the total input of data.

transmission, serial—To move data in sequence, one character at a time as contrasted with parallel transmission.

transmission speed—The number of information elements sent per unit of time, usually expressed as bits, characters, word groups, or records per second (or per minute).

transmission system codes—Method of using a character parity check as well as a block check to detect errors.

transmission system, information—A system which receives and delivers information without changing it.

transmission terminal card—The machine doing the transmitting reads data from punched cards and transmits it over telephone circuits to a receiving machine.

transmission "tones" — Standard telephone company data sets at each end of the telephone line convert signals from the RTU and CTU into "tones" for transmission over the line. Conversely, the data set converts "tones" received from the lines into signals for the terminal units.

transmit—1. To transfer information to a new location, replacing the information previously stored in this location and clearing the source. 2. To copy information from one storage medium or area to another. 3. To move data from one location to another.

transmit mode (communications)—In the transmit mode, T-level data are read from the input paper tape and transmitted. The interlaced parity level is added to the data transmitted. At the end of each block of data the transmitter will pause for a fixed delay and check the transmission line for an error signal. If no error signal is detected, the next block of data is transmitted. Detection of a transmission error causes the unit to stop, and the transmit-error indicator will be illuminated.

To correct the error, the operator must back up the tape to the previous gap. The receiver will signal when ready to receive information again, which will extinguish the transmit-error indicator. The error circuits are cleared by the transmit-receive switch, and the data retransmitted (some systems).

transmitted-data circuit—Signals in this circuit are originated by the data-terminal equipment for transmission on the data-communication channel. This circuit is not required for receive-only service.

transmitter—In telephony, a device to convert sound to electrical energy. In radio and television, a device to generate and radiate electrical energy.

transmitter, distributor—The device in a teletypewriter that makes and breaks the teletype line in timed sequence. Modern usage of the term refers to a paper-tape transmitter.

transmitter-distributor, tape—*Same as* tape reader.

transmitter-start code—Usually a two-letter call that is sent to an outlying machine that automatically turns on its tape transmitter.

transport—1. To convey as a whole from one storage device to another. 2. A device that moves tape past a head. (Synonymous with tape transport.)

transportation, document—The phase in the reading process in character recognition which makes the effective delivery of the source document to the read station.

transport mechanism, tape—*See* tape transport.

transport, tape—The mechanism that moves magnetic or paper tape past sensing and recording heads, and is usually associated with data-processing equipment. (Synonymous with tape transport, tape drive, and tape feed; related to tape unit, magnetic-tape unit, and paper-tape unit.)

transport unit—A specific piece of peripheral equipment or media handling device, such as a card feed.

transverse check—A system of error control based on some preset rules for the formation of characters.

trap—1. A special form of a conditional breakpoint that is activated by the hardware itself, by conditions imposed by the operating system, or by a combination of the two. Traps are an outgrowth of the old idea of switch-controlled halts or jumps. Frequently, a number of internal triggers or traps exist in a computer. Since these traps are usually set only by unexpected or unpredictable occurrences, and since the execution time and number of instructions for testing them can be burdensome, it is usual for these triggers to cause an automatic transfer of control, or jump to a known location. The location from which the transfer occurred, and the cause of the transfer are recorded in other standard locations. Some trapping features can also be enabled or inhibited under program control, e.g., an overflow trap. (Related to tracing routine.) 2. A routine to determine indirectly the setting of internal triggers in the computer.

trap, arithmetic mask—The bit, in the program status doubleword, that indicates whether (if 1) or not (if 0) the fixed-point arithmetic trap is in effect.

trap control settings—Trap control settings which interrupt signals will be allowed to interrupt a program in process. If a trap is armed, then the associate interrupt conditions will be permitted to interrupt the main program when they occur. A trap that has not been armed, or has been disarmed, inhibits the occurrence of interrupt signals.

trap, data transmission—*See* data transmission trap.

trap, dedicated cells—The executive of a time-sharing system regains control when an interrupt occurs by prestoring in the dedicated trap cells. The program then jumps to the appropriate interrupt processing subroutines. The dedicated cells are in a protected area of core memory and cannot be modified by a user program. Arming and enabling operations are usually privileged instructions forbidden to user programs. Exceptions to this may be certain program faults, such as arithmetic overflow.

trapped-program interrupt—Normally, any condition that causes an interrupt should be identified as soon as possible. However, in some cases it may be more convenient to ignore this condition. To allow for this possibility, the interrupt traps may be armed or disarmed by program control. An interrupt trap is associated with each interrupt event; an interrupt may occur only if its corresponding trap is armed. Any trap may be individually armed or disarmed and its condition may be stored in memory or tested under program control. The seven events that may cause an interrupt to occur are: (1) add overflow, (2) operator-interrupt switch, (3) memory-parity fail, (4) power fail, (5) programmed input/output channel, (6) nonpriority external device, and (7) priority external device.

trapping — A feature of some computers whereby an unscheduled (nonprogrammed) jump is made to a predetermined location in response to a machine condition (e.g., a tagged instruction, or an abnormal arithmetic situation). Such a feature is commonly used by monitor routines to provide automatic checking, or for communication between input/output routines and their programs.

trapping mode—A scheme used mainly in program-diagnostic procedures for certain computers. If the trapping mode flip-flop is set and the program includes any one of certain instructions, the instruction is not performed but the next instruction is taken from location 0. Program-counter contents are saved in order to resume the program after executing the diagnostic procedure.

trap settings—Trap settings that control interrupt signals will be allowed to interrupt a program in process. If a trap is armed, then the associated interrupt conditions will be permitted to interrupt the main program when they occur. A trap that has not been armed, or has been disarmed, prevents the occurrence of interrupt signals.

traps, interrupt—For each type of interrupt there is a program-controlled trap that may prevent or allow the corresponding interrupts. If a trap is in the "1" condition, the corresponding interrupt is allowed. If it is a "0," the corresponding interrupt is prevented. The following is a list of traps and their corresponding interrupt events: programmed I/O (input/output) trap— programmed I/O interrupt; operator trap —operator interrupt; add-overflow trap— add-overflow interrupt; power-fail trap— power-fail interrupt; external-device trap —nonpriority external-device interrupts; priority external-device trap—priority external-device interrupts; and memory-parity fail trap—memory-parity fail interrupt.

If the ED (external device) trap is a "1," standard external-device interrupts are allowed. Priority interrupts are prevented if the priority trap is a 0. Setting a trap to the 1 condition is sometimes referred to as arming the trap. Conversely, clearing a trap to the 0 condition may be called disarming the trap (some systems) .

traverse—The area through which a punched card is transported through the machine.

tray—The flat file drawer used to store punched cards.

tree—This term is often used for some types of decoders because their diagrammatic representation can resemble the branches and trunk of a tree.

trend—To print or record variable values.

triad—A group of three bits or three pulses

usually in sequence on one wire or simultaneously on three wires.

trial divisor—An initial approximation in the dividing arithmetic process.

trial run—The procedure which is used to check for accuracy of methods. A sample card deck or part of the actual-run data may be used for the check.

tributary circuit—A circuit that connects as an individual drop, or drops, to a switching center.

trigger—A bistable electronic device used to store information, to generate gates, and to condition AND and OR circuits, etc.

TRIM—A program for simulating a real inventory control system. Test Rules for Inventory Management (TRIM) permits lower investments in inventories. Assembly-line balancing provides a systematic method for analyzing the man-work relationship in assembly-line operations. The program helps reduce cycle and idle time, increases production and labor efficiency.

triple address—*Same as* address, three.

triple-length working—The use of three machine words to represent a number to enhance precision.

triple precision—The retention of three times as many digits of a quantity as the computer normally handles; e.g., a computer whose basic word consists of 10-decimal digits is called upon to handle 30-decimal digit quantities.

trouble-location problem — A test problem that, when incorrectly solved, supplies information on the location of the faulty component. It is used after a check problem has shown that a fault exists.

troubleshoot—1. To search for errors in order to correct them. 2. To isolate and remove the mistakes in a program caused by the malfunction of a computer. (Related to diagnostic routine.)

trouble shooter problem—*See* problem, trouble shooter.

true complement—*Same as* complement.

true time—*Same as* time, real.

true-time operation—*See* operation, real-time, on-line.

truncate—1. The reduction of precision by dropping one or several of the least significant digits; in contrast with rounding off. 2. To drop digits of a number or terms of a series, thus lessening precision; e.g., the number 3.14159265 is truncated to five figures in 3.1415, whereas one may round off to 3.1416. 3. To terminate a computational process in accordance with some rule.

truncation—The process of dropping one or more digits of a number, either at the left or the right, without altering any of the remaining digits. For example, in most operations the number 3847.39 would become 3847.3 when truncated one place at the right, while it would become 3847.4 when rounded correspondingly.

truncation error—1. Error resulting from the use of only a finite number of terms of an infinite series. 2. The approximation of operations in the infinite-serial calculus by a calculus of finite differences.

trunk—1. One or more conductors used for distributing a-c signals or power from one or more sources to one or more destinations. (Synonymous with bus.) 2. A path for the transfer of data or signals.

trunk circuit—A circuit that connects two data-switching centers.

trunk (communications)—A trunk is a telephone line between two central offices that is used to provide communications between subscribers.

trunk, digit transfer—A set of wires used to transfer numbers (electrical pulses) which represent data and instructions to various registers and counters. However, on-off and similar transfer lines or control signals are not considered digit transfer trunks.

trunks, input/output—The basic system is equipped with many input/output telephone-trunk lines, each of which can be connected to a peripheral control. For instance a peripheral control that handles both reading and writing (e.g., a magnetic-tape control) is connected to a pair of trunk lines. Data is transferred between the main memory and the read/write channel of a recorder via a trunk line specified in the instruction routine that initiated the transfer. Additional peripheral devices can be connected to the system simply by adding more input/output trunk lines to the basic configuration. The number of peripheral devices in a system depends only on the number of input/output trunk lines available.

trunks, peripheral—See peripheral trunks.

truth table—See table, truth.

tube—A tube in EDP (electronic data-processing) systems refers usually to a cathode-ray tube that is used to display data.

tube, cathode-ray (CRT)—1. A vacuum tube in which its electron beam can be focused to a small diameter on a luminescent screen. The concentrated beam can be varied in position and intensity to produce a visible pattern. 2. A storage tube. 3. An oscilloscope tube. 4. A picture tube.

tube, display—A cathode-ray tube used to display information.

tube, NIXIE—See NIXIE light.

tube, Williams—A cathode-ray tube used as an electrostatic-storage device and of the type designed by F C. Williams, University of Manchester, England. (Synonymous with Williams-tube storage.)

Turing machine—See machine, Turing.

turnaround document—See document, turnaround.

turnaround system—In character recognition, a system in which the input data to be read are printed by the computer with which the reader is associated.

turnaround time—The particular amount of time that is required for a computation task to get from the programmer to the computer, onto the machine for a test or production run, and back to the programmer in the form of the desired results. Important problems occur when the turnaround time is excessive, especially in scientific installations.

turning, page—See page turning.

twelve edge—The upper edge of an 80-column card or the edge least likely to enter the equipment first, except for interpreting equipment which requires a twelve-edge feed.

twelve punch—1. A punch in the top row of a Hollerith card. 2. A punch position 12 of an 80-column card. It is often used for additional control or selection, or to indicate a positive number as if it were a plus sign. (Synonymous with Y punch.)

twenty-nine feature code—See code, twenty-nine feature.

twin check—A continuous duplication check achieved by the duplication of hardware and/or an automatic comparison of data.

twin-drum (sorting)—In a multidrum computer configuration, the use of two drums for storing a file of data. The elapsed time required to sort is significantly reduced by alternating the moving of one drum head with the reading and writing of data from another drum.

two-address—An instruction that includes an operation and specifies the location of an operand and the result of the operation. See multiple-address code.

two-address code—A specific instruction code containing two operand addresses.

two-addressed machines—See machines, two addressed.

two-address instruction—See multiple-address instruction.

two-address instruction system—A machine-language instruction that has two addresses, but both may reference data.

two input adder—Same as half adder.

two-input subtracter—Same as subtracter, half.

two-level address—See address, indirect.

two-out-of-five code—A code in which each decimal digit is represented by five binary digits of which two are ones and three are zeros, or vice versa.

two-pass assembler—An assembler which requires scanning of the source program twice. The first pass constructs a symbol table. The second does the translation.

two-phase modulation—A method of phase modulation in which the two significant conditions differ.

two plus one address—See address format.

two-plus-one address instruction—See instruction, two-plus-one address.

twos complement—See complement.

two-state variable—A variable which assumes values in a set containing exactly two elements, often symbolized as 0 and 1. This is often confused with double-value variable, i.e., $y = \pm \sqrt{x}$. (Synonymous with binary variable.)

two sum, modelo—*Same as:* nonequivalence, exclusive-OR operation, intersection, collation.

two-, three- or four-address instruction—An instruction consisting of an operation and 2, 3, or 4 addresses respectively. The addresses may specify the location of operands, results or other instructions.

two-valued—*Same as* binary variable.

two-wire channel—A channel for transmission in only one direction at a time.

TWX—A Bell system which provides subscribers with two-way communications via teleprinter equipment connected to the general-switched telephone network. TWX offers both 60 wpm and 100 wpm source.

type bar—*See* printer type bar.

type bar, fixed—A type bar on a printer which cannot be removed by an operator and thus giving to that printer unit a fixed alphabet.

type bar interchangeable—A printer type bar which can be removed by the operator to change from one alphabet to another.

type drum—One example of a type drum has 128 bands of printing characters along its length. Each band contains the 51-character print set around the circumference of the drum. Characters are arranged on the drum in a checkerboard pattern so that they are separated from characters on adjacent bands by approximately $\frac{1}{8}$ inch; this space reduces the possibility of smudging by characters on a band adjacent to the one being printed.

type face—In optical character recognition (OCR), a character style with given relative dimensions and line thicknesses. (Contrasted with type font.)

type font—A type face of a given size, such as 12-point Gothic.

type font, optical—This font was developed as a medium that could be read by both people and machines—a major advance in simplifying the creation of input for data-processing systems.

typeout key respond—A particular push button on a console inquiry keyboard which locks the typewriter keyboard and permits the automatic processing to continue.

type, page time-sharing—*See* time sharing, page type.

typewriter, console—The availability of a typewriter attached to or part of the control unit or programmer desk of a computer, the typewriter being capable of both entering and receiving information.

typewriter, console monitor—The primary function of the typewriter is to monitor system and program operations. Such system conditions as ADD OVERFLOW, EXPONENT OVERFLOW, etc, and program conditions as SYNTAX ERROR, SYMBOL LENGTH, INTEGER SIZE, etc. are brought to the operator's attention via the typewriter. The typewriter also may be programmed to request information from the operator. The typewriter also may be used to enter programs and data into the central processor and to type out the results in lieu of other peripheral equipment specifically designed for these functions.

typewriter, electric—A hand-operated, electric-powered, individual-character printing device having the property that almost every operation of the machine, after the keys are touched by human fingers, is performed by electric power instead of manual power; a typewriter powered by electricity, in all other respects the same as a manually powered typewriter.

typewriter, on-line—The on-line typewriter, a standard feature of the computer, provides monitor control of operating programs. It operates on a character at a time basis under program control and communicates directly with the accumulator. Data communication is through the programmed input/output channel.

typewriter output routine (TYPOUT)—TYPOUT is contained in the monitor for outputting messages to the operator. TYPOUT is used by the monitor, the system loader, and library subroutines for error diagnostics. It may be used by any program to output messages since it is in memory with the monitor. The output device used by TYPOUT is the operator-message device—normally a console typewriter, but it may be a line printer. TYPOUT additionally outputs the message on the system-output (SO) device if it is different from the operator-message device (some systems) .

typing reperforator—A reperforator which is designed to type on chadless tape in such a way that each printed character is located about one-half inch past the punching to which it corresponds.

U

UA—Abbreviation for user area.

UDC—Abbreviation for universal decimal classification.

ultraprecision CRT display—This is a 5-inch random-position, print-plotting cathode-ray tube designed to meet the particular needs of those requiring a high degree of accuracy stability and resolution. It is especially suited for photographic recording of digital output data and for use in combination with a photomultiplier as a precision programmed spot scanner for the input of photographic data to digital computers. Discrete points may be plotted at a 20 kilocycle rate in any sequence on its 3-inch by 3-inch raster. (DEC)

unallowable code—See check, forbidden combination.

unallowable code check—Same as check, forbidden combination.

unallowable instruction digit—See instruction digit, unallowable.

unattended communication data sets—See communication data sets, unattended.

unattended communications—See communications, unattended.

unattended operation, CLT—See CLT unattended operation.

unattended standby time—See time, standby unattached.

unbalanced error—See error, unbalanced.

unblind (blind)—The selective controlling of a transmission printer or reperforator. Used, for example, to prevent prices from typing on a receiving teletypewriter.

unblocking—The process of separating and obtaining one or more records from a block in the memory.

UNCOL—An abbreviation for universal computer oriented language.

uncommitted storage list—Blocks of storage that are chained together and not allocated at any specific moment.

unconditional—1. Subject to a specific instruction only. 2. Without any conditions; e.g., an unconditional statement is executed whenever it is encountered during a routine or program.

unconditional branch—An instruction of basic importance that develops a deviation from the program-execution sequence despite existing conditions.

unconditional jump—Same as unconditional branch.

unconditional transfer—Same as unconditional branch.

unconditional transfer of control—Same as unconditional branch.

underflow—1. In an arithmetical operation, the generation of a quantity too small to be stored by the register or location that is to receive the result. 2. The generation of a quantity smaller than the accepted minimum, e.g., floating-point underflow.

underflow characteristic—A situation developed in floating-point arithmetic if an attempt is made to develop a characteristic less than −99.

underpunch—A punch in one of the lower rows, 1-9, of an 80-column 12-row punch card.

undetected-error rate—The ratio of the number of bits (unit elements, characters, blocks) incorrectly received but undetected or uncorrected by the error-control equipment, to the total number of bits, unit elements, characters, and blocks that are sent.

undisturbed-one output—The 1 output of a magnetic cell. A partial-read pulse has not been applied to this cell since it was last selected for writing.

undisturbed-zero output—The 0 output of a magnetic cell. A partial-write pulse has not been applied to this cell since it was last selected for reading.

UNICOMP—Universal compiler, FORTRAN compatible.

unidirectional—A connection between telegraph sets, one of which is a transmitter and the other a receiver.

uniformity, ink—See ink uniformity.

uniform system—See system, uniterm.

union catalogue—Often means a compiled list of the contents of two or more tape libraries.

union gate—Same as gate, OR.

unipolar (in contrast with bipolar)—1. When both true and false inputs are represented by the same electrical voltage polarity, the signal is defined as unipolar. 2. When a logical true input is represented by an electrical-voltage polarity opposite to that representing a logical false input, the signal is defined as unipolar.

unipunch—Also called a spot punch, it is used for making single holes in punched card or paper tapes, and is operated directly by hand.

uniset—It functions as a general-purpose remote input/output device, it allows rapid and accurate interrogation of the computer. Basically, the uniset is comprised of an alphanumeric keyboard, a format control panel, printer, card mount, and data keys. The keyboard is the principal medium for inserting transaction data. In addition to printing responses as they are received from the computer, the printer part of the uniset provides a printed copy of the input transaction data entered on the keyboard. (UNIVAC)

uniset console—The uniset console is a keyboard device specifically designed to meet point-of-sale operating requirements. Connected on-line with the computer, this device interrogates the system for desired information. Indicator lamps display requested information as well as the computer's reply. Relevant information is stored on a series of transparent cards. When inserted in the uniset console by its operator, this information is identified to the computer. (UNIVAC)

unit, AND—Same as gate, AND.

unit anticoincidence—Same as gate, exclusive OR.

unit, arithmetic—The portion of the hardware of a comptuer in which arithmetic and logic operations are performed. The arithmetic unit generally consists of an accumulator, some special registers for the storage of operands, and results supplemented by the shifting and sequencing circuitry for implementing multiplication, division, and other pertinent operations. Synonymous with ALU (arithmetic and logic unit).

unitary code—A code having only one digit; the number of times it is repeated determines the quantity it represents.

unit, assembly—1. A device that performs the function of associating and joining several parts or piecing together a program. 2. A portion of a program that is capable of being assembled into a larger whole program.

unit, audio-response—See audio-response unit.

unit, card-punch—See punch, card.

unit, card-reader—An input device consisting of a mechanical punch-card reader and related electronic circuitry that transcribes data from punch cards to memory or secondary memory (magnetic tape).

unit, card reader-punch—Same as read punch unit.

unit, card sending-punching—See card sensing-punching unit.

unit, central processing (CPU)—The central processor of the computer system. It contains the main storage, arithmetic unit and special register groups.

unit, code-element—The signal elements in which different arrangements of an equal-length multiunit telegraph code form an alphabet.

unit, computing—See computing unit.

unit, control—The portion of a computer that directs the sequence of operations, interprets the coded instructions, and initiates the proper instructions to the computer circuits.

unit, control (part of the communications system)—A unit associated with a teleprinter and containing the necessary auxiliary equipment for operating this instrument on a switching network. (Same as dialing unit, signalling unit.)

unit, control register system—See control unit register system.

unit, data—A set of one or more related characters that is treated as a whole group. Often used in place of a field (memory) to specify a particular unit of information.

unit data adapter (communications)—See data adapter unit communications.

unit, diagnostics—A unit diagnostic program is used to detect malfunctions in such units as the input/output and the arithmetic circuitry.

unit, digital multiplier—See digital multiplier unit.

unit, display—Generic term used to describe any of the scores of output devices which provide visual representation of data.

unit element—Alphabetic-signal element having a duration equal to the unit interval of time.

unit, equality—A device with output signals that represent 1 when signals representing

identical n-bit numbers are applied to both inputs.

unit, equipment—The hardware or apparatus as contrasted to the programs, routines, or methods of use, i.e., the readily detachable parts of the gear are termed to be equipment units.

uniterm—A word, symbol, or number used as a descriptor for the retrieval of information from a storage collection; especially, a descriptor used in the coordinate-indexing system. (Related to aspect card, descriptor, coordinate indexing, docuterm.)

uniterm indexing—A system of coordinate indexing that utilizes single terms, called uniterms, to define a document uniquely. (Related to uniterm system.)

uniterming—The selection of words, considered to be important and descriptive of the contents of a paper, for later retrieval of the articles, reports, or other documents. The selected words are then included in a uniterm index.

uniterm system—An information-retrieval system that uses uniterm cards. Cards representing words of interest in a search are selected and compared visually. If identical numbers are found to appear on the uniterm card undergoing comparison these numbers represent documents (cards) to be examined in connection with the search. (Related to aspect card, and uniterm indexing.)

unit, functional—See functional unit.

unit, hypertape—Magnetic tape units which use cartridges, house the supply and take up reels, and perform automatic loading.

unit hypertape control—See hypertape control unit.

unit, identity—See identity unit.

unit, indexing applicatons—See indexing unit applications.

unit, input—See input unit.

unit, input/output teletype—See teletype, input/output unit.

unit interval—The length of time of the signal element in an equal length code signaling system. Usually, the duration of the shortest signal element in a coding system using isochronous modulation.

unit, linear—See linear unit.

unit, logic—Same as unit, arithmetic.

unit, magnetic tape—See magnetic tape unit.

unit manual input—See input unit, manual.

unit, monitor—See monitor unit.

unit, on-line—Input/output device or auxiliary equipment under direct control of the computer.

unit, operational—A combination of devices or a circuitry which performs a computer process.

unit, OR—Same as gate, OR.

unit, output—The unit which delivers information in acceptable language to a point outside the computer.

unit, processing—A part of a computing system which is the primary arithmetic and logical performing module.

unit, read-punch—*See* read-punch unit.

unit record—1. Historically, a card containing one complete record; currently, the punched card. 2. A printed line with a maximum of 120 characters; a punched card with a maximum of 72 characters, a BCD (binary-coded decimal) tape record with a maximum of 120 characters.

unit-record equipment—*See* record equipment, unit.

unit, reproducing—*See* reproducing unit.

unit, segregating—*See* segregating unit.

units position—The furthermost right position or the low order location. In the number 1054, the 4 is in the units position.

unit string—A string of characters but one which has only one member, much like a null string which has no members.

units, visual-display—*See* visual display units.

unit tape—*See* tape unit.

unit, tape-processing—*See* tape processing unit.

unit, transport—A specific piece of peripheral equipment or media handling device such as a card feed.

unit, verifying—*See* verifying unit.

universal button box—A coined term for a set of push buttons whose functions are determined by the computer program.

universal decimal classification—An expansion of the Dewey decimal classification started by P. Otlet in Brussels; sometimes referred to as the Brussels system.

universal-interconnecting device—This unit is designed for use with multiple systems where it is desirable to switch peripheral units from one system to another. Any unit which is to be switched between systems must be connected by cable to the interconnector. When switching magnetic files, between systems, it is possible to switch an entire trunk line or up to eight magnetic files with one module. Switching is done automatically by the solenoid-operated switches which are actuated by pushbuttons located on the console panel of the computer. No cables need be manually shifted.

universal Turing machine—A Turing machine that can simulate any other Turing machine.

unload—To remove information in massive quantities as in unloading the storage contents onto a magnetic tape.

unmodified instruction—*See* instruction unmodified.

unpack—1. To decompose packed information into a sequence of separate words or elements. 2. To recover the original data from packed data. 3. To separate combined items of information each into a separate machine word.

unscheduled maintenance—*See* maintenance, corrective.

unscheduled maintenance time—*Same as* maintenance time.

unused combination—*Same as* check, forbidden combination

unused command—*Same as* character illegal.

unused time—That time which is available for machine operations but which is left unused and most often unattended by any computer system personnel, i.e., since 7 twenty-four hour periods per week total 168 hours, total time is the addition of attended time and unused time, i.e., just rest time.

unwind—To code, explicitly, at length and in full all the operations of a cycle, thus eliminating all red-tape operations in the final problem coding. Unwinding may be performed automatically by the computer during assembly, generation, or compilation of a program.

update—1. To modify a master file with current information according to a specified procedure. 2. To apply all current changes, additions, and deletions (substitutions) to a new file. 3. To modify an instruction so that the address numbers it contains are increased by a stated amount each time the instruction is performed. 4. During the checkout period, the updating run deletes and adds programs, corrections, test data, etc. to the master program file.

update, program master-file—Programs from the old master file are deleted, corrected, or left unchanged and new programs are added from the transaction tape. Updating can include changing of program job assignments. A new program master file is produced.

upper curtate—*See* curtate.

up time—The time during which equipment is either producing work or is available for productive work. (Contrasted with down time.)

usage, error—*See* error usage.

user—The person or company using a remote terminal in a time-shared computer system for the purpose of entering a program for execution by the computer.

user area (UA)—The area on a disk where semipermanent data may be stored. This area is also used to store programs, subprograms, and subroutines. This area is contrasted with reserved areas that contain compilers, track and sector information, etc., which may not be written into.

user file, time-sharing—*See* time sharing, user file.

user modes, time-sharing—*See* time sharing, user modes.

user number—*See* number, user.

user-oriented languages, time-sharing—*See* time sharing user-oriented languages.

user's group—Organizations made up of users of various computing systems to give the users an opportunity to share knowledge they have gained in using a digital computing system and exchange programs they have developed.

user tasks scheduling, time-sharing—*See* time sharing, scheduling user tasks.

user time sharing—*See* time sharing, user.

user, time sharing—*See* time sharing, user. ADP contracts, the time during which the equipment is in operation, exclusive of idle time, standby time, maintenance time, or rerun time due to machine failure, is called the use time. Components not programmed for use in a specific computer run are not considered to be in use even though connected into the computer system.

utilities, executive-system—Included within the utilities section of the executive system are diagnostic routines, program file-manipulation routines, file-utility routines, and cooperative routines for aiding the user in performing such functions as reading cards, printing line images on a printer, transferring files from device to device, and carrying out housekeeping functions required for file residence on mass-storage devices.

utility control console—A computer console that is primarily used to control utility and maintenance programs.

utility functions—Auxiliary operations such as tape searching, tape-file copying, media conversion, and dynamic memory and tape dumps.

utility program—A standard routine used to assist in the operation of the computer, e.g., a conversion routine, a sorting routine, a printout routine, or a tracing routine.

utility programmer—This individual develops subroutines and special software. He also develops programming techniques and trains the programming staff in the use of these programming data.

utility routine—1. A standard routine, usually a service or housekeeping routine. 2. A subroutine for controlling machine functions or machine-produced conditions that have little relation to the actual processing of data.

utility routines, complex (CUR)—The complex-utility routine, during the course of its operation, performs various checks on the validity of its output. Messages are produced that inform the programmer of the nature of the trouble when any of these checks fail. Some errors are forgivable and CUR attempts to continue to run; others

are disastrous and result in bypassing the remainder of the operation cards and aborting the run. These will indicate, in general, failures in the hardware or bugs in the system itself.

utility routines, executive-control—Utility routines are contained as an integral part of the executive system. These are programs that are useful for data conversion, editing, etc. A description of the individual utility routines provided with the executive system is given in the individual write-ups of the utility routines. Utility routines are loaded and executed from the master file by an executive-control statement. Frequently used programs may be added to the system as utility routines. These programs may then be called, through the executive, from the master file.

utility routines (Honeywell)—Update and select program. A program under control of input director cards, this program performs master-file update, program selection and directory listing.

utility routines (UNIVAC)—Utility routines are provided which aid in systems operation. These routines include: card-to-tape, tape-to-card, tape-to-print, snap drum, trace, tape file maintenance, and inspect and change routines. Peripherals incorporated into the utility system include all available magnetic-tape systems, all available drum systems, high-speed printer, intercomputer synchronizer, and communications equipment.

utility system—A system or program that is developed to perform miscellaneous or utility functions such as card-to-tape, tape-to-printer, and other peripheral operations or suboperations.

utilization loggers system—A program or a device that collects statistical information about how the system is operating.

utilization ratio, data-transmission—The data-transmission ratio of useful or acceptable data output to the total input of data.

utilization time—The arrangement of a program which allows processing to continue while records necessary for processing are being located in file and read into core and working storage.

V

VAB (voice answer back)—Audio response unit is a device which can link a computer system to a telephone network to provide voice responses to inquiries made from telephone-type terminals. The audio response is composed from a vocabulary prerecorded

in a digital-coded voice or a disk-storage device.

vacuum servo—That peripheral device which maintains a magnetic tape reservoir, maintained by the absence of air pressure on one side of the tape. *See also* tape reservoir.

validity—1. Correctness; especially the degree of the closeness by which the repeated results approach the correct result. 2. A relative measure of the quality of being sound, correct, efficient, etc.

validity check—1. A check for accuracy of character representation. 2. A checking technique based on known reasonable limits on data or computed results. For instance: a man cannot work 400 hours in one week, a month does not have 32 days, an hourly classified man very seldom has a net pay greater than $350.00 per week, etc. Also called a reasonableness check.

validity, data—See data validity.

value—A value designed to serve as a minimum or maximum control value and often compared with the value of some index, count, or signal to determine if the anticipated maximum or minimum has been attained.

value, absolute—A particular quantity, the magnitude of which is known by the computer but the algebraic sign is not relevent.

value, index field—The contents of the 3-bit index (X) field of an instruction word (bit 12-14), designating one of the current general registers 1-7 as an index register.

value, place—The representation of quantities by a positional value system.

valve control amplifier—See amplifier, valve control.

variable—1. A symbol whose numeric value changes from one repetition of a program to the next, or changes within each repetition of a progam. 2. In COBOL, a data item in storage that assumes different values during execution of the object program.

variable address—An address that is to be modified or has been modified by an index register or similar device.

variable binary—See binary variable.

variable, binary-state—See binary variable.

variable block—The number of characters in a block of memory is determined by the programmer and is usually between some practical limits.

variable connector—See connector, variable.

variable, controlled—A quantity, condition, or part of a system which is subject to mainipulation, regulation, or control by computer.

variable-cycle operation—See operation, variable-cycle.

variable, dependent—A variable whose value is determined by some function of another quantity or representation, i.e., the standard expression is y = f (x), where y is considered the dependent variable because its value is determined by the value of x and the nature of the function to be performed.

variable field length—A data field that may have a variable number of characters. This requires item separators to indicate the end of each item.

variable field storage—An indefinite limit of length for the storage field.

variable format—See format, variable.

variable (FORTRAN)—A variable is a symbolic representation (name) that will assume a value. This value may change either for different executions of the program, or at different stages within the program. For example, in the following statement, both I and K are variables: K = 3 I.

variable, integer (FORTRAN)—1. An integer variable usually consists of a series of not more than six alphameric characters (except special characters), of which the first is I, J, K, L, M, or N. 2. The value of I will be assigned by a preceding statement and may change from time to time, and the value of K will vary whenever this computation is performed with a new value of I. As with constants, a variable may be integer or real, depending on whether the value that it will represent is to be integer or real, respectively. In order to distinguish between variables that will derive their value from an integer as opposed to those that will derive their value from a real number, the rules for naming each type of variable are different.

variable length—See length variable.

variable-length fields—Information is stored in variable-length memory areas called fields. A field is defined as a group of consecutive memory locations whose contents are treated as a unit. Each location within a field stores either six binary digits or one alphanumeric character. Since fields can be of any length (from one memory location up to virtually the maximum number of locations), information units of varying lengths can be stored without wasting memory capacity.

variable-length instructions—A feature which increases core efficiency by using only the amount necessary for the application and increases speed because the machine interprets only the fields relevant to the application. Halfword (2 byte), two-halfword (4 bytes), or three-halfword (6 bytes) instructions are used.

variable length record—See record, variable length.

variable-length record file—A file containing a set of records that vary in length.

variable length word—A computer word in which the number of characters is not fixed but is variable and subject to the discretion of the programmer, i.e., storage locations, registers, parallel logic wiring, and gating are arranged in such a way as to handle a character or digit singly, but in storage each character is addressable and thus may be considered a word.

variable, local—A variable whose name is known only to the subprogram to which it belongs.

variable, manipulated—In a process that is desired to regulate some condition, a quantity is altered by the computer in order to initiate a change in the value of the regulated condition.

variable name—*See* name, variable.

variable point—Pertaining to a number system in which the location of the point is indicated by a special character at that location.

variable-point representation—A specific radix notation in which each number is represented by a single set of digits, the position of the radix point explicitly indicated by the inclusion of an appropriate character.

variable-precision coding compaction—A data compaction procedure accomplished using precision, which is reduced in relation to the magnitude of the function, the time, the independent variable, or some other parameter.

variable quantity—A quantity that may assume a succession of values.

variables, integer (FORTRAN)—An integer variable consists of a series of not more than six alphanumeric characters (except special characters), of which the first is I, J, K, L, M, or N.

variables, real (FORTRAN)—A real variable consists of a series of not more than six alphanumeric characters (except special characters), of which the first is alphabetic but not one of the integer indicators, i.e., I, J, K, L, M or N.

variable time—*See* time scale.

variable time scale—*See* time scale, extended.

variable time scaler—*See* time scale, extended.

variable, two-state—*See* binary variable.

variable, two-valued—*See* binary variable.

variable word—The specific feature in which the number of characters handled in the unit is not constant. For contrast, *see* fixed word.

variable word length—1. A phase referring to a computer in which the number of characters addressed is not a fixed number but is varied by the data or instruction. 2. The number of positions in a storage field is determined by the programmer.

variable word length computer—*See* computer, variable word length.

variation indicator — An instruction that changes an operand or command.

variations, calculus of—A specific calculus which relates to the maxima/minima theory of definite integrals. The integrands are functions of dependent variables, independent variables, and their derivatives.

varioplex—A device, used in conjunction with a time-sharing multiplex system, that enables the multiplexed channels to be distributed between the users in a variable manner, according to the number of users who are transmitting at a given time.

variplotter—A large, high-accuracy graphic recording device which plots curves on either a 30″ ×30″ or a 45″ × 60″ surface. Single- and dual-arm models are available for use as horizontal table units or as mounted-vertical units. The plotters feature solid-state circuitry, backlighted plotting surface, vacuum-paper hold-down, continuously variable scale factor and parallax controls. (ESI)

VATE (Versatile Automatic Test Equipment)—VATE is a project that presents a new concept for computer-controlled checkout of complex instrumentation systems. The overall system consists of equipment, test programs, and trained people. VATE tests Air Force inertial-guidance systems, including those on the Titan and Minuteman missiles. The latter system is put on a platform, and flying conditions are simulated during test. The operator at the VATE console receives instructions on each step in the testing procedure by means of a 35-millimeter slide viewed. The computer-controlled random-access slide viewer form the upper portion of the operator's console and displays a succession of instructions to the operator. When a fault is discovered, an illustration of the malfunction is displayed. Then, as VATE isolates the fault, the exact location of it is shown.

vector—A line denoting magnitude and direction, as contrasted with a scalar denoting magnitude only.

vector-continue mode (display)—The vector continue mode of DEC (Digital Equipment Corp.) X-Y plotter is an extension of the vector mode. Its word format is the same. This mode is used when it is desirable to draw a vector from any point to the edge of the screen. The vector specified is automatically extended until the edge of the screen is encountered. Upon violation of the screen edge, automatic return is made to the parameter mode. This mode is particularly useful for drawing long, straight lines (for example, grid lines and graph axes) rapidly and efficiently. (DEC)

vector mode — This mode of DEC (Digital Equipment Corp.) X-Y plotter provides a rapid means for displaying straight lines between two points without specifying any in-between points. A single, 18-bit word causes automatic plotting of the vector. Once the X-Y plotter has been programmed to the vector mode, all subsequent data is interpreted as vector-mode data. Data is received in the form of 18-bit words. Each word consists of 8 bits of delta-X information, 8 bits of delta-Y information, an intensify bit, and an escape bit. Delta-X and delta-Y each comprise 7 magnitude bits and 1 sign bit. Since the display area consists of a 1024 × 1024 point matrix, the maximum length vector that can be drawn with a single instruction is $\pm\frac{1}{8}$ of the display width. There is no limitation for a minimum length vector. Plotting time is $1\frac{1}{2}$ microseconds per individual point. (DEC)

vector, transfer—A table that contains a list of transfer instructions of all the programs that are in core, which enables transfers of control to be made from one program to another program.

Veitch chart—*See* chart, Veitch.

venn diagram—A diagram in which sets are represented by closed regions.

verb—In COBOL, an instruction word that specifies one or more operations to be performed by a data processor.

verbs, processor—Verbs which specify to the processor the procedures by which a source program is to be translated into an object program. Such verbs do not cause action at object time.

verbs, program—Verbs which cause the processor to generate machine instructions that will be executed by the object program.

verge perforated card—*Same as* card, edge-punched.

verge-punched card—*Same as* card, edge-punched.

verification—That act which attempts to make analytical comparisons of data and which indicates or rejects two sets of data which fail to compare accurately.

verifier—1. A manually operated punch-card machine that reports, by means of visual signals, whether a card is punched as intended. 2. A device, similar to a card punch, for checking the inscribing of data by rekeying. 3. A device used to verify the results of keypunching.

verifier, tape—A device designed for checking the accuracy of punched tape by comparing previously punched tape with a second manual punching of the same data, with the machine signalling discrepancies.

verify—1. To check, usually with an automatic machine, one typing or recording of data against another in order to minimize the number of human errors or mistakes in the data transcription. 2. In preparing data for a computer, to make certain that the data prepared is correct. 3. To check a data transfer or transcription, especially those involving manual processes.

verifying, card—A means of checking the accuracy of keypunching. A duplication check. A second operator verifies the original punching by depressing the keys of a verifier while reading the same source data. The machine compares the depressed key with the hole already punched in the card.

verifying unit—Verifying is the process of checking punched data to prove that it has been transcribed correctly. This machine is used in conjunction with any punch equipped with the verifying attachment, and eliminates the human element as completely as possible from the verifying process. Original and verify-punched entries are compared for each card and the errors noted by interfiling signal cards of contrasted color. By simply stacking the verified decks of cards, all those showing discrepancies are "flagged" by the error-indicating cards. A small hole perforated in the right margin of each card indicates the card has passed through the mechanical verifying process.

verify, key—*See* key verify.

vertical feed—Indicates the attitude in which a card is placed in the hopper, enters, and traverses the card track.

vertical format—Pertaining to the vertical arrangement of data, as viewed by an observer of a document.

vertical parity check—*Same as* check, even parity.

vertical redundance—An error condition that exists when a character fails a parity check; i,e., has an even number of bits in an odd-parity system, or vice versa.

video-data interrogator—A terminal unit that is comprised of a keyboard and separable associated display, providing a terminal facility for conventional communications lines.

video display units, data transmission—Any type of input/output equipment with a special feature of displaying information on a screen.

videograph—High-speed cathode-ray printer.

video processor (radar)—*See* processor, radar video.

videoscan optical character reader—A unit that combines OCR (optical character reader) with mark sense and card read. It can read printing and marks in the same pass. It can read holes in cards.

violation subroutines—*See* subroutines, violation.

VIP—Abbreviation for variable information processing, a generalized information storage and retrieval system for small nonformalized files, which provides for retrieval techniques without programming effort, i.e., it is organized by file, using mnemonic codes or abbreviations and plain text language, with no limits on characters.

virgin coil — Tape completely devoid of punches.

virgin medium—That storage medium in which no data is recorded, i.e., paper which is completely unmarked, or paper tape which has no holes punched in it.

virtual—Apparent, as contrasted with actual or absolute.

virtual address—The immediate address or real-time address.

virtual address, effective—The virtual address value after only indirect addressing and/or indexing modifications have been accomplished, but before memory mapping is performed.

virtual addressing—*Same as* addressing, immediate.

virtual memory—*See* memory, virtual.

virtual memory address—*See* memory address, virtual.

visible file—The grouping or systematic arrangement of forms, cards, or documents, so that data placed on the margin may serve as an index which the user can quickly see without the necessity of withdrawing each item.

visual-display console—*See* console display.

visual-display units—*See* display units, visual.

visual-error representation—When a transmission has not been properly received after three successive tries, the third transmission will be printed. The line will be transmitted again and may be printed for comparison with the third transmission.

visual inquiry-display terminal—Inquiry-display terminal (control unit) provides the system with the means to visually display on a cathode-ray tube inquiries from an attached keyboard. With the unit, input data from the keyboard is displayed as it is written, permitting visual verification before release of the message to the computer. It is ideal for applications requiring the instantaneous response of large quantities of data. The unit contains the automatic 20-second time-out clock and the necessary circuits to attach to the System/360 and has these features: complete records, up to 1200 characters in length, can be displayed in a matter of seconds; up to sixty displays can be controlled from one control unit; data is displayed as a dark image against a light background; viewing area of the tube-face is 4″ × 4″, providing 30 lines of 40 characters each; horizontal spacing is ten characters per inch; data remains displayed until erased by the operator; and optimum reading conditions are assured by a soft, glare-free light. (IBM)

visual inquiry station—Usually an input/output unit which permits the interrogation of an automatic data processing system by the immediate processing of data from a human or terminal (automatic) source, together with the display of the results of the processing. . .in many cases, on a Cathode Ray Tube (CRT).

visual operator console—*See* console, visual display.

visual scanner—1. A device that scans optically and usually generates an analog or digital signal. 2. A device that optically scans printed or written data and generates their representation.

visual supervisory control—The P-C (processor-controller) communicates messages and commands to the operator and, if desired, directly to the process equipment and instrumentation. The sensors that measure process conditions are continuously monitored by the P-C. The P-C program analyzes this information and then generates the required output information. Messages from the P-C to the operator may be displayed by several methods in the operator's working area. These messages guide the operator in adjusting the status of instruments located at the point of control. Data messages based upon visual observation of the process and its instrumentation are sent back to the P-C or the

process operator. These messages are evaluated by the P-C to provide additional output, if required, for continued process-operator guidance. Communication between the control-room operator and the process is maintained through the P-C. When the P-C supervisory program computes new set point values, it may—at the discretion of the operator—automatically adjust the set points of the controlling instrumentation to the new values (some systems).

vocabulary—1. A list of operating codes or instructions available to the programmer for writing the program for a given problem for a specific computer. 2. A group of characters occupying one storage location. This unit of information is treated and transported by the computer circuits as an entity; it is treated by the control unit as an instruction, and by the arithmetic unit as a quantity.

vocabulary, sophisticated—An advanced and elaborate set of instructions. Some computers can perform only the more common mathematical calculations such as addition, multiplication, and subtraction. A computer with a sophisticated vocabulary can go beyond this and perform operations such as linearization, extract square root, and select highest number.

voice answer back—*Same as* VAB.

voice frequency—A frequency lying within a part of the human audio range. Voice frequencies used for commercial transmission of speech usually lie within the range of 200 to 3500 cycles per second.

voice-grade channel—A channel which is suitable for transmission of speech, digital or analog data, or facsimile.

voice-grade service (voice channel)—This term originally referred to a service provided by the common carriers that included a circuit capable of carrying a voice transmission. Now, when used in reference to the transmission of data, it also refers to a circuit of sufficient bandwidth to permit a data-transfer rate up to 2400 bits per second. Primarily the term distinguishes this service from teleprinter grade service in reference to regulatory agencies' tariffs.

void—In character recognition, the undesired absence of ink within the outline of a character as might occur in magnetic ink characters or optical characters and is most often due to defects in the inks, paper, or printing process.

volatile—A characteristic of becoming lost or erased when power is removed, i.e., the loss of data where it is not returned or recovered when power is restored. Some such units, as tape units, are in a volatile condition if such a power loss occurs.

volatile file—A temporary or rapidly changing program or file.

volatile memory—A storage medium in which information is destroyed when power is removed from the system.

volatile storage—A storage device in which stored data are lost when the applied power is removed, e.g., an acoustic delay line.

volatility—The aspect of loss or alteration of electrical energy in storage.

volatility of storage—The tendency of a storage device to lose data when the electric power is cut off. Storage media may be classed as volatile (e.g., electrostatic storage tubes) or nonvolatile (e.g., magnetic tape).

volume statistics—The groups of various pertinent facts in relation to the nature and level of operations of an area under consid-eration expressed in numbers (e.g., number of sellers, number of different items, orders, purchases, etc.), plus, or including, sub-classifications of these data to obtain a clear understanding of the pattern of the operations.

volume test—The processing of a volume of actual data to check for program malfunctions.

von Neumann sort—A technique used in a sort program to merge strings of sequenced data. The power of the merge is equal to T/2.

W

WADS (Wide Area Data Service)—This is similar to WATS (Wide Area Telephone Service) used today. AT&T is now asking the Federal Communications Commission for approval to lease teletype-grade circuits on an unlimited dial-up basis from any point in the country. Teletype grade represents the lowest type circuit in terms of speed, cost, and accuracy.

wait—The condition a real-time program meets when it requires information from a file-storage unit and is forced to "wait" until the required-file record is accessed and brought into the main memory. File-oriented systems have this characteristic that leads to multiprogrammed approaches by interleaving and overlapping "wait" times for one program to achieve process time for another program.

waiting lines (queuing theory)—When a flow of goods (or customers) is bottlenecked at a particular servicing point, losses accumulate in the form of lost business, idle equipment, and unused labor. Minimizing such costs involved in waiting lines, or queues, is the object of queuing theory, an O/R (operations research) technique for the most efficient handling of a waiting line at a particular service point.

waiting list—A procedure for organizing and controlling the data of unprocessed operational programs. These lines are ordinarily maintained by the control program.

waiting mode time sharing—*See* time sharing, waiting mode.

waiting state—The state of an interrupt level that is armed and has received an interrupt trigger signal, but is not yet allowed to become active.

waiting time—*Same as* latency, the time interval between the instant the control unit signals the details, addresses, etc., of a transfer of data to or from the storage unit and the instant the transfer commences.

WAIT, macroinstruction—In multithread processing, the presentation of a request on one message that causes a delay so that no processing can go on. A WAIT macro is given which shifts control to a supervisory program so that work may continue on other messages. Work on the delayed message will continue only when the cause of the delay is removed.

walk, random—*See* random walk.

warning marker, destination (DWM)—A reflective spot on the back of a magnetic tape, 18 feet from the physical end of the tape, which is sensed photoelectrically to indicate that the physical end of the tape is approaching.

waste instruction—*Same as* instruction, dummy.

watchdog—*Same as* invigilator.

watchdog timer—A timer set by the program to prevent the system from looping endlessly or becoming idle because of program errors or equipment faults.

WATS (Wide Area Telephone Service)—1. A service that provides a special line allowing the customer to call a certain zone (or band), on a direct-distance dialing basis, for a flat monthly charge. The continental United States is divided into six bands for the purpose of rates. 2. A service provided by AT&T that provides a special tie line allowing the subscriber to make unlimited calls to any location in a specific zone on a direct-distance dialing basis for a flat monthly charge.

waveform generator—A circuit driven by pulses from the master clock; it operates in conjunction with the operation decoder to generate timed pulses needed by other machine circuits to perform the various operations.

way-operated circuit—A circuit shared by three or more stations on a party-line basis. One of the stations may be a switching center.

way station—A telegraphic term for one of the stations on a multipoint network.

WDPC (Western Data Processing Center)—Established in November 1956, it is the first and one of the largest university-computing centers specifically oriented to business applications.

wear resistance—Manufacturers of printing ribbons advise that they have built-in resistance to resist severe reduction to produce images after first-runs and normal use.

weighted, average—A moving average performed on data in which some of the values are more heavily valued than others.

wheel, printer—*See* printer wheel.

wheels, type—*Same as* print wheel.

Whirlwind I—First large machine using ferromagnetic cores in its main memory. It was built at M.I.T. *See* magnetic core.

Wide Area Telephone Service—*See* WATS.

Williams tube—A cathode-ray tube used as an electrostatic storage device of the type designed by F. C. Williams, Manchester University.

Williams-tube storage—*See* Williams tube.

winding—A conductive path, usually of wire, that is inductively coupled to a magnetic device.

window-machine controller—This component furnishes the electronic control for the accounting machine, to supplement the mechanical operations built into it. Functionally, it is part of the accounting machine, but it is packaged in a separate cabinet that fits under the accounting machine.

wing panel—*See* panel, wing.

wire board—*See* board.

wired-program computer—*See* computer, wired-program.

wire, magnetic—A wire made of, or coated with, a magnetic material and used for magnetic recording.

wire printer—*See* printer, wire.

wire wrap—A method of making an electrical connection in an electrical circuit by wrapping wires around specially designed terminals.

wiring board—*See* control panel.

WIZ—The algebraic compiler, further down the scale, is a very fast algebraic compiler. Unlike most scientific compilers which require two or three passes, WIZ requires only one—and its language is considerably easier to learn. Used primarily for engineering, scientific, and other complex mathematical problems, this coding system accepts a program written in easily-understood algebraic format and translates it—in one pass—into a program of machine instructions, punched on cards or paper tape, and ready to run.

WIZ permits engineers and mathematicians to write their own programs in a language familiar to them. As with GECOM, the WIZ user need not be concerned with the complex details of the computer—he can state his problem in its own element. (GE)

word—1. A set of characters that occupies one storage location and is treated by the computer circuits as a unit and transported as such. Ordinarily a word is treated by the control unit as an instruction, and by the arithmetic unit as a quantity. Word lengths are fixed or variable, depending on the particular computer. 2. A unit of data. A set of characters that may be of any length and occupies one storage location. A word is usually treated as a unit by a data processing machine. Quantities, dollar amounts and names are examples of words. 3. In telegraphy, 5 characters plus 1 space, or 6 keystrokes.

word, alphabetic—A specific word entirely of characters of an alphabet or special signs and symbols—hyphens, semicolons, etc.

word arrangement, communications — The standard communication subsystem accommodates four types of computer input/output words. They are the function word, input-data word, output-data word, and output-data request word.

word, banner—The first word in a file record.

word, call—That set of characters designed to identify, label, or place a subroutine or data into the subroutine itself or into a program of which a subroutine is a part. The call word acts as the identifier.

word capacity—The selection of one of the word lengths of the equipment as a datum and thus to classify different operations as partial or multiples of these lengths for working.

word, check—A machine word is often used to represent a check symbol and this is appended and printed to the block, thus signifying the check.

word, communications status—The status word is sent to the central processor in the same manner as the input data word, except that an external interrupt signal is generated after the channel synchronizer has placed the word on the input data lines. In this way, the central processor can distinguish status words from input data words.

word, computer—A group of characters (bits) which is treated as a unit and which is stored in one computer storage location; each word being addressable, such words being instruction words with address and operation parts or a data word with alphanumeric characters of fixed or real numbers. Parts of computer words are syllables, bytes, etc.

word, connective—A COBOL reserved term to denote the presence of a qualifier. It may also be used to form a compound condition.

word, control—A word in the memory, usually the first or last of a record, or first or last word of a block, that carries indicative information for the following words, records, or blocks.

word, duoprimed—A computer word containing a representation of the 6, 7, 8, and 9 rows of information from an 80-column card.

word, ERROR status—This status word indicates that the remote computing system has detected an error.

word, external-interrupt status—A status word is accompanied by an external-interrupt signal. This signal informs the computer that the word on the data lines is a status word; the computer, interpreting this signal, automatically loads this word in a reserved address in core memory. If the programmer or operator desires a visual indication of the status word, it must be programmed.

word, fixed—The limitation of equipment as to the constant number of characters which the equipment will handle.

word, fixed-length—See fixed-length word.

word generator, manual—Same as generator, manual number.

word-half—A group of characters that represent half of a computer word for addressing purposes as a unit in storage.

word index—The contents of a storage position or register that may be used to automatically modify the effective address of any given instruction.

word, information—See information word.

word instruction—See instruction word.

word key—See key.

word, length—The number of bits or characters which are handled as a unit by the equipment, as a size of the field.

word length computer, variable—A computer designed to treat information having a variable number of bits.

word length, data—Same as word capacity.

word length, double—Many arithmetic instructions produce two word results. With fixed-point multiplication, a double-length product is stored in two A registers of control storage for integer and fractional operations. Integer and fractional division is performed upon a double-length dividend with the remainder and the quotient retained in the A registers.

word location, effective—The storage location pointed to by the effective virtual address of a word-addressing instruction.

word, long—The longest or lengthiest computer word which a particular computer can handle. They may be made up of full words, two full words, or a double-length word.

word, machine—A unit of information of a standard number of characters which a machine regularly handles in each transfer; e.g., a machine may regularly handle numbers or instructions in units of 36 binary digits. This is then the machine word.

word-mark—An indicator to signal the beginning or end of a word.

word, memory—See memory word.

word, numerical—A word which consists entirely of digits of some numeration system, as a decimal system, and not of characters of an alphabet, which is not normally used to assign number value.

word, operational—A COBOL term used to denote a word that improves readability of the language but need not be on the reserved list.

word, optional—Words introduced in a COBOL program to improve readability.

word-oriented—Refers to the type of memory system used in early computers. The memory system is divided into sections called "words," each of which has a location number and contains enough bits of binary digits to hold about 10 numeric positions.

word, parameter—A word in a subroutine which contains one or more parameters which specify the action of the subroutine or words which contain the address of such parameters.

word, partial—A programming device which permits the selection of a portion of a machine word for processing.

word period—The size or magnitude of the time interval between the occurance of signals representing digits occupying corresponding positions in consecutive words.

word, ready status—This status word indicates that the remote computing system is waiting for a statement entry from the terminal.

words, constant—Descriptive data that is fixed and does not generally appear as an element of input.

word, selectable-length—The ability of a programmer to assign a number of characters to each item of data. The words must be long enough to handle the longest item, and spaces not used are filled with blanks or zeros.

word-select memory—A computer with a fast memory has been designed to provide a total memory-cycle time in microseconds. This fast memory speed is mainly the result of the word-select technique with diode steering that is used for memory addressing. This replaces the more conventional method of X- and Y-axis half-read and half-write currents which is much slower. The memory also has a positive, automatic restoration feature that prevents an accidental loss of memory information.

word separator—A character in machine coding that segregates fields.

word, serial operation—The specific feature of certain handling equipment in which words are read one immediately after another in groups.

words, function—The function word contains the operating instructions for the peripheral units; its format depending upon the particular subsystem.

word, shortest—A word of the shortest length a computer can use, and which is most often half of the word length of the full length word.

words, mask—The mask word modifies both the identifier word and the input word which is called up for a search comparison in a logical AND operation.

word space—The actual area or space occupied by a word in serial digital devices such as drums, disks, tapes, and serial lines.

words, reserved—The words which are set aside in COBOL language which cannot be used as data names, file names, or procedure names, and are of three types: connected, optional, and key words.

word, status—This status word indicates that the remote computing system has deleted some information.

word status device (DSW)—*See* device, status word.

Word Terminal Synchronous — The Word Terminal Synchronous (WTS) complements the communications subsystem by enabling the central processor to be used more efficiently for high-speed data transmission over a single communications line. Since data characters are transferred to and from main storage on a full-word basis (six 6-bit characters per word), the input/output transfer time and the size of the area required for buffering are both considerably reduced. However, the most significant advantage of the WTS is that it minimizes the manipulation of the data by the central processor. This is accomplished by having the WTS, rather than the central processor, add character and message parity to outgoing messages and checking character and message parity on incoming messages. If an error in parity is detected, an external interrupt is presented to the central processor (some systems) .

word time—1. The time required to transfer a machine word from one storage position to another. 2. Especially in reference to words stored serially, the time required to transport one word from one storage device to another. *See* access time.

word time comparator—That circuitry which compares the word time counter with the specified word time at the moment of coincident pulse. This is done in order to verify that the correct word is being read.

word transfer — Transmission is of entire words (24 bits in parallel). The 24 bits are transferred between the computer and the external device at one time. This means that no breakdown of words into characters, on output, or assembling of characters into words, on input, takes place. This provides an increase of four times the input/output speed over character transfer, assuming the external device can accept or send words at that rate (some systems) .

word, variable-length—A computer word in which the number of characters is not fixed but is variable and subject to the discretion of the programmer, i.e., storage locations, registers, parallel logic wiring and gating are arranged in such a way as to handle a character or digit singly, but in storage each character is addressable and thus may be considered a word.

work cycle—The series or sequence that is necessary to perform a task, job, or execution and yield a unit of production, and which recurs in similar order for each task

or unit of work. As the last element of the task is completed, the first part of the series is started anew for the succeeding job or unit of production.

work-distribution chart—1. A listing or inventory of the duties, responsibilities, and sequence of the personnel in the job or task force under study. 2. The establishment of each duty relationship performed by the individual in relation to the specific task or function, which includes brief volumes-of-occurrence indicators, and the estimated and projected times to perform each item of work.

work file—A CRAM deck (magnetic cards) or magnetic tape used as a buffer or for interim storage within a run, such as a sort. The final file can be called the destination file.

work flow—Operations designed so that several tasks may be conducted simultaneously. This is opposite from serial development, in which tasks must wait until the completion of one before another can begin.

working area—*See* storage, working.

working data files—*See* data files.

working, double-length—*Same as* double precision.

working equipment—The basic or primary set of equipment for modules in which more than one set is available and the other sets are standby equipment in the event of a failure of the working equipment.

working memory—The internal memory which stores information for processing.

working, multiple length—Refers to the use of two or more machine words to represent a number and to thus increase precision, i.e., the use of double-length procedures, double precision, etc.

working, on-line—The performance of operations on data in such a way that the circuits of the equipment operating are under the control of central processor or mainframe, i.e., when on-line, data from the connected peripheral equipment or from another system is processed as soon as it is received and without manual intervention.

working, psuedo-off-line—A type of operation on data in such a way that the operations are completed on equipment connected to the mainframe, but under the control of a separate routine which is running in parallel or concurrently with the mainframe, i.e., the transfer of data from cards to tape while under mainframe control, but for later use.

working ratio, real-time—*See* time scale, extended.

working, real-time—*Same as* real-time operation.

working routine—That routine which produces the results of the problem or program as it was designed, as contrasted with the routines which are designed for support, housekeeping, or to compile, assemble, translate, etc.

working, simultaneous — *Same as* simultaneous operations.

working space—A portion of the internal storage reserved for the data upon which operations are being performed. (Synonymous with temporary storage, and contrasted with program storage.)

working standard—A specified combination of a transmitting and receiving system, or subscriber's lines and feeding circuits (or equivalent systems), connected by means of a distortionless variable attenuator, and employed under specific conditions to determine, by comparison, the transmission quality of other telephone systems or parts of systems.

working storage—*See* storage, working.

working, synchronous—*See* synchronous computer.

working triple-length—The use of three machine words to represent a number to enhance precision.

work-in-process queue—Items that have had some processing and are queued by and for the computer to complete the needed processing.

work load—The assigned amount of work to be performed in a given period.

work measurement—A procedure or set of rules for the establishment of a relationship between the quantity of work performed and the man (and/or machine) power used. Some systems also measure this relationship with a quality base, or a productivity quantum or ratio.

work process schedule—Under general direction, schedules operating time of the over-all electronic data processing activity in order to ensure that the data-processing equipment is effectively and efficiently utilized.

work queue, input—A list or line of jobs ready or submitted for processing but not yet begun or in process. Usually, these tasks are input on a first-come, first-served basis such as an input queue consists of programs, data, and control cards settled and waiting in the input job stream. Schedulers and special operating systems handle and control such queues differently.

work queue, output—Various data which are output are often not immediately printed or punched into final form, but are stored on some type of auxiliary storage device and become part of a queue which is programmed with control information for disposition of this information. Often the computer system is printer-bound or can operate only as fast as the printer can perform.

work, serial—*Same as* serial flow.

work-time, machine spoiled—*See* time, machine spoiled.

worst-case design—The worst-case design approach is an extremely conservative one in which the circuit is designed to function normally even though all component values have simultaneously assumed the worst possible condition that can be caused by initial tolerance, aging, and a temperature range of 0°C to 100°C. Worst-case techniques are also applied to obtain conservative derating of transient and speed specifications.

worst-case noise pattern—Sometimes called a checkerboard or double-checkerboard pattern. Maximum noise appearing when half of the half-selected cores are in a 1 state and the other half are in a zero state.

write—1. To transfer information to an output medium; to copy, usually from internal storage to external storage; to record information in a register, location, or other storage device or medium. 2. To transfer information usually from main storage to an output device.

write, gather—*See* gather, write.

write head—A head used to transfer data to a storage device, such as a drum, disk, tape or magnetic card.

write interval—The determination of the interval during machine operation when output data is available for an output operation, i.e., the net time exclusive of transmission which it takes to perform an output operation such as printing or writing on tape.

write key—A code in the program status doubleword that is used in conjunction with a memory lock to determine whether or not a program may write into a specific page of actual addresses.

write key field—The portion of the program status doubleword that contains the write key.

write lockout—*See* lockout, write.

write, memory lock—A 2-bit write-protect field optionally provided for each 512-word page of core memory addresses (some computers) .

write-only—The operation of transferring information from logic units or files.

write operation, scatter—*See* scatter write operation.

write-process-read—The process of reading in one block of data, while simultaneously processing the preceding block and writing out the results of the previously processed block. Some special processors can perform concurrently on any two or three of these operations, others are limited to read/write.

write-read head—A small electromagnet used for reading, recording, or erasing polarized spots that represent information on magnetic tape, disk, or drum.

writer, output—A service program which moves data from the output work queue to a particular output device, i.e., a printer, card punch, or terminal. The output writer thus transfers the actual output, often from an output work queue to an output device, after it has determined the normal rate of speed of the device to be used.

write time—The amount of time it takes to record information.

writing-while-read—Reading a record or group of records into storage from a tape at the same time another record or group of records is written from storage onto tape.

X

xerography—A dry copying process involving the photoelectric discharge of an electrostatic charge on the plate. The copy is made by tumbling a resinous powder over the plate; the remaining electrostatic charge is discharged, and the resin is transferred to paper or an offset printing master.

X punch—1. A punch in the X or 11 row of an 80-column card. 2. A punch in position 11 of a column. The X punch is often used to control or select, or to indicate a negative number as if it were a minus sign.

XY plotter—A device used in conjunction with a computer to plot coordinate points in the form of a graph.

Y

Y punch—1. A punch in the Y or 12 row of an 80-column card, i.e., the top row of the card. 2. A punch in position 12 of a column. It is often used for additional control or

selection, or to indicate a positive number as if it were a plus sign. (Synonymous with twelve (12) punch.)

Z

zatacode indexing—*Same as* coordinate indexing.

zatacoding—A system developed by C. N. Moores of superimposing codes by edge-notched cards.

zatocoding system—A system of coordinate indexing.

zero—1. Nothing; positive-binary zero is usually indicated by the absence of digits or pulses in a word; negative-binary zero in a computer operating on one's complements by a pulse in every pulse position in a word; in a coded-decimal machine, decimal zero and binary zero may not have the same representation. In most computers, there exists distinct and valid representation both for plus and for minus zero. 2. The combination of coded bits that the computer recognizes as zero. In most computers distinct and valid bit structures are used for positive and negative zero.

zero access—*See* access, zero.

zero-access addition—*See* addition, zero-access.

zero-access storage—The storage for which the latency (waiting time) is small. Though once widely used, this term is becoming less acceptable, since it constitutes a misnomer.

zero address code—An instruction code

which contains no instruction code for the next address.

zero-address instruction—Any of a number of techniques used to eliminate the storage of nonsignificant leading zeros.

zero-address instruction format—*Same as* addressless instruction format.

zero balancing (accounting)—Zero balancing is an effective method of verification when both detail items (e.g., accounts payable distribution cards or records) and their summary (e.g., an accounts payable disbursement card or record) are processed together. Each detail item is accumulated minus, and the summary plus. The result is a zero balance if both are correct.

zero, binary—*See* binary zero.

zero complement—*Same as* complement, radix.

zero compression—That process which eliminates the storage of insignificant leading zeros, and these are to the left of the most significant digits. For clarification see zero suppression.

zero condition—Relating to a magnetic cell, the state of representing one.

zero control, floating—The bit, in the program status doubleword, that indicates whether (if 0) or not (if 1) the result of a floating-operation is stored if the characteristic is reduced below zero.

zero, count interrupt—An interrupt level that is triggered when an associated (clock) counter pulse interrupt has produced a zero result in a clock counter.

zero elimination—*See* zero suppression.

zeroize—The procedure to fill storage space or to replace representations with zeros, i.e., the storage location may be cleared to zero, although doing so may not necessarily be the same as the meaning of zeroize. For example, if an "excess" code is used such as excess-3.

zero. kill—A specific feature of some sorters which determines that only zeros remain in the high order positions of documents while the documents are being sorted in lower order positions, i.e., this permits the machine operator to remove documents that are fully sequenced earlier in the sorting operation.

zero-level address—An instruction address in which the address part of the instruction is the operand.

zero-level addressing—*Same as* addressing, immediate.

zero-match gate—*Same as* gate, NOR.

zero proof—A procedure or process of checking computations by adding positive and negative values so that if all computations are accurate the total of such proof would be zero, i.e., wage deduction plus net pay less gross pay would be equal to zero.

zero state—The condition of a magnetic core in which the direction of the flux through a specified cross-sectional area has a negative value as determined by an arbitrarily specified direction for the negative normal to that area.

zero suppression—The elimination of insignificant zeros (those to the left of a quantity in a field or word) during a printing operation.

zero transmission-level reference point—An arbitrary chosen point in a circuit to which all relative transmission levels are referred. The transmission level at the transmitting switchboard is frequently taken as the zero transmission-level reference point.

zone—1. The 12, 11, or 0 punches in a Hollerith card-code. 2. That portion of a character code that is used with the numeric codings to represent nonnumeric information. 3.

In processors, two bits used in conjunction with four numeric bits to represent alphanumeric characters. The zone bits may be used separately to represent signs, to identify index registers, and for other purposes. 4. For punched cards, the 11 and 12 punches used with numeric punches 0 and 9 to represent alphabetic and special symbols. Zone punches may be used independently and for special control purposes. 5. A portion of internal storage allocated for a particular purpose.

zone bits—The bits other than the four used to represent the digits in a dense binary code.

zoned format—A binary-coded decimal format in which one decimal digit consists of zone bits and numeric bits and occupies an entire byte of storage.

zone, minus—That set of characters in a particular code which is associated with the adjacent bit which represents a minus sign.

zone, neutral—A range of values in the parameters of a control system in which no control action occurs.

zone, plus—A set of characters in a particular code which is associated with the adjacent bit which represents a plus sign.

zone punch—An additional punch, or punches, in a card column for purposes of expanding the number of characters that may be represented.

ZOOM—1. An assembler or compiler routine [part of GAP (General Assembly Program)], that writes statements (called macrostatements) which can be translated into more than one machine instruction—or, one can write single GAP mnemonics. In other words, ZOOM statements that wil generate several machine instructions can be combined with those which generate only one instruction, forming a highly-workable "shorthand" coding system. This allows a high degree of flexibility and provides near-optimum coding. For the experienced programmer, ZOOM provides a condensed and readable input and near-optimum output. (General Electric) 2. A highly-workable "shorthand" coding system for the experienced programmer. ZOOM provides a condensed and readable input and near-optimum output, thus aiding the programmer in gaining a highly-efficient and flexible program.

Memoranda

Memoranda

Memoranda

Memoranda